LEGAL ENVIRONMENT

JEFFREY F. BEATTY
Boston University

SUSAN S. SAMUELSON
Boston University

THOMSON

SOUTH-WESTERN

WEST

Australia · Canada · Mexico · Singapore · Spain · United Kingdom · United States

THOMSON

SOUTH-WESTERN

WEST

Legal Environment, 2e
Jeffrey F. Beatty and Susan S. Samuelson

VP/Editorial Director:
Jack W. Calhoun

VP/Editor-in-Chief:
George Werthman

Acquisitions Editor:
Rob Dewey

Developmental Editor:
Bob Sandman

Marketing Manager:
Steven H. Silverstein

Production Editor:
Lora Arduser

Manufacturing Coordinator:
Rhonda Utley

Senior Design Project Manager:
Michelle Kunkler

Production House:
Navta Associates, Inc.

Cover and Internal Designer:
Knapke Design
Cincinnati, OH

Cover Image:
© SAS / Alamy

Printer:
Quebecor World
Versailles, KY

CHAPTER-OPENING SCENARIO

YOU BE THE JUDGE

Selected Chapter Elements. To see examples of the many attention-grabbing features in **Legal Environment,** use these lists on the inside front and back covers. After these samples catch your interest, you can look at any chapter in the text to see more.

ECONOMICS & THE LAW

UPDATE

ROLE REVERSAL

SEE THE INSIDE BACK COVER FOR MORE EXAMPLES OF EXCITING FEATURES.

Preface

When we began work on the first edition of this textbook, our publisher warned us that our undertaking was risky because there were already so many Legal Environment texts. Despite these warnings, we were convinced that there was a market for a Legal Environment book that was different from all the others. Our goal was to capture the passion and excitement, the sheer enjoyment, of the law. Business law is notoriously complex, and as authors we are obsessed with accuracy. Yet this intriguing subject also abounds with human conflict and hard-earned wisdom, forces that can make a law book sparkle.

Now, as the second edition goes to press, we think of the students who have said to us, "This is the best textbook I have ever read," and "I had no idea business law could be so interesting." We recall the faculty who have told us, "Until I read your book I never really understood UCC 2-207" and "With your book, we have great class discussions." Comments such as these never cease to thrill us and to make us feel grateful that we persisted in our vision to write a Legal Environment text like no other — a book that is precise and authoritative *yet a pleasure to read.*

Strong Narrative.   The law is full of great stories, and we use them. Your students and ours should come to class excited. In Chapter 3, on dispute resolution (page 49), we explain litigation by tracking a double-indemnity lawsuit. An executive is dead. Did he drown accidentally, obligating the insurance company to pay? Or did the businessman commit suicide, voiding the policy? The student follows the action from the discovery of the body, through each step of the lawsuit, to the final appeal. The chapter offers a detailed discussion of dispute resolution, but it does so by exploiting the human drama that underlies litigation.

Students read stories and remember them. Strong narratives provide a rich context for the remarkable quantity of legal material presented. When students care about the material they are reading, they persevere. We have been delighted to find that they also arrive in class eager to question, discuss and learn.

Precise.   The great joy of using English accurately is the power it gives us to attack and dissect difficult issues, rendering them comprehensible to any lay reader. This text takes on the most complex legal topics of the day, yet it is appropriate for *all college and graduate level students.* Accessible prose goes hand in hand with legal precision. We take great pride in walking our readers through the most serpentine mazes this tough subject can offer. UCC section 2-207, on "battle of forms" conflicts, is hardly sexy material, but it is important. We spotlight the real-world need for section 2-207, and then use pinpoint directions to guide our readers through its many switchbacks, arriving at a full understanding with sanity and good humor intact. (See page 239.)

As we explore this extraordinary discipline, we lure readers along with quirky anecdotes and colorful diagrams. (Notice that the color display on page 496 clarifies the complex rules of the duty of care in the business judgment rule.) However, before the trip is over we insist that students:

- gauge policy and political considerations,
- grapple with legal and social history,
- spot the nexus between disparate doctrines, and
- confront tough moral choices.

Beyond that, we ask students to figure out how to avoid the very problems that have generated our law.

Authoritative. We insist, as you do, on a lawbook that is indisputably accurate. A professor must teach with assurance, confident that every paragraph is the result of exhaustive research and meticulous presentation. Dozens of tough-minded people spent thousands of hours reviewing this book, and we are delighted with the stamp of approval we have received from trial and appellate judges, working attorneys, scholars and teachers.

We reject the cloudy definitions and fuzzy explanations that can invade judicial opinions and legal scholarship. To highlight the most important rules, we use bold print, and then follow with vivacious examples written in clear, forceful English. (See, for example, the description of assault, on page 142.) We cheerfully venture into contentious areas, relying on very recent appellate decisions. (Can computer software be patented? See page 598.) Where there is doubt about the current (or future) status of a doctrine, we say so. In areas of particularly heated debate, we footnote our work: we want you to have absolute trust in this book.

Comprehensive. Staying comprehensive means staying current. Look, for example, at the important field of corporate governance. All texts cover par value, and so do we. Yet a future executive is far likelier to face conflicts over board composition, executive compensation, and shareholder proposals. We present a clear path through this thicket of new issues. We want tomorrow's business leaders to anticipate the challenges that await them and then use their knowledge to avert problems.

This book also provides full coverage of rapidly evolving issues such as cyber-law, securities law, UCC revisions, and countless other topics. However, we have kept the strong narrative flow from the earlier edition. Like you, we are here to teach. We do not use boxes because, in our experience, they disrupt the flow of the text. Students inform us that a box indicates peripheral material, that is, material they routinely skip; we prefer to give them an uncluttered whole. Each chapter also contains several Internet addresses, offering students a quick link to additional knowledge. These addresses, however, are woven into the body of the text, to reinforce the point that new technology and research methods are an integral part of a lively discipline. For example, page 394 in Chapter 14 on employment law contains the address of the Web site where the Labor Department answers questions about the Family and Medical Leave Act. We believe that a well-written chapter is seamless and cohesive.

A Book for Students.   We have written this book as if we were speaking directly to our students. We provide black letter law, but we also explain concepts in terms that hook students. Over the years, we have learned how much more successfully we can teach when our students are intrigued. No matter what kind of a show we put on in class, *they are only learning when they want to learn.*

Every chapter begins with a story, either fictional or real, to illustrate the issues in the chapter and provide context. Chapter 20 on Cyberlaw begins with the true story of a college student who discovers nude pictures of himself online. These photos had been taken in the locker room without his knowledge. What privacy rights do any of us have? Does the Internet jeopardize them? Students want to know—right away.

Most of today's undergraduates were not yet born when Jimmy Carter was president. They come to college with varying levels of preparation; many now arrive from other countries. We have found that to teach business law most effectively we must provide its context. Chapter 18 on securities regulation begins with a brief but graphic description of the 1929 stock market crash and the Great Depression (page 513). Only with this background do students grasp the importance and impact of our securities laws.

At the same time, we enjoy offering "nuts and bolts" information that grabs students: how much money corporate directors earn or how scam artists create car accidents in order to file fraudulent insurance claims. In Chapter 23, on consumer law, we bring home the issue of credit history by providing phone numbers and Web sites that students can use to check their own credit reports (page 667).

Students respond enthusiastically to this approach. One professor asked a student to compare our book with the one that the class was then using. This was the student's reaction: "I really enjoy reading the [Beatty & Samuelson] textbook and I have decided that I will give you this memo ASAP, but I am keeping the book until Wednesday so that I may continue reading. Thanks! :-)"

Along with other professors, we have used this text in courses for undergraduates, MBAs and executive MBAs, the students ranging in age from 18 to 55. The book works, as some unsolicited comments indicate:

- An undergraduate wrote, "This is the best textbook I have had in college, on any subject."

- A business law professor stated that the "clarity of presentation is superlative. I have never seen the complexity of contract law made this readable."

- An MBA student commented, "I think the textbook is great. The book is relevant, easy to understand and interesting."

- A state supreme court justice wrote that the book is "a valuable blend of rich scholarship and easy readability. Students and professors should rejoice with this publication."

- A Fortune 500 vice-president, enrolled in an Executive MBA program, commented, "I really liked the chapters. They were crisp, organized and current. The information was easy to understand and enjoyable."

- An undergraduate wrote, "The textbook is awesome. A lot of the time I read more than what is assigned—I just don't want to stop."

Humor. Throughout the text we use humor—judiciously—to lighten and enlighten. Not surprisingly, students have applauded—but is wit appropriate? How dare we employ levity in this venerable discipline? We offer humor because we take law seriously. We revere the law for its ancient traditions, its dazzling intricacy, its relentless though imperfect attempt to give order and decency to our world. Because we are confident of our respect for the law, we are not afraid to employ some levity. Leaden prose masquerading as legal scholarship does no honor to the field.

Humor also helps retention. We have found that students remember a contract problem described in a fanciful setting, and from that setting recall the underlying principle. By contrast, one widget is hard to distinguish from another.

Features

We chose the features for our book with great care. As mentioned above, all features are considered an essential part of the text, and are woven into its body. Also, each feature responds to an essential pedagogical goal. Here are some of those goals and the matching feature.

YOU BE THE JUDGE

GOAL: Get them thinking independently. When reading case opinions, students tend to accept the court's "answer." Judges, of course, try to reach decisions that appear indisputable, when in reality they may be controversial—or wrong. From time to time we want students to think through the problem and reach their own answer. Virtually every chapter contains a *You Be The Judge* feature, providing the facts of the case and conflicting appellate arguments. The court's decision, however, appears only in the Instructor's Manual.

Since students do not know the result, discussions tend to be more free-flowing. For instance, many commentators feel that *Smith v. Van Gorkom*, the landmark case on the business judgment rule, was wrongly decided. However, when students read the court's opinion, they rarely consider the opposing side. Now, with the case presented as *You Be the Judge* in Chapter 17 (page 496), the students disagree with the court at least half the time. They are thinking.

ECONOMICS & THE LAW

GOAL: Understand the economic impact of the law. This feature helps students understand how laws do (or, in some cases, do not) make economic sense. For example in Chapter 18 on securities (page 534) we explain why insider trading causes harm and therefore why the law prohibits it. Conversely, Chapter 24 on environmental law (page 691) explains why political considerations often interfere with the most rational environmental decisions.

NEWSWORTHY

GOAL: Prove that the law touches each of us every day. Students are intrigued to see the relevancy of what they are learning. Each chapter contains at least one Newsworthy feature—a newspaper or magazine article illustrating the legal issue under discussion. Thus, in Chapter 13 on agency law (page 362), an article about an American diplomat killed by terrorists demonstrates that an agency relationship exists only when the principal has control over its agent.

CYBERLAW

GOAL: Master the present and anticipate the future. The computer has changed all of our lives forever, and the courts and statute books are full of fascinating cyberlaw issues. Do employers have the right to read workers' e-mail? When does an electronic signature satisfy the statute of frauds? Can a company hold its shareholder meetings in cyberspace? Cyberlaw is fully discussed in Chapter 20: Cyberlaw and Chapter 21: Intellectual Property. Finally, throughout the text we discuss still more cyberlaw issues as they relate to the particular topic; icons highlight those sections.

AT RISK

GOAL: Help managers stay out of court. As every lawyer knows, the best lawsuit is the one that never happens. Some of our students are already in the workforce, and the rest soon will be, so we offer ideas on avoiding legal disputes. Sometimes we provide detailed methods to avoid the particular problem; other times we challenge the students to formulate their own approach to dispute prevention. For example, this feature in Chapter 7 on crime (page 180) helps future managers transform the general principles of compliance programs into concrete steps that can reduce or eliminate potential criminal liability.

ETHICS

GOAL: Make ethics real. We ask ethical questions about cases, legal issues, and commercial practices. Is it fair for one party to void a contract by arguing, months after the fact, that there was no consideration? Do managers have ethical obligations to older workers for whom employment opportunities may be limited? What is wrong with bribery? What is the ethical obligation of developed nations to dispose of toxic waste from computers? We do not have definitive answers but believe that asking the questions and encouraging discussion reminds students that ethics is an essential element of justice, and of a satisfying life.

UPDATE

GOAL: To keep students current. As we go to press, this book is accurate and up-to-date. Inevitably, however, during the book's three-year life span some laws will change. Courts will decide cases, legislatures will pass statutes. When we can foresee that the law is likely to change in a particular area, we ask the students to research the latest developments. For example, more than five years ago, Disney shareholders sued the company and its board in protest over a gigantic severance package awarded to the ex-President. The Delaware courts have already issued two opinions, with more to come in the future. Because this case is so important in the area of corporate governance, we have asked students to research its outcome (Chapter 17, page 502).

CASES

GOAL: Let the judges speak. Each case begins with a summary of the facts and a statement of the issue. Next comes a tightly edited version of the decision, in the court's own language, so that students "hear" the law developing in the diverse voices of our many judges. We cite cases using a modified bluebook form. In the principal cases in each chapter, we provide the state or federal citation, the regional citation, and the LEXIS or Westlaw citation. We also give students a brief description of the court. Because many of our cases are so recent, some will have only a regional reporter and a LEXIS or Westlaw citation.

PRACTICE TESTS

GOAL: Encourage students to practice! At the end of the chapters we challenge the students with ten or more problems, including the following:

- *Internet Research Problem.* This question sends students to an Internet address where they can explore issues from the chapter.
- *You Be The Judge Writing Problem.* The students are given appellate arguments on both sides of the question and must prepare a written opinion.
- *Ethics.* This question highlights the ethical issues of a dispute and calls upon the student to formulate a specific, reasoned response.
- *CPA Questions.* For topics covered by the CPA exam, administered by the American Institute of Certified Public Accountants, the practice tests include questions from previous CPA exams.
- *Role Reversal.* Students are asked to formulate their own test questions. Crafting questions is a good way to reinforce what they already understand, and recognize areas that they need to review.

Answers to the odd-numbered questions are available on the Beatty *Legal Environment* Web site at http://beatty.westbuslaw.com/. Here is why. Students often ask us how to study for exams. Reviewing the problems in the end-of-chapter practice tests is helpful, but without the answers students have no way of being sure they are on the right track. The answers to the even-numbered questions appear only in the Instructor's Manual so that faculty can assign them for written or oral presentation.

Teaching Materials

For more information about any of these ancillaries, contact your Thomson Learning/West Legal Studies in Business Sales Representative for more details, or visit the Beatty *Legal Environment* Web site at http://beatty.westbuslaw.com/.

Student Study Guide. (ISBN: [0-324-20629-1]) Students may purchase a study guide that includes a chapter outline, chapter objectives, and practice questions.

Students can find further practice problems in the Online Quiz at http://beatty. westbuslaw.com/.

Instructor's Manual. (ISBN: [0-324-20630-5]) We have included special features to enhance class discussion and student progress:

- Dialogues. These are a series of questions-and-answers on pivotal cases and topics. The questions provide enough material to teach a full session. In a pinch, you could walk into class with nothing but the manual and use the Dialogues to conduct an exciting class.

- Action learning ideas: interviews, quick research projects, drafting exercises, classroom activities, commercial analyses, and other suggested assignments that get students out of their chairs and into the diverse settings of business law.

- Skits. Various chapters have lively skits that students can perform in class, with no rehearsal, to put legal doctrine in a real-life context.

- A chapter theme and a quote of the day.

- Updates of text material.

- New cases and examples.

- Answers to You Be the Judge cases from the text and to the Practice Test questions found at the end of each chapter.

Test Bank. (ISBN: [0-324-20631-3]) The test bank offers hundreds of essay, short answer and multiple choice problems, and may be obtained in hard copy or electronic format.

ExamView Testing Software—Computerized Testing Software. (ISBN: [0-324-20632-1]) This testing software contains all of the questions in the printed test bank. This easy-to-use test creation software program is compatible with Microsoft Windows. Instructors can add or edit questions, instructions, and answers; and select questions by previewing them on the screen, selecting them randomly, or selecting them by number. Instructors can also create and administer quizzes online, whether over the Internet, a local area network (LAN), or a wide area network (WAN).

Microsoft PowerPoint Lecture Review Slides. PowerPoint slides are available for use by students as an aid to note-taking and by instructors for enhancing their lectures. Download these slides at http://beatty.westbuslaw.com/.

InfoTrac College Edition is an online library that contains hundreds of scholarly and popular periodicals, including *American Business Law Journal*, *Journal of International Business Studies, Environmental Law,* and *Ethics*. New copies of this text include a package that provides students access to InfoTrac College Edition. Contact your local Thomson Learning/West Legal Studies Sales Representative to learn more.

eCoursepacks provide a tailor fit, easy to use, and online companion for your course. eCoursepacks give educators access to content from thousands of current popular, professional, and academic periodicals; business and industry information from Gale; and the ability to easily add your own material. Permissions for all eCoursepack content are already secured, saving you the time and worry from securing rights. eCoursepacks online publishing tools also save you time, allowing you to quickly search the databases and make selections, organize all your content, and publish the final online product in a clean, uniform, and full color format. eCoursepacks are the best way to provide your audience with current information easily, quickly, and inexpensively. To learn more visit http://ecoursepacks.swlearning.com.

Videos are available to qualified adopters using this text. You may be eligible to access the entire library of West videos, a vast selection covering most business law issues. There are some restrictions, and if you have questions, please contact your local Thomson Learning/West Legal Studies Sales Representative or visit http://www.westbuslaw.com/video_library.html.

Enron Web Project.   West Legal Studies in Business and South-Western have created a special Web project entitled "Inside Look," focusing on Enron. You will find in-depth articles and expert analysis concerning the events leading to Enron's collapse and the continuing investigation of that company. Inside Look provides analysis from all angles by using an interdisciplinary approach emphasizing accounting, business law, and Management. For more information, visit http://insidelook.westbuslaw.com.

Interaction with the Authors.   This is our standard: Every professor who adopts this book must have a superior experience. We are available to help in any way we can. Adopters of this text often call us or E-mail us to ask questions, obtain a syllabus, offer suggestions, share pedagogical concerns, or inquire about ancillaries. One of the pleasures of working on this project has been our discovery that the text provides a link to so many colleagues around the country. We value those connections, are eager to respond, and would be happy to hear from you.

TO THE STUDENT

Each Practice Test contains one **Role Reversal** feature, in which we challenge you to create your own exam question. Your professor may ask you to submit the questions in writing or electronically, or to prepare an overhead slide. The goal is to think creatively and accurately. The question should be challenging enough that the average student will need to stop and think, but clear enough that there is only one answer. Questions can be formatted as essay, short answer or multiple choice.

For a multiple choice question, the first step is to isolate the single issue that you want to test. For example, in the unit on contract law, you do not want to ask a question that concerns five different aspects of forming an agreement. A good question will focus exclusively on one issue, for example, whether a job offer has to be in writing (some do, others do not). Create a realistic fact pattern that raises the issue. Provide one answer that is clearly correct. Add additional answers that might seem plausible but are definitely incorrect.

Some exam questions are very direct, and test whether a student knows a definition. Other questions require deeper analysis. Here are two multiple choice questions. The first is direct.

Question: Which contract is governed by the Uniform Commercial Code?

a.   An agreement for an actor to appear in a movie for a $600,000 fee.

b. An agreement for an actor to appear in a movie for a fee of $600,000 plus 2% of box office.

c. An agreement for the sale of a house.

d. An agreement for the sale of 22,000 picture frames.

e. An agreement for the rental of an apartment.

As you will learn later on, the correct answer is (D), because the Code applies to the sale of goods, not to employment contracts or real estate deals.

The next question is more difficult, requiring the student to spot the issue of law involved (product liability), remember how damages are awarded in such cases (generally, without regard to fault), and make a simple calculation.

Question: Lightweight Corp. manufactures strings of Christmas tree lights and sells 3.5 million sets per year. Every year, between 10 and 20 of the company's strings have a manufacturing defect that causes a consumer injury. Maxine receives a severe shock from a Lightweight string of lights. She sues. The evidence at trial is that: 1) Lightweight's safety record is the best in the industry; 2) all competing companies have a higher rate of injuries; 3) the lights that injured Maxine arrived at her house in the factory box, untouched by anyone outside of Lightweight; 4) Maxine operated the lights properly. Maxine's medical bills amount to $200,000; her lost income is $100,000; and her pain and suffering amounts to $600,000. What is the probable outcome at trial?

a. Maxine will win $200,000.

b. Maxine will win $100,000.

c. Maxine will win $900,000.

d. Maxine will win nothing.

e. Lightweight might win damages for a frivolous lawsuit.

As you will learn, the correct answer is (C). Lightweight is responsible under product liability law regardless of its careful work and excellent record. Maxine is entitled to all of her damages. Notice that the same question could be used in essay format, simply by deleting the multiple choice answers.

ACKNOWLEDGMENTS

We are grateful to the following reviewers who gave such helpful comments on the manuscript of this book:

Teri Elkins
    University of Houston
Paul Fiorelli
    Xavier University
Gary Greene
    Manatee Community College

Russ Meade
    Gardner-Webb University
Bruce L. Rockwood
    Bloomsburg University
Daphyne Saunders Thomas
    James Madison University

Jeffrey F. Beatty
    Phone: (617) 353-6397
    E-mail: jfbeatty@bu.edu

Boston, Massachusetts
December, 2003

Susan S. Samuelson
    Phone: (617) 353-2033
    E-mail: ssamuels@bu.edu

Contents: Overview

Contents

UNIT **3** AGENCY & EMPLOYMENT

CHAPTER 13 AGENCY

THE LEGAL ENVIRONMENT

UNIT 1

Introduction
to Law

Law is powerful. Law is essential. And law is fascinating. We hope this book will persuade you of all three ideas. ◆

Three Important Ideas About Law

POWER

The law displays its muscle every day, to corporate executives, homeless people—and presidents. A driver dies in an automobile accident and the jury concludes that the car had a design defect. The jurors award $8 million to the victim's family. A senior vice-president congratulates himself on a cagey stock purchase but is horrified to receive, not profits, but a prison sentence. A homeless person, ordered by local police to stop panhandling, ambles into court and walks out with an order permitting him to beg on the city's streets. A criminal inquiry spreads until a grand jury hears testimony from an unprecedented source—a sitting president of the United States. The strong reach of the law touches us all. To understand something that powerful is itself power.

Suppose, some years after graduation, you are a mid-level manager at Sublime Corp., which manufactures and distributes video games and related hardware and software. You are delighted with this important position in an excellent company—and especially glad you bring legal knowledge to the job. Sarah, an expert at computer-generated imagery, complains that Rob, her boss, is constantly touching her and making lewd comments. That is sexual harassment, and your knowledge of *employment law* helps you respond promptly and carefully. You have dinner with Jake, who has his own software company. Jake wants to manufacture an exciting new video game in cooperation with Sublime, but you are careful not to create a binding deal. (*Contract law.*) Jake mentions that a similar game is already on the market. Do you have the right to market one like it? That answer you already know. (*Intellectual property law.*)

The next day a letter from the Environmental Protection Agency asks how your company disposes of toxic chemicals used to manufacture computer drives. You can discuss it efficiently with in-house counsel, because you have a working knowledge of *environmental law* and *administrative law*. You may think your corporation is about to surge ahead in its field, and you would like to invest in its stock. But wait! Are you engaging in "insider trading"? Your training in *securities law* will distinguish the intelligent investment from the felony. LuYu, your personnel manager, reports that a silicon chip worker often seems drowsy; she suspects drug use. Does she have the right to test him? (*Constitutional law* and *employment law*.) On the other hand, if she fails to test him, could Sublime Corp. be liable for any harm the worker does? (*Tort law* and *agency law*.)

In a mere week you might use your legal training a dozen times, helping Sublime to steer clear of countless dangers. During the coming year you encounter many other legal issues, and you and your corporation benefit from your skills.

It is not only as a corporate manager that you will confront the law. As a voter, investor, juror, entrepreneur, and community member, you will influence and be affected by the law. Whenever you take a stance about a legal issue, whether in the corporate office, the voting booth, or as part of local community groups, you help to create the social fabric of our nation. Your views are vital. This book will offer you knowledge and ideas from which to form and continually reassess your legal opinions and values.

Importance

Law is also essential. Every society of which we have any historical record has had some system of laws. Naturally, the systems have varied enormously.

An extraordinary example of a detailed written law comes from the Visigoths, a nomadic European people who overran much of present-day France and Spain during the fifth and sixth centuries C.E. Their code admirably required judges to be "quick of perception, clear in judgment, and lenient in the infliction of penalties." It detailed dozens of crimes. For example, a freeman who kidnapped the slave of another had to repay the owner with four slaves and suffer 100 lashes. If he did not have four slaves to give, the kidnapper was himself reduced to slavery. Sadly, the code explicitly permitted torture of slaves and lower-class freemen, while prohibiting it for nobles.[1] The Iroquois Native Americans, disregarded by many historians, in fact played a role in the creation of our own government. Five major nations made up the Iroquois group: the Mohawk, Cayuga, Oneida, Onondaga, and Seneca. Each nation governed itself as to domestic issues. But each nation also elected "sachems" to a League of the Iroquois. The league had authority over any matters that were common to all, such as relations with outsiders. Thus, by the fifteenth century, the Iroquois had solved the problem of *federalism*: how to have two levels of government, each with specified powers. Their system impressed Benjamin Franklin and others and influenced the drafting of our Constitution, with its powers divided between state and federal governments.[2] As European nations today seek to create a more united Europe, they struggle with the same problem.

The greatest of all Chinese lawgivers disliked written law altogether. Confucius, who lived from 551 to 479 B.C., understood law within a broader social perspective. He considered good rulers, strong family ties, and an enlightened nobility to be the surest methods to a good society. "As a judge, I decide disputes, for that is my duty; but the best thing that could happen would be to eliminate the causes for litigation!" Although he spoke 2,500 years ago, the distinction Confucius described is still critically important in our society: Which do we trust more—a written law or the people who enforce it?

Fascination

Law is intriguing. When the jury awarded $8 million against an auto manufacturer for a defective car design, it certainly demonstrated the law's power. But was the jury's decision right? Should a company have to pay that much for one car accident? Maybe the jury was reacting emotionally. Or perhaps the anger caused by terrible trauma *should* be part of a court case. What about the government's role in auto safety? Would we prefer that a federal agency or a jury make decisions about car design? These are not abstract speculations for philosophers. Verdicts such as this may cause each of us to pay more for our next automobile. Then again, we may be driving safer cars. Legal issues can be complex, but they are never *theoretical*. The law affects us and we know it.

In 1835 the young French aristocrat Alexis de Tocqueville traveled through the United States, observing the newly democratic people and the qualities that made them unique. One of the things that struck de Tocqueville most forcefully was the

---

[1] S. P. Scott, *Visigothic Code (Forum Judicum)* (Littleton, CO: Fred B. Rothman & Co., 1982), pp. 3, 45.
[2] Jack Weatherford, *Indian Givers* (New York: Fawcett Columbine, 1988), pp. 133–150.

American tendency to file suit: "Scarcely any political question arises in the United States that is not resolved, sooner or later, into a judicial question."[3] De Tocqueville got it right: for better or worse, we do expect courts to solve many problems.

Not only do Americans litigate—they watch each other do it. Every television season offers at least one new courtroom drama to a national audience breathless for more cross-examination. Almost all of the states permit live television coverage of real trials. The most heavily viewed event in the history of the medium was the O. J. Simpson murder trial. Nonetheless, cameras in the courthouse are still controversial. Federal courts generally prohibit them. Only a small (but growing) number of foreign countries allows coverage of some judicial proceedings, including Australia, Canada, France, Hong Kong, Israel, Italy, the Netherlands, Norway, the Philippines and Spain. Proponents urge that televising trials increases awareness of social ills and reduces the chances of judicial unfairness. Opponents argue that the camera transforms a dignified search for truth into a carnival show of publicity gimmicks.

Regardless of where we allow cameras, it is an undeniable benefit of the electronic age that we can obtain information so quickly. From time to time we will mention Web sites of interest. Some of these are for nonprofit groups while others are commercial sites. We do not endorse or advocate on behalf of any group or company, but simply wish to alert you to what is out there. The commercial site of a cable television company devoted to trial broadcasts, http://www.courttv.com/, includes up-to-the-minute information on current cases, often including trial testimony, appeal briefs, and other timely data.

The law is a big part of our lives, and it is wise to know something about it. Within a few weeks you will probably find yourself following legal events in the news with keener interest and deeper understanding. In this chapter we develop the background for our study. We look at where law comes from: its history and its present-day institutions. In the section on jurisprudence, we examine different theories about what "law" really means. And finally we see how courts—and students—analyze a case.

Origins of Our Law

It would be nice if we could look up "the law" in one book, memorize it, and then apply it. But the law is not that simple, and *cannot* be that simple, because it reflects the complexity of contemporary life. In truth, there is no such thing as "the law." Principles and rules of law actually come from many different sources. Why is this so? In part because we inherited a complex structure of laws from England. We will see that by the time of the American Revolution, English law was already an intricate system.

Additionally, ours is a nation born in revolution and created, in large part, to protect the rights of its people from the government. The Founding Fathers created a national government but insisted that the individual states maintain control in many areas. As a result, each state has its own government with exclusive power over many important areas of our lives. To top it off, the Founders guaranteed many rights to the people alone, ordering national *and* state governments to

---

[3] Alexis de Tocqueville, *Democracy in America* (1835), Vol. 1, Ch. 16.

keep clear. This has worked, but it has caused a multilayered system, with 50 state governments and one federal government all creating and enforcing law.

A summary of English legal history will show the origin of our legal institutions. This brisk survey will also demonstrate that certain problems never go away. Anglo-Saxon England, about 1,000 years ago, was a world utterly different from our own. Yet we can see uncanny foreshadowings of our own unfinished efforts to create a peaceful world.

ENGLISH ROOTS

England in the tenth century was a rustic agricultural community with a tiny population and very little law or order. Danes and Swedes invaded repeatedly, terrorizing the Anglo-Saxon peoples. Criminals were hard to catch in the heavily forested, sparsely settled nation. The king used a primitive legal system to maintain a tenuous control over his people.

England was divided into shires, and daily administration was carried out by a "shire reeve," later called a sheriff. The shire reeve collected taxes and did what he could to keep peace, apprehending criminals and acting as mediator between feuding families. Two or three times a year, a shire court met; lower courts met more frequently.

Contemporary law: Mediation lives on. As we discuss in Chapter 3, on dispute resolution, lawsuits have grown ever more costly. Increasingly, companies are turning to mediation to settle disputes. The humble shire reeve's work is back in vogue.

Because there were so few officers to keep the peace, Anglo-Saxon society created an interesting method of ensuring public order. Every freeman (nonslave) belonged to a group of 10 freemen known as a "tithing," headed by a "tithing-man." If anyone injured a person outside his tithing or interfered with the king's property, all 10 men of the tithing could be forced to pay.

Contemporary law: Today we still use this idea of collective responsibility. In a business partnership, all partners are personally responsible for the debts of the partnership. They could potentially lose their homes and all assets because of the irresponsible conduct of one partner.

When cases did come before an Anglo-Saxon court, the parties would often be represented either by a clergyman, by a nobleman, or by themselves. There were few professional lawyers. Each party produced "oath helpers," usually 12, who would swear that one version of events was correct. The court explicitly gave greater credence to oath helpers from the nobility.

Contemporary law: The Anglo-Saxon oath helpers are probably forerunners of our modern jury of 12 persons. But as to who is telling the truth, that is a question that will never disappear. We deny giving a witness greater credence because of his or her status. But is that accurate? Some commentators believe that jurors are overly impressed with "expert witnesses," such as doctors or engineers, and ignore their own common sense when faced with such "pedigreed" people.

In 1066, the Normans conquered England. William the Conqueror made a claim never before made in England: that he owned all of the land. The king then granted sections of his lands to his favorite noblemen, as his tenants in chief, creating the system of feudalism. These tenants in chief then granted parts of their land to *tenants in demesne*, who actually occupied a particular estate. Each tenant in demesne owed fidelity to his lord (hence "landlord"). So what? Just this: land became the most valuable commodity in all of England, and our law still reflects that.

Contemporary law: One thousand years later, American law still regards land as special. The statute of frauds, which we study in the section on contracts, demands that contracts for the sale or lease of property be in writing. And landlord-tenant law, vital to students and many others, still reflects its ancient roots. Some of a landlord's rights are based on the 1,000-year-old tradition that land is uniquely valuable.

In 1250, Henry de Bracton (d. 1268) wrote a legal treatise that still influences us. *De Legibus et Consuetudinibus Angliae (On the Laws and Customs of England),* written in Latin, summarized many of the legal rulings in cases since the Norman Conquest. De Bracton was teaching judges to rule based on previous cases. He was helping to establish the idea of *precedent.* **The doctrine of precedent, which developed gradually over centuries, requires that judges decide current cases based on previous rulings.**

Contemporary law: This vital principle is the heart of American common law. Precedent ensures predictability. Suppose a 17-year-old student promises to lease an apartment from a landlord, but then changes her mind. The landlord sues to enforce the lease. The student claims that she cannot be held to the agreement because she is a minor. The judge will look for precedent, that is, older cases dealing with the same issue, and he will find many holding that a contract generally may not be enforced against a minor. That precedent is binding on this case, and the student wins. The accumulation of precedent, based on case after case, makes up the **common law.**

During the next few centuries, judges and lawyers acquired special training and skills. Some lawyers began to plead cases full-time and gained unique skill—and power. They represented only those who could pay well.

Parliament passed an ever greater number of laws, generally called **statutes,** the word we still use to mean a law passed by a legislative body. Parliament's statutes swelled in number and complexity until they were unfathomable to anyone but a lawyer.

Contemporary law: Our society still struggles with unequal access to legal talent. Rich people often fare better in court than poor. And many Americans regard law as Byzantine and incomprehensible. A primary purpose of this text is to remove the mystique from the law and to empower you to participate in legal matters.

As lawyers became more highly skilled, they searched ever wider for ways to defeat the other side. One method was by attacking the particular writ in the case. The party bringing the case was called the plaintiff. His first task was to obtain a **writ,** which was a letter from the central government ordering a court to hear the case. Each type of lawsuit required a different writ. For example, a landlord's lawsuit against a tenant required one kind of writ, while a claim of assault needed a different one. If a court decided that the plaintiff's lawyer had used the wrong writ, it would dismiss the lawsuit. This encouraged lawyers for the defendant to attack the writ itself, claiming it was inappropriate. By doing that, they could perhaps defeat the case without ever answering who did what to whom.

Contemporary law: This is the difference between procedure and substance, which will become clear during the course. **Substantive** rules of law state the rights of the parties. For example, it is substantive law that if you have paid the purchase price of land and accepted the deed, you are entitled to occupy the property. **Procedural** rules tell how a court should go about settling disputes. For example, what evidence can be used to establish that you *did* pay for the property? How much evidence is necessary? Who may testify about whether you paid?

Those are all issues of procedural law. To this day, lawyers attack procedural aspects of an opponent's case before dealing with the substantive rights.

Here is an actual case from more than six centuries ago, in the court's own language. The dispute illustrates that some things have changed but others never do. The plaintiff claims that he asked the defendant to heal his eye with "herbs and other medicines." He says the defendant did it so badly that he blinded the plaintiff in that eye.

THE OCULIST'S CASE (1329)

LI MS. Hale 137 (1), fo. 150, Nottingham[4]

ATTORNEY LAUNDE [FOR DEFENDANT]: Sir, you plainly see how [the plaintiff claims] that he had submitted himself to [the defendant's] medicines and his care; and after that he can assign no trespass in his person, inasmuch as he submitted himself to his care: but this action, if he has any, sounds naturally in breach of covenant. We demand [that the case be dismissed].

EXCERPTS FROM JUDGE DENUM'S DECISION: I saw a Newcastle man arraigned before my fellow justice and me for the death of a man. I asked the reason for the indictment, and it was said that he had slain a man under his care, who died within four days afterwards. And because I saw that he was a [doctor] and that he had not done the thing feloniously but [accidentally] I ordered him to be discharged. And suppose a blacksmith, who is a man of skill, injures your horse with a nail, whereby you lose your horse: you shall never have recovery against him. No more shall you here.

Afterwards the plaintiff did not wish to pursue his case any more. ◢

This case from 1329 is an ancient medical malpractice case. Defendant's lawyer makes a procedural argument. Attorney Launde does not deny that his client blinded the plaintiff. He claims that the plaintiff has brought the wrong kind of lawsuit. Launde argues that the plaintiff should have brought a case of "covenant," that is, a lawsuit about a contract.

Judge Denum decides the case on a different principle. He gives judgment to the defendant because the plaintiff voluntarily sought medical care. He implies that the defendant would lose only if he had attacked the plaintiff. As we will see when we study negligence law, this case might have a different outcome today. Note also the informality of the judge's ruling. He rather casually mentions that he came across a related case once before and that he would stand by that outcome. The idea of precedent is just beginning to take hold.

Sometimes a judge refused to hear a case, ruling that no such claims were legal. The injured party might then take his case to the Chancellor, in London, whose status in the king's council gave him unique, flexible powers. This *Court of Chancery* had no jury. The court's duty was to accomplish what "good conscience" required, that is, an *equitable* result, and so this more creative use of a court's power became known as **equity**.

Contemporary law: In present-day America judges still exercise equity powers, based on those cases the Chancery court accepted. For example, a court today

---

[4] J. Baker and S. Milsom, *Sources of English Legal History* (London: Butterworth & Co., 1986).

might issue an injunction requiring a factory owner to stop polluting the air. The injunction (order to stop) is an equitable remedy. Only a judge can exercise equitable powers because, historically, Chancery had no jury. If a judge grants an injunction, she is said to be exercising equitable powers.

Parliament added statutes on more and more matters, at times conflicting with common law rulings of the various judges. What should a court do when faced with a statute that contradicts well-established precedent? In the seventeenth century, one of England's greatest judges, Lord Coke, addressed the problem. In *Dr. Bonham's Case*,[5] Lord Coke ruled that "when an Act of Parliament is against Common right and reason, or repugnant, or impossible to be performed, the Common Law will control it and adjudge such Act to be void."

Audacious man! In a decision of breathtaking strength, Lord Coke declared that a single judge could overrule the entire Parliament, based on what the judge might consider "common right and reason." This same tension carries on today between elected officials, such as state legislators, and courts, which sometimes declare acts of the legislatures void.

Of course, by the time Lord Coke was on the bench, in the seventeenth century, English common law had also spread across the ocean to the newly created colonies. We will pick up the story in America.

LAW IN THE UNITED STATES

The colonists brought with them a basic knowledge of English law, some of which they were content to adopt as their own. Other parts, such as religious restrictions, were abhorrent to them. Many had made the dangerous trip to America precisely to escape persecution, and they were not interested in re-creating their difficulties in a new land. Finally, some laws were simply irrelevant or unworkable in a world that was socially and geographically so different. American law ever since has been a whitewater river created from two strong currents: one carries the ancient principles of English common law, the other, a zeal and determination for change.

During the nineteenth century, the United States changed from a weak, rural nation into one of vast size and potential power. Cities grew, factories appeared, and sweeping movements of social migration changed the population. Changing conditions raised new legal questions. Did workers have a right to form industrial unions? To what extent should a manufacturer be liable if its product injured someone? Could a state government invalidate an employment contract that required 16-hour workdays? Should one company be permitted to dominate an entire industry?

In the twentieth century, the rate of social and technological change increased, creating new legal puzzles. Were some products, such as automobiles, so inherently dangerous that the seller should be responsible for injuries even if no mistakes were made in manufacturing? Who should clean up toxic waste if the company that had caused the pollution no longer existed? If a consumer signed a contract with a billion dollar corporation, should the agreement be enforced even if the consumer never understood it? As we venture into this millennium, new and startling questions are certain to confront us. Before we can begin to examine the answers, we need to understand the sources of contemporary law.

---

[5] Eng. Rep. 638 (C.P. 1610).

Sources of Contemporary Law

During the colonial period there were few trained lawyers and fewer law books in America. After the Revolution, that changed, and law became a serious, professional career. The first great legal achievement was the adoption of the United States Constitution.

CONSTITUTIONS

United States Constitution

The United States Constitution, adopted in 1789 by the original 13 colonies, is the supreme law of the land.[6] Any law that conflicts with it is void. This Federal Constitution, as it is also known, does three basic things. First, it establishes the national government of the United States, with its three branches. The Constitution creates the Congress, with a Senate and a House of Representatives, and prescribes what laws Congress may pass. The same document establishes the office of the president and the duties that go with it. And it creates the third branch of government, the federal courts, describing what cases they may hear.

Second, the Constitution ensures that the states retain all power not given to the national government. This simple idea has meant that state governments play an important role in all of our lives. Major issues of family law, criminal law, property law, and many other areas are regulated predominantly by the various states.

Third, the Constitution guarantees many basic rights to the American people. Most of these rights are found in the amendments to the Constitution. The First Amendment guarantees the rights of free speech, free press, and the free exercise of religion. The Fourth, Fifth, and Sixth Amendments protect the rights of any person accused of a crime. Other amendments ensure that the government treats all people equally and that it pays for any property it takes from a citizen. Merely by creating a limited government of three branches and guaranteeing basic liberties to all citizens, the Constitution became one of the most important documents ever written.

State Constitutions

In addition to the Federal Constitution, each state has a constitution that establishes its own government. All states have an executive (the governor), a legislature, and a court system. Thus there are two entire systems of government affecting each of us: a federal government, with power over the entire country, and a state government, exercising those powers that the United States Constitution did not grant to the federal government. This is federalism at work.

STATUTES

The second important source of law is statutory law. The Constitution gave to the United States Congress the power to pass laws on various subjects. These laws are statutes, like those passed by the English Parliament. For example, the Constitution allows Congress to pass statutes about the military: to appropriate money, reorganize divisions, and close bases. You can find any federal statute, on any subject, at the Web site of the United States House of Representatives, which is http://www.house.gov/.

---

[6] The complete text of the Constitution appears in Appendix A.

State legislatures also pass statutes. Each state constitution allows the legislature to pass laws on a wide variety of subjects. All state legislatures, for example, may pass statutes about family law issues such as divorce and child custody.

COMMON LAW

As we have seen, the common law originated in England as lawyers began to record decisions and urge judges to follow earlier cases. As judges started to do that, the earlier cases, called *precedent*, took on steadily greater importance. Eventually, judges were *obligated* to follow precedent. **The principle that precedent is binding on later cases is** *stare decisis*, **which means "let the decision stand."** *Stare decisis* makes the law predictable, and this in turn enables businesses and private citizens to plan intelligently.

Equity

Principles of equity, created by the Chancellor in England, traveled to the colonies along with the common law rules. All states permit courts to use equitable powers. An example of a contemporary equitable power is an *injunction*, a court order that someone stop doing something. Suppose a music company is about to issue a new CD by a well-known singer, but a composer claims that the recording artist has stolen his song. The composer, claiming copyright violation, could seek an injunction to prevent the company from issuing the CD Every state has a trial court that can issue injunctions and carry out other equitable relief. As was true in medieval England, there is no jury in an equity case.

ADMINISTRATIVE LAW

In a society as large and diverse as ours, the executive and legislative branches of government cannot oversee all aspects of commerce. Congress passes statutes about air safety, but U.S. senators do not stand around air traffic towers, serving coffee to keep everyone awake. The executive branch establishes rules concerning how foreign nationals enter the United States, but presidents are reluctant to sit on the dock of the bay, watching the ships come in. **Administrative agencies** do this day-to-day work.

Most administrative agencies are created by Congress or by a state legislature. Familiar examples at the federal level are the Federal Communications Commission (FCC), which regulates most telecommunications; the Federal Trade Commission (FTC), which oversees interstate trade; and the Immigration and Naturalization Service (INS), which controls our nation's borders. At the state level, regulators set insurance rates for all companies in the state, control property development and land use, and regulate many other issues.

OTHER SOURCES OF LAW

Treaties

The Constitution authorizes the president to make treaties with foreign nations. These must then be ratified by the United States Senate. When they are ratified, they are as binding upon all citizens as any federal statute. In 1994 the Senate ratified the North American Free Trade Agreement (NAFTA) with Mexico and Canada. NAFTA was controversial then and remains so today—but it is now the law of the land.

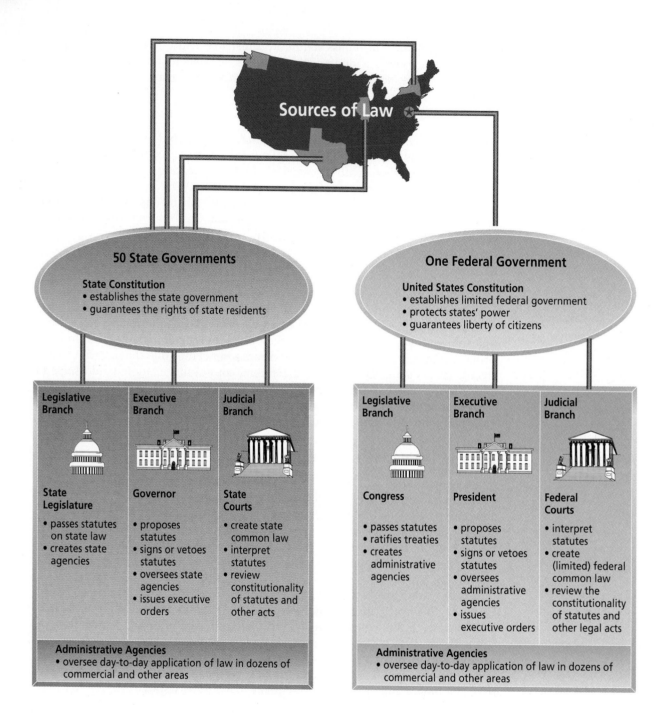

Sources of Law

50 State Governments

State Constitution
- establishes the state government
- guarantees the rights of state residents

Legislative Branch	**Executive Branch**	**Judicial Branch**
State Legislature	**Governor**	**State Courts**
• passes statutes on state law • creates state agencies	• proposes statutes • signs or vetoes statutes • oversees state agencies • issues executive orders	• create state common law • interpret statutes • review constitutionality of statutes and other acts

Administrative Agencies
- oversee day-to-day application of law in dozens of commercial and other areas

One Federal Government

United States Constitution
- establishes limited federal government
- protects states' power
- guarantees liberty of citizens

Legislative Branch	**Executive Branch**	**Judicial Branch**
Congress	**President**	**Federal Courts**
• passes statutes • ratifies treaties • creates administrative agencies	• proposes statutes • signs or vetoes statutes • oversees administrative agencies • issues executive orders	• interpret statutes • create (limited) federal common law • review the constitutionality of statutes and other legal acts

Administrative Agencies
- oversee day-to-day application of law in dozens of commercial and other areas

Federal Form of Government. Principles and rules of law come from many sources. The government in Washington creates and enforces law throughout the nation. But 50 state governments exercise great power in local affairs. And citizens enjoy constitutional protection from both state and federal government. The Founding Fathers wanted this balance of power and rights, but the overlapping authority creates legal complexity.

Executive Orders

In theory, all statutes must originate in Congress or a state legislature. But in fact executives also legislate by issuing executive orders. For example, in 1970 Congress authorized President Nixon to issue wage-price controls in an effort to stabilize the economy. This was a colossal grant of power, allowing the president personally to regulate the nation's economy. Critics charge that Congress should not give away the powers that the people have granted to it, and such delegations of authority have led to extensive lawsuits.

Classifications of Law

We have seen where law comes from. Now we need to classify the law into different types. There are three main classifications that we use throughout this book: criminal and civil law, substantive and procedural law, and public and private law.

CRIMINAL AND CIVIL LAW

It is a crime to embezzle money from a bank, to steal a car, to sell cocaine. **Criminal law concerns behavior so threatening that society outlaws it altogether.** Most criminal laws are statutes, passed by Congress or a state legislature. The government itself prosecutes the wrongdoer, regardless of what the bank president or car owner wants. A district attorney, paid by the government, brings the case to court. The injured party, for example the owner of the stolen car, is not in charge of the case, although she may appear as a witness. The government will seek to punish the defendant with a prison sentence, a fine, or both. If there is a fine, the money goes to the state, not to the injured party.

Civil law is different, and most of this book is about civil law. **Civil law regulates the rights and duties between parties.** Tracy agrees in writing to lease you a 30,000-square-foot store in her shopping mall. She now has a *legal duty* to make the space available. But then another tenant offers her more money, and she refuses to let you move in. Tracy has violated her duty, but she has not committed a crime. The government will not prosecute the case. It is up to you to file a civil lawsuit. Your case will be based on the common law of contract. You will also seek equitable relief, namely, an injunction ordering Tracy not to lease to anyone else. You should win the suit, and you will get your injunction and some money damages. But Tracy will not go to jail.

Some conduct involves both civil and criminal law. Suppose Tracy is so upset over losing the court case that she becomes drunk and causes a serious car accident. She has committed the crime of driving while intoxicated, and the state will prosecute. She has also committed negligence, and the injured party will file a lawsuit against her, seeking money.

SUBSTANTIVE AND PROCEDURAL LAW

We saw this distinction in *The Oculist's Case*, and it remains important today. **Substantive law defines the rights of people.** Substantive law requires that a landlord who has signed a lease must deliver the store to her tenant. Most of this book concerns substantive law. **Procedural law establishes the processes for**

settling disputes. Procedural law requires that, to get an injunction against Tracy, you must first notify her in writing of your claims and the time and place of the hearing on the injunction.

PUBLIC AND PRIVATE LAW

Public law refers to the rights and obligations of governments as they deal with the nation's citizens. For example, when the FTC prohibits deceptive advertising, that is public law. **Private law** regulates the duties between individuals. Landlord-tenant law is private law.

Jurisprudence

We have had a glimpse of legal history and a summary of the present-day sources of American law. But what *is* law? That question is the basis of a field known as **jurisprudence**. How do we distinguish a moral rule from a legal rule? What is the real nature of law? Can there be such a thing as an "illegal" law?

LAW AND MORALITY

Law is different from morality, yet the two are obviously linked. There are many instances when the law duplicates what all of us would regard as a moral position. It is negligence to drive too fast in a school district, and few would dispute the moral value of that law. And similarly with contract law: if the owner of land agrees in writing to sell property to a buyer at a stated price, the seller must go through with the deal, and the legal outcome matches our moral expectations.

On the other hand, we have had laws that we now clearly regard as immoral. At the turn of the century, a factory owner could typically fire a worker for any reason at all—including, for example, his religious or political views. Today, we would say it is immoral to fire a worker because she is Jewish—and the law prohibits it.

Finally, there are legal issues where the morality is not so clear. You are walking down a country lane and notice a three-year-old child playing with matches near a barn filled with hay. Are you obligated to intervene? No, says the law, though many think that is preposterous. (See Chapter 4, on common law.) A company buys property and then discovers, buried under the ground, toxic waste that will cost $300,000 to clean up. The original owner has gone bankrupt. Should the new owner be forced to pay for the cleanup? If the new owner fails to pay for the job, who will? (See Chapter 24, on environmental law.)

LEGAL POSITIVISM

This philosophy can be simply stated: law is what the sovereign says it is. The **sovereign** is the recognized political power whom citizens obey, so in the United States, both state and federal governments are sovereign. A legal positivist holds that whatever the sovereign declares to be the law is the law, whether it is right or wrong.

The primary criticism of legal positivism is that it seems to leave no room for questions of morality. A law permitting a factory owner to fire a worker because she is Catholic is surely different from a law prohibiting arson. Do citizens in a democracy have a duty to consider such differences?

NEWSWORTHY

Most states allow citizens to pass laws directly at the ballot box, a process called voter referendum. California voters often do this, and during the 1990s, they passed one of the state's most controversial laws. Proposition 187 was designed to curb illegal immigration into the state by eliminating social spending for undocumented aliens. Citizens debated the measure fiercely but passed it by a large margin. One section of the new law forbade public schools from educating illegal immigrants. The law obligated a principal to inquire into the immigration status of all children enrolled in the school and to report undocumented students to immigration authorities. Several San Diego school principals rejected the new rules, stating that they would neither inquire into immigration status nor report undocumented aliens. Their statements produced a heated response. Some San Diego residents castigated the school officials as lawbreakers, claiming that:

- A school officer who knowingly disobeyed a law was setting a terrible example for students, who would assume they were free to do the same

- The principals were advocating permanent residence and a free education for anyone able to evade our immigration laws; and

- The officials were scorning grass-roots democracy by disregarding a law passed by popular referendum.

Others applauded the principals' position, asserting that:

- The referendum's rules would transform school officials from educators into border police, forcing them to cross-examine young children and parents

- The new law was foolish because it punished innocent children for violations committed by their parents; and

- Our nation has long respected civil disobedience based on humanitarian ideals, and these officials were providing moral leadership to the whole community.

Ultimately, no one had to decide whether to obey Proposition 187. A federal court ruled that only Congress had the power to regulate immigration and that California's attempt was unconstitutional and void. The debate over immigration reform—and ethics—did not end, however. Congress periodically considers proposals to cut social benefits for illegal immigrants. ▪

NATURAL LAW

St. Thomas Aquinas (1225–1274) answered the legal positivists even before they had spoken. In his *Summa Theologica*, he argued that an unjust law is no law at all and need not be obeyed. It is not enough that a sovereign makes a command. The law must have a moral basis.

Where do we find the moral basis that would justify a law? Aquinas says that "good is that which all things seek after." Therefore, the fundamental rule of all laws is that "good is to be done and promoted, and evil is to be avoided." This sounds appealing, but also vague. Exactly which laws promote good and which do not? Is it better to have a huge corporation dominate a market or many smaller companies competing? Did the huge company get that way by being better than its competitors? If Wal-Mart moves into a rural area, establishes a mammoth store, and sells inexpensive products, is that "good"? Yes, if you are a consumer who cares only about prices. No, if you are the owner of a Main Street store driven into bankruptcy. Maybe, if you are a resident who values small town life but wants lower prices.

Natural law debates are eternal. One of the greatest of the ancient Greek dramatists, Sophocles (496–406 B.C.E.), touches upon the subject in his famous play, *Antigone*. Oedipus's two sons, Eteocles and Polyneices, have arranged to rule Thebes in rotation, but when Eteocles refuses to give up the throne, Polyneices and his many supporters attack the city. Both brothers are killed in the battle. Creon, who inherits the crown, declares that Eteocles will receive a hero's burial but that Polyneices must lie exposed in the dust. Anyone attempting to bury him will be executed. Antigone, the sister of the dead men, is horrified. Declaring that religious beliefs compel her to rescue her brother's soul from perpetual torment, she attempts to bury Polyneices. Antigone admits to Creon that she understood his ruling, but retorts, in the language of natural law:

> [Your] order did not come from God. Justice,
> That dwells with the gods below, knows no such law.
> I did not think your edicts strong enough
> To overrule the unwritten unalterable laws
> Of God and heaven, you being only a man.
> They are not of yesterday or to-day, but everlasting,
> Though where they came from, none of us can tell.[7]

Creon, a legal positivist, responds simply and forcefully that "Our country is our life." Any attack upon the city-state warrants death, as does any disobedience of its laws. Ultimately, he orders Antigone to her death and then, inevitably, regrets his decision.

Two thousand five hundred years later, we still debate the meaning and significance of natural law. Court cases and political debates about abortion, stem cell research, school prayer, evolution, and euthanasia all echo the themes disputed by Creon and Antigone.

What does natural law tell us about abortion? Abortion supporters, or those advocating free choice, will say that natural law protects a woman's reproductive rights and that it is violent and unnatural for any government to tell a woman what to do with her body. Opponents of abortion reach the opposite conclusion, arguing that no good can come from terminating the life of a fetus and that a law permitting abortion is no law at all. What do you think?

LEGAL REALISM

Legal realists take a very different tack. They claim it does not matter what is written as law. What counts is who enforces that law and by what process. All of us are biased by issues such as income, education, family background, race, religion, and many other factors. These personal characteristics, the legal realists say, determine which contracts will be enforced and which ignored, why some criminals receive harsh sentences while others get off lightly, and so on.

Judge Jones hears a multimillion-dollar lawsuit involving an airplane crash. Was the airline negligent? The law is the same everywhere, but legal realists say that Jones's background will determine the outcome. If she spent 20 years

---

[7] *Antigone* from *The Theban Plays* by Sophocles, translated by E. F. Watling (London: Penguin Classics, 1947) Copyright © E.F. Watling, 1947.

representing insurance companies, she will tend to favor the airline. If her law practice consisted of helping the "little guy," she will favor the plaintiff.

Other legal realists argue, more aggressively, that those in power use the machinery of the law to perpetuate their control. The outcome of a given case will be determined by the needs of those with money and political clout. A court puts "window dressing" on a decision, they say, so that society thinks there are principles behind the law. A problem with legal realism, however, is its denial that any lawmaker can overcome personal bias. Yet clearly some do act unselfishly.

Summary of Jurisprudence	
Legal Positivism	Law is what the sovereign says.
Natural Law	An unjust law is no law at all.
Legal Realism	*Who* enforces the law counts more than *what* is in writing.

No one school of jurisprudence is likely to seem perfect. We urge you to keep the different theories in mind as you read cases in the book. Ask yourself which school of thought is the best fit for you.

Working With the Book's Features

In this section we introduce a few of the book's features, and discuss how you can use them effectively. We will start with cases.

ANALYZING A CASE

A law case is the decision a court has made in a civil lawsuit or criminal prosecution. Cases are the heart of the law and an important part of this book. Reading them effectively takes practice. The following decision in a civil suit is a good place to start.

This case begins with violence outside a nightclub. Lindie Osborne, an innocent young woman out for a night on the town, is viciously struck by a drunken karate expert. Obviously the thug who attacked her is responsible for the harm done. But is the nightclub also liable? That is no theoretical question, because the hooligan is likely to have little or no money.

OSBORNE V. STAGES MUSIC HALL, INC.

312 Ill. App. 3d 141; 726 N.E.2d 728; 2000 Ill. App. LEXIS157; 244 Ill. Dec. 753
Illinois Court of Appeals, 2000

FACTS: Stages Music Hall owned the Metro Club in Chicago. Karl Trujillo and his friend Daniel Hosneola became intoxicated while at the Metro and got into a violent fight with eight of the club's bouncers. Trujillo, trained in the martial arts, knocked down two of the employees, but the bouncers finally ejected the young men, who remained outside the door, clamoring for readmission.

Meanwhile, Lindie Osborne and her friend Michelle Becht were leaving the Metro. As Becht exited, one of the young men slapped her in the face. Osborne hurried outside but as she approached her friend, Trujillo spun on his heel and kicked her in the face. Osborne fell to the ground. The two men left the scene but were later arrested.

Osborne suffered two facial fractures that required permanent plates and pins to be inserted in her jaw, which was wired shut for six weeks. She sued Stages, but the trial court gave a directed verdict for Stages, meaning that it dismissed the case. The court declared that Stages had no duty to protect Osborne because the incident took place on a public sidewalk, and because Trujillo's assault was not foreseeable. Osborne appealed.

ISSUE: Did Stages have a duty to protect Osborne from Trujillo's attack?

EXCERPTS FROM JUDGE WOLFSON'S DECISION:

Without the existence of a duty, there can be no recovery. Whether a duty exists is an inquiry shaped by public policy, since we must decide whether defendant and plaintiff stand in such a relationship to one another that the law imposes on defendant an obligation of reasonable conduct for the benefit of plaintiff . Accordingly, we consider not only the reasonable (1) foreseeability and (2) likelihood of injury, but also (3) the magnitude of the burden on defendant in guarding against injury and (4) the consequences of placing that burden on defendant. Where injury results from freakish, bizarre or fantastic circumstances, no duty is present and no negligence claim can be asserted.

The first matter to be addressed is the location of the attack. Whether the assault takes place in or outside the actual premises of the business owner, the dispositive factor remains the reasonable foreseeability of the actions taken by the third party. Based on [earlier cases], we cannot say the fact that the assault in this case took place on a public side-

walk just outside the Metro club disposes of the duty issue. We go on, then, to determine whether, under the facts of this case, the assault on Osborne was reasonably foreseeable so as to give rise to a legal duty to Metro to protect her.

Unlike Osborne and Becht, Metro's bouncers knew the two men outside the club were intoxicated, combative, and angry. Though the bouncers could observe the two men's behavior from inside the club, they did nothing after locking the Metro doors. After ejecting the two men from the club, the bouncers did not supervise or concern themselves with the area in front of the bar—an area over which the club had earlier exercised control by erecting barriers or "horses" to control the flow of traffic.

In short, the bouncers exported the club's problems to the sidewalk and then ignored the troublemakers while allowing two female patrons to leave through locked doors into the path of potentially dangerous men.

Because of what the bouncers knew about the two men, it could be said it was reasonably foreseeable that a patron would be attacked upon exiting the club and, therefore, it was incumbent on the club to guard against such an occurrence.

We do not impose a great burden on Stages when we conclude it owed Osborne a duty. Measures easily could have been taken to protect her against the apparent danger. Whether a simple warning would have been enough in this case is something we need not decide, but it certainly would not be asking too much of the cadre of bouncers.

We conclude the trial court erred when it directed a verdict against Osborne. We reverse the trial court's judgment and remand for a new trial. ◢

Analysis

Let's take it from the top. The case is called *Osborne v. Stages Music Hall, Inc.* Lindie Osborne is the plaintiff, the person who is suing. Stages Music Hall, Inc., which owns the Metro Club, is being sued, and is called the defendant. In this example, the plaintiff's name happens to appear first but that is not always true. When a defendant loses a trial and files an appeal, *some* courts reverse the names of the parties.

The next line gives the legal citation, which indicates where to find the case in a law library. We explain in the footnote how to locate a book if you plan to do research.[8]

The *Facts* section provides a background to the lawsuit, written by the authors of this book. The court's own explanation of the facts is often many pages long and may involve complex matters irrelevant to the subject covered in this book, so we relate only what is necessary.

The *Issue* section is very important. It tells you what the court had to decide—and also why you are reading the case. In giving its decision, a court may digress. If you keep in mind the issue and relate the court's discussion to it, you will not get lost.

Excerpts from Judge Wolfson's Decision begins the court's discussion. This is called the *holding*, meaning a statement of who wins and who loses. The holding also includes the court's *rationale*, which is the reasoning behind the decision.

The holding that we provide is an edited version of the court's own language. Some judges write clear, forceful prose; others do not. Either way, their words give you an authentic feel for how judges think and rule, so we bring it to you in the original. Occasionally we use brackets [ ] to substitute our language for that of the court, either to condense or to clarify. Notice the brackets in the second paragraph of the *Osborne* decision. Judge Wolfson actually discussed a different case, called *Shortall v. Hawkeye Bar and Grill*, in which the court ruled that a tavern owner could not necessarily escape liability for a criminal attack merely because it occurred outside. In order to keep the *Osborne* case to a manageable length, we have deleted the discussion of *Shortall*.

We omit a great deal. A court's opinion may be three pages or it may be 75. We do not use ellipses (. . .) to indicate these deletions, because there is more taken out than kept in, and we want the text to be clean. When a court quotes an earlier decision verbatim but clearly adopts those words as its own, we generally delete the quotation marks, as well as the citation to the earlier case. If you are curious about the full holding, you can always look it up.

Let us look at a few of Judge Wolfson's points. The holding begins with a discussion of *duty*. The court explains that a person can only be liable for harm to another if he had a duty to her. Judge Wolfson then goes on to describe the *public policy* that helps a court decide whether to impose a duty on one party. He mentions foreseeability—the dominant issue in this case—along with three other factors. The judge is emphasizing that courts do not reach decisions arbitrarily. They attempt to

---

8 If you want to do legal research, you need to know where to find particular legal decisions. A case citation guides you to the correct volume(s). The full citation of our case is *Osborne v. Stages Music Hall, Inc.*, 312 Ill. App. 3d 141, 726 N.E.2d 728, 2000 Ill. App. LEXIS 157. The string of numbers identifies three different books in which you can find the full text of this decision. The first citation is to "Ill. App. 3d," which means the official court reporter of the state of Illinois, third set. Illinois, like most states, reports its law cases in a series of numbered volumes. After the volumes reach number 999, most reporters start over with a second set of volumes and then a third. This case appears in volume 312 of the third set of Illinois reporters. If you go to a law library and find that book, you can then turn to page 141 and—*voila!*—you have the case. The decision is also reported in another set of volumes, called the regional reporters. This series of law reports is grouped by geographic region. Illinois is included in the northeast region, so our case appears in volume 726 of the second set of the northeast reporter, at page 728. Finally, most cases are now available online. The third citation is to the electronic law library operated by LEXIS. Once you are connected to the LEXIS service, typing "2000 Ill. App. LEXIS 157" in the appropriate box will bring the Metro Club and its rowdy patrons right into your computer.

make reasoned choices, consistent with earlier rulings, that make good sense for the general public. He adds that if the injury resulted from conduct that was truly bizarre, there would be no liability, since the damage was not foreseeable.

The court then focuses on the defendant's claim that it should not be liable for harm occurring on a "public sidewalk." Judge Wolfson rather summarily dismisses that suggestion, insisting that the real issue is whether the attack was foreseeable, not whether it occurred on one side of the doorway or the other. Notice that in the next paragraph he comes back to this point. He describes the wooden "horses" that the club placed on the sidewalk for crowd control. He is suggesting that if a club takes the liberty of treating the sidewalk as its own for purposes of regulating admission, it keeps responsibility for that area all night long.

Having decided that foreseeability is the crux of this case, the court inquires whether this defendant should in fact have been able to foresee that Lindie Osborne or another patron might be harmed by the drunken oafs on the sidewalk. The answer is a resounding "yes," and Judge Wolfson lists some of the reasons: Metro created the hazard by thrusting its drunken patrons onto the sidewalk; the club knew the two men were combative; and the bouncers could see the two outside, while Osborne and Becht only became aware of them at the last minute.

The court concludes that an attack was foreseeable. Notice that the court *does not* specify what the bouncers should have done. Judge Wolfson merely says that, at the very least, the bouncers should have warned the young women of the danger.

Finally, the court rules. "We conclude the trial court erred when it directed a verdict against Osborne. We reverse the trial court's judgment and remand for a new trial." The first sentence tells us that the trial court got it wrong. Then the court *reverses*, meaning that it *undoes* the result. The lower court's dismissal is now invalid. The court *remands* the dispute to the trial court, meaning it *sends the case back down*. The trial court will have to start all over, with a new jury, and give Lindie Osborne a trial. In contrast, if the appeals court had agreed with the lower court's ruling, the appeals court would have *affirmed* the trial court's decision, leaving it unchanged.

Why does Judge Wolfson not specify what Metro should have done? He is leaving that decision to the jury. He has ruled that the Metro Club *did* have a duty to Osborne and that harm to her *was* foreseeable. The jury will still have some questions to answer: what would a reasonable club have done to prevent the harm? Did the Metro Club do enough? (Almost certainly not, since they did nothing.) How severe were Osborne's injuries? How much money does Metro owe her? The jury will answer all of these questions if the parties go through with the second trial. In all likelihood, though, now that an appeals court has ruled that Metro *did* have a duty, the defendant will be eager to settle out of court. The most important issue of the case is decided: Metro does not escape liability because the attack occurred outside.

Update

In this feature we ask students to find a current article on an issue discussed in the text. The goal is for you to apply the principles of this course to current events— this material is very real! You may use periodicals from the library or articles from any electronic database. The article should be dated within the past two months.

Find an article on nightclub liability. What did the club allegedly do or fail to do? Is this a civil or criminal case? What outcome do you anticipate? How could the owner have avoided the problem?

"YOU BE THE JUDGE"

Many cases involve difficult decisions for juries and judges. Often both parties have legitimate, opposing arguments. Most chapters in this book will have a feature called "You Be the Judge," in which we present the facts of a case but not the court's holding. We offer you two opposing arguments based on the kinds of claims the lawyers made in court. We leave it up to you to debate and decide which position is stronger or to add your own arguments to those given. The following case is another negligence lawsuit, with issues similar to those in the *Osborne* case. A suicide caused a distraught family to sue a rock singer and music producer. Once again the defendants asked the judge to dismiss the case. They pointed out, correctly, that a negligence case requires a plaintiff to prove that the defendant *could have foreseen the type of harm that occurred*. Could Ozzy Osbourne have foreseen this sad outcome to one of his songs? You be the judge.

YOU BE THE JUDGE

MCCOLLUM V. CBS, INC.

202 Cal. App. 3d 989, 249 Cal. Rptr. 187, 1988 Cal. App. LEXIS 909
California Court of Appeal, 1988

FACTS: John McCollum, 19 years old, was an alcoholic with serious emotional problems. He listened over and over to music recorded by Ozzy Osbourne on CBS records, particularly two albums called *Blizzard of Oz* and *Diary of a Madman*. He usually listened to the music on the family stereo in the living room because the sound was most intense there. One Friday evening, though, he went to his bedroom and lay on his bed, listening to more Osbourne music. He placed a loaded .22-caliber handgun to his right temple and pulled the trigger.

McCollum's parents sued Osbourne and CBS records, claiming that they negligently aided and encouraged John to commit suicide. The parents' argument was that Osbourne's songs were designed to appeal to unstable youths and that the message of some of his music explicitly urged death. One of the songs John had listened to before his death was "Suicide Solution," which included these lyrics:

Wine is fine but whiskey's quicker
Suicide is slow with liquor
Take a bottle drown your sorrows
Then it floods away tomorrows

Now you live inside a bottle
The reaper's travelling at full throttle
It's catching you but you don't see
The reaper is you and the reaper is me

Breaking law, knocking doors
But there's no one at home
Made your bed, rest your head
But you lie there and moan
Where to hide, Suicide is the only way out
Don't you know what it's really about.[9]

The trial court dismissed the lawsuit, ruling that the plaintiff had not made out a valid negligence claim. The court ruled that the First Amendment's free speech provision protected the

---

[9] Words and music by John Osbourne, Robert Daisley and Randy Rhoads. TRO © Copyright 1981 Essex Music International, Inc., New York, New York and Jet Music Ltd., London England. Used by permission.

rights of Osbourne and CBS to publish any music they wanted. In addition, the court found that the defendants could not have foreseen that anyone would respond to the lyrics by taking his own life. With no foreseeability, the court ruled, the plaintiffs' case must fail. The parents appealed.

YOU BE THE JUDGE: Was McCollum's suicide foreseeable?

ARGUMENT FOR THE PARENTS: Your honors, for years Ozzy Osbourne has been well known as the "madman" of rock and roll. The words and music of his songs revolve around bizarre, antisocial beliefs, emphasizing death and satanic worship. Many of his songs suggest that life is hopeless and that suicide is not only acceptable but desirable. Now one of his devoted fans has acted on Osbourne's advice and killed himself. The defendants share responsibility for this tragic death.

Osbourne and CBS knew that many of Osbourne's fans struggled with self-identity, alienation, and substance abuse. Both defendants aggressively targeted this market and reaped enormous profits. They realized that the confused youths who adored Osbourne were precisely those most vulnerable to vicious advice. Yet in spite of their knowledge, both defendants churned out songs such as "Suicide Solution," urging troubled, chemically addicted young people to kill themselves. Not only was it *foreseeable* that one of Osbourne's fans would sooner or later take his life,

it was *inevitable*. The only way to ensure that this doesn't occur again is to permit a jury to hear the parents' case and, if it is persuaded by the evidence, to award the grieving parents damages.

ARGUMENT FOR OSBOURNE AND CBS: Your honors, we all agree that this death was tragic and unnecessary. But the plaintiffs delude themselves if they think that Mr. Osbourne and CBS bear any responsibility. The fact is that John McCollum was deeply troubled and alcoholic. He was responsible for his life—and for his own death. Next to the young man himself, of course, those who bear the greatest responsibility for his sad life and gruesome end are his parents, the plaintiffs in this case. Mr. Osbourne and CBS sympathize with the parents' bereavement, but not with their attempt to foist responsibility onto others.

If the plaintiffs' far-fetched foreseeability argument were the law—which it is not—every singer, writer, film and television producer would be at risk of several thousand lawsuits every year. Under their theory, a producer who made a bank robbery movie would be liable for every robbery that took place afterward, as would every author or singer who ever mentioned the subject. The First Amendment was written to ensure that we *do* have access to arts and entertainment, and to prohibit efforts at silencing artists with outlandish lawsuits. This death was never foreseeable and no jury should ever hear the case. ▰

Chapter Conclusion

We depend upon the law to give us a stable nation and economy, a fair society, a safe place to live and work. These worthy goals have occupied Anglo-Saxon kings and twenty-first-century lawmakers alike. But while law is a vital tool for crafting the society we want, there are no easy answers about how to create it. In a democracy, we all participate in the crafting. Legal rules control us, yet we create *them*. A working knowledge of the law can help build a successful career—and a solid democracy.

Chapter Review

1. There is no one source of the law. Our federal system of government means that law comes from a national government in Washington, D.C., and from 50 state governments.

2. The history of law foreshadows many current legal issues, including mediation, partnership liability, the jury system, the role of witnesses, the special value placed on land, the idea of precedent, and the difference between substantive and procedural law.

3. The primary sources of contemporary law are:

   - United States Constitution and state constitutions

   - Statutes, which are drafted by legislatures

   - Common law, which is the body of cases decided by judges, as they follow earlier cases, known as precedent; and

   - Administrative law, the rules and decisions made by federal and state administrative agencies.

4. Other sources of contemporary law include:

   - Treaties

   - Executive orders

5. Criminal law concerns behavior so threatening to society that it is outlawed altogether. Civil law deals with duties and disputes between parties, not outlawed behavior.

6. Substantive law defines the rights of people. Procedural law describes the processes for settling disputes.

7. Jurisprudence is concerned with the basic nature of law. Three theories of jurisprudence are:

   - Legal positivism: The law is what the sovereign says it is.

   - Natural law: An unjust law is no law at all.

   - Legal realism: Who enforces the law is more important than what the law says.

Practice Test

1. Can one person really understand all of the legal issues mentioned at the beginning of this chapter? For example, can a business executive know about insider trading and employment law and environmental law and tort law and all of the others? Will a court really hold one person to such knowledge?

2. Why does our law come from so many different sources?

3. The stock market crash of 1929 and the Great Depression that followed were caused in part because so many investors blindly put their money into stocks they knew nothing about. During the 1920s, it was often impossible for an investor to find out what a corporation was planning to do with its money, who was running the corporation, and many other vital things. Congress responded by passing the Securities Act of 1933, which required a corporation to divulge more information about itself before it could seek money for a new stock issue. What *kind* of law did Congress create? Explain the relationship between voters, Congress, and the law.

4. Union organizers at a hospital wanted to distribute leaflets to potential union members, but hospital rules prohibited leafletting in areas of patient care, hallways, cafeterias, and any areas open to the public. The National Labor Relations Board (NLRB) ruled that these restrictions violated the law and ordered the hospital to permit the activities in the cafeteria and coffee shop. The NLRB cannot create common law or statutory law. What kind of law was it creating?

5. Leslie Bergh and his two brothers, Milton and Raymond, formed a partnership to help build a fancy saloon and dance hall in Evanston, Wyoming. Later, Leslie met with his friend and drinking buddy, John Mills, and tricked Mills into investing in the saloon. Leslie did not tell Mills that no one else was investing cash or that the entire enterprise was already insol-

vent. Mills mortgaged his home, invested $150,000 in the saloon—and lost every penny of it. Mills sued all three partners for fraud. Milton and Raymond defended on the ground that they didn't commit the fraud, only Leslie did. The defendants lost. Was that fair? By holding them liable, what general idea did the court rely on? What Anglo-Saxon legal custom did the ruling resemble?

6. **ETHICS** Confucius did not esteem written laws, believing instead that good rulers were the best guarantee of justice. Does our legal system rely primarily on the rule of law or the rule of people? Which do you instinctively trust more? Legal realists argue that the "rule of law" is a misleading term. What point are they making, and how does it relate to Confucius's principles? Confucius himself was an extraordinarily wise man, full of wisdom about life and compassion for his fellow citizens. Since he was extraordinary, what does that tell us about other rulers by contrast? How does that affect Confucius's own views?

7. Tommy Parker may have been involved in some unsavory activities as an officer in a failed savings and loan institution. A federal agency, the Office of Thrift Supervision (OTS), ordered Tommy not to spend or waste any of his own assets while it was investigating him. Later, Tommy and his wife, Billie, got divorced and divided their property. On February 18, the OTS filed papers in court asking for an order that *Billie* not spend any of her assets. Billie received a copy of the papers on February 20, and the hearing took place on February 24, without Billie in attendance. The court ordered Billie not to spend any assets except for essential living expenses. Billie appealed, claiming that under court rules she was entitled to five days' notice before the hearing took place and that weekend days are not counted. She had had only two business days' notice. Assume that her counting of the days was correct (which it was). Explain the difference between procedural law and substantive law. Which type of law was Billie relying on? Should her appeal be granted?

8. Plaintiff Miss Universe, Inc., owns the trademark "Miss U.S.A." For decades, the company has produced the *Miss U.S.A.* beauty pageant seen by many millions of people in the United States. William Flesher and Treehouse Fun Ranch began to hold a nude beauty pageant in California. They called this the "Miss Nude U.S.A." pageant. Most of the contestants were from California; the majority of states were not represented in the contest. Miss Universe sued Flesher and Treehouse, claiming that the public would be confused and misled by the similar names. The company sought an *equitable remedy* in this lawsuit. What does "equitable" mean? What equitable remedy did Miss Universe seek? Should it win?

9. Jack and Jill go up a hill to fetch a pail of water. Jill heads back down with the water. Jack meets a stranger, who introduces herself as Katrina. Jack sells a kilo of cocaine to Katrina, who then mentions that she enjoys her job at the Drug Enforcement Agency. Jill, halfway down the hill, meets Freddy, a motorist whose car has overheated. Freddy is late for a meeting where he expects to make a $3 million profit; he's desperate for water for his car. He promises to pay Jill $500 tomorrow if she will give him the pail of water, which she does. The next day, Jack is in jail and Freddy refuses to pay for Jill's water. Explain the criminal law/civil law distinction and what it means to Jack and Jill. Who will do what to whom, with what results?

10. **YOU BE THE JUDGE WRITING PROBLEM** Should trials be televised? Here are a few arguments to add to those in the chapter. You be the judge. **Argument against Live Television Coverage:** We have tried this experiment and it has failed. Trials fall into two categories: those that create great public interest and those that do not. No one watches dull trials, so we do not need to broadcast them. The few that are interesting have all become circuses. Judges and lawyers have shown that they cannot resist the temptation to play to the camera. Trials are supposed to be about justice, not entertainment. If a citizen seriously wants to follow a case, she can do it by reading the daily newspaper. **Argument for Live Television Coverage:** It is true that some televised trials have been unseemly affairs, but that is the fault of the presiding judges, not the media. Indeed, one of the

virtues of television coverage is that millions of people now understand that we have a lot of incompetent people running our courtrooms. The proper response is to train judges to run a tight trial by prohibiting the grandstanding in which some lawyers may engage. Access to accurate information is the foundation on which a democracy is built, and we must not eliminate a source of valuable data just because some judges are ill-trained.

11. In his most famous novel, *The Red and the Black,* the French author Stendhal (1783–1842) wrote: "There is no such thing as 'natural law': this expression is nothing but old nonsense. Prior to laws, what is natural is only the strength of the lion, or the need of the creature suffering from hunger or cold, in short, need." What do you think?

12. **ROLE REVERSAL** Each Practice Test contains one Role Reversal feature, in which we challenge you to create your own exam question. The goal is to think creatively and accurately. Crafting questions is a good way to reinforce what you understand and recognize the areas you need to review. Your professor may ask you to submit the questions in writing or electronically or to prepare an overhead slide.

The question should be challenging enough that the average student will need to stop and think, but clear enough that there is only one answer. Useful questions can be formatted as essay, short answer, or multiple choice. Notice that some exam questions are very direct, while others require deeper analysis. Here are two examples. The first focuses on a definition.

Question: Legal positivism is:

(a) A decision by an appeals court *affirming* the trial court.

(b) A decision by an appeals court *reversing* a trial court.

(c) A theory of jurisprudence insisting that the law is what the sovereign says it is.

(d) A theory of law requiring that current cases be decided based on earlier decisions.

(e) A theory of law requiring that current cases be decided by a majority vote of the judges.

As you know, the correct answer is "c."

The next question demands that the student spot the issue of law involved (foreseeability) and correctly apply it to the facts provided.

Question: Marvin asks Sheila, a qualified auto mechanic, to fix his engine, which constantly stalls (stops) while driving. When Marvin returns, Sheila informs him that the engine is now "Perfect—runs like a top." Marvin drives home along Lonesome Highway. Suddenly, the car stalls. Sheila has not fixed it. Marvin pulls over and begins the long walk to the nearest telephone. A blimp flies overhead, advertising "Top" brand tires. Tragically, the blimp suddenly plummets to earth and explodes 20 feet from Marvin, seriously injuring him. Marvin sues Sheila. Sheila's best defense is that:

(a) The falling blimp is so bizarre that Sheila could never have foreseen it.

(b) Sheila made *reasonable efforts* to fix the engine.

(c) Marvin should have checked the engine himself.

(d) Marvin should have carried a cell phone with him in case of emergencies.

(e) Sheila is a qualified mechanic, and her work is presumptively sufficient.

The correct answer is "a." Notice that the same facts could be used as an essay question, simply by deleting the multiple-choice answers. Now it is your turn for Role Reversal: draft a multiple-choice question focusing on *legal realism*.

Internet Research Problem

Take a look at http://www.courttv.com. Find two current cases that interest you: one civil, one criminal. Explain the different roles played by each type of law, and summarize the issues in the respective cases.

You can find further practice problems in the Online Quiz at http://beatty.westbuslaw.com **or in the Study Guide that accompanies this text.**

Business Ethics and Social Responsibility

"Remember," Sheldon Baskin told himself, "you're the landlord. You're the bad guy."

So last fall, when his company sent letters to about 140 of his tenants—most of them poor and elderly—saying they might be forced out of their government-subsidized apartments, Mr. Baskin knew he would appear to be playing the part. He sympathized with his renters, he said, but felt he was in a predicament, too. Twenty years ago, he and his partners had signed a contract with the federal government, promising to build and maintain an apartment building for low-income Chicagoans on the city's north side. In exchange, Mr. Baskin and his investors received a steady stream of government-guaranteed rent.

But the contract for that building, known as Rienzi Plaza, was set to expire in the fall. Then he would be free to sell the building, convert it to condominiums, or start renting to unsubsidized tenants who would pay more rent. The implications of Mr. Baskin's dilemma reach far beyond Rienzi Plaza. About 125,000 units of federally subsidized apartments—known as Section 8 units, a reference to the relevant housing law—have been lost nationwide, as landlords chose not to renew their government contracts.

Demand for Section 8 apartments is rising, in part because big cities such as Chicago are tearing down their old public-housing projects and telling residents to find Section 8 apartments instead. Thousands of families are being forced to double up with relatives or turn to homeless shelters.

Market-rate tenants at Rienzi today pay up to $1,644 a month for two-bedroom apartments. Section 8 tenants pay 30 percent of their income, with certain adjustments, and the government supplies the rest. If forced to leave the building, the Section 8 tenants would have trouble finding anything they could afford in the same neighborhood.

Mr. Baskin's letter last fall caught a lot of tenants by surprise. "It was like the floor dropped out," said Arthur Haupt, a 79-year-old retired waiter who lives with his black cat, Max, in a tidy 650-square-foot apartment on the fifth floor. "At this age, you figure you finally found a measure of security for your remaining years—your few remaining years." Mr. Haupt works 20 hours a week, shelving books at Loyola University's law library, earning $6.95 an hour. He also gets social security and two modest pensions. His total income last year was $18,713. His monthly rent: $352.

The tenants and community groups began looking for a white knight—someone who would buy the building and preserve Rienzi's low-income housing. Two for-profit organizations that specialize in investing in "affordable" housing expressed interest in buying Rienzi, but neither made an immediate offer.

Meanwhile, Mr. Baskin asked government officials how much more rent they would pay if he extended his contract for five years. The government has changed several rules in recent years in an attempt to stop the exodus of Section 8 landlords. One of those changes makes it possible for owners to receive increased rent payments on buildings in affluent neighborhoods. Officials said they would have to hire an outside consultant to do a market study, a task that would take months—long past the deadline by which federal regulations require Mr. Baskin to announce his decision.[1] ◾

Business is an enormously powerful tool that corporate managers can use to accomplish many goals. They may wish to earn a good living, even to become wealthy, but they can also use their business skills to cure the ill, feed the hungry, entertain the bored, and in many other ways affect their community, their country, and their world.

This book is primarily about the impact of law on business. But law is only one set of rules that governs business; ethics is another. **Ethics is the study of how people ought to act.** Law and ethics are often in harmony. Most reasonable people agree that murder should be prohibited. But law and ethics are not always compatible. In some cases it might be *ethical* to commit an *illegal* act; in others it might be *unethical* to be *legal*. Here are two examples in which law and ethics might conflict:

> George Hart, a 75-year-old man confined to a wheelchair, robbed a bank in San Diego of $70 so that he could buy heart medicine. He entered a branch of the HomeFed Bank, where he had $4 in his account, and apologized while demanding $70 from a teller,

---

[1] Jonathan Eig, "Landlord's Dilemma: Help Poor Tenants or Seek More Profits," *The Wall Street Journal*, July 17, 2001, p. 1. Republished with permission of The Wall Street Journal; permission conveyed through the Copyright Clearance Center, Inc.

threatening to blow up the bank if she did not comply. Mr. Hart was arrested minutes later when he tried to buy a $69 bottle of heart medicine at a nearby drugstore. Mr. Hart said he "hated to have to go to this extreme," but insisted he had tried every other way to find money to buy the medicine.[2]

In 1963, Martin Luther King, Jr., was arrested in Birmingham, Alabama, for leading illegal sit-ins and marches to protest laws that discriminated against African Americans. When eight local clergymen criticized his activities, King offered this defense:

> We know through painful experience that freedom is never voluntarily given by the oppressor; it must be demanded by the oppressed. . . . Perhaps it is easy for those who have never felt the stinging darts of segregation to say "Wait.". . . [W]hen you see the vast majority of your 20 million Negro brothers smothering in an air-tight cage of poverty in the midst of an affluent society; when you suddenly find your tongue twisted as you seek to explain to your six-year-old daughter why she can't go to the public amusement park that has just been advertised on television, and see tears welling up when she is told that Funtown is closed to colored children. . . . [W]hen you take a cross-country drive and find it necessary to sleep night after night in the uncomfortable corners of your automobile because no motel will accept you. . . . How can [we] advocate breaking some laws and obeying others? The answer lies in the fact that there are two types of laws: just and unjust. I agree with St. Augustine that "an unjust law is not law at all."[3]

Could one argue in the case of the bank robber that his actions, while illegal, were ethical? Would the argument be stronger if he had been stealing the money to help someone else? In the case of Martin Luther King, Jr., would it be reasonable to conclude not only that breaking the law was ethical, but also that *obeying* the law would have been *unethical*? Were the eight clergymen who criticized King behaving unethically by upholding these odious laws?

The other chapters of this book focus on legal issues, but this chapter concentrates on ethics. In all of the examples in this chapter, the activities are *legal*, but are they *ethical*?

Why Bother with Ethics?

Business schools teach students how to maximize the profitability of an enterprise, large or small. Does ethical behavior maximize profitability? Some people argue that, in the *long run*, ethical behavior does indeed pay. But they must mean the very long run, because to date there is little evidence that ethical behavior necessarily pays financially, either in the short or the long run.

For example, when a fire destroyed the Malden Mills factory in Lawrence, Massachusetts, its 70-year-old owner, Aaron Feuerstein, could have shut down the business, collected the insurance money, and sailed off into retirement. But a layoff of the factory's 3,000 employees would have been a major economic blow to the region. So instead Feuerstein kept the workers on the payroll while he rebuilt the factory. These actions gained him a national reputation as a business hero.

---

[2] "Bank Robber in Wheelchair Has an Alibi: His Medicine," *The New York Times*, Jan. 18, 1991, p. A16.
[3] Martin Luther King, Jr., "Letter from Birmingham Jail," *The Christian Century*, June 12, 1963.

Many consumers promised to buy more of the company's patented Polartec fabric. In the end, however, the story did not have a fairy-tale ending: five years after the fire, Malden Mills filed bankruptcy papers. The company was not able to pay off the loans it had incurred to keep the business going.

In contrast, unethical companies may perform well financially. The Morgan Fun Shares fund purchases stock in tobacco, alcohol, and gambling companies on the theory that money can be made from vices, particularly if other investors shun the companies. Even for individuals, unethical behavior is no bar to financial success. The first antitrust laws in America were designed, at least in part, to restrain John D. Rockefeller's unethical activities. Yet four generations later, his name is still synonymous with wealth, and his numerous heirs can live comfortably on their inheritance from him.[4]

If ethical behavior does not necessarily pay and unethical behavior sometimes does, why bother with ethics?

SOCIETY AS A WHOLE BENEFITS FROM ETHICAL BEHAVIOR

John Akers, the former chairman of IBM, argues that, without ethical behavior, a society cannot be economically competitive. He puts it this way:

> Ethics and competitiveness are inseparable. We compete as a society. No society anywhere will compete very long or successfully with people stabbing each other in the back; with people trying to steal from each other; with everything requiring notarized confirmation because you can't trust the other fellow; with every little squabble ending in litigation; and with government writing reams of regulatory legislation, tying business hand and foot to keep it honest. That is a recipe not only for headaches in running a company, it is a recipe for a nation to become wasteful, inefficient, and noncompetitive. There is no escaping this fact: the greater the measure of mutual trust and confidence in the ethics of a society, the greater its economic strength.[5]

PEOPLE FEEL BETTER WHEN THEY BEHAVE ETHICALLY

Every businessperson has many opportunities to be dishonest. Consider how one person felt when he resisted temptation:

> Occasionally a customer forgot to send a bill for materials shipped to us for processing. . . . It would have been so easy to rationalize remaining silent. After all, didn't they deserve to lose because of their inefficiency? However, upon instructing our staff to inform the parties of their errors, I found them eager to do so. They were actually bursting with pride. . . . Our honesty was beneficial in subtle ways. The "inefficient" customer remained loyal for years. . . . [O]ur highly moral policy had a marvelously beneficial effect on our employees. Through the years, many an employee visited my office to let me know that they liked working for a "straight" company.[6]

---

[4] Chapter 19, on antitrust, discusses Rockefeller's career at greater length.
[5] David Grier, "Confronting Ethical Dilemmas," unpublished manuscript of remarks at the Royal Bank of Canada, Sept. 19, 1989.
[6] Hugh Aaron, "Doing the Right Thing in Business," *The Wall Street Journal*, June 21, 1993, p. A10.

Profitability is generally not what motivates managers to care about ethics. Managers want to feel good about themselves and the decisions they have made; they want to sleep at night. Their decisions—to lay off employees, install safety devices in cars, burn a cleaner fuel—affect peoples' lives. When two researchers asked businesspeople why they cared about ethics, the answers had little to do with the profitability:

> The businesspeople we interviewed set great store on the regard of their family, friends, and the community at large. They valued their reputations, not for some nebulous financial gain but because they took pride in their good names.[7]

The Web site http://www.yourtruehero.org offers examples of ordinary people who have inspired others with their ethical behavior.

UNETHICAL BEHAVIOR CAN BE VERY COSTLY

Unethical behavior is a risky business strategy—it may lead to disaster. An engaged couple made a reservation, and put down a $1,500 deposit, to hold their wedding reception at a New Hampshire restaurant. Tragically, the bride died of asthma four months before the wedding. Invoking the terms of the contract, the restaurant owner refused to return the couple's deposit. In a letter to the groom, he admitted, "Morally, I would of course agree that the deposit should be returned." When newspapers reported this story, customers deserted the restaurant and it was forced into bankruptcy—over a $1,500 disagreement.[8] Unethical behavior does not always damage a business, but it certainly has the potential of destroying a company overnight. So why take the risk?

Even if unethical behavior does not devastate a business, it can cause other subtler damage. In one survey, a majority of those questioned said that they had witnessed unethical behavior in their workplace and that this behavior had reduced productivity, job stability, and profits. Unethical behavior in an organization creates a cynical, resentful, and unproductive workforce.

So why bother with ethics? Because society benefits when managers behave ethically. Because ethical managers have happier, more satisfying lives. And because unethical behavior can destroy a business faster than a snake can bite.

What Is Ethical Behavior?

It is one thing to decide, in theory, that being ethical is good; in practice, it can be much more difficult to make the right decisions. Supreme Court Justice Potter Stewart once said that he could not define pornography, but he knew it when he saw it. Many people feel the same way about ethics—that somehow, instinctively, they know what is right and wrong. In real life, however, ethical dilemmas are often not black and white, but many shades of gray. The purpose of this section is to analyze the following ethics checklist as an aid to managers in making tough decisions:

---

[7] Amar Bhide and Howard H. Stevenson, "Why Be Honest if Honesty Doesn't Pay?" *Harvard Business Review*, Sept.–Oct. 1990, pp. 121–129, at 127.
[8] John Milne, "N.H. Restaurant Goes Bankrupt in Wake of Wedding Refund Flap," *Boston Globe*, Sept. 9, 1994, p. 25.

- What are the facts?
- What are the critical issues?
- Who are the stakeholders?
- What are the alternatives?
- What are the ethical implications of each alternative?
    - Is it legal?
    - How would it look in the light of day?
    - What are the consequences?
    - Does it violate important values?
    - Does it violate the Golden Rule?
    - Is it just?
    - Has the process been fair?
- Is more than one alternative right?
    - Which values are in conflict?
    - Which of these values are most important?
    - Can you find an alternative that is consistent with your values?

ANALYZING THE ETHICS CHECKLIST

What Are the Facts?

Although this question seems obvious, people often forget in the heat of battle to listen to (and, more importantly, to *hear*) all the different viewpoints. Instead of relying on hearsay and rumor, it is crucial to discover the facts, firsthand, from the people involved. It may be easy to condemn a bank robber, until learning the money was needed to buy medicine.

What Are the Critical Issues?

In analyzing ethical dilemmas, expand your thinking to include *all* the important issues. Avoid a narrow focus that encompasses only one or two aspects. In the case of the New Hampshire restaurant that refused to refund a deposit, the owner focused on the narrow legal issue. His interpretation of the *contract* was correct. But if the owner had expanded his thinking to include consideration for his customers, he might have reached a different decision.

Who Are the Stakeholders?

Stakeholders are all the people potentially affected by the decision. That list might include subordinates, bosses, shareholders, suppliers, customers, members of the community in which the business operates, society as a whole, or even more remote stakeholders, such as future generations. The interests of these stakeholders often conflict. Current shareholders may benefit from a company's decision to manufacture a product that contributes to global warming, while future generations are left to contend with a potential environmental nightmare.

What Are the Alternatives?

The next step is to list the reasonable alternatives. A creative manager may find a clever solution that is a winner for everyone. What alternatives might be available to Sheldon Baskin, the landlord who faced a dilemma in this chapter's opening scenario?

What Are the Ethical Implications of Each Alternative?

Is the Alternative Legal?   Illegal may not always be synonymous with unethical, but, as a general rule, you need to think long and hard about the ethics of any illegal activities.

How Would the Alternative Look in the Light of Day?   If your activities were reported on the evening news, how would you feel? Proud? Embarrassed? Horrified? Undoubtedly, sexual harassment would be virtually eliminated if people thought that their parents, spouse, or partner would shortly see a video replay of the offending behavior.

What Are the Consequences of This Alternative?   Ask yourself: Am I hurting anyone by this decision? Which alternative will cause the greatest good (or the least harm) to the most people? For example, you would like to fire an incompetent employee. That decision will clearly have adverse consequences for him. But the other employees in your division will benefit and so will the shareholders of your company. Overall, your decision will cause more good than harm.

You should look with a particularly critical eye if an alternative benefits you while harming others. Suppose that you become CEO of a company whose headquarters are located in a distant suburb. You would like to move the headquarters closer to your home to cut your commuting time. Of course, such a decision would be expensive for shareholders and inconvenient for other employees. Do you simply impose your will on the company or consider the consequences for everyone?

This approach to decision making was first developed by two nineteenth-century English philosophers, Jeremy Bentham and John Stuart Mill. It is called **utilitarianism** because Bentham and Mill argued that all decisions should be evaluated according to how much **utility** they create. Some commentators have criticized this approach on practical grounds—benefit and harm are difficult to measure. Others also argue that not all utility is equal. A band of robbers may receive more benefit from stealing money than the victim suffers harm, but most people would nonetheless argue that the decision to steal is wrong. Despite these criticisms, it is wise at least to consider the costs and benefits of a decision.

Does the Alternative Violate Important Values?   In addition to consequences, consider fundamental values. It is possible to commit an act that does not harm anyone else, but is still the wrong thing to do. Suppose, for example, that you are away from home and have the opportunity to engage in a temporary sexual liaison. You are absolutely certain that your spouse will never find out and your partner for the night will have no regrets or guilt. There would be no negative consequences, but you believe that infidelity is wrong, *regardless of the consequences*, so you resist temptation.

Some people question whether, as a diverse, heterogeneous society (not to mention, world), we have common values. But throughout history, and across many different cultures, common values do appear. The following values are almost universal:

- *Consideration* means being aware of and concerned about other people's feelings, desires, and needs. The considerate person is able to imagine how he would feel in someone else's place.

- *Courage* is the strength to act in the face of fear and danger. Courage can require dramatic action (saving a buddy on a battlefield) or quiet strength (doing what you think is right, despite opposition from your boss).

- *Integrity* means being sincere, honest, reliable, and loyal. If you have integrity, you do not criticize others behind their back or take credit for their ideas and efforts.

- *Self-control* is the ability to resist temptation. The person with self-control does not drink or eat too much, party too hard, watch too much television, or spend too much money.

Although reasonable people may disagree about a precise list of important values, most would agree that values matter. Try compiling your own list of values and then check it periodically to see if you are living up to it in your business and personal life.

Does the Alternative Violate the Golden Rule? We all know the Golden Rule: do unto others as you would have them do unto you. If one of the alternatives you are considering would be particularly unpleasant when done to you, reconsider.

Immanuel Kant, an eighteenth-century German philosopher, took the Golden Rule one step further with a concept he called the **categorical imperative**. According to Kant, you should not do something unless you would be willing for everyone else to do it, too (and not just to you). Imagine that you could cheat on an exam without getting caught. You might gain some short-term benefit—a higher grade. But what would happen if everyone cheated? The professor would have to make the exams harder or curve everyone's grade down. If your school developed a reputation for cheating, you might not be able to find a job after graduation. Cheating works only if most people are honest. To take advantage of everyone else's honesty is contemptible.

Is the Alternative Just? Are you respecting individual rights such as liberty (privacy, free speech, and religious freedom), welfare (employment, housing, food, education), and equality? Would it be just to fire an employee because her political views differ from your own?

Has the Process Been Fair? Unequal outcomes are acceptable, provided they are the result of a fair process. At the end of a poker game, some players have won and others lost, but no one can complain that the result was unfair, unless players cheated. In a business context, a fair process means applying the same set of rules to everyone. If three of your subordinates are vying for the same promotion, it would be unfair to let one state her case to you but not the others.

Is More Than One Alternative Right?

Thus far, the ethics checklist has served two purposes. It helps to clarify the issues at stake. It also filters out decisions that are downright wrong. Have you considered lying to a customer about product specifications? For a start, such an action violates principles of integrity, not to mention the Golden Rule. Nor would you want your activity to be revealed on the front page of the local newspaper.

Often, the most difficult decisions arise not in cases of right versus wrong but in situations of right versus right.[9] President Harry Truman's decision to drop atomic bombs on two Japanese cities is a classic example of right versus right. He argued that if he had not ended the war by using nuclear weapons, more Americans and Japanese would have died during a land invasion. Looking simply at the consequences, he concluded that the terrible suffering by the Japanese people was justified because, ultimately, fewer people died overall. At the same time, Truman's decision violated the Golden Rule and Kant's categorical imperative. Indeed, since the end of World War II, the United States has worked hard to ensure that no one else ever deploys nuclear weapons. The ethics checklist presents no clear-cut answer. In the end, Truman decided that the most right (or least wrong) choice was to end the war quickly.

Nuclear weapons make a dramatic example, but what about a more typical business decision? AT&T adopted a policy of cutting costs to maximize its stock price. To implement this policy, the company laid off 40,000 people, despite record profits. Even as workers suffered, shareholders benefited because the company's stock price rose in response to the layoff announcement. But is stock price the only issue? Does the company have an obligation to protect employee jobs? Is one right more important than another?

Which Values Are in Conflict?　There are many ways to justify a decision to lay off workers, even 40,000 of them. If managers avoid layoffs, profits suffer, stock prices fall, companies merge, and executives lose their own jobs. In business school and on the job, managers learn how to analyze, compete, and win. Competing— and winning—are important. But what about other values, such as compassion and caring? Do the individual people affected by this decision matter, too?

Which of These Values Are Most Important?　Suppose that, growing up, you had seen family members or neighbors suffering through bouts of unemployment. That experience might have taught you that compassion is a high priority. Managers must determine which values are important in their own lives.

Can You Find an Alternative That Is Consistent with Your Values?　The decision you make not only determines the kind of person you are now, but also sets your course for the future. Can you reach a decision that is consistent with the kind of person you are or want to be? Instead of announcing massive layoffs, some companies offer generous severance packages, retraining programs, and other voluntary methods of reducing the workforce. Shareholders may receive less benefit, but employees suffer less harm.

The following article discusses the importance of values in achieving personal fulfillment.

ECONOMICS & THE LAW

Once upon a time, there was a game that Wall Street traders and investment bankers liked to play—often on the commute home to Greenwich, Connecticut, or Short Hills, New Jersey, after a particularly profitable or trying day. It was called

---

[9] For a thoughtful discussion of right versus right, see Joseph L. Badaracco, Jr., *Defining Moments: When Managers Must Choose between Right and Right* (Boston: Harvard Business School Press, 1997).

"What's Your Number?" The answer—in millions of dollars—was the amount you had to have socked away before ditching your high-pressure job and leading the life you really wanted.

The breathtaking part of this game was not the numbers. And it was not that the question was asked by men and women in their twenties, thirties, and forties. No, the remarkable part of this diversion was that the number kept growing. There never seemed to be a high enough answer to "How much is enough?"

And there was a price to pay for all this money. "If your sense of accomplishment is all wrapped up in a bank account, it's going to affect your relationships," said Dr. Stephen Goldbart, a co-director of the Money, Meaning & Choices Institute, a consulting and training firm in San Francisco. "Absorption with money is going to make the human side of you unavailable. Our society has mixed up what it means to feel fulfilled and successful with making a lot of money."

As you might have guessed, this fable seems to have a moral. After the World Trade Center attacks, many of Wall Street's gold hoarders say they now know what is really important: family, friends, and health. But meaningful work and personal fulfillment can't be ordered like pizza. They don't come conveniently attached to certain jobs or careers. The hardest thing about abandoning money as a scorecard for success and fulfillment is that there is no handy replacement, no way to advertise your newfound virtue. The second hardest thing is realizing that if your fulfillment needs to be advertised, you have simply traded one game for another.[10]

Applying the Ethics Checklist: Making Decisions

An organization has responsibilities to customers, employees, shareholders, and society generally, both here and overseas. Employees also have responsibilities to their organizations. The purpose of this section is to apply the ethics checklist to actual business dilemmas. The checklist does not lead to one particular solution; rather it is a method to use in thinking through ethics problems. The goal is for you to reach a decision that satisfies you.

ORGANIZATION'S RESPONSIBILITY TO SOCIETY

Facts.   In the United States, teenagers routinely list alcohol commercials among their favorite advertisements. Adolescents who frequently see ads for alcohol are more likely to believe that drinkers are attractive, athletic, and successful. They are also more likely to drink, drink excessively, and drink in hazardous situations such as driving a car.

While Secretary of Health and Human Services, Louis W. Sullivan publicly denounced the test marketing of Uptown, a high-tar cigarette targeted at African Americans. He called it "contemptible that the tobacco industry has sought to increase their market" among minorities because this population was "already bearing more than its fair share of smoking-related illness and mortality." More pointed was comedian Jay Leno's jest that R. J. Reynolds named the cigarette Uptown "because the word 'Genocide' was already taken."[11]

---

[10] Ellen Sprague, "When Numbers Cease to Matter," *The New York Times*, Oct. 7, 2001, §4, p. 8. Copyright © 2001 by The New York Times Co. Reprinted by permission.

[11] Richard W. Pollay, Jung S. Lee, and David Carter-Whitney, "Separate, But Not Equal: Racial Segmentation in Cigarette Advertising," *Journal of Advertising*, Mar. 1992, vol. 21, no. 1, p. 45.

A promotion for Request Jeans shows a man pinning a naked woman against a shower wall. In Canada, an advertisement features childlike model Kate Moss lying naked on a couch. Above the couch is a picture of the product being promoted—Calvin Klein's Obsession for Men. In England, an ad for a stereo shows a picture of a woman with these words, "She's terrific in bed, she's witty and intelligent, but she didn't have a Linn hi-fi. Her sister did and I married her sister."

In Peru, a television commercial features Africans who are ready to devour white tourists until diverted by the offer of Nabisco pudding. In another Latin American ad, a man compares the thickness of Goodyear tires to the lips of his black partner.

Critical Issues. What are the obligations of advertising executives and marketing managers to those who see their ads? Is it ethical to sell jeans by glorifying rape? Are men more likely to commit rape as a result of seeing one of these advertisements? Is it ethical to entice teenagers into drinking or African Americans into smoking? An advertising executive asserts that Latin American audiences find racial stereotypes amusing. Does that justify racist ads?

Stakeholders. Ad designers are primarily responsible to their firms and the firms' clients. After all, designers are paid to sell product, not to make the world a better place. But what about the people who see the advertisements? Do the designers have any responsibility to them? Or to society as a whole?

Alternatives. Firms have at least four alternatives in dealing with issues of ethics in advertising. They can:

- Ignore ethics and simply strive to create promotions that sell the most product, whatever the underlying message

- Try, in a general way, to minimize racism, sexism, and other exploitation

- Include, as part of the development process, a systematic, focused review of the underlying messages contained in their advertisements; or

- Refuse to create any ads that are potentially demeaning, insensitive, or dangerous, recognizing that such a stand may lead to a loss of clients.

Ethical Implications. All of these alternatives are perfectly legal. And, far from the ad executives being embarrassed if the ads see the light of day, the whole purpose of ads is to be seen. As for the consequences, the ads may help clients sell their products. But the ads may also harm those who see them by encouraging, among other things, drinking, smoking, sexual assault, racism, and promiscuity. A manager might question whether these ads violate fundamental values. Are they showing consideration for others? Do they encourage self-control? As for the Golden Rule, how would an advertising executive feel about an ad in which he was being sexually assaulted? Or a promotion in which he was assumed to be less valuable than a stereo system? Are these ads just? Do they violate principles of equality? Is the process by which they have been created fair? Have those who may be adversely affected by them had an opportunity to be heard?

Right versus Right. Most people using an ethics checklist would agree that an advertisement making fun of a black man's thick lips is offensive and wrong. But what about subtler issues? In a country with rampant anorexia among teenage girls, is it ethical to run ads with emaciated girls as role models? What about ads for lottery tickets? These tickets are largely purchased by those who can least afford to gamble. If you worked in an advertising agency or marketing department, you might feel a strong sense of loyalty to your company. But what about consideration for those who could be harmed by your ads? You must decide which values are important to you and look for solutions that enable you to live by these values.

Some of the ads described in this section appear stunningly tasteless. They could have been worse, however. The Ad Graveyard (http://www.zeldman.com/classics) offers examples of proposed ads that never saw the light of day, for very obvious reasons.

ORGANIZATION'S RESPONSIBILITY TO ITS CUSTOMERS

In this chapter's opening scenario, Sheldon Baskin faces a dilemma: now that his contract with the federal government has expired, he can raise rents by as much as 500 percent at Rienzi Plaza, home to 140 poor and elderly tenants. Moving would be difficult for the elderly tenants, especially since they are unlikely to find another apartment in the neighborhood. They might end up in homeless shelters. But what about Baskin's partners? Is it fair to them if he decides to subsidize the rents of low-income tenants? Does he owe his partners the highest return on their investment?

What would you do if you were Sheldon Baskin? He is concerned about several important stakeholders—his partners and his tenants. What about the community? Does it benefit from having elderly members? Will the community be harmed if some of these elderly become homeless? How will Baskin feel about himself if he puts these elderly tenants out on the street? Or if *The Wall Street Journal* runs a front-page article about his eviction plans? On the other hand, could he argue that it is the government's responsibility to house the poor and elderly? What decision would be best for Baskin? The tenants? His partners? The community?

ORGANIZATION'S RESPONSIBILITY TO ITS EMPLOYEES

Which deal would you rather have? *Non Profit 4.*

- *Plan A:* Your company has a 401(k) pension plan. Federal law permits you to contribute a certain amount tax free each year. You can then invest that money in a choice of mutual funds. In addition, for every dollar you put in, your employer will contribute a dollar of company stock. However, you cannot sell this company stock until you are 50 years old. The good news is that if the stock market—and your company—prosper, your retirement years will indeed be golden. The downside is that if the stock market or your company declines, you could be like one of the tenants in Rienzi Plaza, unable to pay your rent.

- *Plan B:* The amount of your pension is guaranteed by the company, regardless of how the market performs. This guarantee is backed up by a federal agency. In addition, as part of your annual bonus, you are given company stock that you can sell at any time. Moreover, when you invest in your special 401(k) plan, the company guarantees a minimum annual return of 12 percent.

 Define Benefit Pension

Enron Corp. offered Plan A to its rank-and-file employees; Plan B was reserved for top executives. At one point, 60 percent of the assets in the Plan A 401(k) was invested in Enron stock. As this stock plummeted in value from $80 a share to under $1, many employees were unable to sell out because they had not yet turned 50. Even worse, as the stock price sank, the company imposed a month-long "blackout" prohibiting all employees from selling any stock in the 401(k) while a new plan administrator took over. Less than a month after the blackout ended, the company filed for bankruptcy. As a result, the 401(k) plans lost $1.3 billion of their $2.1 billion worth.

During a time when most employees were not permitted to sell Enron stock, top executives of the company sold shares with a market value of more than $600 million. The CEO, Kenneth Lay, unloaded Enron stock worth $28 million (in addition to hundreds of millions worth of Enron stock he had sold earlier, after being warned of the company's financial troubles).

The fate of Enron raises two issues:

1. **Equality of treatment within the company.** Is it ethical for top executives to set up two such different pension/savings plans for company employees? Should top executives be entitled to guaranteed retirement pay while rank-and-filers are at the mercy of stock market fluctuations?

    Alternatively, could one argue that offering top executives a better pension is no more unfair than paying them higher wages? What difference does it make if the difference in pay between the top and bottom takes the form of higher current compensation, a better pension, or a fancier executive dining room?

2. **The ethics of pension plans versus 401(k) plans.** A traditional pension plan (such as top Enron officials had) guarantees a certain annual payment for the life of the employee. Under federal law, companies must set aside money to meet these promises. If, for whatever reason, the company fails to do so, a federal agency guarantees the payments (up to certain limits). These traditional pension plans are expensive for companies to operate because the company must fund the plan primarily with cash, not company stock. To avoid this financial commitment, many companies have switched to 401(k) plans, where all the risk is borne by the employee.

    Supporters of 401(k) plans argue that these plans are better than nothing, which is what companies would offer if 401(k) plans were not available. These plans are good for employees: the matching employer contributions entice many workers into saving money that they might otherwise just spend. And the plans are good for employers: a company can meet its obligations with transfers of company stock, which are much cheaper to make than the cash payments required by traditional plans. In some circumstances companies even receive extra tax breaks for contributing their own stock to their 401(k) plans. Moreover, companies like having their stock in the friendly hands of employees. The younger employees whom companies want to attract rarely object to a 401(k) pension plan because they do not appreciate the significant disadvantages (and companies have not been eager to educate them).

After the Enron disaster, many proposals were made to modify the rules on 401(k) plans. As this book goes to press, it is not clear which, if any, of these changes will be adopted. But that is beside the point for this chapter. Regardless of what the law permits, what will you do when you become a top executive in a large company? Will you do more than meet the minimum requirements of the pension laws? Should the employee plan look like yours? Does your obligation to shareholders require you to save money by offering the cheapest possible pension plan to employees? Would a generous pension plan for all employees benefit the company by attracting valuable workers or harm the company by decreasing its profits?

ORGANIZATION'S RESPONSIBILITY TO ITS SHAREHOLDERS

Ford Motor Company was founded by William C. Ford, Jr.'s great-grandfather, Henry. The younger Ford is an avid environmentalist and also head of the company that bears his name. He shares the concern of many environmentalists that automobile exhaust contributes to global warming. Ford Motor recently announced that it would increase the fuel economy of its sport-utility vehicles (SUVs) by 25 percent (about five miles per gallon). This decision comes shortly after Congress, partly in response to lobbying by automobile manufacturers, refused to increase national fuel economy standards.

Ford Motor has been a leader in the development of SUVs, which comprise about a fifth of its output each year. Because these heavy cars are gas inefficient, Ford has barely been able to meet existing federal standards. To achieve the higher fuel economy it has announced, the company will make more auto parts out of lighter aluminum and will redesign the SUV engines. The cost of implementing these changes could be substantial, but the company has decided not to pass the costs on to consumers. The plan is controversial within the company itself, because some insiders believe that consumers would prefer more powerful cars to more gas efficient ones.

Milton Friedman, a Nobel Laureate in economics, famously observed, "The one and only social responsibility of business is to increase its profits."[12] Is it wrong for companies to be socially responsible? When a company donates funds to support a reading program in the local public schools, encourages employees to spend company time raising funds for the United Way, or builds a cleaner factory than the law requires, shareholders ultimately foot the bill for these initiatives. If you were a shareholder of Ford Motor Company, would you support the fuel efficiency initiative? What if you do not share a concern about global warming? Perhaps you would prefer to earn higher returns on your stock so that you could give money to other projects you consider more compelling (finding an AIDS vaccine, for example). Should William Ford, who inherited his company stock, have the right to spend company funds to support his pet projects? If the air needs to be cleaner or the schools richer, why shouldn't private donors or public institutions be responsible, not one company's shareholders?[13]

Ford officials argue that their fuel economy initiative may be profitable—it might increase sales enough to make up for the lower profit per car. Moreover, an environmentally friendly image may help sales on all of its cars, not just SUVs. By voluntarily increasing its own fuel standards, Ford may head off tighter federal regulation.

---

[12] Milton Friedman, "The Social Responsibility of Business Is to Increase Its Profits," *The New York Times Magazine*, Sept. 13, 1970, p. 32.

[13] See, for example, David Henderson, "Misguided Virtue: False Notions of Corporate Social Responsibility," Hobart Paper 142, Institute of Economic Affairs, London, cited in *The Economist*, Nov. 17, 2001, p. 70.

What would you do if you were William C. Ford, Jr.? How would you feel if you were a Ford shareholder?

 Was Ford successful in its efforts to improve the fuel economy of its SUVs? Did other automobile manufacturers (here and abroad) followed Ford's lead? Did Ford sales increase enough to offset the cost of making these design changes? Did Ford's stock price rise or fall after the company announced its intention to increase fuel economy? ▪

ORGANIZATION'S RESPONSIBILITY OVERSEAS

An American company's ethical obligations do not end at the border. What ethical duties does an American manager owe to stakeholders in countries where the culture and economic circumstances are very different?

Here is a typical story from Guatemala:

> My father left home a long time ago. My mother supported me and my five brothers and sisters by selling tortillas and corn. Our house was a tin shack on the side of the road. We were crowded with all of us in one room, especially when it rained and the roof and sides leaked. There were hundreds of squatters in the neighborhood, but one day the police came and cleared us all out. The owners of the land said we couldn't come back unless we paid rent. How could we afford that? I was 12 and my mother said it was time for me to work. But most people won't hire children. Lots of other kids shine shoes or beg, but I heard that the maquila [clothing factory] was willing to hire children if we would work as hard as older people.
>
> I can keep up with the grown-ups. We work from 6:00 in the morning to 6:30 at night, with half an hour break at noon. We have no other breaks the whole rest of the day. If I don't work fast enough, they hit me, not too hard, and threaten to fire me. Sometimes, if there is too much work to do, they'll lock the doors and not let us out until everything is finished.
>
> I'm always really tired at the end of the day and in the morning, too. But I earn $30 a week and without that money, we would not have enough to eat. My mother hopes all of my brothers and sisters can get jobs in the factory, too.
>
> Of course, I'd rather be in school where I could wear a uniform and have friends. Then I could get a job as a clerk at the medical clinic. I would find people's files and tell them how long before the doctor could see them.

This description paints a distasteful picture indeed: children being beaten as they work 12-hour days. Should American companies (and consumers) buy goods that are produced in sweatshop factories? Jeffrey Sachs, a leading economist and adviser to developing nations, says, "My concern is not that there are too many sweatshops but that there are too few."[14] Why would he support sweatshops and child labor?

Historically, poor children have worked. Indeed, for many people and for many centuries, the point of having children was to create a supply of free labor to help support the family. In England in 1860, almost 40 percent of 14-year-old boys worked, and that was not just a few hours at Burger Box, but more likely 60 hours a week. That percentage is higher than in Africa or India today. For a child

---

[14] Allen R. Meyerson, "In Principle, A Case for More 'Sweatshops,'" *The New York Times*, June 22, 1997, p. E5.

in a desperately poor family, the choice is not work or school, it is work, starvation, or prostitution. (For a history of sweatshops in America, work your way over to http://americanhistory.si.edu/sweatshops/.)

Industrialization has always been the first stepping stone out of dire poverty—it was in England, it is now in the Third World. Eventually, higher productivity leads to higher wages. In China, factory managers have complained that their employees want to work even *longer* hours to earn more money. The results in China have been nothing short of remarkable—if each of China's provinces were counted as a separate country, then 20 of the world's fastest growing economies between 1978 and 1995 would have been Chinese. During the Industrial Revolution in England, per capita output doubled in 58 years. In China, it has taken only 10 years.

During the past 50 years, Taiwan and South Korea welcomed sweatshops. During the same period, India resisted what it perceived to be foreign exploitation. Although all three countries started at the same economic level, Taiwan and South Korea today have much lower levels of infant mortality and much higher levels of education than India.[15]

When governments or customers try to force Third World factories to pay higher wages, the factory owners typically either relocate to lower wage countries or mechanize, thereby reducing the need for workers. In either case, the local economy suffers.

The difference, however, between the twenty-first and the nineteenth centuries is that now there are wealthy countries able to help their poorer neighbors. In the nineteenth century, England was among the richest countries, so it was on its own to solve its economic problems. Is America ethically obligated to assist the people around the world who live in abject poverty? Already, owing to pressure from activists, many companies have introduced better conditions in their factories. Workers are less likely to be beaten. They can go to the bathroom without asking permission. They might even receive rudimentary medical care. Manufacturing processes use fewer dangerous chemicals. Factories are cleaner, with better lighting and more ventilation. But hours are still long and wages low.

Companies argue that higher wages lead to increased prices, which, in their turn, drive away customers. Many of these sweatshops produce clothing. As a consumer, how much would be you willing to pay in higher clothing prices to eliminate sweatshops and child labor? As a taxpayer, how much are you willing to pay in taxes to subsidize Third World incomes so that sweatshops and child labor are no longer necessary?

EMPLOYEES' RESPONSIBILITY TO THEIR ORGANIZATION

Joya is the head of the personal insurance division of a large insurance company. She is one of the few women in her industry to reach such a high level. Six months before, she was almost promoted to vice president, but she lost out to Bill. He is now her boss, and she is determined to make the best of it. She and other department heads have an annual meeting with Bill to award raises and bonuses to all the mid-level managers in their departments. At this year's meeting, they will also

---

[15] The data in this and the preceding paragraph are from Nicholas D. Kristof and Sheryl WuDunn, "Two Cheers for Sweatshops," *The New York Times*, Sunday Magazine, Sept. 24, 2000, p. 70.

discuss who should be promoted to head the marine insurance division. This decision is important to the firm because the marine division is large and profitable. The decision is also important to other department heads because they all work closely together. One difficult person can make everyone's life miserable. The promotion will mean a substantial raise to the person chosen.

In Joya's opinion, Ichiro is the most qualified person for this position. However, she knows that Bill will not support him. In Bill's view, Ichiro has two strikes against him: he is Japanese and a relatively recent immigrant to the United States. The CEO of the company has taken Ichiro with him several times on trips to Japan to explore the possibility of entering the Japanese market. Bill resents what he perceives as special treatment for Ichiro.

Although Joya is well aware of Bill's biases, she is nonetheless astonished by his behavior at the meeting. When Ichiro's name comes up as a potential candidate for promotion, Bill announces that the middle managers in the marine insurance division strongly object to Ichiro because of his drinking problem. Joya knows that this is all nonsense—Ichiro does not have a drinking problem, and the mid-managers in his department think he would be a terrific choice. In her view Bill is outright lying.

Based on Bill's false information, the other department heads agree that the promotion should go to Jim, who happens to be a friend of Bill's. Joya knows that Jim is unpopular in his division because of his harsh, demanding style. She thinks that his appointment as department head will be disastrous. At the end of the meeting, a satisfied Bill says that he will report the sense of the meeting to the CEO. He is confident that Jim will get the job.

Joya knows the CEO (they exchange pleasantries when passing in the hallways), but they have no regularly scheduled meetings. Nor is Joya likely to have the opportunity to mention Bill's behavior in a casual way. She is concerned that if she reports Bill is lying, the CEO will think she is causing trouble out of jealousy that Bill got the job she wanted.

What should Joya do?

Chapter Conclusion

Even employees who are ethical in their personal lives may find it difficult to uphold their standards at work if those around them behave differently. Managers wonder what they can do to create an ethical environment in their companies. To help foster a sense of ethics within their organizations, many U.S. companies have developed their own formal ethics codes. For example, Johnson & Johnson's corporate credo states that managers must take actions that are "just and ethical" and all employees must be "good citizens." (For a closer look at this credo, go to http://www.jnj.com/careers/ourcredo.html.) Many companies have also instituted formal ethics training programs for their employees.

In the end, however, the surest way to infuse ethics throughout an organization is for top executives to behave ethically themselves. Few employees will bother to "do the right thing" unless they observe that their bosses value and support such behavior. To ensure a more ethical world, managers must be an example for others, both within and outside their organizations.

For further discussion and updates on ethical issues, check in at http://ethics.acusd.edu/index.html.

Chapter Review

1. There are at least three reasons to be concerned about ethics in a business environment:

   - Society as a whole benefits from ethical behavior.

   - People feel better when they behave ethically.

   - Unethical behavior can be very costly.

2. The ethics checklist:

   - What are the facts?

   - What are the critical issues?

   - Who are the stakeholders?

   - What are the alternatives?

   - What are the ethical implications of each alternative?

     - Is it legal?

     - How would it look in the light of day?

     - What are the consequences?

     - Does it violate important values?

     - Does it violate the Golden Rule?

     - Is it just?

     - Has the process been fair?

   - Is more than one alternative right?

     - Which values are in conflict?

     - Which of these values are most important?

     - Can you find an alternative that is consistent with your values?

Practice Test

1. A Harvard Business School alumna told this story about her life as an MBA student in the 1980s:

   During the spring of my first year, I took a Business Policy class. One of the young men in the class hung a bigger than life-size poster in the back of the room. It was a naked woman chained to a tree next to a Paul Bunyan-type man, fully clothed in a flannel jacket, with a chain saw. He was starting to de-limb her. The class broke up. The professor was standing there doubled over in laughter. There were 85 men guffawing away as if it were the funniest thing they'd ever seen. The women just sat there with their mouths open.

   Did this professor and these students behave ethically? What would you consider to be ethical behavior in this circumstance for the men, the women, and the professor?

2. An executive gave this account of the dilemma he faced in hiring undocumented workers:

   We have a big temporary workforce. At a time when the labor market was very tight, a guy came to us who runs a temporary agency for Vietnamese workers. He told us he could supply 40 Vietnamese any time. We hired them and, in fact, they were fabulous employees, they had twice the productivity of our best workers. We loved them. But when we asked him if every one of them was legally able to work here, he couldn't produce green cards.

   At that time, it was legal to hire workers without green cards. Would it have been ethical?

3. Executives were considering the possibility of moving their company to a different state. They wanted to determine if employees would be willing to relocate, but they did not want the employees to know the company was contemplating a move because the final decision had not yet been made. Instead of asking the employees directly, the company hired a firm to carry out a telephone survey. When calling the employees, these "pollsters" pretended to be conducting a public opinion poll and identified themselves as working for the new state's Chamber of Commerce. Has this company behaved in an ethical manner? Would there have been a better way to obtain this information?

4. Mark is an executive for a multinational office equipment company that would like to enter the potentially vast Chinese market. The official tariffs on office equipment imported into China are so high that these goods are uncompetitive in the local market. Mark discovers, however, that many companies sell their goods to importers offshore. These importers then negotiate "special" tariff rates with Chinese officials. Because these custom officials are under pressure to meet revenue targets, sometimes they are willing to negotiate lower, unofficial rates. What would you do if you were Mark?

5. Rap artist Ice-T and his band, Body Count, recorded a song called *Cop Killer* in which the singer gleefully anticipates slitting a police officer's throat. (The lyrics to this song are available at http://www.cleat.org/remember/TimeWarner/lyrics.html.) Time Warner, Inc., produced this song and other gangsta rap recordings with violent and sexually degrading lyrics. Recorded music is an important source of profits for the company, which is struggling with a $15 billion debt and a depressed stock price. If Time Warner renounces rap albums, its reputation in the music business—and future profits—might suffer. This damage could spill over into the multimedia market, which is crucial to Time Warner's future. The company is concerned about several important stakeholders—shareholders, consumers, suppliers (rap musicians). What decision would you make if you were CEO of Time Warner?

6. H. B. Fuller Co. of St. Paul is a leading manufacturer of industrial glues. Its mission statement says the company "will conduct business legally and ethically." It has endowed a university chair in business ethics and donates 5 percent of its profits to charity. But now it is under attack for selling its shoemakers' glue, Resistol, in Central America. Many homeless children in these countries have become addicted to Resistol's fumes. So widespread is the problem that glue-sniffers in Central America are called "resistoleros." Glue manufacturers in Europe have added a foul-smelling oil to their glue that discourages abusers. Fuller fears that the smell may also discourage legitimate users. What should Fuller do?

7. According to the Electronic Industries Association, questionable returns have become the toughest problem plaguing the consumer electronics industry. Some consumers purchase electronic equipment to use once or twice for a special occasion and then return it—a radar detector for a weekend getaway or a camcorder to videotape a wedding. Or a customer might return a cordless telephone because he cannot figure out how it works. The retailer's staff lacks the expertise to help, so they refund the customer's money and ship the phone back to the manufacturer labeled as defective. Excessive and unwarranted returns force manufacturers to repackage and reship perfectly good products, imposing extra costs that squeeze their profits and raise prices to consumers. One retailer returned a cordless telephone that was two years old and had been chewed up by a dog. What ethical obligations do consumers and retailers have in these circumstances?

8. Consider this complaint from an ethics professor:

   I make my living teaching and writing about ethics. . . . But in our own world—in our departments of philosophy and religious studies and medical humanities and ethics institutes—what happens?

   • Job openings [for instructors] are announced for positions that are already earmarked for specific persons. . . . [O]ver half the positions announced in the official employment newsletter for the American Academy of Religion were not "real."

   • It is extremely common for letters of application, even those responding to announced openings, to go without acknowledgment.

   • There are numerous instances of candidates who are brought to campus for interviews and who wait in vain to hear anything from their prospective employers. When the candidates finally call, embarrassed but desperate, they are told, "Oh, that position has been filled."

   Do recruiters have any ethical obligations to job candidates?

9. Six months ago, Todd, David, and Stacey joined a large, prestigious accounting firm in

Houston. On paper these three novices look similar, and each graduated from a top MBA program. All three were assigned to work for the same client, a national restaurant chain. They quickly became friends and often lunched together. One day, a senior manager in the firm stopped by the conference room where Todd and David were working to ask if they would like to join him for lunch at the posh Hunter Club nearby. David said, "Thanks, that'd be great, but we usually eat lunch with Stacey. Could she come, too?" The manager hemmed and hawed for a minute, shifted his weight from one foot to the other, and finally said, "The Hunter Club doesn't allow women at lunch." What should Todd and David do?

10. Genentech, Inc., manufactures Protropin, a genetically engineered version of the human growth hormone. This drug's purpose is to enhance the growth of short children. Protropin is an important product for Genentech, accounting for more than one-third of the company's total revenue of $217 million. Although the drug is approved for the treatment of children whose bodies make inadequate quantities of growth hormone, many doctors prescribe it for children with normal amounts of growth hormone who simply happen to be short. There is no firm evidence that the drug actually increases growth for short children with normal growth hormone. Moreover, many people question whether it is appropriate to prescribe such a powerful drug for cosmetic reasons, especially when the drug may not work. Nor is there proof that it is safe over the long term. Is Genentech behaving ethically? Should it discourage doctors from prescribing the drug to normal, short children?

11. ROLE REVERSAL Write one or two paragraphs that could be used as an essay question describing an ethical dilemma that you have faced in your own life.

Internet Research Problem

Go to http://www.mapnp.org/library/ethics/ethxgde .htm and click on *Ethics Tools: Resolving Ethical Dilemmas (with Real-to-Life Examples)*. Outline the steps you would take to resolve one of these dilemmas. Use the ethics checklist in this chapter to guide you.

You can find further practice problems in the Online Quiz at http://beatty.westbuslaw.com **or in the Study Guide that accompanies this text.**

Dispute
Resolution

Tony Caruso had not returned for dinner, and his wife, Karen, was nervous. She put on some sandals and hurried across the dunes, a half mile to the ocean shore. She soon came upon Tony's dog, Blue, tied to an old picket fence. Tony's shoes and clothing were piled neatly nearby. Karen and friends searched frantically throughout the evening. A little past midnight, Tony's body washed ashore, his lungs filled with water. A local doctor concluded he had accidentally drowned.

Karen and her friends were not the only ones distraught. Tony had been partners with Beth Smiles in an environmental consulting business, Enviro-Vision. They were good friends, and Beth was emotionally devastated. When she was able to focus on business issues, Beth filed an insurance claim with the Coastal Insurance Group. Beth hated to think about Tony's death in financial terms, but she was relieved that the struggling business would receive $2 million on the life insurance policy.

Several months after filing the claim, Beth received this reply from Coastal: "Under the policy issued to Enviro-Vision, we are conditionally liable in the amount of $1 million in the event of Mr. Caruso's death. If his death is accidental, we are conditionally liable to pay double indemnity of $2 million. But pursuant to section H(5) death by suicide is not covered. After a thorough investigation, we have concluded that Anthony Caruso's death was an act of suicide, as defined in section B(11) of the policy. Your claim is denied in its entirety." Beth was furious. She was convinced Tony was incapable of suicide. And her company could not afford the $2 million loss. She decided to consult her lawyer, Chris Pruitt. ▪

Three Fundamental Areas of Law

This case is a fictionalized version of several real cases based on double indemnity insurance policies. In this chapter we follow Beth's dispute with Coastal from initial interview through appeal, using it to examine three fundamental areas of law: alternative dispute resolution, the structure of our court systems, and civil lawsuits. But first we need to look at the best sort of dispute—the kind that is avoided.

DISPUTE PREVENTION

Over the years, one of the important services that attorney Chris Pruitt has done for Enviro-Vision is *prevent disputes*. It is vital to understand and apply this concept in business and professional work and in everyday life. There is an old saying that you have a chance to go broke twice in your life: once when you lose a lawsuit, the other time when you win. The financial and emotional costs of litigation are extraordinarily high.

You can avoid disputes in many different ways. Throughout the text we specify an array of preventive steps as they relate to the different legal problems posed. Here we can mention a few of the potential disputes Enviro-Vision avoided by thinking ahead.

When Beth and Tony started Enviro-Vision, Chris pointed out that, as business partners, the best way to protect both their friendship and their business was with a detailed partnership agreement. Although Beth and Tony found it tedious to create, the agreement helped them avoid problems such as those concerning capital contributions to the partnership, about who owns what, and about hiring and firing employees. Further, Enviro-Vision avoids unjustified firings by giving all employees written job descriptions. It educates employees about sexual harassment. When drafting a contract, Beth has learned to be sure that the client knows exactly what it is getting, when the work is due, what the risks are, and how much it will cost. Each of these practices has prevented potential lawsuits. ▪

When Beth Smiles meets with her lawyer, Chris Pruitt brings a second attorney from his firm, Janet Booker, who is an experienced litigator, that is, a lawyer who handles court cases. If they file a lawsuit, Janet will be in charge, so Chris wants her there for the first meeting. Janet probes about Tony's home life, the status of the business, his personal finances, everything. Beth becomes upset that Janet doesn't seem sympathetic, but Chris explains that Janet is doing her job: she needs all the information, good and bad.

LITIGATION VERSUS ALTERNATIVE DISPUTE RESOLUTION

Janet starts thinking about the two methods of dispute resolution: litigation and alternative dispute resolution. **Litigation** refers to lawsuits, the process of filing claims in court, and ultimately going to trial. **Alternative dispute resolution** is any other formal or informal process used to settle disputes without resorting to a trial. It is increasingly popular with corporations and individuals alike because it is generally cheaper and faster than litigation.

Alternative Dispute Resolution

Janet Booker knows that even after expert legal help, vast expense, and years of work, litigation may leave clients unsatisfied. If she can use alternative dispute resolution (ADR) to create a mutually satisfactory solution in a few months, for a fraction of the cost, she is glad to do it. We will look at different types of ADR and analyze their strengths and weaknesses.

NEGOTIATION

In most cases the parties negotiate, whether personally or through lawyers. Fortunately, the great majority of disputes are resolved this way. Negotiation often begins as soon as a dispute arises and may last a few days or several years.

MEDIATION

Mediation is the fastest growing method of dispute resolution in the United States. Here, a neutral person, called a mediator, attempts to coax the two disputing parties toward a voluntary settlement. (In some cases there may be two or more mediators, but we will use the singular.) Generally, the two disputants voluntarily enter mediation, although some judges order the parties to try this form of ADR before allowing a case to go to trial.

A mediator does not render a decision in the dispute, but uses a variety of skills to prod the parties toward agreement. Often a mediator will shuttle between the antagonists, hearing their arguments, sorting out the serious issues from the less important, prompting the parties and lawyers alike to consider new perspectives, and looking for areas of agreement. Mediators must earn the trust of both parties, listen closely, try to diffuse anger and fear, and build the will to settle. Good mediators do not need a law degree, but they must have a sense of humor and low blood pressure.

Mediation has several major advantages. Because the parties maintain control of the process, the two antagonists can speak freely. They need not fear conceding too much, because no settlement takes effect until both parties sign. All discussions are confidential, further encouraging candid talk. This is particularly helpful in cases involving proprietary information that might be revealed during a trial.

Of all forms of dispute resolution, mediation probably offers the strongest "win–win" potential. Since the goal is voluntary settlement, neither party needs to fear that it will end up the loser. This is in sharp contrast to litigation, where one party is very likely to lose. Removing the fear of defeat often encourages thinking and talking that are more open and realistic than negotiations held in the midst of a lawsuit. Studies show that over 75 percent of mediated cases do reach a voluntary settlement. Such an agreement is particularly valuable to parties that wish to preserve a long-term relationship. Consider two companies that have done business successfully for 10 years but now are in the midst of a million-dollar trade dispute. A lawsuit could last three or more years and destroy any chance of future trade. However, if the parties mediate the disagreement, they might reach an amicable settlement within a month or two and could quickly resume their mutually profitable business.

This form of ADR works for disputes both big and small. Two college roommates who cannot get along may find that a three-hour mediation session restores tranquillity in the apartment. On a larger scale, consider the work of former United States Senator George Mitchell, who mediated the Anglo-Irish peace agreement, setting Northern Ireland on the path to peace for the first time in three centuries. Like most good mediators, Mitchell was remarkably patient. In an early session, Mitchell permitted the head of one militant party to speak without interruption—for seven straight hours. The diatribe yielded no quick results, but Mitchell believed that after Northern Ireland's tortured history, any nonviolent discussions represented progress.

ARBITRATION

In this form of ADR, the parties agree to bring in a neutral third party, but with a major difference: the arbitrator has the power to impose an award. The arbitrator allows each side equal time to present its case and, after deliberation, issues a binding decision, generally without giving reasons. Unlike mediation, arbitration ensures that there will be a final result, although the parties lose control of the outcome. Arbitration is generally faster and cheaper than litigation.

Parties in arbitration give up many rights that litigants retain, including discovery and class action. *Discovery*, as we see below, allows the two sides in a lawsuit to obtain, before trial, documentary and other evidence from the opponent. Arbitration permits both sides to keep secret many files that would have to be divulged in a court case, potentially depriving the opposing side of valuable evidence. A party may have a stronger case than it realizes, and the absence of discovery may permanently deny it that knowledge. A *class action* is a suit in which one injured party represents a large group of people who have suffered similar harm. For example, in an employment discrimination case, a large group of employees who claim similar injury might band together to bring the case, giving themselves much greater clout. Arbitration eliminates this possibility, since injured employees face the employer one at a time. Finally, the fact that an arbitrator may not provide a written, public decision bars other plaintiffs, and society generally, from learning what happened.

Mandatory Arbitration

This variation contains one big difference: the parties agree *in advance* to arbitrate any disputes that may arise. For example, a consumer who purchases a computer or hires a real estate agent may sign an agreement requiring arbitration of any disputes; a customer opening an account with a stockbroker or bank—or health plan—may sign a similar form, often without realizing it. The good news is fewer lawsuits; the bad news is you might be the person kept out of court.

Assume that you live in Miami. Using the Internet, you order a $2,000 ThinkLite laptop computer, which arrives in a carton, loaded with six fat instructional manuals and many small leaflets. You read some of the documents and ignore others. For four weeks you struggle to make your computer work, to no avail. Finally, you telephone ThinkLite and demand a refund, but the company refuses. You file suit in your local court, at which time the company points out that buried among the hundreds of pages it mailed you was a *mandatory arbitration form.* This document prohibits you from filing suit against the company and states that if you have any complaint with the company, you must fly to Chicago; pay a $2,000 arbitrator's fee; plead your case before an arbitrator selected by the Laptop Trade Association of America; and, in the event you lose, pay ThinkLite's attorney's fees, which could be several thousand dollars. Is that mandatory arbitration provision valid? It is too early to say with finality, but thus far the courts that have faced such clauses have enforced them.[1]

OTHER FORMS OF ADR

Several hybrid forms of ADR offer advantages in particular kinds of disputes. In a *mini-trial*, the parties agree to stage a short trial before a panel of three "judges." Two of the "judges" are actually executives of the corporate parties; the third is a neutral adviser. Lawyers present shortened versions of their cases. The "judges" then discuss settlement, with the corporate officers relying on the neutral party to act as mediator. This method is useful in commercial disputes where the respective executives interpret the facts very differently.

A *summary jury trial* is initiated and supervised by a court. When a case between two corporations is nearly ready for trial, the judge chooses a mock jury of perhaps six people. With the judge presiding, each lawyer summarizes what the witnesses would say in a real trial. A trial that might take two months can be summarized in a day or two. The "jury" then deliberates. They are asked to reach a consensus if possible, but they may make individual decisions if unavoidable. Each juror fills out a form explaining his impression of the case. The assumption is that once all parties and lawyers learn how jurors might react, their views of the lawsuit should converge, leading to settlement. If this doesn't happen, the parties proceed to a real trial.

Critics argue that summary jury trials can be misleading because juries do not see real witnesses. A lawyer's *summary* of a corporate officer's testimony might sound convincing, but the executive himself might be unpersuasive on the witness stand.

ADR is controversial, but its surging popularity demonstrates great dissatisfaction with ordinary litigation. A corporate executive faced with a serious legal issue must at least consider the options available. Whatever route she chooses, she should be able to justify the choice in terms of time, cost, and likely satisfaction. Information about ADR is readily available on the Internet; a good place to begin a search is http://www.findlaw.com/01topics/11disputeres/.

To return to our hypothetical case, Janet Booker proposes to Coastal Insurance that they use ADR to expedite a decision in their dispute. Coastal rejects the offer. Coastal's lawyer, Rich Stewart, says that suicide is apparent. He does not want a neutral party to split the difference and award $1 million to Enviro-Vision. Janet reports this explanation to Beth, but adds that she does not believe it. She thinks that Coastal wants the case to drag on as long as possible in the hopes that Enviro-Vision will ultimately settle cheap.

It is a long way to go before trial, but Janet has to prepare her case. The first thing she thinks about is where to file the lawsuit.

---

[1] See, e.g., *Hill v. Gateway 2000*, 105 F.3d 1147, 1997 U.S. App. LEXIS 1877 (7th Cir. 1997), upholding a similar clause.

Court Systems

The United States has over 50 *systems* of courts. One nationwide system of *federal* courts serves the entire country. In addition, each *state* has its court system. The state and federal courts are in different buildings, have different judges, and hear different kinds of cases. Each has special powers and certain limitations.

STATE COURTS

The typical state court system forms a pyramid, as Exhibit 3.1 shows. You may use the Internet to learn the exact names and powers of the courts in your state. Go to http://findlaw.com and under the heading "Legal Professionals" click on U.S. State Resources, and then select your state.

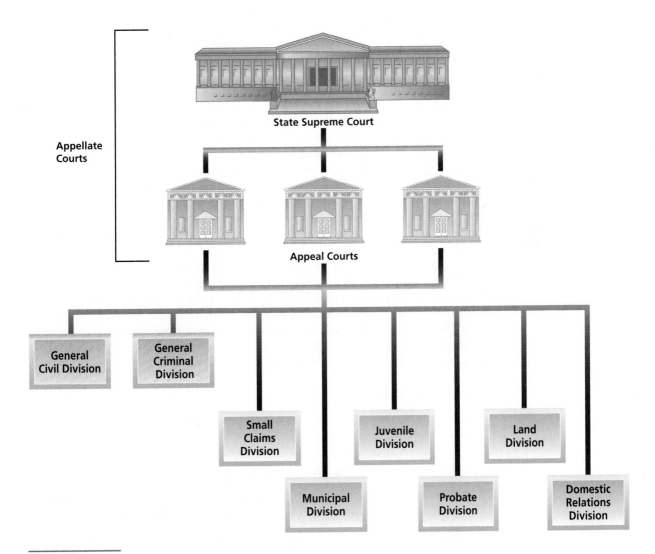

Exhibit 3.1

Trial Courts

Almost all cases start in trial courts, the ones endlessly portrayed on television and film. There is one judge and there will often (but not always) be a jury. This is the only court to hear testimony from witnesses and receive evidence. **Trial courts determine the facts of a particular dispute and apply to those facts the law given by earlier appellate court decisions.**

In the Enviro-Vision dispute, the trial court will decide all important facts that are in dispute. Did Tony Caruso die? Did he drown? Assuming he drowned, was his death accidental or suicide? Once the jury has decided the facts, it will apply the law to those facts. If Tony Caruso died accidentally, contract law provides that Beth Smiles is entitled to double indemnity benefits. If the jury decides he killed himself, Beth gets nothing.

Facts are critical. That may sound obvious, but in a course devoted to legal principles, it is easy to lose track of the key role that factual determinations play in the resolution of any dispute. In the Enviro-Vision case, we will see that one bit of factual evidence goes undetected, with costly consequences.

Jurisdiction refers to a court's power to hear a case. In state or federal court, a plaintiff may start a lawsuit only in a court that has jurisdiction over that kind of case. Some courts have very limited jurisdiction, while others have the power to hear almost any case.

Trial Courts of Limited Jurisdiction. These courts may hear only certain types of cases. Small claims court has jurisdiction only over civil lawsuits involving a maximum of, say, $2,500 (the amount varies from state to state). Municipal court has jurisdiction over traffic citations and minor criminal matters. A juvenile court hears only cases involving minors. Probate court is devoted to settling the estates of deceased persons, though in some states it will hear certain other cases as well. Land court focuses on disputes about title to land and other real property issues. Domestic relations court resolves marital disputes and child custody issues.

Trial Courts of General Jurisdiction. Trial courts of general jurisdiction, however, can hear a very broad range of cases. The most important court, for our purposes, is the general civil division. This court may hear virtually any civil lawsuit. In one day it might hear a $450 million shareholders' derivative lawsuit, an employment issue involving freedom of religion, and a foreclosure on a mortgage. Most of the cases we study start in this court.[2] If Enviro-Vision's case against Coastal goes to trial in a state court, it will begin in the trial court of general jurisdiction.

Appellate Courts

Appellate courts are entirely different from trial courts. Three or more judges hear the case. There are no juries, ever. These courts do not hear witnesses or take new

---

[2] Note that the actual name of the court will vary from state to state. In many states it is called superior court, because it has power superior to the courts of limited jurisdiction. In New York it is called supreme court (anything to confuse the layperson); in some states it is called court of common pleas; in Oregon and other states it is a circuit court. They are all civil trial courts of general jurisdiction. Within this branch, some states are beginning to establish specialized business courts, to hear complex commercial disputes. At least one state has created a cybercourt, for high-tech cases. Lawyers will argue their cases by teleconference and present evidence via streaming video.

evidence. They hear appeals of cases already tried below. **Appeal courts generally accept the facts given to them by trial courts and review the trial record to see if the court made errors of law.**

Generally, an appeal court will accept a factual finding unless there was *no evidence at all* to support it. If the jury decides that Tony Caruso committed suicide, the appeal court will normally accept that fact, even though the appeal judges consider the jury's conclusion dubious. On the other hand, if a jury concluded that Tony had been murdered, an appeal court would overturn that finding if neither side had introduced any evidence of murder during the trial.

An appeal court reviews the trial record to make sure that the lower court correctly applied the law to the facts. If the trial court made an **error of law**, the appeal court may require a new trial. Suppose the jury concludes that Tony Caruso committed suicide, but votes to award Enviro-Vision $1 million because it feels sorry for Beth Smiles. That is an error of law: if Tony committed suicide, Beth is entitled to nothing. An appellate court will reverse the decision. Or suppose that the trial judge permitted a friend of Tony's to state that he was certain Tony would never commit suicide. Normally, such opinions are not permissible in trial, and it was a legal error for the judge to allow the jury to hear it.

Court of Appeals.   The party that loses at the trial court may appeal to the intermediate court of appeals. The party filing the appeal is the **appellant**. The party opposing the appeal (because it won at trial) is the **appellee**.

This court allows both sides to submit written arguments on the case, called **briefs**. Each side then appears for oral argument, usually before a panel of three judges. The appellant's lawyer has about 15 minutes to convince the judges that the trial court made serious errors of law and that the decision should be **reversed**, that is, nullified. The appellee's lawyer has the same time to persuade the court that the trial court acted correctly and that the result should be **affirmed**, that is, permitted to stand.

State Supreme Court.   This is the highest court in the state, and it accepts some appeals from the court of appeals. In most states, there is no absolute right to appeal to the Supreme Court. If the high court regards a legal issue as important, it accepts the case. It then takes briefs and hears oral argument just as the appeal court did. If it considers the matter unimportant, it refuses to hear the case, meaning that the court of appeals's ruling is the final word on the case.[3]

In most states seven judges, or justices, sit on the Supreme Court. They have the final word on state law.

FEDERAL COURTS

As discussed in Chapter 1, federal courts are established by the United States Constitution, which limits what kinds of cases can be brought in any federal court. See Exhibit 3.2. For our purposes, two kinds of civil lawsuits are permitted in federal court: federal question cases and diversity cases.

---

[3] In some states with smaller populations, there is no intermediate appeals court. All appeals from trial courts go directly to the state supreme court.

United States Supreme Court

Appellate
Courts

United States Courts of Appeals (12 Circuits)

United States Court of Appeals for the Federal Circuit

| U.S. District Courts | U.S. Bankruptcy Courts | U.S. Tax Courts | | U.S. Court of International Trade | U.S. Claims Courts | U.S. Patent & Trademark Office |

Trial Courts

Primary Trial Court   *Limited*

Trial Courts

Various Federal Agencies

Administrative Agencies

Exhibit 3.2

Federal Question Cases

A claim based on the United States Constitution, a federal statute, or a federal treaty is called a federal question case.[4] Federal courts have jurisdiction over these cases. If the Environmental Protection Agency orders Logging Company not to cut in a particular forest, and Logging Company claims that the agency has wrongly deprived it of its property, that suit is based on a federal statute and is thus a federal question. If Little Retailer sues Mega Retailer, claiming that Mega has established a monopoly, that claim is also based on a statute—the Sherman Antitrust Act—and creates federal question jurisdiction. Enviro-Vision's potential suit merely concerns an insurance contract. The federal district court has no federal question jurisdiction over the case.

---

[4] 28 U.S.C. §1331 governs federal question jurisdiction and 28 U.S.C. §1332 covers diversity jurisdiction.

Diversity Cases

Even if no federal law is at issue, federal courts have jurisdiction when (1) the plaintiff and defendant are citizens of different states *and* (2) the amount in dispute exceeds $75,000. The theory behind diversity jurisdiction is that courts of one state might be biased against citizens of another state. To ensure fairness, the parties have the option of federal court.

Enviro-Vision is located in Oregon, and Coastal Insurance is incorporated in Georgia.[5] They are citizens of different states, and the amount in dispute far exceeds $75,000. Janet could file this case in United States District Court based on diversity jurisdiction.

Trial Courts

United States District Court. This is the primary trial court in the federal system. The nation is divided into about 94 districts, and each has a district court. States with smaller populations have one district. States with larger populations have several districts; Texas is divided geographically into four districts.

Other Trial Courts. There are other, specialized trial courts in the federal system. Bankruptcy Court, Tax Court, and the United States Court of International Trade all handle name-appropriate cases. The United States Claims Court hears cases brought against the United States, typically on contract disputes.

Judges. The president of the United States nominates all federal court judges, from district court to Supreme Court. The nominees must be confirmed by the Senate.

Appellate Courts

United States Courts of Appeals. These are the intermediate courts of appeals. As the map on the following page shows, they are divided into "circuits," which are geographical areas. There are 11 numbered circuits, hearing appeals from district courts. For example, an appeal from the Northern District of Illinois would go to the Court of Appeals for the Seventh Circuit. You will find an interactive map of the District and Circuit Courts at http://www.uscourts.gov/links.html.

A twelfth court, the Court of Appeals for the District of Columbia, hears appeals only from the district court of Washington, D.C. This is a particularly powerful court because so many suits about federal statutes begin in the district court for the District of Columbia. Also in Washington is the thirteenth Court of Appeals, known as the Federal Circuit. It hears appeals from specialized trial courts, as shown in Exhibit 3.2.

Within one circuit there are many circuit judges, up to about 30 judges in the largest circuit, the Ninth. When a case is appealed, three judges hear the appeal, taking briefs and hearing oral argument.

United States Supreme Court. This is the highest court in the country. There are nine justices on the Court. One justice is the chief justice, and the other eight are

---

[5] For diversity purposes, a corporation is a citizen of the state in which it is incorporated and the state in which it has its principal place of business.

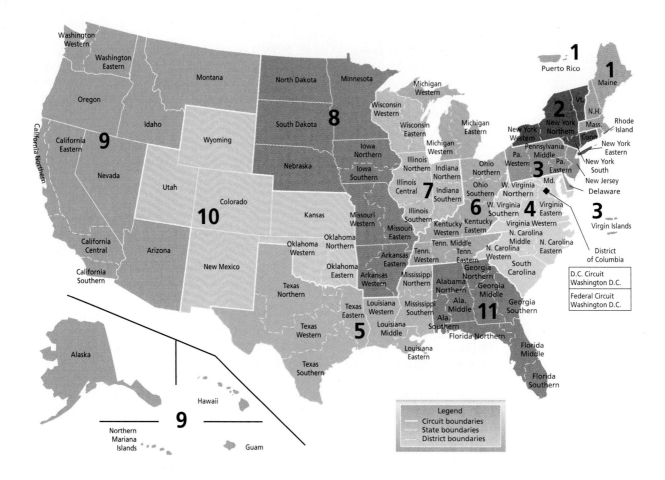

associate justices. When they decide a case, each justice casts an equal vote. The chief justice's special power comes from his authority to assign opinions to a given justice. The justice assigned to write an opinion has an opportunity to control the precise language and thus to influence the voting by other justices. To learn more about the Supreme Court, visit its official web site: http://www.supremecourtus.gov.

The Supreme Court has the power to hear appeals in any federal case and in certain cases that began in state courts. Generally, it is up to the Court whether or not it will accept a case. A party that wants the Supreme Court to review a lower court ruling must file a **writ of certiorari**, asking the Court to hear the case. The Court receives about 8,000 of these writs every year but currently accepts fewer than 100. Most cases accepted involve either an important issue of constitutional law or an interpretation of a major federal statute.

Litigation

Janet Booker decides to file the Enviro-Vision suit in the Oregon trial court. She thinks that a state court judge may take the issue more seriously than a federal district court judge.

PLEADINGS

The documents that begin a lawsuit are called the **pleadings**. These consist of the complaint, the answer, and sometimes a reply.

Complaint

The plaintiff files in court a **complaint**, which is a short, plain statement of the facts she is alleging and the legal claims she is making. The purpose of the complaint is to inform the defendant of the general nature of the claims and the need to come into court and protect his interests.

Janet Booker files the complaint, as shown below. Since Enviro-Vision is a partnership, she files the suit on behalf of Beth, personally.

STATE OF OREGON
CIRCUIT COURT

Multnomah County   Civil Action No. _____

Elizabeth Smiles,
Plaintiff

                                                          JURY TRIAL DEMANDED

v.

Coastal Insurance Company, Inc.,
Defendant

COMPLAINT

Plaintiff Elizabeth Smiles states that:

1. She is a citizen of Multnomah County, Oregon.
2. Defendant Coastal Insurance Company, Inc., is incorporated under the laws of Georgia and has as its usual place of business 148 Thrift Street, Savannah, Georgia.
3. On or about July 5, 2003, plaintiff Smiles ("Smiles"), Defendant Coastal Insurance Co, Inc. ("Coastal") and Anthony Caruso entered into an insurance contract ("the contract"), a copy of which is annexed hereto as Exhibit "A." This contract was signed by all parties or their authorized agents, in Multnomah County, Oregon.
4. The contract obligates Coastal to pay to Smiles the sum of two million dollars ($2 million) if Anthony Caruso should die accidentally.
5. On or about September 18, 2003, Anthony Caruso accidentally drowned and died while swimming.
6. Coastal has refused to pay any sum pursuant to the contract.
7. Coastal has knowingly, willingly, and unreasonably refused to honor its obligations under the contract.

WHEREFORE, plaintiff Elizabeth Smiles demands judgment against defendant Coastal for all monies due under the contract; demands triple damages for Coastal's knowing, willing, and unreasonable refusal to honor its obligations; and demands all costs and attorney's fees, with interest.

ELIZABETH SMILES,
By her attorney,
    [Signed]
Janet Booker
Pruitt, Booker & Bother
983 Joy Avenue
Portland, OR
October 18, 2003

Service

When she files the complaint in court, Janet gets a summons, which is a paper ordering the defendant to answer the complaint within 20 days. A sheriff or constable then serves the two papers by delivering them to the defendant. Coastal's headquarters are in Georgia, so the state of Oregon has required Coastal to specify someone as its agent for receipt of service in Oregon.

Answer

Once the complaint and summons are served, Coastal has 20 days in which to file an answer. Coastal's answer, shown below, is a brief reply to each of the allegations in the complaint. The answer tells the court and the plaintiff exactly what issues are in dispute. Since Coastal admits that the parties entered into the contract that Beth claims they did, there is no need for her to prove that in court. The court can focus its attention on the disputed issue: whether Tony Caruso died accidentally.

STATE OF OREGON
CIRCUIT COURT

Multnomah County   Civil Action No. 03-5626

Elizabeth Smiles,
Plaintiff
v.
Coastal Insurance Company, Inc.,
Defendant

ANSWER

Defendant Coastal Insurance Company, Inc., answers the complaint as follows:
1. Admit.
2. Admit.
3. Admit.
4. Admit.
5. Deny.
6. Admit.
7. Deny.
COASTAL INSURANCE COMPANY, INC.,
By its attorney,
[Signed]
Richard B. Stewart
Kiley, Robbins, Stewart & Glote
333 Victory Boulevard
Portland, OR
October 30, 2003

If the defendant fails to answer in time, the plaintiff will ask for a **default judgment**, meaning a decision that the plaintiff wins without a trial.

Counter-Claim

Sometimes a defendant does more than merely answer a complaint, and files a **counter-claim**, meaning a second lawsuit by the defendant against the plaintiff.

Suppose that after her complaint was filed in court, Beth had written a letter to the newspaper, calling Coastal a bunch of "thieves and scoundrels who spend their days mired in fraud and larceny." Coastal would not have found that amusing. The company's answer would have included a counter-claim against Beth for libel, claiming that she falsely accused the insurer of serious criminal acts. Coastal would have demanded money damages.

If Coastal counter-claimed, Beth would have to file a **reply**, which is simply an answer to a counter-claim. Beth's reply would be similar to Coastal's answer, admitting or denying the various allegations.

Class Actions

Suppose Janet uncovers evidence that Coastal denies 80 percent of all life insurance claims, calling them suicide. She could ask the court to permit a **class action**. If the court granted her request, she would represent the entire group of plaintiffs, including those who are unaware of the lawsuit or even unaware they were harmed. Class actions can give the plaintiffs much greater leverage, since the defendant's potential liability is vastly increased. In the back of her mind, Janet has thoughts of a class action *if* she can uncover evidence that Coastal has used a claim of suicide to deny coverage to a large number of claimants.

ECONOMICS & THE LAW

From his small town in Maine, Ernie decides to get rich quickly. On the Internet he advertises "Energy Breakthrough! Cut your heating costs 15 percent for only $25." One hundred thousand people send him their money. In return, they receive a photocopied graph, illustrating that if you wear two sweaters instead of one, you will feel 15 percent warmer. Ernie has deceitfully earned $2,500,000 in pure profit. What can the angry homeowners do? Under the laws of fraud and consumer protection, they have a legitimate claim to their $25, and perhaps even to treble damages ($75). But few will sue, because the time and effort required would be greater than the money recovered.

Economists analyze such legal issues in terms of *efficiency*. The laws against Ernie's fraud are clear and well intended, but they will not help in this case because it is too expensive for 100,000 people to litigate such a small claim. The effort would be hugely *inefficient*, both for the homeowners and for society generally. The economic reality may permit Ernie to evade the law's grasp.

That is one reason we have class actions. A dozen or so "heating plan" buyers can all hire the same lawyer. This attorney will file court papers in Maine on behalf of *everyone*, nationwide, who has been swindled by Ernie—including the 99,988 people who have yet to be notified that they are part of the case. Now the con artist, instead of facing a few harmless suits for $25, must respond to a multimillion-dollar claim being handled by an experienced lawyer. Treble damages become menacing: three times $25 times 100,000 is no joke, even to a cynic like Ernie. He may also be forced to pay for the plaintiffs' attorney, as well as all costs of notifying class members and disbursing money to them. With one lawyer representing an entire class, the legal system has become fiercely efficient. ∎

Judgment on the Pleadings

A party can ask the court for a judgment based simply on the pleadings themselves, by filing a motion to dismiss. A **motion is a formal request to the court** that the court take some step or issue some order. During a lawsuit the parties file many motions. A **motion to dismiss** is a request that the court terminate a case without permitting it to go further. Suppose that a state law requires claims on life insurance contracts to be filed within three years, and Beth files her claim four years after Tony's death. Coastal would move to dismiss based on this late filing. The court might well agree, and Beth would never get into court.

Discovery

Few cases are dismissed on the pleadings. Most proceed quickly to the next step. **Discovery is the critical, pre-trial opportunity for both parties to learn the strengths and weaknesses of the opponent's case.**

The theory behind civil litigation is that the best outcome is a negotiated settlement and that parties will move toward agreement if they understand the opponent's case. That is likeliest to occur if both sides have an opportunity to examine most of the evidence the other side will bring to trial. Further, if a case does go all the way to trial, efficient and fair litigation cannot take place in a courtroom filled, like a piñata, with surprises. On television dramas, witnesses say astonishing things that amaze the courtroom (and keep viewers hooked through the next commercial). In real trials the lawyers know in advance the answers to practically all questions asked because discovery has allowed them to see the opponent's documents and question its witnesses. The following are the most important forms of discovery.

Interrogatories. These are written questions that the opposing party must answer, in writing, under oath.

Depositions. These provide a chance for one party's lawyer to question the other party, or a potential witness, under oath. The person being questioned is the **deponent**. Lawyers for both parties are present. During depositions, and in trial, good lawyers choose words carefully and ask questions calculated to advance their cause. A fine line separates ethical, probing questions from those that are tricky, and a similar line divides answers that are merely unhelpful from perjury. To see how one attorney prepares witnesses for deposition, go to www.hurtworker.com/english/deposition.htm.

Production of Documents and Things. Each side may ask the other side to produce relevant documents for inspection and copying; to produce physical objects, such as part of a car alleged to be defective; and for permission to enter on land to make an inspection, for example, at the scene of an accident.

Physical and Mental Examination. A party may ask the court to order an examination of the other party if his physical or mental condition is relevant, for example, in a case of medical malpractice.

Requests for Admission. Either party can insist that the opposing party admit or deny certain facts, to avoid wasting time on points not in dispute. In a medical malpractice case, the plaintiff would request that the doctor admit he performed the surgery and admit what would be the normal level of care a surgeon would provide for such a case (while not expecting the surgeon to admit that he erred).

Janet Booker begins her discovery with interrogatories. Her goal is to learn Coastal's basic position and factual evidence and then follow up with more detailed questioning during depositions. Her interrogatories ask for every fact Coastal relied on in denying the claim. She asks for the names of all witnesses, the identity of all documents, the description of all things or objects that they considered. She requests the names of all corporate officers who played any role in the decision and of any expert witnesses Coastal plans to call. Interrogatory No. 18 demands extensive information on all *other* claims in the past three years that Coastal has denied based on alleged suicide. Janet is looking for evidence that would support a class action.

Beth remarks on how thorough the interrogatories are. "This will tell us what their case is." Janet frowns and looks less optimistic: she's done this before.

Coastal has 30 days to answer Janet's interrogatories. Before it responds, Coastal mails to Janet a notice of deposition, stating its intention to depose Beth Smiles. Beth and Janet will go to the office of Coastal's lawyer, and Beth will answer questions under oath. But at the same time Coastal sends this notice, it sends *25 other notices of deposition*. It will depose Karen Caruso as soon as Beth's deposition is over. Coastal also plans to depose all seven employees of Enviro-Vision; three neighbors who lived near Tony and Karen's beach house; two police officers who participated in the search; the doctor and two nurses involved in the case; Tony's physician; Jerry Johnson, Tony's tennis partner; Craig Bergson, a college roommate; a couple who had dinner with Tony and Karen a week before his death; and several other people.

Beth is appalled. Janet explains that some of these people might have relevant information. But there may be another reason that Coastal is doing this: the company wants to make this litigation hurt. Janet will have to attend every one of these depositions. Costs will skyrocket.

Janet files a **motion for a protective order**. This is a request that the court limit Coastal's discovery by decreasing the number of depositions. Janet also calls Rich Stewart and suggests that they discuss what depositions are really necessary. Rich insists that all of the depositions are important. This is a $2 million case, and Coastal is entitled to protect itself.

Before Beth's deposition date arrives, Rich sends Coastal's answers to Enviro-Vision's interrogatories. The answers contain no useful information whatsoever. For example, Interrogatory No. 10 asked, "If you claim that Anthony Caruso committed suicide, describe every fact upon which you rely in reaching that conclusion." Coastal's answer simply says, "His state of mind, his poor business affairs, and the circumstances of his death all indicate suicide."

Janet calls Rich and complains that the interrogatory answers are a bad joke. Rich disagrees, saying that it is the best information they have so early in the case. After they debate it for 20 minutes, Rich offers to settle the case for $100,000. Janet refuses and makes no counteroffer.

Janet files a **motion to compel answers to interrogatories**, in other words, a formal request that the court order Coastal to supply more complete answers. Janet submits a **memorandum** with the motion, which is a supporting argument. Although it is only a few pages long, the memorandum takes several hours of library research and writing to prepare—more costs. Janet also informs Rich Stewart that Beth will not appear for the deposition, since Coastal's interrogatory answers are inadequate.

Rich now files *his* motion to compel, asking the court to order Beth Smiles to appear for her deposition. The court hears all of the motions together. Janet argues that Coastal's interrogatory answers are hopelessly uninformative and defeat the whole purpose of discovery. She claims that Coastal's large number of depositions creates a huge and unfair expense for a small firm.

Rich claims that the interrogatory answers are the best that Coastal can do thus far and that Coastal will supplement the answers when more information becomes available. He argues against Interrogatory No. 18, the one in which Janet asked for the names of other policyholders whom Coastal considered suicides. He claims that Janet is engaging in a fishing expedition that would violate the privacy of Coastal's insurance customers and provide no information relevant to this case. He demands that Janet make Beth available for a deposition.

These discovery rulings are critical because they will color the entire lawsuit. A trial judge has to make many discovery decisions before a case reaches trial. At times the judge must weigh the need of one party to see documents against the other side's need for privacy. One device a judge can use in reaching a discovery ruling is an **in camera inspection**, meaning that the judge views the requested documents alone, with no lawyers present, and decides whether the other side is entitled to view them. The following case illustrates a common discovery problem: refusal by one side to play fair. The decision also demonstrates why such aggressive conduct can be a dangerous ploy.

KLUPT V. KRONGARD

126 Md. App. 179; 728 A.2d 727; 1999 Md. App. LEXIS 86
Court of Special Appeals of Maryland, 1999

FACTS: Carle Klupt invented a disposable cardboard videocassette. He formed a corporation, Sharbar, Inc., to develop and market the product. Alvin Krongard and a few associates paid $115,000 to Klupt for a chance to participate in the manufacture and sale of the cassette. Three years later, Krongard and his associates sued Klupt and Sharbar, claiming that the defendants had fraudulently persuaded them to enter into the deal, in other words, had lied in order to get their investment. Klupt filed a counter-claim against the plaintiffs, asserting that the Krongard group had actually attempted to seize control of the business in violation of their agreement.

The plaintiffs served requests on Klupt for all documents (in writing or any other medium) relating to oral or written communications between the parties. The plaintiffs also scheduled a deposition of Klupt, but the defendant repeatedly objected to dates. Klupt also changed lawyers from time to time, causing further delay. When the trial court ordered him to appear on a specific date, Klupt claimed he had another deposition scheduled for the same date, but that later turned out to be false.

When he finally appeared for deposition, Klupt produced only four pages of notes from phone conversations with the plaintiffs. He then managed to delay the deposition six more months. When it resumed, Klupt was forced to concede that in fact he had tape-recorded all of his phone calls for many years and had possessed hundreds of recorded calls between the parties. However, in the gap between depositions, he had destroyed the tapes.

Claiming that this was gross abuse of the discovery process, the plaintiffs moved to dismiss Klupt's counter-claims. The trial court granted the motion, and Klupt appealed.

ISSUE: Did the trial court abuse its discretion by dismissing Klupt's counter-claims?

EXCERPTS FROM JUDGE THIEME'S DECISION: Appellate courts are reluctant to second-guess the decision of a trial judge to impose sanctions for a failure of discovery. Accordingly, we may not reverse unless we find an abuse of discretion.

Klupt admitted that he had smashed the tapes with a hammer. Neither was there any question about the discoverability of the evidence. For the purposes of discovery sanctions discoverable evidence is anything reasonably calculated to lead to the discovery of admissible evidence, reasonably likely to be requested during discovery, and/or which is the subject of a pending discovery request. The court in the present case found that the destroyed tapes were subject to [the plaintiffs' request for production of documents].

Discretion does, however, require some commensuration between the abusive conduct and the sanction, particularly when the sanction is of the most severe type. The dismissal of a claim is among the gravest of sanctions, and as such, is warranted only in cases of egregious misconduct such as willful or contemptuous behavior.

In the present case, the court explicitly found that appellant Klupt had acted "willfully and contumaciously." The court noted in particular that Klupt deliberately concealed the existence of the tapes, even from his own counsel, made various memoranda from the tapes, including a backdated set of such memoranda, and then physically destroyed the tapes during a time when the litigation had been ongoing for several months. We find no abuse of discretion in the court's dismissal of the appellants' claims.

[Affirmed.] ◢

The judge rules that Coastal must furnish more complete answers to the interrogatories, especially as to the factual basis of its denial. However, he rules against Interrogatory No. 18, the one concerning other claims Coastal has denied. This simple ruling kills Janet's hope of making a class action of the case. He orders Beth to appear for the deposition. As to future depositions, Coastal may take any 10, but then may take additional depositions only by demonstrating to the court that the deponents have useful information.

Rich proceeds to take Beth's deposition. It takes two full days. He asks about Enviro-Vision's past and present. He learns that Tony appeared to have won their biggest contract ever from Rapid City, Oregon, but that he then lost it when he had a fight with Rapid City's mayor. He inquires into Tony's mood, learns that he was depressed, and probes in every direction he can to find evidence of suicidal motivation. Janet and Rich argue frequently over questions and whether Beth should have to answer them. At times Janet is persuaded and permits Beth to answer; other times she instructs Beth not to answer. For example, toward the end of the second day, Rich asks Beth whether she and Tony had been sexually involved. Janet instructs Beth not to answer. This fight necessitates another trip into court to determine whether Beth must answer. The judge rules that Beth must discuss Tony's romantic life only if Coastal has some evidence that he was involved with someone outside his marriage. The company lacks any such evidence.

Crucial Clue.   Now limited to 10 depositions, Rich selects his nine other deponents carefully. For example, he decides to depose only one of the two nurses; he chooses to question Jerry Johnson, the tennis partner, but not Craig Bergson, the former roommate; and so forth. When we look at the many legal issues this case raises, his choices seem minor. In fact, unbeknownst to Rich or anyone else, his choices may determine the outcome of the case. As we will see later, Craig Bergson has evidence that is possibly crucial to the lawsuit. If Rich decides not to depose him, neither side will ever learn the evidence and the jury will never hear it. A jury can only decide a case based on the evidence presented to it. *Facts are elusive—and often controlling.*

In each deposition Rich carefully probes with his questions, sometimes trying to learn what he actually does not know, sometimes trying to pin down the witness to a specific version of facts so that Rich knows how the witness will testify at trial. Neighbors at the beach testify that Tony seemed tense; one testifies about seeing Tony, unhappy, on the beach with his dog. Another testifies he had never before seen Blue tied up on the beach. Karen Caruso admits that Tony had been somewhat tense and unhappy the last couple of months. She reluctantly discusses their marriage, admitting there were problems.

Other Discovery.   Rich sends Requests to Produce Documents, seeking medical records about Tony. Once again, the parties fight over which records are relevant, but Rich gets most of what he wants. Rich sends Requests for Admission, forcing Beth to commit herself to certain positions, for example, that Tony had lost the Rapid City contract and had been depressed about it.

Plaintiff's Discovery.   Janet does less discovery than Rich because most of the witnesses she will call are friendly witnesses. She can interview them privately without giving any information to Coastal. With the help of Beth and Karen, Janet builds her case just as carefully as Rich, choosing the witnesses who will bolster the view that Tony was in good spirits and died accidentally.

She deposes all of the officers of Coastal who participated in the decision to deny insurance coverage. She is particularly aggressive in pinning them down as to the limited information they had when they denied Beth's claim.

Summary Judgment

When discovery is completed, both sides may consider seeking summary judgment. **Summary judgment is a ruling by the court that no trial is necessary because there are no essential facts in dispute.** The purpose of a trial is to determine the facts of the case, that is, to decide who did what to whom, why, when, and with what consequences. If there are no relevant facts in dispute, then there is no need for a trial.

Suppose Joe sues EZBuck Films, claiming that the company's new movie, *Lover Boy*, violates the copyright of a screenplay that he wrote, called *Love Man*. Discovery establishes that the two stories are suspiciously similar. But EZBuck's lawyer also learns that Joe sold the copyright for *Love Man* to HotShot Pix. EZBuck may or may not have violated a copyright, but there is no need for a trial because Joe *cannot win* even if there is a copyright violation. He does not own the copyright. The court will grant summary judgment for EZBuck.

In the following case, the defendant won summary judgment, meaning that the case never went to trial. And yet, this was only the beginning of trouble for that defendant, William Jefferson Clinton.

JONES V. CLINTON

990 F. Supp. 657, 1998 U.S. Dist. LEXIS 3902
United States District Court for the Eastern District of Arkansas, 1998

FACTS: In 1991 Bill Clinton was governor of Arkansas. Paula Jones worked for a state agency, the Arkansas Industrial Development Commission (AIDC). When Clinton became president, Jones sued him, claiming that he had sexually harassed her. She alleged that, in May 1991, the governor arranged for her to meet him in a hotel room in Little Rock, Arkansas. When they were alone, he put his hand on her leg and slid it toward her pelvis. She escaped from his grasp, exclaimed, "What are you doing?" and said she was "not that kind of girl." She was upset and confused, and sat on a sofa near the door. She claimed that Clinton approached her, "lowered his trousers and underwear, exposed his penis and told her to kiss it." Jones was horrified, jumped up and said she had to leave. Clinton responded by saying, "Well, I don't want to make you do anything you don't want to do," and pulled his pants up. He added that if she got in trouble for leaving work, Jones should "have Dave call me immediately and I'll take care of it." He also said, "You are smart. Let's keep this between ourselves." Jones remained at AIDC until February 1993, when she moved to California because of her husband's job transfer.

President Clinton denied all of the allegations. He also filed for summary judgment, claiming that Jones had not alleged facts that justified a trial. Jones opposed the motion for summary judgment.

ISSUE: Was Clinton entitled to summary judgment, or was Jones entitled to a trial?

EXCERPTS FROM JUDGE WRIGHT'S DECISION: [To establish this type of a sexual harassment case, a plaintiff must show that her refusal to submit to unwelcome sexual advances resulted in a tangible job detriment, meaning that she suffered a specific loss. Jones claims that she was denied promotions, given a job with fewer responsibilities, isolated physically, required to sit at a workstation with no work to do, and singled out as the only female employee not to be given flowers on Secretary's Day.]

There is no record of plaintiff ever applying for another job within AIDC, however, and the record shows that not only was plaintiff never downgraded, her position was reclassified upward from a Grade 9 classification to a Grade 11 classification, thereby increasing her annual salary. Indeed, it is undisputed that plaintiff received every merit increase and cost-of-living allowance for which she was eligible during her nearly two-year tenure with the AIDC and consistently received satisfactory job evaluations.

Although plaintiff states that her job title upon returning from maternity leave was no longer that of purchasing assistant, her job duties prior to taking maternity leave and her job duties upon returning to work both involved data input. That being so, plaintiff cannot establish a tangible job detriment. A transfer that does not involve a demotion in form or substance and involves only minor changes in working conditions, with no reduction in pay or benefits, will not constitute an adverse employment action, otherwise every trivial personnel action that an irritable employee did not like would form the basis of a discrimination suit.

Finally, the Court rejects plaintiff's claim that she was subjected to hostile treatment having tangible effects when she was isolated physically, made to sit in a location from which she was constantly watched, made to sit at her workstation with no work to do, and singled out as the only female employee not to be given flowers on Secretary's Day. Plaintiff may well have perceived hostility and animus on the part of her supervisors, but these perceptions are merely conclusory in nature and do not, without more, constitute a tangible job detriment. Although it is not clear why plaintiff failed to receive flowers on Secretary's Day in 1992, such an omission does not give rise to a federal cause of action.

In sum, the Court finds that a showing of a tangible job detriment or adverse employment action is an essential element of plaintiff's sexual harassment claim and that plaintiff has not demonstrated any tangible job detriment or adverse employment action for her refusal to submit to the Governor's alleged advances. The President is therefore entitled to summary judgment [on this claim]. ◢

In other words, the court acknowledged that there were factual disputes, but concluded that even if Jones proved each of her allegations, she would *still* lose the case, because her allegations fell short of a legitimate case of sexual harassment. Jones appealed the case. Later the same year, as the appeal was pending and the House of Representatives was considering whether to impeach President Clinton, the parties settled the dispute. Clinton, without acknowledging any of the allegations, agreed to pay Jones $850,000 to drop the suit.

Janet and Rich each consider moving for summary judgment, but both correctly decide that they would lose. There is one major fact in dispute: Did Tony Caruso commit suicide? Only a jury may decide that issue. As long as there is *some evidence* supporting each side of a key factual dispute, the court may not grant summary judgment.

Final Preparation

The vast majority of litigation never proceeds to this stage. Well over 90 percent of all lawsuits are settled before trial. But the parties in the Enviro-Vision dispute cannot seem to compromise, so each side gears up for trial. The attorneys make lists of all witnesses they will call. They then prepare each witness very carefully, rehearsing the questions they will ask. It is considered ethical and proper to rehearse the questions, provided the answers are honest and come from the witness. It is unethical and illegal for a lawyer to tell a witness what to say. The lawyers also have colleagues cross-examine each witness so that the witnesses are ready for the questions the other side's lawyer will ask.

This preparation takes hours and hours, for many days. Beth is frustrated that she cannot do the work she needs to for Enviro-Vision, because she is spending so much time preparing the case. Other employees have to prepare as well, especially for cross-examination by Rich Stewart, and it is a terrible drain on the small firm. More than a year after Janet filed her complaint, they are ready to begin trial.

Trial

ADVERSARY SYSTEM

Our system of justice assumes that the best way to bring out the truth is for the two contesting sides to present the strongest case possible to a neutral factfinder. Each side presents its witnesses, and then the opponent has a chance to cross-examine. The adversary system presumes that by putting a witness on the stand and letting both lawyers "go at" her, the truth will emerge.

The judge runs the trial. Each lawyer sits at a large table near the front. Beth, looking tense and unhappy, sits with Janet. Rich Stewart sits with a Coastal executive. In the back of the courtroom are benches for the public. On one bench sits Craig Bergson. He will watch the entire proceeding with intense interest and a strange feeling of unease. He is convinced he knows what really happened.

Janet has demanded a jury trial for Beth's case, and Judge Rowland announces that they will now impanel the jury.

RIGHT TO JURY TRIAL

Not all cases are tried to a jury. As a general rule, both plaintiff and defendant have a right to demand a jury trial when the lawsuit is one for money damages. For example, in a typical contract lawsuit, such as Beth's insurance claim, both plaintiff and defendant have a jury trial right whether they are in state or federal court. Even in such a case, though, the parties may waive the jury right, meaning they agree to try the case to a judge.

If the plaintiff is seeking an equitable remedy, such as an injunction, there is no jury right for either party. Equitable rights come from the old Court of Chancery in England, where there was never a jury. Even today, only a judge may give an equitable remedy.

VOIR DIRE

The process of selecting a jury is called *voir dire*, which means "to speak the truth."[6] The court's goal is to select an impartial jury; the lawyers will each try to get a jury as favorable to their side as possible.

Potential jurors are questioned individually, sometimes by the judge and sometimes by the two lawyers, as each side tries to ferret out potential bias. Each lawyer may make any number of **challenges for cause**, claiming that a juror has demonstrated probable bias. For example, if a prospective juror in the Enviro-Vision case works for an insurance company, the judge will excuse her on the assumption that she would be biased in favor of Coastal. If the judge perceives no bias, the lawyer may still make a limited number of **peremptory challenges**, entitling him to excuse that juror for virtually any reason, which need not be stated in court. For example, if Rich Stewart believes that a juror seems hostile to him personally, he will use a peremptory challenge to excuse that juror even if the judge sensed no animosity. The process continues until 14 jurors are seated. Twelve will comprise the jury; the other two are alternates who hear the case and remain available in the event one of the impaneled jurors is taken ill. For a discussion of the jury's responsibility, see http://www.placer.ca.gov/courts/ and click on "Jury Duty: An American Responsibility."

Although jury selection for a case can sometimes take many days, in the Enviro-Vision case the first day of the hearing ends with the jury selected. In the hallway outside the court, Rich offers Janet $200,000 to settle. Janet reports the offer to Beth and they agree to reject it. Craig Bergson drives home, emotionally confused. Only three weeks before his death, Tony had accidentally met his old roommate and they had had several drinks. Craig believes that what Tony told him answers the riddle of this case.

OPENING STATEMENTS

The next day, each attorney makes an opening statement to the jury, summarizing the proof he or she expects to offer, with the plaintiff going first. Janet focuses on Tony's successful life, his business and strong marriage, and the tragedy of his accidental death.[7]

Rich works hard to establish a friendly rapport with the jury. He expresses regret about the death. Nonetheless, suicide is a clear exclusion from the policy. If insurance companies are forced to pay claims they didn't bargain for, everyone's insurance rates will go up.

---

[6] Students of French note that *voir* means "to see" and assume that *voir dire* should translate, "to see, to speak." However, the legal term is centuries old and derives not from modern French but from *Old* French, in which voir meant "truth."

[7] Janet Booker has dropped her claim for triple damages against Coastal. To have any hope of such a verdict, she would have to show that Coastal had no legitimate reason at all for denying the claim. Discovery has convinced her that Coastal will demonstrate some rational reasons for what it did.

BURDEN OF PROOF

In civil cases, the plaintiff has the burden of proof. That means that the plaintiff must convince the jury that its version of the case is correct; the defendant is not obligated to disprove the allegations.

The plaintiff's burden in a civil lawsuit is to prove its case by a **preponderance of the evidence**. It must convince the jury that its version of the facts is at least *slightly more likely* than the defendant's version. Some courts describe this as a "51–49" persuasion, that is, that plaintiff's proof must "just tip" credibility in its favor. By contrast, in a criminal case, the prosecution must demonstrate **beyond a reasonable doubt** that the defendant is guilty. The burden of proof in a criminal case is much tougher because the likely consequences are also tougher. See Exhibit 3.3.

PLAINTIFF'S CASE

Since the plaintiff has the burden of proof, Janet puts in her case first. She wants to prove two things. First, that Tony died. That is easy, since the death certificate clearly demonstrates it and since Coastal does not seriously contest it. Second, in order to win double indemnity damages, she must show that the death was accidental. She will do this with the testimony of the witnesses she calls, one after the other. Her first witness is Beth. When a lawyer asks questions of her own witness, it is **direct examination**. Janet brings out all the evidence she wants the jury to hear: that the business was basically sound, though temporarily troubled, that Tony was a hard worker, why the company took out life insurance policies, and so forth.

Then Rich has a chance to **cross-examine** Beth, which means to ask questions of an opposing witness. He will try to create doubt in the jury's mind. He asks Beth only questions for which he is certain of the answers, based on discovery. Rich gets Beth to admit that the firm was not doing well the year of Tony's death; that Tony had lost the best client the firm ever had; that Beth had reduced salaries; and that Tony had been depressed about business.

RULES OF EVIDENCE

The lawyers are not free simply to ask any question they want. The law of **evidence** determines what questions a lawyer may ask and how the questions are to be phrased, what answers a witness may give, and what documents may be introduced. The goal is to get the best evidence possible before the jurors so that they can decide what really happened. In general, witnesses may only testify about things they saw or heard.

Exhibit 3.3
Burden of Proof. In a civil lawsuit, a plaintiff wins with a mere preponderance of the evidence. But the prosecution must persuade a jury beyond a reasonable doubt in order to win a criminal conviction.

These rules are complex, and a thorough explication of them is beyond the scope of this chapter; however, they can be just as important in resolving a dispute as the underlying substantive law. Suppose a plaintiff's case depends upon the jury hearing about a certain conversation, but the rules of evidence prevent the lawyer from asking about it. That conversation might just as well never have occurred.

Janet calls an expert witness, a marine geologist, who testifies about the tides and currents in the area where Tony's body was found. The expert testifies that even experienced swimmers can be overwhelmed by a sudden shift in currents. Rich objects strenuously that this is irrelevant, because there is no testimony that there *was* such a current at the time of Tony's death. The judge permits the testimony.

Karen Caruso testifies that Tony was in "reasonably good" spirits the day of his death and that he often took Blue for walks along the beach. Karen testifies that Blue was part Newfoundland. Rich objects that testimony about Blue's pedigree is irrelevant, but Janet insists it will show why Blue was tied up. The judge allows the testimony. Karen says that whenever Blue saw them swim he would instinctively go into the water and pull them to shore. Does that explain why Blue was tied up? Only the jury can answer.

Cross-examination is grim for Karen. Rich slowly but methodically questions her about Tony's state of mind and brings out the problems with the company, his depression, and tension within the marriage. Janet's other witnesses testify essentially as they did during their depositions.

MOTION FOR DIRECTED VERDICT

At the close of the plaintiff's case, Rich moves for a **directed verdict**, that is, a ruling that the plaintiff has entirely failed to prove some aspect of her case. Rich is seeking to win without even putting in his own case. He argues that it was Beth's burden to prove that Tony died accidentally and that she has entirely failed to do that.

A directed verdict is permissible only if the evidence so clearly favors the defendant that reasonable minds could not disagree on it. If reasonable minds could disagree, the motion must be denied. Here, Judge Rowland rules that the plaintiff has put in enough evidence of accidental death that a reasonable person could find in Beth's favor. The motion is denied.

DEFENDANT'S CASE

Rich now puts in his case, exactly as Janet did, except that he happens to have fewer witnesses. He calls the examining doctor, who admits that Tony could have committed suicide by swimming out too far. On cross-examination, Janet gets the doctor to acknowledge that he has no idea whether Tony intentionally drowned. Rich also questions several neighbors as to how depressed Tony had seemed and how unusual it was that Blue was tied up. Some of the witnesses Rich deposed, such as the tennis partner Jerry Johnson, have nothing helpful to Coastal's case, so he does not call them.

Craig Bergson, sitting in the back of the courtroom, thinks how different the trial would have been had he been called as a witness. When he and Tony had the fateful drink, Tony had been distraught: business was terrible, he was involved in an extramarital affair that he could not end, and he saw no way out of his problems. He had no one to talk to and had been hugely relieved to speak with Craig. Several times Tony had said, "I just can't go on like this. I don't want to, anymore."

Craig thought Tony seemed suicidal and urged him to see a therapist Craig knew and trusted. Tony had said that it was good advice, but Craig is unsure whether Tony sought any help.

This evidence would have affected the case. Had Rich Stewart known of the conversation, he would have deposed Craig and the therapist. Coastal's case would have been far stronger, perhaps overwhelming. But Craig's evidence will never be heard. Facts are critical. Rich's decision to depose other witnesses and omit Craig may influence the verdict more than any rule of law.

CLOSING ARGUMENT

Both lawyers sum up their case to the jury, explaining how they hope the jury will interpret what they have heard. Janet summarizes the plaintiff's version of the facts, claiming that Blue was tied up so that Tony could swim without worrying about him. Rich claims that business and personal pressures had overwhelmed Tony. He tied up his dog, neatly folded his clothes, and took his own life.

JURY INSTRUCTIONS

Judge Rowland instructs the jury as to its duty. He tells them that they are to evaluate the case based only on the evidence they heard at trial, relying on their own experience and common sense.

He explains the law and the burden of proof, telling the jury that it is Beth's obligation to prove that Tony died. If Beth has proven that Tony died, she is entitled to $1 million; if she has proven that his death was accidental, she is entitled to $2 million. However, if Coastal has proven suicide, Beth receives nothing. Finally, he states that if the jury is unable to decide between accidental death and suicide, there is a legal presumption that it was accidental. Rich asks Judge Rowland to rephrase the "legal presumption" part, but the judge declines.

VERDICT

The jury deliberates informally, with all jurors entitled to voice their opinion. Some deliberations take two hours; some take two weeks. Many states require a unanimous verdict; others require only, for example, a 10–2 vote in civil cases.

This case presents a close call. No one saw Tony die. Yet even though they cannot know with certainty, the jury's decision will probably be the final word on whether he took his own life. After a day and a half of deliberating, the jury notifies the judge that it has reached a verdict. Rich Stewart quickly makes a new offer: $350,000. Beth hesitates but turns it down.

The judge summons the lawyers to court, and Beth goes as well. The judge asks the foreman if the jury has reached a decision. He states that it has: the jury finds that Tony Caruso drowned accidentally and awards Beth Smiles $2 million.

MOTIONS AFTER THE VERDICT

Rich immediately moves for a **judgment** *non obstante veredicto* (judgment n.o.v.), meaning a judgment notwithstanding the jury's verdict. He is asking the judge to overturn the jury's verdict. Rich argues that the jury's decision went against all of the evidence. He also claims that the judge's instructions were wrong and misled the jury.

Judge Rowland denies the judgment n.o.v. Rich immediately moves for a new trial, making the same claim, and the judge denies the motion. Beth is elated that the case is finally over—until Janet says she expects an appeal. Craig Bergson, leaving the courtroom, wonders if he did the right thing. He felt sympathy for Beth and none for Coastal. Yet now he is neither happy nor proud.

Appeals

Two days later, Rich files an appeal to the court of appeal. The same day, he phones Janet and increases his settlement offer to $425,000. Beth is tempted but wants Janet's advice. Janet says the risks of an appeal are that the court will order a new trial, and they would start all over. But to accept this offer is to forfeit over $1.5 million. Beth is unsure what to do. The firm desperately needs cash now. Janet suggests they wait until oral argument, another eight months.

Rich files a brief arguing that there were two basic errors at the trial: first, that the jury's verdict is clearly contrary to the evidence; and second, that the judge gave the wrong instructions to the jury. Janet files a reply brief, opposing Rich on both issues. In her brief, Janet cites many cases that she claims are **precedent**: earlier decisions by the state supreme court on similar or identical issues. Although the following case is from a different jurisdiction, it is an example of the kind of case that she will rely on.

PONCE V. SANDOVAL

2001 Tex. App. LEXIS 7425
Texas Court of Appeals, 2001

FACTS: Judith Ponce ran over Maria Sandoval's left foot. The victim went to an emergency room, but the medical staff determined the accident had caused minimal damage. The doctors found that Sandoval suffered from preexisting foot and knee injuries, along with high blood pressure. She returned several times to the hospital, including its intensive care unit, for problems relating to the hypertension. Sandoval sued Ponce.

Sandoval's expert witness, Dr. Philips, stated that "to a reasonable medical probability," the accident caused Sandoval's hypertension. He testified that her past expenses of $8,167, mostly for hospital visits, were reasonable and were a result of the accident. He anticipated future costs of about $15,300 for hypertension treatment. However, on cross-examination he acknowledged that while accident trauma could cause an episode of high blood pressure, it would typically not induce chronic hypertension.

The jury awarded Sandoval $1,600 for her medical expenses. Sandoval moved for a judgment notwithstanding the verdict. The trial judge granted the motion, stating that the jury award was against the weight of the evidence. He ruled that the undisputed evidence for past expenses was $8,167, and for future costs was $15,300. He awarded those amounts to Sandoval, and Ponce appealed.

ISSUE: Did the trial court err by granting plaintiff a judgment notwithstanding the verdict?

EXCERPTS FROM JUDGE JOHNSON'S DECISION: If the trial court disregards a jury finding and enters judgment nov and such action is challenged on appeal, the appellate standard of review is whether the jury finding was supported by legally sufficient evidence. A jury finding is not based on legally sufficient evidence if there is a complete absence of evidence to support the finding. In assessing personal injury damages, the trier of fact has great discretion in fixing the amount of the damage award.

Evidence in the record would have supported a finding by the jury that Sandoval's past medical expenses resulting from the occurrence were greater than $1,600. But, evidence also was legally sufficient to support a finding that Sandoval's past medical expenses resulting from the occurrence were $1,600, even though the trial court and Sandoval could not fathom the exact mental processes of the jury in reaching its finding. The questions of existence of preexisting conditions, aggravation of any such preexisting conditions, and whether Sandoval failed to properly care for her injuries, if any, from the occurrence were properly entrusted to the jury by the court's charge.

The opinion and judgment of Dr. Philips, as an expert witness, was not conclusive on the issues of the causal relationship of all of Sandoval's medical conditions or expenses to the occurrence—either those in the past, or those in the future. The jury was free to disregard his opinion on such matters as they considered, and weighed all of the evidence and judged the appearance and credibility of the witnesses, including Dr. Philips, and the weight to give the different parts of the evidence and testimony.

We conclude that the jury's finding of $1,600 for past medical expenses is supported by legally sufficient evidence. We likewise conclude the evidence is not conclusive as to whether she would incur future medical expense as a result of the occurrence, or the amount of any such expenses. Accordingly, the trial court erred in disregarding the findings of the jury as to Sandoval's medical expenses in the past and those which she would incur in the future. We remand the case to the trial court for entry of judgment in accordance with this opinion. ◢

Eight months later, the lawyers representing Coastal and Enviro-Vision appear in the court of appeal to argue their case. Rich, the appellant, goes first. The judges frequently interrupt his argument with questions. Relying on decisions like *Ponce*, they show little sympathy for his claim that the verdict was against the facts. They seem more sympathetic with his second point, that the instructions were wrong.

When Janet argues, all of their questions concern the judge's instructions. It appears they believe the instructions were in error. The judges take the case under advisement, meaning they will decide some time in the future—maybe in two weeks, maybe in five months.

APPEAL COURT OPTIONS

The court of appeal can **affirm** the trial court, allowing the decision to stand. The court may **modify** the decision, for example, by affirming that the plaintiff wins but decreasing the size of the award. (That is unlikely here; Beth is entitled to $2 million or nothing.) The court might **reverse and remand**, nullifying the lower court's decision and returning the case to the trial court. Or it could simply **reverse**, turning the loser (Coastal) into the winner, with no new trial.

What will it do here? On the factual issue it will probably rule in Beth's favor. There *was* evidence from which a jury could conclude that Tony died accidentally. It is true that there was also considerable evidence to support Coastal's position, but that is probably not enough to overturn the verdict. As we saw in the *Ponce* case, if reasonable people could disagree on what the evidence proves, an appellate court generally refuses to change the jury's factual findings. The court of appeal is likely to rule that a reasonable jury *could* have found accidental death, even if the appellate judges personally suspect that Tony may have killed himself.

The judge's instructions raise a more difficult problem. Some states would require a more complex statement about "presumptions."[8]

What does a court of appeal do if it decides the trial court's instructions were wrong? If it believes the error rendered the trial and verdict unfair, it will remand the case, that is, send it back to the lower court for a new trial. However, the court may conclude that the mistake was **harmless error**. A trial judge cannot do a perfect job, and not every error is fatal. The court may decide the verdict was fair in spite of the mistake.

Janet and Beth talk. Beth is very anxious and wants to settle. She does not want to wait four or five months, only to learn that they must start all over. Janet urges that they wait a few weeks to hear from Rich: they don't want to seem too eager.

A week later, Rich telephones and offers $500,000. Janet turns it down, but says she will ask Beth if she wants to make a counter-offer. She and Beth talk. They agree that they will settle for $1 million. Janet then calls Rich and offers to settle for $1.7 million. Rich and Janet debate the merits of the case. Rich later calls back and offers $750,000, saying he doubts that he can go any higher. Janet counters with $1.4 million, saying she doubts she can go any lower. They argue, both predicting that they will win on appeal.

Rich calls, offers $900,000 and says, "That's it. No more." Janet argues for $1.2 million, expecting to nudge Rich up to $1 million. He doesn't nudge, instead saying, "Take it or leave it." Janet and Beth talk it over. Janet telephones Rich and accepts $900,000 to settle the case.

If they had waited for the court of appeal decision, would Beth have won? It is impossible to know. It is certain, though, that whoever lost would have appealed. Months would have passed waiting to learn if the state supreme court would accept the case. If that court had agreed to hear the appeal, Beth would have endured another year of waiting, brief writing, oral argument, and tense hoping. The high court has all of the options discussed: to affirm, modify, reverse and remand, or simply reverse.

Chapter Conclusion

No one will ever know for sure whether Tony took his own life. Craig Bergson's evidence might have tipped the scales in favor of Coastal. But even that is uncertain, since the jury could have found him unpersuasive. After two years the case ends with a settlement and uncertainty—both typical lawsuit results. The missing witness is less common but not extraordinary. The vaguely unsatisfying feeling about it all is only too common and indicates why litigation is best avoided—by dispute prevention.

---

[8] Judge Rowland probably should have said, "The law presumes that death is accidental, not suicide. So if there were no evidence either way, the plaintiff would win because we presume accident. But if there is competing evidence, the presumption becomes irrelevant. If you think that Coastal Insurance has introduced some evidence of suicide, then forget the legal presumption. You must then decide what happened based on what you have seen and heard in court, and on any inferences you choose to draw." Note that the judge's instructions were different, though similar.

Chapter Review

1. Alternative dispute resolution (ADR) is any formal or informal process to settle disputes without a trial. Mediation, arbitration, and other forms of ADR are growing in popularity.

2. There are many *systems* of courts, one federal and one in each state. A federal court will hear a case only if it involves a federal question or diversity jurisdiction.

3. Trial courts determine facts and apply the law to the facts; appeal courts generally accept the facts found by the trial court and review the trial record for errors of law.

4. A complaint and an answer are the two most important pleadings, that is, documents that start a lawsuit.

5. Discovery is the critical pre-trial opportunity for both parties to learn the strengths and weaknesses of the opponent's case. Important forms of discovery include interrogatories, depositions, production of documents and objects, physical and mental examinations, and requests for admission.

6. A motion is a formal request to the court.

7. Summary judgment is a ruling by the court that no trial is necessary because there are no essential facts in dispute.

8. Generally both plaintiff and defendant may demand a jury in any lawsuit for money damages.

9. *Voir dire* is the process of selecting jurors in order to obtain an impartial panel.

10. The plaintiff's burden of proof in a civil lawsuit is preponderance of the evidence, meaning that its version of the facts must be at least slightly more persuasive than the defendant's. In a criminal prosecution, the government must offer proof beyond a reasonable doubt in order to win a conviction.

11. The rules of evidence determine what questions may be asked during trial, what testimony may be given, and what documents may be introduced.

12. The verdict is the jury's decision in a case. The losing party may ask the trial judge to overturn the verdict, seeking a judgment *non obstante veredicto* or a new trial. Judges seldom grant either.

13. An appeal court has many options. The court may affirm, upholding the lower court's decision; modify, changing the verdict but leaving the same party victorious; reverse, transforming the loser into the winner; and/or remand, sending the case back to the lower court.

Practice Test

1. You plan to open a store in Chicago, specializing in beautiful rugs imported from Turkey. You will work with a native Turk who will purchase and ship the rugs to your store. You are wise enough to insist on a contract establishing the rights and obligations of both parties and would prefer an ADR clause. But you want to be sensitive to different cultures and do not want a clause that will magnify a problem or alienate the parties. Is there some way you can accomplish all of this?

2. Solo Serve Corp. signed a lease for space in a shopping center. The lease contained this clause: "Neither Landlord nor tenant shall engage in or permit any activity at or around the Demised Premises which violates any applicable law, constitutes a nuisance, or is likely to bring discredit upon the Shopping Center, or discourage customers from patronizing other occupants of the Shopping Center by other than activities customarily engaged in by reputable businesses." Westowne Associates, the landlord, later leased other space in the center to The Finish Line, an off-track betting business that also had a license to sell food and liquor. Solo Serve sued, claiming that Westowne had breached the lease. Solo Serve requested either a permanent injunction barring The Finish Line from using the center or that The Finish Line pay the cost of relocating its own business.

   The case raises two questions. The minor

one is, did Westowne violate the lease? The major one is, how could this dispute have been prevented? It ultimately went to the United States Court of Appeals, costing both sides much time and money.

3. State which court(s) have jurisdiction as to each of these lawsuits:

    (a) Pat wants to sue his next-door neighbor Dorothy, claiming that Dorothy promised to sell him the house next door.

    (b) Paula, who lives in New York City, wants to sue Dizzy Movie Theatres, whose principal place of business is Dallas. She claims that while she was in Texas on holiday, she was injured by their negligent maintenance of a stairway. She claims damages of $30,000.

    (c) Phil lives in Tennessee. He wants to sue Dick, who lives in Ohio. Phil claims that Dick agreed to sell him 3,000 acres of farmland in Ohio, worth over $2 million.

    (d) Pete, incarcerated in a federal prison in Kansas, wants to sue the United States government. He claims that his treatment by prison authorities violates three federal statutes.

4. Probationary schoolteachers sued the New Madrid, Missouri, school district, claiming that the school district refused to give them permanent jobs because of their union organizing activity. The defendant school district claimed that each plaintiff was refused a permanent job because of inferior teaching. During discovery the plaintiffs asked for the personnel files of probationary teachers who *had* been offered permanent jobs. The school district refused to provide them, arguing that the personnel files did not indicate the union status of the teachers and therefore would not help the plaintiffs. The trial court ruled that the school district need not release the files. On appeal, the plaintiffs argue that this hindered their ability to prove the real reasons they had been fired. How should the appeal court rule?

5. Students are now suing schools for sexual harassment. The cases raise important issues about the limits of discovery. In a case in Petaluma, California, a girl claimed that she was harassed for years and that the school knew about it and failed to act. According to press reports, she alleges that a boy stood up in

class and asked, "I have a question. I want to know if [Jane Doe] has sex with hot dogs." In discovery, the school district sought the parents' therapy records, the girl's diary, and a psychological evaluation of the girl. Should they get those things?

6. British discovery practice differs from that in the United States. Most discovery in Britain concerns documents. The lawyers for the two sides, called solicitors, must deliver to the opposing side a list of all relevant documents in their possession. Each side may then request to look at and copy those it wishes. Depositions are rare. What advantages and disadvantages are there to the British practice?

7. **ETHICS** Trial practice also is dramatically different in Britain. The parties' solicitors do not go into court. Courtroom work is done by different lawyers, called barristers. The barristers are not permitted to interview any witnesses before trial. They know the substance of what each witness intends to say, but do not rehearse questions and answers, as in the United States. Which approach do you consider more effective? More ethical? What is the purpose of a trial? Of pre-trial preparation?

8. Claus Scherer worked for Rockwell International and was paid over $300,000 per year. Rockwell fired Scherer for alleged sexual harassment of several workers, including his secretary, Terry Pendy. Scherer sued in United States District Court, alleging that Rockwell's real motive in firing him was his high salary.

    Rockwell moved for summary judgment, offering deposition transcripts of various employees. Pendy's deposition detailed instances of harassment, including comments about her body, instances of unwelcome touching, and discussions of extramarital affairs. Another deposition, from a Rockwell employee who investigated the allegations, included complaints by other employees as to Scherer's harassment. In his own deposition, which he offered to oppose summary judgment, Scherer testified that he could not recall the incidents alleged by Pendy and others. He denied generally that he had sexually harassed anyone. The district court granted summary judgment for Rockwell. Was its ruling correct?

9. Lloyd Dace worked for ACF Industries as a supervisor in the punchpress department of a carburetor factory. ACF demoted Dace to an hourly job on the assembly line, and Dace sued, claiming that ACF discriminated on the basis of age. At trial, Dace showed that he had been 53 years old when demoted and had been replaced by a man aged 40. He offered evidence that ACF's benefits supervisor had attended the meeting at which his demotion was decided and that the benefits supervisor was aware of the cost savings of replacing Dace with a younger man.

At the end of Dace's case, ACF moved for a directed verdict, and the trial court granted it. The judge reasoned that Dace's entire case was based on circumstantial evidence. He held that it was too speculative for the jury to infer age discrimination from the few facts that Dace had offered. Was the trial court correct?

10. **YOU BE THE JUDGE WRITING PROBLEM** Apache Corp. and El Paso Exploration Co. operated a Texas gas well that exploded, burning out of control for over a year. More than 100 plaintiffs sued the two owners, claiming damage to adjoining gas fields. The plaintiffs also sued Axelson, Inc., which manufactured a valve whose failure may have contributed to the explosion. Axelson, in turn, sued Apache and El Paso. Axelson sought discovery from both companies about an internal investigation they had conducted, before the blowout, concerning kickbacks (illegal payments) at the gas field. Axelson claimed that the investigation could shed light on what caused the explosion, but the trial court ruled that the material was irrelevant, and denied discovery. Axelson appealed. Is the investigation discoverable? **Argument for Axelson:** If the companies investigated kickbacks, they were concerned about corruption and mismanagement—both of which can cause employees to cut corners, ignore safety concerns, fabricate reports, and so forth. All of those activities have the potential to cause a serious accident. All parties are entitled to discover material that may lead to relevant evidence, and that could easily happen here. **Argument for Apache and El Paso:** This is a fishing expedition. The investigation was completed before the explosion and is completely unrelated. Any internal investigation has the potential (a) to reveal valuable business or trade secrets and (b) to prove embarrassing to the companies investigated. Axelson's motive is to force the two owners to settle in order to avoid such revelations. Discovery is not supposed to be a weapon.

11. Imogene Williams sued the U.S. Elevator Corp. She claimed that when she entered one of the company's elevators, it went up three floors but failed to open, fell several floors, stopped, and then continued to erratically rise and fall for about 40 minutes. She claimed physical injuries and emotional distress. At trial, U.S. Elevator disputed every allegation. When the judge instructed the jury, he asked them to decide whether the company had been negligent. If it had, the jury was to decide what physical injuries Williams had suffered. The judge also instructed them that she could receive money for emotional damages only if the emotional damages resulted from her physical injury. The jury found for U.S. Elevator, deciding that it had not been negligent.

On appeal, Williams argues that the judge was wrong in stating that the emotional injuries had to result from the physical injuries. The court of appeal agreed that the instruction was incorrect. There could be emotional damages even if there were no physical injuries. What appellate remedy is appropriate?

12. **ROLE REVERSAL** Write a multiple-choice question that illustrates the unique significance of summary judgment: that there is no need for a trial because there are no essential facts in dispute.

Internet Research Problem

You may be called for jury duty before long. Read the summary of the juror's responsibilities at http://www.placer.ca.gov/courts/jury.htm. Some people try hard to get out of jury duty. Why is that a problem in a democratic society?

You can find further practice problems in the Online Quiz at http://beatty.westbuslaw.com **or in the Study Guide that accompanies this text.**

Common Law,
Statutory Law, and
Administrative Law

Jason observes a toddler wander onto the railroad tracks and hears a train approaching. He has plenty of time to pull the child from the tracks with no risk to himself, but chooses to do nothing. The youngster is killed. The child's family sues Jason for his callous behavior, and a court determines that Jason owes—nothing.

"Why can't they just fix the law?" students and professionals often ask, in response to Jason's impunity and countless other legal oddities. Their exasperation is understandable. This chapter cannot guarantee intellectual tranquillity, but it should diminish the sense of bizarreness that law can instill. We will look at three sources of law: common law, statutory law, and administrative law. Most of the law you learn in this course comes from one of these sources. The substantive law will make more sense when you have a solid feel for *how* it was created. ▪

Common Law

Jason and the toddler present a classic legal puzzle: What, if anything, must a bystander do when he sees someone in danger? We will examine this issue to see how the common law works.

The common law is judge-made law. It is the sum total of all the cases decided by appellate courts. The common law of Pennsylvania consists of all cases decided by appellate courts in that state. The Illinois common law of bystander liability is all of the cases on that subject decided by Illinois appellate courts. Two hundred years ago, almost all of the law was common law. Today most new law is statutory. But common law still predominates in tort, contract, and agency law, and it is very important in property, employment, and some other areas.

We focus on appellate courts because they are the only ones to make rulings of *law*, as discussed in Chapter 3. In a bystander case, it is the job of the state's highest court to say what legal obligations, if any, a bystander has. The trial court, on the other hand, must decide *facts*: Was this defendant able to see what was happening? Was the plaintiff really in trouble? Could the defendant have assisted without peril to himself?

STARE DECISIS

Nothing perks up a course like Latin. *Stare decisis* means "let the decision stand." It is the essence of the common law. The phrase indicates that once a court has decided a particular issue, it will generally apply the same rule in future cases. Suppose the highest court of Arizona must decide whether a contract for a new car, signed by a 16-year-old, can be enforced against him. The court will look to see if there is **precedent**, that is, whether the high court of Arizona has already decided a similar case. The Arizona court looks and finds several earlier cases, all holding that such contracts may not be enforced against a minor. The court will apply that precedent and refuse to enforce the contract in this case. Courts do not always follow precedent but they generally do: *stare decisis.*

Two words explain why the common law is never as easy as we might like: *predictability* and *flexibility*. The law is trying to accommodate both goals. The need for predictability is apparent: people must know what the law is. If contract law changed daily, an entrepreneur who leased factory space and then started buying machinery would be uncertain if the factory would actually be available when she was ready to move in. Will the landlord slip out of the lease? Will the machinery be ready on time? The need for predictability created the doctrine of *stare decisis.*

Yet there must also be flexibility in the law, some means to respond to new problems and changing social mores. In this new millennium, we cannot be encumbered by ironclad rules established before electricity was discovered. These two ideas may be obvious but they also conflict: the more flexibility we permit, the less predictability we enjoy. We will watch the conflict play out in the bystander cases.

BYSTANDER CASES

This country inherited from England a simple rule about a bystander's obligations: you have no duty to assist someone in peril unless you created the danger.

In *Union Pacific Railway Co. v. Cappier*,[1] through no fault of the railroad, a train struck a man, severing an arm and a leg. Railroad employees saw the incident happen but did nothing to assist him. By the time help arrived, the victim had died. In this 1903 case, the court held that the railroad had no duty to help the injured man:

> With the humane side of the question courts are not concerned. It is the omission or negligent discharge of legal duties only which come within the sphere of judicial cognizance. For withholding relief from the suffering, for failure to respond to the calls of worthy charity, or for faltering in the bestowment of brotherly love on the unfortunate, penalties are found not in the laws of men but in [the laws of God].

As harsh as this judgment might seem, it was an accurate statement of the law at that time in both England and the United States: bystanders need do nothing. Contemporary writers found the rule inhumane and cruel, and even judges criticized it. But—*stare decisis*—they followed it. With a rule this old and well established, no court was willing to scuttle it. What courts did do was seek openings for small changes.

Eighteen years after the Kansas case of *Cappier*, the court in nearby Iowa found the basis for one exception. Ed Carey was a farm laborer, working for Frank Davis. While in the fields, Carey fainted from sunstroke and remained unconscious. Davis simply hauled him to a nearby wagon and left him in the sun for an additional four hours, causing serious permanent injury. The court's response:

> It is unquestionably the well-settled rule that the master is under no legal duty to care for a sick or injured servant for whose illness or injury he is not at fault. Though not unjust in principle, this rule, if carried unflinchingly and without exception to its logical extreme, is sometimes productive of shocking results. To avoid this criticism [we hold that where] a servant suffers serious injury, or is suddenly stricken down in a manner indicating the immediate and emergent need of aid to save him from death or serious harm, the master, if present is in duty bound to take such reasonable measures as may be practicable to relieve him, even though such master be not chargeable with fault in bringing about the emergency.[2]

And this is how the common law changes: bit by tiny bit. In Iowa a bystander could now be liable *if* he was the employer and *if* the worker was suddenly stricken and *if* it was an emergency and *if* the employer was present. That is a small change but an important one.

For the next 50 years, changes in bystander law came very slowly. Consider *Osterlind v. Hill*, a case from 1928.[3] Osterlind rented a canoe from Hill's boatyard, paddled into the lake, and promptly fell into the water. For *30 minutes* he clung to the side of the canoe and shouted for help. Hill heard the cries but did nothing; Osterlind drowned. Was Hill liable? No, said the court: a bystander has no liability. Not until half a century later did that same state supreme court reverse its position and begin to require assistance in extreme cases—a long time for Osterlind to hold on.[4]

In the 1970s changes came more quickly.

---

1 66 Kan. 649, 72 P. 281 (1903).
2 *Carey v. Davis*, 190 Iowa 720, 180 N.W. 889 (1921).
3 263 Mass. 73, 160 N.E. 301 (1928).
4 *Pridgen v. Boston Housing Authority*, 364 Mass. 696, 308 N.E.2d 467 (1974).

TARASOFF V. REGENTS OF THE UNIVERSITY OF CALIFORNIA

17 Cal. 3d 425, 551 P.2d 334, 131 Cal. Rptr. 14
Supreme Court of California, 1976

FACTS: On October 27, 1969, Prosenjit Poddar killed Tatiana Tarasoff. Tatiana's parents claimed that two months earlier Poddar had confided his intention to kill Tatiana to Dr. Lawrence Moore, a psychologist employed by the University of California at Berkeley. They sued the university, claiming that Dr. Moore should have warned Tatiana and/or should have arranged for Poddar's confinement.

ISSUE: Did Dr. Moore have a duty to Tatiana Tarasoff, and did he breach that duty?

EXCERPTS FROM JUSTICE TOBRINER'S DECISION: Although under the common law, as a general rule, one person owed no duty to control the conduct of another, nor to warn those endangered by such conduct, the courts have carved out an exception to this rule in cases in which the defendant stands in some special relationship to either the person whose conduct needs to be controlled or in a relationship to the foreseeable victim of that conduct. Applying this exception to the present case, we note that a relationship of defendant therapists to either Tatiana or Poddar will suffice to establish a duty of care.

We recognize the difficulty that a therapist encounters in attempting to forecast whether a patient presents a serious danger of violence. Obviously we do not require that the therapist, in making that determination, render a perfect performance; the therapist need only exercise that reasonable degree of skill, knowledge, and care ordinarily possessed and exercised by members of [the field] under similar circumstances.

In the instant case, however, the pleadings do not raise any question as to failure of defendant therapists to predict that Poddar presented a serious danger of violence. On the contrary, the present complaints allege that defendant therapists did in fact predict that Poddar would kill, but were negligent in failing to warn.

In our view, once a therapist does in fact determine, or under applicable professional standards reasonably should have determined, that a patient poses a serious danger of violence to others, he bears a duty to exercise reasonable care to protect the foreseeable victim of that danger.

[The Tarasoffs have stated a legitimate claim against Dr. Moore.]

The *Tarasoff* exception applies when there is some special relationship, such as therapist-patient. What if there is no such relationship? The 1983 case of *Soldano v. O'Daniels*[5] arose when a patron in Happy Jack's bar saw Villanueva threaten Soldano with a gun. The patron dashed next door into the Circle Inn bar, told the bartender what was happening, and urged him to call the police. The bartender refused. The witness then asked to use the phone to call the police himself, but the bartender again refused. Tragically, the delay permitted Villanueva to kill Soldano.

As in the earlier cases we have seen, this case presented an emergency. But the exception created in *Carey v. Davis* applied only if the bystander was an employer, and that in Tarasoff only for a doctor. In *Soldano*, the bystander was neither. Should the law require him to act, that is, should it carve a new exception? Here is what the California court decided:

> Many citizens simply "don't want to get involved." No rule should be adopted [requiring] a citizen to open up his or her house to a stranger so that the latter may use the

---

[5] 141 Cal. App. 3d 443, 190 Cal. Rptr. 310, 1983 Cal. App. LEXIS 1539 (1983).

telephone to call for emergency assistance. As Mrs. Alexander in Anthony Burgess' *A Clockwork Orange* learned to her horror, such an action may be fraught with danger. It does not follow, however, that use of a telephone in a public portion of a business should be refused for a legitimate emergency call.

We conclude that the bartender owed a duty to [Soldano] to permit the patron from Happy Jack's to place a call to the police or to place the call himself. It bears emphasizing that the duty in this case does not require that one must go to the aid of another. That is not the issue here. The employee was not the good samaritan intent on aiding another. The patron was.

Do these exceptions mean that the bystander rule is gone? *Parra v. Tarasco*[6] provides a partial answer. Ernesto Parra was a customer at the Jiminez Restaurant when food became lodged in his throat. The employees did not use the Heimlich maneuver or any other method to try to save him. Parra choked to death. Was the restaurant liable? No, said the Illinois Appeals Court. The restaurant had no obligation to do anything.

The bystander rule, that hardy oak, is alive and well. Various initials have been carved into its bark—the exceptions we have seen and a variety of others—but the trunk is strong and the leaves green. Perhaps someday the proliferating exceptions will topple it, but the process of the common law is slow and that day is nowhere in sight. In the meantime, it is nice to be reminded that even without a legal obligation, some citizens do choose to get involved.

NEWSWORTHY

As the freight train rumbled through rural Indiana, conductor Robert Mohr looked ahead and saw what seemed to be a puppy. Then the "puppy" sat up straight and shook her blond curls. Nineteen-month-old Emily Marshall had wandered away from her mother and was playing on the tracks, dead ahead. Engineer Rodney Lindley jammed on the brakes, but could not possibly stop the 96-car, 6,000-ton train. There was no time to jump off and sprint ahead to the girl. Mohr, aged 49, hustled onto the engine's catwalk and clambered forward, as Lindley slowed the train to 10 miles per hour. Gripping a guard rail, Mohr leaned perilously far forward, waited until the engine loomed directly above the child—and deftly booted her to safety. Emily bounced up with nothing worse than a chipped tooth and forehead cuts, and Mohr, the merrier, was a Hoosier hero.

Statutory Law

Most new law is statutory law. Statutes affect each of us every day in our business, professional, and personal lives. When the system works correctly, this is the one part of the law over which we the people have control. We elect the local legislators who pass state statutes; we vote for the senators and representatives who create federal statutes. If we understand the system, we can affect the largest source of contemporary law. If we live in ignorance of its strengths and pitfalls, we delude ourselves that we participate in a democracy.

As we saw in Chapter 1, there are many systems of government operating in the United States: a national government and 50 state governments. Each level of government has a legislative body. In Washington, D.C., Congress is our national

---

[6] 9230 Ill. App. 3d 819, 595 N.E.2d 1186, 1992 Ill. App. LEXIS 935 (1992).

legislature. Congress passes the statutes that govern the nation. In addition, each state has a legislature, which passes statutes for that state only. In this section we look at how Congress does its work creating statutes. State legislatures operate similarly, but the work of Congress is better documented and obviously of national importance.[7]

BILLS

Congress is organized into two houses, the House of Representatives and the Senate. Either house may originate a proposed statute, which is called a **bill**. The bill must be voted on and approved by both houses. Once both houses pass the bill, they will send it to the president. If the president signs the bill, it becomes law and is then a statute. If the president opposes the bill, he will veto it, in which case it is not law.[8]

Committee Work

If you visit either house of Congress, you will probably find half a dozen legislators on the floor, with one person talking and no one listening. This is because most of the work is done in committees. Both houses are organized into dozens of committees, each with special functions. The House currently has about 27 committees (further divided into about 150 subcommittees), and the Senate has approximately 20 committees (with about 86 subcommittees). For example, the armed services committee of each house oversees the huge defense budget and the workings of the armed forces. Labor committees handle legislation concerning organized labor and working conditions. Banking committees develop expertise on financial institutions. Judiciary committees review nominees to the federal courts. There are dozens of other committees, some very powerful, because they control vast amounts of money, and some relatively weak.

When a bill is proposed in either house, it is referred to the committee that specializes in that subject. Why are bills proposed in the first place? For any of several reasons:

- *New Issue, New Worry.* If society begins to focus on a new issue, Congress may respond with legislation. We consider below, for example, the congressional response to employment discrimination.

- *Unpopular Judicial Ruling.* If Congress disagrees with a judicial interpretation of a statute, the legislators may pass a new statute to modify or "undo" the court decision. For example, if the Supreme Court misinterprets a statute about

---

[7] See the chart of state and federal governments in Chapter 1. A vast amount of information about Congress is available on the Internet. The House of Representatives has a Web page at http:// www.house.gov/. The Senate's site appears at http://www.senate.gov. Each page provides links to current law, pending legislation, votes, committees, and more. If you do not know the name of your representative or senator (shame!), the Web page will provide that information. Most state legislatures have Web sites, which you can reach from links found at http://www.ncsl.org/public/ sitesleg.htm. These sites typically permit you to read statutes, research legislative history, examine the current calendar, and note upcoming events. For example, the Web site http://housegop .state.il.us/ brings you to the Republican caucus in the Illinois House of Representatives, while the site http://www.housedem.state.il.us/ will take you to the same body's Democratic caucus. Many of these Web sites enable you to e-mail your local representatives.

[8] Congress may, however, attempt to override the veto. See the discussion that follows.

musical copyrights, Congress may pass a new law correcting the Court's error. However, the legislators have no such power to modify a court decision based on the Constitution. When the Supreme Court ruled that lawyers had a right *under the First Amendment* to advertise their services, Congress lacked the power to change the decision.

- *Criminal Law.* Statutory law, unlike common law, is prospective. Legislators are hoping to control the future. And that is why almost all criminal law is statutory. A court cannot retroactively announce that it *has been* a crime for a retailer to accept kickbacks from a wholesaler. Everyone must know the rules in advance because the consequences—prison, a felony record—are so harsh.

DISCRIMINATION: CONGRESS AND THE COURTS

The civil rights movement of the 1950s and 1960s convinced most citizens that African Americans continued to suffer relentless discrimination in jobs, housing, voting, schools, and other basic areas of life. Demonstrations and boycotts, marches and counter-marches, church bombings and killings persuaded the nation that the problem was vast and urgent.

In 1963 President Kennedy proposed legislation to guarantee equal rights to African Americans in these areas. The bill went to the House Judiciary Committee, which heard testimony for weeks. Witnesses testified that blacks were often unable to vote because of their race, that landlords and home sellers adamantly refused to sell or rent to blacks, that education was still grossly unequal, and that blacks were routinely denied good jobs in many industries. Eventually the Judiciary Committee approved the bill and sent it to the full House.

The bill was dozens of pages long and divided into "titles," with each title covering a major issue. Title VII concerned employment. We will consider the progress of Title VII in Congress and in the courts. Here is one section of Title VII, as reported to the House floor[9]:

> Sec. 703(a). It shall be an unlawful employment practice for an employer—
>
> (1) to fail or refuse to hire or to discharge any individual, or otherwise to discriminate against any individual with respect to his compensation, terms, conditions, or privileges of employment, because of such individual's race, color, religion, or national origin; or
>
> (2) to limit, segregate, or classify his employees in any way which would deprive or tend to deprive any individual of employment opportunities or otherwise adversely affect his status as an employee, because of such individual's race, color, religion, or national origin.

DEBATE

The proposed bill was intensely controversial and sparked angry argument throughout Congress. Here are some excerpts from one day's debate on the House floor, on February 8, 1964[10]:

---

[9] The section number in the House bill was actually 704(a); we use 703 here because that is the number of the section when the bill became law and the number to which the Supreme Court refers in later litigation.

[10] The order of speakers is rearranged, and the remarks are edited.

MR. WAGGONNER. I speak to you in all sincerity and ask for the right to discriminate if I so choose because I think it is my right. I think it is my right to choose my social companions. I think it is my right if I am a businessman to run it as I please, to do with my own as I will. I think that is a right the Constitution gives to every man. I want the continued right to discriminate and I want the other man to have the right to continue to discriminate against me, because I am discriminated against every day. I do not feel inferior about it.

I ask you to forget about politics, forget about everything except the integrity of the individual, leaving to the people of this country the right to live their lives in the manner they choose to live. Do not destroy this democracy for a Socialist government. A vote for this bill is no less.

MR. CONTE. If the serious cleavage which pitted brother against brother and citizen against citizen during the tragedy of the Civil War is ever to be justified, it can be justified in this House and then in the other body with the passage of this legislation which can and must reaffirm the rights to all individuals which are inherent in our Constitution.

The distinguished poet Mark Van Doren has said that "equality is absolute or no, nothing between can stand," and nothing should now stand between us and the passage of strong and effective civil rights legislation. It is to this that we are united in a strong bipartisan coalition today, and when the laws of the land proclaim that the 88th Congress acted effectively, judiciously, and wisely, we can take pride in our accomplishments as free men.

Other debate was less rhetorical and aimed more at getting information. The following exchange anticipates a 30-year controversy on quotas:

MR. JOHANSEN. I have asked for this time to raise a question and I would ask particularly for the attention of the gentleman from New York [MR. GOODELL] because of a remark he made—and I am not quarreling with it. I understood him to say there is no plan for balanced employment or for quotas in this legislation. . . . I am raising a question as to whether in the effort to eliminate discrimination—and incidentally that is an undefined term in the bill—we may get to a situation in which employers and conceivably union leaders, will insist on legislation providing for a quota system as a matter of self-protection.

Now let us suppose this hypothetical situation exists with 100 jobs to be filled. Let us say 150 persons apply and suppose 75 of them are Negro and 75 of them are white. Supposing the employer . . . hires 75 white men and 25 Negroes. Do the other 50 Negroes or anyone of them severally have a right to claim they have been discriminated against on the basis of color?

MR. GOODELL. It is the intention of the legislation that if applicants are equal in all other respects there will be no restriction. One may choose from among equals. So long as there is no distinction on the basis of race, creed, or color it will not violate the act.

The debate on racial issues carried on. Later in the day, Congressman Smith of Virginia offered an amendment that could scarcely have been smaller—or more important:

Amendment offered by MR. SMITH of Virginia: On page 68, line 23, after the word "religion," insert the word "sex."

In other words, Smith was asking that discrimination on the basis of sex also be outlawed, along with the existing grounds of race, color, national origin, and religion. Congressman Smith's proposal produced the following comments:

Mr. Celler. You know, the French have a phrase for it when they speak of women and men. They say "vive la difference." I think the French are right. Imagine the upheaval that would result from adoption of blanket language requiring total equality. Would male citizens be justified in insisting that women share with them the burdens of compulsory military service? What would become of traditional family relationships? What about alimony? What would become of the crimes of rape and statutory rape? I think the amendment seems illogical, ill timed, ill placed, and improper.

Mrs. St. George. Mr. Chairman, I was somewhat amazed when I came on the floor this afternoon to hear the very distinguished chairman of the Committee on the Judiciary [Mr. Celler] make the remark that he considered the amendment at this point illogical. I can think of nothing more logical than this amendment at this point.

There are still many States where women cannot serve on juries. There are still many States where women do not have equal educational opportunities. In most States and, in fact, I figure it would be safe to say, in all States—women do not get equal pay for equal work. That is a very well known fact. And to say that this is illogical. What is illogical about it? All you are doing is simply correcting something that goes back, frankly to the Dark Ages.

The debate continued. Some supported the "sex" amendment because they were determined to end sexual bias. But politics is complex. Some *opponents* of civil rights supported the amendment because they believed that it would make the legislation less popular and cause Congress to defeat the entire Civil Rights bill.

That strategy did not work. The amendment passed, and sex was added as a protected trait. And, after more debate and several votes, the entire bill passed the House. It went to the Senate, where it followed a similar route from Judiciary Committee to full Senate. Much of the Senate debate was similar to what we have seen. But some senators raised a new issue, concerning §703(2), which prohibited *segregating or classifying* employees based on any of the protected categories (race, color, national origin, religion, or sex). Senator Tower was concerned that §703(2) meant that an employee in a protected category could never be given any sort of job test. So the Senate amended §703 to include a new subsection:

Sec. 703(h). Notwithstanding any other provision of this title, it shall not be an unlawful employment practice for an employer . . . to give and to act upon the results of any professionally developed ability test provided that such test . . . is not designed, intended or used to discriminate because of race, color, religion, sex or national origin.

gender

With that amendment, and many others, the bill passed the Senate. *1964*

Conference Committee

Civil rights legislation had now passed both houses, but the bills were no longer the same due to the many amendments. This is true with most legislation. The next step is for the two houses to send representatives to a House–Senate Conference Committee. This committee examines all of the differences between the two bills and tries to reach a compromise. With the Civil Rights bill, Senator Tower's amendment was left in; other Senate amendments were taken out. When the Conference Committee had settled every difference between the two versions, the new, modified bill was sent back to each house for a new vote.

The House of Representatives and the Senate again angrily debated the compromise language reported from the Conference Committee. Finally, after years of violent public demonstrations and months of debate, each house passed the same bill. President Johnson promptly signed it. The Civil Rights Act of 1964 was law. See Exhibit 4.1.

Title VII of the Civil Rights Act obviously prohibited an employer from saying to a job applicant, "We don't hire blacks." In some parts of the country, that had been common practice; after the Civil Rights Act passed, it became rare. Employers who routinely hired whites only, or promoted only whites, found themselves losing lawsuits.

A new group of cases arose, those in which some job standard was set that appeared to be racially neutral, yet had a discriminatory effect. In North Carolina, the Duke Power Co. required that applicants for higher paying, promotional positions meet two requirements: they must have a high school diploma, and they must pass a standardized written test. There was no evidence that either requirement related to successful job performance. Blacks met the requirements in lower percentages than whites, and consequently whites obtained a disproportionate share of the good jobs.

Title VII did not precisely address this kind of case. It clearly outlawed overt discrimination. Was Duke Power's policy overt discrimination, or was it protect-

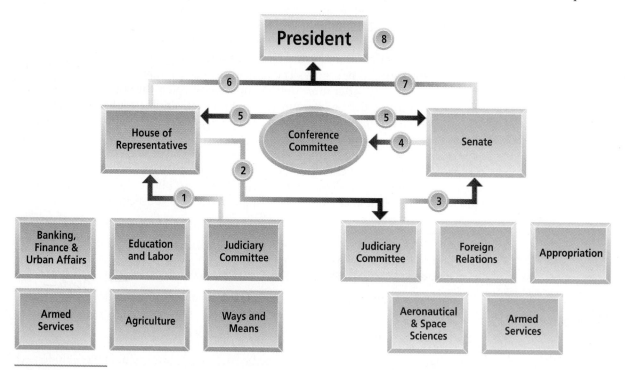

Exhibit 4.1
The two houses of Congress are organized into dozens of committees, a few of which are shown here. The path of the 1964 Civil Rights Act (somewhat simplified) was as follows: (1) The House Judiciary Committee approved the bill and sent it to the full House; (2) the full House passed the bill and sent it to the Senate, where it was assigned to the Senate Judiciary Committee; (3) the Senate Judiciary Committee passed an amended version of the bill and sent it to the full Senate; (4) the full Senate passed the bill with additional amendments. Since the Senate version was now different from the bill the House passed, the bill went to a Conference Committee. The Conference Committee (5) reached a compromise and sent the new version of the bill back to both houses. Each house passed the compromise bill (6 and 7) and sent it to the president, who signed it into law (8).

ed by Senator Tower's amendment, §703(h)? The case went all the way to the Supreme Court, where the Court had to interpret the new law.

STATUTORY INTERPRETATION

Courts are often called upon to interpret a statute, that is, to explain precisely what the language means and how it applies in a given case. There are three primary steps in a court's statutory interpretation:

- *Plain Meaning Rule.* When a statute's words have ordinary, everyday significance, the court will simply apply those words. Section 703(a)(1) of the Civil Rights Act prohibits firing someone because of her religion. Could an employer who had fired a Catholic because of her religion argue that Catholicism is not really a religion, but more of a social group? No. The word "religion" has a plain meaning and courts apply its commonsense definition.

- *Legislative History and Intent.* If the language is unclear, the court must look deeper. Section 703(a)(2) prohibits classifying employees in ways that are discriminatory. Does that section prevent an employer from requiring high school diplomas, as Duke Power did? The explicit language of the statute does not answer the question. The court will look at the law's history to determine the intent of the legislature. The court will examine committee hearings, reports, and the floor debates that we have seen.

- *Public Policy.* If the legislative history is unclear, courts will rely on general public policies, such as reducing crime, creating equal opportunity, and so forth. They may include in this examination some of their own prior decisions. Courts assume that the legislature is aware of prior judicial decisions, and if the legislature did not change those decisions, the statute will be interpreted to incorporate them.

Here is how the Supreme Court interpreted the 1964 Civil Rights Act.

GRIGGS V. DUKE POWER CO.

401 U.S. 424, 91 S. Ct. 849, 1971 U.S. LEXIS 134
United States Supreme Court, 1971

EXCERPTS FROM MR. CHIEF JUSTICE BURGER'S DECISION: The objective of Congress in the enactment of Title VII is plain from the language of the statute. It was to achieve equality of employment opportunities and remove barriers that have operated in the past to favor an identifiable group of white employees over other employees. Under the Act, practices, procedures, or tests neutral on their face, and even neutral in terms of intent, cannot be maintained if they operate to "freeze" the status quo of prior discriminatory employment practices.

The Act proscribes not only overt discrimination but also practices that are fair in form, but discriminatory in operation. The touchstone is business necessity. If an employment practice which operates to exclude Negroes cannot be shown to be related to job performance, the practice is prohibited.

On the record before us, neither the high school completion requirement nor the general intelligence test is shown to bear a demonstrable relationship to successful performance of the jobs for which it was used.

Senator Tower offered an amendment which was adopted verbatim and is now the testing provision of section 703(h). Speaking for the supporters of Title VII, Senator Humphrey endorsed the amendment, stating: "Senators on both sides of the aisle who were deeply interested in Title VII have examined the text of this amendment and have found it to be in accord with the intent and purpose of that title." The amendment was then adopted.

From the sum of the legislative history relevant in this case, the conclusion is inescapable that the . . . requirement that employment tests be job related comports with congressional intent. ◢

And so the highest Court ruled that if a job requirement had a discriminatory impact, the employer could use that requirement only if it was related to job performance. Many more cases arose. For almost two decades courts held that, once workers showed that a job requirement had a discriminatory effect, the employer had the burden to prove that the requirement was necessary for the business. The requirement had to be essential to achieve an important goal. If there was any way to achieve that goal without discriminatory impact, the employer had to use it.

Changing Times

But things changed. In 1989 a more conservative Supreme Court decided *Wards Cove Packing Co. v. Atonio*.[11] The plaintiffs were nonwhite workers in salmon canneries in Alaska. The canneries had two types of jobs: skilled and unskilled. Nonwhites (Filipinos and native Alaskans) invariably worked as low-paid, unskilled workers, canning the fish. The higher paid, skilled positions were filled almost entirely with white workers, who were hired during the off-season in Washington and Oregon.

There was no overt discrimination. But plaintiffs claimed that various practices led to the racial imbalances. The practices included failing to promote from within the company, hiring through separate channels (cannery jobs were done through a union hall, skilled positions were filled out of state), nepotism, and an English language requirement. Once again the case reached the Supreme Court, where Justice White wrote the Court's opinion.

If the plaintiffs succeeded in showing that the job requirements led to racial imbalance, said the Court, the employer now only had to demonstrate that the requirement or practice "serves, in a significant way, the legitimate employment goals of the employer . . . . [T]here is no requirement that the challenged practice be 'essential' or 'indispensable' to the employer's business." In other words, the Court removed the "business necessity" requirement of *Griggs* and replaced it with "legitimate employment goals."

VOTERS' ROLE

The response to *Wards Cove* was quick. Liberals decried it; conservatives hailed it. Everyone agreed that it was a major change that would make it substantially harder for plaintiffs to bring successful discrimination cases. Why had the Court changed its interpretation? Because the *Court* was different. The Court of the 1980s was more conservative, with a majority of justices appointed by Presidents Nixon and Reagan. And so, the voters' political preference had affected the high Court, which in turn changed the interpretation of a statute passed in response to voter concerns of the 1960s. See Exhibit 4.2.

---

[11] 490 U.S. 642, 109 S. Ct. 2115, 1989 U.S. LEXIS 2794 (1989).

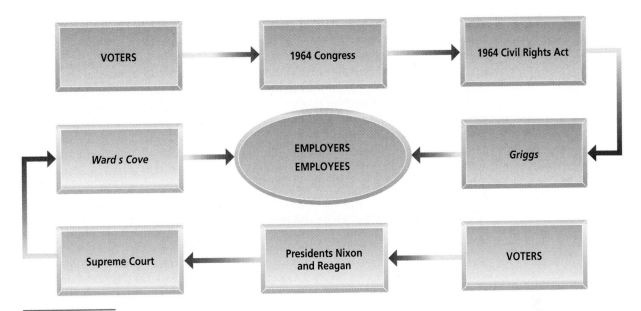

Exhibit 4.2
Statutory interpretation can be just as volatile as the common law, because voters, politicians, and courts all change over time.

Democrats introduced bills to reverse the interpretation of *Wards Cove*. President George H. W. Bush strongly opposed any new bill. He said it would lead to "quotas," that is, that employers would feel obligated to hire a certain percentage of workers from all racial categories to protect themselves from suits. This was the issue that Congressman Johansen had raised in the original House debate in 1964, but it had not been mentioned since.

Both houses passed bills restoring the "business necessity" holding of *Griggs*. Again there were differences, and a Conference Committee resolved them. After acrimonious debate, both houses passed the compromise bill in October 1990. Was it therefore law? No. President Bush immediately vetoed the bill. He said it would compel employers to adopt quotas.

CONGRESSIONAL OVERRIDE

When the president vetoes a bill, Congress has one last chance to make it law: an override. If both houses repass the bill, each by a two-thirds margin, it becomes law over the president's veto. Congress attempted to pass the 1990 Civil Rights bill over the Bush veto, but it fell short in the Senate by one vote.

Civil rights advocates tried again, in January 1991, introducing a new bill to reverse the *Wards Cove* rule. Again both houses debated and bargained. The new bill stated that, once an employee proves that a particular employment practice causes a discriminatory impact, the employer must "demonstrate that the challenged practice is job related for the position in question and consistent with business necessity."

Now the two sides fought over the exact meanings of two terms: "job related" and "business necessity." Each side offered definitions, but the two sides could not reach agreement. It appeared that the entire bill would founder over those terms. So Congress did what it often does when faced with a problem of definition: it dropped the issue. Liberals and conservatives agreed not to define the troublesome terms. They would leave that task to courts to perform through statutory interpretation.

With the definitions left out, the new bill passed both houses. In November 1991, President Bush signed the bill into law. The president stated that the new bill had been improved and no longer threatened to create racial quotas. His opponents charged he had reversed course for political reasons, anticipating the 1992 presidential election.

And so, the Congress restored the "business necessity" interpretation to its own 1964 Civil Rights Act. No one would say, however, that it had been a simple process.

THE OTHER PLAYER: MONEY

No description of the legislative process would be complete, or even realistic, without mentioning money. Campaign contributions and spending have aroused controversy for decades. In 1971 Congress passed the Federal Election Campaign Act (FECA), which limited how much of his own money a federal candidate could spend. Three years later, the statute was amended to place two more limitations on federal campaigns: how much a campaign as a whole could spend, and how much anyone *else* could spend to promote a candidate. One goal was to reduce the power and influence of donors, who gave money expecting favors in return; another purpose was to permit candidates of modest means to compete with millionaire office seekers.

In 1976 the Supreme Court unsettled things in *Buckley v. Valeo*,[12] by ruling that mandatory *spending* limits violate the First Amendment. The Court permitted Congress to limit campaign *contributions*, from individuals and groups, but not to cap the amount that a candidate could spend. This decision was a windfall for wealthy candidates, who could now spend as much of their own money as they chose. It is no coincidence that most members of Congress are very rich.

In 1979 Congress amended the FECA to permit unlimited donations to *political parties* for use in "party building." Initially, party building meant only minor activities like get-out-the-vote drives and distribution of bumper stickers and buttons. Both parties, however, eventually discovered that it was easy to use party-building money in ways that would directly benefit candidates. These funds came to be known as *soft money*. Since the law placed no limit on soft money, the parties went after it feverishly, raising and spending hundreds of millions of dollars every election, effectively destroying any distinction between party building and campaigning.

In 2002 Congress passed legislation designed to curtail the influence of campaign donations by eliminating soft money and regulating campaign advertising.

UPDATE

As this book goes to press, the new reform law has been challenged in court for going too far and criticized by others for doing too little. What is the status of the lawsuits attacking the legislation? Are there any indications of the law's effectiveness? Several nonprofit, nonpartisan groups monitor the corrosive effect of campaign money. The nonprofit Center for Public Integrity has brought to light many money scandals in Washington. To see what a sharp spotlight will reveal, glance at the center's Web page http://www.publicintegrity.org/dtaweb/home.asp.

---

[12] 424 U.S. 1, 96 S. Ct. 612, 1976 U.S. LEXIS 16 (1976).

Common Cause, which you can visit at http://www.commoncause.org, works hard for campaign finance reform. The Center for Responsive Politics, at http://www.crp.org/, includes in its Web site a dollar-by-dollar description of recent elections, demonstrating which candidates took how much from whom.

ECONOMICS & THE LAW

When a contributor gives money to a member of Congress or senator, what is she hoping to accomplish? Does she merely want to assist an incumbent whose views match her own, in the hope of securing his reelection? Or is she attempting to influence the office holder's position on a particular issue? Economists agree that this is an important question, but disagree on the answer. One study concluded that campaign donors do hope to influence votes on particular issues. This economist charted the *timing* of donations. He discovered that disproportionate sums were donated, not during election campaigns, but during legislative sessions, as important bills were coming up for vote. The donors tended to be those directly affected by the proposed legislation. The author of the study concluded that a substantial number of campaign donors attempt to influence a legislator's vote on a particular bill—regardless of whether they succeed.[13]

A second study reached a different conclusion. The authors compared how a legislator voted after he had announced his retirement (but still held office) with his voting pattern while he was an incumbent seeking reelection. These economists reasoned that if campaign donations influence a politician's views, then once the office holder announces his retirement and stops fund raising, his votes should shift back to his own honest positions. But they discovered no such voting shift. The authors concluded that most politicians vote their conscience.[14] Which study do you find more persuasive?

Administrative Law

Before beginning this section, please return your seat to its upright position. Stow the tray firmly in the seat back in front of you. Turn off any radios, CD players, or other electronic equipment. Sound familiar? Administrative agencies affect each of us every day in hundreds of ways. They have become the fourth branch of government. Supporters believe that they provide unique expertise in complex areas; detractors regard them as unelected government run amok.

Many administrative agencies are familiar. The Federal Aviation Agency, which requires all airlines to ensure that your seats are upright before takeoff and landing, is an administrative agency. The Internal Revenue Service haunts us every April 15. The Environmental Protection Agency regulates the water quality of the river in your town. The Federal Trade Commission oversees the commercials that shout at you from your television set.

Other agencies are less familiar. You may never have heard of the Bureau of Land Management, but if you go into the oil and gas industry, you will learn that this powerful agency has more control over your land than you do. If you develop real estate in Palos Hills, Illinois, you will tremble every time the Appearance Commission of the City of Palos Hills speaks, since you cannot construct a new

---

[13] Stratman, "The Market for Congressional Votes: Is Timing of Contributions Everything?" *Journal of Law and Economics*, 1998, vol. 41, p. 85.

[14] Bronars and Lott, "Campaign Donations," *Journal of Law and Economics*, 1997, vol. 40, p. 317.

building without its approval. If your software corporation wants to hire an Argentine expert on databases, you will get to know the complex workings of the Immigration and Naturalization Service. No one lawfully enters this country without its nod of approval.

BACKGROUND

By the 1880s, the amazing iron horse crisscrossed America. But this technological miracle became an economic headache. Congress worried that the railroads' economic muscle enabled a few powerful corporations to reap unfair profits. The railroad industry needed closer regulation. Who would do it? Courts decide individual cases; they do not regulate industries. Congress itself passes statutes, but it has no personnel to oversee the day-to-day workings of a huge industry. For example, Congress lacks the expertise to establish rates for freight passing from Kansas City to Chicago, and it has no personnel to enforce rates once they are set.

A new entity was needed. Congress passed the Interstate Commerce Act, creating the Interstate Commerce Commission (ICC), the first administrative agency. The ICC began regulating freight and passenger transportation over the growing rail system and continued to do so for over 100 years. Congress gave the ICC power to regulate rates and investigate harmful practices, to hold hearings, issue orders, and punish railroads that did not comply.

The ICC was able to hire and develop a staff that was expert in the issues that Congress wanted controlled. The agency had enough flexibility to deal with the problems in a variety of ways: by regulating, investigating, and punishing. And that is what has made administrative agencies an attractive solution for Congress; one entity, focusing on one industry, can combine expertise and flexibility. However, the ICC also developed great power, which voters could not reach, and thereby started the great and lasting conflict over the role of agencies.

During the Great Depression of the 1930s, the Roosevelt administration and Congress created dozens of new agencies. Many were based on social demands, such as the need of the elderly population for a secure income. Political and social conditions dominated again in the 1960s, as Congress created agencies, such as the Equal Employment Opportunity Commission, to combat discrimination.

Then during the 1980s, the Reagan administration made an effort to decrease the number and strength of the agencies. For several years some agencies declined in influence, though others did not. As we begin a new millennium, there is still controversy about how much power agencies should have, but there is no doubt that administrative agencies are a permanent part of our society.

CLASSIFICATION OF AGENCIES

Agencies exist at the federal, state, and local level. We will focus on federal agencies because they have national impact and great power. Most of the principles discussed apply to state and local agencies as well. Virtually any business or profession you choose to work in will be regulated by at least one administrative agency, and it may be regulated by several.

Executive-Independent

Some federal agencies are part of the executive branch, while others are independent agencies. This is a major distinction. The president has much greater control of executive agencies for the simple reason that he can fire the agency head at any time. An executive agency will seldom diverge far from the president's preferred policies. Some familiar executive agencies are the Internal Revenue Service (part of the Treasury Department); the Federal Bureau of Investigation (Department of Justice); the Food and Drug Administration (Department of Health and Human Services); and the Nuclear Regulatory Commission (Department of Energy).

The president has no such removal power over independent agencies. The Federal Communications Commission (FCC) is an independent agency. For many corporations involved in broadcasting, the FCC has more day-to-day influence on their business than Congress, the courts, and the president combined. Other powerful independent agencies are the Federal Trade Commission, the Securities and Exchange Commission, the National Labor Relations Board, and the Environmental Protection Agency.

Enabling Legislation

Congress creates a federal agency by passing **enabling legislation**. The Interstate Commerce Act was the enabling legislation that established the ICC. Typically the enabling legislation describes the problems that Congress believes need regulation, establishes an agency to do it, and defines the agency's powers.

Critics argue that Congress is delegating to another body powers that only the legislature or courts are supposed to exercise. This puts administrative agencies above the voters. But legal attacks on administrative agencies invariably fail. Courts acknowledge that agencies have become an integral part of a complex economy. As long as there are some limits on an agency's discretion, a court will uphold its powers.

The Administrative Procedure Act

This act is a major limitation on how agencies do their work. Congress passed the Administrative Procedure Act (APA) in 1946 in an effort to bring uniformity and control to the many federal agencies. The APA regulates how federal agencies make rules, conduct investigations, hold meetings and hearings, reach decisions, and obtain and release information. How much power should agencies have? How much control should we impose on them? These are two of the major questions that businesses and courts face as we enter a new century.

POWER OF AGENCIES

Administrative agencies use three kinds of power to do the work assigned to them: they make rules, they investigate, and they adjudicate.

Rulemaking

One of the most important functions of an administrative agency is to make rules. In doing this, the agency attempts, prospectively, to establish fair and uniform behavior for all businesses in the affected area. **To create a new rule is to promulgate it.** Agencies promulgate two types of rules: legislative and interpretive.

Legislative Rules. These are the most important agency rules, and they are much like statutes. Here, an agency is changing the law by requiring businesses or private citizens to act in a certain way. For example, the FCC promulgated a rule requiring all cable television systems with more than 3,500 subscribers to develop the capacity to carry at least 20 channels and to make some of those channels available to local community stations. This legislative rule has a heavy financial impact on many cable systems. As far as a cable company is concerned, it is more important than most statutes passed by Congress. Legislative rules have the full effect of a statute.

Interpretive Rules. These rules do not change the law. They are the agency's interpretation of what the law already requires. But they can still affect all of us.

In 1977 Congress passed the Clean Air Act in an attempt to reduce pollution from factories. The act required the Environmental Protection Agency (EPA) to impose emission standards on "stationary sources" of pollution. But what did "stationary source" mean? It was the EPA's job to define that term. Obscure work, to be sure, yet the results could be seen and even smelled, because the EPA's definition would determine the quality of air entering our lungs every time we breathe. Environmentalists wanted the term defined to include every smokestack in a factory so that the EPA could regulate each one. The EPA, however, developed the "bubble concept," ruling that "stationary source" meant an entire factory, but not the individual smokestacks. As a result, polluters could shift emission among smokestacks in a single factory to avoid EPA regulation. Environmentalists howled that this gutted the purpose of the statute, but to no avail. The agency had spoken, merely by interpreting a statute.[15]

How Rules Are Made. Corporations fight many a court battle over whether an agency has the right to issue a particular rule and whether it was promulgated properly. The critical issue is this: How much participation is the public entitled to before an agency issues a rule? There are two basic methods of rulemaking.[16]

Informal Rulemaking. On many issues, agencies may use a simple "notice and comment" method of rulemaking. The agency must publish a proposed rule in advance and permit the public a comment period. During this period the public may submit any objections and arguments, with supporting data. The agency will make its decision and publish the final rule.

For example, the Department of Transportation may use the informal rulemaking procedure to require safety features for all new automobiles. The agency must listen to objections from interested parties, notably car manufacturers, and it must give a written response to the objections. The agency is required to have rational reasons for the final choices it makes. However, it is not obligated to satisfy all parties or do their bidding.

Formal Rulemaking. In the enabling legislation, Congress may require that an agency hold a hearing before promulgating rules. Congress does this to make the agency more accountable to the public. After the agency publishes its proposed rule, it must hold a public hearing. Opponents of the rule, typically affected businesses, may cross-examine the agency experts about the need for the rule and may

---

[15] An agency's interpretation can be challenged in court, and this one was.

[16] Certain rules may be made with no public participation at all. For example, an agency's internal business affairs and procedures can be regulated without public comment, as can its general policy statements. None of these directly affect the public, and the public has no right to participate.

testify against it. When the agency makes its final decision about the rule, it must prepare a formal, written response to everything that occurred at the hearing.

When used responsibly, these hearings give the public access to the agency and can help formulate sound policy. When used irresponsibly, hearings can be manipulated to stymie needed regulation. The most famous example concerns peanut butter. The Food and Drug Administration (FDA) began investigating peanut butter content in 1958. It found, for example, that Jif peanut butter, made by Procter & Gamble, had only 75 percent peanuts and 20 percent of a Crisco-type base. P&G fought the investigation, and any changes, for years. Finally, in 1965, the FDA proposed a minimum of 90 percent peanuts in peanut butter; P&G wanted 87 percent. The FDA wanted no more than 3 percent hydrogenated vegetable oil; P&G wanted no limit.

The hearings dragged on for months. One day, the P&G lawyer objected to the hearing going forward because he needed to vote that day. Another time, when an FDA official testified that consumer letters indicated the public wanted to know what was really in peanut butter, the P&G attorney demanded that the official bring in and identify the letters—all 20,000 of them. Finally, in 1968, a decade after beginning its investigation, the FDA promulgated final rules requiring 90 percent peanuts but eliminating the 3 percent cap on vegetable oil.[17]

Hybrid Rulemaking. In an effort to avoid the agency paralysis made famous in the peanut butter case, some agencies use hybrid rulemaking, following the informal model but adding a few elements of the formal. The agency may give notice and a comment period, deny the right to a full hearing, but allow limited cross-examination on one or two key issues.

Investigation

Agencies do an infinite variety of work, but they all need broad factual knowledge of the field they govern. Some companies cooperate with an agency, furnishing information and even voluntarily accepting agency recommendations. For example, the United States Product Safety Commission investigates hundreds of consumer products every year and frequently urges companies to recall goods that the agency considers defective. Many firms comply. (For an up-to-the-minute report on dangerous products and company compliance, proceed carefully to http://www.cpsc.gov/index.html.)

Other companies, however, jealously guard information, often because corporate officers believe that disclosure would lead to adverse rules. To force disclosure, agencies use subpoenas and searches.

Subpoenas. A **subpoena** is an order to appear at a particular time and place to provide evidence. A **subpoena** *duces tecum* requires the person to appear and bring specified documents. Businesses and other organizations intensely dislike subpoenas and resent government agents plowing through records and questioning employees. What are the limits on an agency's investigation? The information sought:

- Must be *relevant* to a lawful agency investigation. The FCC is clearly empowered to investigate the safety of broadcasting towers, and any documents

---

[17] For an excellent account of this high-fat hearing, see Mark J. Green, *The Other Government* (New York: W. W. Norton & Co., 1978), pp. 136–150.

about tower construction are obviously relevant. Documents about employee racial statistics might indicate discrimination, but the FCC lacks jurisdiction on that issue and thus may not demand such documents.

- Must not be *unreasonably burdensome*. A court will compare the agency's need for the information with the intrusion on the corporation.

- Must not be *privileged*. The Fifth Amendment privilege against self-incrimination means that a corporate officer accused of criminal securities violations may not be compelled to testify about his behavior.

In the following case, a company was determined not to reveal information about its famous sweepstakes. You may read the decision without subscribing to any magazines.

STATE OF IOWA EX REL. THOMAS J. MILLER V. PUBLISHERS CLEARING HOUSE, INC.

633 N.W.2d 732; 2001 Iowa Sup. LEXIS 96
Supreme Court of Iowa, 2001

FACTS: The Iowa attorney general began an investigation into Publishers Clearing House (PCH), to determine if the company was inducing elderly Iowa residents to buy magazine subscriptions in the mistaken belief that doing so would improve their chances of winning the firm's various sweepstakes. For example, some of PCH's letters identified the recipients as "on our Best Customer List," and not "the type of person who wants something for nothing." For example, an 83-year-old woman, believing the "Prize Patrol" would soon visit her, had purchased many videotapes, although she owned no VCR, and had subscribed to over 40 magazines, including *Men's Journal, PC World* (she had no computer), *Sailing, Sports Illustrated for Kids,* and *Cat Fancy* (zero cats).

The attorney general served a subpoena on PCH, requesting for a two-year period: "A list of all Iowa customers who made purchases exceeding $200.00, including the person's name, mailing address, phone number, dollar amount of purchases by year, whether that person is on your active mailing category, and, if not, the date removed. In addition, for anyone whose purchases exceeded $2,500.00 in any year, an itemization of that person's purchases by item, cost, and date of purchase."

PCH claimed the subpoena was overly burdensome. The company delivered only a single list of customers who had spent over $1,000, but PCH refused to itemize their purchases or to disclose whether they were current customers. PCH also claimed it was "self-evident" that such information was "confidential proprietary information that can be used by others to obtain an economic benefit."

The trial court ruled that PCH had "substantially complied" with the subpoena and agreed that much of the information was a trade secret entitled to protection. The attorney general appealed.

ISSUE: Must PCH fully comply with the subpoena?

EXCERPTS FROM JUSTICE LARSON'S OPINION: Agency subpoenas are enforced if they are (1) within the statutory authority of the agency, (2) reasonably specific, (3) not unduly burdensome and (4) reasonably relevant to the matters under investigation. We reject the argument that substantial compliance excuses the subpoenaed party from furnishing all of the information. To adopt PCH's argument would allow it, rather than the attorney general, to determine the scope of the discovery.

In determining whether the discovery is unduly burdensome or expensive, the court may take into account the needs of the case, the amount in controversy, limitations on the parties' resources, and the importance of the issues at stake in the litigation. A certain amount of inconvenience inheres in discovery and must be tolerated by the parties.

Here, the district court found the cost of compliance would be "just under $10,000" in addition to approximately $13,000 already spent in providing information. In light of the 1900 Iowans who have spent $1000 or more on PCH merchandise, or a total Iowa income for PCH exceeding $1.9 million, it is clearly not an undue burden in terms of expense to require compliance.

The attorney general wants information on these customers spending over $1000 to assess the success of PCH's remedial programs aimed at preventing elderly people from spending excessively on products they do not need. We believe PCH has failed to carry its burden of showing that compliance with this subpoena would threaten to unduly disrupt or seriously hinder normal operations of its business.

The district court ruled that PCH's customer list and the other material [sought was a trade secret and should be appropriately protected]. Because of the courts' strong interest in the free flow of information on one hand and protection from commercial damage and abuse of discovery on the other, we have insisted on "a particular and specific demonstration of fact, as distinguished from stereotyped and conclusory statements in order to establish good cause [for a protective order]." PCH did not present particular or specific facts to support its trade-secret claim by merely stating that the trade-secret status of the information was "self-evident."

We reverse and remand with instructions to the court to enforce the attorney general's subpoena. ◢

Search and Seizure. At times an agency will want to conduct a surprise **search** of an enterprise and **seize** any evidence of wrongdoing. May an agency do that? Yes, although there are limitations. When a particular industry is *comprehensively regulated*, courts will assume that companies know they are subject to periodic, unannounced inspections. In those industries, an administrative agency may conduct a search without a warrant and seize evidence of violations. For example, the mining industry is minutely regulated, with strict rules covering equipment, mining depths, transport and safety structures, air quality, and countless other things. Mining executives know that they are closely watched, and for good reason: mine safety is a matter of life and death, and surprise is an essential element of effective inspection. Accordingly, the Bureau of Mines may make unannounced, warrantless searches to ensure safety.[18] Today, it is a rare case that finds a warrantless search by an administrative agency to have been illegal.

Adjudication *—review my case— Due process — informal process*

To **adjudicate** a case is to hold a hearing about an issue and then decide it. Agencies adjudicate countless cases. The FCC adjudicates which applicant for a new television license is best qualified. The Occupational Safety and Health Administration (OSHA) holds adversarial hearings to determine whether a manufacturing plant is dangerous.

Hearing Officer

Most adjudications begin with a hearing before an **administrative law judge** (ALJ). There is no jury. An ALJ is an employee of the agency but is expected to be impartial in her rulings. All parties are represented by counsel. The rules of evidence are informal, and an ALJ may receive any testimony or documents that will help resolve the dispute.

After all evidence is taken, the ALJ makes a decision. The losing party has a right to appeal to an appellate board within the agency. The appellate board has the power to make a *de novo* **decision**, meaning it may ignore the ALJ's decision. A party unhappy with that decision may appeal to federal court.

---

[18] *Donovan v. Dewey*, 452 U.S. 594, 101 S. Ct. 2534, 1980 U.S. LEXIS 58 (1981).

Exhaust a remedies

Limits on Agency Power

There are four primary methods of reining in these powerful creatures: statutory, political, judicial, and informational.

STATUTORY CONTROL

As discussed, the enabling legislation of an agency provides some limits. It may require that the agency use formal rulemaking or investigate only certain issues. The APA imposes additional controls by requiring basic fairness in areas not regulated by the enabling legislation.

POLITICAL CONTROL

The president's influence is greatest with executive agencies. Congress, though, controls the purse. No agency—executive or independent—can spend money it does not have. An agency that angers Congress risks having a particular program defunded or its entire budget cut. Further, Congress may decide to defund an agency as a cost-cutting measure. In its effort to balance the budget, Congress abolished the Interstate Commerce Commission, transferring its functions to the Transportation Department.

Congress has additional control because it must approve presidential nominees to head agencies. Before approving a nominee, Congress will attempt to determine her intentions. And, finally, Congress may amend an agency's enabling legislation, limiting its power.

JUDICIAL REVIEW

An individual or corporation directly harmed by an administrative rule, investigation, or adjudication may generally have that action reviewed in federal court.[19] The party seeking review, for example, a corporation, must have suffered direct harm; the courts will not listen to theoretical complaints about an agency action.[20] And that party must first have taken all possible appeals within the agency itself.[21]

Standard on Review.   Suppose OSHA promulgates a new rule limiting the noise level within steel mills. Certain mill operators are furious because they will have

---

[19] In two narrow groups of cases, a court may *not* review an agency action. In a few cases, courts hold that a decision is "committed to agency discretion," a formal way of saying that courts will keep hands off. This happens only with politically sensitive issues, such as international air routes. In some cases, the enabling legislation makes it absolutely clear that Congress wanted no court to review certain decisions. Courts will honor that.

[20] The law describes this requirement by saying that a party must have *standing* to bring a case. A college student who has a theoretical belief that the EPA should not interfere with the timber industry has no standing to challenge an EPA rule that prohibits logging in a national forest. A lumber company that was ready to log that area has suffered a direct economic injury: it has standing to sue.

[21] This is the doctrine of **exhaustion of remedies**. A lumber company may not go into court the day after the EPA publishes a proposed ban on logging. It must first *exhaust* its administrative remedies by participating in the administrative hearing and then pursuing appeals within the agency before venturing into court.

to retool their mills in order to comply. After exhausting their administrative appeals, they file suit seeking to force OSHA to withdraw the new rule. How does a court decide the case? Or, in legal terms, what standard does a court use in reviewing the case? Does it simply substitute its own opinion for that of the agency? No, it does not. The standard a court uses must take into account:

- *Facts.* Courts generally defer to an agency's fact finding. If OSHA finds that human hearing starts to suffer when decibels reach a particular level, a court will probably accept that as final. The agency is presumed to have expertise on such subjects. As long as there is *substantial evidence* to support the fact decision, it will be respected.

- *Law.* Courts often—but not always—defer to an agency's interpretation of the law, as the following case illustrates.

HOLLY FARMS CORP. V. NATIONAL LABOR RELATIONS BOARD

517 U.S. 392, 116 S. Ct. 1396, 1996 U.S. LEXIS 2801
United States Supreme Court, 1996

FACTS: Holly Farms was a vertically integrated poultry producer, meaning that the company performed many different operations to produce commercial chicken. The company hatched broiler chicks and delivered them to independent farms, where they were raised. When the broilers were seven weeks old, the company sent its live-haul crews to reclaim the birds. The crew included chicken catchers, forklift operators, and "live-haul" drivers. At the farms the chicken catchers entered the coops, manually captured the broilers, and loaded them into cages. The forklift operator lifted the caged chickens onto the bed of the truck, and the live-haul driver returned the truck, with the loaded cases and the crew, to Holly Farms' processing plant. After that, the chickens . . . well, never mind.

A group of Holly Farms workers organized a union, and the National Labor Relations Board permitted the union to include the company's live-haul employees. Holly Farms objected to the new union, claiming that these laborers were actually agricultural workers, who by law were outside the board's authority.

Labor law defines agriculture this way:

Agriculture includes . . . the raising of livestock, bees, fur-bearing animals, or poultry, and any practices performed by a farmer or on a farm as an incident to or in conjunction with such farming operations, including preparation for market, delivery to storage or to market or to carriers for transportation to market.

Several United States Courts of Appeals had split over the issue of whether the National Labor Relation Board's (NLRB's) jurisdiction reached live-haul workers, and the dispute reached the United States Supreme Court.

ISSUE: Did the NLRB accurately interpret labor law by ruling that live-haul workers were employees rather than agricultural workers?

EXCERPTS FROM JUSTICE GINSBURG'S DECISION: Holly Farms argues that under the plain language of the statute, the catching and loading of broilers qualifies as work performed "on a farm as an incident to" the raising of poultry. The corporation emphasizes that [the definition] enumerates "preparation for market" and "delivery to storage or to market" among activities that count as "agriculture." The live-haul employees' work, Holly Farms concludes, enjoys no NLRA protection.

We find Holly Farms' position to be a plausible, but not an inevitable, construction of [this definition]. Hence, we turn to the Board's position, examining only its reasonableness as an interpretation of the governing legislation.

While agreeing that the chicken catchers and forklift operators work "on a farm," the Board contends that their catch and cage work is not incidental to farming operations. Rather, the work is tied to Holly Farms' slaughtering and processing operations, activities that do not constitute "farming" under the statute.

We find the Board's answer reasonable. Once the broilers have grown on the farm for seven weeks, the growers' contractual obligation to raise the birds ends, and the work of the live-haul crew begins. The record reflects minimal overlap between the work of the live-haul crew and the independent growers' raising activities. The growers do not assist the live-haul crews in catching or loading the chickens; their only responsibilities are to move certain equipment from the chicken coops prior to the crews' arrival, and to be present when the crews are on the farms.

Again, we stress that the reviewing court's function is limited. For the Board to prevail, it need not show that its construction is the best way to read the statute; rather, courts must respect the Board's judgment so long as its reading is a reasonable one. Regardless of how we might have resolved the question as an initial matter, the Board's decision here reflects a reasonable interpretation of the law and, therefore, merits our approbation. The judgment of the Court of Appeals is accordingly

Affirmed.

EXCERPTS FROM JUSTICE O'CONNOR'S DISSENTING OPINION: As we said in *Chevron U.S.A. Inc. v. Natural Resources Defense Council, Inc.* [a 1984 case], "First, always, is the question whether Congress has directly spoken to the precise question at issue. If the intent of Congress is clear, that is the end of the matter; for the court, as well as the agency, must give effect to the unambiguously expressed intent of Congress." None of our precedents sanction blind adherence to the Board's position when it is directly contrary to the plain language of the relevant statute.

[Labor law] defines agriculture as "farming in all its branches," including "the raising of . . . poultry," as well as "any practices . . . performed by a farmer or on a farm as an incident to or in conjunction with such farming operations." The coverage intended by Congress is best determined by consulting the language of the statute at issue. Because the relevant portions are perfectly plain and directly speak to the precise question at issue, I would hold that the chicken catchers and forklift operators are agricultural laborers and that the Board's contrary conclusion does not deserve deference. ◢

INFORMATIONAL CONTROL AND THE PUBLIC

We started this section describing the pervasiveness of administrative agencies. We should end it by noting one way in which all of us have some direct control over these ubiquitous authorities: information.

> A popular government, without popular information, or the means of acquiring it, is but a Prologue to a Farce or a Tragedy—or perhaps both. Knowledge will forever govern ignorance, and a people who mean to be their own Governors must arm themselves with the power which knowledge gives.
>
> *James Madison*, President, 1809–1817

Two federal statutes arm us with the power of knowledge.

Freedom of Information Act

Congress passed this landmark statute (known as "FOIA") in 1966. It is designed to give all of us—citizens, businesses, and organizations alike—access to the information that federal agencies are using. The idea is to avoid government by secrecy.

Any citizen or executive may make a "FOIA request" to any federal government agency. It is simply a written request that the agency furnish whatever information it has on the subject specified. Two types of data are available under FOIA. Anyone is entitled to information about how the agency operates, how it spends its money, and what statistics and other information it has collected on a given subject. People routinely obtain records about agency policies, environmental hazards, consumer product safety, taxes and spending, purchasing decisions, and agency forays into foreign affairs. A corporation that believes that OSHA is making more inspections of its textile mills than it makes of the competition could demand all relevant information, including OSHA's documents on the mill itself, comparative statistics on different inspections, OSHA's policies on choosing inspection sites, and so forth.

All citizens are entitled to any records the government has *about them*. You are entitled to information that the Internal Revenue Service or the Federal Bureau of Investigation has collected about you.

FOIA does not apply to Congress, the federal courts, or the executive staff at the White House. Note also that, since FOIA applies to federal government agencies, you may not use it to obtain information from state or local governments or private businesses. For a step-by-step guide explaining how to make a FOIA request, see http://www.aclu.org/library/foia.html. For dramatic proof of FOIA's power, see http://www.gwu.edu/~nsarchiv, a Web site devoted to government documents that have been declassified as a result of FOIA requests.

Exemptions. An agency officially has 10 days to respond to the request. In reality, most agencies are unable to meet the deadline but are obligated to make good faith efforts. FOIA exempts altogether nine categories from disclosure. The most important exemptions permit an agency to keep confidential information that relates to national security, criminal investigations, internal agency matters such as personnel or policy discussions, trade secrets or financial institutions, or an individual's private life.

Privacy Act

This 1974 statute prohibits federal agencies from giving information about an individual to other agencies or organizations without written consent. There are exceptions, but overall this act has reduced the government's exchange of information about us "behind our back."

Chapter Conclusion

"Why can't they just fix the law?" They can, and sometimes they do—but it is a difficult and complex task. "They" includes a great many people and forces, from common law courts to members of Congress to campaign donors to administrative agencies. The courts have made the bystander rule slightly more humane, but it has been a long and bumpy road. Congress managed to restore the legal interpretation of its own 1964 Civil Rights Act, but it took months of debate and compromising. The FDA squeezed more peanuts into a jar of Jif, but it took nearly a decade to get the lid on.

A study of law is certain to create some frustrations. This chapter cannot prevent them all. However, an understanding of how law is made is the first step toward controlling that law.

Chapter Review

1. *Stare decisis* means "let the decision stand" and indicates that once a court has decided a particular issue, it will generally apply the same rule in future cases.

2. The common law evolves in awkward fits and starts because courts attempt to achieve two contradictory purposes: predictability and flexibility.

3. The common law bystander rule holds that, generally, no one has a duty to assist someone in peril unless the bystander himself created the danger. Courts have carved some exceptions during the last 100 years, but the basic rule still stands.

4. Bills originate in congressional committees and go from there to the full House of Representatives or Senate. If both houses pass the bill, the legislation normally must go to a Conference Committee to resolve differences between the two versions. The compromise version then goes from the Conference Committee back to both houses, and if passed by both, to the president. If the president signs the bill, it becomes a statute; if he vetoes it, Congress can pass it over his veto with a two-thirds majority in each house.

5. Courts interpret a statute by using the plain meaning rule; then, if necessary, legislative history and intent; and finally, if necessary, public policy.

6. Campaign contributions and spending are largely uncontrolled.

7. Congress creates federal administrative agencies with enabling legislation. The Administrative Procedure Act controls how agencies do their work.

8. Agencies may promulgate legislative rules, which generally have the effect of statutes, or interpretive rules, which merely interpret existing statutes.

9. Agencies have broad investigatory powers and may use subpoenas and, in some cases, warrantless searches to obtain information.

10. Agencies adjudicate cases, meaning that they hold hearings and decide issues. Adjudication generally begins with a hearing before an administrative law judge and may involve an appeal to the full agency or ultimately to federal court.

11. The four most important limitations on the power of federal agencies are statutory control in the enabling legislation and the APA; political control by Congress and the president; judicial review; and the informational control created by the Freedom of Information Act and the Privacy Act.

Practice Test

1. **ETHICS** Suppose you were on a state supreme court and faced with a choking case in a restaurant. Should you require restaurant employees to know and employ the Heimlich maneuver to assist a choking victim? If they do a bad job, they could cause additional injury. Should you permit them to do nothing at all? Is there a compromise position? What social policies are most important?

2. **YOU BE THE JUDGE WRITING PROBLEM** An off-duty, out-of-uniform police officer and his son purchased some food from a 7-11 store and were still in the parking lot when a carload of teenagers became rowdy. The officer went to speak to them, and the teenagers assaulted him. The officer shouted to his son to get the 7-11 clerk to call for help. The son entered the store, told the clerk that a police officer needed help, and told the clerk to call the police. He returned 30 seconds later and repeated the request, urging the clerk to say it was a Code 13. The son claimed that the clerk laughed at him and refused to do it. The police officer sued the store. **Argument for the**

Store: We sympathize with the policeman and his family, but the store has no liability. A bystander is not obligated to come to the aid of anyone in distress unless the bystander created the peril, and obviously the clerk did not do so. The police officer should prosecute *and* sue those who attacked him. **Argument for the Police Officer:** We agree that in general a bystander has no obligation to come to the aid of one in distress. However, when a business that is open to the public receives an urgent request to call the police, the business should either make the call or permit someone else to do it.

3. You sign a two-year lease with a landlord for an apartment. The rent will be $1,000 per month. A clause in the lease requires payment on the first of every month. The clause states that the landlord has the right to evict you if you are even one day late with the payment. You forget to pay on time and deliver your check to the landlord on the third day of the month. He starts an eviction case against you. Who should win? If we enforce the contract, what social result does that have? If we ignore the clause, what effect does that have on contract law?

4. Federal antitrust statutes are complex, but the basic goal is straightforward: to prevent a major industry from being so dominated by a small group of corporations that they destroy competition and injure consumers. Does major league baseball violate the antitrust laws? Many observers say that it does. A small group of owners not only dominate the industry, but actually *own* it, controlling the entry of new owners into the game. This issue went to the United States Supreme Court in 1922. Justice Holmes ruled, perhaps surprisingly, that baseball is exempt from the antitrust laws, holding that baseball is not "trade or commerce." Suppose that a member of Congress dislikes this ruling and dislikes the current condition of baseball. What could he do?

5. Until recently, every state had a statute outlawing the burning of American flags. But in *Texas*

v. Johnson,[22] the Supreme Court declared such statutes unconstitutional, saying that flag burning is symbolic speech, protected by the First Amendment. Does Congress have the power to overrule the Court's decision?

6. Whitfield, who was black, worked for Ohio Edison. Edison fired him, but then later offered to rehire him. At about that time, another employee, representing Whitfield, argued that Edison's original termination of Whitfield had been race discrimination. Edison rescinded its offer to rehire Whitfield. Whitfield sued Edison, claiming that the rescission of the offer to rehire was in retaliation for the other employee's opposition to discrimination. Edison defended by saying that Title VII of the 1964 Civil Rights Act did not protect in such cases. Title VII prohibits, among other things, an employer from retaliating against *an employee who has opposed* illegal discrimination. But it does not explicitly prohibit an employer from retaliating against one employee based on *another employee's* opposition to discrimination. Edison argued that the statute did not protect Whitfield. Outcome?

Background for Questions 7 through 9. The following three questions begin with a deadly explosion. In 1988 terrorists bombed Pan Am Flight 103 over Lockerbie, Scotland, killing all passengers on board. Congress sought to remedy security shortcomings by passing the Aviation Security Improvement Act of 1990, which, among other things, ordered the Federal Aviation Authority (FAA) to prescribe minimum training requirements and minimum staffing levels for airport security. The FAA promulgated rules according to the informal rulemaking process. However, the FAA refused to disclose certain rules, concerning training at specific airports. *Public Citizen, Inc. v. FAA.*[23]

7. Explain what "promulgated rules according to the informal rulemaking process" means.

8. A public interest group called Public Citizen, Inc., along with family members of those who had died at Lockerbie, wanted to know the details of airport security. What steps should

---

[22] 491 U.S. 397, 109 S. Ct. 2533, 1989 U.S. LEXIS 3115 (1989).
[23] 988 F.2d 186, 1993 U.S. App. LEXIS 6024 (D.C. Cir. 1993).

they take to obtain the information? Are they entitled to obtain it?

9. The Aviation Security Improvement Act (ASIA) states that the FAA can refuse to divulge information about airport security. The FAA interprets this to mean that it can withhold the data in spite of FOIA. Public Citizen and the Lockerbie family members interpret FOIA as being the controlling statute, requiring disclosure. Is the FAA interpretation binding?

10. Hiller Systems, Inc., was performing a safety inspection on board the *M/V Cape Diamond*, an ocean-going vessel, when an accident occurred involving the fire extinguishing equipment. Two men were killed. OSHA, a federal agency, attempted to investigate, but Hiller refused to permit any of its employees to speak to OSHA investigators. What could OSHA do to pursue the investigation? What limits were there on what OSHA could do?

11. ROLE REVERSAL Write a multiple-choice question that highlights the path of legislation from the first congressional committee to the president's desk.

Internet Research Problem

Research some pending legislation in Congress. Go to http://www.senate.gov and click on "Legislation & Records." Choose some keywords that interest you, and see what your government is doing. Read the summary of the bill, if one is provided, or go to the text of the bill, and scan the introduction. What do the sponsors of this bill hope to accomplish? Do you agree or disagree with their goals?

You can find further practice problems in the Online Quiz at http://beatty.westbuslaw.com **or in the Study Guide that accompanies this text.**

Constitutional Law

Suppose you want to dance naked in front of 75 strangers. Do you have the *right* to do it? May the police interrupt your show and insist that you don a few garments? You may consider these odd questions, as relatively few business law students contemplate a career as a nude dancer. Yet the answers to these questions will affect you every day of your life, even if you choose a more prosaic line such as investments or retailing (it is good to have a backup plan).

Consider a very different—yet related—question. A state government wants to reduce the consumption of alcohol by making it expensive. On the theory that competitive ads drive prices down and make drinking more affordable, the legislators pass a statute prohibiting liquor stores from publishing their prices. The new law might have the desired effect, but is it fair? May a state forbid any conduct that it regards as harmful to its citizens? What if the same state passes a law preventing new construction along the coastline? This measure will protect the environment, but in the process it may render some very expensive beach-front property worthless. Whose interest is more important—that of the public or the property owners?

These seemingly unrelated questions all involve the same critical issue: power. Does your state have the *power* to prohibit nude dancing? If so, does that mean it could outlaw a campaign poster on your front lawn? Prohibit political protest? Is the state entitled to abolish liquor ads, for a well-intended purpose? Outlaw beachfront development?

Questions about regulating nude dancing affect all of us because the answers reveal how much control the government may exercise. Constitutional law is a series of variations on one vital theme: government power. ▪■

Government Power

ONE IN A MILLION

The Constitution of the United States is the greatest legal document ever written. No other written constitution has lasted so long, governed so many, or withstood such challenge. This amazing work was drafted in 1787, when two weeks were needed to make the horseback ride from Boston to Philadelphia, a pair of young cities in a weak and disorganized nation. Yet today, when that trip requires less than two hours by jet, the same Constitution successfully governs the most powerful country on earth. This longevity is a tribute to the wisdom and idealism of the Founding Fathers.

The Constitution is not perfect. The original document contained provisions that were racist.[1] Other sections were unclear, and some needed early amendment. Overall, however, the Constitution has worked astonishingly well and has become the model for many constitutions around the world.

The Constitution is short and relatively easy to read. This brevity is potent. The Founding Fathers, also called the Framers, wanted it to last for centuries, and they understood that would happen only if the document permitted interpretation and "fleshing out" by later generations. The Constitution's versatility is striking, as we can see from the fact that the document can be used to resolve the crazy quilt of questions posed above. The *First Amendment* governs the two issues of nude dancing and liquor advertising. Courts will use the *Takings Clause* to decide when a state's efforts to protect the environment have unfairly injured property owners.

This chapter is organized around the issue of power. The first section provides an overview of the Constitution, discussing how it came to be and how it is organized. The second section describes the power given to the three branches of government. The third section is the flip side of power, explaining what individual rights the Constitution guarantees to citizens.

---

[1] Two provisions explicitly endorsed slavery, belying the proposition that all people are created equal. The "Three-Fifths Clause," in Article I, section 2, required that for purposes of taxation and representation, a slave must be counted as three-fifths of a person. Article I, section 9, ensured that southern states would be permitted to continue importing slaves into the country at least until 1808.

Overview

Thirteen American colonies gained independence from Great Britain in 1783. The new status was exhilarating. This was the first nation in modern history founded on the idea that the people could govern themselves, democratically. The idea was daring, brilliant, and fraught with difficulties. The states were governing themselves under the Articles of Confederation, but these articles gave the central government no real power. The government could not tax any state or its citizens and had no way to raise money. A government without the ability to raise money does not govern, it panhandles. The national government also lacked the power to regulate commerce between the states or between foreign nations and any state. This was disastrous. States began to impose taxes on goods entering from other states. The young "nation" was a collection of poor relations, threatening to squabble themselves to death.

By 1787 the articles were largely deemed a failure, and the states sent a group of 55 delegates to Philadelphia to amend them. These delegates—the Framers of our Constitution—were not a true cross section of the populace. There were no women or blacks, artisans or small farmers. Most were wealthy; all were powerful within their states.

Rather than amend the old document, the Framers set out to draft a new one, to create a government that had never existed before. It was hard going. What structure should the government have? How much power? Representatives like Alexander Hamilton urged a strong central government. They were the *federalists*. The new government must be able to tax and spend, regulate commerce, control the borders, and do all things that national governments routinely do. But Patrick Henry and other *anti-federalists* feared a powerful central government. They had fought a bitter war precisely to get rid of autocratic rulers; they had seen the evil that a distant government could inflict. The anti-federalists insisted that the states retain maximum authority, keeping political control closer to home.

Another critical question was how much power the *people* should have. Most of the aristocratic delegates had little love for the common people and feared that extending this idea of democracy too far would lead to mob rule. Anti-federalists again disagreed. The British had been thrown out, they insisted, to guarantee individual liberty and a chance to participate in the government. Power corrupted. It must be dispersed amongst the people to avoid its abuse.

How to settle these basic differences? By compromise, of course. **The Constitution is a series of compromises about power.** We will see many provisions granting power to one branch of the government while at the same time limiting the power given.

SEPARATION OF POWERS

One method of limiting power was to create a national government divided into three branches, each independent and equal. Each branch would act as a check on the power of the other two, avoiding the despotic rule that had come from London. Article I of the Constitution created a Congress, which was to have legislative power. Article II created the office of president, defining the scope of executive power. Article III established judicial power by creating the Supreme Court and permitting additional federal courts.

Consider how the three separate powers balance one another: Congress was given the power to pass statutes, a major grant of power. But the president was permitted to veto legislation, a nearly equal grant. Congress, in turn, had the right to override the veto, ensuring that the president would not become a dictator. The president was allowed to appoint federal judges and members of his cabinet, but only with a consenting vote from the Senate.

FEDERALISM

The national government was indeed to have considerable power, but it would still be *limited power*. Article I, section 8, enumerates those issues on which Congress may pass statutes. If an issue is not on the list, Congress has no power to legislate. Thus Congress may create and regulate a post office because postal service is on the list. But Congress may not pass statutes regulating child custody in a divorce: that issue is not on the list. Only the states may legislate child custody issues.

INDIVIDUAL RIGHTS

The original Constitution was silent about the rights of citizens. This alarmed many citizens, who feared that the new federal government would have unlimited power over their lives. So in 1791 the first 10 amendments, known as the Bill of Rights, were added to the Constitution, guaranteeing many liberties directly to individual citizens.

In the next two sections, we look in more detail at the two sides of the great series of compromises: power granted and rights protected.

Power Granted

CONGRESSIONAL POWER

Article I of the Constitution creates the Congress with its two houses. Representation in the House of Representatives is proportionate with a state's population, but each state elects two senators. The article establishes who is qualified to serve in Congress, setting only three requirements: age, citizenship, and residence.

Congress may perform any of the functions enumerated in Article I, section 8, such as imposing taxes, spending money, creating copyrights, supporting the military, declaring war, and so forth. One of the most important items on this list of congressional powers concerns trade.

Interstate Commerce

"The Congress shall have power to regulate commerce with foreign nations, and among the several states." This is the **Commerce Clause**. With it, the Framers were accomplishing several things in response to the commercial chaos that existed under the Articles of Confederation:

1. *International Commerce—Exclusive Power*. As to international commerce, the Commerce Clause is clear: only the federal government may regulate it. The

federal government must speak with one voice when regulating commercial relations with foreign governments.[2]

2. *Domestic Commerce—Concurrent Power.* As to domestic commerce, the clause gives *concurrent power*, meaning that both Congress and the states may regulate it. Congress is authorized to regulate trade between states; each state regulates business within its own borders. Conflicts are inevitable, and they are important to all of us; *how* business is regulated depends upon *who* does it.

- **Positive Aspect: Congressional Power.** The Framers wanted to give power to Congress to bring coordination and fairness to trade between the states. This is the positive aspect of the Commerce Clause: **Congress is authorized to regulate interstate commerce.**

- **Negative or Dormant Aspect: A Limit on the States.** The Framers also wanted to stop the states from imposing the taxes and regulations that were wrecking the nation's domestic trade. This is the negative, or dormant, aspect of the Commerce Clause: **the power of the states to regulate interstate commerce is severely restricted.**

Substantial Effect Rule

An early test of the Commerce Clause's positive aspect came in the depression years of the 1930s, in *Wickard v. Filburn.*[3] The price of wheat and other grains had fluctuated wildly, severely harming farmers and the national food market. Congress sought to stabilize prices by limiting the bushels per acre that a farmer could grow. Filburn grew more wheat than federal law allowed and was fined. In defense, he claimed that Congress had no right to regulate him. None of his wheat went into interstate commerce. He sold some locally and used the rest on his own farm as food for livestock and as seed. The Commerce Clause, Filburn claimed, gave Congress no authority to limit what he could do.

The Supreme Court disagreed and held that **Congress may regulate any activity that has a substantial economic effect on interstate commerce.** Filburn's wheat affected interstate commerce because the more he grew for use on his own farm, the less he would need to buy in the open market of interstate commerce. Congress could regulate his farm. Since this ruling, most federal statutes based on the Commerce Clause have been upheld. Congress has used the Commerce Clause to regulate such diverse issues as the working conditions in a factory, discrimination in a motel, and the environmental aspects of coal mining.[4] Each of these has substantial effect on interstate commerce.

In *United States v. Lopez,*[5] however, the Supreme Court ruled that Congress had exceeded its power under the Commerce Clause. Congress had passed a criminal statute called the "Gun-Free School Zones Act," which forbade any individual from possessing a firearm in a school zone. The goal of the statute was obvious: to

---

[2] *Michelin Tire Corp. v. Wages, Tax Commissioner,* 423 U.S. 276, 96 S. Ct. 535, 1976 U.S. LEXIS 120 (1976).

[3] 317 U.S. 111, 63 S. Ct. 82, 1942 U.S. LEXIS 1046 (1942).

[4] *Maryland v. Wirts,* 392 U.S. 183, 88 S. Ct. 2017, 1968 U.S. LEXIS 2981 (1968); *Heart of Atlanta Motel v. United States,* 379 U.S. 241, 85 S. Ct. 348, 1964 U.S. LEXIS 2187 (1964); *Hodel v. Indiana,* 452 U.S. 314, 101 S. Ct. 2376, 1981 U.S. LEXIS 34 (1981).

[5] 514 U.S. 549, 115 S. Ct. 1624, 1995 U.S. LEXIS 3039 (1995).

keep schools safe. Lopez was convicted of violating the act and appealed his conviction all the way to the high Court, claiming that Congress had no power to pass such a law. The government argued that the Commerce Clause gave it the power to pass the law, but the Supreme Court was unpersuaded.

> The possession of a gun in a local school zone is in no sense an economic activity that might, through repetition elsewhere, substantially affect any sort of interstate commerce. [Lopez] was a local student at a local school; there is no indication that he had recently moved in interstate commerce, and there is no requirement that his possession of the firearm have any concrete tie to interstate commerce. To uphold the Government's contentions here, we would have to pile inference upon inference in a manner that would bid fair to convert congressional authority under the Commerce Clause to a general police power of the sort retained by the States. [The statute was unconstitutional and void.]

Congress's power is great—but still limited.

State Legislative Power

The "dormant" or "negative" aspect of the Commerce Clause governs state efforts to regulate interstate commerce. **The dormant aspect holds that a state statute that discriminates against interstate commerce is invariably unconstitutional.** The following case illustrates the dormant aspect at work.

CAMPS NEWFOUND/OWATONNA, INC. V. TOWN OF HARRISON, MAINE

520 U.S. 564, 117 S. Ct. 1590, 1997 U.S. LEXIS 3227
United States Supreme Court, 1997

FACTS: Under a Maine statute, charitable institutions incorporated in that state were potentially exempt from real estate taxes. However, if the charitable organization operated principally for the benefit of nonresidents of the state, it only qualified for a limited tax break; further, if the organization charged more than $30 per week for its services, it had to pay full real estate taxes. Camps Newfound and Owatonna were Christian Science organizations that operated summer camps in Maine for children of that faith. The campers paid fees of $400 per week, and about 95 percent of them came from out of state. As a result, Maine law required Newfound and Owatonna to pay full real estate taxes.

The camps filed suit, claiming that Maine's tax laws violated the dormant aspect of the Commerce Clause by favoring intrastate institutions over those that engaged in interstate commerce. The Maine trial court agreed with the camps but the Maine Supreme Court reversed, noting that the statute treated all Maine nonprofit companies alike, and that all had an opportunity to qualify for a tax exemption by dispensing their charities in-state. The camps appealed to the United States Supreme Court.

ISSUE: Did the Maine statute violate the dormant aspect of the Commerce Clause?

EXCERPTS FROM JUSTICE STEVENS'S DECISION: During the first years of our history as an independent confederation, the National Government lacked the power to regulate commerce among the States. Because each State was free to adopt measures fostering its own local interests without regard to possible prejudice to nonresidents, what Justice Johnson [in an 1824 case] characterized as a "conflict of commercial regulations, destructive to the harmony of the States" ensued. In his view, this "was the immediate cause that led to the forming of a [constitutional] convention."

It is not necessary to look beyond the text of this statute to determine that it discriminates against interstate commerce. The Maine law expressly distinguishes between entities that serve a principally interstate clientele and those that primarily serve an intrastate market, singling out camps that serve mostly in-staters for beneficial tax treatment, and penalizing those camps that do a principally interstate business. As a practical matter, the statute encourages affected entities to limit their out-of-state clientele, and penalizes the principally nonresident customers of businesses catering to a primarily interstate market.

If such a policy were implemented by a statutory prohibition against providing camp services to nonresidents, the statute would almost certainly be invalid. We have consistently held that the Commerce Clause precludes a state from mandating that its residents be given a preferred right of access, over out-of-state consumers, to natural resources located within its borders or to the products derived therefrom.

Avoiding this sort of "economic Balkanization," and the retaliatory acts of other States that may follow, is one of the central purposes of our negative Commerce Clause jurisprudence. And, as we noted in [an earlier case:] "Economic protectionism is not limited to attempts to convey advantages on local merchants; it may include attempts to give local consumers an advantage over consumers in other States." By encouraging economic isolationism, prohibitions on out-of-state access to in-state resources serve the very evil that the dormant Commerce Clause was designed to prevent.

The judgment of the Maine Supreme Judicial Court is reversed. ◢

Supremacy Clause

What happens when both the federal and state governments pass regulations that are permissible, but conflicting? For example, Congress passed the federal Occupational Safety and Health Act (OSHA) establishing many job safety standards, including those for training workers who handle hazardous waste. Congress had the power to do so under the Commerce Clause. Later, Illinois passed its own hazardous waste statutes, seeking to protect both the general public and workers. The state statute did not violate the Commerce Clause because it imposed no restriction on interstate commerce.

Each statute specified worker training and employer licensing. But the requirements differed. Which statute did Illinois corporations have to obey? Article VI of the Constitution contains the answer. **The Supremacy Clause states that the Constitution, and federal statutes and treaties, shall be the supreme law of the land.**

- If there is a conflict between federal and state statutes, the federal law **preempts** the field, meaning it controls the issue. The state law is void.

- Even in cases where there is no conflict, if Congress demonstrates that it intends to exercise exclusive control over an issue, federal law preempts.

Thus state law controls only when there is no conflicting federal law *and* Congress has not intended to dominate the issue. In the Illinois case, the Supreme Court concluded that Congress intended to regulate the issue exclusively. Federal law therefore preempted the field, and local employers were obligated to obey only the federal regulations.

EXECUTIVE POWER

Article II of the Constitution defines the executive power. Once again the Constitution gives powers in general terms. The basic job of the president is to enforce the nation's laws. Three of his key powers concern appointment, legislation, and foreign policy.

Appointment

Administrative agencies play a powerful role in business regulation, and the president nominates the heads of most of them. These choices dramatically influence what issues the agencies choose to pursue and how aggressively they do it. For example, a president who believes that it is vital to protect our natural resources may appoint a forceful environmentalist to run the Environmental Protection Agency, whereas a president who dislikes federal regulations will choose a more passive agency head.[6]

Legislation

The president and his advisers propose bills to Congress. During the last 50 years, a vast number of newly proposed bills have come from the executive branch. Some argue that *too many* proposals come from the president and that Congress has become overly passive. The president, of course, also has the power to veto bills.[7]

Foreign Policy

The president conducts the nation's foreign affairs, coordinating international efforts, negotiating treaties, and so forth. The president is also the commander in chief of the armed forces, meaning that he heads the military. But Article II does not give him the right to declare war—only the Senate may do that. Thus a continuing tension between president and Congress has resulted from the president's use of troops overseas *without* a formal declaration of war. Once again the Founding Fathers' desire to create a balanced government leads to uncertain application of the law.

JUDICIAL POWER

Article III of the Constitution creates the Supreme Court and permits Congress to establish lower courts within the federal court system.[8] Federal courts have two key functions: adjudication and judicial review.

Adjudicating Cases

The federal court system hears criminal and civil cases. All prosecutions of federal crimes begin in United States District Court. That same court has limited jurisdiction to hear civil lawsuits, a subject discussed in Chapter 3, on dispute resolution.

Judicial Review

One of the greatest "constitutional" powers appears nowhere in the Constitution. In 1803, the Supreme Court decided *Marbury v. Madison.*[9] Congress had passed a relatively minor statute that gave certain powers to the Supreme Court, and Marbury wanted the Court to use those powers. The Court refused. In an opinion written by Chief Justice John Marshall, the Court held that the statute violated the

---

[6] For a discussion of administrative agency power, see Chapter 4, on administrative law.

[7] For a discussion of the president's veto power and Congress's power to override a veto, see Chapter 4, on statutory law.

[8] For a discussion of the federal court system, see Chapter 3, on dispute resolution.

[9] 5 U.S. (1 Cranch) 137 (1803).

Constitution because Article III of the Constitution did not grant the Court those powers. The details of the case were insignificant, but the ruling was profound: because the statute violated the Constitution, said the Court, it was void. **Judicial review refers to the power of federal courts to declare a statute or governmental action unconstitutional and void.**

This formidable grab of power has produced two centuries of controversy. The Court was declaring that it alone had the right to evaluate acts of the other two branches of government—the Congress and the executive—and to decide which were valid and which void. The Constitution nowhere grants this power. Undaunted, Marshall declared that "[I]t is emphatically the province and duty of the judicial department to say what the law is." In later cases the Supreme Court expanded on the idea, holding that it could also nullify state statutes, rulings by state courts, and actions by federal and state officials. In this chapter we have already encountered examples of judicial review, for example, in the *Camps Newfound/Owatonna* case, in which the Supreme Court prohibited the state of Maine from giving preferential tax treatment to summer camps that benefited local residents, and in the *Lopez* case, where the justices declared that Congress lacked the power to pass local gun regulations.

Is judicial review good for the nation? Those who oppose it argue that federal court judges are all appointed, not elected, and that we should not permit judges to nullify a statute passed by elected officials because that diminishes the people's role in their government. Those who favor judicial review insist that there must be one cohesive interpretation of the Constitution and the judicial branch is the logical one to provide it. This dispute about power simmers continuously beneath the surface and occasionally comes to the boil.

YOUNGSTOWN SHEET & TUBE CO. V. SAWYER

343 U.S. 579, 72 S. Ct. 863, 1952 U.S. LEXIS 2625
United States Supreme Court, 1952

FACTS: During the Korean War, steel companies and the unions were unable to reach a contract. The union notified the companies that they would strike, beginning April 9, 1952. President Truman declared steel essential to the war effort and ordered his Secretary of Commerce, Charles Sawyer, to take control of the steel mills and keep them running. Sawyer immediately ordered the presidents of the various companies to serve as operating managers for the United States.

On April 30, the federal district court issued an injunction to stop Sawyer from running the mills. That same day the United States Court of Appeals "stayed" the injunction, that is, it permitted Sawyer to keep operating the mills. The Supreme Court quickly granted *certiorari*, heard argument May 12, and issued its decision June 2 (at least five years faster than most cases reach final decision).

ISSUE: Did President Truman have the constitutional power to seize the steel mills?

EXCERPTS FROM JUSTICE BLACK'S DECISION: It is clear that if the President had authority to issue the order he did, it must be found in some provision of the Constitution. And it is not claimed that express constitutional language grants this power to the President. The contention is that presidential power should be implied from the aggregate of his powers under the Constitution [including the clauses stating that "the executive power shall be vested in a President," that "he shall take care that the laws be faithfully executed," and that he "shall be Commander in Chief."]

The order cannot properly be sustained as an exercise of the President's military power as Commander in Chief. We cannot with faithfulness to our constitutional system hold that the Commander in Chief has the ultimate power as such to take possession of private property in order to keep labor disputes from stopping production. This is a job for the Nation's lawmakers, not for its military authorities.

Nor can the seizure order be sustained because of the several constitutional provisions that grant executive power to the President. In the framework of our Constitution, the President's power to see that the laws are faithfully executed refutes the idea that he is to be a lawmaker. The Constitution limits his functions in the lawmaking process to the recommending of laws he thinks wise and the vetoing of laws he thinks bad. And the Constitution is neither silent nor equivocal about who shall make laws which the President is to execute. The first section of the first article says that "All legislative powers herein granted shall be vested in a Congress of the United States." The Constitution did not subject this lawmaking power of Congress to presidential or military supervision or control.

The Founders of this Nation entrusted the lawmaking power to the Congress alone in both good and bad times. It would do no good to recall the historical events, the fears of power and the hopes for freedom that lay behind their choice. Such a review would but confirm our holding that this seizure order cannot stand.

[The district court's injunction is *affirmed*.] ◢

President Truman disliked anyone telling him what to do, and he disliked even more having the Supreme Court limit his powers during wartime. But he obeyed the Court's order.

Judicial Activism/Judicial Restraint. The power of judicial review is potentially dictatorial. The Supreme Court nullifies statutes passed by Congress (*Marbury v. Madison, United States v. Lopez*) and executive actions (*Youngstown Sheet & Tube*). May the Court strike down any law it dislikes? In theory, no. The Court should nullify only laws that violate the Constitution. But of course that is circular, since it is the Court that will tell us which laws are violative.

Judicial activism refers to a court's willingness, or even eagerness, to become involved in major issues and to decide cases on constitutional grounds. **Judicial restraint** is the opposite, an attitude that courts should leave lawmaking to legislators and nullify a law only when it unquestionably violates the Constitution.

From the 1950s through the 1970s, the Supreme Court took an active role, deciding many major social issues on constitutional grounds. The landmark 1954 decision in *Brown v. Board of Education*[10] ordered an end to racial segregation in public schools, not only changing the nation's educational systems but altering forever its expectations about race. The Court also struck down many state laws that denied minorities the right to vote. Beginning with *Miranda v. Arizona*,[11] the Court began a sweeping reappraisal of the police power of the state and the rights of criminal suspects during searches, interrogations, trials, and appeals. And in *Roe v. Wade*[12] the Supreme Court established certain rights to abortion, most of which remain after 30 years of continuous litigation and violence.

Beginning in the late 1970s, and lasting to the present, the Court has pulled back from its activism. Some justices believe that the Founding Fathers never intended the judicial branch to take so prominent a role in sculpting the nation's laws and its social vision. Simple numbers tell part of the story of a changing

---

[10] 347 U.S. 483, 74 S. Ct. 686, 1954 U.S. LEXIS 2094 (1954).
[11] 384 U.S. 436, 86 S. Ct. 1602, 1966 U.S. LEXIS 2817 (1966).
[12] 410 U.S. 113, 93 S. Ct. 705, 1973 U.S. LEXIS 159 (1973).

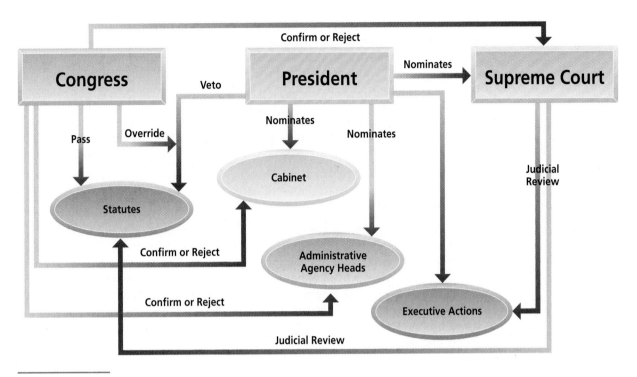

Exhibit 5.1
The Constitution established a federal government of checks and balances. Congress may pass statutes; the president may veto them; and Congress may override the veto. The president nominates cabinet officers, administrative heads, and Supreme Court justices, but the Senate must confirm his nominees. Finally, the Supreme Court (and lower federal courts) exercise judicial review over statutes and executive actions. Unlike the other checks and balances, judicial review is not provided for in the Constitution, but is a creation of the Court itself in *Marbury v. Madison*.

Court. Every year roughly 8,000 requests for review are made to the Court. In the early 1970s, the Supreme Court accepted almost 200 of these cases, but by the new millennium, it was taking fewer than 100. The Court's practice of judicial restraint means that major social issues will increasingly be left to state legislatures and Congress. For a look at the current justices, the full text of famous cases, and a calendar of pending cases, see http://supct.law.cornell.edu/supct/index/html.

Exhibit 5.1 illustrates the balance among Congress, the president, and the Court.

 UPDATE Find an article that describes a recent Supreme Court decision declaring a statute unconstitutional. What was the purpose of the statute? Why did the justices nullify the law? Do you agree with the Court's decision? ▪

Protected Rights

The amendments to the Constitution protect the people of this nation from the power of state and federal governments. The First Amendment guarantees rights of free speech, free press, and religion; the Fourth Amendment protects against illegal searches; the Fifth Amendment ensures due process; the Sixth Amendment demands fair treatment for defendants in criminal prosecutions; and the

Fourteenth Amendment guarantees equal protection of the law. We consider the First, Fifth, and Fourteenth Amendments in this chapter and the Fourth, Fifth, and Sixth Amendments in Chapter 7, on crime.

The "people" who are protected include citizens and, for most purposes, corporations. Corporations are considered persons and receive most of the same protections. The great majority of these rights also extend to citizens of other countries who are in the United States.

Constitutional rights generally protect only against governmental acts. The Constitution generally does not protect us from the conduct of private parties, such as corporations or other citizens.

INCORPORATION

Constitutional protections apply to federal, state, and local governments. Yet that is not what the Bill of Rights explicitly states. The First Amendment declares that *Congress* shall not abridge the right of free speech. The Fourteenth Amendment explicitly limits the power only of *state* governments. But a series of Supreme Court cases has extended virtually all of the important constitutional protections to all levels of national, state, and local government. This process is called **incorporation** because rights explicitly guaranteed at one level are incorporated into rights that apply at other levels.

FIRST AMENDMENT: FREE SPEECH

The First Amendment states that "Congress shall make no law . . . abridging the freedom of speech . . . ." In general, we expect our government to let people speak and hear whatever they choose. The Founding Fathers believed democracy would only work if the members of the electorate were free to talk, argue, listen, and exchange viewpoints in any way they wanted. The people could only cast informed ballots if they were informed. "Speech" also includes symbolic conduct, as the following case flamingly illustrates.

TEXAS V. JOHNSON

491 U.S. 397, 109 S. Ct. 2533, 1989 U.S. LEXIS 3115
United States Supreme Court, 1989

FACTS: Outside the Republican National Convention in Dallas, Gregory Johnson participated in a protest against policies of the Reagan administration. Participants gave speeches and handed out leaflets. Johnson burned an American flag. He was arrested and convicted under a Texas statute that prohibited desecrating the flag, but the Texas Court of Criminal Appeals reversed on the grounds that the conviction violated the First Amendment. Texas appealed to the United States Supreme Court.

ISSUE: Does the First Amendment protect flag burning?

EXCERPTS FROM JUSTICE BRENNAN'S DECISION: The First Amendment literally forbids the abridgment only of "speech," but we have long recognized that its protection does not end at the spoken or written word. While we have rejected the view that an apparently limitless variety of conduct can be labeled "speech," we have acknowledged that conduct may be sufficiently imbued with elements of communication to fall within the scope of the First and Fourteenth Amendments.

In deciding whether particular conduct possesses sufficient communicative elements to bring the First Amendment into play, we have asked whether an intent to convey a particularized message was present, and [whether] the likelihood was great that the message would be understood by those who viewed it. Hence, we have recognized the expressive nature of students' wearing of black armbands to protest American military involvement in Vietnam; of a sit-in by blacks in a "whites only" area to protest segregation; of the wearing of American military uniforms in a dramatic presentation criticizing American involvement in Vietnam; and of picketing about a wide variety of causes.

[The Court concluded that burning the flag was in fact symbolic speech.]

It remains to consider whether the State's interest in reserving the flag as a symbol of nationhood and national unity justifies Johnson's conviction. Johnson was prosecuted because he knew that his politically charged expression would cause "serious offense."

If there is a bedrock principle underlying the First Amendment, it is that the Government may not prohibit the expression of an idea simply because society finds the idea itself offensive or disagreeable. Nothing in our precedents suggests that a State may foster its own view of the flag by prohibiting expressive conduct relating to it.

Could the Government, on this theory, prohibit the burning of state flags? Of copies of the Presidential seal? Of the Constitution? In evaluating these choices under the First Amendment, how would we decide which symbols were sufficiently special to warrant this unique status? To do so, we would be forced to consult our own political preferences, and impose them on the citizenry, in the very way that the First Amendment forbids us to do.

The way to preserve the flag's special role is not to punish those who feel differently about these matters. It is to persuade them that they are wrong. We can imagine no more appropriate response to burning a flag than waving one's own, no better way to counter a flagburner's message than by saluting the flag that burns, no surer means of preserving the dignity even of the flag that burned than by—as one witness here did—according its remains a respectful burial. We do not consecrate the flag by punishing its desecration, for in doing so we dilute the freedom that this cherished emblem represents.

The judgment of the Texas Court of Criminal Appeals is therefore *affirmed*. ◢

Flag burning is an issue that will not go away. For additional thoughts on the subject, ignite http://www.esquilax.com/flag/, an irreverent page that strongly supports the rights of free speech. To read an anti-flag burning Web site, extinguish all matches and go to http://www.cfa-inc.org/.

Political Speech

Because the Framers were primarily concerned with enabling democracy to function, political speech has been given an especially high degree of protection. Such speech may not be barred even when it is offensive or outrageous. A speaker, for example, could accuse a U.S. senator of being insane and could use crude, violent language to describe him. The speech is still protected. The speech lacks protection only if it is *intended and likely to create imminent lawless action*.[13] For example, suppose the speaker said, "The senator is inside that restaurant. Let's get some matches and burn the place down." Speech of this sort is not protected. The speaker could be arrested for attempted arson or attempted murder.

---

[13] *Brandenburg v. Ohio*, 395 U.S. 444, 89 S. Ct. 1827, 1969 U.S. LEXIS 1367 (1969).

Time, Place, and Manner

Even when speech is protected, the government may regulate the *time, place,* and *manner* of such speech. A town may require a group to apply for a permit before using a public park for a political demonstration. The town may insist that the demonstration take place during daylight hours and that there be adequate police supervision and sanitation provided. However, the town may not prohibit such demonstrations outright.

The Supreme Court is frequently called upon to balance the rights of the general public with the rights of those seeking to publicize their causes. In *Madsen v. Women's Health Center, Inc.,*[14] the Court ruled that a local judge could limit protesters' access to a family planning clinic. The protesters, opposed to abortion, had repeatedly blocked access to the clinic, harassed patients and doctors at the clinic and at their homes, and paraded with graphic signs and bullhorns. The Court upheld the order prohibiting the protesters from coming within 36 feet of the clinic and also the order that prohibited excessive noise. But the Court overturned a part of the order that had forbidden protesters from displaying graphic images that could be seen inside the clinic. The Court said that the proper remedy was for the clinic to close its curtains.

Morality and Obscenity

The regulation of morality and obscenity presents additional problems. Obscenity has never received constitutional protection. The Supreme Court has consistently held that it does not play a valued role in our society and has refused to give protection to obscene works. That is well and good, but it merely forces the question: What is obscene? (For a list of books that have been—and in some cases still are—banned by local, state, or foreign governments, see http://onlinebooks.library .upenn.edu/banned-books.html/.

In *Miller v. California,*[15] the Court created a three-part test to determine if a creative work is obscene. The basic guidelines for the factfinder are:

- Whether the average person, applying contemporary community standards, would find that the work, taken as a whole, appeals to the prurient interest

- Whether the work depicts or describes, in a patently offensive way, sexual conduct specifically defined by the applicable state law; and

- Whether the work, taken as a whole, lacks serious literary, artistic, political, or scientific value.

If the trial court finds that the answer to all three of those questions is "yes," it may judge the material obscene; the state may then prohibit the work. If the state fails to prove any one of the three criteria, though, the work is not obscene. A United States District Court ruled that "As Nasty As They Wanna Be," recorded by 2 Live Crew, was obscene. The appeals court, however, reversed, finding that the state had failed to prove lack of artistic merit.[16]

---

[14] 511 U.S. 1016, 114 S. Ct. 1395, 1994 U.S. LEXIS 2671 (1994).
[15] 413 U.S. 15, 93 S. Ct. 2607, 1973 U.S. LEXIS 149 (1973).
[16] *Luke Records, Inc. v. Navarro,* 960 F.2d 134, 1992 U.S. App. LEXIS 9592 (11th Cir. 1992).

What if sexual conduct is not obscene? Let's go back to the chapter's starting point, nude dancing.

YOU BE THE JUDGE

BARNES V. GLEN THEATRE, INC.

501 U.S. 560, 111 S. Ct. 2456, 1991 U.S. LEXIS 3633
United States Supreme Court, 1991

FACTS: Indiana's public indecency statute prohibits any person from appearing nude in a public place. State courts have interpreted this to mean that a dancer in a theater or bar must wear pasties and a G-string. A nightclub called the Kitty Kat Lounge and several dancers who wished to perform nude filed suit, seeking an order that the statute was unconstitutional. The United States District Court ruled that the dancing was not expressive conduct and therefore was not entitled to First Amendment protection. The Court of Appeals reversed, declaring that it was nonobscene expressive conduct and thus protected by the First Amendment.

Indiana did not argue that the dancing was obscene. (If that were the issue, the *Miller* test would have determined the outcome.) Instead, Indiana claimed that its general police powers, including the power to protect social order, allowed it to enforce such a statute.

YOU BE THE JUDGE: Does Indiana's public indecency statute violate the First Amendment?

ARGUMENT FOR INDIANA: Your honors, the State of Indiana has no wish to suppress ideas or censor speech. We are not trying to outlaw eroticism or any other legitimate form of expression. We are simply prohibiting nudity in public. We have outlawed all public nudity, not just nightclub performances. Nudity on the beach, in the park, or anywhere in public is prohibited.

We do this to protect societal order, to foster a stable morality. It is well established that the police power of the state includes the right to regulate the public health, safety, and morals. Our citizens disapprove of people appearing in the nude in public places. The citizens of virtually all states feel the same. Decent dress has been a part of good society since time immemorial. Our voting public is entitled to have that standard upheld.

We also enforce this statute because experience has shown that nightclubs such as these are often associated with criminal behavior. Prostitution, illegal drugs, and violence appear too frequently in the vicinity. It is a reasonable step for the State to maintain control over the performances and the people they will attract.

ARGUMENT FOR KITTY KAT: It is apparent beyond debate that dance is expressive conduct. As an art form it has existed for at least several thousand years. Eroticism, also, is not exactly news. Erotic dance is clearly expressive conduct. Indeed, the present dancing derives its strength from its eroticism. If the State did not consider it erotic, doubtless it would have left the dancers alone. This dancing is expressive conduct and deserves the full protection of the First Amendment.

Indiana is choosing a certain type of expression and outlawing it. The state has not outlawed all nudity, since quite obviously nudity in private is beyond the State's reach. Nor has it prohibited all nude performances. Testimony of police at trial indicated that no arrests have ever been made for nudity as part of a play or ballet. Nudity is no longer anything novel in musicals, ballets, stage plays, or film. Indiana permits nudity in all of them and enforces its moralizing law only against nightclubs.

This is an obvious value judgment on the part of the State. The State is saying that if you can afford to pay for a Broadway show that happens to have nudity, you are free to enjoy it; if your taste or pocketbook leads you to the Kitty Kat Lounge, we deny your right to witness nudity. If the State is allowed to make that appraisal, then it is free to censor any expression—artistic, political, or any other—that it finds inferior. It was *precisely* to prevent states from outlawing unpopular expression that the Founding Fathers added the First Amendment. ▌

 Concerned that pornography on the Internet was easily available to minors, Congress passed the Communications Decency Act (CDA), making it illegal for any person or company to send "obscene or indecent" communications to anyone under 18. Various plaintiffs, including library associations, booksellers, Internet service providers, and others, filed suit, claiming that the law would diminish the extraordinary opportunities for research and education that the Internet provides. The Supreme Court agreed, striking down the law as a violation of the First Amendment. The justices declared that the law failed to define "indecent." The CDA ignored the obscenity standard provided in *Miller v. California* and outlawed material that *did* have socially redeeming value. The Court noted that the law would deny adults access to a vast amount of material that they were legally entitled to obtain. Finally, the Court pointed out that concerned parents could purchase software to screen out objectionable items, avoiding the need for such far-reaching censorship.[17] ▪

Commercial Speech

This refers to speech that has a **dominant theme to propose a commercial transaction**. For example, most advertisements on television and in the newspapers are commercial speech. This sort of speech is protected by the First Amendment, but the government is permitted to regulate it more closely than other forms of speech. **Commercial speech that is false or misleading may be outlawed altogether.** However, regulations on commercial speech must be reasonable and directed to a legitimate goal, as the following case shows.

44 LIQUORMART, INC. V. RHODE ISLAND

517 U.S. 484, 116 S. Ct. 1495, 1996 U.S. LEXIS 3020
United States Supreme Court, 1996

FACTS: Rhode Island passed a statute that prohibited liquor stores from advertising prices, and a second law that barred the media from publicizing such ads. The legislature's goal was to reduce drinking by eliminating the competitive advertising that decreased prices and made alcohol more easily available. Liquor stores filed suit, claiming that the prohibition violated the First Amendment. The United States District Court declared that the laws violated the First Amendment, but the Court of Appeals reversed, holding that the state's theory was logical. The case reached the highest court.

---

[17] *Reno v. American Civil Liberties Union*, 521 U.S. 844, 117 S. Ct. 2329, 1997 U.S. LEXIS 4037 (1997).

ISSUE: Did Rhode Island violate the First Amendment by banning advertisements containing liquor prices?

EXCERPTS FROM JUSTICE STEVENS'S DECISION:

In evaluating the ban's effectiveness in advancing the State's interest, we note that a commercial speech regulation "may not be sustained if it provides only ineffective or remote support for the government's purpose." For that reason, the State bears the burden of showing not merely that its regulation will advance its interest, but also that it will do so "to a material degree."

Without any findings of fact, or indeed any evidentiary support whatsoever, we cannot agree with the assertion that the price advertising ban will significantly advance the State's interest in promoting temperance.

The State also cannot satisfy the requirement that its restriction on speech be no more extensive than necessary. It is perfectly obvious that alternative forms of regulation that would not involve any restriction on speech would be more likely to achieve the State's goal of promoting temperance. As the State's own expert conceded, higher prices can be maintained either by direct regulation or by increased taxation. Per capita purchases could be limited as is the case with prescription drugs. Even educational campaigns focused on the problems of excessive, or even moderate, drinking might prove to be more effective.

As a result, even under the less than strict standard that generally applies in commercial speech cases, the State has failed to establish a "reasonable fit" between its abridgment of speech and its temperance goal.

The judgment of the Court of Appeals is therefore reversed. ◢

NEWSWORTHY

Business idea: Commit violent crime, sell movie rights, use First Amendment to protect profits. Will it work? Ask Barry Keenan. He and Joseph Amsler kidnapped Frank Sinatra, Jr., the son of the legendary singer, and forced his father to pay a large ransom. The criminals were caught and imprisoned. Years later, the felons worked with various journalists to print a tabloid article about the kidnapping. Columbia Pictures promptly paid $1.5 million for the movie rights. Sinatra, Jr., filed suit under a California "Son of Sam" statute. (The law derives its title from a similar New York statute that was in turn named after a notorious killer who had called himself "Son of Sam.") The California law required that when a convicted felon creates a book, article, film or other work, his proceeds must be paid to victims of the crime. How much did Sinatra receive? Nothing. The California Supreme Court declared the statute unconstitutional.

The justices ruled that any law restricting speech *because of its content* must be very narrowly tailored to achieve a compelling purpose. This Son of Sam law failed that test (as had the earlier New York version). The statute applied to income from any work that described the illegal conduct. The law would discourage the dissemination of ideas having almost no connection to the underlying crime. Such a policy might have applied to *The Autobiography of Malcolm X*, because Malcolm mentioned crimes he had committed as a young man; to the writings of Martin Luther King, Jr., who described his protests and arrests; to Thoreau's *Civil Disobedience* and even to the *Confessions of Saint Augustine*. The First Amendment will not tolerate such suppression.

The court did hint, however, that the legislature might achieve its goals if it redrafted the law to avoid any reference to the *content* of the felon's speech. ▪

Has the California legislature redrafted its Son of Sam statute? ▪

UPDATE

FIFTH AMENDMENT: DUE PROCESS AND THE TAKINGS CLAUSE

You are a third-year student in a combined business/law program at a major state university. You feel great about a difficult securities exam you took in Professor Watson's class. The Dean's Office sends for you, and you enter curiously, wondering if your exam was so good that the dean is awarding you a prize. Not quite. The exam proctor has accused you of cheating. Based on the accusation, Watson has flunked you. You protest that you are innocent and demand to know what the accusation is. The dean says that you will learn the details at a hearing if you wish to have one. She reminds you that if you lose the hearing you will be expelled from the university. Three years of work and your entire career are suddenly on the line.

The hearing is run by Professor Holmes, who will make the final decision. Holmes is a junior faculty member in Watson's department. (Next year, Watson will decide Holmes's tenure application.) At the hearing the proctor accuses you of copying from a student sitting in front of you. Both Watson and Holmes have already compared the two papers and concluded that they are strongly similar. Holmes tells you that you must convince him the charge is wrong. You examine the papers, acknowledge that there are similarities, but plead as best you can that you never copied. Holmes doesn't buy it. The university expels you, placing on your transcript a notation of cheating.

Have you received fair treatment? To answer that, we must look to the Fifth Amendment, which provides several vital protections. We here consider two related provisions, the Due Process Clause and the Takings Clause. Together, they state: "No person shall be . . . deprived of life, liberty, or property without due process of law; nor shall private property be taken for public use, without just compensation." These clauses prevent the government from arbitrarily taking the most valuable possessions of a citizen or corporation. Here we discuss the civil law aspects of these clauses, but due process also applies to criminal law. The reference to "life" refers to capital punishment. The criminal law issues of this subject are discussed in Chapter 7, on crime.

In civil law proceedings, the government does have the right to take a person's liberty or property. But there are three important limitations:

- *Procedural Due Process*. Before depriving anyone of liberty or property, the government must go through certain procedures to ensure that the result is fair.

- *The Takings Clause*. When the government takes property for public use, such as to build a new highway, it has to pay a fair price.

- *Substantive Due Process*. Some rights are so fundamental that the government may not take them from us at all.

Procedural Due Process

The government deprives citizens or corporations of their property in a variety of ways. The Internal Revenue Service may fine a corporation for late payment of taxes. The Customs Service may seize goods at the border. As to liberty, the government may take it by confining someone in a mental institution or by taking a child out of the home because of parental neglect. **The purpose of procedural due**

process is to ensure that before the government takes liberty or property, the affected person has a fair chance to oppose the action.

There are two steps in analyzing a procedural due process case:

- Is the government attempting to take liberty or property?

- If so, how much process is due? (If the government is *not* attempting to take liberty or property, there is no due process issue.)

Is the Government Attempting to Take Liberty or Property?   Liberty interests are generally easy to spot: confining someone in a mental institution and taking a child from her home are both deprivations of liberty. A property interest may be obvious. Suppose that, during a civil lawsuit, the court **attaches** a defendant's house, meaning it bars the defendant from selling the property at least until the case is decided. This way, if the plaintiff wins, the defendant will have assets to pay the judgment. The court has clearly deprived the defendant of an important interest in his house, and the defendant is entitled to due process. However, a property interest may be subtler than that. A woman holding a job with a government agency has a "property interest" in that job, because her employer has agreed not to fire her without cause, and she can rely on it for income. If the government does fire her, it is taking away that property interest, and she is entitled to due process. A student attending any public school has a property interest in that education. If a public university suspends a law/business student, as described above, it is taking her property, and she, too, should receive due process.

How Much Process Is Due?   Assuming that a liberty or property interest is affected, a court must decide how much process is due. Does the person get a formal trial, or an informal hearing, or merely a chance to reply in writing to the charges against her? If she gets a hearing, must it be held before the government deprives her of her property, or is it enough that she can be heard shortly thereafter? **What sort of hearing the government must offer depends upon how important the property or liberty interest is and on whether the government has a competing need for efficiency.** The more important the interest, the more formal the procedures must be.

Neutral Factfinder.   Regardless of how formal the hearing, one requirement is constant: the factfinder must be neutral. Whether it is a superior court judge deciding a multimillion-dollar contract suit or an employment supervisor deciding the fate of a government employee, the factfinder must have no personal interest in the outcome. In *Ward v. Monroeville*,[18] the plaintiff was a motorist who had been stopped for traffic offenses in a small town. He protested his innocence and received a judicial hearing. But the "judge" at the hearing was the town mayor. Traffic fines were a significant part of the town's budget. The motorist argued that the town was depriving him of procedural due process because the mayor had a financial interest in the outcome of the case. The United States Supreme Court agreed and reversed his conviction.

---

[18] 409 U.S. 57, 93 S. Ct. 80, 1972 U.S. LEXIS 11 (1972).

Attachment of Property.   As described above, a plaintiff in a civil lawsuit often seeks to *attach* the defendant's property. This protects the plaintiff, but it may also harm the defendant if, for example, he is about to close a profitable real estate deal. Attachments used to be routine. In *Connecticut v. Doehr*, the Supreme Court required more caution.[19] Based on Doehr, when a plaintiff seeks to attach at the beginning of the trial, a court must look at the plaintiff's likelihood of winning. Generally, the court must grant the defendant a hearing *before* attaching the property. The defendant, represented by a lawyer, may offer evidence as to how attachment would harm him and why it should be denied.

Government Employment.   A government employee must receive due process before being fired. Generally this means some kind of hearing, but not necessarily a formal court hearing. The employee is entitled to know the charges against him, to hear the employer's evidence, and to have an opportunity to tell his side of the story. He is not entitled to have a lawyer present. The hearing "officer" need only be a neutral employee. Further, in an emergency, where the employee is a danger to the public or the organization, the government may suspend with pay, before holding a hearing. It then must provide a hearing before the decision becomes final.

Academic Suspension.   There is still a property interest here, but it is the least important of those discussed. When a public school concludes that a student has failed to meet its normal academic standards, such as by failing too many courses, it may dismiss him without a hearing. Due process is served if the student receives notice of the reason and has some opportunity to respond, such as by writing a letter contradicting the school's claims.

In cases of disciplinary suspension or expulsion, courts generally require schools to provide a higher level of due process. In the hypothetical at the beginning of this section, the university has failed to provide adequate due process.[20] The school has accused the student of a serious infraction. The school must promptly provide details of the charge and cannot wait until the hearing to do so. The student should see the two papers and have a chance to rebut the charge. Moreover, Professor Holmes has demonstrated bias. He appears to have made up his mind in advance. He has placed the burden on the student to disprove the charges. And he probably feels obligated to support Watson's original conclusion, since Watson will be deciding his tenure case next year.

The Takings Clause

Florence Dolan ran a plumbing store in Tigard, Oregon. She and her husband wanted to enlarge it on land they already owned. But the city government said that they could expand only if they dedicated some of their own land for use as a public bicycle path and for other public use. Does the city have the right to make them do that? For an answer we must look to a different part of the Fifth Amendment.

The Takings Clause is closely related to the Due Process Clause. **The Takings Clause prohibits a state from taking private property for public use without just compensation.** A town wishing to build a new football field may boot you out of your house. But the town must compensate you. The government takes your land

---

[19] 501 U.S. 1, 111 S. Ct. 2105, 1991 U.S. LEXIS 3317 (1991).

[20] See, e.g., *University of Texas Medical School at Houston v. Than*, 901 S.W.2d 926, 1995 Tex. LEXIS 105 (Tex. 1995).

through the power of *eminent domain*. Officials must notify you of their intentions and give you an opportunity to oppose the project and to challenge the amount the town offers to pay. But when the hearings are done, the town may write you a check and grind your house into goalposts, whether you like it or not.

More controversial issues arise when a local government does not physically take the property but passes regulations that restrict its use. Tigard is a city of 30,000 in Oregon. The city developed a comprehensive land use plan for its downtown area in order to preserve green space, to encourage transportation other than autos, and to reduce its flooding problems. Under the plan, when a property owner sought permission to build in the downtown section, the city could require some of her land to be used for public purposes. This has become a standard method of land use planning throughout the nation. States have used it to preserve coastline, urban green belts, and many environmental features.

When Florence Dolan applied for permission to expand, the city required that she dedicate a 15-foot strip of her property to the city as a bicycle pathway and that she preserve, as greenway, a portion of her land within a floodplain. She sued, and though she lost in the Oregon courts, she won in the United States Supreme Court. The Court held that Tigard City's method of routinely forcing all owners to dedicate land to public use violated the Takings Clause. The city was taking the land, even though title never changed hands.[21]

The Court did not outlaw all such requirements. What it required was that, **before a government may require an owner to dedicate land to a public use, it must show that this owner's proposed building requires this dedication of land.** In other words, it is not enough for Tigard to have a general plan, such as a bicycle pathway, and to make all owners participate in it. Tigard must show that it needs *Dolan's* land *specifically for a bike path and greenway*. This will be much harder for local governments to demonstrate than merely showing a city-wide plan. Some observers consider the decision a major advance for the interests of private property. They say that now the government cannot so easily demand that you give up land for public use. Property you have purchased with hard-earned money should truly be yours. Others decry the Court's ruling. In their view it harms our nation's effort to preserve the environment and gives a freer hand to those who value short-term profit over long-term planning.

In the following case, state regulations prohibited commercial development of a large waterfront property. However, the owner knew about the regulations when he obtained the land. Does his awareness of the regulations prevent him from raising the Takings Clause? Has he lost the entire value of his property?

PALAZZOLO V. RHODE ISLAND

533 U.S. 606; 121 S. Ct. 2448; 150 L. Ed. 2d 592; 2001 U.S. LEXIS 4910; 69 U.S.L.W. 4605
Supreme Court of the United States, 2001

FACTS: In 1959 Shore Gardens, Inc. (SGI), bought a large parcel of waterfront property in Westerly, Rhode Island, a popular vacation area. The land was almost entirely salt marsh, subject to tidal flooding.

SGI failed in its early efforts to develop the parcel. In the 1970s, Rhode Island created a Coastal Resources Management Council to protect the state's extensive shoreline. The council published regulations that

---

21 *Dolan v. City of Tigard*, 512 U.S. 374, 114 S. Ct. 2309, 1994 U.S. LEXIS 4826 (1994).

sharply limited development of coastal wetlands such as SGI's property. Later, SGI transferred the property to Anthony Palazzolo. In the 1980s the new owner proposed a 74-lot residential subdivision and private beach club.

The council rejected his plan, and Palazzolo filed suit, claiming a violation of the Takings Clause. He sought $3,150,000, the value of the parcel if it were developed. The Rhode Island Supreme Court held that he could not even raise such claims, because when he took the property he had notice of the restrictive regulations. The state court also held that Palazzolo had not been deprived of the land's use, because he was permitted to build a large, single-family house on an upland portion of the property worth about $200,000. Palazzolo appealed.

ISSUES: Was Palazzolo barred from making the claim because he took the property with notice of the development regulations? Was he entirely deprived of the use of his property?

EXCERPTS FROM JUSTICE KENNEDY'S DECISION: The Takings Clause of the Fifth Amendment prohibits the government from taking private property for public use without just compensation. The clearest sort of taking occurs when the government encroaches upon or occupies private land for its own proposed use. In [a 1922 case] the Court recognized that there will be instances when government actions do not encroach upon or occupy the property yet still affect and limit its use to such an extent that a taking occurs. In Justice Holmes' well-known, if less than self-defining, formulation, "while property may be regulated to a certain extent, if a regulation goes too far it will be recognized as a taking."

Since [then], we have given some, but not too specific, guidance to courts confronted with deciding whether a particular government action goes too far and effects a regulatory taking. First, we have observed that a regulation which "denies all economically beneficial or productive use of land" will require compensation under the Takings Clause. Where a regulation places limitations on land that fall short of eliminating all economically beneficial use, a taking nonetheless may have occurred, depending on a complex of factors including the regulation's economic effect on the landowner, the extent to which the regulation interferes with reasonable investment-backed expectations, and the character of the government action. [This is known as the "Penn Central" analysis, based on a case of that name.]

The state court held the postregulation acquisition of title was fatal to the claim for deprivation of all economic use, and to the Penn Central claim. Were we to accept the State's rule, the postenactment transfer of title would absolve the State of its obligation to defend any action restricting land use, no matter how extreme or unreasonable. A State would be allowed, in effect, to put an expiration date on the Takings Clause. This ought not to be the rule. Future generations, too, have a right to challenge unreasonable limitations on the use and value of land.

[The Rhode Island Supreme Court held] that all economically beneficial use was not deprived because the uplands portion of the property can still be improved. On this point, we agree with the court's decision. Petitioner accepts the Council's contention and the state trial court's finding that his parcel retains $200,000 in development value under the State's wetlands regulations. He asserts, nonetheless, that he has suffered a total taking and contends the Council cannot sidestep [earlier cases] by the simple expedient of leaving a landowner a few crumbs of value.

Assuming a taking is otherwise established, a State may not evade the duty to compensate on the premise that the landowner is left with a token interest. This is not the situation of the landowner in this case, however. A regulation permitting a landowner to build a substantial residence on an 18-acre parcel does not leave the property "economically idle."

The court did not err in finding that petitioner failed to establish a deprivation of all economic value, for it is undisputed that the parcel retains significant worth for construction of a residence. The claims under the Penn Central analysis were not examined, and for this purpose the case should be remanded. The judgment of the Rhode Island Supreme Court is affirmed in part and reversed in part, and the case is remanded for further proceedings not inconsistent with this opinion. ◢

Substantive Due Process

This doctrine is part of the Due Process Clause, but it is entirely different from procedural due process and from government taking. During the first third of the twentieth century, the Supreme Court frequently nullified state and federal laws, asserting that they interfered with basic rights. For example, in a famous 1905 case, *Lochner v. New York*,[22] the Supreme Court invalidated a New York statute that had limited the number of hours that bakers could work in a week. New York had passed the law to protect employee health. But the Court declared that private parties had a basic constitutional right to contract. In this case the statute interfered with the rights of the employer and the baker to make any bargain they wished. Over the next three decades, the Court struck down dozens of state and federal laws that were aimed at working conditions, union rights, and social welfare generally. This was called **substantive due process** because the Court was looking at the substantive rights being affected, such as the right to contract, not at any procedures.

Critics complained that the Court was interfering with the desires of the voting public by nullifying laws that the justices personally disliked (judicial activism). During the Great Depression, however, things changed. Beginning in 1934, the Court completely reversed itself and began to uphold the types of laws it earlier had struck down. How does the Court now regard substantive due process issues? It treats economic and social regulations differently from cases involving fundamental rights.

Economic and Social Regulations.   Generally speaking, the Court will now *presume valid* any statute that regulates economic or social conditions. If the *Lochner* case were heard today, the legislation would be upheld. State or federal laws regulating wages, working conditions, discrimination, union rights, and any similar topics are presumed valid. The Court will invalidate such a law only if it is *arbitrary or irrational*. Almost all statutes have some minimal rationality, and most are now upheld.

Fundamental Rights.   The standard of review is different for laws that affect **fundamental rights**. The Constitution expressly provides some of these rights, such as the right of free speech, the right to vote, and the right to travel. Other rights do not explicitly appear in the Constitution, but the Supreme Court has determined that they are implied. One of the most important of these is the right to privacy. The Court has decided that the Bill of Rights, taken together, implies a right of privacy for all persons. This includes the right to contraception, to marriage, and, most controversially, to abortion.

Any law that infringes upon a fundamental right is presumed invalid and will be struck down unless it is necessary to a compelling government interest. For example, because it is a fundamental right, no state may outlaw abortion altogether. But the state may require a minor to obtain the consent of a parent or a judge. Although this infringes upon a fundamental right, the government has a compelling interest in regulating the welfare of minors, and this regulation is necessary to achieve that goal.

---

[22] 198 U.S. 45, 25 S. Ct. 539, 1905 U.S. LEXIS 1153 (1905).

Fourteenth Amendment: Equal Protection Clause

Shannon Faulkner wanted to attend The Citadel, a state-supported military college in South Carolina. She was a fine student who met every admission requirement that The Citadel set except one: she was not a male. The Citadel argued that its long and distinguished history demanded that it remain all male. The state government claimed that Ms. Faulkner had no need to attend this particular school. Faulkner responded that she was a citizen of the state and ought to receive the benefits that others got, including the right to a military education. Could the school exclude her on the basis of gender?

The Fourteenth Amendment provides that "No State shall . . . deny to any person within its jurisdiction the equal protection of the laws." This is the **Equal Protection Clause**, and it means that, generally speaking, **governments must treat people equally**. Unfair classifications among people or corporations will not be permitted. A notorious example of unfair classification would be race discrimination: permitting only white children to attend a public school violates the Equal Protection Clause.

Yet clearly, governments do make classifications every day. Rich people pay a higher tax rate than poor people. Some corporations are permitted to deal in securities; others are not. To determine which classifications are constitutionally permissible, we need to know what is being classified. There are three major groups of classifications. The outcome of a case can generally be predicted by knowing which group it is in.

- *Minimal Scrutiny: Economic and Social Relations.* Government actions that classify people or corporations on these bases are almost always upheld.

- *Intermediate Scrutiny: Gender.* Government classifications are sometimes upheld.

- *Strict Scrutiny: Race, Ethnicity, and Fundamental Rights.* Classifications based on any of these are almost never upheld.

Minimal Scrutiny: Economic and Social Regulation

Just as with the Due Process Clause, laws that regulate economic or social issues are presumed valid. They will be upheld if they are *rationally related to a legitimate goal.* This means a statute may classify corporations and/or people and the classifications will be upheld if they make any sense at all. The New York City Transit Authority excluded all methadone users from any employment. The United States District Court concluded that this violated the Equal Protection Clause by unfairly excluding all those who were on methadone. The court noted that even those who tested free of any illegal drugs and were seeking non-safety-sensitive jobs, such as clerks, were turned away. That, said the district court, was irrational)

Not so, said the United States Supreme Court. The Court admitted that the policy might not be the wisest. It would probably make more sense to test individually for illegal drugs rather than automatically exclude methadone users. But, said the Court, it was not up to the justices to choose the best policy. They were only to decide if the policy was rational. Excluding methadone users related rationally to the safety of public transport and therefore did not violate the Equal Protection Clause.[23]

---

[23] *New York City Transit Authority v. Beazer*, 440 U.S. 568, 99 S. Ct. 1355, 1979 U.S. LEXIS 77 (1979).

Intermediate Scrutiny: Gender

Classifications based on sex must meet a tougher test than those resulting from economic or social regulation. Such laws must *substantially relate to important government objectives*. Courts have increasingly nullified government sex classifications as societal concern with gender equality has grown.

At about the same time Shannon Faulkner began her campaign to enter The Citadel, another woman sought admission to the Virginia Military Institute (VMI), an all-male state school. The Supreme Court held that Virginia had violated the Equal Protection Clause by excluding women from VMI. The Court ruled that gender-based government discrimination requires an "exceedingly persuasive justification," and that Virginia had failed that standard of proof. The Citadel promptly opened its doors to women.[24]

ETHICS

Today over 800 high school girls wrestle competitively. Some join female clubs but others have no such opportunity and compete with boys—or seek to. Some schools allow girls to join the boys' wrestling team, but others refuse, citing moral reasons, concern for the girls' safety, and the possibility of sexual harassment. If a particular school has no female team, should girls be permitted to wrestle boys? Do they have an equal protection right to do so?

Strict Scrutiny: Race, Ethnicity, and Fundamental Rights

Any government action that intentionally discriminates against racial or ethnic minorities, or interferes with a fundamental right, is presumed invalid. In such cases, courts will look at the statute or policy with *strict scrutiny*; that is, courts will examine it very closely to determine whether there is compelling justification for it. The law will be upheld only if it is *necessary to promote a compelling state interest*. Very few meet that test.

- *Racial and Ethnic Minorities.* Any government action that intentionally discriminates on the basis of race or ethnicity is presumed invalid. For example, in *Palmore v. Sidoti*,[25] the state had refused to give child custody to a mother because her new spouse was racially different from the child. The practice was declared unconstitutional. The state had made a racial classification, it was presumed invalid, and the government had no *compelling need* to make such a ruling.

- *Fundamental Rights.* A government action interfering with a fundamental right also receives strict scrutiny and will likely be declared void. For example, New York State gave an employment preference to any veteran who had been a state resident when he entered the military. Newcomers who were veterans were less likely to get jobs, and therefore this statute interfered with the right to travel, a fundamental right. The Supreme Court declared the law invalid.[26]

INDIVIDUAL RIGHTS AND STATE ACTION

All of the rights discussed thus far offer protection only from government action, not from the conduct of private citizens or corporations. Suppose it is Sunday

---

[24] *United States v. Virginia*, 518 U.S. 515, 116 S. Ct. 2264, 1996 U.S. LEXIS 4259 (1996).
[25] 466 U.S. 429, 104 S. Ct. 1879, 1984 U.S. LEXIS 69 (1984).
[26] *Attorney General of New York v. Soto-Lopez*, 476 U.S. 898, 106 S. Ct. 2317, 1986 U.S. LEXIS 59 (1986).

morning. You are happily reading the newspaper, sipping coffee, while your nine-year-old niece, visiting for the weekend, plays hopscotch on your front walk. There is a knock at the front door. The Neighborhood Association has arrived with a stern message: "Get the kid out of the neighborhood; she's not allowed." Astonished and enraged, you call your lawyer. But her answer leaves you dazed: You may not have children in your house. "But this is America!" you shout. "The Constitution," she replies, "does not apply."

Like 50 million other Americans, you live in a *common interest development* (CID). Yours happens to be a gated community of single-family homes, all of which were built by a developer. When you bought the house, you automatically joined the Neighborhood Association. Other CIDs take different forms: condominiums, co-ops, or retirement or vacation communities. CIDs are increasingly common, and some observers predict that, soon, about 25 percent of all Americans will live in one.

Some CIDs ban children from living in the development or even visiting. Some prohibit signs on the lawns or windows; others outlaw pets, certain flowers, laundry drying in the sun, day-care centers, or pickup trucks. But various features make CIDs attractive to prospective residents. CIDs are often gated or locked in other ways, so they may be safer than surrounding neighborhoods. The community collects its own fees and operates many services, such as water and sewer, road maintenance, garbage collection, and other work traditionally done by towns and cities. Because they are privately managed by boards elected by the residents, CIDs often do this work more promptly and efficiently than public agencies.

Towns or cities also find CIDs desirable since the CID does much of the municipal work itself, using fees collected from residents. While costing a local political unit no extra money, the CID offers an expanded tax base—a happy combination for local governments chronically short of revenue.

However, the price that residents pay is more than cash: they do indeed forfeit constitutional rights. The Constitution protects citizens from government action, and the local CID is not a government. As the law currently stands, you are probably giving up constitutional protections when you enter a CID. If the Neighborhood Association demands that your niece leave, you will probably have to drive her home. Suppose the nasty Neighborhood Association official also notices that your cat looks heavy. "No cats over 20 pounds," he snarls. "Read the rules." The pet-weight rule is also probably enforceable: get that cat off the sofa and onto a treadmill, fast.

State Action

In some cases the Supreme Court has found that a private organization has taken on all the characteristics of a government and thus should be treated as such for constitutional purposes. In *Marsh v. Alabama*,[27] a private company owned an entire town, where its employees lived and worked. The company brought a trespass case against someone distributing religious literature. However, since the company property had "all the characteristics of any other American town," the Supreme Court ruled that it must be *treated* as a town, meaning that constitutional protections must apply. The First Amendment protected the right to distribute

---

[27] 326 U.S. 501, 66 S. Ct. 276, 1946 U.S. LEXIS 3097 (1946).

religious material. This is the state action doctrine. But there are limits. In 1976 the Court ruled that the state action doctrine does *not* apply to shopping centers because they do not possess all of the attributes of a town.

Before too long the Court will probably have to decide whether a CID is free to make unlimited rules or is subject to the state action doctrine. Like the town in *Marsh*, many CIDs look and act like towns. But in *Marsh* the company owned the town; a CID is a group of owners banding together by agreement. The Court will have to decide whether that agreement can nullify constitutional rights.

Chapter Conclusion

The legal battle over power never stops. The obligation of a state to provide equal educational opportunity for both genders relates to whether Tigard, Oregon, may demand some of Ms. Dolan's store lot for public use. Both issues are governed by one amazing document. That same Constitution determines what tax preferences are permissible, and even whether a state may require you to wear clothing. As social mores change in step with broad cultural developments, as the membership of the Supreme Court changes, the balance of power between federal government, state government, and citizens will continue to evolve. There are no easy answers to these constitutional questions because there has never been a democracy so large, so diverse, or so powerful.

Chapter Review

1. The Constitution is a series of compromises about power.

2. Article I of the Constitution creates the Congress and grants all legislative power to it. Article II establishes the office of president and defines executive powers. Article III creates the Supreme Court and permits lower federal courts; the article also outlines the powers of the federal judiciary.

3. Under the Commerce Clause, Congress may regulate any activity that has a substantial effect on interstate commerce.

4. A state may not regulate commerce in any way that will interfere with interstate commerce.

5. Under the Supremacy Clause, if there is a conflict between federal and state statutes, the federal law preempts the field. Even without a conflict, federal law preempts if Congress intended to exercise exclusive control.

6. The president's key powers include making agency appointments, proposing legislation, conducting foreign policy, and acting as commander in chief of the armed forces.

7. The federal courts adjudicate cases and also exercise judicial review, which is the right to declare a statute or governmental action unconstitutional and void.

8. Freedom of speech includes symbolic acts. Political speech is protected unless it is intended and likely to create imminent lawless action.

9. The government may regulate the time, place, and manner of speech.

10. Obscene speech is not protected.

11. Commercial speech that is false or misleading may be outlawed; otherwise, regulations on this speech must be reasonable and directed to a legitimate goal.

12. Procedural due process is required whenever the government attempts to take liberty or property. The amount of process that is due depends upon the importance of the liberty or property threatened.

13. The Takings Clause prohibits a state from taking private property for public use without just compensation.

14. A substantive due process analysis presumes that any economic or social regulation is valid, and presumes invalid any law that infringes upon a fundamental right.

15. The Equal Protection Clause generally requires the government to treat people equally. Courts apply strict scrutiny in any equal protection case involving race, ethnicity, or fundamental rights; intermediate scrutiny to any case involving gender; and minimal scrutiny to an economic or a social regulation.

16. Generally, constitutional rights protect citizens only from the action of the government, although under the state action doctrine, a private organization *may* be treated like the government if it has *all* the characteristics of one.

Practice Test

1. Michigan's Solid Waste Management Act (SWMA) generally prohibited Michigan counties from accepting for disposal solid waste that had been generated outside that county. Fort Gratiot operated a sanitary landfill in St. Clair County, Michigan. The county denied Fort Gratiot permission to bring in solid waste from out of state, and Fort Gratiot sued. This case involves the negative, or dormant, aspect of the Commerce Clause. What is the difference between that aspect and the positive aspect? What is the evil that the dormant aspect is designed to avoid? How would you rule in this case?

2. **YOU BE THE JUDGE WRITING PROBLEM** Scott Fane was a CPA licensed to practice in New Jersey and Florida. He built his New Jersey practice by making unsolicited phone calls to executives. When he moved to Florida, the Board of Accountancy there prohibited him (and all CPAs) from personally soliciting new business. Fane sued. Does the First Amendment force Florida to forgo foreclosing Fane's phoning? **Argument for Fane:** The Florida regulation violates the First Amendment, which protects commercial speech. Fane was not saying anything false or misleading, but was just trying to secure business. This is an unreasonable regulation, designed to keep newcomers out of the marketplace and maintain steady business and high prices for established CPAs. **Argument**

for the Florida Board of Accountancy: Commercial speech deserves—and gets—a lower level of protection than other speech. This regulation is a reasonable method of ensuring that the level of CPA work in our state remains high. CPAs who personally solicit clients are obviously in need of business. They are more likely to bend legal and ethical rules to obtain clients and keep them happy, and will lower the standards throughout the state.

3. Dairy farming in Massachusetts became more expensive than in other states. In order to help its dairy farmers, the state began taxing all milk sales in the state, whether the milk was produced in state or out of state. The money went into a fund that was then distributed among Massachusetts milk producers as a subsidy for their milk. Discuss.

4. President George Bush insisted that he had the power to send American troops into combat in the Middle East, without congressional assent. Yet before authorizing force in Operation Desert Storm, he secured congressional authorization. President Clinton stated that he was prepared to invade Haiti without a congressional vote. Yet he bargained hard to avoid an invasion, and ultimately American troops entered without the use of force. Why the seeming double-talk by both presidents?

5. In the early 1970s, President Nixon became embroiled in the Watergate dispute. He was accused of covering up a criminal break-in at the national headquarters of the Democratic Party. Nixon denied any wrongdoing. A United States District Court judge ordered the president to produce tapes of conversations held in his office. Nixon knew that complying with the order would produce damaging evidence, probably destroying his presidency. He refused, claiming executive privilege. The case went to the Supreme Court. Nixon strongly implied that even if the Supreme Court ordered him to produce the tapes, he would refuse. What major constitutional issue did this raise?

6. **ETHICS** In the landmark 1965 case of *Griswold v. Connecticut*, the Supreme Court examined a Connecticut statute that made it a crime for any person to use contraception. The majority declared the law an unconstitutional violation of the right of privacy. Justice Black dissented, saying, "I do not to any extent whatever base my view that this Connecticut law is constitutional on a belief that the law is wise or that its policy is a good one. [It] is every bit as offensive to me as it is to the majority. [There is no criticism by the majority of this law] to which I cannot subscribe—except their conclusion that the evil qualities they see in the law make it unconstitutional." What legal doctrines are involved here? Why did Justice Black distinguish between his personal views on the statute and the power of the Court to overturn it? Should a federal court act as a "superlegislature," nullifying statutes with which it disagrees? If a court aggressively takes on social issues, what dangers—and what advantages—does that present to society?

7. You begin work at Everhappy Corp. at the beginning of November. On your second day at work, you wear a political button on your overcoat, supporting your choice for governor in the upcoming election. Your boss glances at it and says, "Get that stupid thing out of this office or you're history, chump." You protest that his statement (a) violates your constitutional rights and (b) uses a boring cliché. Are you right?

8. Gilleo opposed American participation in the war in the Persian Gulf. She displayed a large sign on her front lawn that read, "Say No to War in the Persian Gulf, Call Congress Now." The city of Ladue prohibited signs on front lawns and Gilleo sued. The city claimed that it was regulating "time, place, and manner." Explain that statement, and decide who should win.

9. A federal statute prohibits the broadcasting of lottery advertisements, except by stations that broadcast in states permitting lotteries. The purpose of the statute is to support efforts of states that outlaw lotteries. Edge Broadcasting operated a radio station in North Carolina (a nonlottery state) but broadcast primarily in Virginia (a lottery state). Edge wanted to advertise Virginia's lottery but was barred by the statute. Did the federal statute violate Edge's constitutional rights?

10. Fox's Fine Furs claims that Ermine owes $68,000 for a mink coat on which she has stopped making payments. Fox goes to court, files a complaint, and also asks the clerk to *garnish* Ermine's wages. A garnishment is a court order to an employer to hold an employee's wages, or a portion of them, and pay the money into court so that there will be money for the plaintiff if she wins. What constitutional issue does Fox's request for garnishment raise?

11. David Lucas paid $975,000 for two residential lots on the Isle of Palms near Charleston, South Carolina. He intended to build houses on them. Two years later the South Carolina legislature passed a statute that prohibited building seaward of a certain line, and Lucas's property fell in the prohibited zone. Lucas claimed that his land was now useless and that South Carolina owed him its value. Explain his claim. Should he win?

12. This case concerns unequal taxes on property. In Pennsylvania, a county tax commissioner appraises land, meaning that he sets a value for the land, and the owner then pays real estate taxes based on that value. A commissioner valued land at its sales price, whenever it was sold. If land did not sell for many years, he

made little or no adjustment in its appraised value. As a result, some property was assessed at 35 times as much as neighboring land. A corporate landowner sued. What constitutional issue is raised? What should the outcome be?

13. **ROLE REVERSAL** Write an exam question that distinguishes between these three important Fifth Amendment protections: procedural due process, the Takings Clause, and substantive due process.

Internet Research Problem

Go to http://onlinebooks.library.upenn.edu and locate the feature on banned books. Find a book that was formerly censored. Find another volume that is currently banned, either in the United States or elsewhere. How have changing mores affected censorship? Will the book that is currently outlawed someday be legal?

You can find further practice problems in the Online Quiz at http://beatty.westbuslaw.com **or in the Study Guide that accompanies this text.**

Torts

In a small Louisiana town, Don Mashburn ran a restaurant called Maison de Mashburn. The *New Orleans States-Item* newspaper reviewed his eatery, and here is what the article said:

"'Tain't Creole, 'tain't Cajun, 'tain't French, 'tain't country American, 'tain't good. I don't know how much real talent in cooking is hidden under the mélange of hideous sauces which make this food and the menu a travesty of pretentious amateurism but I find it all quite depressing. Put a yellow flour sauce on top of the duck, flame it for drama and serve it with some horrible multi-flavored rice in hollowed-out fruit and what have you got? A well-cooked duck with an ugly sauce that tastes too sweet and thick and makes you want to scrape off the glop to eat the plain duck. [The stuffed eggplant was prepared by emptying] a shaker full (more or less) of paprika on top of it. [One sauce created] trout à la green plague [while another should have been called] yellow death on duck."

Mashburn sued, claiming that the newspaper had committed libel, damaging his reputation and hurting his business.[1] Trout à la green plague will be the first course on our menu of tort law. Mashburn learned, as you will, why filing such a lawsuit is easier than winning it. ▰

---

[1] *Mashburn v. Collin*, 355 So. 2d 879 (La. 1977).

This odd word "tort" is borrowed from the French, meaning "wrong." And that is what it means in law: a tort is a wrong. More precisely, **a tort is a violation of a duty imposed by the civil law**. When a person breaks one of those duties and injures another, it is a tort. The injury could be to a person or her property. Libel is one example of a tort where, for example, a newspaper columnist falsely accuses someone of being an alcoholic. A surgeon who removes the wrong kidney from a patient commits a different kind of tort, called negligence. A business executive who deliberately steals a client away from a competitor, interfering with a valid contract, commits a tort called interference with a contract. A con artist who tricks money out of you with a phony offer to sell you a boat commits fraud, yet another tort.

Because tort law is so broad, it takes a while to understand its boundaries. To start with, we must distinguish torts from two other areas of law: criminal law and contract law.

It is a crime to steal a car, to embezzle money from a bank, to sell cocaine. As discussed in Chapter 1, society considers such behavior so threatening that the government itself will prosecute the wrongdoer, whether or not the car owner or bank president wants the case to go forward.

In a tort case, it is up to the injured party, the plaintiff, to seek compensation. She must hire her own lawyer, who will file a lawsuit. Her lawyer must convince the court that the defendant breached some legal duty and ought to pay money damages to the plaintiff. The plaintiff has no power to send the defendant to jail. Bear in mind that a defendant's action might be both a crime *and* a tort. The con artist who tricks money out of you with a fake offer to sell you a boat has committed the tort of fraud. You may file a civil suit against him and will collect

---

Differences between Contract, Tort, and Criminal Law

Type of Obligation	Contract	Tort	Criminal Law
How the obligation is created	The parties agree on a contract, which creates duties for both.	The civil law imposes duties of conduct on all persons.	The criminal law prohibits certain conduct.
How the obligation is enforced	Suit by plaintiff.	Suit by plaintiff.	Prosecution by government.
Possible result	Money damages for plaintiff.	Money damages for plaintiff.	Punishment for defendant, including prison and/or fine.
Example	Raul contracts to sell Deirdre 5,000 pairs of sneakers at $50 per pair, but fails to deliver them. Deirdre buys the sneakers elsewhere for $60 per pair and receives $50,000, her extra expense.	A newspaper falsely accuses a private citizen of being an alcoholic. The plaintiff sues and wins money damages to compensate for her injured reputation.	Leo steals Kelly's car. The government prosecutes Leo for grand theft, and the judge sentences him to two years in prison. Kelly gets nothing.

money damages if you can prove your case. The con artist has also committed the crime of fraud. The state will prosecute, seeking to imprison and fine him.

A tort is also different from a contract dispute. A contract case is based on an agreement two people have already made. For example, Deirdre claims that Raul promised to sell her 10,000 pairs of sneakers at a good price but has failed to deliver them. She files a contract lawsuit. In a tort case, there is usually no "deal" between the parties. Don Mashburn had never met the restaurant critic who attacked his restaurant and obviously had never made any kind of contract. The plaintiff in a tort case claims that *the law itself* creates obligations that the defendant has breached.

Tort law itself is divided into categories. We begin by considering **intentional torts,** that is, harm caused by a deliberate action. Then we will examine **negligence** and **strict liability**, which are injuries caused by neglect.

Intentional Torts

DEFAMATION

Defamation refers to false statements that harm someone's reputation. Defamatory statements can be written or spoken. Written defamation is **libel**. Suppose a newspaper accuses a local retail store of programming its cash registers to overcharge customers, when the store has never done so. That is libel. Oral defamation is **slander**. If Professor Wisdom, in class, refers to Sally Student as a drug dealer, and Sally has never sold anything stronger than Arm & Hammer, he has slandered her.

There are four elements to a defamation case. **An element is a fact that a plaintiff must prove to win a lawsuit.** In *any* kind of lawsuit, the plaintiff must prove *all* of the elements to prevail. The elements in a defamation case are:

- *Defamatory Statement.* These are words likely to harm another person's reputation. When Professor Wisdom accuses Sally of dealing drugs, that will clearly harm her reputation.

- *Falseness.* The statement must be false. If Sally Student actually sold marijuana to a classmate, then Professor Wisdom has a defense to slander.

- *Communicated.* The statement must be communicated to at least one person other than the plaintiff. If Wisdom speaks only to Sally and accuses her of dealing drugs, there is no slander.

- *Injury.* In slander cases, the plaintiff generally must show some injury. Sally's injury would be lower reputation in the school, embarrassment, and humiliation. But in libel cases, the law is willing to assume injury. Since libel is written, and more permanent, courts award damages even without proof of injury.[2]

---

[2] When defamation by radio and television became possible, the courts chose to consider it libel, analogizing it to newspapers because of the vast audience. This means that in broadcasting cases, a plaintiff generally does not have to prove damages.

Opinion

Opinion is generally a valid defense in a defamation suit because it cannot be proven true or false. Suppose that a television commentator says, "Frank Landlord certainly does less than many rich people do for our community." Is that defamation? Probably not. Who are the "rich people"? How much do they do? How do we define "does less"? These vague assertions indicate the statement is one of opinion. Even if Frank works hard feeding homeless families, he will probably lose a defamation case.

A related defense involves cases where a supposed statement of fact should not be taken literally. "Reverend Wilson's sermons go on so long, many parishioners suffer brain death before receiving communion." Brain death is a tragic fact of medical science, but this author obviously exaggerates to express her opinion. No defamation.

Mr. Mashburn, who opened the chapter suing over his restaurant review, lost his case. The court held that a reasonable reader would have understood the statements to be opinion only. "A shaker full of paprika" and "yellow death on duck" were not to be taken literally but were merely the author's expression of his personal dislike.

What about a crude description of a college official, appearing in the school's newspaper? You be the judge.

YOU BE THE JUDGE

YEAGLE V. COLLEGIATE TIMES

255 Va. 293, 497 S.E.2d 136, 1998 Va. LEXIS 32
Virginia Supreme Court, 1998

FACTS: Sharon Yeagle was assistant to the Vice President of Student Affairs at the Virginia Polytechnic Institute and State University. The state had an academic honors program called the Governor's Fellows Program, and one of Yeagle's duties was to help students apply. The school newspaper, the *Collegiate Times*, published an article describing the university's success at placing students in the Fellows Program. The article included a block quotation in larger print, attributed to Yeagle. Underneath Yeagle's name was the phrase, "Director of Butt Licking."

Yeagle sued the *Collegiate Times*, alleging that the vulgar phrase defamed her. The trial court dismissed the case, ruling that no reasonable person would take the words literally, and that the phrase conveyed no factual information. Yeagle appealed to the Virginia Supreme Court.

YOU BE THE JUDGE: Was the phrase defamatory, or was it deliberate exaggeration that no reasonable person would take literally?

ARGUMENT FOR YEAGLE: The disgusting phrase that the *Collegiate Times* used to describe Ms. Yeagle is defamatory for several reasons. The conduct described by the words happens to be a crime in Virginia, a violation of the state sodomy statute. Thus the paper is accusing her of criminal offenses that she has never committed.

If, however, defendants argue that the phrase must be interpreted figuratively, then the newspaper has accused Ms. Yeagle of currying favor, or directing others to do so, in a uniquely degrading fashion. The *Collegiate Times* is informing its readers that she performs her job in a sleazy, unprofessional manner evidently because she cannot succeed by merit.

Finally, the *Collegiate Times* is holding Ms. Yeagle up to ridicule and scorn, for no legitimate reason, and with the sole purpose of harming her reputation. The student editors may find it amusing to damage someone's career for their own idle purposes, but hardworking adults will not share the laughter.

Argument for Collegiate Times: Statements are only defamatory if a reasonable reader would understand them as asserting facts that can be proven true or false. There is no such statement in this case, and no defamation. No reasonable reader, after finishing an article about the Fellows Program, would believe that Ms. Yeagle was actually the director as described, or even that there is such a job. From the bluntness of the phrase, it is obvious that the words are hyperbole and have no meaning that can be proven true or false.

The paper chose to inject humor into its coverage of a mundane issue, for the entertainment of its readers. What Ms. Yeagle really objects to is the vulgarity of the phrase, and to that claim the paper pleads guilty. There are two responses. First, the great majority of the paper's readers appreciate lively language that is at times irreverent. Second, vulgarity is not defamation. Freedom of speech is more important than the hurt feelings of an overly sensitive reader. For any reader who is quick to take offense, the proper recourse is not to file suit, but to put down the paper. /

Public Personalities

The rules of the game change for those who play in public. Public officials and public figures receive less protection from defamation. An example of a **public official** is a police chief. A **public figure** is a movie star, for example, or a multimillionaire playboy constantly in the news. In the landmark case *New York Times Co. v. Sullivan*,[3] the Supreme Court ruled that the free exchange of information is vital in a democracy and is protected by the First Amendment to the Constitution. A public official or public figure can win a defamation case only by proving actual malice by the defendant. **Actual malice means that the defendant knew the statement was false or acted with reckless disregard of the truth.** If the plaintiff merely shows that the defendant newspaper printed incorrect statements, even very damaging ones, he loses. In the *New York Times* case, the police chief of Birmingham, Alabama, claimed that the *Times* falsely accused him of racial violence in his job. He lost the suit because he could not prove that the *Times* had acted with actual malice. If he had demonstrated that the *Times* knew its accusation was false, he would have won.

Should have knew the statement was false

Defam false

Kenneth Zeran awoke one day to learn he had become notorious. An unidentified person had posted a message on an AOL bulletin board advertising "Naughty Oklahoma T-Shirts." The shirts featured deeply offensive slogans relating to the 1995 bombing of a federal building in Oklahoma City, in which hundreds of innocent people died. Those interested in purchasing such a T-shirt were instructed to call "Ken" at Zeran's home telephone number. Zeran had nothing to do with the posting or the T-shirts. He was quickly inundated with phone messages from furious callers, some of whom made death threats.

Zeran could not change his number because he ran his business from his home. A radio station in Oklahoma City learned of the alleged offer, and angrily urged its listeners to call Zeran, which they did. Over the next few days, additional similar

---

3 376 U.S. 254, 84 S. Ct. 710, 1964 U.S. LEXIS 1655 (1964).

messages were posted, and before long Zeran was receiving an abusive call every two minutes. Zeran phoned AOL on the first day. The company promised to remove the messages immediately, but did not promptly delete the postings or close the responsible account. Zeran sued AOL for defamation—and lost.

The court held that AOL was immune from a defamation suit based on a third-party posting, based on the Communications Decency Act (CDA). Section 230 of the CDA creates this immunity for any Internet service provider, the court declared, adding:

> Lawsuits seeking to hold a service provider liable for its exercise of a publisher's traditional editorial functions, such as deciding whether to publish, withdraw, postpone or alter content, are barred. . . . Congress' purpose in providing the §230 immunity was thus evident. Interactive computer services have millions of users. The amount of information communicated via interactive computer services is therefore staggering. The specter of tort liability in an area of such prolific speech would have an obvious chilling effect. It would be impossible for service providers to screen each of their millions of postings for possible problems. Faced with potential liability for each message republished by their services, interactive computer service providers might choose to severely restrict the number and type of messages posted. Congress considered the weight of the speech interests implicated and chose to immunize service providers to avoid any such restrictive effect.[4]

What if the defamatory speech is posted not by an anonymous Internet user but by a paid contributor to the Internet service provider? Does the Internet service provider become liable? For a full discussion of this rapidly evolving area, see Chapter 20 on cyberlaw. ▪

Privilege

Defendants receive additional protection from defamation cases when it is important for them to speak freely. **Absolute privilege** exists in courtrooms and legislative hearings. Anyone speaking there, such as a witness in a trial, can say anything at all and never be sued for defamation. Courts extend an absolute privilege in those few instances when candor is essential to a functioning democracy.[5]

Qualified privilege exists when two people have a legitimate need to exchange information. Suppose Trisha Tenant lives in a housing project. She honestly believes that her neighbor is selling guns illegally. She reports this to the manager of the project, who investigates and discovers the guns were toys, being sold legally. Trisha is not liable for slander because she had a good faith reason to report this, and the manager needed to hear it. As long as Trisha acts in good faith and talks only to someone who ought to know about the activity, she is protected by qualified privilege.

FALSE IMPRISONMENT

False imprisonment is the intentional restraint of another person without reasonable cause and without consent. A bank teller became seriously ill and wanted to go to the doctor, but the bank forbade her to leave until she made a final tally

---

[4] *Zeran v. America Online, Inc.*, 129 F.3d 327, 1997 U.S. App. LEXIS 31791 (4th Cir. 1997).

[5] A witness who lies is guilty of perjury but not liable for slander.

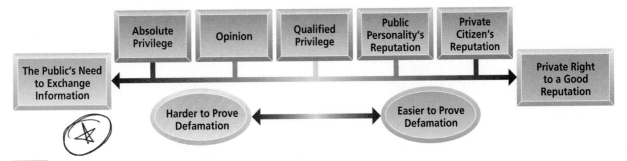

Defamation cases show a tension between the public's need for information and a citizen's right to protect his reputation.

of her accounts. Officials barred her from leaving the bank. That was false imprisonment. The restraint was unreasonable because her accounts could have been verified later.[6]

False imprisonment cases most commonly arise in retail stores, which sometimes detain employees or customers for suspected theft. Most states now have statutes governing the detention of suspected shoplifters. **Generally, a store may detain a customer or worker for alleged shoplifting provided there is a reasonable basis for the suspicion and the detention is done reasonably.** To detain a customer in the manager's office for 20 minutes and question him about where he got an item is lawful. To chain that customer to a display counter for three hours and humiliate him in front of other customers is unreasonable, and false imprisonment.

INTENTIONAL INFLICTION OF EMOTIONAL DISTRESS

What should happen when a defendant's conduct hurts a plaintiff emotionally but not physically? Most courts allow a plaintiff to recover for emotional injury that a defendant intentionally caused.

The intentional infliction of emotional distress results from extreme and outrageous conduct that causes serious emotional harm. A credit officer was struggling vainly to locate Sheehan, who owed money on his car. The officer phoned Sheehan's mother, falsely identified herself as a hospital employee, and said she needed to find Sheehan because his children had been in a serious auto accident. The mother provided Sheehan's whereabouts, which enabled the company to seize his car. But Sheehan spent seven hours frantically trying to locate his supposedly injured children, who in fact were fine. The credit company was liable for the intentional infliction of emotional distress.[7]

By contrast, a muffler shop, trying to collect a debt from a customer, made six phone calls over three months, using abusive language. The customer testified that this caused her to be upset, to cry, and to have difficulty sleeping. The court ruled that the muffler shop's conduct was neither extreme nor outrageous and sent the customer home for another sleepless night.[8]

---

[6] *Kanner v. First National Bank of South Miami*, 287 So. 2d 715, 1974 Fla. App. LEXIS 8989 (Fla. Dist. Ct. App. 1974).

[7] *Ford Motor Credit Co. v. Sheehan*, 373 So. 2d 956, 1979 Fla. App. LEXIS 15416 (Fla. Dist. Ct. App. 1979).

[8] *Midas Muffler Shop v. Ellison*, 133 Ariz. 194, 650 P.2d 496, 1982 Ariz. App. LEXIS 488 (Ariz. Ct. App. 1982).

The following case arose in a setting that guarantees controversy: an abortion clinic.

JANE DOE AND NANCY ROE V. LYNN MILLS

212 Mich. App. 73, 536 N.W. 2d 824, 1995 Mich. App. LEXIS 313
Michigan Court of Appeals, 1995

FACTS: Late one night, an anti-abortion protestor named Robert Thomas climbed into a dumpster located behind an abortion clinic. He found documents indicating that Doe and Roe (not their real names) were soon to have abortions at the clinic. Thomas gave the information to Lynn Mills. She and another woman created signs, using the women's names, indicating that they were about to undergo abortions, and urging them not to "kill their babies." Doe and Roe sued, claiming intentional infliction of emotional distress. The trial court gave summary judgment for the defendants, stating that they had a right to express their views on abortion. The plaintiffs appealed.

ISSUE: Have the plaintiffs made a valid claim of intentional infliction of emotional distress?

EXCERPTS FROM THE COURT'S *PER CURIAM*[9] DECISION: Liability for the intentional infliction of emotional distress has been found only where the conduct complained of has been so outrageous in character, and so extreme in degree, as to go beyond all possible bounds of decency. Liability does not extend to mere insults, indignities, threats, annoyances, petty oppressions, or other trivialities, [but to cases where] an average member of the community would exclaim "Outrageous!"

The trial court observed that defendants have a constitutional right to "protest peaceably against abortion." However, the objectionable aspect of defendants' conduct does not relate to their views on abortion but, rather, to the fact that defendants gave unreasonable or unnecessary publicity to purely private matters involving plaintiffs.

We believe this is the type of case that might cause an average member of the community, upon learning of defendants' conduct, to exclaim, "Outrageous!" Because reasonable men may differ with regard to whether defendants' conduct may be considered sufficiently outrageous and extreme so as to subject them to liability for intentional infliction of emotional distress, this matter should be determined by the trier of fact.

[Summary judgment for the defendants is reversed, and the case is remanded for trial.] ◢

ADDITIONAL INTENTIONAL TORTS

Battery is an intentional touching of another person in a way that is unwanted or offensive. There need be no intention to *hurt* the plaintiff. If the defendant intended to do the physical act, and a reasonable plaintiff would be offended by it, battery has occurred.

Suppose an irate parent throws a chair at a referee during his daughter's basketball game, breaking the man's jaw. It is irrelevant that the father did not intend to injure the referee. But a parent who cheerfully slaps the winning coach on the back has not committed battery, because a reasonable coach would not be offended.

Assault occurs when a defendant does some act that makes a plaintiff fear an imminent battery. It is assault even though the battery never occurs. Suppose Ms. Wilson shouts "Think fast!" at her husband and hurls a toaster at him. He turns and sees it flying at him. His fear of being struck is enough to win a case of assault, even if the toaster misses.

---

[9] A *per curiam* decision is one made by the entire court but not attributed to a specific justice.

Fraud is injuring another person by deliberate deception. It is fraud to sell real estate knowing that there is a large toxic waste deposit underground of which the buyer is ignorant. Fraud is a tort that typically occurs during contract negotiation, and it is discussed in detail in Chapter 9, on contracts.

Damages

COMPENSATORY DAMAGES

Mitchel Bien, who is deaf, enters the George Grubbs Nissan dealership, where folks sell cars aggressively—*very* aggressively. Maturelli, a salesman, and Bien communicate by writing messages back and forth. Maturelli takes Bien's own car keys, and the two then test drive a 300ZX. Bien says he does not want the car, but Maturelli escorts him back inside and fills out a sales sheet. Bien repeatedly asks for his keys, but Maturelli only laughs, pressuring him to buy the new car. Minutes pass. Hours pass. Bien becomes frantic, writing a dozen notes, begging to leave, threatening to call the police. Maturelli mocks Bien and his physical disabilities. Finally, after four hours, the customer escapes.

Bien sues for the intentional infliction of emotional distress. Two former salesmen from Grubbs testify they have witnessed customers cry, yell, and curse as a result of the aggressive tactics. Doctors state that the incident has traumatized Bien, dramatically reducing his confidence and self-esteem and preventing his return to work even three years later.

The jury awards Bien damages. But how does a jury calculate the money? For that matter, why should a jury even try? Money can never erase pain or undo a permanent injury. The answer is simple: money, however inexact and ineffective, is the only thing a court has to give.

A successful plaintiff generally receives **compensatory damages**, meaning an amount of money that the court believes will restore him to the position he was in before the defendant's conduct caused an injury. Here is how compensatory damages are calculated.

First, a plaintiff receives money for medical expenses that he has proven by producing bills from doctors, hospitals, physical therapists, and psychotherapists. Bien receives all the money he has paid. If a doctor testifies that Bien needs future treatment, he will offer evidence of how much that will cost. **The single recovery principle requires a court to settle the matter once and for all, by awarding a lump sum for past and future expenses.** A plaintiff may not return in a year and say, "Oh, by the way, there are some new bills."

Second, the defendants are liable for lost wages. The court takes the number of days or months that Bien missed work and multiplies that times his salary. If Bien is currently unable to work, a doctor estimates how many more months he will miss work, and the court adds that to his damages.

Third, a plaintiff is paid for pain and suffering. Bien testifies about how traumatic the four hours were and how the experience has affected his life. He may state that he now fears shopping, suffers nightmares, and seldom socializes. To bolster the case, a plaintiff uses expert testimony, such as the psychiatrists who testified for Bien. Awards for pain and suffering vary enormously, from a few dollars to many millions, depending on the injury and depending on the jury. In some lawsuits, physical and psychological pain are momentary and insignificant; in other cases, the pain is the biggest part of the verdict. In Bien's case, the jury returns with its verdict: $573,815, calculated as in the table that follows.[10]

Past medical	$ 70.00
Future medical	6,000.00
Past rehabilitation	3,205.00
Past lost earning capacity	112,910.00
Future lost earning capacity	34,650.00
Past physical symptoms and discomfort	50,000.00
Future physical symptoms and discomfort	50,000.00
Past emotional injury and mental anguish	101,980.00
Future emotional injury and mental anguish	200,000.00
Past loss of society and reduced ability to socially interact with family, former fiancee, and friends, and hearing (i.e., nondeaf) people in general	10,000.00
Future loss of society and reduced ability to socially interact with family, former fiancee, and friends, and hearing people	5,000.00
TOTAL	$573,815.00

PUNITIVE DAMAGES

Here we look at a different kind of award, one that is more controversial and potentially more powerful: punitive damages. The purpose is not to compensate the plaintiff for harm, because compensatory damages will have done that. Punitive damages are intended to punish the defendant for conduct that is extreme and outrageous. Courts award these damages in relatively few cases. When an award of punitive damages is made, it is generally in a case of intentional tort, although they occasionally appear in negligence suits.

The idea behind punitive damages is that certain behavior is so unacceptable that society must make an example of it. A large award of money should deter the defendant from repeating the mistake and others from ever making it. This is social engineering in an extreme form. Predictably, some believe punitive damages represent the law at its most avaricious[11] while others attribute to them great social benefit. Large verdicts make headlines, but in fact punitive damages are rare and generally modest. One study indicated that courts award them in only 6 percent of those cases that plaintiffs win.

---

[10] The compensatory damages are described in *George Grubbs Enterprises v. Bien*, 881 S.W.2d 843, 1994 Tex. App. LEXIS 1870 (Tex. Ct. App. 1994). In addition to the compensatory damages described, the jury awarded $5 million in punitive damages. The Texas Supreme Court reversed the award of punitive damages, but not the compensatory. *Id.*, 900 S.W.2d 337, 1995 Tex. LEXIS 91 (Tex. 1995). The high court did not dispute the appropriateness of punitive damages, but reversed because the trial court failed to instruct the jury properly as to how it should determine the assets actually under the defendants' control, an issue essential to punitive damages but not compensatory.

[11] Lawyers normally take personal injury cases on a contingency basis, meaning that they receive no money up-front from their client. Their fee will be a percentage of the plaintiff's judgment *if* she wins. Lawyers often take about one-third of the award. But if the defendant wins, the plaintiff's lawyer will have worked several years for no pay.

When plaintiffs suffer serious personal injuries, high awards may occur. Lana and Pamela Ammerman were riding in a Ford Bronco II when the automobile rolled over. Pamela suffered a crushed pelvis, skull fractures, and brain damage; Lana incurred broken bones and permanent cranial injury giving her face a "caved-in" appearance. The jury concluded that Ford knew the Bronco had an excessively high rollover tendency but rushed the vehicle into production, ignoring repeated warnings of its own engineers. The court gave a compensatory award of more than $4 million (total) to the two women and over $13 million in punitive damages.[12] However, when a plaintiff has suffered only economic harm and no personal injury, a court will not permit such a high award.

The United States Supreme Court has declared that in awarding punitive damages, a court must consider three "guideposts":

- The reprehensibility of the defendant's conduct;

- The ratio between the harm suffered and the award; and

- The difference between the punitive award and any civil penalties used in similar cases.[13]

The Court has refused to provide a definitive ratio between compensatory and punitive damages, but has given additional guidance to lower courts:

- A trial court generally should not permit a punitive award more than 9 times higher than the compensatory damages.

- The trial court may not use the defendant's wealth as an excuse to award an unreasonably high award.

When an insurance company intentionally deceived a vulnerable married couple, a Utah jury was so outraged it awarded $1 million compensatory and $145 million punitive damages. The Supreme Court reversed, ruling that the pair had suffered only economic harm and that the 145:1 ratio was irrational and intolerable.[14]

UPDATE

Although most plaintiffs never obtain one dollar in punitive damages, the verdicts can be large in toxic tort cases. When Captain Joseph Hazelwood's negligence caused the *Exxon Valdez* to run aground off the coast of Alaska, the ship dumped 11 million gallons of oil into the sea, damaging 3,000 square miles of vulnerable ecosystem. The oil spill forced fishermen into bankruptcy, disrupted entire communities, and killed hundreds of thousands of birds and marine animals. A decade later, many of the damaged species had not recovered. The jury decided that Exxon had been reckless by allowing Hazelwood to pilot the ship when the company knew he was an alcoholic. The jury awarded compensatory damages of $286 million and punitive damages of *$5 billion*. Exxon appealed, claiming that the company had voluntarily spent over $2 billion to clean up the spill and $1.3 billion in civil settlements. The appellate court reversed, declaring the punitive damages excessive under the Supreme Court's standard discussed above, and remanded the case with instructions to set a lower judgment. What is the status of the case? Do you agree that $5 billion was exorbitant? What is a fair figure? ◾

---

12 Ford Motor Co. V. Ammerman, 705 N.E.2d 539 (Ind.App. 1999).
13 BMW of North America, Inc. v. Gore, 517 U.S. 559, 116 S. Ct. 1589, 1996 U.S. LEXIS 3390 (1996).
14 *State Farm Mutual Automobile Insurance Co. v. Campbell*, —U.S.—, 2003 WL 1791206 (2003).

ECONOMICS
& THE LAW

We know that damages should be based on such issues as medical expenses, lost wages, and so forth. Is it important whether the judge who presided over the trial was elected or appointed? Yes, it probably does matter, according to economists.

Judges are elected in 23 states and appointed in 27. Injured plaintiffs generally sue in the state where they reside; defendants are frequently out-of-state companies. Substantial data indicate that tort damages against out-of-state defendants are much higher in states where judges are elected than they are in states with appointed judges. Why would that be? Elected judges keep their jobs at the pleasure of local voters. A large tort award against a foreign company will bring money into the state. Voters may perceive such a judgment as a valuable redistribution of wealth. Also, elected judges need to raise money to run for office—and lawyers are generally their largest campaign contributors. One study found that in states with elected judges, verdicts against out-of-state defendants averaged $240,000 more than similar verdicts in states with appointed judges.[15]

Business Torts

In this section we look at four intentional torts that occur almost exclusively in a commercial setting: interference with a contract, interference with a prospective advantage, and the rights to privacy and publicity. Patents, copyrights, and trademarks are discussed in Chapter 21, on intellectual property, as are Lanham Act violations.

TORTIOUS INTERFERENCE WITH BUSINESS RELATIONS

Competition is the essence of business. Successful corporations compete aggressively, and the law permits and expects them to. But there are times when healthy competition becomes illegal interference. This is called tortious interference with business relations. It can take one of two closely related forms: interference with a contract or interference with a prospective advantage.

Tortious Interference with a Contract

Tortious interference with a contract exists only if the plaintiff can establish the following four elements:

- There was a contract between the plaintiff and a third party

- The defendant knew of the contract

- The defendant improperly induced the third party to breach the contract or made performance of the contract impossible; and

- There was injury to the plaintiff.

There is nothing wrong with two companies bidding against each other to buy a parcel of land, and nothing wrong with one corporation doing everything possible to convince the seller to ignore all competitors. But once a company has

---

[15] Tabarrok and Helland, "Court Politics: The Political Economy of Tort Awards," *Journal of Law and Economics*, 1999, vol. 42, p. 157.

signed a contract to buy the land, it is improper to induce the seller to break the deal. The most commonly disputed issues in these cases concern elements one and three: Was there a contract between the plaintiff and another party? Did the defendant *improperly* induce a party to breach it?

A defendant may also rely on the defense of **justification**, that is, a claim that special circumstances made its conduct fair. To establish justification, a defendant must show that:

- it was acting to protect an *existing economic interest*, such as its own contract with the third party,

- it was acting in the *public interest*, for example, by reporting to a government agency that a corporation was overbilling for government services; or

- the existing contract could be *terminated at will* by either party, meaning that although the plaintiff had a contract, the plaintiff had no long-term assurances, because the other side could end it an any time.

Texaco v. Pennzoil. One of the largest verdicts in the history of American law came in a case of contract interference. Pennzoil made an unsolicited bid to buy 20 percent of Getty Oil at $112.50 per share, and the Getty board approved the agreement. Before the lawyers for both sides could complete the paperwork for the deal, Texaco appeared and offered Getty stockholders $128 per share for the entire company. Getty officers turned their attention to Texaco, but Pennzoil sued, claiming tortious interference. Texaco replied that it had not interfered because there was no binding contract.

The jury bought Pennzoil's argument, and they bought it big: $7.53 billion in actual damages, and $3 billion more in punitive damages. After appeals and frantic negotiations, the two parties reached a settlement. Texaco agreed to pay Pennzoil $3 billion as settlement for having wrongfully interfered with Pennzoil's agreement to buy Getty. *resolve before going to appeal*

Tortious Interference with a Prospective Advantage

"Interference with a prospective advantage" is an awkward name for a tort that is simply a variation on interference with a contract. The difference is that, for this tort, there need be no contract; the plaintiff is claiming outside interference with an expected economic relationship. Obviously, the plaintiff must show more than just the hope of a profit. **A plaintiff who has a definite and reasonable expectation of obtaining an economic advantage may sue a corporation that maliciously interferes and prevents the relationship from developing.**

Suppose that Jump Co. and Block Co. both hope to purchase a professional basketball team. The team's owners reject the offer from Block. They informally agree to a price with Jump, but refuse to make a binding deal until Jump leases a stadium. Block owns the only stadium in town and refuses to lease to Jump, meaning that Jump cannot buy the team. Block has interfered with Jump's prospective advantage.[16]

---

[16] Or, to rephrase it, Jump, having courted the owners, must now jump into court and block Block's attempt to bounce Jump off its court. For a case with similar facts, see *Fishman v. Estate of Wirtz*, 807 F.2d 520 (7th Cir. 1986).

PRIVACY AND PUBLICITY

We live in a world of dazzling technology, and it is easier than ever—and more profitable—to spy on someone. For example, the Web page http://www.the smokinggun.com specializes in publishing revealing data about celebrities. Does the law protect us? What power do we have to limit the intrusion of others into our lives and to prohibit them from commercially exploiting information about us? Privacy and publicity law involves four main issues: intrusion, disclosure, false information, and commercial exploitation.

Intrusion

Intrusion into someone's private life is a tort if a reasonable person would find it offensive. Peeping through someone's windows or wiretapping his telephone are obvious examples of intrusion. In a famous case involving a "paparazzo" photographer and Jacqueline Kennedy Onassis, the court found that the photographer had invaded her privacy by making a career out of photographing her. He had bribed doormen to gain access to hotels and restaurants she visited, had jumped out of bushes to photograph her young children, and had driven power boats dangerously close to her. The court ordered him to stop.[17] Nine years later the paparazzo was found in contempt of court for again taking photographs too close to Ms. Onassis. He agreed to stop once and for all—in exchange for a suspended contempt sentence.

Robert Konop, a pilot for Hawaiian Airlines, was distressed with the demands his company was making on employees, and also with his union's response. On a private Web site he criticized both parties and urged fellow pilots to switch to a different union. Konop gave his colleagues passwords to the site, while denying access to management and union officials. Hawaiian Airlines Vice-President James Davis surreptitiously visited the site by using the name and password of two pilots, with their consent. Davis entered the site at least 20 times in this fashion. Konop sued, claiming a violation of two important statutes:

- The **Electronic Communications Privacy Act**, which prohibits the unauthorized interception or disclosure of wire and electronic communications[18]; and

- The **Stored Communications Act**, which prohibits unauthorized access to a facility through which an electronic service is provided.[19]

The district court dismissed the claims, but the appellate court reversed, holding that Konop had raised legitimate—and novel—issues under both statutes. He deserved a trial to demonstrate that Davis had in fact violated these two laws.[20]

The explosive growth of electronic commerce inevitably fosters a burgeoning docket of novel litigation. For a more detailed look at the statutes and issues involved, see Chapter 20 on cyberlaw. ◾

---

[17] *Galella v. Onassis*, 487 F.2d 986, 1973 U.S. App. LEXIS 7901 (2d Cir. 1973).

[18] 18 U.S.C. §2511.

[19] 18 U.S.C. §2701.

[20] *Konop v. Hawaiian Airlines, Inc.*, 236 F.3d 1035, 2001 U.S. App. LEXIS 191 (9th Cir. 2001).

Disclosure of Embarrassing Private Facts

A defendant (such as a media organization) is liable if it discloses to the public facts that a reasonable person would consider very embarrassing, and in which the public has no legitimate interest. Suppose a local newspaper reports that a particular high school student had a baby out of wedlock. The public has no need of that information, and the paper has committed a tort. By contrast, consider the case of a most unusual body surfer. He agreed to an interview with *Sports Illustrated* but then sued when the magazine divulged odd personal facts, including that he put out cigarettes in his mouth, dove off stairs to impress women, hurt himself so he could collect unemployment, and ate insects. *Sports Illustrated* won. The court held that, bizarre as these revelations were, they were not sensationally embarrassing. Further, they were a legitimate part of a news story about an eccentric and daring body surfer.[21]

False Light

Like defamation, this tort involves false information about the plaintiff. Unlike defamation, this tort can arise without harm to a plaintiff's reputation. **If false information portrays the plaintiff in a way that most people would find offensive, it is "false light."** A model named Robyn Douglass posed nude for a photographer and authorized him to publish the photos in *Playboy Magazine*. The photographer sold some to *Playboy* but later sold other photographs to *Hustler Magazine*. The court agreed with Douglass that this placed her in a false light by making her seem to be the sort of person who would pose for *Hustler*. A reasonable person might find that while *Playboy* is mildly erotic, *Hustler* concentrates on sex in ways that are crude and degrading. Douglass won $600,000.[22]

Commercial Exploitation

This right prohibits the use of someone's likeness or voice for commercial purposes. This business tort is the flip side of privacy and covers the right to make money from publicity. For example, it would be illegal to run a magazine ad showing actress Sharon Stone holding a can of soda, without her permission. The ad would imply that she endorses the product. Someone's identity is her own, and it cannot be exploited unless she permits it.

Negligence – Un intentional Tort

Party time! A fraternity at the University of Arizona welcomed new members, and the alcohol flowed freely. Several hundred people danced and shrieked and drank, and no one checked for proof of age. A common occurrence—but one that ended tragically. A minor student drove away, intoxicated, and slammed into another car. The other driver, utterly innocent of wrongdoing, was gravely injured.

The drunken student was obviously liable, but his insurance did not cover the huge medical bills. The injured man also sued the fraternity. Should that organi-

---

[21] *Virgil v. Sports Illustrated*, 424 F. Supp. 1286, 1976 U.S. Dist. LEXIS 11779 (S.D. Cal. 1976).
[22] *Douglass v. Hustler Magazine, Inc.*, 769 F.2d 1128, 1985 U.S. App. LEXIS 19980 (7th Cir. 1985).

zation be legally responsible? The question leads to other similar issues. Should a restaurant that serves an intoxicated adult be liable for resulting harm? If *you* give a party, should you be responsible for any damage caused by your guests?

These are moral questions—but very practical ones, as well. They are typical issues of negligence law. In this contentious area, courts continually face one question: *When someone is injured, how far should responsibility extend?*

We might call negligence the "unintentional" tort because it concerns harm that arises by accident. A person, or perhaps an organization, does some act, neither intending nor expecting to hurt anyone, yet someone is harmed. Should a court impose liability? The fraternity members who gave the party never wanted—or thought—that an innocent man would suffer terrible damage. But he did. Is it in society's interest to hold the fraternity responsible?

Before we can answer this question, we need some background knowledge. Things go wrong all the time, and society needs a means of analyzing negligence cases consistently and fairly. One of America's greatest judges, Benjamin Cardozo, offered such an analysis more than 70 years ago. His decision still dominates negligence thinking today, so we will let him introduce us to Helen Palsgraf.

PALSGRAF V. LONG ISLAND RAILROAD CO.

248 N.Y. 339, 162 N.E.99, 1928 N.Y. LEXIS 1269
New York Court of Appeals, 1928

FACTS: Ms. Palsgraf was waiting on a railroad platform. As a train began to leave the station, a man carrying a package ran to catch it. He jumped aboard but looked unsteady, so a guard on the car reached out to help him as another guard, on the platform, pushed from behind. The man dropped the package, which struck the tracks and exploded—since it was packed with fireworks. The shock knocked over some heavy scales at the far end of the platform, and one of them struck Palsgraf. She sued the railroad.

The jury found that the guards had acted negligently, and held the railroad liable. The company appealed.

ISSUE: Assuming the guards did a bad job assisting the passenger, was the railroad liable for the injuries to Ms. Palsgraf?

EXCERPTS FROM JUDGE CARDOZO'S DECISION: The conduct of the defendant's guard, if a wrong in its relation to the holder of the package, was not a wrong in its relation to the plaintiff, standing far away. Relatively to her it was not negligence at all. Nothing in the situation gave notice that the falling package had in it the potency of peril to persons thus removed. Negligence is not actionable unless it involves the invasion of a legally protected interest, the violation of a right. Proof of negligence in the air, so to speak, will not do.

In every instance, before negligence can be predicated of a given act, back of the act must be sought and found a duty to the individual complaining, the observance of which would have averted or avoided the injury. What the plaintiff must show is "a wrong" to herself; i.e., a violation of her own right, and not merely a wrong to someone else, nor conduct "wrongful" because unsocial.

There was nothing in the situation to suggest to the most cautious mind that the parcel wrapped in newspaper would spread wreckage through the station. If the guard had thrown it down knowingly and willfully, he would not have threatened the plaintiff's safety, so far as appearances could warn him. Liability can be no greater where the act is inadvertent. [Reversed.] ◢

To win a negligence case, the plaintiff must prove five elements:

- Duty of Due Care. The defendant had a duty of due care to this plaintiff.

- Breach. The defendant breached her duty.

- Factual Cause. The defendant's conduct actually caused the injury.

- Foreseeable Harm. It was foreseeable that conduct like the defendant's might cause this type of harm.

- Injury. The plaintiff has actually been hurt.

DUTY OF DUE CARE

The first issue may be the most difficult in all of tort law: Did the defendant have a duty of due care *to the injured person?* The test is generally "foreseeability." **If the defendant could have foreseen injury to a particular person, she has a duty to him.** If she could not have foreseen the harm, there is usually no duty. Let us apply this principle to the fraternity case.

HERNANDEZ V. ARIZONA BOARD OF REGENTS

177 Ariz. 244, 866 P.2d 1330, 1994 Ariz. LEXIS 6
Arizona Supreme Court, 1994

FACTS: At the University of Arizona, the Epsilon Epsilon chapter of Delta Tau Delta fraternity gave a welcoming party for new members. The fraternity's officers knew that the majority of its members were under the legal drinking age, but permitted everyone to consume alcohol. John Rayner, who was under 21 years of age, left the party. He drove negligently and caused a collision with an auto driven by Ruben Hernandez. At the time of the accident, Rayner's blood alcohol level was .15, exceeding the legal limit. The crash left Hernandez blind, severely brain damaged, and quadriplegic.

Hernandez sued Rayner, who settled the case, based on the amount of his insurance coverage. The victim also sued the fraternity, its officers and national organization, all fraternity members who contributed money to buy alcohol, the university, and others. The trial court granted summary judgment for all defendants, and the court of appeals affirmed. Hernandez appealed to the Arizona Supreme Court.

Issue: Did the fraternity and the other defendants have a duty of due care to Hernandez?

EXCERPTS FROM JUDGE FELDMAN'S DECISION: Before 1983, this court arguably recognized the common-law rule of non-liability for tavern owners and, presumably, for social hosts. Traditional authority held that when "an able-bodied man" caused harm because of his intoxication, the act from which liability arose was the consuming not the furnishing of alcohol. However, the common law also provides that:

> One who supplies [a thing] for the use of another whom the supplier knows or has reason to know to be likely because of his youth, inexperience, or otherwise to use it in a manner involving unreasonable risk of physical harm to himself and others is subject to liability for physical harm resulting to them.

We perceive little difference in principle between liability for giving a car to an intoxicated youth and liability for giving drinks to a youth with a car. A growing number of cases have recognized that one of the very hazards that makes it negligent to furnish liquor to a minor is the foreseeable prospect that the [youthful] patron will become drunk and injure himself or others. Accordingly, modern authority has increasingly recognized that one who furnishes liquor to a minor breaches a common law duty owed to innocent third parties who may be injured.

Furnishing alcohol to underaged drinkers violates numerous statutes. The conduct in question violates well-established common-law principles that recognize a duty to avoid furnishing dangerous items to those known to have diminished capacity to use them safely. We join the majority of other states and conclude that as to Plaintiffs and the public in general, Defendants had a duty of care to avoid furnishing alcohol to underage consumers.

Arizona courts, therefore, will entertain an action for damages against [one] who negligently furnishes alcohol to those under the legal drinking age when that act is a cause of injury to a third person. [Reversed and remanded.] ◢

Let us move the liability question away from the fraternity house. Should a *social host* (home owner) be liable for serving alcohol to a guest who then causes an accident? Many states do hold a social host liable for serving a *minor*. New Jersey is one of the few states to go further, and hold a home owner liable even for serving an *adult*. Finally, many states now have some type of **dram act**, making liquor stores, bars, and restaurants liable for serving drinks to intoxicated customers who later cause harm. Which of these rules do you find persuasive? ▪▪

Economists often analyze legal issues by looking at **externalities: costs or benefits of one person's activity that affect someone else**. For example, a factory that pollutes the air imposes *negative externalities*, because the sullied atmosphere makes life unpleasant and unhealthy for those who live nearby. By contrast, a corporation that landscapes its headquarters to include a duck pond with waterfall creates *positive externalities*, by making the neighborhood more attractive for local residents.

Bars and restaurants can generate negative externalities because innocent people may be injured or killed by drivers who become intoxicated in those establishments. **Dram shop laws** are a response. These acts make liquor stores, bars and restaurants liable for serving drinks to intoxicated customers who later cause harm. (Historically, a dram was a small serving of alcohol.) These statutes force a financial dilemma on such firms. The more a tavern or café encourages its customers to drink, the greater its revenue—but also the larger its risk of a liability lawsuit. The goal of dram shop laws is to force businesses serving liquor to consider these externalities. In states without a dram shop statute, the threat of a lawsuit is removed, and the establishment has an incentive to maximize alcohol consumption, despite the external costs.

Do dram shop acts work? Yes, answer the authors of one economic study. In states with such statutes, bars monitor underage drinking more aggressively, refuse drinks earlier to an intoxicated customer, check the references of their own employees more carefully, and prohibit their workers from drinking on the job. These economists conclude that dram shop laws are a promising way to reduce drunk driving accidents.[23] ▪▪

BREACH OF DUTY

The second element of a plaintiff's negligence case is **breach of duty**. Courts apply the reasonable person standard: **a defendant breaches his duty of due care by**

[23] Sloan, Liang, Stout, and Whetten-Goldstein, "Liability, Risk Perceptions, and Precautions at Bars," *Journal of Law and Economics*, 2000, vol. 43, p. 473.

failing to behave the way a reasonable person would under similar circumstances. Reasonable "person" means someone of the defendant's occupation. A taxi driver must drive as a reasonable taxi driver would. A heart surgeon must perform bypass surgery with the care of a trained specialist in that field.

Two medical cases from Texas will illustrate the reasonable person standard. In *Gooden v. Tips*, the plaintiff, Gooden, was struck by an automobile driven by Dr. Tips's patient, who was under the influence of prescription Quaaludes at the time of the accident. The court ruled that the doctor had breached his duty of due care by failing to warn his patient not to drive while taking the drug.[24]

In *Casarez v. NME Hospitals, Inc.*,[25] Dr. Vasquez admitted to a hospital a patient who was terminally ill with AIDS. In his admission instruction, the doctor stated that the patient was HIV positive; he also told the nurses of the patient's condition. Dr. Vasquez did not, however, instruct anyone on the procedures to use with the patient. Casarez, a certified nursing assistant, was caring for the patient when he involuntarily spewed blood on Casarez's mouth, eyes, and arm. The patient died the next day. Casarez tested HIV positive.

Casarez sued Dr. Vasquez (among others), claiming that the doctor negligently failed to instruct him how to handle an AIDS patient. The court was unpersuaded. Vasquez was indeed obligated to take precautions with an AIDS patient, but he did everything reasonably required by ensuring that the staff knew of the patient's illness. He had no obligation to instruct staff in special procedures for such a patient because all hospital staff were already trained. Casarez and all others knew precisely what precautions to take, and Vasquez was not liable.

Crime and Tort: Negligent Hiring

In a recent one-year period, more than 1,000 homicides and 2 million attacks occurred in the workplace. Companies must beware because they can be liable for hiring or retaining violent employees. A mailroom clerk with a previous rape and robbery conviction followed a secretary home after work and fatally assaulted her. Even though the murder took place off the company premises, the court held that the defendant would be liable if it knew or should have known of the mail clerk's criminal history.[26] In other cases, companies have been found liable for failing to check an applicant's driving record, to contact personal references, and to search criminal records.

AT RISK

What can an employer do to diminish the likelihood of workplace violence? Many things.

- Make workplace safety a priority. Many employers still do not believe that violence can occur in their company. They are seriously mistaken.

- Evaluate the workplace for unsafe physical features. Install adequate lighting in parking lots and common areas, hire security guards if necessary, and use closed-circuit television and identification cards.

- Ensure that the company uses thorough pre-hire screening, contacts all former employers, and checks all references and criminal records. Nursing homes

---

24 651 S.W.2d 364, 1983 Tex. App. LEXIS 4388 (Tex. Ct. App. 1983).
25 883 S.W.2d 360, 1994 Tex. App. LEXIS 2091 (Tex. Ct. App. 1994).
26 *Gaines v. Monsanto*, 655 S.W.2d 568, 1983 Mo. LEXIS 3439 (Mo. Ct. App. 1983).

have paid huge sums for negligently hiring convicted assailants who later attack elderly residents.

- Respond quickly to dangerous behavior. In many cases of workplace violence, the perpetrator had demonstrated repeated bizarre, threatening, or obsessive behavior on the job, but his supervisors had not taken it seriously.

Negligence Per Se

In certain areas of life, courts are not free to decide what a "reasonable" person would have done, because the state legislature has made the decision for them. **When a legislature sets a minimum standard of care for a particular activity, in order to protect a certain group of people, and a violation of the statute injures a member of that group, the defendant has committed negligence per se.** A plaintiff who can show negligence per se need not prove breach of duty.

In Minnesota, the state legislature became alarmed about children sniffing glue, and passed a statute prohibiting the sale to a minor of any glue containing toluene. About one month later, 14-year-old Steven Zerby purchased glue containing toluene from a store in his hometown. Steven inhaled the glue and died from injury to his central nervous system. A reasonable person might have made the same error, but that is irrelevant: the clerk violated the statute and the store was liable.[27]

FACTUAL CAUSE AND FORESEEABLE HARM

A plaintiff must also show that the defendant's breach of duty caused the plaintiff's harm. Courts look at two issues to settle causation: Was the defendant's behavior the *factual cause* of the harm? Was *this type of harm foreseeable?*[28]

Factual Cause

Nothing mysterious here. **If the defendant's breach physically led to the ultimate harm, it is the factual cause.** Suppose that Dom's Brake Shop tells Customer his brakes are now working fine, even though Dom knows that is false. Customer drives out of the shop, cannot stop at a red light, and hits Bicyclist crossing at the intersection. Dom is liable to Bicyclist. Dom's unreasonable behavior was the factual cause of the harm. Think of it as a row of dominoes. The first domino (Dom's behavior) knocked over the next one (failing brakes), which toppled the last one (the cyclist's injury).

Suppose, alternatively, that just as Customer is exiting the repair shop, Bicyclist hits a pothole and tumbles off her cycle, avoiding Customer's auto. Bicyclist's injuries stem from her fall, not from the auto. Customer's brakes still fail, and Dom has breached his duty to Customer, but Dom is not liable to Bicyclist. She would have been hurt anyway. This is a row of dominoes that veers off to the side, leaving the last domino (cyclist's injury) untouched. No factual causation.

---

[27] Zerby v. Warren, 297 Minn. 134, 210 N.W.2d 58 (1973).

[28] Courts often refer to these two elements, grouped together, as *proximate cause* or *legal cause*. But, as many judges acknowledge, those terms have created confusion, so we use *factual cause* and *foreseeable type of harm*, the issues on which most decisions ultimately focus.

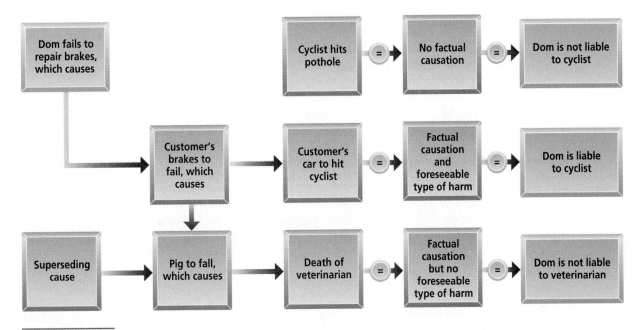

Exhibit 6.1

Foreseeable Type of Harm

For the defendant to be liable, the *type of harm* must have been reasonably foreseeable. In the case above, Dom could easily foresee that bad brakes would cause an automobile accident. He need not have foreseen exactly what happened. He did not know there would be a cyclist nearby. What he could foresee was this general type of harm involving defective brakes.

By contrast, assume the collision of car and bicycle produces a loud crash. Two blocks away, a pet pig, asleep on the window ledge of a twelfth-story apartment, is startled by the noise, awakens with a start, and plunges to the sidewalk, killing a veterinarian who was making a house call. If the vet's family sues Dom, should it win? Dom's negligence was the factual cause: it led to the collision, which startled the pig, which flattened the vet. Most courts would rule, though, that Dom is not liable. The type of harm is too bizarre. Dom could not reasonably foresee such an extraordinary chain of events, and it would be unfair to make him pay for it. See Exhibit 6.1.

Another way of stating that Dom is not liable to the vet's family is by calling the falling pig a *superseding cause.* When one of the "dominoes" in the row is entirely unforeseeable, courts will consider it a superseding cause, letting the defendant off the hook. Negligence cases often revolve around whether the chain of events leading from the defendant's conduct to the injury was broken by a superseding cause.

In *Kowkabany v. The Home Depot, Inc.,*[29] Mr. and Ms. Remseyer bought four 8-foot landscape timbers at a Home Depot store. Mr. Remseyer and a Home Depot employee loaded the timbers into the back seat of Remseyer's car, leaving them protruding about three feet out the front passenger window. After 20 minutes of driving, Remseyer approached Eva Kowkabany and another girl, both on bicycles.

---

[29] 606 So. 2d 716, 1992 Fla. App. LEXIS 10835 (Fla. Dist. Ct. App. 1992).

Remseyer thought he could pass the girls safely, but an approaching car "squeezed him" and the timber struck Eva Kowkabany, severely injuring her. Kowkabany sued The Home Depot.

The Home Depot defended by saying that Remseyer's negligent driving caused the accident. Remseyer had indeed been negligent. Was his negligence a "superseding cause"? No, held the court, stating that a superseding cause should only be found where the circumstances are highly unusual, extraordinary, or bizarre. Remseyer's poor judgment in driving was foreseeable.

Res Ipsa Loquitur

Normally, a plaintiff must prove factual cause and foreseeable type of harm in order to establish negligence. But in a few cases, a court may *infer* that the defendant caused the harm, under the doctrine of **res ipsa loquitur** ("the thing speaks for itself"). Suppose a pedestrian is walking along a sidewalk when an air-conditioning unit falls on his head from a third-story window. The defendant, who owns the third-story apartment, denies any wrongdoing, and it may be difficult or impossible for the plaintiff to prove why the air conditioner fell. In such cases, many courts will apply *res ipsa loquitur* and declare that **the facts imply that the defendant's negligence caused the accident**. If a court uses this doctrine, then the defendant must come forward with evidence establishing that it did not cause the harm.

Because *res ipsa loquitur* dramatically shifts the burden of proof from plaintiff to defendant, it applies only when (1) the defendant had exclusive control of the thing that caused the harm, (2) the harm normally would not have occurred without negligence, and (3) the plaintiff had no role in causing the harm. In the air conditioner example, most states would apply the doctrine and force the defendant to prove she did nothing wrong.

YOU BE THE JUDGE

GRIFFITH V. VALLEY OF SUN RECOVERY, INC.

126 Ariz. 227, 613 P.2d 1283
Arizona Court of Appeals, 1980

FACTS: Don Gorney was a repossession agent, authorized to take cars from owners who are behind on payments. A repossessor is allowed to drive away in such a car, provided he can do it peacefully. Gorney worked for Valley of Sun Recovery. He sought a car belonging to Linda Marsalek and Bob Williams. Gorney knew that there had been other failed efforts to repossess the car, including a violent confrontation involving attack dogs. He thought he could do better.

Gorney went to the car at 4:00 in the morning. He unscrewed the bulb in an overhead street lamp. He unlocked the car, setting off its alarm, and quickly hid. The alarm aroused the neighborhood. Williams and a neighbor, Griffith, investigated and concluded it was an attempted theft. They called the police. Gorney watched all of this from his hiding place. When everyone had gone, Gorney entered the car, again setting off the alarm and arousing the neighborhood. Williams and Griffith again emerged, as did another neighbor, dressed in his underwear and carrying a shotgun. They all believed they had caught a thief. Williams shouted for the gun, and the neighbor passed it to him, but it went off accidentally and severely injured Griffith.

Griffith sued Valley of Sun. The trial court granted summary judgment for Valley of Sun, and Griffith appealed.

YOU BE THE JUDGE:

- Did Valley of Sun have a *duty* to Griffith?

- If so, did the company *breach* its duty?

- If so, was the breach the *factual cause* of the injury?

- If so, was *this type of injury foreseeable*?

ARGUMENT FOR GRIFFITH: Your honors, Mr. Griffith should be allowed to make his case to a jury and let it decide whether Valley of Sun's repossession led to his injury. Valley of Sun had a duty to everyone in the area, because repossessions always involve antagonism and a chance of injury. Gorney breached his duty by acting as though he were Harrison Ford in an adventure film. Had it not been for his preposterous game playing, no neighbors would have been outside, no guns present—and no accidental shooting. This harm was easily foreseeable.

ARGUMENT FOR VALLEY OF SUN RECOVERY: Your honors, there was no duty, no breach and no causation. Surely Valley of Sun does not have a legal duty to the whole neighborhood. Is a repossession company to become an insurer of the entire city? Even if there had been a duty, there was no breach. Mr. Gorney attempted to repossess when it was least likely anyone would see him. Causation? The car owner created this situation by failing to pay, and the neighbor added a superseding cause by recklessly using a firearm. There is no case for a jury to hear.

INJURY

Finally, a plaintiff must prove that he has been injured. In some cases, injury is obvious. For example, Ruben Hernandez, struck by the intoxicated fraternity member, obviously suffered grievous harm. In other cases, though, injury is unclear. **The plaintiff must persuade the court that he has suffered a harm that is genuine, not speculative.**

Among the most vexing are suits involving future harm. Exposure to toxins or trauma may lead to serious medical problems down the road—or it may not. A woman's knee is damaged in an auto accident, causing severe pain for two years. She is clearly entitled to compensation for her suffering. After two years, all of her troubles may cease. Yet there is a chance that in 15 years the trauma will lead to painful arthritis. A court must decide today the full extent of present *and future* damages.

The following lawsuit concerns a woman's fear of developing AIDS. This worry can be overwhelming. A court must still decide, however, whether the cause of the unhappiness is genuine injury or speculation.

REYNOLDS V. HIGHLAND MANOR, INC.

24 Kan. App. 2d 859, 954 P.2d 11, 1998 Kan. App. LEXIS 20
Kansas Court of Appeals, 1998

FACTS: Angelina Reynolds and her family checked into a Holiday Inn, but since the air conditioner did not work they requested a room change. As they were repacking their luggage, Reynolds felt for items left under the bed, and picked up what she thought was a candy wrapper. Reynolds felt a "gush" as she retrieved the item, which unfortunately turned out to be a wet condom. She screamed and quickly washed her hands. There was a second condom under the bed. Reynolds and her husband rushed to an emergency room, taking the condoms with them. Hospital staff said that they were unable to test the contents of the condoms. A doctor examined Reynolds's hand, which had a burn on the middle finger and bloody cuticles, but told her that there was nothing he could do if she had been exposed to infectious diseases.

The condom never was tested. Reynolds sued the motel, claiming among other things that she feared she would die of AIDS. The trial court dismissed the case, ruling that there was no showing of injury. Reynolds appealed.

ISSUE: Has Reynolds demonstrated injury?

EXCERPTS FROM JUDGE PENLAND'S DECISION:
Plaintiff testified that after the incident, she feared she would die from AIDS. As a result of this anxiety, she claimed to have suffered headaches, diarrhea, and nausea. She could not say that she ever vomited and conceded that one type of medication she took caused her digestive problems. Plaintiff also testified to crying and shaking, and feeling overwhelmed with stress. Dr. Elias Chediak, the psychiatrist who treated plaintiff following the incident, testified that most of the time he saw her, "she was feeling pretty anxious, crying, feeling distressed," and she reported headaches and tense muscles. Dr. Chediak stated plaintiff had seen a neurologist who performed tests that turned out

negative. According to Dr. Chediak, the neurologist concluded that any problems plaintiff had experienced were due to stress. Plaintiff also testified that because of her mental state, her sexual relations with her husband had decreased, but they continued to have unprotected sex after the incident, despite her purported fear she might have HIV.

[In an earlier case,] our Supreme Court held that a plaintiff may recover for anxiety based on reasonable fear that an existing injury will lead to the occurrence of a disease or condition in the future. For the fear to be reasonable, the court held the plaintiff must show that a substantial probability exists that such condition or disease will occur. Anxiety about a disease or condition developing from a physical injury is not recoverable as an element of mental distress where the medical evidence indicates the chance of such occurring is slight.

The uncontroverted evidence established that plaintiff took an HIV test four times following the incident, the last occurring more than 1 year after the incident. When an individual tests negative for HIV more than 1 year after exposure, a greater than 99% probability exists that HIV will not appear. Plaintiff has failed to establish even a minimal possibility, much less a substantial or even significant probability, that she will contract AIDS due to her contact with the condom in the motel. Because her fear of contracting the disease is unreasonable as a matter of law, she may not recover damages.

Affirmed. ◢

DAMAGES

The plaintiff's damages in a negligence case are generally compensatory damages. In unusual cases, a court may award punitive damages, that is, money intended not to compensate the plaintiff but to punish the defendant. We discussed both forms of damages earlier in this chapter.

Contributory and Comparative Negligence

Joe is a mental patient in a hospital. The hospital knows he is dangerous to himself and others, but it permits him to wander around unattended. Joe leaves the hospital and steals a gun. Shawn drives by Joe, and Joe waves the gun at him. Shawn notices a police officer a block away. But instead of informing the cop, Shawn leans out his window and shouts, "Hey, knucklehead, what are you doing pointing guns at people?" Joe shoots and kills Shawn.

Shawn's widow sues the hospital for negligently permitting Joe to leave. But the hospital, in defense, claims that Shawn's foolishness got him killed. Who wins? It depends on whether the state in which the suit is heard uses a legal theory called **contributory negligence**. This used to be the law throughout the nation, but it remains in effect in only a few states. It means that, even assuming the defendant is negligent, **if the plaintiff is even *slightly* negligent himself, he recovers nothing**. So if Shawn's homicide occurs in a contributory negligence state, the hospital is not liable regardless of how negligent it was.

Critics attacked the rule as unreasonable. A plaintiff who was 1 percent negligent could not recover from a defendant who was 99 percent negligent. So most states threw out the contributory negligence rule, replacing it with comparative negligence. **In a comparative negligence state, a plaintiff may generally recover even if she is partially negligent.** A jury will be asked to assess the relative negligence of plaintiff and defendant.

Suppose we are in a comparative negligence state, and the jury believes the hospital was 80 percent responsible for Shawn's death, and Shawn himself was 20 percent responsible. It might conclude that the total damages for Shawn's widow are $2 million, based on Shawn's pain in dying and the widow's loss of his income. If so, the hospital would owe $1.6 million, or 80 percent of the damages. See Exhibit 6.2.

Today, most states have adopted some form of comparative negligence. Critics of comparative negligence claim that it rewards a plaintiff for being careless. Suppose, they say, a driver speeds to beat an approaching train, and the railroad's mechanical arm fails to operate. Why should we reward the driver for his foolishness? In response to this complaint, some comparative negligence states do not permit a plaintiff to recover anything if he was more than 50 percent responsible for his injury.

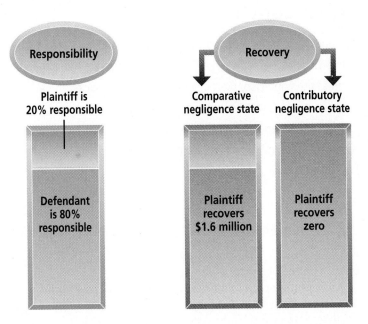

Exhibit 6.2
Defendant's negligence injures plaintiff, who suffers $2 million in damages.

Strict Liability

Some activities are so naturally dangerous that the law places an especially high burden on anyone who engages in them. A corporation that produces toxic waste can foresee dire consequences from its business that a stationery store cannot. This higher burden is **strict liability**. There are two main areas of business that incur strict liability: *ultrahazardous activity* and *defective products*. Defective products are discussed in Chapter 11, on products liability.

ULTRAHAZARDOUS ACTIVITY

Ultrahazardous activities include using harmful chemicals, operating explosives, keeping wild animals, bringing dangerous substances onto property, and a few similar activities where the danger to the general public is especially great. **A defendant engaging in an ultrahazardous activity is virtually always liable for any harm that results.** Plaintiffs do not have to prove duty or breach or foreseeable harm. Recall the deliberately bizarre case we posed earlier of the pig falling from a window ledge and killing a veterinarian. Dom, the mechanic whose negligence caused the car crash, could not be liable for the veterinarian's death because the plunging pig was a superseding cause. But if the pig was jolted off the window ledge by Sam's Blasting Co., which was doing perfectly lawful blasting for a new building down the street, Sam is liable. Even if Sam took extraordinary care, it will do him no good at trial. The "reasonable person" rule is irrelevant in a strict liability case.

Chapter Conclusion

This chapter has been a potpourri of sin, a bubbling cauldron of conduct best avoided. Although tortious acts and their consequences are diverse, two generalities apply. First, the boundaries of torts are imprecise, the outcome of a particular case depending to a considerable extent upon the factfinder who analyzes it. Second, the thoughtful executive and the careful citizen, aware of the shifting standards and potentially vast liability, will strive to ensure that his or her conduct never provides that factfinder an opportunity to give judgment.

Chapter Review

1. A tort is a violation of a duty imposed by the civil law.

2. Defamation involves a false statement, likely to harm another's reputation, which is uttered to a third person, and causes an injury. Opinion and privilege are valid defenses. Public personalities can win a defamation suit only by proving actual malice.

3. False imprisonment is the intentional restraint of another person without reasonable cause and without consent.

4. The intentional infliction of emotional distress involves extreme and outrageous conduct that causes serious emotional harm.

5. Battery is an intentional touching of another person in a way that is offensive. Assault

involves an act that makes the plaintiff fear an imminent battery.

6. Compensatory damages are the normal remedy in a tort case. In unusual cases, the court may award punitive damages, to punish the defendant.

7. Tortious interference with business relations involves the defendant harming an existing contract or a prospective relationship that has a definite expectation of success.

8. The related torts of privacy and publicity involve unreasonable intrusion into someone's private life, disclosure of embarrassing private facts in which the public has no legitimate interest, placing the plaintiff in a false light, or unfair commercial exploitation by using someone's name, likeness, or voice without permission.

9. The five elements of negligence are duty of due care, breach, factual causation, foreseeable type of harm, and injury.

10. If the defendant could foresee that misconduct would injure a particular person, he probably has a duty to her.

11. A defendant breaches his duty of due care by failing to behave the way a reasonable person would under similar conditions.

12. Employers may be liable for negligent hiring.

13. If a legislature sets a minimum standard of care for a particular activity in order to protect a certain group of people, and a violation of the statute injures a member of that group, the defendant has committed negligence per se.

14. If an event physically leads to the ultimate harm, it is the factual cause.

15. For the defendant to be liable, the type of harm must have been reasonably foreseeable.

16. The plaintiff must persuade the court that he has suffered a harm that is genuine, not speculative.

17. In a contributory negligence state, a plaintiff who is even slightly responsible for his own injury recovers nothing; in a comparative negligence state, the jury may apportion liability between plaintiff and defendant.

18. A defendant is strictly liable for harm caused by an ultrahazardous activity or a defective product. Strict liability means that if the defendant's conduct led to the harm, the defendant is liable, even if she exercised extraordinary care.

Practice Test

1. Benzaquin had a radio talk show in Boston. On the program, he complained about an incident earlier in the day, in which state trooper Fleming had stopped his car, apparently for lack of a proper license plate and safety sticker. Even though Benzaquin explained that the license plate had been stolen and the sticker had fallen onto the dashboard, Fleming refused to let him drive the car away, and Benzaquin and his daughter and two young grandsons had to find other transportation. On the show, Benzaquin angrily recounted the incident, then made the following statements about Fleming and troopers generally: "arrogants wearing troopers' uniforms like tights"; "little monkey, you wind him up and he does his thing"; "we're not paying them to be dictators and Nazis"; "this man is an absolute barbarian, a lunkhead, a meathead." Fleming sued Benzaquin for defamation. Comment.

2. Caldwell, carrying a large purse, was shopping in a K-Mart store. A security guard observed her look at various small items such as stain, hinges, and antenna wire. On occasion she bent down out of sight of the guard. The guard thought he saw Caldwell put something in her purse. Caldwell removed her glasses from her purse and returned them a few times. After she left, the guard approached her in the parking lot and said that he believed she had store merchandise in her purse but was unable to say what he thought was put there.

Caldwell opened the purse, and the guard testified he saw no K-Mart merchandise in it. The guard then told Caldwell to return to the store with him. They walked around the store for approximately 15 minutes, while the guard said six or seven times that he saw her put something in her purse. Caldwell left the store after another store employee indicated she could go. Caldwell sued. What kind of suit did she file, and what should the outcome be?

3. Fifteen-year-old Terri Stubblefield was riding in the back seat of a Ford Mustang II when the car was hit from behind. The Mustang was engulfed in a ball of fire, and Terri was severely burned. She died. Terri's family sued Ford, alleging that the car was badly designed—and that Ford knew it. At trial, Terri's family introduced evidence that Ford knew the fuel tank was dangerous and that it could have taken measures to make the tank safe. There was evidence that Ford consciously decided not to remedy the fuel tanks in order to save money. The family sought two different kinds of damages from Ford. What were they?

4. **ETHICS** In the *Stubblefield* case in Question 3, the jury awarded $8 million in punitive damages to the family. Ford appealed. Should the punitive damages be affirmed? What are the obligations of a corporation when it knows one of its products may be dangerous? Is an automobile company ethically obligated to make a *totally safe* car? Should we require a manufacturer to improve the safety of its cars if doing so will make them too expensive for many drivers? What would you do if you were a mid-level executive and saw evidence that your company was endangering the lives of consumers to save money? What would you do if you were on a *jury* and saw such evidence?

5. Caudle worked at Betts Lincoln-Mercury dealer. During an office party, many of the employees, including president Betts, were playing with an electric auto condenser, which gave a slight electric shock when touched. Some employees played catch with the condenser. Betts shocked Caudle on the back of his neck and then chased him around, holding the condenser. The shock later caused Caudle to suffer headaches, to pass out, and eventually to require surgery on a nerve in his neck. Even after surgery, Caudle had a slight numbness on one side of his head. He sued Betts for battery. Betts defended by saying that it was all horseplay and that he had intended no injury. Please rule.

6. **YOU BE THE JUDGE WRITING PROBLEM** Johnny Carson was for many years the star of a well-known television program, *The Tonight Show*. For about 20 years, he was introduced nightly on the show with the phrase, "Here's Johnny!" A large segment of the television watching public associated the phrase with Carson. A Michigan corporation was in the business of renting and selling portable toilets. The company chose the name "Here's Johnny Portable Toilets," and coupled the company name with the marketing phrase, "The World's Foremost Commodian." Carson sued, claiming that the company's name and slogan violated his right to commercial exploitation. Who should win? **Argument for Carson:** The toilet company is deliberately taking advantage of Johnny Carson's good name. He worked hard for decades to build a brilliant career and earn a reputation as a creative, funny, likable performer. No company has the right to use his name, his picture, or anything else closely identified with him, such as the phrase "Here's Johnny." The pun is personally offensive and commercially unfair. **Argument for Here's Johnny Portable Toilets:** Johnny Carson doesn't own his first name. It is available for anyone to use for any purpose. Further, the popular term "john," meaning toilet, has been around much longer than Carson or even television. We are entitled to make any use of it we want. Our corporate name is amusing to customers who have never heard of Carson, and we are entitled to profit from our brand recognition.

7. Jason Jacque was riding as a passenger in a car driven by his sister, who was drunk and driving 19 mph over the speed limit. She failed to negotiate a curve, skidded off the road, and collided with a wooden utility pole erected by the Public Service Company of Colorado (PSC). Jacque suffered severe brain injury. He sued PSC for negligently installing the pole too close to the highway at a dangerous curve where an accident was likely to happen. The

trial court gave summary judgment for PSC, ruling that PSC owed no duty to Jacque. He appealed. Please rule.

8. Ryder leased a truck to Florida Food Service; Powers, an employee, drove it to make deliveries. He noticed that the door strap used to close the rear door was frayed, and he asked Ryder to fix it. Ryder failed to do so in spite of numerous requests. The strap broke, and Powers replaced it with a nylon rope. Later, when Powers was attempting to close the rear door, the nylon rope broke and he fell, sustaining severe injuries to his neck and back. He sued Ryder. The trial court found that Powers's attachment of the replacement rope was a superseding cause, relieving Ryder of any liability, and granted summary judgment for Ryder. Powers appealed. How should the appellate court rule?

9. A new truck, manufactured by General Motors Corp. (GMC) stalled in rush hour traffic on a busy interstate highway because of a defective alternator, which caused a complete failure of the truck's electrical system. The driver stood nearby and waved traffic around his stalled truck. A panel truck approached the GMC truck, and immediately behind the panel truck, Davis was driving a Volkswagen fastback. Because of the panel truck, Davis was unable to see the stalled GMC truck. The panel truck swerved out of the way of the GMC truck, and Davis drove straight into it. The accident killed him. Davis's widow sued GMC. GMC moved for summary judgment, alleging (1) no duty to Davis, (2) no factual causation, and (3) no foreseeable harm. Comment.

10. A prison inmate bit a hospital employee. The employee sued the state for negligence and lack of supervision, claiming a fear of AIDS. The plaintiff had tested negative for HIV three times, and there was no proof that the inmate was HIV positive. Comment on the probable outcome.

11. **ETHICS** Swimming pools in private homes often have diving boards, but those in public parks, hotels, and clubs rarely do. Why is that? Is it good or bad?

12. There is a collision between cars driven by Candy and Zeke, and both drivers are partly at fault. The evidence is that Candy is about 25 percent responsible, for failing to stop quickly enough, and Zeke about 75 percent responsible, for making a dangerous turn. Candy is most likely to win:

(a) A lawsuit for battery

(b) A lawsuit for negligence, in a comparative negligence state

(c) A lawsuit for negligence, in a contributory negligence state

(d) A lawsuit for strict liability; or

(e) A lawsuit for assault.

13. Van Houten owned a cat and allowed it to roam freely outside. In the three years he had owned it, it had never bitten anyone. The cat entered Pritchard's garage. Pritchard attempted to move it outside his garage, and the cat bit him. As a direct result of the bite, Pritchard underwent four surgeries, was fitted with a plastic finger joint, and spent more than $39,000 in medical bills. He sued Van Houten, claiming both strict liability and ordinary negligence. Evaluate his claims.

14. **ROLE REVERSAL** Write a multiple-choice question about defamation in which one and only one element is missing from the plaintiff's case. Choose a set of answers that forces the student to isolate the missing element.

Internet Research Problem

Take a look at http://response.restoration.noaa.gov/index.html. What are some of the long-term problems associated with oil spills? View some of the photos in the "gallery." Are punitive damages for oil spills appropriate or excessive?

You can find further practice problems in the Online Quiz at http://beatty.westbuslaw.com or in the Study Guide that accompanies this text.

Crime

Crime can take us by surprise. Stacey tucks her nine-year-old daughter, Beth, into bed. Promising her husband, Mark, that she will be home by 11:00 P.M., she jumps into her car and heads back to Be Patient, Inc. She puts a CD in the player of her $85,000 sedan and tries to relax. Be Patient is a health care organization that owns five geriatric hospitals. Most of its patients use Medicare, and Stacey supervises all billing to their largest client, the federal government.

She parks in a well-lighted spot on the street and walks to her building, failing to notice two men, collars turned up, watching from a parked truck. Once in her office she goes straight to her computer and works on billing issues. Tonight's work goes more quickly than she expected, thanks to new software she helped develop. At 10:30 she emerges from the building with a quick step and a light heart, walks to her car—and finds it missing.

A major crime has occurred during the 90 minutes Stacey was at her desk, but she will never report it to the police. It is a crime that costs Americans countless dollars each year, yet Stacey will not even mention it to friends or family. Stacey is the criminal. ∎

When we think of crime, we imagine the drug dealers and bank robbers endlessly portrayed on television. We do not picture corporate executives sitting at polished desks. "Street crimes" are indeed serious threats to our security and happiness. They deservedly receive the attention of the public and the law. (For a look at the FBI's 10 most wanted list, see http://www.fbi.gov.) But when measured only in dollars, street crime takes second place to white-collar crime, which costs society *tens of billions* of dollars annually.

The hypothetical about Stacey is based on many real cases and is used to illustrate that crime does not always dress the way we expect. Her car was never stolen; it was simply towed. Two parking bureau employees, watching from their truck, saw Stacey park illegally and did their job. It is Stacey who committed a crime—Medicare fraud. Stacey has learned the simple but useful lesson that company profits rise when she charges the government for work Be Patient has never done. For months she billed the government for imaginary patients. Then she hired a computer hacker to worm into the Medicare computer system and plant a "Trojan horse," a program that seemed useful to Medicare employees but actually contained a series of codes opening the computer to Stacey. Stacey simply entered the Medicare system and altered the calculations for payments owed to Be Patient. Every month, the government paid Be Patient about $10 million for imaginary work. Stacey's scheme was quick and profitable—and a distressingly common crime.

What do we do about cases like these? These questions involve multifarious fact issues and important philosophical values. In this chapter we look first at the big picture of criminal law and then focus on that part of it that most affects business—white-collar crime. We examine four major issues:

- *Crime, Society, and Law.* What makes conduct criminal? We enumerate the basic elements that the prosecution must establish to prove that a crime has been committed, and also some of the most common defenses.

- *Crimes That Harm Business.* We look at specific crimes, such as fraud and embezzlement, that cost businesses enormous sums every year.

- *Crimes Committed by Business.* We analyze "white-collar crimes," which are generally committed by businesspeople and may be directed at consumers, other businesses, or the government.

- *Criminal Process and Constitutional Protections.* We examine how the Bill of Rights protects citizens subjected to search, interrogation, and trial. And we pay a final visit to Stacey.

Crime, Society, and Law

CIVIL LAW/CRIMINAL LAW

Most of this book concerns the civil law—the rights and liabilities that exist between private parties. As we have seen, if one person claims that another has caused her a civil injury, she must file a lawsuit and convince a court of her damages.

The criminal law is different. Conduct is **criminal** when society outlaws it. When a state legislature or Congress concludes that certain behavior threatens the population generally, it passes a statute forbidding that behavior, in other words, declaring it criminal. Medicare fraud, which Stacey committed, is a crime because Congress has outlawed it. Money laundering is a crime because Congress concluded it was a fundamental part of the drug trade and prohibited it.

Prosecution

Suppose the police arrest Roger and accuse him of breaking into a video store and stealing 25 video cameras, videos, and other equipment. The owner of the video store is the one harmed, but **it is the government that prosecutes crimes**. The local prosecutor will decide whether or not to charge Roger and bring him to trial.

Jury Right

The facts of the case will be decided by a judge or jury. A criminal defendant has a right to a trial by jury for any charge that could result in a sentence of six months or longer. The defendant may demand a jury trial or may waive that right, in which case the judge will be the factfinder.

Punishment

In a civil lawsuit, the plaintiff seeks a verdict that the defendant is liable for harm caused to her. But in a criminal case, the government asks the court to find the defendant **guilty** of the crime. The government wants the court to **punish** the defendant. If the judge or jury finds the defendant guilty, the court will punish him with a fine and/or a prison sentence. The fine is paid to the government, not to the injured person (although the court will sometimes order **restitution**, meaning that the defendant must reimburse the victim for harm suffered). It is almost always the judge who imposes the sentence. If the jury is not persuaded of the defendant's guilt, it will acquit him, that is, find him not guilty.

Felony/Misdemeanor

A **felony** is a serious crime, for which a defendant can be sentenced to one year or more in prison. Murder, robbery, rape, drug dealing, money laundering, wire fraud, and embezzlement are felonies. A **misdemeanor** is a less serious crime, often punishable by a year or less in a county jail. Public drunkenness, driving without a license, and simple possession of one marijuana cigarette are considered misdemeanors in most states.

PUNISHMENT

Why punish a defendant? Sometimes the answer is obvious. If a defendant has committed armed robbery, we want that person locked up. Other cases are not so apparent.

You are the judge in charge of sentencing Jason. He is a 61-year-old minister who has devoted 40 years to serving his community, leading his church, and helping to rehabilitate schools. Fifteen years ago he founded a children's hospital and has raised enormous sums to maintain it. He has labored with local government to rebuild abandoned housing and established a center for battered women. Jason suffers from a terminal illness and will die in three to four years. But the jury has just found that in his zeal to get housing built, Jason took kickbacks from construction firms run by gangsters. The construction companies padded their bills, some of which were paid with state and city money. They kicked back a small amount of this illegal profit to Jason, who gave the money to his charities. Jason thought of himself as Robin Hood, but the law regards him as a felon. You can fine Jason and/or sentence him to prison for a maximum of five years.

A flood of letters urges you to allow Jason to continue raising money and helping others. You need to understand the rationale of punishment. Over the past several centuries, philosophers in many countries—and judges in this country—have proposed various reasons for punishing the guilty.

Restraint

A violent criminal who appears likely to commit more crimes must be physically restrained. Here there is no pretense of prison being anything but a cage to protect the rest of society. (An online group that sees little good and much evil in our system of incarceration gives examples of perceived abuses at http://www.prison-activist.org.) In Jason's case, there is clearly no reason to restrain him.

Deterrence

Imprisonment may deter future crimes in two ways. **Specific deterrence** is intended to teach *this defendant* that crime carries a heavy price tag, in the hope that he will never do it again. **General deterrence** is the goal of demonstrating to *society generally* that crime must be shunned. Notice that both ideas of deterrence are utilitarian; that is, they are *means to an end*. Specific and general deterrence both assume that by imprisoning someone, the law achieves a greater good for everyone. Jason almost certainly requires no specific deterrence. Is general deterrence a reason to imprison him?

Retribution

The German philosopher Immanuel Kant (1724–1804) rejected the idea of deterrence. He argued that human beings were supremely important and as a result must always be treated as ends in themselves, *never as a means to an end*. Kant would argue that, if deterrence were legitimate, then it would be all right to torture prisoners—even innocent prisoners—if this deterred massive amounts of crime.

For Kant there is only one valid reason to punish: the prisoner deserves it. This is the idea of **retribution**—giving back to the criminal precisely what he deserves. A moral world, said Kant, requires that the government administer to all prisoners a punishment exactly equal to the crime they committed. A murderer must be put to death (even if he is dying from an illness and would live only a few days); an executive who bribes a government official must suffer a punishment equal to the harm he caused. To Kant, all of Jason's good deeds would be irrelevant, as would his terminal illness. If three years is the appropriate imprisonment for the crime of fraud, then he must serve three years, even if he dies in prison, even if it stops him from raising $10 million for charity.

Related to the idea of retribution is **vengeance**. When a serious crime has occurred, society wants the perpetrator to suffer. If we punish no one, people lose faith in the power and effectiveness of government and may take the law into their own hands.

Rehabilitation

To rehabilitate someone is to provide training so that he may return to a normal life. Most criminal justice experts believe that little or no rehabilitation occurs in a prison, though other forms of punishment may achieve this worthy goal.

Jason's Case. What is your decision? Restraint and specific deterrence are unnecessary. You may imprison him for general deterrence or for retribution. Should you let him go free so that he can raise more money for good causes? In a similar case, a federal court judge decided that general deterrence was essential. To allow someone to go free, he said, would be to send a message that certain people can get away with crime. The judge sentenced the defendant to a prison term, though he shortened the sentence based on the defendant's age and ill health.[1]

THE PROSECUTION'S CASE

In all criminal cases, the prosecution faces several basic issues.

Conduct Outlawed

Virtually all crimes are created by statute. The prosecution must demonstrate to the court that the defendant's alleged conduct is indeed outlawed by a statute. Returning to Roger, the alleged video thief, the state charges that he stole video cameras from a store, a crime clearly defined by statute as burglary.

Burden of Proof

In a civil case, the plaintiff must prove her case by a preponderance of the evidence.[2] But in a criminal case, the government must prove its case **beyond a reasonable doubt**. This is because the potential harm to a criminal defendant is far greater. Roger, the video thief, can be fined and/or sent to prison. The stigma of a criminal conviction will stay with him, making it more difficult to obtain work and housing. Therefore, in all criminal cases, if the jury has any significant doubt at all that Roger stole the video cameras, it *must* acquit him. This high standard of proof in a criminal case reflects a very old belief, inherited from English law, that it is better to set 10 guilty people free than to convict a single innocent one. We will see that our law offers many protections for the accused.

Actus Reus

Actus reus means the "guilty act." **The prosecution must prove that the defendant voluntarily committed a prohibited act.** Suppose Mary Jo files an insurance claim for a stolen car, knowing that her car was not stolen. That is insurance fraud. Filing the claim is the *actus reus*: Mary Jo voluntarily filled out the insurance claim and mailed it. At a bar, Mary Jo describes the claim to her friend, Chi Ling, who laughs and replies, "That's great. It'll serve the company right." Has Chi Ling committed a crime? No. There is no *actus reus*, because Chi Ling has done nothing illegal. Her cynical attitude may contribute to higher premiums for all of us, but criminal law punishes acts, not thoughts or omissions.

---

[1] *United States v. Bergman*, 416 F. Supp. 496, 1976 U.S. Dist. LEXIS 14577 (S.D.N.Y. 1976).
[2] See the earlier discussion in Chapter 3, on dispute resolution.

Mens Rea

The prosecution must also show *mens rea*, **a "guilty state of mind,"** on the defendant's part. This is harder to prove than *actus reus*—it requires convincing evidence about something that is essentially psychological. Precisely what "state of mind" the prosecution must prove varies, depending on the crime. We will discuss the exact *mens rea* requirement for various crimes later in this chapter. In general, however, there are four mental states that a prosecutor may be required to prove, depending on the crime:

General Intent.   Most crimes require a showing of general intent, meaning that the defendant intended to do the prohibited physical action (the *actus reus*). Suppose Miller, a customer in a bar, picks up a bottle and smashes it over the head of Bud. In a trial for criminal assault, the *mens rea* would simply be the intention to hit Bud. The prosecution need not show that Miller intended serious harm, only that he intended the blow.

How will a prosecutor prove what was in Miller's mind? By circumstantial evidence: a witness will describe how Miller picked up the bottle and what he did with it. A jury is free to conclude that Miller intended physical contact since there would be no other reason for his action.

Specific Intent.   Some crimes require the prosecution to prove that the defendant willfully intended to do something beyond the physical act. For example, burglary requires proof that the defendant entered a building at night and intended to commit a felony inside, such as stealing property.

Reckless or Negligent Conduct.   For a few crimes, the prosecution is concerned more with the defendant's irresponsible conduct than with what the defendant was thinking. **Criminal recklessness** means consciously disregarding a substantial risk of injury. One pedestrian who jokingly points a gun at another commits criminal recklessness. The danger of the gun going off is obvious, and the defendant is guilty even if no shot is fired. A slightly lesser crime, **criminal negligence**, refers to gross deviations from reasonable conduct. A hunter who sees movement and shoots at it, without bothering to determine whether the target is a turkey or a professor, commits criminal negligence.

Strict Liability.   In strict liability cases, the prosecution must only prove *actus reus*. If the defendant committed the act, he is guilty, regardless of mental state or irresponsibility. For example, in an effort to improve the environment, many states now hold corporate defendants strictly liable for discharging certain pollutants into the air. If an oil refinery discharges toxic fumes, it is strictly liable, regardless of what efforts it may have taken to control emissions. Thus, strict liability crimes are the easiest for a prosecutor to prove and potentially the most dangerous to corporations.

DEFENSES

A criminal defendant will frequently dispute the facts that link her to the crime. For example, she might claim mistaken identity (that she merely resembles the real criminal) or offer an alibi (that she can prove she was elsewhere when the crime was committed). In addition, a defendant may offer **legal defenses**. Many of these are controversial, as we will see.

Insanity

A defendant who can prove that he was **insane** at the time of the criminal act will be declared not guilty. This reflects the moral basis of our criminal law. Insane people, though capable of great harm, historically have not been considered responsible for their acts. A defendant found to be insane will generally be committed to a mental institution. If that hospital determines he is no longer a danger to society, he will, in theory, be released. Some people applaud this as deeply humane, while others see it as muddled thinking that allows guilty people to walk free.

Two basic tests determine whether a defendant is insane. Some states recognize just one; others allow both.

M'Naghten Rule. The defendant must show (1) that he suffered a serious, identifiable mental disease and that because of it (2) he did not understand the nature of his act or did not know that it was wrong. Suppose Jerry, a homeless man, stabs Phil. At trial, a psychiatrist testifies that Jerry suffers from chronic schizophrenia, that he does not know where he is or what he is doing, and that when he stabbed Phil he believed he was sponging down his pet giraffe. If the jury believes the psychiatrist, it may find Jerry not guilty by reason of insanity.

"Irresistible Impulse." Under this test, the defendant must convince a jury that a mental defect left him unable to control his behavior. Jerry testifies that when he stabbed Phil he knew it was wrong but he could not stop himself. His psychiatrist asserts that Jerry's chronic dementia leaves him physically unable to repress violent impulses. If the jury believes the testimony, it may find Jerry not guilty.

What if the alleged mental defect is a result of the defendant's own behavior? You be the judge.

YOU BE THE JUDGE

BIEBER V. PEOPLE

856 P.2d 811, 1993 Colo. LEXIS 630
Supreme Court of Colorado, 1993

FACTS: Donald Bieber walked up to a truck in which William Ellis was sitting and shot Ellis, whom he did not know, in the back of his head. He threw Ellis's body from the truck and drove away. Shortly before and after the killing, Bieber encountered various people in different places. He sang "God Bless America" and the "Marine Hymn" to them and told them he was a prisoner of war and was being followed by communists. He told people he had killed a communist on "War Memorial Highway." The police arrested him.

Bieber had a long history of drug abuse. As a teenager, he began using drugs, including amphetamines. As an adult, he continued his heavy drug use, while making money selling drugs. Several years before the homicide, Bieber voluntarily sought treatment for mental impairment, entering a hospital and saying he thought he was going to hurt someone. He was later released into a long-term drug program.

Bieber was charged with first-degree murder. He pleaded not guilty by reason of insanity. An expert witness testified that he was insane, suffering from "amphetamine delusional disorder" (ADD), a recognized psychiatric illness resulting from long-term use of amphetamines and characterized by delusions. At trial, Bieber's attorney argued that he was not intoxicated at the time of the crime but that he was insane due to ADD. The trial court refused to instruct that Bieber could be legally insane due to ADD, and the jury found Bieber guilty of first-degree murder. He appealed.

YOU BE THE JUDGE: May a jury find that a defendant with ADD is legally insane?

ARGUMENT FOR BIEBER: Your honors, Mr. Bieber acknowledges the rule that someone who becomes voluntarily intoxicated and commits an offense is liable for the crime. That rule is irrelevant here, since Mr. Bieber was not intoxicated at the time of this homicide. He was insane.

The state of Colorado has long held that insanity is a valid defense to a criminal charge. It is morally and legally proper to distinguish between people who commit a crime out of viciousness and those who suffer serious mental illness. Mr. Bieber suffered from amphetamine delusional disorder, a serious psychotic illness recognized by the American Psychiatric Association. There was overwhelming evidence that he was out of control and did not know what he was doing at the time of the homicide.

The fact that ADD is brought about by years of amphetamine use should make no difference in an insanity case. This man's reason was destroyed by a serious illness. He should not be treated the same as a cold-blooded killer.

ARGUMENT FOR THE STATE: Your honors, there is no qualitative difference between a person who drinks or takes drugs knowing that he or she will be momentarily "mentally defective" as an immediate result and one who drinks or takes drugs knowing that he or she may be "mentally defective" as an eventual, long-term result. In both cases, the person is aware of the possible consequences of his or her actions. We do not believe that in the latter case, such knowledge should be excused simply because the resulting affliction is more severe.

It is a matter of common knowledge that the excessive use of liquor or drugs impairs the perceptual, judgmental, and volitional faculties of the user. Also, because the intoxication must be "self-induced," the defendant necessarily must have had the conscious ability to prevent this temporary incapacity from coming into being at all. Self-induced intoxication by its very nature involves culpability.

As a matter of public policy, therefore, we must not excuse a defendant's actions, which endanger others, based upon a mental disturbance or illness that he or she actively and voluntarily contracted. There is no principled basis to distinguish between the short-term and long-term effects of voluntary intoxication by punishing the first and excusing the second. If anything, the moral blameworthiness would seem to be even greater with respect to the long-term effects of many, repeated instances of voluntary intoxication occurring over an extended period of time. We ask that you affirm. ◢

Jury Role. The insanity defense creates fear and confusion in the public, but most experts believe the concern is unwarranted. A Connecticut study showed that the defense was invoked in only one-tenth of 1 percent of criminal prosecutions in that state, and that in over 90 percent of *those* cases it still failed. Juries are reluctant to acquit based on insanity, probably fearing that the defendant will soon be back on the streets. But just the opposite is true. Most defendants acquitted by reason of insanity spend more time in a mental hospital than convicts spend in prison for the same act.

Entrapment

You go to a fraternity party where you meet a friendly new frat member, Joey. After a drink or two, Joey asks if you can get him some marijuana. You tell him you never use drugs. A week later you accidentally meet Joey in the cafeteria, and he repeats the question, promising a very large profit if you will supply him with an ounce. You again say "no thanks." About once a week Joey bumps into you, in the school hallways, in the bookstore, at parties. He continues to ask you to "get him some stuff," and his offers grow more lucrative. Finally, after six requests, you speak to someone who is reputed to deal in drugs. You buy an ounce, then offer it to Joey at a large markup. Joey gratefully hands over the money, takes your package—and flashes his badge in your face, identifying himself as an undercover agent of the State Police. You are speechless, which is fine, since Joey informs you that you have the right to remain silent.

Drugs are a deadly serious problem in our society, involved directly or indirectly in more than half of all street crime. We need creative police efforts. Has this one gone too far? The issue is **entrapment. When the government induces the defendant to break the law, the prosecution must prove beyond a reasonable doubt that the defendant was predisposed to commit the crime.**

If the government cannot prove predisposition, the defendant is not guilty. In other words, the goal is to separate the cases where the defendant was innocent before the government tempted him from those where the defendant was only too eager to break the law.

JACOBSON V. UNITED STATES

503 U.S. 540, 112 S. Ct. 1535, 1992 U.S. LEXIS 2117
United States Supreme Court, 1992

FACTS: In 1984 Keith Jacobson, a 56-year-old Nebraska farmer, ordered two magazines from a California adult bookstore: *Bare Boys I* and *Bare Boys II*. The magazines showed photos of nude preteen and teenage boys. At that time, the magazines were legal. The pictures startled Jacobson, who had expected pictures of young men 18 and over. Later, federal law changed, making it illegal to receive through the mail any sexual pictures of children.

Postal inspectors found Jacobson's name on the customer list of the California bookstore and began a two and one-half year campaign to entice him into ordering material that had become illegal. A postal inspector sent him a letter from the "American Hedonist Society," a fictitious organization, urging that members had the right to "read what we desire." Jacobson joined and answered a questionnaire about his sexual preferences. Two more fictitious organizations, both the creation of the postal service, began mailing him information and questionnaires. Jacobson responded, saying that he liked "good looking young guys (in their late teens and early 20's) doing their thing together," and that he was opposed to pedophilia. After

26 months of periodic contacts, a third fictitious agency began to solicit Jacobson. Finally, Jacobson ordered some sexual material, which depicted young boys engaged in sexual activities. He was arrested and convicted of violating federal law.

ISSUE: Did the government entrap Jacobson?

EXCERPTS FROM JUSTICE WHITE'S DECISION: By the time petitioner finally placed his order, he had already been the target of 26 months of repeated mailings and communications from Government agents and fictitious organizations.

The sole piece of preinvestigation evidence is petitioner's order and receipt of the Bare Boys magazines. But this is scant if any proof of petitioner's predisposition to commit an illegal act, the criminal character of which a defendant is presumed to know. It may indicate a predisposition to view sexually-oriented photographs that are responsive to his sexual tastes; but evidence that merely indicates a generic inclination to act within a broad range, not all of which is criminal, is of little probative value in establishing predisposition. Furthermore, petitioner was acting within the law at the time he received these magazines.

Law enforcement officials go too far when they implant in the mind of an innocent person the disposition to commit the alleged offense and induce its commission in order that they may prosecute. When the Government's quest for convictions leads to the apprehension of an otherwise law-abiding citizen who, if left to his own devices, likely would have never run afoul of the law, the courts should intervene.

We *reverse* the Court of Appeals' judgment affirming the conviction of Keith Jacobson.

EXCERPTS FROM JUSTICE O'CONNOR'S DISSENTING OPINION:

Keith Jacobson was offered only two opportunities to buy child pornography through the mail. Both times, he ordered. Both times, he asked for opportunities to buy more.

The first time the Government sent Mr. Jacobson a catalog of illegal materials, he ordered a set of photographs advertised as picturing "young boys in sex action fun." He enclosed the following note with his order: "I received your brochure and decided to place an order. If I like your product, I will order more later." The second time the Government sent a catalog of illegal materials, Mr. Jacobson ordered a magazine called "Boys Who Love Boys," described as: "11 year old and 14 year old boys get it on in every way possible. Oral, anal sex and heavy masturbation. If you love boys, you will be delighted with this."

It was the jury's task, as the conscience of the community, to decide whether or not Mr. Jacobson was a willing participant in the criminal activity here or an innocent dupe. The jury is the traditional "defense against arbitrary law enforcement." There is no dispute that the jury in this case was fully and accurately instructed on the law of entrapment, and nonetheless found Mr. Jacobson guilty. Because I believe there was sufficient evidence to uphold the jury's verdict, I respectfully *dissent*. ◢

Final Note on Entrapment. In the hypothetical on the fraternity undercover agent buying marijuana from a reluctant seller, most courts would agree that this was entrapment. The seller said "no" five times. Unless the government has other evidence that the defendant was involved in dealing drugs, there appears to be no predisposition, and the entrapment defense is valid.

Duress

A defendant may plead duress if she can show that a threat by a third person caused her fear of imminent serious physical harm. The threatened harm must be physical. If Roger, the video thief, could show that a drug addict threatened to kill him if he did not steal the videos, he would have a valid duress defense.

By contrast, assume that Roger, a former accountant, stole the videos because he had been out of work for 14 months. A bank foreclosed his suburban home, and he had exhausted his savings during his job search. He and his two children were subsisting in an abandoned station wagon as his wife lay in a sanitorium, weak with tuberculosis. Roger was desperate for money to make a deposit on an apartment. His claim—and all claims—of economic duress will fail because there is no imminent physical harm.

Self Defense reasonable

Crimes That Harm Business

Three major crimes involve taking money from businesses: larceny, fraud, and embezzlement. In each case the criminal ends up with money or property that belongs to someone else.

LARCENY *Shoplifting*

Cable service

It is holiday season at the mall, the period of greatest profits—and the most crime. At the Foot Forum, a teenager limps in wearing ragged sneakers and sneaks out wearing Super Rags, valued at $145. Down the aisle at a home furnishing store, a man is so taken by a $375 power saw that he takes it. Sweethearts swipe sweaters; pensioners pocket produce. All are committing larceny.

Larceny is the trespassory taking of personal property with the intent to steal it. "Trespassory taking" means that someone else originally has the property. The Super Rags are personal property (not real estate), they were in the possession of the Foot Forum, and the teenager deliberately left without paying, intending never to return the goods. That is larceny. By contrast, suppose Fast Eddie leaves Bloomingdale's in New York, descends to the subway system, and jumps over a turnstile without paying. Larceny? No. He has "taken" a service—the train ride—but not personal property.

Every day in the United States, over $25 million in merchandise is stolen from retail stores. Economists estimate that *12 cents out of every dollar* spent in retail stores covers the cost of shoplifting. Some criminal experts believe that drug addicts commit over half of all shoplifting to support their habits. Stores have added electronic surveillance, security patrols, and magnetic antitheft devices, but the problem will not disappear.

FRAUD

Robert Dorsey owned Bob's Chrysler in Highland, Illinois. He ordered cars from the manufacturer, the First National Bank of Highland paid Chrysler, and Dorsey—supposedly—repaid the loans as he sold autos. Dorsey, though, began to suffer financial problems, and the bank suspected he was selling cars without repaying his loans. A state investigator notified Dorsey that he planned to review all dealership records. One week later a fire engulfed the dealership. An arson investigator discovered that an electric iron, connected to a timer, had been placed on a pile of financial papers doused with accelerant.

The saddest part of this true story is that it is only too common. Some experts suggest that 1 percent of corporate revenues are wasted on fraud alone. Dorsey was convicted and imprisoned for committing two crimes that cost business billions of dollars annually—fraud and arson.[3]

Fraud refers to various crimes, all of which have a common element: **the deception of another person for the purpose of obtaining money or property from him.** Robert Dorsey's precise violation was bank fraud, a federal crime. It is **bank fraud** to use deceit to obtain money, assets, securities, or other property under the control of any financial institution. The maximum penalty is a fine of $1 million and/or a prison term of 30 years.[4]

Wire fraud and **mail fraud** are additional federal crimes, involving the use of interstate mail, telegram, telephone, radio, or television to obtain property by deceit.[5] For example, if Marsha makes an interstate phone call to sell land that she does not own, that is wire fraud.

Insurance fraud is another common crime. A Ford suddenly swerves in front of a Toyota, causing it to brake hard. A Mercedes, unable to stop, slams into the

---

[3] *United States v. Dorsey*, 27 F.3d 285, 1994 U.S. App. LEXIS 15010 (7th Cir. 1994).
[4] 18 U.S.C. §1344.
[5] 18 U.S.C. §§1341–1346.

Toyota, as the Ford races away. Regrettable accident? No: a "swoop and squat" fraud scheme. The Ford and Toyota drivers were working together, hoping for an accident. The "injured" Toyota driver now goes to a third member of the fraud team—a dishonest doctor—who diagnoses serious back and neck injuries and predicts long-term pain and disability. The driver files a claim against the Mercedes's driver, whose insurer may be forced to pay tens or even hundreds of thousands of dollars for an accident that was no accident. Insurance companies investigate countless cases like this each year, trying to distinguish the honest victim from the criminal.

Finally, Stacey, the hospital executive described in the chapter-opening scenario, committed a fourth type of fraud. **Medicare fraud** includes using false statements, bribes, or kickbacks to obtain Medicare payments from the federal or state government.[6]

UPDATE

Find a current news article describing a case of *wire*, *mail*, or *insurance fraud*. What did the perpetrator do? Was the scheme subtly crafted or crudely executed? How did authorities discover the crime? What was the outcome of the case? Were there steps that a concerned businessperson or insurance executive should have taken to avoid the problem? Now be fiendishly clever: If you were a criminal, how would you "improve" on this scheme to avoid detection? What should a business executive learn from your scheming?

ARSON

Robert Dorsey, the Chrysler dealer, committed a second serious crime. **Arson** is the malicious use of fire or explosives to damage or destroy any real estate or personal property. It is both a federal and a state crime. Dorsey used arson to conceal his bank fraud. Most arsonists hope to collect on insurance policies. Every year thousands of buildings burn, particularly in economically depressed neighborhoods, as owners try to make a quick kill or extricate themselves from financial difficulties. We involuntarily subsidize their immorality by paying higher insurance premiums.

EMBEZZLEMENT

This crime also involves illegally obtaining property, but with one big difference: the culprit begins with legal possession. **Embezzlement is the fraudulent conversion of property already in the defendant's possession.**

Professor Beach, in North Dakota, asks his work-study student, Sandy, to drive his car to the repair shop. Sandy drives halfway and then hears on the car radio a forecast of snow. "I don't like snow," she thinks. Sandy turns south and never stops until she reaches Key West, Florida. "This is nicer," she murmurs. Sandy is innocent of larceny because she took the car keys with Beach's permission, but guilty of embezzlement because she converted the auto to her own use.

Wherever money abounds, embezzlement tempts. Banks are prime targets. A loan officer embezzled money simply by creating false loans and taking the money for himself. He paid off earlier loans by taking out new ones and managed to stay ahead of the game until he had embezzled over $5 million. He was eventually caught by a suspicious teller.[7]

---

[6] 18 U.S.C. §§1320 et seq. (1994).

COMPUTER CRIME

A 29-year-old computer whiz stole a car—using his keyboard. The man infiltrated a telephone company network and rigged a radio station's call-in promotion, winning himself a splendid new Porsche. He also damaged court-ordered wiretaps of alleged gangsters and may even have jammed the phones on an *Unsolved Mysteries* television episode in which *he was the featured fugitive!* A teenage boy crippled the airport control tower in Worcester, Massachusetts, by breaking into a telephone network and causing a computer crash that eliminated all power at the airport. ▪▪

The ascent of the Internet inevitably brings with it new forms of crime. Various federal statutes criminalize this behavior.

- The **Computer Fraud and Abuse Act** prohibits using a computer to commit theft, espionage, trespass, fraud, and damage to another computer.[8] This statute is the focal point of the case below.

- The **Access Device Fraud Act** outlaws the fraudulent use of cards, codes, account numbers, and other devices to obtain money, goods, or services.[9] For example, it is a violation of this act to reprogram a cell phone so that calls are charged to an improper account.

- The **Identity Theft and Assumption Deterrence Act** bars the use of false identification to commit fraud or other crime.[10] A waiter who uses stolen credit card numbers to buy airline tickets has violated this act. The Federal Trade Commission receives about 100,000 complaints of identity theft every year, so you should guard identifying data carefully.

- The **Wire and Electronic Communications Interception Act** makes it a crime to intercept most wire, oral, and electronic communications.[11] (This law does not prohibit recording your *own* conversations.) We *warned* you not to tape your roommate's conversations!

As the following case illustrates, those who know you the best may be the most likely to intrude electronically.

UNITED STATES V. MIDDLETON

231 F.3d 1207, 2000 U.S. App. LEXIS 29131
Ninth Circuit Court of Appeals, 2000

FACTS: Nicholas Middleton was the personal computer administrator at Slip.net, an Internet service provider. Unhappy with his job, he quit and then began to send threatening e-mails to his former employer. Later, he managed to log into one of the company's "test account" computers and from there gained access to the firm's main system. Middleton created false business accounts and

---

[7] *Peoples State Bank v. American Casualty Co. of Reading, Mich.*, No. Ed-8425-11, *Lawyers Weekly*, May 17, 1993, p. 6A.
[8] 18 U.S.C. §1030.
[9] 18 U.S.C. §1029.
[10] 18 U.S.C. §1028.
[11] 18 U.S.C. §2511.

used them to access an even higher level computer, called "Lemming." Once inside Lemming, Middleton changed all of the administrative passwords, altered the computer's registry, deleted the entire billing system including its support software, and destroyed other databases.

Slip.net spent 150 hours repairing the damage. Middleton was convicted of violating the Computer Fraud and Abuse Act (the CFAA, 18 U.S.C. §1030). He appealed, claiming that the statute prohibited harm to an "individual," but not a corporation.

ISSUE: Does the CFAA prohibit harm to a corporation?

EXCERPTS FROM JUDGE GRABER'S DECISION: Title
18 U.S.C. §1030 prohibits a person from knowingly transmitting "a program, information, code, or command, and as a result of such conduct, intentionally causing damage without authorization, to a protected computer." A "protected computer" is a computer "which is used in interstate or foreign commerce or communication." Defendant concedes that Slip.net's computers fit within that definition. The statute defines "damage" to mean "any impairment to the integrity or availability of data, a program, a system, or information, that causes loss aggregating at least $5,000 in value during any 1-year period to one or more individuals." Defendant argues that Congress intended the phrase "one or more individuals" to exclude corporations. We disagree.

Congress has consciously broadened the statute consistently since its original enactment. The Senate Report on the 1996 amendments notes:

> As intended when the law was originally enacted, the Computer Fraud and Abuse statute facilitates addressing in a single statute the problem of computer crime. . . . As computers continue to prolifer-

ate in businesses and homes, and new forms of computer crimes emerge, Congress must remain vigilant to ensure that the Computer Fraud and Abuse statute is up-to-date and provides law enforcement with the necessary legal framework to fight computer crime.

The report instructs that "the definition of 'damage' is amended to be sufficiently broad to encompass the types of harm against which people should be protected." The report notes that the interaction between the provision that prohibits conduct causing damage and the provision that defines damage will prohibit a hacker from stealing passwords from an existing log-on program, when this conduct requires "all system users to change their passwords, and requires the system administrator to devote resources to resecuring the system. . . . If the loss to the victim meets the required monetary threshold, the conduct should be criminal, and the victim should be entitled to relief." The reference to a "system administrator" suggests that a corporate victim is involved. That is, if Congress intended to limit the definition of the crime to conduct causing financial damage to a natural person only, its report would not use the example of a "system administrator" devoting resources to fix a computer problem as illustrative of the "damage" to be prevented and criminalized. The Senate Report's reference to the proliferation of computers in businesses as well as homes provides additional evidence of the Senate's intent to extend the statute's protections to corporate entities.

On the basis of the statutory text taken in context and the statute's purpose and legislative history, we conclude that 18 U.S.C. §1030 criminalizes computer crime that damages natural persons and corporations alike. The district court did not err in so ruling.

Affirmed. ◢

Crimes Committed by Business

A corporation can be found guilty of a crime based on the conduct of any of its **agents**, who include anyone undertaking work on behalf of the corporation. An agent can be a corporate officer, an accountant hired to audit a statement, a sales clerk, or almost any other person performing a job at the company's request.

If an agent commits a criminal act within the scope of his employment and with the intent to benefit the corporation, the company is liable.[12] This means that the agent himself must first be guilty. The normal requirements of *actus reus* and *mens rea* apply. If the agent is guilty, the corporation is, too.

Critics believe that the criminal law has gone too far. It is unfair, they argue, to impose *criminal* liability on a corporation, and thus penalize the shareholders, unless high-ranking officers were directly involved in the illegal conduct. The following case concerns a corporation's responsibility for an employee's death.

WISCONSIN V. KNUTSON, INC.

196 Wis. 2d 86, 537 N.W.2d 420, 1995 Wis. App. LEXIS 1223
Wisconsin Court of Appeals, 1995

FACTS: Richard Knutson, Inc. (RKI) was constructing a sanitary sewer line for the city of Oconomowoc. An RKI crew attempted to place a section of corrugated metal pipe in a trench in order to remove groundwater. The backhoe operator misjudged the distance from the backhoe's boom to the overhead power lines and failed to realize he had placed the boom in contact with the wires. A crew member attempted to attach a chain to the backhoe's bucket and was instantly electrocuted.

The state charged RKI with negligent vehicular homicide under a statute that says: "Whoever causes the death of another human being by the negligent operation or handling of a vehicle is guilty of a Class E felony." The jury convicted, and RKI appealed, claiming that a corporation could not be held guilty under the statute.

ISSUE: May a corporation be guilty of vehicular homicide under the statute?

EXCERPTS FROM JUDGE ANDERSON'S DECISION: Here, the statute does not provide a definition of "whoever." We will thus employ extrinsic aids to uncover the legislature's intent.

LaFave and Scott [authors of a leading treatise] summarize the persuasive policy considerations supporting corporate criminal liability. Among those considerations is the factor that the corporate business entity has become a way of life in this country and the imposition of criminal liability is an essential part of the regulatory process. Another consideration centers on the premise that it would be unjust to single out one or more persons for criminal punishment when it is the corporate culture that is the origin of the criminal behavior. Also, the size of many corporations makes it impossible to adequately allocate responsibility to individuals.

An additional consideration is the indirect economic benefits that may accrue to the corporation through crimes against the person. To get these economic benefits, corporate management may shortcut expensive safety precautions, respond forcibly to strikes, or engage in criminal anticompetitive behavior. It has also been suggested that the free market system cannot be depended upon to guide corporate decisions in socially acceptable ways, and the threat of imposition of criminal liability is needed to deter inappropriate (criminal) corporate behavior. We agree that if a penal statute is intended to inhibit an act, a corporation is included within the class of perpetrators if to do so is within the spirit and purpose of the act. [The court concluded that a corporation may be guilty of vehicular homicide.]

SUFFICIENCY OF THE EVIDENCE: Homicide by negligent use of a vehicle has three elements: (1) that the defendant cause death (2) by criminal negligence (3) in the operation of a vehicle. Criminal negligence differs from ordinary negligence in two respects. First, the risk is more serious—death or great bodily harm as opposed to simple harm.

---

[12] *New York Central & Hudson River R.R. Co. v. United States*, 212 U.S. 481, 29 S. Ct. 304, 1909 U.S. LEXIS 1832 (1909). And note that what counts is the *intention* to benefit, not actual benefit. A corporation will not escape liability by showing that the scheme failed.

Second, the risk must be more than an unreasonable risk—it must also be substantial.

RKI's management took no action to have the power lines de-energized or barriers erected; rather, management elected to merely warn employees about the overhead lines.

The evidence supports the conclusion that if RKI had enforced the written safety regulations of OSHA, had abided by its own written safety program and had complied with the contract requirements for construction on Wisconsin Electric's property, the electrocution death would likely not have happened. The finder of fact was justified in concluding that RKI operated vehicles in close proximity to the overhead power lines without recognizing the potential hazard to its employees in the vicinity of the vehicles. The jury could reasonably find that RKI's failure to take elementary precautions for the safety of its employees was a substantial cause of the electrocution death.

Judgment *affirmed*. ◢

PUNISHING A CORPORATION

Fines

The most common punishment for a corporation is a fine. This makes sense in that the purpose of a business is to earn a profit, and a fine, theoretically, hurts. But most fines are modest by the present standards of corporate wealth.

Odwalla, Inc., sold fruit juices and nutritional shakes throughout much of the United States. A batch of its apple juice, which contained the highly toxic *E. coli* bacteria, killed a 16-month-old girl and seriously harmed 70 other people. Federal officials prosecuted, charging the company with violating food safety laws. Eventually, the company pleaded guilty, agreed to pay a $1.5 million fine, and submitted to a court-supervised probation for five years. Some public interest law groups applauded the punishment. Critics, though, complained that a million dollar fine is petty change for a large corporation and may have no deterrent effect on other companies. Odwalla has also paid millions of dollars to settle civil lawsuits brought by the injured consumers.

Imprisonment

The corporation itself cannot, of course, be imprisoned—or can it? Federal Judge Doumar found the Allegheny Bottling Co. guilty of price-fixing.[13] Allegheny, a Pepsi distributor, had agreed with a Coca-Cola distributor to fix an artificially high price for both drinks, earning an illegal profit of at least $10 million. Judge Doumar fined the company $1 million and *sentenced the corporation to three years in prison*. He threatened to lock Allegheny's doors and bar the employees from entering for that period. Ultimately, he suspended the sentence, meaning that he would not carry it out provided that Allegheny obeyed the law. His creative approach to sentencing may influence future corporate punishments.

Compliance Programs

The **Federal Sentencing Guidelines** are the detailed rules that judges must follow when sentencing defendants convicted of crimes in federal court. The guidelines instruct judges to determine whether, at the time of the crime, the corporation had in place a serious **compliance program**, that is, a plan to prevent and detect criminal conduct at all levels of the company. A company that can point to a detailed,

---

[13] *United States v. Allegheny Bottling Co.*, 695 F. Supp. 856, 1988 U.S. Dist. LEXIS 10693 (E.D. Va. 1988).

functioning compliance program may benefit from a dramatic reduction in the fine or other punishment meted out. Indeed, a tough compliance program may even convince federal investigators to curtail an investigation and to limit any prosecution to those directly involved, rather than attempting to get a conviction against high-ranking officers or the company itself.

AT RISK

To persuade prosecutors or judges that it seriously intended to follow the law, a company must demonstrate a thorough and effective compliance plan:

- The program must be reasonably capable of reducing the prospect of criminal conduct.

- Specific, high-level officers must be responsible for overseeing the program.

- The company must not place in charge any officers it knows or should have known, from past experience, that are likely to engage in illegal conduct.

- The company must effectively communicate the program to all employees and agents.

- The company must ensure compliance by monitoring employees in a position to cheat and by promptly disciplining any who break the law.

SELECTED CRIMES COMMITTED BY BUSINESS

Workplace Crimes

The workplace can be dangerous. Working on an assembly line exposes factory employees to fast-moving machinery. For a roofer, the first slip may be the last. The invisible radiation in a nuclear power plant can be deadlier than a bullet. The most important statute regulating the workplace is the federal Occupational Safety and Health Act of 1970 (OSHA),[14] which sets safety standards for many industries.[15] May a state government go beyond standards set by OSHA and use the criminal law to punish dangerous conditions? In *People v. O'Neill*,[16] the courts of Illinois answered that question with a potent "yes," permitting a *murder prosecution* against corporate executives. Notice that whereas Wisconsin prosecuted RKI *Corporation* for vehicular homicide, Illinois brought this case against the corporate executives themselves.

NEWSWORTHY

Film Recovery Systems was an Illinois corporation in business to extract silver from used X-ray film and then resell it. Steven O'Neill was president of Film Recovery, Charles Kirschbaum was its plant manager, and Daniel Rodriguez the foreman. To extract the silver, workers at Film Recovery soaked the X-ray film in large, open, bubbling vats that contained sodium cyanide.

A worker named Stefan Golab became faint. He left the production area and walked to the lunchroom, where workers found him trembling and foaming at the mouth. He lost consciousness. Paramedics were unable to revive him. They rushed him to a hospital where he was pronounced dead on arrival. The Cook County medical examiner determined that Golab died from acute cyanide poisoning caused by inhalation of cyanide fumes in the plant.

---

[14] 29 U.S.C. §§651 et seq. (1982).
[15] See Chapter 30, on employment law.
[16] 194 Ill. App. 3d 79, 550 N.E.2d 1090, 1990 Ill. App. LEXIS 65 (Ill. App. Ct. 1990).

Illinois indicted Film Recovery and several of its managers for murder. The indictment charged that O'Neill and Kirschbaum committed murder by failing to disclose to Golab that he was working with cyanide and other potentially lethal substances and by failing to provide him with appropriate and necessary safety equipment.

The case was tried to a judge without a jury. Workers testified that O'Neill, Kirschbaum, and other managers never told them they were using cyanide or that the fumes they inhaled could be harmful; that management made no effort to ventilate the factory; that Film Recovery gave the workers no goggles or protective clothing; that the chemicals they worked with burned their skin; that breathing was difficult in the plant because of strong, foul orders; and that workers suffered frequent dizziness, nausea, and vomiting.

The trial judge found O'Neill, Kirschbaum, and others guilty of murder. Illinois defines murder as performing an act that the defendant *knows will create a strong probability of death* in the victim, and the judge found they had done that. He found Film Recovery guilty of involuntary manslaughter. Involuntary manslaughter is *recklessly* performing an act that causes death. He sentenced O'Neill, Kirschbaum, and Rodriguez to 25 years in prison.

The defendants appealed, contending that the verdicts were inconsistent. They argued, and the Illinois Court of Appeals agreed, that the judge had made contradictory findings. Murder required the specific intent of *knowing there was a strong probability of death*, whereas the manslaughter conviction required *reckless* conduct. The appeals court reversed the convictions and remanded for a new trial.

Moments before the new trial was to start, O'Neill, Kirschbaum, and Rodriguez all pleaded guilty to involuntary manslaughter. They received sentences of three years, two years, and four months, respectively. ∎

RICO

The **Racketeer Influenced and Corrupt Organizations Act (RICO)**[17] is one of the most powerful and controversial statutes ever written. Congress passed the law primarily to prevent gangsters from taking money they earned illegally and investing it in legitimate businesses. But RICO has expanded far beyond the original intentions of Congress and is now used more often against ordinary businesses than against organized criminals. Some regard this wide application as a tremendous advance in law enforcement, but others view it as an oppressive weapon used to club ethical companies into settlements they should never have to make.

RICO creates both criminal and civil law liabilities. The government may prosecute both individuals and organizations for violating RICO. For example, the government may prosecute a mobster, claiming that he has run a heroin ring for years. It may also prosecute an accounting firm, claiming that it lied about corporate assets in a stock sale to make the shares appear more valuable than they really were. If the government proves its case, the defendant can be hit with large fines and a prison sentence of up to 20 years. RICO also permits the government to seek forfeiture of the defendant's property. A court may order a convicted defendant to hand over any property or money used in the criminal acts or derived from them.

---

[17] 18 U.S.C. §§1961–1968.

RICO creates civil liability as well. The government, organizations, and individuals all have the right to file civil lawsuits, seeking damages and, if necessary, injunctions. For example, shareholders claiming that they were harmed by the accounting firm's lies could sue the firm for money lost in buying and selling the stock. RICO is powerful (and for defendants, frightening) in part because a civil plaintiff can recover **treble damages**, that is, a judgment for three times the harm actually suffered, and can also recover attorney's fees.

What is a violation of this law? **RICO prohibits using two or more racketeering acts to accomplish any of these goals: (1) investing in or acquiring legitimate businesses with criminal money; (2) maintaining or acquiring businesses through criminal activity; or (3) operating businesses through criminal activity.**

What does that mean in English? It is a two-step process to prove that a person or an organization has violated RICO. We will assume that this is a criminal prosecution, though the steps are similar in a civil lawsuit.

- The prosecutor must show that the defendant committed two or more **racketeering acts,** which are any of a long list of specified crimes: embezzlement, arson, mail fraud, wire fraud, and so forth. Thus, if a gangster ordered a building torched in January and then burned a second building in October, that would be two racketeering acts. If a stockbroker told two customers that Bronx Gold Mines was a promising stock, when she knew that it was worthless, that would be two racketeering acts.

- The prosecutor must show that the defendant used these racketeering acts to accomplish one of the three *purposes* listed above. If the gangster committed two arsons and then used the insurance payments to buy a dry cleaning business, that would violate RICO. If the stockbroker gave fraudulent advice and used the commissions to buy advertising for her firm, that would violate RICO.

MONEY LAUNDERING

Money laundering consists of taking the proceeds of certain criminal acts and either (1) using the money to promote crime, or (2) attempting to conceal the source of the money.[18]

Money laundering is an important part of major criminal enterprises. Successful criminals earn enormous sums, and they strive to filter their profits back into the flow of commerce so that their crimes go undetected. Laundering is an essential part of the corrosive traffic in drugs. Profits, all in cash, mount so swiftly that the most difficult step for a successful dealer can be to use the money without attracting the government's attention. However, as we will see, it is not only drug dealers who seek to launder their wrongfully obtained cash.

A prosecution under this law frequently involves the RICO statute as well, because most of the criminal acts that give rise to a charge of money laundering are RICO *racketeering acts*. In the case below, the government charged that the defendants laundered money obtained from embezzlement and wire fraud (both RICO racketeering acts). The defendants were clever enough to operate a complex business enterprise. Were they slippery enough to evade the money laundering statute?

---

[18] 18 U.S.C. §1956 et seq.

UNITED STATES V. MORELLI

169 F.3d 798, 1999 U.S. App. LEXIS 3617
United States Court of Appeals for the Third Circuit, 1999

FACTS: Anthony Morelli and Igor Roizman ran a complex series of businesses designed to sell fuel without paying costly excise taxes. The two formed an organization, which they called "The Association," consisting of a chain of companies. The firm at the top sold petroleum products down the chain. The transactions were structured so that a business in the middle, nicknamed the "burn company," would be legally responsible for paying excise taxes to the government. The sales continued down the chain to the "street company," which sold the product to a legitimate service station, typically at a price slightly below market value (including excise taxes). The revenues were then wired back up the chain. The burn company would disappear in smoke, without ever paying the government. All proceeds found their way to Morelli and Roizman.

A jury convicted the two of wire fraud and money laundering. The defendants appealed, claiming that their conduct did not violate the money laundering statute, because the money was not technically "proceeds," and because there had never been a "wire fraud."

ISSUE: Was the scheme money laundering?

EXCERPTS FROM JUDGE BECKER'S DECISION: This case forces us to decide whether the funds involved in the alleged money laundering transaction were "proceeds of specified unlawful activity" [as required by the money laundering statute]. Morelli contends that the money did not become proceeds until *after* it passed through the burn company. The government only proved financial transactions, i.e., wirings of money up the daisy chain, occurring *before* the money reached the burn company. Accordingly, if the money did not become proceeds until after it passed through the burn company, as Morelli contends, the government's proof of money laundering would have failed because it would not have proved a financial transaction involving proceeds.

In essence, he contends that since the duty to pay the taxes lay with the burn company, no fraud occurred until the burn company itself failed to collect and pay the taxes. Hence, before the burn company failed to do so, the money was entirely legitimate. But the taxes were not, as Morelli claims, collected and passed on, and then diverted. They were never collected. The paperwork that indicated that the taxes had been collected was falsified. The transactions going down the chain—purporting to represent sales of fuel—were fraudulent, and the payments going back up the chain were proceeds of that fraud.

The entire chain of companies was operated by the Association; it was all part of the conspiracy. Once the money entered the control of the street company, it entered the control of the Association. The Association never had any intention of paying the taxes. Although in a paperwork sense the taxes were not embezzled until they passed the burn company, the reality is that the taxes were embezzled as soon as the funds entered the chain. Legally, the money was the proceeds of fraud as soon as it entered the hands of the street company.

Morelli [also] contends that, even if the money became proceeds of some illegal activity at the time it came into the possession of the street company, it was only the proceeds of tax fraud [which is not a racketeering act, and not of *wire* fraud, which is a racketeering act and gives rise to a money laundering charge. We disagree.]

Each wiring concealed and promoted each and every fraudulent series of transactions by making the entire scheme less detectable. Without the wirings to make it appear as if a series of distinct transactions between independent companies had occurred, the taxing authorities would have had a much easier time tracking down the perpetrators of the tax fraud scheme. As soon as one wiring took place, the entire tax fraud scheme became a wire fraud scheme. Since the very first series of transactions involved a wiring of the funds, every fraudulent acquisition of funds thereafter was an acquisition of funds through wire fraud.

Affirmed. ◢

OTHER CRIMES

Additional crimes that affect business appear elsewhere in the text. An increasing number of federal and state statutes are designed to punish those who harm the environment. (See Chapter 24, on environmental law.) Antitrust violations, in which a corporation establishes a monopoly, can lead to criminal prosecutions. The *Allegheny Bottling* case, earlier in this chapter, in which the judge threatened to lock up the company, was an antitrust case based on price-fixing. (See Chapter 19, on antitrust law.) Finally, securities fraud is a crime and can lead to severe prison sentences. (See Chapter 18, on securities regulation.)

ECONOMICS & THE LAW

Reputational Penalty. Businesses convicted of criminal conduct often pay more than just a fine. Many economists have concluded that companies suffer significant *reputational penalties* as well. Studies indicate that several negative consequences generally follow a criminal conviction.

First, stock prices fall significantly, reducing shareholder wealth. The angry shareholders may seek compensation from the executives who committed the crime. Second, executives are often forced out of the offending company.

Finally, business relationships often suffer, especially for crimes such as fraud or overcharging in a contract. Suppose that Integrity Motors promises to sell to PlaneMaker 1,000 aircraft engines that have been tested for quality control. When too many of the engines fail, the state government convicts Integrity of falsifying test results. PlaneMaker will never buy another engine from Integrity, and other aircraft manufacturers may also turn away from the convicted company. One study concluded that these reputational penalties are much more likely to occur when the crime is committed against customers, as in the fraud case, rather than against the general public, as in a case of environmental damage.[19]

Constitutional Protections *Bill of Rights — state/Local Gov*

The police arrest Jake and charge him with armed robbery and rape. They claim that he entered a convenience store, took all the money from the cash register, robbed the clerk of her wristwatch, and then raped her. Jake refuses to talk, but the police are absolutely certain he is guilty. The community is outraged and wants a conviction. Should the police be allowed to question Jake for hours without stopping? May they lock him in a walk-in freezer? Beat him? After five hours of interrogation, followed by 10 hours in a freezer and a severe beating, Jake confesses. He tells the police where to find the money and the clerk's watch. Does his guilt render the police conduct acceptable?

These are issues of **criminal procedure**. We are no longer looking at the elements of particular crimes, as we have thus far, but at the *process of investigating, interrogating, and trying* a criminal defendant. The first 10 amendments to the United States Constitution, known as the Bill of Rights, control the behavior of all

---

[19] Alexander, "On the Nature of the Reputational Penalty for Corporate Crime: Evidence," *Journal of Law and Economics*, 1999, vol. 42, p. 489.

law enforcement officers.[20] In this section we look at some of the protections these amendments offer.

THE CRIMINAL PROCESS

In order to understand constitutional safeguards, we need to know how the police do their work. The exact steps will vary from case to case, but the summary in Exhibit 7.1 highlights the important steps.

Informant

Yasmin is a secretary to Stacey, the Be Patient executive who opened this chapter. On her lunch break, Yasmin gets up the courage to telephone an FBI office and speaks to Moe, an agent. She reports that Stacey routinely charges the government for patients who do not exist. Moe arranges to interview Yasmin at her apartment that evening. He tape-records everything she says, including her own job history, her duties at Be Patient, and how she knows about the fraud. Yasmin has not only seen the false bills, she has entered some of them on computers. The next day, Moe prepares an affidavit for Yasmin to sign, detailing everything she told him. An **affidavit** is simply a written statement signed under oath.

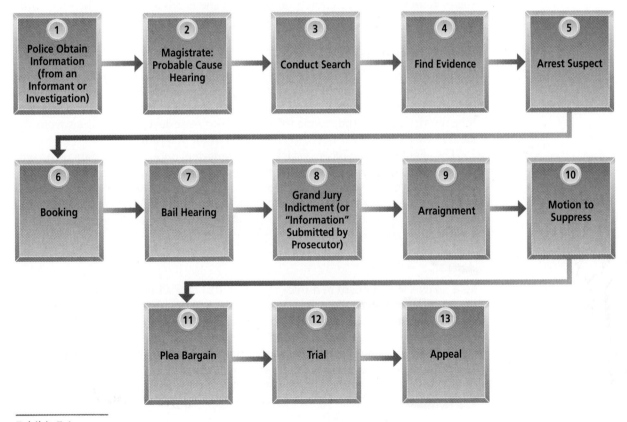

Exhibit 7.1

---

[20] As discussed in Chapter 5, on constitutional law, most of the protections as written apply only to state government or the federal government. But through the process of **incorporation**, almost all important criminal procedure rights have been expanded to apply to federal, state, and local governments.

Warrant

Moe takes Yasmin's affidavit to a United States magistrate, an employee of the federal courts who is similar to a judge. Moe asks the magistrate to issue search warrants for Be Patient's patient records. A **search warrant** is written permission from a neutral official, such as the magistrate, to conduct a search. **A warrant must specify with reasonable certainty the place to be searched and the items to be seized.** This warrant application names all five of Be Patient's hospitals and asks to look through their admission notes, surgery and doctor reports, and discharge data. It states that the records will be copied so that they can be compared with the bills the government has received.

Probable Cause

The magistrate will issue a warrant only if there is probable cause. **Probable cause** means that based on all of the information presented **it is likely that evidence of crime will be found in the place mentioned.** The magistrate will look at Yasmin's affidavit to determine (1) whether the informant (Yasmin) is reliable and (2) whether she has a sound basis for the information. If Yasmin is a five-time drug offender whose information has proven wrong in the past, the warrant should not issue. Here, Yasmin's career record is good, she has no apparent motive to lie, and she is in an excellent position to know what she is talking about. The magistrate issues the warrant, specifying exactly what records may be examined.

Search and Seizure

Armed with the warrants, Moe and other agents arrive at the various hospitals, show the warrants, and take away the appropriate records. The **search** may not exceed what is described in the warrant. Even if Moe suspects that Dr. Narkem is illegally drugging certain patients, he may not seize test tube samples from the lab. He may take only the records described in the warrant.

The agents cart the records back to headquarters and enter the data on a computer. The computer compares the records of actual patients with the bills submitted to the government and indicates that 10 percent of all bills are for fictional patients. Moe summarizes the new data on additional affidavits and presents the affidavits to the magistrate, who issues **arrest warrants**, authorizing the FBI to arrest Stacey and others involved in the overbilling.

Arrest

Moe arrives at Be Patient and informs Stacey that she is under arrest. He reads her the *Miranda* warnings, discussed later. He drives Stacey to FBI headquarters where she is **booked**; that is, her name, photograph, and fingerprints are entered in a log, along with the charges. She is entitled to a prompt **bail hearing**. A judge or magistrate will set an amount of bail that she must pay in order to go free pending the trial. The purpose of bail is to ensure that Stacey will appear for all future court hearings.

Indictment

federal Court

Moe turns all of his evidence over to Larry, the local prosecutor for the United States. Larry presents the evidence to a **grand jury**, which is a group of ordinary citizens, like a trial jury. But the grand jury holds hearings for several weeks at a time, on many different cases. It is the grand jury's job to determine whether there is probable cause that this defendant committed the crime with which she is

right to sue
testimonial evidence
5th Amendment

just prosecution   ∮ cross examine
∮ Defense

charged. Larry shows the computer comparison of the bills with the actual patient lists, and the grand jury votes to indict Stacey. An **indictment** is the government's formal charge that the defendant has committed a crime and must stand trial. The grand jury is persuaded that there is probable cause that Stacey billed for 1,550 nonexistent patients, charging the government for $290 million worth of services that were never performed. The grand jury indicts her for (1) Medicare fraud, (2) mail fraud, (3) computer crimes, and (4) RICO violations.[21] It also indicts Be Patient, Inc., and other employees.

Arraignment

Stacey is ordered back to court. A clerk reads her the formal charges of the indictment. The judge asks whether Stacey has a lawyer, and of course she does. If she did not, the judge would urge her to get one quickly. If a defendant cannot afford a lawyer, the court will appoint one to represent her free of charge. The judge now asks the lawyer how Stacey pleads to the charges. Her lawyer answers that she pleads not guilty to all charges.

Discovery

During the months before trial, both prosecution and defense will prepare the most effective case possible. There is less formal discovery than in civil trials. The prosecution is obligated to hand over any evidence favorable to the defense that the defense attorney requests. The defense has a more limited obligation to inform the prosecution. In most states, for example, if the defense will be based on an alibi, counsel must explain the alibi to the government before trial. In Stacey's case most of the evidence is data that both sides already possess.

Motion to Suppress

If the defense claims that the prosecution obtained evidence illegally, it will move to suppress it. A **motion to suppress** is a request that the court exclude certain evidence because it was obtained in violation of the Constitution. We look at those violations later.

Plea Bargaining

Sometime before trial the two attorneys will meet to consider a plea bargain. A **plea bargain** is an agreement between prosecution and defense that the defendant will plead guilty to a reduced charge, and the prosecution will recommend to the judge a relatively lenient sentence. Based on the RICO violations alone, Stacey faces a possible 20-year prison sentence, along with a large fine and a devastating forfeiture order. The government makes this offer: Stacey will plead guilty to 100 counts of mail fraud; Be Patient will repay all $290 million and an additional $150 million in fines; the government will drop the RICO and computer crime charges and recommend to the judge that Stacey be fined only $1 million and sentenced to three years in prison. In the federal court system, about 75 percent of all prosecutions end in a plea bargain. In state court systems the number is often higher.

---

[21] In federal court, when the defendant is charged with a felony, formal charges may be made only by indictment. In many state court cases, the prosecutor is not required to seek an indictment. Instead, she may file an **information**, which is simply a formal written accusation. In state courts, most cases now begin by information.

Stacey agrees to the government's offer. The judge accepts the plea, and Stacey is fined and sentenced accordingly. A judge need not accept the bargain, but usually does.

Trial and Appeal

When there is no plea bargain, the case must go to trial. The mechanics of a criminal trial are similar to those for a civil trial, described in Chapter 3, on dispute resolution. It is the prosecution's job to convince the jury beyond a reasonable doubt that the defendant committed every element of the crime charged. The defense counsel will do everything possible to win an acquittal. In federal courts, prosecutors obtain a conviction in about 80 percent of cases; in state courts, the percentage is slightly lower. Convicted defendants have a right to appeal, and again, the appellate process is similar to that described in Chapter 3.

THE FOURTH AMENDMENT

The Fourth Amendment prohibits the government from making illegal searches and seizures. This amendment protects individuals, corporations, partnerships, and other organizations.

In general, the police must obtain a warrant before conducting a search. There are six exceptions to this rule, in which the police **may search without a warrant:**

- *Plain View*. Police may search if they see a machine gun, for example, sticking out from under the front seat of a parked car.

- *Stop and Frisk*. If police have an articulable reason for suspecting that someone may be armed and dangerous, they may pat him down.

- *Emergencies*. If police pursue a store robber and catch him, they may search.

- *Automobiles*. If police have lawfully stopped a car and observe evidence of other crimes in the car, such as burglary tools, they may search.

- *Lawful Arrest*. Police may always search a suspect they have arrested.

- *Consent*. If someone in lawful occupancy of a home gives consent to a search, the police may do so.

Apart from those six cases, a warrant is required. If the police search without one, they have violated the Fourth Amendment. Even a search conducted with a warrant can violate the amendment. **A search with a warrant violates the Fourth Amendment if:**

- There was no probable cause to issue the warrant

- The warrant does not specify the place to be searched and the things sought; or

- The search extends beyond what is specified in the warrant.

Exclusionary Rule

Under the exclusionary rule, evidence obtained illegally may not be used at trial against the victim of the search. If the police conduct a warrantless search that is not one of the six exceptions, any evidence they find will be excluded from the trial.

Suppose when Yasmin called the FBI, Moe simply drove straight to one of Be Patient's hospitals and grabbed patient records. Moe lacked a warrant, and his search would be illegal. Stacey's lawyer would file a **motion to suppress** the evidence. Before the trial starts, the judge would hold a hearing. If he agreed that the search was illegal, he would **exclude** the evidence, that is, refuse to allow it in trial. The government could go forward with the prosecution only if it had other evidence.[22]

Is the exclusionary rule a good idea? The Supreme Court created the exclusionary rule to ensure that police conduct legal searches. The theory is simple: if police know in advance that illegally obtained evidence cannot be used in court, they will not be tempted to make improper searches.

Opponents of the rule argue that a guilty person may go free because one police officer bungled. They are outraged by cases like *Coolidge v. New Hampshire*.[23] Pamela Mason, a 14-year-old baby-sitter, was brutally murdered. Citizens of New Hampshire were furious, and the state's attorney general personally led the investigation. Police found strong evidence that Edward Coolidge had done it. They took the evidence to the attorney general who personally issued a search warrant. The search of Coolidge's car uncovered incriminating evidence, and he was found guilty of murder and sentenced to life in prison. But the United States Supreme Court reversed the conviction. The warrant had not been issued by a neutral magistrate. A law officer may not lead an investigation and simultaneously decide what searches are permissible.

After the Supreme Court reversed Coolidge's conviction, New Hampshire scheduled a new trial, attempting to convict him with evidence lawfully obtained. Before the trial began, Coolidge pleaded guilty to second-degree murder. He was sentenced and remained in prison until his release 27 years later.

In fact, very few people do go free because of the exclusionary rule. For example, a study by the General Accounting Office showed that suppression motions were filed in 10.5 percent of all federal prosecutions. But in 80 to 90 percent of those motions, the judge declared that the search was legal. Evidence was actually excluded in only 1.3 percent of all prosecutions. And in about one-half of *those* cases, the court convicted the defendant on other evidence. Only in 0.7 percent of all prosecutions did the defendant go free after the evidence was suppressed. Other studies reveal similar results.[24]

---

[22] There are two important exceptions to the exclusionary rule:

Inevitable Discovery Exception. Suppose that Moe's search of Be Patient is declared illegal. But then officials in the Medicare office testify that they were already aware of Be Patient's fraud, had already obtained some proof, and were about to seek a search warrant for the same records that Moe took. If the court believes the testimony, it will allow the evidence to be used. The inevitable discovery exception permits the use of evidence that would inevitably have been discovered even without the illegal search.

Good Faith Exception. Suppose the police use a search warrant believing it to be proper, but it later proves to have been defective. Is the search therefore illegal? No, said the Supreme Court in *United States v. Leon*, 468 U.S. 897, 104 S. Ct. 3405, 1984 U.S. LEXIS 153 (1984). As long as the police reasonably believed the warrant was valid, the search is legal. It would violate the Fourth Amendment if, for example, it was later shown that the police knew the affidavit used to obtain the warrant was filled with lies. In such a case, the search would be illegal and the evidence obtained would be excluded.

[23] 403 U.S. 443, 91 S. Ct. 2022, 1971 U.S. LEXIS 25 (1971).

[24] See the discussion in *United States v. Leon* (Justice Brennan, dissenting), cited at footnote 22.

October

No Independ Judicial Review

The Patriot Act of 2001

In response to the devastating attacks of September 11, 2001, Congress passed a sweeping anti-terrorist law known as the Patriot Act. The statute was designed to give law enforcement officials greater power to investigate and prevent potential terrorist assaults. The bill raced through Congress nearly unopposed. Proponents hailed it as a vital weapon for use against continuing lethal threats. Opponents argued that the law was passed in haste and threatened the liberties of the very people it purported to shield. They urged that the statute gave law officers too much power, permitting them to conduct searches, intercept private Internet communications, and examine financial and academic records—all with little or no judicial oversight. Supporters of the law responded that its most controversial sections were scheduled to expire in four years. In the meantime, they said, constitutional protections governed the law as they did all others.

It is too soon to assess the full impact of the Patriot Act. In an early legal test, a federal judge permitted the government to use secret evidence in its effort to freeze the assets of Global Relief Foundation, a religious organization suspected of terrorist activity. The group, which claimed to be purely humanitarian, asserted that it could hardly defend itself against unseen evidence. Finding "acute national security concerns," the judge allowed the government to introduce the evidence in private, without the foundation ever seeing it.

UPDATE

Find a recent case involving the Patriot Act. What were the precise issues? How did the court rule and why?

THE FIFTH AMENDMENT

The Fifth Amendment includes three important protections for criminal defendants: due process, double jeopardy, and self-incrimination.

Due Process

Due process requires fundamental fairness at all stages of the case. The basic elements of due process are discussed in Chapter 5, on constitutional law. In the context of criminal law, due process sets additional limits. The requirement that the prosecution disclose evidence favorable to the defendant is a due process rule. Similarly, if a witness says that a tall white male robbed the liquor store, it would violate due process for the police to place the male suspect in a lineup with four short women and two rabbits.

Double Jeopardy

The prohibition against **double jeopardy** means that a criminal defendant may be prosecuted only once for a particular criminal offense. The purpose is to guarantee that the government may not destroy the lives of innocent citizens with repetitive prosecutions. Assume that Roger, the video thief, goes to trial. But the police officer cannot remember what the suspect looked like, and the jury acquits. Later, the prosecutor learns that a second witness actually *videotaped* Roger hauling VCRs from the store. Too late. The Double Jeopardy Clause prohibits the state from retrying Roger for the same offense.

Self-Incrimination

The Fifth Amendment bars the government from forcing any person to testify against himself. In other words, the police may not use mental or physical coercion to force a confession out of someone. (This clause applies only to people; corporations and other organizations are not protected.) Society does not want a government that engages in torture. Such abuse might occasionally catch a criminal, but it would grievously injure innocent people and make all citizens fearful of the government that is supposed to represent them. Also, confessions that are forced out of someone are inherently unreliable. The defendant may confess simply to end the torture. So Jake, the rape-robbery suspect who confessed at the beginning of this section, will never hear his confession used against him in court. Unless the police have other evidence, he will walk free.

When the FBI arrests Stacey for Medicare fraud, she may refuse to answer any questions. The privilege against self-incrimination covers any statement that might help to prosecute her. So, if the FBI agent asks Stacey, "Did you commit Medicare fraud?" she will refuse to answer. If the agent asks, "What are your duties here?" she will also remain silent.

Miranda

In *Miranda v. Arizona*,[25] the Supreme Court ruled that a confession obtained from a custodial interrogation may not be used against a defendant unless he was first warned of his Fifth Amendment rights. A "custodial interrogation" means that the police have prevented the defendant from leaving (usually by arresting him) and are asking him questions. If they do that, and obtain a confession from the defendant, they may use that confession in court only if they first warned him of his Fifth Amendment rights. He must be told that:

- He has the right to remain silent

- Anything he says can be used against him at trial

- He has the right to a lawyer; and

- If he cannot afford a lawyer, the court will appoint one for him.

Exclusionary Rule (Again). If the police fail to give these warnings before interrogating a defendant, the exclusionary rule prohibits the prosecution from using any confession. The rationale is the same as for Fourth Amendment searches: suppressing the evidence means that the police will not attempt to get it illegally. But remember that the confession is void only if it results from custodial questioning. Suppose a police officer, investigating a bank robbery, asks a pedestrian if he noticed anything peculiar. The pedestrian says, "You mean after I robbed the bank?" Result? No custodial questioning, and the confession *may* be used against him.

THE SIXTH AMENDMENT

The Sixth Amendment guarantees the right to a lawyer at all important stages of the criminal process. Stacey, the hospital administrator, is entitled to have her

---

[25] 384 U.S. 436, 86 S. Ct. 1602, 1966 U.S. LEXIS 2817 (1966).

lawyer present during custodial questioning and all court hearings. Because of this right, the government must appoint a lawyer to represent, free of charge, any defendant who cannot afford one.

THE EIGHTH AMENDMENT

The Eighth Amendment prohibits cruel and unusual punishment. The most dramatic issue litigated under this clause is the death penalty. The Supreme Court has ruled that capital punishment is not inherently unconstitutional. Most state statutes bifurcate (divide in half) a capital case, so that the jury first considers only guilt or innocence, and then, if the defendant is found guilty, deliberates on the death penalty. As part of that final decision, the jury must consider aggravating and mitigating circumstances that may make the ultimate penalty more or less appropriate.[26] However, other "cruel and unusual" issues are now coming to the forefront.

Three Strikes Laws

Angry at recidivists (ex-convicts who commit new crimes), voters in many states have demanded so-called **three strikes law**s, which provide long, mandatory prison sentences for defendants convicted of a third serious offense. California passed such a law very quickly after a paroled criminal kidnapped and murdered 12-year-old Polly Klaas. While many citizens applaud the tougher laws, others fear that they are being applied indiscriminately, resulting in harsh penalties for minor crimes. Gary Ewing already had a record of burglary convictions when he was convicted of stealing three golf clubs; under the California law, he received a sentence of 25 years to life (meaning he must actually serve 25 years). In the same state, Leandro Andrade, a heroin addict with a criminal record, stole videotapes from two different stores—and received a sentence of 50 years to life.

The United States Supreme Court affirmed both sentences, ruling that neither violated the Eighth Amendment. The Court acknowledged that the prison terms were very long, but declared that a state could reasonably decide to combat recidivism by incapacitating repeat offenders.[27]

Find a three-strikes case from the past six months. What crimes did the defendant commit? In your view, is the prison term reasonable or unduly severe? What factors should a state legislature weigh when setting criminal penalties? How expensive is it to incarcerate a felon for decades? Are there any reasonable alternatives to imprisonment?

Forfeiture Laws

The Eighth Amendment also outlaws excessive fines. Forfeiture is the most controversial topic under this clause. **Forfeiture** is a *civil* law proceeding that is permitted by many different *criminal* statutes. Once a court has convicted a defendant under certain criminal statutes—such as RICO or a controlled substance law—the government may seek forfeiture of property associated with the criminal act. *How*

---

[26] *Gregg v. Georgia*, 428 U.S. 153, 96 S. Ct. 2909, 1976 U.S. LEXIS 82 (1976).

[27] *Lockyer v. Andrade*, —U.S.—, 123 S.Ct. 1166 (2003); *Ewing v. California*, —U.S.—, 123 S.Ct. 1179 (2003).

much property can the government take? To determine if forfeiture was fair, courts generally look at three factors: whether the property was used in committing the crime, whether it was purchased with proceeds from illegal acts, and whether the punishment is disproportionate to the defendant's wrongdoing. Neal Brunk pleaded guilty to selling 2.5 ounces of marijuana, and the government promptly sought forfeiture of his house on 90 acres, worth about $99,000. The court found forfeiture was legitimate, because Brunk had used drug money to buy the land, and then sold narcotics from the property.[28] By contrast, Hosep Bajakajian attempted to leave the United States without reporting $375,000 cash to customs officials as the law requires. The government demanded forfeiture of the full sum, but the Supreme Court ruled that seizure of the entire amount would be grossly disproportionate to the minor crime of failing to report cash movement.[29]

Chapter Conclusion

Business crime appears in unexpected places, with surprising suspects. A corporate executive aware of its protean nature is in the best position to prevent it. Classic fraud and embezzlement schemes are often foiled with commonsense preventive measures. Federal Sentencing Guidelines make it eminently worthwhile for corporations to establish aggressive compliance programs. Sophisticated computer and money laundering crimes can be thwarted only with determination and the cooperation of citizens and police agencies. We can defeat business crime if we have the knowledge and the will.

Chapter Review

1. The rationales for punishment include restraint, deterrence, retribution, and rehabilitation.

2. In all prosecutions, the government must establish that the defendant's conduct was outlawed, that the defendant committed the *actus reus*, and that he had the necessary *mens rea*.

3. In addition to factual defenses, such as mistaken identity or alibi, a defendant may offer various legal defenses, including insanity, entrapment, justification, and duress.

4. Larceny is the trespassory taking of personal property with the intent to steal.

5. Fraud refers to a variety of crimes, all of which involve the deception of another person for the purpose of obtaining money or property.

6. Arson is the malicious use of fire or explosives to damage or destroy real estate or personal property.

7. Embezzlement is the fraudulent conversion of property already in the defendant's possession.

8. Computer crime statutes prohibit computer trespass and fraud; wrongful use of cards, codes, and identification; and most intercepting or taping of conversations.

9. If a company's agent commits a criminal act within the scope of her employment and with the intent to benefit the corporation, the company is liable.

10. RICO prohibits using two or more racketeering acts to invest in legitimate business or carry on certain other criminal acts. RICO permits civil lawsuits as well as criminal prosecutions.

---

[28] *U.S. v. Brunk*, 2001 U.S. App. LEXIS 7566 (4 Cir. 2001).
[29] *U.S. v. Bajakajian*, 524 U.S. 321, 118 S. Ct. 2028, 1998 U.S. LEXIS 4172 (1998).

11. Money laundering consists of taking profits from a criminal act and either using them to promote crime or attempting to conceal their source.

12. The Fourth Amendment prohibits the government from making illegal searches and seizures.

13. The Fifth Amendment requires due process in all criminal procedures and prohibits double jeopardy and self-incrimination.

14. The Sixth Amendment guarantees criminal defendants the right to a lawyer.

15. Information obtained in violation of the Fourth, Fifth, or Sixth Amendment is generally excluded from trial.

16. The Eighth Amendment prohibits excessive fines and cruel and unusual punishments.

Practice Test

1. Arnie owns a two-family house in a poor section of the city. A fire breaks out, destroying the building and causing $150,000 damage to an adjacent store. The state charges Arnie with arson. Simultaneously, Vickie, the store owner, sues Arnie for the damage to her property. Both cases are tried to juries, and the two juries hear identical evidence of Arnie's actions. But the criminal jury acquits Arnie, while the civil jury awards Vickie $150,000. How did that happen?

2. **YOU BE THE JUDGE WRITING PROBLEM** An undercover drug informant learned from a mutual friend that Philip Friedman "knew where to get marijuana." The informant asked Friedman three times to get him some marijuana, and Friedman agreed after the third request. Shortly thereafter Friedman sold the informant a small amount of the drug. The informant later offered to sell Friedman three pounds of marijuana. They negotiated the price and then made the sale. Friedman was tried for trafficking in drugs. He argued entrapment. Was Friedman entrapped? **Argument for Friedman:** The undercover agent had to ask three times before Friedman sold him a small amount of drugs. A real drug dealer, predisposed to commit the crime, leaps at an opportunity to sell. If the government spends time and money luring innocent people into the commission of crimes, all of us are the losers. **Argument for the Government:** Government officials suspected Friedman of being a sophisticated drug dealer, and they were right. When he had a chance to buy three pounds, a quantity only a dealer would purchase, he not only did so, but bargained with skill, showing a working knowledge of the business. Friedman was not entrapped—he was caught.

3. **ETHICS** Nineteen-year-old David Lee Nagel viciously murdered his grandparents, stabbing them repeatedly and slitting their throats, all because they denied him use of the family car. He was tried for murder and found not guilty by reason of insanity. He has lived ever since in mental hospitals. In 1994 he applied for release. The two psychiatrists who examined him stated that he was no longer mentally ill and was a danger neither to society nor to himself. Yet the Georgia Supreme Court refused to release him, seemingly because of the brutality of the killings. Comment on the court's ruling. What is the rationale for treating an insane defendant differently from others? Do you find the theory persuasive? If you do, what result must logically follow when psychiatrists testify that the defendant is no longer a danger? Should the brutality of the crime be a factor in deciding whether to prolong the detention? If you do not accept the rationale for treating such defendants differently, explain why not.

4. National Medical Enterprises (NME) is a large for-profit hospital and health corporation. One of its hospitals, Los Altos Hospital, in Long Beach, California, paid one doctor $219,275, allegedly for consulting work. In fact, the government claimed, the payment was in exchange for the doctor's referring to the hospital a large number of Medicare patients. Other NME hospitals engaged in similar practices, said the government. What crime is the government accusing NME of committing?

5. Kathy Hathcoat was a teller at a Pendleton, Indiana, bank. In 1990 she began taking home money that belonged in her cash drawer. Her branch manager, Mary Jane Cooper, caught

her. But rather than reporting Hathcoat, Cooper joined in. The two helped cover for each other by verifying that their cash drawers were in balance. They took nearly $200,000 before bank officials found them out. What criminal charge did the government bring against Hathcoat?

6. Federal law requires that all banks file reports with the IRS any time a customer engages in a cash transaction in an amount over $10,000. It is a crime for a bank to "structure" a cash transaction, that is, to break up a single transaction of more than $10,000 into two or more smaller transactions (and thus avoid the filing requirement). In *Ratzlaf v. United States*,[30] the Supreme Court held that in order to find a defendant guilty of structuring, the government must prove that he specifically intended to break the law, that is, that he knew what he was doing was a crime and meant to commit it. Congress promptly passed a law "undoing" *Ratzlaf*. A bank official can now be convicted on evidence that he structured a payment, even with no evidence that he knew it was a crime. The penalties are harsh. (1) Why is structuring so serious? (2) Why did Congress change the law about the defendant's intent?

7. Conley owned video poker machines. They are outlawed in Pennsylvania, but he placed them in bars and clubs. He used profits from the machines to buy more machines. Is he guilty of money laundering?

8. Northwest Telco Corp. (Telco) provides long-distance telephone service. Customers dial a general access number, then enter a six-digit access code and then the phone number they want to call. A computer places the call and charges the account. On January 10, 1990, Cal Edwards, a Telco engineer, noticed that Telco's general access number was being dialed exactly every 40 seconds. After each dialing, a different six-digit number was entered, followed by a particular long-distance number. This continued from 10 p.m. to 6 a.m. Why was Edwards concerned?

9. Under a new British law, a police officer must now say the following to a suspect placed under arrest: "You do not have to say anything. But if you do not mention now something which you later use in your defense, the court may decide that your failure to mention it now strengthens the case against you. A record will be made of anything you say and it may be given in evidence if you are brought to trial." What does a police officer in the United States have to say, and what difference does it make at the time of an arrest?

10. After graduating from college, you work hard for 15 years, saving money to buy your dream property. Finally, you spend all your savings to buy a 300-acre farm with a splendid house and pool. Happy, an old college friend, stops by. She is saving *her* money to make a down payment on a coffee shop in town. You let her have a nice room in your big house for a few months, until she has the funds to make her down payment. But odd acquaintances stop by almost daily for short visits, and you realize that Happy is saving money from marijuana sales. You are unhappy with this, but out of loyalty you permit it to go on for a month. Why is that a big mistake?

11. **ROLE REVERSAL** Write a short-answer question that focuses on the elements of a RICO violation.

Internet Research Problem

A Web site devoted to Internet crime is http://ifccfbi.gov. Find a current crime that might victimize you. What steps should you take to avoid harm?

You can find further practice problems in the Online Quiz at http://beatty.westbuslaw.com or in the Study Guide that accompanies this text.

---

[30] 510 U.S. 135, 114 S. Ct. 655, 1994 U.S. LEXIS 936 (1994)

International
Law

The day after Anfernee graduates from business school, he opens a shop specializing in sports caps and funky hats. Sales are brisk, but Anfernee is making little profit because his American-made caps are expensive. Then an Asian company offers to sell him identical merchandise for 45 percent less than the American suppliers charge. Anfernee is elated, but quickly begins to wonder. Why is the new price so low? Are the foreign workers paid a living wage? Could the Asian company be using child labor? The sales representative expects Anfernee to sell no caps except his. Is that legal? He also requests a $50,000 cash "commission" to smooth the export process in his country. That sounds suspicious. The questions multiply without end. Will the contract be written in English or a foreign language? Must Anfernee pay in dollars or some other currency? The foreign company wants a letter of credit. What does that mean? What law will govern the agreement? If the caps are defective, how will disputes be resolved—and where?

Anfernee should put this lesson under his cap: the world is now one vast economy, and negotiations quickly cross borders. Transnational business grows with breathtaking speed. The United States now exports more than $720 billion worth of goods each year, and an additional $280 billion worth of services. Leading exports include industrial machinery, computers, aircraft and other transportation equipment, electronic equipment, and chemicals.

Here are the leading trading partners of the United States:

Rank	Country	Total Trade (Exports Plus Imports), 2001 in Billions of U.S. Dollars
1	Canada	$381
2	Mexico	233
3	Japan	184
4	China	122
5	Germany	89
6	United Kingdom	82
7	Republic of Korea	57
8	Taiwan	51
9	France	50
10	Italy	34

Source: United States Census Bureau, http://www.census.gov.

The end is nowhere in sight. By the year 2010, a dozen developing countries with a total population 10 times that of the United States will account for 40 percent of all export opportunities. In China alone roughly 300 million people are entering the economic middle class—and the rank of potential consumers.

Who are the people who do all of this trading? Anfernee's modest sports cap concern is at one end of the spectrum. At the other are **multinational enterprises (MNEs)**, that is, companies doing business in several countries simultaneously. ▪

MNEs and Power

An MNE can take various forms. It may be an Italian corporation with a wholly owned American subsidiary that manufactures electrical components in Alabama and sells them in Brazil. Or it could be a Japanese company that licenses a software company in India to manufacture computer programs for sale throughout Europe. One thing is constant: the power of these huge enterprises. Each of the top 10 MNEs earns annual revenue greater than the gross domestic product of *two-thirds of the world's nations*. Over 200 MNEs have annual sales exceeding $1 billion and more cash available at any one time than the majority of countries do. Money means power. This corporate might can be used to create jobs, train workers, and build lifesaving medical equipment. Such power can also be used to corrupt government officials, rip up the environment, and exploit already impoverished workers. International law is vital.

Trade Regulation

Nations regulate international trade in many ways. In this section we look at export and import controls that affect trade out of and into the United States. **Exporting** is shipping goods or services out of a country. The United States, with its huge farms, is the world's largest exporter of agricultural products. **Importing** is shipping goods and services into a country. The United States suffers trade deficits every year because the value of its imports exceeds that of its exports, as the following table demonstrates.

U.S International Trade in Goods and Services (in Millions of Dollars)									
	Exports			Imports			Balance		
Year	Total	Goods	Services	Total	Goods	Services	Total	Goods	Services
1999	957,353	684,553	272,800	1,219,191	1,029,987	189,204	−261,838	−345,434	85,596
2000	1,065,702	772,210	293,492	1,441,441	1,224,417	217,024	−375,739	−452,207	76,468
2001	1,003,744	720,831	282,913	1,350,013	1,147,446	202,567	−346,269	−426,615	80,346

Source: United States Census Bureau, http://www.census.gov.

EXPORT CONTROLS

You and a friend open an electronics business, intending to purchase goods in this country for sale abroad. A representative of TaiLectron stops in to see you. TaiLectron is a Taiwanese electronics company, and the firm wants you to obtain for it a certain kind of infrared dome. The representative explains that this electronic miracle helps helicopters identify nearby aircraft. You find a Pennsylvania company that manufactures the domes, and you realize that you can buy and sell them to TaiLectron for a handsome profit. Any reason not to? As a matter of fact, there is.

All nations limit what may be exported. In the United States, several statutes do this. The **Export Administration Act of 1985**[1] is one. This statute balances the need for free trade, which is essential in a capitalist society, with important requirements of national security. The statute permits the federal government to restrict exports if they endanger national security, harm foreign policy goals, or drain scarce materials.

The Secretary of Commerce makes a **Controlled Commodities List** of those items that meet any of these criteria. No one may export any commodity on the list without a license, and the license may well be denied. A second major limitation comes from the **Arms Export Control Act (AECA)**.[2] This statute permits the president to create a second list of controlled goods, all related to military weaponry. Again, no person may export any listed item without a license.

---

[1] 50 U.S.C. §2402 (1994).
[2] 22 U.S.C. §2778 (1994).

The AECA will prohibit you from exporting the infrared domes to the Taiwan company. They are used in the guidance system of one of the most sophisticated weapons in the American defense arsenal. The Taiwanese government has attempted to obtain the equipment through official channels, but the American government has placed the domes on the list of restricted military items. When a U.S. citizen did send such goods to Taiwan, he was convicted and imprisoned.[3]

Suppose a shipper sends controlled goods to a buyer in a neutral nation who then transports them to an embargoed country. Will there be problems? Ask Randy Reyes—*if* he can come to the phone.

U.S. V. REYES

270 F.3d 1158, 2001 U.S. App. LEXIS 24031
Seventh Circuit Court of Appeals, 2001

FACTS: Randy Reyes was vice president of sales and marketing for Siraj International, Inc., an American broker of commercial and military aircraft component parts. Reyes made contact with a customer named Texam Holding, Ltd., located in Geneva, Switzerland. Reyes maintained Texam as his own client and handled all transactions with the company.

Reyes shipped aircraft parts to Texam in Geneva. The parts appeared on an American "Munitions List" of goods that could not be exported without license, because they were designed for use exclusively in military aircraft. (Additional regulations flatly prohibited granting a license to ship such items to Iran.) The United States Customs Service seized the goods at JFK airport because the shipment was unlicensed. Customs agents then searched Siraj's offices and seized a number of documents relating to Siraj's business dealings with Texam. The government prosecuted Reyes for attempting to ship controlled commodities to Iran (via Geneva) in violation of the AECA and the regulations. Reyes claimed that he was unaware that Texam intended to ship the goods to Iran. Reyes was convicted and sentenced to 41 months in prison. He appealed.

ISSUE: Was there sufficient evidence to prove that Reyes violated the AECA and related regulations?

EXCERPTS FROM JUDGE COFFEY'S DECISION: Conviction required that the government prove beyond a reasonable doubt that Reyes willfully exported or attempted to export an item on the United States Munitions List without having first obtained a license. At trial, the prosecution submitted a mountain of evidence to establish that Reyes was aware of his legal duty not to export Munitions List articles to Iran or any foreign country without a license. This evidence included expert testimony establishing that the aircraft parts Reyes attempted to export were designed exclusively for use on a TF-30 military aircraft engine (which is used on F-111 and F-14 military aircraft), as well as many documents (several with Reyes' handwritten notes on them) seized from Reyes' private office, that helped to establish Reyes' knowledge of the Munitions List and the law restricting exports of items on that list. The evidence also included the tape-recorded phone conversation between Reyes and [another business executive] in which Reyes explicitly acknowledges both the illegality of shipping to Iran without a license and his awareness of the fact that Texam was shipping the parts it ordered to Iran.

During Agent Heyer's interview with Reyes, he acknowledged that he was aware of the illegality of shipping parts to a customer who in turn forwarded them to an Iranian destination, and he falsely stated that he had never been told by anyone, and had no reason to suspect, that shipments sent to Texam Holding were subsequently being forwarded to Iran. The government also introduced a document faxed to Siraj from Texam's Swiss bank, bearing the notation "F/A Iran Aircraft Industries, Tehran, Texam Holding Ltd., Geneva," and referencing Texam's

---

[3] *United States v. Tsai*, 954 F.2d 155, 1992 U.S. App. LEXIS 601 (3d Cir. 1992).

payment for a shipment to Texam. Another damaging piece of evidence was a fax from Texam to its Swiss bank (and on which Siraj was copied) containing a "re" line reading "Air shipment from Geneva/Switzerland to Tehran/Iran." The government also offered evidence through the use of expert computer forensics testimony demonstrating that the fax machine at Siraj received two faxes (again from Texam to its Swiss bank and on which Siraj had been copied) containing a "re" line stating "Air shipment from Geneva/Switzerland to Tehran/Iran."

We hold that when considering the totality of the evidence offered by the prosecution, it was sufficient for the jury to find that Reyes attempted to export parts to Texam without a license and that he had knowledge that the aircraft parts would be forwarded to Iran.

Affirmed. ◢

IMPORT CONTROLS

Tariffs

Tariffs are the most widespread method of limiting what may be imported into a nation. **A tariff is a duty (a tax) imposed on goods when they enter a country.** Nations use tariffs primarily to protect their domestic industries. Because the company importing the goods must pay this duty, the importer's costs increase, making the merchandise more expensive for consumers. This renders domestic products more attractive. High tariffs unquestionably help local industry, but they proportionately harm local buyers. Consumers benefit from zero tariffs, because the unfettered competition drives down prices.

Tariffs change frequently and vary widely from one country to another. Even within one nation, tariffs may be low on some products and high on others. When American companies ship goods to Russia, they pay tariffs averaging about 11 percent. However, the duties imposed on sugar and automobiles are 25 percent or more. Average tariffs for American goods entering Turkey have dropped from 11 percent to 6 percent in the last decade, because of Turkey's desire to expand trade and ultimately join the European Union. However, duties on fruit imported into Turkey are often over 100 percent and are more than 200 percent on meats. At the other extreme, two-thirds of all U.S. products entering Mexico are duty-free. Almost all trade between Canada and the United States is done with zero tariffs, which is partly why the two nations do more bilateral commerce than any others in the world.[4]

Classification. The U.S. Customs Service imposes tariffs at the point of entry into the United States. A customs official inspects the merchandise as it arrives and **classifies** it, in other words, decides precisely what the goods are. This decision is critical because the tariff will vary depending on the classification, as Nissan's experience demonstrates.

◢

MARUBENI AMERICA CORP. V. UNITED STATES

35 F.3d 530, 1994 U.S. App. LEXIS 24288
United States Court of Appeals for the Federal Circuit, 1994

FACTS: One of Japan's major auto manufacturers, Nissan, found itself in the late 1980s behind the competition in the market for four-wheel drive sport utility vehicles. In order to catch up quickly, Nissan used its Hardbody truck line as the basis for designing and building its Pathfinder sport utility vehicle.

---

[4] Tariff statistics come from the Office of the United States Trade Representative, http://www.ustr.gov.

The Pathfinder incorporated the Hardbody's frame side rails, front cab, and front suspension.

When the 1989 models arrived in the United States, the Customs Service had to classify them. The service uses a **tariff schedule** to do this, which is a long list of goods, carefully described, with each type of good assigned a particular duty. The tariff schedule gave the Customs Service two possible classifications:

> Section 8704.31.00: Motor vehicle for the transport of goods.

> Section 8703.23.00: Motor cars and other motor vehicles principally designed for the transport of persons, including stations wagons and racing cars.

The "transport of persons" tariff was 2.5 percent, but the "transport of goods" duty was exactly *10 times higher*. The Customs Service concluded that the Pathfinder was similar to a pickup truck, declared it a "transport of goods" vehicle, and imposed the 25 percent duty, ruining Nissan's hope for profits. The company appealed. Customs appeals go first to the **Court of International Trade (CIT)** in Washington. The CIT trial included test drives of the Pathfinder and comparison vehicles (including the Hardbody), as well as videotapes of competing vehicles and expert testimony about engineering, design, and marketing. (Indeed, the court's work was so thorough, the next time your car needs servicing, you might ask the CIT to take a look at it.) The CIT reversed the Customs Service, declaring the Pathfinder a passenger car. The service appealed to the federal court of appeals.

ISSUE: Is the Pathfinder a vehicle for passengers or for the transport of goods?

EXCERPTS FROM JUDGE RICH'S DECISION: The CIT recognized that the Pathfinder was basically

derived from Nissan's Hardbody truck line yet the Pathfinder was based upon totally different design concepts than a truck. The CIT correctly pointed out these differences and more importantly, the reasons behind the design decisions, including the need for speed and economy in manufacturing to capture the changing market, a market into which Nissan was a late entrant. The fact that a vehicle is derived in part from a truck or from a sedan is not, without more, determinative of its intended principal design objectives which were passenger transport and off-road capability.

Substantial structural changes were necessary to meet the design criterion of transporting passengers. The addition of the rear passenger seat required that the gas tank be moved to the rear and the spare tire relocated. This effectively reduces the cargo carrying capacity. Of particular importance was the design of a new rear suspension that was developed specifically to provide a smooth ride for passengers. New and different cross beams, not present on the Hardbody frame, were added to the Pathfinder's frame to accommodate the above changes.

Other design aspects that point to a principal design for passengers include: the spare tire and the rear seat when folded down intrude upon the cargo space; the cargo area is carpeted; a separate window opening in the pop-up tailgate accommodates passengers loading and unloading small packages without having to lower the tailgate. In contrast, the Hardbody truck bed can accommodate loading with a fork lift, clearly a design feature for cargo.

We hold that the court applied the correct legal standards, and that the evidence of record supports the CIT's decision that the Pathfinder is principally designed for the transport of persons. ◢

Valuation. After classifying the imported goods, customs officials impose the appropriate duty *ad valorem*, meaning "according to the value of the goods." In other words, the service must determine the value of the merchandise before it can tax a percentage of that value. This step can be equally contentious, since goods will have different prices at each stage of manufacturing and delivery. The question is supposed to be settled by the **transaction value** of the goods, meaning the price actually paid for the merchandise when sold for export to the United States (plus shipping and other minor costs). But there is often room for debate, so importers use customs agents to help negotiate the most favorable valuation.

Duties for Dumping and Subsidizing

Dumping means selling merchandise at one price in the domestic market and at a cheaper, unfair price in an international market. Suppose a Singapore company, CelMaker, makes cell phones for $20 per unit and sells them in the United States for $12 each, vastly undercutting domestic American competitors. CelMaker may be willing to suffer short-term losses in order to drive out competitors for the American market. Once it has gained control of that market, it will raise its prices, more than compensating for its initial losses. And CelMaker may get help from its home government. Suppose the Singapore government prohibits foreign cell phones from entering Singapore. CelMaker may sell its phones for $75 at home, earning such high profits that it can afford the temporary losses in America.

In the United States, the Commerce Department investigates suspected dumping. If the Department concludes that the foreign company is selling items at **less than fair value**, and that this harms an American industry, it will impose a **dumping duty** sufficiently high to put the foreign goods back on fair footing with domestic products.

Subsidized goods are also unfair. Suppose the Singapore government permits CelMaker to pay no taxes for 10 years. This enormous benefit will enable the company to produce cheap phones and undersell competitors. Again, the United States imposes a tariff on subsidized goods, called **countervailing duties**. If CelMaker sells phones for $15 that would cost an unsubsidized competitor $21 to make, it will pay a $6 countervailing duty on every phone entering the United States.

Nontariff Barriers

All countries use additional methods to limit imports. A **quota** is a limit on the quantity of a particular good that may enter a nation. For example, the United States, like most importing nations, has agreements with many developing nations, placing a quota on imported textiles. In some cases, textile imports from a particular country may grow by only a small percentage each year. Without such a limit, textile imports from the developing world would increase explosively because costs are so much lower there. As part of the GATT treaty (discussed below), the wealthier nations pledged to increase textile imports from the developing countries, but whether that has occurred is open to dispute.

An **import ban** means that particular goods are flatly prohibited. Some nations prohibit alcohol imports for religious reasons. The United States bars the importation of narcotic drugs. Virtually all countries from time to time halt certain goods for political purposes, for example, to protest the behavior of the exporting country. The United States has increasingly used economic sanctions in an effort to advance its foreign policy goals. During one three-year period, it threatened or imposed sanctions 60 times, against 35 nations. Sanctions were aimed at Colombia for permitting drug trafficking; the Netherlands, Switzerland, and other European nations for trading with Cuba; and Taiwan for environmental violations. Proponents of such sanctions consider them essential components of an ethical foreign policy. Opponents regard them as hypocritical attempts at moral superiority.

Money and politics are a volatile mix, as demonstrated by all recorded history from 3000 B.C.E. to the present. As long as nations have existed, they have engaged in disputes about quotas and import bans. And that is why more than 100 countries negotiated and signed the GATT treaty, the subject of the next section.

GENERAL AGREEMENT ON TARIFFS AND TRADE (GATT)

What is GATT? The greatest boon to American commerce in a century. The worst assault on the American economy in 200 years. It depends on whom you ask. Let's start where everyone agrees.

GATT is the General Agreement on Tariffs and Trade. This massive international treaty has been negotiated on and off since the 1940s to eliminate trade barriers and bolster commerce. GATT has already had considerable effect. In 1947 the worldwide average tariff on industrial goods was about 40 percent. Now it is about 4 percent (although agricultural duties still average over 40 percent). The world's economies have exploded over that half century. Proponents of GATT applaud the agreement. Opponents scoff that both lower duties and higher trade would have arrived without GATT.

The most recent round of bargaining took seven hard years. Finally, in 1994, the United States and 125 other countries signed the treaty. A **signatory**, that is, a nation that signs a treaty, is still not bound by the agreement until it is **ratified**, that is, until the nation's legislature votes to honor it. In the United States, Congress voted to ratify GATT. If the latest round of cuts is fully implemented, average duties in all signatories should drop to about 3.7 percent. Further, nearly half of all trade in industrial goods will be duty-free, at least in developed countries. That must be good—or is it?

Trade

Leading supporters of GATT suggest that its lower tariffs vastly increase world trade. The United States should be one of the biggest beneficiaries because for decades this country has imposed lower duties than most other nations. American companies will for once compete on equal footing. A typical American family's annual income will increase due to the more vigorous domestic economy.

But opponents claim that the United States will be facing nations with unlimited pools of exploited labor. These countries will dominate labor-intensive merchandise such as textiles, eliminating millions of American jobs. It is not fair for U.S. companies to struggle against companies from countries that have no labor standards and dirt-cheap pay. This country will lose millions of jobs. And because the job losses will come in low-end employment, those put out of work will be precisely the ones least able to find a new job. The chasm between rich and poor will widen, and we will all be the losers.

World Trade Organization and the Environment

GATT created the **World Trade Organization (WTO)** to resolve trade disputes. The WTO is empowered to hear arguments from any signatory nation about tariff violations or nontariff barriers. This international "court" may order compliance from any nation violating GATT and may penalize countries by imposing trade sanctions. Proponents say that it is high time to have one international body to resolve complex issues impartially and create an international body of trade law that corporations can rely on when planning business.

Opponents fear the WTO. GATT generally prohibits nontariff barriers, and the WTO may well rule that some American economic sanctions, discussed above, violate the treaty.

Here is how the WTO decides a trade dispute. Suppose that the United States believes that Brazil is unfairly restricting trade. The United States uses the WTO offices to request a consultation with Brazil's trade representative. In the majority of cases, these discussions lead to a satisfactory settlement. If the consultation does not resolve the problem, the United States asks the WTO's Dispute Settlement Body (DSB) to form a panel, which consists of three nations uninvolved in the dispute. After the panel hears testimony and arguments from both countries, it releases its report. The DSB generally approves the report, unless either nation appeals. If there is an appeal, the WTO Appellate Body hears the dispute and generally makes the final decision, subject to approval by the entire WTO. No single nation has the power to block final decisions. If a country refuses to comply with the WTO's ruling, affected nations may retaliate by imposing punitive tariffs. (The official Web site of the WTO, http://www.wto.org/, includes libraries on all sorts of international trade topics, from goods and services to dispute settlement and legal texts.)

Opponents of the agreement argue that GATT may exacerbate environmental problems. Developing nations will be hard-pressed to pay for newly available goods. To bankroll the new expenses, these nations will sell off natural resources, eviscerating their future for short-term gains. Some statistics substantiate this argument. For example, the Costa Rican government decided to export more beef to the United States. To increase grazing land, the government has permitted over 80 percent of all Costa Rican rain forests to be leveled in just 20 years. The Philippines, in order to increase breeding areas for shrimp, has nearly destroyed its vast supply of mangrove swamps, which are essential spawning grounds for many species of ocean fish. But GATT supporters respond that such ecological damage has gone on independently of GATT and must be controlled accordingly.

Child labor is an even more wrenching issue. The practice exists to some degree in all countries and is common throughout the developing world. The International Labor Organization, an affiliate of the United Nations, estimates that 120 million children between the ages of 5 and 14 work full-time, and 130 million more labor part-time. As the world generally becomes more prosperous, this ugly problem has actually increased. Children in developing countries typically work in agriculture and domestic work, but many toil in mines and others in factories, making rugs, glass, clothing, and other goods.

The rug industry illustrates the international nature of this tragedy. In the 1970s, the Shah of Iran banned child labor in rug factories, but many manufacturers simply packed up and moved to southern Asia. Today, in India and Pakistan, tens of millions of children, some as young as four, toil in rug workrooms, seven days a week, 12 hours a day. Many, shackled to the looms they operate, are essentially slaves, working for pennies a day or, in some cases, for no money at all.

ETHICS Child labor raises compelling moral questions—and economic ones as well. No American company can compete with an industry that uses slave labor. As discussed above, the United States is relatively quick to impose trade sanctions in response to moral issues. In 1997 Congress passed a statute prohibiting the import of goods created by forced or indentured child labor. The first suit under the new law targeted the carpet factories of southern Asia and sought an outright ban on most rugs from that area. Is this statute humane legislation or cultural imperialism dressed as a nontariff barrier? Should the voters of this country or the WTO decide the issue? In answering such difficult questions, we must bear in mind that child labor is truly universal. The United Farm Workers union estimates that

800,000 underage children help their migrant parents harvest U.S. crops—work that few Americans are willing to do.

Our response to such a troubling moral issue need not take the form of a statute or lawsuit. Duke University is one of the most popular names in sports apparel, and the school sells about $20 million worth of T-shirts, sweatshirts, jackets, caps, and other sportswear bearing its logo. To produce its clothing, the university licenses about 700 companies in the United States and 10 foreign countries. In response to the troubling issue of child labor, Duke adopted a code of conduct that prohibits its manufacturers from using forced or child labor and requires all of the firms to pay a minimum wage, permit union organizing, and maintain a safe workplace. The university plans to monitor the companies producing its apparel and terminate the contract for any firm that violates its rules. ∎

Intellectual Property

Some foreign countries, particularly developing nations, have long ignored U.S. copyrights and patents. GATT changes things. It allows this country to halt duty-free imports from, and assess tariffs against, a nation that refuses to honor American copyrights or patents.

In addition, GATT creates certain new types of intellectual property. Rock bands and many performing artists have long complained of "bootlegging." When someone attending a concert makes an unauthorized recording or videotape and then sells it, that is a bootlegged version. Bootlegging is a common practice, earning millions of dollars for people who have contributed nothing to the performance. Under GATT, bootlegging is, for the first time, clearly outlawed in all signatory countries. For most musicians, however, bootlegging is a modest problem compared to that of file sharing on the Internet. It is generally as easy to share music files—and violate copyrights—around the world as it is across the street. We discuss this issue in Chapter 21, on intellectual property.

WTO Summary

The WTO continues to grow, adding China (and a quarter of the world's population) early in the new millennium. The agency has enjoyed many successes. Under WTO supervision, the leading economic powers negotiated a new telecommunications treaty, opening a $600 billion industry to international competition for the first time. And the WTO has resolved many trade disputes that otherwise might have caused bitter tariff wars. The United States has been the most active user of the dispute settlement process, bringing almost one-quarter of all cases to the WTO. The United States has prevailed in the majority of its cases, though not all. Many have been settled in the consultative stage. For example, as a result of WTO consultations, Japan changed its law to grant full copyright protection to sound recordings, a case worth about $500 million annually to the American recording industry. Portugal agreed to give full protection to foreign patents, and Turkey dropped discriminatory taxes on box-office receipts for foreign films.

In a case that did not settle, India was ordered to eliminate import bans on 2,700 types of goods, including consumer products, textiles, agricultural products, petrochemicals, and other commodities. On the other hand, Japan prevailed in another case brought by the United States, when a WTO panel determined, contrary to assertions made on behalf of Eastman Kodak, that Japan did not discriminate against imported film.

UPDATE

Find a current trade dispute that the United States has brought to the WTO. What are the issues and respective positions? ▪

It will be many years before we can fairly evaluate this enormous treaty. In all likelihood, some of the most extreme claims will prove false, and the agreement's effects will evolve somewhere in the middle. Unquestionably, some industries will suffer, forcing workers into unemployment. Others will discover and exploit lucrative opportunities. Certainly, the environment must be guarded far more carefully than it currently is, whether the WTO survives a decade or a century. Perhaps the final cost/benefit analysis of the WTO will be decided not by the letter of its rulings but by the spirit and goodwill of those who implement them.

REGIONAL AGREEMENTS

Many regional agreements also regulate international trade. We will briefly describe some that affect the United States.

The European Union

The European Union (EU) used to be known as the Common Market. The original six members—Belgium, France, Luxembourg, the Netherlands, West Germany, and Italy—were joined by Ireland, Denmark, the United Kingdom, Greece, Portugal, Spain, Austria, Finland, and Sweden. One of the key goals of the EU has been **enlargement**, that is, the addition of new member countries to further unify and stabilize the continent. Thirteen additional nations in eastern and southern Europe have applied for membership. Ten of these states will join the EU in May, 2004: Cyprus, the Czech Republic, Estonia, Hungary, Latvia, Lithuania, Malit, Poland, the Slovak Republic, and Slovenia. Bulgaria and Romania hope to enter the EU by 2007. Turkey has applied for membership but is unlikely to join soon.

Already a powerful association, the EU is growing larger and stronger. The expanded 25 member nations have a generally prosperous population of more than 460 million people. The organization's sophisticated legal system sets Union-wide standards for tariffs, dumping, subsidies, antitrust, transportation, and many other issues. The first goals of the EU were to eliminate trade barriers between member nations, establish common tariffs with respect to external countries, permit the free movement of citizens across its borders, and coordinate its agricultural and fishing policies for the collective good. The EU has largely achieved these goals. Most but not all of the member countries have adopted a common currency, the euro. During the next decade the EU will focus on further economic integration and effective coordination of foreign policy.

NAFTA

In 1993, the United States, Canada, and Mexico signed the **North American Free Trade Agreement (NAFTA)**. The principal goal was to eliminate almost all trade barriers—tariff and nontariff—between the three nations. Like GATT, this trilateral (three-nation) compact has been controversial, and there will probably never be agreement on NAFTA's value because the treaty has enriched some while impoverishing others. Unquestionably, trade between the three nations has increased enormously. Mexico now sells more to the United States than do China and Germany combined.

Current EU Members
1. Belgium
2. France
3. Luxembourg
4. The Netherlands
5. Germany
6. Italy
7. Ireland
8. Denmark
9. The United Kingdom
10. Greece
11. Portugal
12. Spain
13. Austria
14. Finland
15. Sweden

Set to Join in May 2004
16. Cyprus
17. The Czech Republic
18. Estonia
19. Hungary
20. Latvia
21. Lithuania
22. Malta
23. Poland
24. The Slovak Republic
25. Slovenia

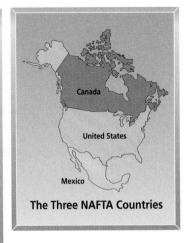

The EU (European Union Countries)

The Three NAFTA Countries

Opponents of the treaty argue that NAFTA costs the United States jobs and lowers the living standards of American workers by forcing them to compete with low-paid labor. For example, Swingline Staplers closed a factory in Queens, New York, after 75 years of operation and moved to Mexico. Instead of paying its American workers $11.58 per hour, Swingline will pay Mexican workers 50 cents an hour to do the same job. Proponents contend that although some jobs are lost, many others are gained, especially in fields with a future, such as high technology. They claim that as new jobs invigorate the Mexican economy, consumers there will be able to afford American goods for the first time, providing an enormous new market. Both Canadian and Mexican law are available online at http://www.lawsource.com/also/.

ASEAN

The Association of South-East Asian Nations (ASEAN) consists of 10 countries: Brunei, Cambodia, Indonesia, Laos, Malaysia, Myanmar, the Philippines, Singapore, Thailand, and Vietnam. The group has negotiated for several years to reduce and eventually eliminate all tariffs among members.

Mercosur

Brazil, Argentina, Uruguay, and Paraguay formed Mercosur to improve commerce among the four South American nations. Trade has in fact increased between Latin America's powerhouse economy, Brazil, and the three other countries. The group is currently considering the creation of a common currency, similar to the euro. You can follow development at http://www.mercosur.com.

International Sales Agreements

Cowboy boots are hot in France. Of course, they can be uncomfortable no matter where you walk, but the point is they are selling fast in the land of Monet and Debussy. Big Heel, Inc., your small company in Tucson, Arizona, makes superb boots with exquisite detailing, and you realize that France could be a bonanza. Your first decision is how to produce and sell the boots in France. For our purposes, Big Heel has three choices:

- **Direct Sales.** You can continue to manufacture the boots in Tucson and sell them directly to French retailers.

- **Indirect Sales.** You can manufacture the boots in Tucson and use a French distributor to wholesale them to French stores.

- **Licensing.** You can license a French manufacturer to make Big Heel boots in France and wholesale them.

DIRECT SALES

You decide to sell the boots directly. Le Pied D'Or, a new, fast-growing French chain of shoe stores, is interested in buying 10,000 pairs of your boots, at about $300 per pair. You must focus on two principal issues: the sales contract and letters of credit. You are wise enough to know that you must have a written contract—$3 million is a lot of money for Big Heel.

This is a contract for the sale of goods. **Goods** are things that can be moved, such as boots, airplanes, pencils, and computers. A sale of goods is governed by different law than the sale of real estate (e.g., a house) or securities (e.g., a share of stock) or services (e.g., accounting).

What Law Governs the Sale of Goods?

Potentially, three conflicting laws could govern your boot contract: Arizona law, French law, and an international treaty. Each is different, and it is therefore essential to negotiate which law will control.

Because this contract is for the sale of goods, Arizona law is its version of the **Uniform Commercial Code (UCC)**. The UCC is discussed throughout Unit 2, on commercial transactions. It is a statute that has taken the common law principles of contract and modified them to meet the needs of contemporary business. Article 2 of the UCC governs the sale of goods. American business lawyers are familiar with the UCC and will generally prefer that it govern. French law is based on **Roman law** and the **Napoleonic Code** and is obviously different. French lawyers and business executives are naturally partial to it. How to compromise? Perhaps by using a neutral law.

The **United Nations Convention on Contracts for the International Sale of Goods (CISG)** is the result of 50 years of work by various international groups, all seeking to create a uniform international law on this important subject. Finally, in 1980, a United Nations conference adopted the CISG, though it became the law in individual nations only if they adopted it. The United States and most of its principal trading partners have adopted this important treaty.

The CISG applies automatically to any contract for the sale of goods between two parties, from different countries, each of which is a signatory. France and the United States have both signed. Thus the CISG automatically applies to the Big Heel–Pied D'Or deal unless the parties *specifically opt out*. If the parties want to be governed by other law, they must state very clearly that they exclude the CISG and elect, for example, the UCC.

Should the parties allow the CISG to govern? They can make an intelligent choice by first understanding how the CISG differs from other law. Here are a few key differences between the CISG and the UCC:

- *Must the contract be written?* Under the UCC, a contract for the sale of goods valued at over $500 generally must be written to be enforceable. But the CISG does not require a writing for any contract. Be advised that discussions you consider informal or preliminary might create a contract under the CISG.

- *When is an offer irrevocable?* The UCC declares that an offer is irrevocable only if it is in writing and states that it will be held open for a fixed period. But the CISG makes some offers irrevocable even if unwritten.

- *What if an acceptance includes new terms?* Under the UCC, an acceptance generally creates a contract, even if it uses new terms. But the CISG insists on an acceptance that is a "mirror image" of the offer. Almost anything else constitutes a rejection.

- *What remedies are available?* The UCC entitles a plaintiff only to money damages for breach of a sales contract. But the CISG permits many plaintiffs to seek specific performance of the contract, that is, to force the other party to perform the contract.

Choice of Forum

The parties must decide not only what law governs, but where disagreements will be resolved. The French and American legal systems are dramatically different. In a French civil lawsuit, generally neither side is entitled to depose the other or to obtain interrogatories or even documents, in sharp contrast to the American system where such discovery methods dominate litigation. American lawyers, accustomed to discovery to prepare a case and advance settlement talks, are unnerved by the French system. Similarly, French lawyers are dismayed at the idea of spending two years taking depositions, exchanging paper, and arguing motions, all at great expense. At trial, the contrasts grow. In a French civil trial, there is generally no right to a jury. The rules of evidence are more flexible (and unpredictable), neither side employs its own expert witnesses, and the parties themselves never appear as witnesses.

Choice of Language and Currency

The parties must select a language for the contract and a currency for payment. Language counts because legal terms seldom translate literally. Currency is vital because the exchange rate may alter between the signing and payment. Suppose the Argentine peso falls 30 percent against the dollar in one week. An Argentine company that contracted on Monday to pay $1 million for U.S. aircraft engines will suddenly have to pay 30 percent more in pesos to meet its contractual obligations. To avoid such calamities, companies engaged in international commerce often purchase from currency dealers a guarantee to obtain the needed currency at a future date for a guaranteed price. Assuming that Big Heel insists on being paid in U.S. dollars, Pied D'Or could obtain a quote from a currency dealer as to the present cost of obtaining $3 million at the time the boots are to be delivered. Pied D'Or might pay a 5 percent premium for this guarantee, but it will have insured itself against disastrous currency changes. (For up-to-the-minute conversion rates between any two currencies, travel no further than http://www.oanda.com/cgi-bin/ncc.)

Choices Made.　The parties agree that the contract price will be paid in U.S. dollars. Pied D'Or is unfamiliar with the UCC and absolutely refuses to make a deal unless either French law or the CISG governs. Your lawyer, Susan Fisher, recommends accepting the CISG, provided that the contract is written in English and that any disputes will be resolved in Arizona courts. Pied D'Or balks at this, but Fisher presses hard, and ultimately those are the terms agreed upon. Fisher is delighted with the arrangement, pointing out that the CISG provisions can all be taken into account as the contract is written, and that by using Arizona courts to settle any dispute, Big Heel has an advantage in terms of familiarity and location.

Letter of Credit

Because Pied D'Or is new and fast growing, you are not sure it will be able to foot the bill. Pied D'Or provides a letter of reference from its bank, La Banque Bouffon, but this is a small bank in Pleasanterie, France, unfamiliar to you. You need greater assurance of payment, and Fisher recommends that payment be made by **irrevocable letter of credit**. Here is how the letter will work.

Big Heel demands that the contract include a provision requiring payment by confirmed, irrevocable letter of credit. Le Pied D'Or agrees. The French company now contacts its bank, La Banque Bouffon, and instructs Bouffon to issue a letter of credit to Big Heel. The letter of credit is a promise *by the bank itself* to pay Big Heel if Big Heel presents certain documents. Banque Bouffon, of course, expects to be repaid by Pied D'Or. The bank is in a good position to assess Pied D'Or's creditworthiness, since it is local and can do any investigating it wants before issuing the credit. It may also insist that Pied D'Or give Bouffon a mortgage on property, or that Pied D'Or deposit money in a separate Bouffon account. Pied D'Or is the **account party** on the letter of credit, and Big Heel is the **beneficiary**.

But at Big Heel you are still not entirely satisfied about getting paid because you don't know anything about Bouffon. That is why you have required a *confirmed* letter of credit. Bouffon will forward its letter of credit to Big Heel's own bank, the Bandito Trust Company of Tucson. Bandito examines the letter and then *confirms* the letter. This is *Bandito's own guarantee* that it will pay Big Heel. Bandito will do this only if it knows, through international banking contacts, that Bouffon is a sound bank. The risk has now been spread to two banks, and at Big Heel, you are confident of payment.

You get busy, make excellent boots, and pack them. When they are ready, you truck them to Galveston, where they are taken alongside a ship, *Le Fond de la Mer*. Your agent presents the goods to the ship's officials, along with customs documents that describe the goods. *Le Fond de la Mer*'s officer in turn issues your agent a **negotiable bill of lading**. This document describes *exactly* the goods received—their quantity, color, quality, and anything else important.

You now take the negotiable bill of lading to Bandito Trust. You also present to Bandito a **draft**, which is simply a formal order to Bandito to pay, based on the letter of credit. Bandito will look closely at the bill of lading, which must specify *precisely* the goods described in the letter of credit. Why so nitpicky? Because the bank is dealing only in paper. It never sees the boots. Bandito is exchanging

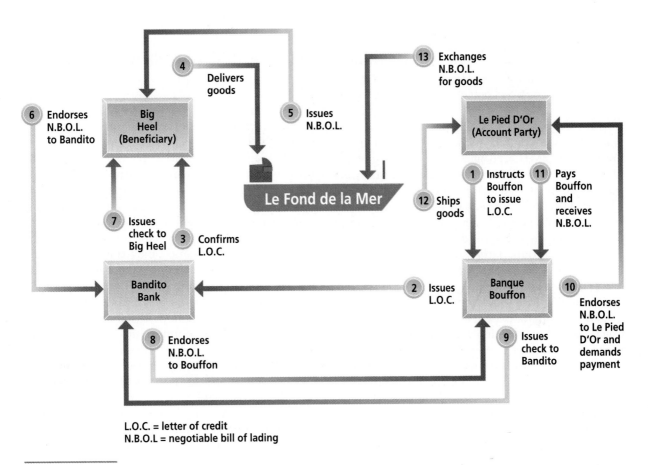

L.O.C. = letter of credit
N.B.O.L = negotiable bill of lading

Exhibit 8.1

$3 million of its own money based on instructions in the letter of credit. The bank should pay only if the bill of lading indicates that *Le Fond de la Mer* received exactly what is described in the letter of credit. Bandito will decide whether the bill of lading is *conforming* or *nonconforming*. If the terms of both documents are identical, the bill of lading is conforming and Bandito must pay. If the terms vary, the bill of lading is nonconforming and Bandito will deny payment. Thus, if the bill of lading indicated 9,000 pairs of boots and 1,000 pairs of sneakers, it is nonconforming and Big Heel would get no money.

Bandito concludes that the documents are conforming, so it issues a check to Big Heel for $3 million. In return, you endorse the bill of lading and other documents over to the Bandito Bank, which endorses the same documents and sends them to Banque Bouffon. Bouffon makes the same minute inspection and then writes a check to Bandito. Bouffon then demands payment from Le Pied D'Or. Pied D'Or pays its bank, receiving in exchange the bill of lading and customs documents. Note that payment in all stages is now complete, though the boots are still rolling on the high seas. Finally, when the boots arrive in Le Havre, Pied D'Or trucks roll up to the wharf and, using the bill of lading and customs documents, collect the boots. See Exhibit 8.1.

Good news: They fit! Not all customers walk away in such comfort, as the following case indicates.

CENTRIFUGAL CASTING MACHINE CO., INC. V. AMERICAN BANK & TRUST CO.

966 F.2d 1348, 1992 U.S. App. LEXIS 13089
United States Court of Appeals for the Tenth Circuit, 1992

FACTS: Centrifugal Casting Machine Co. (CCM) entered into a contract with the State Machinery Trading Co. (SMTC), an agency of the Iraqi government. CCM agreed to manufacture cast iron pipe plant equipment for a total price of $27 million. The contract specified payment of the full amount by confirmed irrevocable letter of credit. The Central Bank of Iraq then issued the letter, on behalf of SMTC (the "account party") to be paid to CCM (the "beneficiary"). The Banca Nazionale del Lavorov (BNL) confirmed the letter.

Following Iraq's invasion of Kuwait on August 2, 1990, President George H.W. Bush issued two executive orders blocking the transfer of property in the United States in which Iraq held any interest. In other words, no one could use, buy, or sell any Iraqi property or cash. When CCM attempted to draw upon the letter of credit, the United States government intervened. The government claimed that like all Iraqi money in the United States, this money was frozen by the executive order. The United States District Court rejected the government's claim, and the government appealed.

ISSUE: Is CCM entitled to be paid pursuant to the letter of credit?

EXCERPTS FROM JUDGE SENTELLE'S DECISION: The United States contends on appeal that the freeze of Iraq's assets furthers national policy to punish Iraq by preventing it from obtaining economic benefits from transactions with American citizens, and by preserving such assets both for use as a bargaining chip in resolving this country's differences with Iraq and as a source of compensation for claims Americans may have against Iraq. We agree that these policy considerations are compelling and that we are therefore required to construe Iraqi property interests broadly. However, we are not persuaded these policies would be furthered by [creating] a property interest on behalf of Iraq that would not otherwise be cognizable under governing legal principles.

Two interrelated features of the letter of credit provide it with its unique value in the marketplace and are of critical importance in our consideration of the United States's claim here. First, the simple result [of a letter of credit] is that the issuer [i.e., the bank] substitutes its credit, preferred by the beneficiary, for that of the account party. Second, the issuer's obligation to pay on a letter of credit is completely independent from the underlying commercial transaction between the beneficiary and the account party. Significantly, the issuer must honor a proper demand even though the beneficiary has breached the underlying contract; even though the insolvency of the account party renders reimbursement impossible; and notwithstanding supervening illegality, impossibility, war or insurrection. This principle of independence is universally viewed as essential to the proper functioning of a letter of credit and to its particular value, i.e., its certainty of payment.

This assurance of payment gives letters of credit a central role in commercial dealings, and gives them a particular value in international transactions, in which sophisticated investors knowingly undertake such risks as political upheaval or contractual breach in return for the benefits to be reaped from international trade. Law affecting such an essential instrument of the economy must be shaped with sensitivity to its special characteristics. Accordingly, courts have concluded that the whole purpose of a letter of credit would be defeated by examining the merits of the underlying contract dispute to determine whether the letter should be paid.

Because of the nature of a letter of credit, we conclude that Iraq does not have a property interest in the money CCM received under the letter. The United States contends in essence that Iraq has a property interest in this money because it was allegedly a contract payment made by Iraq, which Iraq should recover because CCM breached the contract. In so arguing, the United States makes a breach of contract claim on behalf of Iraq that Iraq has never made, creates a remedy for the contracting parties in derogation of the remedy they themselves provided and, most importantly, disregards the controlling legal principles with respect to letters of credit.
Affirmed. ◢

INDIRECT SALES THROUGH A DISTRIBUTOR

You might also have decided that Big Heel would be better off doing business through a French shoe distributor, on the theory that the local company would have superior market knowledge and easier access to valuable retailers. The questions you face regarding choice of law, forum, and method of payment are identical to those you face in direct sales; they must be worked out in advance. But there is one additional problem that deserves close attention.

Suppose you choose Voleurs Freres, a French fashion distributor, to do all of Big Heel's work in France. Voleurs Freres will be an **exclusive dealer**, meaning that it will take on no other accounts of cowboy boots. In return you will give it an **exclusive distributorship**, indicating that no other French distributors will get a chance at Big Heel boots. This is a common method of working. Voleurs Freres benefits because no one else in France may distribute the valuable boots. Big Heel in turn need not worry that Voleurs Freres will devote more energy to a competing boot. It is a tidy relationship, but does it violate antitrust laws?

Antitrust laws make it illegal to destroy competition and capture an entire market. The United States and the EU both have strong antitrust laws that can potentially be applied domestically and in foreign countries.

EU Antitrust Law

The European Union law is found in Articles 85 and 86 of the Treaty of Rome. From the American point of view, the former is more important. **Article 85 outlaws any agreement, contract, or discussion that distorts competition within EU countries.** In other words, any attempt to gain a market edge by *avoiding* competition is going to be suspect. Suppose three Italian cosmetic firms agree to act in unison to increase earnings. They set common prices for makeup and agree that none will undersell the others. This greatly reduces competition, leaving the consumer with fewer options and more expensive products. Their deal violates Article 85.

Will Big Heel's contract with Voleurs Freres violate Article 85? There is no quick answer. You will need to do a careful market analysis and consult with French lawyers, who undoubtedly will have many questions. How popular are Big Heel boots in Europe? How many competitors would like to distribute them? How many other boot companies want Voleurs Freres to sell *their* products? Does the exclusive arrangement between Big Heel and Voleurs Freres diminish competition? Will consumers pay more because of the contract? These questions are a nuisance and an expense, but it is easier and cheaper to make the inquiry now than to face years of antitrust litigation.

American Antitrust Law

In the United States, the primary antitrust law is the **Sherman Act**.[5] This statute controls anticompetitive conduct that harms the American market. It will probably not affect the Big Heel–Voleurs Freres contract, since that deal is likely to have consequences only in Europe. But it is important to understand the Sherman Act when facing foreign competition. In effect, this statute is the American counterpart to Article 85. Any conduct that eliminates competition in the United States

---

[5] See Chapter 19, on antitrust law.

and enables one company, or group of companies, to control a market probably violates this law. And "any conduct" means that anticompetitive acts taking place in a foreign country may still violate the Sherman Act. A company doing business in the United States **may sue a competitor based on its conduct in a foreign country**, provided the local firm can show (1) that the foreign competitor *intends* to affect the U.S. market, and (2) that the foreign conduct has a *direct and substantial effect* on the U.S. market.

Let's look again at the Italian cosmetics makers. Suppose they decide to act in unison in the United States. They set common prices and agree not to compete with each other. That agreement is illegal. It violates the Sherman Act *even if all arrangements were made in Milan*. The companies intend to affect the U.S. market. When an American cosmetics firm demonstrates that the agreement caused it direct and substantial harm, the company may file suit in the United States against all three Italian corporations and expect to recover large damages.

International Comity

But what if the foreign corporation is doing business in a way that is entirely legal in its native country? May U.S. antitrust law still penalize the company's conduct if it harms American business? That was the question presented in the following case, which raises the issue of **international comity**. The word "comity" in this context means concomitant jurisdiction, meaning that two courts have the right to hear a particular case. When those two courts are in different nations, the laws of the two countries may conflict. **In the event of a conflict, international comity requires one court to respect the other legal system and decline to hear a suit if it would more logically be resolved in the foreign country.** Does that principle govern the following case? The plaintiffs wanted the case heard in the United States under the Sherman Act, while the defendants wanted any dispute settled in Britain, where they believed British law would find them innocent of any wrongdoing.

YOU BE THE JUDGE

HARTFORD FIRE INSURANCE CO. V. CALIFORNIA

509 U.S. 764, 113 S. Ct. 2891, 1993 U.S. LEXIS 4404
United States Supreme Court, 1993

FACTS: Nineteen states and many private plaintiffs filed 36 separate lawsuits against various insurance companies, alleging several conspiracies to violate the Sherman Act. The conspiracies related to commercial general liability (CGL) insurance, which covers the insured against accident and damage claims by customers, other companies, or the general public. The defendants were "reinsurance" companies. When a primary insurer issues a CGL policy to a corporation, it usually obtains for itself insurance to cover at least a portion of the risk it is assuming. The availability of reinsurance strongly affects the ability of primary insurers to provide coverage.

Lloyd's of London is a major reinsurance center. Various English syndicates, working through Lloyd's, provide reinsurance for companies throughout the world. The plaintiffs alleged that reinsurers at Lloyd's forced American primary insurers to change the terms of their standard CGL insurance. These changes shortened the time during which a customer could file a claim under its policy, and eliminated certain claims altogether. These changes made CGL less valuable to the insured and more profitable to the reinsurers. The reinsurers were able to impose these changes because (1) there are only a few reinsurers worldwide and (2) all of the reinsurers worked in collusion to limit the coverage. They thus behaved in a monopolistic fashion, controlling the market and reducing customers' insurance coverage.

The United States District Court concluded that since the reinsurers' conduct was legal in Britain, international comity prevented an American court from hearing claims against the London defendants. The court dismissed the case against them. The United States Court of Appeals reversed, holding that the case should go forward in this country. The London reinsurers appealed to the United States Supreme Court.

YOU BE THE JUDGE: Does the principle of international comity prevent an American court from hearing these antitrust claims against London reinsurers?

ARGUMENT FOR THE LONDON REINSURERS: Your honors, for several reasons we urge American courts not to hear these antitrust claims against any London reinsurer. Lloyd's of London has been one of the world's most respected insurance organizations since 1688. Beginning in 1879, Parliament has directly regulated Lloyd's, and continues to control it today, pursuant to the Insurance Companies Act of 1982 and appropriate regulations. Under British law, insurance companies and reinsurance companies are *expressly exempt* from antitrust regulation. Everything that the defendants are alleged to have done in this case is *entirely legal* in Britain. It is an extraordinarily dangerous idea to permit the courts of one nation to subject foreign nationals to phenomenally expensive litigation for alleged conduct that was absolutely legal and proper where it was done.

Further, even though plaintiffs allege that the defendants' conduct technically violated American laws, there can be no suggestion that any of the reinsurers intended to harm any American corporation or citizen. This is not some shady conspiracy forged on a foggy night in an abandoned shack. The London reinsurers simply attempted to limit their own liability. They chose a lawful means to do it. They were doing, in other words, precisely what the plaintiffs in this case do when they buy insurance!

As this Court well knows, British courts have repeatedly expressed hostility to the extraterritorial application of American antitrust laws. So strong is the antagonism from earlier cases that English law now prohibits companies from supplying evidence and documents for use in antitrust proceedings in the United States. Even if this Court were to permit the suit to go forward, it would be nearly impossible for the plaintiffs to obtain documentary evidence to support their case from the only place from which it can come, England.

For all of these reasons, we urge the Court to rely on international comity and dismiss the case.

ARGUMENT FOR THE PLAINTIFFS: Your honors, the defendants all engaged in conduct that they knew violated American antitrust laws. They did it for one reason: to increase their profits. That, of course, is why any corporation attempts to control a market. Here, by fixing deals with other major reinsurers, the Lloyd's syndicates were able to dictate the terms of American primary insurance and reduce coverage to the plaintiffs.

The defendants argue that they have obeyed British law, and that a so-called conflict in the laws requires American courts to stay away. But there is in fact no conflict between American and British law. It may be true that the reinsurers' monopolistic practices do not *violate* British law. But that does not mean that British law *requires* them to behave this way. It is black letter law that American antitrust laws may be applied against conduct that is lawful in a foreign nation. There would be a conflict only if British insurance law *required* Lloyd's firms to act collusively and attempt to control the American market. Obviously, it does not. The Lloyd's reinsurers are free to obey American law and British law, and that is what they ought to have done. They didn't, and we ask a chance to prove that in court.

These reinsurers are some of the most sophisticated business people in the world. They entered the American insurance market to make a profit and have stayed here many decades because they *are* earning money. But the profits were not vast enough, so they engaged in monopolistic, collusive practices to cut back the customer's ability to make a claim. And now, in dominating the American market, they claim they should not be governed by American law. Not fair, your honors. They can't have it both ways. If they enter this market, they must be governed by its laws the same as anyone else. ∎

LICENSING A FOREIGN MANUFACTURER

Big Heel has a third option when selling abroad, which is to license a French manufacturer to produce Big Heel boots. It should do this only if it is convinced the manufacturer will maintain sufficiently high standards. Even so, there are two major issues.

First, Big Heel must ensure that all of its patents and trademarks are protected. In fact, France will honor both forms of American intellectual property, and there should be no problems. But some nations may ignore American intellectual property rights, and no company should establish a licensing arrangement without investigating. As mentioned earlier, the WTO should increase respect worldwide for the intellectual property rights created by all nations.

Second, if Big Heel grants an exclusive license to any French manufacturer, it could encounter exactly the same antitrust problems as those discussed above. It must analyze both EU and American antitrust law before taking the risk.

Investing Abroad

Foreign investment is another major source of international commerce. Assume that Ambux is an American communications corporation that decides to invest in a growing overseas market. The president of Ambux is particularly interested in building telephone systems in the former republics of the Soviet Union, reasoning that these economies offer great opportunity for growth. She wants you to report to her on the most important issues concerning possible investment in Uzbekistan and other former Soviet republics. You quickly realize that such an investment presents several related issues:

- Repatriation of profits
- Expropriation
- Sovereign immunity
- Act of State doctrine
- Foreign corrupt practices

REPATRIATION OF PROFITS

Repatriation of profits occurs when an investing company pulls its earnings out of a foreign country and takes them back home. If Ambux builds a telephone system in Uzbekistan, it will plan to make money and then repatriate the profit to its headquarters in the United States. But Ambux must not assume an automatic right to do so. Many countries impose a much higher tax on repatriated profits than on normal income in order to keep the money in domestic commerce. Others bar repatriation altogether. Developing countries in particular want the money for further growth, and they tend to regard repatriation of rapidly earned profit as a close relative of exploitation. Thus, before Ambux invests anywhere, it must ensure that it can repatriate profits or be prepared to live with any limitations the foreign country might impose.

Fortunately, investing in Uzbekistan is relatively secure. Uzbekistan and the United States have signed a trade treaty guaranteeing unlimited repatriation for American investors. This treaty should suffice. But Ambux might still feel cautious. Uzbekistan is a new nation, and the mechanisms for actually getting the money out of Uzbekistan banks may be slow or faulty. The solution is to get a written agreement from the Minister of Commerce explicitly permitting Ambux to repatriate all profits and providing a clear mechanism to do it through the local banks.

EXPROPRIATION

Many nations, both developed and developing, **nationalize** property, meaning that they declare the national government to be the new owner. For example, during the 1940s and 1950s, Great Britain nationalized its coal, steel, and other heavy industries. The state assumed ownership and paid compensation to the previous owners. In the United States, nationalization is rare, but local governments often take land by eminent domain, to be used for roads or other public works. The United States Constitution requires that the owners be fairly compensated.

When a government takes property owned by foreign investors, it is called **expropriation**. Again, this practice is common and legal, provided there is adequate compensation. The U.S. government historically has acknowledged that the expropriation of American interests is legal, provided the host government pays the owners *promptly and fully, in dollars*. But if compensation is inadequate or long delayed, or made in a local currency that is hard to exchange, the taking is **confiscation**.

The courts of almost all nations concede that confiscation is illegal. But it can be difficult or impossible to prevent because courts of the host country may be partial to their own government. And any attempt to obtain compensation in an American court will encounter two separate problems: sovereign immunity and the Act of State doctrine.

SOVEREIGN IMMUNITY

Sovereign immunity holds that the courts of one nation lack the jurisdiction (power) to hear suits against foreign governments. Most nations respect this principle. In the United States, the **Foreign Sovereign Immunities Act (FSIA)** states that American courts generally cannot entertain suits against foreign governments. This is a difficult hurdle for a company to overcome when seeking compensation for foreign expropriation. There are three exceptions.

Waiver. A lawsuit is permitted against a foreign country that waives its immunity, that is, voluntarily gives up this protection. Suppose the Czech government wishes to buy fighter planes from an American manufacturer. The manufacturer might insist on a waiver in the sales contract, and the Czech Republic might be willing to grant one to get the weapons it desires. If the planes land safely but the checks bounce, the manufacturer may sue.

Commercial Activity.   A plaintiff in the United States can sue a foreign country engaged in commercial activity, as opposed to political. Suppose the government of Iceland hires an American ecology-consulting firm to help its fishers replenish depleted fishing grounds. Since fishing is a for-profit activity, the contract is commercial, and if Iceland refuses to pay, the company may sue in American courts.

Violation of International Law.   A plaintiff in this country may sue a foreign government that has confiscated property in violation of international law, provided that the property either ends up in the United States or is involved in commercial activity that affects someone in the United States. Suppose a foreign government confiscates a visiting American ship, with no claim of right, and begins to use it for shipping goods for profit. Later, the ship carries some American produce. The taking was illegal, and it now affects American commerce. The original owner may sue.

Act of State Doctrine

A second doctrine, annoyingly similar to sovereign immunity, could also affect Ambux or any company whose property is confiscated. The **Act of State doctrine** requires an American court to **abstain from any case in which a court order would interfere with the ability of the president or Congress to conduct foreign affairs.**

In the 1960s, Cuba expropriated American sugar interests, providing little or no compensation to the previous owners. The American owners sued, but in *Banco Nacional de Cuba v. Sabbatino,*[6] the United States Supreme Court refused to permit such suits in American courts. The Court ruled that even where there was strong evidence that the expropriation was illegal, American courts should not be involved because the executive and legislative branches must be free to conduct our foreign policy.

Investment Insurance

Companies eager to do business abroad but anxious about expropriation should consider publicly funded insurance. In 1971, Congress established the **Overseas Private Investment Corporation (OPIC)** to insure U.S. investors against overseas losses due to political violence and expropriation. OPIC insurance is available to investors at relatively low rates for investment in almost any country. The agency has had remarkable success at no cost to the U.S. government. Every year, OPIC participates in overseas ventures worth many billions of dollars, earning insurance fees that have paid the agency's entire budget and left a substantial surplus.

Should Ambux investigate OPIC insurance before investing in Uzbekistan? Absolutely. While the Uzbekistan government has the best of intentions with respect to foreign investment, the nation is young and the government has no track record. A government can change course as quickly as a gnat, and often with less planning. Why take unnecessary risks?

---

[6] 376 U.S. 398, 84 S. Ct. 923, 1964 U.S. LEXIS 2252 (1964).

FOREIGN CORRUPT PRACTICES ACT

Suppose that while you are investigating Uzbekistan, an official from a nearby country contacts you. This official, Dr. J., says that Ambux is the perfect company to install a new, nationwide telephone system for his young republic. You are delighted with his enthusiasm. Over lunch, Dr. J. tells you that he can obtain an exclusive contract for Ambux to do the work, but you will have to pay him a commission of $750,000. Such a deal would be worth millions of dollars for Ambux, and a commission of $750,000 is economically sensible. Should you pay it?

The Foreign Corrupt Practices Act (FCPA)[7] **makes it illegal for an American businessperson to give "anything of value" to any foreign official in order to influence an official decision.** The classic example of an FCPA violation is bribing a foreign official to obtain a government contract. You must find out exactly why Dr. J. needs so much money, what he plans to do with it, and how he will obtain the contract.

You ask these questions, and Dr. J. responds, "I am a close personal friend of the Minister of the Interior. In my country, you must know people to make things happen. The minister respects my judgment, and some of my fee will find its way to him. Do not trouble yourself with details."

Bad advice. A prison sentence is not a detail. The FCPA permits fines of $100,000 for individuals and $1 million for corporations, as well as prison sentences of up to five years. If you pay money that "finds its way to the minister," you have violated the act.

It is sad but true that in many countries bribery is routine and widely accepted. When Congress investigated foreign bribes to see how common they were, more than 300 U.S. companies admitted paying hundreds of millions of dollars in bribes to foreign officials. Legislators concluded that such massive payments distorted competition between American companies for foreign contracts, interfered with the free market system, and undermined confidence everywhere in our way of doing business. The statutory response was simple: foreign bribery is illegal, plain and simple. The FCPA has two principal requirements:

- *Bribes.* The statute makes it illegal for U.S. companies and citizens to bribe foreign officials to influence a governmental decision. The statute prohibits giving anything of value and also bars using third parties as a conduit for such payments.

- *Record Keeping.* All publicly traded companies—whether they engage in international trade or not—must keep detailed records that prevent hiding or disguising bribes. These records must be available for U.S. government officials to inspect.

Lockheed Corp. secured a $79 million contract to sell C-130 Hercules transport aircraft to Egypt, anticipating a $12 million profit. One expense of obtaining the contract was a $1 million payment, made to a Swiss bank account, for the benefit of a former Lockheed consultant who had since become a member of the Egyptian parliament. Big mistake. In federal court, Lockheed later pleaded guilty to violating the FCPA, acknowledging that it had falsified records to cover up the bribe. The company paid a $24.8 million fine—double its profit. The Lockheed executive directly involved in the bribe, Suleiman Nassar, vice-president of international marketing, received a fine of $125,000 and an 18-month prison sentence.

---

[7] 15 U.S.C. §78 et seq.

Not all payments violate the FCPA. A **grease or facilitating payment is legal**, provided the company is paying a foreign official only to expedite performance of a routine function. Grease payments are common in many foreign countries to obtain a permit, process governmental papers, or obtain utility service. For example, the cost of a permit to occupy an office building might be $100, but the government clerk suggests that you will receive the permit faster (within this lifetime) if you pay $150, one-third of which he will pocket. Such small payments are legal. Further, a payment **does not violate the FCPA if it was legal under the written laws** of the country in which it was made. Since few countries establish written codes *permitting* officials to receive bribes, this defense is unlikely to help many Americans who hand out gifts.

Some illegal bribes are blatant. A suitcase full of cash is a ticket to jail. But some payments are subtler. Your company is bidding for the right to build a power station in rural Mexico, and an Italian company is your primary competitor. The Italian company offers to fly all of the relevant Mexican officials and their families to Venice for an all-expenses-paid holiday. Should you match the offer? Such a gift, clearly made to obtain an important contract, would only be lawful if *written* Mexican law permitted it. It is unlikely there is such a law. Never give any gift without checking with a lawyer to assure that local *written* law permits the payment.

Transparency International, an international nonprofit agency based in Germany, publishes a "Corruption Perception Index," gauging how much dishonesty businesspeople and scholars encounter in different nations. In 2001, the agency listed 91 nations on its index. The 10 highest-ranking countries (perceived *least* corrupt) were Finland, Denmark, New Zealand, Iceland, Singapore, Sweden, Canada, the Netherlands, Luxembourg, and Norway. The agency listed the United States as the sixteenth least corrupt nation. The 10 countries ranking lowest (perceived *most* corrupt) were Bangladesh, Nigeria, Uganda, Indonesia, Kenya, Cameroon, Bolivia, Azerbaijan, Ukraine, and Tanzania. The full index is available from Transparency International at http://www.transparency.org.

But corruption is a two-sided coin. Of the more than 200 nations in the world, very few aggressively prevent their nationals from bribing foreign officials. Further, in some countries, a bribe paid to a foreign official may be treated as a tax deduction!

American executives have long complained that the FCPA puts their companies at a competitive disadvantage, and political leaders have lobbied for an international agreement. Finally, the efforts are reaching fruition. The Organization for Economic Cooperation and Development (OECD) produced a "Convention of Combatting Bribery of Foreign Public Officials in International Business Transactions." The 29 nations of the OECD include most of the world's economic powers. Five nonmembers of the OECD also signed. The Convention requires signatories to enact criminal penalties for offering or giving bribes to foreign officials. The Convention also compels signatories to enact record-keeping laws that will prevent companies from disguising bribes. The Convention has various weaknesses, and it remains to be seen whether signatories will implement it aggressively, but the agreement is clearly a bold step on an ethical path.

The best way for a company to avoid liability under the FCPA is to hire a compliance officer. This employee should conduct background checks on foreign agents and consultants to ensure that they are not making secret payments to obtain business. The compliance officer should insist on internal company auditing designed to deter and detect illicit payments. She must train all employees in the nuances of the law and create a system for reporting and investigating suspected breaches of the law.

Chapter Conclusion

Overseas investment, like sales abroad, offers potentially great rewards but significant pitfalls. A working knowledge of international law is essential to any entrepreneur or executive seriously considering foreign commerce. Issues such as choice of law, currency protection, antitrust statutes, and expropriation can mean the difference between profit and loss. As the WTO lowers barriers, international trade will increase, and your awareness of these principles will grow still more valuable.

Chapter Review

1. Several statutes restrict exports from the United States that would harm national security, foreign policy, or certain other goals.

2. A tariff is a duty (tax) imposed on goods when they enter a country. The U.S. Customs Service classifies goods when they enter the United States and imposes appropriate tariffs.

3. Most countries, including the United States, impose duties for goods that have been dumped (sold at an unfairly low price in the international market) and for subsidized goods (those benefiting from government financial assistance in the country of origin).

4. The General Agreement on Tariffs and Trade (GATT) is lowering the average duties worldwide. Proponents see it as a boon to trade; opponents see it as a threat to workers and the environment.

5. GATT created the World Trade Organization (WTO), which resolves disputes between signatories to the treaty.

6. A sales agreement between an American company and a foreign company may be governed by the Uniform Commercial Code (UCC), by the law of the foreign country, or by the United Nations Convention on Contracts for the International Sale of Goods (CISG). The CISG differs from the UCC in several important respects.

7. A confirmed irrevocable letter of credit is an important means of facilitating international sales contracts, because the seller is assured of payment by a local bank as long as it delivers the specified goods.

8. Antitrust laws exist in the United States, the European Union (EU), and other countries. International merchants must be careful not to make agreements that would distort competition.

9. International comity requires a local court to respect the legal system of a foreign country and dismiss a lawsuit if the dispute would more logically be resolved in the other nation.

10. A foreign government may restrict repatriation of profits.

11. Expropriation refers to a government taking property owned by foreign investors. U.S. courts regard this as lawful, provided the country pays the American owner promptly and fully, in dollars.

12. Sovereign immunity means that, in general, American courts lack jurisdiction to hear suits against foreign governments, unless the foreign nation has waived immunity, is engaging in commercial activity, or has violated international law.

13. The Act of State doctrine requires an American court to abstain from any case in which a court order would interfere with the ability of the president or Congress to conduct foreign affairs.

14. The Foreign Corrupt Practices Act (FCPA) makes it illegal for an American businessperson to bribe foreign officials.

Practice Test

1. Arnold Mandel exported certain high-tech electronic equipment. Later, he was in court arguing that the equipment he shipped should not have been on the Department of Commerce's Commodity Control List. What items may be on that list, and why does Mandel care?

2. Sports Graphics, Inc., imports consumer goods, including "Chill" brand coolers, which come from Taiwan. Chill coolers have an outer shell of vinyl, with handles and pockets, and an inner layer of insulation. In a recent federal lawsuit, the issue was whether Chill coolers were technically "luggage" or "articles used for preparing, serving or storing food or beverages." Who were the parties to this dispute likely to be, and why did they care about such a technical description of these coolers?

3. **ETHICS** Hector works in Zoey's importing firm. Zoey overhears Hector on the phone say, "OK, 30,000 ski parkas at $80 per parka. You've got yourself a deal. Thanks a lot." When Hector hangs up, Zoey is furious, yelling, "I told you not to make a deal on those Italian ski parkas without my permission! I think I can get a better price elsewhere." "Relax, Zoey," replies Hector. "I wanted to lock them in, to be sure we had some in case your deal fell through. It's just an oral contract, so we can always back out if we need to." Is that ethical? How far can a company go to protect its interests? Does it matter that another business might make serious financial plans based on the discussion? Apart from the ethics, is Hector's idea smart?

4. **YOU BE THE JUDGE WRITING PROBLEM** Continental Illinois National Bank issued an irrevocable letter of credit on behalf of Bill's Coal Co. for $805,000, with the Allied Fidelity Insurance Co. as beneficiary. Bill's Coal Co. then went bankrupt. Allied then presented to Continental documents that were complete and conformed to the letter of credit. Continental refused to pay. Since Bill's Coal was bankrupt, there was no way Continental would collect once it had paid on the letter. Allied filed suit. Who should win? **Argument for Allied Fidelity:** An irrevocable letter of credit serves one purpose: to assure the seller that it will be paid if it performs the contract. Allied has met its obligation. The company furnished documents demonstrating compliance with the agreement. Continental *must* pay. Continental's duty to pay is an independent obligation, unrelated to the status of Bill's Coal. The bank issued this letter knowing the rules of the game and expecting to make a profit. It is time for Continental to honor its word. **Argument for Continental Bank:** In this transaction, the bank was merely a middleman, helping to facilitate payment of a contract. Allied has fulfilled its obligations under the contract, and we understand the company's desire to be paid. Regrettably, Bill's Coal is bankrupt. No one is going to be paid on this deal. Allied should have researched Bill's financial status more thoroughly before entering into the agreement. While we sympathize with Allied's dilemma, it has only itself to blame and cannot expect the bank to act as some sort of insurance company for a deal gone awry.

5. Jean-François, a French wine exporter, sues Bob Joe, a Texas importer, claiming that Bob Joe owes him $2 million for wine. Jean-François takes the witness stand to describe how the contract was created. Where is the trial taking place?

6. Zenith and other American manufacturers of television sets sued Matsushita and 20 other Japanese competitors, claiming that the Japanese companies had conspired to drive Zenith and the Americans out of the American market. Supposedly, the Japanese companies agreed to maintain artificially high prices in Japan and artificially low prices in the United States. The goal of the low prices in the United States was to destroy American competition, and the goal of the high prices in Japan was to earn sufficient profits at home so that the companies could tolerate the temporary losses in the United States. Is the conduct of Matsushita in Japan subject to the Sherman Act?

7. The Kyrgyz Republic is another of the new nations that broke away from the old Soviet Union. In September 1994, the government of Kyrgyzstan made two independent announcements: (1) it was abolishing all taxes on repatriation; (2) the government was resigning and would shortly be replaced. Explain the significance of these announcements for an American company considering a major investment in Kyrgyzstan.

8. The Instituto de Auxilios y Viviendas is a government agency of the Dominican Republic. Dr. Marion Fernandez, the general administrator of the Instituto and Secretary of the Republic, sought a loan for the Instituto. She requested that Charles Meadows, an American citizen, secure the Instituto a bank loan of $12 million. If he obtained a loan on favorable terms, he would receive a fee of $240,000. Meadows secured a loan on satisfactory terms, which the Instituto accepted. He then sought his fee, but the Instituto and the Dominican government refused to pay. He sued the government in United States District Court. The Dominican government claimed immunity. Comment.

9. Environmental Tectonics Corp. and W. S. Kirkpatrick & Co. were both competing for a valuable contract with the Nigerian government. Kirkpatrick got it. Tectonics then sued Kirkpatrick in the United States, claiming that Kirkpatrick got the contract only because it bribed Nigerian officials. Kirkpatrick acknowledged that the district court had jurisdiction but argued that it should abstain from hearing the case. What doctrine does Kirkpatrick rely on, and what should the trial court do?

10. Blondek and Tull were two employees of an American company called Eagle Bus. They hoped that the Saskatchewan provincial government would award Eagle a contract for buses. To bolster their chances, they went to Saskatchewan and paid $50,000 to two government employees. Back in the United States, they were arrested and charged with a crime. Suppose they argue that even if they did something illegal, it occurred in Canada, and that is the only nation that can prosecute them. Comment on the defense.

11. Richard Johnson, an American citizen, was a highly trained electrical engineer who had worked for Hughes Aircraft and Norcroft Corp. He strongly believed in the cause of the Provisional Irish Republican Army (PIRA), which at the time was attacking British civilian and military targets in Northern Ireland and England. Johnson researched and developed explosives to be exported to Ireland and used by the PIRA. Christina Reid, an electrical engineer, worked with Johnson on IRA projects. She served as a courier of electronic components for remote-control bombs that the two sent to Northern Ireland. What legal problems did they risk by engaging in these transactions?

12. **ROLE REVERSAL** Write an essay or short-answer question that involves a dispute brought to the WTO on one of these issues: dumping, nontariff barriers, or intellectual property.

Internet Research Problem

At http://www.sweatshops.org, read about the worldwide problem of sweatshops. Is this a serious problem? If so, what role should the law play in its resolution? What can one student do about it?

You can find further practice problems in the Online Quiz at http://beatty.westbuslaw.com or in the Study Guide that accompanies this text.

CONTRACTS & THE UCC

UNIT 2

Introduction
to Contracts

Have a seat. Great to see you. Here, grab a menu. Yes, you're right: the tables at this café are jammed together. In fact, *that's why I chose* the spot. Listen to the conversations around us. Oh, go on, don't worry—eavesdropping is acceptable for academic purposes. To our right, a famous director is chatting with Katrina, the glamorous actress. He is trying to sign her up for a new film, *Body Work*, but she seems hesitant.

Katrina (doubtful): I'm intrigued with the character, Bob, and I'd love to work with you. I *am* concerned about the nude scenes. The one on the toboggan run was OK. But that scene in the poultry factory—very explicit. I don't work fully nude.

Bob: We'll solve it—what am I, a sleaze? This is fine art, don't give it another thought. We're talking $2.5 million, Katrina. $600,000 up front, the rest deferred, the usual percentages.

Katrina: As you know, my fee is $3 million. I should talk with my agent. I'd need something in writing about the nudity, the percentages, all of it.

Bob: I have to settle this fast. Julia is seriously considering the role.

Katrina (worried): *Julia!* Are you kidding? Bob, I said I'm interested.

Oh, my look at that. Katrina hesitates, Bob nods encouragingly, then sticks out his hand and . . . Katrina shakes! It's a wrap—I guess. Now bend your ear toward the table on our left. The man wants to quit his job and accept a position with a competing company, but the woman, his boss, is insisting he stay.

Emily: I taught you everything you know about computer encryption, Jake, and you're not taking that sophisticated training to my number one competitor.

Jake: Emily, their offer is just too good to turn down. I deserve a chance to expand my horizons. Come on, be human!

Emily (waving a document): Look here, my friend. Page four of your employment contract: "I agree that if I leave the company for any reason, I will not work for a competing firm anywhere in the United States for a period of three years." And here is your lovely, rounded signature. You work for me, Jake, or you go flip burgers.

Gee, that Emily is tough. I guess poor Jake is stuck in his present job. We need something cheerier. Listen to the two women behind you. While I was waiting, they have been bargaining over a vacation condo.

Li-Li: I don't think I can go lower than 485.

Maria: Well . . . $450,000. I guess.

Li-Li: Maria, it has the best ocean view in the whole complex. And you would be on the top floor!

Maria: 460.

Li-Li: 475. My final offer. Do you happen to have the time?

Maria: The time? What's the hurry? Oh . . . OK 475. Shake, partner.

Li-Li: It's a deal. That's great. I'm so happy for you. You're going to love it. Do we need to put this in writing?

Maria: Are you kidding? How long have we known each other, since we were six?

Li-Li: Five and a half! You're right, why spend the money on lawyers and boring documents? Let's spend it on champagne. Waiter!

The café is a hotbed of contract negotiations—but then, so is our society. These three conversations demonstrate why it is important to understand contract law. Bob and Katrina think they have an agreement, but in fact *they do not*, because the parties have not achieved a meeting of the minds. Jake, if he reads this chapter, will be delighted to learn that *he is free to change jobs*: a court will not enforce Emily's noncompetition agreement. Finally, Li-Li should skip the champagne and instead scratch a simple contract onto a napkin. Without Maria's signature, Li-Li *cannot enforce her friend's promise* to pay.

INTRODUCTION TO CONTRACTS

The Purpose of a Contract

Parties enter into contracts attempting to control their future. **Contracts exist to make business matters more predictable.** Most contracts work out precisely as the parties intended because the parties fulfill their obligations. Most—but not all. We will study contracts that have gone wrong. We look at these errant deals to learn how to avoid the problems they manifest.

JUDICIAL ACTIVISM VERSUS JUDICIAL RESTRAINT

In most contract cases judges do their best simply to enforce whatever terms the parties agreed to. Even if the contract results in serious harm to one party, a court will generally enforce it. This is **judicial restraint**. On the other hand, some courts practice **judicial activism**. In contract law, this means that a court will ignore certain provisions of a contract, or an entire agreement, if the judge believes that enforcing the deal would be unjust. A court may even be willing to create a contract where none existed if it appears necessary to avoid injustice. Judicial activism makes the law **more flexible but less predictable**.

ISSUES (AND ANSWERS)

The three contract negotiations above illustrate several basic principles, and we will consider each. **A contract has four elements:**

1. **Agreement.** One party must make a valid offer, and the other party must accept it. (Bob failed to make a clear offer to Katrina.)

2. **Consideration.** There has to be bargaining that leads to an exchange between the parties.

3. **Legality.** The contract must be for a lawful purpose. (Emily's noncompetition agreement is probably illegal.)

4. **Capacity.** The parties must be adults of sound mind.

Contract cases often raise several other important issues, which we examine throughout this chapter the next:

• **Consent.** Neither party may trick or force the other into the agreement.

• **Written Contracts.** Some contracts must be in writing to be enforceable. (Neither Li-Li nor Maria may enforce the condo contract unless there is a signed agreement.)

• **Third Party Interests.** Some contracts affect people other than the parties themselves.

• **Performance and Discharge.** If a party fully accomplishes what the contract requires, his duties are discharged.

• **Remedies.** A court will award money or other relief to a party injured by a breach of contract.

CONTRACTS DEFINED

A contract is a promise that the law will enforce. As we look more closely at the elements of contract law, we will encounter some intricate issues, but remember that we are usually interested in answering three basic questions of common sense, all relating to promises:

- Is it certain that the defendant promised to do something?

- If she did promise, is it fair to make her honor her word?

- If she did *not* promise, are there unusual reasons to hold her liable anyway?

Types of Contracts

BILATERAL AND UNILATERAL CONTRACTS

In a bilateral contract, both parties make a promise. Suppose a producer says to Gloria, "I'll pay you $2 million to star in my new romantic comedy, *A Promise for a Promise*, which we are shooting three months from now in Santa Fe." Gloria says, "It's a deal." That is a bilateral contract. Each party has made a promise to do something. The producer is now bound to pay Gloria $2 million, and Gloria is obligated to show up on time and act in the movie. The vast majority of contracts are bilateral contracts.

In a unilateral contract, one party makes a promise that the other party can accept only by *doing* something. These contracts are less common. Suppose the movie producer says to Leo, "I'll give you a hundred bucks if you mow my lawn this weekend." Leo is not promising to do it. If he mows the lawn, he has accepted the offer and is entitled to his hundred dollars. If he spends the weekend at the beach, neither he nor the producer owes anything.

EXPRESS AND IMPLIED CONTRACTS

In an express contract, the two parties explicitly state all important terms of their agreement. *The great majority* of binding agreements are express contracts. The contract between the producer and Gloria is an express contract, because the parties explicitly state what Gloria will do, where and when she will do it, and how much she will be paid. Some express contracts are oral, as that one was, and some are written.

In an implied contract, the words and conduct of the parties indicate that they intended an agreement. Suppose every Friday, for two months, the producer asks Leo to mow his lawn, and loyal Leo does so each weekend. Then for three more weekends, Leo simply shows up without the producer asking, and the producer continues to pay for the work done. But on the twelfth weekend, when Leo rings the doorbell to collect, the producer suddenly says, "I never asked you to mow it. Scram." The producer is correct that there was no express contract, because the parties had not spoken for several weeks. But a court will probably rule that the conduct of the parties has *implied* a contract. Not only did Leo mow the lawn every weekend, but the producer even paid on three weekends when they had not spoken. It was reasonable for Leo to assume that he had a weekly deal to mow and be paid. Naturally, there is no implied contract thereafter.

Today, the hottest disputes about implied contracts often arise in the employment setting. Many employees have "at-will" agreements. This means that the employees are free to quit at any time and the company has the right to fire them at any time, for virtually any reason. Courts routinely enforce at-will contracts. But often a company provides its workers with personnel manuals that guarantee certain rights. The company may assure all workers that they will have a hearing and a chance to present evidence on their behalf before being fired. The legal issue then becomes whether the handbook implies a contract guaranteeing a right to a hearing or whether the company is still at liberty to fire any worker at will.

YOU BE THE JUDGE

FEDERAL EXPRESS CORP. V. DUTSCHMANN

846 S.W.2d 282, 1993 Tex. LEXIS 9
Supreme Court of Texas, 1993

FACTS: When Marcie Dutschmann began working as a courier at Federal Express, she received an Employment Handbook and Personnel Manual stating that her employment was at-will and "would continue as long as it was mutually satisfactory to both parties." The manual specified that it created no contractual rights. But it also described a "Guaranteed Fair Treatment Policy" (GFTP). According to the GFTP, any employee who was terminated would have a hearing at a Board of Review, at which he could appear and present evidence.

Federal Express fired Dutschmann in October 1987, claiming that she had falsified delivery records. She responded that her termination was in retaliation for her complaints of sexual harassment. She attempted to appeal her termination through the GFTP, but Federal Express did not allow her the kind of hearing that the handbook described. Dutschmann was not allowed to present the documents that she offered, call her own witnesses, cross-examine the company witnesses, or discuss her claims of harassment.

Dutschmann sued. At trial, Federal Express argued that Dutschmann was an employee at-will and that the company was free to fire her at any time without a hearing. Dutschmann contended that the employee handbook and manual created an implied contract that she was entitled to a full, fair hearing. The jury found that the handbooks did create an implied contract and that Federal

Express had not given her a fair hearing. The court of appeals affirmed. Federal Express appealed to the Texas Supreme Court.

YOU BE THE JUDGE: Did the employee handbook and manual create an implied contract guaranteeing a fair hearing?

ARGUMENT FOR FEDERAL EXPRESS: Your honors, when Federal Express created its employee manuals, it was well aware that some state courts have ruled that these handbooks *may* create an implied contract. And that is why Federal Express wrote employee manuals including the following statements: "The employee's employment is at-will and will continue as long as it is mutually satisfactory to both parties." "This manual does not create any contractual rights. Its use is intended only as a reference." That manual states that it is intended "solely as a guide for management and employees and is not a contract of employment and that no such contract may be implied from its provisions." We think that language is about as clear as it is possible to be, but we didn't stop there. At the inception of Ms. Dutschmann's employment, she signed an agreement stating that she understood the employee manuals *did not constitute a contract.* Freedom to contract means freedom, among other things, to create at-will employment. That is what both parties here voluntarily chose to do.

ARGUMENT FOR MS. DUTSCHMANN: Your honors, the manuals do state that the employment is at-will. But those manuals then go on to say that *all employees are guaranteed* certain rights, including the rights to a fair, thorough termination hearing. The company refused to hear her evidence and refused to see her documents, because they knew she could prove sexual harassment. So they just fired her, pretending that there was no booklet and no guarantee of a hearing.

Federal Express is trying to have it both ways. The company creates these handsome, glossy booklets, filled with assurances of fair dealing. But then Federal Express comes into court and argues that those words don't really mean anything.

Federal Express knew that guaranteeing fair treatment was a proven way to attract and retain good employees. Would Ms. Dutschmann have gone to work for Federal Express if she had been told she might be sexually harassed and then fired without a fair hearing? Of course not. When a company hands out a booklet and tells employees to rely on it, the company must also keep its part of the bargain. ▌

EXECUTORY AND EXECUTED CONTRACTS

A contract is **executory** when one or more parties have not fulfilled their obligations. Recall Gloria, who agrees to act in the producer's film beginning in three months. The moment Gloria and the producer strike their bargain, they have an executory bilateral express contract. A contract is **executed** when all parties have fulfilled their obligations. When Gloria finishes acting in the movie and the producer pays her final fee, their contract will be fully executed.

VALID, UNENFORCEABLE, VOIDABLE, AND VOID AGREEMENTS

A **valid contract** is one that satisfies all of the law's requirements. A court will therefore enforce it. The contract between Gloria and the producer is a valid contract, and if the producer fails to pay Gloria, she will win a lawsuit to collect the unpaid fee.

An **unenforceable agreement** occurs when the parties intend to form a valid bargain but a court declares that some rule of law prevents enforcing it. Suppose Gloria and the producer orally agree that she will star in his movie, which he will start filming in 18 months. The statute of frauds requires that this contract be in writing, because it cannot be completed within one year. If the producer signs up another actress two months later, Gloria has no claim against him.

A **voidable contract** occurs when the law permits one party to terminate the agreement. This happens, for example, when the other party has committed fraud or misrepresentation. Suppose that Klene Corp. induces Smart to purchase 1,000 acres of Klene land by telling Smart that there is no underground toxic waste, even though Klene knows that just under the topsoil lies an ocean of bubbling purple sludge. Klene is committing fraud. Smart may void the contract, that is, terminate it and owe nothing.

A **void agreement** is one that neither party can enforce, usually because the purpose of the deal is illegal or because one of the parties had no legal authority to make a contract.

Remedies Created by Judicial Activism

Now we turn away from true contracts and consider two remedies created by judicial activism: promissory estoppel and quasi-contract. Each of these remedies has grown in importance over the last 100 years. In each case, a sympathetic plaintiff can demonstrate an injury. But the crux of the matter is this: there is no contract. The plaintiff must hope for more "creative" relief. The two remedies can be confusingly similar. The best way to distinguish them is this:

- In **promissory estoppel** cases, the defendant made a promise that the plaintiff relied on.

- In **quasi-contract** cases, the defendant did not make any promise, but did receive a benefit from the plaintiff.

PROMISSORY ESTOPPEL

A fierce fire swept through Dana and Derek Andreason's house in Utah, seriously damaging it. The good news was that agents for Aetna Casualty promptly visited the Andreasons and helped them through the crisis. The agents reassured the couple that all of the damage was covered by their insurance, instructed them on which things to throw out, and helped them choose materials for repairing other items. The bad news was that the agents were wrong: the Andreasons' policy had expired six weeks before the fire. When Derek Andreason presented a bill for $41,957 worth of meticulously itemized work that he had done under the agents' supervision, Aetna refused to pay.

The Andreasons sued—but not for breach of contract, since the insurance agreement had expired. They sued Aetna under the legal theory of promissory estoppel: **Even when there is no contract, a plaintiff may use promissory estoppel to enforce the defendant's promise if he can show that:**

- The defendant made a promise knowing that the plaintiff would likely rely on it

- The plaintiff did rely on the promise; and

- The only way to avoid injustice is to enforce the promise.

Aetna made a promise to the Andreasons, namely, its assurance that all of the damage was covered by insurance. The company knew that the Andreasons would rely on that promise, which they did by ripping up a floor that might have been salvaged, throwing out some furniture, and buying materials to repair the house. Is enforcing the promise the only way to avoid injustice? Yes, ruled the Utah Court of Appeals.[1] The Andreasons' conduct was reasonable, based on what the Aetna agent said. Under promissory estoppel, the Andreasons received virtually the same amount they would have obtained had the insurance contract been valid.

---

[1] *Andreason v. Aetna Casualty & Surety Co.*, 848 P.2d 171, 1993 Utah App. LEXIS 26 (Utah App. 1993).

QUASI-CONTRACT

Don Easterwood leased over 5,000 acres of farmland in Jackson County, Texas, from PIC Realty for one year. The next year he obtained a second one-year lease. During each year, Easterwood farmed the land, harvested the crops, and prepared the land for the following year's planting. Toward the end of the second lease, after Easterwood had harvested his crop, he and PIC began discussing the terms of another lease. As they negotiated, Easterwood prepared the land for the following year, cutting, plowing, and disking the soil. But the negotiations for a new lease failed, and Easterwood moved off the land. He sued PIC Realty for the value of his work preparing the soil.

Did Easterwood have an express contract? Clearly not. The lease had expired. Did he have an implied contract? No. The parties were actively trying to create a new express contract, so their conduct would not create any kind of an implied agreement. How could he make any legal claim? By relying on the theory of a quasi-contract: **Even when there is no contract, a court may use quasi-contract to compensate a plaintiff who can show that:**

- The plaintiff gave some benefit to the defendant

- The plaintiff reasonably expected to be paid for the benefit and the defendant knew this; and

- The defendant would be unjustly enriched if he did not pay.

If a court finds all of these elements present, it will generally award the value of the goods or services that the plaintiff has conferred. The damages awarded are called *quantum meruit*, meaning that the plaintiff gets "as much as he deserved." The court is awarding money that it believes the plaintiff *morally ought to have*, even though there was no valid contract entitling her to it. This is judicial activism. The purpose is justice; the term is contradictory.

Don Easterwood testified that in Jackson County, it was common for a tenant farmer to prepare the soil for the following year but then move. In those cases, he claimed, the landowner compensated the farmer for the work done. Other witnesses agreed. The court ruled that indeed there was no contract, but that all elements of quasi-contract had been satisfied. Easterwood gave a benefit to PIC because the land was ready for planting. Easterwood reasonably assumed he would be paid, and PIC Realty knew it. Finally, said the court, it would be unjust to let PIC benefit without paying anything. The court ordered PIC to pay the fair market value of Easterwood's labors.

Sources of Contract Law

COMMON LAW

Express and implied contracts, promissory estoppel, and quasi-contract were all crafted, over centuries, by appellate courts deciding one contract lawsuit at a time. In this country, the basic principles are similar from one state to another, but there have been significant differences concerning most important contract doctrines. In part because of these differences, the twentieth century saw the rise of two major new sources of contract law: the **Uniform Commercial Code** and the **Restatement of Contracts**.

UNIFORM COMMERCIAL CODE

Business methods changed quickly during the first half of the twentieth century. Executives used new forms of communication, such as telephone and wire, to make deals. Transportation speeded up. Corporations routinely conducted business across state borders and around the world. Executives, lawyers, and judges wanted a body of law for commercial transactions that reflected modern business methods and provided uniformity throughout the United States. That desire gave birth to the Uniform Commercial Code (UCC), created in 1952. The drafters intended the UCC to facilitate the easy formation and enforcement of contracts in a fast-paced world. The Code governs many aspects of commerce, including the sale and leasing of goods, negotiable instruments, bank deposits, letters of credit, investment securities, secured transactions, and other commercial matters. Every state has adopted at least part of the UCC to govern commercial transactions within that state. For our purposes in studying contract, the most important part of the Code is Article 2. The entire UCC is available online at http://www.law.cornell.edu/ucc/ucc.table.html.

UCC Article 2 governs the sale of goods. "Goods" means anything movable, except for money, securities, and certain legal rights. Goods include pencils, commercial aircraft, books, and Christmas trees. Goods do not include land or a house, because neither is movable, nor do they include a stock certificate. A contract for the sale of 10,000 sneakers is governed by the UCC; a contract for the sale of a condominium in Los Angeles is governed by the California common law and its statute of frauds. Thus, when analyzing any contract problem as a student or business executive, you must note whether the agreement concerns the sale of goods.

Article 2 Alert. For more than a decade, the drafters of the UCC have analyzed and debated significant revisions to Article 2 (and other articles). As this book goes to press, the drafters are debating final changes to their proposals, so the exact provisions are unavailable. Even when they agree upon final language, those suggestions will not become law until state legislatures choose to adopt them. It will be months or possibly years before we know which states will adopt the proposals and in precisely what language (a state legislature may adopt a proposal but change its wording).

Find the status of Article 2 proposals and whether your home state has adopted the revisions, by going to http://www.nccusl.org and clicking on "Legislative status."

RESTATEMENT (SECOND) OF CONTRACTS

In 1932, the American Law Institute (ALI), a group of lawyers, scholars, and judges, drafted the Restatement of Contracts, attempting to codify what its members regarded as the best rulings of contract law. In 1979, the ALI issued a new version, the Restatement (Second) of Contracts. Like its predecessor, the Restatement (Second) is not the law anywhere, and in this respect it differs from the common law and the UCC. However, judges often refer to the Restatement (Second) when they decide cases so we, too, will seek its counsel from time to time.

AGREEMENT

Meeting of the Minds

Two parties can form a contract only if they have had a meeting of the minds. This requires that they (1) understood each other and (2) intended to reach an agreement. Recall the café conversation between Katrina and Bob, concerning the new film. Was there a meeting of the minds? Judges make an *objective* assessment of each party's intent. A court will not try to get inside Katrina's head and decide what she was thinking as she shook hands. It will look at the handshake *objectively*, deciding how a reasonable person would interpret the words and conduct. Katrina may honestly have meant to conclude a deal for $3 million with no nude scenes, while Bob might in good faith have believed he was committing himself to $2.5 million and absolute control of the script. Neither belief will control the outcome. A reasonable person observing their discussion would not have known what terms they agreed to, and hence there is no agreement.

Offer

Bargaining begins with an offer. An offer is a serious matter because it permits the other party to create a contract by accepting. **An offer is an act or a statement that proposes definite terms and permits the other party to create a contract by accepting those terms.**

The person who makes an offer is the **offeror**. The person to whom he makes that offer is the **offeree**. The terms are annoying but inescapable because, like handcuffs, all courts use them. In most contract negotiations, two parties bargain back and forth, maybe for minutes, perhaps for months. Each may make several offers, revoke some proposals, suggest counteroffers, and so forth. For our purposes, the offeror remains the one who made the first offer.

Two questions determine whether a statement is an offer:

- Did the offeror *intend* to make a bargain?
- Are the terms of the offer definite?

PROBLEMS WITH INTENT

Zachary says to Sharon, "Come work in my English language center as a teacher. I'll pay you $500 per week for a 35-hour week, for six months starting Monday." This is a valid offer. Zachary intends to make a bargain and his offer is definite. If Sharon accepts, the parties have a contract that either one can enforce. By contrast, we will consider several categories of statements that are *generally not* valid offers.

Invitations to Bargain

An invitation to bargain is not an offer. Suppose Martha telephones Joe and leaves a message on his answering machine, asking if Joe would consider selling his vacation condo on Lake Michigan. Joe faxes a signed letter to Martha saying,

"There is no way I could sell the condo for less than $150,000." Martha promptly sends Joe a cashier's check for that amount. Does she own the condo? No. Joe's fax is not an offer. It is merely an invitation to bargain. Joe is indicating that he would be happy to receive an offer from Martha. He is not promising to sell the condo for $150,000 or for any amount.

Letters of Intent

In complex business negotiations, the parties may spend months bargaining over dozens of interrelated issues. Because each party wants to protect itself during the discussions, ensuring that the other side is serious without binding itself to premature commitments, it *may* make sense during the negotiations to draft a **letter of intent**. The letter can help summarize the progress made thus far and assist the parties in securing necessary financing. But a letter of intent contains a built-in danger: one party may regard it as less than binding. Yet if it is not binding, what is it?

Jones Brothers Construction was the general contractor on a job to expand American Airlines' facilities at O'Hare International Airport. The company invited bids from subcontractors. Quake Construction bid on part of the project, and Jones Brothers orally informed the company that it had won the bid and would soon receive a contract. Jones Brothers wanted the license numbers of the subcontractors that Quake would be using, but Quake could not furnish those numbers until it had assured its subcontractors that they had the job. Quake did not want to give that assurance until it was certain of obtaining the work. So Jones Brothers sent a letter of intent stating that:

- Jones was awarding the contract to Quake

- Quake would begin the specified work immediately

- Jones would pay a lump sum price of $1,060,568

- A contract agreement with detailed terms would be prepared shortly; and

- Jones reserved the right to cancel the letter of intent if the parties could not reach a final agreement.

The parties never signed the full contract, and ultimately Jones Brothers hired another company. Quake sued, seeking to recover the money it had spent in preparation and its loss of anticipated profit. The legal issue: Was the letter of intent a valid offer?

The Illinois Supreme Court declared that the letter was ambiguous and sent the case back to the trial court. The document contained many phrases that made it seem like a firm contract. The letter awarded the work to Quake and authorized the work to begin quickly. On the other hand, the document referred to a future, formal contract, indicating that the parties did not yet consider themselves bound, and it permitted Jones to cancel the letter of intent.[2]

So after several years of litigation, Jones Brothers and Quake had to go *back* to the trial court to establish whether they intended the letter to be binding. Every year there are countless cases just like *Quake*. The problem is that both

---

[2] *Quake Construction v. American Airlines*, 141 Ill. 2d 281, 565 N.E.2d 990, 1990 Ill. LEXIS 151 (Ill. 1990).

sides permit ambiguity and vagueness to enter their negotiations. Sometimes parties do this accidentally, by paying too little attention to what they are saying. The solution is simple: think carefully before offering or responding.

At other times, with sophisticated businesspeople, ambiguity may not be so accidental, as one party is trying to get a commitment from the other side without obligating itself. A party may feel *almost* ready to commit, yet still have reservations. It wants the other party to make a commitment so that planning can go forward. This is understandable, but dangerous.

If you were negotiating for Jones Brothers and wanted to clarify negotiations without committing your company, how could you do it? From Quake's point of view, how should you proceed?

Advertisements

An advertisement is generally not an offer. An advertisement is merely a request for offers. The consumer makes the offer by selecting merchandise in a store and taking it to the cashier. The seller is free to reject the offer. However, while the common law regards advertisements as mere solicitations, consumers do have protection from those shopkeepers intent upon deceit. Every state has some form of **consumer protection statute**. These statutes outlaw false advertising. For example, an automobile dealer who advertises a remarkably low price but then has only one automobile at that price has probably violated a consumer protection statute because the ad was published in bad faith, to trick consumers into coming to the dealership.

PROBLEMS WITH DEFINITENESS

It is not enough that the offeror intends to enter into an agreement. **The terms of the offer must be definite.** If they are vague, then even if the offeree "accepts" the deal, a court does not have enough information to enforce it and there is no contract.

You want a friend to work in your store for the holiday season. This is a definite offer: "I offer you a job as a salesclerk in the store from November 1 through December 29, 40 hours per week at $10 per hour." But suppose, by contrast, you say: "I offer you a job as a salesclerk in the store from November 1 through December 29, 40 hours per week. We will work out a fair wage once we see how busy things get." Your friend replies, "That's fine with me." This offer is indefinite. What is a fair wage? $5 per hour? $15 per hour? How will the determination be made? There is no binding agreement.

TERMINATION OF OFFERS

As we have seen, the great power that an offeree has is to form a contract by accepting an offer. But this power is lost when the offer is terminated, which can happen in several ways:

Revocation. In general, the offeror may revoke the offer any time before it has been accepted. Revocation is effective as soon as the offeree receives it.

Rejection. If an offeree rejects an offer, the rejection immediately terminates the offer. Suppose a major accounting firm telephones you and offers a job, starting at $80,000. You respond, "Nah. I'm gonna work on my surfing for a year or two."

The next day you come to your senses and write the firm, accepting its offer. No contract. Your rejection terminated the offer and ended your power to accept.

Counteroffer.   Frederick faxes Kim, offering to sell a 50 percent interest in the Fab Hotel in New York for only $135 million. Kim faxes back, offering to pay $115 million. Moments later, Kim's business partner convinces her that Frederick's offer was a bargain, and she faxes an acceptance of his $135 million offer. Does Kim have a binding deal? No. A counteroffer is a rejection. The parties have no contract at any price.

Expiration.   When an offer specifies a time limit for acceptance, that period is binding. If the offer specifies no time limit, the offeree has a reasonable period in which to accept.

Destruction of the subject matter.   A used car dealer offers to sell you a rare 1938 Bugatti for $75,000 if you bring cash the next day. You arrive, suitcase stuffed with century notes, just in time to see the dealer fall out of a blimp, dropping 3,000 feet through the air and crushing the Bugatti. The dealer's offer terminated.

Acceptance

As we have seen, when there is a valid offer outstanding, the offeree can create a contract by accepting. **The offeree must say or do something to accept.** Silence, though golden, is not acceptance. Marge telephones Vick and leaves a message on his answering machine: "I'll pay $75 for your law textbook from last semester. I'm desperate to get a copy, so I will assume you agree unless I hear from you by 6:00 tonight." Marge hears nothing by the deadline and assumes she has a deal. She is mistaken. Vick neither said nor did anything to indicate that he accepted.

When the offer is for a bilateral contract, the offeree generally must accept by making a promise. An employer calls you and says, "If you're able to start work two weeks from today, we can pay you $5,000 per month. Can you do it?" That is an offer for a bilateral contract. You must accept by promising to start in two weeks.

When the offer is for a unilateral contract, the offeree must accept by performing. A newspaper telephones you: "If you write us a 5,000-word article on iguanas that can play bridge, and get it to us by Friday at noon, we'll pay you $750." The newspaper does not want a promise, it wants the article. If—and only if—your work is ready on time, you get paid.

MIRROR IMAGE RULE

If only he had known! A splendid university, an excellent position as department chair—gone. And all because of the mirror image rule. The Ohio State University wrote to Philip Foster offering him an appointment as a professor and chair of the art history department. His position was to begin July 1, and he had until June 2 to accept the job. On June 2, Foster telephoned the Dean and left a message accepting the position, **effective July 15**. Later, Foster thought better of it and wrote the university, accepting the school's starting date of July 1. Too late! Professor Foster never did occupy that chair at Ohio State. The court held that since his acceptance varied the starting date, it was a counteroffer. And a counteroffer, as we know, is a rejection.[3]

The common law mirror image rule requires that acceptance be on precisely the same terms as the offer. If the acceptance contains terms that add to or contradict the offer, even in minor ways, courts generally consider it a counteroffer. The rule worked reasonably well in the nineteenth century, when parties would write an original contract and exchange it, penciling in any changes. But now that businesses use standardized forms to purchase most goods and services, the rule creates enormous difficulties. Sellers use forms they have prepared, with all conditions stated to their advantage, and buyers employ their own forms, with terms they prefer. The forms are exchanged in the mail (or electronically), with neither side clearly agreeing to the other party's terms.

The problem is known as the "battle of forms." Once again, the UCC has entered the fray, attempting to provide flexibility and common sense for those contracts involving the sale of goods. But for contracts governed by the common law, such as Professor Foster's, the mirror image rule is still the law.

UCC AND THE BATTLE OF FORMS

UCC §2-207 dramatically modifies the mirror image rule for the sale of goods. Under this provision, an acceptance that adds additional or different terms *will often create a contract*. The rule is intricate, but may be summarized this way:

> For the sale of goods, the most important factor is whether the parties believe they have a binding agreement. If their conduct indicates that they have a deal, they probably do.

> If the offeree *adds new* terms to the offer, acceptance by the offeror generally creates a binding agreement.

> If the offeree *changes* the terms of the offer, a court will probably rely on general principles of the UCC to create a fair contract.

> If a party wants a contract on its terms only, with no changes, it must clearly indicate that.

Suppose Wholesaler writes to Manufacturer, offering to buy "10,000 wheelbarrows at $50 per unit. Payable on delivery, 30 days from today's date." Manufacturer writes back, "We accept your offer of 10,000 wheelbarrows at $50 per unit, payable on delivery. Interest at normal trade rates for unpaid balances." Manufacturer clearly intends to form a contract. The company has added a new term, but there is still a valid agreement.

Clickwraps and Shrinkwraps. You want to purchase Attila brand software and download it to your computer. You type in your credit card number and other information, agreeing to pay $99. Attila also requires that you "read and agree to" all of the company's terms. You click "I agree," without having read one word of the terms. Three frustrating weeks later, tired of trying to operate defective

---

[3] *Foster v. Ohio State University*, 41 Ohio App. 3d 86, 534 N.E.2d 1220, 1987 Ohio App. LEXIS 10761 (Ohio Ct. App. 1987).

Attilaware, you demand a refund and threaten to sue. The company breezily replies that you are barred from suing, because the terms you agreed to included an arbitration clause. To resolve any disputes, you must travel to Attila's hometown, halfway across the nation, use an arbitrator that the company chooses, pay one-half the arbitrator's fee, and also pay Attila's legal bills if you should lose. The agreement makes it financially impossible for you to get your money back. Is that contract enforceable?

You have entered into a "clickwrap" agreement. Similar agreements, called "shrinkwraps," are packaged inside many electronic products. A shrinkwrap notice might require that before inserting a purchased CD into you computer, you must read and agree to all terms in the brochure. Clickwraps and shrinkwraps often include arbitration clauses. They frequently limit the seller's liability if anything goes wrong, saying that the manufacturer's maximum responsibility is to refund the purchase price (even if the software destroys your hard drive).

Most of the courts that have analyzed these issues have ruled that clickwrap and shrinkwrap agreements are indeed binding, even against consumers. Some of the judges have relied on §2-207 to reach that conclusion (holding that any additional terms did not materially alter the agreement), while others have used different UCC provisions. The courts have emphasized that sellers are entitled to offer a product on any terms they wish, and that shrinkwrap and clickwrap are the most efficient methods of including complicated terms in a small space. At least one court has *refused* to enforce such contracts against a consumer, stating that the buyer never understood or agreed to the shrinkwrapped terms. However, the trend is toward enforcement of these agreements. Think before you click![4]

CONSIDERATION

We have all made promises that we soon regretted. Mercifully, the law does not hold us accountable for everything we say. Yet some promises must be enforced. Which ones? The doctrine of consideration exists for one purpose: to distinguish promises that are binding from those that are not.

Consideration is a required element of any contract. **Consideration means that there must be bargaining that leads to an exchange between the parties.** (See Exhibit 9.1) *Bargaining* indicates that each side is obligating itself in some way to *induce the other side to agree*. Generally, a court will enforce one party's promise only if the other party did something or promised something in exchange.

If one party makes a promise without some kind of bargaining, there is generally no contract. Carol Kelsoe had worked at International Wood Products for many years. One day, her supervisor surprised her by promising her 5 percent of the company's stock. Unfortunately, he never gave her those shares. Heartbroken, Kelsoe sued—and lost.[5] Kelsoe had given nothing in exchange for

---

[4] *ProCD, Inc. v Zeidenberg*, 86 F.3d 1447 (7th Cir. 1996) is the leading case to enforce shrinkwrap agreements (and by extension, clickwraps). *Klocek v. Gateway*, 104 F. Supp. 1332 (D. Kan. 2000) is one of the few cases to reject such contracts. *Klocek*, however, was later dismissed for failure to reach the federal court $75,000 jurisdictional level.

[5] *Kelsoe v. International Wood Products, Inc.*, 588 So. 2d 877, 1991 Ala. LEXIS 1014 (Supreme Court of Alabama, 1991).

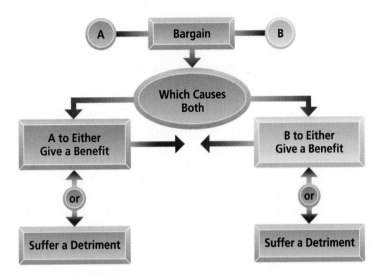

Exhibit 9.1
There is consideration to support a contract when A and B bargain, and their bargaining causes both A and B either to give a benefit to the other or to suffer a detriment.

her supervisor's words. There was no consideration on her part, and she could not enforce his promise. If Kelsoe had assured him that she would remain at International Wood for three extra years (or three extra days) in exchange for the stock, that would have been consideration, and she would have collected her shares.

The thing bargained for can be another promise or action. Usually one party bargains for another promise. Jennifer says to Ben, "I'm supposed to fly to Chicago in a week, to give a speech. Will you do it for me? I'll give you $15,000." "Sure," Ben responds, "I'll do that for $15,000." The very next day Jennifer changes her mind. Too late. Ben's *promise* to go to Chicago was consideration. The parties have a deal that either one can enforce.

The thing bargained for can be action, rather than a promise. Manny tells Sandra, "I need someone to hook up my cable TV by tonight at 8:00. If you get it done, I'll give you $200." Manny seeks action, not a promise. If Sandra connects the television on time, her work is consideration and the parties have a binding deal.

The thing bargained for can be a promise to do something or a promise to refrain from doing something. Megan promises to *deliver 1,000* canoes in two months if Casey agrees to pay $300 per canoe. Megan's promise to act is consideration. The most famous of all consideration lawsuits involved a promise to refrain. The case began in 1869, when a well-meaning uncle made a promise to his nephew. Ever since the nephew responded, generations of American law students have dutifully inhaled the facts and sworn by its wisdom; now you, too, may drink it in.

HAMER V. SIDWAY

124 N.Y.538, 27 N.E.256, 1891 N.Y. LEXIS 1396
New York Court of Appeals, 1891

FACTS: This is a story with two Storys. William Story wanted his nephew to grow up healthy and prosperous. He promised the 15-year-old boy (also William Story) $5,000 if the lad would refrain from drinking liquor, using tobacco, swearing, and playing cards or billiards for money until his twenty-first birthday. (In that wild era—can you believe it?—the nephew had a legal right to do all those things.) The nephew agreed and, what is more, he kept his word. When he reached his twenty-first birthday, the nephew notified his uncle that he had honored the agreement. The uncle congratulated the young man and promised to give him the money, but said he would wait a few more years before handing over the cash, until the nephew was mature enough to handle such a large sum. The uncle died in 1887 without having paid, and his estate refused to honor the promise. Because the nephew had transferred his rights in the money, it was a man named Hamer who eventually sought to collect from the uncle's estate. The estate argued that since the nephew had given no consideration for the uncle's promise, there was no enforceable contract. The trial court found for the plaintiff, and the uncle's estate appealed.

ISSUE: Did the nephew give consideration for the uncle's promise?

EXCERPTS FROM JUSTICE PARKER'S DECISION: The defendant contends that the contract was without consideration to support it, and therefore invalid. He asserts that the promisee, by refraining from the use of liquor and tobacco, was not harmed, but benefited; that that which he did was best for him to do, independently of his uncle's promise,—and insists that it follows that, unless the promisor was benefited, the contract was without consideration,— a contention which, if well founded, would seem to leave open for controversy in many cases whether that which the promisee did or omitted to do was in fact of such benefit to him as to leave no consideration to support the enforcement of the promisor's agreement. Such a rule could not be tolerated, and is without foundation in the law. Courts will not ask whether the thing which forms the consideration does in fact benefit the promisee or a third party, or is of any substantial value to any one. It is enough that something is promised, done, forborne, or suffered by the party to whom the promise is made as consideration for the promise made to him.

Now applying this rule to the facts before us, the promisee used tobacco, occasionally drank liquor, and he had a legal right to do so. That right he abandoned for a period of years upon the strength of the promise of the testator [that is, the uncle] that for such forbearance he would give him $5,000. We need not speculate on the effort which may have been required to give up the use of those stimulants. It is sufficient that he restricted his lawful freedom of action within certain prescribed limits upon the faith of his uncle's agreement, and now, having fully performed the conditions imposed, it is of no moment whether such performance actually proved a benefit to the promisor, and the court will not inquire into it. ◢

ILLUSORY PROMISE

Annabel calls Jim and says, "I'll sell you my bicycle for 325 bucks. Interested?" Jim says, "I'll look at it tonight in the bike rack. If I like what I see, I'll pay you three and a quarter in the morning." At sunrise, Jim shows up with the $325 but Annabel refuses to sell. Can Jim enforce their deal? No. He said he would buy the bicycle *if he liked it*, keeping for himself the power to get out of the agreement for any reason at all. He is not committing himself to do anything, and the law considers his promise illusory, that is, not really a promise at all. **An illusory promise is not consideration.** Because he has given no consideration, there is no contract and *neither party* can enforce the deal.

LEGALITY

Soheil Sadri, a California resident, did some serious gambling at Caesar's Tahoe casino in Nevada. And lost. To keep gambling, he wrote checks to Caesar's and then signed two memoranda pledging to repay money advanced. After two days, with his losses totaling more than $22,000, he went home. Back in California, Sadri stopped payment on the checks and refused to pay any of the money he owed Caesar's. The casino sued, and recovered . . . nothing. Sadri relied on an important legal principle to defeat the suit: **a contract that is illegal is void and unenforceable.** We will examine a variety of contracts that may be void.

Gambling is one of America's fastest growing businesses, but a controversial one. Because our citizens—and our states—are divided over the ethics of wagering, conflicts such as the dispute between Sadri and Caesar's are inevitable. The basic rule, however, is clear: **a gambling contract is illegal unless it is specifically authorized by state statute.** In California, as in many states, gambling on credit is not allowed. In other words, it is illegal to lend money to help someone wager. A contract based on a gambling debt is unenforceable. However, in Nevada, gambling on credit is legal, and debt memoranda such as Sadri's are enforceable contracts. Caesar's sued Sadri in California (where he lived). The court admitted that California's attitude toward gambling had changed, and that bingo, poker clubs, and lotteries were common. Nonetheless, the court denied that the new tolerance extended to wagering on credit, stating: "The judiciary cannot protect pathological gamblers from themselves, but we can refuse to participate in their financial ruin."[6]

Caesar's lost and Sadri kept his money. The dispute is a useful starting place from which to examine contract legality because it illustrates two important themes. First, morality is a significant part of contract legality. In refusing to enforce an obligation that Sadri undeniably had made, the California court relied on the human and social consequences of gambling and on the ethics of judicial enforcement of gambling debts. Second, "void" really means just that: **a court will not assist either party to an illegal agreement**, even if its refusal leaves one party obviously shortchanged.

RESTRAINT OF TRADE

Free trade is the basis of the American economy, and any bargain that restricts it is suspect. Most restraint of free trade is barred by antitrust law. But it is the common law that still regulates one restriction on trade: agreements to refrain from competition. Some of these agreements are legal, some are void. They are *very* common. Many readers of this book will read such a clause in their own employment contract.

---

[6] *Metropolitan Creditors Service of Sacramento v. Sadri*, 15 Cal. App. 4th 1821, 1993 Cal. App. LEXIS 559, 19 Cal. Rptr. 2d 646 (Cal. Ct. App. 1993).

To be valid, an agreement not to compete must be ancillary to a legitimate bargain. "Ancillary" means that the noncompetition agreement must be part of a larger agreement. Suppose Cliff sells his gasoline station to Mina and the two agree that Cliff will not open a competing gas station within five miles anytime during the next two years. Cliff's agreement not to compete is ancillary to the sale of his service station. His noncompetition promise is enforceable. But suppose that Cliff and Mina already had the only two gas stations within 35 miles. They agree between themselves not to hire each other's workers. Their agreement might be profitable to them, because each could now keep wages artificially low. But their deal is ancillary to no legitimate bargain, and it is therefore void.

The two most common settings for legitimate noncompetition agreements are the *sale of a business* and an *employment relationship*.

Sale of a Business

Kory has operated a real estate office, Hearth Attack, in a small city for 35 years, building an excellent reputation and many ties with the community. She offers to sell you the business and its goodwill for $300,000. But you need assurance that Kory will not take your money and promptly open a competing office across the street. With her reputation and connections, she would ruin your chances of success. You insist on a noncompete clause in the sale contract. In this clause, Kory promises that for one year she will not open a new real estate office or go to work for a competing company within a 10-mile radius of Hearth Attack. Suppose, six months after selling you the business, Kory goes to work for a competing realtor, two blocks away. You seek an injunction to prevent her from working. Who wins?

When a noncompete agreement is ancillary to the sale of a business, it is enforceable if reasonable in time, geographic area, and scope of activity. In other words, a court will not enforce a noncompete agreement that lasts an unreasonably long time, covers an unfairly large area, or prohibits the seller of the business from doing a type of work that she never had done before. Measured by this test, Kory is almost certainly bound by her agreement. One year is a reasonable time to allow you to get your new business started. A 10-mile radius is probably about the area that Hearth Attack covers, and realty is obviously a fair business from which to prohibit Kory. A court will grant the injunction, barring Kory from her new job.

If, on the other hand, the noncompetition agreement had prevented Kory from working anywhere within 200 miles of Hearth Attack, and she started working 50 miles away, a court would refuse to enforce the contract.

Employment

When you sign an employment contract, the document may well contain a noncompete clause. Employers have legitimate worries that employees might go to a competitor and take with them trade secrets or other proprietary information. Some employers, though, attempt to place harsh restrictions on their employees, perhaps demanding a blanket agreement that the employee will never go to work for a competitor. Once again, courts look at the reasonableness of restrictions placed on an employee's future work. Because the agreement now involves the very livelihood of the worker, a court scrutinizes the agreement more closely.

A noncompete clause in an employment contract is generally reasonable— and enforceable—only to the extent necessary to protect (1) trade secrets,

(2) confidential information, or (3) customer lists developed over an extended period. In general, other restrictions on future employment are unenforceable.[7] Suppose that Gina, an engineer, goes to work for Fission Chips, a silicon chip manufacturer that specializes in defense work. She signs a noncompete agreement promising never to work for a competitor. Over a period of three years, Gina learns some of Fission's proprietary methods of etching information onto the chips. She acquires a great deal of new expertise about chips generally. And she periodically deals with Fission Chips' customers, all of whom are well-known software and hardware manufacturers. Gina accepts an offer from WriteSmall, a competitor. Fission Chips races into court, seeking an injunction to block Gina from working for WriteSmall.

This injunction threatens Gina's career. If she cannot work for a competitor, or use her general engineering skills, what *will* she do? And for exactly that reason, no court will grant such a broad order. The court will allow Gina to work for competitors, including WriteSmall. It will order her not to use or reveal any trade secrets belonging to Fission. She will, however, be permitted to use the general expertise she has acquired, and she may contact former customers since anyone could get their names from the yellow pages.

The following chart summarizes the factors that courts look at in noncompete agreements.

The Legality of Noncompete Clauses	
Type of Noncompete Agreement	**When Enforceable**
Not ancillary to a sale of business or employment	Never
Ancillary to a sale of business	If reasonable in time, geography, and scope of activity
Ancillary to employment	Contract is *more* likely to be enforced when it involves: • Trade secrets or confidential information: these are almost always protected • Customer lists developed over extended period of time and carefully protected • Limited time and geographical scope • Vital to protect the employer's business Contract is *less* likely to be enforced when it involves: • Employee who already had the skills when he arrived, or merely developed general skills on the job • Customer lists that can be derived from public sources • Excessive time or geographical scope • Unduly harsh on the employee or contrary to public interest

Back with more law in a minute, but first how about something to eat?

---

[7] If the agreement restricts the employee from *starting a new business*, a court may apply the more lenient standard used for the sale of a business; the noncompete clause will be enforced if reasonable in time, geography, and scope of activity.

LIAUTAUD V. LIAUTAUD

221 F.3d 981
United States Court of Appeals for the Seventh Circuit, 2000

FACTS: Jim Liautaud owned and operated a chain of gourmet submarine sandwich shops in Illinois called Jimmy John's, Inc. When his cousin, Michael, inquired about opening his own sandwich shop in Madison, Wisconsin, Jim agreed to provide his "secrets of success." Jim sent Michael this letter, outlining their agreement:

> I want to confirm at this time exactly what we agreed on so that it is clear and understood by both parties. The agreement:
>
> 1. Mike will open up a sub shop in Madison using Jimmy John's products and systems.
>
> 2. Mike can open up as many shops [as] he would like in Madison only.
>
> 3. If you want to expand the sub/club business beyond Madison you will do so using Jimmy John's sub shops as a partner or franchisee. This is subject to 100% agreement on both parties. If you don't use Jimmy John's Inc. you will not expand the sub/club business beyond Madison.
>
> 4. You will not disclose to any one: recipes, products or systems that are given to you. (Except your managers who run your store).
>
> I believe thats [sic] what we agreed on. If I have made any misrepresentations of our agreement please correct them in the margin of this letter and return a copy to me. If I don't receive a copy I'll assume this letter to be the agreement.

Jim then helped Michael open the shop in Madison. A few years later, Michael opened a sandwich shop outside that city, in LaCrosse, Wisconsin. Jim sued to enforce their agreement. The district court found the agreement unreasonable and void, and Jim appealed.

ISSUE: Was the noncompetition agreement valid?

EXCERPTS FROM JUDGE RIPPLE'S DECISION: For this restrictive covenant to be reasonable, its terms (1) must not be greater than necessary to protect Jim, (2) must not be oppressive to Michael, and (3) must not be injurious to the general public.

Jim asserts first that, given the nature of his business and the trade secrets involved, the restraint on Michael's expansion was necessary to protect his business interests. He explains that his trade secrets are the fundamental elements of his business success. According to Michael, Jim does not have a legitimate business interest in preventing Michael from establishing submarine sandwich shops where Jim is not located.

Here, Michael is prevented from expanding anywhere in the world outside of Madison. Jim's articulated legitimate business interest, protection of his trade secrets, does not show why Michael should not be able to expand to locations other than Madison, even when Jim is not in those locations. Jim has not indicated that he plans to expand into the markets where Michael is located.

Moreover, the agreement is oppressive to Michael because it restricts him from expanding his sandwich business, regardless of whether he continues to use Jim's trade secrets. According to the terms of the agreement, Michael could not open *any* kind of sandwich shop outside Madison without Jim's approval. Finally, the complete ban on expansion is injurious to the public because it completely restricts competition. Although it seems "fair" that Jim should receive some compensation for Michael's use of Jim's trade secrets, this noncompetition agreement, without any geographic limitations, is not the reasonable means of accomplishing that end.

The agreement also fails to provide any limits on time. Instead, the agreement, as written, merely states that Michael may not expand his business. Read literally, this means that Michael may not expand his business beyond Madison for the rest of his life. Jim has not shown that he needs to prevent Michael from ever expanding beyond Madison in order to protect his business interests. Also, as stated above, under the agreement, Michael is prevented from ever expanding his shops, even if he develops his own recipes and business strategies. Finally, this infinite agreement injures the public because it stifles competition. We conclude that, in light of the severe and unnecessary restrictions on Michael, this covenant not to compete is unreasonable and is, therefore, void as against public policy.

Affirmed. ◢

EXCULPATORY CLAUSES

You decide to capitalize on your expert ability as a skier and open a ski school in Colorado, "Pike's Pique." But you realize that skiing sometimes causes injuries, so you require anyone signing up for lessons to sign this form:

> I agree to hold Pike's Pique and its employees entirely harmless in the event that I am injured in any way or for any reason or cause, including but not limited to any acts, whether negligent or otherwise, of Pike's Pique or any employee or agent thereof.

The day your school opens, Sara Beth, an instructor, deliberately pushes Toby over a cliff because Toby criticized her color combinations. Eddie, a beginning student, "blows out" his knee attempting an advanced racing turn. And Maureen, another student, reaches the bottom of a steep run and slams into a snowmobile that Sara Beth parked there. Maureen, Eddie, and Toby's families all sue Pike's Pique. You defend based on the form you had them sign. Does it save the day?

The form on which you are relying is an **exculpatory clause**, that is, one that attempts to release you from liability in the event of injury to another party. Exculpatory clauses are common. Ski schools use them and so do parking lots, landlords, warehouses, and day-care centers. All manner of businesses hope to avoid large tort judgments by requiring their customers to give up any right to recover. Is such a clause valid? Sometimes. Courts frequently—but not always—ignore exculpatory clauses, finding that one party was forcing the other party to give up legal rights that no one should be forced to surrender.

An exculpatory clause is generally unenforceable when it attempts to exclude an intentional tort or gross negligence. When Sara Beth pushes Toby over a cliff, that is the intentional tort of battery. A court will not enforce the exculpatory clause. Sara Beth is clearly liable.[8] As to the snowmobile at the bottom of the run, if a court determines that was gross negligence (carelessness far greater than ordinary negligence), then the exculpatory clause will again be ignored. If, however, it was ordinary negligence, then we must continue the analysis.

An exculpatory clause is generally unenforceable when the affected activity is in the public interest, such as medical care, public transportation, or some essential service. What about Eddie's suit against Pike's Pique? Eddie claims that he should never have been allowed to attempt an advanced maneuver. His suit is for ordinary negligence, and the exculpatory clause probably does bar him from recovery. Skiing is a recreational activity. No one is obligated to do it, and there is no strong public interest in ensuring that we have access to ski slopes.

An exculpatory clause is generally unenforceable when the parties have greatly unequal bargaining power. When Maureen flies to Colorado, suppose that the airline requires her to sign a form contract with an exculpatory clause. Because the airline almost certainly has much greater bargaining power, it can afford to offer a "take it or leave it" contract. But because the bargaining power is so unequal, the clause is probably unenforceable.

An exculpatory clause is generally unenforceable unless the clause is clearly written and readily visible. Thus, if Pike's Pique gave all ski students an eight-page contract, and the exculpatory clause was at the bottom of page seven in small print, the average customer would never notice it. The clause would be void.

---

[8] Note that Pike's Pique is probably not liable under agency law principles that preclude an employer's liability for an employee's intentional tort.

Unconscionable Contracts

Gail Waters was young, naive, and insecure. A serious injury when she was 12 years old left her with an annuity, that is, a guaranteed annual payment for many years. When Gail was 21, she became involved with Thomas Beauchemin, an ex-convict, who introduced her to drugs. Beauchemin suggested that Gail sell her annuity to some friends of his, and she agreed. Beauchemin arranged for a lawyer to draw up a contract, and Gail signed it. She received one $50,000 payment for her annuity, which at that time had a cash value of $189,000 and was worth, over its remaining 25 years, $694,000. Gail later decided this was not an excellent bargain. Was the contract enforceable? That depends on the law of unconscionability.

An unconscionable contract is one that a court refuses to enforce because of fundamental unfairness. Historically, a contract was considered unconscionable if it was "such as no man in his senses and not under delusion would make on the one hand, and as no honest and fair man would accept on the other."[9] The two factors that most often lead a court to find unconscionability are (1) **oppression**, meaning that one party used its superior power to force a contract on the weaker party, and (2) **surprise**, meaning that the weaker party did not fully understand the consequences of its agreement.

Gail Waters won her case. The Massachusetts high court ruled:

> Beauchemin introduced the plaintiff to drugs, exhausted her credit card accounts to the sum of $6,000, unduly influenced her, suggested that the plaintiff sell her annuity contract, initiated the contract negotiations, was the agent of the defendants, and benefited from the contract between the plaintiff and the defendants. The defendants were represented by legal counsel; the plaintiff was not. The cash value of the annuity policy at the time the contract was executed was approximately four times greater than the price to be paid by the defendants. For payment of not more than $50,000 the defendants were to receive an asset that could be immediately exchanged for $189,000, or they could elect to hold it for its guaranteed term and receive $694,000.
>
> The defendants assumed no risk and the plaintiff gained no advantage. We are satisfied that the disparity of interests in this contract is so gross that the court cannot resist the inference that it was improperly obtained and is unconscionable.[10]

Capacity and Consent

For Kevin Green, it was love at first sight. She was sleek, as quick as a cat, and a beautiful deep blue. He paid $4,600 cash for the used Camaro. The car soon blew a gasket, and Kevin demanded his money back. But the Camaro came with no guarantee, and Star Chevrolet, the dealer, refused. Kevin repaired the car himself. Next, some unpleasantness on the highway left the car a worthless wreck. Kevin received the full value of the car from his insurance company. Then he sued the dealer, seeking a refund of his purchase price. The dealer pointed out that it was not responsible for the accident, and that the car had no warranty of any kind. Yet the court awarded Kevin the full value of his car. How can this be?

---

[9] *Hume v. United States*, 132 U.S. 406, 411, 10 S. Ct. 134, 1889 U.S. LEXIS 1888 (1889), quoting *Earl of Chesterfield v. Janssen*, 38 Eng. Rep. 82, 100 (Ch. 1750).

[10] *Waters v. Min Ltd.*, 412 Mass. 64, 587 N.E.2d 231, 1992 Mass. LEXIS 66 (1992).

The automobile dealer ignored *legal capacity*. Kevin Green was only 16 years old when he bought the car, and a minor, said the court, has the right to cancel any agreement he made anytime he wants to, for any reason.

Capacity concerns the legal ability of a party to enter a contract. Someone may lack capacity because of his young age or mental infirmity. Consent refers to whether a contracting party truly understood what he was getting into and whether he made the agreement voluntarily. Consent issues arise most often in cases of fraud and mistake.

Capacity

Capacity is the legal ability to enter into a contract. An adult of sound mind has the legal capacity to contract. Generally, any deal she enters into will be enforced if all elements we have seen—agreement, consideration, and so forth—are present. But two groups of people usually lack legal capacity: minors and those with a mental impairment.

MINORS

A minor is someone under the age of 18. Because a minor lacks legal capacity, she normally can create only a voidable contract. **A voidable contract may be canceled by the party who lacks capacity.** Notice that *only the party lacking capacity* may cancel the agreement. So a minor who enters into a contract generally may choose between enforcing the agreement or negating it. The other party, however, has no such right.

DISAFFIRMANCE

A minor who wishes to escape from a contract generally may **disaffirm** it, that is, he may notify the other party that he refuses to be bound by the agreement. Because Kevin was 16 when he signed, the deal was voidable. When the Camaro blew a gasket and the lad informed Star Chevrolet that he wanted his money back, he was disaffirming the contract, which he could do for any reason at all. Kevin was entitled to his money back. If Star Chevrolet had understood the law of capacity, it would have towed the Camaro away and returned the young man's $4,600. At least the dealership would have had a repairable automobile.

RESTITUTION

A minor who disaffirms a contract must return the consideration he has received, to the extent he is able. Restoring the other party to its original position is called **restitution**. The consideration that Kevin Green received in the contract was, of course, the Camaro. If Star Chevrolet had delivered a check for $4,600, Kevin would have been obligated to return the car.

What happens if the minor is not able to return the consideration because he no longer has it or it has been destroyed? Most states hold that the minor is still entitled to his money back. Kevin Green got his money and Star Chevrolet received a fine lesson.

MENTALLY IMPAIRED PERSONS

A person suffers from a mental impairment if by reason of mental illness or defect he is unable to understand the nature and consequences of the transaction.[11] The mental impairment can be insanity that has been formally declared by a court or mental illness that has never been ruled on but is now evident. The impairment may also be due to some other mental illness, such as schizophrenia, or to mental retardation, brain injury, senility, or any other cause that renders the person unable to understand the nature and consequences of the contract.

A party suffering a mental impairment generally creates only a voidable contract. The impaired person has the right to disaffirm the contract just as a minor does. But again, the contract is voidable, not void. The mentally impaired party generally has the right to full performance if she wishes. Similar rules apply in cases of drug or alcohol **intoxication**. When one party is so intoxicated that he cannot understand the nature and consequences of the transaction, the contract is voidable.

Reality of Consent

Smiley offers to sell you his house for $300,000, and you agree in writing to buy. After you move in, you discover that the house is sinking into the earth at the rate of six inches per week. In 12 months, your only access to the house will be through the chimney. You sue, asking to **rescind, which means to cancel the agreement**. You argue that when you signed the contract you did not truly consent because you lacked essential information. In this section, we look at issues of misrepresentation, fraud, and mistake.

MISREPRESENTATION AND FRAUD

Misrepresentation occurs when a party to a contract says something that is factually wrong. "This house has no termites," says a homeowner to a prospective buyer. If the house is swarming with the nasty pests, the statement is a misrepresentation. The misrepresentation might be innocent or fraudulent. If the owner believes the statement to be true and has a good reason for that belief, he has made an **innocent misrepresentation**. If the owner knows that it is false, the statement is **fraudulent misrepresentation**. To explain these concepts, we will assume that two people are discussing a possible deal. One is the "maker," that is, the person who makes the statement that is later disputed. The other is the "injured person," the one who eventually claims to have been injured by the statement. In order to rescind the contract, the injured person must show that the maker's statement was either fraudulent or a material misrepresentation. She does not have to show both. Innocent misrepresentation and fraud each make a contract voidable. **To rescind a contract based on misrepresentation or fraud, a party must show three things: (1) there was a false statement of fact; (2) the statement was fraudulent or material; and (3) the injured person justifiably relied on the statement.**

---

[11] Restatement (Second) of Contracts §15.

Element One: False Statement of Fact

The injured party must show a false statement of fact. Notice that this does not mean the statement was a lie. If a homeowner says that the famous architect Stanford White designed his house, but Bozo Loco actually did the work, it is a false statement. The owner might have a good reason for the error. Perhaps a local history book identifies the house as a Stanford White. Or the owner's words might be an intentional lie. In either case, it is a false statement of fact.

An **opinion**, though, is not a statement of fact. A realtor says, "I think land values around here will be going up 20 or 30 percent for the foreseeable future." That statement is pretty enticing to a buyer, but it is not a false statement of fact. The maker is clearly stating her own opinion, and the buyer who relies on it does so at his peril. A close relative of opinion is something called puffery. A statement is **puffery** when a reasonable person would realize that it is a sales pitch, representing the exaggerated opinion of the seller. Puffery is not a statement of fact and is never a basis for rescission.

Element Two: Fraud or Materiality

This is the heart of the case. The injured party must demonstrate that the statement was fraudulent or material:

- The statement was *fraudulent* if the maker intended to induce the other party to contract, either knowing that her words were false or uncertain that they were true.

- The statement was *material* if the maker expected the other party to rely on her words in reaching an agreement.

So the injured party can win by showing either of two very different things. Fraud indicates a bad faith statement, whereas material misrepresentation signifies that the words were inaccurate—and effective.

Consider the examples in the chart on the following page.

Element Three: Justifiable Reliance

The injured party must also show that she actually did rely on the false statement and that her reliance was reasonable. Suppose the seller of a gas station lies through his teeth about the structural soundness of the building. The buyer believes what he hears but does not much care, because he plans to demolish the building and construct a day-care center. There was fraud but no reliance, and the buyer may not rescind.

Plaintiff's Remedy for Misrepresentation or Fraud

Both innocent and fraudulent misrepresentation permit the injured party to rescind the contract. In other words, the injured party who proves all three elements will get her money back. She will, of course, have to make restitution to the other party. If she bought land and now wants to rescind, she must return the property to the seller.

But the injured party is not forced to rescind the deal if it makes financial sense to go forward with it. After signing a contract to buy a new house, Nancy learns that the building has a terrible heating system. A new one will cost $12,000. If the

Statement. In each case, the words are false.	Owner's Belief	Legal Result	Explanation
1. "The heating system is perfect."	Owner knows this is false.	Fraud.	Owner knew the statement was false and intended to induce the buyer to enter into a contract.
2. "The house is built on solid bedrock."	Owner has no idea what is under the surface.	Fraud.	Owner was not certain the statement was true and intended to induce the buyer to enter into a contract.
3. "The roof is only six years old."	Owner believes the statement is accurate, because when he bought the house six years ago, he was told the roof was new.	Material misrepresentation.	Owner acted in good faith, but the statement is material because owner expects the buyer to rely on it.
4. "The pool is 30 feet long."	Owner believes the statement is accurate because he measured the pool himself, though in fact it is only 29 feet long.	Not a material misrepresentation.	Although this is a misrepresentation, it is not material, since a reasonable buyer would not make a decision based on a one-foot error in the pool length.

The Difference between Fraud and Misrepresentation

seller told her the system was "like new," Nancy may rescind the deal. But it may be economically harmful for her to do so. She might have sold her old house, hired a mover, taken a new job, and so forth. She has the option of fully performing the contract and moving into the new house. What are her other remedies? That will depend on whether the misstatement ("the system is like new") was fraudulent or simply a material misrepresentation.

If the maker's statement is fraudulent, the injured party generally has a choice of rescinding the contract or suing for damages. If the seller's mistake was fraudulent, Nancy will generally be allowed to carry out the contract and sue for damages. She could move into the new house and sue for the difference between what she got and what was promised, which is probably about $12,000, the cost of replacing the heating system. But if the seller's mistake was innocent, and Nancy can prove only material misrepresentation, she has no remedy other than rescission. If she goes forward with the contract, she must accept the house as she finds it.

Special Problem: Silence

We know that a party negotiating a contract may not misrepresent a material fact. But what about silence? Suppose the seller knows the roof is in dreadful condition (since she sleeps under an umbrella) but the buyer never asks. Must the seller disclose what she knows?

This is perhaps the hottest topic today in the law of misrepresentation. A seller who knows something that the buyer does not know is often required to divulge it. The Restatement (Second) of Contracts offers guidance:

Nondisclosure of a fact amounts to misrepresentation only in these four cases:

Where disclosure is necessary *to correct a previous assertion*. During the course of negotiations, one party's perception of the facts may change. When an earlier statement later appears inaccurate, the change generally must be reported.

Where disclosure would correct *a basic mistaken assumption* that the other party is relying on. When one party knows that the other is negotiating with a mistaken assumption about an important fact, the party who knows of the error must correct it.

Where disclosure would correct the other party's mistaken understanding about *a writing* (such as a deed or map).

Where there is *a relationship of trust* between the two parties, for example when a parent is selling to a child.[12]

Most courts require a property seller to disclose hidden defects. The judge in the following case states the rule somewhat differently, but the reasoning and outcome are the same.

FIMBEL V. DECLARK

695 N.E.2d 125
Indiana Court of Appeals, 1998

FACTS: Ronald and Patricia Fimbel bought two lakefront lots on Lake Latonka in Indiana, intending to build a summer cottage. However, they discovered that the soil was not suitable for a septic system. They would have to hire an engineer at a substantial expense to determine if it was even possible to construct an alternative system. They decided to sell the land.

The Fimbels met with several interested buyers, including Thomas and Joan DeClark. The Fimbels said nothing about the septic problems. The DeClarks bought the property and, one week later, learned that the property was unbuildable. They sued, and the trial court granted them rescission. The Fimbels appealed.

ISSUE: Did the Fimbels have a duty to disclose the septic problems?

EXCERPTS FROM JUDGE STATON'S DECISION: Initially, the Fimbels contend that they cannot be held liable in fraud for failing to disclose the soil condition of the lots since they were under no duty to do so. Ordinarily a seller is not bound to disclose any material facts unless there exists a relationship for which the law imposes a duty of disclosure. Courts have found such a relationship, and therefore a duty to disclose, where the buyer makes inquiries about a condition on, the qualities of, or the characteristics of the property. When a buyer makes such inquiries, it becomes incumbent upon the seller to fully declare any and all problems associated with the subject of the inquiry.

The evidence supports the conclusion that the DeClarks and Fimbels had conversations which imposed a duty upon the Fimbels to disclose the unsuitability of the lots for home construction. Mr.

---

[12] Restatement (Second) of Contracts §162.

DeClark testified that, while viewing the lots, he asked Mr. Fimbel if he had ever intended to build a home on them. According to Mr. DeClark, Mr. Fimbel stated that he was going to build, but he ultimately decided that he preferred some property he owned in Minnesota, noting its peacefulness and that he had a friend that lives there. Mr. DeClark told Mr. Fimbel that he wanted to build a home on the lots. The above inquiry and statement sufficiently introduced the issue of home construction into the parties' transaction such that a duty was imposed on the Fimbels to disclose the information they had regarding the suitability of the lots for residential construction.

The Fimbels also contend that they made no misrepresentation of fact as to whether a home could be constructed on the lots. True, the Fimbels never expressly stated whether or not a home could be constructed on the lots. However, this does not insulate the Fimbels from a judgment in fraud. If a seller undertakes to disclose facts within his knowledge, he must disclose the whole truth without concealing material facts and without doing anything to prevent the other party from making a thorough inspection. For, if in addition to his silence, there is any behavior of the seller which points affirmatively to a suppression of the truth or to a withdrawal or distraction of the other parties' attention to the facts, the concealment becomes fraudulent.

In this case, Mr. Fimbel told Mr. DeClark that the reason he never built on the lots was that he preferred other property. The record is unclear as to whether this was indeed a factor as to the Fimbels' decision not to build on Lake Latonka. Nevertheless, the preference for the other property is, at best, only one reason for not building on Lake Latonka: the other being the inability to place a septic system on the land. One cannot be allowed, under the law, to *partially* disclose the facts as he knows them to be, yet create a false impression in the mind of the hearer by failing to fully reveal the true state of affairs. At best, Mr. Fimbel's response was only a partial disclosure of the reasons he did not build at Lake Latonka, and, at worst, the response was a misrepresentation of the true reason a home was never erected on the site.

The statement by Mr. DeClark at closing that he intended to build on the lots appears to have been met with silence. Given the circumstances, this silence can also support a judgment for fraud. Silence accompanied by deceptive conduct, results in active concealment, and is actionable.

Affirmed. ◢

ETHICS

There are various disclosure rules that a state *could* adopt:

- *Caveat emptor*—let the buyer beware.
- Seller has a duty to disclose only if asked.
- Seller has a duty to disclose regardless of whether asked.
- Seller's only duty is to notify buyer of important considerations that *buyer* may wish to investigate (soil condition, building laws, problems with neighboring property, etc.).

Which rule do you prefer, and why? As you answer this question, apply these concepts from the Chapter 2 ethics checklist: What are the alternatives? What outcome does the Golden Rule require? ▪

MISTAKE   *Bilateral. Courts allowed to be rescinded*

Most contract principles come from appellate courts, but in the area of "legal mistake" a cow wrote much of the law. The cow was Rose 2d of Aberlone, a gentle animal that lived in Michigan in 1886. Rose's owner, Hiram Walker & Sons, had bought her for $850. After a few years, the company concluded that Rose could have no calves. As a barren cow she was worth much less, so Walker contracted to sell her to T. C. Sherwood for $80. But when Sherwood came to collect Rose, the parties realized she was pregnant. Walker refused to part with the happy mother, and Sherwood sued. Walker defended, claiming that both parties had made a mistake and that the contract was voidable.

Bilateral Mistake

A **bilateral mistake** occurs when both parties negotiate based on the same factual error. Sherwood and Walker both thought Rose was barren, both negotiated accordingly, and both were wrong. The Michigan Supreme Court gave judgment for Walker, the seller, permitting him to rescind the contract because the parties were both wrong about the essence of what they were bargaining for.

If the parties contract based on an important factual error, the contract is voidable by the injured party. Sherwood and Walker were both wrong about Rose's reproductive ability, and the error was basic enough to cause a tenfold difference in price. Walker, the injured party, was entitled to rescind the contract. Note that the error must be *factual*. Suppose Walker sold Rose thinking that the price of beef was going to drop, when in fact the price rose 60 percent in five months. He made a mistake, but it was simply a business prediction that proved wrong. Walker would have no right to rescind.

Conscious Uncertainty. No rescission is permitted where one of the parties knows he is taking on a risk, that is, he realizes there is uncertainty about the quality of the thing being exchanged. Rufus offers 10 acres of mountainous land to Priscilla. "I can't promise you anything about this land," he says, "but they've found gold on every adjoining parcel." Priscilla, panting with gold lust, buys the land, digs long and hard, and discovers—mud. She may not rescind the contract. She understood her risk, and there was no mutual mistake.

Unilateral Mistake

Sometimes only one party enters a contract under a mistaken assumption, a situation called **unilateral mistake**. In these cases, it is more difficult for the injured party to rescind a contract. To rescind for unilateral mistake, a party must demonstrate that she entered the contract because of a basic factual error and that either (1) enforcing the contract would be unconscionable or (2) the nonmistaken party knew of the error.

Chapter Conclusion

Contracts govern countless areas of our lives, from intimate family issues to multibillion dollar corporate deals. Understanding contract principles is essential for a successful business or professional career and is invaluable in private life. As we enter a new century, this knowledge is especially important because courts no longer rubber-stamp any agreement that two parties have made. If we know the issues that courts scrutinize, the agreement we draft is likelier to be enforced. We thus achieve greater control over our affairs—the very purpose of a contract.

Chapter Review

1. A contract is a promise that the law will enforce. Contracts are intended to make business matters more predictable.

2. The common law governs contracts for services, employment, and real estate. The Uniform Commercial Code (UCC), Article 2, governs contracts for the sale of goods.

3. In an express contract, the two parties explicitly state all important terms of their agreement. In an implied contract, the words and conduct of the parties indicate that they intended an agreement.

4. A claim of promissory estoppel requires that the defendant made a promise knowing that the plaintiff would likely rely, the plaintiff did rely, and it would be wrong to deny recovery.

5. A claim of quasi-contract requires that the defendant received a benefit, knowing that the plaintiff would expect compensation, and it would be unjust not to grant it.

6. The parties can form a contract only if they have a meeting of the minds.

7. An offer is an act or a statement that proposes definite terms and permits the other party to create a contract by accepting. The terms of the offer must be definite.

8. The offeree must say or do something to accept. The common law mirror image rule requires acceptance on precisely the same terms as the offer.

9. A promise is normally binding only if it is supported by consideration, which requires a bargaining and exchange between the parties.

10. Illegal contracts are void and unenforceable. Claims of illegality often arise concerning non-compete clauses, exculpatory clauses, and unconscionable clauses.

11. Minors and mentally impaired persons generally may disaffirm contracts.

12. Fraud and material misrepresentation are grounds for disaffirming a contract. The injured party must prove a false statement of fact, fraud or materiality, and justifiable reliance.

13. In a bilateral mistake, either party may rescind the contract. In a case of unilateral mistake, the injured party may rescind only in limited circumstances.

Practice Test

1. Interactive Data Corp. hired Daniel Foley as an assistant product manager at a starting salary of $18,500. Over the next six years, Interactive steadily promoted Foley until he became Los Angeles branch manager at a salary of $56,116. Interactive's officers repeatedly told Foley that he would have his job as long as his performance was adequate. In addition, Interactive distributed an employee handbook that specified "termination guidelines," including a mandatory seven-step pre-termination procedure. Two years later, Foley learned that his recently hired supervisor, Robert Kuhne, was under investigation by the FBI for embezzlement at his previous job. Foley reported this to Interactive officers. Shortly thereafter, Interactive fired Foley. He sued, claiming that Interactive could only fire him for good cause, after the seven-step procedure. What kind of a claim is he making? Should he succeed?

2. The Hoffmans owned and operated a successful small bakery and grocery store. They spoke with Lukowitz, an agent of Red Owl Stores, who told them that for $18,000 Red Owl would build a store and fully stock it for them. The Hoffmans sold their bakery and grocery store and purchased a lot on which Red Owl was to build the store. Lukowitz then told Hoffman that the price had gone up to $26,000. The Hoffmans borrowed the extra money from relatives, but then Lukowitz informed them that

the cost would be $34,000. Negotiations broke off and the Hoffmans sued. The court determined that there was no contract because too many details had not been worked out—the size of the store, its design, and the cost of constructing it. Can the Hoffmans recover any money?

3. Academy Chicago Publishers (Academy) approached the widow of author John Cheever about printing some of his unpublished stories. She signed a contract, which stated:

> The Author will deliver to the Publisher on a mutually agreeable date one copy of the manuscript of the Work as finally arranged by the editor and satisfactory to the Publisher in form and content. . . .
>
> Within a reasonable time and a mutually agreeable date after delivery of the final revised manuscript, the Publisher will publish the Work at its own expense, in such style and manner and at such price as it deems best, and will keep the Work in print as long as it deems it expedient.

Within a year, Academy located and delivered to Mrs. Cheever more than 60 unpublished stories. She refused to go ahead with the project. Academy sued for the right to publish. The trial court ruled that the agreement was valid; the appeals court affirmed; and the case went to the Illinois Supreme Court. Was the contract enforceable?

4. Rebecca, in Honolulu, faxes a job offer to Spike, in Pittsburgh, saying, "We can pay you $55,000 per year, starting June 1." Spike faxes a reply, saying, "Thank you! I accept your generous offer, though I will also need $3,000 in relocation money. See you June 1. Can't wait!" On June 1, Spike arrives, to find that his position is filled by Gus. He sues Rebecca.

(a) Spike wins $55,000.

(b) Spike wins $58,000.

(c) Spike wins $3,000.

(d) Spike wins restitution.

(e) Spike wins nothing.

5. An aunt saw her eight-year-old nephew enter the room, remarked what a nice boy he was, and said, "I would like to take care of him now." She promptly wrote a note, promising to pay the boy $3,000 upon her death. Her estate refused to pay. Is it obligated to do so?

6. Brockwell left his boat to be repaired at Lake Gaston Sales. The boat contained electronic equipment and other personal items. Brockwell signed a form stating that Lake Gaston had no responsibility for any loss to any property in or on the boat. Brockwell's electronic equipment was stolen and other personal items were damaged, and he sued. Is the exculpatory clause enforceable?

7. Guyan Machinery, a West Virginia manufacturing corporation, hired Albert Voorhees as a salesman and required him to sign a contract stating that if he left Guyan he would not work for a competing corporation anywhere within 250 miles of West Virginia for a two-year period. Later, Voorhees left Guyan and began working at Polydeck Corp., another West Virginia manufacturer. The only product Polydeck made was urethane screens, which comprised half of 1 percent of Guyan's business. Is Guyan entitled to enforce its noncompete clause?

8. **ETHICS** Richard and Michelle Kommit traveled to New Jersey to have fun in the casinos. While in Atlantic City, they used their MasterCard to withdraw cash from an ATM conveniently located in the "pit," which is the gambling area of a casino. They ran up debts of $5,500 on the credit card and did not pay. The Connecticut National Bank sued for the money. What argument should the Kommits make? Which party, if any, has the moral high ground here? Should a casino offer ATM services in the gambling pit? If a credit card company allows customers to withdraw cash in a casino, is it encouraging them to lose money? Do the Kommits have any ethical right to use the ATM, attempt to win money by gambling, and then seek to avoid liability?

9. The McAllisters had several serious problems with their house, including leaks in the ceiling, a buckling wall, and dampness throughout. They repaired the buckling wall by installing I-beams to support it. They never resolved the leaks and the dampness. When they decided to

sell the house, they said nothing to prospective buyers about the problems. They stated that the I-beams had been added for reinforcement. The Silvas bought the house for $60,000. Soon afterwards, they began to have problems with leaks, mildew, and dampness. Are the Silvas entitled to any money damages? Why or why not?

10. **YOU BE THE JUDGE WRITING PROBLEM** Susan Gould was appointed to a three-year probationary position as a teacher at Sewanhaka High School. Normally, after three years, the school board either grants tenure or dismisses the teacher. The Sewanhaka school board notified Gould she would not be rehired. To keep the termination out of her file, Gould agreed to resign. In fact, because Gould had previously taught at a different New York school, state law required that she be given a tenure decision after only two years. If the board failed to do that, the teacher was automatically tenured. When she learned this, Gould sued to rescind her agreement to resign. Is Gould entitled to rescind the contract (i.e., her agreement to resign)? **Argument for Gould:** Both parties assumed that Gould was on probation and could be dismissed after three years. Neither party understood that after three years, Gould actually *had* tenure under New York State law. Gould would never have resigned had she understood she was entitled to tenure. The misunderstanding goes to the essence of the resignation agreement, and she should be permitted to rescind. **Argument for the School Board**: The school board has done nothing wrong here. It is unfair to penalize the school system for an honest mistake. If Gould is serious about her career, she should understand the tenure process and should take the trouble to inform the board about unusual rules that pertain to her case. She failed to do that, causing both parties to negotiate under a misperception, and she must bear the loss.

11. **ROLE REVERSAL** Write one multiple-choice question with two noncompete clauses, one of which is valid and the other void.

Internet Research Problem

Visit http://www.law.cornell.edu/states/listing.html. Select a state. Then click on "Judicial Opinions." Search for a case concerning "quasi-contract." What are the details of the quasi-contract dispute? Who won and why?

You can find further practice problems in the Online Quiz at http://beatty.westbuslaw.com **or in the Study Guide that accompanies this text.**

CHAPTER 10

Conclusion
to Contracts

Oliver and Perry were college roommates, two sophomores with contrasting personalities. They were sitting in the cafeteria with some friends, Oliver chatting away, Perry slumped on a plastic bench. Oliver suggested that they buy a lottery ticket, as the prize for that week's drawing was $3 million. Perry muttered, "Nah. You never win if you buy just one ticket." Oliver bubbled up, "OK, we'll buy a ticket every week. We'll keep buying them from now until we graduate. Come on, it'll be fun. This month, I'll buy the tickets. Next month, you will, and so on." Other students urged Perry to do it and, finally, grudgingly, he agreed. The two friends carefully reviewed their deal. Each party was providing consideration, namely, the responsibility for purchasing tickets during his month. The amount of each purchase was clearly defined at one dollar. They would start that week and continue until graduation day, two and a half years down the road. Finally, they would share equally any money won. As three witnesses looked on, they shook hands on the bargain. That month, Oliver bought a ticket every week, randomly choosing numbers, and won nothing. The next month, Perry bought a ticket with equally random numbers—and won $52 million. Perry moved out of their dorm room into a suite at the Ritz and refused to give Oliver one red cent. Oliver sued, seeking $26 million, and the return of an Eric Clapton CD that he had loaned to Perry.

If the former friends had read this chapter, they would never have slid into such a mess. In the last chapter, we covered the basics of contract law, and now we put the icing on the

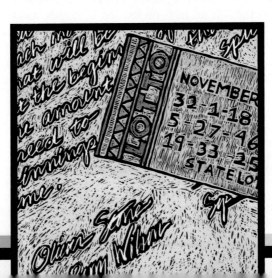

cake. We will examine which contracts must be in writing, when third parties have rights or obligations under an agreement, what problems arise in the performance of contracts, and the remedies available when a deal goes awry. Oliver and Perry's case involves the statute of frauds, which tells us which contracts must be written. ▪

WRITTEN CONTRACTS

The rule we examine in this chapter is not exactly news. Parliament passed the original statute of frauds in 1677. The purpose was to prevent lying (fraud) in civil lawsuits. The statute required that in several types of cases, a contract would be enforced only if it was in writing. Almost all states in our own country later passed their own statutes making the same requirements. It is important to remember, as we examine the rules and exceptions, that Parliament and the state legislatures all had a commendable, straightforward purpose in passing their respective statutes of fraud: *to provide a court with the best possible evidence of whether the parties intended to make a contract.*

The **statute of frauds: A plaintiff may not enforce any of the following agreements, unless the agreement, or some memorandum of it, is in writing and signed by the defendant. The agreements that must be in writing are those:**

• For any interest in **land**

• That **cannot be performed within one year**

• To pay the **debt of another**

• Made by an **executor of an estate**

• Made **in consideration of marriage**; and

• For the **sale of goods worth $500 or more**.

Unenforceable (Sorry, Oliver)

In other words, when two parties make an agreement covered by any one of these six topics, it must be in writing to be enforceable. Oliver and Perry made a definite agreement to purchase lottery tickets during alternate months and share the proceeds of any winning ticket. But their agreement was to last two and one-half years. As the second item on the list indicates, a contract must be in writing if it cannot be performed within one year. The good news is that Oliver gets back his Eric Clapton CD. The bad news is that he gets none of the lottery money. Even though three witnesses saw the deal made, it is unlikely to be enforced in any state. Perry the pessimist will probably walk away with all $52 million.[1]

---

[1] Perry might also raise *illegality* as a defense, claiming that a contract for gambling is illegal. That defense is likely to fail. Courts appear to distinguish between the simple purchase of a legal lottery ticket, which friends often share, and the more traditional—and socially dangerous—gambling contracts involving horse racing or casino betting. See, for example, *Pando v. Fernandez*, 118 A.D.2d 474, 499 N.Y.S.2d 950, 1986 N.Y. App. Div. LEXIS 54345 (N.Y. App. Div. 1986), finding no illegality in an agreement to purchase a lottery ticket, even where the purchaser was a minor! Since an illegality defense would probably fail Perry, it is all the more unfortunate that Oliver did not jot down their agreement in writing.

Contracts That Must Be in Writing

AGREEMENTS FOR AN INTEREST IN LAND

A contract for the sale of any interest in land must be in writing to be enforceable. Notice the phrase "interest in land." This means *any legal right* regarding land. A house on a lot is an interest in land. A mortgage, an easement, and a leased apartment are all interests in land. As a general rule, leases must therefore be in writing, although many states have created an exception for short-term leases of a year or less.

Exception: Full Performance by the Seller

If the seller completely performs her side of a contract for an interest in land, a court is likely to enforce the agreement even if it was oral. Adam orally agrees to sell his condominium to Maggie for $150,000. Adam delivers the deed to Maggie and expects his money a week later, but Maggie fails to pay. Most courts will allow Adam to enforce the oral contract and collect the full purchase price from Maggie.

Exception: Part Performance by the Buyer

The buyer of land may be able to enforce an oral contract if she paid part of the purchase price *and either* entered upon the land or made improvements to it. Suppose that Eloise sues Grover to enforce an alleged oral contract to sell a lot in Happydale. She claims they struck a bargain in January. Grover defends based on the statute of frauds, saying that even if the two did reach an oral agreement, it is unenforceable. Eloise proves that she paid 10 percent of the purchase price and that in February she began excavating on the lot, to build a house, and that Grover knew of the work. Eloise has established part performance and will be allowed to enforce her contract.

Exception: Promissory Estoppel

The other exception to the writing requirement is our old friend promissory estoppel. **If a promisor makes an oral promise that reasonably causes the promisee to rely on it, the promisee *may* be able to enforce the promise, despite the statute of frauds, if that is the only way to avoid injustice.** However, this is an exception to the rule; courts are generally reluctant to erase the writing requirement. In the following case, the plaintiffs make three valiant efforts to evade the piercing grasp of the statute of frauds. They argue that their contract is not really for the sale of land, that they partly performed, and that they relied on the seller's promise.

HERSHON V. CANNON

1993 U.S. Dist. LEXIS 689
United States District Court, District of Maryland, 1993

FACTS: Mary Drysdale and her husband, Simon Hershon, lived in Washington, D.C. They wanted to buy Tulip Hill, an eighteenth-century mansion located on 54 acres in Anne Arundel County, Maryland, property that was owned by an estate and managed by Jonathan Cannon. Drysdale and Hershon orally agreed with Cannon on a purchase price of $1.2 million. Cannon promised that while the lawyers were drafting the written purchase agreement, he would not seek offers from anyone else. Also, if he received an unsolicited offer, he agreed to give Drysdale and Hershon the opportunity to match it.

Drysdale and Hershon applied for a mortgage to buy Tulip Hill. They also met with the Maryland Historical Commission to discuss improvements to the property. Meanwhile, Cannon sold Tulip Hill to someone else. Drysdale and Hershon sued.

ISSUE: Did Drysdale and Hershon have an enforceable contract for Tulip Hill?

EXCERPTS FROM JUDGE HARGROVE'S DECISION:
Plaintiffs make no allegation that they entered into a written contract regarding Tulip Hill, nor do they allege or present a writing of any sort. Plaintiffs contend that their claim is not barred by the statute of frauds for two reasons. First, the plaintiffs argue that they do not seek to enforce an oral purchase agreement. To the contrary, they seek to enforce Cannon's agreement not to solicit other offers for the property and Cannon's agreement that if another offer arose, the plaintiffs would have the right of first refusal. The court finds this argument unpersuasive and believes that the promise the plaintiffs seek to enforce is indeed unenforceable under the statute of frauds, absent a sufficient "writing" or "memorandum."

Second, the plaintiffs contend that Maryland law recognizes exceptions to the statute of frauds where necessary to avoid injustice, including the doctrines of part-performance and estoppel. Part performance of oral agreements can remove the bar of the statute of frauds if the part performance consists of acts that would not have been done but for the existence of the contract. Even if the plaintiffs' allegations are taken as true, their activities are insufficient to create an issue of material fact as to part performance. While the plaintiffs' actions in meeting with officials from the Maryland Historical Trust, preparing design alternatives for Tulip Hill, applying for mortgages to finance the purchase, and liquidating assets, were consistent with the existence of the alleged agreements, they were also consistent with the absence of the alleged agreements. Plaintiffs' activities could have been undertaken in anticipation of a contract for the sale of Tulip Hill.

[As to promissory estoppel] a court must determine if the plaintiff's action or forbearance is definite and substantial in comparison to the remedy sought. [Drysdale and Hershon's reliance was very slight. If the statute of frauds is enforced, and they are unable to buy Tulip Hill, they will not suffer any great injustice.] The court agrees and finds that the plaintiffs' claim based on promissory estoppel fails as a matter of law. [The case is dismissed.] ◢

AGREEMENTS THAT CANNOT BE PERFORMED WITHIN ONE YEAR

Contracts that cannot be performed within one year are unenforceable unless they are in writing. This one-year period begins on the date the parties make the agreement. The critical phrase here is *"cannot be performed* within one year." If a contract *could* be completed within one year, it need not be in writing. Betty gets a job at Burger Brain, throwing fries in oil. Her boss tells her she can have Fridays off for as long as she works there. That oral contract *is* enforceable, whether Betty stays one week or five years. It *could* have been performed within one year if, say, Betty quit the job after six months. Therefore it does not need to be in writing.[2]

---

[2] This is the majority rule. In most states, if a company hires an employee "for life," the contract need not be in writing because the employee could die within one year. "Contracts of uncertain duration are simply excluded [from the statute of frauds]; the provision covers only those contracts whose performance cannot possibly be completed within a year." Restatement (Second) of Contracts §130, Comment a, at 328 (1981). However, a few states disagree. The Illinois Supreme Court ruled that a contract for lifetime employment is enforceable only if written. *McInerney v. Charter Golf, Inc.*, 176 Ill. 2d 482, 680 N.E.2d 1347, 1997 Ill. LEXIS 56 (Ill. 1997).

If the agreement will *necessarily* take longer than one year to finish, it must be in writing to be enforceable. If Betty is hired for three years as manager of Burger Brain, the agreement is unenforceable unless put in writing. She cannot perform three years of work in one year.

Type of Agreement	Enforceability
Cannot be performed within one year. *Example:* An offer of employment for three years.	Must be in writing to be enforceable.
Might be performed within one year, although could take many years to perform. *Example:* "As long as you work here at Burger Brain, you may have Fridays off."	Enforceable whether it is oral or written, since the employee might quit working a month later.

PROMISE TO PAY THE DEBT OF ANOTHER

When one person agrees to pay the debt of another as a favor to that debtor, it is called a **collateral promise**, and it must be in writing to be enforceable. A student applies for a $10,000 loan to help pay for college, and her father agrees to repay the bank if the student defaults. The bank will insist that the father's promise be in writing, since his oral promise alone is unenforceable.

PROMISE MADE BY AN EXECUTOR OF AN ESTATE

An executor is the person who is in charge of an estate after someone dies. The executor's job is to pay debts of the deceased, obtain money owed to him, and disburse the assets according to the will. In most cases, the executor will use only the estate's assets to pay those debts, but occasionally might offer her own money. **An executor's promise to use her own funds to pay a debt of the deceased must be in writing to be enforceable.**

PROMISE MADE IN CONSIDERATION OF MARRIAGE

Barney is a multimillionaire with the integrity of a gangster and the charm of a tax collector. He proposes to Li-Tsing, who promptly rejects him. Barney then pleads that if Li-Tsing will be his bride, he will give her an island he owns off the coast of California. Li-Tsing begins to see his good qualities and accepts. After they are married, Barney refuses to deliver the deed. Li-Tsing will get nothing from a court either, since **a promise made in consideration of marriage must be in writing to be enforceable.**

What the Writing Must Contain

Each of the five types of contract described above must be in writing in order to be enforceable. What must the writing contain? It may be a carefully typed contract, using precise legal terminology, or an informal memorandum scrawled on the back of a paper napkin at a business lunch. The writing may consist of more than one document, written at different times, with each document making a piece of the puzzle. However, there are some general requirements. **The contract or memorandum:**

- **Must be signed by the defendant, and**

- **Must state with reasonable certainty the name of each party, the subject matter of the agreement, and all of the essential terms and promises.**[3]

SIGNATURE

A statute of frauds typically states that the writing must be "signed by the party to be charged therewith," in other words, the defendant. Judges define "signature" very broadly. Using a pen to write one's name, though sufficient, is not required. A secretary who stamps an executive's signature on a letter fulfills this requirement. Any other mark or logo placed on a document to indicate acceptance, even an "X," will likely satisfy the statute of frauds. Electronic commerce creates new methods of signing—and new controversies, discussed in the Cyberlaw feature later in this chapter.

REASONABLE CERTAINTY

Suppose Garfield and Hayes are having lunch, discussing the sale of Garfield's vacation condominium. They agree on a price and want to make some notation of the agreement even before their lawyers work out a detailed purchase and sales agreement. A perfectly adequate memorandum might say, "Garfield agrees to sell Hayes his condominium at 234 Baron Boulevard, apartment 18, for $350,000 cash, payable on June 18, 2004, and Hayes promises to pay the sum on that day." They should make two copies of their agreement and sign both. By doing that, they will avoid the problem that Drysdale and Hershon encountered when trying to purchase Tulip Hill, described earlier. Notice that although Garfield's memo is short, it states all essential terms.

Sale of Goods

The UCC requires a writing for the sale of goods worth $500 or more. This is the sixth and final contract that must be written, although the Code's requirements are easier to meet than those of the common law. In some cases, the Code dispenses altogether with the writing requirement. To read the UCC online, go to http://www.law.cornell.edu/ucc/ucc.table.html. The basic statute of frauds rule is Section 2-201(1). Important exceptions are found at Section 2-201 (2) and (3).

The basic UCC rule: **A contract for the sale of goods worth $500 or more is not enforceable unless there is some writing, signed by the defendant, indicating that the parties reached an agreement.** The key difference between the common law rule and the UCC rule is that the Code does not require all of the terms of the agreement to be in writing. The Code demands only an *indication that the parties*

---

[3] Restatement (Second) of Contracts §131.

reached an agreement. The two things that *are* essential are the signature of the defendant and the quantity of goods being sold. The quantity of goods is required because this is the one term for which there will be no objective evidence. Suppose a short memorandum between textile dealers indicates that Seller will sell to Buyer "grade AA 100% cotton, white athletic socks." If the writing does not state the price, the parties can testify at court about what the market price was at the time of the deal. But how many socks were to be delivered? One hundred pairs or 100,000? The quantity must be written. (A basic sale of goods contract appears at http://www.lectlaw.com/forms/f124.htm.)

Today, many contracts are created without paper. An "electronic signature" could mean any of the following: a name typed at the bottom of an e-mail message; a retinal or vocal scan; a name signed by electronic pen on a writing tablet; a magnetic card using a personal identification number; or a public-key digital signature. Are electronic signatures valid? Yes, generally. State legislatures and Congress are struggling to create clear rules, and the job is incomplete, but here are the rules so far:

- **The Uniform Electronic Transaction Act (UETA).** This proposed legislation was drafted by the National Conference of Commissioners on Uniform State Laws, who also draft the UCC. As this book goes to press, UETA is the law in 39 states, with more likely to adopt it soon. **UETA declares that a contract or signature may not be denied enforceability simply because it is in electronic form.** In other words, the normal rules of contract law apply, but one party may not avoid such a deal simply because it originated in cyberspace. An electronic signature is binding against a person if her action created it. Any evidence that she did so is acceptable.

 - **The Electronic Signatures in Global and National Commerce Act (E-Sign).** This federal statute, which applies in any state that has not adopted UETA, also states that contracts will not be denied enforcement simply because they are in electronic form, or signed electronically. Under this statute, an electronic signature is any "electronic sound, symbol or process, attached to or logically associated with a contract or other record." That is a *very* broad definition. An e-mail message satisfies it. Could the definition be interpreted to include simple voice assent over the telephone?

With cyberlaw in its early stages, how can an executive take advantage *now* of the Internet's commercial opportunities? Be cautious about "electronic signatures." Assume that any commitments you make electronically *can* be enforced against you. Paradoxically, if the contract is important, do *not* assume that the other party's promises, if made electronically, are enforceable unless your lawyer has given you assurance. If in doubt, get a hard copy, signed in ink. ▪

Parol Evidence

Tyrone agrees to buy Martha's house for $800,000. The contract obligates Tyrone to make a 10 percent down payment immediately and pay the remaining $720,000 in 45 days. As the two parties sign the deal, Tyrone discusses his need for financing. Unfortunately, at the end of 45 days, he has been unable to get a mortgage for the full amount. He claims that the parties orally agreed that he would get his deposit back if he could not obtain financing. But the written agreement says no such thing, and Martha disputes the claim. Who will win? Probably Martha, because of the parol evidence rule. To understand this rule, you need to know two terms. **Parol evidence** refers to anything (apart from the written contract itself) that was said, done, or written before the parties signed the agreement or as they signed it. Martha's conversation with Tyrone about financing the house was parol evidence because it occurred as they were signing the contract. The other important term is **integrated contract**, which means a writing that the parties intend as the final, complete expression of their agreement. Now for the rule.

The parol evidence rule: When two parties make an integrated contract, neither one may use parol evidence to contradict, vary, or add to its terms. Negotiations may last for hours, weeks, or even months. Almost no contract includes everything that the parties said. When parties consider their agreement integrated, any statements they made before or while signing are irrelevant. If a court determines that Martha and Tyrone intended their agreement to be integrated, it will prohibit testimony about Martha's oral promises.

THIRD PARTIES

A contract may affect a third party who had no role in forming it. Sometimes the two contracting parties *intend* to benefit a third person. Those are cases of third party beneficiary. In other cases, one of the contracting parties may actually *transfer his rights or responsibilities* to a third party, raising issues of assignment or delegation. We consider these issues one at a time.

Third Party Beneficiary

The two parties who make a contract always intend to benefit themselves. Oftentimes their bargain will also benefit someone else. **A third party beneficiary is someone who was not a party to the contract but who stands to benefit from it.** Many contracts create third party beneficiaries. Problems arise when one of the parties fails to perform the contract as expected. The issue is this: *May the third party beneficiary enforce the contract?*

The outcome depends upon the intentions of the two contracting parties. If they intended to benefit the third party, she will probably be permitted to enforce their contract. If they did not intend to benefit her, she probably has no power to enforce the agreement. The Restatement uses a bit more detail to analyze these cases. We must first recall the terms "promisor" and "promisee." The **promisor** is the one who makes the promise that the third party beneficiary is seeking to enforce. The **promisee** is the other party to the contract.

According to the **Restatement (Second) of Contracts §302: A beneficiary of a promise is an intended beneficiary and may enforce a contract if the parties** *intended* **her to benefit** *and if either* (a) enforcing the promise will satisfy a duty of the promisee to the beneficiary, or (b) the promisee intended to make a gift to the beneficiary.

Any beneficiary who is not an intended beneficiary is an **incidental beneficiary** and may not enforce the contract. In other words, a third party beneficiary must show two things in order to enforce a contract that two other people created. First, she must show that the two contracting parties were aware of her situation and knew that she would receive something of value from their deal. Second, she must show that the promisee wanted to benefit her for one of two reasons: either to satisfy some duty owed or to make her a gift. Contrasting examples should clarify.

Robert Starrett borrowed money from the Commercial Bank of Georgia, using as security a house that he and his wife, Jerry, owned. Several years later, the couple divorced. They amicably divided their assets in a "settlement agreement," which a court approved. The parties agreed to sell the house and disburse the proceeds in this order: first, to pay taxes and costs of the sale; second, to pay in full Robert Starrett's loan from Commercial; and third, to divide the remaining money, 65 percent to Jerry and 35 percent to Robert. The couple never did sell the property, and Robert Starrett died two years later. Robert's estate gave his 50 percent interest in the house to Commercial, but the bank could make no use of it as long as Jerry was half owner. Commercial filed suit, seeking full title. The estate argued that the bank was only an incidental beneficiary. Who wins? The bank. In their settlement agreement, Robert and Jerry clearly *intended* to benefit the bank, since they stated the bank would be paid before any money was divided between them. Did Robert have a *duty* to the bank? Of course: to repay the loan. Both parts of the test are satisfied, and the bank is an intended beneficiary, entitled to its money.[4]

Now suppose a city contracts to purchase from Seller 20 acres of an abandoned industrial site in a rundown neighborhood for a new domed stadium. The owner of a pizza parlor on the edge of Seller's land might benefit enormously. A once marginal operation could become a gold mine of cheese and pepperoni. However, if the city breaks its agreement to buy the land, will the frustrated pizza owner recover lost profits? No. A stadium is a multimillion dollar investment, and it is most unlikely that the city and the seller of the land were even aware of the owner's existence, let alone that they intended to benefit him. He probably cannot prove either the first element or the second element, and certainly not both.

Assignment and Delegation

A contracting party may transfer his rights under the contract, which is called an **assignment of rights**. Or a contracting party may transfer her duties pursuant to the contract, which is a **delegation of duties**. Frequently, a party will do both simultaneously.

For our purposes, the Restatement serves as a good summary of common law provisions. The UCC rules are generally similar. Our first example is a sale of goods case, governed by the UCC, but the outcome would be the same under the Restatement.

Lydia needs 500 bottles of champagne. Bruno agrees to sell them to her for $10,000, payable 30 days after delivery. He transports the wine to her. Bruno happens to owe Doug $8,000 from a previous deal, so he says to Doug, "I don't have the money, but I'll give you my claim to Lydia's $10,000." Doug agrees. Bruno then *assigns* to Doug *his rights* to Lydia's money, and in exchange Doug gives up his

---

[4] *Starrett v. Commercial Bank of Georgia*, 226 Ga. App. 598, 486 S.E.2d 923, 1997 Ga. App. LEXIS 708 (Ga Ct. App. 1997).

claim for $8,000. Bruno is the **assignor, the one making an assignment, and Doug is the assignee, the one receiving an assignment.**

Why would Bruno offer $10,000 when he owed Doug only $8,000? Because all he has is a *claim* to Lydia's money. Cash in hand is often more valuable. Doug, however, is willing to assume some risk for a potential $2,000 gain.

Bruno notifies Lydia of the assignment. Lydia, who owes the money, is called the **obligor**, that is, the one obligated to do something. At the end of 30 days, Doug arrives at Lydia's doorstep, asks for his money, and gets it, since Lydia is obligated to him.

Lydia bought the champagne because she knew she could sell it at a profit. She promptly agrees to sell and deliver the 500 bottles to Coretta, at a mountaintop wilderness camp. Lydia has no four-wheel drive cars, so she finds Keith, who is willing to deliver the bottles for $1,000. Lydia *delegates her duty* to Keith to deliver the bottles to Coretta. Keith is now obligated to deliver the bottles to Coretta, the **obligee**, that is, the one who has the obligation coming to her. Lydia also remains obligated to Coretta, the obligee, to ensure that the bottles are delivered.

Assignment and delegation can each create problems. We will examine the most common ones.

ASSIGNMENT

What Rights Are Assignable?

Any contractual right may be assigned unless assignment

(a) would substantially change the obligor's rights or duties under the contract, or

(b) is forbidden by law or public policy, or

(c) is validly precluded by the contract itself.[5]

Substantial Change.   Assignment is prohibited if it would substantially change the obligor's situation. For example, Bruno may assign to Doug the payment from Lydia because it makes no difference to Lydia whether she writes a check to one or the other. But suppose Erica, who lives on a quarter-acre lot in Hardscrabble, hires Keith to mow her lawn once per week for the summer, for a total fee of $700. Erica pays up front, before she leaves for the summer. May she assign her right to weekly lawn care to Lloyd, who enjoys a three-acre estate in Halcyon, 60 miles distant? No. The extra travel and far larger yard would dramatically change Keith's obligations.

Public Policy.   Some assignments are prohibited by public policy. For example, someone who has suffered a personal injury in an automobile accident may not assign her claim to a third person.

Contract Prohibition.   Finally, one of the contracting parties may try to prohibit assignment in the agreement itself. Most landlords include in the written lease a clause prohibiting the tenant from assigning the tenancy without the landlord's written permission. Such clauses are generally, but not always, enforced by a court.

---

[5] Restatement (Second) of Contracts §317(2). And note that UCC §2-210(2) is, for our purposes, nearly identical.

How Rights Are Assigned

An assignment may be written or oral, and no particular formalities are required. However, when someone wants to assign rights governed by the statute of frauds, she must do it in writing. Suppose City contracts with Seller to buy Seller's land for a domed stadium and then brings in Investor to complete the project. If City wants to assign to Investor its rights to the land, it must do so in writing.

Rights of the Parties after Assignment

Once the assignment is made and the obligor notified, the assignee may enforce her contractual rights against the obligor. If Lydia fails to pay Doug for the champagne she gets from Bruno, Doug may sue to enforce the agreement. The law will treat Doug as though he had entered into the contract with Lydia.

But the reverse is also true. **The obligor may generally raise all defenses against the assignee that she could have raised against the assignor.** Suppose Lydia opens the first bottle of champagne—silently. "Where's the pop?" she wonders. All 500 bottles have gone flat. Bruno has failed to perform his part of the contract, and Lydia may use Bruno's nonperformance as a defense against Doug. If the champagne was indeed worthless, Lydia owes Doug nothing.

DELEGATION OF DUTIES

Garret has always dreamed of racing stock cars. He borrows $250,000 from his sister, Maybelle, in order to buy a car and begin racing. He signs a promissory note in that amount, guaranteeing that he will repay Maybelle the full amount, plus interest, on a monthly basis over 10 years. Regrettably, during his first race, on a Saturday night, Garret discovers that he has a speed phobia. He finally finishes the race at noon on Sunday and quits the business. Garret transfers the car and equipment to Brady, who agrees in writing to pay all money owed to Maybelle. For a few months Brady sends a check, but he is killed while watching bumper cars at a local carnival. Maybelle sues Garret, who defends based on the transfer to Brady. Will his defense work?

Most duties are delegable. But delegation does not by itself relieve the delegator of his own liability to perform the contract.

Garret was the **delegator** and Brady was the **delegatee**. Garret has legally delegated to Brady his duty to repay Maybelle. However, Garret remains personally obligated. When Maybelle sues, she will win. Garret, like many debtors, would have preferred to wash his hands of his debt, but the law is not so obliging.

Garret's delegation to Brady was typical in that it included an assignment at the same time. If he had merely transferred ownership, that would have been only an assignment. If he had convinced Brady to pay off the loan without getting the car, that would have been merely a delegation. He did both at once.

What Duties Are Delegable

The rules concerning what duties may be delegated mirror those about the assignment of rights.

An obligor may delegate his duties unless

(1) delegation would violate public policy, or

(2) the contract prohibits delegation, or

(3) the obligee has a substantial interest in personal performance by the obligor.[6]

Public Policy. Delegation may violate public policy, for example, in a public works contract. If City hires Builder to construct a subway system, state law may prohibit Builder from delegating his duties to Subcontractor. A public agency should not have to work with parties that it never agreed to hire.

Contract Prohibition. The parties may forbid almost any delegation, and the courts will enforce the agreement. Hammer, a contractor, is building a house and hires Spot as his painter, including in his contract a clause prohibiting delegation. Just before the house is ready for painting, Spot gets a better job elsewhere and wants to delegate his duties to Brush. Hammer may refuse the delegation even if Brush is equally qualified.

Substantial Interest in Personal Performance. Suppose Hammer had omitted the "nondelegation" clause from his contract with Spot. Could Hammer still refuse the delegation on the grounds that he has a substantial interest in having Spot do the work? No. Most duties are delegable. There is nothing so special about painting a house that one particular painter is required to do it. But some kinds of work do require personal performance, and obligors may not delegate these tasks. The services of lawyers, doctors, dentists, artists, and performers are considered too personal to be delegated. There is no single test that will perfectly define this group, but generally when the work will test *the character, skill, discretion, and good faith* of the obligor, she *may not* delegate her job.

Novation

As we have seen, a delegator does not get rid of his duties merely by delegating them. But there is one way a delegator can do so. **A novation is a three-way agreement in which the obligor delegates all duties to the delegatee and the obligee agrees to look only to the delegatee for performance. The obligee releases the obligor from all liability.**

Recall Garret, the forlorn race car driver. When he wanted to get out of his obligations to Maybelle, he should have proposed a novation. He would assign all rights and delegate all duties to Brady, and Maybelle would agree that only Brady was obligated by the promissory note, releasing Garret from his responsibility to repay. Why would Maybelle do this? She might conclude that Brady was a financially better bet than Garret who, in turn, might refuse to bring Brady into the deal until Maybelle permits a novation. In the example given, Garret failed to obtain a novation, and hence he and Brady (or Brady's estate) were both liable on the promissory note.

Since a novation has the critical effect of releasing the obligor from liability, you will not be surprised to learn that two parties to a contract sometimes fight over whether some event was a simple delegation of duties or a novation. Here is one such contest. Would you like it in a cone or cup?

---

[6] Restatement (Second) of Contracts §318. And see UCC §2-210, establishing similar limits.

YOU BE THE JUDGE

ROSENBERG V. SON, INC.

491 N.W.2d 71, 1992 N.D. LEXIS 202
Supreme Court of North Dakota, 1992

FACTS: The Rosenbergs owned a Dairy Queen in Grand Forks, North Dakota. They agreed in writing to sell the Dairy Queen to Mary Pratt. The contract required her to pay $10,000 down and $52,000 over 15 years, at 10 percent interest. Two years later, Pratt assigned her rights and delegated her duties under the sales contract to Son, Inc. The agreement between Pratt and Son contained a "Consent to Assignment" clause that the Rosenbergs signed. Pratt then moved to Arizona and had nothing further to do with the Dairy Queen. The Rosenbergs never received full payment for the Dairy Queen. They sued Mary Pratt.

The trial court gave summary judgment for Pratt, finding that she was no longer obligated on the original contract. The Rosenbergs appealed.

YOU BE THE JUDGE: Did Pratt obtain a novation relieving her of her duties under the original sales contract?

ARGUMENT FOR THE ROSENBERGS: Your honors, a party cannot escape contract liability merely by assigning its rights and delegating its duties to a third party. It is evident from the express language of the agreement between Pratt and Son, Inc. that the parties only intended an assignment, not a novation. The agreement made no mention of discharging Pratt from liability. It would be odd to write a novation and make no mention of discharge, which happens to be the primary point of a true novation. It is true that the Rosenbergs signed a consent to the assignment, but merely by permitting Son, Inc. to become involved they did not discharge their principal obligor—Pratt.

ARGUMENT FOR MS. PRATT: Your honors, it is obvious from the contract that Ms. Pratt intended to rid herself entirely of this business. She planned to move out of state, and wanted to terminate all rights and responsibilities in the business. Why would she go to the trouble of assigning rights *and* delegating duties if she still expected to be involved in the business? If that weren't enough, she went one step further, by asking the Rosenbergs to acknowledge the new arrangement—which the Rosenbergs did. If Son, Inc. failed to keep its end of the bargain, then the Rosenbergs should sue that company—not an innocent woman who is long out of the business. ▰

PERFORMANCE AND DISCHARGE

A party is discharged when she has no more duties under a contract. Most contracts are discharged by full performance. In other words, the parties generally do what they promise. Sally agrees to sell Arthur 300 tulip-shaped wine glasses for his new restaurant. Right on schedule, Sally delivers the correct glasses and Arthur pays in full. Contract, full performance, discharge, end of case.

Sometimes the parties discharge a contract by agreement. For example, the parties may agree to **rescind** their contract, meaning that they terminate it by mutual agreement. At times, a court may discharge a party who has not performed. When things have gone amiss, a judge must interpret the contract and issues of public policy to determine who in fairness should suffer the loss. We will analyze the most common issues of performance and discharge.

Performance

Caitlin has an architect draw up plans for a monumental new house, and Daniel agrees to build it by September 1. Caitlin promises to pay $900,000 on that date. The house is ready on time but Caitlin has some complaints. The living room ceiling was supposed to be 18 feet high but it is only 17 feet; the pool was to be azure yet it is aquamarine; the maid's room was not supposed to be wired for cable television but it is. Caitlin refuses to pay anything for the house. Is she justified? Of course not; it would be absurd to give her a magnificent house for free when it has only tiny defects. And that is how a court would decide the case. But in this easy answer lurks a danger. How much leeway will a court permit? Suppose the living room is only 14 feet high, or 12 feet, or 5 feet? What if Daniel finishes the house a month late? Six months late? Three years late? At some point, a court will conclude that Daniel has so thoroughly botched the job that he deserves little or no money. Where is that point? That is a question that businesses—and judges—face everyday.

STRICT PERFORMANCE AND SUBSTANTIAL PERFORMANCE

Strict Performance

Courts dislike strict performance because it enables one party to benefit without paying, and sends the other one home empty-handed. **A party is generally not required to render strict performance unless the contract expressly demands it and such a demand is reasonable.** Caitlin's contract never suggested that Daniel would forfeit all payment if there were minor problems. Even if Caitlin had insisted on such a clause, a court would be unlikely to enforce it, because the requirement is unreasonable.

In some cases, strict performance does make sense. Marshall agrees to deliver 500 sweaters to Leo's store, and Leo promises to pay $20,000 cash on delivery. If Leo has only $19,000 cash and a promissory note for $1,000, he has failed to perform, and Marshall need not give him the sweaters. Leo's payment represents 95 percent of what he promised, but there is a big difference between cash and a promissory note.

Substantial Performance

Daniel, the house builder, won his case against Caitlin because he fulfilled most of his obligations, even though he did an imperfect job. Courts often rely on the substantial performance doctrine, especially in cases involving services as opposed to those concerning the sale of goods or land. **In a contract for services, a party that substantially performs its obligations will receive the full contract price, minus the value of any defects.** Daniel receives $900,000, the contract price, minus the value of a ceiling that is one foot too low, a pool the wrong color, and so forth. It will be for the trial court to decide how much those defects are worth. If the court decides the low ceiling is a $10,000 damage, the pool color worth $5,000 and the cable television worth $500, then Daniel receives $884,500.

On the other hand, a party that fails to perform substantially receives nothing on the contract itself and will only recover the value of the work if any. If the foundation cracks in Caitlin's house and the walls collapse, Daniel will not receive his $900,000. In such a case, he collects only the market value of the work he has done, which is probably zero.

When is performance substantial? There is no perfect test, but courts look at these issues:

- How much benefit has the promisee received?

- If it is a construction contract, can the owner use the thing for its intended purpose?

- Can the promisee be compensated with money damages for any defects?

- Did the promisor act in good faith?

The following case deals with the first three of these issues.

FOLK V. CENTRAL NATIONAL BANK & TRUST CO.

210 Ill. App. 3d 43, 1991 Ill. App. LEXIS 308
Illinois Court of Appeals, 1991

FACTS: Byron Dragway, a drag strip located in Byron, Illinois, needed work. Byron's insurance company insisted that the dragstrip be equipped with concrete retaining walls. Ronald Leek, Byron's president, decided to use the occasion to make other repairs, including resurfacing the 25-year-old surface. The drag strip's starting area (the "starting pads") had a concrete surface, while the remainder of the track was asphalt. Leek hired Randy Folk to do all of the work. When Folk finished, Leek refused to pay, claiming that the work was shabby and would need to be entirely redone. Folk sued. The trial court gave judgment for Folk in the amount of $140,000, finding that, although there were problems, he had substantially performed. Byron Dragway appealed.

ISSUE: Did Folk substantially perform?

EXCERPTS FROM JUSTICE WOODWARD'S DECISION: A contractor is not required to perform perfectly, but rather is held only to the duty of substantial performance in a workmanlike manner. Whether substantial performance has been given will depend upon the relevant facts of each case. However, the burden is on the contractor to prove the elements of substantial performance.

Duane Nichols, president of the United Drag Racers Association (UDRA), testified that the association is the largest owners and drivers association in the nation. It sponsors racing events throughout the country, featuring pro stock cars, super-charged funny cars, dragsters, and exhibition cars, which travel between 180 and 260 miles per hour. Inspecting the new track, Nichols observed that the new concrete [starting] pads were extremely smooth, plus there were significant dips in the concrete surface. Nichols particularly noted a dip where the concrete met the asphalt, an imperfection which would cause cars' tires to spin sideways. He observed several puddles in both asphalt lanes, where the surface dipped. Also, in fall 1987, Nichols attended a local meet held at Byron. Cars were having problems getting down the track, and several of them lost control, with one crashing. Nichols stated that no future UDRA events should be held at the track until the surface was repaired.

As to plaintiff's workmanship, the evidence points convincingly to its poor quality. [One expert] stated the defects of both the concrete starting pads and the asphalt surface were so severe that the total replacement of both was necessary. John Berg of Rockford Blacktop thought that the new asphalt surface would have to be ground off prior to the installation of a new surface.

[Folk did not substantially perform. Judgment reversed, in favor of Byron Dragway.] ◢

PERSONAL SATISFACTION CONTRACTS

Sujata, president of a public relations firm, hires Ben to design a huge multimedia project for her company, involving computer software, music, and live actors, all designed to sell frozen bologna sandwiches to supermarkets. His contract guarantees him two years' employment, provided all of his work "is acceptable in the sole judgment of Sujata." Ben's immediate supervisor is delighted with his work, and his colleagues are impressed—all but Sujata. Three months later she fires him, claiming that his work is "uninspired." Does she have the right to do that?

This is a **personal satisfaction contract, in which the promisee makes a personal, subjective evaluation of the promisor's performance.** In resolving disputes like Ben and Sujata's, judges must decide: When is it fair for the promisee to claim that she is not satisfied? May she make that decision for any reason at all, even on a whim?

A court applies a subjective standard only if assessing the work involves personal feelings, taste, or judgment *and* the contract explicitly demands personal satisfaction. A "subjective standard" means that the promisee's personal views will greatly influence her judgment, even if her decision is foolish and unfair. Artistic or creative work, or highly specialized tasks designed for a particular employer, may involve subtle issues of quality and personal preference. Ben's work combines several media and revolves around his judgment. Accordingly, the law applies a subjective standard to Sujata's decision. Since she concludes that his work is uninspired, she may legally fire him, even if her decision is irrational.

In all other cases, a court applies an objective standard to the promisee's decision. An objective standard means that the promisee's judgment of the work must be reasonable.

GOOD FAITH

The parties to a contract must carry out their obligations in good faith. The Restatement (Second) of Contracts §205 states: **"Every contract imposes upon each party a duty of good faith and fair dealing in its performance and its enforcement."** The UCC establishes a similar requirement for all contracts governed by the Code.[7] How far must one side go to meet its good faith burden? The Restatement emphasizes that the parties must remain faithful to the "agreed common purpose and justified expectations of the other party."

Barbara Thomas's employer had a group life insurance policy with Principal Mutual. The policy covered all employees and their dependents, and defined "dependents" to include an unmarried child between 19 and 25 "provided he is attending school on a full-time basis and is dependent upon the [insured parent] for his principal support and maintenance."

Ms. Thomas's 21-year-old daughter, Melinda Warren, enrolled as a cosmetology student. She paid full tuition and attended full-time for more than a year, when tragically she became disabled by ovarian cancer, which left her bedridden. She died of the disease 18 months later, at age 24. Thomas filed a $1,000 life insurance claim with Principal Mutual, but the insurer refused to pay. The company claimed that Warren was not a dependent at the time of her death, since she was not in school. Barbara Thomas sued, claiming not only benefits under the policy but additional damages for bad faith denial of the claim.

---

[7] UCC §1-203.

At trial, the company's officers were unable to provide a sensible explanation for the denial, or even any standards used in making the decision. The jury found that the company had rejected the claim for irrational, grossly unfair reasons. The state supreme court affirmed the verdict of $1,000 on the initial claim—and $750,000 for the company's bad faith denial.[8]

TIME OF THE ESSENCE CLAUSES

> Go, sir, gallop, and don't forget that the world was made in six days. You can ask me for anything you like, except time.
>
> *Napoleon*, to an aide, 1803

A time of the essence clause will generally make contract dates strictly enforceable. Jackie owns the Starburst Hotel. She agrees in writing to sell it to Eduardo, provided that he demonstrates to her by July 2 that he has obtained all financing. Jackie includes a clause stating that "Owner considers that time is of the essence in the performance of this contract." On July 1, Eduardo asks for a one-month extension to obtain financing, and Jackie promptly sells the hotel elsewhere. Eduardo is out of luck. The time of the essence clause notified him that he must be prompt, and such a clause is reasonable in a real estate agreement. Notice that without the clause, Jackie would be legally obligated to allow Eduardo a reasonable extension.

Breach

When one party *materially* breaches a contract, the other party is discharged. A material breach is one that substantially harms the innocent party. The discharged party has no obligation to perform and may sue for damages. Edwin promises that on July 1 he will deliver 20 tuxedos, tailored to fit male chimpanzees, to Bubba's circus for $300 per suit. After weeks of delay, Edwin concedes he hasn't a cummerbund to his name. This is a material breach and Bubba is discharged. Notice that a trivial breach, such as a one-day delay in delivering the tuxedos, would not have discharged Bubba.

ANTICIPATORY BREACH

Sally will receive her bachelor's degree in May and already has a job lined up for September—a two-year contract as window display designer for Surebet Department Store. The morning of graduation she reads in the paper that Surebet is going out of business that very day. Sally need not wait until September to learn her fate. Surebet has committed an anticipatory breach by making it unmistakably clear that it will not honor the contract. Sally is discharged and may immediately seek other work. She is also entitled to file suit for breach of contract.

STATUTE OF LIMITATIONS

A party injured by a breach of contract should act promptly. **A statute of limitations begins to run at the time of injury and will limit the time within which**

---

[8] *Thomas v. Principal Financial Group*, 566 So. 2d 735, 1990 Ala. LEXIS 614 (Ala. Sup. Ct, 1990).

the injured party may file suit. Statutes of limitation vary widely. In some states, for example, an injured party must sue on oral contracts within three years, on a sale of goods contract within four years, and on some written contracts within five years. Failure to file suit within the time-limits discharges the breaching party.

Impossibility

"Your honor, my client wanted to honor the contract. He just couldn't. Honest." Does the argument work? It depends. A court will discharge an agreement if performing a contract was truly impossible, but not if honoring the deal merely imposed a financial burden.

TRUE IMPOSSIBILITY

These cases are easy—and rare. **True impossibility means that something has happened making it utterly impossible to do what the promisor said he would do.** Francoise owns a vineyard that produces Beaujolais Nouveau wine. She agrees to ship 1,000 cases of *her wine* to Tyrone, a New York importer, as soon as this year's vintage is ready. Tyrone will pay $50 per case. But a fungus wipes out her entire vineyard. Francoise is discharged. It is theoretically impossible for Francoise to deliver wine from her vineyard, and she owes Tyrone nothing.

True impossibility is generally limited to these three causes:

- *Destruction of the Subject Matter.* This happened with Francoise's vineyard.

- *Death of the Promisor in a Personal Services Contract.* When the promisor agrees personally to render a service that cannot be transferred to someone else, her death discharges the contract.

- *Illegality.* If the purpose of a contract becomes illegal, that change discharges the contract.

COMMERCIAL IMPRACTICABILITY AND FRUSTRATION OF PURPOSE

It is rare for contract performance to be truly impossible, but common for it to become a financial burden to one party. Suppose Bradshaw Steel in Pittsburgh agrees to deliver 1,000 tons of steel beams to Rice Construction in Saudi Arabia at a given price, but a week later the cost of raw ore increases 30 percent. A contract once lucrative to the manufacturer is suddenly a major liability. Does that change discharge Bradshaw? Absolutely not. Rice signed the deal *precisely to protect itself against price increases.* The whole purpose of contracts is to enable the parties to control their future.

Yet there may be times when a change in circumstances is so extreme that it would be unfair to enforce a deal. What if a strike made it impossible for Bradshaw to ship the steel to Saudi Arabia, and the only way to deliver would be by air, at five times the sea cost? Must Bradshaw fulfill its deal? What if war in the Middle East meant that any ships or planes delivering the goods might be fired upon? Other changes could make the contract undesirable for Rice. Suppose the builder wanted steel for a major public building in Riyadh, but the Saudi government decided not to go forward with the construction. The steel would then be worthless to Rice. Must the company still accept it?

None of these hypothetical situations involves true impossibility. It is physically possible for Bradshaw to deliver the goods and for Rice to receive. But in some cases it may be so dangerous or costly to enforce a bargain that a court will discharge it instead. Courts use the related doctrines of commercial impracticability and frustration of purpose to decide when a change in circumstances should permit one side to escape its duties.

Commercial impracticability means some event has occurred that neither party anticipated and *fulfilling the contract would now be extraordinarily difficult and unfair to one party.* If a shipping strike forces Bradshaw to ship by air, the company will argue that neither side expected the strike and that Bradshaw should not suffer a fivefold increase in shipping cost. Bradshaw will probably win the argument.

Frustration of purpose means some event has occurred that neither party anticipated and *the contract now has no value for one party.* If Rice's building project is canceled, Rice will argue that the steel now is useless to the company. Frustration cases are hard to predict. Some states would agree with Rice, but others would hold that it was Rice's obligation to protect itself with a government guarantee that the project would be completed. Courts consider the following factors in deciding impracticability and frustration claims:

- Mere financial difficulties will never suffice to discharge a contract.

- The event must have been truly unexpected.

- If the promisor must use a different means to accomplish her task, at a greatly increased cost, she probably does have a valid claim of impracticability.

- The UCC, like the common law, permits discharge only for major, unforeseen disruptions.

REMEDIES

A remedy is the method a court uses to compensate an injured party. The most common remedy, used in the great majority of lawsuits, is money damages.

The first step that a court takes in choosing a remedy is to decide what interest it is trying to protect. An **interest** is a legal right in something. Someone can have an interest in property, for example, by owning it, or renting it to a tenant, or lending money to buy it. He can have an interest in a *contract* if the agreement gives him some benefit. There are four principal contract interests that a court may seek to protect:

- *Expectation Interest.* This refers to what the injured party reasonably thought she would get from the contract.

- *Reliance Interest.* The injured party may be unable to demonstrate expectation damages, but may still prove that he expended money in reliance on the agreement.

- *Restitution Interest.* An injured party may only be able to demonstrate that she has conferred a benefit on the other party. Here, the objective is to restore to the injured party the benefit she has provided.

- *Equitable Interest.* In some cases, something more than money is needed, such as an order to transfer property to the injured party (specific performance) or an order forcing one party to stop doing something (an injunction).

We will look at all four interests. The first two, expectation and reliance, create what are known as *legal* remedies, because they developed in English courts of *law*. The other interests lead to what are termed *equitable* remedies. Historically, when law courts were unable to help a plaintiff, the injured party would sometimes appeal to the Chancellor in London, who had more flexible authority. The Chancellor's powers became known as equitable remedies, a term still used today.

Expectation Interest

This is the most common remedy. **The expectation interest is designed to put the injured party in the position she would have been in had both sides fully performed their obligations.** A court tries to give the injured party the money she would have made from the contract. If accurately computed, this should take into account all the gains she reasonably expected and all the expenses and losses she would have incurred. The injured party should not end up better off than she would have been under the agreement, nor should she suffer serious loss.

William Colby was a former director of the CIA. He wanted to write a book about his 15 years of experiences in Vietnam. He paid James McCarger $5,000 for help in writing an early draft and promised McCarger another $5,000 if the book was published. Then he hired Alexander Burnham to co-write the book. Colby's agent secured a contract with Contemporary Books, which included a $100,000 advance. But Burnham was hopelessly late with the manuscript, and Colby missed his publication date. Colby fired Burnham and finished the book without him. Contemporary published *Lost Victory* several years late, and the book flopped, earning no significant revenue. Because the book was so late, Contemporary paid Colby a total of only $17,000. Colby sued Burnham for his lost expectation interest. The court awarded him $23,000, calculated as follows:

	$ 100,000	advance, the only money Colby was promised
	− 10,000	agent's fee
	= 90,000	fee for the two authors, combined
divided by 2	= 45,000	Colby's fee
	− 5,000	owed to McCarger under the earlier agreement
	= 40,000	Colby's expectation interest
	− 17,000	fee Colby received from Contemporary
	= 23,000	Colby's expectation damages, that is, the amount he would have received had Burnham finished on time[9]

---

[9] *Colby v. Burnham*, 31 Conn. App. 707, 627 A.2d 457, 1993 Conn. App LEXIS 299 (Conn. App. Ct. 1993).

The *Colby* case presented an easy calculation of damages. Other contracts are complex. Courts typically divide the expectation damages into three parts: (1) compensatory (or "direct") damages, which represent harm that flowed directly from the contract's breach; (2) consequential (or "special") damages, which represent harm caused by the injured party's unique situation; and (3) incidental damages, which are minor costs such as storing or returning defective goods, advertising for alternative goods, and so forth. The first two—compensatory and consequential—are the important ones.

COMPENSATORY DAMAGES

Compensatory damages are the most common monetary awards for the expectation interest. Courts also refer to these as "direct damages." **Compensatory damages are those that flow directly from the contract.** In other words, these are the damages that inevitably result from the breach. Suppose Ace Productions hires Reina to star in its new movie, *Inside Straight*. Ace promises Reina $3 million, providing she shows up June 1 and works until the film is finished. But in late May, Joker Entertainment offers Reina $6 million to star in its new feature, and on June 1 Reina informs Ace that she will not appear. Reina has breached her contract, and Ace should recover compensatory damages.

What are the damages that flow directly from the contract? Ace obviously has to replace Reina. If Ace hires Kween as its star and pays her a fee of $4 million, Ace is entitled to the difference between what it expected to pay ($3 million) and what the breach forced it to pay ($4 million), or $1 million in compensatory damages. Suppose the rest of the cast and crew are idle for two weeks because of the delay in hiring a substitute, and the lost time costs the producers an extra $2.5 million. Reina is also liable for those expenses. Both the new actress and the delay are inevitable.

Reasonable Certainty

The injured party must prove the breach of contract caused damages that can be quantified with reasonable certainty. What if *Inside Straight*, now starring Kween, bombs at the box office. Ace proves that each of Reina's last three movies grossed over $60 million, but *Inside Straight* grossed only $28 million. Is Reina liable for the lost profits? No. Ace cannot prove that it was Reina's absence that caused the film to fare poorly. The script may have been mediocre, or Kween's co-stars dull, or the publicity efforts inadequate. Mere "speculative damages" are worth nothing.

CONSEQUENTIAL DAMAGES

In addition to compensatory damages, the injured party may seek consequential damages or, as they are also known, "special damages." **Consequential damages are those resulting from the unique circumstances of *this injured party*.** The rule concerning this remedy comes from a famous 1854 case, *Hadley v. Baxendale*, which all American law students read. Now it is your turn.

HADLEY V. BAXENDALE

9 Ex. 341, 156 Eng. Rep. 145
Court of Exchequer, 1854

FACTS: The Hadleys operated a flour mill in Gloucester. The crankshaft broke, causing the mill to grind to a halt. The Hadleys employed Baxendale to cart the damaged part to a foundry in Greenwich, where a new one could be manufactured. Baxendale promised to make the delivery in one day, but he was late transporting the shaft, and as a result the Hadleys' mill was shut for five extra days. They sued, and the jury awarded damages based in part on their lost profits. Baxendale appealed.

ISSUE: Should the defendant be liable for profits lost because of his delay in delivering the shaft?

EXCERPTS FROM JUDGE ALDERSON'S DECISION:
Where two parties have made a contract which one of them has broken, the damages which the other party ought to receive in respect of such breach of contract should be such as may fairly and reasonably be considered either arising naturally, i.e., according to the usual course of things, from such breach of contract itself, or such as may reasonably be supposed to have been in the contemplation of both parties, at the time they made the contract, as the probable result of the breach of it. Now, if the special circumstances under which the contract was actually made were communicated by the plaintiffs to the defendants, and thus known to both parties, the damages resulting from the breach of such a contract, which they would reasonably contemplate, would be the amount of injury which would ordinarily follow from a breach of contract under these special circumstances so known and communicated.

But, on the other hand, if these special circumstances were wholly unknown to the party breaking the contract, he, at the most, could only be supposed to have had in his contemplation the amount of injury which would arise generally, and in the great multitude of cases not affected by any special circumstances, from such a breach of contract.

Now, in the present case, if we are to apply the principles above laid down, we find that the only circumstances here communicated by the plaintiffs to the defendants at the time the contract was made, were, that the article to be carried was the broken shaft of a mill, and that the plaintiffs were the millers of that mill. But how do these circumstances shew [sic] reasonably that the profits of the mill must be stopped by an unreasonable delay in the delivery of the broken shaft by the carrier to the third person? Suppose the plaintiffs had another shaft in their possession put up or putting up at the time, and that they only wished to send back the broken shaft to the engineer who made it; it is clear that this would be quite consistent with the above circumstances, and yet the unreasonable delay in the delivery would have no effect upon the intermediate profits of the mill. It follows, therefore, that the loss of profits here cannot reasonably be considered such a consequence of the breach of contract as could have been fairly and reasonably contemplated by both the parties when they made this contract.

[The court ordered a new trial, in which the jury would not be allowed to consider the plaintiffs' lost profits.] ◢

The rule from *Hadley v. Baxendale* has been unchanged ever since: **the injured party may recover consequential damages only if the breaching party should have foreseen them.**

Let us return briefly to *Inside Straight*. Suppose that, long before shooting began, Ace had sold the film's soundtrack rights to Spinem Sound for $2 million. Spinem believed it would make a profit only if Reina appeared in the film, so it demanded the right to discharge the agreement if Reina dropped out. When Reina quit, Spinem terminated the contract. Now, when Ace sues Reina, it will also seek $2 million in consequential damages for the lost music revenue. If Reina knew about Ace's contract with Spinem when she signed to do the film, she is liable for $2 million. If she never realized she was an essential part of the music contract, she owes nothing for the lost profits.

INCIDENTAL DAMAGES

Incidental damages are the relatively minor costs that the injured party suffers when responding to the breach. When Reina, the actress, breaches the film contract, the producers may have to leave the set and fly back to Los Angeles to hire a new actress. The cost of travel, renting a room for auditions, and other related expenses are incidental damages.

Reliance Interest

George plans to manufacture and sell silk scarves during the holiday season. In the summer, he contracts with Cecily, the owner of a shopping mall, to rent a high-visibility stall for $100 per day. George then buys hundreds of yards of costly silk and gets to work cutting and sewing. Then in September, Cecily refuses to honor the contract. George sues and easily proves Cecily breached a valid contract. But what is his remedy?

George cannot establish an expectation interest in his scarf business. He hoped to sell each scarf for a $40 gross profit, and wanted to make $2,000 per day. But how much would he actually have earned? Enough to retire on—or enough to buy a salami sandwich for lunch? A court cannot give him an expectation interest, so George will ask for *reliance damages*. **The reliance interest is designed to put the injured party in the position he would have been in had the parties never entered into a contract.** This remedy focuses on the time and money the injured party spent performing his part of the agreement.

Assuming he is unable to sell the scarves to a retail store (which is probable because retailers will have made purchases long ago), George should be able to recover the cost of the silk fabric he bought and perhaps something for the hours of labor he spent cutting and sewing. However, reliance damages can be difficult to win because *they are harder to quantify*. Judges dislike vague calculations. How much was George's time worth in making the scarves? How good was his work? How likely were the scarves to sell? If George has a track record in the industry, he will be able to show a market price for his services. Without such a record, his reliance claim becomes a tough battle.

In one type of case, courts use reliance damages exclusively. Recall the doctrine of promissory estoppel, which sometimes permits a plaintiff to recover damages even without a valid contract. The plaintiff must show that the defendant made a promise knowing that the plaintiff would likely rely on it, that the plaintiff did rely, and that the only way to avoid injustice is to enforce the promise. In promissory estoppel cases, a court will generally award *only* reliance damages. It would be unfair to give expectation damages for the full benefit of the bargain when, legally, there has been no bargain. Lou says to Costas, who lives in Philadelphia, "You're a great chef. Come out to Los Angeles. My new restaurant needs you, and

I can double your salary if not more." Costas quits his job and travels west, but Lou has no job for him. There is no binding contract, because the terms were too vague; however, the chef will *probably* obtain some reliance damages based on lost income and moving costs.

Costas's reliance damages are uncertain. How should he have protected himself?

Restitution Interest

Jim and Bonnie Hyler bought an expensive recreational vehicle (RV) from Autorama. The salesman promised the Hylers that a manufacturer's warranty covered the entire vehicle for a year. The Hylers had a succession of major problems with their RV, including windows that wouldn't shut, a door that fell off, a loose windshield, and defective walls. Then they learned that the manufacturer had gone bankrupt. In fact, the Autorama salesman knew of the bankruptcy when he made the sales pitch.

The Hylers returned the RV to Autorama and demanded their money back. They wanted restitution.

The restitution interest is designed to return to the injured party a benefit that he has conferred on the other party, which it would be unjust to leave with that person. Restitution is a common remedy in contracts involving fraud, misrepresentation, mistake, and duress. In these cases, restitution often goes hand-in-hand with **rescission,** which means to "undo" a contract and put the parties where they were before they made the agreement. The court declared that Autorama had misrepresented the manufacturer's warranty by omitting the small fact that the manufacturer itself no longer existed. Autorama was forced to return to the Hylers the full purchase price plus the value of the automobile they had traded. The dealer, of course, was allowed to keep the defective RV and stare out the ill-fitting windows.[10]

Courts also award restitution in cases of quasi-contract, which we examined in Chapter 9. In quasi-contract cases, the parties never made a contract, but one side did benefit the other. A court may choose to award restitution where one party has conferred a benefit on another and it would be unjust for the other party to retain the benefit. Suppose Owner asks Supplier to install a new furnace in her home. Supplier forgets to ask Owner to sign a contract. If the furnace works properly, it would be unfair to let Owner keep it for free, and a court might order full payment as restitution, even though there was no valid contract.

Other Equitable Interests

In addition to restitution, the other three equitable powers that concern us are specific performance, injunction, and reformation.

---

[10] *Hyler v. Garner,* 548 N.W.2d 864, 1996 Iowa Sup. LEXIS 322 (Iowa, 1966).

SPECIFIC PERFORMANCE

Leona Claussen owned Iowa farmland. She sold some of it to her sister-in-law, Evelyn Claussen, and, along with the land, granted Evelyn an option to buy additional property at $800 per acre. Evelyn could exercise her option anytime during Leona's lifetime or within six months of Leona's death. When Leona died, Evelyn informed the estate's executor that she was exercising her option. But other relatives wanted the property and the executor refused to sell. Evelyn sued and asked for *specific performance*. She did not want an award of damages; she wanted the land itself. The remedy of specific performance forces the two parties to perform their contract.

A court will award specific performance, ordering the parties to perform the contract, only in cases involving the sale of land or some other asset that is unique. Courts use this equitable remedy when money damages would be inadequate to compensate the injured party. If the subject is unique and irreplaceable, money damages will not put the injured party in the same position she would have been in had the agreement been kept. So a court will order the seller to convey the rare object and the buyer to pay for it.

Historically, every parcel of land has been regarded as unique, and therefore specific performance is always available in real estate contracts. Evelyn Claussen won specific performance. The Iowa Supreme Court ordered Leona's estate to convey the land to Evelyn, for $800 per acre.[11] Generally speaking, either the seller or the buyer may be granted specific performance.

Other unique items, for which a court will order specific performance, include such things as rare works of art, secret formulas, patents, and shares in a closely held corporation. By contrast, a contract for a new Jeep Grand Cherokee is not enforceable by specific performance. An injured buyer can use money damages to purchase a virtually identical auto.

INJUNCTION

You move into your new suburban house on two acres of land, and the fresh air is exhilarating. But the wind shifts to the west, and you find yourself thinking of farm animals, especially pigs. Your next-door neighbor just started an organic bacon ranch, and the first 15 porkers have checked in. You check out the town's zoning code, discover that it is illegal to raise livestock in the neighborhood, and sue. Money damages will not suffice, because you want the bouquet to disappear. You seek the equitable remedy of injunction. **An injunction is a court order that requires someone to do something or refrain from doing something.**

The court will order your neighbor immediately to cease and desist raising any pigs or other farm animals on his land. "Cease" means to stop, and "desist" means to refrain from doing it in the future. The injunction will not get you any money, but it will move the pigs out of town, and that was your goal. (The Web site http://www.kinseylaw.com/ATTY%20SERV/civil/complaints/injunction.html provides a sample complaint requesting an injunction.)

In the increasingly litigious world of professional sports, injunctions are commonplace. Brian Shaw was playing professional basketball in Italy when the Boston Celtics flipped him a contract offer. In January, Shaw inked a five-year deal

---

[11] *In re Estate of Claussen*, 482 N.W.2d 381, 1992 Iowa Sup. LEXIS 52 (Iowa 1992).

with the Celtics, to begin playing the following October. The player grabbed a $450,000 bonus and a guaranteed salary of over $1 million per year. In June, Shaw reversed direction, informing the Celtics that he would remain with his Italian team. Boston ran a fast break into federal court, seeking an injunction. Shaw argued that when he signed the Celtics' contract he had been homesick for America, and depressed by criticism in the Italian press. He added that no agent had been available to assist him. The court rejected his claims, noting that Shaw was a college graduate and the contract was a simple, standard-form agreement. The judge granted the injunction, blocking Shaw from playing anywhere except Boston.[12]

REFORMATION

The final remedy, and perhaps the least common, is **reformation**, in which a court will partially "rewrite" a contract. Courts seldom do this, because the whole point of a contract is to enable the parties to control their own futures. However, a court may reform a contract if it believes a written agreement includes a simple mistake. Suppose that Roger orally agrees to sell 35 acres to Hannah for $600,000. The parties then draw up a written agreement, accidentally stating the price as $60,000. Most courts would reform the agreement and enforce it.

Special Issues of Damages

MITIGATION OF DAMAGES

Note one limitation on *all* contract remedies: **a party injured by a breach of contract may not recover for damages that he could have avoided with reasonable efforts.** In other words, when one party perceives that the other has breached or will breach the contract, the injured party must try to prevent unnecessary loss. A party is expected to **mitigate** his damages, that is, to keep damages as low as he reasonably can.

LIQUIDATED DAMAGES

It can be difficult or even impossible to prove how much damage the injured party has suffered. So lawyers and executives negotiating a deal may include in the contract a **liquidated damages clause, a provision stating in advance how much a party must pay if it breaches.** Is that fair? The answer depends on two factors: **a court will generally enforce a liquidated damages clause if (1) at the time of creating the contract it was very difficult to estimate actual damages,** *and* **(2) the liquidated amount is reasonable.** In any other case, the liquidated damage will be considered a penalty and will prove unenforceable.

In the following case, a private school provided special tutoring in liquidated damages—but not for free.

---

[12] *Boston Celtics Limited Partnership v. Shaw*, 908 F.2d 1041, 1990 U.S. App. LEXIS 12117 (U.S. C App. 1st Cir. 1990).

LAKE RIDGE ACADEMY V. CARNEY

66 Ohio St. 3d 376, 613 N.E.2d 183, 1993 Ohio LEXIS 1210
Supreme Court of Ohio, 1993

FACTS: In March, Mr. Carney reserved a spot in the fourth grade class at Lake Ridge Academy for his son, Michael. He paid a $630 deposit and agreed in writing to pay the balance of the tuition, $5,610, later that year. The contract permitted Carney to cancel the agreement and withdraw his son with no further obligation provided he did so before August 1. If he failed to notify the school before that date, he became liable for the full tuition.

Carney wrote a letter notifying Lake Ridge that Michael would not attend. He dated the letter August 1, mailed it August 7, and the school received it August 14. Lake Ridge demanded its full tuition, Carney refused, and the school sued. One of the disputed issues was whether the liquidated damages clause was a penalty. The trial court found for Carney, but the court of appeals reversed, finding that the clause was valid. Carney appealed to the state's highest court.

ISSUE: Was the liquidated damages clause enforceable?

EXCERPTS FROM JUSTICE WRIGHT'S DECISION:
Contracting parties may provide in advance for damages to be paid in the event of a breach as long as the provision does not disregard the principle of compensation. Determining whether stipulated damages are punitive or liquidated is not always easy. It is necessary to look to the whole instrument, its subject-matter, the ease or difficulty of measuring the breach in damages, and the amount of the stipulated sum, not only as compared with the value of the subject of the contract, but in proportion to the probable consequences of the breach.

We conclude that the damages in this case are liquidated damages [and thus enforceable].

When Carney and Lake Ridge entered into their contract the damages that Lake Ridge might suffer as a result of a breach by Carney were "uncertain as to amount and difficult of proof." Lake Ridge goes through a long budgeting process which begins each year in January and ends in the fall. The tuition money paid by students is pooled and goes towards staff salaries and benefits, department budgets, student materials, maintenance, improvements, and utilities. Trial testimony reveals that the school budget process is often an uncertain science; it is quite clear that Lake Ridge would be unable to calculate and prove the precise damages caused by the loss of one student's tuition.

Nor is the contract as a whole unreasonable. The headmaster testified that August 1 was chosen as the day before which notice of cancellation had to be given simply because the school had to know in order to meet its financial commitments. Carney had almost five months after he signed the contract to decide whether to cancel it. Because Lake Ridge's financial commitments became more firm as the school year approached, it is reasonable to assume that by August 1 the school was relying on Carney's full tuition payment. ◢

ECONOMICS & THE LAW

Some economists think that even *penalty clauses* should be enforced, suggesting that they can be a form of cheap insurance. Vivian has organized a reunion for 35 family members, all of whom will fly on a chartered aircraft from Chicago to San Diego, where they will stay at a luxurious resort. This is a once-in-a-lifetime event for the family, with huge costs and great emotional benefits for parents, grandparents, and others. Vivian wants to be sure the charter flight actually gets everyone to California on time, since she has committed to pay for all rooms, meals, and side trips. She insists on a contract that cancels her charter fee if the plane arrives in San Diego more than four hours late, and forces the company to pay a penalty of $5,000 for every day of delay until the entire family is assembled at the resort. The charter company agrees to the clause but demands a higher than usual fee from Vivian. The parties have agreed to a kind of "emotional insurance," based on the unique significance of the event. Vivian might have purchased such insurance from a third party, but the costs would have been higher because the insurer would have had less confidence in the charter company's ability to perform on time, and would also have insisted on making a profit for its risk.

Notice a second, related reason to enforce such contracts. When the charter company, during contract negotiation, agrees to the high liquidated damages clause, it is saying in the most effective way possible, "We are the best company for this job." By putting its money on the line, the company makes itself more attractive to Vivian, and probably forces its competitors to improve their own performance. The result could be better air service for everyone. ▪

Chapter Conclusion

A moment's caution! Often that is the only thing needed to avoid years of litigation. Yes, the broad powers of a court may enable it to compensate an injured party, but problems of proof demonstrate that the best solution is a carefully drafted contract and socially responsible behavior.

Chapter Review

1. Contracts that must be in writing to be enforceable concern:

   - The sale of any interest in land

   - Agreements that cannot be performed within one year

   - Promises to pay the debt of another

   - Promises made by an executor of an estate

   - Promises made in consideration of marriage; and

   - The sale of goods over $500

2. The writing must be signed by the defendant and must state the name of all parties, the subject matter of the agreement, and all essential terms and promises.

3. A third party beneficiary is an intended beneficiary and may enforce a contract *only* if the parties intended her to benefit from the agreement *and* (1) enforcing the promise will satisfy a debt of the promisee to the beneficiary, or (2) the promisee intended to make a gift to the beneficiary.

4. An assignment transfers the assignor's contract rights to the assignee. A delegation transfers the delegator's duties to the delegatee.

5. A party generally may assign contract rights unless doing so would substantially change the obligor's rights or duties; is forbidden by law; or is validly precluded by the contract.

6. Duties are delegable unless delegation would violate public policy; the contract prohibits delegation; or the obligee has a substantial interest in personal performance by the obligor.

7. Unless the obligee agrees otherwise, delegation does not discharge the delegator's duty to perform.

8. A condition is an event that must occur before a party becomes obligated.

9. Strict performance, which requires one party to fulfill its duties perfectly, is unusual. In construction and service contracts, substantial performance is generally sufficient to entitle the promisor to the contract price, minus the cost of defects.

10. Good faith performance is required in all contracts.

11. True impossibility means that some event has made it impossible to perform an agreement. Commercial impracticability means that some unexpected event has made it extraordinarily difficult and unfair for one party to perform its obligations.

12. A remedy is the method a court uses to compensate an injured party.

13. The expectation interest puts the injured party in the position she would have been in had both sides fully performed. It has three components: compensatory, consequential, and incidental damages.

14. The reliance interest puts the injured party in the position he would have been in had the parties never entered into a contract.

15. The restitution interest returns to the injured party a benefit that she has conferred on the other party, which it would be unjust to leave with that person.

16. Specific performance, ordered only in cases of a unique asset, requires both parties to perform the contract.

17. An injunction is a court order that requires someone to do something or refrain from doing something.

Practice Test

1. **CPA QUESTION** Able hired Carr to restore Able's antique car for $800. The terms of their oral agreement provided that Carr was to complete the work within 18 months. Actually, the work could be completed within one year. The agreement is:

   (a) Unenforceable because it covers services with a value in excess of $500

   (b) Unenforceable because it covers a time period in excess of one year

   (c) Enforceable because personal service contracts are exempt from the statute of frauds

   (d) Enforceable because the work could be completed within one year

2. **ETHICS** Jacob Deutsch owned commercial property. He orally agreed to rent it for six years to Budget Rent-A-Car. Budget took possession, began paying monthly rent, and over a period of several months, expended about $6,000 in upgrading the property. Deutsch was aware of the repairs. After a year, Deutsch attempted to evict Budget. Budget claimed it had a six-year oral lease, but Deutsch claimed that such a lease was worthless. Please rule. Is it ethical for Deutsch to use the statute of frauds in attempting to defeat the lease? Assume that, as landlord, you had orally agreed to rent premises to a tenant, but then for business reasons preferred not to carry out the deal. Would you evict a tenant if you thought the statute of frauds would enable you to do so? How should you analyze the problem? What values are most important to you?

3. Intercontinental Metals Corp. (IMC) contracted with the accounting firm of Cherry, Bekaert & Holland to perform an audit. Cherry issued its opinion about IMC, giving all copies of its report directly to the company. IMC later permitted Dun & Bradstreet to examine the statements, and Raritan River Steel Company saw a report published by Dun & Bradstreet. Relying on the audit, Raritan sold IMC $2.2 million worth of steel on credit, but IMC promptly went bankrupt. Raritan sued Cherry, claiming that IMC was not as sound as Cherry had reported, and that the accounting firm had breached its contract with IMC. Comment on Raritan's suit.

4. Nationwide Discount Furniture hired Rampart Security to install an alarm in its warehouse. A fire would set off an alarm in Rampart's office, and the security company was then supposed to notify Nationwide immediately. A fire did break out, but

Rampart allegedly failed to notify Nationwide, causing the fire to spread next door and damage a building owned by Gasket Materials Corp. Gasket sued Rampart for breach of contract, and Rampart moved for summary judgment. Comment.

5. Pizza of Gaithersburg, Maryland, owned five pizza shops. Pizza arranged with Virginia Coffee Service to install soft-drink machines in each of its stores and maintain them. The contract made no mention of the rights of either party to delegate. Virginia Coffee delegated its duties to the Macke Co., leading to litigation between Pizza and Macke. Pizza claimed that Virginia Coffee was barred from delegating because Pizza had a close working relationship with the president of Virginia Coffee, who personally kept the machines in working order. Was the delegation legal?

6. Evans built a house for Sandra Dyer, but the house had some problems. The garage ceiling was too low. Load-bearing beams in the "great room" cracked and appeared to be steadily weakening. The patio did not drain properly. Pipes froze. Evans wanted the money promised for the job, but Dyer refused to pay. Comment.

7. Omega Concrete had a gravel pit and factory. Access was difficult, so Omega contracted with Union Pacific Railroad (UP) for the right to use a private road that crossed UP property and tracks. The contract stated that use of the road was solely for Omega employees and that Omega would be responsible for closing a gate that UP planned to build where the private road joined a public highway. In fact, UP never constructed the gate. Omega had no authority to construct the gate. Mathew Rogers, an Omega employee, was killed by a train while using the private road to reach Omega. Rogers's family sued Omega, claiming, among other things, that Omega failed to keep the gate closed as the contract required. Is Omega liable based on that failure?

8. **YOU BE THE JUDGE WRITING PROBLEM** Kuhn Farm Machinery, a European company, signed an agreement with Scottsdale Plaza Resort, of Arizona, to rent 190 guest rooms for its North American dealers' convention during March 1991. Kuhn invited its top 200 independent dealers from the United States and Canada and about 25 of its own employees from the United States, Europe, and Australia, although it never mentioned those plans to Scottsdale.

On August 2, 1990, Iraq invaded Kuwait, and on January 16, 1991, the United States and allied forces were at war with Iraq. Iraqi leaders threatened terrorist acts against the United States and its allies. Kuhn became concerned about the safety of those traveling to Arizona, especially its European employees. By mid-February, 11 of the top 50 dealers with expense-paid trips had either canceled their plans to attend or failed to sign up. Kuhn postponed the convention. The resort sued. The trial court discharged the contract under the doctrines of commercial impracticability and frustration of purpose. The resort appealed. Did commercial impracticability or frustration of purpose discharge the contract? **Argument for Scottsdale Plaza Resort:** The resort had no way of knowing that Kuhn anticipated bringing executives from Europe, and even less reason to expect that if anything interfered with their travel, the entire convention would become pointless. Most of the dealers could have attended the convention. **Argument for Kuhn:** The parties never anticipated the threat of terrorism. Kuhn wanted this convention so that its European executives, among others, could meet top North American dealers. That is now impossible. As a result, the contract has no value at all to Kuhn, and its obligations should be discharged by law.

9. Racicky was in the process of buying 320 acres of ranch land. While that sale was being negotiated, Racicky signed a contract to sell the land to Simon. Simon paid $144,000, the full price of the land. But Racicky then went bankrupt, before he could complete the purchase of the land, let alone its sale. Which of these remedies should Simon seek: expectation, restitution, or specific performance?

10. **ETHICS** The National Football League owns the copyright to the broadcasts of its games. It licenses local television stations to

telecast certain games and maintains a "black-out rule," which prohibits stations from broadcasting home games that are not sold-out 72 hours before the game starts. Certain home games of the Cleveland team were not sold-out, and the NFL blocked local broadcast. But several bars in the Cleveland area were able to pick up the game's signal by using special antennas. The NFL wanted the bars to stop showing the games. What did it do? Was it unethical of the bars to broadcast the games that they were able to pick up? Apart from the NFL's legal rights, do you think it had the moral right to stop the bars from broadcasting the games?

11. **ROLE REVERSAL** Write a short-answer question that highlights the difference between an assignment and a novation.

Internet Research Problem

You represent a group of neighborhood residents in a large city who are protesting construction of a skyscraper that will violate building height limitations. Draft a complaint, requesting an appropriate injunction. You may use the sample injunction complaint found at http://www.kinseylaw.com/ATTY%20SERV/civil/complaints/injunction.html.

You can find further practice problems in the Online Quiz at http://beatty.westbuslaw.com **or in the Study Guide that accompanies this text.**

Sales, Product Liability, and Negotiable Instruments

He Sued, She Sued. Harold and Maude made a great couple because both were compulsive entrepreneurs. One evening they sat on their penthouse roof deck, overlooking the twinkling Chicago skyline. Harold sipped a decaf coffee while negotiating, over the phone, with a real estate developer in San Antonio. Maude puffed a cigar as she bargained on a different line with a toy manufacturer in Cleveland. They hung up at the same time. "I did it!" shrieked Maude, "I made an incredible deal for the robots—five bucks each!" "No, I did it!" triumphed Harold, "I sold the 50 acres in Texas for $300,000 more than it's worth." They dashed indoors.

Maude quickly scrawled a handwritten memo, which read, "Confirming our deal— 100,000 Psychopath Robots—you deliver Chicago—end of summer." She didn't mention a price, or an exact delivery date, or when payment would be made. She signed her memo and faxed it to the toy manufacturer. Harold took more time. He typed a thorough contract, describing precisely the land he was selling, the $2.3 million price, how and when each payment would be made, and the deed conveyed. He signed the contract and faxed it, along with a plot plan showing the surveyed land. Then the happy couple grabbed a bottle of champagne, returned to the deck—and placed a side bet on whose contract would prove more profitable. The loser would have to cook and serve dinner for six months.

Neither Harold nor Maude ever heard again from the other parties. The toy manufacturer sold the robots to another retailer at a higher price. Maude was forced to buy comparable toys elsewhere for $9 each. She sued. And the Texas property buyer changed his mind, deciding to develop a Club Med in Greenland and refusing to pay Harold for his land. He sued. Only one of the two plaintiffs succeeded. Which one? ▪

SALES

The adventures of Harold and Maude illustrate the Uniform Commercial Code (UCC) in action. The Code is the single most important source of law for people engaged in commerce and controls the vast majority of contracts made every day in every state. The Code is old in origin, contemporary in usage, admirable in purpose, and flawed in application. "Yeah, yeah, that's fascinating," snaps Harold, "but who wins the bet?" Relax, Harold, we'll tell you in a minute.

Development of the UCC

Throughout the first half of the twentieth century, commercial transactions changed dramatically in this country, as advances in transportation and communication revolutionized negotiation and trade. The nation needed a modernized business law to give nationwide uniformity and predictability in a new and faster world. In 1942, two groups of scholars, the American Law Institute (ALI) and the National Conference of Commissioners on Uniform State Laws (NCCUSL), began the effort to draft a modern, national law of commerce. The scholars debated and formulated for nearly a decade. Finally, in 1952, the lawyers published their work—the Uniform Commercial Code. The entire Code is available online at http://www.law.cornell.edu/ucc/ucc.table.html.

The ALI and the NCCUSL have revised the Code several times since then, with the most recent major revisions coming in 2001.

Remember that the UCC in a sense is artificial because it is the creation of scholars, not legislators. No section of the Code, new or old, has any legal effect until a state legislature adopts it. In fact, all 50 states and the District of Columbia have adopted the UCC, but some have adopted the early versions from the 1950s and partially revised them, while other states have adopted more recent texts. Louisiana, with its French law heritage, has not adopted Articles 2, 2A, or 6 in any form. The drafters have proposed significant revisions to Articles 1 and 2, but as this book goes to press, the suggested changes have not been adopted by any state. The drafters have not achieved nationwide uniformity, but they have brought commercial law much closer to that goal.

This chapter is designed to:

- illustrate key elements of the Code *that have changed the common law rules* of contracts

- survey the leading doctrines of product liability; and

- highlight important features of negotiable instruments.

Article 1: *General Provisions*	The purpose of the Code, general guidance in applying it, and definitions.
✓ **Article 2:** *Sale of Goods*	The sale of *goods*, such as a new car, 20,000 pairs of gloves, or 101 dalmatians. This is one of the two most important articles in the UCC.
Article 2A: *Leases*	A temporary exchange of goods for money, such as renting a car.
✓ **Article 3:** *Negotiable Instruments*	The use of checks, promissory notes, and other negotiable instruments.
Article 4: *Bank Deposits and Collections*	The rights and obligations of banks and their customers.
Article 4A: *Funds Transfers*	An instruction, given by a bank customer, to credit a sum of money to another's account.
Article 5: *Letters of Credit*	The use of credit, extended by two or more banks, to facilitate a contract between two parties who do not know each other and require guarantees by banks they trust.
Article 6: *Bulk Transfers*	The sale of a major part of a company's inventory or equipment.
Article 7: *Warehouse Receipts, Bills of Lading, and Other Documents of Title*	Documents proving ownership of goods that are being transported or stored.
Article 8: *Investment Securities*	Rights and liabilities concerning shares of stock or other ownership of an enterprise.
✓ **Article 9:** *Secured Transaction*	A sale of goods in which the seller keeps a financial stake in the goods he has sold, such as a car dealer who may repossess the car if the buyer fails to make payments. This is one of the two most important articles in the Code.

We focus on *changes* the Code makes because in many areas the UCC virtually duplicates the common law. Our discussion reflects recent Code revisions that states have *actually adopted*. At the beginning of the new millenium, the drafters have made substantial—and controversial—recommendations for revision of many of the Code's core articles. However, those revisions have not yet been widely adopted. They will not be allowed an appearance in this book yet and must hover in the wings, hoping for a role in a few years.

HAROLD AND MAUDE, REVISITED

Harold and Maude each negotiated what they believed was an enforceable agreement, and both filed suit: Harold for the sale of his land, Maude for the purchase of toy robots. Only one prevailed. The difference in outcome demonstrates why everyone in business needs a working knowledge of the Code. As we revisit the happy couple, Harold is clearing the dinner dishes. Maude sits back in her chair, lights a cigar, and compliments her husband on the apple tart.

Harold's contract was for the sale of land and was governed by the common law of contracts, which requires any agreement for the sale of land to be in writing and *signed by the defendant*, in this case the buyer in Texas. Harold signed it, but the buyer never did, so Harold's meticulously detailed document was worth less than a five-cent cigar.

Maude's quickly scribbled memorandum, concerning robot toys, was for the sale of goods and was governed by Article 2 of the UCC. The Code requires less detail and formality in a writing. Because Maude and the seller were both merchants, the document she scribbled could be enforced *even against the defendant*, who had never signed anything. The fact that Maude left out the price and other significant terms was not fatal to a contract under the UCC, though under the common law, such omissions would have made the bargain unenforceable.

SCOPE OF ARTICLE 2

Because the UCC changes the common law, it is essential to know whether the Code applies in a given case. Negotiations may lead to an enforceable agreement when the UCC applies, even though the same bargaining would create no contract under the common law.

UCC §2-102: Article 2 applies to the sale of goods.[1] Goods are things that are movable, other than money and investment securities. Hats are goods, and so are railroad cars, lumber, books, and bottles of wine. Land is not a good, nor is a house. Article 2 regulates sales, which means that one party transfers title to the other in exchange for money. If you sell your motorcycle to a friend, that is a sale of goods.[2]

MERCHANTS

The UCC evolved to provide merchants with rules that would meet their unique business needs. However, while the UCC offers a contract law that is more flexible than the common law, it also requires a higher level of responsibility from the merchants it serves. Those who make a living by crafting agreements are expected to understand the legal consequences of their words and deeds. Thus many sections of the Code offer two rules: one for "merchants" and one for everybody else.

UCC §2-104: A merchant is someone who routinely deals in the particular goods involved, or who appears to have special knowledge or skill in those goods, or who uses agents with special knowledge or skill in those goods. A used car dealer is a "merchant" when it comes to selling autos, because he routinely deals in them. He is not a merchant when he goes to a furniture store and purchases a new sofa.

---

[1] Officially, Article 2 tells us that it applies to *transactions* in goods, which is a slightly broader category than sale of goods. But most sections of Article 2, and most court decisions, focus exclusively on sales, and so shall we.

[2] Because leasing is so important, the drafters of the Code added Article 2A to cover the subject. Article 2A is similar to Article 2, but there are important differences, and anyone engaging in a significant amount of commercial leasing must become familiar with Article 2A. For our purposes, leasing law is a variation on the theme of Article 2, and we will concentrate on the principal melody of sales.

The UCC frequently holds a merchant to a higher standard of conduct than a non-merchant. For example, a merchant may be held to an oral contract if she received written confirmation of it, even though the merchant herself never signed the confirmation. That same confirmation memo, arriving at the house of a non-merchant, would *not* create a binding deal.

Contract Formation

The common law expected the parties to form a contract in a fairly predictable and traditional way: the offeror made a clear offer that included all important terms, and the offeree agreed to all terms. Nothing was left open. The drafters of the UCC recognized that businesspeople frequently do not think or work that way and that the law should reflect business reality.

FORMATION BASICS: SECTION 2-204

UCC §2-204 provides three important rules that enable parties to make a contract quickly and informally:

1. *Any Manner That Shows Agreement.* The parties may make a contract in any manner sufficient to show that they reached an agreement. They may show the agreement with words, writings, or even their conduct. Lisa negotiates with Ed to buy 300 barbecue grills. The parties agree on a price, but other business prevents them from finishing the deal. Then six months later Lisa writes, "Remember our deal for 300 grills? I still want to do it if you do." Ed doesn't respond, but a week later a truck shows up at Lisa's store with the 300 grills, and Lisa accepts them. The combination of their original discussion, Lisa's subsequent letter, Ed's delivery, and her acceptance all adds up to show that they reached an agreement. The court will enforce their deal, and Lisa must pay the agreed-upon price.

2. *Moment of Making Is Not Critical.* The UCC will enforce a deal even though it is difficult, in common law terms, to say exactly when it was formed. Was Lisa's deal formed when they orally agreed? When he delivered? She accepted? The Code's answer: it doesn't matter. The contract is enforceable.

3. *One or More Terms May Be Left Open.* The common law insisted that the parties clearly agree on all important terms. The Code changes that. **Under the UCC, a court may enforce a bargain even though one or more terms were left open.** Lisa's letter never said when she required delivery of the barbecue grills or when she would pay. Under the UCC, the omission is not fatal. As long as there is some certain basis for giving damages to the injured party, the court will do just that. If Lisa refused to pay, a court would rule that the parties assumed she would pay within a commercially reasonable time, such as 30 days.

[handwritten margin note: substitute w/ reasonable terms]

STATUTE OF FRAUDS

UCC §2-201 requires a writing for any sale of goods worth $500 or more. However, under the UCC, the writing need not completely summarize the agreement. The Code only requires a writing *sufficient to indicate* that the parties made a contract. In other words, the writing need not be a contract. A simple memo, or a letter or informal note, mentioning that the two sides reached an agreement, is enough.

In general, the writing must be signed by the defendant, that is, whichever party is claiming there was no deal. Dick signs and sends to Shirley a letter saying, "This is to acknowledge your agreement to buy all 650 books in my rare book collection for $188,000." Shirley signs nothing. A day later, Louis offers Dick $250,000. Is Dick free to sell? No. He signed the memo, it indicates a contract, and Shirley can enforce it against him.

Now reverse the problem. Suppose that after Shirley receives Dick's letter, she decides against rare books in favor of original scripts from the *South Park* television show. Dick sues. Shirley wins because she signed nothing.

Enforceable Only to Quantity Stated

Since the writing only has to indicate that the parties agreed, it need not state every term of their deal. But one term is essential: quantity. **The Code will enforce the contract only up to the quantity of goods stated in the writing.** This is logical, since a court can surmise other terms, such as price, based on market conditions. Buyer agrees to purchase pencils from Seller. The market value of the pencils is easy to determine, but a court would have no way of knowing whether Buyer meant to purchase 1,000 pencils or 100,000; the quantity must be stated.

Merchant Exception

This is a major change from the common law. **When two merchants make an oral contract, and one sends a confirming memo to the other within a reasonable time, and the memo is sufficiently definite that it could be enforced against the sender herself, then the memo is also valid against the merchant who receives it, unless he objects within 10 days.** Laura, a tire wholesaler, signs and sends a memo to Scott, a retailer, saying, "Confm yr order today—500 tires cat #886—cat price." Scott realizes he can get the tires cheaper elsewhere and ignores the memo. Big mistake. Both parties are merchants, and Laura's memo is sufficient to bind her. So it also satisfies the statute of frauds against Scott, unless he objects within 10 days.

The following case illustrates the merchant exception.

Issue	Relevant Code Selection
1. Was this farmer a "merchant"?	UCC §2-104: A merchant is anyone who routinely deals in the goods involved (or has special knowledge or an agent with such knowledge).
2. Did the memo satisfy the status of frauds?	UCC §2-201(2), the "merchant exception": When two merchants make an oral contract, and one sends a confirming memo to the other within a reasonable time, and the memo is sufficiently definite that it could be enforced against the sender herself, then the memo is also valid against the merchant who receives it, unless he objects within 10 days.

Code Provisions Discussed in this Case

SMITH V. GENERAL MILLS, INC.

291 Mont. 426, 968 P.2d 723
Montana Supreme Court, 1998

FACTS: Jack Smith operated a farm owned by his mother, Monica. General Mills sued the Smiths, claiming that Jack had orally agreed to sell the company 20,000 bushels of wheat and had received a confirming memo from the company, but that he had neither responded to the memo nor delivered the grain. Jack denied making the oral contract, and also claimed that even if he had, he was not a merchant and could not be bound by an oral contract. The jury found in favor of General Mills and the Smiths appealed.

ISSUES: Had the parties made an oral agreement? Was Jack a merchant? Was the confirming memo sufficient to bind the parties?

EXCERPTS FROM CHIEF JUDGE TURNAGE'S DECISION: Although the question of whether a farmer may be deemed a merchant for purposes of [UCC §2-104] is a matter of first impression for this Court, there are a number of other jurisdictions which have had occasion to address it. Despite the split of authority on this issue, a majority of courts have held that under the Uniform Commercial Code, a farmer may be included under the definition of "merchant" in some instances. However, whether a particular farmer qualifies as a merchant cannot be determined through application of a per se rule; rather, it is a conclusion that must be reached on a case by case basis.

Among the considerations given weight by the District Court were the fact that Jack had an operative knowledge of the grain marketing system, including how the buying and selling worked, how competition moved the market, and what factors affected price. He was familiar with all facets of marketing the grain, including knowledge of the product, how to produce it, how to store it, where and how to sell it, and how to negotiate the best terms possible for its disposition. Jack's experience in marketing grain spanned a period of many years, and he had even been entrusted with the marketing of grain in a fiduciary capacity for his mother and his brother's estate. Furthermore, Jack acknowledged in writing as part of [a different] contract that he was a merchant for purposes of marketing the grain he produced.

Our review of the record supports the District Court's conclusion that Jack was a dealer in grain or otherwise by his occupation held himself out as having knowledge or skill peculiar to the marketing of grain. We therefore affirm the ruling of the District Court that the confirmation sent to Jack was sufficient to satisfy the statute of frauds under [section 2-201(2)].

Monica contends that the evidence in this case does not support the jury's findings that an oral contract existed between Jack and General Mills' Joplin elevator. We disagree. Jack's testimony indicates that on the day the oral contract was formed he was out in the field combining barley, and so could not have placed the phone call to the Joplin elevator for the sale of the feed wheat. However, the testimony of the manager of the Joplin elevator was that Jack did in fact place such a call and that a contract was negotiated on that day. Furthermore, the secretary at the Joplin elevator testified that she overheard the telephone conversation between Jack and the elevator manager and shortly thereafter prepared the contract documents in conformity with the substance of the conversation.

When conflicting evidence exists, it is the province of the jury to judge the credibility and weight of the evidence; this Court will not retry a case or reweigh evidence on appeal. We therefore hold that there is substantial credible evidence in the record to support the jury's verdict that a contract was formed between Jack and General Mills' Joplin elevator for the sale of 20,000 bushels of feed wheat.

[Affirmed.]

ADDED TERMS: SECTION 2-207

Under the common law's mirror image rule, when one party makes an offer, the offeree must accept those exact terms. If the offeree adds or alters any terms, the acceptance is ineffective, and the offeree's response becomes a counteroffer. In one of its most significant modifications of contract law, the UCC changes that outcome. **Under §2-207, an acceptance that adds or alters terms will often create a contract.** The Code has made this change in response to the *battles of the form.* Every day, corporations buy and sell millions of dollars of goods using preprinted forms. The vast majority of all contracts involve such documents. Typically, the buyer places an order by using a preprinted form, and the seller acknowledges with its own preprinted acceptance form. Because each form contains language favorable to the party sending it, the two documents rarely agree. The Code's drafters concluded that the law must cope with real practices.

Intention

The parties must still *intend* to create a contract. Section 2-207 is full of exceptions, but there is no change in this basic requirement of contract law. If the differing forms indicate that the parties never reached agreement, there is no contract.

Additional or Different Terms

An offeree may include a new term in his acceptance and still create a binding deal. Suppose Breeder writes to Pet Shop, offering to sell 100 guinea pigs at $2 each. Pet Shop faxes a memo saying, "We agree to buy 100 g.p. We receive normal industry credit for any unhealthy pig." Pet Shop has added a new term, concerning unhealthy pigs, but the parties have created a binding contract because the writings show they intended an agreement. Now the court must decide what the terms of the contract are, since there is some discrepancy. The first step is to decide whether the new language is an *additional term* or a *different term.*

  Additional terms are those that raise issues not covered in the offer. The "unhealthy pig" issue is an additional term because the offer said nothing about it. **When both parties are *merchants*, additional terms generally become part of the bargain.**[3] Both Pet Shop and Breeder are merchants, and the additional term about credit for unhealthy animals does become part of their agreement.

  Different terms *contradict* those in the offer. Suppose Brilliant Corp. orders 1,500 cell phones from Makem Co., for use by Brilliant's sales force. Brilliant places the order by using a preprinted form stating that the product is fully warranted for normal use and that seller is liable for compensatory *and consequential* damages. This means, for example, that Makem would be liable for lost profits if a salesperson's phone fails during a lucrative sales pitch. Makem responds with its own memo stating that in the event of defective phones, Makem is liable only to repair or replace, and *is not liable for consequential damages, lost profits, or any other damages.*

---

[3] There are three circumstances in which additional terms do *not* become part of the agreement: when the original offer *insisted on its own terms;* when the additional term *materially alters* the offer, that is, makes a dramatic change in the proposal; and when the offeror *promptly objects* to the new terms.

Makem's acceptance has included a different term because its language contradicts the offer. **Different terms cancel each other out. The Code then supplies its own terms, called gap-fillers,** which cover prices, delivery dates and places, warranties, and other subjects. The Code's gap-filler about warranties *does* permit recovery of compensatory and consequential damages. Therefore, Makem *would* be liable for lost profits.

AT RISK

Section 2-207 is a noble but imperfect attempt to cope with battles of form. How can you avoid a disastrous surprise?

First, *read all terms on both contracts*. Know everybody's terms, and figure out the important differences. This may sound obvious, but many merchants never read the fine print on *either* form. Second, if some of the terms on your contract are essential, insist that the other party accept them in writing. Third, if the other side refuses to accept terms that you consider vital, *calculate your potential loss*. If your potential liability is more than you consider acceptable, your choices are to terminate the negotiations or to obtain insurance.

Performance and Remedies

The Code's practical, flexible approach also shapes its rules about contract performance and remedy. Once again, our goal in this chapter is to highlight doctrines that demonstrate a *change or an evolution in common law principles*.

BUYER'S REMEDIES

A seller is expected to deliver what the buyer ordered. **Conforming goods satisfy the contract terms.** Non-conforming goods do not.[4] Frame Shop orders from Wholesaler a large quantity of walnut wood, due on March 15, to be used for picture frames. If Wholesaler delivers, on March 8, high quality *cherry* wood, it has shipped non-conforming goods.

A buyer has the right to **inspect the goods** before paying or accepting,[5] and may **reject non-conforming goods** by notifying the seller within a reasonable time.[6] Frame Shop may lawfully open Wholesaler's shipping crates before paying, and is entitled to refuse the cherry wood. However, when the buyer rejects non-conforming goods, **the seller has the right to cure**, by delivering conforming goods before the contract deadline.[7] If Wholesaler delivers walnut wood by March 15, Frame Shop must pay in full. The Code even permits the seller to cure *after* the delivery date if doing so is reasonable. Notice the UCC's eminently pragmatic goal: to make contracts work.

Cover

If the seller breaches, the buyer may *cover* by reasonably obtaining substitute goods; it may then obtain the difference between the contract price and its cover

---

[4] UCC §2-106(2).
[5] UCC §2-513.
[6] UCC §§2-601, 602.
[7] UCC §2-508.

price, plus incidental and consequential damages, minus expenses saved.[8] Retailer orders 10,000 pairs of ballet shoes from Shoemaker, at $55 per pair, to be delivered August 1. When no shoes dance through the door, Shoemaker explains that its workers in Europe are on strike, and no delivery date can be guaranteed. Retailer purchases comparable shoes elsewhere for $70, and files suit. Retailer will win $150,000, representing the increased cost of $15 per pair.

Incidental and Consequential Damages

An injured buyer is generally entitled to incidental and consequential damages. Incidental damages cover such costs as advertising for replacements, sending buyers to obtain new goods, and shipping the replacement goods. Consequential damages are those resulting from the unique circumstances of *this injured party*. They can be much more extensive and may include lost profits. **A buyer expecting to resell goods may obtain the loss of profit caused by the seller's failure to deliver.** In the ballet shoes case, suppose Retailer has contracts to resell the goods to ballet companies at an average profit of $10 per pair. Retailer is also entitled to those lost profits.

SELLER'S REMEDIES

Of course, a seller has rights, too. Sometimes a buyer breaches before the seller has delivered the goods, for example, by failing to make a payment due under the contract. If that happens, **the seller may refuse to deliver the goods.**[9]

If a buyer unjustly refuses to accept or pay for goods, the injured seller may resell them. **If the resale is commercially reasonable, the seller may recover the difference between the resale price and contract price, plus incidental damages, minus expenses saved.**[10] Incidental damages are expenses the seller incurs in holding the goods and reselling them, costs such as storage, shipping, and advertising for resale. The seller must deduct expenses saved by the breach. For example, if the contract required the seller to ship heavy machinery from Detroit to San Diego, and the buyer's breach enables the seller to market its goods profitably in Detroit, the seller must deduct from its claimed losses the transportation costs that it saved.

Finally, the seller may simply sue **for the contract price** if the buyer has accepted the goods *or if* the goods are conforming and resale is impossible.[11] If the goods were manufactured to the buyer's unique specifications, there might be no other market for them, and the seller should receive the contract price.

WARRANTIES AND PRODUCT LIABILITY

You are sitting in a fast-food restaurant in Washington, D.C. Your friend Ben, who works for a member of Congress, is eating with one hand and gesturing with the other. "We want product liability reform and we want it now," he proclaims,

---

[8] UCC §2-712.
[9] UCC §2-705.
[10] UCC §2-706
[11] UCC §2-709.

stabbing the air with his free hand. "It's absurd, these multimillion dollar verdicts, just because something has a *slight defect*." He waves angrily at the absurdity, takes a ferocious bite from his burger—and with a loud CRACK breaks a tooth. Ben howls in pain and throws down the bun, revealing a large piece of bone in the meat. As he tips back in misery, his defectively manufactured chair collapses, and Ben slams into the tile, knocking himself unconscious. Hours later, when he revives in the hospital, he refuses to speak to you until he talks with his lawyer. They will discuss **product liability**, which refers to goods that have caused an injury. The harm may be physical, as it was in Ben's case. Or it can be purely economic, as when a corporation buys a computer so defective it must be replaced, costing the buyer lost time and profits. The injured party may have a choice of possible remedies, including:

- *Warranty*, which is an assurance provided in a sales contract
- *Negligence*, which refers to unreasonable conduct by the defendant; and
- *Strict liability*, which prohibits defective products whether the defendant acted reasonably or not.

We discuss each of these remedies in this chapter. What all product liability cases have in common is that a person or business has been hurt by goods. We begin with warranties.

Express Warranties

A warranty is a contractual assurance that goods will meet certain standards. It is normally a manufacturer or a seller who gives a warranty, and a buyer who relies on it. A warranty might be explicit and written: "The manufacturer warrants that the lightbulbs in this package will provide 100 watts of power for 2,000 hours." Or a warranty could be oral: "Don't worry, this machine can harvest any size of wheat crop ever planted in the state."

An express warranty is one that the seller creates with his words or actions.[12] Whenever a seller *clearly indicates* to a buyer that the goods being sold will meet certain standards, she has created an express warranty. For example, if the sales-clerk for a paint store tells a professional house painter that "this exterior paint will not fade for three years, even in direct sunlight," that is an express warranty and the store is bound by it. The store is also bound by express warranty if the clerk gives the painter a brochure making the same promise, or a sample that indicates the same thing.

The seller may **disclaim** a warranty. **A disclaimer is a statement that a particular warranty *does not* apply.** The seller may disclaim an oral express warranty by including in the sales contract a statement such as "sold as is," or "any oral promises are disclaimed." Written express warranties generally *cannot* be disclaimed.

---

[12] UCC §2-313.

Implied Warranties

Emily sells Sam a new jukebox for his restaurant, but the machine is so defective it never plays a note. When Sam demands a refund, Emily scoffs that she never made any promises. She is correct that she made no express warranties, but is liable nonetheless. Many sales are covered by implied warranties.

Implied warranties are those created by the Code itself, not by any act or statement of the seller.

IMPLIED WARRANTY OF MERCHANTABILITY

This is the most important warranty in the Code. **Unless excluded or modified, a warranty that the goods shall be merchantable is implied in a contract for their sale, if the seller is a merchant with respect to goods of that kind.** *Merchantable* means that the goods are fit for the ordinary purposes for which they are used.[13] This rule contains several important principles:

- *Unless excluded or modified* means that the seller does have a chance to escape this warranty. A seller may disclaim this warranty provided he actually mentions the word *merchantability*. A seller also has the option to disclaim *all* warranties, by stating that the goods are sold "as is" or "with all faults."

- *Merchantability* requires that goods be fit for their normal purposes. A ladder, to be merchantable, must be able to rest securely against a building and support someone who is climbing it. The ladder need not be serviceable as a boat ramp.

- *Implied* means that the law itself imposes this liability on the seller.

- *A merchant with respect to goods of that kind* means that the seller is someone who routinely deals in these goods or holds himself out as having special knowledge about these goods.

Dacor Corp. manufactured and sold scuba diving equipment. Dacor ordered air hoses from Sierra Precision, specifying the exact size and couplings so that the hose would fit safely into Dacor's oxygen units. Within a year, customers returned a dozen Dacor units, complaining that the hose connections had cracked and were unusable. Dacor recalled 16,000 units and refit them at a cost of $136,000. Dacor sued Sierra and won its full costs. Sierra was a merchant with respect to scuba hoses, because it routinely manufactured and sold them. The defects were life-threatening to scuba divers, and the hoses could not be used for normal purposes.[14]

The scuba equipment was not merchantable, because a properly made scuba hose should never crack under normal use. But what if the product being sold is food, and the food contains something that is harmful—yet quite normal?

---

[13] UCC §2-314(1).

[14] *Dacor Corp. v. Sierra Precision*, 1993 U.S. Dist. LEXIS 8009 (N.D. Ill. 1993).

GOODMAN V. WENCO FOODS, INC.

333 N.C. 1, 423 S.E.2d 444, 1992 N.C.LEXIS 671
Supreme Court of North Carolina, 1992

FACTS: Fred Goodman and a friend stopped for lunch at a Wendy's restaurant in Hillsborough, North Carolina. Goodman had eaten about half of his double hamburger when he bit down and felt immediate pain in his lower jaw. He took from his mouth a triangular piece of cow bone, about one-sixteenth to one-quarter inch thick and one-half inch long, along with several pieces of his teeth. Goodman's pain was intense and his dental repairs took months.

The restaurant purchased all of its meat from Greensboro Meat Supply Company (GMSC). Wendy's required its meat to be chopped and "free from bone or cartilage in excess of 1/8 inch in any dimension." GMSC beef was inspected continuously by state regulators and was certified by the United States Department of Agriculture (USDA). The USDA considered any bone fragment less than three-quarters of an inch long to be "insignificant."

Goodman sued, claiming a breach of the implied warranty of merchantability. The trial court dismissed the claim, ruling that the bone was natural to the food and that the hamburger was therefore fit for its ordinary purpose. The appeals court reversed this, holding that a hamburger could be unfit even if the bone occurred naturally. Wendy's appealed to the state's highest court.

ISSUE: Was the hamburger unfit for its ordinary purpose because it contained a harmful but natural bone?

EXCERPTS FROM JUDGE EXUM'S DECISION: We hold that when a substance in food causes injury to a consumer of the food, it is not a bar to recovery against the seller that the substance was "natural" to the food, provided the substance is of such a size, quality or quantity, or the food has been so processed, or both, that the substance's presence should not reasonably have been anticipated by the consumer.

A triangular, one-half-inch, inflexible bone shaving is indubitably "inherent" in or "natural" to a cut of beef, but whether it is so "natural" to hamburger as to put a consumer on his guard—whether it "is to be reasonably expected by the consumer"—is, in most cases, a question for the jury. We are not requiring that the respondent's hamburgers be perfect, only that they be fit for their intended purpose. It is difficult to conceive of how a consumer might guard against the type of injury present here, short of removing the hamburger from its bun, breaking it apart and inspecting its small components.

Wendy's argues that the evidence supported its contention that its hamburger complied with [federal and state] standards. Wendy's reasons that [state and federal regulators permit] some bone fragments in meat and that its hamburgers are therefore merchantable as a matter of law. The court of appeals rejected this argument, noting that compliance "with all state and federal regulations is only some evidence which the jury may consider in determining whether the product was merchantable." We agree.

We thus conclude, as did the court of appeals majority, that a jury could reasonably determine the meat to be of such a nature, i.e., hamburger, and the bone in the meat of such a size that a consumer of the meat should not reasonably have anticipated the bone's presence. The court of appeals therefore properly reversed the directed verdict for Wendy's on plaintiff's implied warranty of merchantability claim. ◢

IMPLIED WARRANTY OF FITNESS FOR A PARTICULAR PURPOSE

The other warranty that the law imposes on sellers is the implied warranty of fitness for a particular purpose. This cumbersome name is often shortened to the *warranty of fitness*. **Where the seller at the time of contracting knows about a** particular purpose for which the buyer wants the goods, and knows that the buyer is relying on the seller's skill or judgment, there is (unless excluded or modified) an implied warranty that the goods shall be fit for such purpose.[15]

Notice that the seller must know about some special use the buyer intends, and realize that the buyer is relying on the seller's judgment. Suppose a lumber sales clerk knows that a buyer is relying on his advice to choose the best wood for a house being built in a swamp. The Code implies a warranty that the wood sold will withstand those special conditions.

Once again, a seller may disclaim this warranty if she clearly states "as is" or "sold with all faults," or some similar language.

Negligence

A buyer of goods may have remedies other than warranty claims. One is negligence. Here we focus on how this law applies to the sale of goods. Negligence is notably different from contract law. In a contract case, the two parties have reached an agreement, and the terms of their bargain will usually determine how to settle any dispute. If the parties agreed that the seller disclaimed all warranties, then the buyer may be out of luck. But in a negligence case, there has been no bargaining between the parties, who may never have met. A consumer injured by an exploding cola bottle is unlikely to have bargained for her beverage with the CEO of the cola company. Instead, the law *imposes* a standard of conduct on everyone in society, corporation and individual alike. The two key elements of this standard, for present purposes, are *duty* and *breach*. A plaintiff injured by goods she bought must show that the defendant, usually a manufacturer or seller of a product, had a duty to her and breached that duty. A defendant has a duty of due care to anyone who could foreseeably be injured by its misconduct. Generally, it is the duty to act as *a reasonable person* would in like circumstances; a defendant who acts unreasonably has breached his duty.

In negligence cases concerning the sale of goods, plaintiffs most often raise one or more of these claims:

- *Negligent Design.* The buyer claims that the product injured her because the manufacturer designed it poorly. Negligence law requires a manufacturer to design a product free of *unreasonable* risks. The product does not have to be absolutely safe. An automobile that guaranteed a driver's safety could be made but would be prohibitively expensive. Reasonable safety features must be built-in if they can be included at a tolerable cost.

- *Negligent Manufacture.* The buyer claims that the design was adequate but that failure to inspect or some other sloppy conduct caused a dangerous product to leave the plant.

- *Failure to Warn.* A manufacturer is liable for failing to warn the purchaser or users about the dangers of normal use and also foreseeable misuse. However, there is no duty to warn about obvious dangers, a point evidently lost on some manufacturers. A Batman costume unnecessarily included this statement: "For play only: Mask and chest plate are not protective; cape does not enable user to fly."

---

[15] UCC §2-315.

Ibrahim Boumelhem, age four, began playing with a Bic disposable lighter that his parents had bought. He started a fire that burned his legs and severely burned his six-month-old brother over 85 percent of his body. Ibrahim's father sued Bic, claiming that the lighter was negligently designed because it could have been child-proof. He also claimed failure to warn, because the lighter did not clearly warn of the danger to children.

The *Boumelhem* court considered evidence and analyses from several other cases against Bic. The court noted that consumers use over 500 million disposable lighters annually in the United States. Each lighter provides 1,000 to 2,000 lights. During one three-year period, children playing with disposable lighters started 8,100 fires annually, causing an average of 180 people to die every year, of whom 140 were children under five. Another 990 people were injured. The average annual cost of deaths, injuries, and property damage from child-play fires was estimated at $310 to $375 million, or 60 to 75 cents per lighter sold. Bic had acknowledged in earlier litigation that it was foreseeable lighters would get into children's hands and injure them. Bic had also agreed that it was feasible to make a more child-resistant lighter.

How should the court rule? Does this case present an irresponsible parent launching a frivolous lawsuit or a callous corporation disregarding children's safety to make a few extra dollars?

The tragic deaths in cases like *Boumelhem* prompted a federal agency, the Consumer Product Safety Commission (CPSC), to take action. What did the CPSC do, and with what results? You can search for news articles online, or go directly to the agency's Web site at http://www.cpsc.gov.

Strict Liability

The other tort claim that an injured person can bring against the manufacturer or seller of a product is strict liability. Like negligence, strict liability is a burden created by the law rather than by the parties. And, as with all torts, strict liability concerns claims of physical harm. But there is a key distinction between negligence and strict liability: in a negligence case, the injured buyer must demonstrate that the seller's conduct was unreasonable. Not so in strict liability.

In strict liability, the injured person need not prove that the defendant's conduct was unreasonable. The injured person must show only that the defendant manufactured or sold a product that was defective and that the defect caused harm. Almost all states permit such lawsuits, and most adopted the summary of strict liability provided by the Restatement (Second) of Torts §402A. Because §402A is the most frequently cited section in all of tort law, we quote it in full:

(1) One who sells any product in a defective condition unreasonably dangerous to the user or consumer or to his property is subject to liability for physical harm thereby caused to the ultimate user or consumer, or to his property, if

    (a) the seller is engaged in the business of selling such a product, and

    (b) it is expected to and does reach the user or consumer without substantial change in the condition in which it is sold.

(2) The rule stated in Subsection (1) applies although

(a) the seller has exercised all possible care in the preparation and sale of his product, and

(b) the user or consumer has not bought the product from or entered into any contractual relation with the seller.

These are the key terms in subsection (1):

- *Defective condition unreasonably dangerous to the user.* The defendant is liable only if the product is defective when it leaves his hands. There must be something wrong with the goods. If they are reasonably safe and the buyer's mishandling of the goods causes the harm, there is no strict liability. If you attempt to open a soda bottle by knocking the cap against a counter, and the glass shatters and cuts you, the manufacturer owes nothing.

  The article sold must be *more dangerous* than the ordinary consumer would expect. A carving knife can produce a lethal wound, but everyone knows that, and a sharp knife is not unreasonably dangerous. On the other hand, prescription drugs may harm in ways that neither a layperson nor a doctor would anticipate. The manufacturer *must provide adequate warnings* of any dangers that are not apparent.

- *In the business of selling.* The seller is liable only if she normally sells this kind of product. Suppose your roommate makes you a peanut butter sandwich and, while eating it, you cut your mouth on a sliver of glass that was in the jar. The peanut butter manufacturer faces strict liability as does the grocery store where your roommate bought the goods. But your roommate is not strictly liable because he does not serve sandwiches as a business.

- *Reaches the user without substantial change.* Obviously, if your roommate put the glass in the peanut butter thinking it was funny, neither the manufacturer nor the store is liable.

And here are the important phrases in subsection (2).

- *Has exercised all possible care.* This is the heart of strict liability, which makes it a potent claim for consumers. *It is no defense that the seller used reasonable care.* If the product is dangerously defective and injures the user, the seller is liable even if it took every precaution to design and manufacture the product safely. Suppose the peanut butter jar did in fact contain a glass sliver when it left the factory. The manufacturer proves that it uses extraordinary care in keeping foreign particles out of the jars and thoroughly inspects each container before it is shipped. The evidence is irrelevant. The manufacturer has shown that it was not negligent in packaging the food, but reasonable care is irrelevant in strict liability.

- *No contractual relation.* This means that the injured party need not have bought the goods directly from the party responsible for the defect. Suppose the manufacturer that made the peanut butter sold it to a distributor, which sold it to a wholesaler, which sold it to a grocery store, which sold it to your roommate. You may sue the manufacturer, distributor, wholesaler, and store, even though you never contracted with any of them.

Restatement (Third) and Contemporary Trends

We saw that under traditional negligence law, a company could be found liable based on design, manufacture, or failure to warn. The same three activities can give rise to a claim of strict liability. It will normally be easier for a plaintiff to win a claim of strict liability, because she does not need to demonstrate that the manufacturer's conduct was unreasonable.

If the steering wheel on a brand new car falls off, and the driver is injured, that is a clear case of defective manufacturing, and the company will be strictly liable. Those are the easy cases. As courts have applied §402A, defective design cases have been more contentious. Suppose a vaccine that prevents serious childhood illnesses inevitably causes brain damage in a very small number of children, because of the nature of the drug. Is the manufacturer liable? What if a racing sailboat, designed only for speed, is dangerously unstable in the hands of a less experienced sailor? Is the boat's maker responsible for fatalities? Suppose an automobile made of lightweight metal uses less fuel but exposes its occupants to more serious injuries in an accident. How is a court to decide whether the design was defective? Often, these design cases also involve issues of warnings: Did drug designer diligently detail dangers to doctors? Should sailboat seller sell speedy sailboat solely to seasoned sailors?

Over the years, most courts have adopted one of two tests for design and warning cases. The first is *consumer expectation*. Here, a court finds the manufacturer liable for defective design if the product is less safe than a reasonable consumer would expect. If a smoke detector has a 3 percent failure rate, and the average consumer has no way of anticipating that danger, effective cautions must be included, though the design may be defective anyway. Many states have moved away from that test, and now use a *risk-utility test*. Here, a court must weigh the benefits for society against the dangers that the product poses. Principal factors in the risk-utility test include:

- The *value* of the product,

- The *gravity* of the danger (how bad will the harm be),

- The *likelihood* that such danger will occur (the odds),

- The mechanical feasibility of a *safer alternative* design, and

- The *adverse consequences* of an alternative design (greater cost, different risks created).

Because of the conflicting court decisions, the American Law Institute drafted the Restatement (Third) of Torts: Product Liability, in an attempt to harmonize judicial opinions about product liability generally and design defects in particular. The new Restatement treats manufacturing cases differently from those involving design defects and failure to warn.

- In manufacturing cases, a product is defective whenever it departs from its intended design, regardless of how much care was taken. This is the traditional standard.

- In design and warnings cases, a product is defective only when the *foreseeable risks* of harm could have been reduced by using a reasonable alternative design or warning. So-called "strict" liability in these cases is beginning to resemble plain old negligence. If courts adopt this new approach, it will become more difficult for plaintiffs to win a design or warning case, because they will need to prove that the manufacturer should have foreseen the danger and could have done something about it.

There is no strong trend in how judges examine these cases: courts tend to pick and choose the analytic tools they use. Most still regard §402A as the basic law for all strict liability lawsuits. In design cases many courts use the risk-utility test, quite a few still examine consumer expectation, and some permit both analyses. Most states consider the availability of alternative designs to be important, and some consider it essential. And finally, as the following case indicates, some courts employ elements of the Restatement Third—with plenty of disagreement.

UNIROYAL GOODRICH TIRE COMPANY V. MARTINEZ

977 S.W.2d 328
Texas Supreme Court, 1998

FACTS: When Roberto Martinez, a mechanic, attempted to mount a 16-inch tire on a 16.5-inch rim (wheel), the tire exploded, causing him serious, permanent injuries. He sued Goodrich, the tire manufacturer; the Budd Company, which made the rim; and Ford Motor Company, which designed it. Budd and Ford settled out of court, and the case proceeded against Goodrich.

The tire had a conspicuous label, advising users never to mount a 16-inch tire on a 16.5-inch rim, warning of the danger of severe injury or death, and including a picture of a worker thrown into the air by an explosion. The label also urged the user never to lean or reach over the assembly while working. Martinez ignored the warnings.

Martinez admitted that the warnings were adequate, but claimed that Goodrich was strictly liable for failing to use a safer "bead" design. The bead, a rubber-encased steel wire, encircles the tire and holds it to the rim. Martinez's expert testified that an alternative design, used by other tire manufacturers, would have prevented his injury. The trial court gave judgment for Martinez in the amount of $10,308,792.45, the Court of Appeals affirmed, and Goodrich appealed to the state's highest court.

ISSUE: When warnings are adequate, is a manufacturer still obligated to use a safer alternative design?

EXCERPTS FROM CHIEF JUSTICE PHILLIPS' DECISION: This Court has adopted the products liability standard set forth in section 402A of the Restatement (Second) of Torts. A product may be unreasonably dangerous because of a defect in manufacturing, design, or marketing. To prove a design defect, a claimant must establish, among other things, that

the defendant could have provided a safer alternative design. [If] there are no safer alternatives, a product is not unreasonably dangerous as a matter of law.

The newly released Restatement (Third) of Torts: Product Liability carries forward this focus on reasonable alternative design:

A broad range of factors may be considered in determining whether an alternative design is reasonable and whether its omission renders a product not reasonably safe. The factors include, among others, the magnitude and probability of the foreseeable risks of harm, the instructions and warnings accompanying the product, and the nature and strength of consumer expectations regarding the product, including expectations arising from product portrayal and marketing. . . . Thus, the likely effects of the alternative design on production costs; the effects of the alternative design on product longevity, maintenance, repair, and esthetics; and the range of consumer choice among products are factors that may be taken into account. . . .

Goodrich urges this Court to depart from this standard by following certain language from Comment j of the Restatement (Second) of Torts. Comment j provides in part: "Where warning is given, the seller may reasonably assume that it will be read and heeded; and a product bearing such a warning, which is safe for use if it is followed, is not in defective condition, nor is it unreasonably dangerous." The new Restatement, however, expressly rejects the Comment j approach [and we refuse to adopt it].

The dissenting justices argue that Goodrich's warning was clear and that it could have been followed, and consequently Martinez was injured only by "[i]gnoring . . . his own good sense." Even if this were true, it is precisely because it is not at all unusual for a person to fail to follow basic warnings and instructions, that we have rejected the superseded Comment j. The dissent also notes that there have been few reported mismatch accidents involving tires with this particular warning label. While this is certainly relevant, and perhaps would persuade many juries, we cannot say that it conclusively establishes that the tire is reasonably safe when weighed against the other evidence. The jury heard firsthand how an accident can occur despite the warning label, and how a redesigned tire would have prevented that accident. The jury also heard evidence that Goodrich's competitors had incorporated the single strand programmed bead by the early 1980s, and that Goodrich itself adopted this design in 1991, a year after manufacturing the tire that injured Martinez.

The Martinezes offered some evidence that their alternative design would have prevented the injury to Martinez. It is undisputed that the single strand programmed bead is more resistant to breaking in mismatch situations. Goodrich expert Tom Conner testified that in a mismatch situation the tape bead may break at 60 psi, while a single strand bead will not break until at least 130 psi. Conner also testified that he has never heard of a single strand bead breaking during the inflating of a mismatched tire. Goodrich representative Stanley Lew testified that the single strand bead is more resistant in a mismatch situation. Lew also testified that if the tire inflated by Martinez had a single strand bead it would not have exploded. Both Conner and Lew testified that they would prefer a tire inflated by their loved one to have a single strand bead.

For the foregoing reasons, we affirm the judgment of the court of appeals. [Affirmed]

EXCERPTS FROM THE DISSENTING OPINION OF JUSTICE HECHT: Although a 16.5" wheel can be designed so that a 16" tire cannot be mounted on it, a 16" tire cannot be designed so that it cannot be mounted on a 16.5" wheel. A tire manufacturer's only options to reduce the risk of injury from attempting to mount a 16" tire on a 16.5" wheel are to place a warning on the tire or to design the bead wire so that it will withstand higher inflation pressure before exploding. The Uniroyal Goodrich Tire Company, which made the tire Martinez was using, chose to put a prominent, pictographic label on it, which, as I have said, Martinez actually saw but did not heed. Had he done so, he would not have been injured. In fact, according to the record, only one other person has ever claimed to have been injured attempting to mount a 16" tire with a warning label like Goodrich's on a 16.5" wheel, although thousands of labeled tires and more than thirty million 16.5" wheels have been manufactured in the past two decades.

[The] Court holds that a product can be found to be defective whenever it could be more safely designed without substantially impairing its utility. This is not, and should not be, the law. As the *Restatement (Third) of Torts: Product Liability* advises, a "broad range of factors" besides the utility of a reasonable alternate design should be considered in determining whether its use is necessary to keep the product reasonably safe, including "the magnitude and probability of the foreseeable risks of harm [and] the instructions and warnings accompanying the product." When the undisputed evidence is that the magnitude and probability of a risk are low, an alternative design could reduce but not eliminate that risk, and the instructions and warnings given do eliminate the risk, the product should be determined not to be defective as a matter of law. ◢

ECONOMICS & THE LAW

Smoking is expensive. In fact, virtually all state governments concluded that tobacco use causes lung cancer, emphysema, heart disease, and other illnesses, and that these ailments are very expensive to treat. The states filed suit against the tobacco industry, which settled most of the cases for a total of about $206 *billion*, to be paid gradually between the years 2000 and 2025. That is a lot of money, even for a profitable industry. (To find out how much your state will receive, go to http://tobaccowars.com, click first on "Legal," and then on "Tobacco Index.")

Ironically, one economist claims that the settlements make little money sense, because cigarettes are self-financing. This expert concedes that tobacco use causes expensive illnesses, yet argues that the increased costs are offset by savings due to earlier mortality! Because smokers die younger than others, states pay less money for nursing homes and pensions. These savings more than offset the increased medical costs of smoking.

If that is correct, then why would the tobacco industry agree to the pricey settlements? This economist suggests that a tobacco industry defense based on earlier mortality would be very risky to make in court. Jurors might find the argument so offensive that they would impose even higher punitive damages.[16]

NEGOTIABLE INSTRUMENTS

The first part of this chapter has covered Articles 2 and 2A of the UCC, dealing with contracts and product liability. Articles 3 and 4 of the Code regulate negotiable instruments. The second half of the chapter focuses on this important topic.

Commercial Paper

In early human history, people lived on whatever they could hunt, grow, or make for themselves. Over time, people improved their standard of living by bartering for goods and services they could not make themselves. But traders needed a method for keeping account of who owed how much to whom. The first currencies—gold and silver—had two disadvantages: they were easy to steal and heavy to carry. Paper currency solved the weight problem, but was even easier to steal than gold. As a result, money had to be kept in a safe place, and banks developed to meet that need. However, money in a vault is not very useful unless it can be readily spent. Society needed a system for transferring paper funds easily. Commercial paper is that system. The UCC's goal is to facilitate commerce by transforming these pieces of paper into something almost as easily transferable and reliable as money. (For more on the history of money, see http://www.ex.ac.uk/~RDavies/arian/llyfr.html.)

Types of Negotiable Instruments

There are two kinds of commercial paper: negotiable and non-negotiable instruments. Article 3 of the Code covers only negotiable instruments; non-negotiable instruments are governed by ordinary contract law. There are also two categories of negotiable instruments: notes and drafts.

A **note** (also called a **promissory note**) is your promise that you will pay money. A promissory note is used in virtually every loan transaction, whether the borrower is buying a multimillion dollar company or a TV set. For example, when you borrow money from Aunt Leila to buy a car, you will sign a note promising

---

[16] W. Kip Viscusi, "The Governmental Composition of the Insurance Costs of Smoking," *Journal of Law and Economics*, 1999, vol. 42, p. 575.

to repay the money. You are the **maker** because you are the one who has made the promise. Aunt Leila is the **payee** because she expects to be paid. (The Web site http://www.legaldocs.com/ provides a sample promissory note with fill-in blanks.)

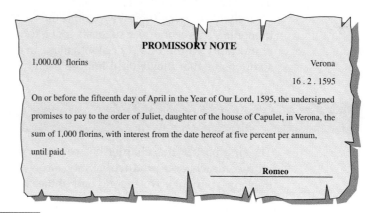

PROMISSORY NOTE

1,000.00 florins   Verona

16 . 2 . 1595

On or before the fifteenth day of April in the Year of Our Lord, 1595, the undersigned promises to pay to the order of Juliet, daughter of the house of Capulet, in Verona, the sum of 1,000 florins, with interest from the date hereof at five percent per annum, until paid.

Romeo

In this note, Romeo is the maker and Juliet is the payee.

A **draft** is an order directing someone else to pay money for you. A **check** is the most common form of a draft—it is an order telling a bank to pay money. In a draft, three people are involved: the **drawer** orders the **drawee** to pay money to the **payee**. Now before you slam the book shut in despair, let us sort out the players. Suppose that Serena Williams wins the River Oaks Club Open. River Oaks writes her a check for $500,000. This check is simply an order by River Oaks (the drawer) to its bank (the drawee) to pay money to Williams (the payee). The terms make sense if you remember that, when you take money out of your account, you *draw* it out. Therefore, when you write a check, you are the draw*er* and the bank is the draw*ee*. The person to whom you make out the check is being paid, so she is called the pay*ee*.

The following table illustrates the difference between notes and drafts. Even courts sometimes confuse the terms *drawer* (the person who signs a check) and *maker* (someone who signs a promissory note). **Issuer** is an all-purpose term that means both maker and drawer.

	Who Pays	Who Plays
Note	You make a promise that you will pay.	Two people are involved: maker and payee.
Draft	You order someone else to pay.	Three people are involved: drawer, drawee, and payee.

The Fundamental "Rule" of Commercial Paper

The possessor of a piece of commercial paper has an unconditional right to be paid, as long as (1) the paper is *negotiable*; (2) it has been *negotiated* to the possessor; (3) the possessor is a *holder in due course*; and (4) the issuer cannot claim a valid *defense*.

NEGOTIABILITY

To work as a substitute for money, commercial paper must be freely transferable in the marketplace, just as money is. In other words, it must be *negotiable*.

The possessor of *non*-negotiable commercial paper has the same rights—no more, no less—as the person who made the original contract. With non-negotiable commercial paper, the transferee's rights are *conditional* because they depend upon the rights of the original party to the contract. If, for some reason, the original party loses his right to be paid, so does the transferee. The value of non-negotiable commercial paper is greatly reduced because the transferee cannot be absolutely sure what his rights are or whether he will be paid at all.

Suppose that Krystal buys a used car from the Trustie Car Lot for her business, Krystal Rocks. She cannot afford to pay the full $15,000 right now, but she is willing to sign a note promising to pay later. As long as Trustie keeps the note, Krystal's obligation to pay is contingent upon the validity of the underlying contract. If, for example, the car is defective, then Krystal might not be liable to Trustie for the full amount of the note. Trustie, however, does not want to keep the note. He needs the cash *now* so that he can buy more cars to sell to other customers. Reggie's Finance Co. is happy to buy Krystal's promissory note from Trustie, but the price Reggie is willing to pay depends upon whether her note is negotiable.

If Krystal's promissory note is non-negotiable, Reggie gets exactly the same rights that Trustie had. As the saying goes, he steps into Trustie's shoes. Suppose that Trustie tampered with the odometer and, as a result, Krystal's car is worth only $12,000. If, under contract law, she owes Trustie only $12,000, then that is all she has to pay Reggie, even though the note *says* $15,000.

The possessor of *negotiable* commercial paper has *more* rights than the person who made the original contract. With negotiable commercial paper, the transferee's rights are *unconditional*. He is entitled to be paid the full amount of the note, regardless of the relationship between the original parties. If Krystal's promissory note is a negotiable instrument, she must pay the full amount to whoever has possession of it, no matter what complaints she might have against Trustie.

Exhibit 11.1 illustrates the difference between negotiable and non-negotiable commercial paper.

Because negotiable instruments are more valuable than non-negotiable ones, it is important for buyers and sellers to be able to tell, easily and accurately, if an instrument is indeed negotiable. To be negotiable:

1. **The Instrument Must Be in *Writing*.**

2. **The Instrument Must Be *Signed* by the Maker or Drawer.**

3. **The Instrument Must Contain an *Unconditional Promise* or *Order to Pay*.** If Krystal's promissory note says, "I will pay $15,000 as long as the car is still in working order," it is not negotiable because it is making a conditional promise. The instrument must also contain a promise or order to pay. It is not enough simply to say, "Krystal owes Trustie $15,000." She has to indicate that she owes the money and also that she intends to pay it. "Krystal promises to pay Trustie $15,000" would work.

4. **The Instrument Must State a *Definite Amount* of Money.** "I promise to pay Trustie one-third of my profits this year" would not work, because the amount

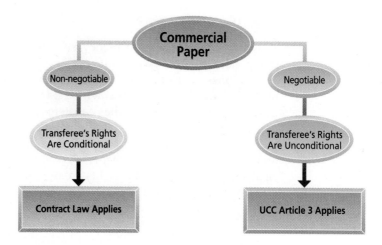

Exhibit 11.1

is unclear. If Krystal's note says, "I promise to pay $15,000 worth of diamonds," it is not negotiable because it does not state a definite amount of *money*.

5. **The Instrument Must Be Payable on *Demand* or at a *Definite Time*.** A demand instrument is one that must be paid whenever the holder requests payment. If an instrument is undated, it is treated as a demand instrument and is negotiable. An instrument can be negotiable even if it will not be paid until some time in the future, provided that the payment date can be determined when the document is made. A graduate of a well-known prep school has written a generous check to his alma mater each year, but for payment date he puts, "The day the headmaster is fired." These checks are not negotiable because they are neither payable on demand nor at a definite time.

6. **The Instrument Must Be Payable to *Order* or to *Bearer*. Order paper** must include the words "Pay to the order of" someone. By including the word "order," the maker is indicating that the instrument is not limited to only one person. "Pay to the order of Trustie Car Lot" means that the money will be paid to Trustie *or to anyone Trustie designates*. If the note is made out "To bearer," it is **bearer paper** and can be redeemed by *any* holder in due course.

The rules for checks are different from other negotiable instruments. All checks are, by definition, negotiable. Most checks are preprinted with the words "Pay to the order of," but sometimes people inadvertently cross out "order of." Even so, the check is still negotiable. Checks are frequently received by consumers who, sadly, have not completed a course on business law. The drafters of the UCC did not think it fair to penalize them when the drawer of the check was the one who made the mistake.

An instrument must be *signed* by the maker or drawer. This sounds straightforward, but what does it mean to sign a note or draft? Many people, for example, pay bills online. How do they sign an online check? How does their bank know the signature is valid? Many states now grant digital signatures the same legal status under the UCC as a traditional paper signature (which is called a "wet"

signature).[17] A computer signature does not look like handwriting; instead, it is a unique series of letters and numbers in code. A digital signature can actually be safer than the traditional wet signature. If the digital document is dishonestly altered, the sender and recipient can tell. ◾

In the following case, a set of notes deviated slightly from the requirements of the UCC. Are the notes negotiable despite the errors?

IN RE BOARDWALK MARKETPLACE SECURITIES LITIGATION

688 F. Supp. 115, 1987 U.S. Dist. LEXIS 15122
United States District Court, District of Connecticut, 1987

FACTS: Investors purchased interests in limited partnerships that were organized to redevelop property in Atlantic City, New Jersey. To finance their purchases, the investors executed promissory notes payable to American Funding Limited. The notes stated, in part:

> I will pay ____ monthly installments of principal and interest, each in the amount of $ ____, commencing on the ____ day of ____ 19 ____ (estimated first payment date). Lender will notify me in writing of the first payment due date, the amount of the first payment, the date of the first payment, the date of the final payment and the amount of the final payment.

In the blanks, someone had handwritten figures representing the number of monthly payments, the amount of each payment, and an estimated date on which the payments were to begin.

American Funding Limited sold these notes to various banks. When the redevelopment plan collapsed, many of the investors ceased making payments on their notes. The investors asserted that the notes were non-negotiable because the payment date was not definite. The banks argued that, whether or not the payment date was definite, equity demanded that the notes be treated as if they were negotiable so that the banks, which were innocent of all wrongdoing, could collect the money owed them. If the notes were non-negotiable, the banks' right to collect might be defeated by claims the investors had against American Funding.

ISSUES: Did these notes comply with UCC requirements for negotiability? If not, should the notes be treated as if they were negotiable?

EXCERPTS FROM JUDGE EGINTON'S DECISION: The investors pose a narrow challenge to the notes' claimed negotiability, alleging that they are neither payable on demand nor at a definite time. The initial question is whether these notes are payable at a "definite time."

The notes do not satisfy the requirements of definite time. Subsection (a) [of the UCC] reads "on or before a stated date or at a fixed period after a stated date." Logically, a note containing an estimated first payment date and a provision which states that the lender will notify the maker of the actual first payment date does not fall within the confines of this subsection.

The overarching concern of the Code and thereby Article Three is to promote the free flow of commerce. The decision was made that a set of formal requisites which the terms of commercial paper must meet would best serve these purposes. One requisite is that the paper be negotiable. The formalities of negotiability arose in history out of the law merchant. There is no particular magic to them; the drafters could have chosen other formalities, although some are obvious.

---

[17] The federal Electronic Signatures in Global and National Commerce Act expanded the definition of electronic signature to include "biometric" identifications such as fingerprints, retina scans, and voiceprints. However, the federal statute does not apply to UCC Articles 3 and 4.

Because the prerequisites to negotiability are formal, it is both simple and necessary to comply with them. To hold that these notes are negotiable would certainly preserve the integrity of these notes and in that limited sense serve the interests of commerce; however, it would reward shoddy drafting and introduce unnecessary doubt into the formalities of negotiability. The reason for employing formalities in legal rules is to preclude the kinds of arguments that the banks offer to circumvent them here. It will not do to argue that the goal of promoting the expansion of commerce with predictably negotiable paper is served by artful reconstruction of the formalities set up initially to serve that same goal.

[The court concluded that the notes were not negotiable.] ◢

Was the result in this case fair? These investors were using a technicality of Article 3 to avoid paying legitimate debt. Why should the banks (and their shareholders or depositors) suffer when they had absolutely no involvement in the investment scheme?

Which of the questions from the Chapter 2 ethics checklist does the court rely on in reaching its decision? Can you argue that this decision violates some of the guidelines on the ethics checklist? Is this a case of Right v. Right? ▰

NEGOTIATION

Negotiation means that an instrument has been transferred to the holder by someone *other than the issuer*. If the issuer has transferred the instrument to the holder, then it has not been negotiated and the issuer can refuse to pay the holder if there was some flaw in the underlying contract. Thus, if Jake gives Madison a promissory note for $2,000 in payment for a new computer, but the computer crashes and burns the first week, Jake has the right to refuse to pay the note. Jake was the issuer and the note was not negotiated. But if, before the computer self-destructs, Madison indorses and transfers the note to Kayla, then Jake is liable to Kayla for the full amount of the note, regardless of his claims against Madison.

To be negotiated, order paper must first be *indorsed* and then *delivered* to the transferee. Bearer paper must simply be *delivered* to the transferee; no indorsement is required.[18]

An indorsement is the signature of the payee. Tess writes a rent check for $475 to her landlord, Larnell. If Larnell signs the back of the check and delivers it to Patty, he has met the two requirements for negotiating order paper: indorsement and delivery. If Larnell delivers the check to Patty but forgets to sign it, the check has not been indorsed and therefore cannot be negotiated—it has no value to Patty.

HOLDER IN DUE COURSE

A holder in due course has an automatic right to receive payment for a negotiable instrument (unless the issuer can claim a valid defense). If the possessor of an instrument is not a holder in due course, then his right to payment depends upon the relationship between the issuer and payee. He inherits whatever claims and defenses arise out of that contract. Clearly, then, holder in due course status dramatically increases the value of an instrument because it enhances the probability of being paid.

---

[18] The UCC spells the word "indorsed." Outside the UCC, the word is more commonly spelled "endorsed."

Requirements for Being a Holder in Due Course

Under §3-302 of the UCC, a holder in due course is a *holder* who has given *value* for the instrument, in *good faith, without notice* of outstanding claims or other defects.

Holder. For order paper, a **holder** is anyone in possession of the instrument if it is payable to or indorsed to her. For bearer paper, a **holder** is anyone in possession. Tristesse gives Felix a check payable to him. Because Felix owes his mother money, he indorses the check and delivers it to her. This is a valid negotiation because Felix has both indorsed the check (which is order paper) and delivered it. Therefore, Felix's mother is a holder.

Value. A holder in due course must give value for an instrument. **Value** means that the holder has *already* done something in exchange for the instrument. Felix's mother has already loaned him money, so she has given value.

Good Faith. There are two tests to determine if a holder acquired an instrument in good faith. The holder must meet *both* of these tests:

- **Subjective Test.** Did the holder *believe* the transaction was honest in fact?

- **Objective Test.** Did the transaction *appear* to be commercially reasonable?

Felix persuades his elderly neighbor, Faith, that he has invented a fabulous beauty cream guaranteed to remove wrinkles. She gives him a $10,000 promissory note, payable in 90 days, in return for exclusive sales rights in Pittsburgh. Felix sells the note to his old friend Dick for $2,000. Felix never delivers the sales samples to Faith. When Dick presents the note to Faith, she refuses to pay on the grounds that Dick is not a holder in due course. She contends that he did not buy the note in good faith.

Dick fails both tests. Any friend of Felix knows he is not trustworthy, especially when presenting a promissory note signed by an elderly neighbor. Dick did not believe the transaction was honest in fact. Also, $10,000 notes are not usually discounted to $2,000; $9,000 would be more normal. This transaction is not commercially reasonable, and Dick should have realized immediately that Felix was up to no good.

Notice of Outstanding Claims or Other Defects. In certain circumstances, a holder is on notice that an instrument has an outstanding claim or other defect:

1. **The Instrument Is Overdue.** An instrument is overdue the day after its due date. At that point, the recipient ought to wonder why no one has bothered to collect the money owed. A check is overdue 90 days after its date. Any other *demand* instrument is overdue (1) the day after a request for payment is made or (2) a reasonable time after the instrument was issued.

2. **The Instrument Is Dishonored.** To dishonor an instrument is to refuse to pay it. For example, once a check has been stamped "Insufficient Funds" by the bank, it has been dishonored, and no one who obtains it afterward can be a holder in due course.

3. **The Instrument Is Altered, Forged, or Incomplete.** Anyone who knows that an instrument has been altered or forged cannot be a holder in due course. Suppose Joe wrote a check to Tony for $200. While showing the check to Liza,

---

PROMISSORY NOTE

$500.00   September 5, 1950

On or before 60 days after date, I promise to pay $500 to
the order of Soames for value received.

_____ *Irene*

The holder of this note should realize that there may be a problem.

Tony cackles to himself and says, "Can you believe what that goof did? Look, he left the line blank after the words 'two hundred.'" Taking his pen out with a flourish, Tony changes the zeroes to nines and adds the words "ninety-nine." He then indorses the check over to Liza, who is definitely not a holder in due course.

4. **The Holder Has Notice of Certain Claims or Disputes.** No one can qualify as a holder in due course if she is on notice that (1) someone else has a claim to the instrument or (2) there is a dispute between the original parties to the instrument. Matt hires Sheila to put aluminum siding on his house. In payment, he gives her a $15,000 promissory note with the due date left blank. They agree that the note will not be due until 60 days after completion of the work. Despite the agreement, Sheila fills in the date immediately and sells the note to Rupert at American Finance Corp., who has bought many similar notes from Sheila. Rupert knows that the note is not supposed to be due until after the work is finished. Usually, before he buys a note from her, he demands a signed document from the home owner certifying that the work is complete. Also, he lives near Matt and can see that Matt's house is only half finished. Rupert is not a holder in due course because he has reason to suspect there is a dispute between Sheila and Matt.

In the following case, the defendant alleged that he was not liable on a promissory note. You be the judge.

YOU BE THE JUDGE

GRANITE MANAGEMENT CORPORATION V. GAAR

1997 U.S. App. LEXIS 27263
United States Court of Appeals for the Second Circuit, 1997

FACTS: Pay Tel Management, Inc., owned pay telephones. An agent of the company convinced Norman Gaar to invest in this business. Gaar agreed to borrow $275,000 from Citytrust and invest that sum in Pay Tel. Gaar would then receive dividends from Pay Tel that were sufficient to repay the Citytrust loan. The Pay Tel agent assured Gaar that he would not have to pay any money out of his own pocket. In reliance on this promise, Gaar signed a promissory note for $275,000, payable to Citytrust. The sums Gaar owed on the note were due on the same dates and in the same amounts as the payments Pay Tel had promised to make to Gaar.

Although Gaar did not know it, Citytrust sold his note to First National Bank (FNB). FNB and Citytrust had been involved in other deals together, but FNB did not participate in the negotiations between Gaar and Citytrust.

You will not be surprised to learn that Pay Tel failed to make the payments that it had promised Gaar (and its other investors). Gaar then stopped paying what he owed on his promissory note to Citytrust.

YOU BE THE JUDGE: Is Gaar liable to FNB for the promissory note he signed?

ARGUMENT FOR GAAR: Pay Tel promised Gaar that this investment would not require him to make any payments out of pocket. The company's payments to him were supposed to equal (in timing and amount) what he owed on the note. Pay Tel has not met these commitments and, therefore, Gaar is not liable. FNB should seek payment from Pay Tel.

FNB had engaged in many deals with Citytrust, and therefore had reason to know that the Gaar transaction was fraudulent. In that case, FNB was not acting in good faith and therefore is not a holder in due course. Any defenses that Gaar could make against Cititrust he can also use to defend against FNB.

ARGUMENT FOR FNB: To win, Gaar must show either (1) FNB believed the transaction between Gaar and PayTel was dishonest or (2) the transaction did not appear to be commercially reasonable. There is simply no evidence that either of these statements is true. The arrangement between PayTel and Gaar may very well have been fraudulent, but that is not FNB's fault and it should not suffer a loss as a result. ▮

God Faith Stand

Defenses against a Holder in Due Course

Negotiable instruments are meant to be a close substitute for money, and, as a general rule, holders expect to be paid. **However, the issuer of a negotiable instrument is not required to pay if:**

1. His signature on the instrument was forged.

2. After signing the instrument, his debts were discharged in bankruptcy.

3. He was a minor at the time he signed the instrument.

4. The amount of the instrument was altered after he signed it. (Although, if he left the instrument blank, he *is* liable for any amounts later filled in.)

5. He signed the instrument under duress, while mentally incapacitated, or as part of an illegal transaction.

6. He was tricked into signing the instrument without knowing what it was and without any reasonable way to find out.

CONSUMER EXCEPTION

In the eighteenth and nineteenth centuries, negotiable instruments often circulated through several hands. The business community treated them as money. The concept of holder in due course was essential because the instruments had little use if they could not be transferred for value. In the modern banking system, however, instruments are much less likely to circulate. Currently, the most common use for negotiable instruments is in consumer transactions. A consumer pays for a refrigerator by giving the store a promissory note. The store promptly sells the note to a finance company. Even if the refrigerator is defective, under Article 3 the consumer must pay full value on the note because the finance company is a holder in due course.

Some commentators have argued that the concept of holder in due course no longer serves a useful purpose and that it should be eliminated once and for all (and with it Article 3 of the UCC). No state has yet taken such a dramatic step. Instead, some states require promissory notes given by a consumer to carry the words "consumer paper." Notes with this legend are non-negotiable.

Meanwhile, the Federal Trade Commission (FTC) has special rules for consumer credit contracts. A **consumer credit contract** is one in which a consumer borrows money from a lender to purchase goods and services from a seller who is affiliated with the lender. If Sears loans money to Gerald to buy a big-screen TV at Sears, that is a consumer credit contract. It is not a consumer credit contract if Gerald borrows money from his cousin Vinnie to buy the TV from Sears. The FTC requires all promissory notes in consumer credit contracts to contain the following language:

NOTICE

ANY HOLDER OF THIS CONSUMER CREDIT CONTRACT IS SUBJECT TO ALL CLAIMS AND DEFENSES WHICH THE DEBTOR COULD ASSERT AGAINST THE SELLER OF GOODS OR SERVICES OBTAINED PURSUANT HERETO OR WITH THE PROCEEDS HEREOF. RECOVERY HEREUNDER BY THE DEBTOR SHALL NOT EXCEED AMOUNTS PAID BY THE DEBTOR HEREUNDER.

Under §3-106(d) of the UCC, no one can be a holder in due course of an instrument with this language. If the language is omitted from a consumer note, it is possible to be a holder in due course, but the seller can be punished by a fine of up to $10,000.

Sometime in your life, you may well sign a promissory note for a consumer loan. Before signing, make sure that the note contains this FTC language.

Chapter Conclusion

The development of the UCC was an enormous and ambitious undertaking. Its goal was to facilitate the free flow of commerce across this large nation. By any measure, the UCC has been a success. Each and every day, thousands of businesspeople comply with the UCC as they sign contracts, write checks, and deliver promissory notes. It is worth remembering, however, that the terms of the UCC are precise and that failure to comply with these exacting provisions can lead to unfortunate consequences. In some ways, the UCC is like a marine drill instructor: rigid, but predictable if you follow the rules.

Chapter Review

1. The Code is designed to modernize commercial law and make it uniform throughout the country. Article 2 applies to the sale of goods.

2. A merchant is someone who routinely deals in the particular goods involved, or who appears to have special knowledge or skill in those goods, or who uses agents with special knowledge or skill.

3. UCC §2-204 permits the parties to form a contract in any manner that shows agreement.

4. For the sale of goods worth $500 or more, UCC §2-201 requires some writing that indicates an agreement.

5. A merchant who receives a signed memo confirming an oral contract may become liable if he fails to object within 10 days.

6. UCC §2-207 governs an acceptance that does not "mirror" the offer. *Additional* terms usually become part of the contract. *Different* terms contradict the offer, and are generally replaced by the Code's own gap-filler terms.

7. An injured seller my resell the goods and obtain the difference between the contract and resale prices. An injured buyer may buy substitute goods and obtain the difference between the contract and cover prices.

8. Product liability may arise in various ways:

    • A party may *create* an express warranty with words or actions. The Code may *imply* a warranty of merchantability or fitness for a particular purpose.

    • A seller will be liable if her conduct is not that of a reasonable person.

    • A seller may be strictly liable for a defective product that reaches the user without substantial change.

9. The possessor of non-negotiable commercial paper has the same rights—no more, no less—as the person who made the original contract. The possessor of negotiable commercial paper has more rights than the person who made the original contract.

10. The possessor of a piece of commercial paper has an unconditional right to be paid, as long as:

    • The paper is negotiable

    • It has been negotiated to the possessor

    • The possessor is a holder in due course; and

    • The issuer cannot claim a valid defense.

11. To be negotiable, an instrument must:

    • Be in writing

    • Be signed by the maker or drawer

    • Contain an unconditional promise or order to pay

    • State a definite amount of money

    • Be payable on demand or at a definite time; and

    • Be payable to order or to bearer.

12. To be negotiated, order paper must first be indorsed and then delivered to the transferee. Bearer paper must simply be delivered to the transferee; no indorsement is required.

13. A holder in due course is a holder who has given value for the instrument, in good faith, without notice of outstanding claims or other defects.

14. The Federal Trade Commission (FTC) requires all promissory notes in consumer credit contracts to contain language preventing any subsequent holder from being a holder in due course.

Practice Test

1. Nina owns a used car lot. She signs and sends a fax to Seth, a used car wholesaler who has a huge lot of cars in the same city. The fax says, "Confirming our agrmt—I pick any 15 cars fr yr lot—30% below blue book." Seth reads the fax, laughs, and throws it away. Two weeks later, Nina arrives and demands to purchase 15 of Seth's cars. Is he obligated to sell?

2. **YOU BE THE JUDGE WRITING PROBLEM** United Technologies advertised a used Beechcraft Baron airplane for sale in an aviation journal. Attorney Thompson Comerford spoke with a United agent who described the plane as "excellently maintained" and said it had been operated "under §135 flight regulations," meaning the plane had been subject to airworthiness inspections every 100 hours. Comerford arrived at a Dallas airport to pick up the plane, where he paid $80,000 for it. He signed a sales agreement stating that the plane was sold "as is" and that there were "no representations or warranties, express or implied, including the condition of the aircraft, its merchantability or its fitness for any particular purpose." Comerford attempted to fly the plane home, but immediately experienced problems with its brakes, steering, ability to climb, and performance while cruising. (Otherwise it was fine.) He sued, claiming breach of express and implied warranties. Did United Technologies breach express or implied warranties? **Argument for Comerford:** United described the airplane as "excellently maintained," knowing that Mr. Comerford would rely. The company should not be allowed to say one thing and put the opposite in writing. **Argument for United Technologies:** Comerford is a lawyer, and we assume he can read. The contract clearly stated that the plane was sold as is. There were no warranties.

3. To satisfy the UCC statute of frauds regarding the sale of goods, which of the following must generally be in writing?

   (a) Designation of the parties as buyer and seller

   (b) Delivery terms

   (c) Quantity of the goods

   (d) Warranties to be made

4. **ETHICS** Texaco, Inc., and other oil companies sold mineral spirits in bulk to distributors, which then resold to retailers. Mineral spirits are used for cleaning and are harmful or fatal if swallowed. Texaco allegedly knew that the retailers, such as hardware stores, frequently packaged the mineral spirits (illegally) in used half-gallon milk containers and sold them to consumers, often with no warnings on the packages. David Hunnings, age 21 months, found a milk container in his home, swallowed the mineral spirits, and died. The Hunningses sued Texaco in negligence. The trial court dismissed the complaint and the Hunningses appealed. What is the legal standard in a negligence case? Have the plaintiffs made out a valid case of negligence? Assume that Texaco knew about the repackaging and the grave risk, but continued to sell in bulk because doing so was profitable. (If the plaintiffs cannot prove those facts, they will lose even if they *do* get to a jury.) Would that make you angry? Should the case go to a jury? Or did the fault still lie with the retailer and/or the parents?

5. **CPA QUESTION** Which of the following factors is least important in determining whether a manufacturer is strictly liable in tort for a defective product?

   (a) The negligence of the manufacturer

   (b) The contributory negligence of the plaintiff

   (c) Modifications to the product by the wholesaler

   (d) Whether the product caused injuries

6. Lewis River Golf, Inc., grew and sold sod. It bought seed from defendant, O. M. Scott & Sons, under an express warranty. But the sod grown from the Scott seeds developed weeds, a breach of Scott's warranty. Several of Lewis River's customers sued, unhappy with the weeds in their grass. Lewis River lost most of its customers, cut back its production from 275 acres to 45 acres, and destroyed all remaining sod grown from Scott's seeds. Eventually, Lewis River sold its business at a large loss. A jury awarded Lewis River $1,026,800, largely for lost profits and loss of goodwill. Scott appealed, claiming that a plaintiff may not recover for lost profits and goodwill. Comment.

7. Gary Culver, a farmer in Missouri, was having financial problems. He agreed to let Nasib Ed Kalliel assume control of the farm's finances. After a few months, Culver urgently asked Kalliel for money. One week later, $30,000 was wire-transferred to Culver from the Rexford State Bank. Culver thought that Kalliel would be responsible for repaying this sum. A man who worked for Kalliel stopped Culver on the street

and asked him to sign a receipt for the $30,000. Culver signed without intending to commit himself to repaying the money. In fact, the document Culver signed was a blank promissory note, payable to Rexford. Someone later filled in the blanks, putting in $50,000 instead of $30,000. Kalliel had received $50,000 before transferring $30,000 to Culver. Is Culver liable on the note?

8. **CPA QUESTION** In order to negotiate bearer paper, one must:

(a) Indorse the paper

(b) Indorse and deliver the paper with consideration

(c) Deliver the paper

(d) Deliver and indorse the paper

9. Gina and Douglas Felde purchased a Dodge Daytona with a 70,000-mile warranty. They signed a loan contract with the dealer to pay for the car in 48 monthly installments of $250. The dealer sold the contract to the Chrysler Credit Corp. Soon, the Feldes complained that the car had developed a tendency to accelerate abruptly and without warning. Neither of two Dodge dealers was able to correct the problem. The Feldes filed suit against Chrysler Credit Corp., but the company refused to rescind the loan contract. The company argued that, as a holder in due course on the note, it was entitled to be paid regardless of any defects in the car. How would you decide this case if you were the judge?

10. **ETHICS** S. J. Littlegreen owned the Lookout Mountain Hotel. In financial trouble, he put the hotel on the market at a price of $850,000. C. Abbott Gardner was his real estate agent. To obtain more time to sell, Littlegreen decided to refinance his debt. Mr. Rupe agreed to lend Littlegreen $300,000. When this loan was ready for closing, Gardner informed Littlegreen that he expected a commission of 5 percent of the amount of the loan, or $15,000. Gardner threatened to block the loan if his demands were not met. Littlegreen needed the proceeds of the loan badly, so he agreed to give Gardner $4,000 in cash and a promissory note for $11,000. On what grounds might Littlegreen claim that the note is invalid? Would this be a valid defense? Even if Gardner was in the right legally, was he in the right ethically? Would he like everyone in town to know that he had squeezed Littlegreen in this way? How would he have felt if he had been in Littlegreen's position? Does might make right?

11. Catherine Wagner suffered serious physical injuries in an automobile accident and became acutely depressed as a result. One morning, she received a check for $17,400 in settlement of her claims arising out of the accident. She indorsed the check and placed it on the kitchen table. She then called Robert Scherer, her long-time roommate, to tell him the check had arrived. That afternoon, she jumped from the roof of her apartment building, killing herself. The police found the check and a note from her, stating that she was giving it to Scherer. Had Wagner negotiated the check to Scherer?

12. **ROLE REVERSAL** Write a multiple-choice question that contrasts the common law rules of contract formation with those of UCC §2-204.

13. **ROLE REVERSAL** Write a multiple-choice question that concerns a holder in due course.

Internet Research Problems

Look at http://www.insure.com/auto/. Which cars are safer than average? Less safe? How important is auto safety to you? Are you willing to pay more for a safe car? Who should be the final judge of auto safety: auto companies, insurance companies, juries, government regulators, or consumers?

Go to http://www.legaldocs.com and fill in the blanks of a promissory note. Who is the maker, and who is the payee of your note? Did you create a demand note?

You can find further practice problems in the Online Quiz at http://beatty.westbuslaw.com or in the Study Guide that accompanies this text.

Secured Transactions
and Bankruptcy

Dear Help-for-All:

Somebody must be crazy. When I got out of school, I paid $18,000 for a used Lexus. I made every payment for over two years. I shelled out over 9,000 bucks for that car. Then I got laid off through no fault of my own. I missed a few payments, and the bank repossessed the car. They auctioned off the Lexus. Now the bank's lawyer phones and says I'm still liable for over $5,000. I owe money for a car I can't drive anymore? If they say I really have to pay all that money, I'm heading straight for Bankruptcy Court.

> Signed,
> Still Sane, I Hope

Dear Still Sane,

I am sympathetic, but unfortunately the bank is entitled to its money. When you bought the car, you signed two documents: a note, in which you promised to pay the full balance owed, and a security agreement, which said that if you stopped making payments, the bank could repossess the vehicle and sell it.

There are two problems. First, even after two years of writing checks, you might still have owed about $10,000 (because of interest). Second, cars depreciate quickly. Your $18,000 vehicle probably had a market value of about $8,000 30 months later. The security agreement allowed the bank to sell the Lexus at auction, where prices are still lower. Your car evidently fetched about $5,000. That leaves a deficiency of $5,000—for which you are legally responsible, regardless of who is driving the car. Bankruptcy law can indeed provide important relief, though the process is not so easy nor the results so absolute as many people think.

Sorry,
Help-for-Almost-All ◾

Secured Transactions and Bankruptcy: Introduction[1]

We can sympathize with "Still Sane," but the bank is entitled to its money. The buyer and the bank had entered into a secured transaction, meaning that one party gave credit to another, insisting on full repayment *and* the right to seize certain property if the debt went unpaid.

It is essential to understand the basics of this law because we live and work in a world economy based solidly—or shakily—on credit. An equally important and closely related topic is bankruptcy law. A debtor unable to pay his bills may end up in Bankruptcy Court, along with a host of creditors clamoring to be paid. We will examine major issues of bankruptcy law in the second half of this chapter, but we begin by looking at secured transactions.

Article 9 of the Uniform Commercial Code (UCC) governs secured transactions in personal property. Article 9 employs terms not used elsewhere, so we must lead off with some definitions:

- **Fixtures** are goods that have become attached to real estate. For example, heating ducts are *goods* when a company manufactures them, but they become *fixtures* when installed in a house.

- **Security interest** means an interest in personal property or fixtures that secures the performance of some *obligation*. If an automobile dealer sells you a new car on credit and retains a security interest, it means she is keeping legal rights *in your car*, including the right to drive it away if you fall behind in your payments. Usually, the obligation is to pay money, such as the money due on the new car, though occasionally the obligation is to perform some other action.

- **Secured party** is the person or company that holds the security interest. The automobile dealer who sells you a car on credit is the secured party.

- **Collateral** is the property subject to a security interest. When a dealer sells you a new car and keeps a security interest, the vehicle is the collateral.

---

[1] In this chapter we use more footnotes than usual, for two reasons. First, Article 9 is a challenging series of interlocking provisions, and many readers will want to peruse the actual Code (in the Appendix) to reinforce the myriad concepts. Second, the revised Article 9 is substantially rewritten and entirely renumbered; experienced practitioners may appreciate guidelines as they encounter new rules and discover familiar concepts in unexpected places. Without Ariadne's thread, Theseus would still be stumbling through the Cretan labyrinth.

- **Debtor and Obligor.** For our purposes, **debtor** refers to a person who has some original ownership interest in the collateral. (Having a security interest in the collateral does not make one a debtor.) If Alice borrows money from a bank and uses her Mercedes as collateral, she is the debtor because she owns the car. **Obligor** means a person who must repay money or perform some other task.

   The obligor and debtor are generally the same person, but not always. When Alice borrows money from a bank and uses her Mercedes as collateral, she is the obligor, because she must repay the loan; as we know, Alice is also the debtor. However, suppose that Toby borrows money from a bank and provides no collateral; Jake co-signs the loan as a favor to Toby, using his Steinway piano as collateral. *Jake* is the only debtor, because he owns the piano. *Both parties* are obligors, because both have agreed to repay the loan.

- **Security agreement** is the contract in which the debtor gives a security interest to the secured party. This agreement protects the secured party's rights in the collateral.

- **Default** occurs when the debtor fails to pay money that is due, for example, on a loan or for a purchase made on credit. Default also includes other failures by the debtor, such as failing to keep the collateral insured.

- **Repossession** occurs when the secured party takes back collateral because the debtor has defaulted.

- **Perfection** is a series of steps the secured party must take to protect its rights in the collateral against people other than the debtor.

- **Financing statement** is a record intended to notify the general public that the secured party has a security interest in the collateral.

- **Record** refers to information written on paper *or* stored in an electronic or other medium.

- **Authenticate** means to sign a document *or* to use any symbol or encryption method that identifies the person and clearly indicates she is adopting the record as her own. You authenticate a security agreement when you sign the papers at an auto dealership. A corporation electronically authenticates a loan agreement by using the Internet to transmit a public-key signature. (See the Cyberlaw feature in Chapter 10 for a discussion of electronic signatures.)

Here is an example using the terms just discussed. A medical equipment company manufactures a CT scanner and sells it to a clinic for $2 million, taking $500,000 cash and the clinic's promise to pay the rest over five years. The clinic simultaneously authenticates a security agreement, giving the manufacturer a security interest in the CT scanner. The manufacturer then electronically files a financing statement in an appropriate state agency. This perfects the manufacturer's rights, meaning that its security interest in the CT scanner is now valid against all the world. Exhibit 12.1 illustrates this transaction.

If the clinic goes bankrupt and many creditors try to seize its assets, the manufacturer has first claim to the CT scanner. The clinic's bankruptcy is of great importance. When a debtor has money to pay all of its debts, there are no concerns about security interests. A creditor insists on a security interest to protect itself in the event the debtor *cannot* pay all of its debts. The secured party intends (1) to give itself a legal interest in specific property of the debtor and (2) to establish a priority claim in that property, ahead of other creditors.

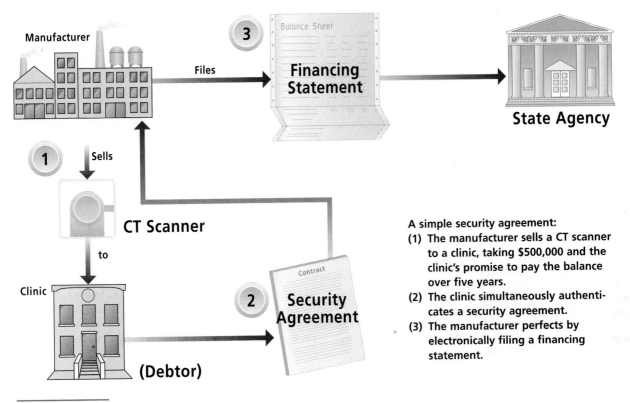

A simple security agreement:
(1) The manufacturer sells a CT scanner to a clinic, taking $500,000 and the clinic's promise to pay the balance over five years.
(2) The clinic simultaneously authenticates a security agreement.
(3) The manufacturer perfects by electronically filing a financing statement.

Exhibit 12.1

ARTICLE 9 REVISIONS

The American Law Institute and the National Conference of Commissioners on Uniform State Laws have rewritten Article 9, and the proposed revisions are now the law in all states. **All citations in this chapter are to the 2000 Revision of Article 9.** The Uniform Commercial Code is available online at http://www.law.cornell.edu/ucc/ucc.table.html.[2] For the actual statutory versions of Article 9 that have been adopted state-by-state, go to http://www.law.cornell.edu/uniform/ucc.html#a9.

SCOPE OF REVISED ARTICLE 9

Article 9 applies to any transaction intended to create a security interest in personal property or fixtures. The personal property that may be used as collateral includes:

- **Goods**, which are things that are movable.

- **Inventory**, meaning goods held by someone for sale or lease, such as all of the beds and chairs in a furniture store.

---

[2] When researching any article of the Code online, be certain that you are reading the most recent revision.

- **Instruments**, such as drafts, checks, certificates of deposit, and notes.

- **Investment Property**, which refers primarily to securities and related rights.

- **Documents of Title**, which are the proof of ownership retained by someone who ships or stores goods.

- **Accounts**, meaning the right to receive payment for goods sold or leased.

- **Deposit accounts**, which refers to money placed in banks.

- **General Intangibles**, a residual category that includes collateral such as copyrights, patents, trademarks, goodwill, and the right to payment of some loans.

- **Chattel Paper**, which is a record that indicates two things: (1) an obligor owes money and (2) a secured party has a security interest in specific goods. Chattel paper most commonly occurs in a consumer sale on credit. If a dealer sells an air conditioner to a customer, who agrees in writing to make monthly payments and also agrees that the dealer has a security interest in the air conditioner, that agreement is chattel paper. The confusing point is that the same chattel paper may be collateral for a second security interest. The dealer who sells the air conditioner could use the chattel paper to obtain a loan. If the dealer gives the chattel paper to a bank as collateral for the loan, the bank has a security interest in the chattel paper, while the dealer continues to have a security interest in the air conditioner. **Electronic chattel paper** is the same thing except that it is an electronic record rather than a writing.

Software. Article 9 takes into account the increasingly important role that computer software plays in all business. The Code distinguishes *software* from *goods*, and this becomes important when competing creditors are fighting over both a computer system and the software inside it. A program embedded in a computer is goods *if* it is customarily considered part of those goods *or if* by purchasing the goods the owner acquires the right to use the program. A program that does *not* meet those criteria is termed *software*, and will be treated differently for some purposes. ◾

In sum, Article 9 applies anytime the parties intended to create a security interest in any of the items listed above.

Attachment of a Security Interest

Attachment is a vital step in a secured transaction. This means that the secured party has taken three steps to create an enforceable security interest:

- The two parties made a security agreement *and either* the debtor has *authenticated a security agreement* describing the collateral *or* the secured party has obtained *possession* or *control*.

---

[3] UCC §9-203.

- The secured party has given value to obtain the security agreement; and

- The debtor has rights in the collateral.[3]

AGREEMENT

Without an agreement there can be no security interest. Generally, the agreement either must be written on paper and signed by the debtor, or electronically recorded and authenticated by the debtor. The agreement must reasonably identify the collateral. For example, a security agreement may properly describe the collateral as "all equipment in the store at 123 Periwinkle Street."[4]

A security agreement at a minimum might:

- State that Happy Homes, Inc. and Martha agree that Martha is buying an Arctic Co. refrigerator, and identify the exact unit by its serial number

- Give the price, the down payment, the monthly payments, and interest rate

- State that because Happy Homes is selling Martha the refrigerator on credit, it has a security interest in the refrigerator; and

- Provide that if Martha defaults on her payments, Happy Homes is entitled to repossess the refrigerator.

An actual security agreement will add many details, such as Martha's obligation to keep the refrigerator in good condition and to deliver it to the store if she defaults; a precise definition of "default"; and how Happy Homes may go about repossessing the goods if Martha defaults.

CONTROL AND POSSESSION

In certain cases, the security agreement need not be in writing if the parties have an oral agreement and the secured party has either **control** or **possession**. For many kinds of collateral it is safer for the secured party actually to take the item than to rely upon a security agreement.

For deposit accounts, electronic chattel paper and certain other collateral, the security interest attaches if the secured party has *control*. Generally speaking, *control means that the secured party has certain exclusive rights to dispose of the collateral.* If Peter deposits $250,000 in Smiley Bank and instructs the bank to dispose of the money as instructed by Wendy, then Wendy has control of the money.

For most other forms of collateral, a security interest attaches if the secured party has *possession*. For example, if you loan your neighbor $175,000 and he gives you a Winslow Homer watercolor as collateral, you have an attached security interest in the painting once it is in your possession.

The court decided the following case based on former Article 9, but the outcome would be the same under the revised Code.

---

[4] A security agreement may not use a **super-generic term** such as "all of Smith's personal property." We will see later that, by contrast, such a super-generic description is legally adequate in a *financing statement.*

IN RE CFLC, INC.

209 B.R. 508, 1997 Bankr. LEXIS 821
United States Bankruptcy Appellate Panel of the Ninth Circuit, 1997

FACTS: Expeditors was a freight company that supervised importing and exporting for Everex Systems, Inc. Expeditors negotiated rates and services for its client and frequently had possession of Everex's goods. During a 17-month period, Expeditors sent over 300 invoices to Everex. Each invoice stated that the customer either had to accept all of the invoice's terms or to pay cash, receiving no work on credit. One of those terms gave Expeditors a security interest in all of the customer's property in its possession. In other words, if the customer failed to pay a bill, Expeditors asserted a right to keep the goods.

Everex filed for bankruptcy, and Expeditors claimed the right to sell Everex's goods, worth about $81,000. The trial judge rejected the claim, ruling that Expeditors lacked a valid security interest. Expeditors appealed.

ISSUE: Did Expeditors have a security interest in Everex's goods?

EXCERPTS FROM JUDGE OLLASON'S DECISION: Under the common law, silence in the face of an offer is not an acceptance, unless there is a relationship between the parties or a previous course of dealing pursuant to which silence would be understood as acceptance.

In this case, Expeditors and Everex had been doing business for about one and one-half years. They had never discussed the terms of the invoice nor negotiated for a security interest. Everex had never expressly acknowledged the invoice terms by accepting or objecting to them, nor did it take actions which acknowledged Expeditors' alleged general lien on the goods. Its only pertinent acts were its payment of the invoices and silence as to the added terms.

The evidence consisting of Everex's receipt and payment of invoices containing terms for a general lien in the goods in favor of Expeditors did not amount to an agreement for such a security interest, pursuant to [revised section 9-102]. As a matter of law, the repetitive sending by Expeditors to Everex of terms which Expeditors wished to be made part of the oral contract was not evidence of course of dealing because an agreement did not exist as to the security interest which could be supplemented by such evidence.

Affirmed.

Expeditors thought—or hoped—that it had a security interest, but the invoices failed to achieve that goal, so the company failed to obtain the money it was owed. How should Expeditors have protected itself?

VALUE

For the security interest to attach, the secured party must give value. Usually, the value will be apparent. If a bank loans $400 million to an airline, that money is the value, and the bank may therefore obtain a security interest in the planes that the airline is buying. The parties may also agree that some of the value will be given in the future. For example, a finance company might extend a $5 million line of credit to a retail store even though the store initially takes only $1 million of the money. The Code considers the entire $5 million line of credit to be value.[5]

---

[5] UCC §9-204(c).

Debtor Rights in the Collateral

The debtor can only grant a security interest in goods if he has some legal right to those goods himself. Typically, the debtor owns the goods. But a debtor may also give a security interest if he is leasing the goods or even if he is a bailee, meaning that he is lawfully holding them for someone else.

Result

Once the security interest has attached to the collateral, the secured party is protected against the debtor. If the debtor fails to pay, the secured party may repossess the collateral.

ATTACHMENT TO FUTURE PROPERTY

The security agreement may specify that the security interest attaches to personal property that the debtor does not yet possess but might obtain in the future.

After-Acquired Property

After-acquired property refers to items that the debtor obtains after the parties have made their security agreement. **The parties may agree that the security interest attaches to after-acquired property.**[6] Basil is starting a catering business, but owns only a beat-up car. He borrows $55,000 from the Pesto Bank, which takes a security interest in the car. But Pesto also insists on an after-acquired clause. When Basil purchases a commercial stove, cooking equipment, and freezer, Pesto's security interest attaches to each item as Basil acquires it.

Proceeds

Proceeds are whatever is obtained by a debtor who sells the collateral or otherwise disposes of it. **The secured party *automatically* obtains a security interest in the proceeds of the collateral.**[7] Suppose the Pesto Bank obtains a security interest in Basil's $4,000 freezer. Basil then decides he needs a larger model and sells the original freezer to his neighbor for $3,000. The $3,000 cash is proceeds, in which Pesto automatically obtains a security interest.

Perfection

NOTHING LESS THAN PERFECTION

Once the security interest has attached to the collateral, the secured party is protected *against the debtor*. Pesto Bank loaned money to Basil and has a security interest in all of his property. If Basil defaults on his loan, Pesto may insist he deliver the goods to the bank. If he fails to do that, the bank can seize the collateral. But Pesto's security interest is valid only against Basil; if a third person claims some interest in the goods, the bank may never get them. For example, Basil might have taken out *another* loan, from his friend Olive, and used the same property as

---

[6] UCC §9-204(a).
[7] UCC §9-203(f).

collateral. Olive knew nothing about the bank's original loan. To protect itself against Olive, and all other parties, the bank must *perfect* its interest.

There are several kinds of perfection:

- Perfection by filing

- Perfection by possession or control

- Perfection of consumer goods

- Perfection of movable collateral and fixtures

In some cases the secured party will have a choice of which method to use; in other cases only one method works.

PERFECTION BY FILING

The most common way to perfect is by filing a financing statement with the appropriate state agency. A **financing statement** gives the names of all parties, describes the collateral, and outlines the security interest, enabling any interested person to learn about it. Suppose the Pesto Bank obtains a security interest in Basil's catering equipment and then perfects by filing with the Secretary of State in the state capital. When Basil asks his friend Olive for a loan, she will check the records to see if anyone has a security interest in the catering equipment. Olive's search uncovers Basil's previous security agreement, and she realizes it would be unwise to make the loan. If Basil were to default, the collateral would go straight to Pesto Bank, leaving Olive empty-handed. See Exhibit 12.2.

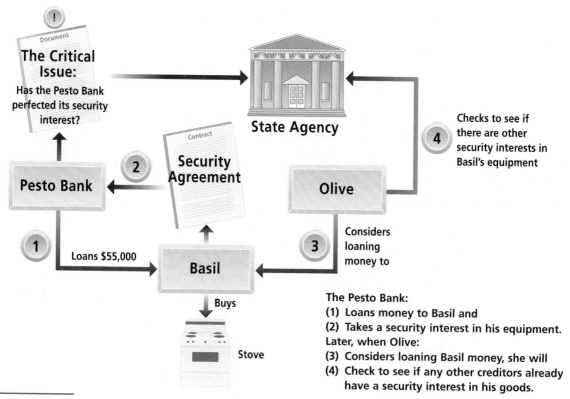

The Critical Issue: Has the Pesto Bank perfected its security interest?

State Agency

Pesto Bank

Security Agreement

Olive

Basil

Loans $55,000

Buys

Stove

Checks to see if there are other security interests in Basil's equipment

Considers loaning money to

The Pesto Bank:
(1) Loans money to Basil and
(2) Takes a security interest in his equipment.
Later, when Olive:
(3) Considers loaning Basil money, she will
(4) Check to see if any other creditors already have a security interest in his goods.

Exhibit 12.2

Article 9 prescribes one form, to be used nationwide for financing statements.[8] The financing form is available online at http://www.ss.ca.gov/business/ucc/ra_9_UCC-1page.htm. Remember that the filing may be done on paper or electronically.

The most common problems that arise in filing cases are (1) whether the financing statement contained enough information to put other people on notice of the security interest, and (2) whether the secured party filed the papers in the right place.

Contents of the Financing Statement

A financing statement is sufficient if it provides the name of the debtor, the name of the secured party, and an indication of the collateral.[9]

The name of the debtor is critical because that is what an interested person will use to search among the millions of other financing statements on file. If the debtor is a "registered organization," such as a corporation, limited partnership or limited liability company, the official, registered name of the company is the only one acceptable. If the debtor is a person or an unregistered organization (such as a club), then the legal name is required. Trade names are not sufficient.

The collateral must be described reasonably so that another party contemplating a loan to the debtor will understand which property is already secured. A financing statement could properly state that it applies to "all inventory in the debtor's Houston warehouse." If the debtor has given a security interest in everything he owns, then it is sufficient to state simply that the financing statement covers "all assets" or "all personal property."

Article 9 devotes considerable space to the "correct name" issue because cases such as the following have been all too familiar. Although the case was decided under former Article 9, the outcome would be the same under the revised Code.

YOU BE THE JUDGE

THE FIRST NATIONAL BANK OF LACON V. STRONG

278 Ill. App. 3d 762, 633 N.E.2d 432, 1996 Ill. App. LEXIS 169
Illinois Court of Appeal, 1996

FACTS: Elmer and Pam Strong leased and operated service stations. They were incorporated as "E. Strong Oil Co.," although they used "Strong Oil Co." as their trade name. The First National Bank of Lacon loaned the couple $75,000. The promissory note named "Strong Oil Co." as the borrower. Both Elmer and Pam signed the note, along with an agreement that gave the bank a security interest in the company's inventory, equipment, accounts, and other assets. The bank filed a financing statement, listing the debtor as "Strong Oil Co."

The Illinois Department of Revenue seized all of the company's assets, claiming $229,000 in unpaid motor fuel taxes. The bank sued, claiming that it was entitled to all of the property, based on its security interest. The issue was whether the bank had perfected its interest. If the bank had

---

[8] UCC §9-521.
[9] UCC §9-502(a).

perfected, it was entitled to the property. If the bank had failed to do so, because it filed under the name Strong rather than "E. Strong," the Department could take everything. The trial court found that the bank had validly perfected its interest, and the Department appealed.

YOU BE THE JUDGE: Did the bank have a perfected security interest in the property?

ARGUMENT FOR THE DEPARTMENT OF REVENUE: Financing statements are designed to permit interested parties to search an index and determine quickly if a debtor has other creditors. Accuracy is essential because the statements are indexed alphabetically by debtor. There are millions of secured transactions annually, and many companies and organizations have similar names. A creditor looking under "E. Strong" would be far from "Strong Oil," where the bank chose to file. Must a searcher also look under "Elmer Strong," "E & P Strong," "Strong Oil," "Strong Gasoline," "Strong Service Stations," and a hundred other permutations? Because the bank could not be bothered to verify the name of its debtor, it failed to perfect and must suffer the loss.

ARGUMENT FOR THE BANK: The Department's greed exceeds its common sense. The purpose of filing is to give a reasonably prudent creditor the chance to check on the credit of its prospective debtor. The company was most widely known as the Strong Oil Co. Any prudent company that considered extending credit to the Strongs would have looked under Strong Oil—exactly where the bank filed. The Code was never intended to elevate nit-picking to the status of policy. ▰

Place and Duration of Filing

Article 9 specifies *where* **a secured party must file.** These provisions may vary from state to state, so it is essential to check local law: a misfiled record accomplishes nothing. Generally speaking, a party must file in a central filing office located in the state where an individual debtor lives or where an organization has its executive office.[10]

Once a financing statement has been filed, it is effective for five years (except for a manufactured home, where it lasts 30 years). After five years the statement will expire and leave the secured party unprotected, unless she files a continuation statement within six months prior to expiration. The continuation statement is valid for an additional five years, and a secured party may file one periodically, forever.[11]

PERFECTION BY POSSESSION OR CONTROL

For most types of collateral, in addition to filing, a secured party generally may perfect by possession or control (described above). So if the collateral is a diamond brooch or 1,000 shares of stock, a bank may perfect its security interest by holding the items until the loan is paid off.

Perfection by possession has some advantages. Notice to other parties is very clear, and if the debtor defaults, a secured party obviously has no difficulties

[10] UCC §9-307.
[11] UCC §9-515.

repossessing. However, both possession and control impose one important duty: **a secured party must use reasonable care in the custody and preservation of collateral in her possession or control.**[12] The following case was decided under the former Code, but the outcome would be the same under revised Article 9. Did the bank do an adequate job of protecting collateral?

HUTHER V. MARINE MIDLAND BANK, N.A.

143 Misc. 2d 697, 541 N.Y.S.2d 902, 1989 N.Y. Misc. LEXIS 649
City Court of New York, 1989

FACTS: In 1985, William Huther borrowed $31,000 from Marine Midland Bank and secured repayment with shares of stock in Eastman Kodak and Mobil Corp. In 1986, Congress enacted a tax reform bill, effective January 1, 1987, that affected capital gains, which are profits earned from the purchase and sale of something, such as shares of stock. Under the new tax law anyone who realized a capital gain during 1986 would save a considerable amount in taxes, compared to someone making that same sale in 1987.

Huther decided to sell his stock before the end of the year and use his capital gains savings to help repay the loan. On December 18, 1986, he telephoned Jack Broomfield, the lending officer at Midland, and arranged for the sale of his stock. Broomfield told Huther that it was "bank policy" to use the bank's own brokerage service to handle the sale of stock when the shares were held as collateral. Huther had his own broker, but since Broomfield insisted, he consented to using the bank's broker for this sale.

On December 24, 1986, Broomfield went to Huther's office to open an account with Marine's brokerage service. Huther signed the application and authorized the sale of his shares. Broomfield then personally took the stock from the bank's vault and sent it by courier to New York City. But the bank's broker failed to sell the stock until January 5, 1987, forcing Huther to pay a significantly increased tax bill. Huther sued Midland.

ISSUE: Did Marine violate its duty to use reasonable care concerning the collateral?

EXCERPTS FROM JUDGE REGAN'S DECISION: A secured lender must use reasonable care in the custody and preservation of the collateral he possesses. And a secured party is liable for "any loss" caused by his failure to meet that obligation.

Under the facts as found, the defendants had four business days left in 1986 to perform the sales contract, and they had reasonable notice that a sale in 1986 was necessary to preserve Mr. Huther's tax advantages. This finding is buttressed by the fact that during December 1986, it was common knowledge throughout the securities industry that stock-owning taxpayers were selling off securities in record-setting volume in order to reap the benefits of the soon-to-expire capital gains income tax treatment.

Accepting these criteria for professional competence, the court holds that it was incumbent upon these defendants to inform Mr. Huther of the choices he had as to the manner in which the stock sale could be accomplished. And it was also incumbent upon them to follow his instructions diligently and correctly. On the brokerage services agreement, Huther indicated that he wanted a "cash" account for this transaction, and that meant delivery on the day of the contract, or on the next business day thereafter. A stockbroker of ordinary acumen would have performed the conditions of this stock sale as "cash" within one or two business days. Yet, the defendants took six days. Because these defendants failed to meet that standard, they are guilty of negligence, and have violated the statutory command of [UCC §9-207].

Plaintiff is entitled to judgment. ◢

---

[12] UCC §9-207.

PERFECTION OF CONSUMER GOODS

The Code gives special treatment to security interests in most consumer goods. Merchants cannot file a financing statement for every bed, television, and stereo for which a consumer owes money. To understand the UCC's treatment of these transactions, we need to know two terms. The first is *consumer goods*, which are those used primarily for personal, family, or household purposes. The second term is *purchase money security interest*.

A purchase money security interest (PMSI) is one taken by the person who sells the collateral or by the person who advances money so the debtor can buy the collateral.[13] Assume the Gobroke Home Center sells Marion a $5,000 stereo system. The sales document requires a payment of $500 down and $50 per month for the next 300 years, and gives Gobroke a security interest in the system. Because the security interest was "taken by the seller," the document is a PMSI. It would also be a PMSI if a bank had loaned Marion the money to buy the system and the document gave the bank a security interest. See Exhibit 12.3.

A purchase money security interest can arise in either of two ways. In the first example, a store sells a stereo to a consumer on credit; the consumer in turn signs a PMSI, giving the store a security interest in the stereo. In the second example, the consumer buys the stereo with money loaned from a bank; the consumer signs a PMSI giving the *bank* a security interest in the stereo

Exhibit 12.3

[13] UCC §9-103.

But aren't all security interests PMSIs? No, many are not. Suppose a bank loans a retail company $800,000 and takes a security interest in the store's present inventory. That is not a PMSI since the store did not use the money to purchase the collateral.

What must Gobroke Home Center do to perfect its security interest? Nothing. **A PMSI in consumer goods perfects automatically, without filing.**[14] Marion's new stereo is clearly consumer goods, because she will use it only in her home. Gobroke's security interest is a PMSI, so the interest has perfected automatically.

The Code provisions about perfecting generally do not apply to motor vehicles, trailers, mobile homes, boats or farm tractors.[15] These types of secured interests are governed by state law, which frequently require a security interest to be noted directly on the vehicle's certificate of title.

A PMSI may be created only in goods, fixtures, or software.[16] No other types of collateral are allowed. Recall that for Article 9 purposes, *software* is defined to mean a computer program that is not embedded in hardware. A seller may obtain a PMSI in software if the debtor is buying the program to run hardware purchased in the same transaction and if the secured party also has a PMSI in that hardware. Merry Bank advances $250,000 to Ben's Books to enable Ben to purchase a new computer system and some separate software to run the computer. Merry may acquire a PMSI in the software, provided it is obtaining a PMSI in the computer as well.

Protection of Buyers

Generally, once a security interest is perfected, it remains effective regardless of whether the collateral is sold, exchanged, or transferred in some other way. Bubba's Bus Co. needs money to meet its payroll, so it borrows $150,000 from Francine's Finance Co., which takes a security interest in Bubba's 180 buses and perfects its interest. Bubba, still short of cash, sells 30 of his buses to Antelope Transit. But even that money is not enough to keep Bubba solvent: he defaults on his loan to Francine and goes into bankruptcy. Francine pounces on Bubba's buses. May she repossess the 30 that *Antelope* now operates? Yes. The security interest continued in the buses even after Antelope purchased them, and Francine can whisk them away.

There are some exceptions to this rule. The Code gives a few buyers special protection.

BUYERS IN ORDINARY COURSE OF BUSINESS

A buyer in ordinary course of business (BIOC) is someone who buys goods in good faith from a seller who routinely deals in such goods.[17] For example, Plato's Garden Supply purchases 500 hemlocks from Socrates' Farm, a grower. Plato is a BIOC: he is buying in good faith and Socrates routinely deals in hemlocks. This is an important status, because a BIOC is generally not affected by

---

[14] UCC §9-309(1).
[15] UCC §9-311(a)(2).
[16] UCC §9-103(b)(c).
[17] UCC §1-201(9).

security interests in the goods. However, if Plato realized that the sale violated another party's rights in the goods, there would be no good faith. If Plato knew that Socrates was bankrupt and had agreed with a creditor not to sell any of his inventory, Plato would not achieve BIOC status.

A buyer in ordinary course of business takes the goods free of a security interest created by his seller even though the security interest is perfected.[18] Suppose that, a month before Plato made his purchase, Socrates borrowed $200,000 from the Athenian Bank. Athenian took a security interest in all of Socrates' trees and perfected by filing. Then Plato purchased his 500 hemlocks. If Socrates defaults on the loan, Athenian will have *no right* to repossess the 500 trees that are now at the Garden Supply. Plato took them free and clear. (Of course, Athenian can still attempt to repossess other trees from Socrates.) The BIOC exception is designed to encourage ordinary commerce. A buyer making routine purchases should not be forced to perform a financing check before buying.

BUYERS OF CHATTEL PAPER, INSTRUMENTS, AND DOCUMENTS

We have seen that debtors often use chattel paper and instruments as collateral. Because each of these is so easily transferred, the Code gives buyers special protection. **A buyer who purchases chattel paper or instruments in good faith in the ordinary course of her business, and then obtains** *possession or control*, **generally takes free of any security interest.**[19]

Priorities among Creditors

What happens when two creditors have a security interest in the same collateral? The party who has **priority** in the collateral gets it. Typically, the debtor lacks assets to pay everyone, so all creditors struggle to be the first in line. After the first creditor has repossessed the collateral, sold it, and taken enough of the proceeds to pay off his debt, there may be nothing left for anyone else. (There may not even be enough to pay the first creditor all that he is due, in which case that creditor will sue for the deficiency.) Who gets priority? There are three principal rules.

The first rule is easy: **a party with a perfected security interest takes priority over a party with an unperfected interest.**[20] This is the whole point of perfecting: to ensure that your security interest gets priority over everyone else's. On August 15 Meredith's Market, an antique store, borrows $100,000 from the Happy Bank, which takes a security interest in all of Meredith's inventory. Happy Bank does not perfect. On September 15 Meredith uses the same collateral to borrow $50,000 from the Suspicion Bank, which files a financing statement the same day. On

---

[18] UCC §9-320(a). In fact, the buyer takes free of the security interest *even if the buyer knew of it.* Yet a BIOC, by definition, must be acting in good faith. Is this a contradiction? No. Plato might know that a third party has a security interest in Socrates' crops, yet not realize that his purchase violates the third party's rights. Generally, for example, a security interest will permit a retailer to sell consumer goods, the presumption being that part of the proceeds will go to the secured party. A BIOC cannot be expected to determine what a retailer plans to do with the money he is paid.

[19] UCC §9-330(a)(b)(d).

[20] UCC §9-322(a)(2).

October 15, as if on cue, Meredith files for bankruptcy and stops paying both creditors. Suspicion wins because it holds a perfected interest, whereas the Happy Bank holds merely an unperfected interest.

The second rule: **if neither secured party has perfected, the first interest to attach gets priority.**[21] Suppose that Suspicion Bank and Happy Bank had both failed to perfect. In that case, Happy Bank would have the first claim to Meredith's inventory, since Happy's interest *attached* first.

And the third rule follows logically: **between perfected security interests, the first to file *or* perfect wins.**[22] Diminishing Perspective, a railroad, borrows $75 million from the First Bank, which takes a security interest in Diminishing's rolling stock (railroad cars) and immediately perfects by filing. Two months later, Diminishing borrows $100 million from Second Bank, which takes a security interest in the same collateral and also files. When Diminishing arrives, on schedule, in bankruptcy court, both banks will race to seize the rolling stock. First Bank gets the railcars because it perfected first.

March 1:	April 2:	May 3:	The Winner:
First Bank loans money and perfects its security interest by filing a financing statement.	Second Bank loans money and perfects its security interest by filing a financing statement.	Diminishing goes bankrupt, and both banks attempt to take the rolling stock.	First Bank, because it perfected first.

The general rules of priority are quite straightforward. However, you will not be surprised to learn that there are some exceptions.

PRIORITY EXCEPTIONS

You may recall that a purchase money security interest (PMSI) is a security interest taken by the seller of the collateral or by a lender whose loan enables the debtor to buy the collateral. A PMSI can be created only in goods, fixtures, and software. **A PMSI that is promptly perfected generally takes priority over a conflicting perfected security interest (even one perfected earlier).** The holder of the PMSI is sometimes required to notify other secured parties of the new PMSI, and generally must perfect before the goods are sold or shortly thereafter, depending on what type of collateral is involved.

On February 1 Tool Shop borrows $100,000 from the Gargoyle Bank, giving Gargoyle a security interest in after-acquired property. Then on November 1, Manufacturer sells a specially built lathe to Tool Shop for $80,000, taking a PMSI in the machine. When the lathe arrives at the Tool Shop, Gargoyle's earlier security interest attaches to the same collateral. Who wins? Manufacturer, provided it promptly perfects its PMSI.

Another significant exception involves perfection by possession or control. **A party that uses possession or control to perfect its interest in deposit accounts, investment property, letter-of-credit rights, or instruments generally obtains priority over a party that perfected earlier by filing.**

[21] UCC §9-322(a)(3).
[22] UCC §9-322(a)(1).

Default and Termination

We have reached the end of the line. Either the debtor has defaulted, or it has performed its obligations and may terminate the security agreement.

DEFAULT

The parties define "default" in their security agreement. **Generally, a debtor defaults when he fails to make payments due or enters bankruptcy proceedings.** The parties can agree that other acts will constitute default, such as the debtor's failure to maintain insurance on the collateral. When a debtor defaults, the secured party has two principal options: (1) it may take possession of the collateral, or (2) it may file suit against the debtor for the money owed. The secured party does not have to choose between these two remedies; it may try one after the other, or both simultaneously.[23]

Taking Possession of the Collateral

When the debtor defaults, the secured party may take possession of the collateral.[24] The secured party may act on its own, without any court order, and simply take the collateral, provided this can be done *without a breach of the peace.* Otherwise, the secured party must file suit against the debtor and request that the court *order* the debtor to deliver the collateral.

Disposition of the Collateral

Once the secured party has obtained possession of the collateral, it has two choices. The secured party may (1) dispose of the collateral or (2) retain the collateral as full satisfaction of the debt. Notice that until the secured party disposes of the collateral, the debtor has the right to **redeem** it, that is, to pay the full value of the debt and retrieve her property.[25]

Disposal of the Collateral. **A secured party may sell, lease, or otherwise dispose of the collateral in any commercially reasonable manner.**[26] Typically, the secured party will sell the collateral in either a private or a public sale. First, however, the debtor must receive *reasonable notice* of the time and place of the sale, so that she may bid on the collateral. The higher the price that the secured party gets for the collateral, the lower the balance still owed by the debtor. Giving the debtor notice of the sale, and a chance to bid, ensures that the collateral will not be sold for an unreasonably low price.

Suppose Bank loans $65,000 to Farmer to purchase a tractor. While still owing $40,000, Farmer defaults. Bank takes possession of the tractor and then notifies Farmer that it intends to sell the tractor at an auction. Farmer has the right to attend and bid on the tractor.

When the secured party has sold the collateral, it applies the proceeds of the sale: first, to its expenses in repossessing and selling the collateral, and second, to

---

[23] UCC §9-601(a)(b)(c).
[24] UCC §9-609.
[25] UCC §9-623.
[26] UCC §9-610.

the debt.[27] Assume Bank sold the tractor for $35,000, and that the process of repossessing and selling the tractor cost $5,000. Bank applies the remaining $30,000 to the debt.

Deficiency or Surplus.   The sale of the tractor yielded $30,000 to be applied to the debt, which was $40,000. The disposition has left a **deficiency**, that is, insufficient funds to pay off the debt. **The debtor is liable for any deficiency.** So the bank will sue the farmer for the remaining $10,000. On the other hand, sometimes the sale of the collateral yields a **surplus**, that is, a sum greater than the debt. In that case, the secured party must pay the surplus to the debtor.[28] Finally, when a secured party disposes of collateral in a *commercially unreasonable* manner, it will be liable to the debtor for the shortfall.

Acceptance of the Collateral.   In many cases, the secured party has the option to satisfy the debt simply by keeping the collateral. **Acceptance refers to a secured party's retention of the collateral as full or partial satisfaction of the debt.** *Partial satisfaction* means that the debtor will still owe some deficiency to the secured party.[29] Generally speaking, a secured party may accept the collateral as full satisfaction unless the debtor objects.

A secured party who wishes to accept the collateral must notify the debtor. If the debtor agrees in an authenticated record, then the secured party may keep the collateral as full *or* partial satisfaction of the debt. If the debtor does not respond within 20 days, the secured party may still accept the collateral as *full* satisfaction but *not* as partial satisfaction. In other words, the debtor's silence does not give the secured party the right to keep the goods and still sue for more money.

Occasionally, the secured party will prefer to ignore its rights in the collateral and simply sue the debtor. **A secured party may sue the debtor for the full debt.**[30]

TERMINATION

Finally, we need to look at what happens when a debtor does not default, but pays the full debt. (You are forgiven if you lost track of the fact that things sometimes work out smoothly.) Once that happens, the secured party must complete a **termination statement**, a document indicating that it no longer claims a security interest in the collateral.[31]

Overview of Bankruptcy

As you may have noticed in the first half of this chapter, many of the cases involving secured transactions are decided in bankruptcy court as part of an overall sorting out of a debtor's financial problems. The U.S. Bankruptcy Code (Code) has three primary goals:

- *To preserve as much of the debtor's property as possible.*

---

[27] UCC §9-615(a).
[28] UCC §9-615(d)
[29] UCC §9-620.
[30] UCC §9-601(a).
[31] UCC §9-513.

- *To divide the debtor's assets fairly between the debtor and creditors.*
- *To divide the debtor's assets fairly among creditors.*

The following options are available under the Bankruptcy Code:

Number	Topic	Description
Chapter 7	Liquidation	The bankrupt's assets are sold to pay creditors. If the debtor owns a business, it terminates. The creditors have no right to the debtor's future earnings.
Chapter 9	Municipal bankruptcies	This chapter is not covered in this book.
Chapter 11	Reorganization	This chapter is designed for businesses and wealthy individuals. Businesses continue in operation, and creditors receive a portion of both current assets and future earnings.
Chapter 12	Family farmers	This chapter is not covered in this book.
Chapter 13	Consumer reorganizations	Chapter 13 offers reorganizations for the typical consumer. Creditors usually receive a portion of the individual's current assets and future earnings.

All of the Code's chapters have one of two objectives—rehabilitation or liquidation. Chapters 11 and 13, for example, focus on rehabilitation. Many debtors can return to financial health provided they have the time and breathing space to work out their problems. These chapters hold creditors at bay while the debtor develops a payment plan. In return for retaining some of their assets, debtors typically promise to pay creditors a portion of their future earnings. However, when debtors are unable to develop a feasible plan for rehabilitation under Chapter 11 or 13, Chapter 7 provides for liquidation (also known as a **straight bankruptcy**). Most of the debtor's assets are distributed to creditors, but the debtor has no obligation to share future earnings.

Debtors are often eligible to file under more than one chapter. No choice is irrevocable because both debtors and creditors have the right to ask the court to convert a case from one chapter to another at any time during the proceedings. (The text of the Bankruptcy Code is available at http://www4.law.cornell.edu/uscode/11/.)

Chapter 7 Liquidation

All bankruptcy cases proceed in a roughly similar pattern, regardless of chapter. We use Chapter 7 as a template to illustrate common features of all bankruptcy cases. Later on, the discussions of the other chapters will indicate how they differ from Chapter 7. The latest news on bankruptcy is available at http://www.abiworld.org.

FILING A PETITION

Any individual, partnership, corporation, or other business organization that lives, conducts business, or owns property in the United States can file under the Code. (Chapter 13, however, is available only to individuals.) The traditional term for someone who could not pay his debts was "**bankrupt**," but the Code uses the term "**debtor**" instead. We use both terms interchangeably.

A case begins with the filing of a bankruptcy petition in federal district court. Debtors may go willingly into the bankruptcy process by filing a **voluntary petition**, or they may be dragged into court by creditors who file an **involuntary petition**. The district court typically refers bankruptcy cases to a specialized bankruptcy judge. Either party can appeal the decision of the bankruptcy judge back to the district court and, from there, to the federal appeals court.

Voluntary Petition

Any debtor may file for bankruptcy. It is not necessary that the debtor's liabilities exceed assets. Debtors sometimes file a bankruptcy petition because cash flow is so tight they cannot pay their debts, even though they are not technically insolvent. The voluntary petition must include the following documents:

Document	Description
Petition	Begins the case. Easy to fill out, it requires checking a few boxes and typing in little more than name, address, and Social Security number.
List of Creditors	The names and addresses of all creditors.
Schedule of Assets and Liabilities	A list of the debtor's assets and debts.
Claim of Exemptions	A list of all assets that the debtor is entitled to keep.
Schedule of Income and Expenditures	The debtor's job, income, and expenses.
Statement of Financial Affairs	A summary of the debtor's financial history and current financial condition. In particular, the debtor must list any recent payments to creditors and any other property held by someone else for the debtor.

Involuntary Petition

Creditors may force a debtor into bankruptcy by filing an involuntary petition. The creditors' goal is to preserve as much of the debtor's assets as possible and to ensure that all creditors receive a fair share. Naturally, the Code sets strict limits—debtors cannot be forced into bankruptcy every time they miss a credit card payment. **An involuntary petition must meet all of the following requirements:**

- The debtor must owe at least $11,625 in unsecured claims to the creditors who file.

- If the debtor has at least 12 creditors, three or more must sign the petition. If the debtor has fewer than 12 creditors, any one of them can file a petition.

- The creditors must allege either that a custodian for the debtor's property has been appointed in the prior 120 days or that the debtor has generally not been paying debts that are due.

What does "a custodian for the debtor's property" mean? *State* laws sometimes permit the appointment of a custodian to protect a debtor's assets. The Code allows creditors to pull a case out from under state law and into federal bankruptcy court by filing an involuntary petition. Creditors also have the right to file an involuntary petition if they can show that the debtor is not paying debts. In the event that a debtor objects to an involuntary petition, the bankruptcy court must hold a trial to determine whether the creditors have met the Code's requirements.

Once a voluntary petition is filed or an involuntary petition approved, the bankruptcy court issues an **order for relief**. This order is an official acknowledgment that the debtor is under the jurisdiction of the court, and it is, in a sense, the start of the whole bankruptcy process. An involuntary debtor must now make all the filings that accompany a voluntary petition. Official bankruptcy forms are available at http://www.uscourts.gov/bankform.

TRUSTEE

The trustee is responsible for gathering the bankrupt's assets and dividing them among creditors. Creditors have the right to elect the trustee, but often they do not bother. In this case, the **U.S. Trustee** makes the selection. The U.S. Attorney General appoints a U.S. Trustee for each region of the country to administer the bankruptcy law. More information about the U.S. Trustee program is available at http://www.usdoj.gov/ust/about_ustp.htm.

CREDITORS

The U.S. Trustee calls a meeting of creditors sometime within 20 to 40 days after the order for relief. At the meeting the bankrupt must answer (under oath) any question the creditors pose about his financial situation. If the creditors want to elect a trustee, they do so at this meeting.

Unsecured creditors must submit a *proof of claim* **within 90 days after the meeting of creditors.** The proof of claim is a simple form stating the name of the creditor and the amount of the claim. **Secured creditors do not file proofs of claim unless the claim exceeds the value of their collateral.** In this case, they are unsecured creditors for the excess amount and must file a proof of claim for it. Suppose that Deborah borrows $750,000 from Morton in return for a mortgage on her house. If she does not repay the debt, he can foreclose. Unfortunately, property values plummet, and by the time Deborah files a voluntary petition in bankruptcy, the house is worth only $500,000. Morton is a secured creditor for $500,000 and need file no proof of claim for that amount. But he is an unsecured creditor for $250,000 and will lose his right to this excess amount unless he files a proof of claim for it.

AUTOMATIC STAY

A fox chased by hounds has no time to make rational long-term decisions. What that fox needs is a safe burrow. Similarly, it is difficult for debtors to make sound financial decisions when hounded night and day by creditors shouting, "Pay me! Pay me!" The Code is designed to give debtors enough breathing space to sort out their affairs sensibly. An automatic stay is a safe burrow for the bankrupt. It goes into effect as soon as the petition is filed. **An automatic stay prohibits creditors from collecting debts that the bankrupt incurred before the petition was filed.** Creditors may not sue a bankrupt to obtain payment nor may they take other steps, outside of court, to pressure the debtor for payment. In the following case, the landlord ate crow instead of Chinese food.

IN RE SECHUAN CITY INC.

96 B.R. 37, 1989 Bankr. LEXIS 103
United States Bankruptcy Court, Eastern District of Pennsylvania, 1989

FACTS: The Sechuan Garden restaurant leased space from North American Motor Inns, Inc. (Hotel). The entrance to the restaurant was in the Hotel lobby. The restaurant did not have a liquor license, but the Hotel bar would deliver drinks to restaurant guests at their tables. Sechuan Garden filed a voluntary petition in bankruptcy. Although the Hotel manager, Jose Garcia, knew that the bankruptcy court had entered an automatic stay, he posted the signs below at all Hotel entrances, in the Hotel lobby, and immediately outside the restaurant doors located in the lobby.

The restaurant's revenues dropped $1,000 a week for three weeks until Garcia finally removed the signs. Garcia testified that he had posted the signs to "shame" and "embarrass" the restaurant's owners into paying their bills.

> **NOTICE**
>
> PLEASE DON'T PATRONIZE THE SECHUAN GARDEN
>
> THIS RESTAURANT UNFAIR TO MANAGEMENT
>
> IT DOES NOT PAY IT'S [sic] BILLS
>
> THANK YOU

> **THE TENANT HAS DISHONORED ITS OBLIGATION FOR PAYMENT TO THE LANDLORD**

> **NOTICE**
>
> NO ALCOHOLIC BEVERAGES ARE ALLOWED
>
> TO BE CONSUMED IN THE RESTAURANT AREA
>
> UNDER PENALTY OF LAW
>
> THANKS
>
> N.A.M.I. MGMT

ISSUE: Did the Hotel violate Sechuan Garden's automatic stay?

EXCERPTS FROM JUDGE FOX'S DECISION:[32] The automatic stay is one of the fundamental debtor protections provided by the bankruptcy laws. It gives the debtor a breathing spell from his creditors. It stops all collection efforts, all harassment, and all foreclosure actions. It permits the debtor to attempt a repayment or reorganization plan or simply to be relieved of the financial pressures that drove him into bankruptcy.

The automatic stay also provides creditor protection. Without it, certain creditors would be able to pursue their own remedies against the debtor's property. Those who acted first would obtain payment of the claims in preference to and to the detriment of other creditors.

The language of [the Code] is very broad, and is designed to prevent creditor coercion and harassment of the debtor. The conduct prohibited ranges from that of an informal nature, such as by telephone contact or by dunning letters to more formal judicial and administrative proceedings.

---

[32] It is no surprise that Judge Fox appreciates the importance of an automatic stay.

Here, I conclude that the Hotel undertook a studied effort to coerce payment of the [restaurant's] prepetition claim. While the lessor did not bring suit against the debtor, its actions were designed to place the debtor in a position of either paying the lessor's prepetition claim or losing business due to defendants' actions. These actions were prohibited by the automatic stay and resulted in clear harm to the debtor.

[The court ordered the hotel to pay the bankruptcy trustee $3,000 in damages and $600 in attorney's fees.] ◢

BANKRUPTCY ESTATE

The filing of the bankruptcy petition creates a new legal entity separate from the debtor—the **bankruptcy estate**. All of the bankrupt's assets pass to the estate, except exempt property and new property that the debtor acquires after the petition is filed.

Exempt Property

The Code permits *individual* debtors (but not organizations) to keep some property for themselves. This exempt property saves the debtor from destitution during the bankruptcy process and provides the foundation for a new life once the process is over.

In this one area of bankruptcy law, the Code defers to state law. Although the Code lists various types of exempt property, it permits states to opt out of the federal system and define a different set of exemptions. A majority of states have indeed opted out of the Code, and for their residents the Code exemptions are irrelevant.

Under the *federal* Code, a debtor is allowed to exempt only $15,000 of the value of her home. If the home is worth more than that, the trustee sells it and returns $15,000 of the proceeds to the debtor. Most *states* exempt items such as the debtor's home, household goods, cars, work tools, disability and pension benefits, alimony, and health aids. Indeed, some states set no limit on the value of exempt property. Both Florida and Texas, for example, permit debtors to keep homes of unlimited value and a certain amount of land. Not surprisingly, these generous exemptions sometimes lead to abuses.

Who could argue with the Texas statute that permits debtors to keep their clothing? Even bankrupts have the right to some last shred of dignity. But what if that clothing includes a Rolex watch? In a section of his opinion entitled "Putting the Cartier before the Horse," Judge Leif M. Clark ruled that a debtor needed his Rolex to preserve "a semblance of dignity."[33]

Many debtors are also living a dignified existence in Florida. Former baseball commissioner Bowie Kuhn sold his (nonexempt) home in New Jersey and bought a million dollar (exempt) mansion in Florida immediately before he filed for bankruptcy. Kuhn is in good company. Former bank president Roy Talmo cruised between bankruptcy court and his 7,000-square-foot mansion in a Rolls-Royce. Marvin L. Warner, former ambassador to Switzerland, bought a 160-acre horse farm in Florida on the eve of bankruptcy.

---

[33] *In re Leva*, 96 B.R. 723, 1989 Bankr. LEXIS 257 (Bankr. W.D. Tex. 1989).

The Florida statute was intended to protect nineteenth-century pioneers who bore the risks of homesteading in wild swampland. Life in Florida may be safer now, but the bankruptcy protection remains. All efforts to change the law have been soundly defeated. ▪

Voidable Preferences

A major goal of the bankruptcy system is to divide the debtor's assets fairly among creditors. It would not be fair, or in keeping with this goal, if debtors were permitted to pay off some of their creditors immediately before filing a bankruptcy petition. Such a payment is called a **preference** because it gives unfair preferential treatment to a creditor. **The trustee can void any transfer to a creditor that took place in the 90-day period before the filing of a petition if the creditor received more from the transfer than she would have received during the bankruptcy process.**

Fraudulent Transfers

Suppose that a debtor sees bankruptcy inexorably approaching across the horizon like a tornado. He knows that, once the storm hits and he files a petition, everything he owns except a few items of exempt property will become part of the bankruptcy estate. Before that happens, he may be tempted to give some of his property to friends or family to shelter it from the tornado. If he succumbs to temptation, however, he is committing a fraudulent transfer.

A transfer is fraudulent if it is made within the year before a petition is filed and its purpose is to hinder, delay, or defraud creditors. The trustee can void any fraudulent transfer. Fraudulent transfers sound similar to voidable preferences, but there is an important distinction: voidable preferences pay legitimate debts, while fraudulent transfers protect the debtor's assets from legitimate creditors. For example, Lawrence Williams and his wife, Diana, enjoyed a luxurious lifestyle while his investment bank flourished. But when the bank failed, Lawrence was faced with debts of $6 million. On the eve of the bankruptcy filing, Diana suddenly announced that she wanted a divorce. In what had to be the most amicable breakup ever, Lawrence willingly transferred all of his assets to her. The court found that the transfer had been fraudulent.[34]

PAYMENT OF CLAIMS

Imagine a crowded delicatessen on Saturday evening. People are pushing and shoving because they know there is not enough food for everyone; some customers will go home hungry. The delicatessen could simply serve whoever pushes to the front of the line, or it could establish a number system to ensure that the most deserving customers are served first. The Code has, in essence, adopted a number system to prevent a free-for-all fight over the bankrupt's assets. Indeed, one of the Code's primary goals is to ensure that creditors are paid in the proper order, not according to who pushes to the front of the line.

All claims are placed in one of three classes: (1) secured claims, (2) priority claims, and (3) unsecured claims. **The trustee pays the bankruptcy estate to the**

---

[34] *In re Williams,* 159 B.R. 648, 1993 Bankr. LEXIS 1482 (Bankr. D.R.I. 1993), *remanded,* 190 B.R. 728, 1996 U.S. Dist. LEXIS 539.

Exhibit 12.4

various classes of claims in order of rank. A higher class is paid in full before the next class receives any payment at all. The debtor is entitled to any funds remaining after all claims have been paid. The payment order is shown in Exhibit 12.4.

Secured Claims

Creditors whose loans are secured by specific collateral are paid first. Secured claims are fundamentally different from all other claims because they are paid by selling a specific asset, not out of the general funds of the estate.

Priority Claims

Each category of priority claims is paid in order, with the first group receiving full payment before the next group receives anything. Priority claims include:

- Administrative expenses (such as fees to the trustee, lawyers, and accountants).

- Back wages to the debtor's employees for work performed during the 90 days prior to the date of the petition.

- Alimony and child support.

- Income and property taxes.

Unsecured Claims

Last, and frequently very much least, unsecured creditors have now reached the delicatessen counter. They can only hope that some food remains.

DISCHARGE

Filing a bankruptcy petition is embarrassing, time-consuming, and disruptive. It can affect the debtor's credit rating for years, making the simplest car loan a challenge. To encourage debtors to file for bankruptcy despite the pain involved, the Code offers a powerful incentive: the **fresh start**. Once a bankruptcy estate has been distributed to creditors, they cannot make a claim against the debtor for money owed before the filing, *whether or not they actually received any payment*. These pre-petition debts are **discharged**. All is forgiven, if not forgotten. As the following case illustrates, however, discharge is sometimes easier said than done.

IN RE VIVIAN

150 B.R. 832; 1992 Bankr. LEXIS 2102
United States Bankruptcy Court for the Southern District of Florida, 1992

FACTS: NationsBank continued to send bills to John and Margaret Vivian for a debt that a bankruptcy court had discharged. Mr. Vivian wrote to the bankruptcy judge angrily demanding that NationsBank be ordered to stop.

ISSUE: Was NationsBank in contempt of court?

EXCERPTS FROM JUDGE CRISTOL'S DECISION:

Following the entry of discharge in bankruptcy to John Coffey Vivian and Margaret Vivian, NationsBank sent them a dunning letter on a debt which had been discharged. NationsBank went to the expense of flying a high executive from North Carolina to Miami to appear and testify that the letter was sent in error and the court was satisfied that no intentional violation of the injunction had occurred. The NationsBank computer had generated the notice and NationsBank wrote a letter of apology to the Vivians and proceeded to appropriately chastise their computer and directed it not to send any more notices to the Vivians.

Only a month went by and the Vivians received a computer generated document from the bank which contained the words, "Please make checks payable to NationsBank and remit with top part of this statement to." Never mind that the document also showed no balance due and no payment due date, the Vivians were annoyed. It appearing to the court that this was not an intentional act of any human at NationsBank but rather the rampage of a rogue computer, the court entered an order suggesting that counsel for the bank communicate with the bank and the Vivians and try and make clear that this was not an intentional violation and it would not happen again.

Lo and behold, another month rolled around and that rogue computer did it again. The account statement showing no balance due and no date to make payment was mailed on NationsBank's red, white and blue stationery to Mr. and Mrs. Vivian. It is this final document that has truly established, beyond any reasonable doubt, that Mr. and Mrs. Vivian have no sense of humor and no gratitude whatsoever for the court's prior efforts on their behalf. They have, in their letter queried "May I ask a question? Why can't you or your Court get these continuing and very annoying letters STOPPED." (The question mark was omitted by the Vivians, not by the court but the court understood what they meant.) The Vivians were so annoyed that they went on to threaten that perhaps they should write to their family friend, a very well known, renowned and respected federal judge, about this serious matter. They then went on to say "May I hear from you or your secretary by return mail?" It is apparent that the Vivians are mad as you know what and they are not going to take it anymore. Likewise, this court is mad as you know what and is not going to take it anymore. Accordingly, and pursuant to Federal Rule of Bankruptcy Procedure 9020, the court determines the NationsBank computer to be in civil contempt of this court. Upon consideration, it is

ORDERED that the NationsBank computer, having been determined in civil contempt, is fined 50 megabytes of hard drive memory and 10 megabytes random access memory. The computer may purge itself of this contempt by ceasing the production and mailing of documents to Mr. and Mrs. Vivian. ◢

Discharge is an essential part of bankruptcy law. Without it, debtors would have little incentive to take part. To avoid abuses, however, the Code limits both the type of debts that can be discharged and the circumstances under which discharge can take place.

Debts that Cannot Be Discharged

The following debts are among those that can never be discharged. The debtor remains liable in full until they are paid:

- Recent income and property taxes.

- Money obtained by fraud.

- Cash advances on a credit card taken out within 60 days before the order of relief.

- Debts omitted from the Schedule of Assets and Liabilities that the debtor filed with the petition if the creditor did not know about the bankruptcy and therefore did not file a proof of claim.

- Money owed for alimony, maintenance, or child support.

- Debts stemming from intentional and malicious injury.

- Student loans guaranteed by the government cannot be discharged for seven years after the due date. The bankruptcy court may discharge these loans only if the student has acted in good faith and payment of the loans would cause undue hardship.

- Debts stemming from a violation of securities laws.

Circumstances That Prevent Debts from Being Discharged

The Code also prohibits the discharge of debts under the following circumstances:

- *Business Organizations.* Under Chapter 7 (but *not* the other chapters), the debts of partnerships and corporations cannot be discharged. Once its assets have been distributed, the organization must cease operation. If the company resumes business again, it becomes responsible for all its pre-filing debts.

- *Repeated Filings for Bankruptcy.* Congress feared that some debtors, attracted by the lure of a fresh start, would make a habit of bankruptcy. Therefore, a debtor who has received a discharge under Chapter 7 or 11 cannot receive another discharge under Chapter 7 for at least six years after the prior filing.

- *Revocation.* A court can revoke a discharge within one year if it discovers the debtor engaged in fraud or concealment.

- *Dishonesty or Bad Faith Behavior.* The court may deny discharge altogether if the debtor has made fraudulent transfers, hidden assets, falsified records, or otherwise acted in bad faith.

Reaffirmation

Sometimes debtors are willing to **reaffirm** a debt, meaning they promise to pay even after discharge. They may want to reaffirm a secured debt to avoid losing the collateral. For example, a debtor who has taken out a loan secured by a car may reaffirm that debt so that the finance company will agree not to repossess it. Sometimes debtors reaffirm because they feel guilty, or they want to maintain a good relationship with the creditor. They may have borrowed from a family member or an important supplier. Because discharge is a fundamental pillar of the bankruptcy process, courts look closely at each reaffirmation to ensure that the creditor has not unfairly pressured the bankrupt. To be valid, either the court must determine that the reaffirmation is in the debtor's best interest and does not impose undue hardship, or the attorney representing the debtor must file an affidavit in court stating that the debtor's consent was informed and voluntary and the agreement does not create a hardship.

ETHICS

At some point in your life, you will borrow money. What *moral* obligation do you have to repay legitimate debts? Should you take the view that, if bankruptcy laws permit you to default on debts, then why not do so? Alternatively, if you get over your head in debt, should you struggle to pay even though you legitimately qualify for bankruptcy protection? Do the laws determine for you what is right and wrong, or should you have your own standard? How would the ethics checklist in Chapter 2 help you answer these questions? What are the consequences of filing for bankruptcy? Who are the stakeholders? How would you feel in the light of day if your neighbors found out about your bankruptcy filing?

Chapter 11 Reorganization

For a business, the goal of a Chapter 7 bankruptcy is euthanasia—putting it out of its misery by shutting it down and distributing its assets to creditors. Chapter 11 has a much more complicated and ambitious goal—resuscitating a business so that it can ultimately emerge as a viable economic concern.

Both individuals and businesses can use Chapter 11. Businesses usually prefer Chapter 11 over Chapter 7 because Chapter 11 does not require them to dissolve at the end as Chapter 7 does. The threat of death creates a powerful incentive to try rehabilitation under Chapter 11. Individuals, however, tend to prefer Chapter 13 because it is specifically designed for them.

A Chapter 11 proceeding follows many of the same steps as Chapter 7: a petition (either voluntary or involuntary), an order for relief, a meeting of creditors, proofs of claim, and an automatic stay. There are, however, some significant differences.

DEBTOR IN POSSESSION

Chapter 11 does not require a trustee. The bankrupt is called the **debtor in possession** and, in essence, serves as trustee. The debtor in possession has two jobs: to operate the business and to develop a plan of reorganization. A trustee is chosen only if the debtor is incompetent or uncooperative. In that case, the creditors can elect the trustee, but if they do not choose to do so, the U.S. Trustee appoints one.

CREDITORS' COMMITTEE

In a Chapter 11 case, the creditors' committee plays a particularly important role because typically there is no neutral trustee to watch over their interests. The committee has the right to help develop the plan of reorganization and to participate in any other way necessary to protect the interests of its constituency. The U.S. Trustee typically appoints the seven largest *un*secured creditors to the committee.

Secured creditors do not serve because their interests require less protection. If the debtor is a corporation, the U.S. Trustee may also appoint a committee of **equity security holders** to represent shareholder interests.

PLAN OF REORGANIZATION

Once the bankruptcy petition is filed, an automatic stay goes into effect to provide the debtor with temporary relief from creditors. The next stage is to develop a plan of reorganization that provides for the payment of debts and the continuation of the business. For the first 120 days after the order for relief, the debtor has the exclusive right to propose a plan. If the shareholders and creditors accept it, then the bankruptcy case terminates. If the creditors or shareholders reject the debtor's plan, they may file their own version. The debtor has a strong incentive to develop a fair plan the first time because the creditors' proposals are likely to be less favorable.

CONFIRMATION OF THE PLAN

All the creditors and shareholders have the right to vote on the plan of reorganization. In preparation for the vote, each creditor and shareholder is assigned to a class. Chapter 11 classifies claims in the same way as Chapter 7: (1) secured claims, (2) priority claims, and (3) unsecured claims. Each secured claim is usually in its own class because each one is secured by different collateral. Shareholders are also divided into classes, depending upon their interests. For example, holders of preferred stock are in a different class from common shareholders.

The bankruptcy court will approve a plan if a majority of *each class* **votes in favor of it.** Even if some classes vote against the plan, the court can still confirm it under what is called a **cramdown** (as in "the plan is crammed down the creditors' throats"). The court will only impose a cramdown if, in its view, the plan is feasible and fair. If the court rejects the plan of reorganization, the creditors must develop a new one.

DISCHARGE

A confirmed plan of reorganization is binding on the debtor, creditors, and shareholders. **The debtor now owns the assets in the bankrupt estate, free of all obligations except those listed in the plan.** Under a typical plan of reorganization, the debtor gives some current assets to creditors and also promises to pay them a portion of future earnings. In contrast, the Chapter 7 debtor typically relinquishes all assets (except exempt property) to creditors but then has no obligation to turn over future income. Exhibit 12.5 illustrates the steps in a Chapter 11 bankruptcy.

ECONOMICS & THE LAW

In America, bankruptcy has come to mean a second chance for bust businesses. On the other side of the Atlantic, when companies stumble, almost as much effort is spent in fingering the guilty as in trying to salvage a viable business. British and French laws, for example, can make a failing company's directors face criminal penalties and personal liability. Moreover, bankers have the power, at the first sign of trouble, to push a company into the arms of the receivers.

As the European Union inches toward greater harmonization, should it try to mimic America? The difference between Europe and America is the choice between two types of mistakes, which economists call type I and type II errors. Type I errors are caused by excessive caution; for example, the court that lets a

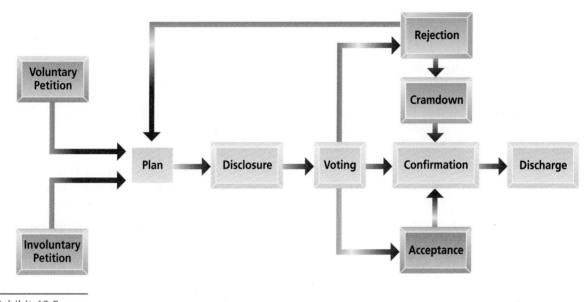

Exhibit 12.5

guilty defendant go free. Type II errors result from excessive zeal; for example, the court that convicts an innocent who is wrongly accused.

America's generous approach to bankruptcy creates type I errors. It occasionally revives firms that should be shut. For example, Eastern Airlines flew for years under Chapter 11, in a better position than its rivals who were burdened with high interest payments on their loans. Less visible are the failures of the European system, which are of the type II variety. Companies that might have been revived are prematurely put down, often amid fire sales. Ironically, this can work against Europeans' oft-stated goal to preserve jobs; a company might be able to survive with reduced debt.

The two strongest forces in a bankruptcy are money and revenge. In America, where failure has long been a routine part of entrepreneurial culture, the emphasis is on money. European law tends to favor revenge. A pity that the different outcomes are so stark.[35]

Chapter 13 Consumer Reorganizations

The purpose of Chapter 13 is to rehabilitate an individual debtor. It is not available at all to businesses or to individuals with more than $290,000 in unsecured debts or $872,000 in secured debts. Under Chapter 13, the bankrupt consumer typically keeps most of her assets in exchange for a promise to repay some of her debts using future income. Therefore, to be eligible, the debtor must have a regular source of income. Individuals usually choose this chapter because it is easier and cheaper than Chapters 7 and 11. Consequently, more money is retained for both creditors and debtor.

---

[35] "Fixing Failed Firms Should Be Based on Economics, Not Revenge," *The Economist*, Dec. 15, 2001, p. 62.

A bankruptcy under Chapter 13 generally follows the same course as Chapter 11: the debtor files a petition, creditors submit proofs of claim, the court imposes an automatic stay, the debtor files a plan, and the court confirms the plan. But there are some differences.

Recently, the number of individuals filing for bankruptcy has been increasing. About 1.5 million Americans file each year. What are the advantages and disadvantages of this method for solving your financial woes?

Good reasons to file:

1. If your car is about to be repossessed, your mortgage foreclosed, or your lease terminated, then by all means file. You need a place to live and a means of getting to work.

2. Bankruptcy experts recommend filing if you expect that it would take you upwards of 5 or 10 years to pay off your debts.

Good reasons to wait a while:

1. You may be able to solve your financial problems without filing. Consult a credit counselor who can suggest alternative approaches, such as setting a budget and eliminating credit cards. You may also find that your credit card companies are willing to negotiate a reduction in the amount you owe them. They have a powerful incentive to be reasonable because, as unsecured creditors, they are likely to get little or nothing from the bankruptcy process. The National Foundation for Consumer Credit offers advice to debtors about bankruptcy—and the alternatives—at http://www.nfcc.org/.

2. A bankruptcy filing stays on your record for a decade. During this time, creditors might lend you money, but only at high rates.

3. A bankruptcy filing does not eliminate all of your debt. You will still be responsible for non-dischargeable items such as student loans, child support, and back taxes.

BEGINNING A CHAPTER 13 CASE

To initiate a Chapter 13 case, the debtor must file a voluntary petition. **Creditors cannot use an involuntary petition to force a debtor into Chapter 13.** In all Chapter 13 cases, the U.S. Trustee appoints a trustee to supervise the debtor although the debtor remains in possession of the bankruptcy estate. The trustee also serves as a central clearinghouse for the debtor's payments to creditors. The debtor pays the trustee who, in turn, transmits these funds to creditors. For this service the trustee is allowed to keep 10 percent of the payments.

PLAN OF PAYMENT

The debtor must file a plan of payment within 15 days after filing the voluntary petition. Only the debtor can file a plan; the creditors have no right to file their own version. Under the plan, the debtor must (1) commit some future earnings to pay off debts, (2) promise to pay all secured and priority claims in full, and (3) treat all remaining classes equally.

Within 30 days after filing the plan of payment, the debtor must begin making payments to the trustee under the plan. The trustee holds these payments until the plan is confirmed and then transmits them to creditors. The debtor continues to make payments to the trustee until the plan has been fully implemented. If the plan is rejected, the trustee returns the payments to the debtor.

Only the bankruptcy court has the authority to confirm or reject a plan of payment. Creditors have no right to vote on it. However, to confirm a plan, the court must ensure that:

- All of the unsecured creditors receive at least as much as they would have under Chapter 7

- The plan is feasible and the bankrupt will be able to make the promised payments

- The plan does not extend beyond three years without good reason and in no event lasts longer than five years; and

- The debtor is acting in good faith, making a reasonable effort to pay obligations.

In the following case, a creditor argued that the debtor's plan was not made in good faith.

IN RE LEMAIRE

898 F.2d 1346, 1990 U.S. App. LEXIS 4374
United States Court of Appeals for the Eighth Circuit, 1990

FACTS: As Paul Handeen got out of his car one Sunday morning, Gregory LeMaire shot at him nine times with a bolt action rifle. Bullets struck Handeen in the mouth, neck, spine, arm, knee, and ankle. LeMaire pleaded guilty to a charge of aggravated assault and served 27 months in prison. After his release he earned a doctorate from the University of Minnesota.

Handeen received a judgment of $50,000 against LeMaire. To avoid paying this judgment, LeMaire filed a bankruptcy petition under Chapter 13. He proposed a plan under which he would pay his creditors 42 percent of their claims. The bankruptcy court confirmed the plan over Handeen's objection. Handeen appealed to the district court, arguing that LeMaire had not filed his plan in good faith. The district court affirmed and, upon appeal, the appeals court also affirmed. Handeen then asked for a rehearing. This time, the appeals court granted a rehearing *en banc*. (Usually, only three judges hear an appeal. "*En banc*" means that all the judges on the court hear it.)

ISSUES: Is a judgment awarded to the victim of an intentional shooting dischargeable under Chapter 13? Did LeMaire file his plan in good faith?

EXCERPTS FROM JUDGE GIBSON'S DECISION: In evaluating LeMaire's motivation and sincerity, the bankruptcy court balanced Handeen's desire to be compensated for his injuries against LeMaire's desire to have a fresh start and found the latter to outweigh the former in importance. The court noted that, while LeMaire had been unable to pay his debt to his victim, he had paid his debt to society by serving a prison sentence and had attempted to reorder his life and make a fresh start. The court found that forcing LeMaire to be burdened the rest of his life with a judgment which would continue to accrue interest, result in endless garnishments, and prevent him from accumulating property would be inimical to such a fresh start. The court concluded that LeMaire had made a wholehearted attempt to pay Handeen as much as possible, and that LeMaire's motivation was proper and his sincerity real.

We do not believe that LeMaire has fulfilled the good faith requirement of Chapter 13. The record here very clearly indicates that LeMaire intended to kill Handeen, and he nearly succeeded in his intention. While pre-filing conduct is not determinative of the good faith issue, it is nevertheless relevant. When we consider the pre-filing conduct here, including the maliciousness of the injury which

LeMaire inflicted upon Handeen, in light of the lack of other factors sufficient to establish good faith, we are persuaded that the bankruptcy court clearly erred in finding that LeMaire proposed his plan in good faith.

We remand this case to the district court with instructions to remand, in turn, to the bankruptcy court for further proceedings consistent with this opinion. ◢

DISCHARGE

Once confirmed, a plan is binding on all creditors, whether they like it or not. **The debtor is washed clean of all pre-petition debts except those provided for in the plan, but, unlike Chapter 7, the debts are not** *permanently* **discharged.** If the debtor violates the plan, all of the debts are revived, and the creditors have a right to recover them under Chapter 7. The debts become permanently discharged only when the bankrupt fully complies with the plan.

If the debtor's circumstances change, the debtor, the trustee, or unsecured creditors can ask the court to modify the plan. Most such requests come from debtors whose income has declined. However, if the debtor's income rises, the creditors or the trustee can, in theory, ask that payments increase, too.

Chapter Conclusion

Borrowed money is the lubricant that keeps a modern economy motoring smoothly. Without it many consumers would never own a home or a car, and many businesses would be unable to grow. But unless these debts are repaid, the economy will falter. Secured transactions are one method for ensuring that creditors are paid.

Bankruptcy law is the safety net that catches those who are not able to meet their financial obligations. Bankruptcy laws cannot create assets where there are none (or not enough), but they can ensure that the debtor's assets, however limited, are fairly divided between the debtor and creditors. Any bankruptcy system that accomplishes this goal must be deemed a success.

Chapter Review

1. Article 9 applies to any transaction intended to create a security interest in personal property or fixtures.

2. Attachment means that (1) the two parties made a security agreement *and either* the debtor has *authenticated a security agreement* describing the collateral or the secured party has obtained *possession or control*; and (2) the secured party gave value in order to get the security agreement; and (3) the debtor has rights in the collateral.

3. Attachment protects against the debtor. Perfection of a security interest protects the

secured party against parties other than the debtor.

4. Filing is the most common way to perfect. For many forms of collateral, the secured party may also perfect by obtaining either possession or control.

5. A purchase money security interest (PMSI) is one taken by the person who sells the collateral or advances money so the debtor can buy the collateral.

6. A buyer in ordinary course of business (BIOC) takes the goods free of a security interest

created by his seller even though the security interest is perfected.

7. Priority among secured parties is generally as follows:

   (a) A party with a perfected security interest takes priority over a party with an unperfected interest.

   (b) If neither secured party has perfected, the first interest to attach gets priority.

   (c) Between perfected security interests, the first to file or perfect wins.

8. When the debtor defaults, the secured party may take possession of the collateral on its own, without a court order, if it can do so without a breach of the peace.

9. A secured party may sell, lease, or otherwise dispose of the collateral in any commercially reasonable way, or it may ignore the collateral and sue the debtor for the full debt.

10. When the debtor pays the full debt, the secured party must complete a termination statement, notifying the public that it no longer claims a security interest in the collateral.

11. The following chart sets out the important elements of each bankruptcy chapter.

	Chapter 7	Chapter 11	Chapter 13
Objective	Liquidation	Reorganization	Consumer reorganization
Who May Use It	Individual or organization	Individual or organization	Individual
Type of Petition	Voluntary or involuntary	Voluntary or involuntary	Only voluntary
Administration of Bankruptcy Estate	Trustee	Debtor in possession (trustee selected only if debtor is unable to serve)	Trustee
Selection of Trustee	Creditors have right to elect trustee; otherwise, U.S. Trustee makes appointment	Usually no trustee	Appointed by U.S. Trustee
Participation in Formulation of Plan	No plan is filed	Both creditors and debtor can propose plans	Only debtor can propose a plan
Creditor Approval of Plan	Creditors do not vote	Creditors vote on plan, but court may approve plan without the creditors' support	Creditors do not vote on plan
Impact on Debtor's Post-petition Income	Not affected; debtor keeps all future earnings	Must contribute toward payment of pre-petition debts	Must contribute toward payment of pre-petition debts

Practice Test

Note to the student: The following cases and problems were decided under the former Article 9. In each instance, the outcome would be the same under the revised laws.

1. **CPA QUESTION** Under the UCC Secured Transactions Article, perfection of a security interest by a creditor provides added protection against other parties in the event the

debtor does not pay its debts. Which of the following parties is not affected by perfection of a security interest?

(a) Other prospective creditors of the debtor

(b) The trustee in a bankruptcy case

(c) A buyer in the ordinary course of business

(d) A subsequent personal injury judgment creditor

2. Eugene Ables ran an excavation company. He borrowed $500,000 from the Highland Park State Bank. Ables signed a note promising to repay the money and an agreement giving Highland a security interest in all of his equipment, including after-acquired equipment. Several years later, Ables agreed with Patricia Myers to purchase a Bantam Backhoe from her for $16,000, which he would repay at the rate of $100 per month, while he used the machine. Ables later defaulted on his note to Highland, and the bank attempted to take the backhoe. Myers and Ables contended that the bank had no right to take the backhoe. Was the backhoe covered by Highland's security interest? Did Ables have sufficient rights in the backhoe for the bank's security interest to attach?

3. Jerry Payne owed the First State Bank of Pflugerville $342,000. The loan was secured by a 9.25-carat diamond ring. The bank claimed a default on the loan and, without notifying Payne, sold the ring. But the proceeds did not pay off the full debt, and the bank sued Payne for the deficiency. Is Payne liable for the deficiency?

4. John and Clara Lockovich bought a 22-foot Chaparrel Villian II boat from Greene County Yacht Club for $32,500. They paid $6,000 cash and borrowed the rest of the purchase money from Gallatin National Bank, which took a security interest in the boat. Gallatin filed a financing statement in *Greene* County, Pennsylvania, where the bank was located. But Pennsylvania law at that time required financing statements to be filed in the county of the debtor's residence, and the Lockoviches lived in *Allegheny* County. The Lockoviches soon washed up in Bankruptcy Court. Other creditors demanded that the boat be sold, claiming that Gallatin's security interest had been filed in the wrong place. Who wins? (Please be advised: this is a trick question.)

5. McMann Golf Ball Co. manufactured, as you might suppose, golf balls. Barwell, Inc., sold McMann a "preformer," a machine that makes golf balls, for $55,000. Barwell delivered the machine on February 20. McMann paid $3,000 down, the remainder to be paid over several years, and signed an agreement giving Barwell a security interest in the preformer. Barwell did not perfect its interest. On March 1 McMann borrowed $350,000 from First of America Bank, giving the bank a security interest in McMann's present and after-acquired property. First of America perfected by filing on March 2. McMann, of course, became insolvent, and both Barwell and the bank attempted to repossess the preformer. Who gets it?

6. **ETHICS** On November 5 The Fred Hawes Organization, Inc., a small subcontractor, opened an account with Basic Distribution Corp., a supplier of construction materials. Hawes promised to pay its bills within 30 days of purchase. Although Hawes purchased a substantial quantity of goods on credit from Basic, it made few payments on the accounts until the following March when it paid Basic over $21,000. On May 14 Hawes filed a voluntary petition under Chapter 7. Does the bankruptcy trustee have a right to recover this payment? Is it fair to Hawes's other creditors if Basic is allowed to keep the $21,000 payment?

7. Mark Milbank built custom furniture in Port Chester, New York. His business was unsuccessful, and he repeatedly borrowed money from his wife and her father. He promised that the loans would enable him to spend more time with his family. Instead, he spent more time in bed with his next-door neighbor. After the divorce, his ex-wife and her father demanded repayment of the loans. When Milbank filed under Chapter 13, his ex-wife and her father asked the court not to discharge Milbank's debts on the grounds that he had acted in bad faith toward them. Should the bankruptcy court discharge Milbank's loans?

8. **CPA QUESTION** Decal Corp. incurred substantial operating losses for the past three

years. Unable to meet its current obligations, Decal filed a petition of reorganization under Chapter 11 of the federal Bankruptcy Code. Which of the following statements is correct?

(a) A creditors' committee, if appointed, will consist of unsecured creditors.

(b) The court must appoint a trustee to manage Decal's affairs.

(c) Decal may continue in business only with the approval of a trustee.

(d) The creditors' committee must select a trustee to manage Decal's affairs.

9. **CPA QUESTION**   A voluntary petition filed under the liquidation provisions of Chapter 7 of the federal Bankruptcy Code:

(a) Is **not** available to a corporation unless it has previously filed a petition under the reorganization provisions of Chapter 11 of the Code

(b) Automatically stays collection actions against the debtor **except** by secured creditors

(c) Will be dismissed unless the debtor has 12 or more unsecured creditors whose claims total at least $5,000

(d) Does **not** require the debtor to show that the debtor's liabilities exceed the fair market value of assets

10. **YOU BE THE JUDGE WRITING PROBLEM** Lydia D'Ettore received a degree in computer programming at Devry Institute of Technology, with a grade-point average of 2.51. To finance her education, she borrowed $20,516.52 from a federal student loan program. After graduation she could not find a job in her field, so she went to work as a clerk at a salary of $12,500. D'Ettore and her daughter lived with her parents free of charge. After setting aside $50 a month in savings and paying bills that included $233 for a new car (a Suzuki Samurai) and $50 for jewelry from Zales, her disposable income was $125 per month. D'Ettore asked the bankruptcy court to discharge the debts she owed Devry. Under the Code these student loans cannot be discharged unless they impose an "undue hardship" on the debtor. Did the debts to Devry Institute impose an undue hardship on D'Ettore? **Argument for D'Ettore:** Lydia D'Ettore lives at home with her parents. Even so, her disposable income is a meager $125 a month. She would have to spend every single penny of her disposable income for nearly 15 years to pay back her $20,000 debt to Devry. That would be an undue hardship. **Argument for the Creditors:** The U.S. government guaranteed D'Ettore's loan. Therefore, if the court discharges it, the American taxpayer will have to pay the bill. Why should taxpayers subsidize an irresponsible student? D'Ettore must also stop buying new cars and jewelry. And why should the government pay her debts while she saves money every month?

11. **ROLE REVERSAL**   Write a multiple-choice question that highlights the difference between Chapters 7 and 11.

Internet Research Problem

Write a security agreement in which your friend gives you a security interest in her $20,000 home entertainment system, in exchange for a loan of $12,000. Because the collateral is something that she uses daily, what special concerns do you have? How will you protect yourself? Next, find the UCC1 financing form at http://www.intercountyclearance.com/ra9/ra9ucc1.pdf. Print the form, then complete it. In what office of your state should you file in order to perfect?

The exemption rules for your state are listed at http://www.bankruptcyaction.com/bankruptcyexemptions.htm. Compared with other jurisdictions, is your state generous or stingy with exemptions? In considering a new bankruptcy statute, Congress has struggled mightily over this issue. What do you think would be a fair exemption?

You can find further practice problems in the Online Quiz at http://beatty.westbuslaw.com **or in the Study Guide that accompanies this text.**

AGENCY
& EMPLOYMENT

UNIT 3

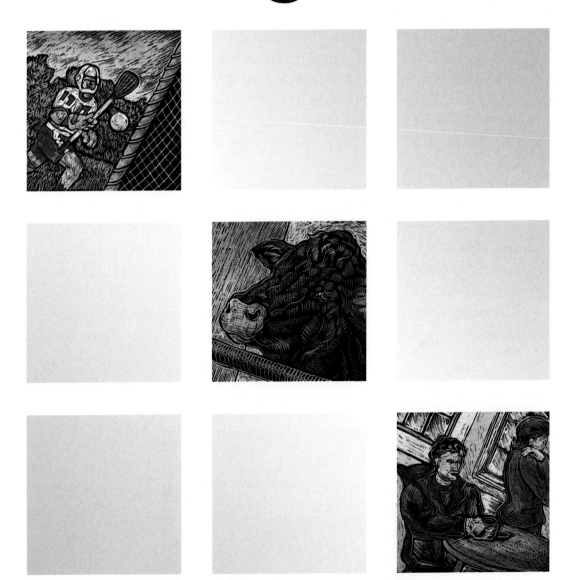

Agency

It was a perfect spring day in Ashland, Ohio. Roger was having a great game as his Ohio State lacrosse team played a close match against Ashland University. Carefully gauging an Ashland pass, Roger stuck his stick out, intercepted the ball, whipped around, and launched a shot on goal. Score! His hands went up in the air. He never saw the Ashland player jump him from behind and knock him to the ground. But he did see the player stand over him, yelling obscenities. He also saw his teammate Brian grab the opponent in a bear hug. And he saw the Ashland player twist violently, throwing Brian to the ground, where he lay motionless. Brian never walked again—the blow to his head as he hit the ground left him a paraplegic. Brian sued Ashland, alleging that the university was responsible for his injury.[1]

Brian's parents hired a real estate broker to find a new house that was handicap accessible. They were so delighted with the one-story bungalow she located that they did not begrudge paying her an $18,000 commission. But after the sale they discovered that the seller of the house had also paid her a commission. They sued for the return of their $18,000.

Nonetheless, the house was perfect for their needs, and they stocked it with all the custom-made items that Brian required. Because these medical devices were so expensive,

---

[1] Based on *Hanson v. Kynast*, 24 Ohio St. 3d 171, 494 N.E.2d 1091, 1986 Ohio LEXIS 667 (Ohio 1986).

they asked their insurance agent to increase their house coverage from $400,000 to $800,000. Brian and his parents suffered a terrible blow a few months later when they returned home from an exhausting visit to the hospital to find their new house burned to the ground. They were even more distressed when they discovered that the insurance agent had misread his notes and only increased their policy to $480,000. They sued him for $320,000. ◼

This example raises several questions of agency law. Thus far, this book has primarily dealt with issues of individual responsibility: What happens if *you* knock someone down or *you* sign an agreement? Agency law, on the other hand, is concerned with your responsibility for the actions of others. What happens if your agent assaults someone or enters into an agreement? Agency law presents a significant trade-off: if you do everything yourself, you have control over the result. But the size and scope of your business (and your life) will be severely limited. Once you hire other people, you can accomplish a great deal more, but your risk of legal liability increases immensely. Though it might be safer to do everything yourself, that is not a practical decision for most business owners (or most people). The alternative is to hire carefully and to limit the risks as much as possible by understanding the law of agency.

Was Ashland University liable for Brian's injuries? It would have been if the Ashland player had been an agent of the university. But, on a similar set of facts, the Ohio Supreme Court held that the Ashland player was not an agent because Ashland had no *control* over him and he was not playing for the school's *benefit*. However, the real estate broker was an agent for Brian's parents. She violated her *duty of loyalty* to them when she acted for both buyer and seller in the same transaction, without disclosing her dual role to both parties. An agent who violates this important duty must forfeit her commission. And the insurance agent violated his *duty of care* when he bought a policy in the wrong amount for Brian's parents. An agent who violates this duty is liable for the harm his carelessness has caused—in this case $320,000.

Creating an Agency Relationship

Principals have substantial liability for the actions of their agents.[2] Therefore, disputes about whether an agency relationship exists are not mere legal quibbles but important issues with potentially profound financial consequences. According to the Restatement of Agency:

> Agency is the fiduciary relation which results from the manifestation of consent by one person to another that the other shall act on his behalf and subject to his control, and consent by the other so to act.[3]

---

[2] The word "principal" is always used when referring to a person. It is not to be confused with the word "principle," which refers to a fundamental idea.

[3] Section 1 of the Restatement (Second) of Agency (1958), prepared by the American Law Institute.

In other words, in an agency relationship, someone (the agent) agrees to perform a task for, and under the control of, someone else (the principal). To create an agency relationship, there must be:

- A **principal** and
- An **agent**
- Who mutually **consent** that the agent will act on behalf of the principal and
- Be subject to the principal's **control**
- Thereby creating a **fiduciary** relationship.

CONSENT

To establish consent, the principal must ask the agent to do something, and the agent must agree. In the most straightforward example, Brian's parents asked their insurance agent to buy a policy on their house, and he agreed. Matters were more complicated, however, when Steven James met some friends one evening at a restaurant. During the two hours he was there, he drank four to six beers. (It is probably a bad sign that he cannot remember how many.) From then on, one misfortune piled upon another. After leaving the restaurant at about 7:00 p.m., James sped down a highway and crashed into a car that had stalled on the roadway, thereby killing the driver. James told the police at the scene that he had not seen the parked car (another bad sign). Evidently, James's lawyer was not as perceptive as the police in recognizing drunkenness. In a misguided attempt to help his client, James's lawyer took him to the local hospital for a blood test. Unfortunately, the test confirmed that James had indeed been drunk at the time of the accident.

The attorney knew that if this evidence was admitted at trial, his client would soon be receiving free room and board from the Massachusetts Department of Corrections. So at trial the lawyer argued that the blood test was protected by the client-attorney privilege because the hospital had been his agent and therefore a member of the defense team. The court disagreed, however, holding that the hospital employees were not agents for the lawyer because they had not consented to act in the role.

The court upheld James's conviction of murder in the first degree by reason of extreme atrocity or cruelty.[4]

CONTROL

Principals are liable for the acts of their agents because they exercise control over the agents. If principals direct their agents to commit an act, it seems fair to hold the principal liable when that act causes harm. In the following example, did Northwest Airlines exercise control over Kuwait Air?

The horse-drawn caisson wound slowly through Arlington National Cemetery and stopped in front of lot number 59, the section reserved for victims of terrorist acts. The flag-draped casket of William L. Stanford, one of the two Agency for International Development auditors killed by plane hijackers in Iran, was carried

---

[4] *Commonwealth v. James*, 427 Mass. 312, 693 N.E.2d 148, 1998 Mass. LEXIS 175.

to the gravesite amid full military honors. Three volleys of rifle fire pierced the unusually warm December air as scores of family, friends, and colleagues lowered their heads and wept. Stanford, 52, was killed as he was traveling to join his wife and 13-year-old daughter in Karachi, Pakistan, where he intended to spend the holidays.[5]

The hijacked plane—with William Stanford aboard—was a Kuwait Airways (KA) flight from Kuwait to Pakistan. Stanford had originally purchased a ticket on Northwest Airlines but had traded in his Northwest ticket for a seat on the KA flight. Stanford's widow sued Northwest on the theory that KA was Northwest's agent. The airlines had an agreement permitting passengers to exchange tickets from one to another. In this case, however, the court found that no agency relationship existed because Northwest had no *control* over KA.[6] Northwest did not tell KA how to fly planes or handle terrorists; therefore it should not be liable when KA made fatal errors. An agent and principal must not only *consent* to an agency relationship, but the principal must also have *control* over the agent.

FIDUCIARY RELATIONSHIP

A fiduciary relationship is a special relationship, with high standards. The beneficiary places special confidence in the fiduciary who, in turn, is obligated to act in good faith and candor, putting his own needs second. The purpose of a fiduciary relationship is for one person to benefit another. **Agents have a fiduciary duty to their principals.** When, in this chapter's opening scenario, Brian's parents hired a real estate broker to find a house for them, she was a fiduciary, obligated to act in their best interest alone. She violated this duty when she also acted for the seller of the house, without telling Brian's parents.

All three elements—consent, control, and a fiduciary duty—are necessary to create an agency relationship. In some relationships, for example, there might be a *fiduciary duty* but no *control*. A trustee of a trust must act for the benefit of the beneficiaries, but the beneficiaries have no right to control the trustee. Therefore, a trustee is not an agent of the beneficiaries. *Consent* is present in every contractual relationship, but that does not necessarily mean that the two parties are agent and principal. If Horace sells his car to Lily, they both expect to benefit under the contract, but neither has a *fiduciary duty* to the other and neither *controls* the other, so there is no agency relationship.

ELEMENTS NOT REQUIRED FOR AN AGENCY RELATIONSHIP

Consent, control, and a fiduciary relationship are necessary to establish an agency relationship. The following elements are **not** required:

- *A Written Agreement.* In most cases an agency agreement does not have to be in writing. An oral understanding is valid, except in one circumstance—the **equal dignities rule.** According to this rule, if an agent is empowered to enter into a contract that must be in writing, then the appointment of the agent must

---

[5] Mary Jordan, "Terrorists' Victim Is Buried," *The Washington Post*, Dec. 18, 1984, p. A14.
[6] *Stanford v. Kuwait Airways Corp.*, 648 F. Supp. 1158, 1986 U.S. Dist. LEXIS 18880 (S.D.N.Y. 1986).

also be written. For example, under the statute of frauds, a contract for the sale of land is unenforceable unless in writing, so the agency agreement to sell land must also be *in writing*.

- *A Formal Agreement.* The principal and agent need not agree formally that they have an agency relationship. They do not even have to think the word "agent." As long as they act like an agent and a principal, the law will treat them as such.

- *Consideration.* An agency relationship need not meet all the standards of contract law. For example, a contract is not valid without consideration, but an agency agreement is valid even *if the agent is not paid*.

Duties of Agents to Principals

Agents owe a fiduciary duty to their principals. In the following example, employees of Steinberg, Moorad & Dunn (SMD) were agents of the firm—they had agreed to act on behalf of SMD and be subject to its control. Did they violate their duty?

NEWSWORTHY

Sports agent Leigh Steinberg, whose story inspired the Tom Cruise film *Jerry Maguire*, is caught up in a legal battle with his former partner that echoes moments from the movie. Steinberg's firm, SMD, has sued David Dunn, claiming Dunn was planning to form his own stable of sports stars while working for SMD. Dunn and agents at his new firm, Athletes First, have said that as many as 80 percent of SMD's clients plan to switch management firms or already have.

SMD plans to ask Los Angeles Superior Court Judge Marilyn Hoffman to order Dunn to stop representing athletes he knew through SMD. "Earlier this year, Dunn orchestrated a despicable raid on [SMD] and its clientele," SMD says in court papers for its suit. Dunn counters that SMD "neglected and lost clients it now accuses Athletes First of stealing."

Overall, about one-third of SMD's former 30-person staff in Newport Beach, California, has since joined Dunn at Athletes First. Steinberg claims that Dunn and his recruits downloaded lists of clients and their specific contract terms and needs, as well as information on prospective clients, while still at SMD.[7] ▪

Search on the Internet for further information about the dispute between Leigh Steinberg and David Dunn. If Dunn won, what were the important factors in the court's decision? If Steinberg was victorious, what penalties were imposed on Dunn? ▪

DUTY OF LOYALTY

The agent must act solely for the benefit of the principal in all matters connected with the agency.[8] The agent has an obligation to put the principal first, to strive to accomplish the principal's goals. If Dunn and his colleagues stole client

---

[7] Joyzelle Davis, "Real-Life Breakup of 'Jerry Maguire' Agency Mirrors Movie," *The Houston Chronicle*, Aug. 12, 2001, Sports, p. 2.

[8] Restatement (Second) of Agency §387.

information from SMD in preparation for their departure to Athletes First, they were violating their duty of loyalty to their principal because they were acting in their own interest, not that of their principal.

An agent is bound by the duty of loyalty, *whether or not the agent and principal have consciously agreed to it.* The agent should know his obligations. However, a principal and agent can change this rule by agreement. SMD could, for example, have given Dunn permission to download the client lists, in which case Dunn would not have been liable, at least for that activity. The various components of the duty of loyalty follow.

Outside Benefits

An agent may not receive profits unless the principal knows and approves. Suppose that Hope is an employee of the agency Big Egos and Talents, Inc. (BEAT). She has been representing Arnold Schwarzenegger in his latest movie negotiations.[9] He often drives her to meetings in his new Hummer military vehicle. He is so thrilled that she has arranged for him to star in the new movie, *Little Men*, that he buys her a Hummer. Can Hope keep this generous gift? Only with BEAT's permission. She must tell BEAT about the Hummer; the company may then take the vehicle itself or allow her to keep it.

Confidential Information

The ability to keep secrets is important in any relationship, but especially a fiduciary relationship. Agents can neither disclose nor use for their own benefit any confidential information they acquire during their agency. As the following case shows, this duty continues even after the agency relationship ends.

ABKCO MUSIC, INC. V. HARRISONGS MUSIC, LTD.

722 F.2d 988, 1983 U.S. App. LEXIS 15562
United States Court of Appeals for the Second Circuit, 1983

FACTS: Bright Tunes Music Corp. (Bright Tunes) owned the copyright to the song "He's So Fine." The company sued George Harrison, a Beatle, alleging that the Harrison composition "My Sweet Lord" copied "He's So Fine." At the time the suit was filed, Allen B. Klein handled the business affairs of the Beatles.

Klein (representing Harrison) met with the president of Bright Tunes to discuss possible settlement of the copyright lawsuit. Klein suggested that Harrison might be interested in purchasing the copyright to "He's So Fine." Shortly thereafter, Klein's management contract with the Beatles expired. Without telling Harrison, Klein began negotiating with Bright Tunes to purchase the copyright to "He's So Fine" for himself. To advance these negotiations, Klein gave Bright Tunes information about royalty income for "My Sweet Lord"—information that he had gained as Harrison's agent.

The trial judge in the copyright case ultimately found that Harrison had infringed the copyright on "He's So Fine" and assessed damages of $1,599,987. After the trial Klein purchased the "He's So Fine" copyright from Bright Tunes and with it, the right to recover from Harrison for the breach of copyright.

---

[9] Do not be confused by the fact that Hope works as an agent for movie stars. As an employee of BEAT, her duty is to the company. She is an agent of BEAT and BEAT works for the celebrities.

ISSUE: Did Klein violate his fiduciary duty to Harrison by using confidential information after the agency relationship terminated?

EXCERPTS FROM JUDGE PIERCE'S DECISION: There is no doubt that the relationship between Harrison and [Klein] prior to the termination of the management agreement was that of principal and agent, and that the relationship was fiduciary in nature. [A]n agent has a duty not to use confidential knowledge acquired in his employment in competition with his principal. This duty exists as well after the employment is terminated as during its continuance. On the other hand, use of information based on general business knowledge or gleaned from general business experience is not covered by the rule, and the former agent is permitted to compete with his former principal in reliance on such general publicly available information. The evidence presented herein is not at all convincing that the information imparted to Bright Tunes by Klein was publicly available.

While the initial attempt to purchase [the copyright to "He's So Fine"] was several years removed from the eventual purchase on [Klein]'s own account, we are not of the view that such a fact rendered [Klein] unfettered in the later negotiations. Taking all of these circumstances together, we agree that [Klein's] conduct did not meet the standard required of him as a former fiduciary. ◢

To listen to the two songs involved in this case, tune in to http://www .copyrightwebsite.com/audio/harrison/harrison.asp.

Klein was angry that the Beatles had failed to renew his management contract. Was it reasonable for him to think that he owed no duty to the principal who had fired him? Should his sense of ethics have told him that his behavior was wrong? Would the ethics checklist in Chapter 2 have helped Klein to make a better decision? ▪

Competition with the Principal

Agents are not allowed to compete with their principal in any matter within the scope of the agency business. If Allen Klein had purchased the "He's So Fine" copyright while he was George Harrison's agent, he would have committed an additional sin against the agency relationship. Owning song rights was clearly part of the agency business, so Klein could not make such purchases without Harrison's consent. Once the agency relationship ends, however, so does the rule against competition. Klein was entitled to buy the "He's So Fine" copyright after the agency relationship ended (as long as he did not use confidential information).

Conflict of Interest between Two Principals

Unless otherwise agreed, an agent may not act for two principals whose interests conflict. Suppose Travis represents both director Steven Spielberg and actress Julia Roberts. Spielberg is casting the title role in his new movie, *Nancy Drew: Girl Detective*, a role that Roberts covets. Travis cannot represent these two clients when they are negotiating with each other, unless they both know about the conflict and agree to ignore it. The following article illustrates the dangers of acting for two principals at once.

Faced with growing health care and retirement costs, the Sisters of Charity decided to sell a 207-acre property that they owned in New Jersey. The order of nuns soon found, however, that the world is not always a charitable place. They agreed to sell the land to Linpro for nearly $10 million. But before the deal closed, Linpro signed a contract to resell the property to Sammis for $34 million. So, you say, the sisters made a bad deal. There is no law against that. But it turned out that the nuns' lawyer, Peter Berkley, also represented Sammis. He knew about the deal between Sammis and Linpro, but never told the sisters. Was that the charitable— or legal—thing to do? For ideas on how Berkley should have handled this delicate situation, look at the discussion on dual agency at **http://www.thbuyers .com/Business/newsbusiness/archivesbusiness.htm**. ▪

Secretly Dealing with the Principal

If a principal hires an agent to arrange a transaction, the agent may not become a party to the transaction without the principal's permission. Matt Damon became an overnight sensation after starring in the movie *Good Will Hunting*. Suppose that he hired Trang to read scripts for him. Unbeknownst to Damon, Trang had written her own script, which she thought would be ideal for him. She may not sell it to him without revealing that she wrote it herself. Damon may be perfectly happy to buy Trang's script, but he has the right, as her principal, to know that she is the person selling it.

Appropriate Behavior

An agent may not engage in inappropriate behavior that reflects badly on the principal. This rule applies even to *off-duty* conduct. For example, two of the flight attendants featured in the following article were fired for inappropriate off-duty behavior; the third was given a warning letter.

The guests at a hotel bar in London were stunned when British Airways flight attendant Shirlie Johns raised her shirt so that colleague Stefania Lanza could caress her breasts while kissing her on the mouth. Johns then lowered her trousers, revealing her underwear. Meanwhile, crew member Matthew Swadling took off his shirt and poured wine down his trousers. All three rubbed up against each other provocatively while downing beer, vodka, and wine. It was, bystanders agreed, a huge embarrassment for British Airways. ▪

OTHER DUTIES OF AN AGENT

In June, Tyler and Taylor Harding left for a five-week trip to England. Before leaving, they hired Angie Warren to sell or rent their vacation house in Grantham, New Hampshire. The regional Multiple Listing Service was the best way to publicize a house for sale. But Angie was busy with one thing or another and never got around to listing the Hardings' house. However, at the end of June, Angie was contacted by the Fords, who happened to be friends of friends. They told her that their son was a contractor who would like to build a house for them in Grantham, but they needed to rent a place to live in the meantime. Angie showed them the Hardings' house as a rental. Although it was not quite right for the Fords (too many stairs, no separate apartment for Mrs. Ford's mother), it was the best they had seen, so they offered to rent it for a year at $750 per month, beginning the first of September.

Angie called Taylor in England and told her that the Fords "were a nice couple who might very well be interested in buying the house after a year's rental." Taylor responded that $750 was too low, especially over the summer months when the house often rented out for as much as $1,000 per *week*. She proposed a contract from September 1 to June 1 at a rent of $800 per month. Angie indicated that the Fords would probably be willing to make a deal on that basis because they loved the house. Taylor told Angie to call back if there was any problem, but otherwise she would sign the lease when she returned home. The following week, the Fords told Angie that they would agree to $800 a month, but insisted on being able to stay from September to September so that they would have time to complete construction on their new house.

Angie had a list of the Hardings' phone numbers in England, but she made no further effort to contact them there. Instead, she left a message on their home answering machine. When the Fords pressed her three or four times for a definite answer, she said she could not get in touch with the Hardings and suggested the Fords look for another house. When Taylor returned home, she called Angie and was told that "the Fords are coming up next week to confirm everything." Taylor called the Fords herself. She then learned the truth about what had happened and also that the Fords were going to Grantham to look at another house, which they ultimately rented.

Although Angie had not violated her *duty of loyalty* to the Hardings, they were still angry at her. Had she violated any of the other duties that agents owe to their principals?

Duty to Obey Instructions

An agent must obey her principal's instructions, unless the principal directs her to behave illegally or unethically. Taylor instructed Angie to call her if the Fords rejected the offer. Angie violated her duty to obey instructions when she neglected to call Taylor back. If, however, the Hardings had asked her to say that the house's basement was dry, when in fact it looked like a rice paddy every spring, Angie would be under no obligation to follow those illegal instructions.

Duty of Care

An agent has a duty to act with reasonable care. In other words, an agent must act as a reasonable person would, under the circumstances. A reasonable person would not have left a message on the Hardings' home answering machine when she knew they were in Europe.

Under some circumstances, an agent is held to a higher—or lower—standard than usual. **An agent with special skills is held to a higher standard because she is expected to use those skills.** A trained real estate agent should know enough to use the "Multiple Listing Service."

But suppose the Hardings had asked their neighbor, Jed, to help them sell their house. Jed is not a trained real estate agent, and he is not being paid, which makes him a *gratuitous agent*. A gratuitous agent is held to a lower standard because he is doing his principal a favor and, as the old saying goes, you get what you pay for—up to a point. **Gratuitous agents are liable if they commit *gross* negligence, but not *ordinary* negligence.** If Jed, as a gratuitous agent, left the Hardings an important message on their answering machine because he forgot they were in England, he would not be liable to them for that ordinary negligence. But if the answering machine had a message that *warned* him the Hardings were away and would not be picking up messages, he would be liable for gross negligence and a violation of his duty.

Duty to Provide Information

An agent has a duty to provide the principal with all information in her possession that she has reason to believe the principal wants to know. She also has a duty to provide accurate information. For example, Oma Grigsby signed up with O.K. Travel for a tour of Israel. O.K. purchased the tour from Trinity Tours. Under state law, tour promoters were required to register and post a financial bond. Although Trinity had not done so, O.K. never warned Grigsby. Matters were far from OK when Grigsby learned a week before her trip that Trinity had gone out of business. In the end, however, she was able to obtain a refund from O.K. because it had violated its duty to tell her that Trinity was unregistered and unbonded.[10] Did Angie violate her duty to proved information to the Hardings?

PRINCIPAL'S REMEDIES WHEN THE AGENT BREACHES A DUTY

A principal has three potential remedies when an agent breaches her duty:

- The principal can recover from the agent any **damages** the breach has caused. Thus, if the Hardings can only rent their house for $600 a month instead of the $800 the Fords offered, Angie would be liable for $2,400—$200 a month for one year.

- If an agent breaches the duty of loyalty, he must turn over to the principal any **profits** he has earned as a result of his wrongdoing. Thus, after Klein violated his duty of loyalty to Harrison, he forfeited profits he would have earned from the copyright of "He's So Fine."

- If the agent has violated her duty of loyalty, the principal may **rescind** the transaction. When Trang sold a script to her principal, Matt Damon, without telling him that she was the author, she violated her duty of loyalty. Damon could rescind the contract to buy the script.[11]

All the agents thus far in this chapter have been people. But do agents have to be human? Or can a *bot* can be your agent? A bot is software that performs automatic tasks.[12] Suppose, for example, you want to buy a vintage lava lamp on eBay. You would be willing to pay as much as $100, but you see one that has a high bid of only $33. You do not want to bid $100 now because you might be able to buy the lamp for much less. But you also do not want to have to keep checking back and rebidding each time another bid comes in. To solve this problem, eBay is willing to place automatic bids for you. It calls this system *proxy bidding*. Here is how the company describes this system on its Web site:

> Proxy bidding means that a bidder can submit a maximum bid amount and our system will bid in their absence, executing their bid for them and trying to keep the bid

---

[10] *Grigsby v. O.K. Travel*, 118 Ohio App. 3d 671, 693 N.E.2d 1142,1997 Ohio App. LEXIS 875 (1997).

[11] A principal can rescind his contract with an agent who has violated her duty, but, as we shall see later in the chapter, the principal might not be able to rescind a contract with a third party when the agent misbehaves.

[12] For a discussion of the legal status of bots, see Stephen T. Middlebrook and John Muller, "Thoughts on Bots: The Emerging Law of Electronic Agents," *The Business Lawyer*, Vol 56, Nov. 2000, p. 341.

price as low as possible. This way a bidder doesn't have to be at the auction every minute.

An easier way to think of this would be to think of the bidding system standing in for you as a bidder at a live auction. Let's say you need to be somewhere and can't be present to bid and you ask a friend to go to the auction and bid for you. You tell your friend that you are willing to pay $25 for an item you saw.

The auctioneer starts the bidding at $5 and your friend bids the $5. Then another bidder bids $6 and your friend then bids $7 on your behalf. Then another bidder bids $12 and your friend bids $13 for you. This would keep going until either your friend wins the item for you at or below $25 or the bidding exceeds the $25 you were willing to pay.[13]

If your friend bid for you, he would be your agent. For that reason, legal commentators argue that this eBay bot is also an agent. However, the eBay User Agreement states: "You and eBay are independent contractors, and no agency . . . relationship is intended or created by this Agreement."[14] So is eBay your agent or not? No cases have yet addressed this issue—what would you decide if you were judge? ▪

Duties of Principals to Agents

In a typical agency relationship, the agent agrees to perform tasks for the principal, and the principal agrees to pay the agent. The range of tasks undertaken by an agent is limited only by the imagination of the principal. Because the agent's job can be so varied, the law has needed to define an agent's duties carefully. The role of the principal, on the other hand, is typically less complicated—often little more than writing a check to pay the agent. Thus the law enumerates fewer duties for the principal. Primarily, the principal must reimburse the agent for reasonable expenses and cooperate with the agent in performing agency tasks. The respective duties of agents and principals can be summarized as follows:

Duties of Agents to Principals	Duty of Principals to Agents
Duty of loyalty	Duty to reimburse
Duty to obey instructions	Duty to cooperate
Duty of care	
Duty to provide information	

DUTY TO REIMBURSE THE AGENT

As a general rule, the principal must **indemnify** (i.e., reimburse) the agent for any expenses she has reasonably incurred. These reimbursable expenses fall into three categories:

---

[13] http://webhelp.ebay.com/cgi-bin/eHNC/showdoc-ebay.tcl?docid=407&queryid=proxy_bidding.

[14] http://pages.ebay.com/help/community/png-user2.html.

- **A principal must indemnify an agent for any expenses or damages reasonably incurred in carrying out his agency responsibilities.** For example, Peace Baptist Church of Birmingham, Alabama, asked its pastor to buy land for a new church. He paid part of the the purchase price out of his own pocket, but the church refused to reimburse him. Although the pastor lost in church, he won in court.[15]

- **A principal must indemnify an agent for tort claims brought by a third party if the principal authorized the agent's behavior and the agent did not realize he was committing a tort.** Marisa owns all the apartment buildings on Elm Street, except one. She hires Rajiv to manage the units and tells him that, under the terms of the leases, she has the right to ask guests to leave if a party becomes too rowdy. But she forgets to tell Rajiv that she does not own one of the buildings, which happens to house a college sorority. One night, when the sorority is having a rambunctious party, Rajiv hustles over and starts ejecting the noisy guests. The sorority is furious and sues Rajiv for trespass. If the sorority wins its suit against Rajiv, Marisa would have to pay the judgment, plus Rajiv's attorney's fees, because she had told him to quell noisy parties, and he did not realize he was trespassing.

- **The principal must indemnify the agent for any liability she incurs from third parties as a result of entering into a contract on the principal's behalf, including attorney's fees and reasonable settlements.** An agent signed a contract to buy cucumbers for Vlasic Food Products Co. to use in making pickles. When the first shipment of cucumbers arrived, Vlasic inspectors found them unsuitable and directed the agent to refuse the shipment. The agent found himself in a pickle when the cucumber farmer sued. The agent notified Vlasic, but the company refused to defend him. He settled the claim himself for $29,000 and, in turn, sued Vlasic. The court ordered Vlasic to reimburse the agent because he had notified them of the suit and had acted reasonably and in good faith.[16]

DUTY TO COOPERATE

Principals have a duty to cooperate with their agent:

- **The principal must furnish the agent with the opportunity to work.** If Lewis agrees to serve as Ida's real estate agent, Ida must allow Lewis access to the house. It is unlikely that Lewis will be able to sell the house without taking anyone inside.

- **The principal cannot unreasonably interfere with the agent's ability to accomplish his task.** Ida allows Lewis to show the house, but she refuses to clean it and then makes disparaging comments to prospective purchasers. "I really get tired of living in such a dank, dreary house," she says. "And the neighborhood children are vicious juvenile delinquents." This behavior would constitute unreasonable interference with an agent.

---

[15] *Lauderdale v. Peace Baptist Church of Birmingham*, 246 Ala. 178, 19 So. 2d 538, 1944 Ala. LEXIS 508 (1944).

[16] *Long v. Vlasic Food Products Co.*, 439 F.2d 229, 1971 U.S. App. LEXIS 11455 (4th Cir. 1971).

- **The principal must perform her part of the contract.** Once the agent has successfully completed the task, the principal must pay him, even if the principal has changed her mind and no longer wants the agent to perform. Ida is a 78-year-old widow who has lived alone for many years in a house that she loves. Her asking price is outrageously high. But, lo and behold, Lewis finds a couple who are happy to pay Ida's price. There is only one problem. Ida does not really want to sell. She put her house on the market because she enjoys showing it to all the folks who move to town. She rejects the offer. Now there is a second problem. The contract provided that Lewis would find a willing buyer at the asking price. Since he has done so, Ida must pay his real estate commission, even if she does not want to sell her house.

Terminating an Agency Relationship

Either the agent or the principal can terminate the agency relationship at any time. In addition, the relationship terminates automatically if the principal or agent can no longer perform their required duties or a change in circumstances renders the agency relationship pointless.

TERMINATION BY AGENT OR PRINCIPAL

The two parties—principal and agent—have five choices in terminating their relationship:

- *Term Agreement.* The principal and agent can agree in advance how long their relationship will last. Alexandra hires Boris to help her purchase exquisite enameled Easter eggs made for the Russian czars by Fabergé. If they agree that the relationship will last five years, they have a term agreement.

- *Achieving a Purpose.* The principal and agent can agree that the agency relationship will terminate when the principal's goals have been achieved. Alexandra and Boris might agree that their relationship will end when Alexandra has purchased 10 eggs.

- *Mutual Agreement.* No matter what the principal and agent agree at the start, they can always change their minds later on, as long as the change is mutual. If Boris and Alexandra originally agree to a five-year term, but after only three years Boris decides he wants to go back to business school and Alexandra runs out of money, they can decide together to terminate the agency.

- *Agency at Will.* If they make no agreement in advance about the term of the agreement, either principal or agent can terminate at any time.

- *Wrongful Termination.* An agency relationship is a *personal* relationship. Hiring an agent is not like buying a book. You might not care which copy of the book you buy, but you do care which agent you hire. If an agency relationship is not working out, the courts will not force the agent and principal to stay together. **Either party always has the *power* to walk out. They may not, however, have the *right*.** If one party's departure from the agency relationship violates the agreement and causes harm to the other party, the wrongful party must pay damages. He will nonetheless be permitted to leave. If Boris has agreed to work for Alexandra for five years but he wants to leave after three, he can leave, provided he pays Alexandra the cost of hiring and training a replacement.

If the agent is a **gratuitous** agent (i.e., is not being paid), he has both the power and the right to quit any time he wants, regardless of the agency agreement. If Boris is doing this job for Alexandra as a favor, he will not owe her damages when he stops work.

PRINCIPAL OR AGENT CAN NO LONGER PERFORM REQUIRED DUTIES

If the principal or the agent is unable to perform the duties required under the agency agreement, the agreement terminates.

- **If either the agent or the principal fails to obtain (or keep) a license necessary to perform duties under the agency agreement, the agreement ends.** Caleb hires Allegra to represent him in a lawsuit. If she is disbarred, their agency agreement terminates because the agent is no longer allowed in court. Alternatively, if Emil hires Bess to work in his gun shop, their agency relationship terminates when he loses his license to sell firearms.

- **The bankruptcy of the agent or the principal terminates an agency relationship only if it affects their ability to perform.** Bankruptcy rarely interferes with an agent's responsibilities. After all, there is generally no reason why an agent cannot continue to act for the principal whether the agent is rich or poor. If Lewis, the real estate agent, becomes bankrupt, he can continue to represent Ida or anyone else who wants to sell a house. The bankruptcy of a principal is different, however, because after filing for bankruptcy, the principal loses control of his assets. A bankrupt principal may be unable to pay the agent or honor contracts that the agent enters into on his behalf. Therefore, the bankruptcy of a principal is more likely to terminate an agency relationship.

- **An agency relationship terminates upon the death or incapacity of either the principal or the agent.** Agency is a personal relationship, and when the principal dies, the agent cannot act on behalf of a nonexistent person.[17] Of course, a nonexistent person cannot act either, so the relationship also terminates when the agent dies. Incapacity has the same legal effect because either the principal or the agent is, at least temporarily, unable to act.

- **If the agent violates her duty of loyalty, the agency agreement automatically terminates.** Agents are appointed to represent the principal's interest; if they fail to do so, there is no point to the relationship. Sam is negotiating a military procurement contract on behalf of his employer, Missiles R Us, Inc. In the midst of these negotiations, he becomes very friendly with Louisa, the government negotiator. One night over drinks, he tells Louisa what Missiles' real costs are on the project and the lowest bid it could possibly make. By passing on this confidential information, Sam has violated his duty of loyalty, and his agency relationship terminates.

---

[17] Restatement (Second) of Agency §120, Comment *a*.

CHANGE IN CIRCUMSTANCES

After the agency agreement is negotiated, circumstances may change. If these changes are significant enough to undermine the purpose of the agreement, then the relationship ends automatically. Andrew hires Melissa to sell his country farm for $100,000. Shortly thereafter, the largest oil reserve in North America is discovered nearby. The farm is now worth 10 times Andrew's asking price. Melissa's authority terminates automatically. Other changes in circumstance that affect an agency agreement are:

- *Loss or Destruction of Subject Matter.* Andrew hired Damian to sell his Palm Beach condominium, but before Damian could even measure the living room, Andrew's creditors attached the condo. Damian is no longer authorized to sell the real estate because Andrew has "lost" the subject matter of his agency agreement with Damian.

- *Change of Law.* If the agent's responsibilities become illegal, the agency agreement terminates. Oscar has hired Marta to ship him succulent avocados from California's Imperial Valley. Before she sends the shipment, Mediterranean fruit flies are discovered, and all fruits and vegetables in California are quarantined. The agency agreement terminates because it is now illegal to ship the California avocados.

EFFECT OF TERMINATION

Once an agency relationship ends, the agent no longer has the authority to act for the principal. If she continues to act, she is liable to the principal for any damages he incurs as a result. The Mediterranean fruit fly quarantine ended Marta's agency. If she sends Oscar the avocados anyway and he is fined for possession of a fruit fly, Marta must pay the fine.

The agent loses her authority to act, but some of the duties of both the principal and agent continue even after the relationship ends:

- *Principal's Duty to Indemnify Agent.* Oscar must reimburse Marta for expenses she incurred before the agency ended. If Marta accumulated mileage on her car during her search for the perfect avocado, Oscar must pay her for gasoline and depreciation. But he owes her nothing for her expenses after the agency relationship ends.

- *Confidential Information.* Remember the "He's So Fine" case earlier in the chapter. George Harrison's agent used confidential information to negotiate, on his own behalf, the purchase of the "He's So Fine" copyright. An agent is not entitled to use confidential information, even after the agency relationship terminates.

Liability

Thus far, this chapter has dealt with the relationship *between* principals and agents. Although an agent can dramatically increase his principal's ability to accomplish her goals, an agency relationship also dramatically increases the risk of legal liability to third parties. A principal may be liable in contract for agreements that the agent signs and also liable in tort for harm the agent causes. Indeed, once a principal hires an agent, she may be liable to third parties for his acts, even if he disobeys instructions. Agents may also find themselves liable to third parties.

PRINCIPAL'S LIABILITY FOR CONTRACTS

Many agents are hired for the primary purpose of entering into contracts on behalf of their principals. Salespeople, for example, may do little other than sign on the dotted line. Most of the time, the principal is delighted to be bound by these contracts. But even if the principal is unhappy (because, say, the agent has disobeyed orders), the principal generally cannot rescind contracts entered into by the agent. After all, if someone is going to be penalized, it should be the principal who hired the disobedient agent, not the innocent third party.

The principal is bound by the acts of an agent if (1) the agent had *authority*, or (2) the principal, for reasons of fairness, is *estopped* from denying that the agent had authority, or (3) the principal *ratifies* the acts of the agent.

To say that the principal is "bound by the acts" of the agent means that the principal is as liable as if he had performed the acts himself. It also means that the principal is liable for statements the agent makes to a third party. In addition, the principal is deemed to know any information that the agent knows or should know.

Authority

A principal is bound by the acts of an agent if the agent has authority. There are three types of authority: express, implied, and apparent. Express and implied authority are categories of actual authority because the agent *is* truly authorized to act for the principal. In apparent authority the principal is liable for the agent's actions even though the agent was *not* authorized.

Express Authority.   The principal grants **express authority** by words or conduct that, reasonably interpreted, cause the agent to believe the principal desires her to act on the principal's account.[18] In other words, the principal asks the agent to do something and the agent does it. Craig calls his stockbroker, Alice, and asks her to buy 100 shares of Banshee Corp. for his account. She has *express authority* to carry out this transaction.

Implied Authority.   **Unless otherwise agreed, authority to conduct a transaction includes authority to do acts that are reasonably necessary to accomplish it.**[19] David has recently inherited a house from his grandmother. He hires Nell to auction off the house and its contents. She hires an auctioneer, advertises the event, rents a tent, and generally does everything necessary to conduct a successful auction. After withholding her expenses, she sends the tidy balance to David. Totally outraged, he calls her on the phone, "How dare you hire an auctioneer and rent a tent? I never gave you permission! I absolutely *refuse* to pay these expenses!"

David is wrong. A principal almost never gives an agent absolutely complete instructions. Unless some authority were implied, David would have had to say,

---

[18] Restatement (Second) of Agency §26.
[19] Restatement (Second) of Agency §35.

"Open the car door, get in, put the key in the ignition, drive to the store, buy stickers, mark an auction number on each sticker" . . . and so forth. To solve this problem, the law assumes that the agent has authority to do anything that is *reasonably necessary* to accomplish her task.

Apparent Authority. **A principal can be liable for the acts of an agent who is not, in fact, acting with authority if the principal's conduct causes a third party reasonably to believe that the agent is authorized.** In the case of *express* and *implied* authority, the principal has authorized the agent to act. Apparent authority is different: the principal has *not* authorized the agent, but has done something to make an innocent third party *believe* the agent is authorized. As a result, the principal is every bit as liable to the third party as if the agent did have authority.

For example, Zbigniew Lambo and Scott Kennedy were brokers at Paulson Investment Co., a stock brokerage firm in Oregon. The two men violated securities laws by selling unregistered stock, which ultimately proved to be worthless. Kennedy and Lambo were liable, but they were unable to repay the money. Either Paulson or its customers would end up bearing the loss. What is the fair result? The law takes the view that the principal is liable, not the third party, because the principal, by word or deed, allowed the third party to believe that the agent was acting on the principal's behalf. The principal could have prevented the third party from losing money.

Although the two brokers did not have *actual* or *implied* authority to sell the stock (Paulson had not authorized them to break the law), the company was nonetheless liable on the grounds that the brokers had *apparent* authority. Paulson had sent letters to its customers notifying them when it hired Kennedy. The two brokers made sales presentations at Paulson's offices. The company had never told customers that the two men were not authorized to sell this worthless stock.[20] Thus the agents *appeared* to have authority, even though they did not. Of course, Paulson had the right to recover from Kennedy and Lambo if it could ever compel them to pay.

Remember that the issue in apparent authority is always what the *principal* has done to make the *third party* believe that the *agent* has authority. Suppose that Kennedy and Lambo never worked for Paulson but, on their own, printed up Paulson stationery. The company would not be liable for the stock the two men sold, because it had never done or said anything that would reasonably make a third party believe that the men were its agents.

Ratification

If a person accepts the benefit of an unauthorized transaction or fails to repudiate it, then he is as bound by the act as if he had originally authorized it. He has *ratified* the act.[21] Many of the cases in agency law involve instances in which one person acts *without* authority for another. To avoid liability, the alleged principal shows that he had not authorized the task at issue. But sometimes, after the fact, the principal decides that he approves of what the agent has done even though it was not authorized at the time. The law would be perverse if it did not permit the principal, under those circumstances, to agree to the deal the agent has

---

[20] *Badger v. Paulson Investment Co.*, 311 Ore. 14, 803 P.2d 1178, 1991 Ore. LEXIS 7 (S.Ct. OR 1991).
[21] Restatement (Second) of Agency §82.

made. The law is not perverse, but it is careful. Even if an agent acts without authority, the principal can decide later to be bound by her actions as long as these requirements are met:

- The "agent" indicates to the third party that she is acting for a principal.
- The "principal" knows all the material facts of the transaction.
- The "principal" accepts the benefit of the whole transaction, not just part.
- The third party does not withdraw from the contract before ratification.

A night clerk at the St. Regis Hotel in Detroit, Michigan, was brutally murdered in the course of a robbery. A few days later, the *Detroit News* reported that the St. Regis management had offered a $1,000 reward for any information leading to the arrest and conviction of the killer. Two days after the article appeared, Robert Jackson turned in the man who was subsequently convicted of the crime. But then it was Jackson's turn to be robbed—the hotel refused to pay the reward on the grounds that the manager who had made the offer had no authority. Jackson still had one weapon left: he convinced the court that the hotel had ratified the offer. One of the hotel's owners admitted he read the Detroit News. The court concluded that if someone reads a newspaper, he is sure to read any articles about a business he owns; therefore, the owner must have been aware of the offer. He accepted the benefit of the reward by failing to revoke it publicly. This failure to revoke constituted a ratification, and the hotel was liable.[22]

Subagents

Many of the examples in this chapter involve a single agent acting for a principal. Real life is often more complex. Daniel, the owner of a restaurant, hires Michaela to manage it. She in turn hires chefs, waiters, and dishwashers. Daniel has never even met the restaurant help, yet they are also his agents, albeit a special category called **subagent**. Michaela is called an **intermediary agent**—someone who hires subagents for the principal.

As a general rule, an agent has no authority to delegate her tasks to another unless the principal authorizes her to do so. But when an agent is authorized to hire a subagent, the principal is as liable for the acts of the subagent as he is for the acts of a regular agent. Daniel authorizes Michaela to hire a restaurant staff. She hires Lydia to serve as produce buyer. When Lydia buys food for the restaurant, Daniel must pay the bill.

AGENT'S LIABILITY FOR CONTRACTS

The agent's liability on a contract depends upon how much the third party knows about the principal. Disclosure is the agent's best protection against liability.

Fully Disclosed Principal

An agent is not liable for any contracts she makes on behalf of a *fully* disclosed principal. A principal is fully disclosed if the third party knows of his *existence* and

---

[22] *Jackson v. Goodman*, 69 Mich. App. 225, 244 N.W.2d 423, 1976 Mich. App. LEXIS 741 (Mich. Ct. App. 1976).

his *identity*. Augusta acts as agent for Parker when he buys Tracey's prize-winning show horse. Augusta and Tracey both grew up in posh Grosse Pointe, Michigan, where they attended the same elite schools. Tracey does not know Parker, but she figures any friend of Augusta's must be OK. She figures wrong—Parker is a charming deadbeat. He injures Tracey's horse, fails to pay the full contract price, and promptly disappears from the face of the earth. Tracey angrily demands that Augusta make good on Parker's debt. Unfortunately for Tracey, Parker was a fully disclosed principal—Tracey knew of his *existence* and his *identity*. Although Tracey partly relied on Augusta's good character when contracting with Parker, Augusta is not liable because Tracey knew who the principal was and could have (should have) investigated him. Augusta did not promise anything herself, and Tracey's only recourse is against the principal, Parker (wherever he may be).

To avoid liability when signing a contract on behalf of a principal, an agent must clearly state that she is an agent and must also identify the principal. Augusta should sign a contract on behalf of her principal, Parker, as follows: "Augusta, as agent for Parker" or "Parker, by Augusta, Agent."

Partially Disclosed Principal

In the case of a *partially* disclosed principal, the third party can recover from either the agent or the principal. A principal is partially disclosed if the third party knew of his *existence* but not his *identity*. Suppose that, when approaching Tracey about the horse, Augusta simply says, "I have a friend who is interested in buying your champion." Any friend of Augusta's is a friend of Tracey's—or so Tracey thinks. Parker is a partially disclosed principal because Tracey knows only that he exists, not who he is. She cannot investigate his creditworthiness because she does not know his name. Tracey relies solely on what she is able to learn from the agent, Augusta. Both Augusta and Parker are liable to Tracey. (They are jointly and severally liable, which means that Tracey can recover from either or both of them. She cannot, however, recover more than the total that she is owed: if her damages are $100,000, she can recover that amount from either Augusta or Parker, or partial amounts from both, but in no event more than $100,000.)

Undisclosed Principal

In the case of an *undisclosed* principal, the third party can recover from either the agent or the principal. A principal is undisclosed if the third party did not know of his existence. Suppose that Augusta simply asks to buy the horse herself, without mentioning that she is purchasing it for Parker. In this case Parker is an undisclosed principal because Tracey does not know that Augusta is acting for someone else. Both Parker and Augusta are jointly and severally liable. As Exhibit 13.1 illustrates, the principal is *always* liable, but the agent is not unless the principal's identity is a mystery.

In some ways the concept of an undisclosed principal violates principles of contract law. If Tracey does not even know that Parker exists, how can they have an agreement or a meeting of the minds? Is such an arrangement fair to Tracey? No matter, a contract with an undisclosed principal is binding. The following incident illustrates why.

William Zeckendorf was a man with a plan. For years he had been eyeing a six-block tract of land along New York's East River. It was a wasteland of slums and slaughterhouses, but he could see its potential. The meat packers had refused to

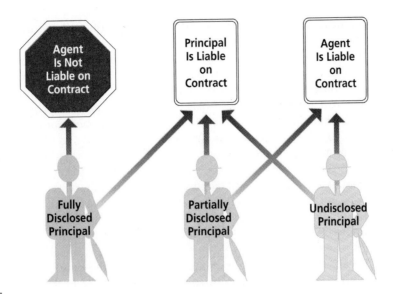

Exhibit 13.1

sell to him, however, because they knew they would never be permitted to build slaughterhouses in Manhattan again. Finally, in 1946 he got the phone call he had been waiting for. The companies were willing to sell—at $17 a square foot, when surrounding land cost less than $5. Undeterred, Zeckendorf immediately put down a $1 million deposit. But to make his investment worthwhile, he needed to buy the neighboring property—once the slaughterhouses were gone, this other land would be much more valuable. Zeckendorf was well-known as a wealthy real estate developer; he had begun his business career managing the Astor family's real estate holdings. If he personally tried to negotiate the purchase of the surrounding land, word would soon get out that he was trying to put together a large parcel. Prices would skyrocket and the project would become too costly. So he hired agents to purchase the land for him. To further conceal his involvement, he went to South America for a month. When he returned, his agents had completed 75 different purchases, and he owned 18 acres of land.

Shortly afterwards, the United Nations began seeking a site for its headquarters. President Truman favored Boston, Philadelphia, or a location in the Midwest. The UN committee suggested Greenwich or Stamford, Connecticut. But John D. Rockefeller settled the question once and for all. He purchased Zeckendorf's land for $8.5 million and donated it to the UN (netting Zeckendorf a profit of $2 million). Without the cooperation of agency law, the UN headquarters would not be in New York today. Discover more about the history of the United Nations at http://www.un.org/Pubs/CyberSchoolBus/unintro/unintro.htm.

The law permits the concept of an undisclosed principal out of commercial necessity. The following article suggests that Harvard behaved unethically when it purchased land secretly. Do you agree?

NEWSWORTHY

Harvard University has bought 52 acres during the past nine years in a secret buying spree that increases the school's land in Allston (across the river from its Cambridge headquarters) by more than a third. Working through the Beal Cos., a prominent real estate development company, Harvard spent $88 million to buy 14 separate parcels. Harvard officials said the university made the purchases without revealing its identity to the sellers, residents, local politicians, or city officials because property owners would have drastically inflated the prices if they knew Harvard was the buyer. "We were really driven by the need to get these properties at fair market value" and avoid "overly inflated acquisition costs," said James H. Rowe, vice president for public affairs at Harvard. But those who were left in the dark—including Mayor Thomas M. Menino—weren't buying it. "That's absurd," Menino scoffed. "Without informing anyone or telling anybody? That's total arrogance." Menino was so incensed that he adopted a mocking singsong tone to express his view of Harvard's attitude, saying: "We're from Harvard, and we're going to do what we want."

"As far as I'm concerned, they practiced a deception," said Ray Mellone, chairman of a neighborhood task force. "There are a lot of people who are going to say we can't trust them. We have to make the process work, and that means making the neighborhood involved, not having deals made in a back room and then coming to us and saying: 'Take it or leave it.'"[23] ◾

Because of concerns about fair play, there are some exceptions to the rule on undisclosed principals. **A third party is not bound to the contract with an undisclosed principal if (1) the contract specifically provides that the third party is not bound to anyone other than the agent, or (2) the agent lies about the principal because she knows the third party would refuse to contract with him.** A cagey property owner, when approached by one of Harvard's agents, could have asked for a clause in the contract providing that the agent was not representing someone else. If the agent told the truth, the owner could have demanded a higher price. If the agent lied, then the owner could have rescinded the contract when the truth emerged.

In the following case, a Degas painting raced around Alabama and New York. In the end, no one wanted it. But someone had to lose the race.

WEIL V. MURRAY

161 F. Supp. 2d 250; 2001 U.S. Dist. LEXIS 4117
United States District Court for the Southern District of New York, 2001

FACTS: Mark Murray, an art dealer in New York, heard that Jean and Robert Weil were interested in selling some of their pictures. He was particularly keen on their painting by Edgar Degas entitled "Aux Courses" ("The Races").[24] Murray discussed this painting with Ian Peck, a fellow art dealer, who expressed an interest in buying it and asked Murray to arrange to have it brought to New York from the Weils' home in Alabama.

Murray alleges that, after Peck saw the painting, Peck agreed to buy it for $1 million. Indeed, Peck's attorney wrote the first draft of the purchase agreement. Murray retyped that draft, changing the name of the buyer from Peck to Murray. Weil then prepared an alternative version. Murray contends that Peck approved the Weil version of the agreement. Peck, on the other hand, claims that there was no discussion of the Weil version, and that

---

[23] Tina Cassidy and Dan Aucoin, "Harvard Reveals Secret Purchases of 52 Acres Worth $88M in Allston," *The Boston Globe*, June 10, 1997, p. A1. Republished with permission of The Boston Globe; permission conveyed through the Copyright Clearance Center, Inc.

[24] A series of Degas racetrack paintings is on view at http://mapage.noos.fr/chevalmaniac/pages/dossier1/art/degas.html.

Murray merely brought it to him so he would know how much to pay.

Murray and Weil both signed the agreement. It stated that the "Buyer" was Mark Murray and further that:

> It is understood that the eventual Buyer is an Undisclosed Principal client of Mark Murray, and that said undisclosed principal shall also be bound by this agreement. Should Sellers not receive full payment by December 8th, Buyer agrees to divulge to the Sellers the exact identity of the Undisclosed Principal, and the Undisclosed Principal must hereby guarantee this purchase and stand in the shoes of the Buyer, should there be cause for non-performance in any particular by said Ultimate Buyer.

When the Weils did not receive the $1 million, they filed suit against Murray and Peck. The Weils and Peck also filed motions for summary judgment.

ISSUE: Are Murray and Peck liable to the Weils for the purchase price of the Degas?

EXCERPTS FROM JUDGE MUKASEY'S DECISION: The contract clearly defines Murray as the "Buyer." Murray advocates a reading of the contract that would make him neither the buyer, nor an agent for the partially disclosed principal, but rather an intermediary whose only contractual obligation was to reveal the identity of the undisclosed principal.

The contract's reference to an undisclosed principal who "shall also be bound by [the] agreement" does not extinguish Murray's obligation as the buyer. Even assuming that Murray was merely signing the contract as an agent for the so-called "undisclosed principal," an agent who enters into an agreement on behalf of a partially disclosed principal is obligated to perform the contract.

Peck argues that he is entitled to summary judgment because the written agreement is explicitly a bilateral agreement between Murray and plaintiffs, and therefore, Peck cannot be bound by it. If the jury were to determine that Murray was acting as Peck's agent, with authority to sign the contract, then Peck could be bound. Furthermore, although Murray signed the contract in his name, not as the agent for Peck or the undisclosed principal, a partially disclosed principal is subject to liability upon an authorized contract in writing although it purports to be the contract of the agent. An agent who enters into an agreement on behalf of an undisclosed or partially disclosed principal is jointly and severally liable with the principal.

For the reasons stated above, plaintiffs' motion for summary judgment against Murray is granted. Peck's motion for summary judgment against plaintiffs is denied. ◢

Unauthorized Agent

Thus far in this section, we have been discussing an agent's liability to a third party for a transaction that was authorized by the principal. Sometimes, however, agents act without the authority of a principal. **If the agent has no authority (express, implied, or apparent), the principal is not liable to the third party and the agent is.** Suppose that Augusta agrees to sell Parker's horse to Tracey. Unfortunately, Parker has never met Augusta and has certainly not authorized this transaction. Augusta is hoping that she can persuade him to sell, but Parker refuses. Augusta, but not Parker, is liable to Tracey for breach of contract.

PRINCIPAL'S LIABILITY FOR TORTS

A master is liable for physical harm caused by the negligent conduct of servants within the scope of employment.[25] This principle of liability is called *respondeat superior*, which is a Latin phrase that means, "let the master answer." Under the theory of *respondeat superior*, the master (i.e., the principal) is liable for the agent's

---

[25] Restatement (Second) of Agency §243.

misbehavior whether or not the principal was at fault. Indeed, the principal is liable even if he forbade or tried to prevent the agent from misbehaving. This sounds like a harsh rule. The logic is that, since the principal controls the agent, he should be able to *prevent* misbehavior. If he cannot prevent it, at least he can *insure* against the risks. Furthermore, the principal may have deeper pockets than the agent or the injured third party and thus be better able to *afford* the cost of the agent's misbehavior.

To apply the principle of *respondeat superior*, it is important to understand each of the following terms: *master and servant, scope of employment, negligent and intentional torts*, and *physical harm*.

Master and Servant

There are two kinds of agents: (1) *servants* and (2) *independent contractors*. **A principal *may be* liable for the torts of a servant but generally is *not* liable for the torts of an independent contractor.** Because of this rule, the distinction between a servant and an independent contractor is important.

Servant or Independent Contractor?   The more control the principal has over an agent, the more likely that the agent will be considered a servant. Therefore, when determining if agents are servants or independent contractors, courts consider whether:

- The principal controls details of the work.

- The principal supplies the tools and place of work.

- The agents work full-time for the principal.

- The agents are paid by time, not by the job.

- The work is part of the regular business of the principal.

- The principal and agents believe they have an employer-employee relationship.

- The principal is in business.[26]

Do not be misled by the term *servant*. A servant does not mean Jeeves, the butler, or Maisie, the maid. In fact, if Mrs. Dillworth hires Jeeves and Maisie for the evening from a catering firm, they are *not* her servants, they are independent contractors. On the other hand, the president of General Motors is a servant of that corporation.

Negligent Hiring   Principals prefer agents to be considered independent contractors not servants because, as a general rule, principals are not liable for the torts of an independent contractor. There is, however, one exception to this rule: **The principal is liable for the physical torts of an independent contractor *only if* the principal has been negligent in hiring or supervising her.** Remember that, under *respondeat superior*, the principal is liable *without fault* for the physical torts of servants. The case of independent contractors is different: the principal is liable only if he was *at fault* by being careless in his hiring or supervising. Was the supermarket at fault in the following case?

---

[26] Restatement (Second) of Agency §220(2).

DURAN V. FURR'S SUPERMARKETS, INC.

921 S.W.2d 778, 1996 Tex. App. LEXIS 1345
Court of Appeals of Texas, 1996

FACTS: Steve Romero was an off-duty police officer working as a security guard for Furr's Supermarkets. He approached a car parked in the supermarket's fire lane and began yelling at a passenger to move it. The passenger, Graciela Duran, asked Romero for his name. He opened the car door and tried to pull her out, all the while threatening to arrest her. Duran ultimately required surgery to repair the injury that Romero's tugs and twists caused to her left arm.

Duran filed suit against Furr's. The supermarket filed a motion for summary judgment on the grounds that it was not responsible for Romero's conduct because he was an independent contractor. Duran argued that Furr's had been negligent in hiring Romero. The trial court granted the motion for summary judgment.

ISSUES: Did the trial court properly grant Furr's motion for summary judgment? Is Duran entitled to a trial?

EXCERPTS FROM JUDGE MCCLURE'S DECISION: The basis of responsibility under the doctrine of negligent hiring is the master's own negligence in hiring or retaining in his employ an incompetent servant whom the master knows or by the exercise of reasonable care should have known was incompetent or unfit and thereby creating an unreasonable risk of harm to others. The evidence showed that Furr's did not require Romero to complete a job application and otherwise made no inquiry into his background as a police officer. Furr's never interviewed Romero or spoke with him before he began working at the store. If Furr's had conducted an investigation of Romero's performance as a police officer, it would have learned that Romero had a prior complaint for using vulgar and abusive language towards a member of the public while on duty as a police officer.

Duran argues that this complaint demonstrates Romero's propensity for aggressive behavior so that Furr's could have reasonably anticipated that Romero might verbally and physically abuse a patron of the store. On the other hand, Furr's argues that even if it had discovered the prior complaint, the information would not have caused Furr's to reasonably anticipate his physical assault upon Duran. In attempting to distinguish between the prior verbal abuse complaint and the physical assault upon Duran, Furr's ignores the evidence showing that Romero first verbally abused Duran during this incident. According to Duran, the verbal abuse escalated into the physical assault. We find that a fact question is raised whether knowledge of this abusive language complaint would put a reasonable person on notice that Romero might verbally abuse a store patron, and that such conduct might escalate into a physical assault. Because of the existence of this fact issue, summary judgment on this ground is improper. ◢

Exhibit 13.2 on the following page illustrates the difference in liability between a servant and an independent contractor.

Scope of Employment

Principals are only liable for torts that a servant commits within the *scope of employment*. If an employee leaves a pool of water on the floor of a store and a customer slips and falls, the employer is liable. But if the same employee leaves water on his own kitchen floor and a friend falls, the employer is not liable because the employee is not acting within the scope of employment. A servant is acting within the scope of employment if the act:

• Is one that servants are generally responsible for

Exhibit 13.2

- Takes place during hours that the servant is generally employed
- Is part of the principal's business
- Is similar to the one the principal authorized
- Is one for which the principal supplied the tools; and
- Is not seriously criminal.

Scope of employment cases raise two major issues: authorization and abandonment.

Authorization.   In authorization cases the agent is clearly working for the principal but commits an act that the principal has not authorized. Although Jane has often told the driver of her delivery van not to speed, Hank ignores her instructions and plows into Bernadette. At the time of the accident, he is working for Jane, delivering flowers for her shop, but his act is not authorized. **An act is within the scope of employment, even if expressly forbidden, if it is of the same general nature as that authorized or if it is incidental to the conduct authorized.**[27] Hank was authorized to drive the van, but not to speed. However, his speeding was of the same general nature as the authorized act, so Jane is liable to Bernadette. In the following case, an employee engaged in unauthorized behavior while on company business. Did his actions fall within the scope of his employment? You be the judge.

---

[27] Restatement (Second) of Agency §229(1).

YOU BE THE JUDGE

CONNER V. MAGIC CITY TRUCKING SERVICE, INC.

592 So. 2d 1048, 1992 Ala. LEXIS 26
Supreme Court of Alabama, 1992

FACTS: Sarah Conner worked for A-Pac, which was building a roadway. A-Pac had hired Magic City to supply dirt. Conner was responsible for punching holes in a ticket to tally the amount of dirt each Magic City truck brought in. When a driver was ready to dump the dirt from the truck, Conner would often release the truck's latch as a courtesy to the driver, who would otherwise have to climb out of the truck to release it.

Magic City employee David King drove up wearing a Halloween mask. Conner punched King's load ticket but ignored the mask. King asked, "You're not going to say anything?" Conner did not comment or respond to this question, and King left. He later returned to Conner's post with a second load of dirt, this time without the mask. Conner punched his load ticket, and King told her to release the latch on his truck quickly or else he would "put [his] friend" on her. Conner attempted to release the latch but could not budge it. Conner told King, who had a tool for forcing the release of the latch, to release it himself. King again threatened to "put [his] friend" on her if Conner did not quickly release the latch. King began chasing Conner with a very large snake. King's Magic City supervisor laughed as Conner ran from King. Eventually, King gave up the chase and threw the snake at Conner. She collapsed with severe medical problems.

YOU BE THE JUDGE: Under *respondeat superior*, is Magic City liable for the actions of its employee, King? Was King acting within the scope of his employment?

ARGUMENT FOR CONNER: An employee is acting within the scope of his employment if the conduct is of the same general nature as that authorized or incidental to that authorized. Sarah Conner would never have met David King if he had not been working for Magic City. He was angry at her because she did not release the latch on his truck. Their interaction was incidental to his job.

Respondeat superior is based on the concept of control. The principal is able to control the agent to prevent him from misbehaving. While David King was tormenting Sarah Conner, King's supervisor stood and *laughed*. He did not even tell King to stop. Sarah Conner has suffered serious injuries as a result of King's behavior on the job. In all fairness, Magic City should bear liability for the harm caused by its employee.

ARGUMENT FOR MAGIC CITY: When King brought in the Halloween mask and snake, he was not acting in furtherance of his employer's goals or business. His employer did not approve of or condone his behavior. Snakes have nothing to do with King's job, and his actions were not within the scope of his employment.

Conner blames Magic City because King's supervisor stood by and laughed. Consciously or not, people often react to bizarre antics with laughter even when they disapprove of the behavior. Magic City is sorry King behaved so badly. But the company did *not* authorize his actions and should not be liable for them. **/**

Abandonment. The second major issue in a *scope of employment* case involves abandonment. **The master is liable for the actions of the servant that occur while the servant is at work, but not for actions that occur after the servant has abandoned the master's business.** Although the rule sounds straightforward, the difficulty lies in determining whether the employee has in fact abandoned the master's business. The employer is liable if the employee is simply on a *detour* from company business, but the employer is not liable if the employee is off on a *frolic of his own*. Suppose that Hank, the delivery van driver, speeds during his afternoon commute home. A servant is generally not acting within the scope of his employment when he commutes to and from work, so his master, Jane, is not liable. Or suppose that, while on the way to a delivery, he stops to view his favorite movie classic, *Dead on Arrival*. Unable to see in the darkened theater, he knocks Anna down, causing grave harm. Jane is not liable because Hank's visit to the movies is outside the scope of his employment. On the other hand, if Hank stops at the Burger King drive-in window en route to making a delivery, Jane is liable when he crashes into Anna on the way out of the parking lot, because this time he is simply making a detour.

Negligent and Intentional Torts

The master is liable if the servant commits a negligent tort that causes physical harm to a person or property. When Hank crashes into Anna, he is committing a negligent tort, and Jane is liable if all the other requirements for *respondeat superior* are met.

A master is *not* liable for the *intentional* torts of the servant *unless* the servant was motivated, at least in part, by a desire to serve the master, or the conduct was reasonably foreseeable. During an NBA basketball game, Kendall pushes Vladimir into some chairs under the basket to prevent him from scoring a breakaway lay-up. Kendall's team is liable for his actions because he was motivated, at least in part, by a desire to help his team. But if Kendall hits Vladimir in the parking lot after the playoffs are over, Kendall's team is not liable because he is no longer motivated by a desire to help the team. His motivation now is personal revenge or frustration.

The courts (of law, not basketball) are generally expansive in their definition of behavior that is intended to serve the master. In one case, a police trainee shot a fellow officer while practicing his quick draw technique. In another, a drunken sailor knocked a shipmate out of bed with the admonition, "Get up, you big son of a bitch, and turn to," after which the two men fought. The courts ruled that both the police trainee and the sailor were motivated by a desire to serve their master and, therefore, the master was liable for their intentional torts.[28]

Physical Harm

In the case of *physical* torts, a master is liable for the negligent conduct of a servant that occurs within the scope of employment. The rule for *nonphysical* torts (i.e., torts that harm only reputation, feelings, or wallet) is different. **Nonphysical torts are treated more like a contract claim, and the principal is liable only if the servant acted with actual, implied, or apparent authority.** For example, the Small Business Administration (SBA) granted Midwest Knitting Mills, Inc. more than $2 million in loans, but the SBA employee in charge of the case never told Midwest. (He was allegedly a drug addict.) The company sued the SBA for the negligence of its employee. Although the conduct had occurred within the scope of employment, it was a nonphysical tort. Since the employee had not acted with actual, implied, or apparent authority, the SBA was not liable.[29]

---

[28] *Nelson v. American-West African Line, Inc.*, 86 F.2d 730, 1936 U.S. App. LEXIS 3841 (2d Cir. 1936), and *Thompson v. United States*, 504 F. Supp. 1087, 1980 U.S. Dist. LEXIS 15834 (D.S.D. 1980).

[29] *Midwest Knitting Mills, Inc. v. United States*, 741 F. Supp. 1345, 1990 U.S. Dist. LEXIS 8663 (E.D. Wis. 1990).

Misrepresentation and defamation are, however, treated differently from other nonphysical torts.

Misrepresentation.

A principal is liable if:

- The agent makes a misrepresentation

- The agent has express, implied, or apparent authority

- The third party relies on the misrepresentation; and

- The third party suffers harm.

This rule applies to any agent, not just a servant. If the agent is authorized to make a *truthful* statement, the principal is liable for any related *false* statement.

Althea hires Morris, a real estate agent, to sell a piece of land. Morris knows that part of the land floods every spring, but when Helen inquires about flooding, Morris lies. He is not authorized to make the false statement, but he is authorized to make statements about the land. Althea is liable to Helen for any harm caused by Morris's misrepresentation, even though Morris is an independent contractor.

Defamation.

A principal is liable if:

- The agent makes a defamatory statement

- The agent has express, implied, or apparent authority; and

- The third party is harmed by the statement.

Again, this rule applies to all agents, not simply to servants. If the agent is authorized to make a *truthful* statement, the principal is liable for any related *defamatory* statements.

A newspaper reporter writes an untrue story alleging that the mayor has been taking kickbacks from contractors who work for the city. The reporter has defamed the mayor, and the newspaper is liable because the reporter is an agent authorized to write the article, even though he is not authorized to write false statements.

Electronic communication has created new risks for employers. They fear that their employees may commit libel by sending flaming e-mails or violate intellectual property laws by downloading copyrighted software from the Internet. Is the company liable in these circumstances? What if an employee posts defamatory information on an Internet bulletin board? Even if the employee is not authorized, she may have *apparent* authority—especially if the posting appears with a company e-mail address. For this reason companies increasingly monitor their employees' e-mail content and Internet usage. Some companies also require employees, when posting on a bulletin board, to include a disclaimer that they do not speak for their company.

AGENT'S LIABILITY FOR TORTS

The focus of this section has been on the *principal's* liability for the agent's torts. But it is important to remember that **agents are always liable for their own torts**. Agents who commit torts are personally responsible, whether or not their principal is also liable. Even if the tort was committed to benefit the principal, the agent is still liable. So the sailor who got into a fistfight while rousting a shipmate from bed is liable even though he thought he was acting for the benefit of his principal.

This rule makes obvious sense. If the agent were not liable, he would have little incentive to be careful. Imagine Hank driving his delivery van for Jane. If he were not personally liable for his own torts, he might think, "If I drive fast enough, I can make it through that light even though it just turned red. And if I don't, what the heck, it'll be Jane's problem, not mine." Agents, as a rule, may have fewer assets than their principal, but it is important that their personal assets be at risk in the event of their negligent behavior.

If the agent and principal are *both* liable, which does the injured third party sue? The principal and the agent are *jointly and severally* liable, which means, as we have seen, that the injured third party can sue either one or both, as she chooses. If she recovers from the principal, he can sue the agent.

Chapter Conclusion

When students enroll in a business law course, they fully expect to learn about torts and contracts, corporations and partnerships. They probably do not think much about agency law; many of them have not even heard the term before. Yet it is an area of the law that affects us all because each of us has been and will continue to be both an agent and a principal many times in our lives.

Chapter Review

1. In an agency relationship, a principal and an agent mutually consent that the agent will act on behalf of the principal and be subject to the principal's control, thereby creating a fiduciary relationship.

2. An agent owes these duties to the principal: duty of loyalty, duty to obey instructions, duty of care, and duty to provide information.

3. The principal has three potential remedies when the agent breaches her duty: recovery of damages the breach has caused, recovery of any profits earned by the agent from the breach, and rescission of any transaction with the agent.

4. The principal has two duties to the agent: to reimburse legitimate expenses, and to cooperate with the agent.

5. Both the agent and the principal have the power to terminate an agency relationship, but they may not have the right. If the termination violates the agency agreement and causes harm to the other party, the wrongful party must pay damages.

6. An agency relationship automatically terminates if the principal or agent can no longer perform the required duties or if a change in circumstances renders the agency relationship pointless.

7. A principal is bound by the contracts of the agent if the agent has express, implied, or apparent authority.

8. The principal grants express authority by words or conduct that, reasonably interpreted, cause the agent to believe that the principal desires her to act on the principal's account.

9. Implied authority includes authority to do acts that are incidental to a transaction, usually accompany it, or are reasonably necessary to accomplish it.

10. Apparent authority means that a principal is liable for the acts of an agent who is not, in fact, acting with authority if the principal's conduct causes a third party reasonably to believe that the agent is authorized.

11. An agent is not liable for any contract she makes on behalf of a fully disclosed principal. The principal is liable. In the case of a partially disclosed or undisclosed principal, both the agent and the principal are liable on the contract.

12. Under *respondeat superior*, a master is liable when a servant acting within the scope of employment commits a negligent tort that causes physical harm to a person or property. Under some limited circumstances, a master is also liable for a servant's intentional torts.

13. The principal is only liable for the physical torts of an independent contractor if the principal has been negligent in hiring or supervising him.

14. A principal is liable for nonphysical torts only if the servant acts with actual, implied, or apparent authority.

15. Agents are always liable for their own torts.

Practice Test

1. The German-American Vocational League was formed in New York during World War II to serve as a propaganda agency for the German Reich. Under U.S. law all foreign agents were required to register. Neither the Vocational League nor its officers registered. When they were charged with violating U.S. law, they argued that they were not agents of the German government because they had no formal agency agreement. Their one written agreement with the German Reich said nothing about being a propaganda agency. Is a formal contract necessary to establish an agency relationship?

2. **ETHICS** Radio TV Reports (RTV) was in the business of recording, transcribing, and monitoring radio and video programming for its clients. The Department of Defense (DOD) in Washington, D.C., was one of RTV's major clients. Paul Ingersoll worked for RTV until August 31. In July the DOD solicited bids for a new contract for the following year. During this same month, Ingersoll formed his own media monitoring business, Transmedia. RTV and Transmedia were the only two bidders on the DOD contract, which was awarded to Transmedia. Did Ingersoll violate his fiduciary duty to RTV? Aside from his legal obligations, did Ingersoll behave ethically? How does his behavior look in the light of day? Was it right?

3. David and Fiona Rookard purchased tickets for a trip through Mexico from a Mexicoach office in San Diego. Mexicoach told them that the trip would be safe. It did not tell them, however, that their tickets had disclaimers written in Spanish warning that, under Mexican law, a bus company is not liable for any harm that befalls its passengers. The Rookards did not read Spanish. They were injured in a bus accident caused by gross negligence on the part of the driver. Did Mexicoach violate its duty to the Rookards?

4. Penny Wilson went to Arlington Chrysler-Plymouth-Dodge to buy an automobile. Penny told Arlington that, as a minor, she could not buy the car unless she obtained credit life insurance that would pay the balance of any loan owing if her mother died. She also disclosed that her mother had cancer. Arlington was an agent for Western Pioneer Life Insurance Co. Western Pioneer reported that a credit insurance policy would be invalid if Mrs. Wilson died within six months. In fact, the policy was invalid if Mrs. Wilson died of cancer within *one year*. Seven months later, Mrs. Wilson died, and Western Pioneer refused to pay. Penny Wilson sued Western Pioneer and Arlington. The trial court found Western Pioneer liable, but not Arlington. Was Western Pioneer liable for Arlington's legal expenses?

5. One Friday afternoon a custodian at the Lazear Elementary School in Oakland, California, raped an 11-year-old student in his office on the school premises. The student sued the school district on a theory of *respondeat superior*. Is the school district liable for this intentional tort by its employee?

6. This article appeared in *The New York Times*:

   A week after criminal charges were announced in the death of tennis star Vitas Gerulaitis, his mother filed suit yesterday against eight defendants, including the owner of the Long Island estate where Mr. Gerulaitis died of carbon monoxide poisoning last fall. Prosecutors have charged that a new swimming pool heater, installed at a cost of $8,000, was improperly vented and sent deadly fumes into a pool house where Mr. Gerulaitis was taking a nap. The lawsuit accuses the companies that manufactured, installed and maintained the pool heater, and the mechanic who installed it, with negligence and reckless disregard for human life. It makes similar charges against the owners of the oceanfront estate, Beatrice Raynes and her son Martin, a real-estate executive.[30]

   Why would the owners of the estate be liable?

7. **CPA QUESTION** A principal will not be liable to a third party for a tort committed by an agent:
   (a) Unless the principal instructed the agent to commit the tort
   (b) Unless the tort was committed within the scope of the agency relationship
   (c) If the agency agreement limits the principal's liability for the agent's tort
   (d) If the tort is also regarded as a criminal act

8. A. B. Rains worked as a broker for the Joseph Denunzio Fruit Co. Raymond Crane offered to sell Rains nine carloads of emperor grapes. Rains accepted the offer on behalf of Denunzio. Later, Rains and Denunzio discovered that Crane was an agent for John Kazanjian. Who is liable on this contract?

9. Roy Watson bought vacuum cleaners from T & F Distributing Co. and then resold them door-to-door. He was an independent contractor. Before hiring Watson, the president of T & F checked with two former employers but could not remember if he called Watson's two references. Watson had an extensive criminal record, primarily under the alias Leroy Turner, but he was listed in FBI records under both Leroy Turner and Roy Watson. T & F granted Watson sales territory that included Neptune City, New Jersey. This city required that all "peddlers" such as Watson be licensed. Applicants for this license were routinely fingerprinted. T & F never insisted that Watson apply for such a license. Watson attacked Miriam Bennett after selling a vacuum cleaner to her at her home in Neptune City. Is T & F liable to Bennett?

10. **YOU BE THE JUDGE WRITING PROBLEM** Sara Kearns went to an auction at Christie's to bid on a tapestry for her employer, Nardin Fine Arts Gallery. The good news is that she purchased a Dufy tapestry for $77,000. The bad news is that it was not the one her employer had told her to buy. In the excitement of the auction, she forgot her instructions. Nardin refused to pay, and Christie's filed suit. Is Nardin liable for the unauthorized act of its agent? **Argument for Christie's:** Kearns executed a bidder form as agent for Nardin. This is a common practice for many purchasers. Christie's cannot possibly ascertain in each case the exact nature of the bidder's authority. Whether or not Kearns had actual authority, she certainly had apparent authority and Nardin is liable. **Argument for Nardin:** Kearns was not authorized to purchase the Dufy tapestry, and therefore Christie's must recover from her, not us.

11. Jack and Rita Powers purchased 312 head of cattle at an auction conducted by Coffeyville Livestock Sales Co. They did not know who owned the cattle they bought. The Powers, in

---

[30] Vivian S. Toy, "Gerulaitis's Mother Files Suit in Son's Carbon Monoxide Death," *The New York Times*, June 1, 1995, p. B5.

turn, sold 159 of this lot to Leonard Hoefling. He sued the Powers, alleging the cattle were diseased and dying in large numbers, and recovered $38,360. Are the Powers entitled to reimbursement from Coffeyville?

12. **ROLE REVERSAL** Write a multiple choice question that deals with the liability of principals for the acts fo their servants.

Internet Research Problem

Acting as an undisclosed principal, William Zeckendorf employed agents to purchase the land in New York on which the United Nations headquarters was ultimately built. Can you find any other examples on the Internet of business dealings in which agents made purchases for an undisclosed principal? Were these business arrangements ethical? What risks did the agents face?

You can find further practice problems in the Online Quiz at http://beatty.westbuslaw.com **or in the Study Guide that accompanies this text.**

Employment Law

"On the killing beds you were apt to be covered with blood, and it would freeze solid; if you leaned against a pillar, you would freeze to that, and if you put your hand upon the blade of your knife, you would run a chance of leaving your skin on it. The men would tie up their feet in newspapers and old sacks, and these would be soaked in blood and frozen, and then soaked again, and so on, until by nighttime a man would be walking on great lumps the size of the feet of an elephant. Now and then, when the bosses were not looking, you would see them plunging their feet and ankles into the steaming hot carcass of the steer . . . . The cruelest thing of all was that nearly all of them—all of those who used knives—were unable to wear gloves, and their arms would be white with frost and their hands would grow numb, and then of course there would be accidents."[1]

---

[1] From Upton Sinclair, *The Jungle* (New York: Bantam Books, 1981), p. 80, a 1906 novel about the meatpacking industry.

Introduction

For most of history, the concept of career planning was unknown. By and large, people were born into their jobs. Whatever their parents had been—landowner, soldier, farmer, servant, merchant, or beggar—they became, too. People not only knew their place, they also understood the rights and obligations inherent in each position. The landowner had the right to receive labor from his tenants, but he also cared for them if they fell ill. Certainly, there were abuses, but at a time when people held religious convictions about their position in life and workers had few expectations that their lives would be better than their parents', the role of law was limited. The primary English law of employment simply established that, in the absence of a contract, an employee was hired for a year at a time. This rule was designed to prevent injustice in an agrarian society. If an employee worked through harvest time, the landowner could not fire him in the unproductive winter. Conversely, a worker could not stay the winter and then leave for greener pastures in the spring.

In the eighteenth and nineteenth centuries, the Industrial Revolution profoundly altered the employment relationship. Many workers left the farms and villages for large factories in the city. Bosses no longer knew their workers personally, so they felt little responsibility toward them. The old laws that had suited an agrarian economy with stable relationships did not fit the new employment conditions. Instead of duties and responsibilities, courts emphasized the freedom to contract. Since employees could quit their factory jobs whenever they wanted, it was only fair for employers to have the same freedom to fire a worker. That was indeed the rule adopted by the courts: unless workers had an explicit employment contract, they were employees at will. **An *employee at will* could be fired for a good reason, a bad reason, or no reason at all.** For nearly a century, this was the basic common law rule of employment. A court explained the rule this way:

> Precisely as may the employee cease labor at his whim or pleasure, and, whatever be his reason, good, bad, or indifferent, leave no one a legal right to complain; so, upon the other hand, may the employer discharge, and, whatever be his reason, good, bad, or indifferent, no one has suffered a legal wrong.[2]

However evenhanded this common law rule of employment may have sounded in theory, in practice it could lead to harsh results. The lives of factory workers were grim.[3] It was not as if they could simply pack up and leave; conditions were no better elsewhere. For the worker, freedom to contract often meant little more than freedom to starve. Courts and legislatures gradually began to recognize that individual workers were generally unable to negotiate fair contracts with powerful employers. Since the beginning of the twentieth century, employment law has changed dramatically. Now, the employment relationship is more strictly regulated by statutes and by the common law. No longer can a boss discharge an employee for any reason whatsoever.

Note that many of the statutes discussed in this chapter were passed by Congress and therefore apply nationally. The common law, however, comes from

---

[2] *Union Labor Hospital Assn. v. Vance Redwood Lumber Co.*, 112 P.886, 888, 1910 Cal. LEXIS 417 (Cal. 1910).

[3] For examples of some truly grim modern jobs, work your way over to http://www.worstjob.com.

state courts and only applies locally. We will look at a sampling of cases that illustrate national trends, even though the law may not be the same in every state.

This chapter covers four topics in employment law: (1) employment security, (2) safety and privacy in the workplace, (3) financial protection, and (4) employment discrimination.

Employment Security

NATIONAL LABOR RELATIONS ACT

Without unions to represent employee interests, employers could simply fire any troublemaking workers who complained about conditions in factories or mines. By joining together, workers could bargain with their employers on more equal terms. Naturally, the owners fought against the unions, firing organizers and even hiring goons to beat them up. Distressed by anti-union violence, Congress passed the **National Labor Relations Act** in 1935. Known as the **NLRA** or the **Wagner Act**, this statute:

- Created the National Labor Relations Board to enforce labor laws

- Prohibits employers from penalizing workers who engage in union activity (e.g., joining a preexisting union or forming a new one); and

- Requires employers to "bargain in good faith" with unions.

  Labor law is covered at greater length in Chapter 15.

FAMILY AND MEDICAL LEAVE ACT

In 1993 Congress passed the Family and Medical Leave Act (FMLA), which guarantees both men and women up to 12 weeks of *unpaid* leave each year for childbirth, adoption, or medical emergencies for themselves or a family member. An employee who takes a leave must be allowed to return to the same or an equivalent job with the same pay and benefits. The FMLA applies only to companies with at least 50 workers and to employees who have been with the company full-time for at least a year—this is about 60 percent of all employees. Each year, about four million workers actually take leave under the FMLA.

When Randy Seale's wife went into premature labor with triplets, he stayed home from his job as a truck driver with Associated Milk Producers, Inc., in Roswell, New Mexico. However, the milk of human kindness did not flow in this company's veins: it promptly fired the expectant father. Since Seale was an employee at will, the company's action would have been perfectly legal without the FMLA. But after the U.S. Department of Labor filed suit, the company agreed to pay Seale $10,000.

According to a survey by the U.S. Department of Labor, 36 percent of employers find complying with the FMLA "difficult," although 90 percent say that it does not reduce their company's profitability. The Labor Department answers questions about the FMLA at http://www.dol.gov/dol/esa/fmla.htm.

WRONGFUL DISCHARGE

Olga Monge was a schoolteacher in her native Costa Rica. After moving to New Hampshire, she attended college in the evenings to earn U.S. teaching credentials.

At night she worked at the Beebe Rubber Co. During the day, she cared for her husband and three children. When she applied for a better job at her plant, the foreman offered to promote her if she would be "nice" and go out on a date with him. When she refused, he assigned her to a lower wage job, took away her overtime, made her clean the washrooms, and generally ridiculed her. Finally, she collapsed at work and he fired her.[4]

Imagine that you are one of the judges who decided this case. Olga Monge has been treated abominably, but she was an employee at will and, as you well know, could be fired for any reason. But how can you let the foreman get away with this despicable behavior? The New Hampshire Supreme Court decided that even an employee at will has rights:

> We hold that a termination by the employer of a contract of employment at will which is motivated by bad faith or malice or based on retaliation is not in the best interest of the economic system or the public good and constitutes a breach of the employment contract.[5]

The employment at will doctrine was created by the courts. Because that rule has sometimes led to absurdly unfair results, the courts have now created a major exception to the rule—**wrongful discharge**. The *Monge* case illustrates this concept. *Wrongful discharge* **prohibits an employer from firing a worker for a *bad reason*.** There are three categories of wrongful discharge claims: public policy, contract law, and tort law.

Public Policy

The *Monge* case is an example of the **public policy rule**. Unfortunately, naming the rule is easier than defining it, because its definition and application vary from state to state. **In essence, the public policy rule prohibits an employer from firing a worker for a reason that violates basic social rights, duties, or responsibilities.** Almost every employee who has ever been fired feels that a horrible injustice has been done. The difficulty, from the courts' perspective, is to distinguish those cases of dismissal that are offensive enough to arouse the community at large from those that outrage only the employee. The courts have primarily applied the public policy rule when an employee refuses to violate the law or insists upon exercising a legal right or performing a legal duty.

Refusing to Violate the Law. Larry Downs went to Duke Hospital for surgery on his cleft palate. When he came out of the operating room, the doctor instructed a nurse, Marie Sides, to give Downs enough anesthetic to immobilize him. Sides refused because she thought the anesthetic was wrong for this patient. The doctor angrily administered the anesthetic himself. Shortly thereafter, Downs stopped breathing. Before the doctors could resuscitate him, he suffered permanent brain damage. When Downs's family sued the hospital, Sides was called to testify. A number of Duke doctors told her that she would be "in trouble" if she testified. She did testify and, after three months of harassment, was fired. When she sued Duke University, the court held:

> It would be obnoxious to the interests of the state and contrary to public policy and sound morality to allow an employer to discharge any employee, whether the employment be

---

[4] *Monge v. Beebe*, 114 N.H. 130, 316 A.2d 549, 1974 N.H. LEXIS 223 (1974).
[5] Id. at 133.

for a designated or unspecified duration, on the ground that the employee declined to commit perjury, an act specifically enjoined by statute. To hold otherwise would be without reason and contrary to the spirit of the law.[6]

As a general rule, employees may not be discharged for refusing to break the law. For example, courts have protected employees who refused to participate in an illegal price-fixing scheme, falsify pollution control records required by state law, pollute navigable waters in violation of federal law, or assist a supervisor in stealing from customers.[7]

ETHICS

Does an employer ever have the right to require workers to participate in an illegal scheme? Suppose that compliance with state pollution control regulations would force a company out of business. When the life of the company is at stake, does the boss have a right to expect a worker to cooperate by fudging records? What guidance does the Chapter 2 Ethics Checklist offer? Is this behavior legal? How would it look in the light of day?

Exercising a Legal Right. **As a general rule, an employer may not discharge a worker for exercising a legal right if that right supports public policy.** Dorothy Frampton injured her arm while working at the Central Indiana Gas Co. Her employer (and its insurance company) paid her medical expenses and her salary during the four months she was unable to work. When she discovered that she also qualified for benefits under the state's workers' compensation plan, she filed a claim and received payment. One month later, the company fired her without giving a reason. In her suit against the gas company, the court held:

> The [Workers' Compensation] Act creates a duty in the employer to compensate employees for work-related injuries and a right in the employee to receive such compensation. If employers are permitted to penalize employees for filing workmen's compensation claims, a most important public policy will be undermined. Employees will not file claims for justly deserved compensation—opting, instead, to continue their employment without incident. The end result, of course, is that the employer is effectively relieved of his obligation.[8]

Performing a Legal Duty. **Courts have consistently held that an employee may not be fired for serving on a jury.** Employers sometimes have difficulty replacing employees who are called up for jury duty and, therefore, prefer that their workers find some excuse for not serving. But jury duty is an important civic obligation that employers are not permitted to undermine.

What about an employee who performs a good deed that is not legally required? Kevin Gardner had just parked his armored truck in front of a bank in Spokane, Washington, when he saw a man with a knife chase the manager out of

---

[6] *Sides v. Duke University*, 74 N.C. App. 331, 328 S.E.2d 818, 1985 N.C. App. LEXIS 3501 (N.C. Ct. App. 1985).

[7] *Tameny v. Atlantic Richfield Co.*, 27 Cal. 3d 167, 610 P.2d 1330, 1980 Cal. LEXIS 171 (1980); *Trombetta v. Detroit*, T. & I. R., 81 Mich. App. 489, 265 N.W.2d 385, 1978 Mich. App. LEXIS 2153 (Mich. Ct. App. 1978); *Sabine Pilot Service, Inc. v. Hauck*, 28 Tex. Sup. J. 339, 687 S.W.2d 733, 1985 Tex. LEXIS 755 (1985); *Vermillion v. AAA Pro Moving & Storage*, 146 Ariz. 215, 704 P.2d 1360, 1985 Ariz. App. LEXIS 592 (Ariz. Ct. App. 1985).

[8] *Frampton v. Central Indiana Gas Co.*, 260 Ind. 249, 297 N.E.2d 425, 1973 Ind. LEXIS 522 (1973).

the bank. While running past the truck, the manager looked directly at Gardner and yelled, "Help me, help me." Gardner got out of his truck and locked the door. By then, the suspect had grabbed another woman, put his knife to her throat, and dragged her into the bank. Gardner followed them in, tackled the suspect, and disarmed him. The rescued woman hailed Gardner as a hero, but his employer fired him for violating a "fundamental" company rule that prohibited drivers from leaving their armored trucks unattended. However, the court held for Gardner on the grounds that, although there is no affirmative legal duty to intervene in such a situation, society values and encourages voluntary rescuers when a life is in danger.[9]

In the following case, the court adopts an expansive view of the public policy rule.

WELLS V. ORMET CORP.

1999 Ohio App. LEXIS 1087
Court of Appeals of Ohio, 1999

FACTS: Mark Wells had worked for the Ormet Corporation for 19 years and was foreman of one of its plants. One evening, he had to cancel an overtime shift when five workers failed to show up. Wells and Lee Smith, one of the company's labor relations specialists, then met with union officials to determine if the employees had legitimate excuses for not working or if they had collaborated to shut the plant down.

After the meeting, Wells and Smith concluded that the employees had had good excuses for their absences and that they had not been part of an organized effort to cause trouble. However, Dunlap, the general manager of the plant, disagreed and suspended the five employees. The union requested a formal hearing. At the hearing, a union official asked Wells if he believed that the absences were part of a concerted plan. After Smith gave Wells permission to answer, Wells responded that he did not believe the employees had collaborated.

Three days later, Dunlap had Wells fired. Wells sued the company, alleging wrongful discharge under the public policy exception to the employment-at-will doctrine. Ormet filed a motion to dismiss, which the trial court granted.

ISSUE: Does the public policy doctrine protect an employee from being fired for disagreeing with his boss at a hearing?

EXCERPTS FROM JUDGE VUKOVICH'S DECISION: [T]he issue before this court is whether there exists a sufficiently clear public policy against the corporate firing of a member of management for answering a question in a way that favors the laborers' position at a grievance hearing. Due to the fact that appellant was a nineteen-year veteran worker at the corporation and the fact that he was only answering the question in a manner that he believed was being directed by the corporation's labor relations specialist, we hold that, as limited to the facts alleged in the complaint, a sufficiently clear public policy was violated by appellant's discharge.

The public policy in the case consists of various established interests of society as a whole. These broad societal interests include a fair workplace, truthful grievance proceedings, job stability for long-term employees, and economic productivity. There is a clear public policy supporting the aforementioned interests, the violation of which is of similar import to the violation of a statute. The adoption of such a policy exception to employment-at-will adequately inures to the benefit of the general public.

---

[9] *Gardner v. Loomis Armored, Inc.*, 913 P.2d 377, 1996 Wash. LEXIS 109 (1996).

Whistleblowing.   No one likes to be accused of wrongdoing even if (or, perhaps, especially if) the accusations are true. **This is exactly what whistleblowers do: they are employees who disclose illegal behavior on the part of their employer.** Not surprisingly, many companies, when faced with such an accusation by an employee, prefer to shoot the messenger. Here is the story of Henry Boisvert.

NEWSWORTHY

FMC Corp. sold 9,000 Bradley Fighting Vehicles to the U.S. Army for as much as $1.5 million each. But the Bradley was controversial from the moment it began rolling off FMC's manufacturing lines. Designed to carry soldiers around battle-fields in Eastern Europe, its ability to "swim" across rivers and lakes was an important part of its job description. But Henry Boisvert, a testing supervisor for FMC, charged that the Bradley swam like a rock. Boisvert said he first encountered problems with the Bradley in the early days of the Army procurement process. He had one driven into a test pond and watched it quickly fill with water. FMC welders who worked on Bradleys claimed they weren't given enough time to do their work properly and so would simply fill gaps with putty. FMC quashed Boisvert's report on the Bradley and fired him when he refused to sign a falsified version. FMC disputes his account, but a jury ultimately agreed with him.[10] ◾

The law on whistleblowers varies across the country. As a general rule, however, whistleblowers are protected in the following situations:

- *The False Claims Act*. Henry Boisvert refused to sign his name to a report he thought was inaccurate. As a result he earned the right to sign a check from FMC for about $20 million. Boisvert recovered under the federal False Claims Act, a statute that permits anyone to bring suit against a "person" (including a company) who defrauds the government. The Act also prohibits employers from firing workers who file suit under the statute. A successful whistleblower receives between 15 and 30 percent of any damages awarded to the government. So far, whistleblowers have recovered $3.5 billion for the government, while their share of the damages has been $550 million.

- *Constitutional Protection for Government Employees*. Employees of federal, state, and local governments have a right to free speech under the United States Constitution. Therefore, the government cannot retaliate against public employees who blow the whistle, as long as the employee is speaking out on a matter of public concern. For example, a New York City child welfare agency received numerous reports that six-year-old Elisa Izquierdo was being abused. After Elisa was beaten to death by her mother, ABC News broadcast an interview with a social worker from the agency. She stated on air that "The workers who are considered the best workers are the ones who seem to be able to move cases out quickly . . . . There are lots of fatalities the press doesn't know anything about." By giving this interview, the social worker violated New York City rules prohibiting employees from disclosing information about families supervised by city agencies. The city suspended the social worker from her job, and she sued. The court acknowledged that the government has the right to prohibit some employee speech. However, if the employee speaks on matters of public concern, the government bears the burden of justifying any

---

[10] Lee Gomes, "A Whistle-Blower Finds Jackpot at the End of His Quest," *The Wall Street Journal*, April 27, 1998, p. B1.

retaliation. In this case, the court held for the social worker. The city reinstated her and gave her back pay.[11]

- *Statutory Protection for Federal Employees.* Congress passed the Civil Service Reform Act in 1978 and the Whistleblower Protection Act in 1989. These two statutes prevent retaliation against federal employees who report wrongdoing. They also permit the award of back pay and attorney's fees to the whistleblower. This statute was used to prevent the National Park Service from disciplining two managers who wrote a report expressing concern over development in Yellowstone National Park.

- *Employees of Publicly Traded Companies.* In response to a series of corporate financial scandals, Congress passed the Sarbanes-Oxley Act of 2002. Among other provisions, this Act protects employees of publicly traded companies who provide evidence of fraud to investigators (whether in or outside the company). A successful plaintiff is entitled to reinstatement, back pay, and attorney's fees.

- *State Statutes.* The good news is that all 50 states have statutes that protect whistleblowers from retaliation by their employers. The bad news is that the scope of this protection varies greatly from state to state. For example, in some states, protection only extends to public employees, while in other states, all employees are covered.

- *Common Law.* Most courts will prohibit the discharge of employees who report illegal activity that relates to their own jobs. For example, a Connecticut court held a company liable when it fired a quality control director for reporting to his boss that some products had failed the quality tests.[12] Sometimes, however, courts have held that employees do not have a right to report wrongdoing if it does not relate to their own job functions. For example, Donald Smith's boss told him to ignore the fact that 73,000 pounds of caustic soda had spilled into the river next to a company warehouse. When Smith instead reported the spill to corporate headquarters, he was fired. The court held that, since Smith had no responsibility for reporting spills, the public's interest "in harmony and productivity in the workplace must prevail over the public's interest in encouraging an employee in Smith's position to express his 'informed view.'"[13]

Thinking about blowing a whistle? The Web site http://www.whistleblower .org/www/Tips.htm offers cautionary advice.

Contract Law

Traditionally, many employers (and employees) thought that only a formal, signed document qualified as an employment contract. Increasingly, however, courts have been willing to enforce an employer's more casual promises, whether written or oral. Sometimes courts have also been willing to *imply* contract terms in the absence of an *express* agreement.

---

[11] Harman v. City of New York, 140 F.3d 111, 1998 U.S. App. LEXIS 5567 (2d Cir. 1998).
[12] *Sheets v. Teddy's Frosted Foods, Inc.*, 179 Conn. 471, 427 A.2d 385, 1980 Conn. LEXIS 690 (1980).
[13] *Smith v. Calgon Carbon Corp.*, 917 F.2d 1338, 1990 U.S. App. LEXIS 19193 (3rd Cir. 1990).

Truth in Hiring. **Oral promises made during the hiring process can be enforceable, even if not approved by the company's top executives.** When the Tanana Valley Medical-Surgical Group, Inc., hired James Eales as a physician's assistant, it promised him that as long as he did his job, he could stay there until retirement age. Six years later the company fired him without cause. The Alaska Supreme Court held that the clinic's promise was enforceable.[14]

In the following case, an insurance company was tackled for a big loss when it failed to disclose information during the hiring process.

While a player with the New York Giants football team, Phil McConkey was used to rough treatment. He expected life in the insurance business to be more civilized. But shortly after Alexander & Alexander hired him, it was acquired by Aon Corp. and the new company sacked him immediately. McConkey filed suit, alleging that Alexander & Alexander should have told him during the hiring process that it was engaged in merger talks (even though those discussions were, at that point, secret). A jury agreed, awarding the downed player $10 million. ◾

Employee Handbooks. The employee handbook at Blue Cross & Blue Shield stated that employees could be fired only for just cause and then only after warnings, notice, a hearing, and other procedures. Charles Toussaint was fired summarily five years after he joined the company. Although this decision was ultimately reviewed by the personnel department, company president, and chairman of the board of trustees, Toussaint was not given the benefit of all of the procedures in the handbook. The court held that **an employee handbook creates a contract**.[15]

AT RISK

Employers are now taking steps to protect themselves from liability for implied contracts. Some employers require new hires to sign a document acknowledging that (1) they are employees at will, (2) they can be terminated at any time for any reason, and (3) no one at the company has made any oral representations concerning the terms of employment. These employers caution interviewers not to make promises. Their employee handbooks now feature stern legal warnings, rather than friendly welcomes. ◾

Covenant of Good Faith and Fair Dealing. A covenant of good faith and fair dealing prohibits one party to a contract from interfering with the other's right to benefit under the contract. All parties are expected to behave in a fair, decent, and reasonable manner. **In some cases, courts will imply a covenant of good faith and fair dealing in an at-will employment relationship.**

When Forrest Fleming went to work for Parametric Technology Corp., the company promised him valuable stock options if he met his sales goals. He would not be able to *exercise* the options (i.e., purchase the stock), however, until several years after they were granted and then only if he was still employed by the company. During his four years with Parametric, Fleming received options to purchase about 18,000 shares for a price as low as 25 cents each. The shares ultimately traded in the market for as much as $50. Although Fleming exercised some options, the company fired him three months before he became eligible to purchase an additional

[14] *Eales v. Tanana Valley Medical-Surgical Group, Inc.*, 663 P.2d 958, 1983 Alas. LEXIS 430 (Alaska 1983).
[15] *Toussaint v. Blue Cross & Blue Shield*, 408 Mich. 579, 292 N.W.2d 880, 1980 Mich. LEXIS 227 (1980).

1,000 shares. The jury awarded him $1.6 million in damages. Although Parametric had not violated the explicit terms of the option agreement, the jury believed it had violated the covenant of good faith and fair dealing by firing Fleming to prevent him from exercising his remaining options.

Tort Law

Workers have successfully sued their employers under the following tort theories:

Defamation. **Employers may be liable for defamation when they give false and unfavorable references about a former employee.** John R. Glennon, Jr., was the branch manager of Dean Witter's Nashville office. Dean Witter fired him and filed a termination notice with the National Association of Securities Dealers saying that Glennon "was under internal review for violating investment-related statutes." This statement was untrue, and Witter had to pay $1.5 million in damages for defamation.

    More than half of the states, however, recognize a qualified privilege for employers who give references about former employees. A **qualified privilege** means that employers are liable only for false statements that they know to be false or that are primarily motivated by ill will. After Becky Chambers left her job at American Trans Air, Inc., she discovered that her former boss was telling anyone who called for a reference that Chambers "does not work good with other people," is a "troublemaker," and "would not be a good person to rehire." Chambers was unable, however, to present compelling evidence that her boss had been primarily motivated by ill will. Neither Trans Air nor the boss was held liable for these statements because they were protected by the qualified privilege.[16]

    Even if the employer wins, a trial is an expensive and time-consuming undertaking. Not surprisingly, companies are leery about offering any references for former employees. The company gains little benefit from giving an honest evaluation and may suffer substantial liability. As a matter of policy, many companies instruct their managers to reveal only a person's salary and dates of employment and not to offer an opinion on job performance. According to one survey, only 55 percent of former employers are totally honest when they give references.

    Employers are afraid of liability if they give a negative reference, but are they liable if they tell less than the whole truth? **Generally, courts have held that employers do not have a legal obligation to disclose information about former employees.** For example, while Jeffrey St. Clair worked at the St. Joseph Nursing Home, he was disciplined 24 times for actions ranging from extreme violence to drug and alcohol use. When he applied for a job with Maintenance Management Corp. (MMC), St. Joseph refused to give any information other than St. Clair's dates of employment. After he savagely murdered a security guard at his new job, the guard's family sued, but the court dismissed the case.[17]

    In some recent cases, however, courts have held that, when a former worker is potentially dangerous, employers do have an obligation to disclose this information. For example, officials from two junior high schools gave Robert

---

[16] *Chambers v. American Trans Air, Inc.*, 577 N.E.2d 612, 1991 Ind. App. LEXIS 1413 (Ind. Ct. App. 1991).

[17] *Moore v. St. Joseph Nursing Home, Inc.*, 184 Mich. App. 766, 459 N.W.2d 100, 1990 Mich. App. LEXIS 285 (Mich. Ct. App. 1990).

Gadams glowing letters of recommendation without mentioning that he had been fired for inappropriate sexual conduct with students. While an assistant principal at a new school, he molested a 13-year-old. Her parents sued the former employers. The court held that the writer of a letter of recommendation owes to third parties (in this case, the student) "a duty not to misrepresent the facts in describing the qualifications and character of a former employee, if making these misrepresentations would present a substantial, foreseeable risk of physical injury to the third persons."[18] As a result of cases such as this, it makes sense to disclose past violent behavior.

To assist employers who are asked for references, Lehigh economist Robert Thornton has written "The Lexicon of Intentional Ambiguous Recommendations" (LIAR). For a candidate with interpersonal problems, he suggests saying, "I am pleased to say that this person is a former colleague of mine." For the lazy worker, "In my opinion, you will be very fortunate to get this person to work for you." For the criminal, he suggests, "He's a man of many convictions" and "I'm sorry we let her get away." For the untrustworthy candidate, "Her true ability is deceiving."[19]

ETHICS

All joking aside, what if someone calls you to check references on a former employee who had a drinking problem? The job is driving a van for junior high school sports teams. What is the manager's ethical obligation in this situation? Many managers say that, in the case of a serious problem such as alcoholism, sexual harassment, or drug use, they will find a way to communicate that an employee is unsuitable. What if the ex-employee says she is reformed? Aren't people entitled to a second chance? Is it right to risk a defamation suit against your company to protect others from harm? What solutions does the Ethics Checklist in Chapter 2 suggest? Would it be just to reveal private information about a former employee? Is the process fair if you provide information that the job applicant has no opportunity to rebut because it is kept secret?

Intentional Infliction of Emotional Distress. **Employers who condone cruel treatment of their workers face liability under the tort of intentional infliction of emotional distress.** For example:

- When a 57-year-old social-work manager at Yale–New Haven Hospital was fired, she was forced to place her personal belongings in a plastic bag and was escorted out the door by security guards in full view of gaping co-workers. A supervisor told her that she would be arrested for trespassing if she returned. A jury awarded her $105,000.

- An employee swore at a co-worker and threatened her with a knife because she rejected his sexual advances. Her superiors fired her for complaining about the incident. A court held that the employer had inflicted emotional distress.[20]

- On the other hand, another court held that an employee who was fired for dating a co-worker did not have a valid claim for infliction of emotional distress.[21]

---

[18] *Randi W. v. Muroc Joint Unified School District*, 14 Cal. 4th 1066, 929 P.2d 582, 1997 Cal. LEXIS 10 (1997), modified, 14 Cal. 4th 1282c, 97 Cal. Daily Op. Service 1439.

[19] *The Wall Street Journal*, Mar. 22, 1994, p. 1.

[20] *Hogan v. Forsyth Country Club Co.*, 79 N.C. App. 483, 340 S.E.2d 116, 1986 N.C. App. LEXIS 2098 (N.C. Ct. App. 1986).

[21] *Patton v. J. C. Penney Co.*, 301 Or. 117, 719 P.2d 854, 1986 Ore. LEXIS 1144 (1986).

Safety and Privacy in the Workplace

WORKPLACE SAFETY

In 1970, Congress passed the Occupational Safety and Health Act (OSHA) to ensure safe working conditions. Under OSHA:

- Employers must comply with specific health and safety standards. For example, health care personnel who work with blood are not permitted to eat or drink in areas where the blood is kept and must not put their mouths on any instruments used to store blood. Protective clothing—gloves, gowns, and laboratory coats—must be impermeable to blood.

- Employers are under a general obligation to keep their workplace "free from recognized hazards that are causing or are likely to cause death or serious physical harm" to employees.

- Employers must keep records of all workplace injuries and accidents.

- The Occupational Safety and Health Administration (also known as OSHA) may inspect workplaces to ensure that they are safe. OSHA may assess fines for violations and order employers to correct unsafe conditions.

OSHA has done a lot to make the American workplace safer. In 1900, roughly 35,000 workers died and 350,000 were injured at work. One hundred years later, the workforce had grown five times larger but the number of annual deaths had fallen to 5,100. You can report hazards at your work site to OSHA online at http://www.osha-slc.gov/as/opa/worker/complain.html.

EMPLOYEE PRIVACY

Upon opening the country's first moving assembly line in the early 1900s, Henry Ford issued a booklet, "Helpful Hints and Advice to Employees," that warned against drinking, gambling, borrowing money, taking in boarders, and practicing poor hygiene. Ford also created a department of 100 investigators for door-to-door checks on his employees' drinking habits, sexual practices, and housekeeping skills. It sounds pretty outrageous, but in modern times employees have been fired or disciplined for such extracurricular activities as playing dangerous sports, dating co-workers, or even having high cholesterol.

The right to hire, fire, and make an honest profit is enshrined in American tradition. But so is the right to privacy. Justice Louis D. Brandeis called it the "right to be let alone—the most comprehensive of rights and the right most valued by civilized men." What protection do workers have against intrusive employers?

Off-Duty Conduct

In an era of rapidly expanding health care costs, employers are concerned about the health of their workers. Some companies have banned off-duty smoking and have even fired employees who show traces of nicotine in their blood. In response, more than half the states have passed laws that protect the right of employees to smoke cigarettes while off-duty. Some of these statutes permit any lawful activity when off-duty, including drinking socially, having high cholesterol, being overweight, or engaging in dangerous hobbies—bungee jumping or roller blading, for example.

Alcohol and Drug Testing

Government employees can be tested for drug and alcohol use only if they show signs of use or if they are in a job where this type of abuse endangers the public. Most states permit private employers to administer alcohol and drug tests. According to one survey, more than 80 percent of large firms test employees for drugs.

Lie Detector Tests

Under the Employee Polygraph Protection Act of 1988, employers may not require, or even *suggest*, that an employee or job candidate submit to a lie detector test, except as part of an "on-going investigation" into crimes that have occurred.

Electronic Monitoring of the Workplace

Technological advances in communications have raised a host of new privacy issues.

About 78 percent of American companies monitor employee use of electronic equipment in the workplace: telephone calls, voice mail, e-mail, and Internet usage. **The Electronic Communications Privacy Act of 1986 (ECPA) permits employers to monitor workers' telephone calls and e-mail messages if (1) the employee consents, (2) the monitoring occurs in the ordinary course of business, or (3) in the case of e-mail, the employer provides the e-mail system.** However, bosses may not disclose any private information revealed by the monitoring.

About 47 percent of companies monitor their employees' e-mail (as compared with the 12 percent that listen to telephone conversations). And beware—an increasing number of companies now monitor instant messages. These chatty words may *seem* to disappear when the messaging session ends, but new software permits an employer to store and read them nonetheless.

Although workers may feel that their e-mail should be private, employers argue that this monitoring improves employee productivity and protects the company from lawsuits. For example, a West Coast company fired a woman "because of a tough economy." When she sued, her attorneys demanded access to the company's e-mail system as part of the discovery process. They found a message from the woman's supervisor saying, "Get that bitch out of here as fast as you can. I don't care what it takes. Just do it." The supervisor had long since erased the message from his computer, but it had remained buried in the system. A few hours after the message was revealed in court, the company settled for $250,000. If the employee had known that his e-mail would be read by others, perhaps he would not have sent such an inflammatory statement.

About 63 percent of companies also monitor employee use of the Internet. They are concerned not only about lawsuits but also that workers may be wasting time. During one month, employees at IBM, Apple Computer, and AT&T logged on to *Penthouse* magazine's Web site 12,823 times, using the equivalent of more than 347 workdays. One company discovered that some of its employees were using their company computers to buy and sell child pornography. Companies fear that even legal logging on to sexually explicit sites may give rise to sexual harassment claims. ◾

In the following case, two employees used company e-mail to trash talk. Could they be fired for their indiscretion?

YOU BE THE JUDGE

MICHAEL A. SMYTH V. THE PILLSBURY CO.

914 F. Supp. 97, 1996 U.S. Dist. LEXIS 776
United States District Court for the Eastern District of Pennsylvania, 1996

FACTS: The Pillsbury Co. repeatedly assured its employees that all company e-mail was confidential. The company promised not to intercept e-mail or use it against employees as grounds for reprimand or termination. One evening at home, Michael Smyth and his supervisor engaged in a series of e-mail exchanges that threatened to "kill the backstabbing bastards" (i.e., company sales managers) and referred to the planned holiday party as the "Jim Jones Koolaid affair." The company found out about these e-mails and fired both men. Smyth sued, alleging that the company had violated his right to privacy.

YOU BE THE JUDGE: Is company e-mail private?

ARGUMENT FOR SMYTH: The public policy doctrine prohibits an employer from firing a worker for a reason that violates basic social rights, duties, or responsibilities. Privacy is a fundamental social right that tort law protects. There are two issues under tort law:

- Did Pillsbury intrude into Smyth's life in a manner that any reasonable person would find offensive?

- Did Smyth have a reasonable expectation of privacy?

The answer to both of these questions is a resounding, "Yes." Today, people use e-mail almost as often as the telephone. They correspond not only with co-workers but also with friends and family members. Sitting in the privacy of their office or home, they do not expect their employer to be reading their e-mail.

Particularly in this case, Smyth had a reasonable expectation of privacy. The company had told him repeatedly that it would not read his e-mail. How could the company make such a promise and then fire him because he believed it?

ARGUMENT FOR PILLSBURY: Smyth behaved in an unprofessional and unacceptable manner. The company had no choice but to fire him after he made death threats against other employees. What if the company had done nothing and he had carried out those threats?

Furthermore, Smyth could not have a reasonable expectation of privacy with an e-mail system that the company established and maintained for the use of its employees. Nor would a reasonable person find this intrusion offensive. No one forced Smyth to share his feelings about the company; he wrote and sent those e-mail messages *voluntarily*. This juvenile and inappropriate behavior demonstrated that he is totally unsuited for employment at Pillsbury. He has no one to blame but himself.

Financial Protection

Congress and the states have enacted laws that provide employees with a measure of financial security. All of the laws in this section were created by statute, not by the courts.

FAIR LABOR STANDARDS ACT

Passed in 1938, the Fair Labor Standards Act (FLSA) regulates wages and limits child labor. The wage provisions do not apply to managerial, administrative, or professional staff, which means that accounting, consulting, and law firms (among others) are free to require as many hours a week as their employees can humanly perform without having to pay overtime or the minimum wage.

Minimum Wage

The current federal minimum wage is $5.15 per hour, although some states have set a higher minimum. Employers can pay students and apprentices under age 20 a training wage of $4.25 per hour. The Department of Labor Web site at http://www.dol.gov lists any changes in the minimum wage and also answers related questions.

Overtime Pay

The FLSA does not limit the number of hours a week that an employee can work (or a student can study!), but it does specify that workers must be paid time and a half for any hours over 40 in one week.

Child Labor

The FLSA prohibits "oppressive child labor," which means that children under 14 may work only in agriculture and entertainment. Fourteen- and 15-year-olds are permitted to work *limited* hours after school in nonhazardous jobs. Sixteen- and 17-year-olds may work *unlimited* hours in nonhazardous jobs.

WORKERS' COMPENSATION

Workers' compensation statutes ensure that employees receive payment for injuries incurred at work. Before workers' comp, injured employees could recover damages only if they sued their employer. It is the brave (or carefree) worker who is willing to risk a suit against his own boss. Lawsuits poison the atmosphere at work. Moreover, employers frequently won these suits by claiming that (1) the injured worker was contributorily negligent, (2) a fellow employee had caused the accident, or (3) the injured worker had assumed the risk of injury. As a result, seriously injured workers (or their families) often had no recourse against the employer.

Workers' comp statutes provide a fixed, certain recovery to the injured employee, no matter who was at fault for the accident. In return, employees are not permitted to sue their employers for negligence. The amounts allowed (for medical expenses and lost wages) under workers' comp statutes are often less than a worker might recover in court, but the injured employee trades the certainty of some recovery for the higher risk of rolling the dice at trial. Payments are approved by an administrative board that conducts an informal hearing into each claim. These payments are funded either through the purchase of private insurance or by a tax on employers—a tax that is based on how many injuries their employees have suffered. Thus employers have an incentive to maintain a safe working environment.

SOCIAL SECURITY

The federal Social Security system began in 1935, during the depths of the Great Depression, to provide a basic safety net for the elderly, ill, and unemployed. **Currently, the Social Security system pays benefits to workers who are retired, disabled, or temporarily unemployed and to the spouses and children of disabled or deceased workers.** It also provides medical insurance to the retired and disabled. The Social Security program is financed through a tax on wages that is paid by employers, employees, and the self-employed.

Although the Social Security system has done much to reduce poverty among the elderly, many worry that it cannot survive in its current form. When workers pay taxes, the proceeds do not go into a savings account for their retirement, but instead are used to pay benefits to current retirees. In 1940 there were 40 workers for each retiree; currently, there are 3.3. By 2030, when the last baby boomers retire, there will be only two workers to support each retiree—a prohibitive burden. No wonder baby boomers are often cautioned not to count on Social Security when making their retirement plans.

The Federal Unemployment Tax Act (FUTA) is the part of the Social Security system that provides support to the unemployed. FUTA establishes some national standards, but states are free to set their own benefit levels and payment schedules. These payments are funded by a tax on employers. While receiving payments, workers must make a good faith effort to look for other employment. No one who quits voluntarily or is fired for just cause is eligible for benefits.

PENSION BENEFITS

In 1974, Congress passed the Employee Retirement Income Security Act (ERISA) to protect workers covered by private pension plans. Under ERISA, employers are not required to establish pension plans, but if they do, they must follow these federal rules. The law was aimed, in particular, at protecting benefits of retired workers if their companies subsequently go bankrupt. The statute also prohibits risky investments by pension plans. In addition, the statute sets rules on the vesting of benefits. (An employer cannot cancel *vested* benefits; *nonvested* benefits are forfeited when the employee leaves.) Before ERISA, retirement benefits at some companies did not vest until the employee retired—if he quit or was fired before retirement, even after years of service, he lost his pension. Under current law, employee benefits vest after five years of employment.

Employment Discrimination

In the last four decades, Congress has enacted important legislation to prevent discrimination in the workplace.

EQUAL PAY ACT OF 1963

Under the Equal Pay Act, an employee may not be paid at a lesser rate than employees of the opposite sex for equal work. "Equal work" means tasks that require equal skill, effort, and responsibility under similar working conditions. If the employee proves that she is not being paid equally, the employer will be found liable unless the pay difference is based on merit, productivity, seniority, or some factor other than sex. A "factor other than sex" includes prior wages, training, profitability, performance in an interview, and value to the company. For example, female agents sued Allstate Insurance Co. because its salary for new agents was based, in part, on prior salary. The women argued that this system was unfair because it perpetuated the historic wage differences between men and women. The court, however, held for Allstate.[22]

To find out how much less women earn than men, in spite of the Equal Pay Act, check out http://www.aflcio.org/yourjobeconomy/women/equalpay/calculate.cfm. This site also calculates how much the pay gap will cost a woman over her lifetime.

TITLE VII

Title VII of the Civil Rights Act of 1964 prohibits employers from discriminating on the basis of race, color, religion, sex, or national origin. (The text of Title VII is available at http://www.eeoc.gov/laws/vii.html.) Originally, "sex" was not included in the statute, but two days before passage, Rep. Howard Smith of Virginia added this word. His intention was not to promote equal opportunity for women, but rather to scuttle the bill. He figured that nobody—but nobody— would vote for a statute that prohibited discrimination against women. He thought wrong, and the most important piece of antidiscrimination legislation in the United States passed.

Title VII prohibits (1) discrimination in the workplace, (2) sexual harassment, and (3) discrimination because of pregnancy. It also permits employers to develop affirmative action plans.

Proof of Discrimination

Discrimination under Title VII means firing, refusing to hire, failing to promote, or otherwise reducing a person's employment opportunities because of race, color, religion, sex, or national origin. This protection applies to every stage of the employment process from job ads to postemployment references and includes placement, wages, benefits, and working conditions.

Plaintiffs in Title VII cases can prove discrimination two different ways: disparate treatment and disparate impact.

Disparate Treatment. To prove a disparate treatment case, the plaintiff must show that she was *treated* differently because of her sex, race, color, religion, or national origin. The required steps in a disparate treatment case are:

Step 1.	The plaintiff presents evidence that the defendant has discriminated against her because of a protected trait. This is called a *prima facie* case. The plaintiff is not required to prove discrimination; she need only create a *presumption* that discrimination occurred.
Step 2.	The defendant must present evidence that its decision was based on *legitimate, nondiscriminatory* reasons.
Step 3.	To win, the plaintiff must now prove that the employer discriminated. She may do so by showing that the reasons offered were simply a *pretext*.

---

[22] *Kouba v. Allstate Insurance Co.*, 691 F.2d 873, 1982 U.S. App. LEXIS 24479 (9th Cir. 1982).

Proving a case of disparate treatment is like a tennis match. Here is how the match goes:

1. The plaintiff serves the ball by making a *prima facie* case. That means she presents evidence that an employer has discriminated against her. At this point, she does not have to *prove* discrimination; she must simply produce evidence that could *indicate* discrimination. She does not have to ace the defendant at this stage; she simply has to put the ball in play. Suppose that Louisa applies for a job coaching a boys' high school ice hockey team. She was an All-American hockey star in college. Although Louisa is obviously qualified for the job, Harry, the school principal, rejects her and continues to interview other people. This is not *proof* of discrimination, because Harry may have a perfectly good, nondiscriminatory explanation. However, his behavior could have been motivated by discrimination.

2. The ball is now in Harry's court. He must show a legitimate, nondiscriminatory reason for rejecting Louisa. He might say, for example, that he wanted someone with prior coaching experience. Although Louisa is clearly a great player, she has never coached before. This is a great return shot, and the ball is back in Louisa's court.

3. Louisa must now prove, by a preponderance of the evidence, that Harry's reason was simply a *pretext* for not hiring her. She might show that he had recently hired a male tennis coach who had no prior coaching experience. Or Harry's assistant might testify that Harry said, "No way I'm going to put a woman on the ice with those guys." If she can present evidence such as this, Louisa wins the point and match.

Disparate Impact. Disparate impact becomes an issue if the employer has a rule that, *on its face*, is not discriminatory, but *in practice* excludes too many people in a protected group. The steps in a disparate impact case are:

Step 1.	The plaintiff must present a *prima facie* case. The plaintiff is not required to prove discrimination; he need only show a disparate impact—that the employment practice in question excludes a disproportionate number of people in a protected group (women and minorities, for example).
Step 2.	The defendant must offer some evidence that the employment practice was a job-related business necessity.
Step 3.	To win, the plaintiff must now prove either that the employer's reason is a pretext or that other, less discriminatory rules would achieve the same results.

Suppose that Harry will only hire teachers who are at least 5 feet 10 inches tall and weigh 170 pounds. He says he is afraid that students will literally push around anyone smaller. When Chou Ping, an Asian male, applies for a job, he cannot meet Harry's physical requirements. Here is what might happen in their legal contest:

1. Chou Ping must show that Harry's rule, *in fact*, eliminates more women or minorities than white males. He might offer evidence that 50 percent of all white males can meet Harry's standard, but only 20 percent of white women and Asian males qualify.

2. Harry must demonstrate that his rule is *job-related*. He might produce evidence, for example, that teachers are regularly expected to wrestle students into their classroom seats. Further, he cites studies showing his standards are essential for this task.

3. Chou Ping will still win if he shows either that Harry's reason is a pretext or that other, less discriminatory rules would achieve the same results. Perhaps all teachers could take a self-defense course or engage in martial arts training.

Is Harry's reason valid? Compare his situation with a case involving police officers. The Illinois Law Enforcement Officers Training Board created an exam to test aspiring police officers. When a higher percentage of minority applicants than white candidates failed the test, some of the unsuccessful aspirants filed suit, alleging that the exam was illegal because it had a disparate impact. In response the board presented evidence that the exam had been very carefully prepared by a consulting company that specialized in creating such exams. The court held that the exam was legal because it was "demonstrably a reasonable measure of job performance."[23] In short, the mere existence of a disparate impact does not mean that an employment practice violates the law.

Religion

Employers must make *reasonable accommodation* **for a worker's religious beliefs unless the request would cause** *undue hardship* **for the business.** Scott Hamby told his manager at Wal-Mart that he could never work on Sunday because that was his Sabbath. It also happened to be one of the store's busiest days. When the manager forced Hamby to quit, he promptly sued on the grounds of religious discrimination. Lawsuits such as his are on the rise as more businesses remain open on Sundays. Wal-Mart denied wrongdoing but settled the case with a cash payment of undisclosed amount. It also established a company-wide training program on religious accommodation.

Defenses to Charges of Discrimination

Under Title VII, the defendant has three possible defenses.

Merit.   A defendant is not liable if he shows that the person he favored was the most qualified. Test results, education, or productivity can all be used to demonstrate merit, provided they relate to the job in question. Harry can show that he hired Bruce instead of Louisa because Bruce has a master's degree in physical education and seven years of coaching experience. On the other hand, the fact that Bruce scored higher on the National Latin Exam in the eighth grade is not a good reason to hire him over Louisa.

ECONOMICS
& THE LAW

It is easy to say that the most qualified person should be hired or promoted. But how do you measure merit? Take the case of Santa Clara, California, for example. No woman had ever held the job of radio dispatcher there. Although Paul Johnson scored higher on the dispatcher exam than Diane Joyce, the county hired Joyce.[24]

---

[23] *Bew v. Chicago*, 252 F.3d 891, 2001 U.S. App. LEXIS 9247 (7th Cir. 2001).
[24] *Johnson v. Transportation Agency*, 489 U.S. 616, 1987 U.S. LEXIS 1387 (1987).

This case ultimately reached the U.S. Supreme Court on the issue of whether a less qualified woman could be promoted over a more qualified man. (The court ruled that she could.)

So do we feel sorry for Paul Johnson? Of course, we feel sorry for anyone who does not get the job of his dreams. It turns out, however, that his score on the dispatcher exam had been 75 out of 100; hers was 73. This two-point difference is simply not persuasive evidence that Johnson would be a better radio dispatcher than Joyce. Indeed, employment tests are typically not very good predictors of on-the-job performance. They are at best blunt instruments. Moreover, a 2-point differential on a 100-point test is meaningless. As an affirmative action case, *Johnson* was unusual only in that the court actually reported the test scores. Typically, in such cases the actual difference in scores is rarely reported or discussed.

The moral of the story? Before concluding that a less qualified applicant has been promoted over a more qualified competitor, it is wise to ask about the validity of the test and the significance of the difference in scores.[25]

Seniority. A legitimate seniority system is legal, even if it perpetuates past discrimination. Suppose that Harry has always chosen the most senior assistant coach to take over as head coach when a vacancy occurs. Since the majority of the senior assistant coaches are male, most of the head coaches are, too. Such a system does not violate Title VII.

Bona Fide Occupational Qualification. An employer is permitted to establish discriminatory job requirements if they are *essential* to the position in question. Such a requirement is called a **bona fide occupational qualification (BFOQ)**. Catholic schools may, if they choose, refuse to hire non-Catholic teachers; mail order companies may refuse to hire men to model women's clothing. Generally, however, courts are not sympathetic to claims of BFOQ. They have, for example, almost always rejected BFOQ claims that are based on customer preference. Thus airlines could not refuse to hire male flight attendants even though travelers prefer female attendants.[26] The major exception to this customer preference rule is sexual privacy: an employer may refuse to hire women to work in a men's bathroom and vice versa. *Female flight attendants –*

Affirmative Action

Affirmative action has become a hot political issue: white males protest that such programs are reverse discrimination against them; political candidates campaign on anti-affirmative action platforms.

Affirmative action is not required by Title VII, nor is it prohibited. Affirmative action programs have three different sources:

- *Litigation.* Courts have the power under Title VII to order affirmative action to remedy the effects of past discrimination.

---

[25] Michael Selmi, "Testing for Equality: Merit, Efficiency, and the Affirmative Action Debate," *UCLA Law Review*, June 1995, vol. 42, p. 1251.

[26] *Diaz v. Pan American World Airways, Inc.*, 442 F.2d 385, 1971 U.S. App. LEXIS 10920 (5th Cir. 1971).

- *Voluntary Action.* Employers can voluntarily introduce an affirmative action plan to remedy the effects of past practices or to achieve equitable representation of minorities and women.

- *Government Contracts.* In 1965, President Johnson signed Executive Order 11246, which prohibits discrimination by federal contractors. This order had a profound impact on the American workplace because one-third of all workers are employed by companies that do business with the federal government. If an employer found that women or minorities were underrepresented in its workplace, it was required to establish goals and timetables to correct the deficiency. In 1995, however, the Supreme Court dramatically limited the extent to which the government can require contractors to establish affirmative action programs. The Court ruled that these programs are permissible only if they serve a "compelling national interest" and are "narrowly tailored" so that they minimize the harm to white males. The government must be able to show that (1) the programs are needed to overcome specific past discrimination, (2) they have time limits, and (3) nondiscriminatory alternatives are not available.[27] This case led to a sharp decrease in the number of federal contracts awarded to companies owned by women and minorities.

Sexual Harassment

When Professor Anita Hill accused Supreme Court nominee Clarence Thomas of sexually harassing her, people across the country were glued to their televisions, watching the Senate hearings on her charges. Thomas was ultimately confirmed to the Supreme Court, but "sexual harassment" became a household phrase. The number of cases—and the size of the damage awards—skyrocketed.

Everyone has heard of sexual harassment, but few people know exactly what it is. Men fear that a casual comment or glance will be met with career-ruining charges; women claim that men "just don't get it." So what is sexual harassment anyway? **Sexual harassment involves unwelcome sexual advances, requests for sexual favors, and other verbal or physical conduct of a sexual nature.** There are two major categories of sexual harassment: (1) *quid pro quo* and (2) hostile work environment.

Quid Pro Quo. From a Latin phrase that means "this for that," *quid pro quo* harassment occurs if any aspect of a job is made contingent upon sexual activity. In other words, when a banker says to a secretary, "You can be promoted to teller if you sleep with me," that is *quid pro quo* sexual harassment.

Hostile Work Environment. This is a more subtle claim and the one that managers worry about most. An employee has a valid claim of sexual harassment if sexual talk and innuendo are so pervasive that they interfere with her (or his) ability to work. Courts have found that offensive jokes, comments about clothes or body parts, and public displays of pornographic pictures create a hostile environment. In the following case, the company president repeatedly insulted and demeaned his female employees.

---

[27] *Adarand Constructors, Inc. v. Pena,* 515 U.S. 200, 115 S. Ct. 2097, 1995 U.S. LEXIS 4037 (1995).

TERESA HARRIS V. FORKLIFT SYSTEMS, INC.

510 U.S. 17, 114 S. Ct. 367, 1993 U.S. LEXIS 7155
United States Supreme Court, 1993

FACTS: Teresa Harris was a manager at Forklift Systems; Charles Hardy was its president. Hardy frequently made inappropriate sexual comments to Harris and other women at the company. For example, he said to Harris, in the presence of others, "You're a woman, what do you know?" and "We need a man as the rental manager." He called her "a dumb ass woman" and suggested that the two of them "go to the Holiday Inn to negotiate her raise." He also asked Harris and other female employees to get coins from his front pants pocket. He insisted that Harris and other women pick up objects he had thrown on the ground. When Harris complained to Hardy, he apologized and claimed he was only joking. A month later, while Harris was arranging a deal with one of Forklift's customers, he asked her, in front of other employees, "What did you do, promise the guy some sex Saturday night?"

Harris sued Forklift, claiming that Hardy had created an abusive work environment. The federal trial court ruled against Harris on the grounds that Hardy's comments might offend a reasonable woman, but they were not severe enough to have a serious impact on Harris's psychological well-being. The appeals court confirmed, and the Supreme Court granted certiorari.

ISSUE: To be a violation of Title VII, must sexual harassment seriously affect the employee's psychological well-being?

EXCERPTS FROM JUSTICE O'CONNOR'S DECISION: Title VII of the Civil Rights Act of 1964 makes it "an unlawful employment practice for an employer to discriminate against any individual with respect to his compensation, terms, conditions, or privileges of employment, because of such individual's race, color, religion, sex, or national origin." [T]his language is not limited to economic or tangible discrimination. The phrase terms, conditions, or privileges of employment evinces a congressional intent to strike at the entire spectrum of disparate treatment of men and women in employment, which includes requiring people to work in a discriminatorily hostile or abusive environment. When the workplace is permeated with discriminatory intimidation, ridicule, and insult, that is sufficiently severe or pervasive to alter the conditions of the victim's employment and create an abusive working environment, Title VII is violated.

This standard takes a middle path between making actionable any conduct that is merely offensive and requiring the conduct to cause a tangible psychological injury. [M]ere utterance of an epithet which engenders offensive feelings in an employee, does not sufficiently affect the conditions of employment to implicate Title VII. Conduct that is not severe or pervasive enough to create an objectively hostile or abusive work environment—an environment that a reasonable person would find hostile or abusive—is beyond Title VII's purview. Likewise, if the victim does not subjectively perceive the environment to be abusive, the conduct has not actually altered the conditions of the victim's employment, and there is no Title VII violation.

But Title VII comes into play before the harassing conduct leads to a nervous breakdown. A discriminatorily abusive work environment, even one that does not seriously affect employees' psychological well-being, can and often will detract from employees' job performance, discourage employees from remaining on the job, or keep them from advancing in their careers. Moreover, even without regard to these tangible effects, the very fact that the discriminatory conduct was so severe or pervasive that it created a work environment abusive to employees because of their race, gender, religion, or national origin offends Title VII's broad rule of workplace equality.

We therefore believe the [trial court] erred in relying on whether the conduct "seriously affected plaintiff's psychological well-being" or led her to "suffer injury." So long as the environment would reasonably be perceived, and is perceived, as hostile or abusive there is no need for it also to be psychologically injurious. ◢

Employees who commit sexual harassment are liable for their own misdeeds. But is their company also liable? The Supreme Court has held that:

- If the victimized employee has suffered a "tangible employment action" such as firing, demotion, or reassignment, the company is liable to her for sexual harassment by a supervisor.

- If the victimized employee has not suffered a tangible employment action, the company is not liable if it can prove that (1) it used reasonable care to prevent and correct sexually harassing behavior, and (2) the employee unreasonably failed to take advantage of the complaint procedure or other preventive opportunities provided by the company.[28]

Corning Consumer Products Co. asks its employees to apply four tests in determining whether their behavior constitutes sexual harassment:

- Would you say or do this in front of your spouse or parents?

- What about in front of a colleague of the opposite sex?

- Would you like your behavior reported in your local newspaper?

- Does it need to be said or done at all?

Procedures and Remedies

Before a plaintiff in a Title VII case brings suit, she must first file a complaint with a federal agency, the Equal Employment Opportunity Commission (EEOC). The EEOC then has the right to sue on behalf of the plaintiff. This arrangement is favorable for the plaintiff because the government pays the legal bill. If the EEOC decides not to bring the case, or does *not* make a decision within six months, it issues a **right to sue letter**, and the plaintiff may proceed on her own in court. Many states also have their own version of the EEOC, but these state commissions are often understaffed.

Remedies available to the successful plaintiff include hiring, reinstatement, retroactive seniority, back pay, reasonable attorney's fees, and damages of up to $300,000. Two recent trends, however, have reduced employees' chances of taking home substantial damages. Concerned about a rise in discrimination lawsuits, employers now often require new hires to agree in advance to arbitrate, not litigate, any future employment claims. The Supreme Court has upheld the employers' right to do so.[29] Typically, employees receive worse results in the arbitrator's office than in the courtroom, largely because arbitrators tend to favor repeat customers (such as management) over one-time users (such as employees). But even if a case does go to trial, plaintiffs in job discrimination cases have a much worse track record than other types of plaintiffs. About 43 percent of all plaintiffs in federal district court win their cases; for discrimination plaintiffs, the win rate is only about 30 percent. Even if discrimination plaintiffs win at trial, they have a 44 percent probability of losing on appeal. Victorious plaintiffs in other types of cases are overturned only 33 percent of the time.

---

[28] *Burlington Industries, Inc. v. Ellerth*, 524 U.S. 742, 118 S. Ct. 2257, 1998 U.S. LEXIS 4217 (1998); *Faragher v. Boca Raton*, 524 U.S. 775, 118 S. Ct. 2275, 1998 U.S. LEXIS 4216 (1998).

[29] *Circuit City Stores, Inc. v. Adams*, 532 U.S. 105, 2001 U.S. LEXIS 2459.

Pregnancy

Under the Pregnancy Discrimination Act of 1978, an employer may not fire or refuse to hire a woman because she is pregnant. An employer must also treat pregnancy as any other temporary disability. If, for example, employees are allowed time off from work for other medical disabilities, women must also be allowed a maternity leave. The United States and Australia are the only industrialized nations that do not require employers to provide paid maternity leave.

AGE DISCRIMINATION

The Age Discrimination in Employment Act (ADEA) of 1967 prohibits age discrimination against employees or job applicants who are at least 40 years old. An employer may not fire, refuse to hire, fail to promote, or otherwise reduce a person's employment opportunities because he is 40 or older. Under this statute, an employer may not require a worker to retire at any age. These retirement rules do not apply to police and top-level corporate executives, who may indeed be forced to retire at a certain age.

The procedure for an age-bias claim is similar to that under Title VII—plaintiffs must first file a charge with the EEOC. If the EEOC does not take action, they can file suit themselves.

During tight economic times, companies often feel great pressure to lower costs. They are sometimes tempted to replace older, higher paid workers with younger, less expensive employees. Courts traditionally held that replacing expensive, older workers with cheaper, younger ones was illegal discrimination under the ADEA. In some recent cases, however, courts have held that an employer is entitled to prefer *lower paid* workers even if that preference results in the company also choosing *younger* workers. As the court put it in one case, "An action based on price differentials represents the very quintessence of a legitimate business decision."[30] The Supreme Court has suggested that the primary goal of the ADEA is to prevent employment decisions based on stereotypes about the productivity and competence of older workers. Further, policies that have the effect of treating older people more harshly do not violate the law as long as the employer is wholly motivated by factors other than age.[31]

ETHICS

A court summed up the age discrimination dilemma thus:

> We are not unmindful of the pain attendant with the loss of any job, particularly when the loss is sustained by an older worker for whom retraining may be more difficult. [W]e are [also] not unmindful that the image of some newly minted whippersnapper MBA who tries to increase corporate profits—and his or her own compensation—by across-the-board layoffs is not a pretty one. Even so, [Congress never] intended the age discrimination laws to inhibit the very process by which a free market economy—decision making on the basis of cost—is conducted and by which, ultimately, real jobs and wealth are created.[32]

Apart from legal issues, does a "newly minted whippersnapper MBA" (or any other manager) have an ethical obligation to older employees for whom opportunities

---

[30] *Marks v. Loral Corp.*, 57 Cal. App. 4th 30, 1997 Cal. App. LEXIS 611 (Cal. Ct. App. 1997).
[31] *Hazen Paper Co. v. Biggins*, 507 U.S. 604, 113 S. Ct. 1701, 1993 U.S. LEXIS 2978 (1993).
[32] *Marks, supra*, note 30.

may be limited? What conclusions can you glean from the Ethics Checklist in Chapter 2? The Golden Rule suggests that you ask yourself how you would like to be treated when you are old. Would a layoff of older employees violate important values? ◼

AMERICANS WITH DISABILITIES ACT

Passed in 1990, the Americans with Disabilities Act (ADA) prohibits employers from discriminating on the basis of disability. (The text of the ADA is available at http://www.eeoc.gov/laws/ada.html. The Justice Department's ADA Web site is http://www.usdoj.gov/crt/ada/adahom1.htm.) As with Title VII, a plaintiff under the ADA must first file a charge with the EEOC. If the EEOC decides not to file suit, the individual may do so himself.

A person with a disability is someone with a physical or mental impairment that substantially limits a major life activity, or someone who is regarded as having such an impairment. This definition includes people with mental illness, visual impairment, epilepsy, dyslexia, and AIDS, or who are *recovered* drug addicts and alcoholics. It does not cover people with sexual disorders, pyromania, exhibitionism, or compulsive gambling.

An employer may not disqualify an employee or job applicant because of disability as long as she can, with *reasonable accommodation*, **perform the** *essential functions* **of the job. An accommodation is not reasonable if it would create** *undue hardship* **for the employer.** In one case, a court held that a welder who could perform 88 percent of a job was doing the essential functions. Reasonable accommodation includes buying necessary equipment, providing readers or interpreters, or permitting a part-time schedule. In determining undue hardship, *relative* cost, not *absolute* cost, is the issue. Even an expensive accommodation—such as hiring a full-time reader—is not considered an undue hardship unless it imposes a significant burden on the overall finances of the company.

An employer may not ask about disabilities before making a job offer. The interviewer may ask only whether an applicant can perform the work. Nor can an employer require applicants to take a medical exam unless the exam is (1) job-related and (2) required of all applicants for similar jobs. However, drug testing is permitted.

After a job offer has been made, an employer may require a medical test, but it must be related to the *essential functions* **of the job.** For example, an employer could not test the cholesterol of someone applying for an accounting job because high cholesterol is no impediment to good accounting.

An employer may not discriminate against someone because of his *relationship* with a disabled person. For example, an employer cannot refuse to hire an applicant because he has a child with Down's syndrome or a spouse with cancer.

In 1997, the EEOC issued rules on the treatment of mental disabilities. These rules were based on an assumption of parity—that physical and mental disabilities should be treated the same. The difficulty is that physical ailments such as diabetes and deafness may be easy to diagnose, but what does a supervisor do when an employee is chronically late, rude, or impulsive? Does this mean the worker is mentally disabled or just a lazy, irresponsible jerk? Among other accommodations, the EEOC rules indicated that employers should be willing to put up barriers to isolate people who have difficulty concentrating, provide detailed day-to-day feedback to those who need greater structure in performing their jobs, or allow workers on antidepressants to come to work later if they are groggy in the morning.

It appears that courts may not be as accommodating of mental illness as the EEOC. In one case, for example, an engineer had been criticized for his "negative attitude." Later his supervisor warned him that he might be terminated if his behavior did not improve. He then told the company that the warning had caused him to be depressed, which, in turn, affected his ability to interact with other people. He asked, as a special accommodation, to be assigned to clerical work that did not require him to run meetings. The company fired him. Although EEOC guidelines state that interacting with others is a major life activity, the court held that it is not. Therefore the engineer was not disabled for purposes of the ADA.[33]

While lauding the ADA's objectives, many managers have been apprehensive about its impact on the workplace. Most acknowledge, however, that society is clearly better off if every member has the opportunity to work. And as advocates for the disabled point out, we are all, at best, only temporarily able-bodied. Even with the ADA, only 29 percent of the disabled population who are of working age are actually employed, while 79 percent of able-bodied persons have jobs.

When cases go to litigation, employers win more than 93 percent of the time. Workers are caught in something of a legal Catch-22: they must prove that they can perform the essential functions of the job, but they must also show that their disability limits a major life activity. In the following case, the Supreme Court takes a close look at the definition of "major life activity."

TOYOTA V. WILLIAMS

534 U.S. 184, 122 S. Ct. 681, 2002 U.S. LEXIS 400
United States Supreme Court, 2002

FACTS: Ella Williams worked in a Toyota manufacturing plant in Georgetown, Kentucky. Her job required her to use pneumatic tools. When her arms and hands began to hurt, she went to see a doctor who diagnosed her with carpal tunnel syndrome. He advised her to avoid using pneumatic tools or lifting more than 20 pounds. Toyota transferred Williams to a position in Quality Control Inspection Operations (QCIO). Employees in this department typically performed four different jobs, but Williams was initially assigned only two tasks. Toyota then changed its policy and required QCIO employees to rotate through all four jobs.

Williams began to perform the "shell body audit." After applying oil to the outside of cars, she visually inspected each car for flaws. To perform this task, she had to hold her hands and arms up around shoulder height for several hours at a time.

A short while after beginning this job, she began to experience pain in her neck and shoulders. She asked permission to perform only the two tasks that she could do without difficulty. Williams claimed that Toyota refused this request. Toyota said that Williams simply began missing work regularly. Ultimately, Williams's doctor told her she should not do any work of any kind. Toyota fired her.

When Williams sued Toyota, alleging that the company had violated the Americans with Disabilities Act, the district court granted summary judgment to Toyota on the grounds that Williams's impairments did not substantially limit any of her major life activities. The Court of Appeals for the Sixth Circuit reversed, finding that the impairments substantially limited Williams in the major life activity of performing manual tasks. The Supreme Court granted *certiorari*.

ISSUES: Was Williams disabled, within the terms of the Americans with Disabilities Act? Did Toyota violate the ADA?

---

[33] *Soileau v. Guildford of Maine*, 105 F.3d 12, 1997 U.S. App. LEXIS 1171 (1st Cir. 1997).

EXCERPTS FROM JUSTICE O'CONNOR'S DECISION, WRITING FOR A UNANIMOUS COURT: When it enacted the ADA in 1990, Congress found that some 43,000,000 Americans have one or more physical or mental disabilities. If Congress intended everyone with a physical impairment that precluded the performance of some isolated, unimportant, or particularly difficult manual task to qualify as disabled, the number of disabled Americans would surely have been much higher. We therefore hold that to be substantially limited in performing manual tasks, an individual must have an impairment that prevents or severely restricts the individual from doing activities that are of central importance to most people's daily lives. The impairment's impact must also be permanent or long-term.

When addressing the major life activity of performing manual tasks, the central inquiry must be whether the claimant is unable to perform the variety of tasks central to most people's daily lives, not whether the claimant is unable to perform the tasks associated with her specific job. In this case, "repetitive work with hands and arms extended at or above shoulder levels for extended periods of time" is not an important part of most people's daily lives. The court, therefore, should not have considered respondent's inability to do such manual work in her specialized assembly line job as sufficient proof that she was substantially limited in performing manual tasks.

[T]he Court of Appeals treated as irrelevant the fact that respondent can tend to her personal hygiene and carry out personal or household chores. Yet household chores, bathing, and brushing one's teeth are among the types of manual tasks of central importance to people's daily lives, and should have been part of the assessment of whether respondent was substantially limited in performing manual tasks.

The District Court noted that at the time respondent sought an accommodation from petitioner, she admitted that she was able to do the manual tasks required by her original two jobs in QCIO. In addition, even after her condition worsened, she could still brush her teeth, wash her face, bathe, tend her flower garden, fix breakfast, do laundry, and pick up around the house. The record also indicates that her medical conditions caused her to avoid sweeping, to quit dancing, to occasionally seek help dressing, and to reduce how often she plays with her children, gardens, and drives long distances. But these changes in her life did not amount to such severe restrictions in the activities that are of central importance to most people's daily lives that they establish a manual-task disability as a matter of law.

Accordingly, we reverse the Court of Appeals' judgment granting summary judgment to respondent and remand the case for further proceedings consistent with this opinion.

So ordered. ◢

Every applicant feels slightly apprehensive before a job interview, but now the interviewer may be even more nervous—fearing that every question is a potential land mine of liability. Most interviewers (and students who have read this chapter) would know better than Delta Airlines interviewers who allegedly asked applicants about their sexual preference, birth control methods, and abortion history. The following list provides guidelines for interviewers.

Don't Even Consider Asking	Go Ahead and Ask
Can you perform this function with or without reasonable accommodation?	Would you need reasonable accommodation in this job?
How many days were you sick last year?	How many days were you absent from work last year?
What medications are you currently taking?	Are you currently using drugs illegally?

Where were you born? Are you a United States citizen?	Are you authorized to work in the United States?
How old are you?	What work experience have you had?
How tall are you? How much do you weigh?	Could you carry a 100-pound weight, as required by this job?
When did you graduate from college?	Where did you go to college?
How did you learn this language?	What languages do you speak and write fluently?
Have you ever been arrested?	Have you ever been convicted of a crime that would affect the performance of this job?
Do you plan to have children? How old are your children? What method of birth control do you use?	Can you work weekends? Travel extensively? Would you be willing to relocate?
What is your corrected vision?	Do you have 20/20 corrected vision?
Are you a man or a woman? Are you single or married? What does your spouse do? What will happen if your spouse is transferred? What clubs, societies, or lodges do you belong to?	Leave well enough alone!

The most common gaffe on the part of interviewers? Asking women about their child-care arrangements. That question assumes the woman is responsible for child care. ▪

Chapter Conclusion

Although managers sometimes feel overwhelmed by the long list of laws that protect workers, the United States guarantees its workers fewer rights than virtually any other industrialized nation. For example, Japan, Great Britain, France, Germany, and Canada all require employers to show just cause before terminating workers. Although American employers are no longer insulated from minimum standards of fairness, reasonable behavior, and compliance with important policies, they still have great freedom to manage their employees.

Chapter Review

1. The traditional common law rule of employment provided that an employee at will could be fired for a good reason, a bad reason, or no reason at all.

2. The National Labor Relations Act (NLRA) prohibits employers from penalizing workers for union activity.

3. The Family and Medical Leave Act (FMLA) guarantees workers up to 12 weeks of unpaid leave each year for childbirth, adoption, or medical emergencies for themselves or a family member.

4. An employer who fires a worker for a *bad* reason is liable under a theory of wrongful discharge.

5. Generally, an employee may not be fired for refusing to break the law, exercising a legal right, or performing a legal duty.

6. Whistleblowers receive some protection under both federal and state laws.

7. Oral promises made during the hiring process may be enforceable, even if not approved by the company's top executives. An employee handbook may create a contract.

8. Employers may be liable for defamation if they give false and unfavorable references.

9. The goal of the Occupational Safety and Health Act (OSHA) is to ensure safe conditions in the workplace.

10. Employees have a limited right to privacy in the workplace.

11. The Fair Labor Standards Act (FLSA) regulates minimum and overtime wages. It also limits child labor.

12. Workers' compensation statutes ensure that employees receive payment for injuries incurred at work.

13. The Social Security system pays benefits to workers who are retired, disabled, or temporarily unemployed and to the spouses and children of disabled or deceased workers.

14. The Employee Retirement Income Security Act (ERISA) regulates private pension plans.

15. Under the Equal Pay Act, an employee may not be paid at a lesser rate than employees of the opposite sex for equal work.

16. Title VII of the Civil Rights Act of 1964 prohibits employers from discriminating on the basis of race, color, religion, sex, or national origin.

17. The Age Discrimination in Employment Act (ADEA) prohibits age discrimination against employees or job applicants who are age 40 or older.

18. The Americans with Disabilities Act (ADA) prohibits employers from discriminating on the basis of disability.

Practice Test

1. When Theodore Staats went to his company's "Council of Honor Convention," he was accompanied by a woman who was not his wife although he told everyone she was. The company fired him. Staats alleged that his termination violated public policy because it infringed upon his freedom of association. He also alleged that he had been fired because he was too successful—his commissions were so high, he out-earned even the highest paid officer of the company. Has Staat's employer violated public policy?

2. This article appeared in *The Wall Street Journal*:

When Michelle Lawrence discovered she was pregnant, she avoided telling Ron Rogers, the owner of the Los Angeles public relations agency where she worked as manager of media relations. "I had heard he wasn't crazy about pregnant women," she says. Instead, she asked her immediate supervisor to pass along the news. Mr. Rogers didn't speak to her for a week. His first comment was, "Congratulations on your pregnancy. My sister vomited for months." A few weeks later, Ms. Lawrence was fired. Mr. Rogers told her the business was shifting away from her area of expertise.[34]

Does Lawrence have a valid claim against Rogers? Under what law?

---

[34] Sue Shellenbarger, "As More Pregnant Women Work, Bias Complaints Rise," *The Wall Street Journal*, Dec. 6, 1993, p. B1.

3. Reginald Delaney managed a Taco Time restaurant in Portland, Oregon. Some of his customers told Mr. Ledbetter, the district manager, that they would not be eating there so often because there were too many black employees. Ledbetter told Delaney to fire Ms. White, who was black. Delaney did as he was told. Ledbetter's report on the incident said: "My notes show that Delaney told me that White asked him to sleep with her and that when he would not that she started causing dissension within the crew. She asked him to come over to her house and that he declined." Delaney refused to sign the report because it was untrue, so Ledbetter fired him. What claim might Delaney make against his former employer?

4. When Walton Weiner interviewed for a job with McGraw-Hill, Inc., he was assured that the company would not terminate an employee without "just cause." Weiner also signed a contract specifying that his employment would be subject to the provisions of McGraw-Hill's handbook. The handbook said, "[The] company will resort to dismissal for just and sufficient cause only, and only after all practical steps toward rehabilitation or salvage of the employee have been taken and failed. However, if the welfare of the company indicates that dismissal is necessary, then that decision is arrived at and is carried out forthrightly." After eight years, Weiner was fired suddenly for "lack of application." Does Weiner have a valid claim against McGraw-Hill?

5. **ETHICS** John Mundorf hired three women to work for Gus Construction Co. as traffic controllers at road construction sites in Iowa. Male members of the construction crew incessantly referred to the women as "f—king flag girls." They repeatedly asked the women if they "wanted to f—k" or engage in oral sex. One crew member held a woman up to the cab window so other men could touch her. Another male employee exposed himself to the women. Male employees also urinated in a woman's water bottle and the gas tank of her car. Mundorf, the supervisor, was present during some of these incidents. He talked to crew members about their conduct, but the abuse continued until the women quit. What claim might the women make against their co-workers? Is Gus Construction Co. liable for the acts of its employees? What procedure must the women follow to pursue their claim? Why do you think these men behaved this way? Why did they want to humiliate their co-workers? What should the supervisor have done when he observed these incidents? What would you have done if you were the supervisor? A fellow employee?

6. **CPA QUESTION** An unemployed CPA generally would receive unemployment compensation benefits if the CPA:

   (a) Was fired as a result of the employer's business reversals

   (b) Refused to accept a job as an accountant while receiving extended benefits

   (c) Was fired for embezzling from a client

   (d) Left work voluntarily without good cause

7. Debra Agis worked in a Ground Round restaurant. The manager, Roger Dionne, informed the waitresses that "there was some stealing going on." Until he found out who was doing it, he intended to fire all the waitresses in alphabetical order, starting with the letter "A." Dionne then fired Agis. Does she have a valid claim against her employer?

8. The Duke Power Co. refused to transfer any employees at its generating plant to better jobs unless they had a high school diploma or could pass an intelligence test. The company was willing to pay two-thirds of the tuition for an employee's high school training. Neither a high school education nor the intelligence test was significantly related to successful job performance. Both requirements disqualified African Americans at a substantially higher rate than white applicants. Is the company in violation of Title VII?

9. The Lillie Rubin boutique in Phoenix would not permit Dick Kovacic to apply for a job as a salesperson. It only hired women to work in sales because fittings and alterations took place in the dressing room or immediately outside. The customers were buying expensive clothes

and demanded a male-free dressing area. Has the Lillie Rubin store violated Title VII? What would its defense be?

10. **YOU BE THE JUDGE WRITING PROBLEM** Nationwide Insurance Co. circulated a memorandum asking all employees to lobby in favor of a bill that had been introduced in the Pennsylvania House of Representatives. By limiting the damages that an injured motorist could recover from a person who caused an accident, this bill would have saved Nationwide significant money. Not only did John Novosel refuse to lobby, but he privately criticized the bill for harming consumers. Nationwide was definitely not on his side—it fired him. Novosel filed suit, alleging that his discharge had violated public policy by infringing his right to free speech. Did Nationwide violate public policy by firing Novosel? **Argument for Novosel:** The United States Constitution and the Pennsylvania Constitution both guarantee the right to free speech. Nationwide has violated an important public policy by firing Novosel for expressing his opinions. **Argument for Nationwide:** For all the high-flown talk about the Constitution, what we have here is an employee who refused to carry out company policy. If the employee prevails in this case, where will it all end? What if an employee for a tobacco company refuses to market cigarettes because he does not approve of smoking? How can businesses operate without loyalty from their employees?

11. When Thomas Lussier filled out a Postal Service employment application, he did not admit that he had twice pleaded guilty to charges of disorderly conduct. Lussier suffered from post-traumatic stress disorder (PTSD) acquired during military service in Vietnam. Because of this disorder, he sometimes had panic attacks that required him to leave meetings. He was also a recovered alcoholic and drug user. During his stint with the Postal Service, he had some personality conflicts with other employees. Once another employee hit him. He also had one episode of "erratic emotional behavior and verbal outburst." In the meantime a postal employee in Ridgewood, New Jersey, killed four colleagues. The Postmaster General encouraged all supervisors to identify workers who had dangerous propensities. Lussier's boss discovered that Lussier had lied on his employment application about the disorderly conduct charges and fired him. Is the Postal Service in violation of the law?

12. **ROLE REVERSAL** Write a short-answer question in which an employee alleges that his discharge violated public policy, but you think a court would not agree.

Internet Research Problem

Go to http://www.eeoc.gov/docs/accommodation.html. The EEOC offers advice on how to comply with some aspects of the Americans with Disabilities Act. Employers sometimes complain that the EEOC unfairly favors workers. What do you think of these EEOC guidelines? Are they fair and even-handed? As an employee, would you like your company to follow these guidelines? If you were in a supervisory role, would your view of these guidelines be different?

You can find further practice problems in the Online Quiz at http://beatty.westbuslaw.com **or in the Study Guide that accompanies this text.**

Labor Law

A strike! For five weeks the union workers have been walking picket lines at JMJ, a manufacturer of small electrical engines. An entire town of 70,000 citizens, most of them blue-collar workers, is sharply divided, right down to the McNally kitchen table. Buddy, age 48, has worked on the assembly lines at JMJ for more than 25 years. Now he's sipping coffee in the house where he grew up. His sister Kristina, age 46, is a vice president for personnel at JMJ. The two have always been close. In high school, Kristina idolized her older brother, the football and track star. Buddy was immensely proud of his kid sister's academic triumphs, boasting to the world that she would "be the first lady president." Today, though, conversation is halting.

"It's time to get back together, Buddy," Kristina murmurs. "The strike is hurting the whole company—and the town."

"Not the *whole* town, Kristina," he tries to quip lightly. "Your management pals still have fat incomes and nice houses."

"Oh yeah?" she attempts to joke, "you haven't seen our porch lately."

"Go talk to Tony Falcione," Buddy replies. "He can't pay his rent."

"Talk to the Ericksons," Kristina snaps back, "they don't even work for JMJ. Their sandwich shop is going under because none of you guys stop in for lunch. Come back to work."

"Not with that clause on the table."

That clause is management's proposal for the new union contract—one that Kristina helped draft. The company officers want the right to subcontract work, that is, to send it out for other companies to perform.

"Buddy, we need the flexibility. K-Ball is underselling us by 35 percent. If we can't compete, there won't be *any* jobs or *any* contract!"

"The way to save money is not by sending our jobs overseas, where a bunch of foreigners will work for 50 bucks a month."

"OK, fine. Tell me how we *should* save money."

"Kristina, I really do not know how you can sit at this table and say these things—in this household. You never would have got a fancy college degree if Dad hadn't made union wages."

"If we can't sell motors to Latin America, we're out of business. *Then* what's your union going to do for you? All we're asking is the right to subcontract some of the smallest components. Everything else gets built here."

"This is just the start. Next it'll be the wiring, then the batteries, then you'll assemble the whole thing over there—and that'll be it for me. You take that clause off the table, we'll be back in 15 minutes."

"Never."

Buddy stands up. They stare silently, sadly, at each other, and then Kristina says, in a barely audible voice, "I have to tell you this. My boss is starting to talk about hiring replacement workers." Buddy walks out. ◾

Some Americans revere unions, believing that organized labor has pulled the working class up from poverty and shielded it from exploitative management. Others loathe organized labor, convinced that unions foment mindless conflicts, decrease productivity, increase costs, and harm corporations and the economy generally. Why do unions exist?

Unions Develop . . . and the Law Responds

During the nineteenth century, as industrialization spread across America, workers found employment conditions increasingly unbearable and wages inadequate. Here is a contemporary account of mining in the American West:

> View their work! Descending from the surface in the shaft-cages, they enter narrow galleries where the air is scarce respirable. By the dim light of their lanterns a dingy rock surface, braced by rotting props, is visible. The stenches of decaying vegetable matter, hot foul water, and human excretions intensify the effects of the heat. The men throw off their clothes at once. Only a light breech-cloth covers their hips, and thick-soled

shoes protect their feet from the scorching rocks and steaming rills of water that trickle over the floor. Except for these coverings they toil naked, with heavy drops of sweat starting from every pore.[1]

Temperatures in the mines were well over 100 degrees. Miners drank more than three gallons of water every day. Some suddenly collapsed, with swollen veins, purple faces, and glazed eyes. Within minutes they were dead, but even before they died, their places in the mine were taken by other workers desperate for pay.

Conditions were equally oppressive in the new factories back east. Workers, often women and sometimes children, worked 60 to 70 hours per week and sometimes more, standing at assembly lines in suffocating, dimly lit factories, performing monotonous yet dangerous work with heavy machinery. A visitor to a factory in Lowell, Massachusetts, in 1855 was shocked by the degrading conditions and the exhausting hours required of all workers.

> I inquired of the agent of a principal factory whether it was the custom of the manufacturers to do anything for the physical, intellectual, and moral welfare of their work-people. "We never do," he said. "As for myself, I regard my work-people just as I regard my machinery. So long as they can do my work for what I choose to pay them, I keep them, getting out of them all I can. What they do or how they fare outside my walls I don't know, nor do I consider it my business to know. When my machines get old and useless, I reject them and get new, and these people are part of my machinery."[2]

Because of the intolerable conditions and impoverishing wages, workers began to band together into unions. But early in the nineteenth century, American courts regarded any coordinated effort by workers as a criminal conspiracy. Courts convicted workers merely for the *act of joining together*, even if no strike took place. In 1842 the Massachusetts high court became the first to reject this use of the criminal law. The court ruled that workers could join together for legitimate economic goals; their efforts would become criminal only if the workers used illegal means to achieve them.[3] Other courts came to agree, and so management resorted to the civil law to curtail unions.

In 1890 Congress passed the Sherman Act to outlaw monopolies.[4] For the next 40 years, courts relied on this statute to issue anti-strike injunctions, declaring that strikes illegally restrained trade. A company could usually obtain an immediate injunction merely by alleging that a strike *might* cause harm. Courts were so quick to issue injunctions that most companies became immune to union efforts. But with the economic collapse of 1929 and the vast suffering of the Great Depression, public sympathy shifted to the workers. Congress responded with the first of several landmark statutes.

In 1932 Congress passed the **Norris-LaGuardia Act**, which prohibited federal court injunctions in nonviolent labor disputes. No longer could management obtain an injunction merely by mentioning the word "strike." By taking away the injunction remedy, Congress was declaring that workers should be permitted to

---

[1] Eliot Lord, *Comstock Mining and Miners* (Washington: G.P.O., 1883), p. 386, *quoted in* Richard E. Lingenfelter, *The Hardrock Miners* (Berkeley: University of California Press, 1974), p. 13.

[2] Massachusetts Senate Dock. no. 21, 1868, p. 23, *quoted in* Norman Ware, *The Industrial Worker* (Chicago: Quadrangle Books, 1964), p. 77.

[3] *Commonwealth v. Hunt*, 45 Mass. 111, 4 Met. 111 (1842).

[4] See Chapter 19, on antitrust law.

organize unions and to use their collective power to achieve legitimate economic ends. The statute led to explosive growth in union membership.

In 1935 Congress passed the Wagner Act, generally known as the **National Labor Relations Act (NLRA)**. This is the most important of all labor laws. A fundamental aim of the NLRA is the establishment and maintenance of industrial peace, to preserve the flow of commerce. The NLRA ensures the right of workers to form unions and encourages management and unions to bargain collectively and productively. For our purposes, Sections 7 and 8 of the NLRA are the most important.

Section 7 guarantees employees the right to organize and join unions, bargain collectively through representatives of their own choosing, and engage in other concerted activities. This is the cornerstone of union power. With the enactment of the NLRA, Congress put an end to any notion that unions were criminal or inherently illegal by explicitly recognizing that workers could join together and bargain as a group, using their collective power to seek better conditions. Section 8 reinforces these rights by outlawing *unfair labor practices*.

Section 8(a) makes it an unfair labor practice (ULP) for an employer:

- To interfere with union organizing efforts

- To dominate or interfere with any union

- To discriminate against a union member, or

- To refuse to bargain collectively with a union.

The NLRA also established the **National Labor Relations Board (NLRB)** to administer and interpret the statute and to adjudicate labor cases. For example, when a union charges that an employer has committed an unfair labor practice—say, by refusing to bargain—the ULP charge goes first to the NLRB.

The NLRB has two primary tasks:

- *Representation*. The Board decides whether a particular union is entitled to represent a group of employees.

- *Unfair Labor Practices*. The Board adjudicates claims by either the employer or workers that the other side has committed a ULP.

To accomplish these tasks, the NLRB has several divisions. Although the agency is headquartered in Washington, D.C., it performs the greatest volume of its work in local offices. **Regional offices**, each headed by a regional director, are located throughout the country. These local offices handle most ULP claims. The General Counsel, a staff of lawyers, investigates such claims. If the General Counsel's office believes that a party has committed a ULP, it prosecutes the case before an administrative law judge (ALJ).

The **Board** itself, which sits in Washington, D.C., has five members, all appointed by the president. The Board makes final agency decisions about representation and ULP cases. But note that the Board has no power to *enforce* its orders. If it is evident that the losing party will not comply, the Board must petition a federal appeals court to enforce the order. Typically, the steps resulting in an appeal follow this pattern: the Board issues a decision, for example, finding that a company has unfairly refused to bargain with a union. The Board orders the company to bargain. The Board then appeals to the United States Court of Appeals to enforce its order, and the company *cross-appeals*, requesting the court not to enforce the Board's order. (The NLRB describes its mission and methods at http://www.nlrb.gov/.)

Throughout the 1930s and 1940s, unions grew in size and power. As strikes became more common, employers complained loudly of union abuse. Unions coerced unwilling workers to join and engaged in *secondary boycotts*, picketing an innocent company to stop it from doing business with an employer the union was fighting. In 1947 Congress responded with the Taft-Hartley Act, also known as the **Labor-Management Relations Act**, designed to curb union abuses. The statute amended Section 8 of the NLRA to outlaw certain unfair labor practices *by unions*.

Section 8(b) makes it an unfair labor practice for a union:

- To interfere with employees who are exercising their labor rights under Section 7

- To encourage an employer to discriminate against a particular employee because of a union dispute

- To refuse to bargain collectively, or

- To engage in an illegal strike or boycott, particularly secondary boycotts.

Finally, in the 1950s the public became aware that certain labor leaders were corrupt. Some officers stole money from large union treasuries, rigged union elections, and stifled opposition within the organization. In response, in 1959 Congress passed the Landrum-Griffin Act, generally called the **Labor-Management Reporting and Disclosure Act (LMRDA)**. The LMRDA requires union leadership to make certain financial disclosures and guarantees free speech and fair elections within a union.

These landmark federal labor laws are outlined below:

Four Key Labor Statutes	
Norris–LaGuardia Act (1932)	Prohibits federal court injunctions in peaceful strikes.
National Labor Relations Act (1935)	Guarantees workers' right to organize unions and bargain collectively. Prohibits an employer from interfering with union organizing or discriminating against union members. Requires an employer to bargain collectively.
Labor-Management Relations Act (1947)	Prohibits union abuses such as coercing employees to join. Outlaws secondary boycotts.
Labor-Management Reporting and Disclosure Act (1959)	Requires financial disclosures by union leadership. Guarantees union members free speech and fair elections.

NEWSWORTHY

Today, labor abuses are less visible—but as ugly as ever. From New York City to Los Angeles, desperately poor, frightened immigrants cut and sew about half of all the garments this country produces, often working in appalling sweatshops where conditions are little better than in nineteenth-century factories. Frequently, the employees are undocumented immigrants who speak no English, know nothing of their rights, and fear that any complaints they make will lead to deportation. Exploitative owners force the workers to toil 50 to 60 hours a week with few breaks in cramped rooms with weak lighting, no ventilation, and inadequate sanitation. Pay is below the minimum wage—and vicious bosses often steal the small

amounts they promised. For a report on sweatshops in the United States, see
http://www.uniteunion.org/sweatshops/sweatshop.html.

STATE LABOR LAW

All states have labor statutes. Some are comprehensive, while others focus on narrow issues. For example, certain states prohibit particular kinds of picketing, while many states outlaw strikes by public employees. A court enforces a state statute when no federal law applies. In general, when a federal law such as the NLRA does apply, it controls the outcome. This is the doctrine of *preemption*, discussed in Chapter 5, on constitutional law. **Preemption: states have no jurisdiction to regulate any labor issue that is governed by federal law.**

In this chapter, we look principally at federal law because it is uniform and because it controls the most fundamental issues of labor policy.

LABOR UNIONS TODAY

Organized labor is shrinking in the United States. In the 1950s about 25 percent of the workforce belonged to a union. Today, only about 13.5 percent of all workers are union members. Employers point to this figure with satisfaction and claim that it shows that unions have failed their memberships. In an increasingly high-tech, service-oriented economy, employers argue, there is no place for organized labor. Union supporters respond that although the country has shed many old factories, workers have not benefited. Throughout the last 20 years, they assert, compensation for executives has soared into the stratosphere, with many CEOs earning several *million* dollars per year, while wages for the average worker, in real dollars, have fallen for two decades.

Whether organized labor is disappearing from the United States or is only retreating temporarily, labor law still affects many. About 16 million workers are union members. The largest unions are national in scope, with hundreds of affiliated **locals** throughout the country. A local is the regional union, which represents workers at a particular company. For example, over 2.2 million teachers belong to the National Education Association, with thousands of locals spread throughout the nation.

Unions are much more common in government offices than private companies. About 37 percent of public workers are organized, while only 9 percent of private employees belong to a union. Full-time workers who are union members average earnings of $718 per week, compared to $575 for their nonunionized counterparts. Union membership is highest in the Northeastern, North Central, and Pacific states, and lowest in the South. Half of all union members live in just six states: California, New York, Illinois, Michigan, Ohio, and Pennsylvania. (For the most recent union statistics, work your way to the Bureau of Labor Statistics Web site, at http://www.bls.gov/.)

Organizing a Union

EXCLUSIVITY

It is difficult to organize a union. When a worker starts to talk about collective action, or when an organizer appears from a national union, many employees are suspicious or fearful; some may be hostile. Management will generally be opposed—sometimes fiercely opposed—to any union organizing effort. The fight can become ugly, and all because of one principle: *exclusivity*.

Under Section 9 of the NLRA, a validly recognized union is the exclusive representative of the employees. This means that the union will represent all of the designated employees, regardless of whether a particular worker *wants* to be represented. The company may not bargain directly with any employee in the group, nor with any other organization representing the designated employees.

A collective bargaining unit is the precisely defined group of employees who will be represented by a particular union. Suppose a hotel workers' union attempts to organize the Excelsior Hotel. The union will seek to represent some of Excelsior's employees, but not all. The union may represent, for example, all maids, porters, and bellhops. Those employees are in the collective bargaining unit. Many other people who work for the hotel will *not* be in the collective bargaining unit. Managers who run the hotel, reservation agents who work in other cities, launderers who work in separate facilities for a different employer—all of these people are *outside* the collective bargaining unit and will be unaffected by the union's bargaining.

It is the union's *exclusive* right to bargain for the unit that gives the organization its power. But some employees may be unhappy with the way a union exercises this power. In the following case, workers believed the union was failing to represent them on a vital issue. Should they be allowed to bargain on their own behalf? You be the judge.

YOU BE THE JUDGE

EMPORIUM CAPWELL CO. V. WESTERN ADDITIONAL COMMUNITY ORGANIZATION

420 U.S. 50, 95 S. Ct. 977, 1975 U.S. LEXIS 134
United States Supreme Court, 1975

FACTS: Emporium Capwell operated a department store in San Francisco. The Department Store Employees Union represented all stock workers. Several black union members complained to the union about racial discrimination in promotions, asserting that highly qualified black workers were routinely passed over in favor of less qualified whites. The union promised to pursue the issue with management, but the black employees were not satisfied with the union's effort. The unhappy workers demanded to speak with top management of the store and then, without the union's permission, picketed the store and handed out leaflets accusing the company of discrimination. Emporium Capwell fired the picketing employees. The resulting case went all the way to the Supreme Court.

In most labor cases, the union is on one side and management is on the other. In this case, the black employees were on one side, with the union on the other. The union argued that exclusivity prohibited any group of workers from demanding to meet separately with management. It claimed that the disgruntled workers violated the NLRA by insisting on separate bargaining, and that it was proper for the company to fire the workers. In other words, the union placed a higher value on exclusivity than on maintaining the jobs of those employees. The black workers, on the other hand, argued that eliminating discrimination was more important than union exclusivity. They insisted that management had no right to fire them and that they were entitled to get their jobs back and to bargain independently.

YOU BE THE JUDGE: Did the picketing employees violate the NLRA by demanding to bargain directly with management?

ARGUMENT FOR THE UNION: Your honors, exclusivity is the core of a union's strength. If management is free to talk with employees individually—or if it can be *compelled* to talk with them—the union has no leverage. An astute manager will quickly use worker conflicts as a tool to divide the union and destroy it. By cutting deals with favored employees, management could demonstrate to all workers that affiliation with the union is a losing tactic, and that the smart worker bargains for himself—and then does what management tells him to do.

Racial discrimination is a terrible evil. It must be eradicated from the workplace. This union is committed to fighting prejudice. But the union must do it *collectively*. If an exception to the principle of exclusivity can be carved out for one important issue, such as race discrimination, then an exception can be carved out for other important issues, such as gender bias, age discrimination, language differences, retirement pay, health benefits . . . and on and on. To allow this group of picketers to pursue a worthy goal with separate bargaining would be to destroy the union—and ensure that no valuable goals are obtained.

ARGUMENT FOR THE PICKETING WORKERS: Congress granted employees the right to organize *for their mutual benefit*, not to advance the cause of unions. A labor organization is a means to an end, not an end in itself. When a union fails to support its members on a vital issue, employees must be free to fend for themselves. Race discrimination is not a simple bargaining issue like retirement benefits; it is a vital matter of human dignity. This union failed to act promptly and vigorously to protect its black members and end discrimination. Why should those employees now be shackled to an organization that has failed them?

It makes no difference *why* the union failed to protect its members. Weak-kneed, docile union leadership can be just as devastating to the cause of racial equality as bad faith. We are not asking that union members be free to pursue every petty complaint directly with management. To equate racial justice with retirement benefits is to ignore the singular evil of discrimination. We merely ask that, when a union fails to protect its members concerning a profound issue such as this, the injured employees be allowed to speak for themselves. ▌

ORGANIZING

A union organizing effort generally involves the following pattern.

Campaign

Union organizers talk with employees—or attempt to talk—and interest them in forming a union. The organizers may be employees of the company, who simply chat with fellow workers about unsatisfactory conditions. Or a union may send nonemployees of the company to hand out union leaflets to workers as they arrive and depart from the factory.

Authorization Cards

Union organizers ask workers to sign authorization cards, which state that the particular worker requests the specified union to act as her sole bargaining representative.

Recognition

If a union obtains authorization cards from a sizable percentage of workers, it seeks **recognition** as the exclusive representative for the bargaining unit. The union may ask the employer to recognize it as the bargaining representative, but most of the time employers refuse to recognize the union voluntarily. The NLRA permits an employer to refuse recognition.

Petition

Assuming that the employer does not voluntarily recognize a union, the union generally petitions the NLRB for an election. It must submit to the NLRB regional office authorization cards signed by at least 30 percent of the workers. The regional office verifies whether there are enough valid cards to warrant an election and looks closely at the proposed bargaining unit to make sure that it is appropriate. If the regional director determines that the union has identified an appropriate bargaining unit and has enough valid cards, it orders an election.

Election

The NLRB closely supervises the election to ensure fairness. All members of the proposed bargaining unit vote on whether they want the union to represent them. If more than 50 percent of the workers vote for the union, the NLRB designates that union as the exclusive representative of all members of the bargaining unit. When unions hold representation elections in private corporations, they win about half the time. Labor organizations claim that management typically uses paid company time to campaign against the union. Employers respond that labor loses elections because workers fear that a union will hurt them, not help. Among public employers, unions generally do much better, winning about 85 percent of representation campaigns. Public employers often do not campaign against the union.

These are some of the issues that most commonly arise during an organizing effort: (1) What may a union do during its organizing campaign? (2) What may the employer do to defeat the campaign? (3) What is an appropriate bargaining unit?

WHAT WORKERS MAY DO

The NLRA guarantees employees the right to talk among themselves about forming a union, to hand out literature, and ultimately to join a union.[5] Workers may urge other employees to sign authorization cards and may vigorously push their cause. When employees hand out leaflets, the employer generally may not limit the content. In one case a union distributed leaflets urging workers to vote against political candidates who opposed minimum wage laws. The employer objected to the union using company property to distribute the information, but the Supreme Court upheld the union's right. Even though the content of the writing was not directly related to the union, the connection was close enough that the NLRA protected the union's activity.[6]

There are, of course, limits to what union organizers may do. The statute permits an employer to restrict organizing discussions if they interfere with discipline

---

[5] NLRA §7.
[6] *Eastex, Inc. v. NLRB*, 434 U.S. 1045, 98 S. Ct. 888, 1978 U.S. LEXIS 547 (1978).

or production. A worker on a moving assembly line has no right to walk away from his task to talk with other employees about organizing a union; the employer may insist that the worker stay at his job and leave discussions until lunch or some other break.[7]

WHAT EMPLOYERS MAY DO

As mentioned above, an employer may prohibit employees from organizing if the efforts interfere with the company's work. In a retail store, for example, management may prohibit union discussions in the presence of customers, because the discussions could harm business.

May the employer speak out against a union organizing drive? Yes. Management is entitled to communicate to the employees why it believes a union will be harmful to the company. But the employer's efforts must be limited to explanation and advocacy. **The employer may vigorously present anti-union views to its employees, but may not use either threats or promises of benefits to defeat a union drive.**[8] Notice that the employer is prohibited not only from threatening reprisals, such as firing a worker who favors the union, but also from offering benefits designed to defeat the union. A company that has vigorously rejected employee demands for higher wages may not suddenly grant a 10 percent pay increase in the midst of a union campaign.

It is an unfair labor practice for an employer to interfere with a union organizing effort. Normally, a union claiming such interference will file a ULP charge. If the Board upholds the union's claim, it will order the employer to stop its interference and permit a fair election. In some cases, though, management's interference is so pervasive and intrusive that the Board may conclude an election would be pointless. **When an employer outrageously interferes with a union organizing campaign, the NLRB may forgo the normal election, certify the union as the exclusive representative, and order the company to bargain.** This *bargaining order* is an extreme measure, and the Board uses it only when an employer has shown extreme anti-union animus. In the following case, the union contended that the employer had done just that.

NLRB AND UNION OF NEEDLETRADES INDUSTRIAL AND TEXTILE EMPLOYEES, LOCAL 76 V. INTERSWEET, INC.

125 F.3d 1064, 1997 U.S. App. LEXIS 25240
United States Court of Appeals for the Seventh Circuit, 1997

FACTS: Intersweet, Inc., manufactured sugar wafers, but conditions in the plant had gone sour. The Needletrades Union conducted three organizational meetings, and 19 of the company's 31 employees signed union representation cards. Later that same month, Intersweet's owner, Julius Meerbaum, suddenly fired all employees. The next day, he recalled 10 of the 31 workers. Eight of the 10 had not signed union cards and the others *claimed* they had not. Meerbaum required the rehired employees to work 50 to 60 hours per week, instead of the normal 40. Workers overheard company supervisors say that no one active in the union would ever be rehired.

---

[7] *NLRB v. Babcock & Wilcox Co.,* 351 U.S. 105, 76 S. Ct. 679, 1956 U.S. LEXIS 1721 (1956).

[8] *NLRB v. Gissel Packing Co.,* 395 U.S. 575, 89 S. Ct. 1918, 1969 U.S. LEXIS 3172 (1969).

802- 386-6882

An administrative law judge ruled that the company had committed outrageous unfair labor practices and ordered the company to bargain with the union, without an election. The NLRB petitioned the court of appeals to enforce its order.

ISSUE: Was the NLRB's order to bargain justified?

EXCERPTS FROM JUDGE ROVNER'S DECISION:
Between the time of the mass terminations and the imposition of the [bargaining] order, Julius Meerbaum, who had been responsible for the shutdown of the plant in 1993, passed away. Intersweet argues that Julius' death obviated the need for the bargaining order by removing any lingering impact of the unfair practices for which he was responsible. Although Julius Meerbaum had passed away, three members of Intersweet's previous management staff, John Meerbaum, Jose Diaz and David Sabin were still running the company. Thus, aside from the fact that Julius was gone, Intersweet's management had not meaningfully changed, and the company was still controlled by the Meerbaum family. In fact, because the individuals that were still present had been responsible for implementing Julius' directive to shut down the plant, the Board found that they may be more closely associated with the terminations than Julius himself, whose involvement was remote and perhaps even unknown to the workers.

The Board did not abuse its discretion in determining that the change in circumstances did not alleviate the need for a bargaining order. Intersweet discharged its entire workforce, rehired only those employees that it believed had not signed union cards, and then openly disclosed to returning employees that the terminations were related to union affiliation. It is difficult to imagine a more egregious attempt to defeat unionization. The management team responsible for these practices remained essentially intact, and there is no reason to believe that the workforce, although expanded, would not continue to be chilled by the earlier actions. The Board considered each of Intersweet's arguments and rejected them in a well-reasoned opinion. We find no abuse of discretion, and the Board's petition for enforcement of its order is GRANTED. ◢

Unlike the company in the *Intersweet* case, the employer in the following dispute admitted a glaring violation of labor law, yet claimed it should pay no damages because the injured worker was in the country illegally.

HOFFMAN PLASTIC COMPOUNDS, INC. V. NATIONAL LABOR RELATIONS BOARD

122 S. Ct. 1275, 152 L. Ed. 2d 271
United States Supreme Court, 2002

FACTS: The United Rubber, Cork, Linoleum and Plastic Workers of America began an organizing campaign at Hoffman Plastic Compounds, Inc. (Hoffman). Jose Castro and others supported this effort and, in retaliation, Hoffman fired them. Several years later (labor cases move very slowly), during hearings concerning his termination, Castro revealed for the first time that he was illegally in the United States. He had used false documents to obtain the job at Hoffman. Despite his illegal status, the NLRB found that Hoffman's retaliatory firing violated the NLRA and ordered the company to pay Castro $66,951, representing backpay from the date of firing until the employer learned that he was ineligible to work. The company appealed and the issue reached the United States Supreme Court.

ISSUE: May an employer who has fired a worker for union organizing be ordered to pay back wages when the employee was illegally in the country?

EXCERPTS FROM MR. CHIEF JUSTICE REHNQUIST'S DECISION: Under the [Immigration Reform and Control Act (IRCA), which regulates immigration into the United States], it is impossible for an undocumented alien to obtain employment in the United States without some party directly contravening explicit congressional policies. Either the

undocumented alien tenders fraudulent identification, which subverts the cornerstone of IRCA's enforcement mechanism, or the employer knowingly hires the undocumented alien in direct contradiction of its IRCA obligations. The Board asks that we overlook this fact and allow it to award backpay to an illegal alien for years of work not performed, for wages that could not lawfully have been earned, and for a job obtained in the first instance by a criminal fraud. We find, however, that awarding backpay to illegal aliens runs counter to policies underlying IRCA, policies the Board has no authority to enforce or administer. Therefore, as we have consistently held in like circumstances, the award lies beyond the bounds of the Board's remedial discretion.

The Board contends that awarding limited backpay to Castro "reasonably accommodates" IRCA, because, in the Board's view, such an award is not "inconsistent" with IRCA. The Board argues that because the backpay period was closed as of the date Hoffman learned of Castro's illegal status, Hoffman could have employed Castro during the backpay period without violating IRCA. The Board further argues that while IRCA criminalized the misuse of documents, "it did not make violators ineligible for backpay awards or other compensation flowing from employment secured by the misuse of such documents." This latter statement, of course, proves little. What matters here, and what sinks both of the Board's claims, is that Congress has expressly made it criminally punishable for an alien to obtain employment with false documents. There is no reason to think that Congress nonetheless intended to permit backpay where but for an employer's unfair labor practices, an alien-employee would have remained in the United States illegally, and continued to work illegally, all the while successfully evading apprehension by immigration authorities. Far from "accommodating" IRCA, the Board's position, recognizing employer misconduct but discounting the misconduct of illegal alien employees, subverts it.

[The NLRB's ruling is reversed.]

EXCERPTS FROM JUSTICE BREYER'S DISSENT: The Court does not deny that the employer in this case dismissed an employee for trying to organize a union—a crude and obvious violation of the labor laws. And it cannot deny that the Board has especially broad discretion in choosing an appropriate remedy for addressing such violations. Nor can it deny that in such circumstances backpay awards serve critically important remedial purposes. Those purposes involve more than victim compensation; they also include deterrence, *i.e.*, discouraging employers from violating the Nation's labor laws.

[Denying backpay] lowers the cost to the employer of an initial labor law violation (provided, of course, that the only victims are illegal aliens). It thereby increases the employer's incentive to find and to hire illegal-alien employees. Were the Board forbidden to assess backpay against a *knowing* employer—a circumstance not before us today—this perverse economic incentive, which runs directly contrary to the immigration statute's basic objective, would be obvious and serious. But even if limited to cases where the employer did not know of the employee's status, the incentive may prove significant—for, as the Board has told us, the Court's rule offers employers immunity in borderline cases, thereby encouraging them to take risks, *i.e.*, to hire with a wink and a nod those potentially unlawful aliens whose unlawful employment (given the Court's views) ultimately will lower the costs of labor law violations. ◢

Appropriate Bargaining Unit

When a union petitions the NLRB for an election, the Board determines whether the proposed bargaining unit is appropriate. **The Board generally certifies a proposed bargaining unit if and only if the employees share a community of interest.** Employers frequently assert that the bargaining unit is inappropriate. If the Board agrees with the employer and rejects the proposed bargaining unit, it dismisses the union's request for an election. The Board pays particular attention to two kinds of employees: managerial and confidential.

Managerial employees must be excluded from the bargaining unit.[9] An employee is managerial if she is so closely aligned with management that her membership in the bargaining unit would create a conflict of interest between her union membership and her actual work. Courts generally find such a conflict only *if the employee is substantially involved in the employer's labor policy.*

For example, a factory worker who spends one-third of his time performing assembly work but two-thirds of his time supervising a dozen other workers is so closely aligned with management that he could not fairly be part of the bargaining unit. There would be constant tension between his supervisory work and his advocacy on behalf of the union. By contrast, an engineer who analyzes production methods and merely reports her findings to management may not be closely aligned with the employer. Unless the engineer has actual control over personnel decisions, she can probably be included in a bargaining unit of other engineers.[10]

Confidential employees are generally excluded from the bargaining unit.[11] A confidential employee is one who works so closely with executives or other management employees that there would be a conflict of interest if the employee were in the bargaining unit. An executive secretary may be so intimately acquainted with her boss's ideas, plans, and other confidential information that it would be unfair to allow her to join a bargaining unit of other secretaries.

Once the Board has excluded managerial and confidential employees, it looks at various criteria to decide whether the remaining employees should logically be grouped in one bargaining unit, that is, whether they share a **community of interest**. The Board looks for:

- Rough equality of pay and benefits, and methods of computing both

- Similar total hours per week and type of work

- Similar skills and training, and

- Previous bargaining history and the number of authorization cards from any different groups within the unit.

Having applied these criteria to all members of the proposed unit, the Board either certifies the bargaining unit or rejects the unit and dismisses the union's petition. Suppose the employees in a public high school decide to organize. The Board will probably find that an appropriate bargaining unit includes all academic teachers and physical education teachers because they do roughly similar work and are paid similarly. The principal and vice principal will not be included in the unit because their work is supervisory and administrative and they are paid on a separate scale.

Collective Bargaining

The goal of bargaining is a contract, which is called a **collective bargaining agreement (CBA)**. As mentioned earlier, Congress passed the NLRA to foster industrial peace, and a CBA is designed to do that. But problems arise as union and

---

9   *NLRB v. Bell Aerospace Co., Div. of Textron, Inc.,* 416 U.S. 267, 94 S. Ct. 1757, 1974 U.S. LEXIS 35 (1974).a

10 See, e.g., *NLRB v. Case Corp.,* 995 F.2d 700, 1993 U.S. App. LEXIS 13246 (7th Cir. 1993).

11 *Ibid.*

employer advocate their respective positions. Three of the most common conflicts are (1) whether an issue is a mandatory subject of bargaining, (2) whether the parties are bargaining in good faith, and (3) how to enforce the agreement. For a Web site devoted to articles and reports on collective bargaining, see http://www.ilr .cornell.edu/depts/ICB/.

SUBJECTS OF BARGAINING

The NLRA *permits* the parties to bargain almost any subject they wish, but *requires* them to bargain certain issues. **Mandatory subjects include wages, hours, and other terms and conditions of employment.** Either side may propose to bargain *other* subjects, but neither side may insist upon bargaining them.

Management and unions often disagree as to whether a particular topic is mandatory or not. Typically, unions attempt to expand the number of mandatory subjects, seeking more input into a greater number of issues, while the company argues that subjects are not mandatory and are none of the union's business. In general, a court is likely to find a given issue mandatory when it *directly relates* to individual workers; when a subject only indirectly affects employees, it is likely to be found not mandatory. In passing the NLRA, Congress never intended a union negotiator to become an equal partner in running the business.

Courts generally find these subjects to be mandatory: pay, benefits, order of layoffs and recalls, production quotas, work rules (such as safety practices), retirement benefits, and in-plant food service and prices (e.g., cafeteria food). Courts usually consider these subjects to be nonmandatory: product type and design, advertising, sales, financing, corporate organization, and location of plants.

Today, some of the angriest disputes between management and labor arise from a company's desire to subcontract work and/or to move plants to areas with cheaper costs. **Subcontracting** means that a manufacturer, rather than producing all parts of a product and then assembling them, contracts for other companies, frequently overseas, to make some of the parts. Is a business free to subcontract work? That depends on management's motive. **A company that subcontracts in order to maintain its economic viability is probably *not* required to bargain first; however, bargaining *is* mandatory if the subcontracting is designed to replace union workers with cheaper labor.**

Dorsey Trailers manufactured dump trucks. During a period of heavy sales, Dorsey subcontracted some of its production work to Bankhead Enterprises, which agreed to manufacture two trucks per week and split the profits. The union filed a ULP charge, claiming that subcontracting was a mandatory subject of bargaining, and that Dorsey had no right to make the deal before negotiating with the union.

The court noted that Dorsey was losing business because it could not fill orders fast enough. The dump truck industry was cyclical, and in a period of strong demand, the company had to be able to manufacture its goods quickly. Dorsey had been unable to hire enough welders and other skilled workers to keep up with demand. The court stated that Dorsey could not survive without the subcontracting. Further, the company had not reduced union jobs; it had simply failed to add more union workers—through no fault of its own. Dorsey was free to subcontract without bargaining the issue.[12]

---

[12] *Dorsey Trailers, Inc. Northumberland PA Plant v. NLRB*, 134 F.3d 125, 1998 U.S. App. LEXIS 764 (3rd. Cir. 1998).

Plant closings, which can result in hundreds or thousands of lost jobs, are also a volatile issue. Although the job losses are potentially greater than those that result from subcontracting, management is not obligated to bargain such a decision. **An employer is not required to bargain over the closing of a plant, only the** *effects* **of the closing.**[13]

The reasoning behind this rule is basic: the company that opened a plant ought to be able to close it. The competing interest of the employees—the need for work—is obviously strong but not strong enough to mandate bargaining. Further, having concluded that the employer has the right to shut down a facility, courts also allow the employer to do so fairly quickly. Management may need speed and flexibility in effecting such major business changes. In contrast, the union will want to slow down or prevent the closing. The two sides will have few things to discuss, and mandated bargaining will gain little for employees while potentially costing the company time and money. When a plant closing will cost jobs, management must bargain such things as the order of layoffs, but it need not bargain the closing itself.

Employer and Union Security

Both the employer and the union will seek clauses making their positions more secure. Management, above all, wants to be sure that there will be no strikes during the course of the agreement. For its part, the union tries to ensure that its members cannot be turned away from work during the CBA's term, and that all newly hired workers will affiliate with the union. We look at several union security issues.

No Strike/No Lockout. Most agreements include some form of no-strike clause, meaning that the union promises not to strike during the term of the contract. In turn, unions insist on a no-lockout clause, meaning that in the event of a labor dispute, management will not prevent union members from working. **No-strike and no-lockout clauses are both legal.**

Closed Shop. A closed shop means the employer must hire only union members. Though obviously very attractive to a union, effectively giving it veto power over new hires, a closed shop is not possible. **A closed shop is illegal.** Indeed, for a union to bargain for a closed shop violates the NLRA .

Union and Agency Shops. In a union shop, membership in the union becomes compulsory *after* the employee has been hired. Thus management retains an unfettered right to hire whom it pleases, but all new employees who fit into the bargaining unit must affiliate with the union. **A union shop is generally legal.** There are two limitations, however. First, new members need not join the union for 30 days. Second, the new members, after joining the union, can only be required to pay initiation fees and union dues. If the new hire decides he does not want to participate in the union, the union may not compel him to do so, and management may not terminate him (pursuant to a CBA) for his refusal. This is a compromise, designed to protect workers from having to play an active role in a union, while ensuring that the union receives normal dues from all employees, whether they participate in union affairs or not. If employees could avoid dues,

---

[13] *First National Maintenance Corp. v. NLRB*, 452 U.S. 666, 101 S. Ct. 2573, 1981 U.S. LEXIS 117 (1981).

they would be "free riders," benefiting from the union's bargaining without paying for it.

An **agency shop** is similar to a union shop. Here, the new hire must pay union fees but need not actually join the organization. In both a union shop and an agency shop, the worker may insist on paying only the percentage of dues that is devoted to collective bargaining, contract administration, and grievances. An employee may refuse to pay, for example, the percentage of union dues devoted to organizing other companies.[14]

Some states have passed so-called **right to work laws**, which restrict or even outlaw union shop and agency shop agreements. These statutes typically prohibit a labor organization from demanding that all employees join the union or pay dues. Right to work laws prompt an intense response from both supporters and opponents of organized labor, and the Internet offers plenty of evidence. At http://www.nrtw.org/, the National Right to Work Legal Defense Foundation explains these statutes and counsels employees about their rights to reject union membership and avoid paying dues. The organization also discusses what it considers to be union abuses. Meanwhile the AFL-CIO, the nation's largest labor organization, offers statistics demonstrating that union workers earn higher pay than their nonunion counterparts in virtually all jobs and professions, and that wages are lower in right to work states than elsewhere in the country. See its Web site at http://www.aflcio.org/.

Hot Cargo Clause.   A hot cargo clause would prohibit an employer from doing business with a specified company. A union might like such a clause to put pressure on the *other* company, where the union already has a dispute. But the effort must fail: **hot cargo clauses are illegal**.

DUTY TO BARGAIN

Both the union and the employer must bargain in good faith with an open mind. However, they are *not* obligated to reach an agreement. This means that the two sides must meet and make a reasonable effort to reach a contract. The goal is good faith bargaining, with the hope that it will lead to a contract and labor peace. Each side must listen to the other's proposals and consider possible compromises. But the NLRA does not require agreement. Suppose a union proposes a 15 percent pay increase, and management offers a 1 percent raise. Each side is required to attend bargaining sessions, listen to the other side's proposal, and consider its supporting argument. But neither side has to agree. Management need not raise its offer to 2 percent, nor must the union drop its demand. However, **if an employer states that it is financially unable to meet the union's demands, the union is entitled to see records that support the claim.** It is an unfair labor practice for an employer to say, "We can't afford a pay raise now," and then refuse to supply its financial data. An employer could easily destroy good faith bargaining if it were allowed to claim financial impossibility without demonstrating it. Similarly, if an employer argues that it must subcontract work to save money, it must furnish the documents it is relying on in making its proposal.

Sometimes an employer will attempt to make changes without bargaining the issues at all. However, **management may not unilaterally change wages, hours,**

---

[14] *Communications Workers of America v. Beck*, 487 U.S. 735, 108 S. Ct. 2641, 1988 U.S. LEXIS 3030 (1988).

or terms and conditions of employment without bargaining the issues to impasse. "Bargaining to impasse" means that both parties must continue to meet and bargain in good faith until it is clear that they cannot reach an agreement. The goal in requiring collective bargaining is to bring the parties together, to reach an agreement that brings labor peace. In one case, the union won an election, but before bargaining could begin, management changed the schedule from five 8-hour days to four 10-hour days a week. The company also changed its layoff policy from one of strict seniority to one based on ability and began laying off employees based on alleged poor performance. The court held that each of these acts violated the company's duty to bargain. The employer ultimately might be allowed to make every one of these changes, but first it had to bargain the issues to impasse.[15]

For the same reasons, though the employer may implement new policies after impasse, it may *implement only what it has proposed at the table*. Again, it would defeat the purpose of the NLRA if a company were free to implement a business decision that it had never proposed; the two sides *could not* have discussed plans that were never offered at the table. Exhibit 15.1 outlines the respective bargaining rights and responsibilities between employers and unions.

Exhibit 15.1

The NLRA requires that the employer and the union meet. They *must* bargain mandatory subjects and *may* bargain permissive subjects. The employer may not make any unilateral change concerning a mandatory subject until bargaining has reached an impasse.

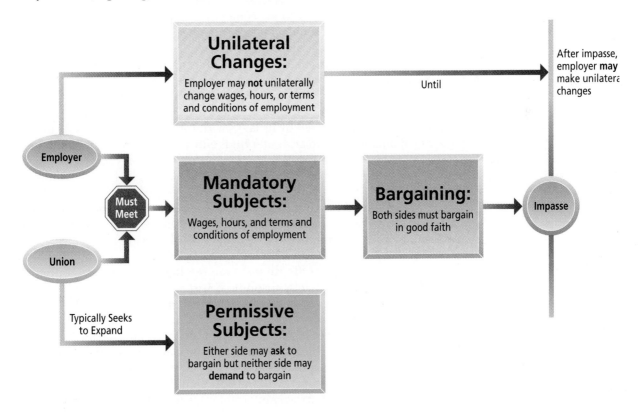

---

[15] *Adair Standish Corp. v. NLRB*, 912 F.2d 854, 1990 U.S. App. LEXIS 14670 (6th Cir. 1990).

Illegal implementation put major league baseball players back on the field after the longest strike in sports history. The CBA had expired, and the players' union bargained with team owners throughout the spring and summer. The two sides could not agree, primarily because the owners demanded a salary cap, which would give all teams equal payrolls. In August the players struck, ending the season without a World Series for the first time in more than 100 years. The two sides continued talking until December, when the owners announced they were implementing their salary cap proposal and changing various aspects of "free agency," the policy that allows a player to seek the highest salary from any team. A federal district court judge ruled that the owners had violated the NLRA by unilaterally imposing new rules concerning a mandatory subject (free agency) that they had never bargained. The judge ordered the owners back to the table, and the parties finally agreed to a new CBA.

ENFORCEMENT

Virtually all collective bargaining agreements provide for their own enforcement, typically through **grievance-arbitration**. Suppose a company transfers an employee from the day shift to the night shift, and the worker believes the contract prohibits such a transfer for any employee with her seniority. The employee complains to the union, which files a **grievance**, that is, a formal complaint with the company, notifying management that the union claims a contract violation. Generally, the CBA establishes some kind of informal hearing, usually conducted by a member of management, at which the employee, represented by the union, may state her case and respond to the company's assertions. The manager has a limited time period—say, seven days—to decide the grievance.

If, after the manager's decision, the employee is still dissatisfied, the union normally has the right to appeal to some kind of formal hearing, perhaps before a top company executive or committee. This appeal hearing is slightly more formal. If this hearing still fails to satisfy the employee, the union typically may file for **arbitration**, that is, a formal hearing before a neutral arbitrator. In the arbitration hearing, each side is represented by its lawyer. The arbitrator is required to decide the case based on the CBA. An arbitrator finds either for the employee, and orders the company to take certain corrective action, or for the employer, and dismisses the grievance. (The American Arbitration Association offers its rules, procedures, and forms at http://www.adr.org/.)

A CBA also permits the company to file a grievance. Its complaint normally goes directly to arbitration. In the vast majority of grievances, the arbitrator's decision is final. In a limited number of cases, however, the losing party attempts to convince a federal court that the arbitration award is unjust. Usually, such an appeal is futile. **Courts generally do not examine the merits of an arbitrator's decision.** The idea of all contracts, including CBAs, is to give the parties a chance to control their own destiny. When a CBA states that grievances should be settled by arbitration, courts seldom undercut the contract by reviewing the arbitrator's award. Of course, a rule would hardly be a rule without an exception. **A court may refuse to enforce an arbitrator's award that is contrary to public policy.** So if an arbitrator's decision encourages either party to violate the law or engage in clearly immoral conduct, a court will probably nullify the award. But like most exceptions, this one is very narrowly interpreted, as the following case illustrates.

UNITED PAPERWORKERS INTERNATIONAL UNION V. MISCO, INC.

484 U.S. 29, 108 S. Ct. 364, 1987 U.S. LEXIS 5028
United States Supreme Court, 1987

FACTS: Misco, Inc. (the Company), operated a paper plant in Louisiana. The Company had a collective bargaining agreement with the United Paperworkers (the Union), which permitted either side to file grievances and take them to final, binding arbitration. The CBA also permitted the Company to post work rules. Rule II.1 notified employees that they could be dismissed for bringing alcohol or drugs onto company premises or arriving for work under the influence of such substances.

Isiah Cooper, an employee covered by the CBA, operated a slitter-rewinder machine, which used sharp blades to cut rolling coils of paper. The machine was hazardous and had caused numerous injuries over the years. Cooper had twice been reprimanded for deficient performance. Two days after the second reprimand, police searched Cooper's house, pursuant to a search warrant, and discovered a large amount of marijuana. Later that day, police apprehended Cooper in the backseat of another worker's car, a white Cutlass, parked in the company lot. There was marijuana smoke in the air and a lighted marijuana cigarette in the ashtray in the front seat. Police arrested Cooper and then searched *his* car, where they found a plastic scales case and some marijuana.

When the Company learned of Cooper's presence in the white Cutlass, it discharged him for having drugs on the premises. He filed a grievance. Eight months later, shortly before the arbitration hearing began, the Company learned that the police had found marijuana in Cooper's own car. The arbitrator found in Cooper's favor, stating that because he was in the backseat of the Cutlass and the marijuana was in the front, the Company had no evidence he had used or possessed an illegal substance on the premises. The arbitrator refused to consider the marijuana found in Cooper's own car because the Company had not known about it when it fired him.

The Company filed suit in United States District Court, which vacated the arbitrator's decision, holding that public policy prohibits the use of marijuana. The court of appeals affirmed the district court, and the union sought review by the Supreme Court.

ISSUE: Was the district court correct in overruling the arbitrator on public policy grounds?

EXCERPTS FROM JUSTICE WHITE'S DECISION: The Court made clear almost 30 years ago that the courts play only a limited role when asked to review the decision of an arbitrator. The courts are not authorized to reconsider the merits of an award even though the parties may allege that the award rests on errors of fact or on misinterpretation of the contract. The federal policy of settling labor disputes by arbitration would be undermined if courts had the final say on the merits of the awards.

The Company's position, simply put, is that the arbitrator committed grievous error in finding that the evidence was insufficient to prove that Cooper had possessed or used marijuana on company property. But the court of appeals, although it took a distinctly jaundiced view of the arbitrator's decision in this regard, was not free to refuse enforcement because it considered Cooper's presence in the white Cutlass, in the circumstances, to be ample proof that Rule II.1 was violated. No dishonesty [on the arbitrator's part] is alleged; only improvident, even silly, factfinding is claimed.

Nor was it open to the court of appeals to refuse to enforce the award because the arbitrator, in deciding whether there was just cause to discharge, refused to consider evidence unknown to the Company at the time Cooper was fired. The parties bargained for arbitration to settle disputes and were free to set the procedural rules for arbitrators to follow if they chose. Article VI of the agreement, entitled "Arbitration Procedure," did set some ground rules for the arbitration process. It forbade the arbitrator to consider hearsay evidence, for example, but evidentiary matters were otherwise left to the arbitrator. Here the arbitrator ruled that in determining whether Cooper had violated

Rule II.1, he should not consider evidence not relied on by the employer in ordering the discharge, particularly in a case like this where there was no notice to the employee or the Union prior to the hearing that the Company would attempt to rely on after-discovered evidence. This, in effect, was a construction of what the contract required when deciding discharge cases: an arbitrator was to look only at the evidence before the employer at the time of discharge.

The parties did not bargain for the facts to be found by a court, but by an arbitrator chosen by them who had more opportunity to observe Cooper and to be familiar with the plant and its problems. Nor does the fact that it is inquiring into a possible violation of public policy excuse a court for doing the arbitrator's task.

The judgment of the court of appeals is *reversed.* ◢

Concerted Action

Concerted action refers to any tactics union members take in unison to gain some bargaining advantage. It is this power that gives a union strength. **The NLRA guarantees the right of employees to engage in concerted action for mutual aid or protection.**[16] The most common forms of concerted action are strikes and picketing.

STRIKES

The NLRA guarantees employees the right to strike, but with some limitations.[17] A union has a guaranteed right to call a strike if the parties are unable to reach a collective bargaining agreement. A union may call a strike to exert economic pressure on management, to protest an unfair labor practice, or to preserve work that the employer is considering sending elsewhere. Note that the right to strike can be waived. Management will generally insist that the CBA include a **no-strike clause**, which prohibits the union from striking while the CBA is in force. A strike is illegal in several other situations as well; here we mention the most important.

Cooling-Off Period

Once the union agrees to a CBA, it may not strike to terminate the agreement, or modify it, without giving management 60 days' notice. Suppose a union contract expires July 1. The two sides attempt to bargain a new contract, but progress is slow. The union may strike as an economic weapon, but must notify management of its intention to do so *and then must wait 60 days*. This cooling-off period is designed to give both sides a chance to reassess negotiations and to decide whether some additional compromise would be wiser than enduring a strike.

Statutory Prohibition

Many states have outlawed strikes by public employees. In some states, the prohibition applies to selected employees, such as firefighters or teachers. In other states, *all* public employees are barred from striking, whether or not they have a contract. The purpose of these statutes is to ensure that unions do not use the public health or welfare as a weapon to secure an unfair bargaining advantage.

---

[16] NLRA §7.
[17] NLRA §13.

However, even employees subject to such a rule may find other tactics to press their cause.

Jen has worked hard throughout high school, achieving a 3.8 GPA and high test scores, and now she is ready to apply to some of the best colleges in the country. All of her teachers think she is an extraordinary student—yet no one will write her a letter of recommendation.

The teacher's union has been bargaining a new contract for a year and a half. The teachers seek a 4 percent raise; the school board has offered 1 percent. The struggle has grown increasingly bitter. There will be no strike—state law prohibits that—but the teachers have decided they will "work to rule," meaning that they will do only what their (expired) contract requires: teach classes, issue grades, and so forth. No teacher will write a letter of recommendation, coach a team, supervise detention, or offer extra help to a student.

"This stinks," wails Jen. "I've never asked for extra assistance. I've tried to be helpful in class, and a lot of times, I've tutored other kids. This is the one time in my life I really need my teachers to be there for me, and they're turning their backs."

"My heart goes out to Jen," responds her American history teacher, "but our problem is simple: as long as we quietly ask for decent pay, no one listens. Students and parents notice us only when they suffer inconvenience."

"This is a moral outrage!" shouts Jen's father. "These so-called teachers have no right to hurt my child over their pay disputes. If they were serious about their profession, they would do everything they could to help the children who are entrusted to them. Our high school normally sends 95 percent of its students to good colleges, and now the teachers are sabotaging everything."

"If the parents were serious about education," the history teacher retorts, "or truly concerned about their children's welfare, they would demand that the town pay respectable salaries. They prefer lower taxes so they can spend more on fancy cars."

Who is right? From the Chapter 2 ethics checklist: What are the alternatives? What are the consequences of each? ▪

Violent Strikes

The NLRA prohibits violent strikes. Violence does sometimes occur on the picket line, when union members attempt to prevent other workers from entering the job site. Or a union may stage a **sit-down strike**, in which members stop working but remain at their job posts, physically blocking replacement workers from taking their places. Any such violence is illegal.

Partial Strikes

A partial strike occurs when employees stop working temporarily, then resume, then stop again, and so forth. This tactic is particularly disruptive because management cannot bring in replacement workers. A union may either walk off the job or stay on it, but it may not alternate.

REPLACEMENT WORKERS

When employees go on strike, management generally wants to replace them to keep the company operating. When replacement workers begin to cross a union picket line, tempers are certain to explode, and entire communities may feel the repercussions. Are replacement workers legal? Yes. **Management has the right to hire replacement workers during a strike.** May the employer offer the replacement workers *permanent* jobs, or must the company give union members their jobs back when the strike is over? It depends on the type of strike.

After an *economic* **strike, an employer may not discriminate against a striker, but the employer is** *not* **obligated to lay off a replacement worker to give a striker his job back.** An economic strike is one intended to gain wages or benefits. When a union bargains for a pay raise but fails to get it and walks off the job, that is an economic strike. During such a strike, an employer may hire permanent replacement workers. When the strike is over, the company has no obligation to lay off the replacement workers to make room for the strikers. However, if the company does hire more workers, it may not discriminate against the strikers.

After a *ULP strike,* **a union member is entitled to her job back, even if that means the employer must lay off a replacement worker.** Suppose management refuses to bargain in good faith by claiming poverty without producing records to substantiate its claim. The union strikes. Management's refusal to bargain was an unfair labor practice, and the strike is a ULP strike. When it ends, the striking workers must get their jobs back. The following case raises the pivotal distinction concerning a strike: Was this one sparked by a ULP—or by money?

NATIONAL LABOR RELATIONS BOARD V. CALIFORNIA ACRYLIC INDUSTRIES, INC.

150 F.3d 1095
Ninth Circuit Court of Appeals, 1998

FACTS: California Acrylic, doing business as Cal Spas, makes spas, gazebos, and other leisure goods at a facility in Pomona, California. The United Electrical, Radio and Machine Workers of America (the Union) began a campaign to organize the production and maintenance workers. The Union alleged that a company security guard videotaped a meeting between employees and Union representatives. Cal Spas denied the videotaping and argued in the alternative that if it occurred, the pictures were necessary to prevent union violence.

A Union representative, Humberto Camacho, addressed a rally, and among other things stated that employees were outraged by the videotaping. A majority of the workers then voted to strike. Employees stopped work and began picketing. Cal Spas hired replacement workers. A month after the strike began, Union officials offered to return to work, but Cal Spas denied jobs to the Union members, stating that they had been permanently replaced. The NLRB found that the videotaping was a ULP and a partial cause of the strike. The Board ruled that the striking workers were entitled to their jobs. The company appealed.

ISSUES: Was the videotaping a ULP? Was the strike a ULP strike?

EXCERPTS FROM JUDGE WIGGINS'S DECISION: We have stated that "[i]n the absence of proper justification, the photographing of pickets violates the Act because it has a tendency to intimidate." Similarly, the photographing of union activity during an organizational campaign tends to create fear among employees of future reprisal. Thus, it chills an employee's freedom to exercise his section 7 rights. The NLRB has extended the prohibition against photographing employees to videotaping employees. We agree with this extension. Absent legitimate justification, Cal Spas' videotape surveillance of protected concerted activity was an unfair labor practice.

Cal Spas argues that its surveillance was justified to document Union trespass and/or violence. The NLRB properly rejected this claim. First, Cal Spas' purported evidence of trespass does not support its contention. That photograph shows Union Representative Camacho standing on a *public* sidewalk, speaking with Cal Spas employees.

Second, Cal Spas' claim that surveillance was justified because of Union violence is also meritless. Employers are not allowed to photograph protected activity simply because they fear "something might happen." Cal Spas argues that it anticipated violence, but it did not show a basis for that purported concern. In sum, the NLRB properly held that Cal Spas' surveillance of protected activity occurred and was an unfair labor practice in violation of section 8(a)(1) of the Act.

The larger and more difficult issue in this case is whether the NLRB erred when it found that the strike was an unfair labor practice strike, rather than an economic strike. The significance of that conclusion is that only unfair labor practice strikers are entitled to reinstatement with backpay, even when they have been replaced.

It is well-established that an unfair labor practice need only be a contributing cause of a strike to produce an unfair labor practice strike. We have noted that a strike based in part on an unfair labor practice is an unfair labor practice strike, even though other reasons [are] also present, since one of the reasons for it [is] to protest an unfair labor practice.

The only evidence used to support the NLRB's conclusion is Camacho's pre-strike mention of the surveillance. Meanwhile, the record is replete with evidence that the strike was not motivated by the unfair labor practice. First, the strike occurred soon after the Regional Director [of the NLRB] postponed the representation election petition hearing—a postponement issued in response to Cal Spas' filing of an unfair labor practice charge

against the Union. In contrast, the strike was some two weeks after the surveillance.

Second, Union literature issued before and after the strike vote enumerated causes and justifications for the work stoppage, but failed altogether to mention the surveillance. Instead, the leaflets focused on economic concerns, including lack of medical insurance and low wages.

Third, Union Representative Camacho appeared before the Pomona City Council during the strike and informed them that "[t]hrough [Cal Spas'] action, our right to vote was taken away. . . . We went on strike because the company denied us that right to vote on a union." All of his comments pertained to economic or Union representation issues. He did not mention the surveillance as a contributing cause.

In sum, the NLRB erred by holding that whenever a union organizer mentions an unfair labor practice prior to a strike vote, any subsequent strike is necessarily an unfair labor practice strike. The proper inquiry is whether the employees actually voted to strike at least in part because of the unfair labor practice. The vast majority of the evidence points to one inescapable conclusion: the strike was motivated solely by economic concerns. To ignore this evidence is to permit union organizers to transform an otherwise economic strike into an unfair labor practice strike simply by invoking a few magic words.

Because we conclude that the strike was an economic strike, Cal Spas may refuse to reinstate [the] strikers if in the interim [it] has taken on permanent replacements. ◢

UPDATE Find a thorough description of a current strike. (The Web site http://www.igc.org/strike/ provides a useful list.) What issues caused the union to walk out? Is this an economic or a ULP strike? In your opinion, which side is making the stronger case, and why? ▪

PICKETING

Picketing the employer's workplace in support of a strike is generally lawful. Striking workers are permitted to establish picket lines at the employer's job site and to urge all others—employees, replacement workers, and customers—not to cross the line. But the picketers are not permitted to use physical force to *prevent* anyone from crossing the line. The NLRA does not authorize or protect violence on the picket line. The company may terminate violent picketers and permanently replace them, regardless of the nature of the strike.

Secondary boycotts are generally illegal. A secondary boycott is a picket line established not at the employer's premises but at the workplace of a *different* company that does business with the union's employer. Such a boycott is designed to put pressure on the union's employer by forcing other companies to stop doing business with it. Suppose Union is on strike against Truck Co. Union is free to picket Truck Co.'s office or terminal. If Truck Co. hires replacement workers, the trucks will be back on the road, making deliveries. Now Union wants to put additional pressure on Truck Co., so it sets up picket lines at a *supermarket* where Truck Co. delivers. Union attempts to persuade customers not to shop at the store and other workers, including delivery drivers, not to enter the premises. If allowed, the picketing might result in the supermarket demanding that Truck Co. compromise with Union. But this is a secondary boycott, so it is illegal. Truck Co. and the supermarket will obtain an injunction, prohibiting the secondary boycott. See Exhibit 15.2.

LOCKOUTS

The workers have bargained with management for weeks, and discussions have turned belligerent. It is 6:00 a.m., the start of another day at the factory. But as 150 employees arrive for work, they are amazed to find the company's gate locked and armed guards standing on the other side. What is this? A lockout.

The power of a union comes ultimately from its potential to strike. But management, too, has weapons. In a lockout, management prohibits workers from entering the premises, denying the employees work and a chance to earn a paycheck. Most, but not all, lockouts are legal.

A defensive lockout is almost always legal. It is one way management can respond to union pressure such as a sit-down strike or a **whipsaw strike**, which may occur when a union is simultaneously bargaining with various employers. Suppose a machinists' union is simultaneously bargaining a contract with three engine manufacturers, attempting to obtain an identical contract from all of the

Exhibit 15.2
A union striking against Truck Co. may lawfully picket the employer, using peaceful means to urge all others to stay away. But if the union attempts to put indirect pressure on Truck Co. by picketing one of the company's customers, it is engaging in an illegal secondary boycott.

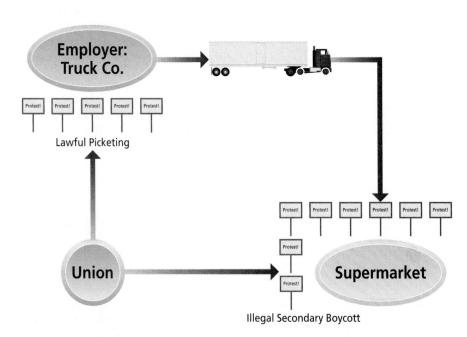

companies. To pressure the companies, the union might choose to strike against only *one* of the manufacturers. This is a whipsaw strike, and it can be very effective because the struck company, losing money while the others profit, will push strongly for a compromise. But management of all three companies may respond by locking out the workers from *all* factories, even those where no strike is under way. That is a defensive lockout, and it is legal.

An offensive lockout is legal if the parties have reached a bargaining impasse. Management, bargaining a new CBA with a union, may wish to use a lockout to advance its position. It is allowed to do so *provided the parties have reached an impasse.* If there is no impasse, a lockout will *probably* be illegal. Most courts consider that a lockout before impasse indicates hostility to the union. That kind of general antagonism to a union is illegal because the NLRA guarantees employees the right to organize. In addition, management usually *must notify the union before locking it out.* Again, the purpose of the NLRA is to bring the parties together through bargaining. A lockout is a legitimate method to pressure a union into compromise, but it can have that effect only if the union is warned and given a chance to bargain.

Regulating Union Affairs

Along with a union's exclusive bargaining power goes a duty of fairness to all of its members. The union's *duty of fair representation* was created by the NLRA and the Labor-Management Reporting and Disclosure Act. **The duty of fair representation requires that a union represent all members fairly, impartially, and in good faith.** A union is not entitled to favor some members over others. No union may discriminate against a member based on impermissible characteristics such as race or sex. A union is allowed to discipline a member for certain acts, such as engaging in an illegal strike or working for wages below union scale. But the union may *not* discipline a member for criticizing union leadership or attempting to replace the leadership through a proper election.

Unions must make reasonable decisions about whether to pursue an employee's grievance. A member may sue his union, claiming that the organization violated its duty of fair representation by deciding not to pursue a grievance on his behalf. But courts generally allow unions a *wide range of latitude* in deciding whether to pursue a grievance. **A union's decision not to file a grievance is illegal only if it was arbitrary, discriminatory, or in bad faith.**

Most employees fail when claiming that a union violated its duty of fair representation. Ramon Hayes worked at the Peoples Gas, Light and Coke Co. Peoples Gas fired him for theft, and the union filed a grievance. Before the grievance could be arbitrated, Hayes was convicted on drug charges. The union, mistakenly believing Hayes had been convicted on the *theft* accusation, withdrew its grievance. Later, the union learned of its error, but refused to pursue the grievance because Peoples Gas had added the drug charge as a reason for the dismissal. A court ruled that the union had probably been inept and negligent in dismissing the original grievance, but had shown no *bad faith* in its belief that the grievance was futile. The union had not violated its duty of fair representation.[18]

---

[18] *Hayes v. People's Gas, Light and Coke Co.,* 1992 U.S. App. LEXIS 30592 (7th Cir. 1992).

Chapter Conclusion

Workers first attempted to organize unions in this country about 200 years ago in response to appalling working conditions. These conditions are generally better today, and contemporary clashes between union and management are less likely to stem from sweltering temperatures in a mine than from a management decision to subcontract work or from a teacher's refusal to write college recommendations. But although the flash points have changed, labor law is still dominated by issues of organizing, collective bargaining, and concerted action.

Chapter Review

1. Section 7 of the National Labor Relations Act (NLRA) guarantees employees the right to organize and join unions, bargain collectively, and engage in other concerted activities.

2. Section 8(a) of the NLRA makes it an unfair labor practice (ULP) for an employer to interfere with union organizing, discriminate against a union member, or refuse to bargain collectively.

3. Section 8(b) of the NLRA makes it a ULP for a union to interfere with employees who are exercising their rights under Section7, to encourage an employer to discriminate against an employee because of a labor dispute, to refuse to bargain collectively, or to engage in an illegal strike or boycott.

4. Section 9 of the NLRA makes a validly recognized union the *exclusive* representative of the employees.

5. During a union organizing campaign, an employer may vigorously present anti-union views to its employees, but it may not use threats or promises of benefits to defeat the union effort.

6. The National Labor Relations Board (NLRB) will certify a proposed bargaining unit only if the employees share a community of interest.

7. The employer and the union *must* bargain over wages, hours, and other terms and conditions of employment. They *may* bargain other subjects, but neither side may insist on doing so.

8. The union and the employer *must* bargain in good faith, but they are not obligated to reach an agreement. Management may not unilaterally change wages, hours, or terms and conditions of employment without bargaining to impasse.

9. The NLRA guarantees employees the right to strike, with some limitations.

10. After an *economic* strike, an employer is not obligated to lay off replacement workers to give a striker her job back, but it may not discriminate against a striker. After a *ULP* strike, the striking worker must get her job back.

11. Picketing the employer's workplace in support of a strike is generally lawful; a secondary boycott is generally illegal.

12. An employer may lock out workers, but only after giving them notice.

13. Multi-employer bargaining and implementation do not violate antitrust laws.

14. The duty of fair representation requires that a union represent all members fairly, impartially, and in good faith.

Practice Test

1. Power, Inc., operated a surface coal mine in central Pennsylvania. Financial losses led it to lay off a number of employees. After that, several employees contacted the United Mine Workers of America (UMWA), which began an organizing drive at the company. Power's general manager and foreman both warned the miners that if the company was unionized, it

would be shut down. An office manager told one of the miners that the company would get rid of union supporters. Shortly before the election was to take place, Power laid off 13 employees, all of whom had signed union cards. One employee, who had not signed a union card, had low seniority but was not laid off. Later, one of Power's lawyers told several miners that anyone caught helping the 13 laid-off workers by contributing to a union hardship fund would "be out there looking for help from somebody else." Comment.

2. Triec, Inc., is a small electrical contracting company in Springfield, Ohio, owned by its executives Yeazell, Jones, and Heaton. Employees contacted the International Brotherhood of Electrical Workers, which began an organizing drive. Six of the 11 employees in the bargaining unit signed authorization cards. The company declined to recognize the union, which petitioned the NLRB to schedule an election. The company then granted several new benefits for all workers, including higher wages, paid vacations, and other measures. When the election was held, only two of the 11 bargaining unit members voted for the union. Did the company violate the NLRA?

3. Q-1 Motor Express was an interstate trucking company. When a union attempted to organize Q-1's drivers, it met heavy resistance. A supervisor told one driver that if he knew what was good for him, he would stay away from the union organizer. The company president told another employee that he had the right to fire everybody, close the company, and then rehire new drivers after 72 hours. He made numerous other threats to workers and their families. Based on the extreme nature of the company's opposition, what exceptional remedy did the union seek before the NLRB?

4. Douglas Kuroda worked for the Hertz Corp. He and his supervisor had a heated argument in which Kuroda told his boss, "You may have a master's degree but you don't know shit." The supervisor instructed Kuroda to punch out for the day, but Kuroda refused to leave until security officers escorted him off the premises. Hertz fired him, and Kuroda filed a grievance. The union represented Kuroda at an arbitra-

tion hearing. During the hearing, the union made no objection to certain evidence that the company offered to demonstrate why it fired Kuroda. The arbitrator ruled in favor of the company. Kuroda sued his union (and also Hertz). What kind of claim is he making against the union? Is he likely to win his claim?

5. Gibson Greetings, Inc., had a plant in Berea, Kentucky, where the workers belonged to the International Brotherhood of Firemen & Oilers. The old CBA expired, and the parties negotiated a new one, but were unable to reach an agreement on economic issues. The union struck. At the next bargaining session, the company claimed that the strike violated the *old* CBA, which had a no-strike clause and which stated that the terms of the old CBA would continue in force as long as the parties were bargaining a *new* CBA. The company refused to bargain until the union at least agreed that by bargaining, the company was not giving up its claim of an illegal strike. The two sides returned to bargaining, but meanwhile the company hired replacement workers. Eventually, the striking workers offered to return to work, but Gibson refused to rehire many of them. In court, the union claimed that the company had committed a ULP by (1) insisting the strike was illegal and (2) refusing to bargain until the union acknowledged the company's position. Why is it very important to the union to establish the company's act as a ULP? *Was* it a ULP?

6. **YOU BE THE JUDGE WRITING PROBLEM** Plainville Ready Mix Concrete Co. was bargaining a CBA with the drivers' union. Negotiations went forward, on and off, over many months, with wages the major source of disagreement. Plainville made its final offer of $9.50 per hour, with step increases of $.25 per hour in a year and another $.25 per hour the following year. The plan also included certain incentive pay. The union refused to accept the offer, and the two sides reached an impasse. Plainville then announced it was implementing its plans. It established a wage rate of $9.50 per hour but eliminated the step increases and incentive pay. Was the company's implementation of the wage increase legal? **Argument for Plainville:** The NLRA only requires the company to bargain in

good faith, which we did. The law does not obligate us to agree to anything. Once the parties reached an impasse, Plainville could implement any plan it wanted. **Argument for the Union:** When the parties reach an impasse, the employer is permitted to implement whatever it proposed at the bargaining table. It would defeat the purpose of collective bargaining if a company could implement plans it had never proposed.

7. Eads Transfer, Inc., was a moving and storage company with a small workforce represented by the General Teamsters, Chauffeurs and Helpers Union. When the CBA expired, the parties failed to reach agreement on a new one, and the union struck. As negotiations continued, Eads hired temporary replacement workers. After 10 months of the strike, some union workers offered to return to work, but Eads made no response to the offer. Two months later, more workers offered to return to work, but Eads would not accept any of the offers. Eventually, Eads notified all workers that they would not be allowed back to work until a new CBA had been signed. The union filed ULP claims against the company. Please rule.

8. Olivetti Office U.S.A., Inc., was located in Newington, Connecticut, and its workers were represented by the United Automobile, Aerospace and Agriculture Implement Workers of America. The company's president reported to the union that Olivetti was losing money. He insisted that unless the union renegotiated certain wage increases in the current CBA, Olivetti would subcontract work to cheaper parts of the country to save money. The union requested to bargain over the proposed subcontracting, and Olivetti agreed. But when the sides met, the company would not permit the union to see the financial data that supported its arguments. After several meetings, the company declared an impasse, implemented its subcontracting proposal, and laid off workers in Connecticut. The union claimed this was a ULP. Was it?

9. Fred Schipul taught English at the Thomaston (Connecticut) High School for 18 years. When the position of English Department chairperson became vacant, Schipul applied, but the Board of Education appointed a less senior teacher. Schipul filed a grievance, based on a CBA provision that required the Board to promote the most senior teacher where two or more applicants were equal in qualification. Before the arbitrator ruled on the grievance, the Board eliminated all department chairpersons. The arbitrator ruled in Schipul's favor. The Board then reinstated all department chairs—all but the English Department. Comment.

10. Labor Day is a national holiday originally intended to celebrate the contributions of working men and women. But for most people today, it simply means a day off from work—or the day before school begins. What are some reasons that unions have declined in membership and power? Are there are any reasons to think that organized labor may rebound and increase its strength?

11. ETHICS   This chapter refers in several places to the contentious issue of subcontracting. Make an argument for management in favor of a company's ethical right to subcontract, and one for unions in opposition.

12. ROLE REVERSAL   Write an essay question involving a union organizing campaign and a management response that includes both permissible advocacy and illegal conduct.

Internet Research Problem

View http://www.uniteunion.org/sweatshops/sweatshop.html. What are sweatshops? Do they exist in the United States? Click on "College Students Against Sweatshops." Describe a current student campaign about this issue. Do you agree or disagree with what the students are doing? Why?

You can find further practice problems in the Online Quiz at http://beatty.westbuslaw.com **or in the Study Guide that accompanies this text.**

BUSINESS ORGANIZATIONS

UNIT 4

Starting
a Business

At long last, Rachel was in love. For years, she had yearned to start her own business, but the perfect concept always eluded her. Then, surfing the Net one day, she found the idea she had been searching for: movie theaters that show only classic films. Sure, you can rent the original *Star Wars* or *Gone with the Wind* anytime, but the little box at home cannot compete with a large screen and digital sound. At home, Atlanta simply does not burn as hot. According to the Internet, these theaters were already a rave success in Paris. Why not in Des Moines?

Rachel began looking for investors. Finally, at her nineteenth lunch meeting, she found Ross, who was as enthusiastic as she. Two days later, they signed a lease on a suitable property. Prospects for the business looked great. Then, while riding his bike on company business, Ross crashed into a pedestrian. Only when Rachel was served with a complaint did she learn that their business was a partnership, which meant that she and Ross were both personally liable for his accident.

In a panic, Rachel resumed surfing the Net, this time looking for legal information. She downloaded a sample corporate charter and formed a corporation, BigScreen, Inc. Now she and Ross enjoyed limited liability and could sell stock to outside investors. Their college friend from Hong Kong, Bing, was the first to buy shares. But other prospective purchasers insisted that BigScreen be organized as an S corporation for tax reasons. Back to the Internet, where Rachel learned that nonresident aliens could not hold stock in S corps. Bing's participation disqualified BigScreen.

By this time, Rachel was surfing in desperation. At last she found an answer: BigScreen could become a limited liability company. This form of business provided all the advantages of an S corp with none of the disadvantages. She and Ross immediately formed an LLC, transferred BigScreen's assets, and sighed in relief—until tax day. The IRS considered their transfer of assets to be a sale. Suddenly, they faced a huge tax bill, with no way to pay it. Ross announced he was withdrawing from the business.

"You promised to stay five years," Rachel insisted.

"Yeah," Ross agreed, "but I never signed the LLC operating agreement, so tough luck for you."

"Ross, I trusted you," Rachel protested.

"Frankly, my dear, I don't give a damn," replied Ross, slamming the door as he left. ◾

Many people dream of starting their own business. They look for exactly the right idea to power a company to success. Creativity is an important ingredient for any successful start-up. So are hard work and finely honed business skills. And so is the law. Legal issues can have as profound an impact on the success of a company as any business decision.

To begin, entrepreneurs must select a form of organization. The correct choice can reduce taxes, liability, and conflict while facilitating outside investment. If entrepreneurs do not make a choice for themselves, the law will automatically select a (potentially undesirable) default option.

At http://www.onlinewbc.gov/docs/starting/test.html, the U.S. Small Business Administration offers advice about starting a business and includes an entrepreneurial test to help you assess your potential as an entrepreneur.

Sole Proprietorships

A sole proprietorship is an unincorporated business owned by a single person. It is the most common form of business organization. For example, Linda runs ExSciTe (which stands for Excellence in Science Teaching), a company that helps teachers prepare hands-on science experiments in the classroom, using such basic items as vinegar, lemon juice, and red cabbage. (Students do *not* have to eat their mistakes.)

Sole proprietorships are easy and inexpensive to create and operate. There is no need to hire a lawyer or register with the government. The company is not even required to file a separate tax return—all profits and losses are reported on the owner's personal return. A very few states and some cities and towns require sole proprietors to obtain a business license. And states generally require sole proprietors to register their business name if it is different from their own. Linda, for example, would file a "d/b/a" or "doing business as" certificate for "ExSciTe."

Sole proprietorships also have some serious disadvantages. First, the owner of the business is responsible for all of the business's debts. If ExSciTe cannot pay its suppliers or if a student is injured by an exploding cabbage, Linda is *personally* liable. She may have to sell her house and car to pay the debt. Second, the owner of a sole proprietorship has limited options for financing her business. Debt is generally her only source of working capital because she has no stock or memberships to sell. If someone else brings in capital and helps with the management of the business, then it is a partnership, not a sole proprietorship. For this reason sole proprietorships work best for small businesses without large capital needs.

General Partnerships

Traditionally, partnerships were regulated by common law, but a lack of consistency among the states became troublesome as interstate commerce grew. To solve this problem, the National Conference of Commissioners on Uniform State Laws proposed the Uniform Partnership Act (UPA) in 1914. Since then there have been several revisions, the most recent in 1997. A majority of states have now passed the latest revisions, so we include them in our discussion of partnership law.

Partnerships have two important advantages: they do not pay *taxes* and they are *easy to form*. Partnerships, however, also have some major disadvantages:

- *Liability.* Each partner is personally liable for the debts of the enterprise whether or not she caused them.

- *Funding.* Financing a partnership may be difficult because the firm cannot sell shares as a corporation does. The capital needs of the partnership must be met by contributions from partners or by borrowing.

- *Management.* Managing a partnership can also be difficult because, in the absence of an agreement to the contrary, all partners have an equal say in running the business.

- *Transferability.* A partner only has the right to transfer the *value* of her partnership interest, not the interest itself. Thus a mother who is a partner in a law firm can pass on to her son the value of her partnership interest, not the right to be a partner in the firm (or even the right to work there).

TAXES

A partnership is not a taxable entity, which means it does not pay taxes itself. All income and losses are passed through to the partners and reported on their personal income tax returns. Corporations, by contrast, are taxable entities and pay income tax on their profits. Shareholders must then pay tax on dividends from the corporation. Thus a dollar is taxed only once before it ends up in a partner's bank account, but twice before it is deposited by a shareholder.

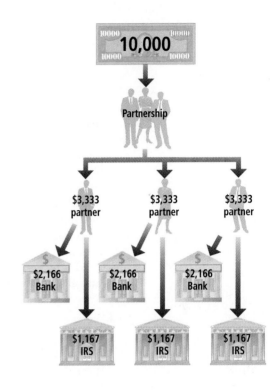

Exhibit 16.1

Exhibit 16.1 compares the single taxation of partnerships with the double taxation of corporations. Suppose, as shown in the exhibit, that a corporation and a partnership each receive $10,000 in additional income. The corporation pays tax at a top rate of 35 percent.[1] Thus the corporation pays $3,500 of the $10,000 in tax. The corporation pays out the remaining $6,500 as a dividend of $2,167 to each of its three shareholders. Then the shareholders are taxed at the special dividend rate of 15 percent, which means they each pay a tax of $325. They are each left with $1,842. Of the initial $10,000, almost 45 percent ($4,475) has gone to the Internal Revenue Service (IRS).

Compare the corporation to a partnership. The partnership itself pays no taxes, so it can pass on $3,333 to each of its partners. At a 35 percent individual rate, they will each pay an income tax of $1,167. As partners, they pocket $2,166, which is $324 more than they could keep as shareholders. Of the partnership's initial $10,000, 35 percent ($3,501) has gone to the IRS—compared with the corporation's 45 percent.

FORMATION

A partnership is an association of two or more co-owners who carry on a business for profit.[2] Each co-owner is called a *general partner*. Like sole proprietorships, partnerships are easy to form. Although, practically speaking, a partnership *should* have a written agreement, UPA does not *require* anything in the way of

---

[1] This is the federal tax rate; most states also levy a corporate tax.
[2] UPA §101 (6).

forms or filings or agreements. If people act like partners—by sharing management and profits—the law will treat them as such, and if they do not act like partners, then nothing they say or write will make them a partnership. (For examples of a partnership agreement, go to http://www.lectlaw.com/formb.htm or http://www.toolkit.cch.com.)

For example, Kevin and Brenda formed an electrical contracting business. The business did so well that Kevin's first wife, Cynthia, asked the court to increase his child support payments. Kevin argued that, because he and Brenda were partners, he was entitled to only half of the business's profits. Therefore his child support should not be increased.

Cynthia claimed that Kevin and Brenda were *not* partners because Kevin had reported all the income from the business on his personal return while Brenda had reported none. Kevin had even put "sole proprietorship" in bold letters on the top of his tax return. No written partnership agreement existed. Kevin and Brenda never informed their accountant that they were a partnership. When Kevin answered interrogatories for Cynthia's lawsuit, he stated that he was sole owner and that Brenda worked for him. Nonetheless, the court held that Brenda and Kevin were partners because Brenda helped manage the business and shared in its profits.[3]

Partnership by Estoppel

Brenda and Kevin wanted to be partners so that they could share the **profits** of their business. In *partnership by estoppel*, non-partners are treated as if they were actually partners and are forced to share *liability*. **Partnership by estoppel applies if:**

- **Participants tell other people that they are partners (even though they are not), or they allow other people to say, without contradiction, that they are partners**

- **A third party relies on this assertion; and**

- **The third party suffers harm.**

Dr. William Martin was held liable under a theory of partnership by estoppel because: he told a patient that he and Dr. John Maceluch were partners (although they were not); the patient relied on this statement and made appointments to see Dr. Maceluch; and she was harmed by Dr. Maceluch's malpractice. He refused to come to the hospital when she was in labor and, as a result, her child was born with brain damage. Although Dr. Martin was out of the country at the time, he was as liable as if he had committed the malpractice himself.[4]

LIABILITY

Under UPA, **every partner is an agent of the partnership**. Thus the entire partnership is liable for the act of one partner in, say, signing a contract. **A partnership is also liable for any torts that a partner commits in the ordinary course of the partnership's business.** Thus, if one partner wields a careless calculator, the whole partnership is liable.

---

[3] *In Re Marriage of Cynthia Hassiepen*, 269 Ill. App. 3d 559, 646 N.E.2d 1348, 1995 Ill. App. LEXIS 101.
[4] *Haught v. Maceluch*, 681 F.2d 290, 1982 U.S. App. LEXIS 17123 (5th Cir. 1982).

It gets worse. **If a partnership does not have enough assets to pay its debts, creditors may go after the personal property of individual partners, whether or not they were in any way responsible for the debt.** Because partners have *joint and several liability,* creditors can sue the partnership and the partners together or in separate lawsuits or in any combination. The partnership and the partners are all individually liable for the full amount of the debt, but, obviously, the creditor cannot keep collecting after he has already received the total amount owed. **Also note that, even if creditors have a judgment against an individual partner, they cannot go after that partner's assets until all the partnership's assets are exhausted.**[5]

Letitia, one of the world's wealthiest people, enters into a partnership with penniless Harry to drill for oil on her estate. While driving on partnership business, Harry crashes into Gus, seriously injuring him. Gus can sue any combination of the partnership, Letitia, and Harry for the full amount, even though Letitia was 2,000 miles away on her Caribbean island when the accident occurred and she had many times cautioned Harry to drive carefully. Even if Gus obtains a judgment against Letitia, however, he cannot recover against her while the partnership still has assets. So, for all practical purposes, he must try to collect first against the partnership. If the partnership is bankrupt and he manages to collect the full amount from Letitia, he cannot then try to recover against Harry.

MANAGEMENT

The management of a partnership can be a significant challenge.

Management Rights

Unless the partnership agrees otherwise, partners share both profits and losses equally, and each partner has an equal right to manage the business.[6] In a large partnership, with hundreds of partners, too many cooks can definitely spoil the firm's profitability. That is why large partnerships are almost always run by one or a few partners who are designated as **managing partners** or **members of the executive committee.** Some firms are run almost dictatorially by the partner who brings in the most business (called a "rainmaker"). Nonetheless, even in relatively autocratic firms, the atmosphere tends to be less hierarchical than in a corporation, where employees are accustomed to the concept of having a boss. Whatever the reality, partners by and large like to think of themselves as being the equal of every other partner.

Management Duties

Partners have a *fiduciary duty* to the partnership. This duty means that:

- *Partners are liable to the partnership for gross negligence or intentional misconduct.*

- *Partners cannot compete with the partnership.* Each partner must turn over to the partnership all earnings from any activity that is related to the partnership's business. Thus law firms would typically expect a partner to turn over any fees

---

[5] UPA §307.
[6] Partnerships have the right to change internal management rules, but they cannot alter the rules governing their relationship with outsiders (such as the rules on liability).

he earned as a director of a company, but he could keep royalties from his novel on scuba diving.

- *A partner may not take an opportunity away from the partnership unless the other partners consent.* If the partnership wants to buy a private plane and a partner hears of one for sale, she must give the partnership an opportunity to buy it before she purchases it herself.

- *If a partner engages in a conflict of interest, he must turn over to the partnership any profits he earned from that activity.* In the following case, one partner bought partnership property secretly. Is that a conflict of interest?

MARSH V. GENTRY

642 S.W.2d 574, 1982 Ky. LEXIS 315
Supreme Court of Kentucky, 1982

FACTS: Tom Gentry and John Marsh were partners in a business that bought and sold racehorses. The partnership paid $155,000 for *Champagne Woman*, who subsequently had a foal named *Excitable Lady*. The partners decided to sell *Champagne Woman* at the annual Keeneland auction, the world's premier thoroughbred horse auction. On the day of the auction, Gentry decided to bid on the horse personally, without telling Marsh. Gentry bought *Champagne Woman* for $135,000. Later, he told Marsh that someone from California had approached him about buying *Excitable Lady*. Marsh agreed to the sale. Although he repeatedly asked Gentry the name of the purchaser, Gentry refused to tell him. Not until 11 months later, when *Excitable Lady* won a race at Churchill Downs, did Marsh learn that Gentry had been the purchaser. Marsh became the Excitable Man.

ISSUE: Did Gentry violate his fiduciary duty when he bought partnership property without telling his partner?

EXCERPTS FROM JUSTICE O'HARA'S DECISION: Admittedly, at an auction sale, the specific identity of a purchaser cannot be ascertained before the sale, but [Kentucky partnership law] required a full disclosure by Gentry to Marsh that he would be a prospective purchaser. As to the private sale of *Excitable Lady*, Marsh consented to a sale from the partnership, at a specified price, to the

prospective purchaser in California. Even though Marsh obtained the stipulated purchase price, a partner has an absolute right to know when his partner is the purchaser. Partners scrutinize buy-outs by their partners in an entirely different light than an ordinary third party sale. This distinction is vividly made without contradiction when Marsh later indicated that he would not have consented to either sale had he known that Gentry was the purchaser. Under these facts, it is obvious that Gentry failed to disclose all that he knew concerning the sales, including his desire to purchase partnership property.

[P]artners, in their relations with other partners, [must] maintain a higher degree of good faith due to the partnership agreement. The requirement of full disclosure among partners as to partnership business cannot be escaped. Had Gentry made a full disclosure to his partner of his intentions to purchase the partnership property, Marsh would not later be heard to complain of the transaction.

Finally, Gentry maintains that it is an accepted practice at auction sales of thoroughbreds for one partner to secretly bid on partnership stock to accomplish a buy-out. We would emphatically state, however, for the benefit of those engaged in such practices, that where an "accepted business practice" conflicts with existing law, the law whether statutory or court ordered, is controlling. To hold otherwise would be chaotic. ◢

TERMINATING A PARTNERSHIP

A partnership begins with an association of two or more people. Appropriately, the end of a partnership begins with a *dissociation*. **A dissociation occurs when a partner quits.**

Dissociation

A partnership is a personal relationship built on trust. All partners are agents for the partnership, and each partner is personally liable for its debts. Under these circumstances, courts will not force someone to remain in a partnership, no matter what the partnership agreement says. **A partner always has the *power* to leave a partnership but may not have the *right*.** In other words, a partner can always dissociate, but she may have to pay damages for any harm that her departure causes.

A dissociation is a fork in the road: **the partnership can either buy out the departing partner(s) and continue in business or wind up the business and terminate the partnership.** Exhibit 16.2 illustrates the dissociation process under UPA. Most large firms provide in their partnership agreement that, upon dissociation, the business continues. If, however, the partnership chooses to terminate the business, it must follow three steps: dissolution, winding up, and termination.

Three Steps to Termination

Dissolution.   The rules on dissolution depend, in part, on the type of partnership. If the partners have agreed in advance how long the partnership will last, it is a **term partnership**. At the end of the specified term, the partnership automatically ends. Otherwise, it is a **partnership at will**, which means that any of the partners can leave at any time, for any reason.

Exhibit 16.2

UPA provides certain circumstances under which a partnership automatically dissolves (although partners can always overrule UPA and decide by unanimous vote to continue the partnership). According to UPA, a partnership dissolves:

- In a partnership at will, when a partner withdraws.

- In a term partnership when:

  - A partner is dissociated and half of the remaining partners vote to wind up the partnership business.

  - All the partners agree to dissolve.

  - The term expires or the partnership achieves its goal.

- In any partnership when:

  - An event occurs that the partners had agreed would cause dissolution.

  - The partnership business becomes illegal.

  - A court determines that the partnership is unlikely to succeed. If the partners simply cannot get along or they cannot make a profit, any partner has the right to ask a court to dissolve the partnership. For example, two men formed a partnership to buy The San Juan Star, Puerto Rico's English-language newspaper. They ended up in court, each bitterly accusing the other of having violated the partnership agreement. Their hostility was so great that the judge ultimately decided he could not tell who was at fault and, furthermore, the two men could never run a business together. The court ordered one partner to buy out the other. If the partners could not agree on a buyout, the judge was prepared to order a sale of the newspaper to outsiders.[7]

Winding Up.   During the winding up process, all debts of the partnership are paid, and the remaining proceeds are distributed to the partners.

Termination.   After the sometimes lengthy and complex winding up, the actual termination of a partnership is anticlimactic. Termination happens automatically once the winding up is finished. The partnership is not required to do anything official; it can go out of the world even more quietly and simply than it came in.

Limited Liability Partnerships

A limited liability partnership (LLP) is a type of general partnership that most states now permit. There is a very important distinction, however, between these two forms of organization: **in an LLP, the partners are not liable for the debts of the partnership.**[8] To form an LLP, the partners must file a statement of qualification with state officials. LLPs must also file annual reports. The other attributes of a partnership remain the same. Thus an LLP is not a taxable entity, and it has the right to choose its duration (that is, it can, but does not have to, survive the dissociation of a member).

---

[7] *Nemazee Capital Corp. v. Angulo Capital Corp.*, 1996 U.S. Dist. LEXIS 10750 (S. Dist. NY, 1996).
[8] UPA §306(c).

With LLPs, however, it is important to bear in mind that the law is still undeveloped. The first major test of the liability provisions may well be the Enron case. Enron was a high-flying company that, as it turned out, owed much of its success to faulty accounting. Investors are seeking compensation from Enron's auditor, Arthur Andersen. As the following article indicates, the cutting edge of the law is not always a comfortable place to be.

Among the life-threatening issues facing Arthur Andersen LLP, one looming especially large for its partners is how effectively those three letters—LLP—shield them from potentially ruinous personal liability. Concerns are growing among Andersen's roughly 1,750 U.S. partners that even those who had nothing to do with the firm's work for Enron Corp. could eventually face personal liability stemming from the botched audit.

Because it is unclear how much protection the LLP structure will provide Andersen partners, partnership and bankruptcy lawyers are expected to be following the matter closely. "As far as I know, there has never been a litigation test of the extent of the LLP shield, and there have been very few LLP cases about liability at all," said Larry Ribstein, a law professor at George Mason University.

In theory, no partner is supposed to lose more than what he or she has invested in the firm. An exception arises when a partner is guilty of professional wrongdoing or negligence, partnership experts said. In those cases, that partner becomes personally liable. The courts haven't yet set clear precedent on the stickier question of who else might be personally liable. The firm's managers? The supervisors of the guilty parties? Every partner in the firm that put its imprint on a corporate audit?[9] ▪

UPDATE

Have any Andersen partners incurred personal liability? If so, what was their role in the Enron audits? ▪

Professional Corporations

Most states now allow professionals to incorporate, but in a special way. These organizations are called "professional corporations" or "PCs." **In many states, PCs provide more liability protection than a partnership.** If a member of a PC commits malpractice, the corporation's assets are at risk, but not the personal assets of the innocent members. If Drs. Sharp, Payne, and Graves form a *partnership*, all the partners will be personally liable when Dr. Payne accidentally leaves her scalpel inside a patient. If the three doctors have formed a *PC* instead, Dr. Payne's Aspen condo and the assets of the PC will be at risk, but not the personal assets of the two other doctors.

Generally, the shareholders of a PC are not personally liable for the contract debts of the organization, such as leases or bank loans. Thus, if Sharp, Payne & Graves, P.C. is unable to pay its rent, the landlord cannot recover from the personal assets of any of the doctors. As partners, the doctors would be personally liable.

---

[9] M. Pacelle and I. J. Dugan, "Partners Forever? Within Andersen, Personal Liability May Bring Ruin," *The Wall Street Journal*, Apr. 2, 2002, p. C1.

PCs have some limitations. First, all shareholders of the corporation must be members of the same profession. For Sharp, Payne & Graves, P.C., that means all shareholders must be licensed physicians. Other valued employees cannot own stock. Second, like other corporations, the required legal technicalities for forming and maintaining a PC are expensive and time-consuming. Third, tax issues can be complicated. A PC is a separate taxable entity, like any other corporation. It must pay tax on its profits, and then its shareholders pay tax on any dividends they receive. *Salaries*, however, are deductible from firm profits. Thus the PC can avoid taxes on its profits by paying out all profits as salary. But any profits remaining in firm coffers *at the end of the year* are taxable. To avoid tax, PCs must be careful to calculate their profits accurately and pay them out before year's end. This chore can be time-consuming, and any error may cause unnecessary tax liability.

Limited Partnerships and Limited Liability Limited Partnerships

The owners of the Montreal Expos asked investment banker Jacques Menard to find a buyer for the baseball team. Instead, he found 11 other people to help him buy the team. They formed a limited partnership, and each purchaser invested between $1 million and $7 million. During their first year of ownership, the Expos lost nearly $5 million and their final 14 home games, finishing in the cellar of their division. Given this dismal showing, management had no choice but to fire the popular team manager. Then a concrete beam in the team's stadium collapsed.

Fortunately, the owners had formed a *limited* partnership. Limited partnerships and general partnerships have similar names but, like many siblings, they operate very differently. Here are the major differences between these two types of organizations.

STRUCTURE

General partnerships have only *general* partners. Limited partnerships have two types of partners—*limited* partners and *general* partners. A limited partnership must have at least one of each.

LIABILITY

All the partners in a general partnership are *personally* liable for the debts of the partnership. **In a limited partnership, however, the limited partners are not *personally* liable.** The limited partners are like corporate shareholders—they risk only their investment in the partnership (which is called their "capital contribution"). No matter how much money the Expos lose, creditors cannot take the personal property of the limited partners.

At this writing, virtually every state provides that general partners are personally liable for the debts of a limited partnership. To avoid this liability, most general partners are, in fact, corporations. Thus Claude Brochu, the Expos' general manager, could form a corporation—Brochu, Inc.—to serve as general partner. Then, only the assets of the corporation, not Brochu's personal assets, would be at risk.

The revised version of the Uniform Limited Partnership Act, however, permits a limited partnership, in its certificate of formation, simply to declare itself a *limited liability* limited partnership.[10] **In a limited liability limited partnership, the general partner is not personally liable for the debts of the partnership.** This provision effectively removes the major disadvantage of limited partnerships. Although, at this writing, no states have yet passed the revised version of the Uniform Limited Partnership Act, this revision would seem to indicate the trend for the future.

TAXES

Limited partnerships, like general partnerships, are not taxable entities. Income is taxed only once before landing in a partner's pocket, and partners can deduct losses against their other income.

FORMATION

General partnerships can be formed very casually, sometimes without the partners even being aware of it. Not so for limited partnerships: the general partners must file a **certificate of limited partnership** with their Secretary of State. Although most limited partnerships do have a partnership agreement, it is not required. (A sample limited partnership agreement is available at http://www.worldlawdirect.com/builddoc.php.) Failure to comply with the necessary formalities can cause serious problems, as the following case illustrates.

YOU BE THE JUDGE

CELLWAVE TELEPHONE SERVICES L.P. V. FCC

30 F.3d 1533, 1994 U.S. App. LEXIS 21834
United States Court of Appeals for the D.C. Circuit, 1994

FACTS: Cellwave Telephone Services Limited Partnership applied to the Federal Communications Commission (FCC) for a license to operate and construct cellular telephone systems in two rural areas. The FCC awards these licenses by lottery. Cellwave won the lottery, but upon investigation, the FCC discovered that Cellwave had never filed its limited partnership certificate with the Secretary of State in Delaware although all the limited partners had signed the limited partnership agreement. The FCC dismissed Cellwave's application on the grounds that the partnership did not exist when the application was filed.

YOU BE THE JUDGE: Did the FCC have the right to dismiss Cellwave's application?

ARGUMENT FOR CELLWAVE: Of all the petty, bureaucratic decisions! The limited partnership was effectively in existence as soon as the limited partners signed the agreement. It is not as if the Secretary of State had to *approve* the certificate in any way. He could not refuse to accept it for filing. The filing simply provides an official record that the partnership exists. But the FCC did not need official notice; it had the original agreement, which is better than a certificate from the Secretary of State.

ARGUMENT FOR THE FCC: The number one priority of the FCC is to ensure adequate service for everyone in America. For many people in rural areas, a cellular phone is the most reliable

---

[10] ULPA §102(9).

means of communication. When it awards a license, the FCC has to be sure that the licensee will be able to develop a telephone system. Without these strict rules, people would sign up for the lottery and then, once they had won, try to put together a company. The FCC cannot take that chance with rural citizens. If Cellwave cannot manage a simple legal task like organizing a limited partnership, how can it run a telephone system?

Cellwave argues that all the limited partners had signed the limited partnership agreement and that is sufficient. The FCC did not make up the rules; it is simply following Delaware law, which says very precisely, "a limited partnership is formed at the time of the filing of the initial certificate of limited partnership in the Office of the Secretary of State." What could be clearer than that? If Cellwave has a problem with the law, it should talk with its legislators. ▰

MANAGEMENT

General partners have the right to manage a limited partnership. Limited partners are essentially passive investors with few management rights beyond the right to be informed about the partnership business. Limited partnership agreements can, however, expand the rights of limited partners. These agreements, for example, often permit a substantial majority (e.g., two-thirds) of the limited partners to remove a general partner. In any event, when *general* partnerships grow large, management becomes difficult. But because *limited* partners are not allowed to manage, a limited partnership can handle a very large number of partners.

TRANSFER OF OWNERSHIP

As is the case with a general partnership, limited partners always have the right to transfer the *value* of their partnership interest, but they can only sell or give away the interest itself if the partnership agreement permits. Thus, if Sadie is a limited partner in the Expos, but decides to invest in basketball instead, she does not have the automatic right to sell her limited partnership interest to Pedro. Although she could sell Pedro the right to receive profit distributions from the Expos, he would not *be* a limited partner, with the right to vote in meetings.

DURATION

Unless the partnership agreement provides otherwise, limited partnerships enjoy perpetual existence—they continue even as partners come and go.

Corporations

Although the concept of a corporation is very old—it began with the Greeks and spread from them through the Romans into English law—corporations were traditionally viewed with deep suspicion. What were shareholders doing to need limited liability? Why did they have to cower behind a corporate shield? For this reason, shareholders originally needed special permission to form a corporation. In England, corporations could be created only by special charter from the king or, later, from Parliament. But with the advent of the Industrial Revolution, large-scale manufacturing enterprises needed huge amounts of capital from investors who were not involved in management and did not want to be personally liable for the debts of an organization that they were not managing. In 1811, New York became the first jurisdiction in the United States to permit routine incorporation.[11]

State laws regulate corporations, but federal statutes determine their tax status. Many states treat small corporations differently and even give them a different name: close corporations. The federal tax code also provides more favorable tax treatment to some small corporations and calls them S corporations. But the two sets of statutes are completely independent. Thus a close corporation or a regular (nonclose) corporation may or may not be an S corporation. Exhibit 16.3 illustrates the difference between state and IRS regulation of corporations.

CORPORATIONS IN GENERAL

When Judy George was a young child, her parents started a plating business using a process her father had invented. Like many entrepreneurs, her parents devoted so much time and energy to this new project that they were rarely at home. Feeling abandoned by her parents, George became obsessed with her surroundings. If she could make her room just the way she wanted it, she would feel safe. As she put it, "Design was a way of fulfilling my own personal fantasy." She also vowed that one day she would start her own business to make money and create beautiful designs. George realized her dream when she started Domain, an upscale, European-style chain of furniture stores.

George's lawyer suggested that she incorporate Domain. He explained that a corporation would offer the protection of limited liability. If Domain flopped and could not pay its bills, George and her backers would lose their investment in the company, but not their other assets.

He also explained that limited liability does not protect against all debts. Individuals are always responsible for their *own* acts. If a Domain employee was in an accident while driving a company van, Domain would be liable for any harm to the other driver, but its shareholders would not be personally liable. If George herself crashed the van, Domain would be liable, and *so would George*. If Domain did not pay the judgment, George would have to, from her personal assets if necessary. A corporation protects managers and investors from personal liability for the debts

Exhibit 16.3
Both a regular and a close corporation can be either a C or an S corporation.

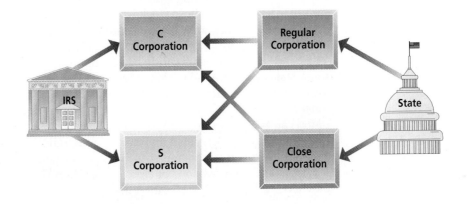

of the corporation and the actions of others, but not against personal negligence (or other torts and crimes).

Corporations have other advantages besides limited liability. They provide flexibility for enterprises small (with one owner) and large (thousands of shareholders). For example, partnership interests are not transferable without the permission of the other partners, whereas corporate stock can be easily bought and sold. Further, when a sole proprietor dies, legally so does the business. But corporations have perpetual existence: they can continue without their founders.

The major disadvantage of a corporation is simply the expense and effort required to create and operate it. Because corporations are taxable entities, they must pay taxes and file returns. The cost of establishing a corporation may exceed $1,000 in legal and filing fees, not to mention the cost of the annual filings that states require. Corporations must also hold annual meetings for both shareholders and directors. Minutes of these meetings must be kept indefinitely in the company minute book.

Judy George knew that she needed at least $3 million to get Domain up and running. She could not borrow that much money, so she needed to sell stock. She chose the corporate form of organization primarily because it would be the most convenient for raising funds.

CLOSE CORPORATIONS

Reynoldo has always been a fabulous cook. He, his son Juan, and Juan's girlfriend Marta have decided to open a restaurant featuring "cucina nueva"—modern, light Latin American food. Reynoldo will do the cooking in the back, while Juan and Marta run the front operation, everything from maitre d' to accountant. They will finance the start-up costs of *Abogado Verde* by borrowing from the local bank; the loan will be secured by a mortgage on their houses. One of the first questions they face is: What form of organization? A sole proprietorship will not work, because there are three of them. They are concerned about the liability of a partnership. A corporation may be the best option, except it seems like an expensive bother. Who would be on their board of directors? Why do they even need a board? They have no plans to sell shares to the public. They want to act like a partnership, with all decisions made equally, but they need the legal protection of a corporation.

Their lawyer suggests that a close corporation might be the best choice. Originally, the terms **"close corporation"** and **"closely held corporation"** referred simply to a company whose stock was not publicly traded on a stock exchange (in other words, a "privately held" company). Most close corporations are small, although some privately held corporations, such as Hallmark Cards, Inc., and Mars, Inc. (maker of Mars candy bars), are huge. Beginning in New York in 1948, some states have amended their corporation statutes to make special provisions for entrepreneurs such as the *Abogado Verde* team. In some cases a corporation must affirmatively elect to be treated as a close corporation; in others, any corporation can take advantage of these special provisions. Now when lawyers refer to close corporations, they usually mean not merely a privately held company, but one that has taken advantage of the close corporation provisions of its state code.

Although the provisions of close corporation statutes vary from state to state, they tend to have certain common themes:

- **Protection of Minority Shareholders.** Marta is concerned that Reynoldo and Juan may form an alliance and vote against her. Close corporations are permitted great leeway to prevent such problems. For example, *Abogado Verde, Inc.*, could require a unanimous vote of all shareholders to choose officers, set salaries, or pay dividends. It could grant each shareholder veto power over all important corporate decisions.

- **Transfer Restrictions.** What would happen if Reynoldo sold some of his shares to his other (irresponsible) children? Or if Marta and Juan broke up, and Juan sold shares to his new girlfriend? Close corporation statutes often limit a shareholder's ability to sell shares without first offering them to the other owners. Similarly, if Reynoldo died, Juan and Marta would have the first option to buy his stock.

- **Flexibility.** Close corporations can typically operate without a board of directors, a formal set of bylaws, or annual shareholder meetings.

- **Dispute Resolution.** The three shareholders are allowed to agree in advance that any one of them can dissolve the corporation if some particular event occurs or, if they choose, for any reason at all. Marta could, for example, insist on the right to dissolve the corporation herself at any time, or if revenues for a month fall below a certain level. Even without such an agreement, a shareholder can ask a court to dissolve a close corporation if the other owners behave "oppressively" or "unfairly." The mere threat of such an action will be some check on Reynoldo and Juan.

The following case illustrates that, no matter how badly a shareholder behaves, her rights in a close corporation are still protected.

MICHAEL L. RETZER V. NANCY B. RETZER

578 So. 2d 580, 1990 Miss. LEXIS 858
Supreme Court of Mississippi, 1990

FACTS: Shortly after Mr. and Mrs. Retzer were married, they moved to Greenville, Mississippi, and opened a McDonald's restaurant. Mr. Retzer managed the restaurant, working 18 hours a day. Mrs. Retzer made little contribution to the business. Mr. Retzer subsequently purchased four additional McDonald's restaurants, transferring ownership of them to Retzer and Retzer, Inc., a Mississippi close corporation. Mr. and Mrs. Retzer each owned 1,600 shares of the corporation.

Mr. Retzer discovered that his wife was having an affair with their attorney. As a condition for salvaging their marriage, Mrs. Retzer agreed to end the affair. She also permitted the corporation to issue 10 additional shares to Mr. Retzer to give him corporate control.

Mrs. Retzer was a profligate spender, often paying more than $3,000 for a dress. When she overdrew her checking account, an officer at the bank would notify Mr. Retzer so that he could replenish her account. Once, when he let her checks bounce, Mrs. Retzer came to his office and began throwing pieces of valuable porcelain. Mr. Retzer called the pastor to calm her down.

Despite the agreement with her husband, Mrs. Retzer continued her affair. The Retzers subsequently divorced on the grounds of Mrs. Retzer's adultery. Their joint net worth was $4 million.

ISSUE: What are Mr. Retzer's obligations to Mrs. Retzer as a minority shareholder in Retzer and Retzer, Inc.?

EXCERPTS FROM JUSTICE HAWKINS'S DECISION: Where divorce has been granted to the husband on the ground of the wife's adultery, this court has consistently denied any alimony, period. Mr. Retzer does have substantial financial obligations to Mrs.

Retzer, however, arising from her ownership of almost half of the shares of Retzer and Retzer, Inc.

Courts look quite differently upon the respective duties existing between majority and minority shareholders in publicly held and close corporations. Retzer and Retzer, Inc., is a very close corporation, which has existed solely for the financial benefit of two people, the Retzers. For almost two decades, and through Mr. Retzer's management, the corporation has indeed furnished them both with large incomes. Now, through ownership of ten more shares than she, Mr. Retzer has control of the management of Retzer and Retzer. As such, under well-settled principles he has a fiduciary obligation to Mrs. Retzer in the management of her property. He has a trustee's duty to preserve, protect and produce income from her corporate shares.

He must manage the corporation prudently, and after paying necessary and reasonable expenses, and setting aside whatever is reasonably necessary for corporate reserves and equipment and facilities, pay her 49.8 percent of the net remaining. He will not be acting at arm's length, but as trustee over her shares. He must keep her currently, fully and accurately informed and abreast of his management, and under regular periodic accounting. While their interest as husband and wife was essentially identical, now they are adverse to each other. This will make his conduct as trustee that much more subject to close scrutiny by a chancery court.

With the hostility existing between them, it would no doubt be preferable if somehow the property of Mr. and Mrs. Retzer were entirely separate, with neither depending on the other. The fact remains that at present they are Siamese twins in Retzer and Retzer. If the burden becomes unduly oppressive for either, the chancery court is not without power to give relief, even to appointing a receivership for the corporation or dissolving it. ◢

This case also alludes to the major disadvantage of a close corporation. Because minority shareholders are given such a strong voice, it is easy for stalemates to develop. In such a case, shareholders may ask a court to dissolve the enterprise. Is your relationship ready for entrepreneurship? The Web site http://entrepreneurs.about.com/cs/familybusiness offers advice to entrepreneurial couples.

S CORPORATIONS

Although entrepreneurs are often optimistic about the likely success of their new enterprise, in truth, the majority of new businesses lose money in their early years. Only about half of all start-ups *survive* as long as eight years. Congress created S corporations (aka "S corps") to encourage entrepreneurship by offering tax breaks. The name "S corporation" comes from the provision of the Internal Revenue Code that created this form of organization.[12] **Shareholders of S corps have the best of all worlds: the limited liability of a corporation and the tax status of a partnership.** Like a partnership, an S corp is not a taxable entity—all of the company's profits and losses pass through to the shareholders, who pay tax at their individual rates. It avoids the double taxation of a regular corporation (called a "C corporation"). If, as is often the case, the start-up loses money, investors can deduct these losses against their other income.

When a group of wealthy investors decided to start a magazine called *Living Alternatives*, their lawyer suggested they organize as an S corp. The investors knew that magazines are risky and that most start-ups fail. But successful magazines are

---

[12] 26 U.S.C. §1361.

very profitable, and these investors believed in the magazine's mission—teaching consumers how to protect the environment. Unfortunately, the magazine failed after a year, but at least the investors could deduct these losses against their other (ample) income. Without this incentive many of them would never have made the initial investment.

If *Living Alternatives* had been profitable, the investors might have decided to continue as an S corporation to avoid the double taxation on dividends. Eventually, however, most companies terminate their S election because of the limitations on this form of organization:

- There can be only one class of stock (although voting rights can vary within the class).

- There can be only 75 shareholders.

- Shareholders must be individuals, estates, charities, pension funds, or trusts, not partnerships or corporations.

- Shareholders must be citizens or residents of the United States, not non-resident aliens.

- All shareholders must agree that the company should be an S corporation.

Although *most* states follow the federal lead on S corporations, a small number treat an S corp like a regular C corporation. In these states, the companies must pay state corporate tax.

Limited Liability Companies

You may be thinking that there are already as many different forms of organization as any entrepreneur could possibly need, but, as you have seen, none of them is perfect. In a continuing search for earthly perfection, states now permit limited liability companies (LLCs). **An LLC offers the limited liability of a corporation and the tax status of a partnership, without the disadvantages of an S corporation.**

An LLC is an extremely useful form of organization increasingly favored by entrepreneurs. It is not, however, as simple as it perhaps should be. Owing to a complex history that involves painful interaction between IRS regulations and state laws (the details of which we will spare you), the specific provisions of state laws vary greatly. To add to the difficulty, there are few court decisions interpreting LLC statutes, and these few cases sometimes disagree. An effort to remedy this confusion—the Uniform Limited Liability Company Act—has not at this point been widely accepted and, in fact, has been heavily criticized. Thus, we can only discuss general trends in state laws. Before forming an LLC, you should carefully review the laws in your particular state.

FORMATION

To organize an LLC, you generally need two documents: a charter and an operating agreement. The charter is short, containing basic information such as name and address. It must be filed with the Secretary of State in your jurisdiction. An operating agreement sets out the rights and obligations of the owners, called members. Although some states do not require an operating agreement, lawyers recommend them as a way to avoid disputes. A sample is shown at http://www.tannedfeet.com/simple_operating_Agreement_for_llc.doc.

LIMITED LIABILITY

As in a corporation, members are not personally liable for debts of the company. They risk only their investment. The following case illustrates the scope of this protection.

ANTHONY V. BLUM

1999 Conn. Super. LEXIS 1037
Superior Court of Connecticut, 1999

FACTS: Leonard C. Blum, an attorney, was negligent in his representation of Louis Anthony, Sr. In settlement of Anthony's claim against him, Blum signed a promissory note for $10,400 on behalf of his law firm, Gladstone, Schwartz, Blum & Woods, LLC. When the law firm did not pay, Anthony filed suit against Blum. In his suit, Anthony alleged that Blum, as a member of the LLC, was personally liable for the promissory note.

ISSUE: Is a member personally liable for the debt of an LLC that was caused by his own negligence?

EXCERPTS FROM JUDGE MELVILLE'S DECISION: Liability of members of limited liability companies is prescribed by statute:

> [A] person who is a member or manager of a limited liability company is not liable, solely by reason of being a member or manager, under a judgment, decree or order of a court, or in any other manner, for a debt, obligation or liability of the limited liability

company, whether arising in contract, tort or otherwise or for the acts or omissions of any other member, manager, agent or employee of the limited liability company.

[This statute further] limits a member's personal liability to the member's own negligent or wrongful acts.

Anthony argues that the negligence of Blum in a prior action constituted the consideration upon which the promissory note was executed. Therefore, Anthony argues that Blum can be held personally liable. However, the present action is not a malpractice action but a breach of contract action. Thus, Anthony seeks payment of a debt arising from a contract, which is a liability that Blum is not personally liable for pursuant to [the statute].

Accordingly, [a] finding that Blum is not personally liable follows from the subordinate facts that Blum executed the promissory note as a member of the LLC and on behalf of the LLC.

TAX STATUS

As in a partnership, income flows through the company to the individual members, avoiding the double taxation of a corporation.

FLEXIBILITY

Unlike S corporations, LLCs can have members that are corporations, partnerships, or nonresident aliens. LLCs can also have different classes of stock. Unlike corporations, LLCs are not required to hold annual meetings or maintain a minute book.

STANDARD FORMS

Corporations are so familiar that the standard documents (such as a charter, by-laws, and shareholder agreement) are well established and widely available. Lawyers can form a corporation easily, and the Internet offers a host of free forms. This is not the case with LLCs. As yet, there are no standard forms to make the formation of an LLC both easy and inexpensive. Free forms are much more difficult to find on the Internet. With state laws varying so widely, standard forms may even be dangerous.

TRANSFERABILITY OF INTERESTS

In corporations, shareholders can generally sell or give their shares to whomever they want. In partnerships, partners generally must obtain the unanimous approval of the other partners before transferring their partnership. In keeping with the flexible approach of LLCs, the members have a choice. If they want, the operating agreement can give them the right to transfer their interests freely to anyone. However, if the operating agreement is silent on this issue, then the members of the LLC must obtain the unanimous permission of the remaining members before transferring their ownership rights.

DURATION

It used to be that LLCs automatically dissolved upon the withdrawal of a member (owing to, for example, death, resignation, or bankruptcy). The current trend in state laws, however, is to permit an LLC to continue in operation even after a member withdraws. Unless the operating agreement provides otherwise, the LLC must pay the departing member the value of her interest.

GOING PUBLIC

Once an LLC goes public, it loses its favorable tax status and is taxed as a corporation, not a partnership.[13] Thus, there is no real advantage to using the LLC form of organization for a publicly traded company. And there are some disadvantages: unlike corporations, LLCs do not enjoy a well-established set of statutory and case law that is relatively consistent across the many states. For this reason, it may well turn out that most privately held companies begin as LLCs but change to corporations when they go public.

CHANGING FORMS

Some companies that are now corporations might prefer to be LLCs. However, the IRS would consider this change to be a sale of the corporate assets and would levy a tax on the value of these assets. For this reason, few corporations have made the change. However, switching from a partnership to an LLC or from an LLC to a corporation is not considered a sale and does not have the same adverse tax impact.

---

[13] 26 U.S.C. §7704.

Joint Ventures

Dutch entertainment giant PolyGram, which has been steadily muscling into the mainstream movie business, announced a key partnership with longtime Hollywood players Tom Pollock and Ivan Reitman. The five-year deal calls for PolyGram, the world's largest recorded-music company, to set up a joint venture in Santa Barbara that will generate three to five films a year. PolyGram, which scored a major hit with *Bean*, will own a third of the yet-to-be-named production company. Pollock, head of Universal Studios' movie operations for a decade, and Reitman, who directed *Animal House, Ghostbusters, Twins,* and *Dave,* will own the rest.

PolyGram did not disclose how much it will invest in the joint venture, which will handle Reitman's movies and seek projects from other directors and producers. The company has made similar joint venture deals with director Tony Scott and actress Jodie Foster. "PolyGram is taking a reasonably conservative approach in these joint ventures with pretty professional names," said Harold Vogel, an analyst at Cowen & Co. in New York.[14] ▪

This newspaper article refers to this business arrangement as both a "partnership" and a "joint venture." What is the difference in meaning? **A joint venture is a partnership for a limited purpose.** PolyGram, Pollock, and Reitman do not intend to work together on all their movies. They have joined together for the limited purpose of making three to five films a year. If they had joined in a full-scale partnership, all three parties would be bound by contracts that any one of them signed. In a joint venture, only contracts relating to the limited purpose are binding on all three. If PolyGram signs a music contract with Sheryl Crow, Pollock and Reitman are not liable on that contract. But if the PolyGram/Pollock/Reitman joint venture enters into a contract with Jennifer Aniston to star in a movie, Pollock and Reitman are liable, too. Nonprofit enterprises do not qualify as joint ventures—the purpose, however limited, must include making a profit.

Franchises

This chapter has presented an overview of the various forms of organization. Franchises are not, strictly speaking, a separate form of organization. They are included here because they represent an important option for entrepreneurs. In the United States, one in 12 small businesses is a franchise. Franchises generate sales of close to $1 trillion each year and provide jobs for more than eight million people. Well-known franchises include Dunkin' Donuts, Midas Muffler, and McDonald's. Most franchisors and franchisees are corporations, although they could legally choose to be any of the forms discussed in this chapter.

Buying a franchise is a compromise between starting one's own business as an entrepreneur and working for someone else as an employee. Franchisees are free to choose which franchise to buy, where to locate it, and how to staff it. But they are not completely on their own. They are buying an established business with all

---

[14] Dave McNary, "PolyGram Sets Up Key Joint Venture," *The Daily News of Los Angeles,* Feb. 14, 1998, p. B2. Reprinted with permission.

the kinks worked out. In case the owner has never boiled water before, the McDonald's operations manual explains everything from how to set the temperature controls on the stove, to the number of seconds that fries must cook, to the length of time they can be held in the rack before being discarded. And a well-known name like McDonald's or Mrs. Fields ought, by itself, to bring customers through the door.

There is, however, a fine line between being helpful and being oppressive. Franchisees sometimes complain that franchisor control is too tight—tips on cooking fries might be appreciated, but rules on how often to sweep the floor are not. Sometimes franchisors, in their zeal to maintain standards, prohibit innovation that appeals to regional tastes. Just because spicy biscuits are unpopular in New England does not mean they should be banned in the South.

Franchises can be very costly to acquire, anywhere from several thousand dollars to several million. That fee is usually payable up front, whether or not a cookie or burger is ever sold. On top of the up-front fee, franchisees also pay an annual fee that is a percentage of *gross sales revenues*, not *profit*. Sometimes the fee seems to eat up all the profits. Franchisees also complain when they are forced to buy supplies from headquarters. In theory, the franchisors can purchase hamburger meat and paper plates more cheaply in bulk. On the other hand, the franchisees are a captive audience, and they sometimes allege that headquarters has little incentive to keep prices low. Franchisees also grumble when they are forced to contribute to expensive "co-op advertising" that benefits all the outlets in the region. The following article illustrates the good news—and bad—about buying a franchise.

NEWSWORTHY

Bellingham, Mass. Stephen Gurwitz is proud that his Hilltop Farms convenience store has long been a fixture here in this small town on the Rhode Island border. His grandfather, Milton Gurwitz, opened the little roadside building in 1955 as a place to sell milk and eggs from his farm. His father, Gary Gurwitz, added a deli counter. Four years ago, Stephen converted half the store to a Subway fast-food franchise.

Mr. Gurwitz, 32, said he felt no shame at trading in the old deli counter for a nationally promoted name and formulaic sandwiches that taste the same as their Subway counterparts around the world. For Mr. Gurwitz, joining Subway was a welcome respite from the myriad decisions he has to make in running the convenience store. "They give you the operations manual, which is as thick as the New York City telephone book, and it tells you within a millimeter how thick to slice the onions," said Mr. Gurwitz.

Indeed, Mr. Gurwitz discovered that many issues were no longer his sole responsibility. "Someone stubs his toe in the store, you call the Subway legal department," he said. "How many convenience stores have a legal department?" Research and development, pricing and menus—all are handled for him. The Subway brand also brings name recognition. Mr. Gurwitz credits it with increasing the traffic in his store by about 1,000 customers a week—roughly a 10 percent gain—more than making up for the 11.5 percent of revenues from the sandwich operation he pays to headquarters.

It seems enticing, but Susan P. Kezios learned to be wary of such a deal. She put all her money into a franchise operation of VR Business Brokers in Chicago Heights, Illinois. While she managed to keep the doors open, she struggled with what she calls "the flaws in the system." They began with the contract, which usually imposes an iron-clad form with no exceptions for a franchisee's particular needs.

"These franchise contracts are often legal works of art with franchisor attorneys determining every possible scenario during the entire length of time you'll own the franchise, to the franchisor's benefit—not yours," she said. When the contract comes up for renewal, the terms often change. "If they were taking a 5 percent royalty, they might change it to 8 percent," she said. Some franchisors force their licensees to purchase from certain vendors at inflated prices, for example. They can open franchise units close by, intensifying competition. Franchisees often find it difficult to sell their businesses if they want out, or to open another business in the same industry because of "noncompete" agreements.

Although Subway allowed Mr. Gurwitz to stray from the standard menu by offering Willow Tree Farms chicken salad, a popular local brand, he has few other opportunities to personalize the business. Still, he said, that is all the sovereignty he needs. "If you're a free-spirited person and want to do it your own way," he advised, "you don't buy a franchise."[15]

Although franchises were once relatively unregulated, the states and the federal government have dramatically increased their supervision and regulation of these businesses. The Federal Trade Commission (FTC) requires that, at least 10 business days prior to the sale, franchisors must give prospective franchisees an **offering circular**. This circular must comply either with FTC rules or with the provisions of the Uniform Franchise Offering Circular (UFOC) Guidelines of the North American Securities Administrators' Association (available at http://www.nasaa.org/nasaa/corpfin/UFOC.doc). Most franchisors choose to comply with the UFOC guidelines, because they are accepted by more states than the FTC rules. As a result, the FTC is considering the possibility of eliminating its own offering circular rules and relying instead on the UFOC. The circular must include the following information:

- Any litigation against the company

- Whether it has gone through bankruptcy proceedings in the prior 10 years

- All fees

- Estimates of the required initial investment

- What goods must be purchased from the franchisor

- The number of franchisees in operation

- How many franchisees have gone out of business in the prior three years

The offering circular must also contain audited financial statements and a sample set of the contracts that a franchisee is expected to sign.

The purpose of the offering circular is to ensure that the franchisor discloses all relevant facts. It is not a guarantee of quality. Under UFOC guidelines the following statement must appear on the cover page of the offering circular:

Registration of this franchise by a state does not mean that the state recommends it or has verified the information in this offering circular. If you learn that anything in the

---

[15] Julie Flaherty, "By the Book: Individuality vs. Franchising; Trading Spark of Creativity for the Safety of Numbers," *The New York Times*, Feb. 17, 2001, §C, p. 1. Copyright © 2001 by The New York Times Co. Reprinted by permission.

offering circular is untrue, contact the Federal Trade Commission and (State or Provincial authority).

Suppose you obtain an offering circular for "Shrinking Cats," a franchise that offers psychiatric services for neurotic felines. The company has lost money on all the outlets it operates itself; it has sold only three franchises, two of which have gone out of business; and all the required contracts are ridiculously favorable to the franchisor. Nevertheless, the FTC will still permit sales as long as the franchisor discloses all the information required in the offering circular. Nor will the FTC investigate to make sure that the information is accurate. After the fact, if the FTC discovers the franchisor has violated the rules, it may sue on your behalf. (You do not have the right to bring suit personally against someone who violates the FTC franchise rules.)

As we have seen, some states also regulate the sale of franchises. They often require franchisors to register and to provide offering circulars, but the franchisor can use the UFOC guidelines to meet the requirements of both the state and the FTC. The states that do regulate franchisors are often stricter than the FTC. California, for example, requires franchisors to file all advertisements ahead of time. Some states will not permit a franchisor to register unless it can meet minimum capital requirements. State laws may also prohibit unfair terms in the franchising contract. Unlike FTC rules, some states permit franchisees themselves to sue for damages or recission anyone who violates franchise laws.

In the following case, a franchisee filed suit under the Illinois Franchise Disclosure Act.

BIXBY'S FOOD SYSTEMS, INC. V. MCKAY

193 F. Supp. 2d 1053, 2002 U.S. Dist. LEXIS 5243
United States District Court for the Northern District of Illinois, 2002

FACT: Phillip McKay was a dentist and his wife, Jan, worked for Ameritech. They were looking for a business to buy when a friend told them about Bixby's, a franchisor of bagel restaurants. This same friend introduced them to Ken Miyamoto, Bixby's president.

Miyamoto gave the McKays a franchise offering circular (FOC), which stated that the initial investment for a franchise, including the initial franchise fee, would be between $143,000 and $198,000. It also stated that, with a store space of between 1,400 and 2,200 square feet, each franchise would have annual sales of $625,000 and would earn an annual profit of $139,450. Miyamoto told the McKays that the FOC figures were conservative, that "existing bagel stores were doing annual sales in excess of $1 million," and that "Bixby's franchises would exceed these revenue figures."

The McKays purchased the right to own a Bixby's franchise. They found a 2,000-square-foot space for lease, but Miyamoto urged them repeatedly to lease an additional space next door, for a total of more than 3,000 square feet. Miyamoto assured them that the site would bring in annual revenues in excess of $1 million. No other Bixby's restaurant nationwide was as large as 3,000 square feet.

At a reception that the McKays attended for existing and prospective Bixby's franchisees, Miyamoto told the guests that the company had 340 franchise agreements. In fact, the company had no more than 15 such agreements. Miyamoto was also quoted in a company newsletter as stating that Bixby's had 340 signed and paid-for agreements, which represented "a $68 million vote of confidence."

The McKays executed a lease for the 3,000-square-foot space and proceeded to renovate the property. Their initial investment was more than $400,000, significantly higher than the estimated investment of between $143,000 and $198,000 in the FOC. Miyamoto assured them that the FOC was accurate, their costs were normal, and that their sales would cover their costs. Miyamoto knew that these statements were false.

After the McKays opened their store, monthly sales ranged from $25,000 to $30,000, far less than Miyamoto had predicted. Because the McKays fell behind on their payments, Bixby's terminated their franchise agreement after only eight months.

Bixby's sued the McKays for violating the franchise agreement. The McKays counter-claimed against Bixby's, alleging that the company had violated the Illinois Franchise Disclosure Act (IFDA). They then filed a motion for summary judgment.

ISSUE: Did Bixby's violate the Illinois Franchise Disclosure Act?

EXCERPTS FROM JUDGE NOLAN'S DECISION: The McKays claim that Miyamoto violated the IFDA by providing false information with respect to the franchise sale. The McKays relied on these representations when they executed their franchise agreement.

To be actionable under the IFDA, the misrepresentation must be an untrue statement of a material fact. A material fact is one in which a buyer would have acted differently knowing the information. In other words, the fact must be essential to the transaction between the parties.

A statement expressing an opinion or that relates to future or contingent events rather than to present facts, however, ordinarily does not constitute an actionable misrepresentation under Illinois law. For example, predictions of future sales or profitability are not considered representations of preexisting material facts.

The McKays have not shown that, contrary to the general rule, Miyamoto's statements about future events, costs, and profitability are actionable misrepresentations under the IFDA, so summary judgment cannot be granted based upon those statements.

The McKays have, however, conclusively shown that Miyamoto falsely claimed that Bixby's had 340 signed and paid-for agreements when no more than fifteen agreements had in fact been executed. Miyamoto's untrue statement was material to the McKays' decision to execute the Bixby's franchise agreement a week later. [T]herefore summary judgment should be granted as to the McKays' claim under the IFDA. ◢

Chapter Conclusion

The process of starting a business is immensely time-consuming. Eighteen-hour days are the norm. Not surprisingly, entrepreneurs are sometimes reluctant to spend their valuable time on legal issues that, after all, do not contribute directly to the bottom line. No customer buys more biscuits because the franchise is a limited liability company instead of a corporation. Wise entrepreneurs know, however, that careful attention to legal issues is an essential component of success. The form of organization affects everything from taxes to liability to management control. The idea for the business may come first, but legal considerations occupy a close second place.

Chapter Review

	Separate Taxable Entity	Personal Liability for Owners	Ease of Formation	Transferable Interests (Easily Bought and Sold)	Perpetual Existence	Other Features
Sole Proprietorship	No	Yes	Very easy	No, can only sell entire business	No	
General Partnership	No	Yes	Easy	No	Depends on the partnership agreement	Supported by law and tradition. Management can be difficult.
Limited Liability Partnership	No	No	Difficult	No	Depends on the partnership agreement	
Professional Corporation	Yes	Yes, for own malpractice, not for malpractice of others or contract debts of organization	Difficult	Shareholders must all be members of same profession	Yes, as long as it has shareholders	Complex tax issues.
Limited Partnership	No	Yes, for general partner No, for limited partners	Difficult	Yes (for limited partners), if partnership agreement permits	Yes	
Limited Liability Limited Partnership	No	No	Difficult	Yes (for limited partners), if partnership agreement permits	Yes	
Corporation	Yes	No	Difficult	Yes	Yes	
Close Corporation	Yes, for C corporation No, for S corporation	No	Difficult	Transfer restrictions	Yes	Protection of minority shareholders. No board of directors required. Stalemates may develop.

table continues on next page

	Separate Taxable Entity	Personal Liability for Owners	Ease of Formation	Transferable Interests (Easily Bought and Sold)	Perpetual Existence	Other Features
S Corporation	No	No	Difficult	Transfer restrictions	Yes	Only 75 shareholders. Only one class of stock. Shareholders must be individuals, estates, trusts, charities, or pension funds and be citizens or residents of the United States. All shareholders must agree to S status.
Limited Liability Company	No	No	Difficult	Yes, if the operating agreement permits	Varies by state, but generally, yes	No limit on the number of shareholders, the number of classes of stock, or the type of shareholder.
Joint Venture	No	Yes	Easy	No	No	Partnership for a limited purpose.
Franchise						Established business. Name recognition. Management assistance. Loss of control. Fees may be high.

Practice Test

1. **ETHICS** Lee McNeely told Hardee's officials that he was interested in purchasing multiple restaurants in Arkansas. A Hardee's officer assured him that any of the company-owned stores in Arkansas would be available for purchase. However, the company urged him to open a new store in Maumelle and sent him a letter estimating first-year sales at around $800,000. McNeely built the Maumelle restaurant, but gross sales the first year were only $508,000. When McNeely asked to buy an existing restaurant, a Hardee's officer refused, informing him that Hardee's rarely sold company-owned restaurants. The franchise offering circular contained no misstatements, but McNeely brought suit alleging fraud in the sale of the Maumelle franchise. Does McNeely have a valid claim against Hardee's? Apart from the legal issues, did Hardee's officers behave ethically? Would they want their behavior to be publicized? Would they like to be treated this way themselves? Is all fair in love, war, and franchising?

2. **CPA QUESTION** Assuming all other requirements are met, a corporation may elect to be treated as an S corporation under the Internal Revenue Code if it has:

(a) Both common and preferred stockholders

(b) A partnership as a stockholder

(c) Seventy-five or fewer stockholders

(d) The consent of a majority of the stockholders

3. Under Delaware law, a corporation cannot appear in court without a lawyer, but a partnership can. Fox Hollow Ventures, Ltd., was a limited liability company. One of its employees, who was not a lawyer, appeared in court to represent the company. Does an LLC more closely resemble a partnership, which may represent itself in court, or a corporation, which requires representation by a lawyer?

4. Glenleigh Falls Development Co. was a limited liability company that hired architects John and Marion Zaugg to design a residential golf course. The Zauggs were to receive partial payment for their services plus part ownership in the LLC. Although the articles of organization had been filed with the Secretary of State in Ohio, the operating agreement had not yet been signed by the members. The Zauggs signed the agreement, but two of the original four members did not. The agreement provided that no member could voluntarily withdraw. When the LLC refused to pay the Zauggs' bill for architectural services, they withdrew from the LLC and filed suit, seeking payment of their bill. The LLC counterclaimed, alleging that the Zauggs had wrongfully withdrawn. Did the Zauggs have the right to withdraw?

5. Alan Dershowitz, a law professor famous for his wealthy clients (O. J. Simpson, Claus von Bulow, Leona Helmsley), joined with other lawyers to open a kosher delicatessen, Maven's Court. Dershowitz met with greater success at the bar than in the kitchen—the deli failed after barely a year in business. One supplier sued for overdue bills. What form of organization would have been the best choice for Maven's Court?

6. **CPA QUESTION** A joint venture is a(n):

(a) Association limited to no more than two persons in business for profit

(b) Enterprise of numerous co-owners in a nonprofit undertaking

(c) Corporate enterprise for a single undertaking of limited duration

(d) Association of persons engaged as co-owners in a single undertaking for profit

7. Mrs. Meadows opened a biscuit shop called The Biscuit Bakery. The business was not incorporated. Whenever she ordered supplies, she was careful to sign the contract in the name of the business, not personally: The Biscuit Bakery by Daisy Meadows. Unfortunately, she had no money to pay her flour bill. When the vendor threatened to sue her, Mrs. Meadows told him that he could only sue the business, because all the contracts were in the business's name. Will Mrs. Meadows lose her dough?

8. **YOU BE THE JUDGE WRITING PROBLEM** Heinz Wartski invented a data collector device to analyze fuel consumption and acceleration in automobiles. He and Terence Bedford formed Fleet Tech, Inc., a close corporation, to develop and market the device. When the venture did not succeed as anticipated, Bedford induced the board of directors to fire Wartski. With Fleet Tech's money all but gone and its debts mounting, the directors voted to authorize Bedford either to sell the company or to file for bankruptcy. Bedford offered to buy the shares for $1. The sale took place, over Wartski's objection. Shortly after buying all the stock, Bedford sold the company to Allied Corp. for $890,267 and a promise of future royalty payments totaling at least $1.2 million. Do Wartski or any of the other shareholders have a right to share in these payments?
Argument for Wartski: Shareholders in a close corporation owe each other a fiduciary duty. Bedford should not be allowed to profit at the expense of the other shareholders.
Argument for Bedford: The directors fired Wartski because he ruined the company. They then authorized Bedford to sell what was left. Everything Bedford did was legal.

9. A bulldozer burned to ashes in Arkansas. For Lawrence Nolen, the good news was that the bulldozer was insured. The bad news was that

Dennis Burnett claimed half the proceeds as Nolen's partner. Nolen and Burnett had not signed a partnership agreement. This is how Nolen testified at trial:

Burnett talked of buying a dozer. I told him I could borrow the money and set up payments on it. Later I told him if he'd come up with his $5,000 that half the dozer was his. That was the deal. I bought the dozer, borrowed the money from the bank. The note was in my name. I bought the insurance on the dozer. I had a bank account in my name and it was used only for the dozer business. In the meantime I paid him for his time. I may have opened an account at the store for N&B Dozer just to keep my purchases at the store separate from my personal purchases.

Others testified that the parties had agreed they would divide all profits on an equal basis, one-half to each, once the bank loan had been paid in full. Had Nolen and Burnett formed a partnership to own and operate the bulldozer?

10. The Logan Wright Foundation (LWF), an Oklahoma nonprofit corporation, was a partner in a partnership formed to operate two Sonic Drive-In restaurants. LWF asked the court to require the IRS to return taxes that LWF had paid on behalf of Sonic. LWF argued that it was not responsible for Sonic's taxes because LWF was merely a limited partner, with limited liability to the partnership's creditors, including the IRS. The partnership had never filed a certificate of limited partnership with the Secretary of State. Is it a valid limited partnership?

11. **ROLE REVERSAL** Write a multiple-choice question that focuses on the difference between an LLC and an S corporation.

Internet Research Problem

At http://www.ftc.gov, the Federal Trade Commission provides information on enforcement cases it has brought against franchisors who violate FTC rules. Do you see a pattern? Are some violations more common than others? How can you avoid falling prey to an unsuitable franchise offering?

You can find further practice problems in the Online Quiz at http://beatty.westbuslaw.com **or in the Study Guide that accompanies this text.**

Corporations

Lindsey and Eben had been good friends since statistics class. Then the dot.com business plan they created for their capstone course won first prize in the school competition. A number of family and friends offered seed funding. Koolsite.com was on its way!

The two entrepreneurs intended to talk with a lawyer, but they were so busy working on their Web site that they kept postponing this chore. They rented space, hired employees, signed contracts. Finally, their investors insisted that they see a lawyer.

The news she had to deliver was not good. Although Eben had been very careful to sign the lease in the name of koolsite.com, Inc., he was nonetheless personally liable for the rent because the business had not actually been incorporated. That was a shock. The lawyer went on to talk about minute books and shareholder meetings and corporate bank accounts. Lindsey and Eben sat in her office thinking, "Blah, blah, blah." The lawyer, however, would not let them leave until the incorporation forms were complete.

For a year, the duo did nothing but work on their business (and play a few rounds of foosball). Then the economy turned down and suddenly the company's survival was in doubt. The financial picture became even darker when an irate customer sued koolsite.com for injuries he received from an item he had ordered through the Web site. As Lindsey rummaged in her desk drawers, looking for the lawyer's telephone number, she reassured Eben,

"At least we're not personally liable, only the corporation is. The customer's welcome to one used foosball game."

The lawyer, however, had a different viewpoint. According to her, the two entrepreneurs might be personally liable. The company did not have enough assets to pay its liabilities, and the two founders had failed to observe the required corporate formalities. They should not have ignored all that "blah, blah" stuff.

Despite these bumps in the road, koolsite.com did survive and even edged into profitability. Eventually, it was able to go public, selling shares in the open market. At that point, Eben sold some of his stock and took (really) early retirement. He was still a shareholder, though, so he kept his eye on the company. Frankly, he was a little distressed by some of Lindsey's decisions. Did she have to move company headquarters closer to her beach house? That decision cost the shareholders a pretty penny. And it seemed that no matter how the stock price performed, her compensation always went up . . . a lot.

Eben was getting pretty annoyed. But what could he do? He had the right to go to shareholder meetings and complain, but what would that accomplish? Only the directors could fire Lindsey, and they all seemed to be friends of hers. Eben might try to organize shareholders to vote out the board, but that would be a difficult and expensive undertaking.

As he stewed, Lindsey continued to make bad decision after bad decision. Clearly, her entrepreneurial skills did not suit a large company. At long last, the board took action. The good news was that it fired Lindsey. The bad news was that it gave her a $100 million severance package. Eben was so furious, he filed suit to prevent the payment.

In this chapter, you will learn how to form a corporation. You will also learn about the rights and responsibilities of corporate managers and shareholders. And you will see why Eben's lawsuit was unsuccessful. Corporate managers have great leeway in running a corporation.

Incorporation Process

Someone who organizes a corporation is called a **promoter. A promoter is personally liable on any contract he signs before the corporation is formed.** In the chapter-opening scenario, Eben signs the lease for koolsite.com before the corporation is formed, only to discover that he is personally responsible. After formation, the corporation can **adopt** the contract, in which case, both it and the promoter are liable. Eben can get off the hook personally only if the landlord agrees to a **novation**, that is, a new contract with the corporation alone.

The mechanics of incorporation are easy: simply fill out the form and mail it (with a check) to the Secretary of State. Nonetheless, this document needs to be completed with some care. The corporate charter defines the corporation, including everything from the company's name to the number of shares it will issue. States use different terms to refer to a charter; some call it the "articles of incorporation," others use "articles of organization," and still others say "certificate" instead of "articles." All of these terms mean the same thing. Similarly, some states use the term "shareholders," and others use "stockholders"; they are both the same.

There is no federal corporation code, which means that a company can incorporate only under state, not federal, law. No matter where a company actually does business, it may incorporate in any state. This decision is important because the organization must live by the laws of whichever state it chooses for incorporation. To encourage similarity among state corporation statutes, the American Bar Association drafted the Model Business Corporation Act (the Model Act) as a guide. Many states do use the Model Act as a guide, although Delaware does not. Therefore, in this chapter we will give examples from both the Model Act and specific states, such as Delaware. Why Delaware? Despite its small size, it has a disproportionate influence on corporate law. More than 300,000 corporations are incorporated there, including 60 percent of Fortune 500 companies.

WHERE TO INCORPORATE?

A company is called a **domestic corporation** in the state where it incorporates and a **foreign corporation** everywhere else. Companies generally incorporate either in the state where they do most of their business or in Delaware. They typically must pay filing fees and franchise taxes in their state of incorporation as well as in any state in which they do business. To avoid this double set of fees, a business that will be operating primarily in one state would probably select that state for incorporation rather than Delaware. But if a company is going to do business in several states, it might consider choosing Delaware (or, perhaps, Ohio, Pennsylvania, Nevada or one of the other states with sophisticated corporate laws). More information about Delaware law is available at http://www.state.de.us/corp/. Or browse http://www.findlaw.com/11stategov/indexcorp.html for links to all state corporation Web sites.

Delaware offers corporations several advantages:

- *Laws that Favor Management.* For example, if the shareholders want to take a vote in writing instead of holding a meeting, many other states require the vote to be unanimous; Delaware requires only a majority to agree. The Delaware legislature also tries to keep up-to-date by changing its code to reflect new developments in corporate law.

- *An Efficient Court System.* Delaware has a special court (called "Chancery Court") that hears nothing but business cases and has judges who are experts in corporate law.

- *An Established Body of Precedent.* Because so many businesses incorporate in the state, its courts hear a vast number of corporate cases, creating a large body of precedent. Thus lawyers feel they can more easily predict the outcome of a case in Delaware than in a state where few corporate disputes are tried each year.

THE CHARTER

Once a company has decided *where* to incorporate, the next step is to prepare and file the charter. The charter must always be filed with the Secretary of State; some jurisdictions also require that it be filed in a county office. Sample articles of incorporation for Delaware are available at http://www.state.de.us/corp.

Name

The Model Act imposes two requirements in selecting a name. First, all corporations must use one of the following words in their name: "corporation," "incorporated," "company," or "limited." Delaware also accepts some additional terms, such as, "association" or "institute." Second, under both the Model Act and Delaware law, a new corporate name must be different from that of any corporation, limited liability company, or limited partnership that already exists *in that state*. If your name is Freddy Dupont, you cannot name your corporation "Freddy Dupont, Inc.," because Delaware already has a company named E. I. Dupont de Nemours & Co. It does not matter that Freddy Dupont is your real name or that the existing company is a large chemical business while you want to open a video arcade. The names are too similar.

Address and Registered Agent

A company must have an official address in the state in which it is incorporated so that the Secretary of State knows where to contact it and so that anyone who wants to sue the corporation can serve the complaint in-state. Since most companies incorporated in Delaware do not actually have an office there, they hire a registered agent to serve as their official presence in the state. Agents typically charge about $100 annually for this service.

Incorporator

The incorporator signs the charter and delivers it to the Secretary of State for filing. Incorporators are not required to buy stock nor do they necessarily have any future relationship with the company. Typically, the lawyer who forms the corporation serves as its incorporator.

Purpose

The corporation is required to give its purpose for existence. Most companies use a very broad purpose clause such as:

> The nature of the business or purposes to be conducted or promoted is to engage in any lawful act or activity for which corporations may be organized under the General Corporation Law of Delaware.

Stock

The charter must provide three items of information about the company's stock.

Number of Shares. Before stock can be sold, it must first be authorized in the charter. The corporation can authorize as many shares as the incorporators choose, but the more shares, the higher the filing fee. In Delaware, the basic price (for stock with no par value) is $.01 per share for the first 20,000 shares (a total of $200); $.005 apiece for up to two million shares; and $.004 each for all shares over two million. If a company wants more shares after incorporation, it simply amends its charter and pays the additional fee.

Stock that has been authorized but not yet sold is called **authorized and unissued**. Stock that has been sold is termed **authorized and issued** or **outstanding**. Stock that the company has sold but later bought back is **treasury stock**.

Par Value. The concept of par value was designed to protect investors. Originally, par value was supposed to be close to market price. A company could not issue stock at a price less than par, which meant that it could not sell to insiders at a sweetheart price well below market value. (Once the stock was *issued*, it could be *traded* at any price.) In modern times, par value does not relate to market value; it is usually some nominal figure such as 1¢ or $1 per share. Companies may even issue stock with no par value.

Classes and Series. Different shareholders often make different contributions to a company. Some may be involved in management, while others may simply contribute financially. Early investors may feel that they are entitled to more control than those who come along later (and who perhaps take less risk). Corporate structure can be infinitely flexible in defining the rights of these various shareholders. Stock can be divided into categories called **classes,** and these classes can be further divided into subcategories called **series.** All stock in a series has the same rights, and all series in a class are fundamentally the same, except for minor distinctions. For example, in a class of preferred stock, all shareholders may be entitled to a dividend, but the amount of the dividend may vary by series. Different classes of stock, however, may have very different rights—a class of preferred stock is different from a class of common stock. Exhibit 17.1 illustrates the concept of class and series.

Defining the rights of a class or series of stock is like baking a cake—the stock can contain virtually any combination of the following ingredients (although the result may not be to everyone's taste):

- *Dividend Rights.* The charter establishes whether the shareholder is entitled to dividends and, if so, in what amount.

- *Voting Rights.* Shareholders are usually entitled to elect directors and vote on charter amendments, among other issues, but these rights can vary among different series and classes of stock. When Ford Motor Co. went public in

Exhibit 17.1

Exhibit 17.2

1956, it issued Class B common stock to members of the Ford family. This class of stock holds about 40 percent of the voting power and, thereby, effectively controls the company. Not surprisingly, the chairman of the company is often named "Ford."

- *Liquidation Rights.* The charter specifies the order in which classes of stockholders will be paid upon dissolution of the company.

These are the ingredients for any class or series of stock. Some stock comes prepackaged like a cake mix. "Preferred" and "common" stock are two classic types. The Model Act does not use these terms, but many states still do.

Owners of *preferred stock* have preference on dividends and also, typically, in liquidation. If a class of preferred stock is entitled to dividends, then it must receive its dividends before common stockholders are paid theirs. If holders of *cumulative* **preferred stock** miss their dividend one year, common shareholders cannot ever receive a dividend until the cumulative preferred shareholders have been paid, no matter how long that takes. Alternatively, holders of *non*-**cumulative preferred stock** lose an annual dividend for good if the company cannot afford it in the year it is due. When a company dissolves, preferred stockholders typically have the right to receive their share of corporate assets before common shareholders. Exhibit 17.2 illustrates the order of payment for dividends.

***Common* stock is last in line for any corporate payouts, including dividends and liquidation payments.** If the company is liquidated, creditors of the company and preferred shareholders are paid before common shareholders.

After Incorporation

DIRECTORS AND OFFICERS

Once the corporation is organized, the incorporators elect the first set of directors. Thereafter, shareholders elect directors. Under the Model Act, a corporation is required to have at least one director, unless (1) *all* the shareholders sign an agreement that eliminates the board, or (2) the corporation has 50 or fewer shareholders. To elect directors, the shareholders may hold a meeting, or, in the more typical case for a small company, they elect directors by **written consent**. A typical written consent looks like this:

Classic American Novels, Inc.

Written Consent

The undersigned shareholders of Classic American Novels, Inc., a corporation organized and existing under the General Corporation Law of the State of Wherever, hereby agree that the following action shall be taken with full force and effect as if voted at a validly called and held meeting of the shareholders of the corporation:

Agreed: That the following people are elected to serve as directors for one year, or until their successors have been duly elected and qualified:

Herman Melville

Louisa May Alcott

Mark Twain

Dated: _____   Signed: _____
                                       Willa Cather

Dated: _____   Signed: _____
                                       Nathaniel Hawthorne

Dated: _____   Signed: _____
                                       Harriet Beecher Stowe

Once the incorporators or shareholders have chosen the directors, the directors must elect the officers of the corporation. They can use a consent form, if they wish. The Model Act is flexible. It simply requires a corporation to have whatever officers are described in the bylaws. The same person can hold more than one office.

The written consents and any records of actual meetings are kept in a **minute book**, which is the official record of the corporation. Entrepreneurs sometimes feel they are too busy to bother with all these details, but, if a corporation is ever sold, the lawyers for the buyers will *insist* on a well-organized and complete minute book. In one case, a company that was seeking a $100,000 bank loan could not find all of its minutes. Many of its early shareholders and directors were not available to re-authorize prior deeds. In the end, the company had to merge itself into a newly created corporation so it could start fresh with a new set of corporate records. The company spent $10,000 on this task, a large chunk out of the $100,000 loan.

BYLAWS

The **bylaws** list all the "housekeeping" details for the corporation. For example, bylaws set the date of the annual shareholders' meeting, define what a quorum is (i.e., what percentage of stock must be represented for a meeting to count), indicate how many directors there will be, give titles to officers, and establish the fiscal (i.e., tax) year of the corporation. A sample set of bylaws is available at http://www.lectlaw.com/forms/f151.htm and http://www.tannedfeet.com/by-laws_for_a_business_corporation.doc. In the following case, the directors' ignorance of company bylaws led to disaster.

IN RE BIGMAR

2002 Del. Ch. LEXIS 45
Court of Chancery, Delaware, 2002

FACTS: Bigmar was a Delaware corporation that manufactured and marketed pharmaceuticals in Europe. While trying to raise additional capital, the company's founder, John Tramontana, met Cynthia May. She lied to him about her education, wealth, and connections in the investment community. Unfortunately, he believed her. The upshot was that May became Bigmar's president and a director of the company. She soon took control of the company's financial records and refused to give Tramontana any information (always a bad sign).[1] When Bigmar ran out of money, Tramontana sent May an e-mail asking for her resignation. She did not respond. (Also a bad sign.)

The company was in desperate financial shape, but Tramontana managed to find a bank willing to buy $1 million of Bigmar stock. He called a special meeting of the board of directors to approve the sale of shares and to fire May. The meeting was to take place by telephone. To establish a quorum necessary for the meeting to be valid, at least five of the nine directors had to take part. May and her three allies on the board refused to participate.

Tramontana testified that, at the appointed time, he met with two directors in his office. They used a speaker feature on a cell phone that Tramontana borrowed from Danilo Graticola to call two other directors, one of whom was in Heathrow Airport in London. The five directors unanimously resolved to issue the stock to the bank. The meeting then adjourned so that they could consult counsel. It was reconvened the next day, at which time they voted to fire May.

The following day, the bank transferred $1 million to Bigmar. Tramontana instructed the company's transfer agent to send stock certificates to the bank, but May contradicted his order. Tramontana and May went to court to determine if the director's meeting was valid and the bank entitled to the shares.

ISSUE: Was the meeting of the Bigmar board of directors valid?

EXCERPTS FROM JUDGE JACOBS'S DECISION: Ms. May attacks the validity of the meeting(s) [claiming that] no meeting at which a quorum of directors was present, ever took place.

There is evidence that the meeting(s) did occur. Minutes of the meetings were prepared, and all but one of the Tramontana directors gave sworn testimony that the meeting(s) took place exactly as the minutes recite. Ordinarily that would be sufficient, but this is not an ordinary case, for several reasons.

First, the minutes were prepared by counsel, who was not present at the meetings, and who simply reduced to writing what Mr. Tramontana told him had occurred. Second, there is no independent documentation or testimony of any third party witness that corroborates the directors' testimony. Moreover, any notes taken at the meeting(s) were destroyed. Further, many of the telephone records whose production was requested were not produced, and the records that were produced either fail to corroborate the Tramontana directors' testimony,[2] or those documents are inconsistent with that testimony.[3]

Third, for the directors' testimony to be accepted, the Court would have to "buy into" a scenario that (to put it charitably) is most improbable. Although Mr. Tramontana had a speaker phone in his office, he testified that he decided to conduct the board meeting on Mr. Graticola's borrowed cellphone. His explanation for that unusual decision was that Mr. Graticola had described his new cellphone's technology in glowing terms and Mr. Tramontana elected to use the telephone to ingratiate his company with Graticola. [T]he story does have some plausibility, however slight. But even that minimal plausibility vanishes when one is told

---

[1] She did, however, send him this e-mail: I wish for GOd's sake that you would GROW [UP] just a little . . . you've F the banking up here in Sweden so I can't get the money that I made [arrangements] for . . . damn idiot . . . take a shower and clean your ears out . . . you can't follow a straight line without having your ego and little hissy fits . . . Get off the play ground . . . before the big boys beat you up . . .

[2] [The] cellphone bills for the [director who is supposed to have received a call in the London airport] do not show any incoming calls to him at Heathrow Airport at 3:00 P.M., London time, which is when the meeting is said to have started. Since [his] cellphone provider was located in Ireland where he lived, [this director] would have incurred a roaming charge for any calls received outside of Ireland, and the roaming charge would have been reflected on his cellphone bill.

[3] For example, Mr. Tramontana's telephone records show that he made an 11-minute telephone call to Mr. Graticola's cellphone number at 7:12 P.M.—a time that Mr. Tramontana claimed to have had Mr. Graticola's cellphone in his possession.

that the same identical scenario occurred a second time, at the adjourned meeting. I find this scenario too implausible for even a gullible fact finder to swallow. Accordingly, the Court is unable to determine that those directors' meetings were validly convened and conducted.

Although the analysis could stop here, that would leave the Court (and perhaps a reader of this Opinion) with a sense of dissatisfaction, because Mr. Tramontana's testimony leaves unanswered questions. In purely human terms, this issue was most difficult and perplexing for the Court.

It is plausible, and the available evidence does indicate, that Mr. Tramontana attempted to assemble all of his colleagues for a telephonic meeting. [But one director] was unavailable, as he was en route from London to Ireland at that time. Because a quorum required the attendance of five directors, [this director's] unavailability meant that the telephonic meeting failed for lack of a quorum. Mr. Tramontana believed, nonetheless, that the problem could be solved by obtaining from himself and his colleagues' individual written consent resolutions taking the actions recited in the minutes. Unfortunately (and unbeknownst to Mr.

Tramontana), Bigmar's by-laws required that any director action by written consent must be unanimous. [When] Mr. Tramontana learned of that unanimity requirement, [he] decided to [say] that a quorum of five directors was present, and that a board meeting was held.

I am persuaded that [Mr. Tramontana and his colleagues acted] in the good-faith belief that unless the issuance of the shares to the Bank was upheld, the Company would fall into the hands of Ms. May, who was incapable of saving the Company. I think it plausible that they believed that at worst, they failed to observe a highly technical legal requirement that, on balance, was too insignificant to justify the ruination of the Company.

The principles of corporate governance, such as those violated here, exist precisely because those procedures enable courts and parties to distinguish between acts that lawfully bind the corporation and its constituents, from those that do not. The directors may have believed in good faith that they had no alternative but to testify as they did, but good faith is not sufficient to validate a procedurally invalid proceeding. ◢

ISSUING DEBT

Most start-up companies begin with some combination of equity and debt. Equity (i.e., stock) is described in the charter; debt is not. Authorizing debt is often one of the first steps a new company takes. There are several types of debt:

- **Bonds** are long-term debt secured by company assets. If the company is unable to pay the debt, creditors have a right to specific assets, such as accounts receivable or inventory.

- **Debentures** are long-term *unsecured* debt. If the company cannot meet its obligations, the debenture holders are paid after bondholders, but before stockholders.

- **Notes** are short-term debt, typically payable within five years. They may be either secured or unsecured.

Death of the Corporation

Sometimes, business ideas are not successful and the corporation fails. This death can be voluntary (the shareholders elect to terminate the corporation) or forced (by court order). Sometimes, a court takes a step that is much more damaging to shareholders than simply dissolving the corporation—it removes the shareholders' limited liability.

PIERCING THE CORPORATE VEIL

One of the major purposes of a corporation is to protect its owners—the share-holders—from personal liability for the debts of the organization. Sometimes, however, a court will **pierce the corporate veil**; that is, the court will hold share-holders personally liable for the debts of the corporation. Courts generally pierce a corporate veil in four circumstances:

- *Failure to Observe Formalities.* If an organization does not act like a corporation, it will not be treated like one. It must, for example, hold required shareholders' and directors' meetings (or sign consents), keep a minute book as a record of these meetings, and make all the required state filings. In addition, officers must be careful to sign all corporate documents with a corporate title, not as an individual. An officer should sign like this:

> Classic American Novels, Inc.
>
> By: _____*Stephen Crane*_____
>
> Stephen Crane, President

- *Commingling of Assets.* Nothing makes a court more willing to pierce a corporate veil than evidence that shareholders have mixed their assets with those of the corporation. Sometimes, for example, shareholders may use corporate assets to pay their personal debts. If shareholders commingle assets, it is genuinely difficult for creditors to determine which assets belong to whom. This confusion is generally resolved in favor of the creditors—*all* assets are deemed to belong to the corporation.

- *Inadequate Capitalization.* If the founders of a corporation do not raise enough capital (either through debt or equity) to give the business a fighting chance of paying its debts, courts may require shareholders to pay corporate obligations.

- *Fraud.* If fraud is committed in the name of a corporation, victims can make a claim against the personal assets of the shareholders who profited from the fraud.

Although it is difficult to feel sorry for shareholders who commit intentional wrongdoing such as fraud, some of these corporate sins involve carelessness more than anything else. That was certainly the case for Lindsey and Eben in the chapter-opening scenario. What about the following case—was the wrongdoing careless or intentional?

RICE V. ORIENTAL FIREWORKS CO.

75 Or. App. 627, 707 P.2d 1250, 1985 Ore. App. LEXIS 3928
Oregon Court of Appeals, 1985

FACTS: J. C. Oriental Fireworks, Inc., was a broker and distributor of professional display fireworks. Gregory Rice filed this claim against Oriental and J. C. Chou for injuries Rice suffered while setting off fireworks. Although Rice bought the fireworks from the corporation, he sought to pierce the corporate veil and obtain a judgment against Chou personally. The trial court, however, granted

Chou's motion to be removed from the case as a defendant. Chou then dismissed Oriental's Oregon lawyer and allowed an uncontested judgment to be entered against the company for $432,000 because the corporation had virtually no assets to pay the judgment.

Chou and his wife owned all the stock of the six-year-old company. Chou was president, treasurer, and chairman of the board; his wife was vice president. The Chous kept no records or minutes of any meetings of the shareholders or directors, except for a signed unanimous consent in lieu of the directors' first meeting. The corporation grossed from $230,000 to $400,000 annually, but its assets never exceeded $13,182. It had never obtained liability insurance, although, as Chou stated, accidents do occur, and lawsuits arise "as a general rule, right after July 4th." Chou also indicated that the lack of liability insurance motivated injured customers to bring actions against other defendants.

ISSUE: Can the plaintiff pierce the corporate veil and hold Chou personally liable?

EXCERPTS FROM JUDGE WARREN'S DECISION: There are three criteria for imposing liability on a shareholder: (1) The shareholder must have controlled the corporation; (2) the shareholder must have engaged in improper conduct in his exercise of control over the corporation; and (3) the shareholder's improper conduct must have caused plaintiff's inability to obtain an adequate remedy from the corporation.

We conclude that plaintiff has demonstrated a *prima facie* case for disregarding the corporate form of Oriental. Chou had complete control over officer and director decisions and, with his wife, has control over shareholder decisions. Chou engaged in improper conduct in the exercise of control over Oriental in two respects. First, he disregarded corporate roles and formalities which serve to protect the rights and define the responsibilities of owners, directors, officers, employees, creditors, government entities and the public at large. Second, Chou failed adequately to capitalize the corporation. A corporation is inadequately capitalized when its assets are insufficient to cover its potential liabilities, which are reasonably foreseeable from the nature of the corporation's business. Finally, there can be no doubt that Chou's failure adequately to capitalize or obtain insurance coverage for Oriental has caused plaintiff to have an inadequate remedy against the corporation.

Reversed and *remanded*. ◢

TERMINATION

Terminating a corporation is a three-step process:

- *Vote*. The directors recommend to the shareholders that the corporation be dissolved, and a majority of the shareholders agree.

- *Filing*. The corporation files "Articles of Dissolution" with the Secretary of State.

- *Winding Up*. The officers of the corporation pay its debts and distribute the remaining property to shareholders. When the winding up is completed, the corporation ceases to exist.

The Secretary of State may dissolve a corporation that violates state law by, for example, failing to pay the required annual fees. Indeed, many corporations, particularly small ones, do not bother with the formal dissolution process. They simply cease paying their required annual fees and let the Secretary of State act. A court may dissolve a corporation if it is insolvent or if its directors and shareholders cannot resolve conflict over how the corporation should be managed. The court will then appoint a receiver to oversee the winding up.

The Role of Corporate Management

Now you know how to avoid some of the legal pitfalls that can ensnare the unwary entrepreneur when organizing a corporation. But what happens as the business grows? In the beginning, many entrepreneurs fund their start-up themselves (with the aid of credit cards), but most expect that the business will ultimately attract outside investors. This concept of outside investors is, in historical terms, relatively new. Before the Industrial Revolution in the eighteenth and nineteenth centuries, a business owner typically supplied both capital and management. However, the capital needs of the great manufacturing enterprises spawned by the Industrial Revolution were larger than any small group of individuals could supply. To find capital, firms sought outside investors, who often had neither the knowledge nor the desire to manage the enterprise. Investors without management skills complemented managers without capital. ("Manager" includes both directors and officers.)

Modern businesses still have the same vast need for capital and the same division between managers and investors. As businesses grow, shareholders are too numerous and too uninformed to manage the enterprises they own. Therefore, they elect directors to manage for them. The directors set policy and then appoint officers to implement corporate goals. The Model Act describes the directors' role thus: "All corporate powers shall be exercised by or under the authority of, and the business and affairs of the corporation managed by or under the direction of, its board of directors. . . ."

Directors have the authority to manage the corporate business, but they also have important responsibilities to shareholders and perhaps to other **stakeholders** who are affected by corporate decisions, such as employees, customers, creditors, suppliers, and neighbors. The interests of these various stakeholders often conflict. What are the rights—and responsibilities—of directors and officers to manage these conflicts?

Managers have a fiduciary duty to act in the best interests of the corporation's shareholders. Since shareholders are primarily concerned about their return on investment, managers must *maximize shareholder value*, which means providing shareholders with the highest possible financial return from dividends and stock price. However, reality is more complicated than this simple rule indicates. It is often difficult to determine which strategy will best maximize shareholder value. And what about stakeholders? A number of states have adopted statutes that permit directors to take into account the interests of stakeholders as well as stockholders. The Indiana Code, for example, permits directors to consider "both the short term and long term best interests of the corporation, taking into account, and weighing as the directors deem appropriate, the effects thereof on the corporation's shareholders and the other corporate constituent groups . . ."[4] The next section looks more closely at directors' responsibilities to their various constituencies.

The Business Judgment Rule

Officers and directors have a fiduciary duty to act in the best interests of their stockholders, but under the **business judgment rule**, the courts allow managers

---

[4] Indiana Code §23-1-35-1.

great leeway in carrying out this responsibility. The business judgment rule is a common law concept that virtually every court in the country recognizes. In addition some states have enacted statutes that codify the business judgment rule. To be protected by the business judgment rule, managers must act in good faith:

Duty of Loyalty	1.	Without a conflict of interest
Duty of Care	2.	With the care that an ordinarily prudent person would take in a similar situation, and
	3.	In a manner they reasonably believe to be in the best interests of the corporation.

The business judgment rule is two shields in one: it protects both the manager and her decision. If a manager has complied with the rule, a court will not hold her personally liable for any harm her decision has caused the company, nor will the court rescind her decision. If the manager violates the business judgment rule, then she has the burden of proving that her decision was fair to the shareholders. If it was not fair, she may be held personally liable, and the decision can be rescinded.

The business judgment rule accomplishes three goals:

- *It permits directors to do their job.* If directors were afraid they would be liable for every decision that led to a loss, they would never make a decision, or at least not a risky one.

- *It keeps judges out of corporate management.* Without the business judgment rule, judges would be tempted, if not required, to second-guess managers' decisions.

- *It encourages directors to serve.* No one in his right mind would serve as a director if he knew that every decision was open to attack in the courtroom.

Analysis of the business judgment rule is divided into two parts. The obligation of a manager to act without a conflict of interest is called the **duty of loyalty**. The requirements that a manager act with care and in the best interests of the corporation are referred to as the **duty of care**.

DUTY OF LOYALTY

The duty of loyalty prohibits managers from making a decision that benefits them at the expense of the corporation.

Self-Dealing

Self-dealing means that a manager makes a decision benefiting either himself or another company with which he has a relationship. While working at the Blue Moon restaurant, Zeke signs a contract on behalf of the restaurant to purchase bread from Rising Sun Bakery. Unbeknownst to anyone at Blue Moon, he is a part owner of Rising Sun. Zeke has engaged in self-dealing, which is a violation of the duty of loyalty.

Once a manager engages in self-dealing, the business judgment rule no longer applies. This does not mean the manager is automatically liable to the corporation or that his decision is automatically void. All it means is that the court will no longer presume that the transaction was acceptable. Instead, the court will scrutinize the deal more carefully. A self-dealing transaction is valid in any one of the following situations:

- **The disinterested members of the board of directors approve the transaction.** Disinterested directors are those who do not themselves benefit from the transaction.

- **The disinterested shareholders approve it.** The transaction is valid if the shareholders who do not benefit from it are willing to approve it.

- **The transaction was entirely fair to the corporation.** In determining fairness, the courts will consider the impact of the transaction on the corporation and whether the price was reasonable.

Exhibit 17.3 illustrates the rules on self-dealing.

Corporate Opportunity

The self-dealing rules prevent managers from *forcing* their companies into unfair deals. The corporate opportunity doctrine is the reverse—it prohibits managers from *excluding* their company from favorable deals. **Managers are in violation of the corporate opportunity doctrine if they compete against the corporation without its consent.**

Charles Guth was president of Loft, Inc., which operated a chain of candy stores. These stores sold Coca-Cola. Guth purchased the Pepsi-Cola Co. personally, without

Exhibit 17.3

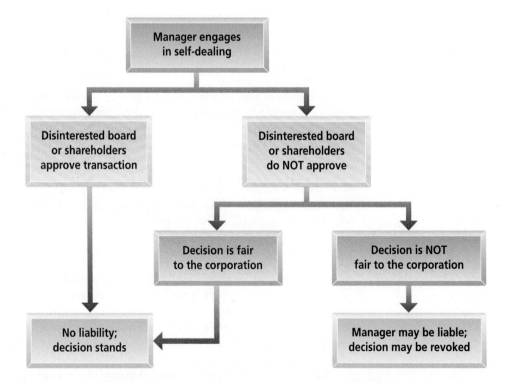

offering the opportunity to Loft. The Delaware court found that Guth had violated the corporate opportunity doctrine and ordered him to transfer all his shares in Pepsi to Loft.[5] That was in 1939, and Pepsi-Cola was bankrupt; today, PepsiCo, Inc. is worth $88 billion.

DUTY OF CARE

In addition to the *duty of loyalty*, managers also owe a *duty of care*. **The duty of care requires officers and directors to act in the best interests of the corporation and to use the same care that an ordinarily prudent person would in the management of her own assets.**

Rational Business Purpose

Courts generally agree in principle that directors and officers are liable for decisions that have no rational business purpose. In practice, however, these same courts have been extremely supportive of managerial decisions, looking hard to find some justification. For decades, the Chicago Cubs baseball team refused to install lights in Wrigley Field. Cubs' fans could only take themselves out to the ball game during the day. A shareholder sued on the grounds that the Cubs' revenues were peanuts and crackerjack compared with those generated by other teams that played at night. The Cubs defended their decision on the grounds that a large night crowd would cause the neighborhood to deteriorate, depressing the value of Wrigley Field (which was not owned by the Cubs). The court rooted for the home team and found that the Cubs' excuse was a "rational purpose" and a legitimate exercise of the business judgment rule.[6]

Legality

Courts are generally unsympathetic to managers who engage in illegal behavior, even if their goal is to help the company. For example, the managing director of an amusement park in New York State used corporate funds to purchase the silence of people who threatened to complain that the park was illegally operating on Sunday. The court ordered the director to repay the money he had spent on bribes, even though the company had earned large profits on Sundays.[7]

Informed Decision

Generally, courts will protect managers who make an *informed* decision, even if the decision ultimately harms the company. Making an informed decision means carefully investigating the facts. However, even if the decision is uninformed, the directors will not be held liable if the decision was entirely fair to the shareholders.

Exhibit 17.4 provides an overview of the duty of care.

---

[5] *Guth v. Loft*, 5 A.2d 503, 23 Del. Ch. 255, 1939 Del. LEXIS 13 (Del. 1939).
[6] *Shlensky v. Wrigley*, 95 Ill. App. 2d 173, 237 N.E.2d 776, 1968 Ill. App. LEXIS 1107 (Ill. App. Ct. 1968).
[7] *Roth v. Robertson*, 64 Misc. 343, 118 N.Y.S. 351, 1909 N.Y. Misc. LEXIS 279 (N.Y. 1909).

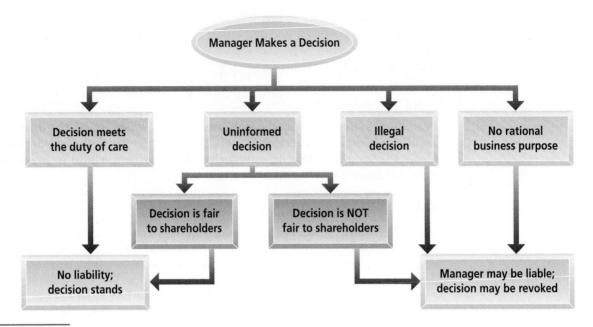

Exhibit 17.4

In the following case, shareholders sued the board of directors for accepting a purchase price that they felt was too low. Did the directors violate their duty of care? You be the judge.

YOU BE THE JUDGE

SMITH V. VAN GORKOM

488 A.2d 858, 1985 Del. LEXIS 421
Supreme Court of Delaware, 1985

FACTS: Trans Union was a publicly traded company in the railcar leasing business. Jerome Van Gorkom had been its chief executive officer for more than 17 years. He was nearing the mandatory retirement age of 65 and was concerned about maximizing the value of his 75,000 shares of Trans Union stock. In the preceding five years, Trans Union's stock had traded at a high of $39.50 and a low of $24.25 per share. The price was now about $37.

Although Trans Union had hundreds of millions of dollars in annual cash flow, it did not have enough income to take advantage of large investment tax credits (ITCs). Van Gorkom fretted that competitors who could efficiently use their ITCs would be able to cut their lease prices and take business away from Trans Union. He believed that Trans Union would be more profitable if it was bought by a company that could use the credits.

On September 13, Van Gorkom met with Jay Pritzker, a well-known corporate takeover specialist, to discuss the potential market for Trans Union. Van Gorkom suggested to Pritzker that a leveraged buyout (LBO) could be done at $55 per share. (In an LBO, the acquiring company buys the target company's stock, using a loan secured by the target's assets.) On Thursday, September

18, Pritzker offered to buy all of Trans Union's stock for $55 per share. The offer expired three days later, on Sunday evening.

On Saturday, Van Gorkom met separately with senior managers and later with the board of directors. Salomon Brothers, the company's investment banker, was not invited to attend. At both meetings, Van Gorkom disclosed the offer and described its terms, but furnished no copies of the proposed agreement. At the first meeting with senior management, the managers' reaction to the Pritzker proposal was completely negative—they feared losing their jobs, they did not like Pritzker, and they thought the price was too low. Nevertheless, Van Gorkom proceeded to the board meeting.

The board was composed of five inside and five outside directors. Of the outside directors, four were corporate CEOs and one was the former Dean of the University of Chicago Business School. None was an investment banker or trained financial analyst. All members of the board were familiar with the company's financial condition and the ITC problem. They had all recently reviewed the company's five-year forecast as well as a comprehensive 18-month study by a well-known consulting firm.

Van Gorkom explained that the issue was not whether $55 per share was the highest price the company could obtain, but whether it was a fair price that the stockholders should be given the opportunity to accept or reject. He also explained that the company had the right to accept a higher offer if one was made. Van Gorkom did not disclose to the board that he had proposed the $55 price in his negotiations with Pritzker. The company's attorney advised the directors that they might be sued if they failed to accept the offer. The company's chief financial officer said that $55 was "in the range of a fair price" for an LBO, but "at the beginning of the range." The board approved the sale.

Van Gorkom executed the agreement at a formal social event that he hosted for the opening of the Chicago Lyric Opera. Neither he nor any other director read the agreement before signing it. The company issued a press release announcing that Trans Union had entered into a "definitive"

agreement with Pritzker. At the same time, it hired Salomon Brothers to solicit other offers. No one else made a firm offer, perhaps because other bidders believed the company was already committed to Pritzker. On February 10, 69 percent of the stockholders of Trans Union voted in favor of the Pritzker proposal.

The plaintiff, Alden Smith, objected to the sale because he did not want to pay tax on the huge profits he realized.

YOU BE THE JUDGE: Did the directors of Trans Union violate their duty of care to the corporation by making an uninformed decision? Did the shareholders consent to the board's decision?

ARGUMENT FOR THE SHAREHOLDERS: The whole procedure for this sale was shockingly casual. Van Gorkom signed the final agreement at a social function. When the directors voted to sell the company, they had not (1) tried to negotiate a higher price with Pritzker, (2) read the agreement, (3) consulted their investment bankers, or (4) determined the intrinsic value of the company. The stock price simply represents the value of a minority stake (one share); a controlling share is worth more, but the board did not know how much more.

The board did not know this important information and neither did the shareholders when they approved the sale. For that reason, the shareholder consent is invalid.

ARGUMENT FOR THE BOARD OF DIRECTORS: Pritzker paid a fair price for the Trans Union stock. It represented a premium of (1) 62 percent over the average of the high and low price in the prior year, (2) 48 percent over the last closing price, and (3) 39 percent over the highest price at which the stock had *ever* traded. The plaintiffs suggest that the "intrinsic value" of the company was higher. The board hired Salomon Brothers to look for better offers and agreed to pay them a fee equal to three-eighths of 1 percent of any increase over $55 that the company received. Salomon would have earned millions of dollars if it had found a buyer willing to pay more than Pritzker.

Jerome Van Gorkom served the company for 24 years, and he knew $55 was a favorable price. He also had an enormous incentive to obtain the highest price available because he personally owned 75,000 shares. The five inside directors had collectively worked for the company for 116 years. The outside directors knew the company well, and they were experienced business people; four of them were CEOs of their own large companies. The board was forced to make a decision quickly because Pritzker's offer expired in three days. What could an expert have discovered in three days that the board did not already know? The Trans Union lawyer warned the directors that if they refused the offer, they would be sued.

Alden Smith's tax problems are not a legitimate reason to hold the board liable. The business judgment rule is meant to protect a board that makes a good faith decision. This board did what it thought best for all of the company's shareholders, not for Alden Smith alone.

Remember that managers are only liable if they make an uninformed decision and the transaction is unfair to the shareholders. If the appeals court in the Trans Union case determined that the directors had violated their duty of care, it would remand the case to the lower court to determine if $55 was a fair price.

Some states have modified their business judgment rule to increase protection for directors. These states either limit liability by statute or permit corporations to include charter provisions that shield directors from personal liability.[8]

Takeovers

The business judgment rule is an important guideline for officers and directors in the routine management of corporations. It also plays a crucial role in the regulation of hostile takeovers. In addition, both Congress and many state legislatures have passed statutes that define the roles of the various combatants in takeovers.

There are three ways to acquire control of a company:

- *Buy the company's assets.* Such a sale must be approved by both the shareholders and the board of directors of the acquired company.

- *Merge with the company.* In a merger, one company absorbs another. The acquired company ceases to exist. A merger must also be approved by the shareholders and the board of directors of the target company. If the current directors object, an acquiring company could buy enough stock to replace the board, but these battles are difficult and often end in defeat for the acquirer.

- *Buy stock from the shareholders.* This method is called a **tender offer** because the acquirer asks shareholders to "tender," or offer their stock for sale. Unlike the other methods of obtaining control, approval from the board of directors of the target company is not strictly necessary. As long as shareholders tender enough stock, the acquirer gains control. A tender offer is called a **hostile takeover** if the board of the target resists.

---

8 For example, the Delaware code permits a corporation to include in its charter a provision limiting a director's personal liability except in certain cases such as intentional misconduct. 8 Del. C. §102(b)(7).

As a shareholder, would you prefer for the law to favor the target or the bidder? Economic research suggests an answer.

ECONOMICS & THE LAW

Suppose you are thinking about buying stock in two companies. The directors and officers of Bright Future, Inc., own 30 percent of the company, while the managers of Dim Bulb Co. own virtually none. You might think that it would be better to invest in a company in which the managers own substantial amounts of stock. In such a case, managers have the same incentives as shareholders—you both benefit from higher stock prices. Moreover, you assume that managers who own lots of stock must have reason to believe that their company's future is promising. Because managers are likely to know more about the inner workings of a company than an ordinary shareholder would, you might legitimately conclude that Bright Future has, well, the brighter future.

It turns out that reality is more complex. If managers own so much stock that they can defeat takeovers, then they tend to become complacent and care less about shareholder value. This phenomenon is called the "entrenchment effect." According to some estimates, the entrenchment effect is most pronounced in companies in which managers own between 5 and 25 percent of the stock.[9] Investors might be wise to investigate such companies carefully. Dim Bulb could be a better choice than Bright Future. ▪

FEDERAL REGULATION OF TENDER OFFERS: THE WILLIAMS ACT

The Williams Act applies only if the target company's stock is publicly traded. Under the Williams Act:

- Any individual or group who together acquire more than 5 percent of a company's stock must file a public disclosure document (called a "Schedule 13D") with the Securities and Exchange Commission (SEC)

- On the day a tender offer begins, a bidder must file a disclosure statement with the SEC

- A bidder must keep a tender offer open for at least 20 business days initially and for at least 10 business days after any substantial change in the terms of the offer

- Any shareholder may withdraw acceptance of the tender offer at any time while the offer is still open

- If the bidder raises the price offered, all selling shareholders must be paid the higher price, regardless of when they tendered; and

- If the stockholders tender more shares than the bidder wants to buy, the bidder must purchase shares pro rata (i.e., it must buy the same proportion from everyone, not first come, first served).

---

[9] R. Morck, A. Schleifer, and R.W. Vishny, "Management Ownership and Market Valuation: An Empirical Analysis," Working Paper No. 23, Institute for Financial Research, Faculty of Business, University of Alberta, *quoted in* P.-O. Bjuggren, "Ownership and Efficiency in Companies Listed on Stockholm Stock Exchange 1985," in M. Faure and R. Van den Bergh, *Essays in Law and Economics* (MAKLU, Antwerp, 1985).

STATE REGULATION OF TAKEOVERS

Common Law of Takeovers

To fend off attack, potential targets often adopt defensive measures known as **anti-takeover devices** or **shark repellents**. (Acquiring companies are sometimes called **sharks**.) **Shareholder rights plans (aka poison pills)** are among the most common antitakeover devices. A target company will, for example, amend its charter to provide that it can issue one share of preferred stock to each of its shareholders. If a shark purchases more than 20 percent of the target's stock and subsequently merges with the target, the preferred stock is convertible into 10 shares of the shark. This device makes a takeover much more expensive for the acquiring company.

Conventional wisdom views antitakeover devices as a mixed blessing—beneficial if used to ensure that shareholders receive the highest possible price for their stock in the event of a sale, but harmful to shareholders if used only to protect management from being fired. However, recent research indicates that the stock prices of companies with few shark repellents significantly outperform those of companies that provide more protection to their managers.[10]

When establishing takeover defenses, shareholder welfare must be the board's primary concern. The directors may institute shark repellents, but they must do so to ensure that bids are high, not to protect their own jobs.

State Antitakeover Statutes

When fighting takeover battles, companies have also found support in state governments. Legislators may not care if a group of directors is thrown into the unemployment line, but they do fear the impact on the local economy if a major employer leaves. When the Belzberg family threatened a hostile takeover of auto parts manufacturer Arvin Industries, the second largest employer in Columbus, Indiana, the state legislature quickly passed a tough antitakeover bill that had been drafted by Arvin's own lawyers. Arvin and the Belzbergs quickly settled.

Most states have now passed laws to deter hostile takeovers. Among the common varieties:

- *Statutes that Automatically Impede Hostile Takeovers.* These statutes, for example, might ban hostile (but not friendly) mergers for five years after the acquirer buys 10 percent of a company.

- *Statutes that Authorize Companies to Fight Off Hostile Takeovers.* These statutes typically permit management, when responding to a hostile takeover, to consider the welfare of company *stake*holders, such as the community, customers, suppliers, and employees. Some even go so far as to allow management to consider the regional or national economy.

Most of these statutes do not totally eliminate hostile takeovers. A determined, well-financed bidder can still be successful. But these state statutes do tip the playing field in favor of management. In the process they prevent some takeovers that shareholders might want, but they also ensure that shareholders receive a high price in those takeovers that are successful.

---

[10] P.A. Gompers, J. Ishii, A. Metrick, "Corporate Governance and Equity Prices," *Quarterly Journal of Economics*, 118(1), Feb. 2003.

Supporters of these state statutes argue that large, publicly traded corporations owe a duty to all of their constituencies. The loss of a large corporate presence can be immensely disruptive to a community. Perhaps a state should have the right to prevent economic upheaval within its borders.

Opponents contend that shareholders own the company, and their interests ought to be paramount. Antitakeover legislation entrenches management and prevents shareholders from obtaining the premium that accompanies a takeover. Opponents also argue that, if other *stake*holders are so concerned with the well-being of the company, let them put their money where their mouths are and buy stock. And if current managers cannot offer shareholders as high a stock price as an outside raider, they ought to be replaced.

Delaware companies can choose not to accept the protection of the antitakeover statute. Is that the ethical choice for directors? What guidance does the Chapter 2 Ethics Checklist offer? Who are the stakeholders? What values are important to a company director? If a director owned stock in another company, how would she wish the directors of that company to respond to a takeover?

The Role of Shareholders

As we have seen, *directors*, not *shareholders*, **have the right to manage the corporate business.** At one time corporate stock was primarily owned by individuals, but now institutional investors—pension plans, mutual funds, insurance companies, banks, foundations, and university endowments—own more than 50 percent of all shares publicly traded in the United States. Traditionally, unhappy shareholders did little more than the "Wall Street walk"—they sold their shares. As the following article illustrates, however, even in the Magic Kingdom, shareholders have begun to rebel against what they perceive as high-handed management.

By any standard, Michael Eisner has had a fabulous run of success at Disney Enterprises Inc. Under his leadership, the market value of the company has soared from $2 billion to $47 billion. Many shareholders have become wealthy on their Disney stock. So why is there trouble in paradise?

For years, Michael Eisner has run Disney as a benign dictatorship. Although he has made many successful decisions, he has also had his share of flops. Eisner has not, for example, had an easy time working with subordinates or grooming a potential successor. And this from a man with a history of heart trouble. Shareholders were infuriated to the point of litigation when he hired his friend Michael Ovitz as company president, only to fire him 14 months later at a cost to the company of $140 million. Some shareholders think that Disney would benefit from a more forceful board of directors instead of the current band, many of whom have long-time connections either with Eisner personally or with the company.

In the past Disney's success permitted Eisner to ignore criticism. His responses were sometimes facetious: "I don't know whether pension funds and law professors really know how these companies are run. I didn't go to business school, so I didn't have the benefit of two years of intensive training in this area."[11]

---

[11] Bruce Orwall and Joann S. Lublin, "The Plutocracy: If a Company Prospers, Should Its Directors Behave by the Book? *The Wall Street Journal*, Feb. 2, 1997, p.1. Reprinted with permission of The Wall Street Journal; permission conveyed through the Copyright Clearance Center, Inc.

The weather in the Magic Kingdom has been even stormier recently as the price of Disney shares has fallen from $43 to $23. This performance is substantially worse than the overall market. In response to the criticism and the declining stock price, the board recently adopted new corporate governance guidelines that would increase its independence, require directors to own more stock in the company, and ban directors from providing paid services to the company. Although shareholders welcome this change in attitude, it still begs the questions: Do the rules of good corporate governance apply only when a company is in trouble? Are the managers of successful companies allowed to behave as they please? ▪

How has Disney stock fared in the past two years, compared with the S&P 500? Can you find an article about recent developments in Disney corporate governance? ▪

What control do shareholders have over Michael Eisner at Disney? The next section of this chapter explores the rights of shareholders (and includes the case in which Disney shareholders sued Michael Eisner). Corporate governance is of such interest to investors that many Web sites contain discussions of these issues. Take a look, for example, at http://www.corpgov.net.

Rights of Shareholders

Shareholders have neither the *right* nor the *obligation* to manage the day-to-day business of the enterprise. If you own stock in Starbucks Corp., your share of stock plus $4.45 entitles you to a cup of mocha Valencia, the same as everyone else. By the same token, if the pipes freeze and the local Starbucks store floods, the manager has no right to call you, as a shareholder, to help clean up the mess. What rights do shareholders have?

RIGHT TO INFORMATION

Under the Model Act, shareholders acting in good faith and with a proper purpose have the right to inspect and copy the corporation's minute book, accounting records, and shareholder lists. A **proper purpose** is one that aids the shareholder in managing and protecting her investment. If, for example, Celeste is convinced that the directors of Devil Desserts, Inc., are mismanaging the company, she might demand a list of other shareholders so that she can ask them to join her in a lawsuit. The company may not *like* this purpose, but it is *proper* and the company is required to give her the list. If, however, Celeste wants to use the shareholder list as a potential source for her new mail-order catalog featuring exercise equipment, the company could legitimately turn her down.

RIGHT TO VOTE

A corporation must have at least one class of stock with voting rights.

Proxies

Shareholders who do not wish to attend a shareholders' meeting may appoint someone else to vote for them. Confusingly, both this person and the document the shareholder signs to appoint the substitute voter are called a **proxy**. Under

SEC rules, companies are not required to solicit proxies. However, a meeting is invalid without a certain percentage of shareholders in attendance, either in person or by proxy. This attendance requirement is referred to as a **quorum**. As a practical matter, if a public company with thousands of investors does not solicit proxies, it will not obtain a quorum. Therefore, virtually all public companies do solicit proxies. Along with the proxy, the company must also give shareholders a **proxy statement** and an **annual report**. The proxy statement provides information on everything from management compensation to a list of directors who miss too many meetings. The annual report contains detailed financial data.

Under SEC rules, companies can offer (but not require) electronic delivery of proxy statements and annual reports. Intel Corp. was one of the first companies to make its proxy statements and annual reports available on its Web site. See http://www.intel.com/intel/finance/savethetrees.htm. You can also read about Intel's policies on corporate governance at http://www.intel.com/intel/finance/corp_gov.htm.

Typically, only the company itself solicits proxies for a shareholder meeting, but sometimes shareholders who disapprove of company policies try to convince other shareholders to appoint them as proxy instead of management. These dissident shareholders must also prepare a proxy statement that discloses, among other information, who they are, how they are financing their opposition, and how many other proxy contests they have participated in. If enough shareholders give their proxies to the dissidents, then the dissidents can elect themselves or their representatives to replace the board of directors.

Shareholder Proposals

Some shareholders who oppose a company policy may not aspire to a board seat or perhaps cannot afford to send material individually to other investors. Such shareholders may use an alternative method, provided by the SEC, for communicating with fellow shareholders. **Under SEC rules, any shareholder who has continuously owned for one year at least 1 percent of the company or $2,000 of stock can require that one proposal be placed in the company's proxy statement to be voted on at the shareholder meeting.** In practice, many of these resolutions have a political agenda: save the environment, withdraw from Myanmar, ban genetically modified ingredients. Others relate to corporate-governance issues: reduce executive compensation and permit secret ballots. Each year, public companies vote on about 450 shareholder proposals. Prior to 1985, only *two* proposals had been approved—ever. Currently, about 10 to 20 receive a majority vote each year, a definite improvement (or deterioration, depending on your perspective). The Web sites at http://www.socialfunds.com and http://www.irrc.org provide information about recent shareholder proposals. If a company refuses to include a shareholder proposal in its proxy material, shareholders can appeal to the SEC.

Despite the long history of shareholder proposals, an essential question remains unanswered: Are shareholder proposals binding on the company? The SEC recommends that proposals be couched in the form of a request or recommendation because state laws sometimes prohibit binding resolutions. Although shareholders traditionally followed this advice, many activists have been angered by companies that refuse to implement proposals that receive a majority vote from shareholders. In response, an increasing number of shareholders have begun to propose binding resolutions. The Supreme Court of Oklahoma provided ammunition when it ruled recently that a shareholder vote on takeover defenses could be binding.[12]

Ironically, companies sometimes implement shareholder proposals that have *not* received support from a majority of the shareholders. The pressure of shareholder proposals is credited with inducing many American companies to withdraw from South Africa in protest against its apartheid regime. Other companies implement shareholder proposals without even putting them up for a vote. Indeed, nearly half of all shareholder proposals are now withdrawn before a vote because the company capitulates. Many companies feel they have little choice but to negotiate, particularly with institutional investors over issues of corporate governance. For example, Colgate-Palmolive Co. agreed to a proposal by institutional investors to permit secret ballots at shareholder meetings.

Whatever shareholder preferences may be, corporate managers like to keep the reins of control firmly in their own hands. And, as the following article illustrates, companies generally view shareholder proposals as a nuisance.

At the General Electric shareholder meeting last month, there were several items of business likely to irritate even the most mild-mannered CEO. First, there was a proposal to limit GE's spending on political contributions, which the resolution's sponsor labeled "nothing more than a thinly disguised bribe." Then there was a proposal to cap the chief executive officer's salary, linking it to the pay of the lowliest janitor in the company. And finally there was Sister Patricia Daly.

Sister Pat stood up to advocate a shareholder resolution on GE's pollution of the Hudson River. She called on the company to publicize the danger of eating fish from the river and to stop fostering misleading studies. And she compared the company's claims that PCBs are harmless with claims made by tobacco industry executives about the harmlessness of smoking.

That is when John F. Welch, Jr., GE's chairman and chief executive, blew up. "That's an outrageous comparison," he shouted at the nun. "You owe it to God to be on the side of truth." As Sister Pat, a Dominican nun from Newton, New Jersey, recalled afterwards, "He totally lost it."

In the end, the resolution was backed by 7.6 percent of the shares voted at the meeting, a figure GE characterized as a resounding defeat but which was sufficient to get it on the proxy ballot again next year. Although Sister Pat's resolution failed, it clearly rattled the company.[13] ▪

Shareholder Meetings

A company must hold an **annual meeting** of shareholders, if for no other reason than to elect directors. Everyone who owns stock on the **record date** must be sent notice of a meeting.

Delaware law has entered cyberspace. It now permits companies to send official notices to their shareholders electronically and even allows shareholders to vote electronically both before and during a meeting. Shareholder meetings can be held

---

12 *International Bhd. of Teamsters Gen. Fund v. Fleming Cos.*, 1999 OK 3, 975 P.2d 907, 1999 Okla. LEXIS 3 (OK, 1999).

13 Elizabeth Kolbert, "It's the Nun Vs. the CEO," *The New York Times*, May 25, 1998, p. B1. Copyright © 1998 by The New York Times Co. Reprinted by permission.

in cyberspace as long as shareholders have a reasonable opportunity to participate in and vote at the meeting. But so far no company has held a meeting online, partly from fear of offending shareholders who suspect that they will not be able to confront corporate managers as effectively online as they can in person. Think of Sister Patricia Daly in the earlier Newsworthy feature. Could she have had the same interaction with the GE CEO if the meeting had been electronic? ▪

Election and Removal of Directors

Shareholders have the right to elect directors and also to remove them from office. Under the Model Act, shareholders generally can remove directors at any time for any reason. In theory, shareholders elect directors and directors then appoint officers. Typically, however, the *real* relationship between directors and shareholders in public companies is very different from this formula. Yes, shareholders elect the directors, but the shareholders almost always vote for nominees chosen by the board itself. And the board's nominating committee rarely chooses candidates that the CEO opposes. The *officers* are really choosing the *directors*, not the other way around.

A recent spate of corporate scandals, involving such high-flying companies as Enron Corp., revealed that some boards of directors have not provided adequate oversight of their companies. In response, Congress passed the Sarbanes-Oxley Act of 2002 (which applies to public companies). Under this statute:

- All members of the board's audit committee must be independent.

- A company's CEO and CFO must certify that the company's financial statements are accurate.

- If a company has to restate its earnings, its CEO and CFO must reimburse the company for any bonus or profits they have received from selling company stock within a year of the release of the flawed financials.

- A company cannot make personal loans to its directors or officers.

- Each company must develop a code of ethics for its senior financial officers.

- A Public Company Accounting Oversight Board was established to develop stricter accounting standards.

In addition, under new rules passed by the New York Stock Exchange, only independent directors can serve on a listed company's audit, compensation, and nominating committees.[14] Moreover, independent directors must comprise a majority of the total board. They also must meet regularly on their own without inside directors.

Compensation for Officers and Directors

NEWSWORTHY

For many children *Pat the Bunny* is their first book. It contains few words but much interaction. "Readers" can pat the bunny, sniff the flowers, and play peekaboo with the blanket. After *Pat the Bunny*, many children graduate to *The Poky*

---

[14] "Independent" means a director who does not earn any compensation from the company outside of the usual director's fees (that is, a director who is not an employee and who has no consulting contracts).

Little Puppy and *Richard Scarry's Busy, Busy Town*, all published by Golden Books Family Entertainment, Inc.

Despite its portfolio of classics, Golden Books was having financial difficulties. The company hired Richard Snyder, an experienced publishing executive, to solve its distribution and sales problems. Such experience does not come cheap. At Golden Books he was the third highest paid executive in the publishing industry. But an executive does not live by pay alone. Snyder relocated the company to posh new quarters, hired a private chef, and used the corporate jet for vacations. He also hired other executives (including his wife) at salaries two to three times the industry average. In return investors expected the stock price to zoom. They just did not expect it to zoom *down*. Not only did the stock price plummet 80 percent, but the company was put up for sale. In the midst of this turmoil, the board doubled Snyder's salary and paid him a $500,000 signing bonus for extending his contract two years. The stock promptly plummeted again. The company ended up filing for bankruptcy protection, not once, but twice, under Snyder's leadership. Ultimately, it was bought out and Snyder received close to $8 million in severance pay for a job well done. This sum was about 11 percent of the total purchase price for the company. ◾

To many investors, sky-high executive compensation has become the symbol of all that is wrong with corporate governance. In 1980, CEOs earned on average 45 times more than an ordinary worker. By 1997, the ratio had risen to 305. In 2000, CEOs at large companies were earning 458 times as much as the typical employee, even though profits had only slightly increased since 1997. As the following case demonstrates, however, shareholders' efforts to challenge executive compensation have met with little success. An officer's salary is presumed to be reasonable unless she voted for it as a director of the company. To be successful in challenging an executive's compensation, shareholders must prove that the board was grossly uninformed or that the amount was so high that it had *no relation* to the value of the services performed and was really a gift. The courts tend to be unsympathetic to this line of argument.

BREHM V. EISNER

746 A.2d 244; 2000 Del. LEXIS 51
Supreme Court of Delaware, 2000

FACTS: Michael Ovitz was an important talent broker in Hollywood. He was also a long-time friend of Disney Chairman and CEO Michael Eisner. Although Ovitz lacked experience managing a diversified public company, Disney hired him to be its president. Eisner unilaterally negotiated Ovitz's employment agreement, and the board approved it.

After 14 months all parties agreed that the experiment had failed, so Ovitz left Disney—but not empty-handed. Under his contract he was entitled to $140 million in severance pay. When the board originally approved this agreement, it had known how the severance payment would be calculated but it had not realized how high the total cost could be. Graef Crystal, the compensation expert who had advised the directors, later said that he wished he had done this calculation for them.

Shareholders of Disney sued to prevent payment or to obtain damages from the directors. After the lower court dismissed their claim, the shareholders appealed to the Supreme Court of Delaware.

ISSUE: Did the Disney directors have the right to pay $140 million to an employee who had worked at the company unsuccessfully and for only 14 months?

EXCERPTS FROM JUSTICE VEASEY'S DECISION: [I]n making business decisions, directors must consider all material information reasonably available, and the directors' process is actionable only if grossly negligent. Merely because Crystal now regrets not having calculated the package is not reason enough to overturn the judgment of the Board then. It is the essence of the business judgment rule that a court will not apply 20/20 hindsight to second guess a board's decision, except in rare cases where a transaction may be so egregious on its face that the board approval cannot meet the test of business judgment. I think it a correct statement of law that the duty of care is still fulfilled even if a Board does not know the exact amount of a severance payout but nonetheless is fully informed about the manner in which such a payout would be calculated. A board is not required to be informed of every fact, but rather is required to be reasonably informed.

Plaintiffs allege that the Board committed a violation constituting waste. Plaintiffs basically quarrel with the Board's judgment in evaluating Ovitz' worth vis a vis the lavish payout to him. [T]he size and structure of executive compensation are inherently matters of judgment. The judicial standard for determination of corporate waste is well developed. Roughly, a waste entails an exchange of corporate assets for consideration so disproportionately small as to lie beyond the range at which any reasonable person might be willing to trade. Such a transfer is in effect a gift. If, however, there is any substantial consideration received by the corporation, and if there is a good faith judgment that in the circumstances the transaction is worthwhile, there should be no finding of waste, even if the fact finder would conclude ex post that the transaction was unreasonably risky. Any other rule would deter corporate boards from the optimal rational acceptance of risk. Courts do not measure, weigh or quantify directors' judgments.

[T]he facts in the Complaint show that Ovitz' performance as president was disappointing at best, that Eisner admitted it had been a mistake to hire him. Plaintiffs may disagree with the Board's judgment as to how this matter should have been handled. But where, as here, there is no reasonable doubt as to the disinterest of or absence of fraud by the Board, mere disagreement cannot serve as grounds for imposing liability based on alleged breaches of fiduciary duty and waste. To rule otherwise would invite courts to become super-directors, measuring matters of degree in business decisionmaking and executive compensation. Such a rule would run counter to the foundation of our jurisprudence. ◢

 Although the Supreme Court of Delaware dismissed most of the plaintiffs' claims, it remanded the case to the trial court with instructions that the plaintiffs could conduct limited additional discovery to find support for one of their allegations. After this additional discovery was completed and the complaint repleaded, the trial court denied Disney's motion to dismiss the complaint and permitted the case to proceed to trial.[15] Has this trial taken place? If so, what was the result?

Directors not only set the salaries of company officers, they also determine their own compensation (unless the charter or bylaws provide otherwise). Directors of Fortune 200 companies are paid on average $137,000 annually, of which about $84,000 is in stock. Directors of small companies earn much less, but they are often granted substantial stock options, which could, in theory, increase dramatically in value.

For more information about executive compensation, pay attention to http://www.paywatch.org. Run by the AFL-CIO labor union, this Web site has an

---

[15] *In Re the Walt Disney Company Derivative Litigation*, 2003 Del. Ch. LEXIS 52, (Del., 2003).

understandably jaundiced view of lavish paychecks. Wondering about your own current or future salary? Check in at http://www.wageweb.com/ to find compensation data for over 150 different types of jobs.

Fundamental Corporate Changes

A corporation must seek shareholder approval before undergoing any of the following fundamental changes: a merger, a sale of major assets, dissolution of the corporation, or an amendment to the charter or bylaws.

RIGHT TO DISSENT

If a corporation (that is not publicly traded) decides to undertake a fundamental change, the Model Act and many state laws require the company to buy back the stock of any shareholders who object. This process is referred to as **dissenters' rights**, and the company must pay "fair value" for the stock. Fundamental changes include a merger or a sale of most of the company's assets.

RIGHT TO PROTECTION FROM OTHER SHAREHOLDERS

Anyone who owns enough stock to control a corporation has a fiduciary duty to minority shareholders. (Minority shareholders are those with less than a controlling interest.) The courts have long recognized that minority shareholders are entitled to extra protection because it is easy (perhaps even natural) for controlling shareholders to take advantage of them. For example:

- The Sinclair Oil Company owned 97 percent of Sinven Co. Sinclair violated its fiduciary duty to Sinven's minority shareholders when it forced Sinven to pay dividends large enough to bankrupt the company.[16]

- A court refused to allow one brother, who was a majority shareholder of the family company, to force the other to sell his shares. According to the court, a minority shareholder can be ejected only for a reason that is fair or has a business purpose.[17]

Enforcing Shareholder Rights

Shareholders in serious conflict with management have three different mechanisms for enforcing their rights: a derivative lawsuit, a direct lawsuit, or a class action.

DERIVATIVE LAWSUITS

A derivative lawsuit is brought by *shareholders* to remedy a wrong to the *corporation*. The suit is brought in the name of the corporation, and all proceeds of the litigation go to the corporation. The shareholders of Disney were upset when the board of directors approved a $140 million severance package for Michael Ovitz. Technically, however, the directors had injured the *corporation*, not the *shareholders*. And who would authorize a suit by the corporation against the directors? The

---

[16] *Sinclair Oil Corp. v. Levien*, 280 A.2d 717, 1971 Del. LEXIS 225 (Del. 1971).
[17] *Lerner v. Lerner*, 306 Md. 771, 511 A.2d 501, 1986 Md. LEXIS 264 (Md. 1986).

directors, of course. Because the directors are unlikely to file suit against themselves, shareholders are permitted to bring a *derivative* action, in the name of the corporation, against managers who have violated their duty to the corporation. All damages, however, go *to the corporation*; the individual shareholders benefit only to the extent that the settlement causes their stock to rise in value.

Litigation is tremendously expensive. How can shareholders afford to sue if they are not entitled to damages? A corporation that loses a derivative suit must pay the legal fees of the victorious shareholders. Most derivative lawsuits are brought by lawyers seeking to earn these fees. (Losing shareholders are generally not required to pay the corporation's legal fees.)

There is a complication, however: **Because a derivative lawsuit is brought in the name of the corporation, shareholders must** *make demand* **on the corporation, unless demand would** *clearly be futile.* That is, before filing a derivative suit, the shareholders must first ask the board to bring the suit itself. Understandably, boards almost always reject this request. Shareholders rarely have luck convincing a court that the board's rejection was a mistake. **Therefore, the shareholders' only real hope is to refuse to make demand on the grounds that such demand would clearly be futile either because the directors had a conflict of interest or because the decision violated the business judgment rule.**

In the *Brehm* case, discussed earlier in this chapter, the Disney shareholders argued that demand would be futile both because Michael Eisner controlled the board of directors and because the directors had violated the business judgment rule by making an uninformed decision. The Supreme Court of Delaware ruled that, on the facts presented, there had not been a conflict of interest and the decision had not violated the business judgment rule. However, as we have seen, the Supreme Court did remand the case to the trial court to permit plaintiffs limited additional discovery. The court cautioned that, "[T]here is a very large—though not insurmountable—burden on stockholders who believe they should pursue the remedy of a derivative suit instead of selling their stock or seeking to reform or oust these directors from office."[18]

DIRECT LAWSUITS

Shareholders are permitted to sue the corporation directly only if their own rights have been harmed. If, for example, the corporation denies shareholders the right to inspect its books and records or to hold a shareholder meeting, they may sue in their own name and keep any damages awarded. The corporation is not required to pay the shareholders' legal fees; winning shareholders can use part of any damage award for this purpose.

CLASS ACTION LAWSUITS

If a group of shareholders all have the same claim, they can join together and file suit as a class action, rather than suing separately. By joining forces, they can share the expense and effort of litigation. It is also far more efficient for the judicial system for one court to try one case than for tens or hundreds of courts all over the country to try the same issue. For obvious reasons, companies tend to resist class actions. In such suits, management is assailed by many small shareholders who otherwise could not afford to (or would not bother to) sue individually.

---

[18] 2000 Del. LEXIS 51, 67.

Chapter Conclusion

Corporations first became prominent in the eighteenth and nineteenth centuries as a means for businesses to raise the outside capital needed for large-scale manufacturing. Shareholders without management skills complemented managers without capital. Although this separation between management and owners makes great economic sense and has contributed significantly to the rise of the American economy, it also creates complex legal issues. How can shareholders ensure that the corporation will operate in their best interest? How can managers make tough decisions without being second-guessed by shareholders? Balancing the interests of managers and shareholders is a complex problem the law has struggled to resolve, without completely satisfying either side.

Chapter Review

1. Promoters are personally liable for contracts they sign before the corporation is formed unless the corporation and the third party agree to a novation.

2. Companies generally incorporate in the state in which they will be doing business. However, if they intend to operate in several states, they may choose to incorporate in a jurisdiction known for its favorable corporate laws, such as Delaware or Nevada.

3. A corporate charter must generally include the company's name, address, registered agent, purpose, and a description of its stock.

4. A court may, under certain circumstances, pierce the corporate veil and hold shareholders personally liable for the debts of the corporation.

5. Termination of a corporation is a three-step process requiring a shareholder vote, the filing of "Articles of Dissolution," and the winding up of the enterprise's business.

6. Officers and directors have a fiduciary duty to act in the best interests of the shareholders of the corporation.

7. The business judgment rule protects managers from liability for their decisions as long as the managers observe the duty of care and the duty of loyalty.

8. Under the duty of loyalty, managers may not take advantage of an opportunity that rightfully belongs to the corporation.

9. If managers enter into an agreement on behalf of their corporation that benefits them personally, then the business judgment rule does not apply. The managers may be liable unless the board of directors or the shareholders have first approved the transaction or it was fair to the corporation.

10. Under the duty of care, managers must make honest, informed decisions that have a rational business purpose.

11. The Williams Act regulates the activities of a bidder in a tender offer for stock in a publicly traded corporation.

12. Virtually all publicly held companies solicit proxies from their shareholders. A proxy authorizes someone else to vote in place of the shareholder.

13. Under certain circumstances public companies must include shareholder proposals in the proxy statement.

14. A shareholder of a privately held company who objects to a fundamental change in the corporation can insist that her shares be bought out at fair value. This protection is referred to as "dissenters' rights."

15. Controlling shareholders have a fiduciary duty to minority shareholders.

16. A derivative lawsuit is brought by shareholders to remedy a wrong to the corporation. The suit is brought in the name of the corporation, and all proceeds of the litigation go to the corporation.

17. If a group of shareholders all have the same claim against the corporation, they can join together and file a class action, rather than suing separately.

Practice Test

1. Michael Ferns incorporated Erin Homes, Inc., to manufacture mobile homes. He issued himself a stock certificate for 100 shares for which he made no payment. He and his wife served as officers and directors of the organization, but, during the eight years of its existence, the corporation held only one meeting. Erin always had its own checking account, and all proceeds from the sales of mobile homes were deposited there. It filed federal income tax returns each year, using its own federal identification number. John and Thelma Laya paid $17,500 to purchase a mobile home from Erin, but the company never delivered it to them. The Layas sued Erin Homes and Michael Ferns, individually. Should the court "pierce the corporate veil" and hold Ferns personally liable?

2. **CPA QUESTION** A corporate stockholder is entitled to which of the following rights?

(a) Elect officers

(b) Receive annual dividends

(c) Approve dissolution

(d) Prevent corporate borrowing

3. An appraiser valued a subsidiary of Signal Co. at between $230 million and $260 million. Six months later, Burmah Oil offered to buy the subsidiary at $480 million, giving Signal only three days to respond. The board of directors accepted the offer, without obtaining an updated evaluation of the subsidiary or determining if other companies would offer a higher price. Members of the board were sophisticated, with a great deal of experience in the oil industry. A Signal Co. shareholder sued to prevent the sale. Is the Signal board protected by the business judgment rule?

4. **YOU BE THE JUDGE WRITING PROBLEM** Asher Hyman and Stephen Stahl formed a corporation named "Ampersand" to produce plays. Both men were employed by the corporation. After producing one play, Stahl decided to write *Philly's Beat*, focusing on the history of rock and roll in Philadelphia. As the play went into production, however, the two men quarreled over Hyman's repeated absences from work and the company's serious financial difficulties. Stahl resigned from Ampersand and formed another corporation to produce the play. Did the opportunity to produce *Philly's Beat* belong to Ampersand? **Argument for Stahl:** Ampersand was formed for the purpose of producing plays, not writing them. When Stahl wrote *Philly's Beat*, he was not competing against Ampersand. **Argument for Hyman:** Ampersand was in the business of producing plays, and it wanted *Philly's Beat*.

5. Davis Ajouelo signed an employment contract with William Wilkerson. The contract stated: ". . . whatever company, partnership, or corporation that Wilkerson may form for the purpose of manufacturing shall succeed Wilkerson and exercise the rights and assume all of Wilkerson's obligations as fixed by this contract." Two months later, Wilkerson formed Auto-Soler Company. Ajouelo entered into a new contract with Auto-Soler providing that the company was liable for Wilkerson's obligations under the old contract. Neither Wilkerson nor the company ever paid Ajouelo the sums owed him under the contracts. Ajouelo sued Wilkerson personally. Does Wilkerson have any obligations to Ajouelo?

6. **ETHICS** Edgar Bronfman, Jr., dropped out of high school to go to Hollywood and write songs and produce movies. Eventually, he left Hollywood to work in the family business—the Bronfmans owned 36 percent of Seagram Co., a liquor and beverage conglomerate. Promoted to president of the company at the age of 32, Bronfman seized a second chance to live his dream. Seagram received 70 percent of its earnings from its 24 percent ownership of DuPont Co. Bronfman sold this stock at *less than market value* to purchase (at an inflated price) 80 percent of MCA, a movie and music company that had been a financial disaster for its prior owners. Some observers thought Bronfman had gone Hollywood, others that he had gone crazy. After the deal was announced, the price of Seagram shares fell 18 percent. Was there anything Seagram shareholders could have done to prevent what to them was not a dream but a nightmare? Apart from legal issues, was Bronfman's decision ethical? What ethical obligations did he owe Seagram's shareholders?

7. Daniel Cowin was a minority shareholder of Bresler & Reiner, Inc., a public company that developed real estate in Washington, D.C. He alleged numerous instances of corporate mismanagement, fraud, self-dealing, and breach of fiduciary duty by the board of directors. He sought damages for the diminished value of his stock. Could Cowin bring this suit as a direct action, or must it be a derivative suit?

8. **CPA QUESTION** Generally, a corporation's articles of incorporation must include all of the following **except** the:

(a) Name of the corporation's registered agent.

(b) Name of each incorporator.

(c) Number of authorized shares.

(d) Quorum requirements.

9. Two shareholders of Bruce Company, Harry and Yolan Gilbert, were fighting management for control of the company. They asked for permission to inspect Bruce's stockholder list so that they could either solicit support for their slate of directors at the upcoming stockholders' meeting, or attempt to buy additional stock from other stockholders, or both. Bruce's board refused to allow the Gilberts to see the shareholder list on the grounds that the Gilberts owned another corporation that competed with Bruce. Do the Gilberts have the right to see Bruce's shareholder list?

10. **ROLE REVERSAL** Write a short-answer question that deals with the duty of care under the business judgment rule.

Internet Research Problems

Think of an idea for a new company, and prepare a corporate charter for your business. You can find a sample Delaware charter at http://www.state.de.us/corp/. For extra credit, find a sample charter for your own state.

Starting at http://www.thecorporatelibrary.com/, find information on a company's shareholder proposals. What were these proposals about? What was the outcome of the shareholder vote? Can you find a proposal that shareholders supported?

You can find further practice problems in the Online Quiz at http://beatty.westbuslaw.com or in the Study Guide that accompanies this text.

CHAPTER 18

Securities
Regulation

In 1926, America was gripped by a fever of stock market speculation. "Playing the market" became a national mania. The most engrossing news on any day's front page was the market. Up and up it soared. The cause of this psychological virus is uncertain, but the focus of the infection was the New York Stock Exchange. Between 1926 and 1929, annual volume leaped from 451 million to over 1.1 billion shares. In one year alone, the price of AT&T went from $179.50 to $335.62.

Much of this feverish trading was done on margin. Customers put down only 10 or 20 percent of a stock's purchase price and then borrowed the rest from their broker. This easy-payment plan excited the gambling instinct of unwary amateurs and professional speculators alike. By September 1929 the volume of these margin loans was equal to about half the entire public debt of the United States.

On September 4, 1929, stock prices began to soften, and for the next month they slid gently. Over the weekend of October 19, brokers sent out thousands of margin calls, asking customers to pay down loans that now exceeded the value of their stock. If customers failed to pay, brokers dumped their stock on the market, causing prices to fall further and brokers to make more margin calls. Soon there was a mad scramble of selling as prices plunged in wild disorder. Tens of thousands of investors across the country were wiped out. On Tuesday, October 29, 1929, the speculative boom completely collapsed. That day, 4 million shares were traded, a record that stood for 30 years. From the peak of the bull market in September to the debacle of October 29, over $32 billion of equity value simply vanished from the earth.

The stock market crash spawned the Great Depression—the most pervasive, persistent, and destructive economic crisis the nation has ever faced. Retail trade fell by one-half, automobile production by two-thirds, steel by three-quarters. In 1933, more businesses failed than in any other year in history. Surviving businesses responded to the crisis by cutting dividends, reducing inventories, laying off workers, slashing wages, and canceling capital investments.

Unemployment statistics were the most poignant of all. In 1932, one in every five people in the labor force was out of a job. Millions of others were underemployed, working only two or three days a week for wages that could not support a family. Distress cut indiscriminately across all economic and social classes. Bankers, insurance agents, architects, and lawyers joined the throng of unemployed. Articles such as the following were common in newspapers across the land:

> *New York, Jan. 6, 1933 (AP)*—After vainly trying to get a stay of dispossession until Jan. 15 from his apartment in Brooklyn, yesterday, Peter J. Cornell, 48 years old, a former roofing contractor out of work and penniless, fell dead in the arms of his wife. A doctor gave the cause of his death as heart disease, and the police said it had at least partly been caused by the bitter disappointment of a long day's fruitless attempt to prevent himself and his family being put out on the streets.[1]

Introduction .

At the time of the great stock market crash, there was no federal securities law, only state law. Congress recognized that the country needed a national securities system if it was to avoid another such catastrophe. In 1933, Congress passed the Securities Act of 1933 (1933 Act) to regulate the issuance of new securities. The next year, it passed the Securities Exchange Act of 1934 (1934 Act) to regulate companies with publicly traded securities. The 1934 Act also established the Securities and Exchange Commission (SEC), the regulatory agency that oversees the securities industry.

---

[1] The material in this section is adapted from Cabell Phillips, *From the Crash to the Blitz* (Toronto: Macmillan, 1969).

THE SECURITIES AND EXCHANGE COMMISSION

The SEC creates law in three different ways:

- **Rules.** The securities statutes are often little more than general guides. Through its rules, the SEC fills in the crucial details.

- **Releases**. These are informal pronouncements from the SEC on current issues. Releases often operate as two-way communication. When the SEC issues a release to announce a proposed change in the rules, it also asks for comments on the proposal.

- **No-Action Letters.** Anyone who is in doubt about whether a particular transaction complies with the securities laws can ask the SEC directly. The response is called a no-action letter because it states that "the staff will recommend that the Commission take no action" if the transaction is done in a specified manner.

In addition to creating laws, the SEC has the power to enforce them. It can bring cease and desist orders against those who violate the securities laws, and it can also levy fines or confiscate profits from illegal transactions. Those accused of wrongdoing can appeal these sanctions to the courts. The SEC does not have the authority to bring a criminal action; it refers criminal cases to the Justice Department.

WHAT IS A SECURITY?

Both the 1933 and the 1934 Acts regulate securities. The official definition of a security includes a note, stock, treasury stock, bond, debenture, evidence of indebtedness, certificate of interest or participation in any profit-sharing agreement, and 17 other equivalents. Courts have interpreted this definition to mean that **a security is any transaction in which the buyer (1) invests money in a common enterprise and (2) expects to earn a profit predominantly from the efforts of others.**

This definition covers investments that are not necessarily called *securities*. For example, they may be called orange trees. W. J. Howey Co. owned large citrus groves in Florida. It sold these trees to investors, most of whom were from out of state and knew nothing about farming. Purchasers were expected to hire someone to take care of their trees. Someone like Howey-in-the-Hills, Inc., a related company that just happened to be in the service business. Customers were free to hire any service company, but 85 percent of the acreage was covered by service contracts with Howey-in-the-Hills. The court held that Howey was selling a security (no matter how orange or tart), because the purchaser was investing in a common enterprise (the orange grove) expecting to earn a profit from Howey's farmwork.

Other courts have interpreted the term "security" to include animal breeding arrangements (chinchillas, silver foxes, or beavers, take your pick); condominium purchases in which the developer promises the owner a certain level of income from rentals; and even investments in whiskey. Life Partners was a company that aimed to help AIDS patients. Was it selling a security?

YOU BE THE JUDGE

SEC V. LIFE PARTNERS, INC.

87 F.3d 536, 1996 U.S. App. LEXIS 16117
United States Court of Appeals for the District of Columbia Circuit, 1996

FACTS: Life Partners, Inc. (LPI), bought life insurance policies from AIDS victims at a discount from face value. It then repackaged these policies and sold them to investors who recovered the full face value of the policy after the patient died. LPI evaluated the patient's medical condition, reviewed his insurance policy, negotiated the purchase price, and prepared the legal documents. Investors could pay as little as $650 and buy as little as 3 percent of the benefits of a policy. Once an investor acquired an interest in a policy, she could avail herself of LPI's ongoing administrative services, which included monitoring the patient's health, assuring that the policy did not lapse, and arranging for resale of the investor's interest if requested.

Although the investment might sound macabre, it offered a valuable benefit to the terminally ill patient who was able to secure much needed income in the final years of life when employment was unlikely and medical bills were overwhelming. This arrangement was known as a "viatical settlement" after the ecclesiastical term "viaticum" (communion given to the dying). The viatical settlement industry developed in response to the AIDS crisis. LPI was the largest viatical settlement organizer in the country, accounting for approximately one-half of the total settlement volume. The SEC

sued LPI, alleging that it was selling a security without registration.

YOU BE THE JUDGE: Was Life Partners selling a security?

ARGUMENT FOR THE SEC: LPI purchases policies from dying patients. The company then pools these policies, sells fractional interests to investors, and pays off investors when the patients die. The investors play no role, other than writing a check. These viatical settlements are clearly a common enterprise in which investors rely completely on the efforts of LPI.

ARGUMENT FOR LPI: The securities laws do not apply to LPI's efforts, which take place *before* the investors make their purchase. At that point, the investors can evaluate LPI for themselves. After the purchase, profitability is determined by the timing of the patient's death, which is outside LPI's control (we hope). After the investment, LPI plays only a clerical role; thus the investors are not earning a profit predominantly from its efforts. In *Howey*, the investors' profit depended on the company's success at growing orange trees. In Life Partners, the profits depended on the patient's life span, not on the company's management efforts. ◢

Securities Act of 1933

The 1933 Act requires that, before offering or selling securities, the issuer must register the securities with the SEC, unless the securities qualify for an exemption. An **issuer** is the company that issues the stock. Registering securities with the SEC in a public offering is a major undertaking, but the 1933 Act exempts some securities and also some particular types of securities transactions from the full-blown registration requirements of a public offering.

It is also important to remember that **when an issuer registers securities, the SEC does not investigate the quality of the offering.** Permission from the SEC to sell securities does not mean that the company has a good product or will be successful. SEC approval simply means that, on the surface, the company has answered all relevant questions about itself and its major products. The guiding principle of the federal securities laws is that investors can make a reasoned decision on whether to buy or sell securities if they have full and accurate information about a company and the security it is selling. For example, the Green Bay Packers football team sold an offering of stock to finance stadium improvements. The prospectus admitted:

> IT IS VIRTUALLY IMPOSSIBLE that any investor will ever make a profit on the stock purchase. The company will pay no dividends, and the shares cannot be sold.

This does not sound like a stock you want in your retirement fund; on the other hand, the SEC will not prevent Green Bay from selling it, or you from buying it, as long as you understand what the risks are.

One last point: **the 1933 Act prohibits fraud in *any* securities transaction.** Anyone who issues fraudulent securities is in violation of the 1933 Act, whether or not the securities are registered. Both the SEC and any purchasers of the stock can sue the issuer.

CYBERLAW

Companies must deliver certain documents to investors and also file them with the SEC. Most companies now make their required SEC filings electronically, using the EDGAR (Electronic Data Gathering, Analysis, and Retrieval) system. Once filed with the SEC, this information is available online at http://www.sec.gov.

Companies can fulfill their SEC filing requirements online with EDGAR, but delivering documents to investors electronically is more difficult because computer literacy and availability among investors vary widely. The SEC does permit issuers to communicate electronically with investors, provided that the following standards are met:

- *Consent.* Although many investors have computers, an issuer cannot assume that all do, or that all want to receive data this way. Therefore, an electronic document is only valid if the investor agrees to receive information in this form.

- *Notice.* A company cannot simply post information on its Internet Web site, because investors will not necessarily know it is there. The issuer must notify investors, via e-mail or snail mail, that information is available.

- *Access.* The recipients must have access to the information for a reasonable period of time and be able to download or print it. The investor can always request the paper version of a document, even after consenting to electronic delivery.

Companies communicate with investors via the Internet, and so does the SEC. Omnigene Diagnostics, Inc., was touted on various online investment bulletin boards, so when the SEC halted trading in this dubious stock, it announced the action on America Online. SEC enforcement officials also regularly surf the Net, looking for illegal activity. ▪

GENERAL EXEMPTION

Before offering securities for sale, the issuer must determine whether they are exempt from registration under the 1933 Act. Typically, exemptions are based on two factors: the type of security and the type of transaction. However, the National Securities Markets Improvement Act of 1996 gave the SEC new authority under both the 1933 and the 1934 Acts to grant exemptions that are "in the public interest" and "consistent with the protection of investors."

EXEMPT SECURITIES

The 1933 Act exempts some types of securities from registration because they (1) are inherently low risk, (2) are regulated by other statutes, or (3) are not really investments. The following securities are exempt from registration:

- **Government securities**, which include any security issued or guaranteed by federal or state government

- **Bank securities**, which include any security issued or guaranteed by a bank

- **Short-term notes**, which are high-quality negotiable notes or drafts that are due within nine months of issuance and are not sold to the general public

- **Nonprofit issues**, which include any security issued by a nonprofit religious, educational, or charitable organization; and

- **Insurance policies and annuity contracts**, which are governed by insurance regulations.[2]

EXEMPT TRANSACTIONS

Section 4(2) of the 1933 Act exempts from registration "transactions by an issuer not involving any public offering." These are simple words to define a complex problem. In effect, the 1933 Act states that an issuer is not required to register securities that are sold in a private offering, that is, an offering with only a few investors or a relatively small amount of money involved. In private offerings, the full-blown disclosure of a public offering is neither necessary nor appropriate. For example, a group of sophisticated investors who know an industry well do not need full disclosure. Or, if the amount at stake is relatively small, it would not make economic sense for the issuer to incur the heavy expense of a public offering.

There is an important distinction between exempt *securities* and exempt *transactions*. Exempt *securities* are always exempt, throughout their lives, no matter how many times they are sold. Stock sold in an exempt *transaction* is exempt only that one time, not necessarily in any subsequent sale. Suppose that Country Bank sells stock to the public. Under the 1933 Act, the bank is never required to register these securities, no matter how many times they are sold. On the other hand, suppose that Tumbleweed, Inc., a quilt maker, sells $5 million worth of stock in a private offering that is exempt from registration. Shamika buys 100 shares of this stock. Seven years later, the company decides to sell stock in a public offering that must be registered. As part of this public offering, Shamika sells her 100 shares. This time, the shares must be registered because they are being sold in a *public offering*.

Most small companies use private, not public, offerings to raise capital. There are three different types of private offerings—intrastate, Regulation D, and Regulation A—each with its own set of rules.

---

[2] Life Partners was selling the rights to already existing policies, not the policies themselves. The insurance companies that issued the policies initially were not required to register them.

Intrastate Offering Exemption

Under SEC Rule 147, an issuer is not required to register securities that are offered and sold only to residents of the state in which the issuer is incorporated and does business. This exemption was designed to provide local financing for local businesses. To qualify under Rule 147, 80 percent of the issuer's revenues and assets must be in-state, and it must also intend to spend 80 percent of the offering's proceeds in-state. Neither the issuer nor any purchaser can sell the securities outside the state for nine months after the offering.

Rule 147 is a **safe harbor**—if an issuer totally complies with it, the offering definitely qualifies as intrastate. But even if the issuer does not comply absolutely with the rule, the SEC or the courts may still consider the offering to be intrastate; however, the issuer cannot be sure in advance how the decision will come out. Sonic was a Utah corporation that sold stock to Utah residents. *Seven* months later, the company sold stock to an Illinois company. Although Sonic violated Rule 147 by making the second sale too early, the court held that the company had nonetheless qualified for an intrastate offering because it had not intended, at the time of the original offering, to sell stock outside Utah.[3] Although Sonic had not totally complied with Rule 147, it had come close enough to avoid liability. A safe harbor is less dangerous, but a voyage outside its boundaries does not necessarily end in disaster.

Regulation D

Three different types of private offerings can be made under Regulation D (often referred to as Reg D) under Rules 504, 505, and 506.

Rule 504.   Under this rule (know as the "seed capital" rule), a company:

- May sell up to $1 million in securities during each 12-month period.

- May advertise the stock and solicit an unlimited number of investors if:

  - The transaction is registered under a state law with disclosure requirements, or

  - Sales are limited to accredited investors. **Accredited investors** are institutions (such as banks and insurance companies) or wealthy individuals (with a net worth of more than $1 million or an annual income of more than $200,000).

If the securities are neither registered under state law nor sold exclusively to accredited investors, they are **restricted** stock, which means they must be purchased for investment purposes. As a general rule, the buyer cannot resell restricted securities, either publicly or privately, for one year.

Rule 505.   This rule permits a company to sell up to $5 million of stock during each 12-month period, subject to the following restrictions:

- The company may not advertise the stock publicly.

- The issuer can sell to as many accredited investors as it wants, but is limited to only 35 unaccredited investors.

---

[3] *Busch v. Carpenter*, 827 F.2d 653, 1987 U.S. App. LEXIS 11034 (10th Cir. 1987).

- The company need not provide information to accredited investors but must make some disclosure to unaccredited investors. This requirement provides issuers with a serious incentive to avoid unaccredited investors because the disclosure requirements, although less demanding than for a public offering, are nonetheless burdensome.

- Stock purchased under this rule is restricted.

Rule 506. This rule is similar to Rule 505. The differences are that:

- There is no limit on the amount of stock a company can sell.

- If an unaccredited purchaser is unsophisticated, he must have a **purchaser representative** to help him evaluate the investment. Is an *unsophisticated* investor someone who does not care for opera? No, it is someone who is unable to assess the risks of the offering himself.

The following table sets out the menu of choices under Reg D:

	Maximum Value of Securities Sold in a 12–Month Period	Maximum Number of Investors		Is Disclosure Required?	Is Public Advertising Permitted?	Are Securities Restricted?
Rule 504 Option 1:	$1 million	No limit on accredited investors	or	Disclosure under state law	Yes	No
Option 2:	$1 million	No limit	and	No	No	Yes
Rule 505	$5 million	No limit on accredited investors; no more than 35 unaccredited investors		Only for unaccredited investors	No	Yes
Rule 506	No limit	No limit on accredited investors; no more than 35 unaccredited investors, who must either be sophisticated or have a purchaser representative		Only for unaccredited investors	No	Yes

Regulation A

Although an offering under Regulation A is *called* a private offering, it really is a small public offering. **Reg A permits an issuer to sell $5 million of securities *publicly* in any 12-month period.** The issuer must give each purchaser an offering circular that provides the same disclosure required for unaccredited investors under Reg D. The following table compares a public offering, Reg A, and Reg D:

	Initial Public Offering	Regulation A	Regulation D
Maximum Value of Securities Sold	No limit	$5 million	$1 million, $5 million, or no limit, depending on the rule
Public Solicitation of Purchasers	Permitted	Permitted	Permitted only under Rule 504
Suitability Requirements for Purchasers	No requirements	No requirements	Must determine if investors are accredited or sophisticated
Disclosure Requirements	Elaborate registration statement, audited financials	Offering circular that is less detailed than a registration statement	Rule 504: may require disclosure under state law Rules 505 and 506: none for accredited investors, the same requirements as Reg A for unaccredited investors
Resale of Securities	Permitted	Permitted	Sometimes permitted under Rule 504, otherwise not permitted for one year
Number of Offerings in 2001	770	50	15,000

Direct Public Offerings

Traditionally, a small company either sold stock to people it knew or hired an investment banker to place the securities. But now, instead of going through Wall Street, many companies trying to raise capital for the first time sell stock to the public themselves through a direct public offering (DPO). In a DPO, the company makes the offering under Regulation A or Rule 504, because both permit public offerings without full-blown registration and disclosure requirements.

The advantages of a DPO are:

- It is much cheaper than a regular public offering done through an underwriter.

- It can be an effective marketing tool—shareholders tend to become even more loyal customers.

The downside:

- Each investor must receive written information about the company. The cost of this disclosure can be prohibitive when dealing with many small investors. Mailing a $10 disclosure document to hundreds of investors who only want to buy $50 worth of stock each may not be an efficient means of raising money.

- Although shareholders are warned that they should view their purchases as long-term investments, some will inevitably want to sell their shares. Setting up a system to permit these trades can be tricky and time-consuming.

Although the companies featured in the following article found their DPOs worthwhile, the process consumed significant management time.

NEWSWORTHY

In 1995, Spring Street Brewery, a New York microbrewery, became the first company to conduct an offering on the Internet. It established a home page that allowed potential investors to examine and download its offering documents. In the end, it raised $1.6 million.

Thanksgiving Coffee Co. of Fort Bragg, California, used both cybertechnology and the old-fashioned face-to-face approach. It had originally planned simply to sell to its loyal customer base. "You think that everybody who knows about you will line up around the block to buy stock, but you have to put the offering in front of potential investors' faces seven times to get them to take action," says Thanksgiving general manager Rick Moon. He did just that. He put offering notices on coffee-bean bags; he hung announcements on bean dispensers. Vendors got the advertisements, as did mail-order customers. Information about the stock sale appeared on the company's Web site, in its catalog, and in advertisements in targeted magazines. Anyone who called about the stock got regular updates on the offering. In the end, the huge effort paid off. By the time the offering closed, Thanksgiving Coffee had sold 20 percent of its stock for $1.25 million.[4]

The Web site http://www.dfdpo.com includes a "screen test" to help you gauge whether you and your company are ready for a DPO. Additional information about DPOs is available at http://www.dpocentral.com.

PUBLIC OFFERINGS

When a company wishes to raise significant amounts of capital from a large number of people, it is time for a public offering. A company's first public sale of securities is called an **initial public offering** or an **IPO**. Here is one company's experience with an IPO.

Shortly after graduating from the Massachusetts Institute of Technology, Daniel Schwinn and Frank Slaughter founded Shiva Corp. (pronounced SHE-va) in Burlington, Massachusetts. The company made hardware and software that allowed personal computers to tie directly into a corporate network from outside the office. Although within a decade sales had reached $42 million and net income was $2.7 million, the company was constantly strapped for cash to fund expansion. Its two founders began thinking about a public offering.

Underwriting

As we have seen, companies can sell stock directly to the public themselves, but they primarily do so if the amounts involved are small. Shiva sought to raise more than $20 million, so it decided to hire an investment bank to serve as underwriter. In a **firm commitment** underwriting, the underwriter buys the stock from the issuer and resells it to the public. The underwriter bears the risk that the stock may sell at a lower price than expected. In a **best efforts** underwriting, the underwriter does not buy the stock but instead acts as the company's agent in selling it. If the stock sells at a low price, the company, not the underwriter, is the loser.

In underwriting, as in life, timing is everything. As it happened, just when Shiva hoped to complete its offering, Wall Street's interest in the high-tech sector suddenly cooled. Investment bankers offered the company only $6 a share for its

---

[4] Stephanie Gruner, "When Mom & Pop Go Public," *INC.*, Dec. 1996, p. 66. Republished with permission of INC Magazine; permission conveyed through the Copyright Clearance Center, Inc.

stock. Shiva decided to wait. Within three months, the market in high-tech stocks picked up again. The company's president, Frank Ingari, and its chief financial officer, Cynthia Deysher, went to New York to sign on with the investment bank Goldman Sachs. Shiva agreed to sell Goldman 2.4 million shares at a tentative price of $12 per share.

Registration Statement

The **registration statement** has two purposes: to notify the SEC that a sale of securities is pending and to disclose information to prospective purchasers. The registration statement must include detailed information about the issuer and its business, a description of the stock, the proposed use of the proceeds from the offering, and audited balance sheets and income statements. Preparing a registration statement is neither quick—it typically takes two to three months—nor inexpensive. Shiva spent $900,000 on audits and other expenses.

Within a month of hiring an investment bank, Shiva filed its *preliminary* draft of the registration statement with the SEC. This preliminary draft is called a **red herring** because it contains a notice in red ink warning that the securities cannot yet be sold.[5] The SEC typically spends between 30 and 100 days reviewing this preliminary draft of the registration statement. Remember that the Commission does not assess the value of the stock or the merit of the investment. Its role is to ensure that the company has disclosed enough to enable investors to make an informed decision.

Prospectus

Typically, buyers never see the registration statement; they are given the **prospectus** instead. (The prospectus is also included in the registration statement that is sent to the SEC.) The prospectus includes all of the important disclosures about the company, while the registration statement includes additional information that is of interest to the SEC but not to the typical investor, such as the names and addresses of the lawyers for the issuer and underwriter. All investors must receive a copy of the prospectus before purchasing the stock.

Sales Effort

The SEC closely regulates an issuer's sales effort.

Quiet Period. The quiet period begins when a company hires an underwriter and ends 25 days after the IPO. During this period, company officers must guard their words carefully to avoid any appearance of hyping the stock. For example, the SEC delayed an offering of stock by Webvan Group Inc. after its officers talked with reporters from *BusinessWeek* and *Forbes* magazines, giving out financial data on recent results that had not been included in the prospectus.

Waiting Period. This is the time after the registration statement has been filed but before the SEC has approved it. The underwriter can publish a **tombstone ad**, that is, a simple, unadorned announcement of the offering that includes the amount and type of security, the name of the underwriter, and the price of stock. You can see many of these ads in *The Wall Street Journal* and also on company Web

---

[5] The term "red herring" is a bit of a joke because, outside securities offerings, it means a false clue.

sites. During the waiting period, the underwriter may distribute the preliminary prospectus. It can also solicit offers, but cannot make sales. The underwriter uses this period to estimate market demand for the stock. It **makes book**, meaning that it talks with traders to determine how many shares it can sell and at what price. It also takes **indications of interest** from traders, but makes no sales.

Road Show. During the waiting period, Goldman and Shiva began the **road show**—the cross-country road trip to convince traders that Shiva was a stock their clients should buy. Ingari and Schwinn spent a grueling two weeks visiting 16 cities. At each stop, they made the same impassioned pitch to influential traders. Sometimes road shows are broadcast on the Internet so that they can be viewed by a larger group that includes wealthy individuals. "We felt like door-to-door salesmen," Ingari said. So strong was the response to Shiva that in the second week of the road show, Goldman suggested raising the price to $15 a share, from $12, and selling an additional 360,000 shares. When the road show ended, orders for the stock exceeded the number of shares by a factor of 30. That the IPO would be hot was certain. But how hot?

Going Effective

Once its review of the preliminary registration statement is complete, the SEC sends the issuer a **comment letter**, listing changes that must be made to the registration statement. An issuer almost always amends the registration statement at least once, and sometimes more than once. After the SEC has approved a final registration statement (which includes, of course, the final prospectus), the issuer then decides on a date to **go effective**, that is, to begin selling the stock. One last step remained: Goldman and Shiva had to agree on an opening price. They decided to raise the price from $12 to $15 per share. Shiva would sell to Goldman at $13.95 per share, and Goldman, in turn, would sell it on the market at $15.

The night before the sale, Shiva executives and the underwriters met for dinner and made bets about the next day's closing price and trading volume. No one guessed nearly high enough. As soon as Goldman sold at $15, the price zoomed to $30.50. The stock closed that day at $31.50 per share. At Goldman, there were hugs, tears of joy, and champagne toasts. But founders Schwinn and Slaughter, with their stock suddenly worth $30 million each, suffered chest pains. And Ingari, the president and chief executive, felt even worse. As the value of his stake in Shiva soared past $14 million, he fled to the men's room. "I was ready to throw up, I was sweating badly, and I could barely stand up. When I looked in the mirror, I had blood coming out of my nose."

In the end, Shiva raised $28 million that day, and its founders and other insiders, who sold about 700,000 shares, took home another $10 million. Goldman earned almost $3 million, or 7 percent of the proceeds. Did Goldman price the offering too low? Pricing an IPO is more art than science. Everyone would like the price to rise gently. At all cost, however, the underwriter wishes to avoid a disaster in which the stock price collapses, leaving it with a large loss. Of course, the underwriter looks bad if the company sells stock for a lot less than it is worth. Shares that Goldman sold in the morning for $15 were trading for twice that amount later in the day. Half of the initial worth of Shiva's stock, or about $43 million, went into the pockets of early buyers who "flipped" the stock, selling it immediately to other investors. In hindsight, Goldman should have priced the stock higher, but it is not clear that it or anyone else could reasonably have predicted the market's reaction.

Frank Slaughter went home after the IPO and spent a day "scrubbing toilets—to retain some humility." He had come through one of the most unnerving, and quintessential, rites of passage of the American capitalist system. The company obtained money to develop new products and build factories. The public got a chance to buy in. And the company's founders, and other key insiders, found a way to cash out.[6]

So what happened to Shiva? Its stock continued an upward climb for two years, reaching a peak of $87 per share. But when the company failed to develop new products, both its business and its stock price faltered. Five years after the public offering, Intel Corp. acquired Shiva at a price of $6 per share.

SALES OF RESTRICTED SECURITIES

After the public offering, Shiva insiders still owned a substantial block of stock. Between them, Schwinn, Slaughter, and Ingari held stock or options for 2.8 million shares. With the stock trading as high as $87 per share, on paper they were worth $245 million, but they could not actually sell their stock, at least not right away. **Rule 144 limits the resale of two types of securities:** *control securities* **and** *restricted securities.*

A **control security** is stock held by any shareholder who owns more than 10 percent of a class of stock or by any officer or director. In any three-month period, such an insider can sell only an amount of stock equal to the average weekly trading volume for the prior four weeks or 1 percent of the number of shares outstanding, whichever is greater. Shiva had 9,589,000 shares outstanding and an (unusually high) average weekly trading volume of roughly 938,000. A Shiva insider could sell at most 938,000 shares during each three-month period. In a company with a more typical trading volume, the number might be a tenth of that. The purpose of this rule is to protect other investors from precipitous declines in stock price. If company insiders sold all of their stock in one day, the price would plunge, causing losses to the other shareholders.

For owners of restricted securities, the rules are more complex. A **restricted security** is any stock purchased in a private offering (such as Regulation D). These securities may not be sold within one year of the offering. After the first year, restricted securities can be sold as long as the sale does not exceed the limitations that apply to control stock: the greater of the average weekly trading volume for the prior four weeks or 1 percent of the number of shares outstanding. After two years, restricted securities can be sold freely, unless they are also control securities, in which case those restrictions still apply. Exhibit 18.1 illustrates the sale of restricted securities under Rule 144.

LIABILITY

Liability for Unregistered Securities

Section 12(a)(1) of the 1933 Act imposes liability on anyone who sells a security that is not registered and not exempt. The purchaser of the security can demand rescission—a return of his money in exchange for the stock—or, if he no longer owns the stock, he can ask for damages.

---

[6] The information about Shiva Corp. is from Glenn Rifkin, "Anatomy of a Highflying IPO, Nosebleeds and All," *The New York Times*, Feb. 19, 1995, p. F7. Copyright © 1995 by The New York Times Co. Reprinted by permission.

Exhibit 18.1
The sale of restricted securites under Rule 144

Fraud

Under §12(a)(2) of the 1933 Act, the seller of a security is liable for making any material misstatement or omission, either oral or written, in connection with the offer or sale of a security. This provision applies to both *public* and *private* offerings if there is some use of interstate commerce, such as the mails, telephone (even for an *intra*state call), or check (which clears). It is difficult to imagine a securities transaction that does not involve interstate commerce. The SEC provides information on how to invest wisely and avoid securities fraud at http://www.sec.gov/investor.shtml. The North American Securities Administrators Association also offers advice on "how to spot a con artist" and popular securities scams (http://www.nasaa.org/nasaa/scripts/prel_display_list.asp?ptid=63). You can obtain disciplinary reports on securities firms or individual brokers at http://www.nasdr.com. To report fraud, contact the SEC at its Complaint Center (http://www.sec.gov/complaint.shtml) or via e-mail at enforcement@sec.gov.

Criminal Liability

Under §24 of the 1933 Act, the Justice Department can prosecute anyone who willfully violates the Act.

Liability for the Registration Statement

Section 11 of the 1933 Act establishes the penalties for any errors in a registration statement. **If a final registration statement contains a material misstatement or omission, the purchaser of the security can recover from everyone who signed the registration statement.** This list of signatories includes the issuer, its directors, and chief officers; experts (such as auditors, engineers, or lawyers); and the underwriters. Everyone who signed the registration statement is jointly and severally liable for any error, except the experts, who are liable only for misstatements in the part of the registration statement for which they were responsible. Thus an auditor is liable for misstatements in the financials but not, say, for omissions about the CEO's criminal past.

Damages. To prevail under §11, the plaintiff need only prove that there was a material misstatement or omission and that she lost money. **Material** means important enough to affect an investor's decision. The plaintiff does not have to prove that she relied on (or even *read*) the registration statement, that she bought the stock from the issuer, or that the defendant was negligent. The plaintiff can recover the difference between what she paid for the stock and its value on the date of the lawsuit. Suppose that Pet Detective, Inc., does an IPO. A week later, Ace Investora buys 1,000 shares at $10 a share. He knows nothing about the company, but he likes the name. This stock turns out to be a dog—Pet Detective has only two agencies, not the 200 stated in the registration statement. When the stock falls to 10 cents, Investora can sue under §11 for $9,900. *— material misstatement*

[margin note: Don't prove you relied on]

Due Diligence. All is not hopeless, however, for those who have signed the registration statement. If the statement contains a material misstatement or omission, the company is liable and has no defense. But everyone else who signed the registration statement can avoid liability by showing that he investigated the registration statement as thoroughly as a "prudent person in the management of his own property." This investigation is called **due diligence**. Its importance cannot be overstated. The SEC does not conduct its own investigation to ensure that the registration statement is accurate. It can only ensure that, on the surface, the issuer has supplied all relevant information. If an issuer chooses to lie, the SEC has no way of knowing. It is the job of the underwriters to check the accuracy of the filing. Thus underwriters typically spend two or three weeks visiting the company, reading all its corporate documents (including minutes back to the beginning), and calling its bankers, customers, suppliers, and competitors to ensure that the registration statement is accurate and no skeletons have been overlooked.

[margin note: Strong Defense for ...]

When §11 was first passed, investment bankers were outraged. Some predicted that this liability provision would cause capital in America to dry up, that grass would grow on Wall Street. In fact, the first case under §11 arose 35 years and 27,000 registration statements later. In this case—*Escott v. Barchris Construction Corp.*—the registration statement was seriously flawed.[7] The underwriter failed to read the minutes of the executive committee meetings that revealed the company to be in serious financial condition. Much of the company's alleged backlog of orders was from nonexistent corporations. Proceeds of the offering were earmarked to pay off debt, not to buy new plant and equipment, as the registration statement had indicated. The company's directors, underwriters, and underwriters' counsel were held liable.

Although *Barchris* still strikes fear in the hearts of underwriters, some commentators now argue that underwriters do not take their due diligence obligations seriously enough. Was there adequate disclosure in the following case?

IN RE DONALD J. TRUMP CASINO SECURITIES LITIGATION

7 F.3D 357, 1993 U.S. APP. LEXIS 26691
United States Court of Appeals for the Third Circuit, 1993

FACTS: Donald J. Trump formed the Taj Mahal Associates Limited Partnership, which sold $675 million in bonds to the public. The partnership used the proceeds to purchase and complete construction on the Taj Mahal, a casino/hotel occupying 17 acres of land on the boardwalk in Atlantic

[margin note: Debt security]

---

[7] 283 F. Supp. 643, 1968 U.S. Dist. LEXIS 3853 (S.D.N.Y. 1968).

City, New Jersey. The Taj Mahal was widely touted as Atlantic City's largest and most lavish casino resort. After the partnership filed for bankruptcy, the purchasers of the bonds filed suit, alleging that the bond prospectus contained material misstatements and omissions.

ISSUE: Did the Taj Mahal prospectus contain material misstatements or omissions?

EXCERPTS FROM JUDGE BECKER'S DECISION: The plaintiffs allege that the prospectus contained material misrepresentations. Their principal claim is that the defendants had neither an honest belief in nor a reasonable basis for one statement in the prospectus: "The Partnership believes that funds generated from the operation of the Taj Mahal will be sufficient to cover all of its debt service (interest and principal)."

The prospectus at issue contained an abundance of warnings and cautionary language which bore directly on the prospective financial success of the Taj Mahal and on the Partnership's ability to repay the bonds. [N]o reasonable investor could believe anything but that the Taj Mahal bonds represented a rather risky, speculative investment which might yield a high rate of return, but which alternatively might result in no return or even a loss. For example, [the prospectus] stated:

> The Taj Mahal has not been completed and, accordingly, has no operating history. The Taj Mahal will be the largest casino/hotel complex in Atlantic City, with approximately twice the room capacity and casino space of many of the existing casino/hotels in Atlantic City. [No] other casino/hotel operator has had experience operating a complex the size of the

Taj Mahal in Atlantic City. Consequently, no assurance can be given that, once opened, the Taj Mahal will be profitable or that it will generate cash flow sufficient to provide for the payment of the debt service.

The prospectus additionally reported that there were risks of delay in the construction of the Taj Mahal and a risk that the casino might not receive the numerous essential licenses and permits from the state regulatory authorities.

In this case the Partnership did not bury the warnings about risks amidst the bulk of the prospectus. Indeed, it was the allegedly misleading statement which was buried amidst the cautionary language. Moreover, an investor would have read the sentence immediately following the challenged statement, which cautioned: "no assurance can be given, however, that actual operating results will meet the Partnership's expectations."

Within this broad context the statement at issue was, at worst, harmless. In other words, cautionary language, if sufficient, renders the alleged omissions or misrepresentations immaterial as a matter of law. Of course, a vague or blanket (boilerplate) disclaimer which merely warns the reader that the investment has risks will ordinarily be inadequate to prevent misinformation. To suffice, the cautionary statements must be substantive and tailored to the specific future projections, estimates or opinions in the prospectus which the plaintiffs challenge.

[W]e think it clear that the accompanying warnings and cautionary language served to negate any potentially misleading effect that the prospectus' statement about the Partnership's belief in its ability to repay the bonds would have on a reasonable investor. ◢

Stuart Wechsler, a New York lawyer representing the bondholders, bemoaned this decision as "another nail in the coffin of prospectus disclosure. The prospectus is becoming a useless document."[8] Is Mr. Wechsler's interpretation of this case correct?

Securities Exchange Act of 1934

Most buyers do not purchase new securities from the issuer in an initial public offering. Rather they buy stock that is publicly traded in the open market. This

---

[8] Edward Felsenthal, "Prospectus Liability," *The Wall Street Journal*, Oct. 18, 1993, p. B8.

stock is, in a sense, *secondhand* because others, perhaps many others, have already owned it. The purpose of the 1934 Act is to maintain the integrity of this secondary market.

GENERAL PROVISIONS OF THE 1934 ACT

Registration Requirements

As we have seen, the 1933 Act requires an issuer to register securities before selling them. That is a onetime effort for the company. The 1933 Act does not require the issuer to provide shareholders with any additional information in later years. Suppose that an automobile company registered and sold securities for the first time in 1946. Purchasers of those securities knew a lot about the firm—in 1946. But how can current investors assess the company? The 1934 Act plugs this hole. It requires issuers with publicly traded stock to continue to make information available to the public so that current—and potential—shareholders can evaluate the company. It is often said that the 1933 Act registers securities, and the 1934 Act registers companies.

Under the 1934 Act, an issuer must register with the SEC if (1) it completes a public offering under the 1933 Act, or (2) its securities are traded on a national exchange (such as the New York Stock Exchange), or (3) it has at least 500 shareholders and total assets that exceed $10 million. A company can *de*register if its number of shareholders falls below 300 or if it has fewer than 500 shareholders and assets of less than $10 million.

Disclosure Requirements—Section 13

Like the 1933 Act, the 1934 Act focuses on disclosure. The difference is that the 1933 Act requires onetime disclosure when a company sells stock to the public. The 1934 Act requires *ongoing*, regular disclosure for any company with a class of stock that is publicly traded. Companies that are required to register under the 1934 Act are called **reporting companies**.

Section 13 requires reporting companies to file the following documents:

- An initial, detailed information statement when the company first registers (similar to the filing required under the 1933 Act)

- Annual reports on Form 10-K, containing audited financial statements, a detailed analysis of the company's performance, and information about officers and directors

- Quarterly reports on Form 10-Q, which are less detailed than 10-Ks and contain unaudited financials

- Form 8-Ks to report any significant developments, such as bankruptcy, a change in control, a purchase or sale of significant assets, the resignation of a director as a result of a policy dispute, or a change in auditing firms

In response to corporate scandals involving Enron Corp. and other companies, Congress passed the Sarbanes-Oxley Act of 2002. It requires each company's CEO and CFO to certify that:

- The information in the quarterly and annual reports is true,

- The company has effective internal controls, and

- The officers have informed the company's audit committee and its auditors of any concerns that they have about the internal control system.

A reporting company must send its annual report to shareholders. All annual reports and other 1934 Act filings are available on the SEC Web site (http://www.sec.gov). The SEC has recently proposed a rule requiring companies to post these reports on their own Web sites as well. For particularly lively examples of this form of literature, check out the filings for Jack in the Box Inc. (http://www.jackinthebox.com/investors/annualreport.php) or Expeditors International of Washington, Inc. (http://www.investor.expeditors.com).

Proxy Requirements—Section 14

As discussed in Chapter 17, most shareholders of public corporations do not attend annual shareholder meetings. Instead, the company solicits their proxies, permitting them to vote by mail rather than in person. If a company solicits proxies, it is required to supply shareholders with a proxy statement that is intended to give them enough information to make informed decisions about the company. The proxy statement contains detailed information about officers and directors, including their experience, relationship with the company, and compensation. (The annual report provides financial information.) Proxy statements must also be filed with the SEC.

Under SEC rules, a company is not *required* to solicit proxies from shareholders, but if it does not, it is unlikely to obtain the quorum needed for the meeting to be held. In any event, a company cannot avoid its responsibility to inform shareholders. Whether or not it solicits proxies, it is still required to furnish shareholders with an information statement that contains essentially the same material as a proxy statement.

Short-Swing Trading—Section 16

During congressional hearings after the 1929 stock market crash, witnesses testified that insiders had manipulated the stock market. For example, insiders would buy a large block of stock, announce a substantial dividend, and then divest before the dividend was reduced. Section 16 was designed to prevent corporate insiders—officers, directors, and shareholders who own more than 10 percent of the company—from taking unfair advantage of privileged information to manipulate the market.

Section 16 takes a two-pronged approach:

- First, insiders must **report** their trades within two days. This report must also reveal their total stock holdings in the company. The filings must be made to the SEC electronically, and both the SEC and the company are required to post them on their respective Web sites within one business day after they are made.

- Second, insiders must **turn over to the corporation** any profits they make from the purchase and sale or sale and purchase of company securities in a six-month period. Section 16 is a strict liability provision. It applies even if the insider did not actually take advantage of secret information or try to manipulate the market; if she bought and sold or sold and bought stock in a six-month period, she is liable.

Suppose that Manuela buys 20,000 shares of her company's stock in June at $10 a share. In September, her (uninsured) summer house in Florida is destroyed by a hurricane. To raise money for rebuilding, she sells the stock at $12 per share, making a profit of $40,000. Her house will have to remain in ruins because she has violated §16 and must turn over the profit to her company.

LIABILITY

Section 18

Under §18, anyone who makes a false or misleading statement in a filing under the 1934 Act is liable to buyers or sellers who (1) acted in reliance on the statement and (2) can prove that the price at which they bought or sold was affected by the false filing. Section 18 applies to all filings under the 1934 Act, including proxy statements and annual reports.

Section 10(b)

Section 18 applies only to *filings* under the 1934 Act. What happens if a company executive makes a false public *statement* about the company? Or writes an untrue statement somewhere other than in a filing? In one case, a corporate officer bought up shares of his company's stock even as he made pessimistic public statements about the company. That is the type of behavior that §10(b) is designed to prevent. **Section 10(b) prohibits fraud in connection with the purchase and sale of any security, whether or not the security is registered under the 1934 Act.**

The SEC adopted Rule 10b-5 to clarify §10(b), but the rule is still a relatively vague, catch-all provision designed to fill any holes left by other sections of the securities laws.[9] Interpretation has largely been left to the courts, which generally have interpreted Rule 10b-5 as follows:

- **A Misstatement or Omission of a Material Fact.** Anyone who fails to disclose material information, or makes incomplete or inaccurate disclosure, is liable. **Material** has the same meaning as under the 1933 Act: important enough to affect an investor's decision. For example, a company repeatedly and falsely denied that it was involved in merger negotiations. It was liable even though the negotiations had only been in a preliminary stage.[10]

- *Scienter.* This is a legal term meaning *willfully*, *knowingly*, or *recklessly*. To be liable under Rule 10b-5, the defendant must have (1) known (or been reckless in not knowing) that the statement was inaccurate and (2) intended for the plaintiff to rely on the statement. Negligence is not enough. A group of shareholders sued the accounting firm Ernst & Ernst because it had failed to discover, during the course of an audit, that a company's chief executive was stealing funds. According to the shareholders, the auditors should have discovered that

---

[9] Rule 10b-5 prohibits any person, in connection with a purchase or sale of any security, from (1) employing any device, scheme, or artifice to defraud; (2) making any untrue statement of a material fact or omitting to state a material fact necessary in order to make the statements made, in light of the circumstances under which they were made, not misleading; or (3) engaging in any act, practice, or course of business that operates or would operate as a fraud or deceit upon any person.

[10] *Basic Inc. v. Levinson*, 485 U.S. 224, 108 S. Ct. 978, 1988 U.S. LEXIS 1197 (1988).

the executive refused to allow anyone else to open his mail and, therefore, should have been suspicious of wrongdoing. The court found Ernst & Ernst not liable. Although it may have been negligent, it had not *intentionally* or even *recklessly* facilitated fraud.[11]

- **Purchase or Sale.** Rule 10b-5 covers both buyers and sellers. It does not include, however, someone who failed to purchase stock because of a material misstatement. In the case of the company executive who spread negative rumors about his company while he bought stock, those who sold because of his false rumors could sue under Rule 10b-5, but not those who simply failed to buy.

- **Reliance.** To bring suit, a plaintiff must show that she relied on the misstatement or omission. In the case of open-market trades, reliance is difficult to prove, so the courts are willing to assume it.

Unfortunately, cyberspace offers new opportunities for fraud. Many investment chat rooms and Web sites are "pump and dump" operations. Con artists post messages hyping stocks, then when viewers buy and the stock price rises, the bad guys sell at a profit. SEC prevention and enforcement efforts are hindered by the sheer size of the Internet—it is too vast to patrol carefully. Moreover, Rule 10b-5 requires *scienter* and this intent is always difficult to prove, especially in the overheated atmosphere of cyberspace chat rooms. For a look at SEC efforts to prevent cyber fraud, click away at http://www.mcwhortle.com.

In the following case, the Supreme Court explains how §10(b) promotes the general goals of the securities acts.

SEC V. ZANDFORD

122 S. Ct. 1899; 2002 U.S. LEXIS 4023
United States Supreme Court, 2002

FACTS: William Wood was an elderly man in poor health whose daughter had a mental disability. He placed $419,255 in a brokerage account, instructing his broker, Charles Zandford, that his principal goal was the "safety of principal and income." Relying on Zandford's promise to "conservatively invest" the money, Wood gave the broker a general power of attorney that permitted him to trade securities in the account without prior approval. Zandford proceeded to transfer the Woods' money into his own personal account. By the time Wood died four years later, all his money was gone.

Zandford was convicted of criminal fraud and sentenced to 52 months in prison.

The SEC filed a civil suit against Zandford alleging that he had violated §10(b). Because of Zandford's criminal conviction, the SEC filed a motion asking for summary judgment in the civil case. Zandford argued that his fraud was not a violation of §10(b) because it was not "connected with the purchase or sale of a security." The trial court granted the SEC's motion for summary judgment, but the court of appeals reversed. The Supreme Court granted certiorari.

---

[11] *Ernst & Ernst v. Hochfelder*, 425 U.S. 185, 96 S. Ct. 1375, 1976 U.S. LEXIS 2 (1976).

ISSUES: What is the scope of §10(b)? What does the term "connected with the purchase or sale of a security" mean?

EXCERPTS FROM JUSTICE STEVENS'S DECISION: The [appeals] court held that [Zandford's] scheme was simply to steal the Woods' assets rather than to engage in manipulation of a particular security. Ultimately, the [appeals] court refused "to stretch the language of the securities fraud provisions to encompass every conversion or theft that happens to involve securities." [The appeals] court held that without some "relationship to market integrity or investor understanding," there is no violation of §10(b).

Among Congress' objectives in passing the [Securities Exchange] Act was "to insure honest securities markets and thereby promote investor confidence" after the market crash of 1929. More generally, Congress sought to substitute a philosophy of full disclosure for the philosophy of *caveat emptor* and thus to achieve a high standard of business ethics in the securities industry. Consequently, the statute should be construed not technically and restrictively, but flexibly to effectuate its remedial purposes.

In its role enforcing the Act, the SEC has consistently adopted a broad reading of the phrase "in connection with the purchase or sale of any security." While the statute must not be construed so broadly as to convert every common-law fraud that happens to involve securities into a violation of §10(b), neither the SEC nor this Court has ever held that there must be a misrepresentation about the value of a particular security in order to run afoul of the Act.

The securities sales and respondent's fraudulent practices were not independent events. [E]ach sale was made to further respondent's fraudulent scheme; each was deceptive because it was neither authorized by, nor disclosed to, the Woods.

[T]he Woods were injured as investors through respondent's deceptions, which deprived them of any compensation for the sale of their valuable securities. Not only does such a fraud prevent investors from trusting that their brokers are executing transactions for their benefit, but it undermines the value of a discretionary account like that held by the Woods. If such individuals cannot rely on a broker to exercise that discretion for their benefit, then the account loses its added value.

Accordingly, the judgment of the Court of Appeals is reversed, and the case is remanded for further proceedings consistent with this opinion. ◢

This case was decided in the midst of widespread scandals involving companies that released inaccurate financial statements and investment banks that aggressively sold stocks to their customers even as they admitted privately (via e-mails) that the stocks were rubbish. In the *Zandford* case, Justice Stevens says, "Congress sought to substitute a philosophy of full disclosure for the philosophy of *caveat emptor* and thus to achieve a high standard of business ethics in the securities industry." How would you characterize the state of ethics on Wall Street now? Has it improved since this case?

The Private Securities Litigation Reform Act of 1995

In 1995, Congress passed an amendment to the 1934 Act intended to discourage fraud suits by shareholders. Under this amendment, companies are liable to shareholders for so-called forward-looking statements (that is, financial projections or statements about future plans) *only if* (1) the company fails to include a warning that the predictions may not come to pass, *and* (2) the shareholders can show that company executives knew the predictions were false. Suppose a pharmaceutical company predicts that a new drug will generate billions in sales, but two years later the drug is a total failure. Before 1995, shareholders would have had a strong case, but now the company would not be liable as long as it had disclosed, at the time of making the prediction, reasons why the drug might not be a success. Even if the company failed to mention these reasons, it would be liable only if executives knew the prediction to be false when they made it.

Thus far, however, this statute has not diminished the number of lawsuits filed under §10(b). (Shareholders even sued Shiva, the company discussed earlier in this chapter, when its stock price fell.) In the past 10 years, companies in the United States have paid out more than $20 billion to settle allegations of incomplete disclosure.[12] For more information about these lawsuits, or to see if you might be eligible to join in, browse at http://securities.stanford.edu or http://www.classactionamerica.com.

INSIDER TRADING

Insider trading is immensely tempting. Anyone with reliable secret information can earn millions of dollars overnight. Costandi Nasser bought shares of Santa Fe International, Inc., after learning that Kuwait Petroleum Co. was set to acquire the company. His profit? $4.6 million in three weeks. The downside? Insider trading is a crime punishable by fines of up to $1.1 million and prison sentences of up to 10 years. The guilty party may also be forced to turn over to the SEC three times the profit made. Ivan Boesky paid $100 million and spent two years in prison. Dennis Levine suffered an $11.6 million penalty and three years in prison.

Why is insider trading a crime? Who is harmed? After all, if you buy or sell stock in a company, presumably you are reasonably content with the price or you would not have traded. Insider trading is illegal because:

- It offends our fundamental sense of fairness. No one wants to be in a poker game with marked cards.

- Investors will lose confidence in the market if they feel that insiders have an unfair advantage.

- Investment banks typically "make a market" in stocks, meaning that they hold extra shares so that orders can be filled smoothly. If an insider buys stock because she knows the company is about to sign an important contract, she earns the profit on that information at the expense of the marketmaker who sold her the stock. These marketmakers expect to earn a certain profit. If they do not earn it from normal stock appreciation, they simply raise the commission they charge for being a marketmaker. As a result, everyone who buys and sells stock pays a slightly higher price because insider trading skims off some of the profits.

In the following feature, economists argue that there is another reason insider trading is illegal.

ECONOMICS & THE LAW

Although economists generally laud free markets, at times markets create inefficient results. The market for information is particularly subject to inefficiencies. Stock markets, for example, tend to create too much information. (And, as we will see in Chapter 21, intellectual property markets have the opposite problem.)

---

[12] Some plaintiffs tried to do an end run around this statute by filing suit in a state court (under more favorable state law). Congress passed the Securities Litigation Uniform Standards Act of 1998 to force plaintiffs in certain types of securities cases to file suit in federal court (under federal law).

Generally, economists think that society benefits when financial information spreads widely and quickly. Investors are thereby able to make more informed decisions. However, insider trading is an exception to this rule. When someone trades on inside information, she can quickly earn vast profits—but she has effectively stolen these profits from uninformed shareholders. The benefit that society gains from having this hidden information indirectly revealed to the market (via her purchase or sale of stock) is less than the harm to the shareholders who trade in ignorance. True, everyone now knows that the stock is more or less valuable than the market thought, but they have learned this information at a high price. Thus, the government prohibits insider trading to prevent society from "paying too much" for this private information.

Recent research supports the view that insider trading harms securities markets. In comparing returns in all 103 stock markets in the world, two economists found that markets in those countries that enforced insider trading laws earned 5 percent higher returns than did markets in countries with no laws or with lax enforcement. Five percent of the world's stock market capitalization amounts to $1.75 trillion.[13]

As noted, Rule 10b-5 is a vaguely worded rule that generally prohibits fraud. The language of the rule never explicitly mentions insider trading, but courts have interpreted it to prohibit this activity. Although the courts are nominally *interpreting* the rule, in fact, they are more or less fashioning this crime out of whole cloth. Insider trading has been described as "the judicial oak that has grown from little more than a legislative acorn." The current rules on insider trading are as follows:

- **Strangers.** The SEC has argued many times that anyone in possession of nonpublic material information must disclose it or refrain from trading. The courts, however, have definitively rejected this approach. The Supreme Court has held that **someone who trades on inside information is liable only if he has a fiduciary duty to the company whose stock he has traded.** Suppose that, while looking in a dumpster, Harry finds correspondence indicating that MediSearch, Inc., will shortly announce a major breakthrough in the treatment of AIDS. Harry buys the stock, which promptly quadruples in value. Harry will be dining at the Ritz, not in the dumpster nor in federal prison, because he has no fiduciary duty to MediSearch.

- **Fiduciaries.** Anyone who works for a company is a fiduciary. **A fiduciary violates Rule 10b-5 if she trades stock of her company while in possession of nonpublic material information.** If the director of research for MediSearch learns of the promising new treatment for AIDS and buys stock in the company before the information is public, she has violated Rule 10b-5. This rule applies not only to employees who work for the company, but also to **constructive insiders**—others who have an indirect employment relationship, such as employees of the company's auditors or law firm. Thus, if a lawyer who works at the firm that is patenting MediSearch's new discovery buys stock before the information is public, she has violated Rule 10b-5.

- *Possession* **versus** *use* **of information.** Suppose that an insider sells stock just after learning that her company is about to report lower earnings but before

---

[13] Hazem Daouk and Utpal Bhattacharya, "The World Price of Insider Trading," *Journal of Finance*, 2002, vol. 57, pp. 75–108. Discussed in *The Economist*, Jan. 22, 2000, p. 75.

this information is public. When challenged by the SEC, she argues that she sold her stock for other reasons—say, to buy a new house or to set her son up in business. The appeals courts were divided on whether the SEC actually had to prove that the insider had traded because of the secret information and not for some other (legitimate) reason. To clarify this murky issue, the SEC issued Rule 10b5-1. **This rule provides that an insider violates Rule 10b-5 if she trades while in possession of material, nonpublic information, unless she has committed in advance to a plan to sell those securities.** Thus, if an insider knows that she will want to sell stock to pay college tuition, she can establish such a sales plan in advance. (And, then, despite any change in circumstances, she must sell according to the plan.) She will then not be liable for the sales, no matter what inside information she ultimately learns.

- **Tippers.** Now things become really complicated. **Insiders who pass on nonpublic, material information are liable under Rule 10b-5, even if they do not trade themselves, as long as (1) they know the information is confidential and (2) they expect some personal gain.** Personal gain is loosely defined. Essentially, any gift to a friend counts as personal gain. W. Paul Thayer was a corporate director, deputy secretary of defense, and former fighter pilot ace who gave stock tips to his girlfriend in lieu of paying her rent. That counted as personal gain, and he spent a year and a half in prison.

- **Tippees.** Those who receive tips—tippees—are liable for trading on inside information, even if they do not have a fiduciary relationship to the company, as long as (1) they know the information is confidential, (2) they know it came from an insider who was violating his fiduciary duty, and (3) the insider expected some personal gain.** Barry Switzer, then head football coach at the University of Oklahoma, went to a track meet to see his son compete. While sunbathing on the bleachers, he overheard someone talking about a company that was going to be acquired. Switzer bought the stock but was acquitted of insider trading charges, because the insider had not breached his fiduciary duty. He had not tipped anyone on purpose—he had simply been careless. Also, Switzer did not know that the insider was breaching a fiduciary duty, and the insider expected no personal gain.[14]

- **Takeovers.** Frustrated by its lack of success under Rule 10b-5, the SEC adopted Rule 14e-3. **This rule prohibits trading on inside information during a tender offer if the trader knows the information was obtained from either the bidder or the target company.** The trader or tipper need not have violated a fiduciary duty. (Tender offers are discussed in Chapter 17, on corporations.)

- **Misappropriation.** In an effort to tighten the insider trading noose further, the SEC developed a new theory—misappropriation. Under this theory, **a person is liable if he trades in securities (1) for personal profit, (2) using confidential information, and (3) in breach of a fiduciary duty to the source of the information.** This theory applies even if that source was not the company whose stock was traded. Foster Winans wrote a column for *The Wall Street Journal* entitled "Heard on the Street" in which he reported rumors he had heard about companies. Frequently, the stock of these companies would rise or

---

[14] *SEC v. Switzer*, 590 F. Supp. 756, 1984 U.S. Dist. LEXIS 15303 (W.D. Okla. 1984). After this case some wags joked, "When Barry Switzer listens, people talk."

fall in response to his story. He began leaking information about his columns in advance to Peter Brant, a stockbroker at Kidder, Peabody & Co. Brant would trade the stock and split the profits with Winans. After the first episode, the SEC noticed the abnormally large trade. When it called the company to find out who was buying, the officers said they could think of no explanation except that the company had been the subject of a "Heard on the Street" column. It was all over for Winans, though the SEC let him pass on information a few more times, to make sure.

But had Winans and Brant violated Rule 10b-5? Not according to traditional insider trading rules. Neither of them had a fiduciary relationship to the company whose stock was traded. When the case went to the Supreme Court, it split 4–4 on the issue of misappropriation (there were only eight judges because one had resigned and his successor had not yet been appointed). However, the Court did find 8–0 that Winans was guilty of mail and wire fraud for having violated *The Wall Street Journal*'s rules about confidentiality.[15] Ten years later, the Supreme Court finally resolved the misappropriation issue.

UNITED STATES V. O'HAGAN

521 U.S. 642, 117 S. Ct. 2199, 1997 U.S. LEXIS 4033
United States Supreme Court, 1997

FACTS: Grand Metropolitan PLC (Grand Met) hired the law firm of Dorsey & Whitney to represent it in a takeover of Pillsbury Co. James O'Hagan, a partner in Dorsey & Whitney, did not work for Grand Met, but he found out about the deal and purchased significant amounts of Pillsbury stock. After Grand Met publicly announced its takeover attempt, the price of Pillsbury stock rose dramatically. O'Hagan sold his stock at a profit of more than $4.3 million. A jury convicted O'Hagan of misappropriation in violation of §10(b), and he was sentenced to prison.[16] The appeals court reversed, ruling that misappropriation is not a violation of §10(b). The Supreme Court granted *certiorari*.

ISSUE: Is misappropriation a violation of §10(b)?

EXCERPTS FROM JUSTICE GINSBURG'S DECISION: Under the "traditional" or "classical theory" of insider trading liability, §10(b) and Rule 10b-5 are violated when a corporate insider trades in the

securities of his corporation on the basis of material, nonpublic information. The classical theory applies not only to officers, directors, and other permanent insiders of a corporation, but also to attorneys, accountants, consultants, and others who temporarily become fiduciaries of a corporation.

The "misappropriation theory" holds that a person commits fraud "in connection with" a securities transaction, and thereby violates §10(b) and Rule 10b-5, when he misappropriates confidential information for securities trading purposes, in breach of a duty owed to the source of the information. Under this theory, a fiduciary's undisclosed, self-serving use of a principal's information to purchase or sell securities, in breach of a duty of loyalty and confidentiality, defrauds the principal of the exclusive use of that information.

The two theories are complementary, each addressing efforts to capitalize on nonpublic information through the purchase or sale of securities. The classical theory targets a corporate insider's breach of duty to shareholders with whom the

---

[15] *Carpenter v. United States*, 484 U.S. 19, 108 S. Ct. 316, 1987 U.S. LEXIS 4815 (1987).

[16] O'Hagan used the profits he gained through this trading to conceal his previous embezzlement of client funds. There is a moral here.

insider transacts; the misappropriation theory outlaws trading on the basis of nonpublic information by a corporate "outsider" in breach of a duty owed not to a trading party, but to the source of the information. The misappropriation theory is thus designed to protect the integrity of the securities markets against abuses by "outsiders" to a corporation who have access to confidential information that will affect the corporation's security price when revealed, but who owe no fiduciary or other duty to that corporation's shareholders.

A company's confidential information qualifies as property to which the company has a right of exclusive use. The undisclosed misappropriation of such information, in violation of a fiduciary duty constitutes fraud akin to embezzlement.

The theory is also well-tuned to an animating purpose of the Exchange Act: to insure honest securities markets and thereby promote investor confidence. Although informational disparity is inevitable in the securities markets, investors likely would hesitate to venture their capital in a market where trading based on misappropriated nonpublic information is unchecked by law. An investor's informational disadvantage vis-à-vis a misappropriator with material, nonpublic information stems from contrivance, not luck; it is a disadvantage that cannot be overcome with research or skill.

It makes scant sense to hold a lawyer like O'Hagan a §10(b) violator if he works for a law firm representing the target of a tender offer, but not if he works for a law firm representing the bidder. The text of the statute requires no such result. The misappropriation at issue here was properly made the subject of a §10(b) charge because it meets the statutory requirement that there be "deceptive" conduct "in connection with" securities transactions. ◢

After the *O'Hagan* case established the principle of misappropriation, it was still not clear how this rule applied to family members. If a wife told her husband that her company was about to be taken over and he then sold company stock as a result, was he in violation of 10b-5? Did he have a fiduciary duty to her? Rule 10b-5-2 establishes that anyone who receives nonpublic, material information from a spouse, parent, child or sibling has a fiduciary duty unless the trader can prove that he did not have a duty of trust or confidence to the family member in question.

If you learn confidential information about a company, what can you do? Of course, it is always safe *not* to trade. If you want to trade anyway, you should wait 24 to 48 hours after the information is disseminated through wire services or in the financial press. ▪

FOREIGN CORRUPT PRACTICES ACT

In the 1970s, more than 450 major U.S. corporations paid millions of dollars in foreign bribes. The Japanese premier and the Italian president both resigned after it was revealed that Lockheed had paid them off. In the Netherlands, members of the royal family were implicated in the scandal. Many of these payments had been labeled "commissions" or other legitimate business expenses and then illegally deducted from the company's income tax. In response Congress passed the Foreign Corrupt Practices Act as an amendment to the 1934 Act.

Under the Foreign Corrupt Practices Act, it is a crime for *any American company* (whether reporting under the 1934 Act or not) to make or promise to make payments or gifts to foreign officials, political candidates, or parties in order to influence a governmental decision, even if the payment is legal under local law. There is one exception: it is legal for a company to make payments to a foreign official to expedite a "routine governmental action." Anyone who violates the law is subject to fines of up to $100,000 and imprisonment for up to five years. The Department of Justice reveals its enforcement guidelines at http://www.usdoj.gov/criminal/fraud/fcpa/dojdocb.htm.

Congress believed that the ready availability of corporate slush funds had facilitated the payment of bribes. Therefore, it also tightened accounting standards for companies that report under the 1934 Act. It requires *reporting companies* to (1) keep books that accurately and fairly reflect the transactions of the issuer, and (2) maintain a system of internal controls that ensures transactions are executed only "in accordance with management's authorization."

For years, American companies complained that they were handicapped when competing against rivals who could bribe their way to success overseas. The U.S. government estimated that American companies lost contracts worth more than $15 billion a year to competitors who paid bribes. But in 1997, 34 developed countries signed a treaty in Paris outlawing bribery of foreign officials.

What's wrong with bribery anyway? Many businesspeople think it is relatively harmless, just a cost of doing business, like New York's high taxes or Germany's high labor costs. Corruption is not a victimless crime. Poor people in poor countries are the losers when officials are on the take: corruption means that good projects are squeezed out by bad ones. And corruption can reduce a country's entire administration to a state of decay. Honest officials give up. Bribes grow ever bigger and more ubiquitous. The trough becomes less well stocked; the snouts plunge deeper.[17] From the Chapter 2 Ethics Checklist: Who are the stakeholders? What are the consequences of corruption?

Which countries are most corrupt? According to Transparency International, an international nonprofit agency, Bangladesh, Nigeria, Uganda, Indonesia, Kenya, Cameroon, Bolivia, Azerbaijan, Ukraine, and Tanzania lead the list of shame. The most honest? Finland, Denmark, New Zealand, Iceland, Singapore, Sweden, Canada, Netherlands, Luxembourg, and Norway. (The United States was sixteenth on the honest list.)

Blue Sky Laws

At the end of the nineteenth century, years before the great stock market crash, states had already begun to regulate the sale of securities. These statutes are called **blue sky laws** (because crooks were willing to sell naive investors a "piece of the great blue sky"). Currently, all states and the District of Columbia have blue sky laws.

To make life easier for issuers of stock, Congress also passed the National Securities Markets Improvement Act (NSMIA) of 1996. Essentially, states may no longer regulate offerings of securities that are:

- Traded on a national exchange
- Exempt under Rule 506, or
- Sold to "qualified purchasers."

Any securities offerings not covered by the NSMIA must comply with state securities laws. Easier said than done. The 50 states have exhibited great creativity in crafting their securities laws and, as a result, have caused many headaches for issuers of securities. To begin, the 1933 Act is primarily concerned with disclosure,

---

[17] "Who Will Listen to Mr. Clean?" *The Economist*, Aug. 2, 1997, p. 52.

but many state statutes focus on the quality of the investment and require a so-called *merit review*. For example, in 1981 the Massachusetts securities commissioner refused to allow Apple Computer Co. to sell its initial public offering in Massachusetts because he believed the stock, selling at 92 times earnings, was too risky. He "protected" Massachusetts residents from this investment.

Typically, states take one of the following approaches to securities offerings:

- *Registration by notification.* Some states permit issuers with an established track record simply to file a notice before offering their securities.

- *Registration by coordination.* Some states permit issuers that have registered with the SEC simply to file copies of the federal registration statement (and perhaps some additional documents) with the state.

- *Registration by qualification.* Some states require issuers to undergo a full-blown registration, complete with a merit review.

All is not bleak, however. For offerings over $5 million that are registered with the SEC, the issuer might be able to take advantage of the Coordinated Equity Review (CER) program. Under this program, the issuer deals with only one state, which takes responsibility for coordinating the comments from all other states. The process is simpler, but state officials still have the right to conduct a merit review.

To facilitate capital financing for small businesses, offerings that are exempt under federal law often receive special treatment under state law:

- **Rule 147** (intrastate exemption). Most states permit a so-called SCOR (small company offering registration) for Rule 147 offerings. The relatively simple form (U-7) is in a question-and-answer format. Any company using a SCOR form can request a coordinated review from the states in which it has filed. Under this system, a designated lead state takes responsibility for coordinating the process with all other states. The result is a faster, simpler process, although, again, the states have the right to conduct a merit review.

- **Rule 504.** Most states also permit SCOR to be used for Rule 504 offerings.

- **Rule 505.** Under the Uniform Limited Offering Exemption, offerings under Rule 505 are largely exempt from state regulation. Most states have adopted this statute.

- **Rule 506.** The NSMIA exempts Rule 506 from state registration requirements.

- **Regulation A.** Most states permit SCOR to be used for Regulation A offerings.

The moral of the story? Securities offerings are exceedingly complex and require professional supervision. Do not attempt this at home!

Chapter Conclusion

The 1929 stock market crash and the Great Depression that followed were an economic catastrophe for the United States. The Securities Act of 1933 and the Securities Exchange Act of 1934 were designed to prevent such disasters from ever occurring again. This country has enjoyed years of prosperity that is based, at least in part, on a reliable and honest securities market. The securities laws deserve some of the credit for that stability.

Chapter Review

1. A security is any transaction in which the buyer invests money in a common enterprise and expects to earn a profit predominantly from the efforts of others.

2. Before any offer or sale, an issuer must register securities with the SEC (Securities and Exhange Commission), unless the securities qualify for an exemption.

3. These securities are exempt from the registration requirement: government securities, bank securities, short-term notes, nonprofit issues, insurance policies, and annuity contracts.

4. The following table compares the different types of securities offerings:

	Public Offering	Intrastate Offering	Regulation A	Regulation D: Rule 504	Regulation D: Rule 505	Regulation D: Rule 506
Maximum Value of Securities Sold	Unlimited	Unlimited	$5 million	$1 million	$5 million	Unlimited
Public Solicitation of Purchasers	Permitted	Permitted	Permitted	Sometimes permitted	Not permitted	Not permitted
Suitability Requirements for Purchasers	No requirements	Must reside in issuer's state	No requirements	May be limited to accredited investors	No limit on accredited investors; no more than 35 unaccredited investors	No limit on accredited investors; no more than 35 unaccredited investors who, if unsophisticated, must have a purchaser representative
Disclosure Requirements	Elaborate registration statement; audited financials	None	Offering circular that is less detailed than a registration statement	May be required under state law	Same requirements as Reg A for unaccredited investors; no disclosure to accredited investors	Same requirements as Reg A for unaccredited investors; no disclosure to accredited investors
Resale of Securities	Permitted	Permitted, but may not be made out of state for nine months	Permitted	Sometimes permitted	Not permitted for one year	Not permitted for one year

5. If a final registration statement contains a material misstatement or omission, the purchaser of a security offered under that statement can recover from everyone who signed it.

6. The 1934 Act requires public companies to make regular filings with the SEC.

7. Under §16, insiders who buy and sell or sell and buy company stock within a six-month

period must turn over to the corporation any profits from the trades. They must also disclose any trades they make in company stock.

8. Section 10(b) prohibits fraud in connection with the purchase and sale of any security, whether or not the issuer is registered under the 1934 Act.

9. Section 10(b) also prohibits insider trading.

10. Under the Foreign Corrupt Practices Act, it is a crime for any U.S. company to make payments to foreign officials to influence a government decision. This statute also requires reporting companies to keep accurate records.

11. The NSMIA prohibits states from regulating securities offerings that are:

- Traded on a national exchange

- Exempt under Rule 506, or

- Sold to "qualified purchasers."

12. Any securities offerings not covered by the NSMIA must comply with state securities laws, which are varied and complex.

Practice Test

1. Christopher Stenger bought 12 Impressionist paintings from R. H. Love Galleries for $1.5 million. Love told Stenger that art investment would produce a safe profit. The two men agreed that Stenger could exchange any painting within five years for any one or two other paintings with the same or greater value. When Stenger's paintings did not increase in value, he sued Love, arguing that the right to trade paintings made them securities. Is Stenger correct?

2. **CPA QUESTION** When a common stock offering requires registration under the Securities Act of 1933:

   (a) The registration statement is automatically effective when filed with the SEC

   (b) The issuer would act unlawfully if it were to sell the common stock without providing the investor with a prospectus

   (c) The SEC will determine the investment value of the common stock before approving the offering

   (d) The issuer may make sales 10 days after filing the registration statement

3. Fluor, an engineering and construction company, was awarded a $1 billion project to build a coal gasification plant in South Africa. Fluor signed an agreement with a South African client that prohibited them both from announcing the agreement until March 10. Accordingly, Fluor denied all rumors that a major transaction was pending. Between March 3 and March 6, the State Teachers Retirement Board pension fund sold 288,257 shares of Fluor stock. After the contract was announced, the stock price went up. Did Fluor violate Rule 10b-5?

4. **CPA QUESTION** Hamilton Corp. makes a $4.5 million securities offering under Rule 505 of Regulation D of the Securities Act of 1933. Under this regulation, Hamilton is:

   (a) Required to provide full financial information to accredited investors only

   (b) Allowed to make the offering through a general solicitation

   (c) Limited to selling to no more than 35 nonaccredited investors

   (d) Allowed to sell to an unlimited number of investors both accredited and nonaccredited

5. Does this excerpt from the *Boston Globe* reveal any potential securities law problems?

   Berkshire Ice Cream's down-home investment strategy is paying off for more than 100 people who last year put up $800 to $1,000 to "own" a company cow. Last month, the company sent out about $32,000 to investors who bought a total of 110 cows a year ago, with the expectation of a 20 percent annual return on their money. [I]nitially, there were 63 investors who agreed to finance the purchase of a cow—

which the company then cares for—in return for a piece of the company's profits.[18]

6. **ETHICS** Ira Waldbaum was president and controlling shareholder of Waldbaum, Inc., a large supermarket chain. After deciding to accept A & P's offer to purchase the chain, he told his sister, Shirley Witkin, about the offer so that she would be ready to sell her shares. He admonished her not to tell anyone, but she told her daughter, Susan Loeb, who passed the word (and the warning) on to her husband, Keith Loeb. The next day, Keith told his broker, Robert Chestman, about the impending sale and ordered some Waldbaum stock. Chestman purchased 11,000 shares of the stock for himself and his clients, at a price of roughly $25 per share. The A&P offer was for $50 per share. Did Chestman violate Rule 10b-5? Whether or not Chestman's trades were legal, did they harm anyone? How do they look in the light of day? Were Loeb's actions right? How might they have affected his wife (and other stakeholders)?

7. **CPA QUESTION** Pace Corp. previously issued 300,000 shares of its common stock. The shares are now actively traded on a national securities exchange. The original offering was exempt from registration under the Securities Act of 1933. Pace has $2.5 million in assets and 425 shareholders. With regard to the Securities Exchange Act of 1934, Pace is:

   (a) Required to file a registration statement because its assets exceed $2 million in value

   (b) Required to file a registration statement even though it has fewer than 500 shareholders

   (c) Not required to file a registration statement because the original offering of its stock was exempt from registration

   (d) Not required to file a registration statement unless insiders own at least 5 percent of its outstanding shares of stock

8. **YOU BE THE JUDGE WRITING PROBLEM** World-Wide Coin Investments Ltd. sold rare coins, precious metals, camera equipment, and Coca-Cola collector items. Its stock was registered with the SEC under the 1934 Act. Joseph Hale was the controlling shareholder, chairman of the board, CEO, and president. World-Wide's independent auditor warned Hale that the company's faulty system of accounting procedures was causing problems with inventory control. Furthermore, the auditor could not document transactions, and it had found that the books and records of the company were inaccurate. Is World-Wide in violation of the Foreign Corrupt Practices Act? **Argument for the SEC:** Without exception, all reporting companies are required to maintain accurate books and records. **Argument for World-Wide:** This is a small company, and the cost of such an elaborate internal control system would bankrupt it.

9. Consider this scenario from the periodical *Investor's Business Daily, Inc.*:

   You're in line at the grocery store when you overhear a stranger say, "That new widget is going to make XYZ Co. a fortune. I can't wait until the product launches tomorrow."

   What do you do? (a) Nothing? (b) Call your broker and buy as much XYZ Co. stock as you possibly can?

10. Malaga Arabian Limited Partnership sold investments in the Spanish Arabian horse industry under Rule 506. James E. Mark, who purchased one of the partnership interests, alleged that the partnership violated Rule 506 because it never gave him any disclosure about the risks of the investment. He was not an accredited investor. At trial the partnership said that it had surveyed investors to ensure that they were either accredited or sophisticated but had not actually read the surveys and did not have them available for the trial court. Is this offering exempt from registration under the 1933 Act?

---

[18] Ellen Labr, "Investors Milk Profits of Ice Cream Firm," *Boston Globe*, July 30, 1995, p. 38.

11. CoolCom, Inc., sends notice to all of its shareholders that its annual report and proxy soliciting materials are on its Web site. It provides investors with the Web address and a telephone number that they may call to request a paper copy. Is CoolCom in compliance with SEC rules?

12. **ROLE REVERSAL** Write a multiple-choice question that focuses on an issue involving Rule 504, restricted securities, or insider trading.

Internet Research Problem

Choose a company, go to the EDGAR database at the SEC (http://www.sec.gov), and look at all filings this company has made during the last year. What filings has it made and why? Extra credit: search EDGAR for a prospectus for an initial public offering.

You can find further practice problems in the **Online Quiz at** http://beatty.westbuslaw.com **or in the Study Guide that accompanies this text.**

GOVERNMENT REGULATION & PROPERTY

UNIT 5

Antitrust

Mike Elliott was not looking for trouble when he brought an order form for Girl Scout cookies to work. Mr. Elliott, an employee at DaimlerChrysler's factory in Dearborn, Michigan, started asking co-workers to buy a few boxes on behalf of his girlfriend's eight-year-old daughter. "I worked for four or five hours, and suddenly this lady came up to me and said that a guy who worked 50 feet down the line from me was selling them cheaper," Mr. Elliott says. "The first thing that everyone thinks is, 'You're trying to rip me off.'"

In an increasingly competitive marketplace, price wars are breaking out over Thin Mints and Peanut Butter Patties. The 36,500-member Michigan Metro Council, citing rising costs and the need to subsidize inner city troops, reluctantly raised its price to $3 a box this year. The neighboring—but much smaller—Macomb County Girl Scout Council stayed at $2.50 a box, setting the stage for a marketing battle. However, most of the troops in this skirmish are not Scouts: they are grown-ups who peddle the cookies at.work. Such scenarios have been repeated in other parts of the country, as many of the nation's 330 Girl Scout councils go through their annual pricing debate. Why don't the councils simply agree on one national price? Because antitrust laws prohibit price-fixing.[1]

---

[1] Rebecca Blumenstein, "Cookie Price War Sends Adult Troops into Marketing Battle," *The Wall Street Journal*, Mar. 8, 1996, p. A1. Republished with permission of The Wall Street Journal; permission conveyed through the Copyright Clearance Center. Inc.

Competition is an essential element of the American economic system. Antitrust laws are the rules that govern that competition. As the chapter-opening scenario illustrates, these laws affect many aspects of our lives—both as consumers and as businesspeople. ◾

In the Beginning

Throughout much of the nineteenth century, competition in America was largely a local affair. The country was so big and transportation so poor that companies primarily competed in small local markets. It was too costly to transport goods great distances. State laws rather than national statutes regulated competition.

By the second half of the nineteenth century, four railroad lines crossed the continent from coast to coast. For the first time, national markets were a real possibility. John D. Rockefeller saw the potential. In 1859, Edwin L. Drake, a retired railroad conductor, drilled the first commercially successful oil well in the United States. Three years later, when the 23-year-old Rockefeller entered the scene, the oil industry was full of producers too small to benefit from economies of scale. Production was inefficient, and prices varied dramatically in different parts of the country.

Rockefeller set out to reorganize the industry. He began by buying refineries, first in Cleveland and then in other cities. He and his partners spread into all segments of the oil industry: buying oil fields, building pipelines, and establishing an efficient marketing system. To unify the management of these companies, they transferred their stock to the Standard Oil Trust. By 1870, Rockefeller had achieved his goal—the Standard Oil Trust controlled virtually all the oil in the country, from producer to consumer. Rockefeller was the wealthiest person in the world.

Some of Rockefeller's tactics were controversial. When a competitor tried to build an oil pipeline, Rockefeller used every weapon short of violence to stop it. He planted stories in the press suggesting the pipes would leak and ruin nearby fields. He flooded local builders with orders for tank cars so no workers would be available to build the pipeline. When the pipeline was finished, he refused to allow his oil to flow through it. These tactics were frightening, especially in an industry as important as oil. What if Rockefeller decided to raise prices unfairly? Or cut off oil altogether? Newspapers began to attack him ferociously.

SHERMAN ACT

With the coming of the railroads, it became clear that large companies might be able to control other industries as well. To prevent extreme concentrations of economic power, Congress passed the **Sherman Act** in 1890. It was one of the first national laws designed to regulate competition. Because this statute was aimed at the Standard Oil Trust and other similar organizations, it was termed **antitrust** legislation. In 1892, the Ohio Supreme Court dissolved the Standard Oil Trust, which was replaced by the Standard Oil Co. But the government was not satisfied until a spring day in 1911, when Supreme Court Chief Justice Edward White quietly read aloud his dramatic 20,000-word opinion ordering the breakup of Standard Oil.[2] The 33 companies that made up Standard Oil were forced to compete as separate

---

[2] *Standard Oil Company of New Jersey v. United States*, 221 U.S. 1, 31 S. Ct. 502, 1911 U.S. LEXIS 1725 (1911).

businesses. Today, descendants of Standard Oil include Amoco, Atlantic Richfield, Chevron, ExxonMobil, and Pennzoil. Imagine what kind of giant they would be if still united.

For the first 70 or so years after the passage of the Sherman Act, most scholars and judges took the view that large concentrations of economic power were suspect, even if they had no obvious impact on competition itself. Big was bad. Big meant too much economic and political power. As Senator John Sherman, sponsor of the Sherman Act, put it, a nation that "would not submit to an emperor should not submit to an autocrat of trade." Fragmented, competitive markets were desirable in and of themselves. Standard Oil should not control the oil markets, even if the company was very efficient and had gained control by completely acceptable methods.

CHICAGO SCHOOL

Beginning in the 1960s and 1970s, however, a group of influential economists and lawyers at the University of Chicago began to argue that the goal of antitrust enforcement should be *efficiency*. Let a company grow as large as it likes provided that this growth is based on a superior product or lower costs, not ruthless tactics. Insist on a clean fight, but do not handicap large successful companies to help the weaker competitors. Some companies will thrive, others will die, but in either case, the consumer will come out ahead. Adherents of the **Chicago School** argued further that the market should decide the most efficient size for each industry. In some cases, such as automobiles or long-distance telephone service, the most efficient size might be very large indeed. Under traditional antitrust analysis, courts often asked, "Has a *competitor* been harmed?" The Chicago School suggests that courts should ask instead, "Has *competition* been harmed?"

At the turn of the twentieth century, President Theodore Roosevelt personally plotted the breakup of Standard Oil. (As one of Rockefeller's compatriots said of Roosevelt, "We bought the son of a bitch, and then he didn't stay bought.") At the turn of the twenty-first century, two descendants of Standard Oil—Exxon and Mobil—announced their intention to merge. This time, not one politician so much as grabbed a microphone to object to the recombination. Where once size alone was cause for concern, now regulators believe that a certain bulk may be necessary if American companies are to compete in the intense global economy.

Antitrust policy, however, continues to evolve. Adherents of the so-called **Post Chicago School** are beginning to recognize that competition alone may not be enough to protect consumers. For example, an industry with a large number of competitors may foster collusion, not competition. Or, activities that appear consumer-friendly, such as giving a product away for free, may in the long run harm consumers. (Take, for example, Microsoft's decision to give away its Internet browser. Although consumers benefited in the short run, the Justice Department alleged that this giveaway harmed consumers by driving competitors out of business.) Now, when deciding whether to take action, federal trustbusters are beginning to focus directly on consumers, asking two questions: Will this action cause consumers to pay higher prices? Are the higher prices sustainable in the face of existing competition? As you read the cases in this chapter, think about which factors the court considered important: size, competition, or the impact on consumers.

It is worth noting that throughout the twentieth century, the United States had stricter antitrust laws than most countries. Now its markets are more competitive than most. No matter what standard of law the government has applied, it managed to prevent the worst competitive abuses.

Overview of Antitrust Laws

The major provisions of the antitrust laws are:

- Section 1 of the Sherman Act prohibits all agreements "in restraint of trade."

- Section 2 of the Sherman Act bans "monopolization"—the wrongful acquisition of a monopoly.

- The Clayton Act prohibits anticompetitive mergers, tying arrangements, and exclusive dealing agreements.

- The Robinson-Patman Act bans price discrimination that reduces competition.

The full text of the antitrust statutes is available at http://www.antitrustinstitute. org/links/codes.cfm.

In 1914, Congress passed the **Clayton Act** in part because the courts were not enforcing the Sherman Act as strictly as it had intended. The purpose of the Clayton Act was to clarify the earlier statute. As a result, the two laws overlap significantly. The **Robinson-Patman Act** (passed in 1936) is an amendment to the Clayton Act. Rather than systematically reviewing the terms of each statute in order, this chapter focuses instead on the *kinds of behavior* that the antitrust laws regulate.

Violations of the antitrust laws are divided into two categories: **per se** and **rule of reason**. As the name implies, *per se* violations are automatic. Defendants charged with this type of violation cannot defend themselves by saying, "But the impact wasn't so bad" or "No one was hurt." The court will not listen to excuses, and the defendants are subject to both *criminal* and *civil* penalties. Typically, the Justice Department has sought criminal sanctions only against *per se* violators.

Rule of reason violations, on the other hand, are illegal only if they have an anticompetitive impact. To determine if an activity is an unreasonable restraint of trade, the courts consider its circumstances, intent, and impact. For example, if competitors join together and agree that they will not deal with a particular supplier, their action is illegal only if it harms competition. Although rule of reason violators may be subject to civil penalties or private lawsuits, traditionally the Justice Department has not sought criminal penalties against them.

Both the Justice Department and the Federal Trade Commission (FTC) have authority to enforce the antitrust laws. However, only the Justice Department can bring criminal proceedings; the FTC is limited to civil injunctions and other administrative remedies. In addition to the government, anyone injured by an antitrust violation has the right to sue for damages. The United States is unusual in this regard— in most other countries, only the government is able to sue antitrust violators. A successful plaintiff can recover treble (that is, triple) damages from the defendant.

In developing a competitive strategy, managers typically consider two different approaches:

- Cooperative strategies that allow companies to work together to their mutual advantage

- Aggressive strategies, designed to create an advantage over competitors

Cooperative Strategies

Three types of cooperative strategies are potentially illegal:

- **Horizontal agreements** among competitors. An agreement between Levi Strauss and Wrangler—both manufacturers of denim jeans—would be a horizontal agreement.

- **Vertical agreements** among participants at different stages of the production process. An agreement between Levi Strauss and Diesel—one company makes jeans, the other sells them—would be a vertical agreement.

- **Mergers and joint ventures** among competitors. Here, companies go beyond simple agreements to combine forces more permanently.

The following table lists the cooperative strategies that will be discussed in this chapter:

Horizontal Strategies	Vertical Strategies	Mergers
Market division	Reciprocal dealing	Horizontal mergers
Price-fixing	Price discrimination	Vertical mergers
Bid-rigging		Joint ventures
Refusal to deal		

HORIZONTAL COOPERATIVE STRATEGIES

Although the term "cooperative strategies" *sounds* benign, these tactics are often harmful to competition. Many horizontal cooperative strategies are *per se* violations of the law and can lead to prison terms, heavy fines, and expensive lawsuits with customers and competitors.

Market Division

Any effort by a group of competitors to divide its market is a *per se* violation of §1 of the Sherman Act. Illegal arrangements include agreements to allocate customers, territory, or products. For example, these business schools would be in violation if:

- Georgetown agreed to accept only men and, in return, George Washington would take only women[3]

- Stanford agreed to accept only students from west of the Mississippi, leaving the east to Yale, or

- Northwestern agreed not to provide courses in entrepreneurship, while the University of Chicago eliminated its international offerings.

---

[3] This, of course, does not mean that all single-sex schools are violating the antitrust laws. They are in violation only if their admissions policy results from an agreement with competitors.

Price-Fixing and Bid-Rigging

When competitors agree on the prices at which they will buy or sell products or services, their price-fixing is a *per se* violation of §1 of the Sherman Act. Bid-rigging is also a *per se* violation. In bid-rigging, competitors eliminate price competition by agreeing on who will submit the lowest bid. In an early case, the defendants argued that price-fixing was only wrong if the prices were *unfair*. The Supreme Court disagreed. In its view, prices should be set by markets, not by competitors—or judges. Moreover, "The reasonable price fixed today may through economic and business changes become the unreasonable price of tomorrow."[4]

For the better part of a century, price-fixing and bid-rigging have been illegal, yet they never seem to go away. Here are some examples:

- *Dairy Industry.* Using a computer to analyze the bids that schools received on their milk contracts, the Florida Attorney General uncovered a pervasive price-fixing scheme. By some estimates, price-fixing raised milk prices in Florida by 14 percent. Forty-three companies were convicted or pleaded guilty; two dozen individuals went to prison. Companies paid fines in excess of $90 million.

- *College Athletics.* Colleges were concerned about the cost of their athletic programs. In particular, the cost of the coaching staffs seemed out of control. Some assistant coaches were being paid as much as $70,000 a year. In response, NCAA schools (that is, members of the National Collegiate Athletic Association) agreed to cap the salaries of assistant coaches at (a very stingy) $12,000. But a court blew the whistle, finding that the NCAA had engaged in illegal price-fixing. A jury awarded the coaches $66 million.

For information about new and interesting price-fixing cases, check out http://www.antitrust.org/. The following article discusses the Justice Department's successful strategy for ensnaring price-fixers.

Meeting clandestinely at an airport hotel outside London, top executives from the leading makers of a crucial raw material for forging steel reached an agreement to fix global prices. The executives were from France, Germany, Japan, and the United States. But the cartel began to unravel after a steelmaker complained to federal investigators about the lack of competition. The U.S. government filed suit and ultimately obtained corporate fines in the case of $437 million. Two executives pleaded guilty, paid large fines, and received prison sentences.

The antitrust division, once a small and sleepy backwater of the Justice Department, has become a power center against white-collar crime. All told, the antitrust division has won fines—corporate and individual—of more than $1.7 billion in the last four years. No one doubts that the global price-fixing collusions it has exposed affected every American consumer. These collusions have raised prices for gasoline, vitamins, soft drinks, and other food products.

The recent takeoff in investigations and prosecutions is a result of a new Justice Department policy that made amnesty automatic if the company came in before an investigation began and permitted broad amnesty afterward to the first company to offer assistance. It also covered all executives from that company who cooperated, a significant inducement because violations of the Sherman Act carry a potential prison sentence of three years for every count, in addition to virtually

---

[4] *United States v. Trenton Potteries Co.*, 273 U.S. 392, 397, 1927 U.S. LEXIS 975 (1927).

limitless fines. Almost immediately, the change could be seen in the quantity and quality of tips coming to prosecutors. Before the new rule, the division reported an average of one amnesty request a year. Since the change, it is one a month.[5] ▪

The ethics discussion in Chapter 2 considered the possibility that illegal behavior could sometimes be ethical. Price-fixing is a *per se* violation of the law. Are there times when it might nonetheless be ethical? For example, every year the Council of Fashion Designers of America puts on a major fashion show under tents in New York's Bryant Park. This show offers an opportunity for up-and-coming designers to mix with more established names—and to attract media attention. The newcomers complained, however, that they could not compete with famous designers and attract vital media attention without hiring top models. But the price of these superstar models was too high: upwards of $10,000 for a three-hour show. Sympathetic to the newcomers' plight, the Council capped modeling fees at $750 an hour for supermodels and $500 for rookies. Is this price-fixing illegal? Is it ethical to protect the inexperienced designers? From the Chapter 2 Ethics Checklist: What are the consequences of this alternative? Does the alternative violate important values? ▪

Refusals to Deal

Every company generally has the right to decide with whom it will or will not do business. **However, a refusal to deal is a rule of reason violation of the Sherman Act, illegal if it harms competition.** In a **refusal to deal**, a group of competitors boycotts a buyer, supplier, or even another competitor. The following case illustrates the dangers of threatening Barbie.

TOYS "R" US, INC. V. FTC

221 F.3d 928, 2000 U.S. App. LEXIS 18304
United States Court of Appeals for the Seventh Circuit, 2000

FACTS: Toys "R" Us (TRU) sells approximately 20 percent of all toys bought in the United States, about 11,000 different items each year. The company buys about 30 percent of the total output of the large, traditional toy manufacturers, and it is typically their most important customer.

Toy customers (i.e., children) typically have very specific product preferences. The child who wants Malibu Barbie is not likely to be satisfied with My First Barbie, and she certainly does not want Ken or Skipper. The boy who has his heart set on a figure of Anakin Skywalker will be disappointed if he receives Jar-Jar Binks, or a truck, or a baseball bat instead. Toys are also a very faddish product, so toy retailers want to carry the latest hot item.

TRU traditionally had a secure market niche, until warehouse clubs came on the scene. At the high end of the market are traditional toy stores and department stores, which mark their product up 40 to 50 percent. TRU sells at an average 30 percent markup, compared with general discounters like Wal-Mart and Target at 22 percent, and the warehouse clubs like Costco at a slender 9 percent or so. TRU competed effectively against Wal-Mart and Target, because those stores did not offer anywhere

---

[5] Stephen Labaton, "The World Gets Tough on Fixing Prices," *The New York Times,* June 3, 2001, §3, p. 1. Copyright © 2001 by The New York Times Co. Reprinted by permission.

near the variety TRU did. The warehouse clubs were a different story—they could offer both variety and lower prices.

To fight the clubs, TRU asked its major suppliers, including Mattel, Hasbro, and Fisher Price, to sell the clubs only unique items or combo packs specifically designed for them and not sold to other customers. Thus, the clubs would not have the same items as TRU. The manufacturers were reluctant to agree, because the clubs were an important and growing market. But TRU was a valuable customer. Ultimately, about 10 manufacturers did agree with TRU, but on the condition that their competitors did so, too. TRU served as the central clearinghouse for complaints about breaches in the agreement.

In the year before the agreement took effect, the clubs' share of toy sales in the United States grew from 1.5 to 1.9 percent. After the agreement, that percentage slipped back to 1.4 percent. The Federal Trade Commission found that TRU had engaged in an illegal boycott.

ISSUE: Did TRU engage in an illegal boycott?

EXCERPTS FROM JUDGE WOOD'S DECISION: TRU sought to eliminate the competitive threat the clubs posed by denying them merchandise, forcing the clubs' customers to buy products they did not want, and frustrating customers' ability to make direct price comparisons of club prices and TRU prices. [T]he boycott was illegal under a full rule of reason analysis because its anticompetitive effects clearly outweighed any possible business justification.

These manufacturers were in effect being asked by TRU to reduce their output (especially of the popular toys), and as is classically true in such cartels, they were willing to do so only if TRU could protect them against cheaters.

Here, TRU was trying to disadvantage the warehouse clubs, its competitors, by coercing suppliers to deny the clubs the products they needed. It accomplished this goal by inducing the suppliers to collude, rather than to compete independently for shelf space in the different toy retail stores.

TRU seems to think that anticompetitive effects in a market cannot be shown unless the plaintiff first proves that it has a large market share. This, however, has things backwards. [T]he share a firm has in a properly defined relevant market is only a way of estimating market power, which is the ultimate consideration. [H]owever TRU's market power as a toy retailer was measured, it was clear that its boycott was having an effect in the market. It was remarkably successful in causing the 10 major toy manufacturers to reduce output of toys to the warehouse clubs, and that reduction in output protected TRU from having to lower its prices to meet the clubs' price levels.

The decision is hereby Affirmed. ◢

VERTICAL COOPERATIVE STRATEGIES

Vertical cooperative strategies are agreements among participants at different stages of the production process.

Reciprocal Dealing Agreements

Under a reciprocal dealing agreement, a buyer refuses to purchase goods from a supplier unless the supplier also purchases items from the buyer. Imagine that you are in the business of processing beets into sugar. During this process, it is easy to separate the seeds, which can then be used to grow more beets. Why not suggest to your beet suppliers that they buy their seeds from you? Why not further suggest that if *they* are not willing, you will find other suppliers who are?[6]

You are proposing a reciprocal dealing agreement. In the past, such arrangements were common. Many major corporations even kept computer records of purchases, sales, and "balance of trade" with other companies. Although these

---

[6] See *Betaseed, Inc. v. U & I, Inc.*, 681 F.2d 1203, 1982 U.S. App. LEXIS 17190 (9th Cir. 1982).

arrangements might have made *business* sense, the government took the view that they were also *rule of reason* violations of the Sherman Act; that is, they were illegal if they had an anticompetitive effect. The government brought suit against several companies, including a beet processor. It also halted a number of mergers that might have resulted in internal reciprocal arrangements. In recent years, however, the government has brought few of these cases. Reciprocal dealing agreements are likely to be a problem now only if they foreclose a *significant share* of the market and if the participants agree not to buy from others.

Price Discrimination

Under the Robinson-Patman Act, it is illegal to charge different prices to different purchasers if:

- The items are the same, and

- The price discrimination lessens competition.

However, it is legal to charge a lower price to a particular buyer if:

- The costs of serving this buyer are lower, or

- The seller is simply meeting competition.

Congress passed the Robinson-Patman Act (RPA) in 1936 to prevent large chains from driving small, local stores out of business. Owners of these "Ma and Pa stores" complained that the large chains could sell goods cheaper because suppliers charged them lower prices. As a result of the RPA, managers who would otherwise like to develop different pricing strategies for specific customers or regions may hesitate to do so for fear of violating this statute. In reality, however, they have little to fear.

Under the RPA, a plaintiff must prove that price discrimination occurred and that it lessened competition. It is now perfectly permissible, for example, for a supplier to sell at a different price to its Texas and California distributors, or to its health care and educational distributors, as long as the distributors are not in competition with each other.

The RPA also expressly permits price variations that are based on differences in cost. Thus Amy's Kitchen would be perfectly within its legal rights to sell its frozen cheese enchiladas to Giant at a lower price than to Corner Grocery if Amy's costs are lower to do so. Giant often buys shipments the size of railroad containers that cost less to deliver than smaller boxes.

During the last decade, the federal government has virtually abandoned its enforcement of the RPA. Between 1937 and 1971, the FTC brought an average of 40 price discrimination cases each year; recently, it has averaged only one or two. Some federal officials have even urged that the RPA be repealed to prevent it from interfering with the smooth operation of the market. This fade-out of government action has left enforcement in the hands of individual plaintiffs, but these cases are receiving little encouragement from the courts.

The Supreme Court has, for example, made it much more difficult for plaintiffs to win damages in price discrimination cases. Chrysler Motors charged the J. Truett Payne dealership more than other car dealers in Birmingham, Alabama. Unable to compete, Payne went out of business. The accepted formula for determining damages in a Robinson-Patman Act case *had been* the difference between the two prices multiplied by the number of units purchased. These numbers were easy to calculate. However, in *Payne*, the Supreme Court held that it is not enough to prove that competitors are able to buy at a lower cost. The plaintiff must also show that these competitors passed their savings on to customers and, as a result, plaintiff lost profits.[7] These are difficult facts to prove. As a result of cases such as this, antitrust lawyers often advise their clients not to worry too much about price discrimination suits because dissatisfied customers will usually not seek damages in court but will instead try to negotiate a better price.

MERGERS AND JOINT VENTURES

The Clayton Act prohibits mergers that are anticompetitive. Companies with substantial assets must notify the FTC *before* consummating a merger.[8] This notification gives the government an opportunity to prevent a merger ahead of time, rather than trying to untangle one after the fact.

Horizontal Mergers

A horizontal merger involves companies that compete in the same market. Traditionally, the government has aggressively sought to prevent horizontal mergers that could lead to a monopoly or even a highly concentrated industry. In the *Von's Grocery* case, decided in 1966, the Supreme Court upheld the Justice Department in its suit to prevent the merger of two grocery chains that represented only 7.5 percent of the grocery market in Los Angeles.[9] Compare that decision with the following case, decided almost 20 years later.

UNITED STATES V. WASTE MANAGEMENT, INC.

743 F.2d 976, 1984 U.S. App. LEXIS 18843
United States Court of Appeals for the Second Circuit, 1984

FACTS: Waste Management, Inc. (WMI), acquired Texas Industrial Disposal, Inc. (TIDI). Both companies were in the trash collection business. In Dallas, their combined market share was 48.8 percent. The trial court held that the merger was illegal and ordered WMI to divest itself of TIDI.

ISSUE: Did WMI violate the Clayton Act by acquiring TIDI?

EXCERPTS FROM JUDGE WINTER'S DECISION: A post-merger market share of 48.8 percent is sufficient to establish *prima facie* illegality under *United States v.*

Philadelphia National Bank and its progeny. That decision held that large market shares are a convenient proxy for appraising the danger of monopoly power resulting from a horizontal merger. Under its rationale, a merger resulting in a large market share is presumptively illegal, rebuttable only by a demonstration that the merger will not have anticompetitive effects.

[In the present case, the *Philadelphia National Bank*] presumption is rebutted by the fact that competitors can enter the Dallas waste hauling market with such ease. WMI argues that it is unable to raise prices over the competitive level

7 *J. Truett Payne Co., Inc. v. Chrysler Motors Corp.*, 451 U.S. 557, 101 S. Ct. 1923, 1981 U.S. LEXIS 49, (1981).

8 If, for example, the acquiring company is purchasing stock or assets of the acquired company that is worth more than $200 million in 2004 dollars.

9 *United States v. Von's Grocery Co.*, 384 U.S. 270, 86 S. Ct. 1478, 1966 U.S. LEXIS 2823 (1966).

because new firms would quickly enter the market and undercut them. A person wanting to start in the trash collection business can acquire a truck, a few containers, drive the truck himself, and operate out of his home. A great deal depends on the individual's personal initiative, and whether he has the desire and energy to perform a high quality of service. If he measures up well by these standards, he can compete successfully with any other company for a portion of the trade, even though a small portion. Over the last 10 years or so a number of companies have started in the commercial trash collection business.

We conclude that the 48.8 percent market share attributed to WMI does not accurately reflect future market power. Since that power is in fact insubstantial, the merger does not, therefore, substantially lessen competition in the relevant market and does not violate the [Clayton Act]. ◢

Traditionally, market share was the most important factor in evaluating mergers. As *Waste Management* indicates, however, market share is no longer the sole issue in merger cases. The government and the courts now also consider how the merger will affect competition and consumers. Thus the government cleared a merger between aircraft giants Boeing and McDonnell Douglas, which together had a virtual monopoly on the American aircraft business. But the aircraft market is global, and American companies faced severe competition from Europe's Airbus consortium. Therefore, the government believed that the merger would not harm competition.

Conversely, the FTC blocked the merger of office supply giants, Staples, Inc., and Office Depot. Nationally, these two retailers controlled only 4 percent of the market for office supplies. Was the FTC harking back to the days of *Von's Grocery*? Not exactly. The office superstores' *national* market share was relatively low because they had no stores at all in many areas of the country. Rather than national market share, the FTC focused instead on their ability to control prices locally. The agency found that, when both stores operated in the same market, prices were significantly lower than when only one store was present. Thus a box of file folders cost $1.72 in Orlando, Florida (where both stores competed) and $4.17 in nearby Leesburg (where Office Depot had a monopoly). In the FTC's view, if the two stores combined, they would have had enough power in local markets to raise prices and harm consumers.

FTC merger guidelines are available at http://www.ftc.gov/bc/docs/horizmer.htm. For a merger simulation game, go to http://www.antitrust.org/simulation.html.

As the following article illustrates, antitrust enforcement is a worldwide issue.

NEWSWORTHY

The United States has always felt perfectly comfortable enforcing its antitrust laws overseas, as long as the activity had some impact within its borders. (Remember the article earlier about the price-fixing charges against foreign companies.) Now the gavel is in the other hand: the European Union scuttled a proposed merger between General Electric and Honeywell International—a marriage between two American companies that had already been approved in Washington. More trouble may be ahead because Europe and the United States each applies a different standard when evaluating mergers. The European Commission considers whether a merger would create or strengthen a *dominant position*. The commission reasoned that since GE makes jet engines and Honeywell manufactures avionics equipment, this portfolio of products together might make them more dominant. To U.S. authorities, the important issue was whether the merger would reduce competition or harm consumers. ▪

Vertical Mergers

A vertical merger involves companies at different stages of the production process—for example, when a producer of a final good acquires a supplier or vice versa. Vertical mergers can also be anticompetitive, especially if they reduce entry into a market by putting a lock on an important supplier or a top distributor. Consider the following example.

International Management Group (IMG) is a management conglomerate that dominates the tennis world. IMG operates tournaments, sets up exhibitions, holds broadcast rights, and manages the careers of more than 100 pros. Recently, IMG acquired the Nick Bolletieri Tennis Academy, training ground for many of the sport's present and future stars. IMG's competitors question whether this acquisition violates the antitrust laws. Says the head coach of another tennis academy, "You name it, IMG owns it, owns tournaments, owns the players, owns the academy. It's impossible to compete at that level, so we don't even bother to try.[10] ▪

IMG's acquisition of the Nick Bolletieri Tennis Academy was a vertical merger—IMG acquired a source of supply for its management group. The Justice Department has not been overly concerned about vertical mergers. The department's guidelines provide that it will challenge vertical mergers only if they are likely to increase entry barriers in a concentrated market.

Joint Ventures

A joint venture is a partnership for a limited purpose—the companies do not combine permanently, they simply work together on a specific project. The government will usually permit a joint venture, even between competitors with significant market power. The FTC approved, over strenuous objections from competitors, a joint venture between General Motors and Toyota to produce cars.

Aggressive Strategies

The goal of an aggressive strategy is to gain an unfair advantage over competitors.

MONOPOLIZATION

Aggressive competition is beneficial for consumers—up until the moment a company develops enough power to control a market. One purpose of the Sherman Act is to prevent this type of control. **Under §2 of the act, it is illegal to monopolize or attempt to monopolize a market.** To monopolize means to acquire a monopoly in the wrong way. *Having* a monopoly is legal unless it is *gained* or *maintained* by using wrongful tactics.

---

[10] Robin Finn, "Mixed Doubles: Players as Business," *The New York Times*, Mar. 16, 1994, p. B17.

ECONOMICS
& THE LAW

What is so bad about a monopoly? Imagine, for example, that you owned the only movie theater in town. Although the price of movie tickets in other towns is $10, you are able to charge $20 or maybe even $30 (for *Star Wars*, Part XVII). Although fewer customers might buy tickets at this expensive price, your profits are still higher because you earn so much on each ticket. There are two things wrong with this picture: fewer people are able to afford the movies and, when they do attend, they have less choice about what to see. The owner of the only theater in town might not be in tune with the tastes of his audiences. Economists believe that it is harmful for the movie theater to have many buyers while the customers have only one seller. ▪

To determine if a defendant has illegally monpolized, we must ask three questions:

• **What is the market?** Without knowing the market, it is impossible to determine if someone is controlling it.

• **Does the company control the market?** Without control, there is no monopoly.

• **How did the company acquire or maintain its control?** Monopolization is illegal only if gained or kept in the wrong way.

What Is the Market?

This question is not as easy to answer as it sounds. Some people refer to the antitrust laws as the "Economists' Full-Employment Acts" because antitrust litigation requires detailed testimony from economic experts.

Suppose that your company sells soft drinks with unusual food flavors—steak and cheese, among others. For some reason, you are the only company that sells food-flavored soft drinks so, by definition, you control 100 percent of the market. But is that the *relevant* market? Perhaps the relevant market is flavored drinks or soft drinks or all beverages. The question economists ask is: **How high can your prices rise before your buyers will switch to a different product?** If a price rise from $1.00 to $1.05 a bottle causes many of your customers to desert to Snapple or Coke, it is clear you are part of a larger market. Moreover, if changes in the prices of other drinks affect your sales, your products and theirs are probably close competitors. However, if you could raise your price to $5.00 per bottle and still hold on to many of your customers, then you might well be in your own market.

Does the Company Control the Market?

You have 100 percent of the food-flavored soft drink market (although only 1 percent of the overall soft drink market and an infinitesimal percentage of the total beverage market). Traditionally, courts considered a share anywhere between 70 and 90 percent to constitute a monopoly. However, under modern antitrust law, market share is not important if other competitors can enter the market anytime they want (or anytime you raise your prices or lower your quality). **No matter what your market share, you do not have a monopoly unless you can exclude competitors or control prices.** In the following case, Judge Kozinski explains this principle and demonstrates a sense of humor—his opinion is larded with movie titles. How many can you find?

UNITED STATES V. SYUFY ENTERPRISES

903 F.2d 659, 1990 U.S. App. LEXIS 7396
United States Court of Appeals for the Ninth Circuit, 1990

FACTS: Raymond Syufy entered the Las Vegas cinema market with a splash by opening a six-screen theater. His theaters are among the finest built and best run in the nation, making him something of a local hero. Syufy's entry into the Las Vegas market caused a stir, precipitating a titanic bidding war. Soon, theaters in Las Vegas were paying some of the highest license fees in the nation, while distributors sat back and watched the easy money roll in. After a hard-fought battle among several contenders, Syufy gained the upper hand. Three of his rivals saw their future as rocky and decided to sell out to Syufy, leaving a small exhibitor of mostly second-run films as Syufy's only competitor in Las Vegas. The Justice Department brought this antitrust suit to force Syufy to disgorge the theaters he had purchased from his former competitors.

ISSUE: Did Syufy have an illegal monopoly?

EXCERPTS FROM JUDGE KOZINSKI'S DECISION:
Monopoly power is the power to exclude competition or control prices. Time after time, we have recognized this basic fact of economic life: A high market share, though it may ordinarily raise an inference of monopoly power, will not do so in a market with low entry barriers or other evidence of a defendant's inability to control prices or exclude competitors.

When Syufy acquired his competitors' theaters he temporarily diminished the number of competitors in the Las Vegas first-run film market. But this does not necessarily indicate foul play; many legitimate market arrangements diminish the number of competitors. It would be odd if they did not, as the nature of competition is to make winners and losers. If there are no significant barriers to entry,

however, eliminating competitors will not enable the survivors to reap a monopoly profit; any attempt to raise prices above the competitive level will lure into the market new competitors able and willing to offer their commercial goods or personal services for less.

Syufy was unable to maintain market share. [In one year], Syufy raked in 93 percent of the gross box office from first-run films in Las Vegas. [Three years later,] that figure had fallen to 75 percent. The government insists that 75 percent is still a large number, and we are hard-pressed to disagree; but that's not the point. The antitrust laws do not require that rivals compete in a dead heat, only that neither is unfairly kept from doing his personal best.

It can't be said often enough that the antitrust laws protect competition, not competitors. The record here conclusively demonstrates that neither acquiring the screens of his competitors nor working hard at better serving the public gave Syufy deliverance from competition.

The Justice Department also alleges that Syufy, top gun in the Las Vegas movie market, had the power to push around Hollywood's biggest players, dictating to them what prices they could charge for their movies. The evidence does not support this view. Syufy has at all times paid license fees far in excess of the national average. While successful, Syufy is in no position to put the squeeze on distributors. It would have been risky business even to try.

By finding that Syufy did not possess the power to set prices or to exclude competition, the district court removed the firing pins from the government's litigation arsenal. Without these essential elements, its lawsuit collapses like a house of cards. ◢

How Did the Company Acquire or Maintain Its Control?

Possessing **a monopoly is not necessarily illegal; using** *"bad acts"* **to acquire or maintain one is.** If the law prohibited the mere possession of a monopoly, it might discourage companies from producing excellent products or offering low prices. Anyone who can produce a better product cheaper is entitled to a monopoly. In your case, you have very cleverly developed a secret method for adding flavors to carbonated water. You also have an efficient factory and highly trained workers, so you can sell your drinks for 5¢ a bottle less than your competitors. If, in fact, you do have a monopoly, it is for all the right reasons. You have demonstrated exactly the kind of innovative, efficient behavior that benefits consumers. If you were sued for a violation of the antitrust laws, you would win.

Some companies use ruthless tactics to acquire or maintain a monopoly. It is these "bad acts" that render a monopoly illegal. In the past, the definition of bad acts was broad, and any company with a monopoly could be in violation unless it showed that, despite its best efforts to duck, a monopoly had been *thrust upon* it. In 1945, a famous judge, with the appropriate name of Learned Hand, found that Alcoa's monopoly in the aluminum industry was illegal because the company had repeatedly expanded capacity to anticipate demand.[11] In his view, the company should have waited to expand until demand actually existed. Alcoa was in violation because it could have easily *avoided* a monopoly—the monopoly had not been thrust upon it.

Everyone makes mistakes. Although Learned Hand is generally considered one of the greatest judges of his era, most commentators now believe that Alcoa was wrongly decided. *Berkey Photo* is a more typical modern case.[12] Berkey accused Eastman Kodak Co. of repeatedly and unnecessarily changing the size of its cameras to confound competitors who manufactured film to fit them. Although Learned Hand most likely would have found such actions to be illegal, the *Berkey* court rejected the view that monopolies are acceptable only if *thrust upon* the defendant and instead held that aggressive competitive strategies are legal even if they have the effect of hindering competitors. In finding Kodak not liable, the court reasoned that the company would not have repeatedly changed camera and film specifications if consumers had objected. The success or failure of Kodak's strategy ought to be determined in the market and not by the courts. .

UPDATE

In a case that has been going on for well over a decade, the Justice Department and some state attorneys general accused the Microsoft Corp. of illegal monopolization of the software market. Not only is this case the most significant antitrust battle of the era, but it is also shaping an industry crucial to the world economy. Microsoft has a substantial share of the world market for software, but as we learned from the *Syufy* case, a large market share is not sufficient evidence of a monopoly. There must also be evidence that the company can control prices or exclude competitors. Does Microsoft control the software market? How did it obtain (or maintain) this control?

Where does the Microsoft case stand now? Has the company settled with the Justice Department? With the states? What were the terms of the settlement? You can start at http://www.usdoj.gov/atr/cases/ms_index.htm and http://www.microsoft.com/presspass/legalnews.asp. ◾

---

[11] *United States v. Aluminum Co. of America*, 148 F.2d 416, 1945 U.S. App. LEXIS 4091 (2d Cir. 1945). Judge Hand's parents did not necessarily foresee his illustrious career when naming him. "Learned" was his mother's maiden name, and it was the tradition in his family to give the mother's name to one of the children.

[12] *Berkey Photo, Inc. v. Eastman Kodak Co.*, 603 F.2d 263, 1979 U.S. App. LEXIS 13692 (2d Cir. 1979), cert. denied, 444 U.S. 1093, 1980 U.S. LEXIS 923 (1980).

Predatory Pricing

Predatory pricing occurs when a company lowers its prices below cost to drive competitors out of business. Once the predator has the market to itself, it raises prices to make up lost profits—and more besides.

Recall that, under §2 of the Sherman Act, it is illegal "to monopolize" and also to "attempt to monopolize." Typically, the goal of a predatory pricing scheme is either to win control of a market or to maintain it. A ban on these schemes prevents monopolization and attempts to monopolize. To win a predatory pricing case, the plaintiff must prove three elements:

- The defendant is selling its products *below cost*.

- The defendant *intends* that the plaintiff go out of business.

- If the plaintiff does go out of business, the defendant will be able to earn sufficient profits to *recoup* its prior losses.

The classic example of predatory pricing is a large grocery store that comes into a small town offering exceptionally low prices subsidized by profits from its other branches. Once all the "Ma and Pa" corner groceries go out of business, MegaGrocery raises its prices to much higher levels.

Predatory pricing offers a good example of how attitudes toward antitrust laws have changed. Formerly, courts took predatory pricing very seriously. The term certainly *sounds* bad. But despite its name, courts generally are not as concerned about predatory pricing now as they used to be. For one thing, consumers benefit from price wars, at least in the short run. For another, the cases are hard to prove. Here is why:

- **The defendant is selling its products below cost.** This rule sounds sensible, but what does "cost" mean? As you know from your economics courses, there are many different kinds of costs—total, average variable, marginal, to name a few. Under current law, any price below *average variable cost* is generally presumed to be predatory.[13] The rule may be easy to state, but, in real life, average variable cost is difficult to calculate. First, plaintiffs must obtain most of the data from the defendant. Even if a defendant has a good idea of what its average variable costs are, it will not willingly tell all in court. Moreover, many of the economic decisions about what items fit into which cost category are subjective. It is difficult for the plaintiff to prove that its subjective view is closer to the truth than the defendant's.

- **The defendant intends that the plaintiff go out of business.** Even if Ma and Pa can calculate MegaGrocery's average variable cost to the satisfaction of a court, they will not necessarily win their case. They must prove that MegaGrocery intended to put them out of business. That is a pretty tall order, short of finding some smoking gun like a strategic plan that explicitly says MegaGrocery wants Ma and Pa gone.

- **If the plaintiff does go out of business, the defendant will be able to earn sufficient profits to recoup its prior losses.** Until Ma and Pa go out of business,

---

13 To calculate average variable cost, add all the firm's costs except its fixed costs and then divide by the total quantity of output.

MegaGrocery will lose money—after all, it is selling food below cost. To win their case, Ma and Pa must show that MegaGrocery will be able to make up all its lost profits once the corner grocery is out of the way. They need to prove, for example, that no other grocery chain will come to town. It is difficult to prove a negative proposition like that, especially in the grocery business where barriers to entry are low.

Recently, plaintiffs have not had much success with predatory pricing suits. For example, Liggett began selling generic cigarettes 30 percent below the price of branded cigarettes. Brown & Williamson retaliated by introducing its own generics at an even lower price. Liggett sued, claiming that Brown's prices were below cost. The Supreme Court agreed that Brown was not only selling below cost but also intended to harm Liggett. Brown still won the case, however, because there was no evidence that it would be able to recover its losses from the below-cost pricing. If Brown raised its prices, other competitors would come back into the market.[14]

TYING ARRANGEMENTS

A tying arrangement is an agreement to sell a product on the condition that the buyer also purchases a different (or tied) product. A tying arrangement is illegal under §3 of the Clayton Act and §1 of the Sherman Act if:

- Two products are clearly separate

- The seller requires the buyer to purchase the two products together

- The seller has significant power in the market for the tying product, and

- The seller is shutting out a significant part of the market for the tied product.

Six more distributors refused to sell individual films to television stations. Instead, they insisted that a station buy an entire package of movies. To obtain classics such as *Treasure of the Sierra Madre* and *Casablanca* (the **tying product**), the station also had to purchase such forgettable films as *Nancy Drew Troubleshooter*, *Gorilla Man*, and *Tugboat Annie Sails Again* (the **tied product**).[15] Is this an illegal tying arrangement? These are the questions to ask:

- **Are the two products clearly separate?** A left and right shoe are not separate products, and a seller can legally require that they be purchased together. *Gorilla Man*, on the other hand, is a separate product from *Casablanca*.

- **Is the seller requiring the buyer to purchase the two products together?** Yes, that is the whole point of these "package deals."

- **Does the seller have significant power in the market for the tying product?** In this case, the tying products are the classic movies. Since they are copyrighted, no one else can show them without the distributor's permission. The six distributors controlled a great many classic movies. So, yes, they do have significant market power.

---

[14] *Brooke Group Ltd. v. Brown & Williamson Tobacco Corp.*, 509 U.S. 209, 113 S. Ct. 2578, 1993 U.S. LEXIS 4245 (1993).

[15] *United States v. Loew's Inc.*, 371 U.S. 38, 83 S. Ct. 97, 1962 U.S. LEXIS 2332 (1962).

- **Is the seller shutting out a significant part of the market for the tied product?** In this case, the tied products are the undesirable films like *Tugboat Annie Sails Again*. Television stations forced to take the unwanted films did not buy "B" movies from other distributors. These other distributors were effectively foreclosed from a substantial part of the market.

In the following case, Mercedes-Benz decided to include floor mats as standard equipment. Is that illegal tying?

YOU BE THE JUDGE

LLOYD DESIGN CORP. V. MERCEDES-BENZ OF NORTH AMERICA, INC.

66 Cal. App. 4th 716, 1998 Cal. App. LEXIS 768
Court of Appeal of California, 1998

FACTS: Mercedes-Benz sells less than 1 percent of all automobiles in this country, but among luxury cars, it holds about a 10 percent market share. Floor mats were originally optional accessories. Mercedes then decided to make floor mats standard equipment because dealers reported that luxury car customers expected floor mats, and a growing number of competitors provided them.

Lloyd Design Corp. had been selling some $250,000 in floor mats to Mercedes dealerships in California, but lost this entire business after the change in policy. Lloyd filed suit against Mercedes, claiming that the decision to deliver the cars with floor mats constituted an illegal tying arrangement.

YOU BE THE JUDGE: Did Mercedes engage in illegal tying when it provided floor mats in its automobiles?

ARGUMENT FOR LLOYD: These two products—cars and floor mats—are clearly separate products. They have traditionally been sold separately.

Mercedes is now requiring that they be purchased together. The company has significant power in the market for luxury cars and is forcing customers to buy a product that they may not want. This is a classic case of illegal tying and, like all tying arrangements, it serves no purpose beyond the suppression of competition.

ARGUMENT FOR MERCEDES: Floor mats are not a separate product; they are a fundamental part of the car. Does Lloyd believe that Mercedes should sell just the engine and the body, and that everything else—including the mirrors, seats, and steering wheel—is a different product?

Moreover, Mercedes controls only 10 percent of the luxury car market; it cannot force consumers to buy a product they do not want. Nor is Mercedes attempting to control the floor mat market. This market is still highly competitive, but now manufacturers are competing to sell to Mercedes, rather than to dealers. There is no harm to competition and no illegal tying. Nor is there any harm to consumers—they are receiving a floor mat for free.

CONTROLLING DISTRIBUTORS AND RETAILERS

The goal of an aggressive strategy is to force competitors out of a market—by undercutting their prices or tying products together, for example. Controlling distributors and retailers is another method for excluding competitors. It is difficult to compete in a market if you are foreclosed from the best distribution channels.

Allocating Customers and Territory

As you saw earlier in this chapter, a *horizontal* agreement by *competitors* to allocate customers and territories is a *per se* violation of §1 of the Sherman Act. **However, a vertical allocation of customers or territory is illegal only if it adversely affects competition in the market as a whole.** It is a rule of reason, not a *per se*, violation.

Suppose that Hot Sound, Inc., produces expensive, high-quality CD players. It grants its distributors the exclusive right to sell in a particular territory or the exclusive right over a particular type of customer (consumers, corporate, automobiles). In return for these exclusive rights, Hot Sound requires the distributors to stock a wide range of inventory, hire highly trained (expensive) sales help, and advertise widely. Such requirements not only increase sales but also enhance distributor loyalty. The distributors have such a large investment in Hot Sound's products that they are reluctant to switch to another manufacturer. A change would mean unloading a large inventory, developing new advertisements, and retraining or laying off some of the sales force.

Hot Sound clearly has good business reasons for adopting such a plan. It is reducing intrabrand competition (among its dealers) but enhancing interbrand competition (between brands). With its committed dealer network, Hot Sound can compete more fiercely against other brands. Vertical allocation is a rule of reason violation, which means that the law will intervene only if Hot Sound's activities have an anticompetitive impact on the market as a whole. But since Hot Sound's plan increases interbrand competition, it is unlikely to have an anticompetitive impact.

EXCLUSIVE DEALING AGREEMENTS

An **exclusive dealing** contract is one in which a distributor or retailer agrees with a supplier not to carry the products of any other supplier. **Under §1 of the Sherman Act and §3 of the Clayton Act, exclusive dealing contracts are subject to a rule of reason and are illegal only if they have an anticompetitive effect.**

Consider the case of Ben & Jerry's. With more than $100 million in sales, it was a major player in the ice cream market. And some of its competitors alleged that it was playing hardball. Just ask Amy Miller. She started Amy's Ice Creams in a small storefront in Austin, Texas. Her ice cream was so popular that she decided to begin producing pints for sale in grocery stores. But when she tried to enter the Houston market, Sunbelt, the dominant distributor in the area, refused to carry her desserts. She thinks Sunbelt turned her down because Ben & Jerry's had forbidden it to carry other premium brands.

Ironically, the ice cream was once in the other bowl, so to speak. When Ben and Jerry were the new boys on the block, they discovered that Pillsbury (owner of Häagen-Dazs) included provisions in its contracts that prohibited distributors from carrying Ben & Jerry's brand. When Ben & Jerry's produced written contracts containing these exclusory clauses, Pillsbury backed down immediately. Thereafter, no one in the industry used written distribution contracts.

Amy Miller threatened to sue Ben & Jerry's for violating the antitrust laws with exclusive dealing contracts. In determining if these agreements had an anticompetitive impact on the market, a court would consider the following factors:

- **The number of other distributors available.** Amy said that no one but Sunbelt would do because only the best distributors were able to preserve her ice cream's quality.

- **The portion of the market foreclosed by the exclusive dealing agreements.** Without Sunbelt, Amy's Ice Creams could not penetrate the Houston market, so it had to shut down its pint production line.

- **The ease with which new distributors could enter the market.** Sunbelt had few, if any, competitors. Presumably, the market was a difficult one to enter.

- **The possibility that Amy could distribute the products herself.** Not a chance. Amy could barely manage to *make* the ice cream.

- **The legitimate business reasons that might have led the distributor to accept an exclusive contract.** Here is what Sunbelt's vice president had to say: "We already had our table full with super premium pints. We felt Amy's was an underfinanced product and we would have had to replace a high-volume product to give it a shot. And we personally did not think the product was very good."[16]

Would an exclusive dealing agreement between Ben & Jerry's and Sunbelt be anticompetitive? If so, would their business reasons justify the contract?

RESALE PRICE MAINTENANCE

NEWSWORTHY

Peter Polites (pronounced po-LEE-tus), owner of a Nine West store in New Jersey, slashed the price of a popular, smart-looking women's shoe last winter, knowing he would attract many more customers—and still earn a smooth 60 percent on each pair. But Mr. Polites's sale irritated some managers at large department stores down the hall in the Mall at Short Hills. One Nordstrom manager, he said, walked into Mr. Polites's small store, picked some shoes off the shelf, looked at the prices, slammed them down, and left without a word.

Mr. Polites said the Nordstrom manager later explained that the flats Mr. Polites had reduced to $49.99 from $60 were included on a confidential list of styles—known as the "off-limits list"—whose prices Nine West Group, Inc., rarely, if ever, lets stores mark down. Mr. Polites's low prices also maddened executives at Nine West, the footwear giant that says it sells one out of every five pairs of shoes sold to women in the United States. Vincent Camuto, chief executive of Nine West, called Mr. Polites and demanded that he end his sale. When Mr. Polites refused, Mr. Camuto told him that in that case, "We can't ship you those shoes."[17] ▪

Is it legal for Nine West to cut off a retailer who refuses to raise his prices? This question is at the heart of an important antitrust conundrum—the validity of **resale price maintenance (RPM)**. RPM means the manufacturer sets *minimum* prices that retailers may charge. In other words, it prevents retailers from discounting. Why does the manufacturer care? After all, once the retailer purchases the shoes, the manufacturer has made its profit. The only way the manufacturer makes more money is to raise its *wholesale* price, not the *retail* price. RPM guarantees a profit margin for the *retailer*.

Manufacturers argue that they ought to have the right to decide how and at what price their products are sold. They may, for example, want to promote an

---

16 Rickie Windle, "Ben & Jerry's Creams Amy's," *Austin Business Journal*, Oct. 4, 1993, vol. 13, no. 33, §1, p. 1.
17 Melody Petersen, "Treading a Contentious Line," *The New York Times*, Jan. 13, 1999, p. C1. Copyright © 1999 by The New York Times Co. Reprinted by permission.

upscale brand image, one that could be destroyed by discount prices. Or the manufacturer may expect its dealers to provide a higher level of service than discounters can afford. Consumer advocates contend, however, that manufacturers such as Nine West are simply protecting dealers from competition. Discounting may or may not harm products, but, they insist, RPM certainly hurts consumers.

To settle this controversy, the Supreme Court has spoken. Spray-Rite was an herbicide dealer selling products manufactured by Monsanto. Spray-Rite claimed that Monsanto terminated the dealership contract because other dealers had complained about Spray-Rite's discount prices. Monsanto countered that Spray-Rite had not spent enough money training its salespeople or promoting the products. The jury, however, found for Spray-Rite and awarded $3.5 million in damages, which were trebled to $10.5 million. Monsanto appealed to the Supreme Court.[18]

Many commentators expected the Supreme Court to decide that RPM was a rule of reason, not a *per se*, violation. The Court ruled unanimously, however, that **RPM is a *per se* violation of the law. A manufacturer may not enter into an agreement with distributors to fix prices.** The Court did create a potential loophole by saying that an agreement cannot be inferred simply because a manufacturer cuts off one distributor after receiving complaints from another. Unilateral action by a manufacturer to set prices is legal; an agreement with distributors about prices is not.[19]

And what happened to Nine West? It agreed to end RPM and to pay a settlement of $34 million to be used for women's health, educational, and safety programs.

VERTICAL MAXIMUM PRICE-FIXING

In *Spray-Rite*, the Supreme Court held that resale price maintenance is a *per se* violation of the Sherman Act. In that case, the manufacturer set the *minimum* prices its distributors could charge. **Vertical *maximum* price fixing (when a manufacturer sets *maximum* prices), however, is a *rule of reason* violation of the Sherman Act.** The defendant is liable only if the price-fixing harms competition. (You remember, from earlier in this chapter, that all *horizontal* price-fixing is a *per se* violation.)

When State Oil Co. leased a gas station to Barkat Khan, it set a maximum price that Khan could charge for gas. Khan sued State Oil, but the Supreme Court ruled in favor of the oil company, on the grounds that cutting prices to increase business is the very essence of competition and, furthermore, low prices benefit consumers.[20]

Chapter Conclusion

The purpose of the antitrust laws in the United States is to keep businesses on a narrow road. On the one hand, they may not swerve to one side and work too closely with competitors. Nor may they swerve to the other side and attack competitors too aggressively. Although managers sometimes resent the constraints imposed on them by antitrust laws, it is these laws that ensure the fair and open competition necessary for a healthy economy. In the end, the antitrust laws benefit us all.

---

[18] *Monsanto Co. v. Spray-Rite Corp.*, 465 U.S. 752, 104 S. Ct. 1464, 1984 U.S. LEXIS 39 (1984).

[19] The court decided that Monsanto had engaged in RPM because it had terminated Spray-Rite as part of an agreement with other distributors.

[20] *State Oil Co. v. Khan*, 522 U.S. 3, 118 S. Ct. 275, 1997 U.S. LEXIS 6705 (1997).

Chapter Review

1. There are two categories of antitrust violations: *per se* and rule of reason. *Per se* violations are automatic; courts do not consider mitigating circumstances. Rule of reason violations, on the other hand, are illegal only if they have an anti-competitive impact.

2. Any effort by a group of competitors to divide their market is a *per se* violation of the Sherman Act. Illegal arrangements include agreements to allocate customers, territory, or products.

3. Price-fixing and bid-rigging are *per se* violations of the Sherman Act.

4. Every company generally has the right to decide with whom it will do business. However, the Sherman Act prohibits competitors from joining together in an agreement to exclude a particular supplier, buyer, or even another competitor if the agreement would hurt competition.

5. Under a reciprocal dealing agreement, a buyer refuses to purchase goods from a supplier unless the supplier also purchases items from the buyer. Reciprocal dealing agreements violate the Sherman Act if they foreclose competitors from a significant part of the market.

6. The Robinson-Patman Act (RPA) prohibits companies from selling the same item at different prices if the sale lessens competition. However, a seller may charge different prices if these prices reflect different costs.

7. Under the Clayton Act, the federal government has the authority to prohibit anticompetitive mergers and joint ventures.

8. Possessing a monopoly need not be illegal; acquiring or maintaining it through "bad acts" is.

9. To determine if a company is guilty of monopolization, ask three questions:
   - What is the market?
   - Does the company control the market?
   - How did the company acquire its control?

10. To win a predatory pricing case, a plaintiff must prove three elements:
    - The defendant is selling its products below cost.
    - The defendant intends that the plaintiff go out of business.
    - If the plaintiff does go out of business, the defendant will be able to earn sufficient profit to recoup its prior losses.

11. A tying arrangement is illegal if:
    - The two products are clearly separate
    - The seller requires that the buyer purchase the two products together
    - The seller has significant power in the market for the tying product; and
    - The seller is shutting out a significant part of the market for the tied product.

12. Efforts by a manufacturer to allocate customers or territory among its distributors are subject to a rule of reason. These allocations are illegal only if they adversely affect competition in the market.

13. An exclusive dealing contract is one in which a distributor or retailer agrees with a supplier not to carry the products of any other supplier. Exclusive dealing contracts are subject to a rule of reason and are prohibited only if they have an anticompetitive effect.

14. When a manufacturer enters into an agreement with distributors or retailers to fix minimum prices, this arrangement is called resale price maintenance (RPM). RPM is a *per se* violation of the law.

15. Vertical maximum price-fixing is a rule of reason violation of the Sherman Act. It is illegal only if it has an adverse impact on competition.

Practice Test

1. Harcourt Brace Jovanovich (HBJ) granted BRG an exclusive license to market HBJ's bar review materials in Georgia and to use HBJ's trade name. HBJ agreed not to compete with BRG in Georgia, and BRG agreed not to compete with HBJ outside the state. HBJ was entitled to receive $100 per student enrolled by BRG and 40 percent of revenues over $350 per student. Did this agreement violate the antitrust laws?

2. Fifty bakeries in New York formed an association. They developed a system of distribution under which stores were only allowed to buy from a single baker. A store that wanted to shift to another baker had to consult the association and pay cash to the former baker. The association also decided to raise the retail price of bread from 75 to 85 cents. All the association's members printed the new price on their bread sleeves. Are the bakeries in violation of the antitrust laws?

3. Fifty restaurants in Boston threatened to stop accepting the American Express card if the company refused to reduce the commission it charged on each purchase. Visa International, one of American Express's rivals, offered to pay the group's legal expenses. American Express then lowered its commission. For restaurants that processed more than $10 million in annual volume, American Express reduced charges from 3.25 percent to 2.75 percent. Rates for restaurants processing less than $10 million but more than $1 million a year fell to 3 percent. The company did not lower rates for restaurants with volume lower than $1 million a year. Have either the restaurants, Visa, or American Express potentially violated the antitrust laws?

4. Reserve Supply Corp., a cooperative of 379 lumber dealers, charged that Owens-Corning Fiberglass Corp. violated the Robinson-Patman Act by selling at lower prices to Reserve's competitors. Owens-Corning had granted lower prices to a number of Reserve's competitors to meet, but not beat, the prices of other insulation manufacturers. Is Owens-Corning in violation of the Robinson-Patman Act?

5. BAR/BRI is a company that prepares law students for bar exams. With branches in 45 states, it has the largest share of the bar review market in the country. Barpassers is a much smaller company located only in Arizona and California. BAR/BRI distributed pamphlets on campuses falsely suggesting Barpassers was near bankruptcy. Enrollments in Barpassers' courses dropped, and the company was forced to postpone plans for expansion. Does Barpassers have an antitrust claim against BAR/BRI?

6. **YOU BE THE JUDGE WRITING PROBLEM** American Academic Suppliers (AAS) and Beckley-Cardy (B-C) both sold educational supplies to schools. B-C's sales began to plummet, and it was rapidly losing market share. The company responded by reducing its catalogue prices 5 to 12 percent. It also offered a discount of 25 to 40 percent in states in which AAS was making substantial gains. What claim might AAS make against B-C? Is it likely to prevail in court? **Argument for AAS:** B-C has committed predatory pricing. The company is selling below cost for the purpose of driving us out of business. **Argument for B-C:** Even if we were to drive AAS out of business, we do not have enough market power to recoup our losses.

7. Two medical supply companies in the San Francisco area provide oxygen to homes of patients. The companies are owned by the doctors who prescribe the oxygen. These doctors make up 60 percent of the lung specialists in the area. Does this arrangement create an antitrust problem?

8. After acquiring the Schick brand name and electric shaver assets, North American Phillips controlled 55 percent of the electric shaver industry in the United States. Remington, a competitor, claimed that the acquisition of such a large market share was a violation of the law because the increased competition from Phillips would decrease Remington's profits. Does Remington have a valid claim?

9. Videos of *Jurassic Park* and *Snow White and the Seven Dwarfs* were due in stores the same

month. The stores ought to have been delight-ed at the prospect of having two blockbusters to sell, but instead they were worried—how to price the videos? Both Disney (*Snow White*) and MCA/Universal (*Jurassic Park*) were longtime proponents of MAP—minimum advertised pricing. In other words, if retailers sold the videos at prices below $14.95, the studios would not subsidize their advertising budgets. Many retailers would have *liked* to sell the videos at $14.95, but they were afraid competi-tors would undercut them. To make matters even more complicated, they had all heard rumors that Disney planned to take other steps against retailers who ignored MAP, such as delaying shipment of the next hit—*The Lion King*. Is MAP legal? What if the studios take "other steps"?

10. **ETHICS** An 18-year-old woman with a men-tal disability and her mother (the Nelsons) brought a malpractice suit against one of the doctors at the Monroe Regional Medical Center. As a result, the Monroe Clinic notified the Nelsons that it would no longer treat them on a nonemergency basis. The patients then went to another local clinic, which was later acquired by Monroe. The merged clinic refused to treat the Nelsons on a nonemergency basis, so the Nelsons were obliged to seek medical treatment in another town 40 miles away. Has Monroe violated the antitrust laws? Whether or not the Monroe clinic has violated the law, is it ethical to deny treatment to a patient?

11. **ROLE REVERSAL** Write a short-answer question based on an article you have found in the newspaper that involves an antitrust issue.

Internet Research Problem

Choose one of the cases featured at http://www.usdoj.gov/atr/cases.html. Read the Information (that is, the complaint) in the case. Then see if you can find out how the case was ultimately resolved. You could try looking on WestLaw or LEXIS, in newspaper reports, at the company Web site, or you could even call the Justice Department or the defen-dant's attorney.

You can find further practice problems in the Online Quiz at http://beatty.westbuslaw.com **or in the Study Guide that accompanies this text.**

Cyberlaw

Jason always said that his computer was his best friend. He was online all the time, sending instant messages to his friends, listening to music, doing research for his courses, and, OK, maybe playing a few games now and again. Occasionally, the computer could be annoying. It would crash once in a while, trashing part of a paper he had forgotten to save. And there was the time that a copy of an e-mail he sent Lizzie complaining about Caroline somehow ended up in Caroline's mailbox. He was pretty irritated when the White Sox tickets he bought in an online auction turned out to be for a Little League team. And he was tired of all the spam advertising pornographic Web sites. But these things happen and, despite the petty annoyances, his computer was an important part of his life.

Then one day, Jason received a panicked instant message from a teammate on the college wrestling squad telling him to click on a certain Web site pronto to see someone they knew. Jason eagerly clicked on the Web site and discovered, to his total horror, that he was featured—in the nude. The Web site was selling videos showing him and other members of the wrestling team in the locker room in various states of undress. Other videos, from other locker and shower rooms, were for sale, too, showing football players and wrestlers from dozens of universities. The videos had titles like "Straight Off the Mat" and "Voyeur Time." No longer trusting technology, Jason pulled on his running shoes and dashed over to the office of his business law professor.

More than two billion people use the Internet[1] worldwide. Computers and the Internet—cyberspace—together comprise one of the great technological developments of the twentieth century. Inevitably, new technologies create the need for new law. In the thirteenth century, England was one of the first countries to develop passable roads. Like the Internet, these roadways greatly enhanced communication, creating social and business opportunities, but also enabled new crimes. Good roads meant that bad guys could sneak out of town without paying their bills. Parliament responded with laws to facilitate the collection of out-of-town debts. Similarly, while the Internet has opened up enormous opportunities in both our business and personal lives, it has also created the need for new laws, both to pave the way for these opportunities and to limit their dangers.

The process of lawmaking never stops. Judges sit and legislatures meet—all in an effort to create better rules and a better society. However, in an established area of law, such as contracts, the basic structure changes little. Cyberlaw is different, because it is still very much in its infancy. Not only are new laws being created almost daily, but whole areas of regulation are, as yet, unpaved roads. Although the process of rule making has progressed well, much debate still surrounds cyberspace law and much work remains to be done. This chapter focuses on the existing rules and also discusses the areas of regulation that are still incomplete and in debate.

Cyberlaw affects many areas of our lives. You will have noticed that this book contains numerous Cyberlaw features throughout. Chapter 10, for example, discusses the validity of electronic contracts and signatures, Chapter 18 deals with cyber-issues in securities law, and Chapter 21 contains a lengthy discussion of cyberlaw and intellectual property. This chapter, however, deals with issues that are unique to the cyberworld, such as online privacy, hacking, and spam. If some of the words confuse you, the Web site at http://www.matisse.net/files/glossary.html provides a glossary of Internet terms.

Before beginning the chapter in earnest, let's return briefly to Jason, the wrestler. What recourse does Jason have for his Internet injuries? The nude video incident actually happened at Illinois State University and seven other colleges. Approximately 30 athletes filed suit against GTE and PSINet for selling the videos online. The outcome of that case is revealed later in this chapter. What about Jason's other computer injuries? Lizzie was not being a good friend, but it was perfectly legal for her to forward Jason's e-mail to Caroline. The seller of the White Sox tickets violated both federal and state fraud statutes. Some states now prohibit spam—unsolicited commercial e-mail—but a lawsuit is a slow and awkward tool for killing such a flourishing weed. Thus far, the available legal tools have been relatively ineffectual (as you can tell from your e-mail in-box).

---

[1] The term "Internet" means "the international computer network of both Federal and non-Federal interoperable packet switched data networks." 47 U.S. §230 (f)(1). It began in the 1960s as a project to link military contractors and universities. Now, it is a giant network that connects smaller groups of linked computer networks. The World Wide Web was created in 1991 by Tim Berners-Lee as a subnetwork of the Internet. It is a decentralized collection of documents containing text, pictures, and sound. Users can move from document to document using links that form a "web" of information.

Privacy

The Internet has vastly increased our ability to communicate quickly and widely. There was a time when intraoffice memos were typed, photocopied, and then hand-delivered by messengers. Catalogue orders were sent via regular mail, a comparatively slow, inefficient, and costly method.

As wonderful as computerized communication can be, though, it is not without its dangers. Consumers enter the most personal data—credit card numbers, bank accounts, lists of friends, medical information, product preferences—on the Internet. Who will have access to this data? Who can see it, use it, sell it? Many people fear that the Internet is a very large window through which the government, employers, business, and criminals can find out more than they should about you and your money, habits, beliefs and health. Even e-mail has its dangers: Who has not been embarrassed by an e-mail that ended up in the wrong mailbox?

Many commentators argue that, without significant changes in the law, our privacy will be obliterated. At the moment, however, privacy on the Internet is very much like the weather—everyone talks about it, but (so far) no one has done much about it. The three major sources of privacy concerns are Internet tracking, the hard drive, and e-mail.

INTERNET TRACKING

Of Cookies and Caches

If you order a book from Amazon.com, you may notice that the next time you log on, you will be greeted with the message, "Hello, [Your Name]. We have recommendations for you." Click on the link and you may find that, because you bought a GMAT study guide the first time, Amazon will entice you with other guides for standardized tests. However did Amazon know? Many Web sites automatically place a cookie on the hard drive of your computer when you visit them. **A cookie is a small file that includes an identification number and may also include personal data such as your address, phone and credit card numbers, and searches you have made or advertisements you have clicked on.**[2]

Some cookies are designed to follow a user from site to site, along the entire Internet trail. Indeed, a whole industry of Internet marketing firms knows how to target Web banners to individual surfers. Thus, if you visit Web sites for hotels in Togo you might, without your knowledge, be invisibly linked to an Internet marketing company that will automatically record this site visit in a cookie on your hard drive. Then, when you visit a travel site, in less time than it takes you to say "click," the marketing company can automatically retrieve your cookie, realize you are interested in Togo, and show you banner ads for travel there. You, meanwhile, are blissfully unaware that you have a dossier in cyberspace.

Other cookies can be used to authenticate who you are, storing such information as your name, address, and credit card number. Amazon.com has patented its so-called "1-Click" system that permits a shopper to buy an item by clicking once on the button. What could be easier than that? One-click buying would not be

---

[2] Legend has it that the term "cookie" refers to the Hansel and Gretel fairy tale. An evil stepmother forced her husband to take his two young children out into the woods and lose them. Anticipating such a plan, the children left a trail of bread crumbs to follow home. Legend does not reveal why these files are called cookies rather than crumbs.

possible without cookies. No doubt, cookies are convenient. And not just for one-click shopping. Consumers benefit from targeted advertisements—for example, long-distance runners see ads for running shoes, not cigarettes. Industry representatives also argue that, without the revenue from cookie-based ads, many Internet sites would not be free to consumers.

But there is no such thing as a free lunch, or even a free snack. Cookies raise privacy issues. When you traipse around the Internet, cookies create a dossier that could come back to haunt you. Although much of the information gathered is anonymous (that is, the consumer is identified only by a computer identification number), this anonymous information can be linked to **personally identifiable information** (PII), such as name and address. One company now markets a databank with the names of 150 million registered voters. Anyone can buy a list of voters that is sliced and diced however they want, say, Republicans between the ages of 45 and 60 with Hispanic surnames and incomes greater than $50,000. This company can also transmit specially tailored banner ads to voters surfing the Net.[3]

If marketers can put together a databank of Hispanic Republican voters, they can also find out that you have visited a Web site for recovering alcoholics or uncovered gamblers or Nazi sympathizers. Do you want information about every Web site you visit to be public?

Even without cookies, your computer creates a dossier about you. When you surf the Net, your computer stores a copy of the Web pages you visit in a cache file on your hard drive. Thus, anyone with access to your hard drive could get a good idea of your regular stopping places. Would you be concerned if your boss knew that you were visiting sites that specialized in job searches, cancer, or, for that matter, *any* non-job-related site?

The State of Privacy on the Internet

Almost since its inception, the Internet has caused persistent worries over privacy. Despite these concerns, Internet users continue to reveal vast quantities of personal data. No other invention has ever created such an incentive to be indiscreet. A recent survey illustrates this point.[4]

Many Internet users feel that their privacy has been violated:	• 28% have received an offensive e-mail from a stranger. • 25% have caught a computer virus, typically from infected e-mail. • 17% know someone who was fired or disciplined because of e-mailing or Web browsing at work. • 4% have been cheated while purchasing online.
Nonetheless, Internet users are still willing to reveal personal data:	• 55% have sought health information. • 48% have used a credit card to purchase an item online. • 43% have looked for financial data, such as stock prices. • 36% have gone to a support-group site that provides information about a specific medical condition or personal situation. • 25% have made friends with someone that they met online.

---

[3] For example, during the 2000 Republican presidential primaries, time was running short for John McCain to obtain enough voter signatures to get his name on the Virginia ballot. For $5,000 his campaign hired a company to send Internet advertisements to registered Republican voters in Virginia. When people in this database went online, they would see a McCain banner asking them to sign his petition.

[4] Pew Research Center. Available at http://www.pewinternet.org.

No matter what the dangers, consumers will inevitably reveal personal information about themselves over the Internet. The benefits of researching, shopping, and meeting others online are too tempting to resist. Who will protect consumers from themselves? At the moment, regulation of privacy over the Internet is incomplete and uncertain, a murky combination of self-regulation and government rules. (The Web site http://www.consumerprivacyguide.org/topthings offers advice on how to protect your privacy.)

SELF-REGULATION OF ONLINE PRIVACY

Voluntary Principles

The Network Advertising Initiative (NAI), an industry group, met with representatives of the Federal Trade Commission (FTC) and the Department of Commerce to negotiate principles of self-regulation for Internet advertisers. The FTC then issued a report supporting the following NAI principles:

1. **Notice.** Before collecting personal information from consumers, a Web site must disclose its privacy policy in a "clear and conspicuous notice." In the case of PII, the notice must be provided before the consumer enters any personal information.

2. **Choice.** Consumers must be able to choose whether their data will be collected. In most cases, consumers have the right to *opt out*; that is, a Web site can collect their data unless the consumer denies permission. In a few situations, however, the Web site cannot collect data unless the consumer *opts in*, that is, grants permission. For example, non-PII (i.e., anonymous) data cannot be linked with PII data unless the consumer opts in.

3. **Access.** A Web site must provide consumers reasonable access to their own data. This requirement sounds reasonable, but implementation is more complicated. Should consumers be entitled to access *all* information about themselves? Data collected years ago? Data now sitting on computer tapes stored in a distant off-site facility? Should consumers have the right to insist on changes to inaccurate information? (No, I didn't buy the *Joy of Sex*, it was the *Joy of Cooking*.)

4. **Security.** Web sites that collect information should ensure that nothing will be revealed without the consumer's permission. But how will companies ensure that only authorized people gain access?

5. **Sensitive Data.** Web sites must not use highly sensitive data (such as Social Security numbers, sexual behavior or preference, medical or financial information) to create profiles of individual consumers. (That is, they will not put together a list of gay men with AIDS who buy international index funds.)

6. **Enforcement.** An independent third party must monitor Web sites for compliance with these principles. Violators may be reported to the FTC. The NAI has hired TRUSTe, a nonprofit organization, to fulfill this role. Consumers can register complaints at http://www.truste.org/users/users_watchdog_intro.html.

The full text of the FTC report is available at http://www.ftc.gov/os/2000/07/onlineprofiling.htm.

Although the NAI principles are an important first step, there is concern that they are insufficient because (1) 10 percent of Internet advertisers are not members of NAI; (2) Web sites that do not run advertisements are not covered by NAI rules; and (3) enforcement mechanisms are weak.

These NAI principles are simply guidelines, not laws. If you ran a Web site, what principles would you follow? What rules would be fair to you and Web users? From the Chapter 2 Ethics Checklist: What values are at stake? Which alternative is just?

Technology: P3P

Even as the NAI struggles to enforce its voluntary principles, new developments in technology may increase privacy protection online. The so-called *Platform for Privacy Preferences* (P3P), at least in theory, permits consumers to choose how much privacy they want. Each Web site answers a complex set of questions about its privacy policies. Then, each consumer indicates in her Web browser the level of privacy protection she desires. Her browser will not visit a Web site whose privacy policy does not meet the minimum standard she has set. For this system to work, Web sites must cooperate and consumers must take the time to configure their Web browsers. Microsoft has included P3P software in its Internet Explorer 6 so, for the first time, P3P will be tested in the real world. To learn more about P3P, sneak over to http://www.w3.org/P3P.

GOVERNMENT REGULATION OF ONLINE PRIVACY

Members of Congress have filed more than 300 bills to regulate online privacy. So intense, however, is the debate between industry and consumer advocates that no consensus—and little law—has emerged. There has, however, been some government regulation.

The FTC

The FTC had originally asked Congress to legislate online privacy. However, in 2001 the chairman of the FTC expressed doubt about the benefits of new legislation and suggested that the FTC should instead use existing consumer statutes to regulate online privacy.[5] He said that "At this time, we need more law enforcement, not more laws."[6] The chairman indicated, for example, that the FTC would take action against Web sites that failed to comply with their posted policies. He made no reference, however, to the NAI principles.

In another action, the FTC intervened when Microsoft introduced its so-called *Passport Internet authentication service.* Under the Passport system, a consumer enters one name and password, which then works at many different sites. Surfing the Net is easier and faster, but the opportunity for privacy abuses is great. The FTC charged that Microsoft had been less than candid about its Passport privacy policies. The company was, for example, collecting more information than it had said it would and was providing less security than it had promised. In its settlement, Microsoft agreed to permit the FTC to supervise the company's privacy practices for 20 years.

---

5 Section 5 of the Federal Trade Commission Act prohibits "unfair and deceptive acts or practices." This statute is discussed at greater length in Chapter 23, on consumer law.
6 Remarks of FTC Chairman Timothy J. Muris, "Protecting Consumers' Privacy: 2002 and Beyond" at http://www.ftc.gov/speeches/muris/privisp1002.htm#N_35_.

Children's Online Privacy Protection Act of 1998

The Children's Online Privacy Protection Act of 1998 (COPPA) prohibits Internet operators from collecting information from children under 13 without parental permission. It also requires sites to disclose how they will use any information they acquire. The standard for obtaining parental consent is on a sliding scale—a higher standard applies if the information will be disclosed publicly. If the Web site only intends to use information *internally*, it can obtain parental consent by e-mail. But if the personal data will be disclosed to third parties, parental consent must be obtained by regular mail, fax, e-mail with an official digital signature, a telephone call from the parent, or it must be accompanied by a credit card number. Enforcement is in the hands of the FTC, which has the option of eliminating the sliding scale and applying the tougher standard to all transactions. (An explanation of the statute is available at http://www.ftc.gov/bcp/conline/pubs/buspubs/coppa.htm.) Children's Web sites claim that the cost of complying with COPPA is upwards of $100,000 per site. As a result, some sites now simply turn away children under 13 (which may have the unintended consequence of diverting them to unregulated, more adult Web pages).

Shortly after COPPA became law, the FTC brought an action against Young Investor (http://www.younginvestor.com). This site asked children about their weekly allowance, spending habits, work history, plans for college, and family finances. In addition, it asked for the child's name, address, age, and e-mail address. The site promised that all answers would be anonymous but, in fact, it could match names with surveys. Under a consent decree, Young Investor agreed to post a privacy policy and obtain parental consent before collecting personal information from children.

Gramm-Leach-Bliley Privacy Act of 1999

The Gramm-Leach-Bliley Privacy Act of 1999 (GLB) requires banks and other financial institutions to disclose to consumers any nonpublic information they wish to reveal to third parties.[7] A financial institution cannot disclose this private information if the consumer opts out (that is, denies permission). The Web site http://www.privacyrights.org offers advice on how to opt out.

GLB also prohibits pretexting, a process by which so-called *information brokers* use deception to find out private financial information. Thus, an FTC investigator contacted a Web site that was offering to sell private financial information. She offered to pay for information about her "fiancé's" bank balances. Someone working for the Web site successfully obtained this information by calling the bank and pretending to be the fiancé. The Web site settled with the FTC and agreed not to violate the GLB in future.

State Regulation

A few states have passed their own online privacy statutes. Minnesota, for example, requires Internet service providers to obtain permission from consumers before disclosing PII.[8]

---

[7] 15 U.S.C. §6801.
[8] 2002 Minn. ALS 395.

The European Directive

The European Union (EU) has established strict privacy rules for the collection of personal data. This directive could have far-reaching impact outside of Europe because it prohibits the transfer of personal data to any countries that do not provide adequate privacy protection. Some countries, such as Canada, have already passed legislation to comply with the directive. Because the United States has not done so, the Department of Commerce reached agreement with the EU on so-called *safe harbor principles*. Any company that complies with the safe harbor rules will be permitted to receive data from European companies.

To be in compliance with the safe harbor principles, a company must:

1. Tell consumers how it intends to use their data and how they can limit its use.

2. Provide consumers with the opportunity to prevent disclosure of their personal data (in other words, to opt out). If the data are particularly sensitive (involving, for example, health or sex), then the data cannot be used unless the consumer opts in.

3. Provide adequate security for the data.

4. Provide customers with reasonable access to their data.

5. Establish a procedure for resolving disputes with customers.

To date, only about 200 U.S. companies, mostly small to medium high-tech businesses, are in compliance with the safe harbor principles. Most American companies have not complied because:

- The rules are cumbersome and require major changes in how companies manage customer data.

- European countries are not aggressively enforcing the rules, even against their own companies.

- If a U.S. company announces that it will comply with the safe harbor principles and then does not, the FTC has the authority to sanction the company. Therefore, companies are better off complying with a weak policy rather than violating a strict one.

YOUR HARD DRIVE AS WITNESS (AGAINST YOU)

Many people confide their deepest secrets to their computers. Would you want everything you have ever typed into your computer to be revealed publicly? Monica Lewinsky certainly did not. Investigators in the President Clinton impeachment case discovered damaging evidence on the hard drive of Lewinsky's computer—evidence she clearly thought was private, including copies of deleted e-mails and drafts of letters she had never sent. What protection do you have for information stored on your computer?

Criminal Law

The Fourth Amendment to the Constitution prohibits unreasonable searches and seizures by the government. In enforcing this provision of the Constitution, the courts ask: Did the person being searched have a legitimate expectation of privacy in the place searched or the item seized? If yes, then the government must obtain a warrant from a court before conducting the search. (For more on this topic, investigate Chapter 7, on crime.) The Fourth Amendment applies to computers.

The architecture professor in the following case would have benefited from a course in business law and perhaps in computer science, too.

UNITED STATES OF AMERICA V. ANGEVINE

281 F.3d 1130, 2002 U.S. App. LEXIS 2746
United States Court of Appeals for the Tenth Circuit, 2002

FACTS: Professor Eric Angevine taught architecture at Oklahoma State University. The university provided him with a computer that was linked to the university network, and through it to the Internet. Professor Angevine used this computer to download more than 3,000 pornographic images of young boys. After viewing the images and printing some of them, he deleted the files. Tipped off by Professor Angevine's wife, police officers seized the computer and turned it over to a police computer expert who retrieved the pornographic files that the professor had deleted.

The Oklahoma State University computer policy states that:

• The contents of all storage media owned or stored on university computing facilities are the property of the university.

• Employees cannot use university computers to access obscene material.

• The university reserves the right to view or scan any file or software stored on a computer or passing through the network, and will do so periodically to audit the use of university resources. The university cannot guarantee confidentiality of stored data.

• System administrators keep logs of file names that may indicate why a particular data file is being erased, when it was erased, and what user identification has erased it.

The trial court held that federal agents did not need a warrant to search Professor Angevine's office computer because he had no expectation of privacy. He was sentenced to 51 months in prison for "knowing possession of child pornography." The professor appealed.

ISSUE: Did Professor Angevine have a reasonable expectation of privacy in his office computer?

EXCERPTS FROM JUDGE BRORBY'S DECISION: Oklahoma State University policies and procedures prevent its employees from reasonably expecting privacy in data downloaded from the Internet onto University computers. The University computer-use policy reserved the right to randomly audit Internet use and to monitor specific individuals suspected of misusing University computers. The policy explicitly cautions computer users that information flowing through the University network is not confidential either in transit or in storage on a University computer. These office practices and procedures should have warned reasonable employees not to access child pornography with University computers.

We are reluctant to find a reasonable expectation of privacy where the circumstances reveal a careless effort to maintain a privacy interest. Professor Angevine downloaded child pornography through a monitored University computer network. The policy explained network administrators actively audit network transmissions for such misuse. While Professor Angevine did attempt to erase the child pornography, the University computer policy warned system administrators kept file logs recording when and by whom files were deleted. Moreover, given his transmission of the pornographic data through a monitored University network, deleting the files alone was not sufficient to establish a reasonable expectation of privacy.

We hold Professor Angevine could not have an objectively reasonable expectation of privacy. ◢

Civil Litigation

Increasingly, computers are fair game in civil litigation. Suppose that you sue your company for wrongful termination. The company counterclaims, alleging that you cheated on your expense account. During litigation, it might subpoena your computer to find support for its allegations. Or suppose that, during the midst of a bitter divorce, your spouse alleges that you have shown pornography to your children. Your computer—with its Web trail—could end up in court. The following article illustrates how fragile privacy is when hard drives become pawns in litigation.

NEWSWORTHY

Each day, Ted Reeve pours his life into his home computer. He spends hours reading news online, and dutifully records monthly payments for his Visa card and Toyota Camry, along with ATM withdrawals. He regularly types up notes from talks with his doctor. It never occurred to him that such personal data could be extracted and shared among strangers. But that's what happened when his computer's hard drive was copied by two investigators retained for his employer, Northwest Airlines. Working right in his living room with a program called EnCase, they excavated every last bit and byte from his desktop hard drive.

Northwest suspected that its flight-attendant union had used the Internet to run an illegal call-in-sick campaign to disrupt the airline. So the airline won a court order to search 20 or so hard drives at flight attendants' homes and union offices. As people commit an ever-growing pile of information to computers, their hard drives are becoming a digital mother lode for lawyers. More federal courts are approving searches of home PCs for evidence in civil cases.[9] ◾

E-MAIL

E-mails may feel ephemeral, but they can do lasting damage. They typically stay stored on your own computer and on your provider's system long after you have hit the delete button. For example, when the Justice Department sued Microsoft for antitrust violations, some of the most damaging evidence against the company was extracted from its own e-mail archives. E-mail that had long since been deleted rose from the dead to haunt the company. Even online chat rooms store all posted comments for years. The Electronic Communications Privacy Act of 1986 (ECPA) is a federal statute that regulates e-mail.

Electronic Communications Privacy Act of 1986

The ECPA prohibits unauthorized interception or disclosure of wire and electronic communications or unauthorized access to stored communications. The definition of electronic communication includes e-mail and transmissions from pagers and cell phones. Violators are subject to both criminal and civil penalties. Under this statute:

1. **Any intended recipient of an e-mail has the right to disclose it.** Thus, if you sound off to a friend about your boss, the (erstwhile) friend may legally forward that e-mail to the boss or anyone else.

2. **Internet service providers (ISPs) are generally prohibited from disclosing electronic messages to anyone other than the addressee**, unless this disclosure

---

[9] Michael J. McCarthy, "In Airline's Suit, PC Becomes Legal Pawn, Raising Privacy Issues," *The Wall Street Journal*, May 24, 2000, p. 1.

is necessary for the performance of their service or for the protection of their own rights or property.

3. **An employer has the right to monitor workers' e-mail messages if (1) the employee consents, (2) the monitoring occurs in the ordinary course of business, or (3) the employer provides the e-mail system.** Chapter 14, on employment law, contains *Smyth v. Pillsbury*, a case brought under the ECPA by an unhappy employee.

4. **The government has the right to access e-mail messages if it first obtains a search warrant or court order.**

Timothy McVeigh learned about the dangers of e-mail the hard way. A highly decorated, 17-year veteran of the U.S. Navy, he was the senior enlisted man on the nuclear submarine U.S.S. *Chicago*. McVeigh sent an e-mail via AOL to Helen Hajne, a civilian organizer of a toy drive for children of the *Chicago* crew. McVeigh used the screen name "boysrch," although he signed the e-mail "Tim." Hajne searched AOL's "member profile directory," where she discovered that boysrch's marital status was "gay." This information ultimately landed on the desk of McVeigh's commanding officer. A Navy paralegal telephoned AOL and asked the identity of boysrch. AOL promptly and willingly revealed that this screen name belonged to McVeigh. The Navy then moved to discharge McVeigh for homosexual conduct. He sued under the ECPA, and a federal court issued an injunction prohibiting the Navy from discharging him. The court held that the Navy should not have asked for information from AOL without obtaining a search warrant or court order.[10]

Common Law Regulation of E-mail Privacy

In addition to the ECPA, some lawsuits have alleged that employers who read their workers' e-mails are violating the common law right of privacy. **Under the common law, intrusion into someone's private life is a tort if a reasonable person would find it offensive.** (For a review of the tort of invasion of privacy, peek at Chapter 6, on torts.) Did Microsoft violate an employee's privacy? You be the judge.

YOU BE THE JUDGE

BILL MCLAREN, JR. V. MICROSOFT CORPORATION

1999 Tex App. LEXIS 4103
Court of Appeals of Texas, 1999

FACTS: Microsoft suspended Bill McLaren from his job pending an investigation into allegations of sexual harassment and "inventory questions." In response, he sent a memorandum requesting that no one tamper with his Microsoft office workstation or his e-mail. Ignoring this request, Microsoft accessed e-mail files in the "personal folders" on McLaren's computer. These files

---

[10] The court would not have granted this request, however, because such a search would have violated the "don't ask, don't tell" policy of the U.S. military. *McVeigh v. Cohen*, 983 F. Supp. 215, 1998 U.S. Dist. LEXIS 790 (1998).

were password protected, but the company "decrypted" McLaren's personal password. The company then fired him.

McLaren filed suit against Microsoft for invasion of privacy. He alleged that he had a reasonable expectation of privacy in password-protected personal e-mail files.

YOU BE THE JUDGE: Would a reasonable person find this intrusion offensive? Does an employee have a reasonable expectation of privacy in his e-mail files?

ARGUMENT FOR MCLAREN: A company might have a legitimate right to read employee e-mails in the general course of events, but these e-mails were different. When Microsoft developed a system that permitted employees to store e-mails in personal folders with password protection, the company was creating an expectation of privacy. The whole point of a password is to safeguard privacy. Microsoft lured McLaren into storing personal messages and then betrayed him by breaking into his folders.

ARGUMENT FOR MICROSOFT: To win this case, McLaren must show that the intrusion on his privacy was unreasonable. These folders were part of an e-mail system owned and administered by Microsoft and made available to McLaren so that he could perform the functions of his job. These files were no more private than a locked file cabinet that Microsoft provided for his office.

McLaren could not have thought that it would take Microsoft more than two seconds to crack his password. Therefore, any expectation of privacy on his part was *un*reasonable. Moreover, these e-mail messages were transmitted over Microsoft's network and, thus, had already been accessible to third parties at some point.

McLaren was under suspicion of sexual harassment and inventory theft. Even if he had a reasonable expectation of privacy, a company's interest in preventing inappropriate and unprofessional conduct, not to mention illegal activity, outweighed his privacy rights. **/**

AT RISK

So what can you do to protect your privacy online? Here are some possibilities:

- Some Net surfers are opting for self-help measures:

  - About a quarter of Internet users have given a fake name or false personal information to a Web site.

  - About 20 percent of online users have used secondary e-mail addresses to disguise their identity.

  - Remember, before you click, to look for a Web site's privacy policy. If you cannot find one, or do not like what you find, you have the right to go elsewhere.

  - If your Web browser uses the P3P system, check the default settings to make sure that they match your privacy preferences.

- The Electronic Privacy Information Center offers a menu of privacy tools at http://www.epic.org/privacy/tools.html.

- The Privacy Council (http://www.privacycouncil.com/) offers advice about shopping and surfing anonymously on the Internet.

Crime on the Internet

Computers and the Internet are responsible for much good—together they have created enormous opportunities for communication, education, and entertainment. They have increased productivity and provided a foundation for many new businesses. However, for the dishonest and unscrupulous, the Internet has also opened new frontiers in crime.

HACKING

Gaining unauthorized access to a computer system is called *hacking.* The Pentagon reports that hackers make more than 250,000 attempts annually on its computers. The goal of hackers is varied; some do it for little more than the thrill of the challenge. The objective for other hackers may be industrial espionage, extortion, or theft of credit card information. Whatever the motive, hacking is a major crime. A survey of U.S. corporations, government agencies, and colleges revealed that 70 percent had experienced computer security breaches within the year. No surprise then that American companies spend more than $6 billion annually on computer security systems.

Hacking is illegal under the federal Computer Fraud and Abuse Act of 1986 (CFAA).[11] This statute applies to any computer attached to the Internet. **The CFAA prohibits:**

- Computer espionage

- Theft of financial information

- Theft of information from the U.S. government

- Theft from a computer

- Computer trespass

- Computer fraud

- Intentional, reckless, and negligent damage to a computer

- Trafficking in computer passwords

- Computer extortion

Some states have also adopted statutes prohibiting computer crime. A list of these statutes is available at http://www.cybercrimes.net/State/state_index.html. For advice on how to report a computer crime, visit http://cybercrimes.net/Reporting/reporting.html.

The CFAA has been an essential tool in fighting cybercrime. Unfortunately, because the Internet is truly international, cybercriminals do not always fall within the jurisdiction of American laws. For example, a computer virus called ILOVEYOU caused an estimated $7 billion worth of damage worldwide. Although the perpetrator would have been subject to prosecution under the CFAA in the United States, he lived in the Philippines, which did not have laws

---

[11] 18 U.S.C. §1030.

prohibiting cybercrime. Nor could the suspect be extradited automatically to the United States because the extradition treaty only applied if both nations had the same law. The Philippines ultimately dropped all charges against the suspect.

FRAUD

Fraud is a growth business on the Internet. The Internet's anonymity and speed facilitate fraud, and computers help criminals identify and contact victims. Common scams include the sale of merchandise that is either defective or nonexistent, the so-called Nigerian letter scam,[12] billing for services that are touted as "free," fraudulent stock offers, fake scholarship search services, business opportunity scams (for a small investment, you will get rich), and credit card scams (for a fee, you can get a credit card, even with a poor credit rating).

Fraud is the deception of another person for the purpose of obtaining money or property from him. It can be prosecuted under state law or the Computer Fraud and Abuse Act. In addition, federal mail and wire fraud statutes prohibit the use of mail or wire communication in furtherance of a fraudulent scheme.[13] The FTC can bring civil cases under §5 of the FTC act. (Chapter 7, on crime, discusses fraud, while Chapter 23, on consumer law, contains a detailed discussion of the FTC act.)

Auctions

Internet auctions are the number one source of consumer complaints about online fraud. Wrongdoers either sell goods they do not own, provide defective goods, or offer fakes. Fewer than 1 percent of online auctions involve fraud, but with upwards of $9 billion worth of goods being auctioned on the Internet each year, even 1 percent begins to add up.

Shilling is an increasingly popular online auction fraud. **Shilling means that a seller either bids on his own goods or agrees to cross-bid with a group of other sellers.** Shilling is prohibited because the owner drives up the price of his own item by bidding on it. Thus, for example, Kenneth Walton, a San Francisco lawyer, put up for auction on eBay an abstract painting purportedly by famous artist Richard Diebenkorn. A bidder offered $135,805 before eBay withdrew the item in response to charges that Walton had placed a bid on the painting himself and had also engaged in cross-bidding with a group of other eBay users. Walton claimed that he had placed the bids for friends.

To date, eBay has generally responded to shillers by suspending them for 30 days on the first offense and indefinitely on the second. Shillers are also subject to suit under general anti-fraud statutes. In addition, some states explicitly prohibit shilling.[14]

---

[12] Victims receive an e-mail from someone alleging to be a Nigerian government official who has stolen money from the government. He needs some place safe to park the money for a short time. The official promises that, if the victim will permit her account to be used for this purpose, she will be allowed to keep a percentage of the stolen money. Instead, of course, once the "official" has the victim's bank information, he cleans out the account. The highest average dollar losses are reported in this Internet scam—$5,575 per victim.

[13] U.S.C. §§1341–1346.

[14] For example, New Mexico law provides that "It shall be unlawful to employ shills or puffers at any such auction sale or to offer or to make or to procure to be offered or made any false bid or offer any false bid to buy or pretend to buy any article sold or offered for sale." N.M. Stat. §61-16-14.

The FTC has initiated *Project Safebid*, under which it educates law enforcement officials and then maintains a national database of Internet auction fraud complaints so that it can refer cases to the appropriate law enforcement agencies. To file a fraud complaint, click on http://www.ifccfbi.gov.

Identity Theft

Identity theft is one of the scariest crimes against property. Although it existed before computers, the Internet has made it much easier. The following article describes what it is like to be a victim of identity fraud.

NEWSWORTHY

I was working at Home Depot, where I'm a manager, when the Discover Card fraud unit called to find out why I'd requested an additional credit card. The Discover agent asked when I had moved to 1919 Madison Avenue, Norfolk, Va. My stomach turned inside out; I live on Long Island. I'd never even been to Virginia. The agent told me to notify the credit bureaus immediately.

A woman at one bureau told me someone had applied for eight cards in my name within the last month. My heart raced as I called each company to confirm my worst fear—they were all carrying large balances in my name. Even though I was able to cancel each card, I was freaking out. Two weeks later, I received more credit reports. He had opened 21 accounts overall. After two computers were delivered to his Norfolk address, I called the Norfolk police. They refused to arrest him. My wife had to stop me from going to sit in front of his house myself. In less than a month, this guy spent more than $40,000, a large chunk on stuff I'd never buy for myself, like Tommy Hilfiger and Nautica clothes and designer shoes.

I finally contacted the F.B.I., which discovered that the address he was using was fake and that the guy had a driver's license in my name. In the end, the F.B.I. nabbed him in a stolen car. Turns out he conned 50 or 60 people out of more than $500,000. He plea-bargained and got six and a half years, but will probably get out earlier. This guy wrecked my credit history. What's worse is that he still knows my Social Security number. What would stop him from doing it again?[15] ◾

Although the owner of a credit card must generally pay only the first $50 that is stolen (as discussed in Chapter 23, on consumer law), the time and effort required to undo the damage can be substantial. And credit cards may be the least of it. Armed with data such as a Social Security number and mother's maiden name, thieves can obtain loans, acquire a passport and driver's license, or even commit (additional) crimes under their new identities. Meanwhile, the victim may find himself unable to obtain a credit card, loan, or job. One victim spent several nights in jail after he was arrested for a crime that his alter ego had committed.

Responding to these concerns, Congress passed the Identity Theft and Assumption Deterrence Act of 1998.[16] **This statute prohibits the use of false identification to commit fraud or other crimes and it also permits the victim to seek restitution in court.**

A number of states have also passed identity theft statutes. California, for example, prohibits the use of Social Security numbers on ID cards or on bank

---

[15] Adam Ray, as told to Liz Welch, "Taken to the Bank," *The New York Times*, June 2, 2002, Sec. 6, p. 106. Copyright © 2002 (1999) by The New York Times Co. Reprinted by permission.
[16] 18 U.S. §1028.

statements or other documents sent by mail. Also, consumers can place a security freeze on their credit reports. When a freeze is in place, thieves cannot obtain a credit card or loan in the consumer's name.

What can you do to prevent the theft of your identity?

- Check your credit reports at least once a year. (The addresses and Web sites for the three largest credit agencies are listed in Chapter 23, on consumer law.)

- Subscribe to a credit monitoring service that will notify you each week if there are any major changes to your credit reports. AOL and Privista.com both offer such a service.

- If you suspect that your identity has been stolen, contact the FTC at 877-IDTHEFT (877-438-4338), or http://www.consumer.gov/idtheft. Also, file a police report immediately and keep a copy to show creditors. Notify the three credit agencies.

The Web site http://www.consumer.gov/knowfraud/index.html offers some additional tips.

FIGHTING INTERNET CRIME

Carnivore. Mark Jakob learned that he who commits a crime by the Internet can be caught by the Internet. One morning, as the stock market opened, a news release announced that Emulex Corp. would have to restate its earnings and was being investigated by the Securities and Exchange Commission (SEC). Within minutes the company's stock plummeted by more than half—from $113 to $43. In an instant $2.45 *billion* in market capitalization vanished. Needlessly. It turned out the press release was a phony. In less than a week, the FBI accused 23-year-old Jakob. He had "sold short" Emulex stock, that is, he had bet the stock would decline. Desperate when the stock went up instead, causing him a $97,000 paper loss, Jakob allegedly issued the phony release. It solved his problems temporarily—his loss turned into a profit of nearly $250,000—but the FBI was able to track the e-mail and the news release and make the arrest.

The good news is: cyberspace has given the government new and better methods for fighting crime. The bad news is: these crime fighting tools may threaten our privacy. As Supreme Court Justice Louis Brandeis famously observed in 1928,

> The progress of science in furnishing the Government with the means of espionage is not likely to stop with wire-tapping. Ways may some day develop by which the Government, without removing papers from secret drawers, can reproduce them in court, and by which it will be enabled to expose to a jury the most intimate occurrences of the home. . . . That places the liberty of every man in the hands of every petty officer.[17]

As the *Jakob* case illustrates, the Internet has been fertile ground for con artists perpetrating securities fraud. Nonetheless, protests greeted the SEC's announcement that it planned to monitor Web sites, bulletin boards, and chat groups for suspicious phrases like "get rich quick." The SEC also intended to track e-mail addresses to discover the identity of anonymous writers.

---

[17] *Olmstead v. U.S.*, 277 US 438; 1928 US LEXIS 694 (US Sup. Ct. 1928).

Then came the news that the FBI was using a computer program called "Carnivore" to intercept e-mail from terrorists, hackers, and other criminals. (Even the FBI acknowledged that the choice of names was unfortunate and now refers to Carnivore as DCS1000, the digital collection system.) Once installed on an Internet service provider, Carnivore (and other "dragnet" programs) works like a wiretap to track e-mail. Carnivore cannot be employed without a court order. The FBI had reportedly used it to intercept e-mail among terrorists around the world. Privacy advocates worry, though, that Carnivore could also be used to monitor the e-mail of political dissidents or others who espouse unpopular views. (For the FBI's view on Carnivore, investigate http://www.fbi.gov/hq/lab/carnivore/carnivore.htm.)

Convention on Cybercrime. The United States has signed the Council of Europe's Convention on Cybercrime treaty. The first international treaty on computer crime, it has provisions dealing with computer fraud, network security, and child pornography. The hope is that this treaty will establish a consistent international law and will also increase cooperation among countries in the fight against cybercrime. Although the treaty has, thus far, been *signed* by 33 countries, it has only been *ratified* by one (Albania). The full text is available at http://conventions.coe.int/Treaty/EN/CadreListeTraites.htm.

Internet Service Providers and Web Hosts

Internet service providers (ISPs) are companies, such as AOL, that provide connection to the Internet. Web hosts post Web pages on the Internet. Both play important roles in the Internet. As the legal structure that supports the Internet develops, so have legal issues involving these players.

SPAM

Spam is officially known as *unsolicited commercial e-mail (UCE)* or *unsolicited bulk e-mail (UBE)*. Whatever it is called, it can be annoying as millions of these messages clog ISP computers and consumer mailboxes. As much as 30 percent of all e-mail is spam. It is estimated that roughly half of all spam is fraudulent—either in content (promoting a scam) or in packaging (the headers or return address are false). At a minimum, bulk e-mail adds to the cost of connecting to the Internet. The European Commission has estimated that for consumers worldwide, spam increases their connection costs by $8.8 billion per year. ISPs must, for example, increase server capacity to handle the millions of spam e-mails. Moreover, both consumers and ISPs must endure the cost of outages caused by an overload of bulk e-mail. ISPs also argue that their reputations as service providers are harmed when consumers blame them for unsolicited advertisements. ISPs typically use filters to block this unwanted mail, but these programs are not foolproof and much spam sneaks through.

Concerned that deceptive bulk e-mails pose a threat to consumer confidence in online commerce, the FTC has advocated federal legislation to require that commercial messages bear accurate headers and domain names, and include accurate contact information in the text of the message. But Congress has not thus far acted. Almost half of the states, however, have passed anti-spam laws. In Virginia, for example, it is illegal to send unsolicited bulk e-mail that contains false information (such as a fake return address).[18] A California statute requires spammers to include "ADV" at the beginning of the subject line or "ADV:ADLT" if the spam is adult in nature.[19] More information about state spam laws is available at http://law.spamcon.org. Although one can only applaud the effort, in truth, the success of anti-spam laws is not assured. Spammers operate in the netherworld of cyberspace where they are difficult to identify and locate. California has not yet prosecuted anyone under its statute. For the optimistic, http://spamcop.net offers a service where you can report spammers.

E-mails promoting a scam can be attacked like any other fraud on the Internet—through state fraud statutes, the CFAA, or by the FTC.

Some observers have expressed concern that the rise of bulk e-mail could hamper the growth of the Internet. The FTC has brought a substantial number of anti-spam cases. For example, a company based in the Caribbean country of Dominca sent bulk e-mail to consumers informing them that their "orders had been received and processed" and their credit cards charged for amounts up to $899. The spam contained a forged header to hide the identity of the actual sender. If the recipients had any questions about the "order," the e-mail advised them to call a particular telephone number in area code 767 to speak with an operator. The consumers did not know that this area code was in Dominca and that, by making the call, they would incur substantial international long-distance charges (which the wrongdoer shared with the telephone company). After dialing the number, the consumer reached an adult entertainment service. Under the terms of the settlement, the defendants were enjoined permanently from falsifying information in the "from" and "subject" lines of e-mails, as well as in the text of the message.[20]

The following case is important because it establishes that individual states have the authority to regulate spam that originates elsewhere. Any other result would seriously handicap state anti-spam statutes.

WASHINGTON V. HECKEL

143 Wn.2d 824, 24 P.3d 404, 2001 Wash. LEXIS 388
Supreme Court of Washington, 2001

FACTS: Jason Heckel wrote an online booklet that described how to make money sending spam. He marketed this booklet by sending between 100,000 and 1,000,000 spam messages per week. Charging $39.95 for the booklet, Heckel made 30 to 50 sales per month. Heckel used one of two subject lines to introduce his solicitations: "Did I get the right e-mail address?" and "For your review—HANDS OFF!" The first subject line falsely suggested that an acquaintance of the recipient was trying to make contact, while the second subject line implied that

the message contained confidential information for the recipient.

Heckel used at least a dozen different return e-mail addresses, none with his name. Instead, his return addresses contained a name and a number, such as "marlin1374," or "cindyt5667." Because his e-mail accounts were usually canceled within two days of a bulk mailing, recipients had little opportunity to reply to the spam. Heckel maintained a personal e-mail account from which he sent no spam, but that e-mail address was not included in

---

[18] Code of Virginia, Chapter 886.
[19] California Business & Professions Code §17538.
[20] *FTC v. Benoit*, No. 3:99 CV 181 (W.D.N.C. filed May 11, 1999).

any of his spam messages. To further cover his tracks, Heckel routed his spam through at least a dozen different domain names, but did not receive permission to do so from the registered owners of those names.

Responding to consumer complaints, the state of Washington's Consumer Protection Division notified Heckel that he was in violation of Washington's anti-spam law. This act provides that anyone sending a commercial e-mail message from a computer located in Washington or to an e-mail address held by a Washington resident may not use a third-party's domain name without permission, misrepresent or disguise in any other way the message's point of origin or transmission path, or use a misleading subject line.

When Heckel continued to send spam, Washington filed suit against him. The trial court struck down the act, ruling that it violated the Commerce Clause of the U.S. Constitution. The state appealed.

ISSUE: Does the Washington anti-spam law violate the Commerce Clause of the Constitution?

EXCERPTS FROM JUSTICE OWENS'S DECISION: The Commerce Clause grants Congress the "power to regulate commerce with foreign nations, and among the several states." [T]he states impermissibly intrude on this federal power when they enact laws that unduly burden interstate commerce. Where the statute regulates evenhandedly to effectuate a legitimate local public interest, and its effects on interstate commerce are only incidental, it will be upheld unless the burden imposed on such commerce is clearly excessive in relation to the putative local benefits.

The [anti-spam] Act applies evenhandedly to in-state and out-of-state spammers: *"No person"* may transmit the proscribed commercial e-mail messages. Thus, just as the statute applied to Heckel, an Oregon resident, it is enforceable against a Washington business engaging in the same practices.

The Act protects the interests of three groups—ISPs, actual owners of forged domain names, and e-mail users. To handle the increased e-mail traffic attributable to deceptive spam, ISPs must invest in more computer equipment.

Operational costs likewise increase as ISPs hire more customer service representatives to field spam complaints and more system administrators to detect accounts being used to send spam.

Along with ISPs, the owners of impermissibly used domain names and e-mail addresses suffer economic harm. For example, the registered owner of "localhost.com" alleged that his computer system was shut down for three days by 7,000 responses to a bulk-mail message in which the spammer had forged the e-mail address "nobody at localhost.com" into his spam's header.

Deceptive spam harms individual Internet users as well. When a spammer distorts the point of origin or transmission path of the message, e-mail recipients cannot promptly and effectively respond to the message (and thereby opt out of future mailings); their efforts to respond take time, cause frustration, and compound the problems that ISPs face in delivering and storing the bulk messages. And the use of false or misleading subject lines further hampers an individual's ability to use computer time most efficiently. Individuals who do not have flat-rate plans for Internet access but pay instead by the minute or hour are harmed more directly, but all Internet users (along with their ISPs) bear the cost of deceptive spam.

We thus recognize that the Act serves the legitimate local purpose of banning the cost-shifting inherent in the sending of deceptive spam. To be weighed against the Act's local benefits, the only burden the Act places on spammers is the requirement of truthfulness, a requirement that does not burden commerce at all but actually facilitates it by eliminating fraud and deception. Spammers must use an accurate, nonmisleading subject line, and they must not manipulate the transmission path to disguise the origin of their commercial messages. While spammers incur no costs in complying with the Act, they do incur costs for noncompliance, because they must take steps to introduce forged information into the header of their message.

We find that the local benefits of the Act outweigh any conceivable burdens the Act places on those sending commercial e-mail messages. Consequently, we hold that the Act does not violate the Commerce Clause of the United States Constitution. ◢

COMMUNICATIONS DECENCY ACT OF 1996

The Internet is an enormously powerful tool for disseminating information. But what if some of this information happens to be false or in violation of our privacy rights? Is an ISP liable for transmitting it to the world?

In 1995, a trial judge in New York held that an ISP, Prodigy Services Company, was potentially liable for defamatory statements that an unidentified person posted on one of its bulletin boards.[21] The message alleged that the president of an investment bank had committed "criminal and fraudulent acts." It was not only a false statement, but it was posted on the most widely read financial computer bulletin board in the country. Although one can only feel sympathy for the target of this slur, the decision nonetheless alarmed many observers who argued that there was no way ISPs could review every piece of information that hurtles through their portals. The next year, Congress overruled the *Prodigy* case by passing the **Communications Decency Act of 1996** (CDA).[22] **Under this statute, ISPs are not liable for information that is provided by someone else.** The following case (on which the chapter-opening scenario was based) illustrates how broadly this statute has been interpreted.

JOHN DOES V. FRANCO PRODUCTIONS

2000 U.S. Dist. LEXIS 8645
United States District Court for the Northern District of Illinois

FACTS: A group of college athletes was secretly videotaped in various states of undress by hidden cameras in restrooms, locker rooms, and showers. These videotapes were sold on Web sites hosted by GTE and PSINet. The Web sites also showed pictures taken from the videotapes. The athletes had not authorized the videotapes and only learned about their existence from a newspaper article. They brought suit against the producers and distributors of the videotapes, and against the Web hosts, GTE and PSINet. The Court dismissed the plaintiffs' complaint against GTE and PSINet, finding that they were ISPs and therefore immune from suit under the CDA. The plaintiffs amended their complaint, alleging that GTE and PSINet were also liable in their capacity as Web site hosts. GTE and PSINet filed a motion to dismiss.

ISSUES: Are GTE and PSINet liable for the posting and sale of unauthorized videos? Should their motion to dismiss be granted?

EXCERPTS FROM JUDGE KOCORAS'S DECISION: [The CDA] provides, "No provider or user of an interactive computer service shall be treated as the publisher or speaker of any information provided by another information content provider." This creates a federal immunity to any cause of action that would make service providers liable for information originating with a third-party user of the service. Plaintiffs have recast the dismissed claims raised in their previous complaint by alleging that they are bringing the instant suit against GTE and PSINet in their capacity as "web site hosts" rather than service providers. In this capacity as web hosts, Plaintiffs claim that GTE and PSINet acted as "information content providers" and would, thus, not be immune from suit under the CDA.

Immunity under the CDA is not limited to service providers who contain their activity to editorial exercises or those who do not engage in web hosting, but rather, Congress provided immunity even where the interactive service provider has an

21 *Stratton Oakmont, Inc. v. Prodigy Services Company*, 1995 N.Y. Misc. LEXIS 229.
22 47 U.S.C. 230.

active, even aggressive role in making available content prepared by others. The deficiency in Plaintiffs' allegations is the notion that involvement in web hosting activities transforms an entity into an information content provider.

Perhaps the Court is obtuse in its consistent misunderstanding of Plaintiffs' cause of action, but it is still at a loss to understand how GTE's and PSINet's roles in the descriptions or presentation of the images on the Web site impact the creation or development of the images and videotapes themselves. Plaintiffs' explain that "the culpable conduct is not only the taking of the videotapes but also disseminating them on the Internet and offering them for sale and selling them." This makes no clearer Plaintiffs' theory that GTE and PSINet were somehow content providers. Plaintiffs do not allege that GTE or PSINet themselves sold or offered for sale the videotapes at issue. Plaintiffs simply allege that GTE and PSINet, as web hosts, provided a medium through which others could sell or offer for sale the videotapes at issue. However, by offering web hosting services which enable someone to create a web page, GTE and PSINet are not magically rendered the creators of those web pages. As such, Plaintiffs' new characterization of GTE and PSINet as web hosts neither prevents these defendants from being deemed service providers protected by immunity under the CDA nor makes them content providers unprotected by the CDA's immunity.

For the reasons set forth above, the Court grants Defendants GTE's and PSINet's motion to dismiss. ◢

1. An employee at AnswerThink Consulting group in Miami posted criticism of his boss on a Yahoo bulletin board. Without telling him, Yahoo revealed his identity to his employer and he was fired.

2. Four New Jersey boarding school students bought the drug DMX from eBay. After taking the drug, they began vomiting and became disoriented.

Internet middlemen are not liable for what happens on their watch (i.e., on their Web site). Courts have generally taken the view that online providers are like the telephone company—simply transmitters of information. But do these companies have a moral obligation? Should eBay review listings before posting them to keep drugs and other illegal items at bay? Should Yahoo at least have notified the employee before revealing his identity? Should GTE and PSINet have asked questions about nude videos of college students? From the Chapter 2 Ethics Checklist: What important values are at stake? What answer would the Golden Rule suggest? ▪

Chapter Conclusion

The Internet has changed our lives in ways that were inconceivable a generation ago. Like a racer coming off a delayed start, the law is rushing to catch up. Not only will laws change, as legislators and courts learn from experience, but new laws will inevitably be needed. Old laws may also be applied in new ways.

Inevitably, the law of cyberspace will become increasingly international. What does Europe accomplish by regulating Internet privacy if its citizens spend a good portion of their time on American Web sites? What will the FTC do if scam artists or spammers operate offshore? Leaders of e-commerce companies around the world have formed the Global Business Dialogue on Electronic Commerce to develop policies and advise governments on cyberspace issues. (To learn more about this organization, travel to http://www.gbd.org.) Effective regulation of cyberspace will require cooperation among nations and between government and industry.

Chapter Review

1. Currently, there is little regulation governing the collection or use of personal data on the Internet. Under principles established by the Federal Trade Commission (FTC) and the Network Advertising Initiative (NAI), Web sites should provide notice, choice, access, security, and enforcement.

2. The Children's Online Privacy Protection Act of 1998 prohibits Internet operators from collecting information from children under 13 without parental permission. It also requires sites to disclose how they will use any information they acquire.

3. The Gramm-Leach-Bliley Privacy Act of 1999 requires banks and other financial institutions to disclose to consumers any nonpublic information they wish to reveal to third parties.

4. The U.S. Department of Commerce and the European Union (EU) have established safe harbor principles for the collection of personal data. Any company that complies with the safe harbor rules will be permitted to receive data from European companies.

5. The Fourth Amendment to the Constitution prohibits unreasonable searches and seizures by government agents. This provision applies to computers.

6. The Electronic Communications Privacy Act of 1986 prohibits unauthorized interception or disclosure of wire and electronic communications or unauthorized access to stored communications. Under this statute:
   - Any intended recipient of an e-mail has the right to disclose it.
   - Internet service providers (ISPs) are generally prohibited from disclosing e-mail messages to anyone other than the addressee, unless this disclosure is necessary for the performance of their service or for the protection of their own rights or property.

   - An employer has the right to monitor workers' e-mail messages if (1) the employee consents, (2) the monitoring occurs in the ordinary course of business, or (3) the employer provides the e-mail system.
   - The government has the right to access e-mail messages if it first obtains a search warrant or court order.

7. Under the common law, intrusion into someone's private life is a tort if a reasonable person would find it offensive.

8. Hacking is illegal under the federal Computer Fraud and Abuse Act of 1986. The CFAA prohibits:
   - Computer espionage
   - Theft of financial information
   - Theft of information from the U.S. government
   - Theft from a computer
   - Computer trespass
   - Computer fraud
   - Intentional, reckless, and negligent damage to a computer
   - Trafficking in computer passwords
   - Computer extortion

9. Fraud is the deception of another person for the purpose of obtaining money or property from him.

10. The Identity Theft and Assumption Deterrence Act of 1998 prohibits the use of false identification to commit fraud or other crimes.

11. Almost half of the states have passed anti-spam laws.

12. Under the Communications Decency Act of 1996, ISPs and Web hosts are not liable for information that is provided by someone else.

Practice Test

1. Three travel agents used fictitious accounts to steal 61 million frequent flyer miles from American Airlines. They traded this mileage in for 546 free tickets, with a value of $1.3 million. As evidence in the criminal trial, prosecutors used electronic communications from the

agents on SABRE, American's computerized travel reservations system. The agents alleged that this search was illegal under the Fourth Amendment to the Constitution. Do you agree?

2. **ETHICS** Matt Drudge published a report on his Web site (http://www.drudgereport.com) that White House aide Sidney Blumenthal "has a spousal abuse past that has been effectively covered up. . . . There are court records of Blumenthal's violence against his wife." The Drudge Report is an electronic publication focusing on Hollywood and Washington gossip. AOL paid Drudge $3,000 a month to make the Drudge Report available to AOL subscribers. Drudge e-mailed his reports to AOL, which then posted them. Before posting, however, AOL had the right to edit content. Drudge ultimately retracted his allegations against Blumenthal, who sued AOL. He alleged that under the Communications Decency Act of 1996, AOL was a "content provider" because it paid Drudge and edited what he wrote. Do you agree? Putting liability aside, what moral obligation did AOL have to its members? To Blumenthal? Should AOL be liable for content it bought and provided to its members?

3. To demonstrate the inadequacies of existing computer security systems, Cornell student Robert Morris created a computer virus. His plan, however, went awry, as plans sometimes do. He thought his virus would be relatively harmless, but it ran amok, crashing scores of computers at universities, military sites, and medical research sites. Under what statute might Morris be charged? Has he committed a crime, or is he liable only for civil penalties? Does it matter that he did not intend to cause damage?

4. **YOU BE THE JUDGE WRITING PROBLEM** Jerome Schneider wrote several books on how to avoid taxes. These books were sold on Amazon.com. Amazon permits visitors to post comments about items for sale. Amazon's policy suggests that these comments should be civil (e.g., no profanity or spiteful remarks). The comments about Schneider's books were not so kind. One person alleged Schneider was a felon. When Schneider complained, an Amazon representative agreed that some of the postings violated its guidelines and promised that they would be removed within one to two business days. Two days later, the posting had not been removed. Schneider filed suit. **Argument for Schneider:** Amazon has editorial discretion over the posted comments: it both establishes guidelines and then monitors the comments to ensure that they comply with the guidelines. These activities make Amazon an information content provider, not protected by the Communications Decency Act. **Argument for Amazon:** The right to edit material is not the same thing as creating the material in the first place.

5. During the course of 10 months, Joseph Melle sent more than 60 million unsolicited e-mail advertisements to AOL members. What charges could AOL bring against him in Washington? In your state? (You can find out more about the spam law in your state at http://law.spamcon.org.)

6. Anthony Davis operated a computer bulletin board system that permitted users to send and receive e-mail, access the Internet, and download software. Davis's system had one attribute that distinguished it from, say, AOL. It specialized in pornography. Alerted by an anonymous tip, the Oklahoma City Police Department obtained a warrant to search his premises for "equipment, order materials, papers, membership lists and other paraphernalia pertaining to the distribution or display of pornographic material." During their raid the officers seized computer equipment that contained 150,000 e-mails in electronic storage, some of which had not been retrieved by the recipients. Alleging that the e-mails had not been included in the warrant, Davis filed suit against the police officers for violations of the Electronic Communications Privacy Act. Does Davis have a valid claim?

7. Nancy Garrity and Joanne Clark worked for John Hancock Mutual Life Insurance Company. On their office computers they regularly received sexually explicit e-mails from friends and from Internet joke sites, which they

then sent to co-workers. When a fellow employee complained, Hancock searched their e-mail folders and, finding inappropriate e-mails, fired the two women. The Hancock e-mail policy states: "Messages that are defamatory, abusive, obscene, profane, sexually oriented, threatening or racially offensive are prohibited. Company management reserves the right to access all E-mail files." The two employees filed suit against Hancock, alleging that the company had invaded their privacy. How would you rule as judge?

8. What can you do to protect your privacy online? Draw up a concrete list of steps that you might reasonably consider. Are there some actions that you would not be willing to take,

either because they are not worth the effort or because they are too sneaky?

9. Craig Hare offered computers and related equipment for sale on various Internet auction Web sites. He accepted payment but not responsibility—he never shipped the goods. Both the FTC and the U.S. attorney general in Florida (that is, the prosecutor for the federal government) brought charges against him. What charges did they bring? Why would these two separate agencies of the federal government both bring suit?

10. **ROLE REVERSAL** Write a short-answer question that deals with an issue involving crime in cyberspace.

Internet Research Problems

1. The FTC offers advice to Web site operators about how to comply with the Children's Online Privacy Protection Act at http:// www.ftc.gov/bcp/conline/edcams/kidzprivacy/ index.html. Find a Web site that does comply and one that does not.

2. The FTC provides an online brochure titled *Site Seeing on the Internet* (at http://www .ftc.gov/) that offers suggestions for safe travel on the Internet. Have you ever violated the FTC's advice on how to protect yourself in cyberspace?

You can find further practice problems in the Online Quiz at http://beatty.westbuslaw.com **or in the Study Guide that accompanies this text.**

Intellectual Property

It is hard to imagine that a Goliath like the $12 billion American music industry could see a 19-year-old college sophomore as a threat to its long-term financial health. But when Brian Matiash, a computer engineering major, boots up the computer in his dorm room at Syracuse University on a typical evening, several hundred e-mail messages will await him, each a request for digital copies of recorded music. He will fire up his computer, which is equipped with a hard drive that holds copies of literally hundreds of songs and a CD burner, a device that allows him to copy those songs onto blank CDs.

Mr. Matiash is part of a thriving underground network of digital music scavengers, mostly college students, who copy and trade music files globally over the Internet in violation of copyright laws. To the recording industry, Mr. Matiash's hobby is deeply disturbing. There are suddenly hundreds if not thousands of people around the globe creating vast electronic libraries of copy-protected music and posting it to the Internet in a format that allows for sound of near-CD quality. That means that potential consumers have a free alternative to buying music.

Mr. Matiash said, "I feel bad sometimes because I know I'm making a mess for the music companies. I know it's technically a crime."

The Recording Industry Association of America employs people to surf the Net looking for sites where copy-protected material is posted and is experimenting with software that automatically searches the Internet for such sites. When sites are found, officials usually notify the Internet service provider, often a university, which then typically asks the site's owner to remove the offending material. So far, that effort does not appear to have slowed the pirates. "I pretty much can guarantee everyone that I can find any song I want on the Internet if you give me a day or two," Mr. Matiash said.[1]

Introduction

For much of history, land was the most valuable form of property. It was the primary source of wealth and social status. Today, intellectual property is a major source of wealth. New ideas—for manufacturing processes, computer programs, medicines, books—bring both affluence and influence.

ECONOMICS & THE LAW

Land and intellectual property, though both valuable assets, are fundamentally different. The value of land lies in the owner's right to exclude, to prevent others from entering or using it. Intellectual property, however, has little economic value unless it is used by many.

The crux of the economic problem is this: intellectual property is typically expensive to *produce* but cheap to *transmit*. Movies or computer software, for example, cost millions to make but can be copied or reproduced for virtually nothing. (How much does it cost to download software?) But if too much intellectual property is transmitted too freely, then those who create ideas will not be paid the full value of their efforts. (Those who simply transmit ideas will tend to be overpaid.) The resulting imbalance creates too many transmitters and not enough producers. So the next time you are tempted to copy a friend's CD or download music free from the Internet, remember that lost royalty payments to musicians ultimately means less music for you.

Because producers of intellectual property are likely to be underpaid in the free market, the government provides three remedies: it *protects* the property rights of producers (with patents and copyrights), *produces* information itself (such as weather reports), and *subsidizes* production by others (via government research grants).

Some commentators suggest that the United States has been a technological leader partly because its laws have provided strong protection for intellectual property since early in the country's history. Indeed, the Constitution provides for patent protection. In contrast, one of the oldest civilizations in the world, China, has been much slower in developing new technology. It did not institute a patent system until 1985, and its protection of patents is weak.

The conflict between those who have intellectual property and those who want to use it has taken on a global dimension. Developing countries argue that American intellectual property laws increase the price of medicines, such as AIDS drugs and

---

[1] Jason Chervokas, "Internet CD Copying Tests Music Industry," *The New York Times*, Apr. 6, 1998, p. D3. Copyright ©1998 by The New York Times Co. Reprinted by permission.

vaccines, that could save lives if only they were cheaper and, therefore, more readily available. "Patents kill" is their slogan. The United States responds that, without patent protection, there would be no innovation, no miracle drugs. In India, for example, biotech entrepreneurs hesitate to sell their new products at home where intellectual property laws offer little protection. Their inventions go overseas.

But even U.S. drug companies admit that patents can sometimes stifle innovation. The pharmaceutical company Bristol-Meyers Squibb says that it cannot conduct research on many cancer-fighting drugs because of patents held by its competitors. Information technology firms make a similar complaint. In a study of the American semiconductor business, researchers found that more patents did not necessarily mean there was more innovation. Instead, some companies were simply more aggressive about patenting every possible aspect of their research. Nor was there any evidence that innovation increased as patent rights were enhanced. And, in a study of developing companies, researchers could find no evidence that patent protection promoted innovation.

The role of intellectual property law is to balance the rights of those who create intellectual property and those who would enjoy it. And as this chapter reveals, such a balancing act is no easy feat.

Patents

A patent is a grant by the government that permits the inventor exclusive use of an invention for 20 years (or 14 years in the case of design patents). During this period, no one may make, use, or sell the invention without permission. In return, the inventor publicly discloses information about the invention that anyone can use upon expiration of the patent.

TYPES OF PATENTS

There are three type of patents: utility patents, design patents, and plant patents.

Utility Patent

Whenever people use the word "patent" by itself, they are referring to a utility patent. This type of patent is available to those who invent (or significantly improve) any of the following:

Type of Invention	Example
Mechanical invention	A hydraulic jack used to elevate heavy aircraft
Electrical invention	A prewired, portable wall panel for use in large, open-plan offices
Chemical invention	The chemical 2-chloroethylphosphonic acid used as a plant growth regulator
Process	A method for applying a chemical compound to an established plant such as rice in order to inhibit the growth of weeds electively; the application can be patented separately from the actual chemical

Type of Invention	Example
Machine	A device that enables a helicopter pilot to control all flight functions (pitch, roll, and heave) with one hand
Composition of matter	A sludge used as an explosive at construction sites; the patent specifies the water content, the density, and the types of solids contained in the mixture

A patent is not available solely for an idea, but only for its tangible application. Thus patents are *not* available for laws of nature, scientific principles, mathematical algorithms, or formulas such as $a^2 + b^2 = c^2$. In recent years, the status of computer software has been controversial: Is it an (unpatentable) mathematical formula or a (patentable) process or machine? The following case answers this question.

STATE STREET BANK & TRUST CO. V. SIGNATURE FINANCIAL GROUP, INC.

149 F.3d 1368, 1998 U.S. App. LEXIS 16869
United States Court of Appeals for the Federal Circuit,[2] 1998

FACTS: Signature Financial Group, Inc., owns a patent on a computer software program that aids in the administration of mutual funds. The so-called Hub and Spoke System allows several mutual funds, or "Spokes," to pool their investment funds into a single portfolio, or "Hub." In this way, the funds can share administrative costs. Each Spoke sells shares to the public, and the cost of these shares depends upon the value of the assets pooled in the Hub. Therefore, each day within hours of the close of the stock market, each fund's administrator must know the value to the nearest penny of its pooled shares. The Signature software makes this calculation.

State Street Bank and Trust Co. negotiated with Signature for a license to use its software. When negotiations broke down, State Street brought suit alleging that the patent was invalid. The trial court granted State Street's motion for summary judgment.

ISSUE: Is data processing software patentable?

EXCERPTS FROM JUDGE RICH'S DECISION: [The Supreme] Court has held that mathematical algorithms are not patentable subject matter to the extent that they are merely abstract ideas. From a practical standpoint, this means that to be patentable an algorithm must be applied in a "useful" way.

Today, we hold that the transformation of data, representing discrete dollar amounts, by a machine through a series of mathematical calculations into a final share price, constitutes a practical application of a mathematical algorithm, formula, or calculation, because it produces "a useful, concrete and tangible result"—a final share price momentarily fixed for recording and reporting purposes.

The question of whether a claim encompasses statutory subject matter should focus on the essential characteristics of the subject matter, in particular, its practical utility. For purpose of our analysis, [this] claim is directed to a machine programmed with the Hub and Spoke software and admittedly produces a "useful, concrete, and tangible result." This renders it statutory subject matter, even if the useful result is expressed in numbers, such as price, profit, percentage, cost, or loss.

Reversed and remanded.

---

[2] Recall from Chapter 3 that the Court of Appeals for the Federal Circuit is the thirteenth United States Court of Appeals. It hears appeals from specialized trial courts.

The *State Street* case could have a profound impact on e-commerce as companies rush to patent techniques for doing business over the Internet. For example, Priceline.com received a patent for the reverse auction system offered on its Web site (http://www.priceline.com). Customers list the price (backed up by a credit card) that they are willing to pay for an airline ticket, hotel room, car, or other item. Priceline then scours its database to find a seller willing to make a deal at that price. Similarly, Amazon.com received a patent for its 1-Click method of instant ordering. The company then obtained an injunction to prevent barnesandnoble.com from using its Express Lane service that was similar to 1-Click. The judge directed barnesandnoble.com to add an additional step to its ordering process.

Proponents of these patents argue that they permit innovators on the Internet to protect their ideas. Otherwise, it is easy for copycats to open a rival Web site overnight. Critics counter that these patents could stifle e-commerce by limiting the use of new ideas. In response to criticism, the Patent and Trademark Office (PTO) altered its evaluation process to ensure that patents were awarded only for real innovation. The PTO has, for example, asked software experts to help train examiners. Each Internet business method patent is now subject to three and, in some cases, four separate examinations before approval. ▪

Design Patent

A design patent protects the appearance, not the function, of an item. It is granted to anyone who invents a new, original, and ornamental design for an article. For example, Braun, Inc., patented the look of its handheld electric blenders. Design patents last only 14 years, not 20.

Plant Patent

Anyone who creates a new type of plant can patent it, *provided that* the inventor is able to reproduce it asexually—such as through grafting, not by planting its seeds. For example, one company patented its unique heather plant.

REQUIREMENTS FOR A PATENT

To obtain a patent, the inventor must show that her invention meets all of the following tests:

- **Novel.** An invention is not patentable if it (1) is known or has already been used in this country, or (2) has been described in a publication here or overseas. For example, an inventor discovered a new use for existing chemical compounds but was not permitted to patent it because the chemicals had already been described in prior publications, though the new uses had not.[3]

- **Nonobvious.** An invention is not patentable if it is obvious to a person with ordinary skill in that particular area. An inventor was not allowed to patent a waterflush system designed to remove cow manure from the floor of a barn because it was obvious.[4]

---

[3] *In re Schoenwald*, 964 F.2d 1122, 1992 U.S. App. LEXIS 10181 (Fed. Cir. 1992).
[4] *Sakraida v. Ag Pro, Inc.*, 425 U.S. 273, 96 S. Ct. 1532, 1976 U.S. LEXIS 146 (1976).

- **Useful.** To be patented, an invention must be useful. It need not necessarily be commercially valuable, but it must have some current use. Being merely of scientific interest is not enough. Thus a company was denied a patent for a novel process for making steroids because they had no therapeutic value.[5]

A searchable database of all patents issued since 1976 is available at the Patent and Trademark Office's Web site: http://www.uspto.gov/patft/index.html. To find out just how creative inventors can be, check out the Wacky Patent of the Month at http://www.colitz.com/site/wacky.htm.

PATENT APPLICATION AND ISSUANCE

To obtain a patent, the inventor must file a complex application with the federal Patent and Trademark Office in Washington, D.C. If a patent examiner determines that the application meets all legal requirements, the PTO will issue the patent. If the examiner denies the patent application, the inventor can appeal that decision to the PTO Board of Appeals and from there to the Court of Appeals for the Federal Circuit in Washington. Alternatively, upon denial of the application, the inventor can file suit against the PTO in the federal district court in Washington.

Priority between Two Inventors

When two people invent the same product, who is entitled to a patent—the first to invent or the first to file an application? Generally, the person who invents and *puts the invention into practice* has priority over the first filer. Having the idea is not enough; the inventor must actually use the product.

Prior Sale

However, an inventor must apply for a patent within one year of selling the product commercially. The purpose of this rule is to encourage prompt disclosure of inventions. It prevents someone from inventing a product, selling it for years, and then obtaining a 20-year monopoly with a patent.

Provisional Patent Application

Investors who are unable to assess the market value of their ideas sometimes hesitate to file a patent application because the process is expensive and cumbersome. To solve this problem, the PTO now permits inventors to file a **provisional patent application (PPA)**. The PPA is a simpler, shorter, cheaper application that gives inventors the opportunity to show their ideas to potential investors without incurring the full expense of a patent application. PPA protection lasts only one year. To maintain protection after that time, the inventor must file a regular patent application.

Duration of a Patent

Patents are valid for 20 years from the date of *filing* the application (except design patents, which are valid for 14 years from date of *issuance*). Currently, approval of a patent takes about 24 months from the date of filing, which means that patent

---

[5] *Brenner v. Manson*, 383 U.S. 519, 86 S. Ct. 1033, 1966 U.S. LEXIS 2907 (1966).

holders effectively receive 18 years of protection (although in the case of exceptional delays, it is possible to request an extension).

Eighteen months after patents are filed, the PTO publishes them. This means that patent applications are often published before they have been approved. Although there is some concern that patent ideas are therefore easier to steal, publication also gives anyone with knowledge in the field an opportunity to provide the PTO with additional information about why the patent should or (more likely) should not be granted.

ECONOMICS & THE LAW

How long should patents last? Holders enjoy a monopoly that protects them from competition and permits them to charge higher prices. But these monopoly profits are not all bad—they also provide inventors with the incentive to spend large sums hoping to develop new products. In theory, the duration of a patent should be individually tailored to each product. The goal is to ensure that a patent creates the right incentive for each product. Take, for example, a complex, lifesaving drug that costs $400 million to develop. No drug company would undertake such a project without assurance that it could recoup its costs. But if the company would make $300 million in the first year of sale, it needs only a short patent life to recoup its costs. On the other hand, if the company would only make $25 million a year, it should have at least a 16-year patent. Likewise, if a product has little value to society, its patent should be of short duration.

Of course, the PTO would be in chaos if examiners had to decide how much protection each individual patent deserved, but Germany has gone some distance along this path. It awards a standard patent for important inventions. Less important products receive a so-called *petty patent* that lasts only three years. Moreover, all patent owners pay an annual maintenance fee. At the beginning, this fee is low, but it increases so much each year that only 5 percent of German patents are maintained for a full term. Most owners abandon ship in less than eight years.[6]

Infringement

A patent holder has the exclusive right to use the invention during the term of the patent. A holder can prohibit others from using any product that is substantially the same, license the product to others for a fee, and recover damages from anyone who uses the product without permission.

International Patent Treaties

Suppose you have a great idea that you want to protect around the world. It used to be that filing an application in other countries was a logistical nightmare because almost every country had its own unique filing procedures and standards. Several treaties now facilitate this process, although it is still not the one-stop (or one-click) effort that inventors desire. These treaties were drafted by the World Intellectual Property Organization (WIPO) of the United Nations and are available on its Web site at http://www.wipo.org.

The Paris Convention for the Protection of Industrial Property requires each member country to grant to citizens of other member countries the same rights

[6] R. Cooter and T. Ulen, *Law and Economics*, 2nd ed. (Reading, Mass.: Addison-Wesley, 1997).

under patent law as its own citizens enjoy. Thus, the patent office in each member country must accept and recognize all patent and trademark applications filed with it by anyone who lives in any member country. For example, the French patent office cannot refuse to accept an application from an American, as long as the American has complied with French law.

The Patent Law Treaty requires that countries use the same standards for the form and content of patent applications (whether submitted on paper or electronically). This treaty reduces the procedural conflicts over issues such as translations and fees. In short, it takes an important first step in standardizing the application *process*. Still to be worked out, however, is an international standard for the *substance* of patent laws. For example, the U.S. "first to invent" rule conflicts with the "first to file" rule used in most other countries. Also, countries often have very different definitions of what constitutes "novelty" under patent law.

Copyrights

The holder of a copyright owns the *particular tangible expression* of an idea, but not the underlying idea or method of operation. Abner Doubleday could copyright a book setting out his particular version of the rules of baseball, but he could not copyright the rules themselves nor could he require players to pay him a royalty. Similarly, the inventor of double-entry bookkeeping could copyright a pamphlet explaining his system but not the system itself.

Unlike patents, the ideas underlying copyrighted material need not be novel. Two movies that came out at the same time—*Armageddon* and *Deep Impact*—were both based on the idea of meteors destroying the earth. Neither violated the other's copyright because their *expressions* of the basic idea were different.

The Copyright Act protects literature, music, drama, choreography, pictures, sculpture, movies, recordings, architectural works, and "computer data bases, and computer programs to the extent that they incorporate authorship in the programmer's expression of original ideas, as distinguished from the ideas themselves."

A copyright is valid until 70 years after the death of the work's only or last living author. In the case of works owned by a corporation—such as Mickey Mouse—the copyright lasts 95 years from publication or 120 years from creation. Once the copyright expires, anyone may use the material. Mark Twain died in 1910, so anyone may now publish *Tom Sawyer* without permission and without paying a copyright fee.

A work is automatically copyrighted once it is in tangible form. For example, once a songwriter puts notes on paper, the work is copyrighted without further ado. But if she whistles a happy tune without writing it down, the song is not copyrighted, and anyone else can use it without permission. Registration with the Copyright Office of the Library of Congress is necessary only if the holder wishes to bring suit to enforce the copyright. Although authors still routinely place the copyright symbol (©) on their works, such a precaution is not necessary in the United States. However, some lawyers still recommend using the copyright symbol because other countries recognize it. Also, the penalties for intentional copyright infringement are heavier than for unintentional violations, and the presence of a copyright notice is evidence that the infringer's actions were intentional.

INFRINGEMENT

Anyone who uses copyrighted material without permission is violating the Copyright Act. **To prove a violation, the plaintiff must present evidence that the work was original** and that either:

- The infringer actually copied the work, or

- The infringer had access to the original and the two works are substantially similar.

A court may (1) prohibit the infringer from committing further violations, (2) order destruction of the infringing material, and (3) require the infringer to pay damages, profits earned, and attorney's fees. The story that opened this chapter illustrates how widespread copyright infringement has become.

FAIR USE

The purpose of copyright laws is to encourage creative work. A writer who can control, and profit from, artistic work will be inclined to produce more. If enforced oppressively, however, the copyright laws could stifle creativity by denying access to copyrighted work. **The doctrine of *fair use* permits limited use of copyrighted material without permission of the author for purposes such as criticism, comment, news reporting, scholarship, or research.** Courts generally do not permit a use that will decrease revenues from the original work by, say, competing with it. A reviewer is permitted, for example, to quote from a book without the author's permission, but, as we see below, online music companies cannot download entire versions of copyrighted songs.

Also under the fair use doctrine, faculty members are permitted to photocopy and distribute copyrighted materials to students, as long as the materials are brief and the teacher's action is spontaneous. If, over his breakfast coffee one morning, Professor Learned spots a terrific article in *Mad Magazine* that perfectly illustrates a point he intends to make in class that day, the fair use doctrine permits him to photocopy the page and distribute it to his class. However, under a misinterpretation of the fair use doctrine, some faculty were in the habit of routinely preparing lengthy course packets of copyrighted material without permission of the authors. In *Basic Books, Inc. v. Kinko's Graphic Corp.*[7], a federal court held that this practice violated the copyright laws because the material was more than one short passage and because it was sold to students. Now, when professors put together course packets, they (or the copy shop) must obtain permission and pay a royalty for the use of copyrighted material.

Parody

Parody has a long history in the United States—some of our most cherished songs have been the basis of parodies. Before Francis Scott Key wrote the words to the *Star-Spangled Banner*, other lyrics that mocked colonial governors had been set to the same music. (The tune was well known as a drinking song.) During the Civil War, this parody of the *Battle Hymn of the Republic* expressed anti-war sentiment:

---

[7] 758 F. Supp. 1522, 1991 U.S. Dist. LEXIS 3804 (S.D.N.Y. 1991). A federal appeals court reached the same result in *Princeton University Press v. Michigan Document Services, Inc.*, 99 F.3d 1381, 1996 U.S. App. LEXIS 29132 (6th Cir. 1996).

> Tell Abe Lincoln of Antietam's bloody dell
> Tell Abe Lincoln where a thousand heroes fell
> Tell Abe Lincoln and his gang to go to hell
> And we'll go marching home.

The Capitol Steps, a singing group in Washington, wrote this version of Rodgers and Hammerstein's song *My Favorite Things* to make fun of George W. Bush's environmental record:

> Strip mines on hillsides and derricks on beaches
> Clear cutting forests and spotted owl quiches
> So many smokestacks it makes your eyes sting
> These are some things favored by the right wing.

(For more parodies by the Capitol Steps, dance over to their Web site: http://www.capsteps.com/.) Have the Capitol Steps violated Rodgers and Hammerstein's copyright? After all, they did use their music. What if the words or opinions expressed in a parody are ones with which the original creators (or whoever now owns the rights) do not agree? The Capitol Steps appear to be on safe ground. The United States has a long history of protecting the expression of unpopular ideas.

The Supreme Court faced this issue in a case involving the rap group 2 Live Crew. The group wanted to record a parody of the song *Oh, Pretty Woman*, but the copyright holder refused permission. Undaunted, 2 Live Crew went ahead anyway, and the group was sued, all the way to the Supreme Court. The following lyrics are excerpted from the Court's decision in this case:

Original:	Parody:
Pretty Woman, walking down the street,	Big hairy woman you need to shave that stuff
Pretty Woman, the kind I like to meet,	Big hairy woman you know I bet it's tough
Pretty Woman, I don't believe you, you're not the truth,	Big hairy woman all that hair it ain't legit
No one could look as good as you Mercy	'Cause you look like "Cousin It" Big hairy woman

The Court decided in favor of 2 Live Crew, holding that **parody is a fair use of copyrighted material as long as the use of the original is not excessive.** The parody may copy enough to remind the audience of the original work but not so much that the parody harms the market for the original. The Supreme Court remanded the case to the trial court to determine if the 2 Live Crew version had copied too much or harmed the market for a nonparody rap version of *Oh, Pretty Woman*.[8] The two sides ultimately settled with 2 Live Crew agreeing to pay royalties.

LINKING

A *link* is a connection between two files on the Web or between two parts of the same file. The ability to link is fundamental to the World Wide Web. In a case that

---

[8] *Campbell v. Acuff-Rose Music, Inc.*, 510 U.S. 569, 114 S. Ct. 1164, 1994 U.S. LEXIS 2052 (1994).

shocked and frightened the computer world, a court recently held that linking could violate copyright law. However, the court then withdrew its opinion, leaving the law unsettled.

Leslie Kelly is a photographer specializing in images of the American West. He posted some of his pictures on his Web site. Arriba Soft Corp. operated an Internet search engine (at http://www.ditto.com) that searched for graphic images. It displayed its results in the form of small pictures called *thumbnails*. By double-clicking on one of these thumbnails, a large version of that same picture was automatically copied from the originating Web page onto Arriba's site, complete with Arriba advertising. The user might have thought that the image was, in fact, on Arriba's Web site. Kelly alleged that Arriba was violating his copyright. Arriba claimed that its activities were protected by the fair use doctrine. The trial court agreed with Arriba. The appeals court decided, however, that while the thumbnails were a fair use, the display of the larger image was a copyright violation.[9]

Critics of this decision argued that it threatened the use of linking, not just for pictures, but for text as well. If search engines were required to obtain the permission of every copyright holder before setting up a link, they would soon be out of business. Other commentators argued, however, that neither Arriba nor anyone else needed permission to create a link to Kelly's site; they were simply forbidden from competing with Kelly by offering his images in the same size and quality.

Seventeen months after its initial decision, the appeals court withdrew this opinion. It agreed that the thumbnails were protected by fair use, but held that the trial court should not have decided if the larger images were also protected because that issue had not been properly before the court.[10] If the trial court should not reach a decision on this issue, then neither should the appellate tribunal. This area of the law is now in a state of confusion, awaiting another case to bring clarity.

DIGITAL MUSIC AND MOVIES

As the chapter opener illustrates, much copyrighted music is now singing (for free) in cyberspace. Movie studios are facing the same issue with digitized movies on DVDs. A fierce war is currently raging in the entertainment world against online entrepreneurs (aka "pirates") who have figured out how to turn music and movies into downloadable files on the Internet.

Online Music

In one of the first cases to challenge this practice of downloading copyrighted files for free, UMG Recordings, Inc., charged MP3.com, Inc., with copyright infringement. MP3.com had uploaded tens of thousands of CDs onto its Web site. A service called My.MP3.com allowed subscribers to download files for free. The subscriber simply had to "prove" he owned a CD by inserting his copy into his CD-ROM drive for a few seconds. Thereafter, he could access this CD via the Internet from any computer in the world. MP3.com argued that it was doing nothing more than storing subscriber CDs and, anyway, its activities were protected

---

[9] *Kelly v. Arriba Soft Corporation*, 280 F.3d 934; 2002 U.S. App. LEXIS 1786, United States Court of Appeals (9th Cir 2002).

[10] *Kelly v. Arriba Soft Corporation*, 2003 U.S. App. LEXIS 13562.

under the fair use doctrine. UMG took a darker view, claiming that MP3.com was, in fact, replaying recordings it had copied without permission.

The court scolded MP3.com, saying "The complex marvels of cyberspatial communication may create difficult legal issues; but not in this case. Defendant's infringement of plaintiff's copyrights is clear." The court dismissed the fair use defense, holding that UMG has the right to decide how its property is used and is entitled to a license fee from MP3.com.[11]

MP3 had copied more than 40,000 CDs for distribution, but its business (and the damage it caused to the recording companies) was minuscule compared with Napster, a truly brilliant—or diabolic—innovation, depending on your perspective. Napster developed a so-called *peer-to-peer* file sharing system. Its software linked individual computers so that anyone could copy any song from any linked computer. Napster also maintained a directory to facilitate finding the right files. If you hankered after your own copy of Cole Porter's *True Love*, you could download versions by 10 different artists in about 10 seconds. At its peak, Napster had 38 million users.

Napster did real damage to the recording industry. For the first time ever, CD sales declined nationally. One study found that the decline was particularly sharp in areas around college campuses. Perhaps even more insidious, Napster convinced a whole generation that music was, and should be, free. While an older sibling might in her teens and twenties have purchased a thousand CDs, her younger brother would buy none at all.

Eighteen music studios sued Napster for copyright violations.[12] In its defense Napster claimed that it was protected under the fair use doctrine. The court disagreed, largely because Napster was competing with the music companies and reducing their revenues. **According to the court, Napster was harming the music market in at least two ways: it reduced audio CD sales among college students, and it raised barriers to entry for the music companies if they wanted to enter the online distribution business.** The court entered an injunction against Napster, and the company ultimately filed for bankruptcy.

No sooner had the music companies killed Napster than, like the multi-headed hydra, other, tougher competitors appeared. Napster was particularly vulnerable to court action because it maintained its directory on a central server that could easily be shut down. Other companies such as Gnutella and KaZaA were more difficult to attack because they did not need a central directory. In theory, for a lawsuit to be effective, the music companies would have to take action against each and every user. The KaZaA software has been downloaded 90 million times. As determined as ever, the Recording Industry Association of America has filed suit against three of these new peer-to-peer services: StreamCast Networks, Grokster, and KaZaA.

Has a verdict been reached in this case? What was the result?

Even if the suit against KaZaA and the others is successful, odds are that new companies will arise in their place. Therefore, the music industry is trying other approaches. Traditionally, it was reluctant to go after individual users (who might

---

[11] *UMG Recordings, Inc. v. MP3.com*, 92 F. Supp. 2d 349; 2000 U.S. Dist. LEXIS 5761 (S.D.N.Y. 2000).
[12] *A&M Records v. Napster*, 239 F.3d 1004, 2001 U.S. App. LEXIS 5446, United States Court of Appeals (9th Cir. 2001).

also be paying customers), but Sony recently asked colleges to take action against students who download copyrighted music. Some colleges have notified their students that if they violate copyright laws, they face the loss of campus computer privileges. The Recording Industry Association of America has also announced that it will begin filing suit against the individuals with the largest offerings of songs on KaZaA and other peer-to-peer services. Music companies have also tried introducing their own online music sites but, as the court observed in the *Napster* case, it is difficult to compete with a free service. Also, the Justice Department has notified the music companies that it is investigating these ventures for possible violation of the antitrust laws.

The Digital Millennium Copyright Act

The good news is that Mary Schmich wrote an influential article in the *Chicago Tribune*. The bad news is that people deleted her name, attributed the article to Kurt Vonnegut, and sent it around the world via e-mail. Tom Tomorrow's cartoon was syndicated to 100 newspapers, but, by the time the last papers received it, the cartoon had already gone zapping around cyberspace. Because his name had been deleted, some editors thought he had plagiarized it.

In response to such incidents, Congress passed the **Digital Millennium Copyright Act** (DMCA), which provides that:

- **It is illegal to delete copyright information, such as the name of the author or the title of the article.** It is also illegal to distribute false copyright information. Thus anyone who e-mailed Schmich's article without her name on it, or who claimed it was his own work, would be violating the law.

- **It is illegal to circumvent encryption or scrambling devices that protect copyrighted works.** For example, some software programs are designed so that they can only be copied once. Anyone who overrides this protective device to make another copy is violating the law. (The statute does permit purchasers of copyrighted software to make one backup copy.) If you buy a Disney DVD that prevents you from fastforwarding through commercials, you are violating the DMCA if you figure out how to do it anyway.

- **It is illegal to distribute tools and technologies used to circumvent encryption devices.** If you tell others how to fastforward through the Disney commercials, you have violated the statute.

The DMCA has been controversial. Its goal was laudable: to protect legitimate businesses from copyright pirates. However, opponents allege that:

- The DMCA interferes with legitimate scientific research. An organization called the Secure Digital Music Initiative (SDMI) developed a technology to encrypt digital music. It issued a public challenge to see if anyone could override the encryption. Edward Felten, a Princeton professor, did manage to circumvent the technology, but when he tried to present his results at an academic conference, the SDMI threatened him with suit for violating the DMCA. He ultimately was able to publish part of his research, but only after filing suit against SDMI.

- The DMCA interferes with legal activities. For example, copy-protected CDs prevent consumers from making copies for their own use. These copies are legal under the fair use doctrine.

With new technologies, finding the proper balance between the rights of those who create and those who purchase copyrighted material is increasingly troublesome. In the following case, movie studios sued under the DMCA to prevent an online magazine from posting a software program that could be used to copy DVDs.

YOU BE THE JUDGE

UNIVERSAL CITY STUDIOS, INC. V. ERIC CORLEY

273 F.3d 429, 2001 U.S. App. LEXIS 25330
United States Court of Appeals for the Second Circuit, 2001

FACTS: In 1996, movie studios developed the Content Scramble System (CSS), an encryption method to prevent the copying of DVDs. In 1997, the studios began releasing movies on DVDs. They quickly became a significant source of revenue. In 1999, Jon Johansen, a Norwegian teenager, created a program called DeCSS, which could bypass CSS. Johansen's goal was not to facilitate the illegal copying of DVDs but rather to develop a DVD player that worked on Linux, an alternative operating system that could not at that time play any DVDs. A DeCSS user could decrypt a DVD's CSS protection and copy the DVD onto his hard drive where it could be copied, manipulated, and transferred just like any other computer file.

Eric Corley published the print magazine *2600: The Hacker Quarterly* and an affiliated Web site, http://www.2600.com. Although the magazine and the Web site covered some issues of general interest to computer users—such as threats to online privacy—the focus of the publications was on computer security systems. Typical articles explained how to steal an Internet domain name and how to break into the computer systems at Federal Express. Corley's audience included serious computer science scholars, computer buffs intrigued by the challenge of trying to circumvent security devices, mischief-makers interested in disrupting computer operations, and thieves, including copyright infringers who wanted to acquire copyrighted material without paying for it.

Corley wrote an article about DeCSS for the magazine and posted it on his Web site. The article included a copy of DeCSS and links to other Web sites where DeCSS could be found. Eight movie studios brought suit against him seeking an injunction under the DMCA that would prohibit him from posting DeCSS on his Web site or from linking to any other Web site containing DeCSS. Corley argued that the DMCA was unconstitutional because computer code is "speech" entitled to protection under the First Amendment to the Constitution.

ISSUE: Was Corley's article entitled to protection under the First Amendment?

ARGUMENT FOR CORLEY: The studios are attempting to censor an article because it contains speech of which they disapprove. The purpose of the First Amendment is to protect speech, even when unpopular.

Censoring this type of free interchange of ideas will, in the long run, have a much greater impact than simply making DVDs more difficult to copy. All sorts of scientific research will be disrupted. After all, Johansen first developed the DeCSS program while working to improve Linux, which many consider to be the best hope for challenging Microsoft's monopoly of operating system software.

If the studios are to censor speech, they must do so by the least restrictive means available. In this case, that would mean going after people who illegally use DeCSS to copy and distribute movies. They are the lawbreakers, not Corley.

Prohibiting a Web site from publishing DeCSS is like prohibiting a newspaper from publishing the addresses of bookstores that happen to sell pornography. This would be a violation of the First Amendment and so is the prohibition against linking.

ARGUMENT FOR THE STUDIOS:

The First Amendment protects speech, but only as long as that speech does not cause unreasonable harm. Thus, it is illegal to distribute child pornography and to shout fire in a crowded theater. The DMCA is designed to prevent real harm to the entire entertainment industry. Corley is aiding and abetting thieves who want to steal intellectual property developed by studios at great expense.

The studios will certainly go after those who use DeCSS to copy movies illegally. But that is a difficult task indeed. If a thief illegally publishes a copyrighted book, it is relatively easy to trace the distribution source back to the printer. But to find every person who privately downloads DeCSS and copies a movie is virtually impossible.

DeCSS software is two things bundled together—both speech and function. What the studios are censoring is the function—the ability to copy illegally. In essence, this software is like a skeleton key that can open any lock. A law prohibiting skeleton keys that unlock jail cells would not be unconstitutional, even if the keys were printed with a slogan or other speech.

Corley argues that, because a newspaper has the right to publish the addresses of bookstores, he has the right to link to sites with DeCSS. The difference is that, if the police want to shut down a pornographic bookstore, they can easily find it. But the task of shutting down Web sites that post DeCSS is much more difficult and may indeed be impossible. ▰

INTERNATIONAL COPYRIGHT TREATIES

The Berne Convention requires member countries to provide automatic copyright protection to any works created in another member country. The protection does not expire until 50 years after the death of the author.[13] The WIPO Copyright Treaty and the WIPO Performances and Phonograms Treaty add computer programs, movies, and music to the list of copyrightable materials.

Trademarks

A trademark is any combination of words and symbols that a business uses to identify its products or services and distinguish them from others. Trademarks are important to both consumers and businesses. Consumers use trademarks to distinguish between competing products. People who feel that Nike shoes fit their feet best can rely on the Nike trademark to know they are buying the shoe they want. A business with a high-quality product can use a trademark to develop a loyal base of customers who are able to distinguish its product from another.

TYPES OF MARKS

There are four different types of marks:

* **Trademarks** are affixed to *goods* in interstate commerce.

---

[13] Under U.S. law, copyrights last 70 years. The United States must grant works created in other signatory countries a copyright that lasts either 50 years or the length of time granted in that country, whichever is longer, but in no case longer than 70 years.

- **Service marks** are used to identify services, not products. Fitness First, Burger King, and Weight Watchers are service marks. In this chapter the terms "trademark" and "mark" are used to refer to both trademarks and service marks.

- **Certification marks** are words or symbols used by a person or an organization to attest that products and services produced by others meet certain standards. The Good Housekeeping Seal of Approval means that the Good Housekeeping organization has determined that a product meets its standards.

- **Collective marks** are used to identify members of an organization. The Lions Club, the Girls Scouts of America, and the Masons are examples of collective marks.

Ownership and Registration

Under common law, the first person to use a mark in trade owns it. Registration with the federal government is not necessary. However, under the federal Lanham Act, the owner of a mark may register it on the Lanham Act Principal Register. A trademark owner may use the symbol ™ at any time, even before registering it, but not until the mark is registered can the symbol ® be placed next to it. Registration has several advantages:

- Even if a mark has been used in only one or two states, registration makes it valid nationally.

- Registration notifies the public that a mark is in use because anyone who applies for registration first searches the Public Register to ensure that no one else has rights to the mark.

- Five years after registration, a mark becomes virtually incontestable because most challenges are barred.

- The damages available under the Lanham Act are higher than under common law.

- The holder of a registered trademark generally has the right to use it as an Internet domain name.

Under the Lanham Act, the owner files an application with the PTO in Washington, D.C. The PTO will accept an application only if the owner has already used the mark attached to a product in interstate commerce or promises to use the mark within six months after the filing. In addition, the applicant must be the *first* to use the mark in interstate commerce. Initially, the trademark is valid for 10 years, but the owner can renew it for an unlimited number of 10-year terms as long as the mark is still in use. Trademark searches are free on PTO's Web site: http://www.uspto.gov/main/trademarks.htm.

Valid Trademarks

Words (Reebok), symbols (Microsoft's flying window logo), phrases ("Just do it"), shapes (a Coca-Cola bottle), sounds (NBC's three chimes), and even scents (plumeria blossoms on sewing thread) can be trademarked. **To be valid, a trademark must**

be distinctive; that is, the mark must clearly distinguish one product from another. There are five basic categories of distinctive marks:

- **Fanciful marks** are made-up words such as Converse or Saucony.

- **Arbitrary marks** use existing words that do *not* describe the product—Prince tennis racquets, for example. No one really thinks that these racquets are designed by or for royalty.

- **Suggestive marks** *indirectly* describe the product's function. Greyhound implies that the bus line is swift, and Coppertone suggests what customers will look like after applying the product.

- Marks with **secondary meaning** cannot, by themselves, be trademarked, unless they have been used so long that they are now associated with the product in the public's mind. When a film company released a movie called *Ape*, it used as an illustration a picture that looked like a scene from *King Kong*—a gigantic gorilla astride the World Trade Center in New York City. The court held that the movie posters of *King Kong* had acquired a secondary meaning in the mind of the public, so the *Ape* producers were forced to change their poster.[14]

- **Trade dress** is the image and overall appearance of a business or product. It may include size, shape, color, or texture. The Supreme Court held that a Mexican restaurant was entitled to protection under the Lanham Act for the shape and general appearance of the exterior of its building as well as the decor, menu, servers' uniforms, and other features reflecting the total image of the restaurant.[15]

The following categories are not distinctive and *cannot* be trademarked:

- **Similar to an Existing Mark.** To avoid confusion, the PTO will not grant a trademark that is similar to one already in existence on a similar product. Once the PTO had granted a trademark for "Pledge" furniture polish, it refused to trademark "Promise" for the same product. "Chat noir" and "black cat" were also too similar because one is simply a translation of the other. Houghton-Mifflin Co. sued to prevent a punk rock band from calling itself Furious George because the name is too similar to Curious George, the star of a series of children's books.

- **Generic Trademarks.** No one is permitted to trademark an item's ordinary name—"shoe" or "book," for example. Sometimes, however, a word begins as a trademark and later becomes a generic name. Zipper, escalator, aspirin, linoleum, thermos, yo-yo, band-aid, ping-pong, and nylon all started out as trademarks, but became generic. Once a name is generic, the owner loses the trademark because the name can no longer be used to distinguish one product from another—all products are called the same thing. That is why, in advertisements for Sanka, people ask for "a cup of Sanka-brand decaffeinated coffee." And why Xerox Corp. encourages people to say, "I'll photocopy this document," rather than "I'll xerox it." Martini, jeep, and rollerblade are trademarks that seem destined for generic status.

---

[14] *Paramount Pictures Corp. v. Worldwide Entertainment Corp.*, 2 Media L. Rep. 1311, 195 U.S.P.Q. (BNA) 539, 1977 U.S. Dist. LEXIS 17931 (S.D.N.Y. 1977).

[15] *Two Pesos, Inc. v. Taco Cabana, Inc.*, 505 U.S. 763, 112 S. Ct. 2753, 1992 U.S. LEXIS 4533 (1992).

- **Descriptive Marks.** Words cannot be trademarked if they simply describe the product—such as "low-fat," "green," or "crunchy." Descriptive words can, however, be trademarked if they do *not* describe that particular product because they then become distinctive rather than descriptive. "Blue Diamond" is an acceptable trademark for nuts as long as the nuts are neither blue nor diamond shaped.

- **Names.** The PTO generally will not grant a trademark in a surname because other people are already using it and have the right to continue. No one could register "Jefferson" as a trademark. However, a surname can be used as part of a longer title— "Jefferson Home Tours," for example. Similarly, no one can register a geographical name such as "Boston" unless it is also associated with another word, such as "Boston Ale."

- **Deceptive Marks.** The PTO will not register a mark that is deceptive. It refused to register a trademark with the words "National Collection and Credit Control" and an eagle superimposed on a map of the United States because this trademark gave the false impression that the organization was an official government agency.

- **Scandalous or Immoral Trademarks.** The PTO refused to register a mark that featured a nude man and woman embracing. In upholding the PTO's decision, the court was unsympathetic to arguments that this was the perfect trademark for a newsletter on sex.[16]

Microsoft introduced its Internet Explorer software to great fanfare. There was only one problem: SyNet, Inc., had trademarked the name a year before. What was Microsoft to do? First, it offered $75,000 to buy the rights to the name, but the owner of SyNet refused to sell. Then Microsoft claimed that Internet Explorer could not be trademarked at all because it was a descriptive mark. Microsoft argued that Internet Explorer simply described software for surfing the Net, just as chocolate fudge describes candy. However, a day after trial began in federal court in Chicago, SyNet accepted Microsoft's $5 million settlement offer.

In the following case, the Supreme Court decided whether a color could be trademarked.

QUALITEX & CO. V. JACOBSON PRODUCTS, INC.

514 U.S. 159, 115 S. Ct. 1300, 1995 U.S. LEXIS 2408
United States Supreme Court, 1995

FACTS: Since the 1950s, Qualitex has used a special shade of green-gold color on the pads that it makes for dry cleaning presses. After Jacobson Products (a Qualitex rival) began to use a similar shade on its own press pads, Qualitex registered its color as a trademark and filed suit against Jacobson for trademark infringement.

ISSUE: Does the Lanham Act permit a color to be trademarked?

EXCERPTS FROM JUSTICE BREYER'S DECISION: The language of the Lanham Act describes [trademarks] in the broadest of terms. It says that trademarks "include any word, name, symbol, or device, or any

---

16 *In re McGinley*, 660 F.2d 481, 211 U.S.P.Q. (BNA) 668, 1981 CCPA LEXIS 177 (C.C.P.A. 1981).

combination thereof." Since human beings might use as a "symbol" or "device" almost anything at all that is capable of carrying meaning, this language, read literally, is not restrictive. If a shape, a sound, and a fragrance can act as symbols why can a color not do the same?

We cannot find in the basic objectives of trademark law any obvious theoretical objection to the use of color alone as a trademark, where that color identifies and distinguishes a particular brand (and thus indicates its "source"). Indeed, the district court, in this case, entered findings that show Qualitex's green-gold press pad color has met these requirements. The green-gold color acts as a symbol. Having developed secondary meaning (for customers identified the green-gold color as Qualitex's), it identifies the press pad's source.

Jacobson says that, if the law permits the use of color as a trademark, it will produce uncertainty and unresolvable court disputes about what shades of a color a competitor may lawfully use. Because lighting (morning sun, twilight mist) will affect perceptions of protected color, competitors and courts will suffer from "shade confusion" as they try to decide whether use of a similar color on a similar product does, or does not, confuse customers and thereby infringe a trademark. We do not believe, however, that color, in this respect, is special. Courts traditionally decide quite difficult questions about whether two words or phrases or symbols are sufficiently similar, in context, to confuse buyers. They have had to compare, for example, such words as "Bonamine" and "Dramamine" (motion-sickness remedies); "Huggies" and "Dougies" (diapers); "Cheracol" and "Syrocol" (cough syrup).

We conclude that the Ninth Circuit erred in barring Qualitex's use of color as a trademark. ◢

INFRINGEMENT

To win an infringement suit, the trademark owner must show that the defendant's trademark is likely to deceive customers about who has made the goods or provided the services. The rightful owner is entitled to (1) an injunction prohibiting further violations, (2) destruction of the infringing material, (3) up to three times actual damages, (4) any profits the infringer earned on the product, and (5) attorney's fees.

Many Web sites give away free information and (try to) make money selling advertisements. To be successful, the sites must attract hordes of visitors. What can they do to lure cybersurfers? Some site operators embed words like "sex" and "nudity" in invisible coding, even if the sites have nothing to do with sex. Although visitors cannot see the words, search engines will still call up the site. Not content with these generic lures, Calvin Designer Label (no relation to Calvin Klein, the clothing designer) embedded the words "Playboy" and "Playmate" in machine-readable code on its Web site. A federal court entered a restraining order preventing Calvin Designer from infringing on Playboy's trademarks.[17] ▪

FEDERAL TRADEMARK DILUTION ACT OF 1995

Before Congress passed the Federal Trademark Dilution Act of 1995, a trademark owner could win an infringement lawsuit only by proving that consumers would be deceived about who had really made the product. **The new statute prevents others from using a trademark in a way that dilutes its value**, even though consumers are not confused about the origin of the product. Thus, for example, Hasbro, Inc., trademarked "Candyland" for use on a children's board game.

---

[17] *Playboy Enterprises, Inc. v. Calvin Designer Label*, 985 F. Supp. 1220, 1997 U.S. Dist. LEXIS 14345 (N.D. Cal. 1997).

Internet Entertainment Group, Ltd., used the name Candyland to identify a sexually explicit Internet site. Although consumers were unlikely to think that Hasbro had developed the Candyland site, the court held that Internet Entertainment had diluted the value of the Candyland trademark.[18]

DOMAIN NAMES

Internet addresses, known as domain names, can be immensely valuable. Suppose you want to buy a new pair of jeans. Without thinking twice, you type in http://www.jcrew.com and there you are, ready to order. What if that address took you to a different site altogether, say, the personal site of one Jackie Crew? The store might lose out on a sale. Companies not only want to own their own domain name, they want to prevent complaint sites such as http://www.untied.com (about United Airlines). Generic domain names can be valuable, too. Shopping.com paid $750,000 to acquire its domain name from the previous (lucky) owner.

Who has the right to a domain name? In the beginning, the National Science Foundation, which maintained the Internet, granted Network Solutions, Inc. (NSI), a private company, the right to allocate domain names. NSI charged no fee for domain names and the rule was "first come, first served." Then so-called "cybersquatters" began to register domain names, not to use, but to sell to others. Someone, for example, tried to sell the name "Bill Gates" for $1 million.

In response to complaints, NSI began suspending any domain name that was challenged by the holder of a registered trademark. For example, NSI would not allow Princeton Review to keep kaplan.com, which Princeton had acquired simply to inconvenience its arch-rival in the test preparation business. Congress then passed the **Anticybersquatting Consumer Protection Act, which permits both trademark owners and famous people to sue anyone who registers their name as a domain name in "bad faith."** The rightful owner of a trademark is entitled to damages of up to $100,000.

Although the goal of this statute was laudable, in practice it sometimes looked like a heavy club in the hands of corporations who used it to threaten innocent holders of domain names. The maker of Pokey toys threatened a boy who had registered his nickname, Pokey, and Archie Comics went after a girl named Veronica. The Web site http://www.chillingeffects.org maintains a database of so-called "cease and desist" letters sent to holders of domain names. To discover if your name has been taken, explore http://www.verisign.com.

As both the value and the number of domain names soared, the U.S. government transferred management of the Internet, including the allocation of names, to a private, nonprofit, international organization, the Internet Corporation for Assigned Names and Numbers (ICANN). Now, disputes over domain names can be decided by arbitration under ICANN's Uniform Domain Name Dispute Resolution Policy rather than by litigation under the Anticybersquatting Consumer Protection Act.

To bring a case under the ICANN policy, the complainant (i.e., the plaintiff) must allege that:

- The domain name creates confusion because it is similar to a registered trademark.

---

[18] *Hasbro, Inc. v. Internet Entertainment Group*, 1996 U.S. Dist LEXIS 11626 (N.D. Wash. 1996).

- The respondent (i.e., the defendant) has no legitimate reason to use the domain name.

- The respondent registered the domain name in bad faith. If the respondent is a competitor of the complainant and has acquired the domain name to disrupt the complainant's business (à la Princeton Review), that is evidence of bad faith. So is an attempt by the respondent to sell the name to the complainant.

If the complainant wins, it is entitled either to take over the domain name or to cancel it.

For example, in a dispute over wal-martsucks.com, the WIPO arbitrator ordered that the name be transferred to Wal-Mart. The respondent had demonstrated his bad faith by attempting to sell the name for $530,000. In a similar case, however, the WIPO arbitrator found for a respondent who had registered Wallmartcanadasucks.com. In this case, the respondent had not tried to sell the name and was using the Web site to criticize Wal-Mart. As the arbitrator stated in his opinion: "Posting defamatory material on a Web site would not justify revocation of a domain name. The Policy should not be used to shut down robust debate and criticism." (These cases, and others, are available at http://arbiter.wipo.int/domains/search/index.html.)

Critics have complained that WIPO arbitrators unfairly favor trademark holders, who win roughly 81 percent of the cases they bring. (A study of this issue is available at http://www.lawbytes.com.) Either party has the option before or after an ICANN arbitration to litigate the issue in court. Of course, litigation is slower and more expensive.

Our discussion thus far has been about registering a trademark as a domain name. Sometimes businesses want to do the opposite—trademark a domain name. The PTO will issue such a trademark only for services offered via the Internet. Thus it trademarked "eBay" for "on-line trading services in which seller posts items to be auctioned and bidding is done electronically." The PTO will not trademark a domain name that is merely an address and does not identify the service provided.

INTERNATIONAL TRADEMARK TREATIES

Under the Madrid Agreement, any trademark registered with the international registry is valid in all signatory countries. (The United States is a signatory.) The Trademark Law Treaty simplifies and harmonizes the process of applying for trademarks around the world.

Trade Secrets

As the following news report indicates, trade secrets can be a company's most valuable asset.

NEWSWORTHY

At Slick 50, Inc., sneakiness is company policy. The handful of employees privy to the secret formula for the fancy engine treatment, which has nearly $80 million in annual sales, must swear a notarized oath of silence. Only those few who need to know are in possession of the combination to the fireproof vault with eight-inch-thick walls in which the sole printed copy of the Slick 50 recipe is housed. They alone are entrusted with the multiple passwords to the specially encoded database where the computer version is filed. When the company ships ingredients to hired blenders around the country, it dispatches them in odd allotments of containers identified only by numbered codes and mixing instructions. Masking chemicals are included in every batch so that chemical analysis to determine exactly what it takes to concoct the stuff is virtually impossible.

Despite the company's precautions, an employee at a Slick processing plant in the Cayman Islands was able to figure out the formula. He threatened to disclose it unless the company paid him $2.5 million. Fortunately for the company, when the extortionist faxed his demands, he included a cover page listing his mailbox address. The police arrested him immediately. As criminals go, he was not very slick.[19] ◾◾

Although a company can patent some types of trade secrets, it may be reluctant to do so because patent registration requires that the formula be disclosed publicly. In addition, patent protection expires after 20 years. Some types of trade secrets cannot be patented—customer lists, business plans, manufacturing processes, and marketing strategies.

It has been estimated that the theft of trade secrets costs U.S. businesses $100 billion a year. In response, the National Conference of Commissioners on Uniform State Laws drafted the Uniform Trade Secrets Act (UTSA), which most states have now adopted. **A trade secret is a formula, device, process, method, or compilation of information that, when used in business, gives the owner an advantage over competitors who do not know it.** In determining if information is a trade secret, courts consider:

- How difficult (and expensive) was the information to obtain? Was it readily available from other sources?

- Does the information create an important competitive advantage?

- Did the company make a reasonable effort to protect it?

Anyone who misappropriates a trade secret is liable to the owner for (1) actual damages, (2) unjust enrichment, or (3) a reasonable royalty. If the misappropriation was willful or malicious, the court may award attorney's fees and double damages. A jury recently awarded Avery Dennison Corp. $40 million in damages from a competitor that had misappropriated secret information about the adhesives used in self-stick stamps.

The following case deals with a typical issue: Are customer lists trade secrets?

MORLIFE, INC. V. PERRY

56 Cal. App. 4th 1514, 1997 Cal. App. LEXIS 648
Court of Appeal of California, 1997

FACTS: Morlife, Inc., repaired roofs on commercial buildings. Carl Bowersmith was production manager, and Lloyd Perry was a sales representative. Perry signed an agreement not to disclose information about Morlife's customers if he ever left the company. When the two men resigned to start a competing business, Perry took with him the collection of business cards he had accumulated while at

---

[19] Anne Reifenberg, "How Secret Formula for Coveted Slick 50 Fell into Bad Hands," *The Wall Street Journal*, Oct. 25, 1995, p. A1. Republished with permission of The Wall Street Journal; permission conveyed through the Copyright Clearance Center, Inc.

Morlife. These cards represented approximately 75 to 80 percent of the company's customers. Perry immediately began soliciting these clients, and 32 switched to him.

Morlife filed suit, claiming that Perry had violated the Uniform Trade Secrets Act. The court found for Morlife, awarded it $39,293.47 in damages, and ordered Perry not to use Morlife's trade secrets.

ISSUE: Did Perry violate the Uniform Trade Secrets Act?

EXCERPTS FROM JUDGE RUVOLO'S DECISION: [W]e acknowledge the important legal right of persons to engage in businesses and occupations of their choosing. Some would count this freedom as one of the most cherished commercial rights we possess. Yet also fundamental to the preservation of our free market economic system is the concomitant right to have the ingenuity and industry one invests in the success of the business or occupation protected from the gratuitous use of that "sweat-of-the-brow" by others.

[C]ourts are reluctant to protect customer lists to the extent they embody information which is "readily ascertainable" through public sources, such as business directories. On the other hand, where the employer has expended time and effort identifying customers with particular needs or characteristics, courts will prohibit former employees from using this information to capture a share of the market. As a general principle, the more difficult information is to obtain, and the more time and resources expended by an employer in gathering it, the more likely a court will find such information constitutes a trade secret.

In the case at bar, Morlife's president testified about the difficulty encountered by sales personnel in getting past the "gatekeepers" and identifying and gaining access to the actual decisionmakers with the authority to purchase roofing services. Morlife developed its customer base by investment in telemarketing, sales visits, mailings, advertising, membership in trade associations, referrals and research. Out of 100 persons contacted by the telemarketing department, only about 10 result in contacts. He estimated an initial visit by a Morlife salesperson costs the company $238.

The record amply supports that reasonable steps were taken by Morlife to protect the information from disclosure. [C]ustomer information was stored on computer with restricted access. Moreover, in its employment contract signed by Perry, Morlife included a confidentiality provision expressly referring to its customer names and telephone numbers. The Morlife employee handbook contained an express statement that employees shall not use or disclose Morlife secrets or confidential information subsequent to their employment including "lists of present and future customers."

The judgment is affirmed. ◢

Only civil penalties are available under the Uniform Trade Secrets Act. To safeguard national security and maintain the nation's industrial and economic edge, Congress passed the **Economic Espionage Act of 1996, which makes a criminal offense of any attempt to steal trade secrets for the benefit of someone other than the owner, including for the benefit of any foreign government.** Kai-Lo Hsu was charged under this statute for his alleged attempt to steal the formula for manufacturing Taxol, an anticancer drug produced by Bristol-Myers. His employer, Yuen Foong Paper Co. in Taiwan, had directed him to steal this information because it sought to diversify into biotechnology and obtain technology from other countries.[20]

 To be protected under the UTSA, the owner of a trade secret must make a reasonable effort to keep the information confidential. For example, a company required employees to sign an agreement promising to keep trade secrets confidential, but the agreement did not list the particular information the firm considered secret. Instead of destroying important diagrams, the company simply put them in the

---

[20] *United States v. Kai-Lo Hsu*, 155 F.3d 189, 1998 U.S. App. LEXIS 20810 (3rd Cir. 1998).

trash. Nor had it marked its technical documents "confidential." The court held that the company had not met the standards of the UTSA and was therefore not entitled to trade secret protection.[21]

In formulating a policy on trade secrets, a company should:

- Identify specific information that is a trade secret.

- Set out the company's trade secret policy in writing (including what is secret) and require employees to sign this agreement. The company cannot simply identify everything as secret. Both employees and courts are less likely to treat a policy seriously if the company makes no effort to distinguish the important from the trivial.

- Allow access only to those employees who need the information to perform their jobs.

- Remind employees who leave the firm that they are still bound by the trade secret agreement.

Chapter Conclusion

Intellectual property takes many different forms. It can be an Internet domain name, a software program, a cartoon character, a formula for motor oil, or a process for making anticancer drugs. Because of its great variety, intellectual property is difficult to protect. Yet, for many individuals and companies, intellectual property is the most valuable asset they will ever own. As its economic value increases, so does the need to understand the rules of intellectual property law.

Chapter Review

	Patent	Copyright	Trademark	Trade Secrets
Protects:	Mechanical, electrical, chemical inventions; processes; machines; composition of matter; designs; plants	The tangible expression of an idea, but not the idea itself	Words and symbols that a business uses to identify its products or services	A formula, device, process, method, or compilation of information that, when used in business, gives the owner an advantage over competitors who do not know it
Requirements for Legal Protection:	Application approved by PTO	An item is automatically copyrighted once it is in tangible form	Use is the only requirement; registration is not necessary but does offer some benefits	Must be kept confidential

table continued on next page

---

[21] *Electro-Craft Corp. v. Controlled Motion, Inc.*, 332 N.W.2d 890, 1983 Minn. LEXIS 1127 (Minn. 1983).

	Patent	Copyright	Trademark	Trade Secrets
Duration:	20 years after the application is filed (14 years from date of issuance for a design patent)	70 years after the death of the work's only or last living author or, for a corporation, 95 years from publication	Valid for 10 years but the owner can renew for an unlimited number of terms as long as the mark is still being used	As long as it is kept confidential

Practice Test

1. For many years, the jacket design for *Webster's Ninth New Collegiate Dictionary* featured a bright red background. The front was dominated by a "bull's eye" logo. The center of the bull's eye was white with the title of the book in blue. Merriam-Webster registered this logo as a trademark. Random House published a dictionary with a red dust jacket, the title in large black and white letters, and Random House's "house" logo—an angular drawing of a house—in white. What claim might Merriam-Webster make against Random House? Would it be successful?

2. "Hey, Paula," a pop hit that spent months on the music charts, was back on the radio 30 years later, but in a form the song's author never intended. Talk-show host Rush Limbaugh played a version with the same music as the original but with lyrics that poked fun at President Bill Clinton's alleged sexual misconduct with Paula Jones. Has Limbaugh violated the author's copyright?

3. From the following description of Jean-Pierre Foissey's activities one evening, can you guess what he is doing and why?

   Mr. Foissey waits until sundown. Then it is time to move. A friend whom he employs drops him off by car near the plum orchard, turning off the headlights as they approach. Mr. Foissey and another operative move quickly through adjacent cornfields and enter the orchard, careful not to leave footprints. Armed with a flashlight, his associate crawls through the orchard reading aloud the numbers on labels attached to the trees by the grower. Mr. Foissey picks leaves off the trees and marks the tree numbers on them. He takes those leaves back to an expert who will examine their size, shape, color, and texture, and also test their DNA.[22]

4. Rebecca Reyher wrote (and copyrighted) a children's book entitled *My Mother Is the Most Beautiful Woman in the World*. The story was based on a Russian folktale told to her by her own mother. Years later, the children's TV show *Sesame Street* televised a skit entitled "The Most Beautiful Woman in the World." The *Sesame Street* version took place in a different locale and had fewer frills, but the sequence of events in both stories was identical. The author of the Sesame Street script denied he had ever seen Reyher's book but said his skit was based on a story told to his sister some 20 years before. Has *Sesame Street* infringed Reyher's copyright?

5. Roger Schlafly applied for a patent for two prime numbers. (A prime number cannot be evenly divided by any number other than itself and 1, for example, 3, 7, 11, 13.) Schlafly's numbers are a bit longer—one is 150 digits, the other is 300. His numbers, when used together, can help perform the type of mathematical operation necessary for exchanging coded messages by computer. Should the PTO issue this patent?

6. DatagraphiX manufactured and sold computer graphics equipment that allowed users to transfer large volumes of information directly from computers to microfilm. Customers were required to keep maintenance documentation on-site for the DatagraphiX service personnel. The service manual carried this legend: "No

---

[22] Thomas Kamm, "Patented Plums Give French Fruit Sleuth His Raison D'être," *The Wall Street Journal*, Sep. 18, 1995, p. A1.

other use, direct or indirect, of this document or of any information derived therefrom is authorized. No copies of any part of this document shall be made without written approval by DatagraphiX." Additionally, on every page of the maintenance manual, the company placed warnings that the information was proprietary and not to be duplicated. Frederick J. Lennen left DatagraphiX to start his own company that serviced DatagraphiX equipment. Can DatagraphiX prevent Lennen from using its manuals?

7. A man asked a question of the advice columnist at his local newspaper. His wife had thought of a clever name for an automobile. He wanted to know if there was any way they could own or register the name so that no one else could use it. If you were the columnist, how would you respond?

8. Babe Ruth was one of the greatest baseball players of all time. After Ruth's death, his daughters registered the words "Babe Ruth" as a trademark. MacMillan, Inc., published a baseball calendar that contained three Babe Ruth photos. Ruth's daughters did not own the specific photographs, but they objected to the use of Ruth's likeness. As holders of the Babe Ruth trademark, do his daughters have the right to prevent others from publishing pictures of Ruth without their permission?

9. Harper & Row signed a contract with former President Gerald Ford to publish his memoirs. As part of the deal, the two agreed that *Time* magazine could print an excerpt from the memoirs shortly before the book was published. *Time* was to pay $25,000 for this right. Before *Time* published its version, *Nation* magazine published an *unauthorized* excerpt. *Time* canceled its article and refused to pay the $25,000. Harper sued *Nation* for copyright infringement. What was *Nation*'s defense? Was it successful?

10. Frank B. McMahon wrote one of the first psychology textbooks to feature a light and easily readable style. He also included many colloquialisms and examples that appealed to a youthful student market. Charles G. Morris wrote a psychology textbook that copied McMahon's style. Has Morris infringed McMahon's copyright?

11. **ETHICS** After Edward Miller left his job as a salesperson at the New England Insurance Agency, Inc., he took some of his New England customers to his new employer. At New England, the customer lists had been kept in file cabinets. Although the company did not restrict access to these files, it claimed there was a "you do not peruse my files and I do not peruse yours" understanding. The lists were not marked "confidential" or "not to be disclosed." Did Miller steal New England's trade secrets? Whether or not he violated the law, was it ethical for him to use this information at his new job?

12. **YOU BE THE JUDGE WRITING PROBLEM** Three inventors developed a software program that generated a particularly clear screen display on a computer. The PTO refused to issue a patent for this software. Do the inventors have a right to a patent? **Argument for the PTO:** This software is merely a series of mathematical formulas that cannot be patented. **Argument for the inventors:** The program is not merely a mathematical concept or an abstract idea, but rather a specific machine to produce a useful, concrete, and tangible result.

13. **ROLE REVERSAL** Draft a multiple-choice question that focuses on an issue of copyright law.

Internet Research Problem

Think of a name for an interesting new product. Click on SEARCH Trademarks at http://www.uspto.gov/main/trademarks.htm to see if this name is available as a trademark. Also look at http://www.verisign.com to see if it is available as an Internet domain name.

You can find further practice problems in the **Online Quiz** at http://beatty.westbuslaw.com **or in the Study Guide that accompanies this text.**

Property

Charley lives in retirement in his modest bungalow, counting pennies to make his meager savings last. Then everything changes—or does it? He is playing bridge with three friends: a rabbi, a bishop, and a banker. As rain beats against the roof and everyone murmurs about possible flooding, the banker suddenly announces to the astonished group that he is obscenely rich and is going to give $100,000 to everyone at the table. "Meet me at the bank tomorrow at 10:00, and the money is yours." Shouts! Hugs! Tears!

That night, as rain continues to lash the house, Charley smiles in his sleep, dreaming that he is floating in a tropical paradise. He awakens to discover that he *is* floating. His bedroom is filled with water, and Charley's head is now pressing against the ceiling. To avoid a flooding catastrophe, the Power Company has released a nearby dam, inundating 150 acres. The flood level on Charley's property is 16 feet and rising. Charley squirms through a broken window and escapes from his uninsured house just as it disappears beneath roiling black water.

The next morning, Charley, sneezing, arrives at the bank, where the bishop and rabbi grimly announce that the banker died before he could sign the three cashier's checks. There is no money. Charley, dazed and distraught, sues the Power Company for the damage to his house compensation and recovers—nothing. The company was *legally entitled* to destroy his house! Desperate, he seeks his $100,000 from the bank. Read on for the result.

A bewildering two days for Charley, but instructive for us, as we have glimpsed two issues of property law. The Power Company was entitled to destroy his house if it chose, because it owned an *easement*. The banker's promise will be settled according to the law of *gifts*. Our survey will focus on three primary topics: real property, landlord-tenant law, and personal property. ▪

REAL PROPERTY

Nature of Real Property

We need to define a few terms. A **grantor** is an owner who conveys his property, or some interest in it, to someone else, called the **grantee**. If you sell your house to Veronica, you are the grantor and she is the grantee. Real property may be any of the following:

- **Land.** Land is the most common and important form of real property. In England, land was historically the greatest source of wealth and social status, far more important than industrial or commercial enterprises. As a result, the law of real property has been of paramount importance for nearly 1,000 years, developing very gradually to reflect changing conditions. Some real property terms sound medieval for the simple reason that they *are* medieval. (For a fascinating look at the English and Roman roots of our property law, dig down to http://www.libertystory.net and find the link to "Ancient Romans contributions to private property rights.")

- **Buildings.** Buildings are real property. Houses, office buildings, and factories all fall (or stand) in this category.

- **Subsurface Rights.** In most states, the owner of the land also owns anything under the surface, down to the center of the earth. In some cases the subsurface rights may be worth far more than the surface land, for example, if there is oil or gold underfoot. Although the landowner generally owns these rights, she may sell them, while retaining ownership of the surface land.

- **Air Rights.** The owner of land owns the air space above the land. Suppose you own an urban parking lot. The owner of an adjacent office building wishes to build a walkway across your parking lot to join her building with a neighboring skyscraper. The office owner needs your permission to build across the air space and will expect to pay you a handsome fee for the privilege.

- **Plant Life.** Plant life growing on land is real property, whether the plants are naturally occurring, such as trees, or cultivated crops. When a landowner sells his property, plant life is automatically included in the sale, unless the parties agree otherwise.

- **Fixtures.** Fixtures are goods that have become attached to real property. A house (which is real property) contains many fixtures. The furnace and heating ducts were goods when they were manufactured and when they were sold to the builder, because they were movable. But when the builder attached them to the house, the items became fixtures. By contrast, neither the refrigerator nor the grand piano is a fixture.

When an owner sells real property, the buyer normally takes the fixtures, unless the parties specify otherwise. Sometimes it is difficult to determine whether something is a fixture. The general rule is this: **an object is a fixture if a reasonable person would consider the item to be a permanent part of the property,** taking into account attachment, adaptation, and other objective manifestations of permanence:

- *Attachment.* If an object is attached to property in such a way that removing it would damage the property, it is probably a fixture. Heating ducts could be removed from a house, but only by ripping open walls and floors, so they are fixtures.

- *Adaptation.* Something that is made or adapted especially for attachment to the particular property is probably a fixture, such as custom-made bookshelves fitted in a library.

- *Other Manifestations of Permanence.* If the owner of the property clearly intends the item to remain permanently, it is probably a fixture. Suppose a home owner constructs a large concrete platform in his backyard, then buys a heavy metal shed and puts it on the platform. His preparatory work indicates that he expects the shed to remain permanently, and a court would likely declare it a fixture.

Estates in Real Property

Use and ownership of real estate can take many different legal forms. A person may own property outright, having the unrestricted use of the land and an unlimited right to sell it. However, someone may also own a lesser interest in real property. For example, you could inherit the *use* of a parcel of land during your lifetime, but have no power to leave the land to your heirs. Or you could retain ownership and possession of some land yet allow a corporation to explore for oil and drill wells. The different rights that someone can hold in real property are known as **estates** or **interests**. Both terms simply indicate specified rights in property.

FREEHOLD ESTATES

The owner of a freehold estate has the present right to possess the property and to use it in any lawful way she wants. The three most important freehold estates are (1) fee simple absolute, (2) fee simple defeasible, and (3) life estate.

Fee Simple Absolute

A fee simple absolute provides the owner with the greatest possible control of the property. This is the most common form of land ownership. Suppose Cecily inherits a fee simple interest in a 30-acre vineyard. She may use the land for any purpose that the law allows. She may continue to raise grapes, or, if she hates wine, she may rip up the vines and build a condominium complex. Although zoning laws may regulate her use, nothing in Cecily's estate itself limits her use of the land. Cecily may pass on to her heirs her entire estate, that is, her full fee simple absolute.

Fee Simple Defeasible

Other estates contain more limited rights than the fee simple absolute. Wily establishes the Wily Church of Perfection. Upon his death, Wily leaves a 100-acre estate to the church for as long as it keeps the name "Wily Church of Perfection." Wily has included a significant limitation in the church's ownership. The church has a fee simple defeasible.

A fee simple defeasible may terminate upon the occurrence of some limiting event. If the congregation decides to rename itself the Happy Valley Church of Perfection, the church automatically loses its estate in the 100 acres. Ownership of the land then **reverts** to Wily's heirs, meaning title goes back to them. Because the heirs might someday inherit the land, they are said to have a *future interest* in the 100 acres. A landowner may create a fee simple defeasible to ensure that property is used in a particular way, or is *not* used in a specified manner. In the following case, a California city was surprised to learn that this ancient doctrine still has plenty of life.

WALTON V. CITY OF RED BLUFF

2 Cal. App. 4th 117, 3 Cal. Rptr. 2d 275, 1991 Cal. App. LEXIS 1474
California Court of Appeal, 1991

FACTS: In 1908 and 1916, Mrs. Elizabeth Kraft and her son, Edward Kraft, granted to the city of Red Bluff two adjoining properties, with buildings, for use as a public library. The grants from the Krafts required continuous use as a public library and stated that the property would return to the Kraft family if the city ever used it for other purposes.

In 1986, Red Bluff decided that the buildings were too small for its needs and moved all of the books to a new building nearby. The city used the Kraft property for other civic purposes such as town meetings, social gatherings, and school tutoring. Herbert Kraft Walton, a descendant and heir, filed suit seeking to have the property reconveyed to him. The trial court found for Red Bluff, and Walton appealed.

ISSUE: Did Red Bluff violate the terms of the grants, so the property must now revert to Walton?

EXCERPTS FROM JUDGE CARR'S DECISION: The grants provide in part: "If the property herein conveyed shall at any time be abandoned by the said Town of Red Bluff, . . . or if the said property shall cease to be used, for library purposes, by said Town, . . . or shall be put to [any] use other [than] the uses and purposes herein specifically referred

to, . . . then the grant and conveyance herein made shall cease and terminate, and the title to the said property and all the improvements thereon shall at once revert to [the Kraft family].

Red Bluff admits all the books were removed from the library as of September 1986. The trial court framed the issue as one of abandonment. But the grantors specified that "if the said property shall cease to be used, for library purposes" the grants terminate.

Whether Red Bluff intended to "abandon" the use purpose of the property or not, it removed the books and stopped using the premises for library purposes. The grants defined library purposes broadly to include various educational endeavors, but there is no evidence any of these other activities took place. It stopped using the grant for library purposes and the property must go back to the Kraft heir.

At oral argument Red Bluff focussed on the "changed conditions" doctrine. The power of termination expires when it becomes "obsolete." In a leading case involving a covenant restricting the use of lots to residential purposes it was said that "where there has been a change in the uses to which the property in the neighborhood is being put, so that such property is no longer residence property, it would be unjust, oppressive, and inequitable to give effect to the restrictions, if such change has resulted from causes other than their breach." In this case the alleged change in circumstance is that Red Bluff needs a bigger, modern library building, not that the present building cannot be used for the purposes of the grant or that the use of surrounding property makes operation of a library impracticable. In these circumstances there is nothing inequitable about enforcing the restriction in the grant.

The judgment is *reversed* with directions to the trial court to enter a judgment [granting title to] Walton. ◢

Life Estate

A life estate is exactly what you would think: **an estate for the life of some named person**. For example, Aretha owns Respect Farm, and in her will she leaves it to Max, for his lifetime. Max is the **life tenant**. He is entitled to live on the property and work it as a normal farm during his lifetime, though he is obligated to maintain it properly. The moment Max dies, the farm reverts to Aretha or her heirs.

CONCURRENT ESTATES

When two or more people own real property at the same time, they have concurrent estates. In a **tenancy in common**, the owners have an equal interest in the entire property. Each co-tenant has the right to sell her interest to someone else, or to leave it to her heirs upon her death. A **joint tenancy** is similar, except that upon the death of one joint tenant (owner), his interest passes *to the surviving joint tenants*, not to his heirs.

To provide special rights for married couples, some states have created **tenancy by the entirety** and **community property**. These forms of ownership allow one spouse to protect some property from the other, and from the other's creditors.

Condominiums and **cooperatives** are most common in apartment buildings with multiple units, though they can be used in other settings, such as a cluster of houses on a single parcel of land. In a condominium, the owner of the apartment typically has a fee simple absolute in his particular unit. He is normally entitled to sell or lease the unit, must pay taxes on it, and may receive the normal tax deduction if he is carrying a mortgage. All unit owners belong to a condominium association, which manages the common areas. In a cooperative, the residents generally do not own their particular unit. Instead, they are shareholders in a corporation that owns the building and leases specified units to the shareholders.

Nonpossessory Interests

All of the estates and interests that we have examined thus far focused on one thing: possession of the land. Now we look at interests that *never* involve possession. These interests may be very valuable, even though the holder never lives on the land.

EASEMENTS

The Alabama Power Co. drove a flatbed truck over land owned by Thomas Burgess, damaging the property. The power company did this to reach its power lines and wooden transmission poles. Burgess had never given Alabama Power permission to enter his land, and he sued for the damage that the heavy trucks caused. He recovered—nothing. Alabama Power had an easement to use Burgess's land.

An easement gives one person the right to enter land belonging to another and make a limited use of it, without taking anything away. Burgess had bought his land from a man named Denton, who years earlier had sold an easement to Alabama Power. The easement gave the power company the right to construct several transmission poles on one section of Denton's land and to use reasonable means to reach the poles. Alabama Power owned that easement forever, and when Burgess bought the land, he took it subject to the easement. Alabama Power drove its trucks across a section of land where the power company had never gone before, and the easement did not explicitly give the company this right. But the court found that the company had no other way to reach its poles, and therefore the easement allowed this use. Burgess is stuck with his uninvited guest as long as he owns the land.[1]

Property owners normally create easements in one of two ways. A **grant** occurs when a landowner expressly intends to convey an easement to someone else. This is how Alabama Power acquired its easement. A **reservation** occurs when an owner sells land but keeps some right to enter the property. A farmer might sell 40 acres to a developer but reserve an easement giving him the right to drive his equipment across a specified strip of the land.

In this chapter's opening scenario, the Power Company had a flood easement on Charley's property. If Charley had read the following case, he might not have bought the land.

CARVIN V. ARKANSAS POWER AND LIGHT

14 F.3d 399, 1993 U.S. App. LEXIS 33986
United States Court of Appeals for the Eighth Circuit, 1993

FACTS: Between 1923 and 1947, Arkansas Power & Light (AP&L) constructed several dams on two Arkansas lakes, Hamilton and Catherine. The company then obtained "flood easements" on property adjoining the lakes. AP&L obtained some of the easements by grant and others by reservation, selling lakeside property and keeping the easement. These flood easements permitted AP&L to "clear of trees, brush and other obstructions and to submerge by water" certain acreage, which was described exactly. AP&L properly recorded the easements, and when the current landowners bought lakeside property, they were aware of the documents.

During one 12-hour period in May 1990, extraordinarily heavy rains fell in the Ouachita River Basin, including both lakes. In some areas, over 10 inches of rain fell, causing the water to reach the highest levels ever recorded, even washing away the equipment designed to measure rainfall. To avoid flooding Lake Hamilton, AP&L opened the gates of a dam called Carpenter. This caused Lake Catherine to flood, with water in some places rising 25 feet. This flood caused massive damage to the plaintiffs' houses, with water in some cases rising to the roof level.

Several dozen landowners sued, claiming that AP&L was negligent in opening one dam without

---

[1] *Burgess v. Alabama Power Co.*, 658 So. 2d 435, 1995 Ala. LEXIS 119 (Ala. 1995).

simultaneously opening another and also in failing to warn home owners of the intended action. The federal district court granted summary judgment for AP&L, based on the flood easements, and the landowners appealed.

Issue: Did the easements relieve AP&L from liability for flooding?

EXCERPTS FROM JUDGE GIBSON'S DECISION: This case involves a variety of easement forms, executed on different dates, but all with the same background. Some expressly reserved the right to "submerge" the land up to 307 feet and to "flood any part" of "said lands." Others conveyed the right to "flood any and all of said lands." Others granted the right to flood to a certain level, varying from 315 feet to 329 feet, elevations clearly much higher than the normal lake level. Two of the three forms used, and the condemnation decree, specifically granted the right to flood the lands "by waters impounded by a dam." The language is plain and specific. The obvious purpose of the flood and flowage rights is to protect AP&L from liability from its management of the lake in circumstances such as occurred in the extremely heavy rainfall in the seven hours on May 19 and 20. When AP&L opened the flood gates during the heaviest rains experienced since the dam was built, with the resultant flooding on the property of the shores in Lake Catherine, it was exercising rights retained by it or granted to it in the documents creating the property interest of the landowners. We can only conclude that protection from liability for flooding of the plaintiffs' land was the very reason the dam owner purchased the easement.

The issues in this case are extremely close. The loss of property is most substantial and the result seems harsh. [However, in view of the property interest created by the documents involving each of the landholders, we cannot place liability on AP&L in such circumstances. [Affirmed.] ◢

PROFIT

A *profit* gives one person the right to enter land belonging to another and take something away. You own 100 acres of vacation property, and suddenly a mining company informs you that the land contains valuable nickel deposits. You may choose to sell a profit to the mining company, allowing it to enter your land and take away the nickel. You receive cash up front, and the company earns money from the sale of the mineral.

LICENSE

A license gives the holder temporary permission to enter upon another's property. Unlike an easement or profit, a license is a *temporary* right. When you attend a basketball game by buying a ticket, the basketball club that sells you the ticket is the licensor and you are the licensee. You are entitled to enter the licensor's premises, namely the basketball arena, and to remain during the game, though the club can revoke the license if you behave unacceptably.

MORTGAGE

Generally, in order to buy a house, a prospective owner must borrow money. The bank or other lender will require security before it hands over its money, and the most common form of security for a real estate loan is a mortgage. **A mortgage is a security interest in real property.** The homeowner who borrows money is the **mortgagor**, because she is *giving* the mortgage to the lender. The lender, in turn, is the **mortgagee**, the party acquiring a security interest. The mortgagee in most cases obtains a **lien** on the house, meaning the right to foreclose on the property if the mortgagor fails to pay back the money borrowed.

Sale of Real Property

For most people, buying or selling a house is the biggest, most important financial transaction they will make. Here we consider several of the key issues that may arise. (For an instructive course on home buying, go to http://mirage.towerauction.net and find the link for homebuyer education.)

SELLER'S OBLIGATIONS CONCERNING THE PROPERTY

Historically, the common law recognized the rule of caveat emptor in the sale of real property—that is, let the buyer beware. If a buyer walked into his new living room and fell through the floor into a lake of toxic waste, it was his tough luck. But the common law changes with the times, and today courts place an increasing burden of fairness on the sellers of real estate. Two of the most significant obligations are the implied warranty of habitability and the duty to disclose defects.

Implied Warranty of Habitability

Most states now impose an implied warranty of habitability on a builder who sells a new home. This means that, whether he wants to or not, the builder is guaranteeing that the new house contains **adequate materials and good workmanship**. The law implies this warranty because of the inherently unequal position of builder and buyer. Some defects might be obvious to a lay observer, such as a room with no roof or a front porch that sways whenever the neighbors sneeze. But only the builder will know if he made the frame with proper wood, if the heating system was second-rate, the electrical work shabby, and so forth. Note that in most states the law implies this warranty to protect buyers of residential, but not commercial, property.

Duty to Disclose Defects

The seller of a home must disclose facts that a buyer does not know and cannot readily observe if they materially affect the property's value. Roy and Charlyne Terrell owned a house in the Florida Keys, where zoning codes required all living areas to be 15 feet above sea level. They knew that their house violated the code because a bedroom and bathroom were on the ground floor. They offered to sell the house to Robert Revitz, assuring him that the property complied with all codes and that flood insurance would cost about $350 per year. Revitz bought the house, moved in, and later learned that because of the code violations, flood insurance would be slightly more expensive—costing just over *$36,000 per year*. He sued and won. The court declared that the Terrells had a duty to disclose the code violations; it ordered a rescission of the contract, meaning that Revitz got his money back. The court mentioned that the duty to disclose was wide-ranging and included leaking roofs, insect infestation, cracks in walls and foundations, and any other problems that a buyer might be unable to discern.[2]

---

[2] *Revitz v. Terrell*, 572 So. 2d 996, 1990 Fla. App. LEXIS 9655 (Fla. Dist. Ct. App. 1990).

SALES CONTRACT AND TITLE EXAMINATION

The statute of frauds requires that an agreement to sell real property must be in writing to be enforceable. A contract for the sale of a house is often several pages of dense legal reading, in which the lawyers for the buyer and seller attempt to allocate risks for every problem that might go wrong. However, the contract *need* not be so thorough. A written contract for the sale of land is generally valid if it includes the names of all parties, a precise description of the property being sold, the price, and signatures.

Once the parties have agreed to the terms and signed a contract, the buyer's lawyer performs a **title examination**, which means that she, or someone she hires, searches through the local land registry for all documents that relate to the property. The purpose is to ensure that the seller actually has valid title to this land, since it is dispiriting to give someone half a million dollars for property and then discover that he never owned it and neither do you. Even if the seller owns the land, his title may be subject to other claims, such as an easement or a mortgage.

CLOSING AND DEEDS

While the buyer is checking the seller's title, she also probably needs to arrange financing, as described earlier in the section on mortgages. When the title work is complete and the buyer has arranged financing, the parties arrange a **closing**, a meeting at which the property is actually sold. The seller brings to the closing a **deed**, which is the document proving ownership of the land. The seller signs the deed over to the buyer in exchange for the purchase price. The buyer pays the price either with a certified check and/or by having her lender pay. If a lender pays part or all of the price, the buyer executes a mortgage to the lender as part of the closing.

RECORDING

Recording the deed means filing it with the official state registry. The registry clerk places a photocopy of the deed in the agency's bound volumes and indexes the deed by the name of the grantor and the grantee. Recording is a critical step in the sale of land, because it puts all the world on notice that the grantor has sold the land. It has little effect between grantor and grantee: once the deed and money are exchanged, the sale is generally final between those two. But recording is vital to protect the general public.

 You have spotted your dream vacation property on a pristine beach in Mexico. The next-door neighbor, a retired U.S. citizen, offers to sell you the property at a fair price. You draw up a contract in English and take the plunge. Mistake! Buying land in any foreign country presents pitfalls that you must consider. You might construct a $700,000 beach house, only to discover that you do not own the sandy soil on which it stands. In Mexico, all land within 66 feet of the high-tide mark is federal property and cannot be sold to anyone. Further, as a foreigner, you have no right to buy Mexican real estate within 31 miles of the ocean. Thousands of innocent U.S. citizens have lost millions of dollars paying for Mexican property they never acquire. Your friendly neighbor may have known of the local law and intended to cheat you, or he may have been equally ignorant and be horrified to learn that his own house stands on slippery ground. Know and respect local laws and customs before you write a check. (And by the way, in Mexico, a contract is binding only if written in Spanish.)

Land Use Regulation

ZONING

Zoning statutes are state laws that permit local communities to regulate building and land use. The local communities, whether cities, towns, or counties, then pass zoning ordinances that control many aspects of land development. For example, a town's zoning ordinance may divide the community into an industrial zone where factories may be built, a commercial zone in which stores of a certain size are allowed, and several residential zones in which only houses may be constructed. Within the residential zones, there may be further divisions, for example, permitting two-family houses in certain areas and requiring larger lots in others.

An owner prohibited by an ordinance from erecting a certain kind of building, or adding on to his present building, may seek a **variance** from the zoning board, meaning an exception granted for special reasons unique to the property. Whether a board will grant a variance generally depends upon the type of the proposed building, the nature of the community, the reason the owner claims he is harmed by the ordinance, and the reaction of neighbors.

Many people abhor "adult" businesses, such as strip clubs and pornography shops. Urban experts agree that a large number of these establishments in a neighborhood often causes crime to increase and property values to drop. Nonetheless, many people patronize such businesses, which can earn a good profit. Should a city have the right to restrict adult businesses? New York City officials determined that the number of sex shops had grown steadily for two decades and that their presence harmed various neighborhoods. With the support of community groups, the city passed a zoning ordinance that prohibited adult businesses from all residential neighborhoods, from some commercial districts, *and* from being within 500 feet of schools, houses of worship, day-care centers, or other sex shops (to avoid clustering). Owners and patrons of these shops protested, claiming that the city was unfairly denying the public access to a form of entertainment that it obviously desired. Are such ordinances good? Are they fair? Why or why not?

Many cities have put their zoning codes online. Find out if your city has done so. If the code is available, check to see if it includes restrictions for adult businesses.

EMINENT DOMAIN

Eminent domain is the power of the government to take private property for public use. A government may need land to construct a highway, an airport, a university, or public housing. All levels of government—federal, state, and local—have this power. But the Fifth Amendment to the United States Constitution states: ". . . nor shall private property be taken for public use, without just compensation." The Supreme Court has held that this clause, the Takings Clause, applies not only to the federal government but also to state and local governments. So, although all levels of government have the power to take property, they must pay the owner a fair price.

A "fair price" generally means the reasonable market value of the land. Generally, if the property owner refuses the government's offer, the government will file suit seeking **condemnation** of the land, that is, a court order specifying what compensation is just and awarding title to the government.

LANDLORD-TENANT LAW

On a January morning in Studio City, California, Alpha Donchin took her small Shih Tzu for a walk. Suddenly, less than a block from her house, two large rottweilers attacked Donchin and her pet. The heavy animals mauled the 14-pound Shih Tzu, and when Donchin picked her dog up, the rottweilers knocked her down, breaking her hip and causing other serious injuries.

Ubaldo Guerrero, who lived in a rented house nearby, owned the two rottweilers, and Donchin sued him. But she also sued Guerrero's *landlord*, David Swift, who lived four blocks away from the rental property. Donchin claimed that the landlord was liable for her injuries, because he knew of the dogs' vicious nature and permitted them to escape from the property he rented to Guerrero. Should the landlord be liable for injuries caused by his tenant's dogs?

As is typical of many landlord-tenant issues, the law in this area is in flux. Under the common law, a landlord had no liability for injuries caused by animals belonging to a tenant, and many states adhere to that rule. But some states are expanding the landlord's liability for injuries caused on or near his property. The California court ruled that Donchin could maintain her suit against Swift. If Donchin could prove that Swift knew the dogs were dangerous and allowed them to escape through a defective fence, the landlord would be liable for her injuries.[3]

One reason for the erratic evolution of landlord-tenant law is that it is really a combination of three venerable areas of law: property, contract, and negligence. The confluence of these legal theories produces results that are unpredictable but interesting and important. (To survey a variety of articles and laws in this rapidly evolving area, visit http://www.law.cornell.edu/topics/landlord_tenant.html.) We begin our examination of landlord-tenant law with an analysis of the different types of tenancy.

Recall that a freehold estate is the right to possess real property and use it in any lawful manner. **When an owner of a freehold estate allows another person temporary, exclusive possession of the property, the parties have created a landlord-tenant relationship.** The freehold owner is the **landlord**, and the person allowed to possess the property is the **tenant**. The landlord has conveyed a **leasehold** interest to the tenant, meaning the right to temporary possession. Courts also use the word "**tenancy**" to describe the tenant's right to possession. A leasehold may be commercial or residential.

THREE LEGAL AREAS COMBINED

Property law influences landlord-tenant cases because the landlord is conveying rights in real property to the tenant. She is also keeping a **reversionary interest** in the property, meaning the right to possess the property when the lease ends. Contract law plays a role because the basic agreement between the landlord and tenant is a contract. **A lease is a contract that creates a landlord-tenant relationship.** And negligence law increasingly determines the liability of landlord and tenant when there is an injury to a person or property. Many states have combined

---

[3] *Donchin v. Guerrero*, 34 Cal. App. 4th 1832, 1995 Cal. App. LEXIS 462 (Cal. Ct. App. 1995).

these three legal issues into landlord-tenant statutes; you can see a typical statute by going to http://www.law.cornell.edu/topics/landlord_tenant.html and, under "State Material," finding the link to the uniform residential landlord tenant act.

LEASE

The statute of frauds generally requires that a lease be in writing. Some states will enforce an oral lease if it is for a short term, such as one year or less, but even when an oral lease is permitted, it is wiser for the parties to put their agreement in writing, because a written lease avoids many misunderstandings. At a minimum, a lease must state the names of the parties, the premises being leased, the duration of the agreement, and the rent. But a well-drafted lease generally includes many provisions, called covenants. A **covenant** is simply a promise by either the landlord or the tenant to do something or refrain from doing something. For example, most leases include a covenant concerning the tenant's payment of a security deposit and the landlord's return of the deposit, a covenant describing how the tenant may use the premises, and several covenants about who must maintain and repair the property, who is liable for damage, and so forth. The parties should also agree about how the lease may be terminated and whether the parties have the right to renew it.

Types of Tenancy

There are four types of tenancy: a tenancy for years, a periodic tenancy, a tenancy at will, and a tenancy at sufferance. The most important feature distinguishing one from the other is how each tenancy terminates. In some cases, a tenancy terminates automatically, while in others, one party must take certain steps to end the agreement.

TENANCY FOR YEARS

Any lease for a stated, fixed period is a tenancy for years. If a landlord rents a summer apartment for the months of June, July, and August of next year, that is a tenancy for years. A company that rents retail space in a mall beginning January 1, 2002, and ending December 31, 2007, also has a tenancy for years. A tenancy for years terminates automatically when the agreed period ends.

PERIODIC TENANCY

A periodic tenancy is created for a fixed period and then automatically continues for additional periods until either party notifies the other of termination. This is probably the most common variety of tenancy, and the parties may create one in either of two ways. Suppose a landlord agrees to rent you an apartment "from month to month, rent payable on the first." That is a periodic tenancy. The tenancy automatically renews itself every month, unless either party gives adequate notice to the other that she wishes to terminate. A periodic tenancy could also be for one-year periods—in which case it automatically renews for an additional year if neither party terminates—or for any other period.

TENANCY AT WILL

A tenancy at will has no fixed duration and may be terminated by either party at any time. Tenancies at will are unusual tenancies.[4] Typically, the agreement is vague, with no specified rental period and with payment, perhaps, to be made in kind. The parties might agree, for example, that a tenant farmer could use a portion of his crop as rent. Since either party can end the agreement at any time, it provides no security for either landlord or tenant.

TENANCY AT SUFFERANCE

A tenancy at sufferance occurs when a tenant remains on the premises, against the wishes of the landlord, after the expiration of a true tenancy. Thus a tenancy at sufferance is not a true tenancy because the tenant is staying without the landlord's agreement. The landlord has the option of seeking to evict the tenant or of forcing the tenant to pay rent for a new rental period.

Landlord's Duties

DUTY TO DELIVER POSSESSION

The landlord's first important duty is to deliver possession of the premises at the beginning of the tenancy, that is, to make the rented space available to the tenant. In most cases, this presents no problems and the new tenant moves in. But what happens if the previous tenant has refused to leave when the new tenancy begins? In most states, the landlord is legally required to remove the previous tenant. In some states, it is up to the new tenant either to evict the existing occupant or begin charging him rent.

QUIET ENJOYMENT

All tenants are entitled to quiet enjoyment of the premises, meaning the right to use the property without the interference of the landlord. Most leases expressly state this covenant of quiet enjoyment. And if a lease includes no such covenant, the law implies the right of quiet enjoyment anyway, so all tenants are protected. If a landlord interferes with the tenant's quiet enjoyment, he has breached the lease, entitling the tenant to damages.

The most common interference with quiet enjoyment is an eviction, meaning some act that forces the tenant to abandon the premises. Of course, some evictions are legal, as when a tenant fails to pay the rent. But some evictions are illegal. There are two types of eviction: actual and constructive.

Actual Eviction

If a landlord prevents the tenant from possessing the premises, he has actually evicted her. Suppose a landlord decides that a group of students are

---

[4] The courts of some states, annoyingly, use the term "tenancy at will" for what are, in reality, periodic tenancies. They do this to bewilder law students and even lawyers, a goal at which they are quite successful. This text uses tenancy at will in its more widely known sense, meaning a tenancy terminable at any time.

"troublemakers." Without going through lawful eviction procedures in court, the landlord simply waits until the students are out of the apartment and changes the locks. By denying the students access to the premises, the landlord has actually evicted them and has breached their right of quiet enjoyment.

Constructive Eviction

If a landlord substantially interferes with the tenant's use and enjoyment of the premises, he has constructively evicted her. Courts construe certain behavior as the equivalent of an eviction. In these cases, the landlord has not actually prevented the tenant from possessing the premises, but has instead interfered so greatly with her use and enjoyment that the law regards the landlord's actions as equivalent to an eviction. Suppose the heating system in an apartment house in Juneau, Alaska, fails during January. The landlord, an avid sled-dog racer, tells the tenants he is too busy to fix the problem. If the tenants move out, the landlord has constructively evicted them and is liable for all expenses they suffer.

To claim a constructive eviction, the tenant must vacate the premises. The tenant must also prove that the interference was sufficiently serious and lasted long enough that she was forced to move out. A lack of hot water for two days is not fatal, but lack of any water for two weeks creates a constructive eviction.

Duty to Maintain Premises

In most states, a landlord has a duty to deliver the premises in a habitable condition and a continuing duty to maintain the habitable condition. This duty overlaps with the quiet enjoyment obligation, but it is not identical. The tenant's right to quiet enjoyment focuses primarily on the tenant's *ability to use* the rented property. The landlord's duty to maintain the property focuses on whether the property *meets a particular legal standard*. The required standard may be stated in the lease, created by a state statute, or implied by law.

Lease

The lease itself generally obligates the landlord to maintain the exterior of any buildings and the common areas. If a lease does not do so, state law may imply the obligation.

Building Codes

Many state and local governments have passed building codes, which mandate minimum standards for commercial and/or residential property. The codes are likely to be stricter for residential property and may demand such things as minimum room size, sufficient hot water, secure locks, proper working kitchens and bathrooms, absence of insects and rodents, and other basics of decent housing. Generally, all rental property must comply with the building code, whether the lease mentions the code or not.

Implied Warranty of Habitability

Students Maria Ivanow, Thomas Tecza, and Kenneth Gearin rented a house from Les and Martha Vanlandingham. The monthly rent was $900. But the roommates failed to pay any rent for the final five months of the tenancy. After they moved out, the Vanlandinghams sued. How much did the landlords recover? Nothing. The landlords had breached the implied warranty of habitability.

The implied warranty of habitability requires that a landlord meet all standards set by the local building code, or that the premises be fit for human habitation. Most states, though not all, *imply* this warranty of habitability, meaning that the landlord must meet this standard whether the lease includes it or not.

The Vanlandinghams breached the implied warranty. The students had complained repeatedly about a variety of problems. The washer and dryer, which were included in the lease, frequently failed. A severe roof leak caused water damage in one of the bedrooms. Defective pipes flooded the bathroom. The refrigerator frequently malfunctioned, and the roommates repaired it several times. The basement often flooded, and when it was dry, rats and opossums lived in it. The heat sometimes failed.

In warranty of habitability cases, a court normally considers the severity of the problems and their duration. In the case of Maria Ivanow and friends, the court abated (reduced) the rent 50 percent. The students had already paid more than the abated rent to the landlord, so they owed nothing for the last five months.[5]

Tenant Remedies for Defective Conditions

Different states allow various remedies for defective conditions. For tenant rights in your state, see http://www.tenantsunion.org/tulist.html, which provides links to tenant organizations throughout the nation. For a useful series of form letters concerning defective conditions, problems with neighbors, interference with quiet enjoyment, and other common tenant concerns, see http://little.nhlink.net/nhlink/housing/cto/letters/letrs.htm. Many states allow a tenant to withhold rent, representing the decreased value of the premises. In some states, if a tenant notifies the landlord of a serious defect and the landlord fails to remedy the problem, the tenant may deduct a reasonable amount of money from the rental payment and have the repair made himself. Also, a landlord who refuses to repair significant defects is breaching the lease and/or state law, and the tenant may simply sue for damages.

DUTY TO RETURN SECURITY DEPOSIT

Most landlords require tenants to pay a security deposit, in case the tenant damages the premises. In many states, a landlord must either return the security deposit soon after the tenant has moved out or notify the tenant of the damage and the cost of the repairs. A landlord who fails to do so may owe the tenant damages of two or even three times the deposit.

Your authors are always grateful when a litigant volunteers to illustrate half a dozen legal issues in one lawsuit. The landlord in the following case demonstrates problems of security deposit, quiet enjoyment, constructive eviction, and . . . well, see how many you can count.

---

[5] *Vanlandingham v. Ivanow*, 246 Ill. App. 3d 348, 615 N.E.2d 1361, 1993 Ill. App. LEXIS 985 (Ill. Ct. App. 1993).

HARRIS V. SOLEY

2000 Me. 150, 756 A.2d 499
Supreme Judicial Court of Maine, 2000

FACTS: Here is an apartment adventure that begins as a horror story but ends happily. The court will tell you what happened.

ISSUE: Are the tenants entitled to such large damages?

EXCERPTS FROM JUSTICE SAUFLEY'S DECISION:

Near Labor Day, Andrea Harris, Kimberly Nightingale, Karen Simard, and Michelle Dussault moved into a large apartment that was located in the Old Port area of Portland and owned by Joseph Soley. Soley had promised the tenants that the apartment, which had previously been condemned by the City of Portland, would be repaired by the time they moved in. When they arrived, the condemnation notice was still on the door. Upon entering the apartment, they found it in an uninhabitable condition. They spoke to Soley's property manager who indicated that if the tenants were willing to clean the apartment themselves, she would credit them with $750 of their $1000 monthly rent for the month of September. They rented a steam cleaner, bought various cleaning supplies, and cleaned the apartment themselves. Soley's property manager also suggested that they buy a new refrigerator and deduct it from the rent because the one in the apartment did not work.

Despite their efforts to clean the apartment, the tenants continued to have problems with infestations of mice and cockroaches, as well as a persistent odor of cat urine. A dead cat was eventually found beneath the floorboards. The apartment had no heat during the month of October. One tenant slept with blankets over her head, not only because of the cold, but also to keep bugs away from her. These problems persisted into November, and the tenants submitted to Soley a list of complaints including a broken skylight, a broken toilet, a broken garbage disposal, a leaking roof, and cockroach infestation. As winter arrived, snow would fall into the living room through the broken skylight. When Soley did not make the needed repairs, the tenants stopped paying rent. Soley telephoned them on several occasions regarding the rent and spoke to the tenants in a rude

and abrasive manner. In February, the property manager told the tenants that Soley had begun eviction proceedings against them.

The tenants eventually found another place to live and had begun moving [when] Soley's agents broke into the apartment and took many of the tenants' remaining belongings. Upon confrontation with the returning tenants and police officers who had been called to the scene, Soley's agents indicated that Soley had directed their actions. Eventually, the officers and one of the tenants went to an apartment nearby and recovered some, but not all, of the missing property.

The tenants then sought out Soley to request that he return their remaining possessions. They located him at his restaurant, the Seamen's Club. According to one of the tenants, he replied that he would return their property only after they paid him $3000. He then ordered them to leave and threatened to call the police and have them forcibly removed. Soley told the tenants that he knew where they were moving and where their families lived, a statement that the tenants took as a threat.

The tenants brought suit against the defendants in a complaint that included claims for conversion [the wrongful taking of property], intentional infliction of emotional distress, punitive damages, breach of contract, wrongful eviction, and wrongful retention of a security deposit. [For months, Soley refused to respond to discovery requests and finally the trial court gave a default judgment for the plaintiffs. The judge instructed the jury that all of the plaintiffs' allegations were deemed true, and that their job was simply to award damages.]

The jury awarded each of the tenants $15,000 as damages for emotional distress. The defendants argue that the evidence does not support an award to each of the tenants in identical amounts. In addition, Soley relies on the fact that the awards are identical to support a claim that the awards are the result of passion and prejudice.

Contrary to Soley's argument, the jury was not required to find that each of the tenants suffered identical emotional distress in order to award the same amount of damages to each; rather, the jury need only have found that the emotional distress suffered by each, regardless of the nature of that distress, warranted comparable monetary compensation. The evidence introduced at trial, including evidence of Soley's conduct and the tenants' testimony regarding their emotional responses, could support a determination that the tenants suffered comparable emotional distress.

Finally, Soley challenges the award of $1 million in punitive damages as excessive. Again, we begin with the facts of the complaint as conclusively established by the default judgment. Among other things, those facts included the following:

> Plaintiffs were shaken up, infuriated, violated, intimidated and in fear for their physical safety. . . . The conduct of Defendants, and each of them, was so extreme and outrageous as to exceed all possible bounds of decency. . . . Defendants acted intentionally, knowingly, willfully, wantonly and with malice.

There can be no question that the jury was justified in deciding that an award of punitive damages was warranted. The tenants had to endure the presence of insect and rodent infestations, dead animals, snow falling into the apartment, and a total lack of response from their landlord after repeated complaints. Soley's continued refusal to repair conditions that rendered the apartment unfit for human occupation, the violent removal of tenants' property before eviction proceedings had proceeded, the retention of property belonging to the tenants, the destruction of their property, and his threatening behavior combined to create a pattern of conduct that must be considered intolerable.

Judgment affirmed. ◢

Tenant's Duties

DUTY TO PAY RENT

> My landlord said he's gonna raise the rent. "Good," I said, " 'cause I can't raise it."
> *Slappy White*, comedian, 1921–1995

Rent is the compensation the tenant pays the landlord for use of the premises, and paying the rent, despite Mr. White's wistful hope, is the tenant's foremost obligation. The lease normally specifies the amount of rent and when it must be paid. Typically, the landlord requires that rent be paid at the beginning of each rental period, whether that is monthly, annually, or otherwise.

If the tenant fails to pay rent on time, the landlord has several remedies. She is entitled to apply the security deposit to the unpaid rent. She may also sue the tenant for nonpayment of rent, demanding the unpaid sums, cost of collection, and interest. Finally, the landlord may evict a tenant who has failed to pay rent.

State statutes prescribe the steps a landlord must take to evict a tenant for nonpayment. Typically, the landlord must serve a termination notice on the tenant and wait for a court hearing. At the hearing, the landlord must prove that the tenant has failed to pay rent on time. If the tenant has no excuse for the nonpayment, the court grants an order evicting him. The order authorizes a sheriff to remove the tenant's goods and place them in storage, at the tenant's expense. However, if the tenant was withholding rent because of unlivable conditions, the court may refuse to evict.

DUTY TO USE PREMISES PROPERLY

A lease normally lists what a tenant may do in the premises and prohibits other activities. For example, a residential lease allows the tenant to use the property for normal living purposes, but not for any retail, commercial, or industrial purpose. **A tenant is liable to the landlord for any significant damage he causes to the property.** The tenant is not liable for normal wear and tear. If, however, he knocks a hole in a wall or damages the plumbing, the landlord may collect the cost of repairs, either by using the security deposit or by suing if necessary.

Injuries

TENANT'S LIABILITY

 # 129

A tenant is generally liable for injuries occurring within the premises she is leasing, whether that is an apartment, a store, or otherwise. If a tenant permits grease to accumulate on a kitchen floor and a guest slips and falls, the tenant is liable. If a merchant negligently installs display shelving that tips onto a customer, the merchant pays for the harm. Generally, a tenant is not liable for injuries occurring in common areas over which she has no control, such as exterior walkways. If a tenant's dinner guest falls because the building's common stairway has loose steps, the landlord is probably liable.

LANDLORD'S LIABILITY

Historically, the common law held a landlord responsible only for injuries that occurred in the common areas, or due to the landlord's negligent maintenance of the property. Increasingly, though, the law holds landlords liable under the normal rules of negligence law. **In many states, a landlord must use reasonable care to maintain safe premises and is liable for foreseeable harm.** For example, most states now have building codes that require a landlord to maintain structural elements in safe condition. States further imply a warranty of habitability, which mandates reasonably safe living conditions.

As always, the common law advances in a disorderly fashion, and state courts disagree about what "reasonable care" requires. The following pair of cases illustrate the diversity of issues—and conflicting arguments—that a landlord must consider before renting units. You make the calls.

YOU BE THE JUDGE

MCGUIRE V. K & G MANAGEMENT CO.

1998 Ohio App. LEXIS 4742
Ohio Court of Appeals, 1998

FACTS: The McGuire family rented a second-story apartment from K & G Management, which managed a residential complex on behalf of Avant Co. Robin McGuire notified K & G that a window screen in her son's bedroom was loose and had fallen out once. Neighbors had also complained about loose-fitting screens. Five days after Robin reported the loose screen, her son, 26-month-old Devin, was playing in his bedroom with his eight-year-old cousin. Somehow, Devin fell or leaned into the window screen, which gave way. Devin fell to the ground and was seriously hurt.

The McGuires filed suit against K & G and Avant, claiming negligence. In Ohio (and most states), a landlord has a statutory duty to "make all repairs and do whatever is reasonably necessary to put and keep the premises in a fit and habitable condition." The trial court granted summary judgment for both defendants, ruling that the defendants had no duty to install screens strong enough to restrain a child. The McGuires appealed.

YOU BE THE JUDGE: Are the McGuires entitled to a trial on their claim of negligence?

ARGUMENT FOR THE MCGUIRES: Both defendants have a statutory duty to keep the apartment fit and habitable, and both failed to do that. The screen was loose and they knew it, but failed to fix it. The danger of a child falling was entirely foreseeable, and the defendants are responsible. No parent can watch a child 24 hours a day. Young children climb and play anywhere they can reach. A landlord who makes a profit renting apartments to families should use reasonable care to protect all family members, young and old.

ARGUMENT FOR K & G AND AVANT: A window screen is not a child restraint. A screen is designed to keep insects and birds out, not to hold children in. A normal window screen, no matter how tightly installed, would not restrain a child. If all landlords throughout the state are suddenly obligated to install child-proof screens, let the legislature announce the new rule and provide time to comply. We do not think that the voters want to pay the additional rent required to cover such a huge expense. /

YOU BE THE JUDGE

MATTHEWS V. AMBERWOOD ASSOCIATES LIMITED PARTNERSHIP, INC.

351 Md. 544, 719 A.2d 199, 1998 Md. LEXIS 807
Maryland Court of Appeals, 1998

FACTS: Shelly Morton leased an apartment owned by Amberwood and operated by Monocle Management. The lease permitted the landlord to evict any tenant who broke the "House Rules," one of which prohibited pets. Morton kept her boyfriend's pit bull, named Rampage, in her apartment. At times, she kept Rampage chained outside the apartment house. When Morton was near the dog, he was not violent, but when she was absent, Rampage would attempt to attack anyone who came near him. Numerous maintenance workers had been unable to perform service work because Rampage barked and lunged at them. The workers reported each of these incidents to Monocle.

Shanita Matthews and her 16-month-old son, Tevin, visited Morton and her child, something they had done many times. As the adults worked on a puzzle in the dining room, the children played in the living room. Morton briefly left the apartment, and suddenly Rampage attacked Tevin. The dog grabbed the boy by the neck and shook him. Matthews was unable to free her son. She yelled for help and called 911. Morton reentered the apartment, could not free the boy, grabbed a knife, and repeatedly stabbed the animal, which finally released Tevin. An ambulance

arrived, but an hour after reaching the hospital, Tevin died from his injuries.

Matthews sued Amberwood and Monocle. The jury awarded her $5,018,750 for the wrongful death of her son. The defendants appealed.

YOU BE THE JUDGE: Does a landlord owe a duty to a social guest of a tenant for an attack within the tenant's apartment?

ARGUMENT FOR MATTHEWS: The House Rules prohibited pets. Monocle knew that Morton was breaking the rule and keeping an especially dangerous animal. Monocle should have acted to protect the other residents and all guests to the complex. The companies' failure to enforce their own rules led directly to the death of a child.

ARGUMENT FOR THE DEFENDANTS: Neither the owner nor the management company has control over the apartment or what goes on inside it. The companies could not have foreseen this attack, nor could they have done anything to stop it. Matthews knew the dog's nature. She had no business leaving her son alone with such a vicious beast. /

CRIME

Landlords may be liable in negligence to tenants or their guests for criminal attacks that occur on the premises. Courts have struggled with this issue and have reached opposing results in similar cases. The very prevalence of crime sharpens the debate. What must a landlord do to protect a tenant? Courts typically answer the question by looking at four factors.

- *Nature of the Crime.* How did the crime occur? Could the landlord have prevented it?

- *Reasonable Person Standard.* What would a reasonable landlord have done to prevent this type of crime? What did the landlord actually do?

- *Foreseeability.* Was it reasonably foreseeable that such a crime might occur? Were there earlier incidents or warnings?

- *Prevalence of Crime in the Area.* If the general area, or the particular premises, has a high crime rate, courts are more likely to hold that the crime was foreseeable and the landlord responsible.

PERSONAL PROPERTY

Personal property means all property other than real property. Real property, as we know, refers to land and things firmly attached to it. All other property is personal: a bus, a toothbrush, a share of stock. Most personal property is goods, meaning something that can be moved. We have already examined the purchase and sale of goods, which are governed by the Uniform Commercial Code (UCC). Now we look at several important aspects of personal property, including gifts, found property, and bailments.

Gifts

A gift is a voluntary transfer of property from one person to another without any consideration. It is the lack of consideration that distinguishes a gift from a contract. Contracts usually consist of mutual promises to do something in the future. Each promise is consideration for the other one, and the mutual consideration makes each promise enforceable. But a gift is a one-way transaction, without consideration. The person who gives property away is the **donor** and the one who receives it is the **donee.**

A gift involves three elements:

- The donor intends to transfer ownership of the property to the donee immediately.

- The donor delivers the property to the donee.

- The donee accepts the property.

INTENTION TO TRANSFER OWNERSHIP

The donor must intend to transfer ownership to the property right away, immediately giving up all control of the item. Notice the two important parts of this element. First, the donor's intention must be to *transfer ownership*, that is, to give title to the donee. Merely proving that the owner handed you property does not guarantee that you have received a gift; if the owner only intended that you use the item, there is no gift and she can demand it back.

Second, the donor must also intend the property to transfer *immediately*. A promise to make a gift in the future is unenforceable. Promises about future behavior are governed by contract law, and a contract is unenforceable without consideration. That is why poor Charley, at the beginning of this chapter, will never collect his $100,000 from the banker. If the banker had handed Charley the cash as he gushed his extravagant words, Charley could keep the money. However, the banker's promise to make the gift the next day is legally worthless. Nor does Charley have an enforceable contract, since there was no consideration for the banker's promise.

A *revocable gift* is a contradiction in terms, because it violates the rule just discussed. It is not a gift and the donee keeps nothing.[6] Suppose Harold tells his daughter Faith, "The mule is yours from now on, but if you start acting stupid again, I'm taking her back." Harold has retained some control over the animal, which means he has not intended to transfer ownership. There is no gift, and Harold still owns the mule.

DELIVERY

Physical Delivery

The donor must deliver the property to the donee. Generally, this involves physical delivery. If Anna hands Eddie a Rembrandt drawing, saying, "I want you to have this forever,"she has satisfied the delivery requirement. This is the element missing from the banker's "gift" to Charley.

Constructive Delivery

Physical delivery is the most common and the surest way to make a gift, but it is not always necessary. **A donor makes constructive delivery by transferring ownership without a physical delivery**. Most courts permit constructive delivery only when physical delivery is impossible or extremely inconvenient. Suppose Anna wants to give her niece Jen a blimp, which is parked in a hangar at the airport. The blimp will not fit through the doorway of Jen's dorm. Instead of flying the aircraft to the university, Anna may simply deliver to Jen the certificate of title and the keys to the blimp. When she has done that, Jen owns the aircraft.

Delivery to an Agent

A donor might deliver the property to an agent, either someone working for him or for the donee. If the donor delivers the property to his own agent, there is no gift. By definition, the agent works for the donor, and thus the donor still has

---

[6] The only exception to this rule is a gift *causa mortis*, discussed below.

control and ownership of the property. But if the donor delivers the property to the donee's agent, the gift is made.

INTER VIVOS GIFTS AND GIFTS CAUSA MORTIS

A gift can be either *inter vivos* or *causa mortis*. **An *inter vivos* gift means a gift made during life, that is, when the donor is not under any fear of impending death.** The vast majority of gifts are *inter vivos*, involving a healthy donor and donee. Shirley, age 30 and in good health, gives her husband Terry an eraser for his birthday. This is an *inter vivos* gift, which is absolute. The gift becomes final upon delivery, and the donor may not revoke it. If Shirley and Terry have a fight the next day, Shirley has no power to erase her gift.

A gift *causa mortis* is one made in contemplation of approaching death. The gift is valid if the donor dies as expected, but is revoked if he recovers. Suppose Lance's doctors have told him he will probably die of a liver ailment within a month. Lance calls Jane to his bedside and hands her a fistful of emeralds, saying, "I'm dying; these are yours." Jane sheds a tear, then sprints to the bank. If Lance dies of the liver ailment within a few weeks, Jane gets to keep the emeralds. The law permits the gift *causa mortis* to act as a substitute for a will, since the donor's delivery of the property clearly indicates his intentions. But note that this kind of gift is revocable. Since a gift *causa mortis* is conditional (upon the donor's death), the donor has the right to revoke it at any time before he dies. If Lance telephones Jane the next day and says that he has changed his mind, he gets the jewels back. Further, if the donor recovers and does not die as expected, the gift is automatically revoked.

ACCEPTANCE

The donee must accept the gift. This rarely leads to disputes, but if a donee should refuse a gift and then change her mind, she is out of luck. Her repudiation of the donor's offer means there is no gift, and she has no rights in the property.

The following case offers a combination of love and anger, alcohol and diamonds—always a volatile mix.

YOU BE THE JUDGE

ALBINGER V. HARRIS

2002 Mont. 118, 2002 WL 1226858
Montana Supreme Court, 2002

FACTS: Michelle Harris and Michael Albinger lived together, on and off, for three years. Their roller-coaster relationship was marred by alcohol abuse and violence. When they announced their engagement, Albinger gave Harris a $29,000 diamond ring, but the couple broke off their wedding plans because of emotional and physical turmoil. Harris returned the ring. Later, they reconciled and resumed their marriage plans, and Albinger gave his fiancee the ring again. This cycle repeated several times over the three years. Each time they broke off their relationship, Harris returned the ring to Albinger, and each time they made up, he gave it back to her.

On one occasion Albinger held a knife over Harris as she lay in bed, threatening to chop off her finger if she didn't remove the ring. He beat her and forcibly removed the ring. Criminal charges were brought but then dropped when, inevitably, the couple reconciled. Another time, Albinger told her to "take the car, the horse, the dog, and the ring and get the hell out." Finally, mercifully, they ended their stormy affair, and Harris moved to Kentucky—keeping the ring.

Albinger sued for the value of the ring. The trial court found that the ring was a conditional gift, made in contemplation of marriage, and ordered Harris to pay its full value. She appealed. The Montana Supreme Court had to decide, in a case of first impression, whether an engagement ring was given in contemplation of marriage. (In Montana and in many states, neither party to a broken engagement may sue for breach of contract, because it is impossible to determine who is responsible for ending the relationship.)

YOU BE THE JUDGE: Who owns the ring?

ARGUMENT FOR HARRIS: The main problem with calling the ring a "conditional gift" is that there is no such thing. The elements of a gift are intent, delivery, and acceptance, and Harris has proven all three. A gift is not a contract, nor is it a loan. Once a gift has been accepted, the donor has no more rights in the property and may not demand its return. Hundreds of years of litigation have resulted in only one exception to this rule—a gift

causa mortis—and despite some cynical claims to the contrary, marriage is not death. If this court carves a new exception to the long-standing rule, other unhappy donors will dream up more "conditions" that supposedly entitle them to their property. What is more, to create a special rule for engagement rings would be blatant gender bias, because the exception would only benefit men. This court should stick to settled law, and permit the recipient of a gift to keep it.

ARGUMENT FOR ALBINGER: The symbolism of an engagement ring is not exactly news. For decades, Americans have given rings—frequently diamond—in contemplation of marriage. All parties understand why the gift is made and what is expected if the engagement is called off: the ring must be returned. Albinger's *intent*, to focus on one element, was conditional—and Michelle Harris understood that. Each time the couple separated, she gave the ring back. She knew that she could wear this beautiful ring in anticipation of their marriage, but that custom and decency required its return if the wedding was off. She knew it, that is, until greed got the better of her and she fled to Kentucky, attempting to profit at the expense of Albinger's generosity. We are not asking for *new* law, but for confirmation of what everyone has known for generations: there is no wedding ring when there is no wedding. ◢

The following chart distinguishes between a contract and a gift:

A Contract and a Gift Distinguished
A Contract:
Lou: I will pay you $2,000 to paint the house if you promise to finish by July 3.   Abby: I agreed to paint the house by July 3, for $2,000.
Lou and Abby have a contract. Each promise is consideration in support of the other promise. Lou and Abby can each enforce the other's promise.
A Gift:
Lou hands Phil two opera tickets, while saying:
Lou: I want you to have these two tickets to *Rigoletto*.   Phil: Hey, thanks.
This is a valid *inter vivos* gift. Lou intended to transfer ownership immediately and deliver the property to Phil, who now owns the tickets.

> **Neither Contract nor Gift:**
> Lou: You're a great guy. Next week, I'm going to give you two tickets to *Rigoletto*.
>
> Jason: Hey, thanks.
>
> There is no gift because Lou did not intend to transfer ownership immediately, and he did not deliver the tickets. There is no contract because Jason has given no consideration to support Lou's promise.

Bailment

A bailment is the rightful possession of goods by one who is not the owner. The one who delivers the goods is the **bailor** and the one in possession is the **bailee**. Bailments are common. Suppose you are going out of town for the weekend and loan your motorcycle to Stan. You are the bailor and your friend is the bailee. When you check your suitcase with the airline, you are again the bailor and the airline is the bailee. If you rent a car at your destination, you become the bailee while the rental agency is the bailor. In each case, someone other than the true owner has rightful, temporary possession of personal property.

The parties generally—but not always—create a bailment by agreement. In each of the examples, the parties agreed to the bailment. In two cases, the agreement included payment, which is common but not essential. When you buy your airline ticket, you pay for your ticket, and the price includes the airline's agreement, as bailee, to transport your suitcase. When you rent a car, you pay the bailor for the privilege of using it. By loaning your motorcycle, you engage in a bailment without either party paying compensation.

A bailment without any agreement is called a constructive, or involuntary, bailment. Suppose you find a wristwatch in your house that you know belongs to a friend. You are obligated to return the watch to the true owner, and until you do so, you are the bailee, liable for harm to the property. This is called a constructive bailment because, with no agreement between the parties, the law is *construing* a bailment.

Because the bailor is the one who delivers the goods to another, the bailor is typically the owner, but he need not be. Suppose that Stan, who borrowed your motorcycle, allows his girlfriend Sheila to try out the bike, and she takes it to a mall where she jumps over a row of six parked cars. Stan, the bailee from you, has become a bailor, and Sheila is his bailee.

CONTROL

To create a bailment, the bailee must assume physical control with intent to possess. A bailee may be liable for loss or damage to the property. But it is not fair to hold him liable unless he has taken physical control of the goods, intending to possess them.

Disputes about whether someone has taken control often arise in parking lot cases. When a car is damaged or stolen, the lot's owner may try to avoid liability by claiming it lacked control of the parked auto and therefore was not a bailee. If the lot is a "park and lock" facility, where the car's owner retains the key and the lot owner exercises no control at all, then there may be no bailment, and no liability for damage. (For a sample automobile bailment form, see http://www.gate.net/ ~legalsvc/autobail.html.)

By contrast, when a driver leaves her keys with a parking attendant, the lot clearly is exercising control of the auto, and the parties have created a bailment. The lot is probably liable for loss or damage. What about cases in the middle, where the driver keeps her keys but the lot owner exercises *some other control*? There is no uniform rule, but the trend is probably toward liability for the lot owner.

RIGHTS OF THE BAILEE

The bailee's primary right is possession of the property. Anyone who interferes with the bailee's rightful possession is liable to her. **The bailee is typically, though not always, permitted to use the property.** Obviously, a customer is permitted to drive a car rented from an agency. When a farmer loans his tractor to a neighbor, the bailee is entitled to use the machine for normal farm purposes. But some bailees have no authority to use the goods. If you store your furniture in a warehouse, the storage company is your bailee, but it has no right to curl up in your bed. The bailee may or may not be entitled to compensation, depending on the parties' agreement.

DUTIES OF THE BAILEE

The bailee is strictly liable to redeliver the goods on time to the bailor or to whomever the bailor designates. Strict liability means there are virtually no exceptions. Rudy stores his $6,000 drum set with Melissa's Warehouse while he is on vacation. Blake arrives at the warehouse and shows a forged letter, supposedly from Rudy, granting Blake permission to remove the drums. If Melissa permits Blake to take the drums, she will owe Rudy $6,000, even if the forgery was a high-quality job.

DUE CARE

The bailee is obligated to exercise due care. **The level of care required depends upon who receives the benefit of the bailment.** There are three possibilities.

- *Sole Benefit of Bailee.* If the bailment is for the sole benefit of the bailee, the bailee is required to use **extraordinary care** with the property. Generally, in these cases, the bailor loans something for free to the bailee. Since the bailee is paying nothing for the use of the goods, most courts consider her the only one to benefit from the bailment. If your neighbor loans you a power lawn mower, the bailment is probably for your sole benefit. You are liable if you are even slightly inattentive in handling the lawn mower and can expect to pay for virtually any harm done.

- *Mutual Benefit.* When the bailment is for the mutual benefit of bailor and bailee, the bailee must use **ordinary care** with the property. Ordinary care is what a reasonably prudent person would use under the circumstances. When you rent a car, you benefit from the use of the car, and the agency profits from the fee you pay. When the airline hauls your suitcase to your destination, both parties benefit. Most bailments benefit both parties, and courts decide the majority of bailment disputes under this standard.

- *Sole Benefit of Bailor.* When the bailment benefits only the bailor, the bailee must use only **slight care**. This kind of bailment is called a **gratuitous bailment**, and the bailee is liable only for **gross negligence**. Sheila enters a greased-pig contest and asks you to hold her $140,000 diamond engagement ring while she competes. You put the ring in your pocket. Sheila wins the $20 first prize, but the ring has disappeared. This was a gratuitous bailment, and you are not liable to Sheila unless she can prove gross negligence on your part. If the ring dropped from your pocket or was stolen, you are not liable. If you used the ring to play catch with friends, you are liable.

Burden of Proof

In an ordinary negligence case, the plaintiff has the burden of proof to demonstrate that the defendant was negligent and caused the harm alleged. In bailment cases, the burden of proof is reversed. **Once the bailor has proven the existence of a bailment and loss or harm to the goods, a presumption of negligence arises, and the burden shifts to the bailee to prove adequate care.** This is a major change from ordinary negligence cases. Georgina's car is struck by another auto. If Georgina sues for negligence, it is her burden to prove that the defendant was driving unreasonably and caused the harm. By comparison, assume that Georgina rents Sam her sailboat for a month. At the end of the month, Sam announces that the boat is at the bottom of Lake Michigan. If Georgina sues Sam, she only needs to demonstrate that the parties had a bailment and that he failed to return the boat. The burden then shifts to Sam to prove that the boat was lost through no fault of his own. If he cannot meet that burden, Georgina recovers the full value of the boat.

In the following case, the court looks at the two principal issues we have examined: whether there was a bailment, and whether the bailee exercised adequate care.

GIN V. WACKENHUT CORP.

741 F. Supp. 1454, 1990 U.S. Dist. LEXIS 8718
United States District Court for the District of Hawaii, 1990

FACTS: Max Gin and Johnnie Fong had a partnership specializing in wholesale jewelry. They often traveled to jewelry shows and conventions to display their wares. Gin left a jewelry show in Miami and went to the airport, where he intended to catch a flight to New Orleans, for another trade show. Gin checked his suitcases with a curbside skycap and proceeded to the departure gate. He held one carry-on bag, containing $140,000 in jewelry.

Wackenhut operated the security checkpoint at the entrance to the departure gate. Like most, this checkpoint had an X-ray machine for baggage and a magnetometer to detect metal carried by passengers. Gin waited at one side until the line of people waiting for the magnetometer had dwindled. He then placed his bag on the conveyor belt and stepped up to the magnetometer. Just at that moment a woman wearing a heavy coat abruptly cut in front of Gin and passed through the magnetometer. She activated the metal detection alarm. The Wackenhut employee who operated the magnetometer motioned for Gin to wait on the terminal side of the machine, while the woman emptied her pockets onto a tray. She passed through the machine again and once more the alarm sounded. She emptied more items from her pockets, but again set off the alarm. Only on the fourth attempt did she proceed through the magnetometer. Gin walked through the machine, went to pick up his jewelry bag, and found it gone. He dashed through the departure lounge searching for the bag and sought police help, but to no avail.

Gin sued, alleging negligent bailment. Wackenhut defended, claiming that no bailment had arisen and that, even if it had, the company used adequate care.

ISSUES: Was there a bailment? If so, did Wackenhut use adequate care?

EXCERPTS FROM JUDGE KING'S DECISION: Although the law of bailments is well settled, the brevity of the alleged bailment makes this case somewhat novel.

This court is convinced that in the instant case a bailment was created. In proceeding through the security checkpoint, plaintiff placed his bag upon the X-ray conveyor belt. From the moment the bag entered the machine the plaintiff surrendered control to the defendant. The defendant could stop the bag in the machine for prolonged examination, could run it through the machine a second time, or could order it opened for an examination of its contents. Further, passengers such as the plaintiff have virtually no control over the length of time they will be separated from their bag. This time could vary from a few seconds to several minutes. It is also noteworthy that plaintiff could not retrieve his bag until the Wackenhut employee operating the magnetometer permitted plaintiff to pass into the concourse area. Due to the orientation of the X-ray machine and the magnetometer, it was impossible for a passenger waiting in line for the magnetometer to see his bag after it emerged from the X-ray machine. Although the period of separation might be brief, the plaintiff had surrendered possession and control of his belongings and a bailment was created.

Negligence: Under Florida law, once a plaintiff has proven the existence of a bailment, and demonstrated the failure of the bailee to return the bailed goods, a presumption of negligence on the part of the bailee arises. In order to avoid liability for the lost goods, the defendant has the burden of showing that he exercised the degree of care required by the nature of the bailment.

The court finds that Wackenhut failed to exercise the requisite degree of care in the instant case. Wackenhut knew passengers could not keep a visual watch over their bags throughout the inspection process. In addition, the defendant's own witness testified that carry-on bags had been lost, either through theft or inadvertence, an average of twice each week over the past several years. Despite this knowledge the defendant evidently made no effort either to more closely coordinate the screening of passengers with their baggage, to reorient the X-ray machine and magnetometer so that passengers could watch their bags during the security check, or to simply post a sign alerting passengers that thefts frequently occurred.

[The court awarded the plaintiffs $140,000.] ◢

Rights and Duties of the Bailor

The bailor's rights and duties are the reverse of the bailee's. The bailor is entitled to the return of his property on the agreed-upon date. He is also entitled to receive the property in good condition and to recover damages for harm to the property if the bailee failed to use adequate care.

LIABILITY FOR DEFECTS

Depending upon the type of bailment, the bailor is potentially liable for known or even unknown defects in the property. **If the bailment is for the sole benefit of the bailee, the bailor must notify the bailee of any known defects.** Suppose Megan lends her stepladder to Dave. The top rung is loose and Megan knows it, but forgets to tell Dave. The top rung crumbles and Dave falls onto his girlfriend's duck. Megan is liable to Dave and the girlfriend unless the defect in the ladder was obvious. Notice that Megan's liability is not only to the bailee, but also to any others injured by the defects. Megan would not be liable if she had notified Dave of the defective rung.

In a mutual-benefit bailment, the bailor is liable not only for known defects but also for unknown defects that the bailor could have discovered with

reasonable diligence. Suppose RentaLot rents a power sander to Dan. RentaLot does not realize that the sander has faulty wiring, but a reasonable inspection would have revealed the problem. When Dan suffers a serious shock from the defect, RentaLot is liable to him, even though it was unaware of the problem.

Chapter Conclusion

Real property law is ancient but forceful, as waterfront property owners discovered when a power company flooded their land and an old-fashioned easement deprived them of compensation. Had the families understood nonpossessory interests, they might have declined to buy the property. Landlord-tenant law, by contrast, is new and rapidly changing, especially as to liability for injuries. Personal property law affects most of us every day, as we park a car, leave goods with a repair shop, or put our suitcases through an X-ray machine. Understanding property law can be worth a lot of money—but never carry all of it with you.

Chapter Review

1. Real property includes land, buildings, air and subsurface rights, plant life, and fixtures. A fixture is any good that has become attached to other real property.

2. A fee simple absolute provides the owner with the greatest possible control of the property, including the right to make any lawful use of it and to sell it. A fee simple defeasible may terminate upon the occurrence of some limiting event. A life estate permits the owner to possess the property during her life, but not to sell it or leave it to heirs.

3. An easement gives a person the right to enter land belonging to another and make a limited use of it, without taking anything away.

4. The implied warranty of habitability means that a builder selling a new home guarantees the adequacy of materials and workmanship.

5. The seller of a home must disclose facts that a buyer does not know and cannot readily observe if they materially affect the property's value.

6. When an owner of a freehold estate allows another person temporary, exclusive possession of the property, the parties have created a landlord-tenant relationship.

7. Any lease for a stated, fixed period is a tenancy for years. A periodic tenancy is created for a fixed period and then automatically continues for additional periods until either party notifies the other of termination. A tenancy at will has no fixed duration and may be terminated by either party at any time. A tenancy at sufferance occurs when a tenant remains, against the wishes of the landlord, after the expiration of a true tenancy.

8. A landlord may be liable for constructive eviction if he substantially interferes with the tenant's use and enjoyment of the premises.

9. The implied warranty of habitability requires that a landlord meet all standards set by the local building code and/or that the premises be fit for human habitation.

10. The tenant is obligated to pay the rent and must pay the landlord for any significant damage he causes to the property.

11. At common law, a landlord had very limited liability for injuries on the premises, but today many courts require a landlord to use reasonable care and hold her liable for foreseeable harm.

12. A gift is a voluntary transfer of property from one person to another without consideration. The elements of a gift are intention to transfer ownership immediately, delivery, and acceptance.

13. A bailment is the rightful possession of goods by one who is not the owner. The one who delivers the goods is the bailor and the one in possession is the bailee. To create a bailment, the bailee must assume physical control with intent to possess.

14. The bailee is obligated to exercise due care. The level of care required depends upon who receives the benefit of the bailment: if the bailee is the sole beneficiary, she must use extraordinary care; if the parties mutually benefit, the bailee must use ordinary care; and if the bailor is the sole beneficiary of the bailment, the bailee must use only slight care.

Practice Test

1. Paul and Shelly Higgins had two wood stoves in their home. Each rested on, but was not attached to, a built-in brick platform. The downstairs wood stove was connected to the chimney flue and was used as part of the main heating system for the house. The upstairs stove, in the master bedroom, was purely decorative. It had no stovepipe connecting it to the chimney. The Higginses sold their house to Jack Everitt, and neither party said anything about the two stoves. Is Everitt entitled to either stove? Both stoves?

2. In 1944, W. E. Collins conveyed land to the Church of God of Prophecy. The deed said: "This deed is made with the full understanding that should the property fail to be used for the Church of God, it is to be null and void and property to revert to W. E. Collins or heirs." In the late 1980s, the church wished to move to another property and sought a judicial ruling that it had the right to sell the land. The trial court ruled that the church owned a fee simple absolute and had the right to sell the property. Comment.

3. **CPA QUESTION** On July 1, 1992, Quick, Onyx, and Nash were deeded a piece of land as tenants in common. The deed provided that Quick owned one-half the property and Onyx and Nash owned one-quarter each. If Nash dies, the property will be owned as follows:

    (a) Quick ½, Onyx ½.

    (b) Quick ⅝, Onyx ⅜.

    (c) Quick ⅓, Onyx ⅓, Nash's heirs ⅓.

    (d) Quick ½, Onyx ¼, Nash's heirs ¼.

4. Summey Building Systems built a condominium project in Myrtle Beach, South Carolina. The project included an adjacent parking deck. Shortly after Summey relinquished control to the condominium association, the deck began to experience problems. Water and caustic materials leaked through the upper deck and dripped onto cars parked underneath. Cracks appeared, and an expert concluded that the bond between the top deck and the structural supports was insufficient. Repairs would cost about $205,000. Summey had never warranted that the deck would be free of all problems. Is the company liable for the repairs?

5. Kenmart Realty sued to evict Mr. and Ms. Alghalabio for nonpayment of rent and sought the unpaid monies, totaling several thousand dollars. In defense, the Alghalabios claimed that their apartment was infested with rats. They testified that there were numerous rat holes in the walls of the living room, bedroom, and kitchen, that there were rat droppings all over the apartment, and that on one occasion they saw their toddler holding a live rat. They testified that the landlord had refused numerous requests to exterminate. Please rule on the landlord's suit.

6. **YOU BE THE JUDGE WRITING PROBLEM** Dominion Bank owned a large office building in Washington, D.C. Because it planned to sell

the building, the bank stopped leasing new space, and five of the 13 floors became vacant. Tenants complained to the bank that vagrants were using the empty spaces for drug deals and prostitution. Jane Doe, a secretary who worked in the building, was dragged to an empty, unlocked floor and raped. She sued the bank. A security expert testified that all vacant offices and floors should have been sealed off. Is the bank liable for Doe's injuries? **Argument for Jane Doe:** The bank created a dangerous situation by gradually abandoning a commercial building. The bank should be held to a "reasonable person" standard, one that it clearly failed to meet. **Argument for Dominion Bank:** The bank is not a police force. The bank's obligation was to keep the rented premises in good working order, which it did.

7. While in her second year at the Juilliard School of Music in New York City, Ann Rylands had a chance to borrow for one month a rare Guadagnini violin, made in 1768. She returned the violin to the owner in Philadelphia, but telephoned her father to ask if he would buy it for her. He borrowed money from his pension fund and paid the owner. Ann traveled to Philadelphia to pick up the violin. She had exclusive possession of the violin for the next 20 years, using it in her professional career. Unfortunately, she became an alcoholic, and during one period when she was in a treatment center, she entrusted the violin to her mother for safekeeping. At about that time, her father died. When Ann was released from the center, she requested return of the violin, but her mother refused. Who owns the violin?

8. **ETHICS** Jane says to Cody, "If you will agree to work as my yard man, I'll pay you $1,000 per week for a normal work week. You can start on Monday, and I'll guarantee you eight months' work." Cody is elated at his good fortune and agrees to start work on Monday. Later that day, Cody, still rejoicing, says to Beth, his girlfriend, "You know those sapphire earrings in the jewelry store that you're wild about? At the end of next week I'm going to buy them for you." On Monday, Jane realizes what a foolish thing she said, and refuses to hire Cody. Cody, in turn, refuses to buy the earrings for Beth.

Cody sues Jane and wins; Beth sues Cody and loses. Why the opposite outcomes? What basic ideas of fairness underlie the two results?

9. Ronald Armstead worked for First American Bank as a courier. His duties included making deliveries between the bank's branches in Washington, D.C. Armstead parked the bank's station wagon near the entrance of one branch in violation of a sign that read "No Parking Rush Hour Zone." In the rear luggage section of the station wagon were four locked bank dispatch bags containing checks and other valuable documents. Armstead had received tickets for illegal parking at this spot on five occasions. Shortly after Armstead entered the bank, a tow truck arrived and its operator prepared to tow the station wagon. Transportation Management, Inc., operated the towing service on behalf of the District of Columbia. Armstead ran out to the vehicle and told the tow truck operator that he was prepared to drive the vehicle away immediately. But the operator drove away with the station wagon in tow. One and one-half hours later, a bank employee paid for the car's release, but one dispatch bag, containing documents worth $107,000, was missing. First American sued Transportation Management and the District of Columbia. The defendants sought summary judgment, claiming they could not be liable. Were they correct?

10. **YOU BE THE JUDGE WRITING PROBLEM** Eileen Murphy often cared for her elderly neighbor, Thomas Kenney. He paid her $25 per day for her help and once gave her a bank certificate of deposit worth $25,000. Murphy alleged that shortly before his death, Kenney gave her a large block of shares in three corporations. He called his broker to instruct him to transfer the shares to Murphy's name, but the broker was unavailable. So Kenney told Murphy to write her name on the shares and keep them, which she did. Two weeks later Kenney died. When Murphy presented the shares to Kenney's broker to transfer ownership to her, the broker refused because Kenney had never signed them over to Murphy. Was Murphy entitled to the $25,000? To the shares? **Argument for Murphy:** The purpose of the

law is to do what a donor intended, and it is obvious that Kenney intended Murphy to have the $25,000 and the shares. **Argument for the Estate:** Murphy is not entitled to the $25,000 because we have no way of knowing what Kenney's intentions were when he gave her the money. She is not entitled to the shares of stock because Kenney's failure to endorse them over to her meant he never delivered them.

11. **ROLE REVERSAL** Write a short-answer question focusing on one of the following: a fixture, an easement, or adverse possession.

12. **ROLE REVERSAL** Write a multiple-choice question highlighting the difference between any two of the following: a contract, an *inter vivos* gift, or a gift *causa mortis*.

Internet Research Problems

Go to http://www.tenantsunion.org/tulist.html, and search for the law of your state concerning a landlord's obligation to provide a habitable apartment. Now assume that you are living in a rental unit with serious defects. Write a letter to the landlord asking for prompt repairs. You may use the form letters provided at http://little.nhlink.net/nhlink/housing/cto/letters/letrs.htm as a guide.

You own a helicopter worth $250,000. A business associate wishes to use it for one week to show prospective clients around various islands in the Caribbean. You are willing to let him use it, for a fee of $15,000. Draft a bailment agreement. Use the form supplied at http://www.gate.net/~legalsvc/autobail.html as a model.

You can find further practice problems in the Online Quiz at http://beatty.westbuslaw.com **or in the Study Guide that accompanies this text.**

Consumer Law

Three women signed up for a lesson at the Arthur Murray dance studio in Washington, D.C. Expecting a session of decorous fun, they instead found themselves in a nightmare of humiliation and coercion:

- "First of all, I did not want the [additional] lesson, and I think it was unpleasant because I had three, maybe four, people, as I say, pressuring me to buy something by a certain time, and I do recall asking that I be let to think, let me think it over, and I was told that the contest would end at 6 o'clock or something to that effect and if I did not sign by a certain time it would be too late. I think we got under the deadline by maybe a minute or two. If I had been given time to think, I would not have signed that contract."

- "I tried to say no and get out of it and I got very, very upset because I got frightened at paying out all that money and having nothing to fall back on. I remember I started crying and couldn't stop crying. All I thought of was getting out of there. So finally after—I don't know how much time, Mr. Mara said, well, I could sign up for 250 hours, which was half the 500 Club, which would amount to $4,300. So I finally signed it. After that, I tried to raise the money from the bank and found I couldn't get a loan for that amount and I didn't have any savings and I had to get a bank loan to pay for it. That was when I went back and asked him to cancel that contract. But Mr. Mara said that he couldn't cancel it."

CHAPTER 23

- "I did not join the carnival. I did not wish to join the carnival, and while it was only an additional $55, I had no desire to join. [My instructor] asked everyone in the room to sit down in a circle around me and he stood me up in that circle, in the middle of the circle, and said, 'Everybody, I want you to look at this woman here who is too cheap to join the carnival. I just want you to look at a woman like that. Isn't it awful?'" ◾

Because of abuses such as these, the Federal Trade Commission (FTC) ordered the Arthur Murray dance studio to halt its high-pressure sales techniques, limit each contract to no more than $1,500 in dance lessons, and permit all contracts to be canceled within seven days.[1]

Introduction

Years ago consumers typically dealt with merchants they knew well. A dance instructor in a small town would not stay in business long if he tormented his elderly, vulnerable clients. As the population of this country grew and cities expanded, however, merchants became less and less subject to community pressure. The law has supplemented, if not replaced, these informal policing mechanisms. Both Congress and the states have passed statutes that protect consumers from the unscrupulous. But the legal system in America is generally too slow and expensive to handle small cases. The women who fell into the web of Arthur Murray had neither the wealth nor the energy to sue the studio themselves. To aid consumers such as these, Congress empowered federal agencies to enforce consumer laws. The Federal Trade Commission is the most important of these agencies.

FEDERAL TRADE COMMISSION

Congress created the FTC in 1915 to regulate business. Although its original focus was on antitrust law, it now regulates a wide range of business activities that affect consumers, everything from advertising to consumer loans to warranties to debt collection practices.[2] It is, if you will, the consumer's best friend in Washington. The FTC has several options for enforcing the law:

- *Voluntary Compliance.* When the FTC determines that a business has violated the law, it first asks the offender to sign a voluntary compliance affidavit promising to stop the prohibited activity.

- *Administrative Hearings and Appeals.* If the company refuses to stop voluntarily, the FTC takes the case to an administrative law judge (ALJ) within the agency. The violator may settle the case at this point by signing a **consent order**. If the case proceeds to a hearing, the ALJ has the right to issue a **cease and desist order**, commanding the violator to stop the offending activity. The FTC issued a cease and desist order against the Arthur Murray dance studio. A defendant can appeal such an order to the five Commissioners of the FTC, from there to a federal appeals court, and ultimately to the United States Supreme Court.

---

[1] *In re Arthur Murray Studio of Washington, Inc.*, 78 F.T.C. 401, 1971 FTC LEXIS 75 (1971).
[2] Chapter 19 discusses the FTC's role in antitrust enforcement.

Both the Commissioners and the Fifth Circuit Court of Appeals confirmed the cease and desist order against Arthur Murray. The case never reached the Supreme Court.

- *Penalties.* The penalty for each violation of a voluntary compliance affidavit, consent order, or cease and desist order is $11,000. The same penalty also applies to each knowing violation of (1) an FTC rule or (2) a cease and desist order issued against *someone else.* For example, the Arthur Murray studio could be liable for violating an FTC cease and desist order prohibiting high-pressure sales by the Fred Astaire studio. In addition, the FTC can file suit in federal court asking for damages on behalf of an injured consumer if (1) the defendant has violated FTC rules and (2) a reasonable person would have known under the circumstances that the conduct was dishonest or fraudulent.

Sales

Section 5 of the Federal Trade Commission Act (FTC Act) prohibits "unfair and deceptive acts or practices." You can report an unfair or deceptive practice to the FTC at its Web site (http://www.ftc.gov).

DECEPTIVE ACTS OR PRACTICES

Many deceptive acts or practices involve advertisements. **Under the FTC Act, an advertisement is deceptive if it contains an important misrepresentation or omission that is likely to mislead a reasonable consumer.** A company advertised that a pain-relief ointment called "Aspercreme" provided "the strong relief of aspirin right where you hurt." From this ad and the name of the product, do you assume that the ointment contains aspirin? Are you a reasonable consumer? Consumers surveyed in a shopping mall believed the product contained aspirin. In fact, it does not. The FTC required the company to disclose that there is no aspirin in Aspercreme.[3]

Is there anything wrong with the following ads?

---

[3] *In re Thompson Medical Co., Inc.,* 104 F.T.C. 648, 1984 FTC LEXIS 6 (1984).

Do not believe a word of them, warns the FTC. It takes more than three minutes a day to get muscle-bound, no matter what equipment you use. As for the #1 Doctor Recommended Ensure, the doctors in the survey were asked which liquid meal they would choose if they were going to recommend one to a patient. In fact, most doctors would not recommend Ensure to the healthy adults pictured in the advertisements. The half-price cars were for lease, not sale. By the end of the lease, owners would have paid only half the value of the cars, but they would also have to return the cars to the dealer. Was the company in the following case deceptive about its treatment for baldness?

FTC V. PANTRON I CORP.

33 F.3d 1088, 1994 U.S. App. LEXIS 22977
United States Court of Appeals for the Ninth Circuit, 1994

FACTS: Pantron I Corp. marketed the Helsinki Formula, a conditioner and shampoo costing $49.95 for a three-month supply. Pantron's advertisements (including late-night infomercials hosted by Robert Vaughn, star of the old TV show the "Man from U.N.C.L.E.") claimed scientific studies proved that the formula promoted growth of new hair on bald men.

At trial, three doctors testified that there was "no reason to believe" from current scientific data that the Helsinki Formula would cure or prevent baldness and that the studies on which Pantron relied did not meet generally accepted scientific standards. Users of the Helsinki Formula (or any other baldness cure) may indeed experience hair regrowth because of the so-called *placebo effect*. Frequently, products with no medicinal value work for psychological reasons. A patient who takes sugar pills believing they are pain relievers may feel better, although the pills themselves are worthless in treating pain. Hair growth products have a particularly strong placebo effect.

Pantron introduced evidence from 18 men who experienced hair regrowth or a reduction in hair loss after using the formula. It also introduced evidence of a "consumer satisfaction survey" that showed positive results in 70 percent of those who had used the product for six months or more. Over half of Pantron's orders came from repeat purchasers; it received very few written complaints; and fewer than 3 percent of its customers asked for their money back.

The trial court decided that Pantron could state, in its advertisements, that the Helsinki Formula was

effective to some extent for some people in treating baldness. However, the ads must disclose that (1) the formula was more likely to stop hair loss than grow new hair, and (2) the claims were not supported by scientific studies that met U.S. standards.

ISSUE: Are the advertisements for the Helsinki Formula deceptive?

EXCERPTS FROM JUDGE REINHARDT'S DECISION: Where, as here, a product's effectiveness arises solely as a result of the placebo effect, a representation that the product is effective constitutes a false advertisement even though some consumers may experience positive results. Under the evidence in the record before us, it appears that massaging vegetable oil on one's head would likely produce the same positive results as using the Helsinki Formula. All that might be required would be for Wesson Oil to [run] infomercials with Mr. Vaughn that promote its product as a baldness cure.

As the FTC has explained, "The Commission cannot accept as proof of a product's efficacy a psychological reaction stemming from a belief which, to a substantial degree, was caused by respondent's deceptions." Indeed, were we to hold otherwise, advertisers would be encouraged to foist unsubstantiated claims on an unsuspecting public in the hope that consumers would believe the ads and the claims would be self-fulfilling. Moreover, allowing advertisers to rely on the placebo effect would not only harm those individuals who were deceived; it would create a substantial economic cost as well, by allowing sellers to fleece large numbers of consumers who, unable to evaluate the efficacy of an inherently useless product, make repeat purchases of that product. [W]e conclude that the district court erred in deciding that the FTC had not shown that Pantron's effectiveness claims were false. ◢

UNFAIR PRACTICES

The FTC Act also prohibits unfair acts or practices. The **Commission considers a practice to be** *unfair* **if it meets all of the following three tests:**

- *It causes a substantial consumer injury.* This can mean physical or financial injury. A furnace repair company that dismantled home furnaces for "inspection" and then refused to reassemble them until the consumers agreed to buy services or replacement parts had caused a substantial consumer injury.

- *The harm of the injury outweighs any countervailing benefit.* A pharmaceutical company sold a sunburn remedy without conducting adequate tests to ensure that it worked. The expense of these tests would have forced the company to raise the product's price. The company had demonstrated that the product was safe, and there was evidence in the medical literature that the ingredients when used in other products were effective. The FTC determined that, although the company was technically in violation of its rules, the benefit to consumers of a cheaper product more than outweighed the risk of injury to them.

- *The consumer could not reasonably avoid the injury.* The FTC is particularly vigilant in protecting susceptible consumers—such as the elderly or the ill—who are less able to avoid injury. For example, the Commission looks especially carefully at those who offer a cure for cancer.

In addition, the FTC may decide that a practice is unfair simply because it violates public policy even if it does not meet these three tests. The Commission refused to allow a mail-order company to file collection suits in states far from where the defendants lived because the practice was unfair, whether or not it met the three tests.

What is the difference between *deceptive* and *unfair*? Consider this case: Audio Communications, Inc. (ACI), ran a telephone service for children. By dialing a 900 number, children could listen to recorded stories or games featuring characters such as Santa Claus and the Easter Bunny. ACI ran advertisements on children's TV shows and in children's magazines. The FTC held that the ads were *deceptive* because they did not reveal that the phone calls cost money. Moreover, the ads promised a free gift in return for one phone call. In reality, callers (who were, after all, young children) could not obtain a gift without following several complicated steps that were explained very rapidly. Often, more than one call was necessary to obtain the gift. This practice was also *unfair* because children often made the calls without parental permission. Parents (who paid the bill) had little control over children (who made the call). In its consent order, the FTC required ACI to include in all of its advertisements the following statement: "Kids, you must ask your mom or dad and get their permission before you call. This call costs money."[4]

---

[4] F.T.C., 56 C.F.R. 22432 (May 15, 1991).

OTHER SALES PRACTICES

Bait and Switch

FTC rules prohibit bait and switch advertisements: a merchant may not advertise a product and then disparage it to consumers in an effort to sell a different item. In addition merchants must have enough stock on hand to meet reasonable demand for any advertised product. Sears, Roebuck and Co. ran many advertisements like the following:

Portable Zig-Zag Sewing Machine
from SEARS
$58

Sews on buttons, sews buttonholes
Does zig-zag or straight stitching
monograms, appliqués, other fancy work
for household linens, gifts
Sews forward and reverse for her convenience

When eager customers went to buy this fabulous item, they were told that the machines were noisy, did not come with Sears's standard sewing machine guarantee, and could neither stitch in reverse nor do buttonholes. Also, the store was out of stock and would not be receiving any new machines for a long time.[5]

This is bait and switch advertising, and it violates FTC rules. The **bait** is an alluring offer that sounds almost too good to be true. Of course, it is. The advertiser does not wish to sell the advertised merchandise; it wants to **switch** consumers to another, higher-priced product. The real purpose of the advertisement is simply to find customers who are interested in buying.

Mail or Telephone Order Merchandise

Many Americans rely on catalogues to buy everything from clothing to medicine to furnishings, so it is important that these merchants deliver as promised. **The FTC has established the following guidelines on mail or telephone order merchandise:**

- Mail-order companies must ship an item within the time stated or, if no time is given, within 30 days after receipt of the order.

---

[5] *In re Sears, Roebuck and Co.*, 89 F.T.C. 229, 1977 FTC LEXIS 225 (1977).

- If a company cannot ship the product when promised, it must send the customer a notice with the new shipping date and an opportunity to cancel. If the new shipping date is within 30 days of the original one, and the customer does not cancel, the order is still on.

- If the company cannot ship within 30 days of the original date, it must send the customer another notice. This time, however, the company must cancel the order unless the customer returns the notice, indicating that he still wants the item.

For example, Dell Computer Corp. advertised that its Dimension computer came with the "Dell Software Suite." In fact for several months the suite was not available. Instead of the software, Dell sent customers a coupon for the suite "when available." The FTC charged Dell with violations of the mail or telephone order rules because the company:

- Knew it could not ship the software within 30 days

- Failed to offer buyers the opportunity to cancel their orders, and

- Did not cancel the orders automatically as it should have under the rules.[6]

Telemarketing

The telephone rings: "Could I speak with Alexander Johannson? This is Denise from Master Chimney Sweeps." It is 7:30 P.M.; you have just straggled in from work and are looking forward to a peaceful dinner of takeout cuisine. You are known as Sandy, your last name is pronounced Yohannson, and you live in a modern apartment without a chimney. A telemarketer has struck again! What can you do to protect your peace and quiet?

More than half the states currently have statutes that prohibit telemarketers from calling any telephone number listed on the state's do-not-call registry. Recently, the FTC has also established a national do-not-call registry. You can register your telephone numbers with the FTC online at http://www.donotcall.gov or by telephone at (888) 382-1222. The FTC is working to coordinate the state and federal registries. FTC rules also prohibit telemarketers from blocking their names and telephone numbers on Caller ID systems.

Unordered Merchandise

Under §5 of the FTC Act, anyone who receives unordered merchandise in the mail can treat it as a gift. She can use it, throw it away, or do whatever else she wants with it.

There you are, watching an infomercial for Anushka products, guaranteed to fight that scourge of modern life—cellulite! Rushing to your phone, you place an order. The Anushka cosmetics arrive, but for some odd reason, the cellulite remains. A month later another bottle arrives, like magic, in the mail. The magic spell is broken, however, when you get your credit card bill and see that, without your authorization, the company has charged you for the new supply of Anushka. Is this a hot new marketing technique? Not exactly. The FTC ordered the company to cease and desist this unfair and deceptive practice. The company improperly

---

6 *United States v. Dell Computer Corp.*, 1998 FTC LEXIS 30 (1998).

billed its customers, said the FTC, and should have notified them that they were free to treat the unauthorized products as a gift, to use or throw out as they wished.[7]

Door-to-Door Sales

Consumers at home need special protection from unscrupulous salespeople. In a store, customers can simply walk out, but at home they may feel trapped. Also, it is difficult at home to compare products or prices offered by competitors. Under the FTC door-to-door rules, **a salesperson is required to notify the buyer that she has the right to cancel the transaction prior to midnight of the third business day thereafter.** This notice must be given both orally and in writing; the actual cancellation must be in writing. The seller must return the buyer's money within 10 days. The following news report illustrates an illegal method of selling magazine subscriptions.

A federal judge assessed a $50,000 civil penalty against a door-to-door magazine sales company. Customers who purchased magazine subscriptions from Tork & Associates were given (partial) receipts that misrepresented their right to cancel. The receipt indicated that a customer wishing to cancel was required to submit a copy of the complete receipt, the canceled check, the salesperson's name, the magazine name, the date of the transaction, and the total cost. Because the salesperson never gave the customer the complete receipt, it was difficult to comply. In two years, Tork generated $2 million in revenues.[8]

ETHICS

A vice president of Grolier, the encyclopedia company, made the following statement:

> The proposition that a buyer should have the right to whimsically change his mind with respect to a transaction which has been formalized by an agreement containing all of the elements of a legally binding contract, is indeed, a revolutionary legal concept. This proposal represents an attack on the basic contractual concepts which are the foundation of the American economic system.[9]

Do you agree with this statement? From the Chapter 2 Ethics Checklist: What answer would the Golden Rule provide? If you were head of Grolier, would you support or resist the FTC door-to-door rule?

Consumer Credit

Historically, the practice of charging interest on loans was banned by most countries and by three of the most prominent religions—Christianity, Islam, and Judaism. As the European economy developed, however, money lending became essential. To compromise, governments began to permit interest charges but limited the maximum rate to 6 percent. European settlers carried this concept to the United States, which soon adopted the 6 percent rule, too.

---

[7] *In the Matter of Synchronal Corp.*, 116 F.T.C. 1189, 1993 FTC LEXIS 280 (1993).

[8] Nancy Stancill, "Door-to-Door Firm Hit with $50,000 Penalty," *Houston Chronicle*, Jan. 28, 1993, p. A17.

[9] *Quoted in* Douglas Whaley, *Problems and Materials on Consumer Law* (Boston: Little, Brown & Co., 1991), at p. 135.

Even in modern times, most states limit the maximum interest rate a lender may charge. The penalty for violating usury statutes varies among the states. Depending upon the jurisdiction, the borrower may be allowed to keep (1) the interest above the usury limit, (2) all of the interest, or (3) all of the loan and the interest.

Before Congress passed the Truth in Lending Act (TILA), lenders found many creative methods to disguise the real interest rate and circumvent the law. For example, they would use a so-called add-on rate. That is, they would charge the permissible interest rate but would insist that the borrower begin to repay the loan in installments immediately. The borrower only had effective use of the money for half the term of the loan. Suppose that a car dealer loaned a customer $3,600 for three years, at 8 percent. The total interest would be .08 × $3,600 × 3 = $864. If the borrower was required to repay $100 of the principal each month, she would be repaying half the loan within 18 months, but would still pay the full $864 in interest. This customer's real interest rate was 16 percent, not 8 percent.

TRUTH IN LENDING ACT

The problem with add-ons and other such devices designed to hide the real rate of interest from the authorities is that they also hide it from the borrower. Before TILA, many consumers had no idea what interest rate they were really paying. Congress passed the statute to ensure that consumers were adequately informed about credit terms before entering into a loan and could compare the cost of credit. TILA does not regulate interest rates or the terms of a loan; these are still set by state law. It simply requires lenders to *disclose* the terms of a loan in an understandable and complete manner.

TILA applies to a transaction only if all of the following tests are met:

- *It is a consumer loan.* That means a loan to an individual for personal, family, or household purposes but not a loan to a business. For example, TILA does not apply to a loan on a truck used to sell produce.

- *The loan has a finance charge or will be repaid in more than four installments.* Sometimes finance charges masquerade as installment plans. Boris can pay for his big-screen TV in six monthly installments of $200 each, or he can pay $900 cash up front. If he chooses the installment plan, he is effectively paying a finance charge of $300. That is why TILA applies to loans with more than four installments.

- *The loan is for less than $25,000 or secured by a mortgage on real estate.* If Boris borrows money to buy a $1 million house, TILA applies, but not if he buys a $50,000 yacht.

- *The loan is made by someone in the business of offering credit.* If Boris borrows $5,000 from his friend Ludmilla to buy a riding mower, TILA does not apply. If he borrows the money from Friendly Neighborhood Loan Depot, Inc., TILA does apply.

REQUIRED DISCLOSURE

In all loans regulated by TILA:

- *The disclosure must be clear and in meaningful sequence.* A finance company violated TILA when it loaned money to Dorothy Allen. The company made all the required disclosures but scattered them throughout the loan document and intermixed them with confusing terms that were not required by TILA.[10] A TILA disclosure statement should not be a game of *Where's Waldo?*

- *The lender must disclose the finance charge.* The finance charge is the amount, in dollars, the consumer will pay in interest and fees over the life of the loan. It is important for consumers to know this amount because otherwise they may not understand the real cost of the loan. Of course, the longer the loan, the higher the finance charge. Someone who borrows $5 for 10 years at 10 percent annual interest will pay $.50 each year for 10 years, for a total finance charge of $5— equal to the principal borrowed. In 25-year mortgages, the finance charge will almost always exceed the amount of the principal.

- *The creditor must also disclose the annual percentage rate (APR).* This number is the actual rate of interest the consumer pays on an annual basis. Without this disclosure, it would be easy in a short-term loan to disguise a very high APR because the finance charge is low. Boris borrows $5 for lunch from his employer's credit union. Under the terms of the loan, he must repay $6 the following week. His finance charge is only $1, but his APR is astronomical—20 percent per week for a year.

All TILA loans must meet these three requirements. TILA requires additional disclosure for two types of loans: open-end credit and closed-end credit.

Open-End Credit. This is a credit transaction in which the lender makes a series of loans that the consumer can repay at once or in installments. The typical Visa or MasterCard account is open-end credit—the cardholder has a choice of paying his balance in full each month or making only the required minimum payment.[11] The lender must disclose credit terms in any advertisements. In addition, before beginning an open-end credit account, the lender must disclose to the consumer when a finance charge will be imposed and how the finance charge will be calculated (e.g., whether it will be based on the account balance at the beginning of the billing cycle, the end, or somewhere in between). **In each statement, the lender must disclose the following:** the amount owed at the beginning of the billing cycle (the previous balance); amounts and dates of all purchases, credits and payments; finance charges; and the date by which a bill must be paid to avoid finance charges. The Federal Reserve Board offers advice on choosing a credit card at http://www.federalreserve.gov/pubs/shop/.

Closed-End Credit. In a closed-end transaction, there is only one loan, and the borrower knows the amount and the payment schedule in advance. Boris enters into a closed-end transaction when he buys a $30,000 car and agrees to make specified monthly payments over five years. Before a consumer enters into a closed-end transaction, the lender must disclose the cash price; the total down payment; the amount financed; an itemized list of all other charges; the number, amount, and due dates of payments; the total amount of payments; late payment charges; penalties for prepaying the loan; and the lender's security interest in the item purchased.[12]

---

[10] *Allen v. Beneficial Fin. Co. of Gary*, 531 F.2d 797, 1976 U.S. App. LEXIS 12935 (7th Cir. 1976).

[11] Open-end credit rules apply to all consumer credit cards, even those that require the balance to be paid every month.

[12] See Chapter 12, on secured transactions and bankruptcy, for a discussion of security interests.

Other TILA Provisions

Home Equity Loans.   Scam artists sometimes prey upon the elderly who are vulnerable to pressure and upon the poor who may not have access to conventional financing. These swindlers offer home equity loans, secured by a second mortgage, to finance fraudulent repairs. (There are, of course, many legitimate lenders in the home equity business.) The following news report shows scam artists at work.

NEWSWORTHY

Mack and Jacqueline Moon of East Baltimore hired a home improvement contractor to install a dropped ceiling, paneling, and cabinets in the unfinished basement of their row house. The couple were determined not to put a second mortgage on their house, anticipating they would need backup money to pay medical expenses for their 10-year-old daughter who had lupus. They signed the contract a few days later after a second salesperson assured them, "We were able to work it out, and you don't have to worry about a mortgage." The Moons were never given copies of the loan documents nor told of the 17 percent interest rate. A year later, when they tried to use their home's equity to pay medical bills for their daughter, who had since died, they discovered they had given a second mortgage to the lender without knowing it.[13]

In response to such scams, TILA was amended to provide additional consumer safeguards for home equity installment loans. If a home equity installment loan:

- Has an APR (interest rate) that is more than 10 percentage points higher than Treasury securities, or

- The consumer must pay fees and points at closing that are higher than $480 (in 2002 dollars) or 8 percent of the total loan amount,

then,

- At least three business days before the loan closing the lender must notify the consumer that (1) he does not have to go through with the loan (even if he has signed the loan agreement) and (2) he could lose his home if he fails to make payments, and

- Loans that are for less than five years may not contain balloon payments (i.e., a payment at the end that is more than twice the regular monthly payment).

Rescission.   This change in the law came too late to help the Moons, but they found relief in a different TILA provision. Under TILA, consumers have the right to rescind a mortgage for up to three business days after the signing. If the lender does not comply with the disclosure provisions of TILA, the consumer can rescind for up to three years from the date of the mortgage.

The Moons were able to rescind the loan because the lender had not made adequate disclosure. This right of rescission does *not* apply to a *first* mortgage used to finance a home purchase or to any refinancing with the consumer's existing lender. The following table summarizes the major provisions of TILA.

---

[13] Lorraine Mirabella, "With Hopes of Improving Their Homes, Many Owners Fall Prey to Loan Scams," *Baltimore Sun*, Sep. 4, 1994, p. 1K.

TILA applies to a transaction only if:	• It is a consumer loan • The loan has a finance charge or will be repaid in more than four installments • The loan is for less than $25,000 or to secure a mortgage on real estate, and • The loan is made by someone in the business of offering credit.
In all loans regulated by TILA:	• The disclosure must be clear and in meaningful sequence, and • The lender must disclose the finance charge and the annual percentage rate (APR).
Consumers have the right to rescind a mortgage:	• For up to three business days after the signing, or • For up to three years from the date of the mortgage if the lender does not comply with TILA disclosure provisions. • This provision does not apply if the mortgage is a first mortgage used to finance a home purchase or a refinancing with the consumer's existing lender.

Advertising. TILA is meant to enable consumers to shop around and compare available financing alternatives. With this goal in mind, the statute requires lenders to advertise their rates accurately. A lender cannot "bait and switch"; that is, it cannot advertise rates unless they are generally available to anyone who applies. Moreover, if the lender advertises any credit terms, it must tell the whole story. For example, if it advertises "Nothing down, 12 months to pay," it must also disclose the APR and other terms of repayment.

Enforcement. The FTC generally has the right to enforce TILA. In addition, consumers who have been injured by any violation (except for the advertising provisions) have the right to file suit.

ECONOMICS & THE LAW

What is the economic impact of TILA? This statute requires lenders to provide a service against their will: detailed information about loans. Although this information is important to consumers, it is relatively expensive for them to produce while being relatively easy for lenders. Without TILA, consumers could compile credit information only by spending hours on the phone, asking questions of each lender. With TILA, all of this information to consumers is available more or less for free. (Although lenders do pass their costs on to consumers, this cost is low compared with the value of the information or the cost to consumers if they had to find out the information on their own.)

Economists believe in efficiency, which means, among other things, that a product should be produced as cheaply as possible. TILA is consistent with this goal: it ensures that loan information is produced cheaply (by lenders) rather than at great cost (by consumers).

Access to detailed loan information permits borrowers to compare competing offers. The ability to comparison shop enhances consumers' market power. Greater customer power leads to lower prices. In short TILA not only protects consumers from entering into loans that are more expensive than they realized, it also lowers the cost of borrowing money. ▪

Special Credit Card Rules.   Your wallet is missing, and with it your cash, your driver's license, a photo of your dog, a coupon for a free video rental and—oh, no!—all your credit cards! It is a disaster, to be sure. But it could have been worse. There was a time when you would have been responsible for every charge the thief rang up. **Now, under TILA, you are liable only for the first $50 in charges the thief makes before you notify the credit card company.** If you call the company before any charges are made, you have no liability at all. But if, by the time you contact the company, the speedy robber has completely furnished her apartment on your card, you are still liable only for $50. Of course, if you carry a wallet full of cards, $50 for each one can add up to a sizable total. If the thief steals just your credit card number, but not the card itself, you are not liable for any unauthorized charges.

Suppose that a credit card company mails a card to you that you did not order and someone steals it out of your mailbox. You know nothing about the card until the bills arrive. If you did not request the card, and it is not a renewal or substitute for a card you already have, you are not liable, even for the $50.

You use your credit card to buy a new computer at ShadyComputers. When you arrive home and start to load software, you discover the hard disk is only 1 gigabyte, not 20 gigabytes as advertised. The computer crashes six times the first day. In short, you have a major, $2,200 problem. But all is not lost. **In the event of a dispute between a customer and a merchant, the credit card company cannot bill the customer if** (1) she makes a good faith effort to resolve the dispute, (2) the dispute is for more than $50, and (3) the merchant is in the same state where she lives or is within 100 miles of her home.

What happens if the merchant and the consumer cannot resolve their dispute? Or if the merchant is not in the same state as the consumer? Clearly, credit card companies do not want to be caught in the middle between consumer and merchant. In practice, they now require all merchants to sign a contract specifying that, in the event of a dispute between the merchant and a customer, the credit card company has the right to charge back the merchant's account. If a customer seems to have a reasonable claim against a merchant, the credit card company will typically transfer the credit it has given the merchant back to the customer's account. Of course, the merchant can try to sue the customer for any money owed.

Debit Cards.   So your wallet is missing, and with it your debit card. No problem, right, it is just like a credit card? Wrong. Debit cards look and feel like credit cards, but legally they are a different plastic altogether. Debit cards work like checks (which is why they are also called **check cards**). When you use your debit card, the bank deducts money directly from your account, which means there is no bill to pay at the end of the month (and no interest charges on unpaid bills). That is the good news. The bad news is that your liability for a stolen debit card is much greater. If you report the loss before anyone uses your card, you are not liable for any unauthorized withdrawals. If you report the theft within two days of discovering it, the bank will make good on all losses above $50. If you wait until after two days, your bank will only replace stolen funds above $500. After 60 days of receipt of your bank statement, all losses are yours: the bank will not repay any stolen funds. If an unauthorized transfer takes place using just your number, not your card, then you are not liable at all as long as you report the loss within 60 days of receiving the bank statement showing the loss. After 60 days, however, you are liable for the full amount.

FAIR CREDIT BILLING ACT

The Fair Credit Billing Act (FCBA) provides additional protection for credit card holders. Is there anyone in America who has not sometime or other discovered an error in a credit card bill? Before Congress passed the FCBA in 1975, a dispute with a credit card company often deteriorated into an avalanche of threatening form letters that ignored any response from the hapless cardholder. **Under the FCBA:**

- If, within 60 days of receipt of a bill, a consumer writes to a credit card company to complain about the bill, the company must acknowledge receipt of the complaint within 30 days.

- Within two billing cycles (but no more than 90 days) the credit card company must investigate the complaint and respond:

    - In the case of an error, by correcting the mistake and notifying the consumer

    - If there is no error, by writing to the consumer with an explanation.

- Whether or not there was a mistake, if the consumer requests it, the credit card company must supply documentary evidence to support its position—for example, copies of the bill signed by the consumer or evidence that the package actually arrived.

- The credit card company cannot try to collect the disputed debt or close or suspend the account until it has responded to the consumer complaint.

- The credit card company cannot report to credit agencies that the consumer has an unpaid bill until 10 days after the response. If the consumer still disputes the charge, the credit card company may report the amount to a credit agency but must disclose that it is disputed.

At http://www.ftc.gov/bcp/conline/pubs/credit/fcb.htm the FTC provides a sample form letter to send to a credit card company if you want to dispute a bill.

In the following case, American Express made a big mistake picking on a law professor. The court's opinion was written by Abner J. Mikva, a highly regarded judge on the federal appeals court. He was clearly exasperated by American Express's arguments and used strong language to reprimand the company—and the lower court. Since Judge Mikva had served in Congress, he could speak with some authority about Congress's approach to consumer legislation.

GRAY V. AMERICAN EXPRESS CO.

743 F.2d 10, 240 U.S. App. D.C. 10, 1984 U.S. App. LEXIS 19033
United States Court of Appeals for the District of Columbia Circuit, 1984

FACTS: In December, Oscar Gray used his American Express credit card to buy airline tickets costing $9,312. American Express agreed that Gray could pay for the tickets in 12 monthly installments. In January, Gray paid $3,500 and then in February an additional $1,156. In March, American Express billed Gray by mistake for the entire remaining balance, which he did not pay. In April, Gray and his wife went out for dinner to celebrate their wedding anniversary. When he tried to pay with his American Express card, the restaurant told him that the credit card company had not only refused to accept the charges for the meal, but had instructed the restaurant to confiscate and destroy the card. While still at the restaurant, Gray spoke to an American Express employee on the telephone who informed him, "Your account is canceled as of now."

Gray wrote to American Express, pointing out the error. For more than a year, the company failed to respond to Gray or to investigate his claim. It then turned the bill over to a collection agency. Gray sued American Express for violating the Fair Credit Billing Act. The trial court granted summary judgment to American Express and dismissed the complaint on the grounds that Gray had waived his rights under the Act.

ISSUE: Is American Express liable to Gray for violating the Fair Credit Billing Act?

EXCERPTS FROM JUDGE MIKVA'S DECISION: The contract between Gray and American Express provides: "We can revoke your right to use [the card] at any time. We can do this with or without cause and without giving you notice." American Express concludes from this language that the cancellation was not of the kind prohibited by the Act, even though the Act regulates other aspects of the relationship between the cardholder and the card issuer.

[T]he Act states that, during the pendency of a disputed billing, the card issuer shall not cause the cardholder's account to be restricted or closed because of the failure of the obligor to pay the amount in dispute. American Express seems to argue that, despite that provision, it can exercise its right to cancellation for cause unrelated to the disputed amount, or for no cause, thus bringing itself out from under the statute. At the very least, the argument is audacious. American Express would restrict the efficacy of the statute to those situations where the parties had not agreed to a "without cause, without notice" cancellation clause, or to those cases where the cardholder can prove that the sole reason for cancellation was the amount in dispute. We doubt that Congress painted with such a faint brush.

The effect of American Express's argument is to allow the equivalent of a "waiver" of coverage of the Act simply by allowing the parties to contract it away. Congress usually is not so tepid in its approach to consumer problems. The rationale of consumer protection legislation is to even out the inequalities that consumers normally bring to the bargain. To allow such protection to be waived by boiler plate language of the contract puts the legislative process to a foolish and unproductive task. A court ought not impute such nonsense to a Congress intent on correcting abuses in the market place.

The district court's order of summary judgment and dismissal is hereby *vacated*. ◢

FAIR CREDIT REPORTING ACT

Gossip and rumor can cause great harm. Bad enough when whispered behind one's back, worse yet when placed in files and distributed to potential creditors. Most adults rely on credit—to acquire a home, credit cards, or overdraft privileges at the bank. A sullied credit report makes life immensely more difficult. The goal of the Fair Credit Reporting Act (FCRA) is to ensure that consumer credit reports are accurate.

The FCRA regulates **consumer reporting agencies**. These are businesses that supply consumer reports to third parties. If an insurance agency or a bank conducts its own investigation to determine whether a consumer is creditworthy, the FCRA does not apply. A **consumer report** is any communication about a consumer's creditworthiness, character, general reputation, or lifestyle that is considered as a factor in establishing credit, obtaining insurance, securing a job, acquiring a government license, or for any other legitimate business need.

Under the FCRA:

- A consumer report can be used only for a legitimate business need, and a consumer reporting agency must be careful not to supply reports that will be used for any other purpose. A nosy neighbor does not have the right to order a report.

- A consumer reporting agency cannot report obsolete information. Ordinary credit information is obsolete after seven years, bankruptcies after 10 years. (But if a consumer is applying for more than $150,000 of credit or life insurance, or for a job that pays more than $75,000 a year, then there is no time limit.) **Investigative reports** that discuss character, reputation, or lifestyle become obsolete in three *months*. Some commentators argue that the type of information contained in investigative reports is not relevant and should not be used at all. Although the FCRA does not limit the kinds of information that can be collected and reported, it does specify that an investigative report cannot be ordered without first informing the consumer.

- A consumer reporting agency cannot report medical information without the consumer's permission.

- An employer cannot request a consumer report on any current or potential employee without the employee's permission. An employer cannot take action because of information in the consumer report without first giving the current or potential employee a copy of the report and a description of the employee's rights under this statute.

- Anyone who makes an adverse decision against a consumer because of a credit report must reveal the name and address of the reporting agency that supplied the information. An "adverse decision" includes denying credit or charging higher rates.

- Upon request from a consumer, a reporting agency must disclose all information in his file, the source of the information (except for investigative reports), the name of anyone to whom a report has been sent in the prior year (two years for employment purposes), and the name of anyone who has requested a report in the prior year.

- If a consumer tells an agency that some of the information in his file is incorrect, the agency must both investigate and forward the data to the information provider. The information provider must investigate and report the results to the agency. If the data is inaccurate, the information provider must so notify all national credit agencies. The consumer also has the right to give the agency a short report telling his side of the story. The agency must then include the consumer's statement with any credit reports it supplies and also, at the consumer's request, send the statement to anyone who has received a report within six months (or two years for employment purposes).

The following article illustrates the usefulness of the FCRA.

NEWSWORTHY

Kimberly Dorcik wanted a new job. An assistant manager at a Lechters housewares store, she applied for the manager's position at Ups 'N Downs, a women's clothing store a dozen doors away in Solano Mall, in Fairfield, California. But her hopes for the job, which paid a few thousand dollars more than she was earning, vanished, she said, when the staff member taking her application whispered: "We're not supposed to tell anybody, but we pull credit reports on people. Is that going to be a problem?"

Ms. Dorcik remembers mumbling a noncommittal response, but she knew that it was going to be a problem. Three years earlier, when she was 19, she had had emergency surgery resulting from complications from pregnancy. Because of what she calls a clerical error, $30,000 in medical bills were still unpaid and in dispute, tainting her credit history. Ms. Dorcik did not get the job, and she said she was almost certain that the deciding factor was her credit history. The FCRA now requires employers to tell applicants like Ms. Dorcik if credit histories are being used as part of hiring. Employers will also have to obtain written permission from applicants before even requesting a credit history. If someone is turned down for a job and a credit report was used in the decision, the applicant can presumably weed out wrong information in the report and reapply.[14] ▪

A survey revealed that 70 percent of credit reports contain errors. About 25 percent of the reports contain serious mistakes. Consumer advocates recommend that every year you check your credit reports from each of the three major reporting agencies: Equifax (800-685-1111; http://www.equifax.com), Experian (888-397-3742; http://www.experian.com/), and Trans Union (800-916-8800; http://www.transunion.com/). A report is free if you have been turned down for credit within 60 days; otherwise, it generally costs $8, although, in some states, it is free. If you find any errors, notify the agency in writing and warn it that failing to make corrections is a violation of the law. At http://www.ftc.gov/bcp/conline/pubs/credit/crdtdis.htm the FTC offers advice on how to dispute credit report errors. ▪

Also, under the Gramm-Leach-Bliley Privacy Act of 1999, banks, other financial institutions, and consumer reporting agencies must notify consumers before disclosing any personal information to a third party.[15] The company cannot disclose this private information if the consumer *opts out* (that is, denies permission).

FAIR DEBT COLLECTION PRACTICES ACT

The introduction to the Fair Debt Collection Practices Act (FDCPA) states that "Abusive debt collection practices contribute to the number of personal bankruptcies, to marital instability, to the loss of jobs, and to invasions of individual privacy."[16] Debt collection practices can also disrupt Super Bowl Sunday. Debt collectors want to catch their prey off guard, and what better time than when the entire nation is at home, glued to the television? If the phone rings, sports fans assume it is a friend calling to gab about the game.

Is that legal? It depends. **The FDCPA provides** that a collector must, within five days of contacting a debtor, send the debtor a written notice containing the amount of the debt, the name of the creditor to whom the debt is owed, and a statement that if the debtor disputes the debt (in writing), the collector will cease all collection efforts until it has sent evidence of the debt. **Also under the FDCPA, collectors may not:**

- Call or write a debtor who has notified the collector in writing that he wishes no further contact

- Call or write a debtor who is represented by an attorney

- Call a debtor before 8:00 A.M. or after 9:00 P.M.

- Threaten a debtor or use obscene or abusive language

---

[14] Anthony Ramirez, "Name, Resumé, References. And How's Your Credit," *The New York Times*, Aug. 31, 1997, p. F8. Copyright © 1997 by The New York Times Co. Reprinted by permission.

[15] 15 U.S.C. §6801.

[16] 15 U.S.C. §1692(a).

- Call or visit the debtor at work if the consumer's employer prohibits such contact

- Imply that they are attorneys or government representatives when they are not, or use a false name

- Threaten to arrest consumers who do not pay their debts

- Make other false or deceptive threats, that is, threats that would be illegal if carried out or which the collector has no intention of doing—such as suing the debtor or seizing property

- Contact acquaintances of the debtor for any reason other than to locate the debtor (and then only once), or

- Tell acquaintances that the consumer is in debt.

Of course, these rules do not prevent the collector from filing suit against the debtor. In the event of a violation of the FDCPA, the debtor is entitled to damages, court costs, and attorney's fees. The FTC also has authority to enforce the Act.

The following case illustrates the types of abuses that the FDCPA was designed to prevent.

GRADISHER V. CHECK ENFORCEMENT UNIT, INC.

2002 U.S. Dist. LEXIS 6003
United States District Court for the Western District of Michigan, 2002

FACTS: Check Enforcement Unit, Inc. (CEU), was in the business of helping merchants collect on bad checks. When a merchant received a dishonored check, it would forward the check directly to CEU, which would then send out a series of notices to the check writer, using the letterhead of the local Sheriff's Department. CEU had permission to use this letterhead, but the Sheriff's Department was not otherwise involved in the collection effort. Only after the three notices had been sent, and no payment received, would CEU notify the Sheriff's Department about a bad check. Even then, the check did not become a criminal matter until the Sheriff's Department assigned a complaint number.

After Sherri Gradisher bounced a check for $81.30 at Doug Born's Smokehouse, she received three notices from CEU. Gradisher filed suit alleging that CEU had violated the FDCPA.

ISSUE: Did CEU violate the FDCPA?

EXCERPTS FROM JUDGE QUIST'S DECISION: CEU admits that the Notice did not contain the exact language required by the statute but contends that it did contain much of the information required, such as the amount of the debt, the name of the creditor, and a telephone number and address which Gradisher could use to contact CEU if she wished to dispute the debt. [But] the Notice does not state [as required by law] that the debtor may dispute the validity of the debt by notifying the debt collector in writing within thirty days after receipt of the Notice.

Gradisher contends that CEU violated [the statute] because CEU's use of the letterhead of the Office of the Sheriff gave the false and misleading impression that the notices were from the Sheriff's Department when they were actually from CEU. In addition, Gradisher contends that CEU violated the FDCPA by failing to disclose its true name.

[The Notices] all conveyed the impression that they were authorized, created, and sent by the Sheriff's Department without any indication that CEU, an independent contractor of the County, was actually the entity that generated the notices. The fact that CEU had an "affiliation" with the Sheriff's

Department is irrelevant because CEU's notices created the false impression that the notices were generated by the Sheriff's Department. Moreover, CEU's notices violated [the statute] because CEU used a name other than its own name.

Gradisher's next claim is that CEU violated the FDCPA by implying that Gradisher would be arrested or imprisoned if she failed to pay the debt. The back side of the Notice stated:

WARNING
Failure To Make Payment Can Result In A
Warrant For Your Arrest

[Any] debtor would conclude after reading CEU's notices that the Sheriff's Department had determined that the debtor committed a crime and arrest or criminal prosecution was certain to occur if the debt was not paid. In fact, the Sheriff's Department had no involvement with the notices sent by CEU and never made any determination regarding violation of the law or arrest. Gradisher has shown that criminal prosecution occurs infrequently on files CEU sends to the Sheriff's Department. Thus, in any given case there is only a slight possibility of criminal prosecution. Under these circumstances, CEU's notices violated [the statute]. ◢

If a debt collector calls you, what can you do? First of all, be sure to write down his name and the name of the agency for which he works. Tell the caller that you are recording the conversation and then do so. Send a letter to the agency, requesting that it not contact you. Report any violations to the FTC at http://www.ftc.gov/bcp/conline/pubs/credit/fdc.htm.

EQUAL CREDIT OPPORTUNITY ACT

The Equal Credit Opportunity Act (ECOA) prohibits any creditor from discriminating against a borrower because of race, color, religion, national origin, sex, marital status, age (as long as the borrower is old enough to enter into a legal contract), or because the borrower is receiving welfare. A lender must respond to a credit application within 30 days. If a lender rejects an application, it must either tell the applicant why or notify him that he has the right to a written explanation of the reasons for the rejection. The following news report illustrates the types of abuses that the ECOA is designed to prevent.

Florence and Joe made an offer to buy a new home at the Meadowood housing development near Tampa. The developer accepted their offer, contingent upon their obtaining a mortgage. When the couple filed an application with Rancho Mortgage and Investment Corp., they were surprised by the hostility of Rancho's loan processor. She requested information they had already supplied and repeatedly questioned them about whether they intended to occupy the house, which was about 80 miles from their jobs. Florence and Joe insisted they wanted to live near their son and daughter-in-law and escape city crime. Rancho turned down their mortgage, refusing to give either an oral or a written explanation. The house was sold to another buyer.

Joe and Florence didn't get mad, they got even. They sued under the ECOA. Rancho was ordered to pay the African American couple $35,000.[17] ◼

In the following case, the lender asked a spouse to co-sign her husband's loan. Did this request violate the ECOA? You be the judge.

---

[17] Robert J. Bruss, "Home Buyers Sue Mortgage Lender for Racial Discrimination," *Tampa Tribune*, Nov. 5, 1994, p. 3.

YOU BE THE JUDGE

AMERICAN SECURITY BANK, N.A. V. YORK

1992 U.S. Dist. LEXIS 14309
United States District Court for the District of Columbia, 1992

FACTS: John York and Michael Lipson borrowed money several times from American Security Bank (ASB) to finance their business deals. When the two men met with their loan officer to request an additional $13.5 million, he told them that their wives would have to sign any additional loan. ASB imposed this requirement before undertaking any study of the two men's creditworthiness. Under ASB's standards, York and Lipson were entitled to the loan on their own merits, without their wives' signatures. In granting the loan, ASB did not actually consider the wives' personal assets or the assets that each couple held jointly.

The two wives signed the loan, the two husbands defaulted, and ASB sued for payment. The two wives counter-claimed, alleging that ASB had violated the Equal Credit Opportunity Act and that, therefore, neither they nor their husbands were required to repay the loan. They also asked for damages. ASB filed a motion for summary judgment, asking the court to dismiss the counter-claim.

YOU BE THE JUDGE: Did ASB violate the Equal Credit Opportunity Act when it insisted that a wife guarantee her husband's loan? What is the appropriate remedy for a violation?

ARGUMENT FOR ASB: There was a time when banks and other lenders would not give credit to a married woman without her husband's permission. The purpose of the ECOA is to permit married women to obtain credit on their own. In this case, the two women are arguing that ASB violated the law by giving them credit. This interpretation stands the law on its head. They are taking a statute designed to prevent the *denial* of credit and saying it applies to the *granting* of a loan. That is clearly not what Congress had in mind.

Even if ASB did violate the ECOA, the loan is still valid. The two women may be entitled to some damages, but this is a $13.5 million loan. Surely, they are not suggesting that their damages for this technical violation equal $13.5 million. If ASB has violated the Act, the court should enforce the loan and impose modest damages.

ARGUMENT FOR MS. YORK AND MS. LIPSON: ASB misreads the ECOA. This statute prevents discrimination because of marital status. These two women had no connection to the loan except that they were married to the men who wanted to borrow money. The two women had no ownership interest in the business and played no role in the loan negotiations. If they had not been married, the ASB would never have asked them to sign the note. The bank discriminated on the basis of marital status when it demanded of a married woman what it would not have asked of a single person.

ASB asked the wives to sign before even checking their husbands' credit status. ASB has admitted that the two husbands were creditworthy on their own. If the men had not been married, ASB would have given them the loan. ASB asked the wives to sign, simply because they were there.

As for the damage question, if ASB had not violated the ECOA, the two wives would not have signed the loan and they would not now be liable. If they have to pay the loan, their damages are indeed $13.5 million. /

CONSUMER LEASING ACT

If you, like many other consumers, lease a car rather than buy it, you are protected under the Consumer Leasing Act (CLA). The CLA does not apply to the rental of real property, that is, to house or apartment leases. **Before a lease is signed, a lessor must disclose the following in writing:**

- All required payments, including deposits, down payments, taxes, and license fees

- The number and amount of each monthly payment and how payments are calculated

- Balloon payments (i.e., payments due at the end of the lease)

- Required insurance payments

- The total amount the consumer will have paid by the end of the lease

- Available warranties

- Maintenance requirements and a description of the lessor's wear and use standards

- Penalties for late payments

- The consumer's right to purchase the leased property and at what price

- The consumer's right to terminate a lease early

- Any penalties for early termination

The government brochure "Keys to Vehicle Leasing" is available at http://www .federalreserve.gov/pubs/leasing/. It lays out the lessor's rights and compares the advantages and disadvantages of leasing versus purchasing a car.

Magnuson-Moss Warranty Act

When Senator Frank E. Moss sponsored the Magnuson-Moss Warranty Act, this is how he explained the need for such a statute:

> [W]arranties have for many years confused, misled, and frequently angered American consumers. . . . Consumer anger is expected when purchasers of consumer products discover that their warranty may cover a 25-cent part but not the $100 labor charge or that there is full coverage on a piano so long as it is shipped at the purchaser's expense to the factory. . . . There is a growing need to generate consumer understanding by clearly and conspicuously disclosing the terms and conditions of the warranty and by telling the consumer what to do if his guaranteed product becomes defective or malfunctions.[18]

The Magnuson-Moss Warranty Act does not require manufacturers or sellers to provide a warranty on their products. **The Act does require any supplier that offers a written warranty on a consumer product that costs more than $15 to disclose the terms of the warranty in simple, understandable language** *before the sale.* This statute covers sales by catalogue or on the Internet. Required disclosure includes the following:

- The name and address of the person the consumer should contact to obtain warranty service

---

[18] *Quoted in* David G. Epstein and Steve H. Nickles, *Consumer Law* (Eagan, Minn.: West, 1981).

- The parts that are covered and those that are not

- What services the warrantor will provide, at whose expense, and for what period of time

- A statement of what the consumer must do and what expenses he must pay

Although suppliers are not required to offer a warranty, if they do offer one, they must indicate whether it is *full* or *limited*. Under a **full warranty**, the warrantor must promise to fix a defective product for a reasonable time without charge; if, after a reasonable number of efforts to fix the defective product, it still does not work, the consumer must have the right to a refund or a replacement without charge; but the warrantor is not required to cover damage caused by the consumer's unreasonable use.

Consumer Product Safety

In 1969, the federal government estimated that consumer products caused 30,000 deaths, 110,000 disabling injuries, and 20 million trips to the doctor. Toys were among the worst offenders, injuring 700,000 children a year. Children were cut by Etch-a-Sketch glass panels, choked by Zulu gun darts, and burned by Little Lady toy ovens. Although injured consumers had the right to seek damages under tort law, the goal of the Consumer Product Safety Act (CPSA) was to prevent injuries in the first place. This Act created the Consumer Product Safety Commission to evaluate consumer products and develop safety standards. The Commission can impose civil and criminal penalties on those who violate its standards. Individuals have the right to sue under the CPSA for damages, including attorney's fees, from anyone who knowingly violates a consumer product safety rule. You can find out about product recalls or file a report on an unsafe product at the Commission's Web site (http://www.cpsc.gov/). The Web site http://www.safetyalerts.com provides consumer-friendly information about product recalls.

Chapter Conclusion

Virtually no one will go through life without reading an advertisement, ordering from a catalogue, borrowing money, needing a credit report, or using a consumer product. It is important to know your rights.

Chapter Review

1. The Federal Trade Commission (FTC) prohibits "unfair and deceptive acts or practices." A practice is unfair if it meets the following three tests:

   - It causes a substantial consumer injury.

   - The harm of the injury outweighs any countervailing benefit.

   - The consumer could not reasonably avoid the injury.

2. The FTC considers an advertisement to be deceptive if it contains an important misrepresentation or omission that is likely to mislead a reasonable consumer.

3. FTC rules prohibit bait and switch advertisements. A merchant may not advertise a product and then disparage it to consumers in an effort to sell a different item.

4. Almost half of the states have statutes that prohibit telemarketers from calling any telephone number listed on the state's do-not-call registry. The FTC has proposed rules that would establish a national do-not-call registry.

5. Consumers may keep as a gift any unordered merchandise that they receive in the mail.

6. Under the FTC door-to-door rules, a salesperson is required to notify the buyer that she has the right to cancel the transaction prior to midnight of the third business day thereafter.

7. In all loans regulated by the Truth in Lending Act (TILA), the disclosure must be clear and in meaningful sequence. The lender must disclose the finance charge and the annual percentage rate (APR).

8. In the case of a high-rate home equity loan, the lender must notify the consumer at least three business days before the closing that (1) he does not have to go through with the loan (even if he has signed the loan agreement) and (2) he could lose his home if he fails to make payments. If the duration of a high-rate home equity loan is less than five years, it may not contain balloon payments.

9. Under TILA, consumers have the right to rescind a mortgage (other than a first mortgage) for three business days after the signing. If the lender does not comply with the disclosure provisions of TILA, the consumer may rescind for up to three years from the date of the mortgage.

10. Under TILA, a *credit* card holder is liable only for the first $50 in unauthorized charges made before the credit card company is notified that the card was stolen. If, however, you wait more than two days to report the loss of a *debit* card, your bank will only reimburse you for losses in excess of $500. If you fail to report the lost debit card within 60 days of receipt of your bank statement, the bank is not liable at all.

11. In the event of a dispute between a customer and a merchant, the credit card company cannot bill the customer if:

- She makes a good faith effort to resolve the dispute

- The dispute is for more than $50, and

- The merchant is in the same state where she lives or is within 100 miles of her home.

12. Under the Fair Credit Billing Act (FCBA), a credit card company must promptly investigate and respond to any consumer complaints about a credit card bill.

13. Under the Fair Credit Reporting Act (FCRA):

- A consumer report can be used only for a legitimate business need

- A consumer reporting agency cannot report obsolete information

- An employer cannot request a consumer report on any current or potential employee without the employee's permission, and

- Anyone who makes an adverse decision against a consumer because of a credit report must reveal the name and address of the reporting agency that supplied the negative information.

14. Under the Fair Debt Collection Practices Act (FDCPA), a debt collector may not harass or abuse debtors.

15. The Equal Credit Opportunity Act (ECOA) prohibits any creditor from discriminating against a borrower on the basis of race, color, religion, national origin, sex, marital status, age, or because the borrower is receiving welfare.

16. The Magnuson-Moss Warranty Act requires any supplier that offers a written warranty on a consumer product costing more than $15 to disclose the terms of the warranty in simple and readily understandable language before the sale.

17. The Consumer Product Safety Commission evaluates consumer products and develops safety standards.

Practice Test

1. In August, Dorothy Jenkins went to First American Mortgage and Loan Association of Virginia (the Bank) to sign a second mortgage on her home. Her first mortgage was with a different bank. She left the closing without a copy of the required Truth in Lending Act disclosure forms. Jenkins defaulted on her loan payments, and, the following May, the Bank began foreclosure proceedings on her house. In June, she notified the Bank that she wished to rescind the loan. Does Jenkins have a right to rescind the loan 10 months after it was made?

2. **YOU BE THE JUDGE WRITING PROBLEM** Process cheese food slices must contain at least 51 percent natural cheese. Imitation cheese slices, by contrast, contain little or no natural cheese and consist primarily of water, vegetable oil, flavoring, and fortifying agents. Kraft, Inc., makes Kraft Singles, which are individually wrapped process cheese food slices. When Kraft began losing market share to imitation slices that were advertised as both less expensive and equally nutritious as Singles, Kraft responded with a series of advertisements informing consumers that Kraft Singles cost more than imitation slices because they are made from five ounces of milk. Kraft does use five ounces of milk in making each Kraft Single, but 30 percent of the calcium contained in the milk is lost during processing. Imitation slices contain the same amount of calcium as Kraft Singles. Are the Kraft advertisements deceptive? **Argument for Kraft:** This statement is completely true—Kraft does use five ounces of milk in each Kraft Single. The FTC is assuming that the only value of milk is the calcium. In fact, people might prefer having milk rather than vegetable oil, regardless of the calcium. **Argument for the FTC:** It is deceptive to advertise more milk if the calcium is the same after all the processing.

3. Joel Curtis was two and his brother, Joshua, was three years old when their father left both children asleep in the rear seat of his automobile while visiting a friend. His cigarette lighter was on the dashboard of the car. After awaking, Joshua began playing with the lighter and set fire to Joel's diaper. Do the parents have a claim against the manufacturer of the lighter under the Consumer Product Safety Act?

4. Josephine Rutyna was a 60-year-old widow who suffered from high blood pressure and epilepsy. A bill collector from Collections Accounts Terminal, Inc., called her and demanded that she pay $56 she owed to Cabrini Hospital Medical Group. She told him that Medicare was supposed to pay the bill. Shortly thereafter, Rutyna received a letter from Collections that stated:

   You have shown that you are unwilling to work out a friendly settlement with us to clear the above debt. Our field investigator has now been instructed to make an investigation in your neighborhood and to personally call on your employer. The immediate payment of the full amount, or a personal visit to this office, will spare you this embarrassment.

   Has Collections violated the law?

5. Thomas Pinner worked at a Sherwin-Williams paint store that was managed by James Schmidt. Pinner and Schmidt had a falling out when, according to Pinner, "a relationship began to bloom between Pinner and one of the young female employees, the one Schmidt was obsessed with." Pinner quit. Schmidt claimed that Pinner owed the company $121.71 for paint he had taken but not paid for. Sherwin-Williams reported this information to Chilton, who ran a credit reporting agency. Pinner's attorney sent a letter to Chilton notifying him that Pinner disputed the accuracy of the Sherwin-Williams charges. Chilton contacted Schmidt who confirmed that Pinner's account remained delinquent. Chilton failed to note in Pinner's file that a dispute was pending. Thereafter, Pinner was denied credit cards at two stores. Have Schmidt and Chilton violated the Fair Credit Reporting Act?

6. Kathleen Carroll, a single woman, applied for an Exxon credit card. Exxon rejected her application without giving any specific reason and without providing the name of the credit bureau it had used. When Carroll asked for a reason for the rejection, she was told that the

credit bureau did not have enough information about her to establish creditworthiness. In fact Exxon had denied her credit application because she did not have a major credit card or a savings account, she had been employed for only one year, and she had no dependents. Did Exxon violate the law?

7. In October, Renie Guimond discovered that her credit report at TransUnion Credit Information Co. incorrectly stated that she was married, used the name "Ruth Guimond," and had a credit card from Saks Fifth Avenue. After she reported the errors, TransUnion wrote her in November to say that it had removed this information. However, in March, TransUnion again published the erroneous information. The following October, TransUnion finally removed the incorrect information from her file. Guimond was never denied credit because of these mistakes. Is TransUnion liable for violating the Fair Credit Reporting Act?

8. The National Coalition for Consumer Education and MasterCard International created the following quiz to help consumers find out how smart they are about buying on credit:

   (a) What's the best way to correct a mistake on your credit card bill?

   (i) Call your credit card issuer immediately and explain the mistake.

   (ii) Circle the mistake in red and return the bill to your card issuer.

   (iii) Immediately write a letter to your credit card issuer and clearly describe the problem.

   (b) How should you handle an unauthorized charge (a purchase that you didn't make) if you see one on your credit card statement?

   (i) Write a letter to the company that accepted your card for payment to absolve yourself of any liability.

   (ii) Call your credit issuer immediately to alert them.

   (iii) Note the error on your credit card bill and refuse to pay it.[19]

9. Thomas Waldock purchased a 1983 BMW 320i from Universal Motors, Inc. It was warranted "to be free of defects in materials or workmanship for a period of three years or 36,000 miles, whichever occurs first." Within the warranty period, the car's engine failed and upon examination was found to be extensively damaged. Universal denied warranty coverage because it concluded that Waldock damaged the engine by over-revving it. Waldock vehemently disputed BMW's contention. He claimed that, while being driven at a low speed, the engine emitted a gear-crunching noise, ceased operation, and would not restart. Is Universal in violation of the law?

10.

> GET ENOUGH BROADLOOM TO CARPET ANY AREA OF YOUR HOME OR APARTMENT UP TO 150 SQUARE FEET CUT, MEASURED, AND READY FOR INSTALLATION FOR ONLY $77. GET 100% DUPONT CONTINUOUS FILAMENT NYLON PILE BROADLOOM.
> CALL COLLECT

When customers called the number provided, New Rapids Carpet Center, Inc., sent salespeople to visit them at home to sell them carpet that was not as advertised—it was not continuous filament nylon pile broadloom, and the price was not $77. Has New Rapids violated a consumer law?

11. **ETHICS** After TNT Motor Express hired Joseph Bruce Drury as a truck driver, it ordered a background check from Robert Arden & Associates. TNT provided Drury's Social Security number and date of birth, but not his middle name. Arden discovered that a Joseph *Thomas* Drury, who coincidentally had the same birth date as Joseph *Bruce* Drury, had served a prison sentence for drunk driving. Not knowing that it had the wrong Drury, Arden reported this information to TNT, which

---

[19] "Give Yourself Some Credit If You Pass This Quiz," *Times-Picayune*, Apr. 7, 1994, p. E5.

promptly fired Drury. When he asked why, the TNT executive merely stated, "We do not discuss these matters." Did TNT violate the law? Whether or not TNT was in violation, did its executives behave ethically? Who would have been harmed or helped if TNT managers had informed Drury of the Arden report?

12. **ROLE REVERSAL** Prepare a short-answer question that focuses on deceptive advertisements. Include a sample ad in the question (either a real ad or one that you have made up.)

Internet Research Problem

The Consumer Product Safety Commission (http://www.cpsc.gov) lists products that have been recalled and provides consumers with a telephone number for contacting the manufacturer. Choose a recalled product and telephone the manufacturer to find out how it is handling the problem. Also, see if you can find the manufacturer's Web site to learn if it has disclosed the recall there. What do you think of the manner in which the manufacturer has handled the recall? Is the manufacturer providing adequate protection to consumers?

You can find further practice problems in the Online Quiz at http://beatty.westbuslaw.com **or in the Study Guide that accompanies this text.**

Environmental Law

"When my mother was left a widow almost 50 years ago, she taught school to support her family. A few years after my father's death, she took her savings and bought a small commercial building on a downtown lot in our little town in Oregon. The building, she said, would offer what my father couldn't—a source of support in her old age. In one half of the building was a children's clothing store, in the other a dry cleaners. The two stores served Main Street shoppers for years.

"Now the building that once represented security has produced a menace with the potential to bankrupt my mother. The discovery of contamination in city park well water triggered groundwater tests in the area. Waste products discarded by dry cleaners were identified as a likely source of contamination. Although a dry cleaner hasn't operated for 20 years on my mother's property, chemicals remain in the soil. Mother knew nothing of this hazard until a letter came from the Oregon Department of Environmental Quality. It said she should decide if she would oversee further testing and cleanup herself or if she would let the government handle it. In either case, my mother would pay the costs.

"The building is worth just under $70,000. Cleanup costs will be at least $200,000. At 84, my mother has enough savings to preserve her independence. She does not have enough money to bear the enormous costs of new community standards. The dry cleaner that operated in my mother's building disposed of chemicals the same way other dry cleaners did.

None of these businesses was operated in a negligent fashion. They followed standards accepted by the community at the time. Now we are learning that we must live more carefully if we are to survive in a world that is safe and clean. My question is: Who will pay? Who will be responsible for cleaning up environmental messes made before we knew better?"[1]

Introduction

The environmental movement in the United States began in 1962 with the publication of Rachel Carson's book, *Silent Spring*. She exposed the deadly—and lingering—impact of DDT and other pesticides. These chemicals spread a wide web, poisoning not only the targeted insects, but the entire food chain: fish, birds, and even humans. Since Carson first sounded the alarm, environmental issues have appeared regularly in the news—everything from acute disasters such as the *Exxon Valdez* tanker oil spill in Alaska to chronic concerns over pesticide residues in food. For more about Rachel Carson (and links to other environmental Web sites), visit http://www.rachelcarson.org/.

The environmental movement began with the fervor of a moral crusade. How could anyone be against a clean environment? It has become clear, however, that the issue is more complex. It is not enough simply to say, "We are against pollution." As the opening scenario reveals, the question is: Who will pay? Who will pay for past damage inflicted before anyone understood the harm that pollutants cause? Who will pay for current changes necessary to prevent damage now and in the future? Are car owners willing to spend $100 or $1,000 more per car to prevent air pollution? Are easterners ready to ban oil drilling in the Arctic National Wildlife Refuge in Alaska if that means higher prices for heating oil? Will loggers in the West give up their jobs to protect endangered species? Are all consumers willing to pay more to insulate their homes? The first President George Bush, a Republican, said, "Beyond all the studies, the figures, and the debates, the environment is a moral issue." But Newt Gingrich, a Republican Speaker of the House of Representatives, called the Environmental Protection Agency "the biggest job-killing agency in inner-city America."[2]

The cost-benefit trade-off is particularly complex in environmental issues because those who pay the cost often do not receive the benefit. If a company dumps toxic wastes into a stream, its shareholders benefit by avoiding the expense of safe disposal. Those who fish or drink the waters pay the real costs without receiving any of the benefit. Economists use the term *externality* to describe the situation in which people do not bear the full cost of their decisions. Externalities prevent the market system from achieving a clean environment on its own. Only government involvement can realign costs and benefits.

ENVIRONMENTAL PROTECTION AGENCY

Thirty-five years ago, environmental abuses were (ineffectively) governed by tort law and a smattering of local ordinances. Now, environmental law is a mammoth

---

[1] Carolyn Scott Kortge, "Taken to the Cleaners," *Newsweek*, Oct. 23, 1995, p. 16. Reprinted with permission.

[2] Both men are *quoted in* Robert V. Percival, Alan S. Miller, Christopher H. Schroeder, and James P. Leape, *Environmental Regulation* (Boston: Little, Brown & Co., 1992), p. 1, and 1995 supp. p. 2.

structure of federal and state regulation. In 1970, Congress created the Environmental Protection Agency (EPA) to consolidate environmental regulation under one roof. Among government agencies, only the military is larger. When Congress passes a new environmental law, the EPA issues regulations to implement it. The agency can bring administrative enforcement action against those who violate its regulations. An administrative law judge (ALJ) within the agency hears these actions. Either party can appeal this decision to a United States Court of Appeals and, from there, to the Supreme Court. Those who violate environmental laws are liable for civil damages. In addition, some statutes, such as the Clean Water Act, the Resource Conservation and Recovery Act, and the Endangered Species Act, provide for *criminal* penalties, including imprisonment. The EPA is not shy about seeking criminal prosecutions of those who knowingly violate these statutes, and of those corporate officers who fail to prevent criminal negligence by their employees.

Air Pollution

On October 26, 1948, almost half of the 10,000 people in Donora, Pennsylvania, fell ill from air pollution. A weather inversion trapped industrial pollutants in the air, creating a lethal smog. Twenty residents ultimately died. Although air pollution rarely causes this type of acute illness, it can cause or increase the severity of diseases that are annoying, chronic, or even fatal—such as pneumonia, bronchitis, emphysema, and cancer. Even apart from the health risks, air pollution can be irritating: it blocks visibility, damages car exteriors, and grimes windowsills.

There are three major sources of air pollution: coal-burning utility plants, factories, and motor vehicles. Residential furnaces, farm operations, forest fires, and dust from mines and construction sites also contribute. Local regulation is ineffective in controlling air pollution. For example, when cities limited pollution from factory smokestacks, plants simply built taller stacks that sent the pollution hundreds, or even thousands, of miles away. Local governments had little incentive to prevent this long-distance migration. Recognizing the national nature of the problem, Congress passed three air pollution laws during the 1950s and 1960s. With little enforcement bite and no EPA to ensure implementation, these statutes had minimal impact.

CLEAN AIR ACT

Dissatisfied by this lack of progress, Congress passed the Clean Air Act of 1970. **The Clean Air Act has four major provisions:**

- **Primary Standards.** Congress directed the EPA to establish **national ambient air quality standards** (known as NAAQSs) for primary pollution, that is, pollution that harms the public health. The EPA's mandate was to set standards that protected public health and provided an adequate margin of safety *without regard to cost*. Pollution may not exceed these limits anyplace in the country. The EPA must regularly update the rules to reflect the latest scientific evidence.

- **Secondary Standards.** Congress also directed the EPA to establish NAAQSs for pollution that may not be a threat to health but has other unpleasant effects, such as obstructing visibility and harming plants or other materials.

- **State Implementation Plans (SIPs).** The Clean Air Act envisioned a partnership between the EPA and the states. After the EPA set primary and secondary standards, states would produce SIPs to meet the primary standards within three years and the secondary standards within a reasonable time. If a SIP was not acceptable, the EPA would produce its own plan for that state. In formulating their SIPs, states were required to identify the major sources of pollution. Each polluter would then be given a pollution limit to bring the area into compliance with national standards. The worse the pollution in a particular area, the tougher the regulations.

- **Citizen Suits.** The Clean Air Act (and many other environmental statutes) permits anyone to file suit against a polluter or against the EPA for failing to enforce the statute. Citizens have often been more assertive than the EPA in enforcing environmental statutes. For example, the Arizona Center for Law in the Public Interest has sued the EPA more than a dozen times for failing to impose sufficiently strict air quality standards on Phoenix and Tucson.

Although air quality throughout the country has improved dramatically, a 1990 EPA study revealed that, 20 years after passage of the Clean Air Act, virtually every American was still breathing unsafe levels of some pollutants. In 1990, Congress amended the Act, setting more realistic goals but also higher penalties for failure. For example, the deadline for Los Angeles was extended, but the penalty for noncompliance was increased—a cutoff of federal highway funds (a serious blow indeed in Los Angeles) and the threat of even stricter controls. Already, everything in California from lawn mowers to bakeries to barbecue grills is subject to increasingly strict standards.

Elsewhere, the good news is that in 2001, Denver became the first major city to meet Clean Air Act standards, despite being one of the fastest growing cities in the nation. Not only did the city *meet* air quality standards, but it was able to *maintain* compliance for three years. The bad news is that it is the only city that has done so since the passage of the Clean Air Act. About 62 million Americans breathe unhealthy air. To find out about the air quality in your community, feel your way over to http://www.scorecard.org/.

In the following case, a power plant argued that the EPA had imposed a solution whose cost far outweighed its benefit. There is only one Grand Canyon. Should visibility there be preserved at any cost?

YOU BE THE JUDGE

CENTRAL ARIZONA WATER CONSERVATION DISTRICT V. EPA

990 F.2d 1531, 1993 U.S. App. LEXIS 5881
United States Court of Appeals for the Ninth Circuit, 1993

FACTS: In the Clean Air Act, Congress directed the EPA to issue regulations that would protect visibility at national landmarks. The Navaho Generating Station (NGS) is a power plant 12 miles from the Grand Canyon. In response to a citizen suit filed by the Environmental Defense Fund under the Clean Air Act, the EPA ordered NGS to reduce its sulfur dioxide emissions by 90 percent. To do so would cost NGS $430 million initially in capital expenditures and then $89.6

million annually. Average winter visibility in the Grand Canyon would be improved by at most 7 percent, but perhaps less. NGS sued to prevent implementation of the EPA's order. A court may nullify an EPA order if it determines that the agency action was arbitrary and capricious.

YOU BE THE JUDGE: Did the EPA act arbitrarily and capriciously in requiring NGS to spend half a billion dollars to improve winter visibility at the Grand Canyon by at most 7 percent?

ARGUMENT FOR NGS: This case is a perfect example of environmentalism run amok. Half a billion dollars for the *chance* of increasing winter visibility at the Grand Canyon by 7 percent? No rational person would choose to spend his own money that way, but the EPA is happy to spend NGS's. Winter visitors to the Grand Canyon would undoubtedly prefer that NGS provide them with a free lunch rather than a 7 percent improvement in visibility. The EPA order is simply a waste of money.

ARGUMENT FOR THE EPA: Under the Clean Air Act, Congress instructed the EPA to protect visibility at national landmarks such as the Grand Canyon. How can NGS, or anyone else, measure the benefit of protecting a national treasure like the Grand Canyon? Even people who never have and never will visit it during the winter sleep better at night knowing that the Canyon is protected. NGS has been causing harm to the Grand Canyon, and now it should remedy the damage.

Courts generally defer to federal agencies, whose experts deal with similar problems all the time. The EPA has greater expertise in these matters than either NGS or this court. ▌

ECONOMICS & THE LAW

Although the Clean Air Act reduced concentrations of some of the most harmful chemicals—carbon monoxide, sulfur dioxide, ground-level ozone—new scientific evidence indicated that the EPA standards were not strict enough. Even lower levels of these chemicals can cause health problems. In response to this new evidence, the EPA tightened its standards, predicting that stricter rules could save 20,000 lives a year and eliminate 250,000 cases of asthma. However, critics argued that the benefits of these regulations were too low to justify the enormous costs. They pointed to a recent study calculating that EPA regulations during the last 10 years cost about $50 million for each year of life saved. (In other words, for each $50 million spent, one person lives one year longer.) In contrast, home smoke alarms cost about $200,000 for each additional year of life, and mammograms for women over 50 cost a mere $17,000 for each year saved. The Clean Air Act directs the EPA to set air quality standards without regard to cost. How much is a year of life worth? What if it is your life?[3] ▪

NEW SOURCES OF POLLUTION

Some states had air so clean that they could have allowed air quality to decline and still have met EPA standards. However, the Clean Air Act declared that one of its purposes was to "protect and enhance" air quality. Using this phrase, the Sierra Club sued the EPA to prevent it from approving any SIPs that met EPA standards but nonetheless permitted a decline in air quality. As a result of this suit, the EPA developed a **prevention of significant deterioration (PSD)** program. **No one may undertake a building project that will cause a major increase in pollution**

---

[3] "Clean Air, Dirty Fight," *The Economist*, Mar. 15, 1997, p. 29.

without first obtaining a permit from the EPA. The agency will grant permits only if an applicant can demonstrate that (1) its emissions will not cause an overall decline in air quality and (2) it has installed the **best available control technology** for every pollutant.

The PSD program prohibits any deterioration in current air quality, **regardless of health impact**. In essence, national policy values a clean environment for its own sake, apart from any health benefits.

ACID RAIN

In some places, rain is now 10 times more acidic than it would naturally be. The results of acid rain are visible in the eastern United States and Canada—damaged forests, crops, and lakes. Acid is primarily created by sulfur emissions from large coal-burning utility plants in the Midwest. Many of these plants were built before the Clean Air Act, when the easiest way to meet state and local standards (while keeping electricity prices low) was to build tall stacks that would send the sulfur dioxide far away. Terrific for Ohio; not so wonderful for Maine.

The Clean Air Act banned the tall-stack solution, leaving coal plants, in theory, with two choices: install (expensive) scrubbers or buy (cheaper) low-sulfur western coal. Under pressure from members who represented states with high-sulfur coal, Congress compromised and required all power plants to install scrubbers regardless of the coal they burned. In this way, western coal would have no advantage.

In 1990, Congress amended the Clean Air Act to require power plants to cut their sulfur dioxide emissions by half. This time, however, Congress did not specify how the goal should be achieved and instead offered new methods for minimizing costs and maximizing economic efficiency. **Power plants have four options for meeting emissions standards: (1) installing scrubbers, (2) using low-sulfur coal, (3) switching to alternative fuels (such as natural gas), or (4) trading emissions allowances.** This last alternative requires some explanation. Each year, every utility receives an emissions allowance, meaning that it is allowed to emit a certain number of tons of pollutants. If a company does not need its entire allowance, because it uses cleaner fuels or has installed pollution control devices, it can sell the leftover allowance to other companies or stockpile the allowance for future use. Plants with high levels of pollution either buy more allowances or reduce their own emissions, depending on which alternative is cheaper. In effect, the government establishes the maximum amount of pollution, and then the market sets the price for meeting the national standard.

The market for sulfur dioxide emissions has become remarkably efficient and effective. Power plants now have a financial incentive to reduce pollution through innovation. In some years, pollution from sulfur dioxide has declined by as much as 25 percent, at a cost one-tenth the original estimate. For more information on the emissions trading program, click on **http://www.epa.gov/airmarkets/trading/index.html**. This Web site reveals who has bought allowances and at what cost. Note that sometimes the highest bidders are organizations such as the Birney Elementary School, which buy emissions allowances simply to keep polluters from using them.

AUTOMOBILE POLLUTION

The Clean Air Act of 1970 directed the EPA to reduce automobile pollution levels by 90 percent within six years. Although the technology to achieve this goal did not then exist, Congress believed that the auto industry would, if forced, be able to develop the necessary innovations. This approach has been referred to as **technology forcing**, in the sense that the industry will be forced to develop the technology. Indeed, by 1975, General Motors developed a catalytic converter that not only reduced harmful emissions but improved fuel economy.

Although new cars are 97 percent cleaner than 1970 models, motor vehicles are still a major source of air pollution, releasing more than 50 percent of the hazardous pollutants in the air. Each car may be cleaner, but Americans are driving more—and bigger—cars more miles on more trips. During 1970, Americans traveled one trillion miles, but by 2000 the total had increased to four trillion miles. To counteract this increase, Congress has required oil companies to produce cleaner gasoline. It has also required automakers to build **low-emission vehicles**, such as cars powered by electricity or natural gas. The most polluted cities must also reduce auto use by encouraging car pools. However, in 2002 the auto industry fought off congressional efforts to increase automobile fuel efficiency requirements.

Plagued as it is by smog, California has been more aggressive than Congress in limiting automobile pollution. In 1990, for example, it passed a statute requiring auto manufacturers, by 2003, to derive at least 10 percent of their sales from vehicles that produce zero (or close to zero) emissions. This would mean about 100,000 vehicles a year. In their efforts to meet these standards, car companies have sold everything from golf carts designed for gated communities to electric SUVs that cost almost twice as much as the conventional kind. Automobile manufacturers have argued that they are being forced to do the impossible. Environmentalists countered that if the companies tried hard enough, they could succeed. General Motors and DaimlerChrysler sued to prevent enforcement of the statute, and a federal court has enjoined it, at least temporarily.

What is the status of the California zero emissions law? What percentage of the vehicles sold in California are zero emission?

SOOT PARTICLES

Produced primarily by power plants and diesel fuel, microscopic soot particles substantially increase the risk of premature death from lung cancer and other breathing and heart disorders. Because of these particles, residing in a city has the same impact on one's lungs as living with a smoker. In 1997, the EPA issued regulations limiting soot. However, a lawsuit by power plant operators and automobile manufacturers delayed the rules until 2002, when the Supreme Court ruled that the EPA had the right to impose these new regulations without conducting a cost-benefit analysis.[4]

AIR TOXICS

Some pollutants are so potent that even tiny amounts cause harm. For instance, the EPA has never been able to establish a safe level of exposure to asbestos. Each year, 2.7 billion pounds of toxics spew into the air in the United States, causing an estimated annual increase of 3,000 cancer deaths. Two-thirds of Americans face an increased cancer risk from exposure to toxic chemicals in the air. Because the Clean Air Act directed the EPA to set safety standards that provided an adequate

---

[4] *Whitman v. American Trucking Associations*, 531 U.S. 457; 2001 U.S. LEXIS 1952.

margin of safety without regard to cost, the agency in theory has no choice except an outright ban on some pollutants. Such a ban would shut down the steel, chemical, and petroleum industries, among others. The EPA does not consider such a strategy to be politically viable.

The Environmental Defense Fund sued the EPA to force compliance with the law. Nevertheless, by 1990 the agency had proposed standards for only seven substances. Although these standards do not eliminate health risks, they are set at the lowest feasible level given existing technology. The courts have upheld these standards.

In 1990 amendments to the Clean Air Act, Congress directed the EPA to set standards for each of 189 specific pollutants and any other toxics the EPA wanted to include. The EPA may base these standards initially on the **maximum achievable control technology (MACT)**. Within eight years of developing MACT rules, the EPA must raise the standards to a level at which the risk of cancer from these substances is no more than one in one million over a lifetime. This two-step process is meant to create an incentive for polluters to continue to develop better technology.

Under the Clean Air Act, the EPA is required to create a Web site showing what would happen if an accident occurred at any of the 66,000 locations around the United States where dangerous chemicals are stored. But the Federal Bureau of Investigation and the Central Intelligence Agency are concerned that this worst-case data would enable a terrorist group to identify the most dangerous industrial sites in the United States with a few clicks on a laptop. The EPA's security consultants estimate that putting this information on a Web site would double the probability of a terrorist attack. ▪

GLOBAL WARMING

During the last 100 years, the average temperature worldwide has increased between 0.5° and 1.1°F. If current trends continue, the world's average temperature during the next 100 years will rise another 2° to 6°F, producing the warmest climate in the history of humankind. (By comparison, the planet is only 5° to 9°F warmer than during the last ice age.) The impact of this climate change is potentially catastrophic: a rise in sea level that would engulf coastal areas, a devastating decline in fishing stocks, the death of major forests, and a loss of farmland worldwide. Although for a long time, the scientific evidence underlying the theory of global warming was subject to doubt and debate, most reasonable scientists now accept that the burning of fossil fuels produces gases—carbon dioxide, methane, and nitrous oxide—that do indeed create a greenhouse effect by trapping heat in the earth's atmosphere.

Identifying the problem, however, does not illuminate the solution. Global warming is the most complex environmental problem of the new millennium because any solution requires international political cooperation coupled with major lifestyle changes. The Energy Department has estimated that, to fight global warming effectively, U.S. gasoline prices would have to rise by nearly $2 a gallon and electricity prices might have to increase by 86 percent.

The United States plays a particularly important role in finding a solution to global warming because with 5 percent of the world's population, it consumes 25 percent of the world's energy. Thus far, however, this country has generally elected to be part of the problem, not part of the solution. It is the only leading industrialized nation that refused to ratify the Kyoto Protocol, an international treaty signed by 178 nations. This treaty requires emissions to be reduced by the year 2012 to a level 5.2 percent below 1990 amounts.

In 2002, the U.S. government sent the U.S. Climate Action Report to the United Nations. In this document the United States acknowledged that the use of fossil fuels causes global warming. The report also conceded that global warming was likely to have a damaging impact on this country—causing severe heat waves, coastal flooding, and water shortages. However, the report also pointed out some potential benefits, such as a longer growing season, at least in the short run. Its proposed solution was not prevention but adaptation. It suggested, for example, that increased use of air-conditioning could mitigate the impact of heat waves. The report stated that "In the real world, no one will forego meeting basic family needs to protect the global commons." (This report is available at http://www.epa.gov. Search the site for Climate Action Report. More information on global warming is available at http://www.law.pace.edu/env/energy/globalwarming.html.)

Water Pollution

One day, thousands of Milwaukeeans suddenly began to suffer nausea, cramps, and diarrhea. The suspected culprit? *Cryptosporidium*, a tiny protozoan that usually resides in the intestines of cattle and other animals. Ironically, the parasite may have entered Milwaukee's water supply at a purification plant on Lake Michigan. Officials suspect that infected runoff from dairy farms spilled into Lake Michigan near the plant's intake pipe. Doctors advised those with a damaged immune system (such as AIDS patients) to avoid drinking municipal water. Most Milwaukeeans were taking no chances—more than 800,000 switched to boiled or bottled water.

Polluted water can cause a number of loathsome diseases, such as typhus and dysentery. But by 1930 most American cities had dramatically reduced outbreaks of waterborne diseases by chlorinating their water. (The parasite that caused the Milwaukee outbreak is relatively immune to chlorine.) However, industrial discharges into the water supply have increased rapidly, with a visible impact on water quality. These industrial wastes may not induce acute illnesses like typhus, but they can cause serious diseases such as cancer. There is more at stake than health alone; clean water is valued for esthetics, recreation, and fishing.

CLEAN WATER ACT

In 1972, Congress passed a statute that is now called the Clean Water Act (CWA). This statute had two ambitious goals: (1) to make all navigable water suitable for swimming and fishing by 1983, and (2) to eliminate the discharge of pollutants into navigable water by 1985. Like the Clean Air Act, the CWA sets goals without regard to cost; leaves enforcement primarily to the states, with oversight by the EPA; and permits citizen suits. Also, like the Clean Air Act, the CWA's goals have not been met.

Industrial Discharges

The CWA prohibits any single producer from discharging pollution into water without a permit from the EPA. Before granting a permit, the EPA must set limits, by industry, on the amount of each type of pollution any single producer (called a **point source**) can discharge. These limits must be based on the **best available technology**. The EPA faces a gargantuan task in determining the best available technology that *each* industry can use to reduce pollution. Furthermore, standards become obsolete quickly as technology changes.

The CWA also requires the EPA to measure water quality broadly to determine if the permit system is working. Until clean water standards are met, every point source is held to the same standard, whether it is discharging into a clean ocean that can handle more pollution or a stagnant lake that cannot. Since determining the impact of a particular discharge may not be possible, especially when it is mingled with others, it is easier for the EPA to set the same standards for everyone. Easier and fairer—Congress did not want states to lure industry with promises of laxer pollution rules.

Water Quality Standards

The CWA requires states to set EPA-approved water quality standards and develop plans to achieve them. The first step in developing a plan is to determine how each body of water is used. Standards may vary depending upon the designated use—higher for recreational lakes than for a river used to irrigate farmland. No matter what the water's designated use, standards may not be set at a level lower than its current condition. Congress is not in the business of permitting *more* pollution.

States are supposed to pay special attention to so-called **non-point sources**, that is, pollutants with no single source, such as water runoff from agricultural land or city streets. This runoff may contain gasoline, pesticides, or bacteria. Congress left non-point source pollution to the states because it is so difficult to regulate. This regulation also involves complex issues such as land use planning that are, in theory, better handled at the local level than by national fiat. However optimistic Congress may have been, to date the states have not successfully implemented this section of the CWA. They appear to lack both the political will and the technological know-how, for which they are not totally to blame. Determining the impact of individual pollutants on the overall quality of a body of water used for many different purposes is a complex problem. Land use planning requires a delicate and volatile mix of consensus and control.

As the ambitious goals set by the CWA have not been met, Congress has granted numerous extensions. At the same time, environmental advocates have filed citizen suits to force the EPA to toughen its enforcement. In the following case, the American Canoe Association challenged the EPA for failing to enforce the CWA.

AMERICAN CANOE ASSOCIATION, INC. V. EPA

30 F. Supp. 2d 908, 1998 U.S. Dist. LEXIS 19785
United States District Court for the Eastern District of Virginia, 1998

FACTS: The American Canoe Society sued the EPA for failing to require the state of Virginia to establish total maximum daily loads (TMDLs) for Virginia's waters. A TMDL is a plan assessing the reduction in pollution that is necessary to meet CWA standards. A TMDL also allocates responsibility among polluters for this reduction. The EPA contends that it is not required to take action until a state submits a TMDL, at which point it must approve or disapprove the plan. The EPA filed a motion to dismiss.

ISSUE: Does the CWA require the EPA to take action against a state that has not submitted a required plan?

EXCERPTS FROM JUDGE ELLIS'S DECISION: Under EPA's reading of the statute, its duty to approve or disapprove TMDLs and promulgate its own lists in the event of disapproval is triggered only by the states' submission of TMDL lists. In EPA's view, inaction by states, for however long a period, imposes no duty on EPA. Plaintiffs respond that Virginia's failure to submit its TMDL lists by the 1979 deadline or in the nearly twenty years following constitutes a constructive submission that no TMDLs are required for the state's water, which the CWA compels EPA to disapprove as inadequate.

Under EPA's theory of the case, a statute creates a[n] enforceable duty only when it provides a date-certain deadline for agency action. Here, EPA alleges, no date-certain deadline exists. [T]he CWA appears to offer such a readily-ascertainable deadline. [It] provides that state TMDL lists must be submitted to the EPA no later than 180 days after EPA's publication of its first water pollutants list (June 26, 1979); that EPA must approve or disapprove the submissions within 30 days after that (July 26, 1979); and that if disapproved, the EPA must promulgate its own TMDL lists within 30 days (August 25, 1979). The deadline for EPA's approval or disapproval of state submissions would appear to be July 26, 1979.

EPA's alternative interpretation of the statute would allow recalcitrant states to short-circuit the Clean Water Act and render it a dead letter. It seems highly likely that Congress intended that EPA should be required to act not only when states promulgate lists that fail to meet the standards, but also when states completely ignore their mandatory statutory responsibilities and fail to promulgate any list at all. Here, the appropriate remedy for the plaintiffs' TMDL complaints would appear to be an order directing EPA to approve or disapprove Virginia's constructive submission within 30 days and, if the submission is disapproved, to proceed to promulgate its own lists. ◢

WETLANDS

Wetlands are the transition areas between land and open water. They may look like swamps, they may even be swamps, but their unattractive appearance should not disguise their vital role in the aquatic world. They are natural habitats for many fish and wildlife. They also serve as a filter for neighboring bodies of water, trapping chemicals and sediments. Moreover, they are an important aid in flood control because they can absorb a high level of water and then release it slowly after the emergency is past.

The CWA prohibits any discharge of dredge and fill material into wetlands without a permit. Although filling in wetlands requires a permit, many other activities that harm wetlands, such as draining them, originally did not. (However, many states require permits for draining wetlands.) After some particularly egregious abuses, the EPA issued regulations to limit the destruction of wetlands. These new regulations were, however, successfully challenged in the courts.[5] The EPA then rewrote the regulations to accomplish the same goal within the parameters set out by the courts. These new regulations will certainly be challenged, too.

Although, in theory, the government's official policy is no net loss of wetlands, the reality has been different. Since the country was settled, about half of the original 230 million acres of wetlands in the continental United States have been destroyed. In 2002, the Bush administration amended the "no net loss" rule so that it could issue waivers in some cases. The Web site http://www.nwi.fws.gov shows an inventory of wetlands in the United States.

---

[5] *National Mining Ass'n v. U.S. Army Corps of Engineers*, 145 F.3d 1399 (D.C. Cir. 1998).

Sewage

Plumbing drains must be attached to either a septic system or a sewer line. A septic system is, in effect, a freestanding waste treatment plant. A sewer line, on the other hand, feeds into a publicly owned wastewater treatment plant, also known as a municipal sewage plant. **Under the CWA, a municipality must obtain a permit for any discharge from a wastewater treatment plant.** To obtain a permit, the municipality must first treat the waste to reduce its toxicity. However, taxpayers have stubbornly resisted the large increases in taxes or fees necessary to fund required treatments. Since the fines imposed by the EPA are almost always less than the cost of treatment, some cities have been slow to comply. The following news report illustrates the complex trade-offs between costs and benefits.

NEWSWORTHY

In the two years since Tom Cox took over as general manager of Constitution Marina, located in one of the sludgiest pockets of Boston's infamously sludgy Inner Harbor, he has seen an entire ecosystem reborn before his eyes. At the mouth of a now-sealed effluent pipe that once poured sewer waste directly into his anchorage, baby herring and krill shrimp feed. "This spring, for the first time in a decade, we even had porpoises in the Inner Harbor, and seals flopping onto my docks. Boston Harbor," Cox says, "is definitely back."[6]

Back? The Boston Harbor? The harbor that was gruesomely swamped with human waste during the disastrous crash of the old Deer Island treatment plant? The harbor that only a few years ago still reeked of 350 years of ill use?

The harbor has passed a vital milestone on its voyage from toilet bowl for 43 cities and towns to tourist attraction and recharging jobs engine. The new $183 million Deer Island sewage-treatment plant received a formal commission, and its predecessor, an obsolete and overburdened albatross that once channeled raw sewage directly in the bay, was bulldozed into dust.

This transformation has not come cheap. Sewer user charges for residents of the greater Boston area have risen more than 560 percent in the past decade, becoming among the highest in the country. These charges are expected to rise an additional 50 to 75 percent in the next few years. In protest, angry ratepayers dumped tea boxes full of sewer bills into the harbor. ◼

OTHER WATER POLLUTION STATUTES

The Safe Drinking Water Act of 1974:

- Requires the EPA to set national standards for contaminants potentially harmful to human health that are found in drinking water

- Assigns enforcement responsibility to the states but permits the EPA to take enforcement action against states that do not adhere to the standards

- Prohibits the use of lead in any pipes through which drinking water flows, and

- Requires community water systems to send every customer an annual *consumer confidence report* disclosing the level of contaminants in the drinking water. (One can only hope that consumers will remain confident after receiving the report.) To find out more about your drinking water, turn on http://www.epa.gov/ogwdw/dwinfo.htm.

---

[6] Tom Mashberg, "Harbor Cleans Up Its Act," *Boston Herald*, July 30, 1995, p. 1.

The **Ocean Dumping Act of 1972** prohibits the dumping of wastes in ocean water without a permit from the EPA.

Congress passed the **Oil Pollution Act of 1990** in response to the mammoth 1989 *Exxon Valdez* tanker oil spill in Prince William Sound, Alaska. To prevent defective boats from leaking oil, this statute sets design standards for ships operating in U.S. waters. It also requires shipowners to pay for damage caused by oil discharged from their ships.

Although few would argue with the concept that those who spill ought to pay, there has been great controversy over how to measure damages. The U.S. government proposed that damages should be based on the subjective value that people assign to an injured area. Suppose that an oil spill prevents 1,000 people from using a beach. The government proposal would base the fine on the value that these people report (in a survey) that they place on a day of swimming or walking on the beach. If sea fowl are injured by the spill, nearby residents would be asked what they would be willing to pay to save a bird from death. Oil companies prefer to pay only the cost of fixing the damage. If 1,000 seagulls are killed by a spill, oil companies contend that the proper fine should equal the cost of cleaning up the area and increasing the number of seagulls. That might mean importing seagulls or augmenting their food supply.

Waste Disposal

The time is 1978. The place is 96th Street in Niagara Falls, New York. Six women are afflicted with breast cancer, one man has bladder cancer, another suffers from throat cancer. A seven-year-old boy suddenly goes into convulsions and dies of kidney failure. Other residents have chromosomal abnormalities, epilepsy, respiratory problems, and skin diseases. This street is three blocks away from Love Canal.

In 1945, Hooker Chemical Co. disposed of 21,800 tons of 82 different chemicals by dumping them into Love Canal or burying them nearby. An internal memorandum warned that this decision would lead to "potential future hazard" and be a "potential source of lawsuits." A year later, the company's lawyer wrote that "children in the neighborhood use portions of the water for swimming and, as a matter of fact, just before we left the site we saw several young children walking down the path with what appeared to be bathing costumes in hand." He suggested that Hooker build a fence around the canal, but the company never did. Instead, it sold the land to the local school board to build an elementary school. When the company's executive vice president recommended against the sale, the company inserted a clause in the deed to eliminate the company's liability.

Schoolchildren tripped over drums of chemicals that worked their way up to the surface. Some children were burned playing with hot balls of chemical residue—what they called "fire stones"—that popped up through the ground. Home owners noticed foul odors in their basements after heavy rains. Finally, a national health emergency was declared at Love Canal, and a joint federal-state program relocated 800 families. In 1994, Occidental Chemical Corp. (which had since bought Hooker) agreed to pay the state of New York $98 million to settle a lawsuit over Love Canal.[7] Two years later, the EPA settled its lawsuit with Occidental for $129 million.

---

[7] William Glaberson, "Love Canal: Suit Focuses on Records from 1940s," *The New York Times*, Oct. 22, 1990, p. B1.

In its time what Hooker did was not unusual. Companies historically dumped waste in waterways, landfills, or open dumps. Out of sight was out of mind. Waste disposal continues to be a major problem in the United States. It has been estimated that the cost of cleaning up existing waste products will exceed $1 *trillion*. At the same time, the country continues to produce more than six billion tons of agricultural, commercial, industrial, and domestic waste each year. Ironically, air and water pollution control devices have added to the problem because the pollutants they remove from the air and water become waste that must be discarded somewhere.

Two major statutes regulate wastes. The Resource Conservation and Recovery Act (RCRA) focuses on *preventing* future Love Canals by regulating the production and disposal of solid wastes, both toxic and otherwise. The Comprehensive Environmental Response, Compensation, and Liability Act (CERCLA), also referred to as **Superfund**, focuses on *cleaning up* existing hazardous waste sites.

RESOURCE CONSERVATION AND RECOVERY ACT

The RCRA establishes rules for treating both hazardous wastes and other forms of solid waste (such as ordinary garbage).

Solid Waste

Before 1895, the city of New York did not collect garbage. Residents simply piled it up in the streets, causing the streets to rise five feet in height over the century. At present, each American generates 4.5 pounds of solid waste a *day*, an increase of 60 percent since 1960.

But most Americans never gave much thought to their garbage until the infamous case of the garbage barge. The trouble arose in 1983 when the New York legislature banned new landfills (garbage dumps) on Long Island. Three years later, the landfill began to fill up in Islip, a bedroom community outside New York City. Lowell Herrelson, an Alabama businessman, offered to put the Islip garbage on a barge and ship it to another state. But once he filled the barge, no other state would take the garbage. Loaded with 3,186 tons of waste, the barge traveled over 6,000 miles in five months and was turned away by six states and three countries before returning to New York and anchoring near the Statue of Liberty. Its movements were reported daily in the newspapers and even became the subject of the *Tonight Show* monologue: "The only town to send its garbage on a 6,000 mile cruise." The garbage was ultimately burned in a Brooklyn incinerator, but not before Herrelson had lost $500,000 in the venture. Islip introduced recycling and built a $38 million garbage incinerator.

The disposal of nonhazardous solid waste has generally been left to the states, but they must follow guidelines set by the RCRA. **The RCRA:**

- Bans new open dumps

- Requires that garbage be sent to sanitary landfills

- Sets minimum standards for landfills

- Requires landfills to monitor nearby groundwater

- Requires states to develop a permit program for landfills; and

- Provides some financial assistance to aid states in waste management.

ECONOMICS & THE LAW

The federal Office of Management and Budget (OMB) objected to the solid waste regulations that the EPA intended to issue under the RCRA because, according to the OMB's calculations, complying with the proposed regulations would have cost more than $19 billion for every life saved. Not worth it, said the OMB. As a result, the EPA's revised regulations are more flexible than the original version.

This dispute typifies the ongoing conflict in environmental law. On the one hand, the EPA argues that scientific data are uncertain and the health risks of pollutants may be much worse than we realize. The EPA's goal is to stop pollution virtually without regard to cost. The OMB, on the other hand, prefers to base decisions on a numerical cost-benefit analysis. The OMB believes that a clean-air-and-water-for-its-own-sake approach makes little economic sense. Is a human life worth $19 billion? Is your life?

ETHICS

Computers and other consumer electronic devices have created the most rapidly growing waste problem in the world. Containing chemicals such as lead and mercury, these products produce not only large volume, but also dangerous toxicity. Industrialized nations have found a simple solution—between 50 and 80 percent of the "e-waste" collected for recycling is sent to countries such as China, India, and Pakistan.

Once in Asia, adults and children, working without any protective clothing or equipment, burn the plastic casings in the open air, dismantle toner cartridges by hand, and melt circuit boards. The ground, air, and water are polluted with the residue of these toxic components. Because this disposal method is so easy and cheap (for the industrialized nations), manufacturers have not attempted to reduce toxic components in electronic products, and governments have not forced them to take responsibility for safe disposal at the end of the product's life.[8]

What is the ethical obligation of developed nations to dispose of toxic e-waste? From the Chapter 2 Ethics Checklist: What would the Golden Rule suggest? What values are at stake?

What will you do with your old computer when you buy a new one? Hewlett Packard will safely recycle e-waste, whether or not HP made it, for a fee of $13 to $34 per item (see http://www.hp.com/go/recycle). Would you be willing to pay that sum?

Underground Storage Tanks

Concerned that underground gasoline storage tanks were leaking into water supplies, Congress required the EPA to issue regulations for detecting and correcting leaks in existing tanks and establishing specifications for new receptacles. Anyone who owns property with an underground storage tank must notify the EPA and comply with regulations that require installation of leak detectors, periodic testing, and, in some cases, removal of old tanks.

Identifying Hazardous Wastes

The EPA must establish criteria for determining what is, and is not, hazardous waste. It must then prepare a list of wastes that qualify as hazardous.

---

[8] The Basel Action Networks, "Exporting Harm: The Techno-Trashing of Asia," Feb. 25, 2002, available at http://www.ban.org.

Tracking Hazardous Wastes

Anyone who creates, transports, stores, treats, or disposes of more than a certain quantity of hazardous wastes must apply for an EPA permit. All hazardous wastes must be tracked from creation to final disposal. They must be disposed of at a certified facility. Any company that generates more than 100 kilograms of hazardous waste in any month (roughly 200,000 firms nationwide) must obtain an identification number for its wastes. When it ships this waste to a disposal facility, it must send along a multicopy manifest that identifies the waste, the transporter, and the destination. The company must notify the EPA if it does not receive a receipt from the disposal site indicating that the waste has been received.

SUPERFUND

In the vignette that opened this chapter, an elderly woman faced financial ruin from the cost of cleaning up pollutants that her dry cleaner tenants had left. The RCRA was designed to ensure safe disposal of current hazardous wastes. In contrast, the goal of Superfund (aka CERCLA) is to clean up hazardous wastes that have been improperly dumped in the past.

The philosophy of Superfund is that "the polluter pays." **Therefore, anyone who has ever owned or operated a site on which hazardous wastes are found, or who has transported wastes to the site, or who has arranged for the disposal of wastes that were released at the site, is liable for (1) the cost of cleaning up the site, (2) any damage done to natural resources, and (3) any required health assessments.**

In a "shovels first, lawyers later" approach, Congress established a $15.2 billion revolving trust fund for the EPA to use in cleaning up sites even before obtaining reimbursement from those responsible for the damage. Any reimbursements go into the trust fund to be used to repair other sites. The trust fund was initially financed by a tax on the oil and chemical industries, which produce the bulk of hazardous waste. In 1995, however, the taxes expired, and Congress has thus far refused to renew them, thereby threatening the viability of the statute. In 1996, the trust fund had $3.8 billion; as of 2002 it had only $28 million.

Since its creation in 1980, Superfund has been hugely controversial. President Carter signed the statute immediately before he left office, but the Reagan administration that followed largely ignored it. During its first five years, the EPA cleaned up only five sites. Congress then took action to strengthen enforcement. However, progress is slow because each of these cleanups typically costs more than $30 billion and has taken on average 11 years per site.

Of the money spent on Superfund cleanups, the trust fund traditionally paid about 80 percent and the government (i.e., taxpayers) contributed the remaining 20 percent. As the trust fund has dwindled, the number of sites being worked on has fallen by half and taxpayers will soon be paying all expenses. There are 1,551 sites on the national priority list, of which 257 are completely cleaned up and 552 are almost completed. During the next decade, up to 500 sites could be added to the list, at an additional cost of $14 billion. Meanwhile, one in four Americans, including 10 million children below the age of 12, lives within four miles of a Superfund site. To find out about hazardous waste sites in your community, click on http://www.epa.gov/oerrpage/superfund/sites/.

Property owners have complained, and litigated, bitterly because:

- Current and former owners are liable, even though they did nothing illegal at the time, and indeed even if they did nothing more than own property where someone else dumped hazardous wastes. In addition, officers or controlling shareholders in closely held corporations can be personally liable for operations of the company.

- Polluters have joint and several liability—each polluter is responsible for the entire cost of cleaning up a site, even if it contributed only a portion of the pollution. A polluter can reduce its liability only by proving that it caused a smaller percentage of the damage, but that proof is often impossible.

- The expense of a Superfund cleanup can be devastating—higher than $100 million on some sites. Property owners have often viewed litigation as a better investment. More than 50 percent of total Superfund spending has gone to administrative and legal expenses.

- Congress requires that land be returned to pristine condition. Owners point to scientific evidence indicating that this goal is often impossible to achieve, given existing knowledge. Once again, cost-benefit analysis enters the picture as property owners argue that the cost of perfection is higher than the benefit. To encourage redevelopment of contaminated land, the EPA has implemented a "Brownsfield" program that bases the cleanup levels for some property on potential risk to human health. However, Superfund proponents counter that, to be safe, all hazardous wastes should be removed. They offer as Exhibit A the Forrest Glen real estate development in upstate New York. The developers knew they could buy the land cheap because it had been used as a hazardous waste dump. Instead of cleaning it up, they slapped on a bucolic name. Now chemicals ooze up on lawns.

AT RISK

Virtually any commercial real estate is at risk for Superfund liability. Before purchasing land, it is important to investigate whether it has ever been used to dispose of hazardous wastes. Consider testing the soil and groundwater. It might also be a good idea to ask the seller for indemnification against Superfund liability or to purchase Superfund insurance.

In the following case, the Supreme Court clarified an important issue of Superfund liability.

UNITED STATES V. BESTFOODS

524 U.S. 51, 118 S. Ct. 1876, 1998 U.S. LEXIS 3733
United States Supreme Court, 1998

FACTS: Ott Chemical Co. was a wholly owned subsidiary of CPC International, Inc. Some of Ott's managers also worked directly for CPC. Ott littered the land around its chemical plant with thousands of leaking and exploding drums of hazardous waste, and the soil and water were saturated with noxious chemicals. The EPA estimated that the cost of cleaning up the site would be tens of millions of dollars. It filed suit under CERCLA (i.e.,

Superfund) against CPC. Ott was bankrupt.

The district court concluded that CPC was liable under CERCLA. The court of appeals reversed, holding that CPC was not liable for the actions of its subsidiary. The Supreme Court granted *certiorari*.

ISSUE: When is a parent company liable under CERCLA for the actions of its subsidiary?

EXCERPTS FROM JUSTICE SOUTER'S DECISION: It is a general principle of corporate law deeply ingrained in our economic and legal systems that a parent corporation is not liable for the acts of its subsidiaries. But there is an equally fundamental principle of corporate law, applicable to the parent-subsidiary relationship as well as generally, that the corporate veil may be pierced and the shareholder held liable for the corporation's conduct when the corporate form would otherwise be misused to accomplish certain wrongful purposes, on the shareholder's behalf. Nothing in CERCLA purports to rewrite this well-settled rule. The Court of Appeals was accordingly correct in holding that when (but only when) the corporate veil may be pierced, may a parent corporation be charged with CERCLA liability for its subsidiary's actions.

[However,] nothing in the statute's terms bars a parent corporation from direct liability for its own actions in operating a facility owned by its subsidiary. The question is not whether the parent operates the subsidiary, but rather whether it operates the facility, and that operation is evidenced by participation in the activities of the facility, not the subsidiary. The District Court emphasized the facts that CPC placed its own high-level officials on Ott's board of directors and in key management positions at Ott, and that those individuals made major policy decisions and conducted day-to-day operations at the facility. In imposing direct liability on these grounds, the District Court failed to recognize that it is entirely appropriate for directors of a parent corporation to serve as directors of its subsidiary, and that fact alone may not serve to expose the parent corporation to liability for its subsidiary's acts. The Government would have to show that, despite the general presumption to the contrary, the officers and directors were acting in their capacities as CPC officers and directors, and not as Ott officers and directors, when they committed those acts.

The District Court found that G.R.D. Williams, CPC's governmental and environmental affairs director, actively participated in and exerted control over a variety of Ott environmental matters. We think that these findings are enough to raise an issue of CPC's operation of the facility through Williams's actions. Prudence thus counsels us to remand for reevaluation of Williams's role, and of the role of any other CPC agent who might be said to have had a part in operating the facility.

It is so ordered. ◢

ECONOMICS & THE LAW

In a perfect world, the EPA would make rational decisions based on sound science, using its limited resources to solve the most severe problems. Reality can be a bit different.

If you were head of the EPA, how would you decide which Superfund sites the EPA should address first? You might think that the environmental agency should focus on the most harmful sites. That may sound sensible, but it is not how the system works. A recent study reveals that the EPA's priorities are largely determined by two actors: the polluters and the local communities. An aggressive defendant can stave off EPA action, or an eager community can persuade the EPA to clean up their town first, even as a neighboring community with a more pressing problem finds itself moved down the waiting list.[9] Likewise, one would expect that decisions about which species to add to the endangered list (discussed later in this chapter) should perhaps be based solely on the rarity and importance of the species in question. In fact, public opinion (whether in favor or against) can dramatically affect the listing decision.[10]

Can you think of any way to render the decision-making process more effective? ▪

---

9 Hilary Sigman, "The Pace of Progress at Superfund Sites: Policy Goals and Interest Group Influence," *Journal of Law and Economics*, April 2001, vol. 44, p. 315.

10 Amy Whritenour Ando, "Waiting to Be Protected Under the Endangered Species Act: The Political Economy of Regulatory Delay," *Journal of Law and Economics*, April 1999, vol. 42, p. 29.

Chemicals

More than 70,000 chemicals are used in food, drugs, cosmetics, pesticides, and other products. Some of these chemicals are known to accumulate in human tissue and cause, among other harm, cancer, birth defects, and neurological damage. However, only 2 percent of these 70,000 chemicals have been adequately tested to determine their total health impact. Almost 70 percent have not been tested at all. Scientists know virtually nothing about their impact on the health of wildlife.

Several federal agencies share responsibility for regulating chemicals. The Food and Drug Administration (FDA) has control over foods, drugs, and cosmetics. The Occupational Safety and Health Administration (OSHA) is responsible for protecting workers from exposure to toxic chemicals. The Nuclear Regulatory Commission (NRC) regulates radioactive substances. The EPA regulates pesticides and other toxic chemicals.

FEDERAL INSECTICIDE, FUNGICIDE, AND RODENTICIDE ACT

The Federal Insecticide, Fungicide, and Rodenticide Act (FIFRA) requires manufacturers to register all pesticides with the EPA. Before registering a pesticide, the EPA must ensure that its benefits exceed its (then-known) risks. However, many of the 50,000 pesticides currently registered with the EPA were approved at a time when little was known about their risks. In 1972, Congress directed the EPA to reevaluate all registered pesticides and cancel those whose risks exceed their benefits. This process has been very slow. Before the EPA cancels a registration, the manufacturer is entitled to a formal hearing, which may take several years. In the event of an emergency, the EPA may order an immediate suspension; otherwise the chemical stays on the market until the hearing. If a pesticide is banned, the EPA must reimburse end users of the chemicals for their useless inventory.

FEDERAL FOOD, DRUG, AND COSMETIC ACT

The Federal Food, Drug, and Cosmetic Act requires the EPA to set maximum levels for pesticide residue in raw or processed food. The FDA can confiscate food with pesticide levels that exceed the EPA standards.

FOOD QUALITY PROTECTION ACT OF 1996

The Food Quality Protection Act requires the EPA to set pesticide standards at levels that are safe for children. If the data for children are unclear, the EPA must reduce levels to one-tenth the amount now permitted in food. The EPA must also consider all sources of exposure. Thus, for example, in setting limits for pesticides on grapes, the EPA must factor in other sources of pesticides, such as drinking water.

This statute is highly controversial. The pesticide industry argues that the EPA could effectively ban many valuable chemicals for years while careful research into their impact on children is conducted. Environmental advocates, on the other hand, are dismayed that the EPA has not demanded more thorough research before setting standards for some pesticides.

TOXIC SUBSTANCES CONTROL ACT

The Toxic Substances Control Act (TSCA) regulates chemicals other than pesticides, foods, drugs, and cosmetics. For example, it regulates lead in gasoline and paints. **Before selling a new chemical (or an old chemical being used for a new purpose), the manufacturer must register it with the EPA.** As part of the registration process, the manufacturer must present evidence of the chemical's impact on health and the environment. The EPA may prohibit the manufacture, sale, or a particular use of any chemical that poses an unreasonable risk.

Natural Resources

Thus far, this chapter has focused on the regulation of pollution. Congress has also passed statutes whose purpose is to preserve the country's natural resources.

NATIONAL ENVIRONMENTAL POLICY ACT

The National Environmental Policy Act of 1969 (NEPA) requires all federal agencies to prepare an *environmental impact statement* **(EIS) for every major federal action significantly affecting the quality of the human environment.** An EIS is a major undertaking—often hundreds, if not thousands, of pages long. It must discuss (1) environmental consequences of the proposed action, (2) available alternatives, (3) direct and indirect effects, (4) energy requirements, (5) impact on urban quality, historic, and cultural resources, and (6) means to mitigate adverse environmental impacts. Once a draft report is ready, the federal agency must hold a hearing to allow for outside comments.

The EIS requirement applies not only to actions *undertaken* by the federal government, but also to activities *regulated* or *approved* by the government. For example, the following projects required an EIS:

- Expanding the Snowmass ski area in Aspen, Colorado—because approval was required by the Forest Service

- Killing a herd of wild goats that was causing damage at the Olympic National Park (outside Seattle)

- Closing a road to create a beachside pavilion in Redondo Beach, California

- Creating a golf course outside Los Angeles—because the project required a government permit to build in wetlands.

The EIS process is controversial. If a project is likely to have an important impact, environmentalists almost always litigate the adequacy of the EIS. Industry advocates argue that environmentalists are simply using the EIS process to delay—or halt—any projects they oppose. In 1976, seven years after NEPA was passed, a dam on the Teton River in Idaho burst, killing 17 people and causing $1 billion in property damage. The Department of the Interior had built the dam in the face of allegations that its EIS was incomplete; it did not, for example, confirm that a large earth-filled dam resting on a riverbed was safe. To environmentalists, this tragedy graphically illustrated the need for a thorough EIS.

Researchers have found that the EIS process generally has a beneficial impact on the environment. The mere prospect of preparing an EIS tends to eliminate the worst projects. Litigation over the EIS eliminates the next weakest group. If an agency does a good faith EIS, honestly looking at the available alternatives, projects tend to be kinder to the environment, at little extra cost.

ENDANGERED SPECIES ACT

The Endangered Species Act (ESA):

- Requires the Secretary of Commerce or the Secretary of the Interior to prepare a list of species that are in danger of becoming extinct,

- Requires the government to develop plans to revive these species

- Requires all federal agencies to ensure that their actions will not jeopardize an endangered species

- Prohibits any sale or transport of these species

- Makes any taking of an endangered animal species unlawful—taking is defined as harassing, harming, killing, or capturing any endangered species or modifying its habitat in such a way that its population is likely to decline—and

- Prohibits the taking of any endangered plant species on federal property.

No environmental statute has been more controversial than the ESA. In theory, everyone is in favor of saving endangered species. There are currently 987 endangered species (388 animals and 599 plants) on the U.S. list, and species are becoming extinct at 100 to 1,000 times the rate one would expect to occur naturally. To quote the House of Representatives Report on the ESA:

> As we homogenize the habitats in which these plants and animals evolved . . . we threaten their—and our own—genetic heritage. . . . Who knows, or can say, what potential cures for cancer or other scourges, present or future, may lie locked up in the structures of plants which may yet be undiscovered, much less analyzed?

In practice, however, the cost of saving a species can be astronomical. One of the earliest ESA battles involved the snail darter—a three-inch fish that lived in the Little Tennessee River. The Supreme Court upheld a decision under the ESA to halt work on a dam that would have blocked the river, flooding 16,500 acres of farmland and destroying the snail darter's habitat. To the dam's supporters, this decision was ludicrous: stopping a dam (on which $100 million in taxpayer money had already been spent) to save a little fish that no one had ever even thought of before the dam (or damn) controversy. The real agenda, they argued, was simply to halt development. Environmental advocates argued, however, that the wanton destruction of whole species will ultimately and inevitably lead to disaster for humankind. In the end, Congress overruled the Supreme Court and authorized completion of the dam. It turned out that the snail darter has survived in other rivers.

The snail darter was the first in a long line of ESA controversies that have included the spotted owl, the gnatcatcher, the island fox, and the pygmy rabbit, among others. Although the government pays out $227 million a year to enforce the ESA, and private citizens spend millions more, only about 55 species have revived enough to be delisted since 1973 when the statute was passed. Much time and money have been spent on litigation. The following case, however, discusses the advantages of the ESA.

GIBBS V. BABBITT

214 F.3d 483, 2000 U.S. App. LEXIS 12280
United States Court of Appeals for the Fourth Circuit, 2000

FACTS: The red wolf used to roam throughout the southeastern United States. Owing to wetlands drainage, dam construction, and hunting, this wolf is now on the endangered species list. The Fish and Wildlife Service (FWS) trapped the remaining red wolves, placed them in a captive breeding program, and then reintroduced them into the wild. Ultimately, the FWS reintroduced 75 wolves into the 120,000-acre Alligator River National Wildlife Refuge in eastern North Carolina and the Pocosin Lakes National Wildlife Refuge in Tennessee.

After reintroduction, about 41 red wolves wandered from federal refuges onto private property. Plaintiff Richard Lee Mann shot a red wolf that he feared might threaten his cattle. Mann pled guilty to violating a provision of the ESA that prohibits the taking of any endangered species without a permit.

Two individuals and two counties in North Carolina filed suit against the U.S. government, alleging that the anti-taking regulation as applied to the red wolves on private land exceeded Congress's power under the interstate Commerce Clause of the U.S. Constitution.

ISSUE: Is the anti-taking provision of the ESA constitutional?

EXCERPTS FROM JUSTICE WILKINSON'S DECISION:
Congress' commerce authority includes the power to regulate those activities having a substantial relation to interstate commerce. Although the connection to economic or commercial activity plays a central role in whether a regulation will be upheld under the Commerce Clause, economic activity must be understood in broad terms.

The red wolves are part of a $29.2 billion national wildlife-related recreational industry that involves tourism and interstate travel. Many tourists travel to North Carolina from throughout the country for "howling events"—evenings of listening to wolf howls accompanied by educational programs. According to a study conducted by Dr. William E. Rosen of Cornell University, the recovery of the red wolf and increased visitor activities could result in a significant regional economic impact. Rosen estimates that northeastern North Carolina could see an increase of between $39.61 and $183.65 million per year in tourism-related activities, and that the Great Smoky Mountains National Park could see an increase of between $132.09 and $354.50 million per year. This is hardly a trivial impact on interstate commerce.

Appellants argue that the tourism rationale relates only to howling events on national park land or wildlife refuges because people do not travel to private land. Yet this argument misses the mark. Indeed, wolves are known to be "great wanderers." Because so many members of this threatened species wander on private land, the regulation of takings on private land is essential to the entire program of reintroduction and eventual restoration of the species. Such regulation is necessary to conserve enough red wolves to sustain tourism.

The regulation of red wolf takings is also closely connected to a second interstate market—scientific research. Scientific research generates jobs. It also deepens our knowledge of the world in which we live. The red wolf reintroduction program has already generated numerous scientific studies. Scientists have studied how the red wolf affects small mammal populations and how the wolves interact with the ecosystem as a whole. Scientific research can also reveal other uses for animals—for instance, approximately 50 percent of all modern medicines are derived from wild plants or animals.

The anti-taking regulation is also connected to a third market—the possibility of a renewed trade in fur pelts. Wolves have historically been hunted for their pelts. Congress had the renewal of trade in mind when it enacted the ESA. In such a case businessmen may profit from the trading and marketing of that species for an indefinite number of years, where otherwise it would have been completely eliminated from commercial channels. The American alligator is a case in point. In 1975, the American alligator was nearing extinction and listed as endangered, but by 1987 conservation efforts restored the species. Now there is a vigorous trade in alligator hides.

Finally, the taking of red wolves is connected to interstate markets for agricultural products and livestock. For instance, appellant landowners find red wolves a menace because they threaten livestock and other animals of economic and commercial value. This effect on commerce, however, still qualifies as a legitimate subject for regulation. It is well-settled under Commerce Clause cases that a regulation can involve the promotion or the restriction of commercial enterprises and development.

It is anything but clear that red wolves harm farming enterprises. They may in fact help them, and in so doing confer additional benefits on commerce.

For instance, red wolves prey on animals like raccoons, deer, and rabbits—helping farmers by killing the animals that destroy their crops.

[I]t is reasonable for Congress to decide that conservation of species will one day produce a substantial commercial benefit to this country and that failure to preserve a species will result in permanent, though unascertainable, commercial loss. If a species becomes extinct, we are left to speculate forever on what we might have learned or what we may have realized. If we conserve the species, it will be available for the study and benefit of future generations. We therefore hold that the anti-taking provision at issue here involves regulable economic and commercial activity as understood by current Commerce Clause jurisprudence. ◢

The government has introduced the Habitat Conservation Plan (HCP) as a blueprint for compromise over the ESA. In an HCP, developers agree to conserve some land in return for developing other property as they want. These deals contain a "no surprises" clause, meaning that the government has no right to retrieve land once it has been approved for development, even if scientists later determine that a particular species needs that habitat for survival. Unfortunately, the natural world is full of surprises, and environmentalists worry about the ultimate impact of these HCPs. In the short run, however, the success has been striking. For example, to save the gnatcatcher, a songbird found near San Diego, federal and local governments agreed to set aside 82,000 acres that they owned. They bought an additional 27,000 acres, at a cost of $300 million, and developers donated 63,000 acres more. In return, the developers earned the right to build on their remaining land without limitation. More than 16 million acres, including 10 percent of timberland in the Pacific Northwest, are now designated HCPs.

In the long run, the real issue is not how much land developers will give up, but how each of us will change our lifestyle. The government recently announced that nine wild salmon species in the Pacific Northwest are threatened. The Columbia River used to be home to 16 million salmon, but dozens of dams now block the river, interfering with the fish's annual migration. Fewer than a million salmon remain. The following article discusses some of the remedies that may be necessary to save the salmon.

NEWSWORTHY

With the salmon crisis, you step out the door and the rain that's running off your front lawn, awash in fertilizer, is a problem. You drive to work (alone) and you are adding to the oil and other chemicals that all eventually drain into the streams. You work for a company that wants to expand its offices into what is a salmon habitat, which describes just about every wetland within a day's drive of Seattle. At home, you turn on a light that is fed cheaply by the very dams that make it nearly impossible for salmon to swim upstream. For us to change this chain of events requires changing our lifestyles, which is something most

Northwesterners have always seemed loath to do. We don't want anyone to tell us what to do with our lot size or with that instrument that is most integral to life here: the sport utility vehicle. All of a sudden being for the salmon means being against building a new home wherever you'd like, being for increased taxes, being prepared to change suburban life.

As this new debate begins, the phrase "putting salmon before people" will be heard over and over. Somehow the people need to line up behind the fish, that the fish are like the canary in the coal mine. Now, the salmon are making us look not just at what we can do with the rivers but at what we can do with the way we commute and choose our homes and shop and live. The question is, Will it be too much of a hassle for us to look at ourselves?[11] ◗

Chapter Conclusion

Environmental laws have a pervasive impact on our lives. The cost has been great—whether it is the higher price for cars with pollution control devices or the time spent filling out environmental impact statements. Some argue that cost is irrelevant, that a clean environment has incalculable value for its own sake. Others insist on a more pragmatic approach and want to know if the benefits outweigh the costs.

What benefits has the country gained from environmental regulation? Since 1970, when Congress created the EPA, the record on common air pollutants, such as lead, has been extraordinarily successful. Total emissions of lead nationwide have declined by 96 percent. Before 1970, emissions of sulfur dioxide had been increasing rapidly. Since then, in spite of strong economic growth and an increase in population, these emissions have dropped. Despite this progress, however, many Americans live in areas that do not meet EPA quality standards.

As for water, wetland acreage continues to decline at a rapid rate. However, the number of Americans whose sewage goes to wastewater treatment facilities has more than doubled. Two-thirds of the nation's waters are safe for fishing and swimming, up from only one-third when the Clean Water Act was passed.

Despite this progress, as a nation we still face many intractable problems. We have not developed a political consensus on global warming. The health effects of pesticides in our food supply are uncertain. Superfund and the Endangered Species Act are mired in a thornbush of litigation.

In short, despite significant progress, much work remains to be done. Although many people, and many politicians, readily acknowledge the importance of the environment to both present and future generations, when the time comes to allocate resources, change lifestyles, make tough choices, the consensus too often breaks down, with the result that resources are spent on litigation, instead of the environment.

---

[11] Robert Sullivan, "And Now, the Salmon War," *The New York Times*, Mar. 20, 1999, p. A15. Copyright © 2002 (1999) by The New York Times Co. Reprinted by permission.

Chapter Review

1. The following table provides a list of environmental statutes:

Air Pollution	Water Pollution	Waste Disposal	Chemicals	Natural Resources
Clean Air Act	Clean Water Act	Resource Conservation and Recovery Act	Federal Insecticide, Fungicide, and Rodenticide Act	National Environmental Policy Act
	Safe Drinking Water Act	Comprehensive Environmental Response, Compensation, and Liability Act (Superfund, or CERCLA)	Federal Food, Drug, and Cosmetic Act	Endangered Species Act
	Ocean Dumping Act			
	Oil Pollution Act		Food Quality Protection Act	
			Toxic Substances Control Act	

2. Under the Clean Air Act of 1970, the Environmental Protection Agency must establish national ambient air quality standards for both primary and secondary pollution. States must produce implementation plans to meet the EPA standards.

3. Under the Clean Air Act, power plants may trade emission allowances.

4. The Clean Water Act (CWA) prohibits the discharge of pollution into water without a permit from the EPA. States must set EPA-approved water quality standards and develop plans to achieve them. The Clean Water Act also prohibits any discharge of dredge and fill material into a wetland without a permit.

5. The Safe Drinking Water Act requires the EPA to set national standards for every contaminant potentially harmful to human health that is found in drinking water.

6. The Ocean Dumping Act prohibits the dumping of wastes in ocean water without a permit from the EPA.

7. The Oil Pollution Act of 1990 sets design standards for ships operating in U.S. waters and requires shipowners to pay for damage caused by oil discharged from their ships.

8. The Resource Conservation and Recovery Act (RCRA) establishes rules for treating hazardous wastes and other forms of solid waste.

9. Under Superfund (CERCLA), anyone who has ever owned or operated a site on which hazardous wastes are found, or who has transported wastes to the site, or who has arranged for the disposal of wastes that were released at the site, is liable for (1) the cost of cleaning up the site, (2) any damage done to natural resources, and (3) any required health assessments.

10. The Federal Insecticide, Fungicide, and Rodenticide Act (FIFRA) requires manufacturers to register all pesticides with the EPA.

11. The Federal Food, Drug, and Cosmetic Act requires the EPA to set maximum levels for pesticide residue in raw or processed food. The Food Quality Protection Act requires the EPA to set pesticide standards at levels that are safe for children.

12. Under the Toxic Substances Control Act (TSCA), manufacturers must register new chemicals with the EPA.

13. The National Environmental Policy Act (NEPA) requires all federal agencies to prepare an environmental impact statement for every major federal action significantly affecting the quality of the environment.

14. The Endangered Species Act (ESA) prohibits activities that cause harm to endangered species.

Practice Test

1. Astro Circuit Corp. in Lowell, Massachusetts, manufactured printed circuit boards. David Boldt was in charge of the production line. In theory, the company pretreated its industrial waste to remove toxic metals, but, in practice, the factory was producing twice as much wastewater as the treatment facility could handle. The company often bypassed the treatment facility and dumped wastewater directly into the city sewer. Once, when caught by the city, Boldt wrote a letter implying that the violation was a temporary aberration. Boldt felt that he was caught "between the devil and the deep blue sea." It was his job to keep the production line moving, but he had no place to put the waste product. Has Boldt violated the law? What penalties might he face?

2. The U.S. Forest Service planned to build a road in the Nez Perce National Forest in Idaho to provide access to loggers. Is the Forest Service governed by any environmental statutes? Must it seek permission before building the road?

3. In 1963, FMC Corp. purchased a manufacturing plant in Virginia from American Viscose Corp., the owner of the plant since 1937. During World War II, the government's War Production Board had commissioned American Viscose to make rayon for airplanes and truck tires. In 1982, inspections revealed carbon disulfide, a chemical used to manufacture this rayon, in groundwater near the plant. American Viscose was out of business. Who is responsible for cleaning up the carbon disulfide? Under what statute?

4. Tariq Ahmad owned Shankman Laboratories. He decided to dispose of some of the lab's hazardous chemicals by shipping them to his home in Pakistan. He sent the chemicals to Castelazo & Associates (in the United States) to prepare the materials for shipment. Ahmad did not tell the driver who picked up the chemicals that they were hazardous. Nor did he give the driver any written documentation. Ahmad had packed the chemicals hurriedly in flimsy containers that were unsafe for transporting hazardous materials. He also grossly misrepresented to Castelazo the amount and type of hazardous material that he was shipping to Pakistan. Has Ahmad violated U.S. law? What penalties might he face?

5. Suppose that you are the manager of the General Motors Hummer plant in Mishawaka, Indiana. Hummers are the successor to the U.S. Army jeep and have become popular recreational vehicles among the rich and famous. Arnold Schwarzenegger has several. The Hummer requires special protective paint that reacts with other chemicals during the application process to create ozone, a pollutant. You want to increase production of Hummers. Are there any legal requirements you must observe?

6. Alcan Aluminum Corp. manufactures aluminum sheet in Oswego, New York. It hired the Mahler Cos. to dispose of an emulsion used during the manufacturing process. This emulsion contained a variety of hazardous substances. Without Alcan's knowledge, Mahler dumped the emulsion into a borehole that connected to deep underground mines along the Susquehanna River in Pennsylvania. You can guess what happened next. Approximately 100,000 gallons of water contaminated with hazardous substances spilled from the borehole into the river. The EPA paid to clean up the river and then sued Alcan along with others who had hired Mahler for hazardous waste disposal. All other defendants settled. The court entered judgment against Alcan in the amount of $473,790.18, which was the difference between the full response costs the government had incurred in cleaning the river and the amount the government had recovered from the settling defendants. Is Alcan required to pay this amount?

7. In 1991, Illinois passed a statute requiring its four largest generating plants to install scrubbers so that they could continue using high-sulfur Illinois coal. What federal law was this Illinois statute designed to overcome? Extra credit: On what grounds did a federal appeals court strike down the Illinois statute?

8. The marbled murrelet is a rare seabird that lives only in old-growth forests on the West

Coast. Logging has destroyed so much of its habitat that its numbers in California have declined from 60,000 to between 2,000 and 5,000. Pacific Lumber Co. wanted to harvest trees from 137 acres of land it owned in the Owl Creek forest in California. It originally received approval to log, on the condition that it would cooperate with regulators to protect the murrelet. But the company sneaked in one weekend and cut down trees before it met the condition. Caught in the act, it promised no more logging until it had a plan to protect the birds. This time it waited until the long weekend over Thanksgiving to take down some more trees. Finally, a federal court ordered a permanent halt to any further logging. There was no evidence that the company had harmed the murrelet. Had it violated the law?

9. **ETHICS** Geronimo Villegas owned a blood-testing lab in Brooklyn, New York. He threw vials of human blood from the lab into the Hudson River. A group of eighth graders on a field trip to Staten Island discovered 70 of these glass vials along the shore. Ten vials contained blood infected with the highly contagious hepatitis-B virus. Did Villegas violate the Clean Water Act? Why had Villegas disposed of the vials in this way? Whether or not he was in violation of the statute, was his behavior ethical?

Did he violate any of the ethical tests from Chapter 2?

10. **YOU BE THE JUDGE WRITING PROBLEM** The Lordship Point Gun Club operated a trap and skeet shooting club in Stratford, Connecticut, for 70 years. During this time, customers deposited close to 5 million tons of lead shot and 11 million pounds of clay target fragments on land around the club and in Long Island Sound. Forty-five percent of sediment samples taken from the Sound exceeded the established limits for lead. Was the Gun Club in violation of the RCRA? **Argument for the Gun Club:** The Gun Club does not *dispose* of hazardous wastes, within the meaning of the RCRA. Congress meant the statute to apply only to companies in the business of manufacturing articles that produce hazardous waste. If the Gun Club happens to produce wastes, that is only *incidental* to the normal use of a product. **Argument for the plaintiff:** Under the RCRA, lead shot is hazardous waste. The law applies to anyone who produces hazardous waste, no matter how.

11. **ROLE REVERSAL** Write a short-answer question that poses an ethics or economics question under the environmental laws.

Internet Research Problem

Using the information provided at http://www.globalwarming.org/index.htm and http://www.law.pace.edu/env/energy/globalwarming.html, write an essay summarizing your views on global warming. What should our own government, and other governments, do? What should you do personally?

You can find further practice problems in the Online Quiz at http://beatty.westbuslaw.com **or in the Study Guide that accompanies this text.**

The Constitution of the United States

Preamble   We the People of the United States, in Order to form a more perfect Union, establish Justice, insure domestic Tranquility, provide for the common defense, promote the general Welfare, and secure the Blessings of Liberty to ourselves and our Posterity, do ordain and establish this Constitution for the United States of America.

ARTICLE I

Section 1.

All legislative Powers herein granted shall be vested in a Congress of the United States, which shall consist of a Senate and House of Representatives.

Section 2.

The House of Representatives shall be composed of Members chosen every second Year by the People of the several States, and the Electors in each State shall have the Qualifications requisite for Electors of the most numerous Branch of the State Legislature.

No Person shall be a Representative who shall not have attained to the Age of twenty five Years, and been seven Years a Citizen of the United States, and who shall not, when elected, be an Inhabitant of that State in which he shall be chosen.

Representatives and direct Taxes shall be apportioned among the several States which may be included within this Union, according to their respective Numbers, which shall be determined by adding to the whole Number of free Persons, including those bound to Service for a Term of Years, and excluding Indians not taxed, three fifths of all other Persons. The actual Enumeration shall be made within three Years after the first Meeting of the Congress of the United States, and within every subsequent Term of ten Years, in such Manner as they shall by Law direct. The number of Representatives shall not exceed one for every thirty Thousand, but each State shall have at Least one Representative; and until such enumeration shall be made, the State of New Hampshire shall be entitled to chuse three, Massachusetts eight, Rhode Island and Providence Plantations one, Connecticut five, New-York six, New Jersey four, Pennsylvania eight, Delaware one, Maryland six, Virginia ten, North Carolina five, South Carolina five, and Georgia three.

When vacancies happen in the Representation from any State, the Executive Authority thereof shall issue Writs of Election to fill such vacancies.

The House of Representatives shall chuse their Speaker and other Officers; and shall have the sole Power of Impeachment.

Section 3.

The Senate of the United States shall be composed of two Senators from each State, chosen by the Legislature thereof, for six Years; and each Senator shall have one Vote.

Immediately after they shall be assembled in Consequence of the first Election, they shall be divided as equally as may be into three Classes. The Seats of the Senators of the first Class shall be vacated at the Expiration of the second Year, of the second Class at the Expiration of the fourth Year, and of the third Class at the Expiration of the sixth Year, so that one third may be chosen every second Year; and if Vacancies happen by Resignation or otherwise, during the Recess of the Legislature of any State, the Executive thereof may make temporary Appointments until the next Meeting of the Legislature, which shall then fill such Vacancies.

No Person shall be a Senator who shall not have attained to the Age of thirty Years, and been nine Years a Citizen of the United States, and who shall not, when elected, be an Inhabitant of that State for which he shall be chosen.

The Vice President of the United States shall be President of the Senate, but shall have no Vote, unless they be equally divided.

The Senate shall chuse their other Officers, and also a President pro tempore, in the Absence of the Vice President, or when he shall exercise the Office of President of the United States.

The Senate shall have the sole power to try all Impeachments. When sitting for that Purpose, they shall be an Oath or Affirmation. When the President of the United States is tried, the Chief Justice shall preside: And no Person shall be convicted without the Concurrence of two thirds of the Members present.

Judgment in Cases of Impeachment shall not extend further than to removal from Office, and disqualification to hold and enjoy any Office of honor, Trust or Profit under the United States: but the Party convicted shall nevertheless be liable and subject to Indictment, Trial, Judgment and Punishment, according to Law.

Section 4.

The Times, Places and Manner of holding Elections for Senators and Representatives, shall be prescribed in each State by the Legislature thereof: but the Congress may at any time by Law make or alter such Regulations, except as to the Places of chusing Senators.

The Congress shall assemble at least once in every Year, and such Meeting shall be on the first Monday in December, unless they shall by Law appoint a different Day.

Section 5.

Each House shall be the Judge of the Elections, Returns and Qualifications of its own Members, and a Majority of each shall constitute a Quorum to do Business; but a smaller Number may adjourn from day to day, and may be authorized to compel the Attendance of absent Members, in such Manner, and under such Penalties as each House may provide.

Each House may determine the Rules of its Proceedings, punish its Members for disorderly Behaviour, and, with the Concurrence of two thirds, expel a Member.

Each House shall keep a Journal of its Proceedings, and from time to time publish the same, excepting such Parts as may in their Judgment require Secrecy; and the Yeas and Nays of the Members of either House on any question shall, at the Desire of one fifth of those Present, be entered on the Journal.

Neither House, during the Session of Congress, shall, without the Consent of the other, adjourn for more than three days, nor to any other Place than that in which the two Houses shall be sitting.

Section 6.

The Senators and Representatives shall receive a Compensation for their Services, to be ascertained by Law, and paid out of the Treasury of the United States. They shall in all Cases, except Treason, Felony and Breach of the Peace, be privileged from Arrest during their Attendance at the Session of their respective Houses, and in going to and returning from the same; and for any Speech or Debate in either House, they shall not be questioned in any other Place.

No Senator or Representative shall, during the Time for which he was elected, be appointed to any civil Office under the Authority of the United States, which shall have been created, or the Emoluments whereof shall have been encreased during such time; and no Person holding any Office under the United States, shall be a Member of either House during his Continuance in Office.

Section 7.

All Bills for raising Revenue shall originate in the House of Representatives; but the Senate may propose or concur with Amendments as on other Bills.

Every Bill which shall have passed the House of Representatives and the Senate, shall, before it become a Law, be presented to the President of the United States; If he approve he shall sign it, but if not he shall return it, with his Objections to that House in which it shall have originated, who shall enter the Objections at large on their Journal, and proceed to reconsider it. If after such Reconsideration two thirds of that House shall agree to pass the Bill, it shall be sent, together with the Objections, to the other House, by which it shall likewise be reconsidered, and if approved by two thirds of that House, it shall become a Law. But in all such Cases the Votes of both Houses shall be determined by Yeas and Nays, and the Names of the Persons voting for and against the Bill shall be entered on the Journal of each House respectively. If any Bill shall not be returned by the President within ten Days (Sundays excepted) after it shall have been presented to him, the Same shall be a Law, in like Manner as if he had signed it, unless the Congress by their Adjournment prevent its Return, in which Case it shall not be a Law.

Every Order, Resolution, or Vote to which the Concurrence of the Senate and House of Representatives may be necessary (except on a question of Adjournment) shall be presented to the President of the United States; and before the Same shall take Effect, shall be approved by him, or being disapproved by him, shall be repassed by two thirds of the Senate and House of Representatives, according to the Rules and Limitations prescribed in the Case of a Bill.

Section 8.

The Congress shall have Power to lay and collect Taxes, Duties, Imposts and Excises, to pay the Debts and provide for the common Defence and general Welfare of the United States; but all Duties, Imposts and Excises shall be uniform throughout the United States;

To borrow Money on the credit of the United States;

To regulate Commerce with foreign Nations, and among the several States, and with the Indian Tribes;

To establish an uniform Rule of Naturalization, and uniform Laws on the subject of Bankruptcies throughout the United States;

To coin Money, regulate the Value thereof, and of foreign Coin, and fix the Standard of Weights and Measures;

To provide for the Punishment of counterfeiting the Securities and current Coin of the United States;

To establish Post Offices and post Roads;

To promote the Progress of Science and useful Arts, by securing for limited Times to Authors and Inventors the exclusive Right to their respective Writings and Discoveries;

To constitute Tribunals inferior to the supreme Court;

To define and punish Piracies and Felonies committed on the high Seas, and Offenses against the Law of Nations;

To declare War, grant Letters of Marque and Reprisal, and make Rules concerning Captures on Land and Water;

To raise and support Armies, but no Appropriation of Money to that Use shall be for a longer Term than two Years;

To provide and maintain a Navy;

To make Rules for the Government and Regulation of the land and naval Forces;

To provide for calling forth the Militia to execute the Laws of the Union, suppress Insurrections and repel Invasions;

To provide for organizing, arming, and disciplining, the Militia, and for governing such Part of them as may be employed in the Service of the United States, reserving to the States respectively, the Appointment of the Officers, and the Authority of training the Militia according to the discipline described by Congress;

To exercise exclusive Legislation in all Cases whatsoever, over such District (not exceeding ten Miles square) as may, by Cession of particular States, and the Acceptance of Congress, become the Seat of the Government of the United States, and to exercise like Authority over all Places purchased by the Consent of the Legislature of the State in which the Same shall be, for the Erection of Forts, Magazines, Arsenals, dock-Yards, and other needful Buildings;—And

To make all Laws which shall be necessary and proper for carrying into Execution the foregoing Powers, and all other Powers vested by this Constitution in the Government of the United States, or in any Department or Officer thereof.

Section 9.

The Migration or Importation of such Persons as any of the States now existing shall think proper to admit, shall not be prohibited by the Congress prior to the Year one thousand eight hundred and eight, but a Tax or Duty may be imposed on such Importation, not exceeding ten dollars for each Person.

The Privilege of the Writ of Habeas Corpus shall not be suspended, unless when in Cases of Rebellion or Invasion the public Safety may require it.

No Bill of Attainder or ex post facto Law shall be passed.

No Capitation, or other direct, Tax shall be laid, unless in Proportion to the Census or Enumeration herein before directed to be taken.

No Tax or Duty shall be laid on Articles exported from any State.

No Preference shall be given by any Regulation of Commerce or Revenue to the Ports of one State over those of another; nor shall Vessels bound to, or from, one State, be obliged to enter, clear, or pay Duties in another.

No Money shall be drawn from the Treasury, but in Consequence of Appropriations made by Laws; and a regular Statement and Account of the Receipts and Expenditures of all public Money shall be published from time to time.

No Title of Nobility shall be granted by the United States: And no Person holding any Office of Profit or Trust under them, shall, without the Consent of the Congress, accept of any present, Emolument, Office, or Title, of any kind whatever, from any King, Prince, or foreign State.

Section 10.

No State shall enter into any Treaty, Alliance, or Confederation; grant Letters of Marque and Reprisal; coin Money; emit Bills of Credit; make any Thing but gold and silver Coin a Tender in Payment of Debts; pass any Bill of Attainder, ex post facto Law, or Law impairing the Obligation of Contracts, or grant any Title of Nobility.

No State shall, without the Consent of the Congress, lay any Imposts or Duties on Imports or Exports, except what may be absolutely necessary for executing its inspection Laws: and the net Produce of all Duties and Imposts, laid by any State on Imports or Exports, shall be for the Use of the Treasury of the United States; and all such Laws shall be subject to the Revision and Controul of the Congress.

No State shall, without the Consent of Congress, lay any Duty of Tonnage, keep Troops, or Ships of War in time of Peace, enter into any Agreement or Compact with another State, or with a foreign Power, or engage in War, unless actually invaded, or in such imminent Danger as will not admit of delay.

ARTICLE II

Sales of Goods

Section 1.

The executive Power shall be vested in a President of the United States of America. He shall hold his Office during the Term of four Years, and, together with the Vice President, chosen for the same Term, be elected, as follows:

Each State shall appoint, in such Manner as the Legislature thereof may direct, a Number of Electors, equal to the whole Number of Senators and Representatives to which the State may be entitled in the Congress: but no Senator or Representative, or Person holding an Office of Trust or Profit under the United States, shall be appointed an Elector.

The Electors shall meet in their respective States, and vote by Ballot for two Persons, of whom one at least shall not be an Inhabitant of the same State with themselves. And they shall make a list of all the Persons voted for, and of the Number of Votes for each; which List they shall sign and certify, and transmit sealed to the Seat of the Government of the United States, directed to the President of the Senate. The President of the Senate shall, in the presence of the Senate and House of Representatives, open all the Certificates, and the Votes shall be counted. The Person having the greatest Number of Votes shall be the President, if such Number be a Majority of the whole Number of Electors appointed; and if there be more than one who have such Majority, and have an equal Number of Votes, then the House of Representatives shall immediately chuse by Ballot one of them for President; and if no Person have a Majority, then from the five highest on the List the said House shall in like Manner chuse the President. But in chusing the President, the Votes shall be taken by States, the Representation from each State having one Vote; A quorum for this Purpose shall consist of a Member or Members from two thirds of the States, and a Majority of all the States shall be necessary to a Choice. In every Case, after the Choice of the President, the Person having the greatest Number of Votes of the Electors shall be the Vice President. But if there should remain two or more who have equal Votes, the Senate shall chuse from them by Ballot the Vice President.

The Congress may determine the Time of Chusing the Electors, and the Day on which they shall give their Votes; which Day shall be the same throughout the United States.

No Person except a natural born Citizen, or a Citizen of the United States, at the time of the Adoption of this Constitution, shall be eligible to the Office of President; neither shall any Person be eligible to that Office who shall not have attained to the Age of thirty five Years, and been fourteen Years a Resident within the United States.

In Case of the Removal of the President from Office, or of his Death, Resignation, or Inability to discharge the Powers and Duties of the said Office, the Same shall devolve on the Vice President, and the Congress may by Law provide for the Case of Removal, Death, Resignation or Inability, both of the President and Vice President, declaring what Officer shall then act as President, and such Officer shall act accordingly, until the Disability be removed, or a President shall be elected.

The President shall, at stated Times, receive for his Services, a Compensation, which shall neither be encreased nor diminished during the Period for which he shall have been elected, and he shall not receive within that Period any other Emolument from the United States, or any of them.

Before he enter on the Execution of his Office, he shall take the following Oath or Affirmation:—"I do solemnly swear (or affirm) that I will faithfully execute the Office of President of the United States, and will to the best of my Ability, preserve, protect and defend the Constitution of the United States."

Section 2.

The President shall be Commander in Chief of the Army and Navy of the United States, and of the Militia of the several States, when called into the actual Service of the United States; he may require the Opinion, in writing, of the principal

Officer in each of the executive Departments, upon any Subject relating to the Duties of their respective Offices, and he shall have Power to grant Reprieves and Pardons for Offenses against the United States, except in Cases of Impeachment.

He shall have Power, by and with the Advice and Consent of the Senate, to make Treaties, providing two thirds of the Senators present concur; and he shall nominate, and by and with the Advice and Consent of the Senate, shall appoint Ambassadors, other public Ministers and Consuls, Judges of the supreme Court, and all other Officers of the United States, whose Appointments are not herein otherwise provided for, and which shall be established by Law: but the Congress may by Law vest the Appointment of such inferior Officers, as they think proper, in the President alone, in the Courts of Law, or in the Heads of Departments.

The President shall have Power to fill up all Vacancies that may happen during the Recess of the Senate, by granting Commissions which shall expire at the End of their next Session.

Section 3.

He shall from time to time give to the Congress Information of the State of the Union, and recommend to their Consideration such Measures as he shall judge necessary and expedient; he may, on extraordinary Occasions, convene both Houses, or either of them, and in Case of Disagreement between them, with Respect to the Time of Adjournment, he may adjourn them to such Time as he shall think proper, he shall receive Ambassadors and other public Ministers; he shall take Care that the Laws be faithfully executed, and shall Commission all the Offices of the United States.

Section 4.

The President, Vice President and all civil Officers of the United States, shall be removed from Office on Impeachment for, and Conviction of, Treason, Bribery, or other high Crimes and Misdemeanors.

ARTICLE III

Section 1.

The judicial Power of the United States, shall be vested in one supreme Court, and in such inferior Courts as the Congress may from time to time ordain and establish. The Judges, both of the supreme and inferior Courts, shall hold their Offices during good Behaviour, and shall, at Times, receive for their Services, a Compensation, which shall not be diminished during their Continuance in Office.

Section 2.

The judicial Power shall extend to all Cases, in Law and Equity, arising under this Constitution, the Laws of the United States, and Treaties made, or which shall be made, under their Authority;—to all Cases affecting Ambassadors, other public Ministers and Consuls;—to all Cases of admiralty and maritime Jurisdiction;—to Controversies to which the United States shall be a Party;—to controversies between two or more States;—between a State and Citizens of another State;—between Citizens of different States;—between Citizens of the same State claiming Lands under Grants of different States; and between a State, or the Citizens thereof, and foreign States, Citizens or Subjects.

In all Cases affecting Ambassadors, other public Ministers and Consuls, and those in which a State shall be Party, the supreme Court shall have original Jurisdiction. In all the other Cases before mentioned, the supreme Court shall have appellate Jurisdiction, both as to Law and Fact, with such Exceptions, and under such Regulations as the Congress shall make.

The Trial of all Crimes, except in Cases of Impeachment, shall be by Jury; and such Trial shall be held in the State where the said Crimes shall have been committed; but when not committed within any State, the Trial shall be at such Place or Places as the Congress may by Law have directed.

Section 3.

Treason against the United States, shall consist only in levying War against them, or in adhering to their Enemies, giving them Aid and Comfort. No Person shall be convicted of Treason unless on the Testimony of two Witnesses to the same overt Act, or on Confession in open Court.

The Congress shall have Power to declare the Punishment of Treason, but no Attainder of Treason shall work Corruption of Blood, or Forfeiture except during the Life of the Person attainted.

ARTICLE IV

Section 1.

Full Faith and Credit shall be given in each State to the public Acts, Records, and judicial Proceedings of every other State. And the Congress may by general Laws prescribe the Manner in which such Acts, Records and Proceedings shall be proved, and the Effect thereof.

Section 2.

The Citizens of each State shall be entitled to all Privileges and Immunities of Citizens in the several States.

A Person charged in any State with Treason, Felony, or other Crime, who shall flee from Justice, and be found in another State, shall on Demand of the executive Authority of the State from which he fled, be delivered up, to be removed to the State having Jurisdiction of the Crime.

No Person held to Service or Labour in one State, under the Laws thereof, escaping into another, shall, in Consequence of any Law or Regulation therein, be discharged from such Service or Labour, but shall be delivered up on Claim of the Party to whom such Service or Labour may be due.

Section 3.

New States may be admitted by the Congress into this Union; but no new State shall be formed or erected within the Jurisdiction of any other State; nor any State be formed by the Junction of two or more States, or Parts of States, without the Consent of the Legislatures of the States concerned as well as the Congress.

The Congress shall have Power to dispose of and make all needful Rules and Regulations respecting the Territory or other Property belonging to the United States; and nothing in this Constitution shall be so construed as to Prejudice any Claims of the United States, or of any particular State.

Section 4.

The United States shall guarantee to every State in this Union a Republican Form of Government, and shall protect each of them against Invasion; and on Application of the Legislature, or of the Executive (when the Legislature cannot be convened) against domestic Violence.

ARTICLE V

The Congress, whenever two thirds of both Houses shall deem it necessary, shall propose Amendments to this Constitution, or, on the Application of the Legislatures of two thirds of the several States, shall call a Convention for proposing Amendments, which, in either Case, shall be valid to all Intents and Purposes, as Part of this Constitution, when ratified by the Legislatures of three fourths of the several States, or by Conventions in three fourths thereof, as the one or the other Mode of Ratification may be proposed by the Congress; Provided that no Amendment which may be made prior to the Year One thousand eight hundred and eight shall in any Manner affect the first and fourth Clauses in the Ninth Section of the first Article; and that no State, without its Consent, shall be deprived of its equal Suffrage in the Senate.

ARTICLE VI

All Debts contracted and Engagements entered into, before the Adoption of this Constitution, shall be as valid against the United States under this Constitution, as under the Confederation.

This Constitution, and the Laws of the United States which shall be made in Pursuance thereof; and all Treaties made, or which shall be made, under the Authority of the United States, shall be the supreme Law of the Land; and the Judges in every State shall be bound thereby, any Thing in the Constitution or Laws of any State to the Contrary notwithstanding.

The Senators and Representatives before mentioned, and the Members of the several State Legislatures, and all executive and judicial Officers, both of the United States and of the Several States, shall be bound by Oath or Affirmation, to support this Constitution; but no religious Test shall ever be required as a Qualification to any Office or public Trust under the United States.

ARTICLE VII

Bill of Rights

The Ratification of the Conventions of nine States, shall be sufficient for the Establishment of this Constitution between the States so ratifying the Same.

Amendment I [1791].

Protects individual

Congress shall make no law respecting an establishment of religion, or prohibiting the free exercise thereof; or abridging the freedom of speech, or the press; or the right of the people peaceably to assemble, and to petition the Government for a redress of grievances.

Amendment II [1791].

A well regulated Militia, being necessary to the security for a free State, the right of the people to keep and bear Arms, shall not be infringed.

Amendment III [1791].

No Soldier shall, in time of peace be quartered in any house, without the consent of the Owner, nor in time of war, but in a manner to be prescribed by law.

Amendment IV [1791].

The right of the people to be secure in their persons, houses, papers, and effects, against unreasonable searches and seizures, shall not be violated, and no Warrants shall issue, but upon probable cause, supported by Oath or Affirmation, and particularly describing the place to be searched, and the persons or things to be seized.

Amendment V [1791].

No person shall be held to answer for a capital, or otherwise infamous crime, unless on a presentment or indictment of a Grand Jury, except in cases arising in the land or naval forces, or in the Militia, when in actual service in time of War or public danger; nor shall any person be subject for the same offense to be twice put in jeopardy of life or limb; nor shall be compelled in any criminal case to be a witness against himself, nor be deprived of life, liberty, or property, without due process of law; nor shall private property be taken for public use, without just compensation.

Amendment VI [1791].

In all criminal prosecutions, the accused shall enjoy the right to a speedy and public trial, by an impartial jury of the State and district wherein the crime shall have been committed, which district shall have been previously ascertained by law, and to be informed of the nature and cause of the accusation; to be confronted with the Witnesses against him; to have compulsory process for obtaining witnesses in his favor, and to have the Assistance of counsel for his defence.

Amendment VII [1791].

In suits at common law, where the value in controversy shall exceed twenty dollars, the right of trial by jury shall be preserved, and no fact tried by a jury, shall be otherwise re-examined in any Court of the United States, than according to the rules of the common law.

Amendment VIII [1791].

Excessive bail shall not be required, no excessive fines imposed, nor cruel and unusual punishments inflicted.

Amendment IX [1791].

The enumeration in the Constitution, of certain rights, shall not be construed to deny or disparage others retained by the people.

Amendment X [1791].

The powers not delegated to the United States by the Constitution, nor prohibited by it to the States, are reserved to the States respectively, or to the people.

Amendment XI [1798].

The judicial power of the United States shall not be construed to extend to any suit in law or equity, commenced or prosecuted against one of the United States by Citizens of another State, or by Citizens or Subjects of any Foreign State.

Amendment XII [1804].

The Electors shall meet in their respective states and vote by ballot for President and Vice-President, one of whom, at least, shall not be an inhabitant of the same state with themselves; they shall name in their ballots the person voted for as President, and in distinct ballots the person voted for as Vice-President, and they shall make distinct lists of all persons voted for as President, and of all persons voted for as Vice-President, and of the number of votes for each, which lists they shall sign and certify, and transmit sealed to the seat of the government of the United States, directed to the President of the Senate;—The President of the Senate shall, in the presence of the Senate and House of Representatives, open all the certificates and the votes shall then be counted;—The person having the greatest number of votes for President, shall be the President, if such number be a majority of the whole number of Electors appointed; and if no person have such majority, then from the persons having the highest numbers not exceeding three on the list of those voted for as President, the House of Representatives shall choose immediately, by ballot, the President. But in choosing the President, the votes shall be taken by states, the representation from each state having one vote; a quorum for this purpose shall consist of a member or members from two-thirds of the states, and a majority of all the states shall be necessary to a choice. And if the House of Representatives shall not choose a President whenever the right of choice shall devolve upon them, before the fourth day of March next following, then the Vice-President shall act as President, as in the case of the death or other constitutional disability of the President. The person having the greatest number of votes as Vice-President, shall be the Vice-President, if such number be a majority of the whole number of Electors appointed, and if no person have a majority, then from the two highest numbers on the list, the Senate shall choose the Vice-President; a quorum for the purpose shall consist of two-thirds of the whole number of Senators, and a majority of the whole number shall be necessary to a choice. But no person constitutionally ineligible to the office of President shall be eligible to that of the Vice-President of the United States.

Amendment XIII [1865].

Section 1. Neither slavery nor involuntary servitude, except as a punishment for crime whereof the party shall have been duly convicted, shall exist within the United States, or any place subject to their jurisdiction.

Section 2. Congress shall have power to enforce this article by appropriate legislation.

Amendment XIV [1868].

Section 1. All persons born or naturalized in the United States, and subject to the jurisdiction thereof, are citizens of the United States and of the State wherein they reside. No State shall make or enforce any law which shall abridge the privileges or immunities of citizens of the United States; nor shall any State deprive any person of life, liberty, or property, without due process of law; nor deny to any person within its jurisdiction the equal protection of the laws.

Section 2. Representatives shall be appointed among the several States according to their respective numbers, counting the whole number of persons in each State, excluding Indians not taxed. But when the right to vote at any election for the choice of electors for President and Vice President of the United States, Representatives in Congress, the Executive and Judicial officers of a State, or the members of the Legislature thereof, is denied to any of the male inhabitants of such State, being twenty-one years of age, and citizens of the United

States, or in any way abridged, except for participation in rebellion, or other crime, the basis of representation therein shall be reduced in the proportion which the number of such male citizens shall bear the whole number of male citizens twenty-one years of age in such State.

Section 3. No person shall be a Senator or Representative in Congress, or elector of President and Vice President, or hold any office, civil or military, under the United States, or under any State, who, having previously taken an oath, as a member of Congress, or as an officer of the United States, or as a member of any State legislature, or as an executive or judicial officer of any State, to support the Constitution of the United States, shall have engaged in insurrection or rebellion against the same, or given aid or comfort to the enemies thereof. But Congress may by a vote of two-thirds of each House, remove such disability.

Section 4. The validity of the public debt of the United States, authorized by law, including debts incurred for payment of pensions and bounties for services in suppressing insurrection or rebellion, shall not be questioned. But neither the United States nor any State shall assume or pay any debt or obligation incurred in aid of insurrection of rebellion against the United States, or any claim for the loss or emancipation of any slave; but all such debts, obligations and claims shall be held illegal and void.

Section 5. The Congress shall have power to enforce, by appropriate legislation, the provisions of this article.

Amendment XV [1870].

Section 1. The right of citizens of the United States to vote shall not be denied or abridged by the United States or by any State on account of race, color, or previous condition of servitude.

Section 2. The Congress shall have power to enforce this article by appropriate legislation.

Amendment XVI [1913].

The Congress shall have power to lay and collect taxes on incomes, from whatever source derived, without apportionment among the several States, and without regard to any census or enumeration.

Amendment XVII [1913].

The Senate of the United States shall be composed of two Senators from each State, elected by the people thereof, for six years; and each Senator shall have one vote. The electors in each State shall have the qualifications requisite for electors of the most numerous branch of the State legislatures.

When vacancies happen in the representation of any State in the Senate, the executive authority of each State shall issue writs of election to fill such vacancies; *Provided*, That the legislature of any State may empower the executive thereof to make temporary appointments until the people fill the vacancies by election as the legislature may direct.

This amendment shall not be construed as to affect the election or term of any Senator chosen before it becomes valid as part of the Constitution.

Amendment XVIII [1919].

Section 1. After one year from the ratification of this article the manufacture, sale, or transportation of intoxicating liquors within, the importation thereof into, or the exportation thereof from the United States and all territory subject to the jurisdiction thereof for beverage purposes is hereby prohibited.

Section 2. The Congress and the several States shall have concurrent power to enforce this article by appropriate legislation.

Section 3. This article shall be inoperative unless it shall have been ratified as an amendment to the Constitution by the legislatures of the several States, as provided in the Constitution, within seven years from the date of the submission hereof to the States by the Congress.

Amendment XIX [1920].

The right of citizens of the United States to vote shall not be denied or abridged by the United States or by any State on account of sex.

Congress shall have power to enforce this article by appropriate legislation.

Amendment XX [1933].

Section 1. The terms of the President and Vice President shall end at noon on the 20th day of January, and the terms of Senators and Representatives at noon on the 3d day of January, of the years in which such terms would have ended if this article had not been ratified; and the terms of their successors shall then begin.

Section 2. The Congress shall assemble at least once in every year, and such meeting shall begin at noon on the 3d day of January, unless they shall by law appoint a different day.

Section 3. If, at the time fixed for the beginning of the term of the President, the President elect shall have died, the Vice President elect shall become President. If a President shall not have been chosen before the time fixed for the beginning of his term, or if the President elect shall have failed to qualify, then the Vice President elect shall act as President until a President shall have qualified; and the Congress may by law provide for the case wherein neither a President elect nor a Vice President elect shall have qualified, declaring who shall then act as President, or the manner in which one who is to act shall be selected, and such person shall act accordingly until a President or Vice President shall have qualified.

Section 4. The Congress may by law provide for the case of the death of any of the persons from whom the House of Representatives may choose a President whenever the right of choice shall have devolved upon them, and for the case of the death of any of the persons from whom the Senate may choose a Vice President whenever the right of choice shall have devolved upon them.

Section 5. Sections 1 and 2 shall take effect on the 15th day of October following the ratification of this article.

Section 6. This article shall be inoperative unless it shall have been ratified as an amendment to the Constitution by the legislatures of three-fourths of the several States within seven years from the date of its submission.

Amendment XXI [1933].

Section 1. The eighteenth article of amendment to the Constitution of the United States is hereby repealed.

Section 2. The transportation or importation into any State, Territory, or possession of the United States for delivery or use therein of intoxicating liquors, in violation of the laws thereof, is hereby prohibited.

Section 3. This article shall be inoperative unless it shall have been ratified as an amendment to the Constitution by conventions in the several States, as provided in the Constitution, within seven years from the date of the submission hereof to the States by the Congress.

Prior to Stockmarket Crash 19 20-1933 Dry time

Amendment XXII [1951].

Section 1. No person shall be elected to the office of the President more than twice, and no person who has held the office of President, or acted as President, for more than two years of a term to which some other person was elected President shall be elected to the office of the President more than once. But this Article shall not apply to any person holding the office of President when this Article was proposed by the Congress, and shall not prevent any person who may be holding the office of President, or acting as President, during the term within which this Article becomes operative from holding the office of President, or acting as President during the remainder of such term.

Section 2. This article shall be inoperative unless it shall have been ratified as an amendment to the Constitution by the legislatures of the several States within seven years from the date of its submission to the States by the Congress.

Amendment XXIII [1961].

Section 1. The District constituting the seat of Government of the United States shall appoint in such manner as the Congress may direct:

A number of electors of President and Vice President equal to the whole number of Senators and Representatives in Congress to which the District would be entitled if it were a State, but in no event more than the least populous State; they shall be in addition to those appointed by the States, but they shall be considered, for the purposes of the election of President and Vice President, to be electors appointed by a State; and they shall meet in the District and perform such duties as provided by the twelfth article of amendment.

Section 2. The Congress shall have power to enforce this article by appropriate legislation.

Amendment XXIV [1964].

Section 1. The right of citizens of the United States to vote in any primary or other election for President or Vice President, for electors for President or Vice President, or for Senator or Representative in Congress, shall not be denied or abridged by the United States or any State by reason of failure to pay any poll tax or other tax.

Section 2. The Congress shall have power to enforce this article by appropriate legislation.

Amendment XXV [1967].

Section 1. In case of the removal of the President from office or of his death or resignation, the Vice President shall become President.

Section 2. Whenever there is a vacancy in the office of the Vice President, the President shall nominate a Vice President who shall take office upon confirmation by a majority vote of both Houses of Congress.

Section 3. Whenever the President transmits to the President pro tempore of the Senate and the Speaker of the House of Representatives his written declaration that he is unable to discharge the powers and duties of his office, and until he transmits to them a written declaration to the contrary, such powers and duties shall be discharged by the Vice President as Acting President.

Section 4. Whenever the Vice President and a majority of either the principal officers of the executive departments or of such other body as Congress may by law provide, transmit to the President pro tempore of the Senate and the Speaker of the House of Representatives their written declaration that the President is unable to discharge the powers and duties of his office, the Vice President shall immediately assume the powers and duties of the office as Acting President.

Thereafter, when the President transmits to the President pro tempore of the Senate and the Speaker of the House of Representatives his written declaration that no inability exists, he shall resume the powers and duties of his office unless the Vice President and a majority of either the principal officers of the executive department or of such other body as Congress may by law provide, transmit within four days to the President pro tempore of the Senate and the Speaker of the House of Representatives their written declaration that the President is unable to discharge the powers and duties of his office. Thereupon Congress shall decide the issue, assembling within forty-eight hours for that purpose if not in session. If the Congress, within twenty-one days after receipt of the latter written declaration, or, if Congress is not in session, within twenty-one days after Congress is required to assemble, determines by two-thirds vote of both Houses that the President is unable to discharge the powers and duties of his office, the Vice President shall continue to discharge the same as Acting President; otherwise, the President shall resume the powers and duties of his office.

Amendment XXVI [1971].

Section 1. The right of citizens of the United States, who are eighteen years of age or older, to vote shall not be denied or abridged by the United States or by any State on account of age.

Section 2. The Congress shall have power to enforce this article by appropriate legislation.

Amendment XXVII [1992].

No law, varying the compensation for the services of the Senators and Representatives, shall take effect, until an election of Representatives shall have intervened.

Uniform Commercial Code

ARTICLE 1

General Provisions

PART 1 SHORT TITLE, CONSTRUCTION, APPLICATION AND SUBJECT MATTER OF THE ACT

§ 1–101. Short Title.

This Act shall be known and may be cited as Uniform Commercial Code.

§ 1–102. Purposes; Rules of Construction; Variation by Agreement.

(1) This Act shall be liberally construed and applied to promote its underlying purposes and policies.

(2) Underlying purposes and policies of this Act are

    (a) to simplify, clarify and modernize the law governing commercial transactions;

    (b) to permit the continued expansion of commercial practices through custom, usage and agreement of the parties;

    (c) to make uniform the law among the various jurisdictions.

(3) The effect of provisions of this Act may be varied by agreement, except as otherwise provided in this Act and except that the obligations of good faith, diligence, reasonableness and care prescribed by this Act may not be disclaimed by agreement but the parties may by agreement determine the standards by which the performance of such obligations is to be measured if such standards are not manifestly unreasonable.

(4) The presence in certain provisions of this Act of the words "unless otherwise agreed" or words of similar import does not imply that the effect of other provisions may not be varied by agreement under subsection (3).

(5) In this Act unless the context otherwise requires

    (a) words in the singular number include the plural, and in the plural include the singular;

    (b) words of the masculine gender include the feminine and the neuter, and when the sense so indicates words of the neuter gender may refer to any gender.

§ 1–103. Supplementary General Principles of Law Applicable.

Unless displaced by the particular provisions of this Act, the principles of law and equity, including the law merchant and the law relative to capacity to contract, principal and agent, estoppel, fraud, misrepresentation, duress, coercion, mistake, bankruptcy, or other validating or invalidating cause shall supplement its provisions.

§ 1–104. Construction Against Implicit Repeal.

This Act being a general act intended as a unified coverage of its subject matter, no part of it shall be deemed to be impliedly repealed by subsequent legislation if such construction can reasonably be avoided.

§ 1–105. Territorial Application of the Act; Parties' Power to Choose Applicable Law.

(1) Except as provided hereafter in this section, when a transaction bears a reasonable relation to this state and also to another state or nation the parties may agree that the law either of this state or of such other state or nation shall govern their rights and duties. Failing such agreement this Act applies to transactions bearing an appropriate relation to this state.

(2) Where one of the following provisions of this Act specifies the applicable law, that provision governs and a contrary agreement is effective only to the extent permitted by the law (including the conflict of laws rules) so specified:

Rights of creditors against sold goods. Section 2–402.

Applicability of the Article on Leases. Sections 2A–105 and 2A–106.

Applicability of the Article on Bank Deposits and Collections. Section 4–102.

Governing law in the Article on Funds Transfers. Section 4A–507.

[Publisher's Editorial Note: If a state adopts the repealer of Article 6—Bulk Transfers (Alternative A), there should not be any item relating to bulk transfers. If, however, a state adopts Revised Article 6—Bulk Sales (Alternative B), then the item relating to bulk sales should read as follows:]

Bulk sales subject to the Article on Bulk Sales. Section 6–103.

Applicability of the Article on Investment Securities. Section 8–110.

Perfection provisions of the Article on Secured Transactions. Section 9–103.

§ 1–106.   Remedies to Be Liberally Administered.

(1) The remedies provided by this Act shall be liberally administered to the end that the aggrieved party may be put in as good a position as if the other party had fully performed but neither consequential or special nor penal damages may be had except as specifically provided in this Act or by other rule of law.

(2) Any right or obligation declared by this Act is enforceable by action unless the provision declaring it specifies a different and limited effect.

§ 1–107.   Waiver or Renunciation of Claim or Right After Breach.

Any claim or right arising out of an alleged breach can be discharged in whole or in part without consideration by a written waiver or renunciation signed and delivered by the aggrieved party.

§ 1–108.   Severability.

If any provision or clause of this Act or application thereof to any person or circumstances is held invalid, such invalidity shall not affect other provisions or applications of the Act which can be given effect without the invalid provision or application, and to this end the provisions of this Act are declared to be severable.

§ 1–109.   Section Captions.

Section captions are parts of this Act.

PART 2   GENERAL DEFINITIONS AND PRINCIPLES OF INTERPRETATION

§ 1–201.   General Definitions.

Subject to additional definitions contained in the subsequent Articles of this Act which are applicable to specific Articles or Parts thereof, and unless the context otherwise requires, in this Act:

(1) "Action" in the sense of a judicial proceeding includes recoupment, counterclaim, set-off, suit in equity and any other proceedings in which rights are determined.

(2) "Aggrieved party" means a party entitled to resort to a remedy.

(3) "Agreement" means the bargain of the parties in fact as found in their language or by implication from other circumstances including course of dealing or usage of trade or course of performance as provided in this Act (Sections 1–205, 2–208, and 2A–207). Whether an agreement has legal consequences is determined by the provisions of this Act, if applicable; otherwise by the law of contracts (Section 1–103). (Compare "Contract".)

(4) "Bank" means any person engaged in the business of banking.

(5) "Bearer" means the person in possession of an instrument, document of title, or certificated security payable to bearer or indorsed in blank.

(6) "Bill of lading" means a document evidencing the receipt of goods for shipment issued by a person engaged in the business of transporting or forwarding goods, and includes an airbill. "Airbill" means a document serving for air transportation as a bill of lading does for marine or rail transportation, and includes an air consignment note or air waybill.

(7) "Branch" includes a separately incorporated foreign branch of a bank.

(8) "Burden of establishing" a fact means the burden of persuading the triers of fact that the existence of the fact is more probable than its non-existence.

(9) "Buyer in ordinary course of business" means a person who in good faith and without knowledge that the sale to him is in violation of the ownership rights or security interest of a third party in the goods buys in ordinary course from a person in the business of selling goods of that kind but does not include a pawnbroker. All persons who sell minerals or the like (including oil and gas) at wellhead or minehead shall be deemed to be persons in the business of selling goods of that kind. "Buying" may be for cash or by exchange of other property or on secured or unsecured credit and includes receiving goods or documents of title under a pre-existing contract for sale but does not include a transfer in bulk or as security for or in total or partial satisfaction of a money debt.

(10) "Conspicuous": A term or clause is conspicuous when it is so written that a reasonable person against whom it is to operate ought to have noticed it. A printed heading in capitals (as: NON-NEGOTIABLE BILL OF LADING) is conspicuous. Language in the body of a form is "conspicuous" if it is in larger or other contrasting type or color. But in a telegram any stated term is "conspicuous". Whether a term or clause is "conspicuous" or not is for decision by the court.

(11) "Contract" means the total legal obligation which results from the parties' agreement as affected by this Act and any other applicable rules of law. (Compare "Agreement".)

(12) "Creditor" includes a general creditor, a secured creditor, a lien creditor and any representative of creditors, including an assignee for the benefit of creditors, a trustee in bankruptcy, a receiver in equity and an executor or administrator of an insolvent debtor's or assignor's estate.

(13) "Defendant" includes a person in the position of defendant in a cross-action or counterclaim.

(14) "Delivery" with respect to instruments, documents of title, chattel paper, or certificated securities means voluntary transfer of possession.

(15) "Document of title" includes bill of lading, dock warrant, dock receipt, warehouse receipt or order for the delivery of goods, and also any other document which in the regular course of business or financing is treated as adequately evidencing that the person in possession of it is entitled to receive, hold and dispose of the document and the

goods it covers. To be a document of title a document must purport to be issued by or addressed to a bailee and purport to cover goods in the bailee's possession which are either identified or are fungible portions of an identified mass.

(16) "Fault" means wrongful act, omission or breach.

(17) "Fungible" with respect to goods or securities means goods or securities of which any unit is, by nature or usage of trade, the equivalent of any other like unit. Goods which are not fungible shall be deemed fungible for the purposes of this Act to the extent that under a particular agreement or document unlike units are treated as equivalents.

(18) "Genuine" means free of forgery or counterfeiting.

(19) "Good faith" means honesty in fact in the conduct or transaction concerned.

(20) "Holder," with respect to a negotiable instrument, means the person in possession if the instrument is payable to bearer or, in the case of an instrument payable to an identified person, if the identified person is in possession. "Holder" with respect to a document of title means the person in possession if the goods are deliverable to bearer or to the order of the person in possession.

(21) To "honor" is to pay or to accept and pay, or where a credit so engages to purchase or discount a draft complying with the terms of the credit.

(22) "Insolvency proceedings" includes any assignment for the benefit of creditors or other proceedings intended to liquidate or rehabilitate the estate of the person involved.

(23) A person is "insolvent" who either has ceased to pay his debts in the ordinary course of business or cannot pay his debts as they become due or is insolvent within the meaning of the federal bankruptcy law.

(24) "Money" means a medium of exchange authorized or adopted by a domestic or foreign government and includes a monetary unit of account established by an intergovernmental organization or by agreement between two or more nations.

(25) A person has "notice" of a fact when
    (a) he has actual knowledge of it; or
    (b) he has received a notice or notification of it; or
    (c) from all the facts and circumstances known to him at the time in question he has reason to know that it exists.
A person "knows" or has "knowledge" of a fact when he has actual knowledge of it. "Discover" or "learn" or a word or phrase of similar import refers to knowledge rather than to reason to know. The time and circumstances under which a notice or notification may cease to be effective are not determined by this Act.

(26) A person "notifies" or "gives" a notice or notification to another by taking such steps as may be reasonably required to inform the other in ordinary course whether or not such other actually comes to know of it. A person "receives" a notice or notification when
    (a) it comes to his attention; or
    (b) it is duly delivered at the place of business through which the contract was made or at any other place held out by him as the place for receipt of such communications.

(27) Notice, knowledge or a notice or notification received by an organization is effective for a particular transaction from the time when it is brought to the attention of the individual conducting that transaction, and in any event from the time when it would have been brought to his attention if the organization had exercised due diligence. An organization exercises due diligence if it maintains reasonable routines for communicating significant information to the person conducting the transaction and there is reasonable compliance with the routines. Due diligence does not require an individual acting for the organization to communicate information unless such communication is part of his regular duties or unless he has reason to know of the transaction and that the transaction would be materially affected by the information.

(28) "Organization" includes a corporation, government or governmental subdivision or agency, business trust, estate, trust, partnership or association, two or more persons having a joint or common interest, or any other legal or commercial entity.

(29) "Party", as distinct from "third party", means a person who has engaged in a transaction or made an agreement within this Act.

(30) "Person" includes an individual or an organization (See Section 1–102).

(31) "Presumption" or "presumed" means that the trier of fact must find the existence of the fact presumed unless and until evidence is introduced which would support a finding of its non-existence.

(32) "Purchase" includes taking by sale, discount, negotiation, mortgage, pledge, lien, issue or re-issue, gift or any other voluntary transaction creating an interest in property.

(33) "Purchaser" means a person who takes by purchase.

(34) "Remedy" means any remedial right to which an aggrieved party is entitled with or without resort to a tribunal.

(35) "Representative" includes an agent, an officer of a corporation or association, and a trustee, executor or administrator of an estate, or any other person empowered to act for another.

(36) "Rights" includes remedies.

(37) "Security interest" means an interest in personal property or fixtures which secures payment or performance of an obligation. The retention or reservation of title by a seller of goods notwithstanding shipment or delivery to the buyer (Section 2–401) is limited in effect to a reservation of a "security interest". The term also includes any interest of a buyer of accounts or chattel paper which is subject to Article 9. The special property interest of a buyer of goods on identification of those goods to a contract for sale under Section 2–401 is not a "security interest", but a buyer may also acquire a "security interest" by complying with Article 9. Unless a consignment is intended as security, reservation of title thereunder is not a "security interest", but a consignment in any event is subject to the provisions on consignment sales (Section 2–326).

Whether a transaction creates a lease or security interest is determined by the facts of each case; however, a transaction creates a security interest if the consideration the lessee is to pay the lessor for the right to possession and use of the goods is an obligation for the term of the lease not subject to termination by the lessee, and

(a) the original term of the lease is equal to or greater than the remaining economic life of the goods,

(b) the lessee is bound to renew the lease for the remaining economic life of the goods or is bound to become the owner of the goods,

(c) the lessee has an option to renew the lease for the remaining economic life of the goods for no additional consideration or nominal additional consideration upon compliance with the lease agreement, or

(d) the lessee has an option to become the owner of the goods for no additional consideration or nominal additional consideration upon compliance with the lease agreement.

A transaction does not create a security interest merely because it provides that

(a) the present value of the consideration the lessee is obligated to pay the lessor for the right to possession and use of the goods is substantially equal to or is greater than the fair market value of the goods at the time the lease is entered into,

(b) the lessee assumes risk of loss of the goods, or agrees to pay taxes, insurance, filing, recording, or registration fees, or service or maintenance costs with respect to the goods,

(c) the lessee has an option to renew the lease or to become the owner of the goods,

(d) the lessee has an option to renew the lease for a fixed rent that is equal to or greater than the reasonably predictable fair market rent for the use of the goods for the term of the renewal at the time the option is to be performed, or

(e) the lessee has an option to become the owner of the goods for a fixed price that is equal to or greater than the reasonably predictable fair market value of the goods at the time the option is to be performed.

For purposes of this subsection (37):

(x) Additional consideration is not nominal if (i) when the option to renew the lease is granted to the lessee the rent is stated to be the fair market rent for the use of the goods for the term of the renewal determined at the time the option is to be performed, or (ii) when the option to become the owner of the goods is granted to the lessee the price is stated to be the fair market value of the goods determined at the time the option is to be performed. Additional consideration is nominal if it is less than the lessee's reasonably predictable cost of performing under the lease agreement if the option is not exercised;

(y) "Reasonably predictable" and "remaining economic life of the goods" are to be determined with reference to the facts and circumstances at the time the transaction is entered into; and

(z) "Present value" means the amount as of a date certain of one or more sums payable in the future, discounted to the date certain. The discount is determined by the interest rate specified by the parties if the rate is not manifestly unreasonable at the time the transaction is entered into; otherwise,

the discount is determined by a commercially reasonable rate that takes into account the facts and circumstances of each case at the time the transaction was entered into.

(38) "Send" in connection with any writing or notice means to deposit in the mail or deliver for transmission by any other usual means of communication with postage or cost of transmission provided for and properly addressed and in the case of an instrument to an address specified thereon or otherwise agreed, or if there be none to any address reasonable under the circumstances. The receipt of any writing or notice within the time at which it would have arrived if properly sent has the effect of a proper sending.

(39) "Signed" includes any symbol executed or adopted by a party with present intention to authenticate a writing.

(40) "Surety" includes guarantor.

(41) "Telegram" includes a message transmitted by radio, teletype, cable, any mechanical method of transmission, or the like.

(42) "Term" means that portion of an agreement which relates to a particular matter.

(43) "Unauthorized" signature means one made without actual, implied, or apparent authority and includes a forgery.

(44) "Value". Except as otherwise provided with respect to negotiable instruments and bank collections (Sections 3–303, 4–210 and 4–211) a person gives "value" for rights if he acquires them

(a) in return for a binding commitment to extend credit or for the extension of immediately available credit whether or not drawn upon and whether or not a charge-back is provided for in the event of difficulties in collection; or

(b) as security for or in total or partial satisfaction of a pre-existing claim; or

(c) by accepting delivery pursuant to a pre-existing contract for purchase; or

(d) generally, in return for any consideration sufficient to support a simple contract.

(45) "Warehouse receipt" means a receipt issued by a person engaged in the business of storing goods for hire.

(46) "Written" or "writing" includes printing, typewriting or any other intentional reduction to tangible form.

§ 1–202. Prima Facie Evidence by Third Party Documents.

A document in due form purporting to be a bill of lading, policy or certificate of insurance, official weigher's or inspector's certificate, consular invoice, or any other document authorized or required by the contract to be issued by a third party shall be prima facie evidence of its own authenticity and genuineness and of the facts stated in the document by the third party.

§ 1–203. Obligation of Good Faith.

Every contract or duty within this Act imposes an obligation of good faith in its performance or enforcement.

§ 1–204. Time; Reasonable Time; "Seasonably".

(1) Whenever this Act requires any action to be taken with-

in a reasonable time, any time which is not manifestly unreasonable may be fixed by agreement.

(2) What is a reasonable time for taking any action depends on the nature, purpose and circumstances of such action.

(3) An action is taken "seasonably" when it is taken at or within the time agreed or if no time is agreed at or within a reasonable time.

§ 1–205. Course of Dealing and Usage of Trade.

(1) A course of dealing is a sequence of previous conduct between the parties to a particular transaction which is fairly to be regarded as establishing a common basis of understanding for interpreting their expressions and other conduct.

(2) A usage of trade is any practice or method of dealing having such regularity of observance in a place, vocation or trade as to justify an expectation that it will be observed with respect to the transaction in question. The existence and scope of such a usage are to be proved as facts. If it is established that such a usage is embodied in a written trade code or similar writing the interpretation of the writing is for the court.

(3) A course of dealing between parties and any usage of trade in the vocation or trade in which they are engaged or of which they are or should be aware give particular meaning to and supplement or qualify terms of an agreement.

(4) The express terms of an agreement and an applicable course of dealing or usage of trade shall be construed wherever reasonable as consistent with each other, but when such construction is unreasonable express terms control both course of dealing and usage of trade and course of dealing controls usage of trade.

(5) An applicable usage of trade in the place where any part of performance is to occur shall be used in interpreting the agreement as to that part of the performance.

(6) Evidence of a relevant usage of trade offered by one party is not admissible unless and until he has given the other party such notice as the court finds sufficient to prevent unfair surprise to the latter.

§ 1–206. Statute of Frauds for Kinds of Personal Property Not Otherwise Covered.

(1) Except in the cases described in subsection (2) of this section a contract for the sale of personal property is not enforceable by way of action or defense beyond five thousand dollars in amount or value of remedy unless there is some writing which indicates that a contract for sale has been made between the parties at a defined or stated price, reasonably identifies the subject matter, and is signed by the party against whom enforcement is sought or by his authorized agent.

(2) Subsection (1) of this section does not apply to contracts for the sale of goods (Section 2–201) nor of securities (Section 8–113) nor to security agreements (Section 9–203).

§ 1–207. Performance or Acceptance Under Reservation of Rights.

A party who with explicit reservation of rights performs or promises performance or assents to performance in a manner demanded or offered by the other party does not thereby prejudice the rights reserved. Such words as "without prejudice", "under protest" or the like are sufficient.

§ 1–208. Option to Accelerate at Will.

A term providing that one party or his successor in interest may accelerate payment or performance or require collateral or additional collateral "at will" or "when he deems himself insecure" or in words of similar import shall be construed to mean that he shall have power to do so only if he in good faith believes that the prospect of payment or performance is impaired. The burden of establishing lack of good faith is on the party against whom the power has been exercised.

§ 1–209. Subordinated Obligations.

An obligation may be issued as subordinated to payment of another obligation of the person obligated, or a creditor may subordinate his right to payment of an obligation by agreement with either the person obligated or another creditor of the person obligated. Such a subordination does not create a security interest as against either the common debtor or a subordinated creditor. This section shall be construed as declaring the law as it existed prior to the enactment of this section and not as modifying it. Added 1966.

Note: This new section is proposed as an optional provision to make it clear that a subordination agreement does not create a security interest unless so intended.

ARTICLE 2

Sales

PART 1   **SHORT TITLE, CONSTRUCTION AND SUBJECT MATTER**

§ 2–101. Short Title.

This Article shall be known and may be cited as Uniform Commercial Code—Sales.

§ 2–102. Scope; Certain Security and Other Transactions Excluded From This Article.

Unless the context otherwise requires, this Article applies to transactions in goods; it does not apply to any transaction which although in the form of an unconditional contract to sell or present sale is intended to operate only as a security transaction nor does this Article impair or repeal any statute regulating sales to consumers, farmers or other specified classes of buyers.

§ 2–103. Definitions and Index of Definitions.

(1) In this Article unless the context otherwise requires

   (a) "Buyer" means a person who buys or contracts to buy goods.

   (b) "Good faith" in the case of a merchant means honesty in fact and the observance of reasonable commercial standards of fair dealing in the trade.

   (c) "Receipt" of goods means taking physical possession of them.

   (d) "Seller" means a person who sells or contracts to sell goods.

(2) Other definitions applying to this Article or to specified Parts thereof, and the sections in which they appear are:

"Acceptance". Section 2–606.
"Banker's credit". Section 2–325.
"Between merchants". Section 2–104.
"Cancellation". Section 2–106(4).
"Commercial unit". Section 2–105.
"Confirmed credit". Section 2–325.
"Conforming to contract". Section 2–106.
"Contract for sale". Section 2–106.
"Cover". Section 2–712.
"Entrusting". Section 2–403.
"Financing agency". Section 2–104.
"Future goods". Section 2–105.
"Goods". Section 2–105.
"Identification". Section 2–501.
"Installment contract". Section 2–612.
"Letter of Credit". Section 2–325.
"Lot". Section 2–105.
"Merchant". Section 2–104.
"Overseas". Section 2–323.
"Person in position of seller". Section 2–707.
"Present sale". Section 2–106.
"Sale". Section 2–106.
"Sale on approval". Section 2–326.
"Sale or return". Section 2–326.
"Termination". Section 2–106.

(3) The following definitions in other Articles apply to this Article:

"Check". Section 3–104.
"Consignee". Section 7–102.
"Consignor". Section 7–102.
"Consumer goods". Section 9–109.
"Dishonor". Section 3–502.
"Draft". Section 3–104.

(4) In addition Article 1 contains general definitions and principles of construction and interpretation applicable throughout this Article.

§ 2–104. Definitions: "Merchant"; "Between Merchants"; "Financing Agency".

(1) "Merchant" means a person who deals in goods of the kind or otherwise by his occupation holds himself out as having knowledge or skill peculiar to the practices or goods involved in the transaction or to whom such knowledge or skill may be attributed by his employment of an agent or broker or other intermediary who by his occupation holds himself out as having such knowledge or skill.

(2) "Financing agency" means a bank, finance company or other person who in the ordinary course of business makes advances against goods or documents of title or who by arrangement with either the seller or the buyer intervenes in ordinary course to make or collect payment due or claimed under the contract for sale, as by purchasing or paying the seller's draft or making advances against it or by merely taking it for collection whether or not documents of title accompany the draft. "Financing agency" includes also a bank or

other person who similarly intervenes between persons who are in the position of seller and buyer in respect to the goods (Section 2–707).

(3) "Between merchants" means in any transaction with respect to which both parties are chargeable with the knowledge or skill of merchants.

§ 2–105. Definitions: Transferability; "Goods"; "Future" Goods; "Lot"; "Commercial Unit".

(1) "Goods" means all things (including specially manufactured goods) which are movable at the time of identification to the contract for sale other than the money in which the price is to be paid, investment securities (Article 8) and things in action. "Goods" also includes the unborn young of animals and growing crops and other identified things attached to realty as described in the section on goods to be severed from realty (Section 2–107).

(2) Goods must be both existing and identified before any interest in them can pass. Goods which are not both existing and identified are "future" goods. A purported present sale of future goods or of any interest therein operates as a contract to sell.

(3) There may be a sale of a part interest in existing identified goods.

(4) An undivided share in an identified bulk of fungible goods is sufficiently identified to be sold although the quantity of the bulk is not determined. Any agreed proportion of such a bulk or any quantity thereof agreed upon by number, weight or other measure may to the extent of the seller's interest in the bulk be sold to the buyer who then becomes an owner in common.

(5) "Lot" means a parcel or a single article which is the subject matter of a separate sale or delivery, whether or not it is sufficient to perform the contract.

(6) "Commercial unit" means such a unit of goods as by commercial usage is a single whole for purposes of sale and division of which materially impairs its character or value on the market or in use. A commercial unit may be a single article (as a machine) or a set of articles (as a suite of furniture or an assortment of sizes) or a quantity (as a bale, gross, or carload) or any other unit treated in use or in the relevant market as a single whole.

§ 2–106. Definitions: "Contract"; "Agreement"; "Contract for Sale"; "Sale"; "Present Sale"; "Conforming" to Contract; "Termination"; "Cancellation".

(1) In this Article unless the context otherwise requires "contract" and "agreement" are limited to those relating to the present or future sale of goods. "Contract for sale" includes both a present sale of goods and a contract to sell goods at a future time. A "sale" consists in the passing of title from the seller to the buyer for a price (Section 2–401). A "present sale" means a sale which is accomplished by the making of the contract.

(2) Goods or conduct including any part of a performance

are "conforming" or conform to the contract when they are in accordance with the obligations under the contract.

(3) "Termination" occurs when either party pursuant to a power created by agreement or law puts an end to the contract otherwise than for its breach. On "termination" all obligations which are still executory on both sides are discharged but any right based on prior breach or performance survives.

(4) "Cancellation" occurs when either party puts an end to the contract for breach by the other and its effect is the same as that of "termination" except that the cancelling party also retains any remedy for breach of the whole contract or any unperformed balance.

§ 2–107. Goods to Be Severed From Realty: Recording.

(1) A contract for the sale of minerals or the like (including oil and gas) or a structure or its materials to be removed from realty is a contract for the sale of goods within this Article if they are to be severed by the seller but until severance a purported present sale thereof which is not effective as a transfer of an interest in land is effective only as a contract to sell.

(2) A contract for the sale apart from the land of growing crops or other things attached to realty and capable of severance without material harm thereto but not described in subsection (1) or of timber to be cut is a contract for the sale of goods within this Article whether the subject matter is to be severed by the buyer or by the seller even though it forms part of the realty at the time of contracting, and the parties can by identification effect a present sale before severance.

(3) The provisions of this section are subject to any third party rights provided by the law relating to realty records, and the contract for sale may be executed and recorded as a document transferring an interest in land and shall then constitute notice to third parties of the buyer's rights under the contract for sale.

PART 2 FORM, FORMATION AND READJUSTMENT OF CONTRACT

§ 2–201. Formal Requirements; Statute of Frauds.

(1) Except as otherwise provided in this section a contract for the sale of goods for the price of $500 or more is not enforceable by way of action or defense unless there is some writing sufficient to indicate that a contract for sale has been made between the parties and signed by the party against whom enforcement is sought or by his authorized agent or broker. A writing is not insufficient because it omits or incorrectly states a term agreed upon but the contract is not enforceable under this paragraph beyond the quantity of goods shown in such writing.

(2) Between merchants if within a reasonable time a writing in confirmation of the contract and sufficient against the sender is received and the party receiving it has reason to know its contents, it satisfies the requirements of subsection (1) against such party unless written notice of objection to its contents is given within ten days after it is received.

(3) A contract which does not satisfy the requirements of subsection (1) but which is valid in other respects is enforceable

(a) if the goods are to be specially manufactured for the buyer and are not suitable for sale to others in the ordinary course of the seller's business and the seller, before notice of repudiation is received and under circumstances which reasonably indicate that the goods are for the buyer, has made either a substantial beginning of their manufacture or commitments for their procurement; or

(b) if the party against whom enforcement is sought admits in his pleading, testimony or otherwise in court that a contract for sale was made, but the contract is not enforceable under this provision beyond the quantity of goods admitted; or

(c) with respect to goods for which payment has been made and accepted or which have been received and accepted (Sec. 2–606).

§ 2–202. Final Written Expression: Parol or Extrinsic Evidence.

Terms with respect to which the confirmatory memoranda of the parties agree or which are otherwise set forth in a writing intended by the parties as a final expression of their agreement with respect to such terms as are included therein may not be contradicted by evidence of any prior agreement or of a contemporaneous oral agreement but may be explained or supplemented

(a) by course of dealing or usage of trade (Section 1–205) or by course of performance (Section 2–208); and

(b) by evidence of consistent additional terms unless the court finds the writing to have been intended also as a complete and exclusive statement of the terms of the agreement.

§ 2–203. Seals Inoperative.

The affixing of a seal to a writing evidencing a contract for sale or an offer to buy or sell goods does not constitute the writing a sealed instrument and the law with respect to sealed instruments does not apply to such a contract or offer.

§ 2–204. Formation in General.

(1) A contract for sale of goods may be made in any manner sufficient to show agreement, including conduct by both parties which recognizes the existence of such a contract.

(2) An agreement sufficient to constitute a contract for sale may be found even though the moment of its making is undetermined.

(3) Even though one or more terms are left open a contract for sale does not fail for indefiniteness if the parties have intended to make a contract and there is a reasonably certain basis for giving an appropriate remedy.

§ 2–205. Firm Offers.

An offer by a merchant to buy or sell goods in a signed writing which by its terms gives assurance that it will be held open is not revocable, for lack of consideration, during the time stated or if no time is stated for reasonable time, but in no event may such period of irrevocability exceed three months; but any such term of assurance on a form supplied by the offeree must be separately signed by the offeror.

§ 2–206. Offer and Acceptance in Formation of Contract.

(1) Unless other unambiguously indicated by the language or circumstances

(a) an offer to make a contract shall be construed as inviting acceptance in any manner and by any medium reasonable in the circumstances;

(b) an order or other offer to buy goods for prompt or current shipment shall be construed as inviting acceptance either by a prompt promise to ship or by the prompt or current shipment of conforming or nonconforming goods, but such a shipment of nonconforming goods does not constitute an acceptance if the seller seasonably notifies the buyer that the shipment is offered only as an accommodation to the buyer.

(2) Where the beginning of a requested performance is a reasonable mode of acceptance an offeror who is not notified of acceptance within a reasonable time may treat the offer as having lapsed before acceptance.

§ 2–207. Additional Terms in Acceptance or Confirmation.

(1) A definite and seasonable expression of acceptance or a written confirmation which is sent within a reasonable time operates as an acceptance even though it states terms additional to or different from those offered or agreed upon, unless acceptance is expressly made conditional on assent to the additional or different terms.

(2) The additional terms are to be construed as proposals for addition to the contract. Between merchants such terms become part of the contract unless:

(a) the offer expressly limits acceptance to the terms of the offer;

(b) they materially alter it; or

(c) notification of objection to them has already been given or is given within a reasonable time after notice of them is received.

(3) Conduct by both parties which recognizes the existence of a contract is sufficient to establish a contract for sale although the writings of the parties do not otherwise establish a contract. In such case the terms of the particular contract consist of those terms on which the writings of the parties agree, together with any supplementary terms incorporated under any other provisions of this Act.

§ 2–208. Course of Performance or Practical Construction.

(1) Where the contract for sale involves repeated occasions for performance by either party with knowledge of the nature of the performance and opportunity for objection to it by the other, any course of performance accepted or acquiesced in without objection shall be relevant to determine the meaning of the agreement.

(2) The express terms of the agreement and any such course of performance, as well as any course of dealing and usage of trade, shall be construed whenever reasonable as consistent with each other; but when such construction is unreasonable, express terms shall control course of performance and course of performance shall control both course of deal-ing and usage of trade (Section 1–205).

(3) Subject to the provisions of the next section on modification and waiver, such course of performance shall be relevant to show a waiver or modification of any term inconsistent with such course of performance.

§ 2–209. Modification, Rescission and Waiver.

(1) An agreement modifying a contract within this Article needs no consideration to be binding.

(2) A signed agreement which excludes modification or rescission except by a signed writing cannot be otherwise modified or rescinded, but except as between merchants such a requirement on a form supplied by the merchant must be separately signed by the other party.

(3) The requirements of the statute of frauds section of this Article (Section 2–201) must be satisfied if the contract as modified is within its provisions.

(4) Although an attempt at modification or rescission does not satisfy the requirements of subsection (2) or (3) it can operate as a waiver.

(5) A party who has made a waiver affecting an executory portion of the contract may retract the waiver by reasonable notification received by the other party that strict performance will be required of any term waived, unless the retraction would be unjust in view of a material change of position in reliance on the waiver.

§ 2–210. Delegation of Performance; Assignment of Rights.

(1) A party may perform his duty through a delegate unless otherwise agreed or unless the other party has a substantial interest in having his original promisor perform or control the acts required by the contract. No delegation of performance relieves the party delegating of any duty to perform or any liability for breach.

(2) Unless otherwise agreed all rights of either seller or buyer can be assigned except where the assignment would materially change the duty of the other party, or increase materially the burden or risk imposed on him by his contract, or impair materially his chance of obtaining return performance. A right to damages for breach of the whole contract or a right arising out of the assignor's due performance of his entire obligation can be assigned despite agreement otherwise.

(3) Unless the circumstances indicate the contrary a prohibition of assignment of "the contract" is to be construed as barring only the delegation to the assignee of the assignor's performance.

(4) An assignment of "the contract" or of "all my rights under the contract" or an assignment in similar general terms is an assignment of rights and unless the language or the circumstances (as in an assignment for security) indicate the contrary, it is a delegation of performance of the duties of the assignor and its acceptance by the assignee constitutes a promise by him to perform those duties. This promise is enforceable by either the assignor or the other party to the original contract.

(5) The other party may treat any assignment which delegates performance as creating reasonable grounds for insecurity and may without prejudice to his rights against the assignor demand assurances from the assignee (Section 2–609).

PART 3 GENERAL OBLIGATION AND CONSTRUCTION OF CONTRACT

§ 2–301. General Obligations of Parties.

The obligation of the seller is to transfer and deliver and that of the buyer is to accept and pay in accordance with the contract.

§ 2–302. Unconscionable Contract or Clause.

(1) If the court as a matter of law finds the contract or any clause of the contract to have been unconscionable at the time it was made the court may refuse to enforce the contract, or it may enforce the remainder of the contract without the unconscionable clause, or it may so limit the application of any unconscionable clause as to avoid any unconscionable result.

(2) When it is claimed or appears to the court that the contract or any clause thereof may be unconscionable the parties shall be afforded a reasonable opportunity to present evidence as to its commercial setting, purpose and effect to aid the court in making the determination.

§ 2–303. Allocation or Division of Risks.

Where this Article allocates a risk or a burden as between the parties "unless otherwise agreed", the agreement may not only shift the allocation, but may also divide the risk or burden.

§ 2–304. Price Payable in Money, Goods, Realty, or Otherwise.

(1) The price can be made payable in money or otherwise. If it is payable in whole or in part in goods each party is a seller of the goods which he is to transfer.

(2) Even though all or part of the price is payable in an interest in realty the transfer of the goods and the seller's obligations with reference to them are subject to this Article, but not the transfer of the interest in realty or the transferor's obligations in connection therewith.

§ 2–305. Open Price Term.

(1) The parties if they so intend can conclude a contract for sale even though the price is not settled. In such a case the price is a reasonable price at the time for delivery if
   (a) nothing is said as to price; or
   (b) the price is left to be agreed by the parties and they fail to agree; or
   (c) the price is to be fixed in terms of some agreed market or other standard as set or recorded by a third person or agency and it is not so set or recorded.

(2) A price to be fixed by the seller or by the buyer means a price for him to fix in good faith.

(3) When a price left to be fixed otherwise than by agreement of the parties fails to be fixed through fault of one party the other may at his option treat the contract as cancelled or himself fix a reasonable price.

(4) Where, however, the parties intend not to be bound unless the price be fixed or agreed and it is not fixed or agreed there is no contract. In such a case the buyer must return any goods already received or if unable so to do must pay their reasonable value at the time of delivery and the seller must return any portion of the price paid on account.

§ 2–306. Output, Requirements and Exclusive Dealings.

(1) A term which measures the quantity by the output of the seller or the requirements of the buyer means such actual output or requirements as may occur in good faith, except that no quantity unreasonably disproportionate to any stated estimate or in the absence of a stated estimate to any normal or otherwise comparable prior output or requirements may be tendered or demanded.

(2) A lawful agreement by either the seller or the buyer for exclusive dealing in the kind of goods concerned imposes unless otherwise agreed an obligation by the seller to use best efforts to supply the goods and by the buyer to use best efforts to promote their sale.

§ 2–307. Delivery in Single Lot or Several Lots.

Unless otherwise agreed all goods called for by a contract for sale must be tendered in a single delivery and payment is due only on such tender but where the circumstances give either party the right to make or demand delivery in lots the price if it can be apportioned may be demanded for each lot.

§ 2–308. Absence of Specified Place for Delivery.

Unless otherwise agreed
   (a) the place for delivery of goods is the seller's place of business or if he has none his residence; but
   (b) in a contract for sale of identified goods which to the knowledge of the parties at the time of contracting are in some other place, that place is the place for their delivery; and
   (c) documents of title may be delivered through customary banking channels.

§ 2–309. Absence of Specific Time Provisions; Notice of Termination.

(1) The time for shipment or delivery or any other action under a contract if not provided in this Article or agreed upon shall be a reasonable time.

(2) Where the contract provides for successive performances but is indefinite in duration it is valid for a reasonable time but unless otherwise agreed may be terminated at any time by either party.

(3) Termination of a contract by one party except on the happening of an agreed event requires that reasonable notification be received by the other party and an agreement dispensing with notification is invalid if its operation would be unconscionable.

§ 2–310.   Open Time for Payment or Running of Credit; Authority to Ship Under Reservation.

Unless otherwise agreed

(a) payment is due at the time and place at which the buyer is to receive the goods even though the place of shipment is the place of delivery; and

(b) if the seller is authorized to send the goods he may ship them under reservation, and may tender the documents of title, but the buyer may inspect the goods after their arrival before payment is due unless such inspection is inconsistent with the terms of the contract (Section 2–513); and

(c) if delivery is authorized and made by way of documents of title otherwise than by subsection (b) then payment is due at the time and place at which the buyer is to receive the documents regardless of where the goods are to be received; and

(d) where the seller is required or authorized to ship the goods on credit the credit period runs from the time of shipment but post-dating the invoice or delaying its dispatch will correspondingly delay the starting of the credit period.

§ 2–311.   Options and Cooperation Respecting Performance.

(1) An agreement for sale which is otherwise sufficiently definite (subsection (3) of Section 2–204) to be a contract is not made invalid by the fact that it leaves particulars of performance to be specified by one of the parties. Any such specification must be made in good faith and within limits set by commercial reasonableness.

(2) Unless otherwise agreed specifications relating to assortment of the goods are at the buyer's option and except as otherwise provided in subsections (1)(c) and (3) of Section 2–319 specifications or arrangements relating to shipment are at the seller's option.

(3) Where such specification would materially affect the other party's performance but is not seasonably made or where one party's cooperation is necessary to the agreed performance of the other but is not seasonably forthcoming, the other party in addition to all other remedies

(a) is excused for any resulting delay in his own performance; and

(b) may also either proceed to perform in any reasonable manner or after the time for a material part of his own performance treat the failure to specify or to cooperate as a breach by failure to deliver or accept the goods.

§ 2–312.   Warranty of Title and Against Infringement; Buyer's Obligation Against Infringement.

(1) Subject to subsection (2) there is in a contract for sale a warranty by the seller that

(a) the title conveyed shall be good, and its transfer rightful; and

(b) the goods shall be delivered free from any security interest or other lien or encumbrance of which the buyer at the time of contracting has no knowledge.

(2) A warranty under subsection (1) will be excluded or modified only by specific language or by circumstances which give the buyer reason to know that the person selling does not claim title in himself or that he is purporting to sell only such right or title as he or a third person may have.

(3) Unless otherwise agreed a seller who is a merchant regularly dealing in goods of the kind warrants that the goods shall be delivered free of the rightful claim of any third person by way of infringement or the like but a buyer who furnishes specifications to the seller must hold the seller harmless against any such claim which arises out of compliance with the specifications.

§ 2–313.   Express Warranties by Affirmation, Promise, Description, Sample.

(1) Express warranties by the seller are created as follows:

(a) Any affirmation of fact or promise made by the seller to the buyer which relates to the goods and becomes part of the basis of the bargain creates an express warranty that the goods shall conform to the affirmation or promise.

(b) Any description of the goods which is made part of the basis of the bargain creates an express warranty that the goods shall conform to the description.

(c) Any sample or model which is made part of the basis of the bargain creates an express warranty that the whole of the goods shall conform to the sample or model.

(2) It is not necessary to the creation of an express warranty that the seller use formal words such as "warrant" or "guarantee" or that he have a specific intention to make a warranty, but an affirmation merely of the value of the goods or a statement purporting to be merely the seller's opinion or commendation of the goods does not create a warranty.

§ 2–314.   Implied Warranty: Merchantability; Usage of Trade.

(1) Unless excluded or modified (Section 2–316), a warranty that the goods shall be merchantable is implied in a contract for their sale if the seller is a merchant with respect to goods of that kind. Under this section the serving for value of food or drink to be consumed either on the premises or elsewhere is a sale.

(2) Goods to be merchantable must be at least such as

(a) pass without objection in the trade under the contract description; and

(b) in the case of fungible goods, are of fair average quality within the description; and

(c) are fit for the ordinary purpose for which such goods are used; and

(d) run, within the variations permitted by the agreement, of even kind, quality and quantity within each unit and among all units involved; and

(e) are adequately contained, packaged, and labeled as the agreement may require; and

(f) conform to the promises or affirmations of fact made on the container or label if any.

(3) Unless excluded or modified (Section 2–316) other implied warranties may arise from course of dealing or usage of trade.

§ 2–315. Implied Warranty: Fitness for Particular Purpose.

Where the seller at the time of contracting has reason to know any particular purpose for which the goods are required and that the buyer is relying on the seller's skill or judgment to select or furnish suitable goods, there is unless excluded or modified under the next section an implied warranty that the goods shall be fit for such purpose.

§ 2–316. Exclusion or Modification of Warranties.

(1) Words or conduct relevant to the creation of an express warranty and words or conduct tending to negate or limit warranty shall be construed wherever reasonable as consistent with each other, but subject to the provisions of this Article on parol or extrinsic evidence (Section 2–202) negation or limitation is inoperative to the extent that such construction is unreasonable.

(2) Subject to subsection (3), to exclude or modify the implied warranty of merchantability or any part of it the language must mention merchantability and in case of a writing must be conspicuous, and to exclude or modify any implied warranty of fitness the exclusion must be by a writing and conspicuous. Language to exclude all implied warranties of fitness is sufficient if it states, for example, that "There are no warranties which extend beyond the description on the face hereof."

(3) Notwithstanding subsection (2)

   (a) unless the circumstances indicate otherwise, all implied warranties are excluded by expressions like "as is", "with all faults" or other language which in common understanding calls the buyer's attention to the exclusion of warranties and makes plain that there is no implied warranty; and

   (b) when the buyer before entering into the contract has examined the goods or the sample or model as fully as he desired or has refused to examine the goods there is no implied warranty with regard to defects which an examination ought in the circumstances to have revealed to him; and

   (c) an implied warranty can also be excluded or modified by course of dealing or course of performance or usage of trade.

(4) Remedies for breach of warranty can be limited in accordance with the provisions of this Article on liquidation or limitation of damages and on contractual modification of remedy (Sections 2–718 and 2–719).

§ 2–317. Cumulation and Conflict of Warranties Express or Implied.

Warranties whether express or implied shall be construed as consistent with each other and as cumulative, but if such construction is unreasonable the intention of the parties shall determine which warranty is dominant. In ascertaining that intention the following rules apply:

   (a) Exact or technical specifications displace an inconsistent sample or model or general language of description.

   (b) A sample from an existing bulk displaces inconsistent general language of description.

   (c) Express warranties displace inconsistent implied warranties other than an implied warranty of fitness for a particular purpose.

§ 2–318. Third Party Beneficiaries of Warranties Express or Implied.

Note: If this Act is introduced in the Congress of the United States this section should be omitted. (States to select one alternative.)

Alternative A A seller's warranty whether express or implied extends to any natural person who is in the family or household of his buyer or who is a guest in his home if it is reasonable to expect that such person may use, consume or be affected by the goods and who is injured in person by breach of the warranty. The seller may not exclude or limit the operation of this section.

Alternative B A seller's warranty whether express or implied extends to any natural person who may reasonably be expected to use, consume or be affected by the goods and who is injured in person by breach of the warranty. A seller may not exclude or limit the operation of this section.

Alternative C A seller's warranty whether express or implied extends to any person who may reasonably be expected to use, consume or be affected by the goods and who is injured by breach of the warranty. A seller may not exclude or limit the operation of this section with respect to injury to the person of an individual to whom the warranty extends. As amended 1966.

§ 2–319. F.O.B. and F.A.S. Terms.

(1) Unless otherwise agreed the term F.O.B. (which means "free on board") at a named place, even though used only in connection with the stated price, is a delivery term under which

   (a) when the term is F.O.B. the place of shipment, the seller must at that place ship the goods in the manner provided in this Article (Section 2–504) and bear the expense and risk of putting them into the possession of the carrier; or

   (b) when the term is F.O.B. the place of destination, the seller must at his own expense and risk transport the goods to that place and there tender delivery of them in the manner provided in this Article (Section 2–503);

   (c) when under either (a) or (b) the term is also F.O.B. vessel, car or other vehicle, the seller must in addition at his own expense and risk load the goods on board. If the term is F.O.B. vessel the buyer must name the vessel and in an appropriate case the seller must comply with the provisions of this Article on the form of bill of lading (Section 2–323).

(2) Unless otherwise agreed the term F.A.S. vessel (which means "free alongside") at a named port, even though used only in connection with the stated price, is a delivery term under which the seller must

   (a) at his own expense and risk deliver the goods alongside the vessel in the manner usual in that port or on a dock designated and provided by the buyer; and

   (b) obtain and tender a receipt for the goods in exchange for which the carrier is under a duty to issue a bill of lading.

(3) Unless otherwise agreed in any case falling within subsection (1)(a) or (c) or subsection (2) the buyer must season-

ably give any needed instructions for making delivery, including when the term is F.A.S. or F.O.B. the loading berth of the vessel and in an appropriate case its name and sailing date. The seller may treat the failure of needed instructions as a failure of cooperation under this Article (Section 2–311). He may also at his option move the goods in any reasonable manner preparatory to delivery or shipment.

(4) Under the term F.O.B. vessel or F.A.S. unless otherwise agreed the buyer must make payment against tender of the required documents and the seller may not tender nor the buyer demand delivery of the goods in substitution for the documents.

§ 2–320. C.I.F. and C. & F. Terms.

(1) The term C.I.F. means that the price includes in a lump sum the cost of the goods and the insurance and freight to the named destination. The term C. & F. or C.F. means that the price so includes cost and freight to the named destination.

(2) Unless otherwise agreed and even though used only in connection with the stated price and destination, the term C.I.F. destination or its equivalent requires the seller at his own expense and risk to

(a) put the goods into the possession of a carrier at the port for shipment and obtain a negotiable bill or bills of lading covering the entire transportation to the named destination; and

(b) load the goods and obtain a receipt from the carrier (which may be contained in the bill of lading) showing that the freight has been paid or provided for; and

(c) obtain a policy or certificate of insurance, including any war risk insurance, of a kind and on terms then current at the port of shipment in the usual amount, in the currency of the contract, shown to cover the same goods covered by the bill of lading and providing for payment of loss to the order of the buyer or for the account of whom it may concern; but the seller may add to the price the amount of premium for any such war risk insurance; and

(d) prepare an invoice of the goods and procure any other documents required to effect shipment or to comply with the contract; and

(e) forward and tender with commercial promptness all the documents in due form and with any indorsement necessary to perfect the buyer's rights.

(3) Unless otherwise agreed the term C. & F. or its equivalent has the same effect and imposes upon the seller the same obligations and risks as a C.I.F. term except the obligation as to insurance.

(4) Under the term C.I.F. or C. & F. unless otherwise agreed the buyer must make payment against tender of the required documents and the seller may not tender nor the buyer demand delivery of the goods in substitution for the documents.

§ 2–321. C.I.F. or C. & F.: "Net Landed Weights"; "Payment on Arrival"; Warranty of Condition on Arrival.

Under a contract containing a term C.I.F. or C. & F.

(1) Where the price is based on or is to be adjusted according to "net landed weights", "delivered weights", "out turn" quantity or quality or the like, unless otherwise

agreed the seller must reasonably estimate the price. The payment due on tender of the documents called for by the contract is the amount so estimated, but after final adjustment of the price a settlement must be made with commercial promptness.

(2) An agreement described in subsection (1) or any warranty of quality or condition of the goods on arrival places upon the seller the risk of ordinary deterioration, shrinkage and the like in transportation but has no effect on the place or time of identification to the contract for sale or delivery or on the passing of the risk of loss.

(3) Unless otherwise agreed where the contract provides for payment on or after arrival of the goods the seller must before payment allow such preliminary inspection as is feasible; but if the goods are lost delivery of the documents and payment are due when the goods should have arrived.

§ 2–322. Delivery "Ex-Ship".

(1) Unless otherwise agreed a term for delivery of goods "ex-ship" (which means from the carrying vessel) or in equivalent language is not restricted to a particular ship and requires delivery from a ship which has reached a place at the named port of destination where goods of the kind are usually discharged.

(2) Under such a term unless otherwise agreed

(a) the seller must discharge all liens arising out of the carriage and furnish the buyer with a direction which puts the carrier under a duty to deliver the goods; and

(b) the risk of loss does not pass to the buyer until the goods leave the ship's tackle or are otherwise properly unloaded.

§ 2–323. Form of Bill of Lading Required in Overseas Shipment; "Overseas".

(1) Where the contract contemplates overseas shipment and contains a term C.I.F. or C. & F. or F.O.B. vessel, the seller unless otherwise agreed must obtain a negotiable bill of lading stating that the goods have been loaded on board or, in the case of a term C.I.F. or C. & F., received for shipment.

(2) Where in a case within subsection (1) a bill of lading has been issued in a set of parts, unless otherwise agreed if the documents are not to be sent from abroad the buyer may demand tender of the full set; otherwise only one part of the bill of lading need be tendered. Even if the agreement expressly requires a full set

(a) due tender of a single part is acceptable within the provisions of this Article on cure of improper delivery (subsection (1) of Section 2–508); and

(b) even though the full set is demanded, if the documents are sent from abroad the person tendering an incomplete set may nevertheless require payment upon furnishing an indemnity which the buyer in good faith deems adequate.

(3) A shipment by water or by air or a contract contemplating such shipment is "overseas" insofar as by usage of trade or agreement it is subject to the commercial, financing or shipping practices characteristic of international deep water commerce.

§ 2–324. "No Arrival, No Sale" Term.

Under a term "no arrival, no sale" or terms of like meaning, unless otherwise agreed,

(a) the seller must properly ship conforming goods and if they arrive by any means he must tender them on arrival but he assumes no obligation that the goods will arrive unless he has caused the non-arrival; and

(b) where without fault of the seller the goods are in part lost or have so deteriorated as no longer to conform to the contract or arrive after the contract time, the buyer may proceed as if there had been casualty to identified goods (Section 2–613).

§ 2–325. "Letter of Credit" Term; "Confirmed Credit".

(1) Failure of the buyer seasonably to furnish an agreed letter of credit is a breach of the contract for sale.

(2) The delivery to seller of a proper letter of credit suspends the buyer's obligation to pay. If the letter of credit is dishonored, the seller may on seasonable notification to the buyer require payment directly from him.

(3) Unless otherwise agreed the term "letter of credit" or "banker's credit" in a contract for sale means an irrevocable credit issued by a financing agency of good repute and, where the shipment is overseas, of good international repute. The term "confirmed credit" means that the credit must also carry the direct obligation of such an agency which does business in the seller's financial market.

§ 2–326. Sale on Approval and Sale or Return; Consignment Sales and Rights of Creditors.

(1) Unless otherwise agreed, if delivered goods may be returned by the buyer even though they conform to the contract, the transaction is

(a) a "sale on approval" if the goods are delivered primarily for use, and

(b) a "sale or return" if the goods are delivered primarily for resale.

(2) Except as provided in subsection (3), goods held on approval are not subject to the claims of the buyer's creditors until acceptance; goods held on sale or return are subject to such claims while in the buyer's possession.

(3) Where goods are delivered to a person for sale and such person maintains a place of business at which he deals in goods of the kind involved, under a name other than the name of the person making delivery, then with respect to claims of creditors of the person conducting the business the goods are deemed to be on sale or return. The provisions of this subsection are applicable even though an agreement purports to reserve title to the person making delivery until payment or resale or uses such words as "on consignment" or "on memorandum". However, this subsection is not applicable if the person making delivery

(a) complies with an applicable law providing for a consignor's interest or the like to be evidenced by a sign, or

(b) establishes that the person conducting the business is generally known by his creditors to be substantially engaged in selling the goods of others, or

(c) complies with the filing provisions of the Article on Secured Transactions (Article 9).

(4) Any "or return" term of a contract for sale is to be treated as a separate contract for sale within the statute of frauds section of this Article (Section 2–201) and as contradicting the sale aspect of the contract within the provisions of this Article on parol or extrinsic evidence (Section 2–202).

§ 2–327. Special Incidents of Sale on Approval and Sale or Return.

(1) Under a sale on approval unless otherwise agreed

(a) although the goods are identified to the contract the risk of loss and the title do not pass to the buyer until acceptance; and

(b) use of the goods consistent with the purpose of trial is not acceptance but failure seasonably to notify the seller of election to return the goods is acceptance, and if the goods conform to the contract acceptance of any part is acceptance of the whole; and

(c) after due notification of election to return, the return is at the seller's risk and expense but a merchant buyer must follow any reasonable instructions.

(2) Under a sale or return unless otherwise agreed

(a) the option to return extends to the whole or any commercial unit of the goods while in substantially their original condition, but must be exercised seasonably; and

(b) the return is at the buyer's risk and expense.

§ 2–328. Sale by Auction.

(1) In a sale by auction if goods are put up in lots each lot is the subject of a separate sale.

(2) A sale by auction is complete when the auctioneer so announces by the fall of the hammer or in other customary manner. Where a bid is made while the hammer is falling in acceptance of a prior bid the auctioneer may in his discretion reopen the bidding or declare the goods sold under the bid on which the hammer was falling.

(3) Such a sale is with reserve unless the goods are in explicit terms put up without reserve. In an auction with reserve the auctioneer may withdraw the goods at any time until he announces completion of the sale. In an auction without reserve, after the auctioneer calls for bids on an article or lot, that article or lot cannot be withdrawn unless no bid is made within a reasonable time. In either case a bidder may retract his bid until the auctioneer's announcement of completion of the sale, but a bidder's retraction does not revive any previous bid.

(4) If the auctioneer knowingly receives a bid on the seller's behalf or the seller makes or procures such a bid, and notice has not been given that liberty for such bidding is reserved, the buyer may at his option avoid the sale or take the goods at the price of the last good faith bid prior to the completion of the sale. This subsection shall not apply to any bid at a forced sale.

PART 4 TITLE CREDITORS AND GOOD FAITH PURCHASERS

§ 2–401. Passing of Title; Reservation for Security; Limited Application of This Section.

Each provision of this Article with regard to the rights, obligations and remedies of the seller, the buyer, purchasers or other third parties applies irrespective of title to the goods except where the provision refers to such title. Insofar as situations are not covered by the other provisions of this Article and matters concerning title became material the following rules apply:

(1) Title to goods cannot pass under a contract for sale prior to their identification to the contract (Section 2–501), and unless otherwise explicitly agreed the buyer acquires by their identification a special property as limited by this Act. Any retention or reservation by the seller of the title (property) in goods shipped or delivered to the buyer is limited in effect to a reservation of a security interest. Subject to these provisions and to the provisions of the Article on Secured Transactions (Article 9), title to goods passes from the seller to the buyer in any manner and on any conditions explicitly agreed on by the parties.

(2) Unless otherwise explicitly agreed title passes to the buyer at the time and place at which the seller completes his performance with reference to the physical delivery of the goods, despite any reservation of a security interest and even though a document of title is to be delivered at a different time or place; and in particular and despite any reservation of a security interest by the bill of lading

(a) if the contract requires or authorizes the seller to send the goods to the buyer but does not require him to deliver them at destination, title passes to the buyer at the time and place of shipment; but

(b) if the contract requires delivery at destination, title passes on tender there.

(3) Unless otherwise explicitly agreed where delivery is to be made without moving the goods,

(a) if the seller is to deliver a document of title, title passes at the time when and the place where he delivers such documents; or

(b) if the goods are at the time of contracting already identified and no documents are to be delivered, title passes at the time and place of contracting.

(4) A rejection or other refusal by the buyer to receive or retain the goods, whether or not justified, or a justified revocation of acceptance revests title to the goods in the seller. Such revesting occurs by operation of law and is not a "sale".

§ 2–402. Rights of Seller's Creditors Against Sold Goods.

(1) Except as provided in subsections (2) and (3), rights of unsecured creditors of the seller with respect to goods which have been identified to a contract for sale are subject to the buyer's rights to recover the goods under this Article (Sections 2–502 and 2–716).

(2) A creditor of the seller may treat a sale or an identification of goods to a contract for sale as void if as against him a retention of possession by the seller is fraudulent under any rule of law of the state where the goods are situated, except that retention of possession in good faith and current course of trade by a merchant-seller for a commercially reasonable time after a sale or identification is not fraudulent.

(3) Nothing in this Article shall be deemed to impair the rights of creditors of the seller

(a) under the provisions of the Article on Secured Transactions (Article 9); or

(b) where identification to the contract or delivery is made not in current course of trade but in satisfaction of or as security for a pre-existing claim for money, security or the like and is made under circumstances which under any rule of law of the state where the goods are situated would apart from this Article constitute the transaction a fraudulent transfer or voidable preference.

§ 2–403. Power to Transfer; Good Faith Purchase of Goods; "Entrusting".

(1) A purchaser of goods acquires all title which his transferor had or had power to transfer except that a purchaser of a limited interest acquires rights only to the extent of the interest purchased. A person with voidable title has power to transfer a good title to a good faith purchaser for value. When goods have been delivered under a transaction of purchase the purchaser has such power even though

(a) the transferor was deceived as to the identity of the purchaser, or

(b) the delivery was in exchange for a check which is later dishonored, or

(c) it was agreed that the transaction was to be a "cash sale", or

(d) the delivery was procured through fraud punishable as larcenous under the criminal law.

(2) Any entrusting of possession of goods to a merchant who deals in goods of that kind gives him power to transfer all rights of the entruster to a buyer in ordinary course of business.

(3) "Entrusting" includes any delivery and any acquiescence in retention of possession regardless of any condition expressed between the parties to the delivery or acquiescence and regardless of whether the procurement of the entrusting or the possessor's disposition of the goods have been such as to be larcenous under the criminal law.

(4) The rights of other purchasers of goods and of lien creditors are governed by the Articles on Secured Transactions (Article 9), Bulk Transfers (Article 6) and Documents of Title (Article 7).

PART 5 PERFORMANCE

§ 2–501. Insurable Interest in Goods; Manner of Identification of Goods.

(1) The buyer obtains a special property and an insurable interest in goods by identification of existing goods as goods to which the contract refers even though the goods so identified are nonconforming and he has an option to return or

reject them. Such identification can be made at any time and in any manner explicitly agreed to by the parties. In the absence of explicit agreement identification occurs

(a) when the contract is made if it is for the sale of goods already existing and identified;

(b) if the contract is for the sale of future goods other than those described in paragraph (c), when goods are shipped, marked or otherwise designated by the seller as goods to which the contract refers;

(c) when the crops are planted or otherwise become growing crops or the young are conceived if the contract is for the sale of unborn young to be born within twelve months after contracting or for the sale of crops to be harvested within twelve months or the next normal harvest season after contracting whichever is longer.

(2) The seller retains an insurable interest in goods so long as title to or any security interest in the goods remains in him and where the identification is by the seller alone he may until default or insolvency or notification to the buyer that the identification is final substitute other goods for those identified.

(3) Nothing in this section impairs any insurable interest recognized under any other statute or rule of law.

§ 2–502. Buyer's Right to Goods on Seller's Insolvency.

(1) Subject to subsection (2) and even though the goods have not been shipped a buyer who has paid a part or all of the price of goods in which he has a special property under the provisions of the immediately preceding section may on making and keeping good a tender of any unpaid portion of their price recover them from the seller if the seller becomes insolvent within ten days after receipt of the first installment on their price.

(2) If the identification creating his special property has been made by the buyer he acquires the right to recover the goods only if they conform to the contract for sale.

§ 2–503. Manner of Seller's Tender of Delivery.

(1) Tender of delivery requires that the seller put and hold conforming goods at the buyer's disposition and give the buyer any notification reasonably necessary to enable him to take delivery. The manner, time and place for tender are determined by the agreement and this Article, and in particular

(a) tender must be at a reasonable hour, and if it is of goods they must be kept available for the period reasonably necessary to enable the buyer to take possession; but

(b) unless otherwise agreed the buyer must furnish facilities reasonably suited to the receipt of the goods.

(2) Where the case is within the next section respecting shipment tender requires that the seller comply with its provisions.

(3) Where the seller is required to deliver at a particular destination tender requires that he comply with subsection (1) and also in any appropriate case tender documents as described in subsections (4) and (5) of this section.

(4) Where goods are in the possession of a bailee and are to be delivered without being moved

(a) tender requires that the seller either tender a negotiable document of title covering such goods or procure acknowledgment by the bailee of the buyer's right to possession of the goods; but

(b) tender to the buyer of a non-negotiable document of title or of a written direction to the bailee to deliver is sufficient tender unless the buyer seasonably objects, and receipt by the bailee of notification of the buyer's rights fixes those rights as against the bailee and all third persons; but risk of loss of the goods and of any failure by the bailee to honor the non-negotiable document of title or to obey the direction remains on the seller until the buyer has had a reasonable time to present the document or direction, and a refusal by the bailee to honor the document or to obey the direction defeats the tender.

(5) Where the contract requires the seller to deliver documents

(a) he must tender all such documents in correct form, except as provided in this Article with respect to bills of lading in a set (subsection (2) of Section 2–323); and

(b) tender through customary banking channels is sufficient and dishonor of a draft accompanying the documents constitutes non-acceptance or rejection.

§ 2–504. Shipment by Seller.

Where the seller is required or authorized to send the goods to the buyer and the contract does not require him to deliver them at a particular destination, then unless otherwise agreed he must

(a) put the goods in the possession of such a carrier and make such a contract for their transportation as may be reasonable having regard to the nature of the goods and other circumstances of the case; and

(b) obtain and promptly deliver or tender in due form any document necessary to enable the buyer to obtain possession of the goods or otherwise required by the agreement or by usage of trade; and

(c) promptly notify the buyer of the shipment.

Failure to notify the buyer under paragraph (c) or to make a proper contract under paragraph (a) is a ground for rejection only if material delay or loss ensues.

§ 2–505. Seller's Shipment Under Reservation.

(1) Where the seller has identified goods to the contract by or before shipment:

(a) his procurement of a negotiable bill of lading to his own order or otherwise reserves in him a security interest in the goods. His procurement of the bill to the order of a financing agency or of the buyer indicates in addition only the seller's expectation of transferring that interest to the person named.

(b) a non-negotiable bill of lading to himself or his nominee reserves possession of the goods as security but except in a case of conditional delivery (subsection (2) of Section 2–507) a non-negotiable bill of lading naming the buyer as consignee reserves no security interest even though the seller retains possession of the bill of lading.

(2) When shipment by the seller with reservation of a security interest is in violation of the contract for sale it consti-

tutes an improper contract for transportation within the preceding section but impairs neither the rights given to the buyer by shipment and identification of the goods to the contract nor the seller's powers as a holder of a negotiable document.

§ 2–506.   Rights of Financing Agency.

(1) A financing agency by paying or purchasing for value a draft which relates to a shipment of goods acquires to the extent of the payment or purchase and in addition to its own rights under the draft and any document of title securing it any rights of the shipper in the goods including the right to stop delivery and the shipper's right to have the draft honored by the buyer.

(2) The right to reimbursement of a financing agency which has in good faith honored or purchased the draft under commitment to or authority from the buyer is not impaired by subsequent discovery of defects with reference to any relevant document which was apparently regular on its face.

§ 2–507.   Effect of Seller's Tender; Delivery on Condition.

(1) Tender of delivery is a condition to the buyer's duty to accept the goods and, unless otherwise agreed, to his duty to pay for them. Tender entitles the seller to acceptance of the goods and to payment according to the contract.

(2) Where payment is due and demanded on the delivery to the buyer of goods or documents of title, his right as against the seller to retain or dispose of them is conditional upon his making the payment due.

§ 2–508.   Cure by Seller of Improper Tender or Delivery; Replacement.

(1) Where any tender or delivery by the seller is rejected because non-conforming and the time for performance has not yet expired, the seller may seasonably notify the buyer of his intention to cure and may then within the contract time make a conforming delivery.

(2) Where the buyer rejects a non-conforming tender which the seller had reasonable grounds to believe would be acceptable with or without money allowance the seller may if he seasonably notifies the buyer have a further reasonable time to substitute a conforming tender.

§ 2–509.   Risk of Loss in the Absence of Breach.

(1) Where the contract requires or authorizes the seller to ship the goods by carrier

(a) if it does not require him to deliver them at a particular destination, the risk of loss passes to the buyer when the goods are duly delivered to the carrier even though the shipment is under reservation (Section 2–505); but

(b) if it does require him to deliver them at a particular destination and the goods are there duly tendered while in the possession of the carrier, the risk of loss passes to the buyer when the goods are there duly so tendered as to enable the buyer to take delivery.

(2) Where the goods are held by a bailee to be delivered without being moved, the risk of loss passes to the buyer

(a) on his receipt of a negotiable document of title covering the goods; or

(b) on acknowledgment by the bailee of the buyer's right to possession of the goods; or

(c) after his receipt of a non-negotiable document of title or other written direction to deliver, as provided in subsection (4)(b) of Section 2–503.

(3) In any case not within subsection (1) or (2), the risk of loss passes to the buyer on his receipt of the goods if the seller is a merchant; otherwise, the risk passes to the buyer on tender of delivery.

(4) The provisions of this section are subject to contrary agreement of the parties and to the provisions of this Article on sale on approval (Section 2–327) and on effect of breach on risk of loss (Section 2–510).

§ 2–510.   Effect of Breach on Risk of Loss.

(1) Where a tender or delivery of goods so fails to conform to the contract as to give a right of rejection the risk of their loss remains on the seller until cure or acceptance.

(2) Where the buyer rightfully revokes acceptance he may to the extent of any deficiency in his effective insurance coverage treat the risk of loss as having rested on the seller from the beginning.

(3) Where the buyer as to conforming goods already identified to the contract for sale repudiates or is otherwise in breach before risk of their loss has passed to him, the seller may to the extent of any deficiency in his effective insurance coverage treat the risk of loss as resting on the buyer for a commercially reasonable time.

§ 2–511.   Tender of Payment by Buyer; Payment by Check.

(1) Unless otherwise agreed tender of payment is a condition to the seller's duty to tender and complete any delivery.

(2) Tender of payment is sufficient when made by any means or in any manner current in the ordinary course of business unless the seller demands payment in legal tender and gives any extension of time reasonably necessary to procure it.

(3) Subject to the provisions of this Act on the effect of an instrument on an obligation (Section 3–310), payment by check is conditional and is defeated as between the parties by dishonor of the check on due presentment.

§ 2–512.   Payment by Buyer Before Inspection.

(1) Where the contract requires payment before inspection non-conformity of the goods does not excuse the buyer from so making payment unless

(a) the non-conformity appears without inspection; or

(b) despite tender of the required documents the circumstances would justify injunction against honor under the provisions of this Act (Section 5–114).

(2) Payment pursuant to subsection (1) does not constitute an acceptance of goods or impair the buyer's right to inspect or any of his remedies.

§ 2–513.   Buyer's Right to Inspection of Goods.

(1) Unless otherwise agreed and subject to subsection (3),

where goods are tendered or delivered or identified to the contract for sale, the buyer has a right before payment or acceptance to inspect them at any reasonable place and time and in any reasonable manner. When the seller is required or authorized to send the goods to the buyer, the inspection may be after their arrival.

(2) Expenses of inspection must be borne by the buyer but may be recovered from the seller if the goods do not conform and are rejected.

(3) Unless otherwise agreed and subject to the provisions of this Article on C.I.F. contracts (subsection (3) of Section 2–321), the buyer is not entitled to inspect the goods before payment of the price when the contract provides

(a) for delivery "C.O.D." or on other like terms; or

(b) for payment against documents of title, except where such payment is due only after the goods are to become available for inspection.

(4) A place or method of inspection fixed by the parties is presumed to be exclusive but unless otherwise expressly agreed it does not postpone identification or shift the place for delivery or for passing the risk of loss. If compliance becomes impossible, inspection shall be as provided in this section unless the place or method fixed was clearly intended as an indispensable condition failure of which avoids the contract.

§ 2–514. When Documents Deliverable on Acceptance; When on Payment.

Unless otherwise agreed documents against which a draft is drawn are to be delivered to the drawee on acceptance of the draft if it is payable more than three days after presentment; otherwise, only on payment.

§ 2–515. Preserving Evidence of Goods in Dispute.

In furtherance of the adjustment of any claim or dispute

(a) either party on reasonable notification to the other and for the purpose of ascertaining the facts and preserving evidence has the right to inspect, test and sample the goods including such of them as may be in the possession or control of the other; and

(b) the parties may agree to a third party inspection or survey to determine the conformity or condition of the goods and may agree that the findings shall be binding upon them in any subsequent litigation or adjustment.

PART 6 BREACH, REPUDIATION AND EXCUSE

§ 2–601. Buyer's Rights on Improper Delivery.

Subject to the provisions of this Article on breach in installment contracts (Section 2–612) and unless otherwise agreed under the sections on contractual limitations of remedy (Sections 2–718 and 2–719), if the goods or the tender of delivery fail in any respect to conform to the contract, the buyer may

(a) reject the whole; or

(b) accept the whole; or

(c) accept any commercial unit or units and reject the rest.

§ 2–602. Manner and Effect of Rightful Rejection.

(1) Rejection of goods must be within a reasonable time after their delivery or tender. It is ineffective unless the buyer seasonably notifies the seller.

(2) Subject to the provisions of the two following sections on rejected goods (Sections 2–603 and 2–604),

(a) after rejection any exercise of ownership by the buyer with respect to any commercial unit is wrongful as against the seller; and

(b) if the buyer has before rejection taken physical possession of goods in which he does not have a security interest under the provisions of this Article (subsection (3) of Section 2–711), he is under a duty after rejection to hold them with reasonable care at the seller's disposition for a time sufficient to permit the seller to remove them; but

(c) the buyer has no further obligations with regard to goods rightfully rejected.

(3) The seller's rights with respect to goods wrongfully rejected are governed by the provisions of this Article on seller's remedies in general (Section 2–703).

§ 2–603. Merchant Buyer's Duties as to Rightfully Rejected Goods.

(1) Subject to any security interest in the buyer (subsection (3) of Section 2–711), when the seller has no agent or place of business at the market of rejection a merchant buyer is under a duty after rejection of goods in his possession or control to follow any reasonable instructions received from the seller with respect to the goods and in the absence of such instructions to make reasonable efforts to sell them for the seller's account if they are perishable or threaten to decline in value speedily. Instructions are not reasonable if on demand indemnity for expenses is not forthcoming.

(2) When the buyer sells goods under subsection (1), he is entitled to reimbursement from the seller or out of the proceeds for reasonable expenses of caring for and selling them, and if the expenses include no selling commission then to such commission as is usual in the trade or if there is none to a reasonable sum not exceeding ten per cent on the gross proceeds.

(3) In complying with this section the buyer is held only to good faith and good faith conduct hereunder is neither acceptance nor conversion nor the basis of an action for damages.

§ 2–604. Buyer's Options as to Salvage of Rightfully Rejected Goods.

Subject to the provisions of the immediately preceding section on perishables if the seller gives no instructions within a reasonable time after notification of rejection the buyer may store the rejected goods for the seller's account or reship them to him or resell them for the seller's account with reimbursement as provided in the preceding section. Such action is not acceptance or conversion.

§ 2–605. Waiver of Buyer's Objections by Failure to Particularize.

(1) The buyer's failure to state in connection with rejection a particular defect which is ascertainable by reasonable

inspection precludes him from relying on the unstated defect to justify rejection or to establish breach

(a) where the seller could have cured it if stated seasonably; or

(b) between merchants when the seller has after rejection made a request in writing for a full and final written statement of all defects on which the buyer proposes to rely.

(2) Payment against documents made without reservation of rights precludes recovery of the payment for defects apparent on the face of the documents.

§ 2–606. What Constitutes Acceptance of Goods.

(1) Acceptance of goods occurs when the buyer

(a) after a reasonable opportunity to inspect the goods signifies to the seller that the goods are conforming or that he will take or retain them in spite of their nonconformity; or

(b) fails to make an effective rejection (subsection (1) of Section 2–602), but such acceptance does not occur until the buyer has had a reasonable opportunity to inspect them; or

(c) does any act inconsistent with the seller's ownership; but if such act is wrongful as against the seller it is an acceptance only if ratified by him.

(2) Acceptance of a part of any commercial unit is acceptance of that entire unit.

§ 2–607. Effect of Acceptance; Notice of Breach; Burden of Establishing Breach After Acceptance; Notice of Claim or Litigation to Person Answerable Over.

(1) The buyer must pay at the contract rate for any goods accepted.

(2) Acceptance of goods by the buyer precludes rejection of the goods accepted and if made with knowledge of a nonconformity cannot be revoked because of it unless the acceptance was on the reasonable assumption that the nonconformity would be seasonably cured but acceptance does not of itself impair any other remedy provided by this Article for non-conformity.

(3) Where a tender has been accepted

(a) the buyer must within a reasonable time after he discovers or should have discovered any breach notify the seller of breach or be barred from any remedy; and

(b) if the claim is one for infringement or the like (subsection (3) of Section 2–312) and the buyer is sued as a result of such a breach he must so notify the seller within a reasonable time after he receives notice of the litigation or be barred from any remedy over for liability established by the litigation.

(4) The burden is on the buyer to establish any breach with respect to the goods accepted.

(5) Where the buyer is sued for breach of a warranty or other obligation for which his seller is answerable over

(a) he may give his seller written notice of the litigation. If the notice states that the seller may come in and defend and that if the seller does not do so he will be bound in any action against him by his buyer by any determination of fact common to the two litigations, then unless the seller after seasonable receipt of the notice does come in and defend he

is so bound.

(b) if the claim is one for infringement or the like (subsection (3) of Section 2–312) the original seller may demand in writing that his buyer turn over to him control of the litigation including settlement or else be barred from any remedy over and if he also agrees to bear all expense and to satisfy any adverse judgment, then unless the buyer after seasonable receipt of the demand does turn over control the buyer is so barred.

(6) The provisions of subsections (3), (4) and (5) apply to any obligation of a buyer to hold the seller harmless against infringement or the like (subsection (3) of Section 2–312).

§ 2–608. Revocation of Acceptance in Whole or in Part.

(1) The buyer may revoke his acceptance of a lot or commercial unit whose non-conformity substantially impairs its value to him if he has accepted it

(a) on the reasonable assumption that its non-conformity would be cured and it has not been seasonably cured; or

(b) without discovery of such non-conformity if his acceptance was reasonably induced either by the difficulty of discovery before acceptance or by the seller's assurances.

(2) Revocation of acceptance must occur within a reasonable time after the buyer discovers or should have discovered the ground for it and before any substantial change in condition of the goods which is not caused by their own defects. It is not effective until the buyer notifies the seller of it.

(3) A buyer who so revokes has the same rights and duties with regard to the goods involved as if he had rejected them.

§ 2–609. Right to Adequate Assurance of Performance.

(1) A contract for sale imposes an obligation on each party that the other's expectation of receiving due performance will not be impaired. When reasonable grounds for insecurity arise with respect to the performance of either party the other may in writing demand adequate assurance of due performance and until he receives such assurance may if commercially reasonable suspend any performance for which he has not already received the agreed return.

(2) Between merchants the reasonableness of grounds for insecurity and the adequacy of any assurance offered shall be determined according to commercial standards.

(3) Acceptance of any improper delivery or payment does not prejudice the aggrieved party's right to demand adequate assurance of future performance.

(4) After receipt of a justified demand failure to provide within a reasonable time not exceeding thirty days such assurance of due performance as is adequate under the circumstances of the particular case is a repudiation of the contract.

§ 2–610. Anticipatory Repudiation.

When either party repudiates the contract with respect to a performance not yet due the loss of which will substantially impair the value of the contract to the other, the aggrieved party may

(a) for a commercially reasonable time await performance by the repudiating party; or

(b) resort to any remedy for breach (Section 2–703 or Section 2–711), even though he has notified the repudiating party that he would await the latter's performance and has urged retraction; and

(c) in either case suspend his own performance or proceed in accordance with the provisions of this Article on the seller's right to identify goods to the contract notwithstanding breach or to salvage unfinished goods (Section 2–704).

§ 2–611. Retraction of Anticipatory Repudiation.

(1) Until the repudiating party's next performance is due he can retract his repudiation unless the aggrieved party has since the repudiation cancelled or materially changed his position or otherwise indicated that he considers the repudiation final.

(2) Retraction may be by any method which clearly indicates to the aggrieved party that the repudiating party intends to perform, but must include any assurance justifiably demanded under the provisions of this Article (Section 2–609).

(3) Retraction reinstates the repudiating party's rights under the contract with due excuse and allowance to the aggrieved party for any delay occasioned by the repudiation.

§ 2–612. "Installment Contract"; Breach.

(1) An "installment contract" is one which requires or authorizes the delivery of goods in separate lots to be separately accepted, even though the contract contains a clause "each delivery is a separate contract" or its equivalent.

(2) The buyer may reject any installment which is nonconforming if the non-conformity substantially impairs the value of that installment and cannot be cured or if the non-conformity is a defect in the required documents; but if the non-conformity does not fall within subsection (3) and the seller gives adequate assurance of its cure the buyer must accept that installment.

(3) Whenever non-conformity or default with respect to one or more installments substantially impairs the value of the whole contract there is a breach of the whole. But the aggrieved party reinstates the contract if he accepts a nonconforming installment without seasonably notifying of cancellation or if he brings an action with respect only to past installments or demands performance as to future installments.

§ 2–613. Casualty to Identified Goods.

Where the contract requires for its performance goods identified when the contract is made, and the goods suffer casualty without fault of either party before the risk of loss passes to the buyer, or in a proper case under a "no arrival, no sale" term (Section 2–324) then

(a) if the loss is total the contract is avoided; and

(b) if the loss is partial or the goods have so deteriorated as no longer to conform to the contract the buyer may nevertheless demand inspection and at his option either treat the contract as avoided or accept the goods with due allowance from the contract price for the deterioration or the deficiency in quantity but without further right against the seller.

§ 2–614. Substituted Performance.

(1) Where without fault of either party the agreed berthing, loading, or unloading facilities fail or an agreed type of carrier becomes unavailable or the agreed manner of delivery otherwise becomes commercially impracticable but a commercially reasonable substitute is available, such substitute performance must be tendered and accepted.

(2) If the agreed means or manner of payment fails because of domestic or foreign governmental regulation, the seller may withhold or stop delivery unless the buyer provides a means or manner of payment which is commercially a substantial equivalent. If delivery has already been taken, payment by the means or in the manner provided by the regulation discharges the buyer's obligation unless the regulation is discriminatory, oppressive or predatory.

§ 2–615. Excuse by Failure of Presupposed Conditions.

Except so far as a seller may have assumed a greater obligation and subject to the preceding section on substituted performance:

(a) Delay in delivery or non-delivery in whole or in part by a seller who complies with paragraphs (b) and (c) is not a breach of his duty under a contract for sale if performance as agreed has been made impracticable by the occurrence of a contingency the non-occurrence of which was a basic assumption on which the contract was made or by compliance in good faith with any applicable foreign or domestic governmental regulation or order whether or not it later proves to be invalid.

(b) Where the causes mentioned in paragraph (a) affect only a part of the seller's capacity to perform, he must allocate production and deliveries among his customers but may at his option include regular customers not then under contract as well as his own requirements for further manufacture. He may so allocate in any manner which is fair and reasonable.

(c) The seller must notify the buyer seasonably that there will be delay or non-delivery and, when allocation is required under paragraph (b), of the estimated quota thus made available for the buyer.

§ 2–616. Procedure on Notice Claiming Excuse.

(1) Where the buyer receives notification of a material or indefinite delay or an allocation justified under the preceding section he may by written notification to the seller as to any delivery concerned, and where the prospective deficiency substantially impairs the value of the whole contract under the provisions of this Article relating to breach of installment contracts (Section 2–612), then also as to the whole,

(a) terminate and thereby discharge any unexecuted portion of the contract; or

(b) modify the contract by agreeing to take his available quota in substitution.

(2) If after receipt of such notification from the seller the buyer fails so to modify the contract within a reasonable time not exceeding thirty days the contract lapses with respect to any deliveries affected.

(3) The provisions of this section may not be negated by agreement except in so far as the seller has assumed a greater obligation under the preceding section.

PART 7   REMEDIES

§ 2–701.   Remedies for Breach of Collateral Contracts Not Impaired.

Remedies for breach of any obligation or promise collateral or ancillary to a contract for sale are not impaired by the provisions of this Article.

§ 2–702.   Seller's Remedies on Discovery of Buyer's Insolvency.

(1) Where the seller discovers the buyer to be insolvent he may refuse delivery except for cash including payment for all goods theretofore delivered under the contract, and stop delivery under this Article (Section 2–705).

(2) Where the seller discovers that the buyer has received goods on credit while insolvent he may reclaim the goods upon demand made within ten days after the receipt, but if misrepresentation of solvency has been made to the particular seller in writing within three months before delivery the ten day limitation does not apply. Except as provided in this subsection the seller may not base a right to reclaim goods on the buyer's fraudulent or innocent misrepresentation of solvency or of intent to pay.

(3) The seller's right to reclaim under subsection (2) is subject to the rights of a buyer in ordinary course or other good faith purchaser under this Article (Section 2–403). Successful reclamation of goods excludes all other remedies with respect to them.

§ 2–703.   Seller's Remedies in General.

Where the buyer wrongfully rejects or revokes acceptance of goods or fails to make a payment due on or before delivery or repudiates with respect to a part or the whole, then with respect to any goods directly affected and, if the breach is of the whole contract (Section 2–612), then also with respect to the whole undelivered balance, the aggrieved seller may

    (a) withhold delivery of such goods;

    (b) stop delivery by any bailee as hereafter provided (Section 2–705);

    (c) proceed under the next section respecting goods still unidentified to the contract;

    (d) resell and recover damages as hereafter provided (Section 2–706);

    (e) recover damages for non-acceptance (Section 2–708) or in a proper case the price (Section 2–709);

    (f) cancel.

§ 2–704.   Seller's Right to Identify Goods to the Contract Notwithstanding Breach or to Salvage Unfinished Goods.

(1) An aggrieved seller under the preceding section may

    (a) identify to the contract conforming goods not already identified if at the time he learned of the breach they are in his possession or control;

    (b) treat as the subject of resale goods which have demonstrably been intended for the particular contract even though those goods are unfinished.

(2) Where the goods are unfinished an aggrieved seller may in the exercise of reasonable commercial judgment for the purposes of avoiding loss and of effective realization either complete the manufacture and wholly identify the goods to the contract or cease manufacture and resell for scrap or salvage value or proceed in any other reasonable manner.

§ 2–705.   Seller's Stoppage of Delivery in Transit or Otherwise.

(1) The seller may stop delivery of goods in the possession of a carrier or other bailee when he discovers the buyer to be insolvent (Section 2–702) and may stop delivery of carload, truckload, planeload or larger shipments of express or freight when the buyer repudiates or fails to make a payment due before delivery or if for any other reason the seller has a right to withhold or reclaim the goods.

(2) As against such buyer the seller may stop delivery until

    (a) receipt of the goods by the buyer; or

    (b) acknowledgment to the buyer by any bailee of the goods except a carrier that the bailee holds the goods for the buyer; or

    (c) such acknowledgment to the buyer by a carrier by reshipment or as warehouseman; or

    (d) negotiation to the buyer of any negotiable document of title covering the goods.

(3)

    (a) To stop delivery the seller must so notify as to enable the bailee by reasonable diligence to prevent delivery of the goods.

    (b) After such notification the bailee must hold and deliver the goods according to the directions of the seller but the seller is liable to the bailee for any ensuing charges or damages.

    (c) If a negotiable document of title has been issued for goods the bailee is not obliged to obey a notification to stop until surrender of the document.

    (d) A carrier who has issued a non-negotiable bill of lading is not obliged to obey a notification to stop received from a person other than the consignor.

§ 2–706.   Seller's Resale Including Contract for Resale.

(1) Under the conditions stated in Section 2–703 on seller's remedies, the seller may resell the goods concerned or the undelivered balance thereof. Where the resale is made in good faith and in a commercially reasonable manner the seller may recover the difference between the resale price and the contract price together with any incidental damages allowed under the provisions of this Article (Section 2–710), but less expenses saved in consequence of the buyer's breach.

(2) Except as otherwise provided in subsection (3) or unless otherwise agreed resale may be at public or private sale including sale by way of one or more contracts to sell or of identification to an existing contract of the seller. Sale may be as a unit or in parcels and at any time and place and on any terms but every aspect of the sale including the method,

manner, time, place and terms must be commercially reasonable. The resale must be reasonably identified as referring to the broken contract, but it is not necessary that the goods be in existence or that any or all of them have been identified to the contract before the breach.

(3) Where the resale is at private sale the seller must give the buyer reasonable notification of his intention to resell.

(4) Where the resale is at public sale

(a) only identified goods can be sold except where there is a recognized market for a public sale of futures in goods of the kind; and

(b) it must be made at a usual place or market for public sale if one is reasonably available and except in the case of goods which are perishable or threaten to decline in value speedily the seller must give the buyer reasonable notice of the time and place of the resale; and

(c) if the goods are not to be within the view of those attending the sale the notification of sale must state the place where the goods are located and provide for their reasonable inspection by prospective bidders; and

(d) the seller may buy.

(5) A purchaser who buys in good faith at a resale takes the goods free of any rights of the original buyer even though the seller fails to comply with one or more of the requirements of this section.

(6) The seller is not accountable to the buyer for any profit made on any resale. A person in the position of a seller (Section 2–707) or a buyer who has rightfully rejected or justifiably revoked acceptance must account for any excess over the amount of his security interest, as hereinafter defined (subsection (3) of Section 2–711).

§ 2–707.   "Person in the Position of a Seller".

(1) A "person in the position of a seller" includes as against a principal an agent who has paid or become responsible for the price of goods on behalf of his principal or anyone who otherwise holds a security interest or other right in goods similar to that of a seller.

(2) A person in the position of a seller may as provided in this Article withhold or stop delivery (Section 2–705) and resell (Section 2–706) and recover incidental damages (Section 2–710).

§ 2–708.   Seller's Damages for Non-Acceptance or Repudiation.

(1) Subject to subsection (2) and to the provisions of this Article with respect to proof of market price (Section 2–723), the measure of damages for non-acceptance or repudiation by the buyer is the difference between the market price at the time and place for tender and the unpaid contract price together with any incidental damages provided in this Article (Section 2–710), but less expenses saved in consequence of the buyer's breach.

(2) If the measure of damages provided in subsection (1) is inadequate to put the seller in as good a position as performance would have done then the measure of damages is the profit (including reasonable overhead) which the seller would have made from full performance by the

buyer, together with any incidental damages provided in this Article (Section 2–710), due allowance for costs reasonably incurred and due credit for payments or proceeds of resale.

§ 2–709.   Action for the Price.

(1) When the buyer fails to pay the price as it becomes due the seller may recover, together with any incidental damages under the next section, the price

(a) of goods accepted or of conforming goods lost or damaged within a commercially reasonable time after risk of their loss has passed to the buyer; and

(b) of goods identified to the contract if the seller is unable after reasonable effort to resell them at a reasonable price or the circumstances reasonably indicate that such effort will be unavailing.

(2) Where the seller sues for the price he must hold for the buyer any goods which have been identified to the contract and are still in his control except that if resale becomes possible he may resell them at any time prior to the collection of the judgment. The net proceeds of any such resale must be credited to the buyer and payment of the judgment entitles him to any goods not resold.

(3) After the buyer has wrongfully rejected or revoked acceptance of the goods or has failed to make a payment due or has repudiated (Section 2–610), a seller who is held not entitled to the price under this section shall nevertheless be awarded damages for non-acceptance under the preceding section.

§ 2–710.   Seller's Incidental Damages.

Incidental damages to an aggrieved seller include any commercially reasonable charges, expenses or commissions incurred in stopping delivery, in the transportation, care and custody of goods after the buyer's breach, in connection with return or resale of the goods or otherwise resulting from the breach.

§ 2–711.   Buyer's Remedies in General; Buyer's Security Interest in Rejected Goods.

(1) Where the seller fails to make delivery or repudiates or the buyer rightfully rejects or justifiably revokes acceptance then with respect to any goods involved, and with respect to the whole if the breach goes to the whole contract (Section 2–612), the buyer may cancel and whether or not he has done so may in addition to recovering so much of the price as has been paid

(a) "cover" and have damages under the next section as to all the goods affected whether or not they have been identified to the contract; or

(b) recover damages for non-delivery as provided in this Article (Section 2–713).

(2) Where the seller fails to deliver or repudiates the buyer may also

(a) if the goods have been identified recover them as provided in this Article (Section 2–502); or

(b) in a proper case obtain specific performance or replevy the goods as provided in this Article (Section 2–716).

(3) On rightful rejection or justifiable revocation of accept-

ance a buyer has a security interest in goods in his possession or control for any payments made on their price and any expenses reasonably incurred in their inspection, receipt, transportation, care and custody and may hold such goods and resell them in like manner as an aggrieved seller (Section 2–706).

§ 2–712.   "Cover"; Buyer's Procurement of Substitute Goods.

(1) After a breach within the preceding section the buyer may "cover" by making in good faith and without unreasonable delay any reasonable purchase of or contract to purchase goods in substitution for those due from the seller.

(2) The buyer may recover from the seller as damages the difference between the cost of cover and the contract price together with any incidental or consequential damages as hereinafter defined (Section 2–715), but less expenses saved in consequence of the seller's breach.

(3) Failure of the buyer to effect cover within this section does not bar him from any other remedy.

§ 2–713.   Buyer's Damages for Non-Delivery or Repudiation.

(1) Subject to provisions of this Article with respect to the proof of market price (Section 2–723), the measure of damages for non-delivery or repudiation by the seller is the difference between the market price at the time when the buyer learned of the breach and the contract price together with any incidental and consequential damages provided in this Article (Section 2–715), but less expenses saved in consequence of the seller's breach.

(2) Market price is to be determined as of the place for tender or, in cases of rejection after arrival or revocation of acceptance, as of the place of arrival.

§ 2–714.   Buyer's Damages for Breach in Regard to Accepted Goods.

(1) Where the buyer has accepted goods and given notification (subsection (3) of Section 2–607) he may recover as damages for any non-conformity of tender the loss resulting in the ordinary course of events from the seller's breach as determined in any manner which is reasonable.

(2) The measure of damages for breach of warranty is the difference at the time and place of acceptance between the value of the goods accepted and the value they would have had if they had been as warranted, unless special circumstances show proximate damages of a different amount.

(3) In a proper case any incidental and consequential damages under the next section may be recovered.

§ 2–715.   Buyer's Incidental and Consequential Damages.

(1) Incidental damages resulting from the seller's breach include expenses reasonably incurred in inspection, receipt, transportation and care and custody of goods rightfully rejected, any commercially reasonable charges, expenses or commissions in connection with effecting cover and any other reasonable expense incident to the delay or other breach.

(2) Consequential damages resulting from the seller's breach include

(a) any loss resulting from general or particular requirements and needs of which the seller at the time of contracting had reason to know and which could not reasonably be prevented by cover or otherwise; and

(b) injury to person or property proximately resulting from any breach of warranty.

§ 2–716.   Buyer's Right to Specific Performance or Replevin.

(1) Specific performance may be decreed where the goods are unique or in other proper circumstances.

(2) The decree for specific performance may include such terms and conditions as to payment of the price, damages, or other relief as the court may deem just.

(3) The buyer has a right of replevin for goods identified to the contract if after reasonable effort he is unable to effect cover for such goods or the circumstances reasonably indicate that such effort will be unavailing or if the goods have been shipped under reservation and satisfaction of the security interest in them has been made or tendered.

§ 2–717.   Deduction of Damages From the Price.

The buyer on notifying the seller of his intention to do so may deduct all or any part of the damages resulting from any breach of the contract from any part of the price still due under the same contract.

§ 2–718.   Liquidation or Limitation of Damages; Deposits

(1) Damages for breach by either party may be liquidated in the agreement but only at an amount which is reasonable in the light of the anticipated or actual harm caused by the breach, the difficulties of proof of loss, and the inconvenience or nonfeasibility of otherwise obtaining an adequate remedy. A term fixing unreasonably large liquidated damages is void as a penalty.

(2) Where the seller justifiably withholds delivery of goods because of the buyer's breach, the buyer is entitled to restitution of any amount by which the sum of his payments exceeds

(a) the amount to which the seller is entitled by virtue of terms liquidating the seller's damages in accordance with subsection (1), or

(b) in the absence of such terms, twenty per cent of the value of the total performance for which the buyer is obligated under the contract or $500, whichever is smaller.

(3) The buyer's right to restitution under subsection (2) is subject to offset to the extent that the seller establishes

(a) a right to recover damages under the provisions of this Article other than subsection (1), and

(b) the amount or value of any benefits received by the buyer directly or indirectly by reason of the contract.

(4) Where a seller has received payment in goods their reasonable value or the proceeds of their resale shall be treated as payments for the purposes of subsection (2); but if the

seller has notice of the buyer's breach before reselling goods received in part performance, his resale is subject to the conditions laid down in this Article on resale by an aggrieved seller (Section 2–706).

§ 2–719. Contractual Modification or Limitation of Remedy.

(1) Subject to the provisions of subsection (2) and (3) of this section and of the preceding section on liquidation and limitation of damages,

    (a) the agreement may provide for remedies in addition to or in substitution for those provided in this Article and may limit or alter the measure of damages recoverable under this Article, as by limiting the buyer's remedies to return of the goods and repayment of the price or to repair and replacement of non-conforming goods or parts; and

    (b) resort to a remedy as provided is optional unless the remedy is expressly agreed to be exclusive, in which case it is the sole remedy.

(2) Where circumstances cause an exclusive or limited remedy to fail of its essential purpose, remedy may be had as provided in this Act.

(3) Consequential damages may be limited or excluded unless the limitation or exclusion is unconscionable. Limitation of consequential damages for injury to the person in the case of consumer goods is prima facie unconscionable but limitation of damages where the loss is commercial is not.

§ 2–720. Effect of "Cancellation" or "Rescission" on Claims for Antecedent Breach.

Unless the contrary intention clearly appears, expressions of "cancellation" or "rescission" of the contract or the like shall not be construed as a renunciation or discharge of any claim in damages for an antecedent breach.

§ 2–721. Remedies for Fraud.

Remedies for material misrepresentation or fraud include all remedies available under this Article for non-fraudulent breach. Neither rescission or a claim for rescission of the contract for sale nor rejection or return of the goods shall bar or be deemed inconsistent with a claim for damages or other remedy.

§ 2–722. Who Can Sue Third Parties for Injury to Goods.

Where a third party so deals with goods which have been identified to a contract for sale as to cause actionable injury to a party to that contract

    (a) a right of action against the third party is in either party to the contract for sale who has title to or a security interest or a special property or an insurable interest in the goods; and if the goods have been destroyed or converted a right of action is also in the party who either bore the risk of loss under the contract for sale or has since the injury assumed that risk as against the other;

    (b) if at the time of the injury the party plaintiff did not bear the risk of loss as against the other party to the contract for sale and there is no arrangement between them for disposition of the recovery, his suit or settlement is subject to his

own interest, as a fiduciary for the other party to the contract;

    (c) either party may with the consent of the other sue for the benefit of whom it may concern.

§ 2–723. Proof of Market Price: Time and Place.

(1) If an action based on anticipatory repudiation comes to trial before the time for performance with respect to some or all of the goods, any damages based on market price (Section 2–708 or Section 2–713) shall be determined according to the price of such goods prevailing at the time when the aggrieved party learned of the repudiation.

(2) If evidence of a price prevailing at the times or places described in this Article is not readily available the price prevailing within any reasonable time before or after the time described or at any other place which in commercial judgment or under usage of trade would serve as a reasonable substitute for the one described may be used, making any proper allowance for the cost of transporting the goods to or from such other place.

(3) Evidence of a relevant price prevailing at a time or place other than the one described in this Article offered by one party is not admissible unless and until he has given the other party such notice as the court finds sufficient to prevent unfair surprise.

§ 2–724. Admissibility of Market Quotations.

Whenever the prevailing price or value of any goods regularly bought and sold in any established commodity market is in issue, reports in official publications or trade journals or in newspapers or periodicals of general circulation published as the reports of such market shall be admissible in evidence. The circumstances of the preparation of such a report may be shown to affect its weight but not its admissibility.

§ 2–725. Statute of Limitations in Contracts for Sale.

(1) An action for breach of any contract for sale must be commenced within four years after the cause of action has accrued. By the original agreement the parties may reduce the period of limitation to not less than one year but may not extend it.

(2) A cause of action occurs when the breach occurs, regardless of the aggrieved party's lack of knowledge of the breach. A breach of warranty occurs when tender of delivery is made, except that where a warranty explicitly extends to future performance of the goods and discovery of the breach must await the time of such performance the cause of action accrues when the breach is or should have been discovered.

(3) Where an action commenced within the time limited by subsection (1) is so terminated as to leave available a remedy by another action for the same breach such other action may be commenced after the expiration of the time limited and within six months after the termination of the first action unless the termination resulted from voluntary discontinuance or from dismissal for failure or neglect to prosecute.

(4) This section does not alter the law on tolling of the statute of limitations nor does it apply to causes of action which have accrued before this Act becomes effective.

ARTICLE 2A

LEASES

PART 1   GENERAL PROVISIONS

§ 2A–101.   Short Title.

This Article shall be known and may be cited as the Uniform Commercial Code—Leases.

§ 2A–102.   Scope.

This Article applies to any transaction, regardless of form, that creates a lease.

§ 2A–103.   Definitions and Index of Definitions.

(1) In this Article unless the context otherwise requires:

(a) "Buyer in ordinary course of business" means a person who in good faith and without knowledge that the sale to him [or her] is in violation of the ownership rights or security interest or leasehold interest of a third party in the goods buys in ordinary course from a person in the business of selling goods of that kind but does not include a pawnbroker. "Buying" may be for cash or by exchange of other property or on secured or unsecured credit and includes receiving goods or documents of title under a pre-existing contract for sale but does not include a transfer in bulk or as security for or in total or partial satisfaction of a money debt.

(b) "Cancellation" occurs when either party puts an end to the lease contract for default by the other party.

(c) "Commercial unit" means such a unit of goods as by commercial usage is a single whole for purposes of lease and division of which materially impairs its character or value on the market or in use. A commercial unit may be a single article, as a machine, or a set of articles, as a suite of furniture or a line of machinery, or a quantity, as a gross or carload, or any other unit treated in use or in the relevant market as a single whole.

(d) "Conforming" goods or performance under a lease contract means goods or performance that are in accordance with the obligations under the lease contract.

(e) "Consumer lease" means a lease that a lessor regularly engaged in the business of leasing or selling makes to a lessee who is an individual and who takes under the lease primarily for a personal, family, or household purpose [, if the total payments to be made under the lease contract, excluding payments for options to renew or buy, do not exceed $].

(f) "Fault" means wrongful act, omission, breach, or default.

(g) "Finance lease" means a lease with respect to which:

(i) the lessor does not select, manufacture, or supply the goods;

(ii) the lessor acquires the goods or the right to possession and use of the goods in connection with the lease; and

(iii) one of the following occurs:

(A) the lessee receives a copy of the contract by which the lessor acquired the goods or the right to possession and use of the goods before signing the lease contract;

(B) the lessee's approval of the contract by which the lessor acquired the goods or the right to possession and use of the goods is a condition to effectiveness of the lease contract;

(C) the lessee, before signing the lease contract, receives an accurate and complete statement designating the promises and warranties, and any disclaimers of warranties, limitations or modifications of remedies, or liquidated damages, including those of a third party, such as the manufacturer of the goods, provided to the lessor by the person supplying the goods in connection with or as part of the contract by which the lessor acquired the goods or the right to possession and use of the goods; or

(D) if the lease is not a consumer lease, the lessor, before the lessee signs the lease contract, informs the lessee in writing (a) of the identity of the person supplying the goods to the lessor, unless the lessee has selected that person and directed the lessor to acquire the goods or the right to possession and use of the goods from that person, (b) that the lessee is entitled under this Article to the promises and warranties, including those of any third party, provided to the lessor by the person supplying the goods in connection with or as part of the contract by which the lessor acquired the goods or the right to possession and use of the goods, and (c) that the lessee may communicate with the person supplying the goods to the lessor and receive an accurate and complete statement of those promises and warranties, including any disclaimers and limitations of them or of remedies.

(h) "Goods" means all things that are movable at the time of identification to the lease contract, or are fixtures (Section 2A–309), but the term does not include money, documents, instruments, accounts, chattel paper, general intangibles, or minerals or the like, including oil and gas, before extraction. The term also includes the unborn young of animals.

(i) "Installment lease contract" means a lease contract that authorizes or requires the delivery of goods in separate lots to be separately accepted, even though the lease contract contains a clause "each delivery is a separate lease" or its equivalent.

(j) "Lease" means a transfer of the right to possession and use of goods for a term in return for consideration, but a sale, including a sale on approval or a sale or return, or retention or creation of a security interest is not a lease. Unless the context clearly indicates otherwise, the term includes a sublease.

(k) "Lease agreement" means the bargain, with respect to the lease, of the lessor and the lessee in fact as found in their language or by implication from other circumstances including course of dealing or usage of trade or course of performance as provided in this Article. Unless the context clearly indicates otherwise, the term includes a sublease agreement.

(l) "Lease contract" means the total legal obligation that results from the lease agreement as affected by this Article and any other applicable rules of law. Unless the context clearly indicates otherwise, the term includes a sublease contract.

(m) "Leasehold interest" means the interest of the lessor or the lessee under a lease contract.

(n) "Lessee" means a person who acquires the right to possession and use of goods under a lease. Unless the context clearly indicates otherwise, the term includes a sublessee.

(o) "Lessee in ordinary course of business" means a person who in good faith and without knowledge that the lease to him [or her] is in violation of the ownership rights or security interest or leasehold interest of a third party in the goods, leases in ordinary course from a person in the business of selling or leasing goods of that kind but does not include a pawnbroker. "Leasing" may be for cash or by exchange of other property or on secured or unsecured credit and includes receiving goods or documents of title under a pre-existing lease contract but does not include a transfer in bulk or as security for or in total or partial satisfaction of a money debt.

(p) "Lessor" means a person who transfers the right to possession and use of goods under a lease. Unless the context clearly indicates otherwise, the term includes a sublessor.

(q) "Lessor's residual interest" means the lessor's interest in the goods after expiration, termination, or cancellation of the lease contract.

(r) "Lien" means a charge against or interest in goods to secure payment of a debt or performance of an obligation, but the term does not include a security interest.

(s) "Lot" means a parcel or a single article that is the subject matter of a separate lease or delivery, whether or not it is sufficient to perform the lease contract.

(t) "Merchant lessee" means a lessee that is a merchant with respect to goods of the kind subject to the lease.

(u) "Present value" means the amount as of a date certain of one or more sums payable in the future, discounted to the date certain. The discount is determined by the interest rate specified by the parties if the rate was not manifestly unreasonable at the time the transaction was entered into; otherwise, the discount is determined by a commercially reasonable rate that takes into account the facts and circumstances of each case at the time the transaction was entered into.

(v) "Purchase" includes taking by sale, lease, mortgage, security interest, pledge, gift, or any other voluntary transaction creating an interest in goods.

(w) "Sublease" means a lease of goods the right to possession and use of which was acquired by the lessor as a lessee under an existing lease.

(x) "Supplier" means a person from whom a lessor buys or leases goods to be leased under a finance lease.

(y) "Supply contract" means a contract under which a lessor buys or leases goods to be leased.

(z) "Termination" occurs when either party pursuant to a power created by agreement or law puts an end to the lease contract otherwise than for default.

(2) Other definitions applying to this Article and the sections in which they appear are:

"Accessions". Section 2A–310(1).
"Construction mortgage". Section 2A–309(1)(d).
"Encumbrance". Section 2A–309(1)(e).
"Fixtures". Section 2A–309(1)(a).
"Fixture filing". Section 2A–309(1)(b).
"Purchase money lease". Section 2A–309(1)(c).

(3) The following definitions in other Articles apply to this

Article:

"Account". Section 9–106.
"Between merchants". Section 2–104(3).
"Buyer". Section 2–103(1)(a).
"Chattel paper". Section 9–105(1)(b).
"Consumer goods". Section 9–109(1).
"Document". Section 9–105(1)(f).
"Entrusting". Section 2–403(3).
"General intangibles". Section 9–106.
"Good faith". Section 2–103(1)(b).
"Instrument". Section 9–105(1)(i).
"Merchant". Section 2–104(1).
"Mortgage". Sect 9–105(1)(j).
"Pursuant to commitment". Section 9–105(1)(k).
"Receipt". Section 2–103(1)(c).
"Sale". Section 2–106(1).
"Sale on approval". Section 2–326.
"Sale or return". Section 2–326.
"Seller". Section 2–103(1)(d).

(4) In addition Article 1 contains general definitions and principles of construction and interpretation applicable throughout this Article.

As amended in 1990.

§ 2A–104. Leases Subject to Other Law.

(1) A lease, although subject to this Article, is also subject to any applicable:

(a) certificate of title statute of this State: (list any certificate of title statutes covering automobiles, trailers, mobile homes, boats, farm tractors, and the like);

(b) certificate of title statute of another jurisdiction (Section 2A–105); or

(c) consumer protection statute of this State, or final consumer protection decision of a court of this State existing on the effective date of this Article.

(2) In case of conflict between this Article, other than Sections 2A–105, 2A–304(3), and 2A–305(3), and a statute or decision referred to in subsection (1), the statute or decision controls.

(3) Failure to comply with an applicable law has only the effect specified therein.

As amended in 1990.

§ 2A–105. Territorial Application of Article to Goods Covered by Certificate of Title.

Subject to the provisions of Sections 2A–304(3) and 2A–305(3), with respect to goods covered by a certificate of title issued under a statute of this State or of another jurisdiction, compliance and the effect of compliance or noncompliance with a certificate of title statute are governed by the law (including the conflict of laws rules) of the jurisdiction issuing the certificate until the earlier of (a) surrender of the certificate, or (b) four months after the goods are removed from that jurisdiction and thereafter until a new certificate of title is issued by another jurisdiction.

§ 2A–106. Limitation on Power of Parties to Consumer Lease to Choose Applicable Law and Judicial Forum.

(1) If the law chosen by the parties to a consumer lease is

that of a jurisdiction other than a jurisdiction in which the lessee resides at the time the lease agreement becomes enforceable or within 30 days thereafter or in which the goods are to be used, the choice is not enforceable.

(2) If the judicial forum chosen by the parties to a consumer lease is a forum that would not otherwise have jurisdiction over the lessee, the choice is not enforceable.

§ 2A–107. Waiver or Renunciation of Claim or Right After Default.

Any claim or right arising out of an alleged default or breach of warranty may be discharged in whole or in part without consideration by a written waiver or renunciation signed and delivered by the aggrieved party.

§ 2A–108. Unconscionability.

(1) If the court as a matter of law finds a lease contract or any clause of a lease contract to have been unconscionable at the time it was made the court may refuse to enforce the lease contract, or it may enforce the remainder of the lease contract without the unconscionable clause, or it may so limit the application of any unconscionable clause as to avoid any unconscionable result.

(2) With respect to a consumer lease, if the court as a matter of law finds that a lease contract or any clause of a lease contract has been induced by unconscionable conduct or that unconscionable conduct has occurred in the collection of a claim arising from a lease contract, the court may grant appropriate relief.

(3) Before making a finding of unconscionability under subsection (1) or (2), the court, on its own motion or that of a party, shall afford the parties a reasonable opportunity to present evidence as to the setting, purpose, and effect of the lease contract or clause thereof, or of the conduct.

(4) In an action in which the lessee claims unconscionability with respect to a consumer lease:

(a) If the court finds unconscionability under subsection (1) or (2), the court shall award reasonable attorney's fees to the lessee.

(b) If the court does not find unconscionability and the lessee claiming unconscionability has brought or maintained an action he [or she] knew to be groundless, the court shall award reasonable attorney's fees to the party against whom the claim is made.

(c) In determining attorney's fees, the amount of the recovery on behalf of the claimant under subsections (1) and (2) is not controlling.

§ 2A–109. Option to Accelerate at Will.

(1) A term providing that one party or his [or her] successor in interest may accelerate payment or performance or require collateral or additional collateral "at will" or "when he [or she] deems himself [or herself] insecure" or in words of similar import must be construed to mean that he [or she] has power to do so only if he [or she] in good faith believes that the prospect of payment or performance is impaired.

(2) With respect to a consumer lease, the burden of establishing good faith under subsection (1) is on the party who exercised the power; otherwise the burden of establishing lack of good faith is on the party against whom the power has been exercised.

PART 2   FORMATION AND CONSTRUCTION OF LEASE CONTRACT

§ 2A–201. Statute of Frauds.

(1) A lease contract is not enforceable by way of action or defense unless:

(a) the total payments to be made under the lease contract, excluding payments for options to renew or buy, are less than $1,000; or

(b) there is a writing, signed by the party against whom enforcement is sought or by that party's authorized agent, sufficient to indicate that a lease contract has been made between the parties and to describe the goods leased and the lease term.

(2) Any description of leased goods or of the lease term is sufficient and satisfies subsection (1)(b), whether or not it is specific, if it reasonably identifies what is described.

(3) A writing is not insufficient because it omits or incorrectly states a term agreed upon, but the lease contract is not enforceable under subsection (1)(b) beyond the lease term and the quantity of goods shown in the writing.

(4) A lease contract that does not satisfy the requirements of subsection (1), but which is valid in other respects, is enforceable:

(a) if the goods are to be specially manufactured or obtained for the lessee and are not suitable for lease or sale to others in the ordinary course of the lessor's business, and the lessor, before notice of repudiation is received and under circumstances that reasonably indicate that the goods are for the lessee, has made either a substantial beginning of their manufacture or commitments for their procurement;

(b) if the party against whom enforcement is sought admits in that party's pleading, testimony or otherwise in court that a lease contract was made, but the lease contract is not enforceable under this provision beyond the quantity of goods admitted; or

(c) with respect to goods that have been received and accepted by the lessee.

(5) The lease term under a lease contract referred to in subsection (4) is:

(a) if there is a writing signed by the party against whom enforcement is sought or by that party's authorized agent specifying the lease term, the term so specified;

(b) if the party against whom enforcement is sought admits in that party's pleading, testimony, or otherwise in court a lease term, the term so admitted; or

(c) a reasonable lease term.

§ 2A–202. Final Written Expression: Parol or Extrinsic Evidence.

Terms with respect to which the confirmatory memoranda of the parties agree or which are otherwise set forth in a writing intended by the parties as a final expression of their agreement with respect to such terms as are included therein may not be contradicted by evidence of any prior agreement or of a contemporaneous oral agreement but may be explained or supplemented:

(a) by course of dealing or usage of trade or by course of performance; and

(b) by evidence of consistent additional terms unless the court finds the writing to have been intended also as a complete and exclusive statement of the terms of the agreement.

§ 2A–203. Seals Inoperative.

The affixing of a seal to a writing evidencing a lease contract or an offer to enter into a lease contract does not render the writing a sealed instrument and the law with respect to sealed instruments does not apply to the lease contract or offer.

§ 2A–204. Formation in General.

(1) A lease contract may be made in any manner sufficient to show agreement, including conduct by both parties which recognizes the existence of a lease contract.

(2) An agreement sufficient to constitute a lease contract may be found although the moment of its making is undetermined.

(3) Although one or more terms are left open, a lease contract does not fail for indefiniteness if the parties have intended to make a lease contract and there is a reasonably certain basis for giving an appropriate remedy.

§ 2A–205. Firm Offers.

An offer by a merchant to lease goods to or from another person in a signed writing that by its terms gives assurance it will be held open is not revocable, for lack of consideration, during the time stated or, if no time is stated, for a reasonable time, but in no event may the period of irrevocability exceed 3 months. Any such term of assurance on a form supplied by the offeree must be separately signed by the offeror.

§ 2A–206. Offer and Acceptance in Formation of Lease Contract.

(1) Unless otherwise unambiguously indicated by the language or circumstances, an offer to make a lease contract must be construed as inviting acceptance in any manner and by any medium reasonable in the circumstances.

(2) If the beginning of a requested performance is a reasonable mode of acceptance, an offeror who is not notified of acceptance within a reasonable time may treat the offer as having lapsed before acceptance.

§ 2A–207. Course of Performance or Practical Construction.

(1) If a lease contract involves repeated occasions for performance by either party with knowledge of the nature of the performance and opportunity for objection to it by the other, any course of performance accepted or acquiesced in without objection is relevant to determine the meaning of the lease agreement.

(2) The express terms of a lease agreement and any course of performance, as well as any course of dealing and usage of trade, must be construed whenever reasonable as consistent with each other; but if that construction is unreasonable, express terms control course of performance, course of performance controls both course of dealing and usage of trade, and course of dealing controls usage of trade.

(3) Subject to the provisions of Section 2A–208 on modification and waiver, course of performance is relevant to show a waiver or modification of any term inconsistent with the course of performance.

§ 2A–208. Modification, Rescission and Waiver.

(1) An agreement modifying a lease contract needs no consideration to be binding.

(2) A signed lease agreement that excludes modification or rescission except by a signed writing may not be otherwise modified or rescinded, but, except as between merchants, such a requirement on a form supplied by a merchant must be separately signed by the other party.

(3) Although an attempt at modification or rescission does not satisfy the requirements of subsection (2), it may operate as a waiver.

(4) A party who has made a waiver affecting an executory portion of a lease contract may retract the waiver by reasonable notification received by the other party that strict performance will be required of any term waived, unless the retraction would be unjust in view of a material change of position in reliance on the waiver.

§ 2A–209. Lessee Under Finance Lease as Beneficiary of Supply Contract.

(1) The benefit of a supplier's promises to the lessor under the supply contract and of all warranties, whether express or implied, including those of any third party provided in connection with or as part of the supply contract, extends to the lessee to the extent of the lessee's leasehold interest under a finance lease related to the supply contract, but is subject to the terms of the warranty and of the supply contract and all defenses or claims arising therefrom.

(2) The extension of the benefit of a supplier's promises and of warranties to the lessee (Section 2A–209(1)) does not: (i) modify the rights and obligations of the parties to the supply contract, whether arising therefrom or otherwise, or (ii) impose any duty or liability under the supply contract on the lessee.

(3) Any modification or rescission of the supply contract by the supplier and the lessor is effective between the supplier and the lessee unless, before the modification or rescission, the supplier has received notice that the lessee has entered into a finance lease related to the supply contract. If the modification or rescission is effective between the supplier and the lessee, the lessor is deemed to have assumed, in addition to the obligations of the lessor to the lessee under the lease contract, promises of the supplier to the lessor and warranties that were so modified or rescinded as they existed and were available to the lessee before modification or rescission.

(4) In addition to the extension of the benefit of the supplier's promises and of warranties to the lessee under subsection (1), the lessee retains all rights that the lessee may have against the supplier which arise from an agreement between the lessee and the supplier or under other law.
As amended in 1990.

§ 2A–210. Express Warranties.

(1) Express warranties by the lessor are created as follows:

(a) Any affirmation of fact or promise made by the lessor to the lessee which relates to the goods and becomes part of the basis of the bargain creates an express warranty that the goods will conform to the affirmation or promise.

(b) Any description of the goods which is made part of the basis of the bargain creates an express warranty that the goods will conform to the description.

(c) Any sample or model that is made part of the basis of the bargain creates an express warranty that the whole of the goods will conform to the sample or model.

(2) It is not necessary to the creation of an express warranty that the lessor use formal words, such as "warrant" or "guarantee," or that the lessor have a specific intention to make a warranty, but an affirmation merely of the value of the goods or a statement purporting to be merely the lessor's opinion or commendation of the goods does not create a warranty.

§ 2A–211. Warranties Against Interference and Against Infringement; Lessee's Obligation Against Infringement.

(1) There is in a lease contract a warranty that for the lease term no person holds a claim to or interest in the goods that arose from an act or omission of the lessor, other than a claim by way of infringement or the like, which will interfere with the lessee's enjoyment of its leasehold interest.

(2) Except in a finance lease there is in a lease contract by a lessor who is a merchant regularly dealing in goods of the kind a warranty that the goods are delivered free of the rightful claim of any person by way of infringement or the like.

(3) A lessee who furnishes specifications to a lessor or a supplier shall hold the lessor and the supplier harmless against any claim by way of infringement or the like that arises out of compliance with the specifications.

§ 2A–212. Implied Warranty of Merchantability.

(1) Except in a finance lease, a warranty that the goods will be merchantable is implied in a lease contract if the lessor is a merchant with respect to goods of that kind.

(2) Goods to be merchantable must be at least such as

(a) pass without objection in the trade under the description in the lease agreement;

(b) in the case of fungible goods, are of fair average quality within the description;

(c) are fit for the ordinary purposes for which goods of that type are used;

(d) run, within the variation permitted by the lease agreement, of even kind, quality, and quantity within each unit and among all units involved;

(e) are adequately contained, packaged, and labeled as the lease agreement may require; and

(f) conform to any promises or affirmations of fact made on the container or label.

(3) Other implied warranties may arise from course of dealing or usage of trade.

§ 2A–213. Implied Warranty of Fitness for Particular Purpose.

Except in a finance lease, if the lessor at the time the lease contract is made has reason to know of any particular purpose for which the goods are required and that the lessee is relying on the lessor's skill or judgment to select or furnish suitable goods, there is in the lease contract an implied warranty that the goods will be fit for that purpose.

§ 2A–214. Exclusion or Modification of Warranties.

(1) Words or conduct relevant to the creation of an express warranty and words or conduct tending to negate or limit a warranty must be construed wherever reasonable as consistent with each other; but, subject to the provisions of Section 2A–202 on parol or extrinsic evidence, negation or limitation is inoperative to the extent that the construction is unreasonable.

(2) Subject to subsection (3), to exclude or modify the implied warranty of merchantability or any part of it the language must mention "merchantability", be by a writing, and be conspicuous. Subject to subsection (3), to exclude or modify any implied warranty of fitness the exclusion must be by a writing and be conspicuous. Language to exclude all implied warranties of fitness is sufficient if it is in writing, is conspicuous and states, for example, "There is no warranty that the goods will be fit for a particular purpose".

(3) Notwithstanding subsection (2), but subject to subsection (4),

(a) unless the circumstances indicate otherwise, all implied warranties are excluded by expressions like "as is," or "with all faults," or by other language that in common understanding calls the lessee's attention to the exclusion of warranties and makes plain that there is no implied warranty, if in writing and conspicuous;

(b) if the lessee before entering into the lease contract has examined the goods or the sample or model as fully as desired or has refused to examine the goods, there is no implied warranty with regard to defects that an examination ought in the circumstances to have revealed; and

(c) an implied warranty may also be excluded or modified by course of dealing, course of performance, or usage of trade.

(4) To exclude or modify a warranty against interference or against infringement (Section 2A–211) or any part of it, the language must be specific, be by a writing, and be conspicuous, unless the circumstances, including course of performance, course of dealing, or usage of trade, give the lessee reason to know that the goods are being leased subject to a claim or interest of any person.

§ 2A–215. Cumulation and Conflict of Warranties Express or Implied.

Warranties, whether express or implied, must be construed as consistent with each other and as cumulative, but if that construction is unreasonable, the intention of the parties determines which warranty is dominant. In ascertaining that intention the following rules apply:

(a) Exact or technical specifications displace an inconsistent sample or model or general language of description.

(b) A sample from an existing bulk displaces inconsistent general language of description.

(c) Express warranties displace inconsistent implied warranties other than an implied warranty of fitness for a particular purpose.

§ 2A–216. Third-Party Beneficiaries of Express and Implied Warranties.

Alternative A A warranty to or for the benefit of a lessee under this Article, whether express or implied, extends to any natural person who is in the family or household of the lessee or who is a guest in the lessee's home if it is reasonable to expect that such person may use, consume, or be affected by the goods and who is injured in person by breach of the warranty. This section does not displace principles of law and equity that extend a warranty to or for the benefit of a lessee to other persons. The operation of this section may not be excluded, modified, or limited, but an exclusion, modification, or limitation of the warranty, including any with respect to rights and remedies, effective against the lessee is also effective against any beneficiary designated under this section.

Alternative B A warranty to or for the benefit of a lessee under this Article, whether express or implied, extends to any natural person who may reasonably be expected to use, consume, or be affected by the goods and who is injured in person by breach of the warranty. This section does not displace principles of law and equity that extend a warranty to or for the benefit of a lessee to other persons. The operation of this section may not be excluded, modified, or limited, but an exclusion, modification, or limitation of the warranty, including any with respect to rights and remedies, effective against the lessee is also effective against the beneficiary designated under this section.

Alternative C A warranty to or for the benefit of a lessee under this Article, whether express or implied, extends to any person who may reasonably be expected to use, consume, or be affected by the goods and who is injured by breach of the warranty. The operation of this section may not be excluded, modified, or limited with respect to injury to the person of an individual to whom the warranty extends, but an exclusion, modification, or limitation of the warranty, including any with respect to rights and remedies, effective against the lessee is also effective against the beneficiary designated under this section.

§ 2A–217. Identification.

Identification of goods as goods to which a lease contract refers may be made at any time and in any manner explicitly agreed to by the parties. In the absence of explicit agreement, identification occurs:

(a) when the lease contract is made if the lease contract is for a lease of goods that are existing and identified;

(b) when the goods are shipped, marked, or otherwise designated by the lessor as goods to which the lease contract refers, if the lease contract is for a lease of goods that are not existing and identified; or

(c) when the young are conceived, if the lease contract is for a lease of unborn young of animals.

§ 2A–218. Insurance and Proceeds.

(1) A lessee obtains an insurable interest when existing goods are identified to the lease contract even though the goods identified are nonconforming and the lessee has an option to reject them.

(2) If a lessee has an insurable interest only by reason of the lessor's identification of the goods, the lessor, until default or insolvency or notification to the lessee that identification is final, may substitute other goods for those identified.

(3) Notwithstanding a lessee's insurable interest under subsections (1) and (2), the lessor retains an insurable interest until an option to buy has been exercised by the lessee and risk of loss has passed to the lessee.

(4) Nothing in this section impairs any insurable interest recognized under any other statute or rule of law.

(5) The parties by agreement may determine that one or more parties have an obligation to obtain and pay for insurance covering the goods and by agreement may determine the beneficiary of the proceeds of the insurance.

§ 2A–219. Risk of Loss.

(1) Except in the case of a finance lease, risk of loss is retained by the lessor and does not pass to the lessee. In the case of a finance lease, risk of loss passes to the lessee.

(2) Subject to the provisions of this Article on the effect of default on risk of loss (Section 2A–220), if risk of loss is to pass to the lessee and the time of passage is not stated, the following rules apply:

(a) If the lease contract requires or authorizes the goods to be shipped by carrier

(i) and it does not require delivery at a particular destination, the risk of loss passes to the lessee when the goods are duly delivered to the carrier; but

(ii) if it does require delivery at a particular destination and the goods are there duly tendered while in the possession of the carrier, the risk of loss passes to the lessee when the goods are there duly so tendered as to enable the lessee to take delivery.

(b) If the goods are held by a bailee to be delivered without being moved, the risk of loss passes to the lessee on acknowledgment by the bailee of the lessee's right to possession of the goods.

(c) In any case not within subsection (a) or (b), the risk of loss passes to the lessee on the lessee's receipt of the goods if the lessor, or, in the case of a finance lease, the supplier, is a merchant; otherwise the risk passes to the lessee on tender of delivery.

§ 2A–220. Effect of Default on Risk of Loss.

(1) Where risk of loss is to pass to the lessee and the time of passage is not stated:

(a) If a tender or delivery of goods so fails to conform to the lease contract as to give a right of rejection, the risk of their loss remains with the lessor, or, in the case of a finance lease, the supplier, until cure or acceptance.

(b) If the lessee rightfully revokes acceptance, he [or she], to the extent of any deficiency in his [or her] effective insurance coverage, may treat the risk of loss as having remained with the lessor from the beginning.

(2) Whether or not risk of loss is to pass to the lessee, if the lessee as to conforming goods already identified to a lease contract repudiates or is otherwise in default under the lease contract, the lessor, or, in the case of a finance lease, the supplier, to the extent of any deficiency in his [or her] effective insurance coverage may treat the risk of loss as resting on the lessee for a commercially reasonable time.

§ 2A–221. Casualty to Identified Goods.

If a lease contract requires goods identified when the lease contract is made, and the goods suffer casualty without fault of the lessee, the lessor or the supplier before delivery, or the goods suffer casualty before risk of loss passes to the lessee pursuant to the lease agreement or Section 2A–219, then:

(a) if the loss is total, the lease contract is avoided; and

(b) if the loss is partial or the goods have so deteriorated as to no longer conform to the lease contract, the lessee may nevertheless demand inspection and at his [or her] option either treat the lease contract as avoided or, except in a finance lease that is not a consumer lease, accept the goods with due allowance from the rent payable for the balance of the lease term for the deterioration or the deficiency in quantity but without further right against the lessor.

PART 3   EFFECT OF LEASE CONTRACT

§ 2A–301. Enforceability of Lease Contract.

Except as otherwise provided in this Article, a lease contract is effective and enforceable according to its terms between the parties, against purchasers of the goods and against creditors of the parties.

§ 2A–302. Title to and Possession of Goods.

Except as otherwise provided in this Article, each provision of this Article applies whether the lessor or a third party has title to the goods, and whether the lessor, the lessee, or a third party has possession of the goods, notwithstanding any statute or rule of law that possession or the absence of possession is fraudulent.

§ 2A–303. Alienability of Party's Interest Under Lease Contract or of Lessor's Residual Interest in Goods; Delegation of Performance; Transfer of Rights.

(1) As used in this section, "creation of a security interest" includes the sale of a lease contract that is subject to Article 9, Secured Transactions, by reason of Section 9–102(1)(b).

(2) Except as provided in subsections (3) and (4), a provision in a lease agreement which (i) prohibits the voluntary or involuntary transfer, including a transfer by sale, sublease, creation or enforcement of a security interest, or attachment, levy, or other judicial process, of an interest of a party under the lease contract or of the lessor's residual interest in the goods, or (ii) makes such a transfer an event of default, gives rise to the rights and remedies provided in subsection (5), but a transfer that is prohibited or is an event of default under the lease agreement is otherwise effective.

(3) A provision in a lease agreement which (i) prohibits the creation or enforcement of a security interest in an interest of a party under the lease contract or in the lessor's residual interest in the goods, or (ii) makes such a transfer an event of default, is not enforceable unless, and then only to the extent that, there is an actual transfer by the lessee of the lessee's right of possession or use of the goods in violation of the provision or an actual delegation of a material performance of either party to the lease contract in violation of the provision. Neither the granting nor the enforcement of a security interest in (i) the lessor's interest under the lease contract or (ii) the lessor's residual interest in the goods is a transfer that materially impairs the prospect of obtaining return performance by, materially changes the duty of, or materially increases the burden or risk imposed on, the lessee within the purview of subsection (5) unless, and then only to the extent that, there is an actual delegation of a material performance of the lessor.

(4) A provision in a lease agreement which (i) prohibits a transfer of a right to damages for default with respect to the whole lease contract or of a right to payment arising out of the transferor's due performance of the transferor's entire obligation, or (ii) makes such a transfer an event of default, is not enforceable, and such a transfer is not a transfer that materially impairs the prospect of obtaining return performance by, materially changes the duty of, or materially increases the burden or risk imposed on, the other party to the lease contract within the purview of subsection (5).

(5) Subject to subsections (3) and (4):

(a) if a transfer is made which is made an event of default under a lease agreement, the party to the lease contract not making the transfer, unless that party waives the default or otherwise agrees, has the rights and remedies described in Section 2A–501(2);

(b) if paragraph (a) is not applicable and if a transfer is made that (i) is prohibited under a lease agreement or (ii) materially impairs the prospect of obtaining return performance by, materially changes the duty of, or materially increases the burden or risk imposed on, the other party to the lease contract, unless the party not making the transfer agrees at any time to the transfer in the lease contract or otherwise, then, except as limited by contract, (i) the transferor is liable to the party not making the transfer for damages caused by the transfer to the extent that the damages could not reasonably be prevented by the party not making the transfer and (ii) a court having jurisdiction may grant other appropriate relief, including cancellation of the lease contract or an injunction against the transfer.

(6) A transfer of "the lease" or of "all my rights under the lease", or a transfer in similar general terms, is a transfer of rights and, unless the language or the circumstances, as in a transfer for security, indicate the contrary, the transfer is a delegation of duties by the transferor to the transferee. Acceptance by the transferee constitutes a promise by the transferee to perform those duties. The promise is enforceable by either the transferor or the other party to the lease contract.

(7) Unless otherwise agreed by the lessor and the lessee, a delegation of performance does not relieve the transferor as against the other party of any duty to perform or of any liability for default.

(8) In a consumer lease, to prohibit the transfer of an interest of a party under the lease contract or to make a transfer an event of default, the language must be specific, by a writing, and conspicuous.

As amended in 1990.

§ 2A–304. Subsequent Lease of Goods by Lessor.

(1) Subject to Section 2A–303, a subsequent lessee from a lessor of goods under an existing lease contract obtains, to the extent of the leasehold interest transferred, the leasehold interest in the goods that the lessor had or had power to transfer, and except as provided in subsection (2) and Section 2A–527(4), takes subject to the existing lease contract. A lessor with voidable title has power to transfer a good leasehold interest to a good faith subsequent lessee for value, but only to the extent set forth in the preceding sentence. If goods have been delivered under a transaction of purchase, the lessor has that power even though:

(a) the lessor's transferor was deceived as to the identity of the lessor;

(b) the delivery was in exchange for a check which is later dishonored;

(c) it was agreed that the transaction was to be a "cash sale"; or

(d) the delivery was procured through fraud punishable as larcenous under the criminal law.

(2) A subsequent lessee in the ordinary course of business from a lessor who is a merchant dealing in goods of that kind to whom the goods were entrusted by the existing lessee of that lessor before the interest of the subsequent lessee became enforceable against that lessor obtains, to the extent of the leasehold interest transferred, all of that lessor's and the existing lessee's rights to the goods, and takes free of the existing lease contract.

(3) A subsequent lessee from the lessor of goods that are subject to an existing lease contract and are covered by a certificate of title issued under a statute of this State or of another jurisdiction takes no greater rights than those provided both by this section and by the certificate of title statute.

As amended in 1990.

§ 2A–305. Sale or Sublease of Goods by Lessee.

(1) Subject to the provisions of Section 2A–303, a buyer or sublessee from the lessee of goods under an existing lease contract obtains, to the extent of the interest transferred, the leasehold interest in the goods that the lessee had or had power to transfer, and except as provided in subsection (2) and Section 2A–511(4), takes subject to the existing lease contract. A lessee with a voidable leasehold interest has power to transfer a good leasehold interest to a good faith buyer for value or a good faith sublessee for value, but only to the extent set forth in the preceding sentence. When goods have been delivered under a transaction of lease the lessee has that power even though:

(a) the lessor was deceived as to the identity of the lessee;

(b) the delivery was in exchange for a check which is later dishonored; or

(c) the delivery was procured through fraud punishable as larcenous under the criminal law.

(2) A buyer in the ordinary course of business or a sublessee in the ordinary course of business from a lessee who is a merchant dealing in goods of that kind to whom the goods were entrusted by the lessor obtains, to the extent of the interest transferred, all of the lessor's and lessee's rights to the goods, and takes free of the existing lease contract.

(3) A buyer or sublessee from the lessee of goods that are subject to an existing lease contract and are covered by a certificate of title issued under a statute of this State or of another jurisdiction takes no greater rights than those provided both by this section and by the certificate of title statute.

§ 2A–306. Priority of Certain Liens Arising by Operation of Law.

If a person in the ordinary course of his [or her] business furnishes services or materials with respect to goods subject to a lease contract, a lien upon those goods in the possession of that person given by statute or rule of law for those materials or services takes priority over any interest of the lessor or lessee under the lease contract or this Article unless the lien is created by statute and the statute provides otherwise or unless the lien is created by rule of law and the rule of law provides otherwise.

§ 2A–307. Priority of Liens Arising by Attachment or Levy on, Security Interests in, and Other Claims to Goods.

(1) Except as otherwise provided in Section 2A–306, a creditor of a lessee takes subject to the lease contract.

(2) Except as otherwise provided in subsections (3) and (4) and in Sections 2A–306 and 2A–308, a creditor of a lessor takes subject to the lease contract unless:

(a) the creditor holds a lien that attached to the goods before the lease contract became enforceable;

(b) the creditor holds a security interest in the goods and the lessee did not give value and receive delivery of the goods without knowledge of the security interest; or

(c) the creditor holds a security interest in the goods which was perfected (Section 9–303) before the lease contract became enforceable.

(3) A lessee in the ordinary course of business takes the leasehold interest free of a security interest in the goods created by the lessor even though the security interest is per-

fected (Section 9–303) and the lessee knows of its existence.

(4) A lessee other than a lessee in the ordinary course of business takes the leasehold interest free of a security interest to the extent that it secures future advances made after the secured party acquires knowledge of the lease or more than 45 days after the lease contract becomes enforceable, whichever first occurs, unless the future advances are made pursuant to a commitment entered into without knowledge of the lease and before the expiration of the 45-day period. As amended in 1990.

§ 2A–308. Special Rights of Creditors.

(1) A creditor of a lessor in possession of goods subject to a lease contract may treat the lease contract as void if as against the creditor retention of possession by the lessor is fraudulent under any statute or rule of law, but retention of possession in good faith and current course of trade by the lessor for a commercially reasonable time after the lease contract becomes enforceable is not fraudulent.

(2) Nothing in this Article impairs the rights of creditors of a lessor if the lease contract (a) becomes enforceable, not in current course of trade but in satisfaction of or as security for a pre-existing claim for money, security, or the like, and (b) is made under circumstances which under any statute or rule of law apart from this Article would constitute the transaction a fraudulent transfer or voidable preference.

(3) A creditor of a seller may treat a sale or an identification of goods to a contract for sale as void if as against the creditor retention of possession by the seller is fraudulent under any statute or rule of law, but retention of possession of the goods pursuant to a lease contract entered into by the seller as lessee and the buyer as lessor in connection with the sale or identification of the goods is not fraudulent if the buyer bought for value and in good faith.

§ 2A–309. Lessor's and Lessee's Rights When Goods Become Fixtures.

(1) In this section:

(a) goods are "fixtures" when they become so related to particular real estate that an interest in them arises under real estate law;

(b) a "fixture filing" is the filing, in the office where a mortgage on the real estate would be filed or recorded, of a financing statement covering goods that are or are to become fixtures and conforming to the requirements of Section 9–402(5);

(c) a lease is a "purchase money lease" unless the lessee has possession or use of the goods or the right to possession or use of the goods before the lease agreement is enforceable;

(d) a mortgage is a "construction mortgage" to the extent it secures an obligation incurred for the construction of an improvement on land including the acquisition cost of the land, if the recorded writing so indicates; and

(e) "encumbrance" includes real estate mortgages and other liens on real estate and all other rights in real estate that are not ownership interests.

(2) Under this Article a lease may be of goods that are fixtures or may continue in goods that become fixtures, but no lease exists under this Article of ordinary building materials incorporated into an improvement on land.

(3) This Article does not prevent creation of a lease of fixtures pursuant to real estate law.

(4) The perfected interest of a lessor of fixtures has priority over a conflicting interest of an encumbrancer or owner of the real estate if:

(a) the lease is a purchase money lease, the conflicting interest of the encumbrancer or owner arises before the goods become fixtures, the interest of the lessor is perfected by a fixture filing before the goods become fixtures or within ten days thereafter, and the lessee has an interest of record in the real estate or is in possession of the real estate; or

(b) the interest of the lessor is perfected by a fixture filing before the interest of the encumbrancer or owner is of record, the lessor's interest has priority over any conflicting interest of a predecessor in title of the encumbrancer or owner, and the lessee has an interest of record in the real estate or is in possession of the real estate.

(5) The interest of a lessor of fixtures, whether or not perfected, has priority over the conflicting interest of an encumbrancer or owner of the real estate if:

(a) the fixtures are readily removable factory or office machines, readily removable equipment that is not primarily used or leased for use in the operation of the real estate, or readily removable replacements of domestic appliances that are goods subject to a consumer lease, and before the goods become fixtures the lease contract is enforceable; or

(b) the conflicting interest is a lien on the real estate obtained by legal or equitable proceedings after the lease contract is enforceable; or

(c) the encumbrancer or owner has consented in writing to the lease or has disclaimed an interest in the goods as fixtures; or

(d) the lessee has a right to remove the goods as against the encumbrancer or owner. If the lessee's right to remove terminates, the priority of the interest of the lessor continues for a reasonable time.

(6) Notwithstanding subsection (4)(a) but otherwise subject to subsections (4) and (5), the interest of a lessor of fixtures, including the lessor's residual interest, is subordinate to the conflicting interest of an encumbrancer of the real estate under a construction mortgage recorded before the goods become fixtures if the goods become fixtures before the completion of the construction. To the extent given to refinance a construction mortgage, the conflicting interest of an encumbrancer of the real estate under a mortgage has this priority to the same extent as the encumbrancer of the real estate under the construction mortgage.

(7) In cases not within the preceding subsections, priority between the interest of a lessor of fixtures, including the lessor's residual interest, and the conflicting interest of an encumbrancer or owner of the real estate who is not the lessee is determined by the priority rules governing conflicting interests in real estate.

(8) If the interest of a lessor of fixtures, including the lessor's residual interest, has priority over all conflicting interests of all owners and encumbrancers of the real estate, the lessor

or the lessee may (i) on default, expiration, termination, or cancellation of the lease agreement but subject to the agreement and this Article, or (ii) if necessary to enforce other rights and remedies of the lessor or lessee under this Article, remove the goods from the real estate, free and clear of all conflicting interests of all owners and encumbrancers of the real estate, but the lessor or lessee must reimburse any encumbrancer or owner of the real estate who is not the lessee and who has not otherwise agreed for the cost of repair of any physical injury, but not for any diminution in value of the real estate caused by the absence of the goods removed or by any necessity of replacing them. A person entitled to reimbursement may refuse permission to remove until the party seeking removal gives adequate security for the performance of this obligation.

(9) Even though the lease agreement does not create a security interest, the interest of a lessor of fixtures, including the lessor's residual interest, is perfected by filing a financing statement as a fixture filing for leased goods that are or are to become fixtures in accordance with the relevant provisions of the Article on Secured Transactions (Article 9).
As amended in 1990.

§ 2A–310. Lessor's and Lessee's Rights When Goods Become Accessions.

(1) Goods are "accessions" when they are installed in or affixed to other goods.

(2) The interest of a lessor or a lessee under a lease contract entered into before the goods became accessions is superior to all interests in the whole except as stated in subsection (4).

(3) The interest of a lessor or a lessee under a lease contract entered into at the time or after the goods became accessions is superior to all subsequently acquired interests in the whole except as stated in subsection (4) but is subordinate to interests in the whole existing at the time the lease contract was made unless the holders of such interests in the whole have in writing consented to the lease or disclaimed an interest in the goods as part of the whole.

(4) The interest of a lessor or a lessee under a lease contract described in subsection (2) or (3) is subordinate to the interest of

(a) a buyer in the ordinary course of business or a lessee in the ordinary course of business of any interest in the whole acquired after the goods became accessions; or

(b) a creditor with a security interest in the whole perfected before the lease contract was made to the extent that the creditor makes subsequent advances without knowledge of the lease contract.

(5) When under subsections (2) or (3) and (4) a lessor or a lessee of accessions holds an interest that is superior to all interests in the whole, the lessor or the lessee may (a) on default, expiration, termination, or cancellation of the lease contract by the other party but subject to the provisions of the lease contract and this Article, or (b) if necessary to enforce his [or her] other rights and remedies under this Article, remove the goods from the whole, free and clear of all interests in the whole, but he [or she] must reimburse any holder of an interest in the whole who is not the lessee and who has not otherwise agreed for the cost of repair of any physical injury but not for any diminution in value of the whole caused by the absence of the goods removed or by any necessity for replacing them. A person entitled to reimbursement may refuse permission to remove until the party seeking removal gives adequate security for the performance of this obligation.

§ 2A–311. Priority Subject to Subordination.

Nothing in this Article prevents subordination by agreement by any person entitled to priority.
As added in 1990.

PART 4 PERFORMANCE OF LEASE CONTRACT: REPUDIATED, SUBSTITUTED AND EXCUSED

§ 2A–401. Insecurity: Adequate Assurance of Performance.

(1) A lease contract imposes an obligation on each party that the other's expectation of receiving due performance will not be impaired.

(2) If reasonable grounds for insecurity arise with respect to the performance of either party, the insecure party may demand in writing adequate assurance of due performance. Until the insecure party receives that assurance, if commercially reasonable the insecure party may suspend any performance for which he [or she] has not already received the agreed return.

(3) A repudiation of the lease contract occurs if assurance of due performance adequate under the circumstances of the particular case is not provided to the insecure party within a reasonable time, not to exceed 30 days after receipt of a demand by the other party.

(4) Between merchants, the reasonableness of grounds for insecurity and the adequacy of any assurance offered must be determined according to commercial standards.

(5) Acceptance of any nonconforming delivery or payment does not prejudice the aggrieved party's right to demand adequate assurance of future performance.

§ 2A–402. Anticipatory Repudiation.

If either party repudiates a lease contract with respect to a performance not yet due under the lease contract, the loss of which performance will substantially impair the value of the lease contract to the other, the aggrieved party may:

(a) for a commercially reasonable time, await retraction of repudiation and performance by the repudiating party;

(b) make demand pursuant to Section 2A–401 and await assurance of future performance adequate under the circumstances of the particular case; or

(c) resort to any right or remedy upon default under the lease contract or this Article, even though the aggrieved party has notified the repudiating party that the aggrieved party would await the repudiating party's performance and assurance and has urged retraction. In addition, whether or not the aggrieved party is pursuing one of the foregoing remedies, the aggrieved party may suspend performance or, if the aggrieved party is the lessor, proceed in accordance with the provisions of this Article on the lessor's right to identify goods to the lease contract notwithstanding default or to salvage unfinished goods (Section 2A–524).

§ 2A–403. Retraction of Anticipatory Repudiation.

(1) Until the repudiating party's next performance is due, the repudiating party can retract the repudiation unless, since the repudiation, the aggrieved party has cancelled the lease contract or materially changed the aggrieved party's position or otherwise indicated that the aggrieved party considers the repudiation final.

(2) Retraction may be by any method that clearly indicates to the aggrieved party that the repudiating party intends to perform under the lease contract and includes any assurance demanded under Section 2A–401.

(3) Retraction reinstates a repudiating party's rights under a lease contract with due excuse and allowance to the aggrieved party for any delay occasioned by the repudiation.

§ 2A–404. Substituted Performance.

(1) If without fault of the lessee, the lessor and the supplier, the agreed berthing, loading, or unloading facilities fail or the agreed type of carrier becomes unavailable or the agreed manner of delivery otherwise becomes commercially impracticable, but a commercially reasonable substitute is available, the substitute performance must be tendered and accepted.

(2) If the agreed means or manner of payment fails because of domestic or foreign governmental regulation:

(a) the lessor may withhold or stop delivery or cause the supplier to withhold or stop delivery unless the lessee provides a means or manner of payment that is commercially a substantial equivalent; and

(b) if delivery has already been taken, payment by the means or in the manner provided by the regulation discharges the lessee's obligation unless the regulation is discriminatory, oppressive, or predatory.

§ 2A–405. Excused Performance.

Subject to Section 2A–404 on substituted performance, the following rules apply:

(a) Delay in delivery or nondelivery in whole or in part by a lessor or a supplier who complies with paragraphs (b) and (c) is not a default under the lease contract if performance as agreed has been made impracticable by the occurrence of a contingency the nonoccurrence of which was a basic assumption on which the lease contract was made or by compliance in good faith with any applicable foreign or domestic governmental regulation or order, whether or not the regulation or order later proves to be invalid.

(b) If the causes mentioned in paragraph (a) affect only part of the lessor's or the supplier's capacity to perform, he [or she] shall allocate production and deliveries among his [or her] customers but at his [or her] option may include regular customers not then under contract for sale or lease as well as his [or her] own requirements for further manufacture. He [or she] may so allocate in any manner that is fair and reasonable.

(c) The lessor seasonally shall notify the lessee and in the case of a finance lease the supplier seasonally shall notify the lessor and the lessee, if known, that there will be delay or nondelivery and, if allocation is required under paragraph (b), of the estimated quota thus made available for the lessee.

§ 2A–406. Procedure on Excused Performance.

(1) If the lessee receives notification of a material or indefinite delay or an allocation justified under Section 2A–405, the lessee may by written notification to the lessor as to any goods involved, and with respect to all of the goods if under an installment lease contract the value of the whole lease contract is substantially impaired (Section 2A–510):

(a) terminate the lease contract (Section 2A–505(2)); or

(b) except in a finance lease that is not a consumer lease, modify the lease contract by accepting the available quota in substitution, with due allowance from the rent payable for the balance of the lease term for the deficiency but without further right against the lessor.

(2) If, after receipt of a notification from the lessor under Section 2A–405, the lessee fails so to modify the lease agreement within a reasonable time not exceeding 30 days, the lease contract lapses with respect to any deliveries affected.

§ 2A–407. Irrevocable Promises: Finance Leases.

(1) In the case of a finance lease that is not a consumer lease the lessee's promises under the lease contract become irrevocable and independent upon the lessee's acceptance of the goods.

(2) A promise that has become irrevocable and independent under subsection (1):

(a) is effective and enforceable between the parties, and by or against third parties including assignees of the parties; and

(b) is not subject to cancellation, termination, modification, repudiation, excuse, or substitution without the consent of the party to whom the promise runs.

(3) This section does not affect the validity under any other law of a covenant in any lease contract making the lessee's promises irrevocable and independent upon the lessee's acceptance of the goods.

As amended in 1990.

PART 5   DEFAULT

A. In General

§ 2A–501. Default: Procedure.

(1) Whether the lessor or the lessee is in default under a lease contract is determined by the lease agreement and this Article.

(2) If the lessor or the lessee is in default under the lease contract, the party seeking enforcement has rights and remedies as provided in this Article and, except as limited by this Article, as provided in the lease agreement.

(3) If the lessor or the lessee is in default under the lease contract, the party seeking enforcement may reduce the party's claim to judgment, or otherwise enforce the lease contract by self-help or any available judicial procedure or nonjudicial procedure, including administrative proceeding, arbitration, or the like, in accordance with this Article.

(4) Except as otherwise provided in Section 1–106(1) or this

Article or the lease agreement, the rights and remedies referred to in subsections (2) and (3) are cumulative.

(5) If the lease agreement covers both real property and goods, the party seeking enforcement may proceed under this Part as to the goods, or under other applicable law as to both the real property and the goods in accordance with that party's rights and remedies in respect of the real property, in which case this Part does not apply.

As amended in 1990.

§ 2A–502. Notice After Default.

Except as otherwise provided in this Article or the lease agreement, the lessor or lessee in default under the lease contract is not entitled to notice of default or notice of enforcement from the other party to the lease agreement.

§ 2A–503. Modification or Impairment of Rights and Remedies.

(1) Except as otherwise provided in this Article, the lease agreement may include rights and remedies for default in addition to or in substitution for those provided in this Article and may limit or alter the measure of damages recoverable under this Article.

(2) Resort to a remedy provided under this Article or in the lease agreement is optional unless the remedy is expressly agreed to be exclusive. If circumstances cause an exclusive or limited remedy to fail of its essential purpose, or provision for an exclusive remedy is unconscionable, remedy may be had as provided in this Article.

(3) Consequential damages may be liquidated under Section 2A–504, or may otherwise be limited, altered, or excluded unless the limitation, alteration, or exclusion is unconscionable. Limitation, alteration, or exclusion of consequential damages for injury to the person in the case of consumer goods is prima facie unconscionable but limitation, alteration, or exclusion of damages where the loss is commercial is not prima facie unconscionable.

(4) Rights and remedies on default by the lessor or the lessee with respect to any obligation or promise collateral or ancillary to the lease contract are not impaired by this Article.

As amended in 1990.

§ 2A–504. Liquidation of Damages.

(1) Damages payable by either party for default, or any other act or omission, including indemnity for loss or diminution of anticipated tax benefits or loss or damage to lessor's residual interest, may be liquidated in the lease agreement but only at an amount or by a formula that is reasonable in light of the then anticipated harm caused by the default or other act or omission.

(2) If the lease agreement provides for liquidation of damages, and such provision does not comply with subsection (1), or such provision is an exclusive or limited remedy that circumstances cause to fail of its essential purpose, remedy may be had as provided in this Article.

(3) If the lessor justifiably withholds or stops delivery of goods because of the lessee's default or insolvency (Section 2A–525 or 2A–526), the lessee is entitled to restitution of any

amount by which the sum of his [or her] payments exceeds:

(a) the amount to which the lessor is entitled by virtue of terms liquidating the lessor's damages in accordance with subsection (1); or

(b) in the absence of those terms, 20 percent of the then present value of the total rent the lessee was obligated to pay for the balance of the lease term, or, in the case of a consumer lease, the lesser of such amount or $500.

(4) A lessee's right to restitution under subsection (3) is subject to offset to the extent the lessor establishes:

(a) a right to recover damages under the provisions of this Article other than subsection (1); and

(b) the amount or value of any benefits received by the lessee directly or indirectly by reason of the lease contract.

§ 2A–505. Cancellation and Termination and Effect of Cancellation, Termination, Rescission, or Fraud on Rights and Remedies.

(1) On cancellation of the lease contract, all obligations that are still executory on both sides are discharged, but any right based on prior default or performance survives, and the cancelling party also retains any remedy for default of the whole lease contract or any unperformed balance.

(2) On termination of the lease contract, all obligations that are still executory on both sides are discharged but any right based on prior default or performance survives.

(3) Unless the contrary intention clearly appears, expressions of "cancellation," "rescission," or the like of the lease contract may not be construed as a renunciation or discharge of any claim in damages for an antecedent default.

(4) Rights and remedies for material misrepresentation or fraud include all rights and remedies available under this Article for default.

(5) Neither rescission nor a claim for rescission of the lease contract nor rejection or return of the goods may bar or be deemed inconsistent with a claim for damages or other right or remedy.

§ 2A–506. Statute of Limitations.

(1) An action for default under a lease contract, including breach of warranty or indemnity, must be commenced within 4 years after the cause of action accrued. By the original lease contract the parties may reduce the period of limitation to not less than one year.

(2) A cause of action for default accrues when the act or omission on which the default or breach of warranty is based is or should have been discovered by the aggrieved party, or when the default occurs, whichever is later. A cause of action for indemnity accrues when the act or omission on which the claim for indemnity is based is or should have been discovered by the indemnified party, whichever is later.

(3) If an action commenced within the time limited by subsection (1) is so terminated as to leave available a remedy by another action for the same default or breach of warranty or indemnity, the other action may be commenced after the expiration of the time limited and within 6 months after the

termination of the first action unless the termination resulted from voluntary discontinuance or from dismissal for failure or neglect to prosecute.

(4) This section does not alter the law on tolling of the statute of limitations nor does it apply to causes of action that have accrued before this Article becomes effective.

§ 2A–507. Proof of Market Rent: Time and Place.

(1) Damages based on market rent (Section 2A–519 or 2A–528) are determined according to the rent for the use of the goods concerned for a lease term identical to the remaining lease term of the original lease agreement and prevailing at the times specified in Sections 2A–519 and 2A–528.

(2) If evidence of rent for the use of the goods concerned for a lease term identical to the remaining lease term of the original lease agreement and prevailing at the times or places described in this Article is not readily available, the rent prevailing within any reasonable time before or after the time described or at any other place or for a different lease term which in commercial judgment or under usage of trade would serve as a reasonable substitute for the one described may be used, making any proper allowance for the difference, including the cost of transporting the goods to or from the other place.

(3) Evidence of a relevant rent prevailing at a time or place or for a lease term other than the one described in this Article offered by one party is not admissible unless and until he [or she] has given the other party notice the court finds sufficient to prevent unfair surprise.

(4) If the prevailing rent or value of any goods regularly leased in any established market is in issue, reports in official publications or trade journals or in newspapers or periodicals of general circulation published as the reports of that market are admissible in evidence. The circumstances of the preparation of the report may be shown to affect its weight but not its admissibility.

As amended in 1990.

B. Default by Lessor

§ 2A–508. Lessee's Remedies.

(1) If a lessor fails to deliver the goods in conformity to the lease contract (Section 2A–509) or repudiates the lease contract (Section 2A–402), or a lessee rightfully rejects the goods (Section 2A–509) or justifiably revokes acceptance of the goods (Section 2A–517), then with respect to any goods involved, and with respect to all of the goods if under an installment lease contract the value of the whole lease contract is substantially impaired (Section 2A–510), the lessor is in default under the lease contract and the lessee may:

    (a) cancel the lease contract (Section 2A–505(1));

    (b) recover so much of the rent and security as has been paid and is just under the circumstances;

    (c) cover and recover damages as to all goods affected whether or not they have been identified to the lease contract (Sections 2A–518 and 2A–520), or recover damages for nondelivery (Sections 2A–519 and 2A–520);

    (d) exercise any other rights or pursue any other remedies provided in the lease contract.

(2) If a lessor fails to deliver the goods in conformity to the lease contract or repudiates the lease contract, the lessee may also:

    (a) if the goods have been identified, recover them (Section 2A–522); or

    (b) in a proper case, obtain specific performance or replevy the goods (Section 2A–521).

(3) If a lessor is otherwise in default under a lease contract, the lessee may exercise the rights and pursue the remedies provided in the lease contract, which may include a right to cancel the lease, and in Section 2A–519(3).

(4) If a lessor has breached a warranty, whether express or implied, the lessee may recover damages (Section 2A–519(4)).

(5) On rightful rejection or justifiable revocation of acceptance, a lessee has a security interest in goods in the lessee's possession or control for any rent and security that has been paid and any expenses reasonably incurred in their inspection, receipt, transportation, and care and custody and may hold those goods and dispose of them in good faith and in a commercially reasonable manner, subject to Section 2A–527(5).

(6) Subject to the provisions of Section 2A–407, a lessee, on notifying the lessor of the lessee's intention to do so, may deduct all or any part of the damages resulting from any default under the lease contract from any part of the rent still due under the same lease contract.

As amended in 1990.

§ 2A–509. Lessee's Rights on Improper Delivery; Rightful Rejection.

(1) Subject to the provisions of Section 2A–510 on default in installment lease contracts, if the goods or the tender or delivery fail in any respect to conform to the lease contract, the lessee may reject or accept the goods or accept any commercial unit or units and reject the rest of the goods.

(2) Rejection of goods is ineffective unless it is within a reasonable time after tender or delivery of the goods and the lessee seasonably notifies the lessor.

§ 2A–510. Installment Lease Contracts: Rejection and Default.

(1) Under an installment lease contract a lessee may reject any delivery that is nonconforming if the nonconformity substantially impairs the value of that delivery and cannot be cured or the nonconformity is a defect in the required documents; but if the nonconformity does not fall within subsection (2) and the lessor or the supplier gives adequate assurance of its cure, the lessee must accept that delivery.

(2) Whenever nonconformity or default with respect to one or more deliveries substantially impairs the value of the installment lease contract as a whole there is a default with respect to the whole. But, the aggrieved party reinstates the installment lease contract as a whole if the aggrieved party accepts a nonconforming delivery without seasonably notifying of cancellation or brings an action with respect only to past deliveries or demands performance as to future deliveries.

§ 2A–511. Merchant Lessee's Duties as to Rightfully Rejected Goods.

(1) Subject to any security interest of a lessee (Section 2A–508(5)), if a lessor or a supplier has no agent or place of business at the market of rejection, a merchant lessee, after rejection of goods in his [or her] possession or control, shall follow any reasonable instructions received from the lessor or the supplier with respect to the goods. In the absence of those instructions, a merchant lessee shall make reasonable efforts to sell, lease, or otherwise dispose of the goods for the lessor's account if they threaten to decline in value speedily. Instructions are not reasonable if on demand indemnity for expenses is not forthcoming.

(2) If a merchant lessee (subsection (1)) or any other lessee (Section 2A–512) disposes of goods, he [or she] is entitled to reimbursement either from the lessor or the supplier or out of the proceeds for reasonable expenses of caring for and disposing of the goods and, if the expenses include no disposition commission, to such commission as is usual in the trade, or if there is none, to a reasonable sum not exceeding 10 percent of the gross proceeds.

(3) In complying with this section or Section 2A–512, the lessee is held only to good faith. Good faith conduct hereunder is neither acceptance or conversion nor the basis of an action for damages.

(4) A purchaser who purchases in good faith from a lessee pursuant to this section or Section 2A–512 takes the goods free of any rights of the lessor and the supplier even though the lessee fails to comply with one or more of the requirements of this Article.

§ 2A–512. Lessee's Duties as to Rightfully Rejected Goods.

(1) Except as otherwise provided with respect to goods that threaten to decline in value speedily (Section 2A–511) and subject to any security interest of a lessee (Section 2A–508(5)):

(a) the lessee, after rejection of goods in the lessee's possession, shall hold them with reasonable care at the lessor's or the supplier's disposition for a reasonable time after the lessee's seasonable notification of rejection;

(b) if the lessor or the supplier gives no instructions within a reasonable time after notification of rejection, the lessee may store the rejected goods for the lessor's or the supplier's account or ship them to the lessor or the supplier or dispose of them for the lessor's or the supplier's account with reimbursement in the manner provided in Section 2A–511; but

(c) the lessee has no further obligations with regard to goods rightfully rejected.

(2) Action by the lessee pursuant to subsection (1) is not acceptance or conversion.

§ 2A–513. Cure by Lessor of Improper Tender or Delivery; Replacement.

(1) If any tender or delivery by the lessor or the supplier is rejected because nonconforming and the time for performance has not yet expired, the lessor or the supplier may seasonably notify the lessee of the lessor's or the supplier's intention to cure and may then make a conforming delivery within the time provided in the lease contract.

(2) If the lessee rejects a nonconforming tender that the lessor or the supplier had reasonable grounds to believe would be acceptable with or without money allowance, the lessor or the supplier may have a further reasonable time to substitute a conforming tender if he [or she] seasonably notifies the lessee.

§ 2A–514. Waiver of Lessee's Objections.

(1) In rejecting goods, a lessee's failure to state a particular defect that is ascertainable by reasonable inspection precludes the lessee from relying on the defect to justify rejection or to establish default:

(a) if, stated seasonably, the lessor or the supplier could have cured it (Section 2A–513); or

(b) between merchants if the lessor or the supplier after rejection has made a request in writing for a full and final written statement of all defects on which the lessee proposes to rely.

(2) A lessee's failure to reserve rights when paying rent or other consideration against documents precludes recovery of the payment for defects apparent on the face of the documents.

§ 2A–515. Acceptance of Goods.

(1) Acceptance of goods occurs after the lessee has had a reasonable opportunity to inspect the goods and

(a) the lessee signifies or acts with respect to the goods in a manner that signifies to the lessor or the supplier that the goods are conforming or that the lessee will take or retain them in spite of their nonconformity; or

(b) the lessee fails to make an effective rejection of the goods (Section 2A–509(2)).

(2) Acceptance of a part of any commercial unit is acceptance of that entire unit.

§ 2A–516. Effect of Acceptance of Goods; Notice of Default; Burden of Establishing Default After Acceptance; Notice of Claim or Litigation to Person Answerable Over.

(1) A lessee must pay rent for any goods accepted in accordance with the lease contract, with due allowance for goods rightfully rejected or not delivered.

(2) A lessee's acceptance of goods precludes rejection of the goods accepted. In the case of a finance lease, if made with knowledge of a nonconformity, acceptance cannot be revoked because of it. In any other case, if made with knowledge of a nonconformity, acceptance cannot be revoked because of it unless the acceptance was on the reasonable assumption that the nonconformity would be seasonably cured. Acceptance does not of itself impair any other remedy provided by this Article or the lease agreement for nonconformity.

(3) If a tender has been accepted:

(a) within a reasonable time after the lessee discovers or should have discovered any default, the lessee shall notify the lessor and the supplier, if any, or be barred from any remedy against the party not notified;

(b) except in the case of a consumer lease, within a reasonable time after the lessee receives notice of litigation for infringement or the like (Section 2A–211) the lessee shall notify the lessor or be barred from any remedy over for liability established by the litigation; and

(c) the burden is on the lessee to establish any default.

(4) If a lessee is sued for breach of a warranty or other obligation for which a lessor or a supplier is answerable over the following apply:

(a) The lessee may give the lessor or the supplier, or both, written notice of the litigation. If the notice states that the person notified may come in and defend and that if the person notified does not do so that person will be bound in any action against that person by the lessee by any determination of fact common to the two litigations, then unless the person notified after seasonable receipt of the notice does come in and defend that person is so bound.

(b) The lessor or the supplier may demand in writing that the lessee turn over control of the litigation including settlement if the claim is one for infringement or the like (Section 2A–211) or else be barred from any remedy over. If the demand states that the lessor or the supplier agrees to bear all expense and to satisfy any adverse judgment, then unless the lessee after seasonable receipt of the demand does turn over control the lessee is so barred.

(5) Subsections (3) and (4) apply to any obligation of a lessee to hold the lessor or the supplier harmless against infringement or the like (Section 2A–211).

As amended in 1990.

§ 2A–517. Revocation of Acceptance of Goods.

(1) A lessee may revoke acceptance of a lot or commercial unit whose nonconformity substantially impairs its value to the lessee if the lessee has accepted it:

(a) except in the case of a finance lease, on the reasonable assumption that its nonconformity would be cured and it has not been seasonably cured; or

(b) without discovery of the nonconformity if the lessee's acceptance was reasonably induced either by the lessor's assurances or, except in the case of a finance lease, by the difficulty of discovery before acceptance.

(2) Except in the case of a finance lease that is not a consumer lease, a lessee may revoke acceptance of a lot or commercial unit if the lessor defaults under the lease contract and the default substantially impairs the value of that lot or commercial unit to the lessee.

(3) If the lease agreement so provides, the lessee may revoke acceptance of a lot or commercial unit because of other defaults by the lessor.

(4) Revocation of acceptance must occur within a reasonable time after the lessee discovers or should have discovered the ground for it and before any substantial change in condition of the goods which is not caused by the nonconformity. Revocation is not effective until the lessee notifies the lessor.

(5) A lessee who so revokes has the same rights and duties with regard to the goods involved as if the lessee had rejected them.

As amended in 1990.

§ 2A–518. Cover; Substitute Goods.

(1) After a default by a lessor under the lease contract of the type described in Section 2A–508(1), or, if agreed, after other default by the lessor, the lessee may cover by making any purchase or lease of or contract to purchase or lease goods in substitution for those due from the lessor.

(2) Except as otherwise provided with respect to damages liquidated in the lease agreement (Section 2A–504) or otherwise determined pursuant to agreement of the parties (Sections 1–102(3) and 2A–503), if a lessee's cover is by a lease agreement substantially similar to the original lease agreement and the new lease agreement is made in good faith and in a commercially reasonable manner, the lessee may recover from the lessor as damages (i) the present value, as of the date of the commencement of the term of the new lease agreement, of the rent under the new lease agreement applicable to that period of the new lease term which is comparable to the then remaining term of the original lease agreement minus the present value as of the same date of the total rent for the then remaining lease term of the original lease agreement, and (ii) any incidental or consequential damages, less expenses saved in consequence of the lessor's default.

(3) If a lessee's cover is by lease agreement that for any reason does not qualify for treatment under subsection (2), or is by purchase or otherwise, the lessee may recover from the lessor as if the lessee had elected not to cover and Section 2A–519 governs.

As amended in 1990.

§ 2A–519. Lessee's Damages for Non-delivery, Repudiation, Default, and Breach of Warranty in Regard to Accepted Goods.

(1) Except as otherwise provided with respect to damages liquidated in the lease agreement (Section 2A–504) or otherwise determined pursuant to agreement of the parties (Sections 1–102(3) and 2A–503), if a lessee elects not to cover or a lessee elects to cover and the cover is by lease agreement that for any reason does not qualify for treatment under Section 2A–518(2), or is by purchase or otherwise, the measure of damages for non-delivery or repudiation by the lessor or for rejection or revocation of acceptance by the lessee is the present value, as of the date of the default, of the then market rent minus the present value as of the same date of the original rent, computed for the remaining lease term of the original lease agreement, together with incidental and consequential damages, less expenses saved in consequence of the lessor's default.

(2) Market rent is to be determined as of the place for tender or, in cases of rejection after arrival or revocation of acceptance, as of the place of arrival.

(3) Except as otherwise agreed, if the lessee has accepted goods and given notification (Section 2A–516(3)), the measure of damages for non-conforming tender or delivery or other default by a lessor is the loss resulting in the ordinary course of events from the lessor's default as determined in any manner that is reasonable together with incidental and consequential damages, less expenses saved in consequence of the lessor's default.

(4) Except as otherwise agreed, the measure of damages for breach of warranty is the present value at the time and place of acceptance of the difference between the value of the use of the goods accepted and the value if they had been as warranted for the lease term, unless special circumstances show proximate damages of a different amount, together with incidental and consequential damages, less expenses saved in consequence of the lessor's default or breach of warranty. As amended in 1990.

§ 2A–520. Lessee's Incidental and Consequential Damages.

(1) Incidental damages resulting from a lessor's default include expenses reasonably incurred in inspection, receipt, transportation, and care and custody of goods rightfully rejected or goods the acceptance of which is justifiably revoked, any commercially reasonable charges, expenses or commissions in connection with effecting cover, and any other reasonable expense incident to the default.

(2) Consequential damages resulting from a lessor's default include:

(a) any loss resulting from general or particular requirements and needs of which the lessor at the time of contracting had reason to know and which could not reasonably be prevented by cover or otherwise; and

(b) injury to person or property proximately resulting from any breach of warranty.

§ 2A–521. Lessee's Right to Specific Performance or Replevin.

(1) Specific performance may be decreed if the goods are unique or in other proper circumstances.

(2) A decree for specific performance may include any terms and conditions as to payment of the rent, damages, or other relief that the court deems just.

(3) A lessee has a right of replevin, detinue, sequestration, claim and delivery, or the like for goods identified to the lease contract if after reasonable effort the lessee is unable to effect cover for those goods or the circumstances reasonably indicate that the effort will be unavailing.

§ 2A–522. Lessee's Right to Goods on Lessor's Insolvency.

(1) Subject to subsection (2) and even though the goods have not been shipped, a lessee who has paid a part or all of the rent and security for goods identified to a lease contract (Section 2A–217) on making and keeping good a tender of any unpaid portion of the rent and security due under the lease contract may recover the goods identified from the lessor if the lessor becomes insolvent within 10 days after receipt of the first installment of rent and security.

(2) A lessee acquires the right to recover goods identified to a lease contract only if they conform to the lease contract.

C. Default by Lessee

§ 2A–523. Lessor's Remedies.

(1) If a lessee wrongfully rejects or revokes acceptance of goods or fails to make a payment when due or repudiates with respect to a part or the whole, then, with respect to any goods involved, and with respect to all of the goods if under an installment lease contract the value of the whole lease contract is substantially impaired (Section 2A–510), the lessee is in default under the lease contract and the lessor may:

(a) cancel the lease contract (Section 2A–505(1));

(b) proceed respecting goods not identified to the lease contract (Section 2A–524);

(c) withhold delivery of the goods and take possession of goods previously delivered (Section 2A–525);

(d) stop delivery of the goods by any bailee (Section 2A–526);

(e) dispose of the goods and recover damages (Section 2A–527), or retain the goods and recover damages (Section 2A–528), or in a proper case recover rent (Section 2A–529);

(f) exercise any other rights or pursue any other remedies provided in the lease contract.

(2) If a lessor does not fully exercise a right or obtain a remedy to which the lessor is entitled under subsection (1), the lessor may recover the loss resulting in the ordinary course of events from the lessee's default as determined in any reasonable manner, together with incidental damages, less expenses saved in consequence of the lessee's default.

(3) If a lessee is otherwise in default under a lease contract, the lessor may exercise the rights and pursue the remedies provided in the lease contract, which may include a right to cancel the lease. In addition, unless otherwise provided in the lease contract:

(a) if the default substantially impairs the value of the lease contract to the lessor, the lessor may exercise the rights and pursue the remedies provided in subsections (1) or (2); or

(b) if the default does not substantially impair the value of the lease contract to the lessor, the lessor may recover as provided in subsection (2).

As amended in 1990.

§ 2A–524. Lessor's Right to Identify Goods to Lease Contract.

(1) After default by the lessee under the lease contract of the type described in Section 2A–523(1) or 2A–523(3)(a) or, if agreed, after other default by the lessee, the lessor may:

(a) identify to the lease contract conforming goods not already identified if at the time the lessor learned of the default they were in the lessor's or the supplier's possession or control; and

(b) dispose of goods (Section 2A–527(1)) that demonstrably have been intended for the particular lease contract even though those goods are unfinished.

(2) If the goods are unfinished, in the exercise of reasonable commercial judgment for the purposes of avoiding loss and of effective realization, an aggrieved lessor or the supplier may either complete manufacture and wholly identify the goods to the lease contract or cease manufacture and lease, sell, or otherwise dispose of the goods for scrap or salvage value or proceed in any other reasonable manner.

As amended in 1990.

§ 2A–525. Lessor's Right to Possession of Goods.

(1) If a lessor discovers the lessee to be insolvent, the lessor may refuse to deliver the goods.

(2) After a default by the lessee under the lease contract of the type described in Section 2A–523(1) or 2A–523(3)(a) or, if agreed, after other default by the lessee, the lessor has the right to take possession of the goods. If the lease contract so provides, the lessor may require the lessee to assemble the goods and make them available to the lessor at a place to be designated by the lessor which is reasonably convenient to both parties. Without removal, the lessor may render unusable any goods employed in trade or business, and may dispose of goods on the lessee's premises (Section 2A–527).

(3) The lessor may proceed under subsection (2) without judicial process if it can be done without breach of the peace or the lessor may proceed by action.

As amended in 1990.

§ 2A–526. Lessor's Stoppage of Delivery in Transit or Otherwise.

(1) A lessor may stop delivery of goods in the possession of a carrier or other bailee if the lessor discovers the lessee to be insolvent and may stop delivery of carload, truckload, planeload, or larger shipments of express or freight if the lessee repudiates or fails to make a payment due before delivery, whether for rent, security or otherwise under the lease contract, or for any other reason the lessor has a right to withhold or take possession of the goods.

(2) In pursuing its remedies under subsection (1), the lessor may stop delivery until

   (a) receipt of the goods by the lessee;

   (b) acknowledgment to the lessee by any bailee of the goods, except a carrier, that the bailee holds the goods for the lessee; or

   (c) such an acknowledgment to the lessee by a carrier via reshipment or as warehouseman.

(3) (a) To stop delivery, a lessor shall so notify as to enable the bailee by reasonable diligence to prevent delivery of the goods.

   (b) After notification, the bailee shall hold and deliver the goods according to the directions of the lessor, but the lessor is liable to the bailee for any ensuing charges or damages.

   (c) A carrier who has issued a nonnegotiable bill of lading is not obliged to obey a notification to stop received from a person other than the consignor.

§ 2A–527. Lessor's Rights to Dispose of Goods.

(1) After a default by a lessee under the lease contract of the type described in Section 2A–523(1) or 2A–523(3)(a) or after the lessor refuses to deliver or takes possession of goods (Section 2A–525 or 2A–526), or, if agreed, after other default by a lessee, the lessor may dispose of the goods concerned or the undelivered balance thereof by lease, sale, or otherwise.

(2) Except as otherwise provided with respect to damages liquidated in the lease agreement (Section 2A–504) or otherwise determined pursuant to agreement of the parties (Sections 1–102(3) and 2A–503), if the disposition is by lease agreement substantially similar to the original lease agreement and the new lease agreement is made in good faith and in a commercially reasonable manner, the lessor may recover from the lessee as damages (i) accrued and unpaid rent as of the date of

the commencement of the term of the new lease agreement, (ii) the present value, as of the same date, of the total rent for the then remaining lease term of the original lease agreement minus the present value, as of the same date, of the rent under the new lease agreement applicable to that period of the new lease term which is comparable to the then remaining term of the original lease agreement, and (iii) any incidental damages allowed under Section 2A–530, less expenses saved in consequence of the lessee's default.

(3) If the lessor's disposition is by lease agreement that for any reason does not qualify for treatment under subsection (2), or is by sale or otherwise, the lessor may recover from the lessee as if the lessor had elected not to dispose of the goods and Section 2A–528 governs.

(4) A subsequent buyer or lessee who buys or leases from the lessor in good faith for value as a result of a disposition under this section takes the goods free of the original lease contract and any rights of the original lessee even though the lessor fails to comply with one or more of the requirements of this Article.

(5) The lessor is not accountable to the lessee for any profit made on any disposition. A lessee who has rightfully rejected or justifiably revoked acceptance shall account to the lessor for any excess over the amount of the lessee's security interest (Section 2A–508(5)).

As amended in 1990.

§ 2A–528. Lessor's Damages for Non-acceptance, Failure to Pay, Repudiation, or Other Default.

(1) Except as otherwise provided with respect to damages liquidated in the lease agreement (Section 2A–504) or otherwise determined pursuant to agreement of the parties (Sections 1–102(3) and 2A–503), if a lessor elects to retain the goods or a lessor elects to dispose of the goods and the disposition is by lease agreement that for any reason does not qualify for treatment under Section 2A–527(2), or is by sale or otherwise, the lessor may recover from the lessee as damages for a default of the type described in Section 2A–523(1) or 2A–523(3)(a), or, if agreed, for other default of the lessee, (i) accrued and unpaid rent as of the date of default if the lessee has never taken possession of the goods, or, if the lessee has taken possession of the goods, as of the date the lessor repossesses the goods or an earlier date on which the lessee makes a tender of the goods to the lessor, (ii) the present value as of the date determined under clause (i) of the total rent for the then remaining lease term of the original lease agreement minus the present value as of the same date of the market rent at the place where the goods are located computed for the same lease term, and (iii) any incidental damages allowed under Section 2A–530, less expenses saved in consequence of the lessee's default.

(2) If the measure of damages provided in subsection (1) is inadequate to put a lessor in as good a position as performance would have, the measure of damages is the present value of the profit, including reasonable overhead, the lessor would have made from full performance by the lessee,

together with any incidental damages allowed under Section 2A–530, due allowance for costs reasonably incurred and due credit for payments or proceeds of disposition.
As amended in 1990.

§ 2A–529. Lessor's Action for the Rent.

(1) After default by the lessee under the lease contract of the type described in Section 2A–523(1) or 2A–523(3)(a) or, if agreed, after other default by the lessee, if the lessor complies with subsection (2), the lessor may recover from the lessee as damages:

(a) for goods accepted by the lessee and not repossessed by or tendered to the lessor, and for conforming goods lost or damaged within a commercially reasonable time after risk of loss passes to the lessee (Section 2A–219), (i) accrued and unpaid rent as of the date of entry of judgment in favor of the lessor, (ii) the present value as of the same date of the rent for the then remaining lease term of the lease agreement, and (iii) any incidental damages allowed under Section 2A–530, less expenses saved in consequence of the lessee's default; and

(b) for goods identified to the lease contract if the lessor is unable after reasonable effort to dispose of them at a reasonable price or the circumstances reasonably indicate that effort will be unavailing, (i) accrued and unpaid rent as of the date of entry of judgment in favor of the lessor, (ii) the present value as of the same date of the rent for the then remaining lease term of the lease agreement, and (iii) any incidental damages allowed under Section 2A–530, less expenses saved in consequence of the lessee's default.

(2) Except as provided in subsection (3), the lessor shall hold for the lessee for the remaining lease term of the lease agreement any goods that have been identified to the lease contract and are in the lessor's control.

(3) The lessor may dispose of the goods at any time before collection of the judgment for damages obtained pursuant to subsection (1). If the disposition is before the end of the remaining lease term of the lease agreement, the lessor's recovery against the lessee for damages is governed by Section 2A–527 or Section 2A–528, and the lessor will cause an appropriate credit to be provided against a judgment for damages to the extent that the amount of the judgment exceeds the recovery available pursuant to Section 2A–527 or 2A–528.

(4) Payment of the judgment for damages obtained pursuant to subsection (1) entitles the lessee to the use and possession of the goods not then disposed of for the remaining lease term of and in accordance with the lease agreement.

(5) After default by the lessee under the lease contract of the type described in Section 2A–523(1) or Section 2A–523(3)(a) or, if agreed, after other default by the lessee, a lessor who is held not entitled to rent under this section must nevertheless be awarded damages for non-acceptance under Section 2A–527 or Section 2A–528.
As amended in 1990.

§ 2A–530. Lessor's Incidental Damages.

Incidental damages to an aggrieved lessor include any commercially reasonable charges, expenses, or commissions incurred in stopping delivery, in the transportation, care and custody of goods after the lessee's default, in connection with return or disposition of the goods, or otherwise resulting from the default.

§ 2A–531. Standing to Sue Third Parties for Injury to Goods.

(1) If a third party so deals with goods that have been identified to a lease contract as to cause actionable injury to a party to the lease contract (a) the lessor has a right of action against the third party, and (b) the lessee also has a right of action against the third party if the lessee:

(i) has a security interest in the goods;

(ii) has an insurable interest in the goods; or

(iii) bears the risk of loss under the lease contract or has since the injury assumed that risk as against the lessor and the goods have been converted or destroyed.

(2) If at the time of the injury the party plaintiff did not bear the risk of loss as against the other party to the lease contract and there is no arrangement between them for disposition of the recovery, his [or her] suit or settlement, subject to his [or her] own interest, is as a fiduciary for the other party to the lease contract.

(3) Either party with the consent of the other may sue for the benefit of whom it may concern.

§ 2A–532. Lessor's Rights to Residual Interest.

In addition to any other recovery permitted by this Article or other law, the lessor may recover from the lessee an amount that will fully compensate the lessor for any loss of or damage to the lessor's residual interest in the goods caused by the default of the lessee.
As added in 1990.

ARTICLE 3

Negotiable instruments

PART 1 GENERAL PROVISIONS AND DEFINITIONS

§ 3–101. Short Title.

This Article may be cited as Uniform Commercial Code—Negotiable Instruments.

§ 3–102. Subject Matter.

(a) This Article applies to negotiable instruments. It does not apply to money or to payment orders governed by Article 4A. A negotiable instrument that is also a certificated security under Section 8–102(1)(a) is subject to Article 8 and to this Article.

(b) In the event of conflict between the provisions of this Article and those of Article 4, Article 8, or Article 9, the provisions of Article 4, Article 8 and Article 9 prevail over those of this Article.

(c) Regulations of the Board of Governors of the Federal Reserve System and operating circulars of the Federal Reserve Banks supersede any inconsistent provision of this Article to the extent of the inconsistency.

§ 3–103. Definitions.

(a) In this Article:

(1) "Acceptor" means a drawee that has accepted a draft.

(2) "Drawee" means a person ordered in a draft to make payment.

(3) "Drawer" means a person that signs a draft as a person ordering payment.

(4) "Good faith" means honesty in fact and the observance of reasonable commercial standards of fair dealing.

(5) "Maker" means a person that signs a note as promisor of payment.

(6) "Order" means a written instruction to pay money signed by the person giving the instruction. The instruction may be addressed to any person, including the person giving the instruction, or to one or more persons jointly or in the alternative but not in succession. An authorization to pay is not an order unless the person authorized to pay is also instructed to pay.

(7) "Ordinary care" in the case of a person engaged in business means observance of reasonable commercial standards, prevailing in the area in which that person is located, with respect to the business in which that person is engaged. In the case of a bank that takes an instrument for processing for collection or payment by automated means, reasonable commercial standards do not require the bank to examine the instrument if the failure to examine does not violate the bank's prescribed procedures and the bank's procedures do not vary unreasonably from general banking usage not disapproved by this Article or Article 4.

(8) "Party" means party to an instrument.

(9) "Promise" means a written undertaking to pay money signed by the person undertaking to pay. An acknowledgment of an obligation by the obligor is not a promise unless the obligor also undertakes to pay the obligation.

(10) "Prove" with respect to a fact means to meet the burden of establishing the fact (Section 1–201(8)).

(11) "Remitter" means a person that purchases an instrument from its issuer if the instrument is payable to an identified person other than the purchaser.

(b) Other definitions applying to this Article and the sections in which they appear are:

"Acceptance" Section 3–409.
"Accommodated party" Section 3–419.
"Accommodation indorsement" Section 3–205.
"Accommodation party" Section 3–419.
"Alteration" Section 3–407.
"Blank indorsement" Section 3–205.
"Cashier's check" Section 3–104.
"Certificate of deposit" Section 3–104.
"Certified check" Section 3–409.
"Check" Section 3–104.
"Consideration" Section 3–303.
"Draft" Section 3–104.
"Fiduciary" Section 3–307.
"Guarantor" Section 3–417.
"Holder in due course" Section 3–302.
"Incomplete instrument" Section 3–115.
"Indorsement" Section 3–204.
"Indorser" Section 3–204.

"Instrument" Section 3–104.
"Issue" Section 3–105.
"Issuer" Section 3–105.
"Negotiable instrument" Section 3–104.
"Negotiation" Section 3–201.
"Note" Section 3–104.
"Payable at a definite time" Section 3–108.
"Payable on demand" Section 3–108.
"Payable to bearer" Section 3–109.
"Payable to order" Section 3–110.
"Payment" Section 3–603.
"Person entitled to enforce" Section 3–301.
"Presentment" Section 3–501.
"Reacquisition" Section 3–207.
"Represented person" Section 3–307.
"Special indorsement" Section 3–205.
"Teller's check" Section 3–104.
"Traveler's check" Section 3–104.
"Value" Section 3–303.

(c) The following definitions in other Articles apply to this Article:

"Bank" Section 4–105.
"Banking day" Section 4–104.
"Clearing house" Section 4–104.
"Collecting bank" Section 4–105.
"Customer" Section 4–104.
"Depositary bank" Section 4–105.
"Documentary draft" Section 4–104.
"Intermediary bank" Section 4–105.
"Item" Section 4–104.
"Midnight deadline" Section 4–104.
"Payor bank" Section 4–105.
"Suspends payments" Section 4–104.

(d) In addition, Article 1 contains general definitions and principles of construction and interpretation applicable throughout this Article.

§ 3–104. Negotiable Instrument.

(a) "Negotiable instrument" means an unconditional promise or order to pay a fixed amount of money, with or without interest or other charges described in the promise or order, if it:

(1) is payable to bearer or to order at the time it is issued or first comes into possession of a holder;

(2) is payable on demand or at a definite time; and

(3) does not state any other undertaking or instruction by the person promising or ordering payment to do any act in addition to the payment of money except that the promise or order may contain (i) an undertaking or power to give, maintain, or protect collateral to secure payment, (ii) an authorization or power to the holder to confess judgment or realize on or dispose of collateral, or (iii) a waiver of the benefit of any law intended for the advantage or protection of any obligor.

(b) "Instrument" means negotiable instrument.

(c) An order that meets all of the requirements of subsection (a) except subparagraph (1) and otherwise falls within the definition of "check" in subsection (f) is a negotiable instrument and a check.

(d) Notwithstanding subsection (a), a promise or order other than a check is not an instrument if, at the time it is issued or first comes into possession of a holder, it contains a conspicuous statement, however expressed, indicating that the writing is not an instrument governed by this Article.

(e) An instrument is a "note" if it is a promise, and is a "draft" if it is an order. If an instrument falls within the definition of both "note" and "draft," the person entitled to enforce the instrument may treat it as either.

(f) "Check" means (i) a draft, other than a documentary draft, payable on demand and drawn on a bank or (ii) a cashier's check or teller's check. An instrument may be a check even though it is described on its face by another term such as "money order."

(g) "Cashier's check" means a draft with respect to which the drawer and drawee are the same bank or branches of the same bank.

(h) "Teller's check" means a draft drawn by a bank (i) on another bank, or (ii) payable at or through a bank.

(i) "Traveler's check" means an instrument that (i) is payable on demand, (ii) is drawn on or payable at or through a bank, (iii) is designated by the term "traveler's check" or by a substantially similar term, and (iv) requires, as a condition to payment, a countersignature by a person whose specimen signature appears on the instrument.

(j) "Certificate of deposit" means an instrument containing an acknowledgment by a bank that a sum of money has been received by the bank, and a promise by the bank to repay the sum of money. A certificate of deposit is a note of the bank.

§ 3–105. Issue of Instrument.

(a) "Issue" means the first delivery of an instrument by the maker or drawer, whether to a holder or nonholder, for the purpose of giving rights on the instrument to any person.

(b) An unissued instrument, or an unissued incomplete instrument (Section 3–115) that is completed, is binding on the maker or drawer, but nonissuance is a defense. An instrument that is conditionally issued or is issued for a special purpose is binding on the maker or drawer, but failure of the condition or special purpose to be fulfilled is a defense.

(c) "Issuer" applies to issued and unissued instruments and means any person that signs an instrument as maker or drawer.

§ 3–106. Unconditional Promise or Order.

(a) Except as provided in subsections (b) and (c), for the purposes of Section 3–104(a), a promise or order is unconditional unless it states (i) an express condition to payment or (ii) that the promise or order is subject to or governed by another writing, or that rights or obligations with respect to the promise or order are stated in another writing; however, a mere reference to another writing does not make the promise or order conditional.

(b) A promise or order is not made conditional (i) by a reference to another writing for a statement of rights with respect to collateral, prepayment, or acceleration, or (ii) because

payment is limited to resort to a particular fund or source.

(c) If a promise or order requires, as a condition to payment, a countersignature by a person whose specimen signature appears on the promise or order, the condition does not make the promise or order conditional for the purposes of Section 3–104(a). If the person whose specimen signature appears on an instrument fails to countersign the instrument, the failure to countersign is a defense to the obligation of the issuer, but the failure does not prevent a transferee of the instrument from becoming a holder of the instrument.

(d) If a promise or order at the time it is issued or first comes into possession of a holder contains a statement, required by applicable statutory or administrative law, to the effect that the rights of a holder or transferee are subject to claims or defenses that the issuer could assert against the original payee, the promise or order is not thereby made conditional for the purposes of Section 3–104(a), but there cannot be a holder in due course of the promise or order.

§ 3–107. Instrument Payable in Foreign Money.

Unless the instrument otherwise provides, an instrument that states the amount payable in foreign money may be paid in the foreign money or in an equivalent amount in dollars calculated by using the current bank-offered spot rate at the place of payment for the purchase of dollars on the day on which the instrument is paid.

§ 3–108. Payable on Demand or at a Definite Time.

(a) A promise or order is "payable on demand" if (i) it states that it is payable on demand or at sight, or otherwise indicates that it is payable at the will of the holder, or (ii) it does not state any time of payment.

(b) A promise or order is "payable at a definite time" if it is payable on elapse of a definite period of time after sight or acceptance or at a fixed date or dates or at a time or times readily ascertainable at the time the promise or order is issued, subject to rights of (i) prepayment, (ii) acceleration, or (iii) extension at the option of the holder or (iv) extension to a further definite time at the option of the maker or acceptor or automatically upon or after a specified act or event.

(c) If an instrument, payable at a fixed date, is also payable upon demand made before the fixed date, the instrument is payable on demand until the fixed date and, if demand for payment is not made before that date, becomes payable at a definite time on the fixed date.

§ 3–109. Payable to Bearer or to Order.

(a) A promise or order is payable to bearer if it:

(1) states that it is payable to bearer or to the order of bearer or otherwise indicates that the person in possession of the promise or order is entitled to payment,

(2) does not state a payee, or

(3) states that it is payable to or to the order of cash or otherwise indicates that it is not payable to an identified person.

(b) A promise or order that is not payable to bearer is payable to order if it is payable (i) to the order of an identified person or (ii) to an identified person or order. A promise or order that is payable to order is payable to the identified person.

(c) An instrument payable to bearer may become payable to an identified person if it is specially indorsed as stated in Section 3–205(a). An instrument payable to an identified person may become payable to bearer if it is indorsed in blank as stated in Section 3–205(b).

§ 3–110. Identification of Person to Whom Instrument Is Payable.

(a) A person to whom an instrument is payable is determined by the intent of the person, whether or not authorized, signing as, or in the name or behalf of, the maker or drawer. The instrument is payable to the person intended by the signer even if that person is identified in the instrument by a name or other identification that is not that of the intended person. If more than one person signs in the name or behalf of the maker or drawer and all the signers do not intend the same person as payee, the instrument is payable to any person intended by one or more of the signers.

(b) If the signature of the maker or drawer of an instrument is made by automated means such as a check-writing machine, the payee of the instrument is determined by the intent of the person who supplied the name or identification of the payee, whether or not authorized to do so.

(c) A person to whom an instrument is payable may be identified in any way including by name, identifying number, office, or account number. For the purpose of determining the holder of an instrument, the following rules apply:

(1) If an instrument is payable to an account and the account is identified only by number, the instrument is payable to the person to whom the account is payable. If an instrument is payable to an account identified by number and by the name of a person, the instrument is payable to the named person, whether or not that person is the owner of the account identified by number.

(2) If an instrument is payable to:

(i) a trust, estate, or a person described as trustee or representative of a trust or estate, the instrument is payable to the trustee, the representative, or a successor of either, whether or not the beneficiary or estate is also named;

(ii) a person described as agent or similar representative of a named or identified person, the instrument is payable either to the represented person, the representative, or a successor of the representative;

(iii) a fund or organization that is not a legal entity, the instrument is payable to a representative of the members of the fund or organization; or

(iv) an office or to a person described as holding an office, the instrument is payable to the named person, the incumbent of the office, or a successor to the incumbent.

(d) If an instrument is payable to two or more persons alternatively, it is payable to any of them and may be negotiated, discharged, or enforced by any of them in possession of the instrument. If an instrument is payable to two or more persons not alternatively, it is payable to all of them and may be negotiated, discharged, or enforced only by all of them. If an

instrument payable to two or more persons is ambiguous as to whether it is payable to the persons alternatively, the instrument is payable to the persons alternatively.

§ 3–111. Place of Payment.

Except as otherwise provided for items in Article 4, an instrument is payable at the place of payment stated in the instrument. If no place of payment is stated, an instrument is payable at the address of the drawee or maker stated in the instrument. If no address is stated, the place of payment is the place of business of the drawee or maker. If a drawee or maker has more than one place of business, the place of payment is any place of business of the drawee or maker chosen by the person entitled to enforce the instrument. If the drawee or maker has no place of business, the place of payment is the residence of the drawee or maker.

§ 3–112. Interest.

(a) Unless otherwise provided in the instrument, (i) an instrument is not payable with interest, and (ii) interest on an interest-bearing instrument is payable from the date of the instrument.

(b) Interest may be stated in an instrument as a fixed or variable amount of money or it may be expressed as a fixed or variable rate or rates. The amount or rate of interest may be stated or described in the instrument in any manner and may require reference to information not contained in the instrument. If an instrument provides for interest but the amount of interest payable cannot be ascertained from the description, interest is payable at the judgment rate in effect at the place of payment of the instrument and at the time interest first accrues.

§ 3–113. Date of Instrument.

(a) An instrument may be antedated or postdated. The date stated determines the time of payment if the instrument is payable at a fixed period after date. Except as provided in Section 4–401(3), an instrument payable on demand is not payable before the date of the instrument.

(b) If an instrument is undated, its date is the date of its issue or, in the case of an unissued instrument, the date it first comes into possession of a holder.

§ 3–114. Contradictory Terms of Instrument.

If an instrument contains contradictory terms, typewritten terms prevail over printed terms, handwritten terms prevail over both, and words prevail over numbers.

§ 3–115. Incomplete Instrument.

(a) "Incomplete instrument" means a signed writing, whether or not issued by the signer, the contents of which show at the time of signing that it is incomplete but that the signer intended it to be completed by the addition of words or numbers.

(b) Subject to subsection (c), if an incomplete instrument is an instrument under Section 3–104, it may be enforced (i) according to its terms if it is not completed, or (ii) according to its terms as augmented by completion. If an incomplete instrument is not an instrument under Section 3–104 but, after completion, the requirements of Section 3–104 are met, the instrument may be enforced according to its terms as augmented by completion.

(c) If words or numbers are added to an incomplete instrument without authority of the signer, there is an alteration of the incomplete instrument governed by Section 3–407.

(d) The burden of establishing that words or numbers were added to an incomplete instrument without authority of the signer is on the person asserting the lack of authority.

§ 3–116. Joint and Several Liability; Contribution.

(a) Except as otherwise provided in the instrument, two or more persons who have the same liability on an instrument as makers, drawers, acceptors, indorsers who are indorsing joint payees, or anomalous indorsers, are jointly and severally liable in the capacity in which they sign.

(b) Except as provided in Section 3–417(e) or by agreement of the affected parties, a party with joint and several liability that pays the instrument is entitled to receive from any party with the same joint and several liability contribution in accordance with applicable law.

(c) Discharge of one party with joint and several liability by a person entitled to enforce the instrument does not affect the right under subsection (b) of a party with the same joint and several liability to receive contribution from the party discharged.

§ 3–117. Other Agreements Affecting an Instrument.

Subject to applicable law regarding exclusion of proof of contemporaneous or prior agreements, the obligation of a party to an instrument to pay the instrument may be modified, supplemented, or nullified by a separate agreement of the obligor and a person entitled to enforce the instrument if the instrument is issued or the obligation is incurred in reliance on the agreement or as part of the same transaction giving rise to the agreement. To the extent an obligation is modified, supplemented, or nullified by an agreement under this section, the agreement is a defense to the obligation.

§ 3–118. Statute of Limitations.

(a) Except as provided in subsection (e), an action to enforce the obligation of a party to pay a note payable at a definite time must be commenced within six years after the payment date or dates stated in the note or, if a payment date is accelerated, within six years after the accelerated payment date.

(b) Except as provided in subsection (d) or (e), if demand for payment is made to the maker of a note payable on demand, an action to enforce the obligation of a party to pay the note must be commenced within six years after the demand. If no demand for payment is made to the maker, an action to enforce the note is barred if neither principal nor interest on the note has been paid for a continuous period of 10 years.

(c) Except as provided in subsection (d), an action to enforce the obligation of a party to an unaccepted draft to pay the draft must be commenced within six years after dishonor of the draft or 10 years after the date of the draft, whichever period expires first.

(d) An action to enforce the obligation of the acceptor of a certified check or the issuer of a teller's check, cashier's check, or traveler's check must be commenced within six years after demand for payment is made to the acceptor or issuer, as the case may be.

(e) An action to enforce the obligation of a party to a certificate of deposit to pay the instrument must be commenced within six years after demand for payment is made to the maker, but if the instrument states a maturity date and the maker is not required to pay before that date, the six-year period begins when a demand for payment is in effect and the maturity date has passed.

(f) This subsection applies to an action to enforce the obligation of a party to pay an accepted draft, other than a certified check. If the obligation of the acceptor is payable at a definite time, the action must be commenced within six years after the payment date or dates stated in the draft or acceptance. If the obligation of the acceptor is payable on demand, the action must be commenced within six years after the date of the acceptance.

(g) Unless governed by other law regarding claims for indemnity or contribution, an action (i) for conversion of an instrument, for money had and received, or like action based on conversion, (ii) for breach of warranty, or (iii) to enforce an obligation, duty, or right arising under this Article and not governed by this section must be commenced within three years after the cause of action accrues.

§ 3–119. Notice of Right to Defend Action.

In an action for breach of an obligation for which a third person is answerable over pursuant to this Article or Article 4, the defendant may give the third person written notice of the litigation, and the person notified may then give similar notice to any other person who is answerable over. If the notice states (i) that the person notified may come in and defend and (ii) that failure to do so will bind the person notified in an action later brought by the person giving the notice as to any determination of fact common to the two litigations, the person notified is so bound unless after seasonable receipt of the notice the person notified does come in and defend.

PART 2 NEGOTIATION, TRANSFER AND INDORSEMENT

§ 3–201. Negotiation.

(a) "Negotiation" means a transfer of possession, whether voluntary or involuntary, of an instrument to a person who thereby becomes its holder if possession is obtained from a person other than the issuer of the instrument.

(b) Except for a negotiation by a remitter, if an instrument is payable to an identified person, negotiation requires transfer of possession of the instrument and its indorsement by the holder. If an instrument is payable to bearer, it may be negotiated by transfer of possession alone.

§ 3–202. Negotiation Subject to Rescission.

(a) Negotiation is effective even if obtained (i) from an infant, a corporation exceeding its powers, or a person without capacity, or (ii) by fraud, duress, or mistake, or in breach of duty or as part of an illegal transaction.

(b) To the extent permitted by law, negotiation may be rescinded or may be subject to other remedies, but those remedies may not be asserted against a subsequent holder in due course or a person paying the instrument in good faith and without knowledge of facts that are a basis for rescission or other remedy.

§ 3–203. Rights Acquired by Transfer.

(a) An instrument is transferred when it is delivered by a person other than its issuer for the purpose of giving to the person receiving delivery the right to enforce the instrument.

(b) Transfer of an instrument, regardless of whether the transfer is a negotiation, vests in the transferee any right of the transferor to enforce the instrument, including any right as a holder in due course, but the transferee cannot acquire rights of a holder in due course by a transfer, directly or indirectly, from a holder in due course if the purchaser engaged in fraud or illegality affecting the instrument.

(c) Unless otherwise agreed, if an instrument is transferred for value and the transferee does not become a holder because of lack of indorsement by the transferor, the transferee has a specifically enforceable right to the unqualified indorsement of the transferor, but negotiation of the instrument does not occur until the indorsement is made.

(d) If a transferor purports to transfer less than the entire instrument, negotiation of the instrument does not occur. The transferee obtains no rights under this Article and has only the rights of a partial assignee.

§ 3–204. Indorsement.

(a) "Indorsement" means a signature, other than that of a maker, drawer, or acceptor, that alone or accompanied by other words, is made on an instrument for the purpose of (i) negotiating the instrument, (ii) restricting payment of the instrument, or (iii) incurring indorser's liability on the instrument, but regardless of the intent of the signer, a signature and its accompanying words is an indorsement unless the accompanying words, the terms of the instrument, the place of the signature, or other circumstances unambiguously indicate that the signature was made for a purpose other than indorsement. For the purpose of determining whether a signature is made on an instrument, a paper affixed to the instrument is a part of the instrument.

(b) "Indorser" means a person who makes an indorsement.

(c) For the purpose of determining whether the transferee of an instrument is a holder, an indorsement that transfers a security interest in the instrument is effective as an unqualified indorsement of the instrument.

(d) If an instrument is payable to a holder under a name that is not the name of the holder, indorsement may be made by the holder in the name stated in the instrument or in the holder's name or both, but signature in both names may be required by a person paying or taking the instrument for value or collection.

§ 3–205. Special Indorsement; Blank Indorsement; Anomalous Indorsement.

(a) If an indorsement is made by the holder of an instrument, whether payable to an identified person or payable to bearer, and the indorsement identifies a person to whom it makes the instrument payable, it is a "special indorsement." When specially indorsed, an instrument becomes payable to the identified person and may be negotiated only by the indorsement of that person. The principles stated in Section 3–110 apply to special indorsements.

(b) If an indorsement is made by the holder of an instrument and it is not a special indorsement, it is a "blank indorsement." When indorsed in blank, an instrument becomes payable to bearer and may be negotiated by transfer of possession alone until specially indorsed.

(c) The holder may convert a blank indorsement that consists only of a signature into a special indorsement by writing, above the signature of the indorser, words identifying the person to whom the instrument is made payable.

(d) "Anomalous indorsement" means an indorsement made by a person that is not the holder of the instrument. An anomalous indorsement does not affect the manner in which the instrument may be negotiated.

§ 3–206. Restrictive Indorsement.

(a) An indorsement limiting payment to a particular person or otherwise prohibiting further transfer or negotiation of the instrument is not effective to prevent further transfer or negotiation of the instrument.

(b) An indorsement stating a condition to the right of the indorsee to receive payment does not affect the right of the indorsee to enforce the instrument. A person paying the instrument or taking it for value or collection may disregard the condition, and the rights and liabilities of that person are not affected by whether the condition has been fulfilled.

(c) The following rules apply to an instrument bearing an indorsement (i) described in Section 4–201(2), or (ii) in blank or to a particular bank using the words "for deposit," "for collection," or other words indicating a purpose of having the instrument collected for the indorser or for a particular account:

(1) A person, other than a bank, that purchases the instrument when so indorsed converts the instrument unless the proceeds of the instrument are received by the indorser or are applied consistently with the indorsement.

(2) A depositary bank that purchases the instrument or takes it for collection when so indorsed converts the instrument unless the proceeds of the instrument are received by the indorser or applied consistently with the indorsement.

(3) A payor bank that is also the depositary bank or that takes the instrument for immediate payment over the counter from a person other than a collecting bank converts the instrument unless the proceeds of the instrument are received by the indorser or applied consistently with the indorsement.

(4) Except as otherwise provided in paragraph (3), a

payor bank or intermediary bank may disregard the indorsement and is not liable if the proceeds of the instrument are not received by the indorser or applied consistently with the indorsement.

(d) Except for an indorsement covered by subsection (c), the following rules apply to an instrument bearing an indorsement using words to the effect that payment is to be made to the indorsee as agent, trustee, or other fiduciary for the benefit of the indorser or another person:

(1) Unless there is notice of breach of fiduciary duty as provided in Section 3–307, a person that purchases the instrument from the indorsee or takes the instrument from the indorsee for collection or payment may pay the proceeds of payment or the value given for the instrument to the indorsee without regard to whether the indorsee violates a fiduciary duty to the indorser.

(2) A later transferee of the instrument or person that pays the instrument is neither given notice nor otherwise affected by the restriction in the indorsement unless the transferee or payor knows that the fiduciary dealt with the instrument or its proceeds in breach of fiduciary duty.

(e) Purchase of an instrument bearing an indorsement to which this section applies does not prevent the purchaser from becoming a holder in due course of the instrument unless the purchaser is a converter under subsection (c).

(f) In an action to enforce the obligation of a party to pay the instrument, the obligor has a defense if payment would violate an indorsement to which this section applies and the payment is not permitted by this section.

§ 3–207.　Reacquisition.

Reacquisition of an instrument occurs if it is transferred, by negotiation or otherwise, to a former holder. A former holder that reacquires the instrument may cancel indorsements made after the reacquirer first became a holder of the instrument. If the cancellation causes the instrument to be payable to the reacquirer or to bearer, the reacquirer may negotiate the instrument. An indorser whose indorsement is canceled is discharged, and the discharge is effective against any later holder.

PART 3　ENFORCEMENT OF INSTRUMENTS

§ 3–301.　Person Entitled to Enforce Instrument.

"Person entitled to enforce" an instrument means (i) the holder of the instrument, (ii) a nonholder in possession of the instrument who has the rights of a holder, or (iii) a person not in possession of the instrument who is entitled to enforce the instrument pursuant to Section 3–309. A person may be a person entitled to enforce the instrument even though the person is not the owner of the instrument or is in wrongful possession of the instrument.

§ 3–302.　Holder in Due Course.

(a) Subject to subsection (c) and Section 3–106(d), "holder in due course" means the holder of an instrument if:

(1) the instrument when issued or negotiated to the holder does not bear such apparent evidence of forgery or alteration or is not otherwise so irregular or incomplete as to call

into question its authenticity, and

(2) the holder took the instrument (i) for value, (ii) in good faith, (iii) without notice that the instrument is overdue or has been dishonored or that there is an uncured default with respect to payment of another instrument issued as part of the same series, (iv) without notice that the instrument contains an unauthorized signature or has been altered, (v) without notice of any claim to the instrument stated in Section 3–306, and (vi) without notice that any party to the instrument has any defense or claim in recoupment stated in Section 3–305(a).

(b) Notice of discharge of a party to the instrument, other than discharge in an insolvency proceeding, is not notice of a defense under subsection (a), but discharge is effective against a person who became a holder in due course with notice of the discharge. Public filing or recording of a document does not of itself constitute notice of a defense, claim in recoupment, or claim to the instrument.

(c) Except to the extent a transferor or predecessor in interest has rights as a holder in due course, a person does not acquire rights of a holder in due course of an instrument taken (i) by legal process or by purchase at an execution, bankruptcy, or creditor's sale or similar proceeding, (ii) by purchase as part of a bulk transaction not in ordinary course of business of the transferor, or (iii) as the successor in interest to an estate or other organization.

(d) If, under Section 3–303(a)(1), the promise of performance that is the consideration for an instrument has been partially performed, the holder may assert rights as a holder in due course of the instrument only to the fraction of the amount payable under the instrument equal to the value of the partial performance divided by the value of the promised performance.

(e) If (i) the person entitled to enforce an instrument has only a security interest in the instrument and (ii) the person obliged to pay the instrument has a defense, claim in recoupment or claim to the instrument that may be asserted against the person who granted the security interest, the person entitled to enforce the instrument may assert rights as a holder in due course only to an amount payable under the instrument which, at the time of enforcement of the instrument, does not exceed the amount of the unpaid obligation secured.

(f) To be effective, notice must be received at such time and in such manner as to give a reasonable opportunity to act on it.

(g) This section is subject to any law limiting status as a holder in due course in particular classes of transactions.

§ 3–303.　Value and Consideration.

(a) An instrument is issued or transferred for value if:

(1) the instrument is issued or transferred for a promise of performance, to the extent the promise has been performed;

(2) the transferee acquires a security interest or other lien in the instrument other than a lien obtained by judicial proceedings;

(3) the instrument is issued or transferred as payment of,

or as security for, an existing obligation of any person, whether or not the obligation is due;

(4) the instrument is issued or transferred in exchange for a negotiable instrument; or

(5) the instrument is issued or transferred in exchange for the incurring of an irrevocable obligation to a third party by the person taking the instrument.

(b) "Consideration" means any consideration sufficient to support a simple contract. The drawer or maker of an instrument has a defense if the instrument is issued without consideration. If an instrument is issued for a promise of performance, the drawer or maker has a defense to the extent performance of the promise is due and the promise has not been performed. If an instrument is issued for value as stated in subsection (a), the instrument is also issued for consideration.

§ 3–304.   Overdue Instrument.

(a) An instrument payable on demand becomes overdue at the earliest of the following times:

(1) on the day after the day demand for payment is duly made;

(2) if the instrument is a check, 90 days after its date; or

(3) if the instrument is not a check, when the instrument has been outstanding for a period of time after its date which is unreasonably long under the circumstances of the particular case in light of the nature of the instrument and trade usage.

(b) With respect to an instrument payable at a definite time the following rules apply: (1) If the principal is payable in installments and a due date has not been accelerated, the instrument becomes overdue upon default under the instrument for nonpayment of an installment, and the instrument remains overdue until the default is cured. (2) If the principal is not payable in installments and the due date has not been accelerated, the instrument becomes overdue on the day after the due date. (3) If a due date with respect to principal has been accelerated, the instrument becomes overdue on the day after the accelerated due date.

(c) Unless the due date of principal has been accelerated, an instrument does not become overdue if there is default in payment of interest but no default in payment of principal.

§ 3–305.   Defenses and Claims in Recoupment.

(a) Except as stated in subsection (b), the right to enforce the obligation of a party to pay the instrument is subject to the following:

(1) A defense of the obligor based on (i) infancy of the obligor to the extent it is a defense to a simple contract, (ii) duress, lack of legal capacity, or illegality of the transaction that nullifies the obligation of the obligor, (iii) fraud that induced the obligor to sign the instrument with neither knowledge nor reasonable opportunity to learn of its character or its essential terms, or (iv) discharge of the obligor in insolvency proceedings.

(2) A defense of the obligor stated in another section of this Article or a defense of the obligor that would be available if the person entitled to enforce the instrument were enforcing a right to payment under a simple contract.

(3) A claim in recoupment of the obligor against the original payee of the instrument if the claim arose from the transaction that gave rise to the instrument. The claim of the obligor may be asserted against a transferee of the instrument only to reduce the amount owing on the instrument at the time the action is brought.

(b) The right of a holder in due course to enforce the obligation of a party to pay the instrument is subject to defenses of the obligor stated in subsection (a)(1), but is not subject to defenses of the obligor stated in subsection (a)(2) or claims in recoupment stated in subsection (a)(3) against a person other than the holder.

(c) Except as stated in subsection (d), in an action to enforce the obligation of a party to pay the instrument, the obligor may not assert against the person entitled to enforce the instrument a defense, claim in recoupment, or claim to the instrument (Section 3–306) of another person, but the other person's claim to the instrument may be asserted by the obligor if the other person is joined in the action and personally asserts the claim against the person entitled to enforce the instrument. An obligor is not obliged to pay the instrument if the person seeking enforcement of the instrument does not have rights of a holder in due course and the obligor proves that the instrument is a lost or stolen instrument.

(d) In an action to enforce the obligation of an accommodation party to pay an instrument, the accommodation party may assert against the person entitled to enforce the instrument any defense or claim in recoupment under subsection (a) that the accommodated party could assert against the person entitled to enforce the instrument, except the defenses of discharge in insolvency proceedings, infancy, or lack of legal capacity.

§ 3–306.   Claims to an Instrument.

A person taking an instrument, other than a person having rights of a holder in due course, is subject to a claim of a property or possessory right in the instrument or its proceeds, including a claim to rescind a negotiation and to recover the instrument or its proceeds. A person having rights of a holder in due course takes free of the claim to the instrument.

§ 3–307.   Notice of Breach of Fiduciary Duty.

(a) This section applies if (i) an instrument is taken from a fiduciary for payment or collection or for value, (ii) the taker has knowledge of the fiduciary status of the fiduciary, and (iii) the represented person makes a claim to the instrument or its proceeds on the basis that the transaction of the fiduciary is a breach of fiduciary duty. Notice of breach of fiduciary duty by the fiduciary is notice of the claim of the represented person. "Fiduciary" means an agent, trustee, partner, corporation officer or director, or other representative owing a fiduciary duty with respect to the instrument. "Represented person" means the principal, beneficiary, partnership, corporation, or other person to whom the duty is owed.

(b) If the instrument is payable to the fiduciary, as such, or to the represented person, the taker has notice of the breach of fiduciary duty if the instrument is (i) taken in payment of or as security for a debt known by the taker to be the personal debt of the fiduciary, (ii) taken in a transaction known by the taker to be for the personal benefit of the fiduciary, or (iii) deposited to an account other than an account of the fiduciary, as such, or an account of the represented person.

(c) If the instrument is made or drawn by the fiduciary, as such, payable to the fiduciary personally, the taker does not have notice of the breach of fiduciary duty unless the taker knows of the breach of fiduciary duty.

(d) If the instrument is made or drawn by or on behalf of the represented person to the taker as payee, the taker has notice of the breach of fiduciary duty if the instrument is (i) taken in payment of or as security for a debt known by the taker to be the personal debt of the fiduciary, (ii) taken in a transaction known by the taker to be for the personal benefit of the fiduciary, or (iii) deposited to an account other than an account of the fiduciary, as such, or an account of the represented person.

§ 3–308. Proof of Signatures and Status as Holder in Due Course.

(a) In an action with respect to an instrument, the authenticity of, and authority to make, each signature on the instrument is admitted unless specifically denied in the pleadings. If the validity of a signature is denied in the pleadings, the burden of establishing validity is on the person claiming validity, but the signature is presumed to be authentic and authorized unless the action is to enforce the liability of the purported signer and the signer is dead or incompetent at the time of trial of the issue of validity of the signature. If an action to enforce the instrument is brought against a person as the undisclosed principal of a person who signed the instrument as a party to the instrument, the plaintiff has the burden of establishing that the defendant is liable on the instrument as a represented person pursuant to Section 3–402(a).

(b) If the validity of signatures is admitted or proved and there is compliance with subsection (a), a plaintiff producing the instrument is entitled to payment if the plaintiff proves entitlement to enforce the instrument under Section 3–301, unless the defendant proves a defense or claim in recoupment. If a defense or claim in recoupment is proved, the right to payment of the plaintiff is subject to the defense or claim except to the extent the plaintiff proves that the plaintiff has rights of a holder in due course which are not subject to the defense or claim.

§ 3–309. Enforcement of Lost, Destroyed, or Stolen Instrument.

(a) A person not in possession of an instrument is entitled to enforce the instrument if (i) that person was in rightful possession of the instrument and entitled to enforce it when loss of possession occurred, (ii) the loss of possession was not the result of a voluntary transfer by that person or a lawful seizure, and (iii) that person cannot reasonably obtain possession of the instrument because the instrument was destroyed, its whereabouts cannot be determined, or it is in the wrongful possession of an unknown person or a person that cannot be found or is not amenable to service of process.

(b) A person seeking enforcement of an instrument pursuant to subsection (a) must prove the terms of the instrument and the person's right to enforce the instrument. If that proof is made, Section 3–308 applies to the case as though the person seeking enforcement had produced the instrument. The court may not enter judgment in favor of the person seeking enforcement unless it finds that the person required to pay the instrument is adequately protected against loss that might occur by reason of a claim by another person to enforce the instrument. Adequate protection may be provided by any reasonable means.

§ 3–310. Effect of Instrument on Obligation for Which Taken.

(a) Unless otherwise agreed, if a certified check, cashier's check, or teller's check is taken for an obligation, the obligation is discharged to the same extent discharge would result if an amount of money equal to the amount of the instrument were taken in payment of the obligation. Discharge of the obligation does not affect any liability that the obligor may have as an indorser of the instrument.

(b) Unless otherwise agreed and except as provided in subsection (a), if a note or an uncertified check is taken for an obligation, the obligation is suspended to the same extent the obligation would be discharged if an amount of money equal to the amount of the instrument were taken.

(1) In the case of an uncertified check, suspension of the obligation continues until dishonor of the check or until it is paid or certified. Payment or certification of the check results in discharge of the obligation to the extent of the amount of the check.

(2) In the case of a note, suspension of the obligation continues until dishonor of the note or until it is paid. Payment of the note results in discharge of the obligation to the extent of the payment.

(3) If the check or note is dishonored and the obligee of the obligation for which the instrument was taken has possession of the instrument, the obligee may enforce either the instrument or the obligation. In the case of an instrument of a third person which is negotiated to the obligee by the obligor, discharge of the obligor on the instrument also discharges the obligation.

(4) If the person entitled to enforce the instrument taken for an obligation is a person other than the obligee, the obligee may not enforce the obligation to the extent the obligation is suspended. If the obligee is the person entitled to enforce the instrument but no longer has possession of it because it was lost, stolen, or destroyed, the obligation may not be enforced to the extent of the amount payable on the instrument, and to that extent the obligee's rights against the obligor are limited to enforcement of the instrument.

(c) If an instrument other than one described in subsection (a) or (b) is taken for an obligation, the effect is (i) that stated in subsection (a) if the instrument is one on which a bank is liable as maker or acceptor, or (ii) that stated in subsection (b) in any other case.

§ 3–311. Accord and Satisfaction by Use of Instrument.

(a) This section applies if a person against whom a claim is asserted proves that (i) that person in good faith tendered an instrument to the claimant as full satisfaction of the claim, (ii) the amount of the claim was unliquidated or subject to a bona fide dispute, and (iii) the claimant obtained payment of the instrument.

(b) Unless subsection (c) applies, the claim is discharged if the person against whom the claim is asserted proves that the instrument or an accompanying written communication contained a conspicuous statement to the effect that the instrument was tendered as full satisfaction of the claim.

(c) Subject to subsection (d), a claim is not discharged under subsection (b) if the claimant is an organization and proves that within a reasonable time before the tender, the claimant sent a conspicuous statement to the person against whom the claim is asserted that communications concerning disputed debts, including an instrument tendered as full satisfaction of a debt, are to be sent to a designated person, office or place, and the instrument or accompanying communication was not received by that designated person, office, or place.

(d) Notwithstanding subsection (c), a claim is discharged under subsection (b) if the person against whom the claim is asserted proves that within a reasonable time before collection of the instrument was initiated, an agent of the claimant having direct responsibility with respect to the disputed obligation knew that the instrument was tendered in full satisfaction of the claim, or received the instrument and any accompanying written communication.

PART 4   LIABILITY OF PARTIES

§ 3–401.   Signature.

(a) A person is not liable on an instrument unless (i) the person signed the instrument, or (ii) the person is represented by an agent or representative who signed the instrument and the signature is binding on the represented person under Section 3–402.

(b) A signature may be made (i) manually or by means of a device or machine, and (ii) by the use of any name, including any trade or assumed name, or by any word, mark, or symbol executed or adopted by a person with present intention to authenticate a writing.

§ 3–402.   Signature by Representative.

(a) If a person acting, or purporting to act, as a representative signs an instrument by signing either the name of the represented person or the name of the signer, the represented person is bound by the signature to the same extent the represented person would be bound if the signature were on a simple contract. If the represented person is bound, the signature of the representative is the "authorized signature of the represented person" and the represented person is liable on the instrument, whether or not identified in the instrument.

(b) If a representative signs the name of the representative to an instrument and that signature is an authorized signature of the represented person, the following rules apply:

(1) If the form of the signature shows unambiguously that the signature is made on behalf of the represented person who is identified in the instrument, the representative is not liable on the instrument.

(2) Subject to subsection (c), if (i) the form of the signature does not show unambiguously that the signature is made in a representative capacity or (ii) the represented person is not identified in the instrument, the representative is liable on the instrument to a holder in due course that took the instrument without notice that the representative was not intended to be liable on the instrument. With respect to any other person, the representative is liable on the instrument unless the representative proves that the original parties to the instrument did not intend the representative to be liable on the instrument.

(c) If a representative signs the name of the representative as drawer of a check without indication of the representative status and the check is payable from an account of the represented person who is identified on the check, the signer is not liable on the check if the signature is an authorized signature of the represented person.

§ 3–403.   Unauthorized Signature.

(a) Except as otherwise provided in this Article, an unauthorized signature is ineffective except as the signature of the unauthorized signer in favor of a person who in good faith pays the instrument or takes it for value. An unauthorized signature may be ratified for all purposes of this Article.

(b) If the signature of more than one person is required to constitute the authorized signature of an organization, the signature of the organization is unauthorized if one of the required signatures is missing.

(c) The civil or criminal liability of a person who makes an unauthorized signature is not affected by any provision of this Article that makes the unauthorized signature effective for the purposes of this Article.

§ 3–404.   Impostors; Fictitious Payees.

(a) If an impostor by use of the mails or otherwise induces the maker or drawer of an instrument to issue the instrument to the impostor, or to a person acting in concert with the impostor, by impersonating the payee of the instrument or a person authorized to act for the payee, an indorsement of the instrument by any person in the name of the payee is effective as the indorsement of the payee in favor of any person that in good faith pays the instrument or takes it for value or for collection.

(b) If (i) a person whose intent determines to whom an instrument is payable (Section 3–110(a) or (b)) does not intend the person identified as payee to have any interest in the instrument, or (ii) the person identified as payee of the instrument is a fictitious person, the following rules apply until the instrument is negotiated by special indorsement:

(1) Any person in possession of the instrument is its holder.

(2) An indorsement by any person in the name of the payee stated in the instrument is effective as the indorsement of the payee in favor of any person that in good faith pays the instrument or takes it for value or for collection.

(c) Under subsection (a) or (b) an indorsement is made in the name of a payee if (i) it is made in a name substantially similar to that of the payee or (ii) the instrument, whether or not indorsed, is deposited in a depositary bank to an account in a name substantially similar to that of the payee.

(d) With respect to an instrument to which subsection (a) or (b) applies, if a person paying the instrument or taking it for value or for collection fails to exercise ordinary care in paying or taking the instrument and that failure substantially contributes to loss resulting from payment of the instrument, the person bearing the loss may recover from the person failing to exercise ordinary care to the extent the failure to exercise ordinary care contributed to the loss.

§ 3–405. Employer Responsibility for Fraudulent Indorsement by Employee.

(a) This section applies to fraudulent indorsements of instruments with respect to which an employer has entrusted an employee with responsibility as part of the employee's duties. The following definitions apply to this section:

(1) "Employee" includes, in addition to an employee of an employer, an independent contractor and employee of an independent contractor retained by the employer.

(2) "Fraudulent indorsement" means (i) in the case of an instrument payable to the employer, a forged indorsement purporting to be that of the employer, or (ii) in the case of an instrument with respect to which the employer is drawer or maker, a forged indorsement purporting to be that of the person identified as payee.

(3) "Responsibility" with respect to instruments means authority (i) to sign or indorse instruments on behalf of the employer, (ii) to process instruments received by the employer for bookkeeping purposes, for deposit to an account, or for other disposition, (iii) to prepare or process instruments for issue in the name of the employer, (iv) to supply information determining the names or addresses of payees of instruments to be issued in the name of the employer, (v) to control the disposition of instruments to be issued in the name of the employer, or (vi) to otherwise act with respect to instruments in a responsible capacity. "Responsibility" does not include the assignment of duties that merely allow an employee to have access to instruments or blank or incomplete instrument forms that are being stored or transported or are part of incoming or outgoing mail, or similar access.

(b) For the purpose of determining the rights and liabilities of a person who, in good faith, pays an instrument or takes it for value or for collection, if an employee entrusted with responsibility with respect to the instrument or a person acting in concert with the employee makes a fraudulent indorsement to the instrument, the indorsement is effective as the indorsement of the person to whom the instrument is payable if it is made in the name of that person. If the person paying the instrument or taking it for value or for collection fails to exercise ordinary care in paying or taking the instrument and that failure substantially contributes to loss resulting from the fraud, the person bearing the loss may recover from the person failing to exercise ordinary care to the extent the failure to exercise ordinary care contributed to the loss.

(c) Under subsection (b) an indorsement is made in the name of the person to whom an instrument is payable if (i) it is made in a name substantially similar to the name of that person or (ii) the instrument, whether or not indorsed, is deposited in a depositary bank to an account in a name substantially similar to the name of that person.

§ 3–406. Negligence Contributing to Forged Signature or Alteration of Instrument.

(a) A person whose failure to exercise ordinary care substantially contributes to an alteration of an instrument or to the making of a forged signature on an instrument is precluded from asserting the alteration or the forgery against a person that, in good faith, pays the instrument or takes it for value.

(b) If the person asserting the preclusion fails to exercise ordinary care in paying or taking the instrument and that failure substantially contributes to loss, the loss is allocated between the person precluded and the person asserting the preclusion according to the extent to which the failure of each to exercise ordinary care contributed to the loss.

(c) Under subsection (a) the burden of proving failure to exercise ordinary care is on the person asserting the preclusion. Under subsection (b) the burden of proving failure to exercise ordinary care is on the person precluded.

§ 3–407. Alteration.

(a) "Alteration" means (i) an unauthorized change in an instrument that purports to modify in any respect the obligation of a party to the instrument, or (ii) an unauthorized addition of words or numbers or other change to an incomplete instrument relating to the obligation of any party to the instrument.

(b) Except as provided in subsection (c), an alteration fraudulently made by the holder discharges any party to whose obligation the alteration applies unless that party assents or is precluded from asserting the alteration. No other alteration discharges any party, and the instrument may be enforced according to its original terms.

(c) If an instrument that has been fraudulently altered is acquired by a person having rights of a holder in due course, it may be enforced by that person according to its original terms. If an incomplete instrument is completed and is then acquired by a person having rights of a holder in due course, it may be enforced by that person as completed, whether or not the completion is a fraudulent alteration.

§ 3–408. Drawee Not Liable on Unaccepted Draft.

A check or other draft does not of itself operate as an assignment of funds in the hands of the drawee available for its payment, and the drawee is not liable on the instrument until the drawee accepts it.

§ 3–409.   Acceptance of Draft; Certified Check.

(a) "Acceptance" means the drawee's signed agreement to pay a draft as presented. It must be written on the draft and may consist of the drawee's signature alone. Acceptance may be made at any time and becomes effective when notification pursuant to instructions is given or the accepted draft is delivered for the purpose of giving rights on the acceptance to any person.

(b) A draft may be accepted although it has not been signed by the drawer, is otherwise incomplete, is overdue, or has been dishonored.

(c) If a draft is payable at a fixed period after sight and the acceptor fails to date the acceptance, the holder may complete the acceptance by supplying a date in good faith.

(d) "Certified check" means a check accepted by the bank on which it is drawn. Acceptance may be made as stated in subsection (a) or by a writing on the check which indicates that the check is certified. The drawee of a check has no obligation to certify the check, and refusal to certify is not dishonor of the check.

§ 3–410.   Acceptance Varying Draft.

(a) If the terms of a drawee's acceptance vary from the terms of the draft as presented, the holder may refuse the acceptance and treat the draft as dishonored. In that case, the drawee may cancel the acceptance.

(b) The terms of a draft are not varied by an acceptance to pay at a particular bank or place in the United States, unless the acceptance states that the draft is to be paid only at that bank or place.

(c) If the holder assents to an acceptance varying the terms of a draft, the obligation of each drawer and indorser that does not expressly assent to the acceptance is discharged.

§ 3–411.   Refusal to Pay Cashier's Checks, Teller's Checks, and Certified Checks.

(a) In this section, "obligated bank" means the acceptor of a certified check or the issuer of a cashier's check or teller's check bought from the issuer.

(b) If the obligated bank wrongfully (i) refuses to pay a cashier's check or certified check, (ii) stops payment of a teller's check, or (iii) refuses to pay a dishonored teller's check, the person asserting the right to enforce the check is entitled to compensation for expenses and loss of interest resulting from the nonpayment and may recover consequential damages if the obligated bank refused to pay after receiving notice of particular circumstances giving rise to the damages.

(c) Expenses or consequential damages under subsection (b) are not recoverable if the refusal of the obligated bank to pay occurs because (i) the bank suspends payments, (ii) the obligated bank is asserting a claim or defense of the bank that it has reasonable grounds to believe is available against the person entitled to enforce the instrument, (iii) the obligated bank has a reasonable doubt whether the person demanding payment is the person entitled to enforce the instrument, or (iv) payment is prohibited by law.

§ 3–412.   Obligation of Maker.

A maker of a note is obliged to pay the note (i) according to its terms at the time it was issued or, if not issued, at the time it first came into possession of a holder, or (ii) if the maker signed an incomplete instrument, according to its terms when completed as stated in Sections 3–115 and 3–407. The obligation is owed to a person entitled to enforce the note or to an indorser that paid the note pursuant to Section 3–415.

§ 3–413.   Obligation of Acceptor.

(a) An acceptor of a draft is obliged to pay the draft (i) according to its terms at the time it was accepted, even though the acceptance states that the draft is payable "as originally drawn" or equivalent terms, (ii) if the acceptance varies the terms of the draft, according to the terms of the draft as varied, or (iii) if the acceptance is of a draft that is an incomplete instrument, according to its terms when completed as stated in Sections 3–115 and 3–407. The obligation is owed to a person entitled to enforce the draft or to the drawer or an indorser that paid the draft pursuant to Section 3–414 or 3–415.

(b) If the certification of a check or other acceptance of a draft states the amount certified or accepted, the obligation of the acceptor is that amount. If (i) the certification or acceptance does not state an amount, (ii) the instrument is subsequently altered by raising its amount, and (iii) the instrument is then negotiated to a holder in due course, the obligation of the acceptor is the amount of the instrument at the time it was negotiated to the holder in due course.

§ 3–414.   Obligation of Drawer.

(a) If an unaccepted draft is dishonored, the drawer is obliged to pay the draft (i) according to its terms at the time it was issued or, if not issued, at the time it first came into possession of a holder, or (ii) if the drawer signed an incomplete instrument, according to its terms when completed as stated in Sections 3–115 and 3–407. The obligation is owed to a person entitled to enforce the draft or to an indorser that paid the draft pursuant to Section 3–415.

(b) If a draft is accepted by a bank and the acceptor dishonors the draft, the drawer has no obligation to pay the draft because of the dishonor, regardless of when or by whom acceptance was obtained.

(c) If a draft is accepted and the acceptor is not a bank, the obligation of the drawer to pay the draft if the draft is dishonored by the acceptor is the same as the obligation of an indorser stated in Section 3–415(a) and (c).

(d) Words in a draft indicating that the draft is drawn without recourse are effective to disclaim all liability of the drawer to pay the draft if the draft is not a check or a teller's check, but they are not effective to disclaim the obligation stated in subsection (a) if the draft is a check or a teller's check.

(e) If (i) a check is not presented for payment or given to a depositary bank for collection within 30 days after its date, (ii) the drawee suspends payments after expiration of the 30-day period without paying the check, and (iii) because of the suspension of payments the drawer is deprived of funds maintained with the drawee to cover payment of the check, the drawer to the extent deprived of funds may discharge its obligation to pay the check by assigning to the person entitled to enforce the check the rights of the drawer against the drawee with respect to the funds.

§ 3–415. Obligation of Indorser.

(a) Subject to subsections (b), (c) and (d) and to Section 3–419(d), if an instrument is dishonored, an indorser is obliged to pay the amount due on the instrument (i) according to the terms of the instrument at the time it was indorsed, or (ii) if the indorser indorsed an incomplete instrument, according to its terms when completed as stated in Sections 3–115 and 3–407. The obligation of the indorser is owed to a person entitled to enforce the instrument or to a subsequent indorser that paid the instrument pursuant to this section.

(b) If an indorsement states that it is made "without recourse" or otherwise disclaims liability of the indorser, the indorser is not liable under subsection (a) to pay the instrument.

(c) If notice of dishonor of an instrument is required by Section 3–503 and notice of dishonor complying with that section is not given to an indorser, the liability of the indorser under subsection (a) is discharged.

(d) If a draft is accepted by a bank after an indorsement was made and the acceptor dishonors the draft, the indorser is not liable under subsection (a) to pay the instrument.

(e) If an indorser of a check is liable under subsection (a) and the check is not presented for payment, or given to a depositary bank for collection, within 30 days after the day the indorsement was made, the liability of the indorser under subsection (a) is discharged.

§ 3–416. Transfer Warranties.

(a) A person that transfers an instrument for consideration warrants to the transferee and, if the transfer is by indorsement, to any subsequent transferee that:

(1) the warrantor is a person entitled to enforce the instrument,

(2) all signatures on the instrument are authentic and authorized,

(3) the instrument has not been altered,

(4) the instrument is not subject to a defense or claim in recoupment stated in Section 3–305(a) of any party that can be asserted against the warrantor, and

(5) the warrantor has no knowledge of any insolvency proceeding commenced with respect to the maker or acceptor or, in the case of an unaccepted draft, the drawer.

(b) A person to whom the warranties under subsection (a) are made and who took the instrument in good faith may recover from the warrantor as damages for breach of warranty an amount equal to the loss suffered as a result of the breach, but not more than the amount of the instrument plus expenses and loss of interest incurred as a result of the breach.

(c) The warranties stated in subsection (a) cannot be disclaimed with respect to checks. Unless notice of a claim for breach of warranty is given to the warrantor within 30 days after the claimant has reason to know of the breach and the identity of the warrantor, the warrantor is discharged to the extent of any loss caused by the delay in giving notice of the claim.

(d) A cause of action for breach of warranty under this section accrues when the claimant has reason to know of the breach.

§ 3–417. Presentment Warranties.

(a) If an unaccepted draft is presented to the drawee for payment or acceptance and the drawee pays or accepts the draft, (i) the person obtaining payment or acceptance, at the time of presentment, and (ii) a previous transferor of the draft, at the time of transfer, warrant to the drawee making payment or accepting the draft in good faith that:

(1) the warrantor is or was, at the time the warrantor transferred the draft, a person entitled to enforce the draft or authorized to obtain payment or acceptance of the draft on behalf of a person entitled to enforce the draft;

(2) the draft has not been altered; and

(3) the warrantor has no knowledge that the signature of the purported drawer of the draft is unauthorized.

(b) A drawee making payment may recover from any warrantor damages for breach of warranty equal to the amount paid by the drawee less the amount the drawee received or is entitled to receive from the drawer because of payment of the draft. In addition the drawee is entitled to compensation for expenses and loss of interest resulting from the breach. The right of the drawee to recover damages under this subsection is not affected by any failure of the drawee to exercise ordinary care in making payment. If the drawee accepts the draft (i) breach of warranty is a defense to the obligation of the acceptor, and (ii) if the acceptor makes payment with respect to the draft, the acceptor is entitled to recover from any warrantor for breach of warranty the amounts stated in the first two sentences of this subsection.

(c) If a drawee asserts a claim for breach of warranty under subsection (a) based on an unauthorized indorsement of the draft or an alteration of the draft, the warrantor may defend by proving that the indorsement is effective under Section 3–404 or 3–405 or the drawer is precluded under Section 3–406 or 4–406 from asserting against the drawee the unauthorized indorsement or alteration.

(d) This subsection applies if (i) a dishonored draft is presented for payment to the drawer or an indorser or (ii) any other instrument is presented for payment to a party obliged to pay the instrument, and payment is received. The person obtaining payment and a prior transferor of the instrument warrant to the person making payment in good faith that the warrantor is or was, at the time the warrantor transferred the instrument, a person entitled to enforce the instrument or authorized to obtain payment on behalf of a person entitled to enforce the instrument. The person making payment may recover from any warrantor for breach of warranty an amount equal to the amount paid plus expenses and loss of interest resulting from the breach.

(e) The warranties stated in subsections (a) and (d) cannot be disclaimed with respect to checks. Unless notice of a claim for breach of warranty is given to the warrantor within 30 days after the claimant has reason to know of the breach and the identity of the warrantor, the warrantor is discharged to the extent of any loss caused by the delay in giving notice of the claim.

(f) A cause of action for breach of warranty under this section accrues when the claimant has reason to know of the breach.

§ 3–418. Payment or Acceptance by Mistake.

(a) Except as provided in subsection (c), if the drawee of a draft pays or accepts the draft and the drawee acted on the mistaken belief that (i) payment of the draft had not been stopped under Section 4–403, (ii) the signature of the purported drawer of the draft was authorized, or (iii) the balance in the drawer's account with the drawee represented available funds, the drawee may recover the amount paid from the person to whom or for whose benefit payment was made or, in the case of acceptance, may revoke the acceptance. Rights of the drawee under this subsection are not affected by failure of the drawee to exercise ordinary care in paying or accepting the draft.

(b) Except as provided in subsection (c), if an instrument has been paid or accepted by mistake and the case is not covered by subsection (a), the person paying or accepting may recover the amount paid or revoke acceptance to the extent allowed by the law governing mistake and restitution.

(c) The remedies provided by subsection (a) or (b) may not be asserted against a person who took the instrument in good faith and for value. This subsection does not limit remedies provided by Section 3–417 for breach of warranty.

§ 3–419. Instruments Signed for Accommodation.

(a) If an instrument is issued for value given for the benefit of a party to the instrument ("accommodated party") and another party to the instrument ("accommodation party") signs the instrument for the purpose of incurring liability on the instrument without being a direct beneficiary of the value given for the instrument, the instrument is signed by the accommodation party "for accommodation."

(b) An accommodation party may sign the instrument as maker, drawer, acceptor, or indorser and, subject to subsection (d), is obliged to pay the instrument in the capacity in which the accommodation party signs. The obligation of an accommodation party may be enforced notwithstanding any statute of frauds and regardless of whether the accommodation party receives consideration for the accommodation.

(c) A person signing an instrument is presumed to be an accommodation party and there is notice that the instrument is signed for accommodation if the signature is an anomalous indorsement or is accompanied by words indicating that the signer is acting as surety or guarantor with respect to the obligation of another party to the instrument. Except as provided in Section 3–606, the obligation of an accommodation party to pay the instrument is not affected by the fact that the person enforcing the obligation had notice when the instrument was taken by that person that the accommodation party signed the instrument for accommodation.

(d) If the signature of a party to an instrument is accompanied by words indicating unambiguously that the party is guaranteeing collection rather than payment of the obligation of another party to the instrument, the signer is obliged to pay the amount due on the instrument to a person entitled to enforce the instrument only if (i) execution of judgment against the other party has been returned unsatisfied, (ii) the other party is insolvent or in an insolvency proceeding, (iii) the other party cannot be served with process, or (iv) it is otherwise apparent that payment cannot be obtained from the party whose obligation is guaranteed.

(e) An accommodation party that pays the instrument is entitled to reimbursement from the accommodated party and is entitled to enforce the instrument against the accommodated party. An accommodated party that pays the instrument has no right of recourse against, and is not entitled to contribution from, an accommodation party.

§ 3–420. Conversion of Instrument.

(a) The law applicable to conversion of personal property applies to instruments. An instrument is also converted if the instrument lacks an indorsement necessary for negotiation and it is purchased or taken for collection or the drawee takes the instrument and makes payment to a person not entitled to receive payment. An action for conversion of an instrument may not be brought by (i) the maker, drawer, or acceptor of the instrument or (ii) a payee or indorsee who did not receive delivery of the instrument either directly or through delivery to an agent or a co-payee.

(b) In an action under subsection (a), the measure of liability is presumed to be the amount payable on the instrument, but recovery may not exceed the amount of the plaintiff's interest in the instrument.

(c) A representative, other than a depositary bank, that has in good faith dealt with an instrument or its proceeds on behalf of one who was not the person entitled to enforce the instrument is not liable in conversion to that person beyond the amount of any proceeds that it has not paid out.

PART 5 DISHONOR

§ 3–501. Presentment.

(a) "Presentment" means a demand (i) to pay an instrument made to the maker, drawee, or acceptor or, in the case of a note or accepted draft payable at a bank, to the bank, or (ii) to accept a draft made to the drawee, by a person entitled to enforce the instrument.

(b) Subject to Article 4, agreement of the parties, clearing house rules and the like,

(1) presentment may be made at the place of payment of the instrument and must be made at the place of payment if the instrument is payable at a bank in the United States; may be made by any commercially reasonable means, including an oral, written, or electronic communication; is effective when the demand for payment or acceptance is received by the person to whom presentment is made; is effective if made to any one of two or more makers, acceptors, drawees or other payors; and

(2) without dishonoring the instrument, the party to whom presentment is made may (i) treat presentment as occurring on the next business day after the day of presentment if the party to whom presentment is made has established a cut-off hour not earlier than 2 p.m. for the receipt and processing of instruments presented for payment or acceptance and presentment is made after the cut-off hour, (ii) require exhibition of the instrument, (iii) require reasonable identification of the person making presentment and evidence of authority to make it if made on behalf of another person, (iv) require a signed receipt on the instrument for any payment made or surrender of the instrument if full payment is made, (v) return the instrument for lack of a necessary indorsement, or (vi) refuse payment or acceptance for failure of the presentment to comply with the terms of the instrument, an agreement of the parties, or other law or applicable rule.

§ 3–502.   Dishonor.

(a) Dishonor of a note is governed by the following rules:

(1) If the note is payable on demand, the note is dishonored if presentment is duly made and the note is not paid on the day of presentment.

(2) If the note is not payable on demand and is payable at or through a bank or the terms of the note require presentment, the note is dishonored if presentment is duly made and the note is not paid on the day it becomes payable or the day of presentment, whichever is later.

(3) If the note is not payable on demand and subparagraph (2) does not apply, the note is dishonored if it is not paid on the day it becomes payable.

(b) Dishonor of an unaccepted draft other than a documentary draft is governed by the following rules:

(1) If a check is presented for payment otherwise than for immediate payment over the counter, the check is dishonored if the payor bank makes timely return of the check or sends timely notice of dishonor or nonpayment under Section 4–301 or 4–302, or becomes accountable for the amount of the check under Section 4–302.

(2) If the draft is payable on demand and subparagraph (1) does not apply, the draft is dishonored if presentment for payment is duly made and the draft is not paid on the day of presentment.

(3) If the draft is payable on a date stated in the draft, the draft is dishonored if (i) presentment for payment is duly made and payment is not made on the day the draft becomes payable or the day of presentment, whichever is later, or (ii) presentment for acceptance is duly made before the day the draft becomes payable and the draft is not accepted on the day of presentment.

(4) If the draft is payable on elapse of a period of time after sight or acceptance, the draft is dishonored if presentment for acceptance is duly made and the draft is not accepted on the day of presentment.

(c) Dishonor of an unaccepted documentary draft occurs according to the rules stated in subparagraphs (2), (3), and (4) of subsection (b) except that payment or acceptance may be delayed without dishonor until no later than the close of the third business day of the drawee following the day on which payment or acceptance is required by those subpara-

graphs.

(d) Dishonor of an accepted draft is governed by the following rules:

(1) If the draft is payable on demand, the draft is dishonored if presentment for payment is duly made and the draft is not paid on the day of presentment.

(2) If the draft is not payable on demand, the draft is dishonored if presentment for payment is duly made and payment is not made on the day it becomes payable or the day of presentment, whichever is later.

(e) In any case in which presentment is otherwise required for dishonor under this section and presentment is excused under Section 3–504, dishonor occurs without presentment if the instrument is not duly accepted or paid.

(f) If a draft is dishonored because timely acceptance of the draft was not made and the person entitled to demand acceptance consents to a late acceptance, from the time of acceptance the draft is treated as never having been dishonored.

§ 3–503.   Notice of Dishonor.

(a) The obligation of an indorser stated in Section 3–415(a) and the obligation of a drawer stated in Section 3–414(c) may not be enforced unless (i) the indorser or drawer is given notice of dishonor of the instrument complying with this section or (ii) notice of dishonor is excused under Section 3–504(c).

(b) Notice of dishonor may be given by any person; may be given by any commercially reasonable means including an oral, written, or electronic communication; is sufficient if it reasonably identifies the instrument and indicates that the instrument has been dishonored or has not been paid or accepted. Return of an instrument given to a bank for collection is a sufficient notice of dishonor.

(c) Subject to Section 3-504(d), with respect to an instrument taken for collection by a collecting bank, notice of dishonor must be given (i) by the bank before midnight of the next banking day following the banking day on which the bank receives notice of dishonor of the instrument, and (ii) by any other person within 30 days following the day on which the person receives notice of dishonor. With respect to any other instrument, notice of dishonor must be given within 30 days following the day on which dishonor occurs.

§ 3–504.   Excused Presentment and Notice of Dishonor.

(a) Presentment for payment or acceptance of an instrument is excused if (i) the person entitled to present the instrument cannot with reasonable diligence make presentment, (ii) the maker or acceptor has repudiated an obligation to pay the instrument or is dead or in insolvency proceedings, (iii) by the terms of the instrument presentment is not necessary to enforce the obligation of indorsers or the drawer, or (iv) the drawer or indorser whose obligation is being enforced waived presentment or otherwise had no reason to expect or right to require that the instrument be paid or accepted.

(b) Presentment for payment or acceptance of a draft is also excused if the drawer instructed the drawee not to pay or accept the draft or the drawee was not obligated to the drawer to pay the draft.

(c) Notice of dishonor is excused if (i) by the terms of the instrument notice of dishonor is not necessary to enforce the obligation of a party to pay the instrument, or (ii) the party whose obligation is being enforced waived notice of dishonor. A waiver of presentment is also a waiver of notice of dishonor.

(d) Delay in giving notice of dishonor is excused if the delay was caused by circumstances beyond the control of the person giving the notice and the person giving the notice exercised reasonable diligence after the cause of the delay ceased to operate.

§ 3–505. Evidence of Dishonor.

(a) The following are admissible as evidence and create a presumption of dishonor and of any notice of dishonor stated:

(1) a document regular in form as provided in subsection (b) which purports to be a protest;

(2) a purported stamp or writing of the drawee, payor bank, or presenting bank on or accompanying the instrument stating that acceptance or payment has been refused unless reasons for the refusal are stated and the reasons are not consistent with dishonor;

(3) a book or record of the drawee, payor bank, or collecting bank, kept in the usual course of business which shows dishonor, even if there is no evidence of who made the entry.

(b) A protest is a certificate of dishonor made by a United States consul or vice consul, or a notary public or other person authorized to administer oaths by the law of the place where dishonor occurs. It may be made upon information satisfactory to that person. The protest must identify the instrument and certify either that presentment has been made or, if not made, the reason why it was not made, and that the instrument has been dishonored by nonacceptance or nonpayment. The protest may also certify that notice of dishonor has been given to some or all parties.

PART 6   DISCHARGE AND PAYMENT

§ 3–601. Discharge and Effect of Discharge.

(a) The obligation of a party to pay the instrument is discharged as stated in this Article or by an act or agreement with the party which would discharge an obligation to pay money under a simple contract.

(b) Discharge of the obligation of a party is not effective against a person acquiring rights of a holder in due course of the instrument without notice of the discharge.

§ 3–602. Payment.

(a) Subject to subsection (b), an instrument is paid to the extent payment is made (i) by or on behalf of a party obliged to pay the instrument, and (ii) to a person entitled to enforce the instrument. To the extent of the payment, the obligation of the party obliged to pay the instrument is discharged even though payment is made with knowledge of a claim to the instrument under Section 3–306 by another person.

(b) The obligation of a party to pay the instrument is not discharged under subsection (a) if:

(1) a claim to the instrument under Section 3–306 is enforceable against the party receiving payment and (i) payment is made with knowledge by the payor that payment is prohibited by injunction or similar process of a court of competent jurisdiction, or (ii) in the case of an instrument other than a cashier's check, teller's check, or certified check, the party making payment accepted, from the person having a claim to the instrument, indemnity against loss resulting from refusal to pay the person entitled to enforce the instrument, or

(2) the person making payment knows that the instrument is a stolen instrument and pays a person that it knows is in wrongful possession of the instrument.

§ 3–603. Tender of Payment.

(a) If tender of payment of an obligation of a party to an instrument is made to a person entitled to enforce the obligation, the effect of tender is governed by principles of law applicable to tender of payment of an obligation under a simple contract.

(b) If tender of payment of an obligation to pay the instrument is made to a person entitled to enforce the instrument and the tender is refused, there is discharge, to the extent of the amount of the tender, of the obligation of an indorser or accommodation party having a right of recourse against the obligor making the tender.

(c) If tender of payment of an amount due on an instrument is made by or on behalf of the obligor to the person entitled to enforce the instrument, the obligation of the obligor to pay interest after the due date on the amount tendered is discharged. If presentment is required with respect to an instrument and the obligor is able and ready to pay on the due date at every place of payment stated in the instrument, the obligor is deemed to have made tender of payment on the due date to the person entitled to enforce the instrument.

§ 3–604. Discharge by Cancellation or Renunciation.

(a) A person entitled to enforce an instrument may, with or without consideration, discharge the obligation of a party to pay the instrument (i) by an intentional voluntary act such as surrender of the instrument to the party, destruction, mutilation, or cancellation of the instrument, cancellation or striking out of the party's signature, or the addition of words to the instrument indicating discharge, or (ii) by agreeing not to sue or otherwise renouncing rights against the party by a signed writing.

(b) Cancellation or striking out of an indorsement pursuant to subsection (a) does not affect the status and rights of a party derived from the indorsement.

§ 3–605. Discharge of Indorsers and Accommodation Parties.

(a) For the purposes of this section, the term "indorser" includes a drawer having the obligation stated in Section 3–414(c).

(b) Discharge of the obligation of a party to the instrument under Section 3–605 does not discharge the obligation of an indorser or accommodation party having a right of recourse against the discharged party.

(c) If a person entitled to enforce an instrument agrees, with or without consideration, to a material modification of the obligation of a party to the instrument, including an extension of the due date, there is discharge of the obligation of an indorser or accommodation party having a right of recourse against the person whose obligation is modified to the extent the modification causes loss to the indorser or accommodation party with respect to the right of recourse. The indorser or accommodation party is deemed to have suffered loss as a result of the modification equal to the amount of the right of recourse unless the person enforcing the instrument proves that no loss was caused by the modification or that the loss caused by the modification was less than the amount of the right of recourse.

(d) If the obligation of a party to an instrument is secured by an interest in collateral and impairment of the value of the interest is caused by a person entitled to enforce the instrument, there is discharge of the obligation of an indorser or accommodation party having a right of recourse against the obligor to the extent of the impairment. The value of an interest in collateral is impaired to the extent (i) the value of the interest is reduced to an amount less than the amount of the right of recourse of the party asserting discharge, or (ii) the reduction in value of the interest causes an increase in the amount by which the amount of the right of recourse exceeds the value of the interest. The burden of proving impairment is on the party asserting discharge.

(e) If the obligation of a party to an instrument is secured by an interest in collateral not provided by an accommodation party and the value of the interest is impaired by a person entitled to enforce the instrument, the obligation of any party who is jointly and severally liable with respect to the secured obligation is discharged to the extent the impairment causes the party asserting discharge to pay more than that party would have been obliged to pay, taking into account rights of contribution, if impairment had not occurred. If the party asserting discharge is an accommodation party not entitled to discharge under subsection (d), the party is deemed to have a right to contribution based on joint and several liability rather than a right to reimbursement. The burden of proving impairment is on the party asserting discharge.

(f) Under subsection (d) or (e) causation of impairment includes (i) failure to obtain or maintain perfection or recordation of the interest in collateral, (ii) release of collateral without substitution of collateral of equal value, (iii) failure to perform a duty to preserve the value of collateral owed, under Article 9 or other law, to a debtor or surety or other person secondarily liable, or (iv) failure to comply with applicable law in disposing of collateral.

(g) An accommodation party is not discharged under subsection (c) or (d) unless the person agreeing to the modification or causing the impairment knows of the accommodation or has notice under Section 3–419(c) that the instrument was signed for accommodation. There is no discharge of any party under subsection (c), (d), or (e) if (i) the party asserting discharge consents to the event or conduct that is the basis of the discharge, or (ii) the instrument or a separate agreement of the party provides for waiver of discharge under this section either specifically or by general language indicating that parties to the instrument waive defenses based on suretyship or impairment of collateral.

ARTICLE 9

Secured Transactions; Sales of Accounts and Chattel Paper

Note: The adoption of this Article should be accompanied by the repeal of existing statutes dealing with conditional sales, trust receipts, factor's liens where the factor is given a non-possessory lien, chattel mortgages, crop mortgages, mortgages on railroad equipment, assignment of accounts and generally statutes regulating security interests in personal property.

Where the state has a retail installment selling act or small loan act, that legislation should be carefully examined to determine what changes in those acts are needed to conform them to this Article. This Article primarily sets out rules defining rights of a secured party against persons dealing with the debtor; it does not prescribe regulations and controls which may be necessary to curb abuses arising in the small loan business or in the financing of consumer purchases on credit. Accordingly there is no intention to repeal existing regulatory acts in those fields by enactment or re-enactment of Article 9. See Section 9–203(4) and the Note thereto.

PART 1 SHORT TITLE, APPLICABILITY AND DEFINITIONS

§ 9–101. Short Title.

This Article shall be known and may be cited as Uniform Commercial Code—Secured Transactions.

§ 9–102. Policy and Subject Matter of Article.

(1) Except as otherwise provided in Section 9–104 on excluded transactions, this Article applies

    (a) to any transaction (regardless of its form) which is intended to create a security interest in personal property or fixtures including goods, documents, instruments, general intangibles, chattel paper or accounts; and also

    (b) to any sale of accounts or chattel paper.

(2) This Article applies to security interests created by contract including pledge, assignment, chattel mortgage, chattel trust, trust deed, factor's lien, equipment trust, conditional sale, trust receipt, other lien or title retention contract and lease or consignment intended as security. This Article does not apply to statutory liens except as provided in Section 9–310.

(3) The application of this Article to a security interest in a secured obligation is not affected by the fact that the obligation is itself secured by a transaction or interest to which this Article does not apply.

§ 9–103. Perfection of Security Interest in Multiple State Transactions.

(1) Documents, instruments and ordinary goods.

(a) This subsection applies to documents and instruments and to goods other than those covered by a certificate of title described in subsection (2), mobile goods described in subsection (3), and minerals described in subsection (5).

(b) Except as otherwise provided in this subsection, perfection and the effect of perfection or non-perfection of a security interest in collateral are governed by the law of the jurisdiction where the collateral is when the last event occurs on which is based the assertion that the security interest is perfected or unperfected.

(c) If the parties to a transaction creating a purchase money security interest in goods in one jurisdiction understand at the time that the security interest attaches that the goods will be kept in another jurisdiction, then the law of the other jurisdiction governs the perfection and the effect of perfection or non-perfection of the security interest from the time it attaches until thirty days after the debtor receives possession of the goods and thereafter if the goods are taken to the other jurisdiction before the end of the thirty-day period.

(d) When collateral is brought into and kept in this state while subject to a security interest perfected under the law of the jurisdiction from which the collateral was removed, the security interest remains perfected, but if action is required by Part 3 of this Article to perfect the security interest,

(i) if the action is not taken before the expiration of the period of perfection in the other jurisdiction or the end of four months after the collateral is brought into this state, whichever period first expires, the security interest becomes unperfected at the end of that period and is thereafter deemed to have been unperfected as against a person who became a purchaser after removal;

(ii) if the action is taken before the expiration of the period specified in subparagraph (i), the security interest continues perfected thereafter;

(iii) for the purpose of priority over a buyer of consumer goods (subsection (2) of Section 9–307), the period of the effectiveness of a filing in the jurisdiction from which the collateral is removed is governed by the rules with respect to perfection in subparagraphs (i) and (ii).

(2) Certificate of title.

(a) This subsection applies to goods covered by a certificate of title issued under a statute of this state or of another jurisdiction under the law of which indication of a security interest on the certificate is required as a condition of perfection.

(b) Except as otherwise provided in this subsection, perfection and the effect of perfection or non-perfection of the security interest are governed by the law (including the conflict of laws rules) of the jurisdiction issuing the certificate until four months after the goods are removed from that jurisdiction and thereafter until the goods are registered in another jurisdiction, but in any event not beyond surrender of the certificate. After the expiration of that period, the goods are not covered by the certificate of title within the meaning of this section.

(c) Except with respect to the rights of a buyer described in the next paragraph, a security interest, perfected in another jurisdiction otherwise than by notation on a certificate of title, in goods brought into this state and thereafter covered by a certificate of title issued by this state is subject to the rules stated in paragraph (d) of subsection (1).

(d) If goods are brought into this state while a security interest therein is perfected in any manner under the law of the jurisdiction from which the goods are removed and a certificate of title is issued by this state and the certificate does not show that the goods are subject to the security interest or that they may be subject to security interests not shown on the certificate, the security interest is subordinate to the rights of a buyer of the goods who is not in the business of selling goods of that kind to the extent that he gives value and receives delivery of the goods after issuance of the certificate and without knowledge of the security interest.

(3) Accounts, general intangibles and mobile goods.

(a) This subsection applies to accounts (other than an account described in subsection (5) on minerals) and general intangibles (other than uncertificated securities) and to goods which are mobile and which are of a type normally used in more than one jurisdiction, such as motor vehicles, trailers, rolling stock, airplanes, shipping containers, road building and construction machinery and commercial harvesting machinery and the like, if the goods are equipment or are inventory leased or held for lease by the debtor to others, and are not covered by a certificate of title described in subsection (2).

(b) The law (including the conflict of laws rules) of the jurisdiction in which the debtor is located governs the perfection and the effect of perfection or non-perfection of the security interest.

(c) If, however, the debtor is located in a jurisdiction which is not a part of the United States, and which does not provide for perfection of the security interest by filing or recording in that jurisdiction, the law of the jurisdiction in the United States in which the debtor has its major executive office in the United States governs the perfection and the effect of perfection or non-perfection of the security interest through filing. In the alternative, if the debtor is located in a jurisdiction which is not a part of the United States or Canada and the collateral is accounts or general intangibles for money due or to become due, the security interest may be perfected by notification to the account debtor. As used in this paragraph, "United States" includes its territories and possessions and the Commonwealth of Puerto Rico.

(d) A debtor shall be deemed located at his place of business if he has one, at his chief executive office if he has more than one place of business, otherwise at his residence. If, however, the debtor is a foreign air carrier under the Federal Aviation Act of 1958, as amended, it shall be deemed located at the designated office of the agent upon whom service of process may be made on behalf of the foreign air carrier.

(e) A security interest perfected under the law of the jurisdiction of the location of the debtor is perfected until the expiration of four months after a change of the debtor's location to another jurisdiction, or until perfection would have ceased by the law of the first jurisdiction, whichever period first expires. Unless perfected in the new jurisdiction before the end of that period, it becomes unperfected thereafter and is deemed to have been unperfected as against a person who became a purchaser after the change.

(4) Chattel paper.

The rules stated for goods in subsection (1) apply to a possessory security interest in chattel paper. The rules stated for accounts in subsection (3) apply to a non-possessory security interest in chattel paper, but the security interest may not be perfected by notification to the account debtor.

(5) Minerals.

Perfection and the effect of perfection or non-perfection of a security interest which is created by a debtor who has an interest in minerals or the like (including oil and gas) before extraction and which attaches thereto as extracted, or which attaches to an account resulting from the sale thereof at the wellhead or minehead are governed by the law (including the conflict of laws rules) of the jurisdiction wherein the wellhead or minehead is located.

(6) Uncertificated securities.

The law (including the conflict of laws rules) of the jurisdiction of organization of the issuer governs the perfection and the effect of perfection or non-perfection of a security interest in uncertificated securities.

§ 9–104.   Transactions Excluded From Article.

This Article does not apply

(a) to a security interest subject to any statute of the United States, to the extent that such statute governs the rights of parties to and third parties affected by transactions in particular types of property; or

(b) to a landlord's lien; or

(c) to a lien given by statute or other rule of law for services or materials except as provided in Section 9–310 on priority of such liens; or

(d) to a transfer of a claim for wages, salary or other compensation of an employee; or

(e) to a transfer by a government or governmental subdivision or agency; or

(f) to a sale of accounts or chattel paper as part of a sale of the business out of which they arose, or an assignment of accounts or chattel paper which is for the purpose of collection only, or a transfer of a right to payment under a contract to an assignee who is also to do the performance under the contract or a transfer of a single account to an assignee in whole or partial satisfaction of a preexisting indebtedness; or

(g) to a transfer of an interest in or claim in or under any policy of insurance, except as provided with respect to proceeds (Section 9–306) and priorities in proceeds (Section 9–312); or

(h) to a right represented by a judgment (other than a judgment taken on a right to payment which was collateral); or

(i) to any right of set-off; or

(j) except to the extent that provision is made for fixtures in Section 9–313, to the creation or transfer of an interest in or lien on real estate, including a lease or rents thereunder; or

(k) to a transfer in whole or in part of any claim arising out of tort; or

(l) to a transfer of an interest in any deposit account (subsection (1) of Section 9–105), except as provided with respect to proceeds (Section 9–306) and priorities in proceeds

(Section 9–312).

§ 9–105.   Definitions and Index of Definitions.

(1) In this Article unless the context otherwise requires:

(a) "Account debtor" means the person who is obligated on an account, chattel paper or general intangible;

(b) "Chattel paper" means a writing or writings which evidence both a monetary obligation and a security interest in or a lease of specific goods, but a charter or other contract involving the use or hire of a vessel is not chattel paper. When a transaction is evidenced both by such a security agreement or a lease and by an instrument or a series of instruments, the group of writings taken together constitutes chattel paper;

(c) "Collateral" means the property subject to a security interest, and includes accounts and chattel paper which have been sold;

(d) "Debtor" means the person who owes payment or other performance of the obligation secured, whether or not he owns or has rights in the collateral, and includes the seller of accounts or chattel paper. Where the debtor and the owner of the collateral are not the same person, the term "debtor" means the owner of the collateral in any provision of the Article dealing with the collateral, the obligor in any provision dealing with the obligation, and may include both where the context so requires;

(e) "Deposit account" means a demand, time, savings, passbook or like account maintained with a bank, savings and loan association, credit union or like organization, other than an account evidenced by a certificate of deposit;

(f) "Document" means document of title as defined in the general definitions of Article 1 (Section 1–201), and a receipt of the kind described in subsection (2) of Section 7–201;

(g) "Encumbrance" includes real estate mortgages and other liens on real estate and all other rights in real estate that are not ownership interests;

(h) "Goods" includes all things which are movable at the time the security interest attaches or which are fixtures (Section 9–313), but does not include money, documents, instruments, accounts, chattel paper, general intangibles, or minerals or the like (including oil and gas) before extraction. "Goods" also includes standing timber which is to be cut and removed under a conveyance or contract for sale, the unborn young of animals, and growing crops;

(i) "Instrument" means a negotiable instrument (defined in Section 3–104), or a certificated security (defined in Section 8–102) or any other writing which evidences a right to the payment of money and is not itself a security agreement or lease and is of a type which is in ordinary course of business transferred by delivery with any necessary indorsement or assignment;

(j) "Mortgage" means a consensual interest created by a real estate mortgage, a trust deed on real estate, or the like;

(k) An advance is made "pursuant to commitment" if the secured party has bound himself to make it, whether or not a subsequent event of default or other event not within his control has relieved or may relieve him from his obligation;

(l) "Security agreement" means an agreement which creates or provides for a security interest;

(m) "Secured party" means a lender, seller or other person in whose favor there is a security interest, including a person to whom accounts or chattel paper have been sold. When the holders of obligations issued under an indenture of trust, equipment trust agreement or the like are represented by a trustee or other person, the representative is the secured party;

(n) "Transmitting utility" means any person primarily engaged in the railroad, street railway or trolley bus business, the electric or electronics communications transmission business, the transmission of goods by pipeline, or the transmission or the production and transmission of electricity, steam, gas or water, or the provision of sewer service.

(2) Other definitions applying to this Article and the sections in which they appear are:

"Account". Section 9–106.
"Attach". Section 9–203.
"Construction mortgage". Section 9–313(1).
"Consumer goods". Section 9–109(1).
"Equipment". Section 9–109(2).
"Farm products". Section 9–109(3).
"Fixture". Section 9–313(1).
"Fixture filing". Section 9–313(1).
"General intangibles". Section 9–106.
"Inventory". Section 9–109(4).
"Lien creditor". Section 9–301(3).
"Proceeds". Section 9–306(1).
"Purchase money security interest". Section 9–107.
"United States". Section 9–103.

(3) The following definitions in other Articles apply to this Article:

"Check". Section 3–104.
"Contract for sale". Section 2–106.
"Holder in due course". Section 3–302.
"Note". Section 3–104.
"Sale". Section 2–106.

(4) In addition Article 1 contains general definitions and principles of construction and interpretation applicable throughout this Article.

§ 9–106. Definitions: "Account"; "General Intangibles".

"Account" means any right to payment for goods sold or leased or for services rendered which is not evidenced by an instrument or chattel paper, whether or not it has been earned by performance. "General intangibles" means any personal property (including things in action) other than goods, accounts, chattel paper, documents, instruments, and money. All rights to payment earned or unearned under a charter or other contract involving the use or hire of a vessel and all rights incident to the charter or contract are accounts.

§ 9–107. Definitions: "Purchase Money Security Interest".

A security interest is a "purchase money security interest" to the extent that it is

(a) taken or retained by the seller of the collateral to secure all or part of its price; or

(b) taken by a person who by making advances or incurring an obligation gives value to enable the debtor to acquire rights in or the use of collateral if such value is in fact so used.

§ 9–108. When After-Acquired Collateral Not Security for Antecedent Debt.

Where a secured party makes an advance, incurs an obligation, releases a perfected security interest, or otherwise gives new value which is to be secured in whole or in part by after-acquired property his security interest in the after-acquired collateral shall be deemed to be taken for new value and not as security for an antecedent debt if the debtor acquires his rights in such collateral either in the ordinary course of his business or under a contract of purchase made pursuant to the security agreement within a reasonable time after new value is given.

§ 9–109. Classification of Goods; "Consumer Goods"; "Equipment"; "Farm Products"; "Inventory".

Goods are

(1) "consumer goods" if they are used or bought for use primarily for personal, family or household purposes;

(2) "equipment" if they are used or bought for use primarily in business (including farming or a profession) or by a debtor who is a non-profit organization or a governmental subdivision or agency or if the goods are not included in the definitions of inventory, farm products or consumer goods;

(3) "farm products" if they are crops or livestock or supplies used or produced in farming operations or if they are products of crops or livestock in their unmanufactured states (such as ginned cotton, wool-clip, maple syrup, milk and eggs), and if they are in the possession of a debtor engaged in raising, fattening, grazing or other farming operations. If goods are farm products they are neither equipment nor inventory;

(4) "inventory" if they are held by a person who holds them for sale or lease or to be furnished under contracts of service or if he has so furnished them, or if they are raw materials, work in process or materials used or consumed in a business. Inventory of a person is not to be classified as his equipment.

§ 9–110. Sufficiency of Description.

For purposes of this Article any description of personal property or real estate is sufficient whether or not it is specific if it reasonably identifies what is described.

§ 9–111. Applicability of Bulk Transfer Laws.

The creation of a security interest is not a bulk transfer under Article 6 (see Section 6–103).

§ 9–112. Where Collateral Is Not Owned by Debtor.

Unless otherwise agreed, when a secured party knows that collateral is owned by a person who is not the debtor, the owner of the collateral is entitled to receive from the secured party any surplus under Section 9–502(2) or under Section 9–504(1), and is not liable for the debt or for any deficiency after resale, and he has the same right as the debtor.

(a) to receive statements under Section 9–208;

(b) to receive notice of and to object to a secured party's proposal to retain the collateral in satisfaction of the indebtedness under Section 9–505;

(c) to redeem the collateral under Section 9–506;

(d) to obtain injunctive or other relief under Section 9–507(1); and

(e) to recover losses caused to him under Section 9–208(2).

§ 9–113. Security Interests Arising Under Article on Sales.

A security interest arising solely under the Article on Sales (Article 2) is subject to the provisions of this Article except that to the extent that and so long as the debtor does not have or does not lawfully obtain possession of the goods

(a) no security agreement is necessary to make the security interest enforceable; and

(b) no filing is required to perfect the security interest; and

(c) the rights of the secured party on default by the debtor are governed by the Article on Sales (Article 2).

§ 9–114. Consignment.

(1) A person who delivers goods under a consignment which is not a security interest and who would be required to file under this Article by paragraph (3)(c) of Section 2–326 has priority over a secured party who is or becomes a creditor of the consignee and who would have a perfected security interest in the goods if they were the property of the consignee, and also has priority with respect to identifiable cash proceeds received on or before delivery of the goods to a buyer, if

(a) the consignor complies with the filing provision of the Article on Sales with respect to consignments (paragraph (3)(c) of Section 2–326) before the consignee receives possession of the goods; and

(b) the consignor gives notification in writing to the holder of the security interest if the holder has filed a financing statement covering the same types of goods before the date of the filing made by the consignor; and

(c) the holder of the security interest receives the notification within five years before the consignee receives possession of the goods; and

(d) the notification states that the consignor expects to deliver goods on consignment to the consignee, describing the goods by item or type.

(2) In the case of a consignment which is not a security interest and in which the requirements of the preceding subsection have not been met, a person who delivers goods to another is subordinate to a person who would have a perfected security interest in the goods if they were the property of the debtor.

PART 2   VALIDITY OF SECURITY AGREEMENT AND RIGHTS OF PARTIES THERETO

§ 9–201. General Validity of Security Agreement.

Except as otherwise provided by this Act a security agreement is effective according to its terms between the parties, against purchasers of the collateral and against creditors. Nothing in this Article validates any charge or practice illegal under any statute or regulation thereunder governing usury, small loans, retail installment sales, or the like, or extends the application of any such statute or regulation to any transaction not otherwise subject thereto.

§ 9–202. Title to Collateral Immaterial.

Each provision of this Article with regard to rights, obligations and remedies applies whether title to collateral is in the secured party or in the debtor.

§ 9–203. Attachment and Enforceability of Security Interest; Proceeds; Formal Requisites.

(1) Subject to the provisions of Section 4–210 on the security interest of a collecting bank, Section 8–321 on security interests in securities and Section 9–113 on a security interest arising under the Articles on Sales and Leases, a security interest is not enforceable against the debtor or third parties with respect to the collateral and does not attach unless:

(a) the collateral is in the possession of the secured party pursuant to agreement, or the debtor has signed a security agreement which contains a description of the collateral and in addition, when the security interest covers crops growing or to be grown or timber to be cut, a description of the land concerned;

(b) value has been given; and

(c) the debtor has rights in the collateral.

(2) A security interest attaches when it becomes enforceable against the debtor with respect to the collateral. Attachment occurs as soon as all of the events specified in subsection (1) have taken place unless explicit agreement postpones the time of attaching.

(3) Unless otherwise agreed a security agreement gives the secured party the rights to proceeds provided by Section 9–306.

(4) A transaction, although subject to this Article, is also subject to . . .*, and in the case of conflict between the provisions of this Article and any such statute, the provisions of such statute control. Failure to comply with any applicable statute has only the effect which is specified therein.

> Note: At * in subsection (4) insert reference to any local statute regulating small loans, retail installment sales and the like.
>
> The foregoing subsection (4) is designed to make it clear that certain transactions, although subject to this Article, must also comply with other applicable legislation.
>
> This Article is designed to regulate all the "security" aspects of transactions within its scope. There is, however, much regulatory legislation, particularly in the consumer field, which supplements this Article and should not be repealed by its enactment. Examples are small loan acts, retail installment selling acts and the like. Such acts may provide for licensing and rate regulation and may prescribe particular forms of contract. Such provisions should remain in force despite the enactment of this Article. On the other hand if a retail installment selling act contains provisions on filing, rights on default, etc., such provisions should be repealed as inconsistent with this Article except that inconsistent provisions as to deficien-

cies, penalties, etc., in the Uniform Consumer Credit Code and other recent related legislation should remain because those statutes were drafted after the substantial enactment of the Article and with the intention of modifying certain provisions of this Article as to consumer credit.

§ 9–204. After-Acquired Property; Future Advances.

(1) Except as provided in subsection (2), a security agreement may provide that any or all obligations covered by the security agreement are to be secured by after-acquired collateral.

(2) No security interest attaches under an after-acquired property clause to consumer goods other than accessions (Section 9–314) when given as additional security unless the debtor acquires rights in them within ten days after the secured party gives value.

(3) Obligations covered by a security agreement may include future advances or other value whether or not the advances or value are given pursuant to commitment (subsection (1) of Section 9–105).

§ 9–205. Use or Disposition of Collateral Without Accounting Permissible.

A security interest is not invalid or fraudulent against creditors by reason of liberty in the debtor to use, commingle or dispose of all or part of the collateral (including returned or repossessed goods) or to collect or compromise accounts or chattel paper, or to accept the return of goods or make repossessions, or to use, commingle or dispose of proceeds, or by reason of the failure of the secured party to require the debtor to account for proceeds or replace collateral. This section does not relax the requirements of possession where perfection of a security interest depends upon possession of the collateral by the secured party or by a bailee.

§ 9–206. Agreement Not to Assert Defenses Against Assignee; Modification of Sales Warranties Where Security Agreement Exists.

(1) Subject to any statute or decision which establishes a different rule for buyers or lessees of consumer goods, an agreement by a buyer or lessee that he will not assert against an assignee any claim or defense which he may have against the seller or lessor is enforceable by an assignee who takes his assignment for value, in good faith and without notice of a claim or defense, except as to defenses of a type which may be asserted against a holder in due course of a negotiable instrument under the Article on Negotiable Instruments (Article 3). A buyer who as part of one transaction signs both a negotiable instrument and a security agreement makes such an agreement.

(2) When a seller retains a purchase money security interest in goods the Article on Sales (Article 2) governs the sale and any disclaimer, limitation or modification of the seller's warranties.

§ 9–207. Rights and Duties When Collateral Is in Secured Party's Possession.

(1) A secured party must use reasonable care in the custody and preservation of collateral in his possession. In the case of an instrument or chattel paper reasonable care includes taking necessary steps to preserve rights against prior parties unless otherwise agreed.

(2) Unless otherwise agreed, when collateral is in the secured party's possession

(a) reasonable expenses (including the cost of any insurance and payment of taxes or other charges) incurred in the custody, preservation, use or operation of the collateral are chargeable to the debtor and are secured by the collateral;

(b) the risk of accidental loss or damage is on the debtor to the extent of any deficiency in any effective insurance coverage;

(c) the secured party may hold as additional security any increase or profits (except money) received from the collateral, but money so received, unless remitted to the debtor, shall be applied in reduction of the secured obligation;

(d) the secured party must keep the collateral identifiable but fungible collateral may be commingled;

(e) the secured party may repledge the collateral upon terms which do not impair the debtor's right to redeem it.

(3) A secured party is liable for any loss caused by his failure to meet any obligation imposed by the preceding subsections but does not lose his security interest.

(4) A secured party may use or operate the collateral for the purpose of preserving the collateral or its value or pursuant to the order of a court of appropriate jurisdiction or, except in the case of consumer goods, in the manner and to the extent provided in the security agreement.

§ 9–208. Request for Statement of Account or List of Collateral.

(1) A debtor may sign a statement indicating what he believes to be the aggregate amount of unpaid indebtedness as of a specified date and may send it to the secured party with a request that the statement be approved or corrected and returned to the debtor. When the security agreement or any other record kept by the secured party identifies the collateral a debtor may similarly request the secured party to approve or correct a list of the collateral.

(2) The secured party must comply with such a request within two weeks after receipt by sending a written correction or approval. If the secured party claims a security interest in all of a particular type of collateral owned by the debtor he may indicate that fact in his reply and need not approve or correct an itemized list of such collateral. If the secured party without reasonable excuse fails to comply he is liable for any loss caused to the debtor thereby; and if the debtor has properly included in his request a good faith statement of the obligation or a list of the collateral or both the secured party may claim a security interest only as shown in the statement against persons misled by his failure to comply. If he no longer has an interest in the obligation or collateral at the time the request is received he must disclose the name and address of any successor in interest known to him and he is liable for any loss caused to the debtor as a result of failure to disclose. A successor in interest is not subject to this section until a request is received by him.

(3) A debtor is entitled to such a statement once every six months without charge. The secured party may require payment of a charge not exceeding $10 for each additional statement furnished.

PART 3   RIGHTS OF THIRD PARTIES; PERFECTED AND UNPERFECTED SECURITY INTERESTS; RULES OF PRIORITY

§ 9–301.   Persons Who Take Priority Over Unperfected Security Interests; Rights of "Lien Creditor".

(1) Except as otherwise provided in subsection (2), an unperfected security interest is subordinate to the rights of

(a) persons entitled to priority under Section 9–312;

(b) a person who becomes a lien creditor before the security interest is perfected;

(c) in the case of goods, instruments, documents, and chattel paper, a person who is not a secured party and who is a transferee in bulk or other buyer not in ordinary course of business or is a buyer of farm products in ordinary course of business, to the extent that he gives value and receives delivery of the collateral without knowledge of the security interest and before it is perfected;

(d) in the case of accounts and general intangibles, a person who is not a secured party and who is a transferee to the extent that he gives value without knowledge of the security interest and before it is perfected.

(2) If the secured party files with respect to a purchase money security interest before or within ten days after the debtor receives possession of the collateral, he takes priority over the rights of a transferee in bulk or of a lien creditor which arise between the time the security interest attaches and the time of filing.

(3) A "lien creditor" means a creditor who has acquired a lien on the property involved by attachment, levy or the like and includes an assignee for benefit of creditors from the time of assignment, and a trustee in bankruptcy from the date of the filing of the petition or a receiver in equity from the time of appointment.

(4) A person who becomes a lien creditor while a security interest is perfected takes subject to the security interest only to the extent that it secures advances made before he becomes a lien creditor or within 45 days thereafter or made without knowledge of the lien or pursuant to a commitment entered into without knowledge of the lien.

§ 9–302.   When Filing Is Required to Perfect Security Interest; Security Interests to Which Filing Provisions of This Article Do Not Apply.

(1) A financing statement must be filed to perfect all security interests except the following:

(a) a security interest in collateral in possession of the secured party under Section 9–305;

(b) a security interest temporarily perfected in instruments or documents without delivery under Section 9–304 or in proceeds for a 10 day period under Section 9–306;

(c) a security interest created by an assignment of a beneficial interest in a trust or a decedent's estate;

(d) a purchase money security interest in consumer goods; but filing is required for a motor vehicle required to be registered; and fixture filing is required for priority over conflicting interests in fixtures to the extent provided in Section 9–313;

(e) an assignment of accounts which does not alone or in conjunction with other assignments to the same assignee transfer a significant part of the outstanding accounts of the assignor;

(f) a security interest of a collecting bank (Section 4–210) or in securities (Section 8–321) or arising under the Articles on Sales and Leases (see Section 9–113) or covered in subsection (3) of this section;

(g) an assignment for the benefit of all the creditors of the transferor, and subsequent transfers by the assignee thereunder.

(2) If a secured party assigns a perfected security interest, no filing under this Article is required in order to continue the perfected status of the security interest against creditors of and transferees from the original debtor.

(3) The filing of a financing statement otherwise required by this Article is not necessary or effective to perfect a security interest in property subject to

(a) a statute or treaty of the United States which provides for a national or international registration or a national or international certificate of title or which specifies a place of filing different from that specified in this Article for filing of the security interest; or

(b) the following statutes of this state; [list any certificate of title statute covering automobiles, trailers, mobile homes, boats, farm tractors, or the like, and any central filing statute]; but during any period in which collateral is inventory held for sale by a person who is in the business of selling goods of that kind, the filing provisions of this Article (Part 4) apply to a security interest in that collateral created by him as debtor; or

(c) a certificate of title statute of another jurisdiction under the law of which indication of a security interest on the certificate is required as a condition of perfection (subsection (2) of Section 9–103).

(4) Compliance with a statute or treaty described in subsection (3) is equivalent to the filing of a financing statement under this Article, and a security interest in property subject to the statute or treaty can be perfected only by compliance therewith except as provided in Section 9–103 on multiple state transactions. Duration and renewal of perfection of a security interest perfected by compliance with the statute or treaty are governed by the provisions of the statute or treaty; in other respects the security interest is subject to this Article. Amended in 1972 and 1977.

§ 9–303.   When Security Interest Is Perfected; Continuity of Perfection.

(1) A security interest is perfected when it has attached and when all of the applicable steps required for perfection have

been taken. Such steps are specified in Sections 9–302, 9–304, 9–305 and 9–306. If such steps are taken before the security interest attaches, it is perfected at the time when it attaches. (2) If a security interest is originally perfected in any way permitted under this Article and is subsequently perfected in some other way under this Article, without an intermediate period when it was unperfected, the security interest shall be deemed to be perfected continuously for the purposes of this Article.

§ 9–304. Perfection of Security Interest in Instruments, Documents, and Goods Covered by Documents; Perfection by Permissive Filing; Temporary Perfection Without Filing or Transfer of Possession.

(1) A security interest in chattel paper or negotiable documents may be perfected by filing. A security interest in money or instruments (other than certificated securities or instruments which constitute part of chattel paper) can be perfected only by the secured party's taking possession, except as provided in subsections (4) and (5) of this section and subsections (2) and (3) of Section 9–306 on proceeds.

(2) During the period that goods are in the possession of the issuer of a negotiable document therefor, a security interest in the goods is perfected by perfecting a security interest in the document, and any security interest in the goods otherwise perfected during such period is subject thereto.

(3) A security interest in goods in the possession of a bailee other than one who has issued a negotiable document therefor is perfected by issuance of a document in the name of the secured party or by the bailee's receipt of notification of the secured party's interest or by filing as to the goods.

(4) A security interest in instruments (other than certificated securities) or negotiable documents is perfected without filing or the taking of possession for a period of 21 days from the time it attaches to the extent that it arises for new value given under a written security agreement.

(5) A security interest remains perfected for a period of 21 days without filing where a secured party having a perfected security interest in an instrument (other than a certificated security), a negotiable document or goods in possession of a bailee other than one who has issued a negotiable document therefor

    (a) makes available to the debtor the goods or documents representing the goods for the purpose of ultimate sale or exchange or for the purpose of loading, unloading, storing, shipping, transshipping, manufacturing, processing or otherwise dealing with them in a manner preliminary to their sale or exchange, but priority between conflicting security interests in the goods is subject to subsection (3) of Section 9–312; or

    (b) delivers the instrument to the debtor for the purpose of ultimate sale or exchange or of presentation, collection, renewal or registration of transfer.

(6) After the 21 day period in subsections (4) and (5) perfection depends upon compliance with applicable provisions of this Article.

§ 9–305. When Possession by Secured Party Perfects Security Interest Without Filing.

A security interest in letters of credit and advices of credit (subsection (2)(a) of Section 5–116), goods, instruments (other than certificated securities), money, negotiable documents, or chattel paper may be perfected by the secured party's taking possession of the collateral. If such collateral other than goods covered by a negotiable document is held by a bailee, the secured party is deemed to have possession from the time the bailee receives notification of the secured party's interest. A security interest is perfected by possession from the time possession is taken without a relation back and continues only so long as possession is retained, unless otherwise specified in this Article. The security interest may be otherwise perfected as provided in this Article before or after the period of possession by the secured party.

§ 9–306. "Proceeds"; Secured Party's Rights on Disposition of Collateral.

(1) "Proceeds" includes whatever is received upon the sale, exchange, collection or other disposition of collateral or proceeds. Insurance payable by reason of loss or damage to the collateral is proceeds, except to the extent that it is payable to a person other than a party to the security agreement. Money, checks, deposit accounts, and the like are "cash proceeds". All other proceeds are "non-cash proceeds".

(2) Except where this Article otherwise provides, a security interest continues in collateral notwithstanding sale, exchange or other disposition thereof unless the disposition was authorized by the secured party in the security agreement or otherwise, and also continues in any identifiable proceeds including collections received by the debtor.

(3) The security interest in proceeds is a continuously perfected security interest if the interest in the original collateral was perfected but it ceases to be a perfected security interest and becomes unperfected ten days after receipt of the proceeds by the debtor unless

    (a) a filed financing statement covers the original collateral and the proceeds are collateral in which a security interest may be perfected by filing in the office or offices where the financing statement has been filed and, if the proceeds are acquired with cash proceeds, the description of collateral in the financing statement indicates the types of property constituting the proceeds; or

    (b) a filed financing statement covers the original collateral and the proceeds are identifiable cash proceeds; or

    (c) the security interest in the proceeds is perfected before the expiration of the ten day period.

    Except as provided in this section, a security interest in proceeds can be perfected only by the methods or under the circumstances permitted in this Article for original collateral of the same type.

(4) In the event of insolvency proceedings instituted by or against a debtor, a secured party with a perfected security interest in proceeds has a perfected security interest only in the following proceeds:

    (a) in identifiable non-cash proceeds and in separate deposit accounts containing only proceeds;

(b) in identifiable cash proceeds in the form of money which is neither commingled with other money nor deposited in a deposit account prior to the insolvency proceedings;

(c) in identifiable cash proceeds in the form of checks and the like which are not deposited in a deposit account prior to the insolvency proceedings; and

(d) in all cash and deposit accounts of the debtor in which proceeds have been commingled with other funds, but the perfected security interest under this paragraph (d) is

(i) subject to any right to set-off; and

(ii) limited to an amount not greater than the amount of any cash proceeds received by the debtor within ten days before the institution of the insolvency proceedings less the sum of (I) the payments to the secured party on account of cash proceeds received by the debtor during such period and (II) the cash proceeds received by the debtor during such period to which the secured party is entitled under paragraphs (a) through (c) of this subsection (4).

(5) If a sale of goods results in an account or chattel paper which is transferred by the seller to a secured party, and if the goods are returned to or are repossessed by the seller or the secured party, the following rules determine priorities:

(a) If the goods were collateral at the time of sale, for an indebtedness of the seller which is still unpaid, the original security interest attaches again to the goods and continues as a perfected security interest if it was perfected at the time when the goods were sold. If the security interest was originally perfected by a filing which is still effective, nothing further is required to continue the perfected status; in any other case, the secured party must take possession of the returned or repossessed goods or must file.

(b) An unpaid transferee of the chattel paper has a security interest in the goods against the transferor. Such security interest is prior to a security interest asserted under paragraph (a) to the extent that the transferee of the chattel paper was entitled to priority under Section 9–308.

(c) An unpaid transferee of the account has a security interest in the goods against the transferor. Such security interest is subordinate to a security interest asserted under paragraph (a).

(d) A security interest of an unpaid transferee asserted under paragraph (b) or (c) must be perfected for protection against creditors of the transferor and purchasers of the returned or repossessed goods.

§ 9–307. Protection of Buyers of Goods.

(1) A buyer in ordinary course of business (subsection (9) of Section 1–201) other than a person buying farm products from a person engaged in farming operations takes free of a security interest created by his seller even though the security interest is perfected and even though the buyer knows of its existence.

(2) In the case of consumer goods, a buyer takes free of a security interest even though perfected if he buys without knowledge of the security interest, for value and for his own personal, family or household purposes unless prior to the purchase the secured party has filed a financing statement covering such goods.

(3) A buyer other than a buyer in ordinary course of business

(subsection (1) of this section) takes free of a security interest to the extent that it secures future advances made after the secured party acquires knowledge of the purchase, or more than 45 days after the purchase, whichever first occurs, unless made pursuant to a commitment entered into without knowledge of the purchase and before the expiration of the 45 day period.

§ 9–308. Purchase of Chattel Paper and Instruments.

A purchaser of chattel paper or an instrument who gives new value and takes possession of it in the ordinary course of his business has priority over a security interest in the chattel paper or instrument

(a) which is perfected under Section 9–304 (permissive filing and temporary perfection) or under Section 9–306 (perfection as to proceeds) if he acts without knowledge that the specific paper or instrument is subject to a security interest; or

(b) which is claimed merely as proceeds of inventory subject to a security interest (Section 9–306) even though he knows that the specific paper or instrument is subject to the security interest.

§ 9–309. Protection of Purchasers of Instruments, Documents and Securities.

Nothing in this Article limits the rights of a holder in due course of a negotiable instrument (Section 3–302) or a holder to whom a negotiable document of title has been duly negotiated (Section 7–501) or a bona fide purchaser of a security (Section 8–302) and the holders or purchasers take priority over an earlier security interest even though perfected. Filing under this Article does not constitute notice of the security interest to such holders or purchasers.

§ 9–310. Priority of Certain Liens Arising by Operation of Law.

When a person in the ordinary course of his business furnishes services or materials with respect to goods subject to a security interest, a lien upon goods in the possession of such person given by statute or rule of law for such materials or services takes priority over a perfected security interest unless the lien is statutory and the statute expressly provides otherwise.

§ 9–311. Alienability of Debtor's Rights: Judicial Process.

The debtor's rights in collateral may be voluntarily or involuntarily transferred (by way of sale, creation of a security interest, attachment, levy, garnishment or other judicial process) notwithstanding a provision in the security agreement prohibiting any transfer or making the transfer constitute a default.

§ 9–312. Priorities Among Conflicting Security Interests in the Same Collateral.

(1) The rules of priority stated in other sections of this Part and in the following sections shall govern when applicable: Section 4–208 with respect to the security interests of col-

lecting banks in items being collected, accompanying documents and proceeds; Section 9–103 on security interests related to other jurisdictions; Section 9–114 on consignments.

(2) A perfected security interest in crops for new value given to enable the debtor to produce the crops during the production season and given not more than three months before the crops become growing crops by planting or otherwise takes priority over an earlier perfected security interest to the extent that such earlier interest secures obligations due more than six months before the crops become growing crops by planting or otherwise, even though the person giving new value had knowledge of the earlier security interest.

(3) A perfected purchase money security interest in inventory has priority over a conflicting security interest in the same inventory and also has priority in identifiable cash proceeds received on or before the delivery of the inventory to a buyer if

    (a) the purchase money security interest is perfected at the time the debtor receives possession of the inventory; and

    (b) the purchase money secured party gives notification in writing to the holder of the conflicting security interest if the holder had filed a financing statement covering the same types of inventory (i) before the date of the filing made by the purchase money secured party, or (ii) before the beginning of the 21 day period where the purchase money security interest is temporarily perfected without filing or possession (subsection (5) of Section 9–304); and

    (c) the holder of the conflicting security interest receives the notification within five years before the debtor receives possession of the inventory; and

    (d) the notification states that the person giving the notice has or expects to acquire a purchase money security interest in inventory of the debtor, describing such inventory by item or type.

(4) A purchase money security interest in collateral other than inventory has priority over a conflicting security interest in the same collateral or its proceeds if the purchase money security interest is perfected at the time the debtor receives possession of the collateral or within ten days thereafter.

(5) In all cases not governed by other rules stated in this section (including cases of purchase money security interests which do not qualify for the special priorities set forth in subsections (3) and (4) of this section), priority between conflicting security interests in the same collateral shall be determined according to the following rules:

    (a) Conflicting security interests rank according to priority in time of filing or perfection. Priority dates from the time a filing is first made covering the collateral or the time the security interest is first perfected, whichever is earlier, provided that there is no period thereafter when there is neither filing nor perfection.

    (b) So long as conflicting security interests are unperfected, the first to attach has priority.

(6) For the purposes of subsection (5) a date of filing or perfection as to collateral is also a date of filing or perfection as to proceeds.

(7) If future advances are made while a security interest is perfected by filing, the taking of possession, or under Section 8–321 on securities, the security interest has the same priority for the purposes of subsection (5) with respect to the future advances as it does with respect to the first advance. If a commitment is made before or while the security interest is so perfected, the security interest has the same priority with respect to advances made pursuant thereto. In other cases a perfected security interest has priority from the date the advance is made.

§ 9–313. Priority of Security Interests in Fixtures.

(1) In this section and in the provisions of Part 4 of this Article referring to fixture filing, unless the context otherwise requires

    (a) goods are "fixtures" when they become so related to particular real estate that an interest in them arises under real estate law

    (b) a "fixture filing" is the filing in the office where a mortgage on the real estate would be filed or recorded of a financing statement covering goods which are or are to become fixtures and conforming to the requirements of subsection (5) of Section 9–402

    (c) a mortgage is a "construction mortgage" to the extent that it secures an obligation incurred for the construction of an improvement on land including the acquisition cost of the land, if the recorded writing so indicates.

(2) A security interest under this Article may be created in goods which are fixtures or may continue in goods which become fixtures, but no security interest exists under this Article in ordinary building materials incorporated into an improvement on land.

(3) This Article does not prevent creation of an encumbrance upon fixtures pursuant to real estate law.

(4) A perfected security interest in fixtures has priority over the conflicting interest of an encumbrancer or owner of the real estate where

    (a) the security interest is a purchase money security interest, the interest of the encumbrancer or owner arises before the goods become fixtures, the security interest is perfected by a fixture filing before the goods become fixtures or within ten days thereafter, and the debtor has an interest of record in the real estate or is in possession of the real estate; or

    (b) the security interest is perfected by a fixture filing before the interest of the encumbrancer or owner is of record, the security interest has priority over any conflicting interest of a predecessor in title of the encumbrancer or owner, and the debtor has an interest of record in the real estate or is in possession of the real estate; or

    (c) the fixtures are readily removable factory or office machines or readily removable replacements of domestic appliances which are consumer goods, and before the goods become fixtures the security interest is perfected by any method permitted by this Article; or

    (d) the conflicting interest is a lien on the real estate obtained by legal or equitable proceedings after the security interest was perfected by any method permitted by this Article.

(5) A security interest in fixtures, whether or not perfected,

has priority over the conflicting interest of an encumbrancer or owner of the real estate where

(a) the encumbrancer or owner has consented in writing to the security interest or has disclaimed an interest in the goods as fixtures; or

(b) the debtor has a right to remove the goods as against the encumbrancer or owner. If the debtor's right terminates, the priority of the security interest continues for a reasonable time.

(6) Notwithstanding paragraph (a) of subsection (4) but otherwise subject to subsections (4) and (5), a security interest in fixtures is subordinate to a construction mortgage recorded before the goods become fixtures if the goods become fixtures before the completion of the construction. To the extent that it is given to refinance a construction mortgage, a mortgage has this priority to the same extent as the construction mortgage.

(7) In cases not within the preceding subsections, a security interest in fixtures is subordinate to the conflicting interest of an encumbrancer or owner of the related real estate who is not the debtor.

(8) When the secured party has priority over all owners and encumbrancers of the real estate, he may, on default, subject to the provisions of Part 5, remove his collateral from the real estate but he must reimburse any encumbrancer or owner of the real estate who is not the debtor and who has not otherwise agreed for the cost of repair of any physical injury, but not for any diminution in value of the real estate caused by the absence of the goods removed or by any necessity of replacing them. A person entitled to reimbursement may refuse permission to remove until the secured party gives adequate security for the performance of this obligation.

§ 9–314. Accessions.

(1) A security interest in goods which attaches before they are installed in or affixed to other goods takes priority as to the goods installed or affixed (called in this section "accessions") over the claims of all persons to the whole except as stated in subsection (3) and subject to Section 9–315(1).

(2) A security interest which attaches to goods after they become part of a whole is valid against all persons subsequently acquiring interests in the whole except as stated in subsection (3) but is invalid against any person with an interest in the whole at the time the security interest attaches to the goods who has not in writing consented to the security interest or disclaimed an interest in the goods as part of the whole.

(3) The security interests described in subsections (1) and (2) do not take priority over

(a) a subsequent purchaser for value of any interest in the whole; or

(b) a creditor with a lien on the whole subsequently obtained by judicial proceedings; or

(c) a creditor with a prior perfected security interest in the whole to the extent that he makes subsequent advances

if the subsequent purchase is made, the lien by judicial proceedings obtained or the subsequent advance under the prior perfected security interest is made or contracted for without knowledge of the security interest and before it is perfected. A purchaser of the whole at a foreclosure sale other than the holder of a perfected security interest purchasing at his own foreclosure sale is a subsequent purchaser within this section.

(4) When under subsections (1) or (2) and (3) a secured party has an interest in accessions which has priority over the claims of all persons who have interests in the whole, he may on default subject to the provisions of Part 5 remove his collateral from the whole but he must reimburse any encumbrancer or owner of the whole who is not the debtor and who has not otherwise agreed for the cost of repair of any physical injury but not for any diminution in value of the whole caused by the absence of the goods removed or by any necessity for replacing them. A person entitled to reimbursement may refuse permission to remove until the secured party gives adequate security for the performance of this obligation.

§ 9–315. Priority When Goods Are Commingled or Processed.

(1) If a security interest in goods was perfected and subsequently the goods or a part thereof have become part of a product or mass, the security interest continues in the product or mass if

(a) the goods are so manufactured, processed, assembled or commingled that their identity is lost in the product or mass; or

(b) a financing statement covering the original goods also covers the product into which the goods have been manufactured, processed or assembled.

In a case to which paragraph (b) applies, no separate security interest in that part of the original goods which has been manufactured, processed or assembled into the product may be claimed under Section 9–314.

(2) When under subsection (1) more than one security interest attaches to the product or mass, they rank equally according to the ratio that the cost of the goods to which each interest originally attached bears to the cost of the total product or mass.

§ 9–316. Priority Subject to Subordination.

Nothing in this Article prevents subordination by agreement by any person entitled to priority.

§ 9–317. Secured Party Not Obligated on Contract of Debtor.

The mere existence of a security interest or authority given to the debtor to dispose of or use collateral does not impose contract or tort liability upon the secured party for the debtor's acts or omissions.

§ 9–318. Defenses Against Assignee; Modification of Contract After Notification of Assignment; Term Prohibiting Assignment Ineffective; Identification and Proof of Assignment.

(1) Unless an account debtor has made an enforceable agreement not to assert defenses or claims arising out of a sale as provided in Section 9–206 the rights of an assignee are subject to

(a) all the terms of the contract between the account debtor and assignor and any defense or claim arising therefrom; and

(b) any other defense or claim of the account debtor against the assignor which accrues before the account debtor receives notification of the assignment.

(2) So far as the right to payment or a part thereof under an assigned contract has not been fully earned by performance, and notwithstanding notification of the assignment, any modification of or substitution for the contract made in good faith and in accordance with reasonable commercial standards is effective against an assignee unless the account debtor has otherwise agreed but the assignee acquires corresponding rights under the modified or substituted contract. The assignment may provide that such modification or substitution is a breach by the assignor.

(3) The account debtor is authorized to pay the assignor until the account debtor receives notification that the amount due or to become due has been assigned and that payment is to be made to the assignee. A notification which does not reasonably identify the rights assigned is ineffective. If requested by the account debtor, the assignee must seasonably furnish reasonable proof that the assignment has been made and unless he does so the account debtor may pay the assignor.

(4) A term in any contract between an account debtor and an assignor is ineffective if it prohibits assignment of an account or prohibits creation of a security interest in a general intangible for money due or to become due or requires the account debtor's consent to such assignment or security interest.

PART 4   FILING

§ 9–401.   Place of Filing; Erroneous Filing; Removal of Collateral.

First Alternative Subsection (1)

(1) The proper place to file in order to perfect a security interest is as follows:

(a) when the collateral is timber to be cut or is minerals or the like (including oil and gas) or accounts subject to subsection (5) of Section 9–103, or when the financing statement is filed as a fixture filing (Section 9–313) and the collateral is goods which are or are to become fixtures, then in the office where a mortgage on the real estate would be filed or recorded;

(b) in all other cases, in the office of the [Secretary of State].

Second Alternative Subsection (1)

(1) The proper place to file in order to perfect a security interest is as follows:

(a) when the collateral is equipment used in farming operations, or farm products, or accounts or general intangibles arising from or relating to the sale of farm products by a farmer, or consumer goods, then in the office of the _____ in the county of the debtor's residence or if the debtor is not a resident of this state then in the office of the _____ in the county where the goods are kept, and in addition when the collateral is crops growing or to be grown in the office of the _____ in the county where the land is located;

(b) when the collateral is timber to be cut or is minerals or the like (including oil and gas) or accounts subject to subsection (5) of Section 9–103, or when the financing statement is filed as a fixture filing (Section 9–313) and the collateral is goods which are or are to become fixtures, then in the office where a mortgage on the real estate would be filed or recorded;

(c) in all other cases, in the office of the [Secretary of State].

Third Alternative Subsection (1)

(1) The proper place to file in order to perfect a security interest is as follows:

(a) when the collateral is equipment used in farming operations, or farm products, or accounts or general intangibles arising from or relating to the sale of farm products by a farmer, or consumer goods, then in the office of the _____ in the county of the debtor's residence or if the debtor is not a resident of this state then in the office of the _____ in the county where the goods are kept, and in addition when the collateral is crops growing or to be grown in the office of the _____ in the county where the land is located;

(b) when the collateral is timber to be cut or is minerals or the like (including oil and gas) or accounts subject to subsection (5) of Section 9–103, or when the financing statement is filed as a fixture filing (Section 9–313) and the collateral is goods which are or are to become fixtures, then in the office where a mortgage on the real estate would be filed or recorded;

(c) in all other cases, in the office of the [Secretary of State] and in addition, if the debtor has a place of business in only one county of this state, also in the office of _____ of such county, or, if the debtor has no place of business in this state, but resides in the state, also in the office of _____ of the county in which he resides.

Note: One of the three alternatives should be selected as subsection (1).

(2) A filing which is made in good faith in an improper place or not in all of the places required by this section is nevertheless effective with regard to any collateral as to which the filing complied with the requirements of this Article and is also effective with regard to collateral covered by the financing statement against any person who has knowledge of the contents of such financing statement.

(3) A filing which is made in the proper place in this state continues effective even though the debtor's residence or place of business or the location of the collateral or its use, whichever controlled the original filing, is thereafter changed.

Alternative Subsection (3)

[(3) A filing which is made in the proper county continues effective for four months after a change to another county of the debtor's residence or place of business or the location of the collateral, whichever controlled the original filing. It becomes ineffective thereafter unless a copy of the financing statement signed by the secured party is filed in the new county within said period. The security interest may also be perfected in the new county after the expiration of the four-month period; in such case perfection dates from the time of perfection in the new county. A change in the use of the collateral does not impair the effectiveness of the original filing.]

(4) The rules stated in Section 9–103 determine whether filing is necessary in this state.

(5) Notwithstanding the preceding subsections, and subject to subsection (3) of Section 9–302, the proper place to file in order to perfect a security interest in collateral, including fixtures, of a transmitting utility is the office of the [Secretary of State]. This filing constitutes a fixture filing (Section 9–313) as to the collateral described therein which is or is to become fixtures.

(6) For the purposes of this section, the residence of an organization is its place of business if it has one or its chief executive office if it has more than one place of business.

Note: Subsection (6) should be used only if the state chooses the Second or Third Alternative Subsection (1).

§ 9–402. Formal Requisites of Financing Statement; Amendments; Mortgage as Financing Statement.

(1) A financing statement is sufficient if it gives the names of the debtor and the secured party, is signed by the debtor, gives an address of the secured party from which information concerning the security interest may be obtained, gives a mailing address of the debtor and contains a statement indicating the types, or describing the items, of collateral. A financing statement may be filed before a security agreement is made or a security interest otherwise attaches. When the financing statement covers crops growing or to be grown, the statement must also contain a description of the real estate concerned. When the financing statement covers timber to be cut or covers minerals or the like (including oil and gas) or accounts subject to subsection (5) of Section 9–103, or when the financing statement is filed as a fixture filing (Section 9–313) and the collateral is goods which are or are to become fixtures, the statement must also comply with subsection (5). A copy of the security agreement is sufficient as a financing statement if it contains the above information and is signed by the debtor. A carbon, photographic or other reproduction of a security agreement or a financing statement is sufficient as a financing statement if the security agreement so provides or if the original has been filed in this state.

(2) A financing statement which otherwise complies with subsection (1) is sufficient when it is signed by the secured party instead of the debtor if it is filed to perfect a security interest in

  (a) collateral already subject to a security interest in another jurisdiction when it is brought into this state, or when the debtor's location is changed to this state. Such a financing statement must state that the collateral was brought into this state or that the debtor's location was changed to this state under such circumstances; or

  (b) proceeds under Section 9–306 if the security interest in the original collateral was perfected. Such a financing statement must describe the original collateral; or

  (c) collateral as to which the filing has lapsed; or

  (d) collateral acquired after a change of name, identity or corporate structure of the debtor (subsection (7)).

(3) A form substantially as follows is sufficient to comply with subsection (1):

Name of debtor (or assignor) _____

Address _____

Name of secured party (or assignee) _____

Address _____

1. This financing statement covers the following types (or items) of property:

(Describe) _____

2. (If collateral is crops) The above described crops are growing or are to be grown on:

(Describe Real Estate) _____

3. (If applicable) The above goods are to become fixtures on*

*Where appropriate substitute either "The above timber is standing on _____" or "The above minerals or the like (including oil and gas) or accounts will be financed at the wellhead or minehead of the well or mine located on _____"

(Describe Real Estate) _____ and this financing statement is to be filed [for record] in the real estate records. (If the debtor does not have an interest of record) The name of a record owner is_____

4. (If products of collateral are claimed) Products of the collateral are also covered.

(use

_____

whichever   Signature of Debtor (or Assignor)

is

_____

applicable)   Signature of Secured Party (or Assignee)

(4) A financing statement may be amended by filing a writing signed by both the debtor and the secured party. An amendment does not extend the period of effectiveness of a financing statement. If any amendment adds collateral, it is effective as to the added collateral only from the filing date of the amendment. In this Article, unless the context otherwise requires, the term "financing statement" means the original financing statement and any amendments.

(5) A financing statement covering timber to be cut or covering minerals or the like (including oil and gas) or accounts subject to subsection (5) of Section 9–103, or a financing statement filed as a fixture filing (Section 9–313) where the debtor is not a transmitting utility, must show that it covers this type of collateral, must recite that it is to be filed [for record] in the real estate records, and the financing statement must contain a description of the real estate [sufficient if it were contained in a mortgage of the real estate to give constructive notice of the mortgage under the law of this

state]. If the debtor does not have an interest of record in the real estate, the financing statement must show the name of a record owner.

(6) A mortgage is effective as a financing statement filed as a fixture filing from the date of its recording if

(a) the goods are described in the mortgage by item or type; and

(b) the goods are or are to become fixtures related to the real estate described in the mortgage; and

(c) the mortgage complies with the requirements for a financing statement in this section other than a recital that it is to be filed in the real estate records; and

(d) the mortgage is duly recorded.

No fee with reference to the financing statement is required other than the regular recording and satisfaction fees with respect to the mortgage.

(7) A financing statement sufficiently shows the name of the debtor if it gives the individual, partnership or corporate name of the debtor, whether or not it adds other trade names or names of partners. Where the debtor so changes his name or in the case of an organization its name, identity or corporate structure that a filed financing statement becomes seriously misleading, the filing is not effective to perfect a security interest in collateral acquired by the debtor more than four months after the change, unless a new appropriate financing statement is filed before the expiration of that time. A filed financing statement remains effective with respect to collateral transferred by the debtor even though the secured party knows of or consents to the transfer.

(8) A financing statement substantially complying with the requirements of this section is effective even though it contains minor errors which are not seriously misleading.

Note: Language in brackets is optional.

Note: Where the state has any special recording system for real estate other than the usual grantor-grantee index (as, for instance, a tract system or a title registration or Torrens system) local adaptations of subsection (5) and Section 9–403(7) may be necessary. See Mass.Gen.Laws Chapter 106, Section 9–409.

§ 9–403. What Constitutes Filing; Duration of Filing; Effect of Lapsed Filing; Duties of Filing Officer.

(1) Presentation for filing of a financing statement and tender of the filing fee or acceptance of the statement by the filing officer constitutes filing under this Article.

(2) Except as provided in subsection (6) a filed financing statement is effective for a period of five years from the date of filing. The effectiveness of a filed financing statement lapses on the expiration of the five year period unless a continuation statement is filed prior to the lapse. If a security interest perfected by filing exists at the time insolvency proceedings are commenced by or against the debtor, the security interest remains perfected until termination of the insolvency proceedings and thereafter for a period of sixty days or until expiration of the five year period, whichever occurs later. Upon lapse the security interest becomes unperfected, unless it is perfected without filing. If the security interest becomes unperfected upon lapse, it is deemed to have been unperfected as against a person who became a purchaser or lien creditor before lapse.

(3) A continuation statement may be filed by the secured party within six months prior to the expiration of the five year period specified in subsection (2). Any such continuation statement must be signed by the secured party, identify the original statement by file number and state that the original statement is still effective. A continuation statement signed by a person other than the secured party of record must be accompanied by a separate written statement of assignment signed by the secured party of record and complying with subsection (2) of Section 9–405, including payment of the required fee. Upon timely filing of the continuation statement, the effectiveness of the original statement is continued for five years after the last date to which the filing was effective whereupon it lapses in the same manner as provided in subsection (2) unless another continuation statement is filed prior to such lapse. Succeeding continuation statements may be filed in the same manner to continue the effectiveness of the original statement. Unless a statute on disposition of public records provides otherwise, the filing officer may remove a lapsed statement from the files and destroy it immediately if he has retained a microfilm or other photographic record, or in other cases after one year after the lapse. The filing officer shall so arrange matters by physical annexation of financing statements to continuation statements or other related filings, or by other means, that if he physically destroys the financing statements of a period more than five years past, those which have been continued by a continuation statement or which are still effective under subsection (6) shall be retained.

(4) Except as provided in subsection (7) a filing officer shall mark each statement with a file number and with the date and hour of filing and shall hold the statement or a microfilm or other photographic copy thereof for public inspection. In addition the filing officer shall index the statement according to the name of the debtor and shall note in the index the file number and the address of the debtor given in the statement.

(5) The uniform fee for filing and indexing and for stamping a copy furnished by the secured party to show the date and place of filing for an original financing statement or for a continuation statement shall be $_____ if the statement is in the standard form prescribed by the [Secretary of State] and otherwise shall be $_____, plus in each case, if the financing statement is subject to subsection (5) of Section 9–402, $_____. The uniform fee for each name more than one required to be indexed shall be $_____. The secured party may at his option show a trade name for any person and an extra uniform indexing fee of $_____; shall be paid with respect thereto.

(6) If the debtor is a transmitting utility (subsection (5) of Section 9–401) and a filed financing statement so states, it is effective until a termination statement is filed. A real estate mortgage which is effective as a fixture filing under subsection (6) of Section 9–402 remains effective as a fixture filing until the mortgage is released or satisfied of record or its effectiveness otherwise terminates as to the real estate.

(7) When a financing statement covers timber to be cut or covers minerals or the like (including oil and gas) or accounts subject to subsection (5) of Section 9–103, or is filed as a fixture filing, [it shall be filed for record and] the filing officer shall index it under the names of the debtor and any owner of record shown on the financing statement in the same fashion as if they were the mortgagors in a mortgage of the real estate described, and, to the extent that the law of this state provides for indexing of mortgages under the of the mortgagee, under the name of the secured party as if he were the mortgagee thereunder, or where indexing is by description in the same fashion as if the financing statement were a mortgage of the real estate described.

Note: In states in which writings will not appear in the real estate records and indices unless actually recorded the bracketed language in subsection (7) should be used.

§ 9–404.   Termination Statement.

(1) If a financing statement covering consumer goods is filed on or after _____, then within one month or within ten days following written demand by the debtor after there is no outstanding secured obligation and no commitment to make advances, incur obligations or otherwise give value, the secured party must file with each filing officer with whom the financing statement was filed, a termination statement to the effect that he no longer claims a security interest under the financing statement, which shall be identified by file number. In other cases whenever there is no outstanding secured obligation and no commitment to make advances, incur obligations or otherwise give value, the secured party must on written demand by the debtor send the debtor, for each filing officer with whom the financing statement was filed, a termination statement to the effect that he no longer claims a security interest under the financing statement, which shall be identified by file number. A termination statement signed by a person other than the secured party of record must be accompanied by a separate written statement of assignment signed by the secured party of record complying with subsection (2) of Section 9–405, including payment of the required fee. If the affected secured party fails to file such a termination statement as required by this subsection, or to send such a termination statement within ten days after proper demand therefor, he shall be liable to the debtor for one hundred dollars, and in addition for any loss caused to the debtor by such failure.

(2) On presentation to the filing officer of such a termination statement he must note it in the index. If he has received the termination statement in duplicate, he shall return one copy of the termination statement to the secured party stamped to show the time of receipt thereof. If the filing officer has a microfilm or other photographic record of the financing statement, and of any related continuation statement, statement of assignment and statement of release, he may remove the originals from the files at any time after receipt of the termination statement, or if he has no such record, he may remove them from the files at any time after one year after receipt of the termination statement.

(3) If the termination statement is in the standard form prescribed by the [Secretary of State], the uniform fee for filing and indexing the termination statement shall be $_____, and otherwise shall be $_____, plus in each case an additional fee of $_____ for each name more than one against which the termination statement is required to be indexed.

Note: The date to be inserted should be the effective date of the revised Article 9.

§ 9–405.   Assignment of Security Interest; Duties of Filing Officer; Fees.

(1) A financing statement may disclose an assignment of a security interest in the collateral described in the financing statement by indication in the financing statement of the name and address of the assignee or by an assignment itself or a copy thereof on the face or back of the statement. On presentation to the filing officer of such a financing statement the filing officer shall mark the same as provided in Section 9–403(4). The uniform fee for filing, indexing and furnishing filing data for a financing statement so indicating an assignment shall be $_____ if the statement is in the standard form prescribed by the [Secretary of State] and otherwise shall be $_____, plus in each case an additional fee of $_____ for each name more than one against which the financing statement is required to be indexed.

(2) A secured party may assign of record all or part of his rights under a financing statement by the filing in the place where the original financing statement was filed of a separate written statement of assignment signed by the secured party of record and setting forth the name of the secured party of record and the debtor, the file number and the date of filing of the financing statement and the name and address of the assignee and containing a description of the collateral assigned. A copy of the assignment is sufficient as a separate statement if it complies with the preceding sentence. On presentation to the filing officer of such a separate statement, the filing officer shall mark such separate statement with the date and hour of the filing. He shall note the assignment on the index of the financing statement, or in the case of a fixture filing, or a filing covering timber to be cut, or covering minerals or the like (including oil and gas) or accounts subject to subsection (5) of Section 9–103, he shall index the assignment under the name of the assignor as grantor and, to the extent that the law of this state provides for indexing the assignment of a mortgage under the name of the assignee, he shall index the assignment of the financing statement under the name of the assignee. The uniform fee for filing, indexing and furnishing filing data about such a separate statement of assignment shall be $_____ if the statement is in the standard form prescribed by the [Secretary of State] and otherwise shall be $_____, plus in each case an additional fee of $_____; for each name more than one against which the statement of assignment is required to be indexed. Notwithstanding the provisions of this subsection, an assignment of record of a security interest in a fixture contained in a mortgage effective as a fixture filing

(subsection (6) of Section 9–402) may be made only by an assignment of the mortgage in the manner provided by the law of this state other than this Act.

(3) After the disclosure or filing of an assignment under this section, the assignee is the secured party of record.

§ 9–406. Release of Collateral; Duties of Filing Officer; Fees.

A secured party of record may by his signed statement release all or a part of any collateral described in a filed financing statement. The statement of release is sufficient if it contains a description of the collateral being released, the name and address of the debtor, the name and address of the secured party, and the file number of the financing statement. A statement of release signed by a person other than the secured party of record must be accompanied by a separate written statement of assignment signed by the secured party of record and complying with subsection (2) of Section 9–405, including payment of the required fee. Upon presentation of such a statement of release to the filing officer he shall mark the statement with the hour and date of filing and shall note the same upon the margin of the index of the filing of the financing statement. The uniform fee for filing and noting such a statement of release shall be $_____ if the statement is in the standard form prescribed by the [Secretary of State] and otherwise shall be $_____, plus in each case an additional fee of $_____ for each name more than one against which the statement of release is required to be indexed.

[§ 9–407. Information From Filing Officer].

[(1) If the person filing any financing statement, termination statement, statement of assignment, or statement of release, furnishes the filing officer a copy thereof, the filing officer shall upon request note upon the copy the file number and date and hour of the filing of the original and deliver or send the copy to such person.]

[(2) Upon request of any person, the filing officer shall issue his certificate showing whether there is on file on the date and hour stated therein, any presently effective financing statement naming a particular debtor and any statement of assignment thereof and if there is, giving the date and hour of filing of each such statement and the names and addresses of each secured party therein. The uniform fee for such a certificate shall be $_____ if the request for the certificate is in the standard form prescribed by the [Secretary of State] and otherwise shall be $_____. Upon request the filing officer shall furnish a copy of any filed financing statement or statement of assignment for a uniform fee of $_____ per page.]

> Note: This section is proposed as an optional provision to require filing officers to furnish certificates. Local law and practices should be consulted with regard to the advisability of adoption.

§ 9–408. Financing Statements Covering Consigned or Leased Goods.

A consignor or lessor of goods may file a financing statement using the terms "consignor," "consignee," "lessor," "lessee" or the like instead of the terms specified in Section 9–402. The provisions of this Part shall apply as appropriate to such a financing statement but its filing shall not of itself be a factor in determining whether or not the consignment or lease is intended as security (Section 1–201(37)). However, if it is determined for other reasons that the consignment or lease is so intended, a security interest of the consignor or lessor which attaches to the consigned or leased goods is perfected by such filing.

PART 5 DEFAULT

§ 9–501. Default; Procedure When Security Agreement Covers Both Real and Personal Property.

(1) When a debtor is in default under a security agreement, a secured party has the rights and remedies provided in this Part and except as limited by subsection (3) those provided in the security agreement. He may reduce his claim to judgment, foreclose or otherwise enforce the security interest by any available judicial procedure. If the collateral is documents the secured party may proceed either as to the documents or as to the goods covered thereby. A secured party in possession has the rights, remedies and duties provided in Section 9–207. The rights and remedies referred to in this subsection are cumulative.

(2) After default, the debtor has the rights and remedies provided in this Part, those provided in the security agreement and those provided in Section 9–207.

(3) To the extent that they give rights to the debtor and impose duties on the secured party, the rules stated in the subsections referred to below may not be waived or varied except as provided with respect to compulsory disposition of collateral (subsection (3) of Section 9–504 and Section 9–505) and with respect to redemption of collateral (Section 9–506) but the parties may by agreement determine the standards by which the fulfillment of these rights and duties is to be measured if such standards are not manifestly unreasonable:

   (a) subsection (2) of Section 9–502 and subsection (2) of Section 9–504 insofar as they require accounting for surplus proceeds of collateral;

   (b) subsection (3) of Section 9–504 and subsection (1) of Section 9–505 which deal with disposition of collateral;

   (c) subsection (2) of Section 9–505 which deals with acceptance of collateral as discharge of obligation;

   (d) Section 9–506 which deals with redemption of collateral; and

   (e) subsection (1) of Section 9–507 which deals with the secured party's liability for failure to comply with this Part.

(4) If the security agreement covers both real and personal property, the secured party may proceed under this Part as to the personal property or he may proceed as to both the real and the personal property in accordance with his rights and remedies in respect of the real property in which case the provisions of this Part do not apply.

(5) When a secured party has reduced his claim to judgment the lien of any levy which may be made upon his collateral by virtue of any execution based upon the judgment shall relate back to the date of the perfection of the security interest in such collateral. A judicial sale, pursuant to such execution, is a foreclosure of the security interest by judicial procedure within the meaning of this section, and the secured party may purchase at the sale and thereafter hold the collateral free of any other requirements of this Article.

§ 9–502. Collection Rights of Secured Party.

(1) When so agreed and in any event on default the secured party is entitled to notify an account debtor or the obligor on an instrument to make payment to him whether or not the assignor was theretofore making collections on the collateral, and also to take control of any proceeds to which he is entitled under Section 9–306.

(2) A secured party who by agreement is entitled to charge back uncollected collateral or otherwise to full or limited recourse against the debtor and who undertakes to collect from the account debtors or obligors must proceed in a commercially reasonable manner and may deduct his reasonable expenses of realization from the collections. If the security agreement secures an indebtedness, the secured party must account to the debtor for any surplus, and unless otherwise agreed, the debtor is liable for any deficiency. But, if the underlying transaction was a sale of accounts or chattel paper, the debtor is entitled to any surplus or is liable for any deficiency only if the security agreement so provides.

§ 9–503. Secured Party's Right to Take Possession After Default.

Unless otherwise agreed a secured party has on default the right to take possession of the collateral. In taking possession a secured party may proceed without judicial process if this can be done without breach of the peace or may proceed by action. If the security agreement so provides the secured party may require the debtor to assemble the collateral and make it available to the secured party at a place to be designated by the secured party which is reasonably convenient to both parties. Without removal a secured party may render equipment unusable, and may dispose of collateral on the debtor's premises under Section 9–504.

§ 9–504. Secured Party's Right to Dispose of Collateral After Default; Effect of Disposition.

(1) A secured party after default may sell, lease or otherwise dispose of any or all of the collateral in its then condition or following any commercially reasonable preparation or processing. Any sale of goods is subject to the Article on Sales (Article 2). The proceeds of disposition shall be applied in the order following to

　(a) the reasonable expenses of retaking, holding, preparing for sale or lease, selling, leasing and the like and, to the extent provided for in the agreement and not prohibited by law, the reasonable attorneys' fees and legal expenses incurred by the secured party;

　(b) the satisfaction of indebtedness secured by the security interest under which the disposition is made;

　(c) the satisfaction of indebtedness secured by any subordinate security interest in the collateral if written notification of demand therefor is received before distribution of the proceeds is completed. If requested by the secured party, the holder of a subordinate security interest must seasonably furnish reasonable proof of his interest, and unless he does so, the secured party need not comply with his demand.

(2) If the security interest secures an indebtedness, the secured party must account to the debtor for any surplus, and, unless otherwise agreed, the debtor is liable for any deficiency. But if the underlying transaction was a sale of accounts or chattel paper, the debtor is entitled to any surplus or is liable for any deficiency only if the security agreement so provides.

(3) Disposition of the collateral may be by public or private proceedings and may be made by way of one or more contracts. Sale or other disposition may be as a unit or in parcels and at any time and place and on any terms but every aspect of the disposition including the method, manner, time, place and terms must be commercially reasonable. Unless collateral is perishable or threatens to decline speedily in value or is of a type customarily sold on a recognized market, reasonable notification of the time and place of any public sale or reasonable notification of the time after which any private sale or other intended disposition is to be made shall be sent by the secured party to the debtor, if he has not signed after default a statement renouncing or modifying his right to notification of sale. In the case of consumer goods no other notification need be sent. In other cases notification shall be sent to any other secured party from whom the secured party has received (before sending his notification to the debtor or before the debtor's renunciation of his rights) written notice of a claim of an interest in the collateral. The secured party may buy at any public sale and if the collateral is of a type customarily sold in a recognized market or is of a type which is the subject of widely distributed standard price quotations he may buy at private sale.

(4) When collateral is disposed of by a secured party after default, the disposition transfers to a purchaser for value all of the debtor's rights therein, discharges the security interest under which it is made and any security interest or lien subordinate thereto. The purchaser takes free of all such rights and interests even though the secured party fails to comply with the requirements of this Part or of any judicial proceedings

　(a) in the case of a public sale, if the purchaser has no knowledge of any defects in the sale and if he does not buy in collusion with the secured party, other bidders or the person conducting the sale; or

　(b) in any other case, if the purchaser acts in good faith.

(5) A person who is liable to a secured party under a guaranty, indorsement, repurchase agreement or the like and who receives a transfer of collateral from the secured party

or is subrogated to his rights has thereafter the rights and duties of the secured party. Such a transfer of collateral is not a sale or disposition of the collateral under this Article.

§ 9–505. Compulsory Disposition of Collateral; Acceptance of the Collateral as Discharge of Obligation.

(1) If the debtor has paid sixty per cent of the cash price in the case of a purchase money security interest in consumer goods or sixty per cent of the loan in the case of another security interest in consumer goods, and has not signed after default a statement renouncing or modifying his rights under this Part a secured party who has taken possession of collateral must dispose of it under Section 9–504 and if he fails to do so within ninety days after he takes possession the debtor at his option may recover in conversion or under Section 9–507(1) on secured party's liability.

(2) In any other case involving consumer goods or any other collateral a secured party in possession may, after default, propose to retain the collateral in satisfaction of the obligation. Written notice of such proposal shall be sent to the debtor if he has not signed after default a statement renouncing or modifying his rights under this subsection. In the case of consumer goods no other notice need be given. In other cases notice shall be sent to any other secured party from whom the secured party has received (before sending his notice to the debtor or before the debtor's renunciation of his rights) written notice of a claim of an interest in the collateral. If the secured party receives objection in writing from a person entitled to receive notification within twenty-one days after the notice was sent, the secured party must dispose of the collateral under Section 9–504. In the absence of such written objection the secured party may retain the collateral in satisfaction of the debtor's obligation.

§ 9–506. Debtor's Right to Redeem Collateral.

At any time before the secured party has disposed of collateral or entered into a contract for its disposition under Section 9–504 or before the obligation has been discharged under Section 9–505(2) the debtor or any other secured party may unless otherwise agreed in writing after default redeem the collateral by tendering fulfillment of all obligations secured by the collateral as well as the expenses reasonably incurred by the secured party in retaking, holding and preparing the collateral for disposition, in arranging for the sale, and to the extent provided in the agreement and not prohibited by law, his reasonable attorneys' fees and legal expenses.

§ 9–507. Secured Party's Liability for Failure to Comply With This Part.

(1) If it is established that the secured party is not proceeding in accordance with the provisions of this Part disposition may be ordered or restrained on appropriate terms and conditions. If the disposition has occurred the debtor or any person entitled to notification or whose security interest has been made known to the secured party prior to the disposition has a right to recover from the secured party any loss caused by a failure to comply with the provisions of this Part. If the collateral is consumer goods, the debtor has a right to recover in any event an amount not less than the credit service charge plus ten per cent of the principal amount of the debt or the time price differential plus 10 per cent of the cash price.

(2) The fact that a better price could have been obtained by a sale at a different time or in a different method from that selected by the secured party is not of itself sufficient to establish that the sale was not made in a commercially reasonable manner. If the secured party either sells the collateral in the usual manner in any recognized market therefor or if he sells at the price current in such market at the time of his sale or if he has otherwise sold in conformity with reasonable commercial practices among dealers in the type of property sold he has sold in a commercially reasonable manner. The principles stated in the two preceding sentences with respect to sales also apply as may be appropriate to other types of disposition. A disposition which has been approved in any judicial proceeding or by any bona fide creditors' committee or representative of creditors shall conclusively be deemed to be commercially reasonable, but this sentence does not indicate that any such approval must be obtained in any case nor does it indicate that any disposition not so approved is not commercially reasonable.

Glossary

A

Accounts Any right to receive payment for goods sold or leased, other than rights covered by chattel paper or instruments. (Chapter 12)

Accredited investor Under the Securities Act of 1933, an accredited investor is an institution (such as a bank or insurance company) or any individual with a net worth of more than $1 million or an annual income of more than $200,000. (Chapter 18)

Acquit To find the defendant not guilty of the crime for which he was tried. (Chapter 7)

Act of State doctrine A rule requiring American courts to abstain from cases if a court order would interfere with the ability of the President or Congress to conduct foreign policy. (Chapter 8)

Actus reus The guilty act. The prosecution must show that a criminal defendant committed some proscribed act. In a murder prosecution, taking another person's life is the actus reus. (Chapter 7)

Adjudicate To hold a formal hearing in a disputed matter and issue an official decision. (Chapter 4)

Administrative law Concerns all agencies, boards, commissions, and other entities created by a federal or state legislature and charged with investigating, regulating, and adjudicating a particular industry or issue. (Chapter 1)

Affidavit A written statement signed under oath. (Chapter 7)

Affirm A decision by an appellate court to uphold the judgment of a lower court. (Chapter 3)

Affirmative action A plan introduced in a workplace for the purpose of either remedying the effects of past discrimination or achieving equitable representation of minorities and women. (Chapter 14)

After-acquired property Items that a debtor obtains after making a security agreement with the secured party. (Chapter 12)

Agent A person who acts for a principal. (Chapter 7, 13)

Alternative dispute resolution Any method of resolving a legal conflict other than litigation, such as: negotiation, arbitration, mediation, mini-trials, and summary jury trials. (Chapter 3)

Annual report Each year, public companies must send their shareholders an annual report that contains detailed financial data. (Chapter 17)

Apparent authority A situation in which conduct of a principal causes a third party to believe that the principal consents to have an act done on his behalf by a person purporting to act for him when, in fact, that person is not acting for the principal. (Chapter 13)

Appellant The party who appeals a lower court decision to a higher court. (Chapter 3)

Appellate court Any court in a state or federal system that reviews cases that have already been tried. (Chapter 3)

Appellee The party opposing an appeal from a lower court to a higher court. (Chapter 3)

Arbitration A form of alternative dispute resolution in which the parties hire a neutral third party to hear their respective arguments, receive evidence, and then make a binding decision. (Chapter 3, 15)

Arson Malicious use of fire or explosives to damage or destroy real estate or personal property. (Chapter 7)

Assault An intentional act that causes the plaintiff to fear an imminent battery. (Chapter 6)

Assignee The party who receives an assignment of contract rights from a party to the contract. (Chapter 10)

Assignment The act by which a party transfers contract rights to a third person. (Chapter 10)

Assignor The party who assigns contract rights to a third person. (Chapter 10)

Attachment A court order seizing property of a party to a civil action, so that there will be sufficient assets available to pay the judgment. (Chapter 5, 12)

Authorized and issued stock Stock that has been approved by the corporation's charter and subsequently sold. (Chapter 17)

Authorized and unissued stock Stock that has been approved by the corporation's charter, but has not yet been sold. (Chapter 17)

B

Bailee A person who rightfully possesses goods belonging to another. (Chapter 22)

Bailment Giving possession and control of personal property to another person. (Chapter 22)

Bailor One who creates a bailment by delivering goods to another. (Chapter 22)

Battery The intentional touching of another person in a way that is unwanted or offensive. (Chapter 6)

Bilateral contract A binding agreement in which each party has made a promise to the other. (Chapter 9)

Bill A proposed statute that has been submitted for consideration to Congress or a state legislature. (Chapter 4)

Blue sky laws State securities laws. (Chapter 18)

Bona fide occupational qualification A job requirement that would otherwise be discriminatory is permitted in situations in which it is essential to the position in question. (Chapter 14)

Bonds Long-term debt secured by some of the issuing company's assets. (Chapter 17)

Brief The written legal argument that an attorney files with an appeal court. (Chapter 3)

Burden of proof The allocation of which party must prove its case. In a civil case, the plaintiff has the burden of proof to persuade the factfinder of every element of her case. In a criminal case, the government has the burden of proof. (Chapter 3)

Business judgment rule A common law rule that protects managers from liability if they are acting without a conflict of interest, and make informed decisions that have a rational business purpose. (Chapter 17)

Buyer in ordinary course of business Someone who buys goods in good faith from a seller who routinely deals in such goods. (Chapter 12)

Bylaws A document that specifies the organizational rules of a corporation or other organization, such as the date of the annual meeting and the required number of directors. (Chapter 17)

C

***Certiorari,* writ of** Formal notice from the United States Supreme Court that it will accept a case for review. (Chapter 3)

Challenge for cause An attorney's request, during voir dire, to excuse a prospective juror because of apparent bias. (Chapter 3)

Chattel paper Any writing that indicates two things: (1) a debtor owes money and (2) a secured party has a security interest in specific goods. The most common chattel paper is a document indicating a consumer sale on credit. (Chapter 12)

Check An instrument in which the drawer orders the drawee bank to pay money to the payee. (Chapter 11)

Chicago School A theory of antitrust law first developed at the University of Chicago. Adherents to this theory believe that antitrust enforcement should focus on promoting efficiency and should not generally be concerned about the size or number of competitors in any market. (Chapter 19)

Civil law The large body of law concerning the rights and duties between parties. It is distinguished from criminal law, which concerns behavior outlawed by a government. (Chapter 1)

Class action A method of litigating a civil lawsuit in which one or more plaintiffs (or occasionally defendants) seek to represent an entire group of people with similar claims against a common opponent. (Chapter 3)

Classification The process by which the Customs Service decides what label to attach to imported merchandise, and therefore what level of tariff to impose. (Chapter 8)

Close corporation A corporation with a small number of shareholders. Its stock is not publicly traded. (Chapter 16)

Collateral The property subject to a security interest. (Chapter 12)

Collateral promise A promise to pay the debt of another person, as a favor to the debtor. (Chapter 10)

Collective bargaining Contract negotiations between an employer and a union. (Chapter 15)

Collective bargaining unit The precisely defined group of employees who are represented by a particular union. (Chapter 15)

Comity A doctrine that requires a court to abstain from hearing a case out of respect for another court that also has jurisdiction. International comity demands that an American court refuse to hear a case in which a foreign court shares jurisdiction if there is a conflict between the laws and if it is more logical for the foreign court to take the case. (Chapter 8)

Commerce clause One of the powers granted by Article I, §8 of the Constitution, it gives Congress exclusive power to regulate international commerce and concurrent power with the states to regulate domestic commerce. (Chapter 5)

Commercial impracticability After the creation of a contract, an entirely unforeseen event occurs which makes enforcement of the contract extraordinarily unfair. (Chapter 16)

Commercial paper Instruments such as checks and promissory notes that contain a promise to pay money. Commercial paper includes both negotiable and non-negotiable instruments. (Chapter 11)

Commercial speech Communication, such as television advertisements, that has the dominant theme of proposing a commercial transaction. (Chapter 5)

Common law Judge-made law, that is, the body of all decisions made by appellate courts over the years. (Chapter 1, 4)

Common stock Certificates that reflect ownership in a corporation. Owners of this equity security are last in line for corporate pay-outs such as dividends and liquidation proceeds. (Chapter 17)

Compensatory damages Those that flow directly from the contract. (Chapter 6, 10)

Complaint A pleading, filed by the plaintiff, providing a short statement of the claim. (Chapter 3)

Concerted action Tactics, such as a strike, used by a union to gain a bargaining advantage. (Chapter 15)

Confiscation Expropriation without adequate compensation of property owned by foreigners. (Chapter 8)

Consent order An agreement entered into by a wrongdoer and an administrative agency (such as the Securities and Exchange Commission or the Federal Trade Commission) in which the wrongdoer agrees not to violate the law in the future. (Chapter 23)

Consequential damages Those resulting from the unique circumstances of this injured party. (Chapter 10)

Consideration In contract law, something of legal value that has been bargained for and given in exchange by the parties. (Chapter 9, 12)

Contract A legally enforceable promise or set of promises. (Chapter 9)

Contributory negligence A rule of tort law that permits a negligent defendant to escape liability if she can demonstrate that the plaintiff's own conduct contributed in any way to the plaintiff's harm. (Chapter 6)

Control security Stock owned by any officer or director of the issuer, or by any shareholder who holds more than 10 percent of a class of stock of the issuer. (Chapter 18)

Cookie A small computer file that identifies the user of a computer. Internet sites typically place cookies on a computer's hard drive to track visitors to their site. (Chapter 20)

Copyright Under federal law, the holder of a copyright owns a particular expression of an idea, but not the idea itself. This ownership right applies to creative activities such as literature, music, drama, and software. (Chapter 21)

Counter-claim A claim made by the defendant against the plaintiff. (Chapter 3)

Criminal law Rules that permit a government to punish certain behavior by fine or imprisonment. (Chapter 1)

Cross-examination During a hearing, for a lawyer to question an opposing witness. (Chapter 3)

D

Damages (1) The harm that a plaintiff complains of at trial, such as an injury to her person, or money lost because of a contract breach. (2) Money awarded by a trial court for injury suffered. (Chapter 13)

De novo The power of an appellate court or appellate agency to make a new decision in a matter under appeal, entirely ignoring the findings and conclusions of the lower court or agency official. (Chapter 4)

Debentures Long-term, unsecured debt, typically issued by a corporation. (Chapter 17)

Defamation The act of injuring someone's reputation by stating something false about her to a third person. Libel is defamation done either in writing or by broadcast. *Slander* is defamation done orally. (Chapter 6, 14)

Debtor A person who owes money or some other obligation to another party. (Chapter 12)

Default The failure to perform an obligation, such as the failure to pay money when due. (Chapter 12)

Default judgment Court order awarding one party everything it requested because the opposing party failed to respond in time. (Chapter 3)

Delegation The act by which a party to a contract transfers duties to a third person who is not a party to the contract. (Chapter 10)

Deponent The person being questioned in a deposition. (Chapter 3)

Deterrence Using punishment, such as imprisonment, to discourage criminal behavior. (Chapter 7)

Direct examination During a hearing, for a lawyer to question his own witness. (Chapter 3)

Directed verdict The decision by a court to instruct a jury that it must find in favor of a particular party because, in the judge's opinion, no reasonable person could disagree on the outcome. (Chapter 3)

Disaffirmance The act of notifying the other party to a contract that the party giving the notice refuses to be bound by the agreement. (Chapter 9)

Discharge (1) A party to a contract has no more duties. (2) A party to an instrument is released from liability. (Chapter 12)

Discovery A stage in litigation, after all pleadings have been served, in which each party seeks as much relevant information as possible about the opposing party's case. (Chapter 3)

Dissociation A dissociation occurs when a partner leaves a partnership. (Chapter 16)

Disclaimer A statement that a particular warranty does not apply. (Chapter 11)

Domestic corporation A corporation is a domestic

corporation in the state in which it was formed. (Chapter 17)

Donee A person who receives a gift. (Chapter 22)

Donor A person who makes a gift to another. (Chapter 22)

Draft The drawer of this instrument orders someone else to pay money. Checks are the most common form of draft. The drawer of a check orders a bank to pay money. (Chapter 8, 11)

Drawee The person who pays a draft. In the case of a check, the bank is the drawee. (Chapter 11)

Drawer The person who issues a draft. (Chapter 11)

Due Process Clause Part of the Fifth Amendment. Procedural due process ensures that before depriving anyone of liberty or property, the government must go through procedures which ensure that the deprivation is fair. Substantive due process holds that certain rights, such as privacy, are so fundamental that the government may not eliminate them. (Chapter 7)

Dumping Selling merchandise at one price in the domestic market and at a cheaper, unfair price in an international market. (Chapter 8)

Duress (1) A criminal defense in which the defendant shows that she committed the wrongful act because a third person threatened her with imminent physical harm. (2) An improper threat made to force another party to enter into a contract. (Chapter 7)

E

Easement The right to enter land belonging to another and make a limited use of it, without taking anything away. (Chapter 22)

Element A fact that a party to a lawsuit must prove in order to prevail. (Chapter 6)

Embezzlement Fraudulent conversion of property already in the defendant's possession. (Chapter 7)

Eminent domain The power of the government to take private property for public use. (Chapter 5, 22)

Employee at will A worker whose job does not have a specified duration. (Chapter 14)

Enabling legislation A statute authorizing the creation of a new administrative agency and specifying its powers and duties. (Chapter 4)

Entrapment A criminal defense in which the defendant demonstrates that the government induced him to break the law. (Chapter 7)

Equal Protection Clause Part of the Fourteenth Amendment, it generally requires the government to treat equally situated people the same. (Chapter 5)

Equity The broad powers of a court to fashion a remedy where justice demands it and no common law remedy exists. An injunction is an example of an equitable remedy. (Chapter 1)

Error of law A mistake made by a trial judge that con-

cerns a legal issue as opposed to a factual matter. Permitting too many leading questions is a legal error; choosing to believe one witness rather than another is a factual matter. (Chapter 3)

Estate The legal entity that holds title to assets after the owner dies and before the property is distributed. (Chapter 22)

Evidence, rules of Law governing the proof offered during a trial or formal hearing. These rules limit the questions that may be asked of witnesses and the introduction of physical objects. (Chapter 3)

Exclusionary rule In a criminal trial, a ban on the use of evidence obtained in violation of the Constitution. (Chapter 7)

Exclusive dealing agreement A potential violation of §1 of the Sherman Act, in which a distributor or retailer agrees with a supplier not to carry the products of any other supplier. (Chapter 19)

Exculpatory clause A contract provision that attempts to release one party from liability in the event the other party is injured. (Chapter 9)

Executed contract A binding agreement in which all parties have fulfilled all obligations. (Chapter 9)

Executory contract A binding agreement in which one or more of the parties has not fulfilled its obligations. (Chapter 9)

Exhaustion of remedies A principle of administrative law that no party may appeal an agency action to a court until she has utilized all available appeals within the agency itself. (Chapter 4)

Expectation interest A remedy in a contract case that puts the injured party in the position he would have been in had both sides fully performed. (Chapter 10)

Export To transport goods or services out of a country. (Chapter 8)

Express authority Conduct of a principal that, reasonably interpreted, causes the agent to believe that the principal desires him to do a specific act. (Chapter 13)

Express contract A binding agreement in which the parties explicitly state all important terms. (Chapter 9)

Express warranty A guarantee, created by the words or actions of the seller, that goods will meet certain standards. (Chapter 11)

Expropriation A government's seizure of property or companies owned by foreigners. (Chapter 8)

F

False imprisonment The intentional restraint of another person without reasonable cause and without her consent. (Chapter 6)

Federal question jurisdiction One of the two main

types of civil cases that a United States district court has the power to hear. It involves a federal statute or a constitutional provision. (Chapter 3)

Fee simple absolute The greatest possible ownership right in real property, including the right to possess, use, and dispose of the property in any lawful manner. (Chapter 22)

Felony The most serious crimes, typically those for which the defendant could be imprisoned for more than a year. (Chapter 7)

Fiduciary duty An obligation to behave in a trustworthy and confidential fashion toward the object of that duty. (Chapter 13)

Financing statement A document that a secured party files to give the general public notice that the secured party has a secured interest in the collateral. (Chapter 12)

Fixtures Goods that are attached to real estate. (Chapter 12)

Foreign corporation A corporation formed in another state. (Chapter 17)

Foreign Sovereign Immunity Act A federal statute that protects other nations from suit in courts of the United States, except under specified circumstances. (Chapter 8)

Fraud Deception of another person to obtain money or property from her. (Chapter 7, 20)

Freehold estate The present right to possess property and to use it in any lawful manner. (Chapter 22)

Frustration of purpose After the creation of a contract, an entirely unforeseen event occurs that eliminates the value of the contract for one of the parties. (Chapter 16)

Fundamental rights In constitutional law, those rights that are so basic that any governmental interference with them is suspect and likely to be unconstitutional. (Chapter 5)

G

GATT See General Agreement on Tariffs and Trade. (Chapter 8)

General deterrence See Deterrence. (Chapter 7)

General intangibles Potential sources of income such as copyrights, patents, trademarks, goodwill and certain other rights to payment. (Chapter 12)

Gift A voluntary transfer of property from one person to another without consideration. (Chapter 22)

Gift causa mortis A gift made in contemplation of approaching death. (Chapter 22)

Goods Anything movable, except for money, securities, and certain legal rights. (Chapter 8, 12)

Grantee The person who receives property, or some interest in it, from the owner. (Chapter 22)

Grantor (1) An owner who conveys property, or some interest in it. (2) Someone who creates a trust. (Chapter 22)

H

Hacking Gaining unauthorized access to a computer system. (Chapter 20)

Harmless error A ruling made by a trial court which an appeals court determines was legally wrong but not fatal to the decision. (Chapter 3)

Holder in due course Someone who has given value for an instrument, in good faith, without notice of outstanding claims or other defenses. (Chapter 11)

Horizontal agreement or merger An agreement or merger between two potential competitors. (Chapter 19)

I

Illusory promise An apparent promise that is unenforceable because the promisor makes no firm commitment. (Chapter 9)

Implied authority When a principal directs an agent to undertake a transaction, the agent has the right to do acts that are incidental to it, usually accompany it, or are reasonably necessary to accomplish it. (Chapter 13)

Implied contract A binding agreement created not by explicit language but by the informal words and conduct of the parties. (Chapter 9)

Implied warranty Guarantees created by the Uniform Commercial Code and imposed on the seller of goods. (Chapter 11)

Import To transport goods or services into a country. (Chapter 8)

In camera "In the judge's chambers," meaning that the judge does something out of view of the jury and the public. (Chapter 3)

Incidental damages The relatively minor costs, such as storage and advertising, that the injured party suffered when responding to a contract breach. (Chapter 16)

Indemnification A promise to pay someone else's obligations. (Chapter 13)

Independent contractor Someone who undertakes tasks for others and whose work is not closely controlled. (Chapter 13)

Indictment The government's formal charge that a defendant has committed a crime. (Chapter 7)

Initial public offering (IPO) A company's first public sale of securities. (Chapter 18)

Injunction A court order that a person either do or stop doing something. (Chapter 1)

Integrated contract A writing that the parties intend as the complete and final expression of their agreement. (Chapter 10)

Intentional tort An act deliberately performed that violates a legally imposed duty and injures someone. (Chapter 6)

Inter vivos gift A gift made "during life," that is, when the donor is not under any fear of impending death. (Chapter 22)

Interest A legal right in something, such as ownership or a mortgage or a tenancy. (Chapter 10)

Inventory Goods that the seller is holding for sale or lease in the ordinary course of its business. (Chapter 12)

Issuer The maker of a promissory note or the drawer of a draft. (Chapter 11)

J

Joint venture A partnership for a limited purpose. (Chapter 16, 19)

Judgment *non obstante verdicto* (n.o.v.) "Judgment notwithstanding the verdict." A trial judge overturns the verdict of the jury and enters a judgment in favor of the opposing party. (Chapter 3)

Judicial activism The willingness shown by certain courts (and not by others) to decide issues of public policy, such as constitutional questions (free speech, equal protection, etc.) and matters of contract fairness (promissory estoppel, unconscionability, etc.). (Chapter 5, 9)

Judicial restraint A court's preference to abstain from adjudicating major social issues and to leave such matters to legislatures. (Chapter 5, 9)

Judicial review The power of the judicial system to examine, interpret, and even nullify actions taken by another branch of government. (Chapter 5)

Jurisdiction The power of a court to hear a particular dispute, civil or criminal, and to make a binding decision. (Chapter 3)

Jurisprudence The study of the purposes and philosophies of the law, as opposed to particular provisions of the law. (Chapter 1)

Justification A criminal defense in which the defendant establishes that he broke the law to avoid a greater harm. (Chapter 6)

L

Larceny Taking personal property with the intention of preventing the owner from ever using it. (Chapter 7)

Lease A contract creating a landlord-tenant relationship. (Chapter 22)

Letter of credit A commercial device used to guarantee payment in international trade, usually between parties that have not previously worked together. (Chapter 8)

Libel See Defamation. (Chapter 6)

License To grant permission to another person (1) to make or sell something or (2) to enter on property. (Chapter 22)

Lien A security interest created by rule of law, often based on labor that the secured party has expended on the collateral. (Chapter 22)

Life estate An ownership interest in real property entitling the holder to use the property during his lifetime, but which terminates upon his death. (Chapter 22)

Limited liability limited partnership In a limited liability limited partnership, the general partner is not personally liable for the debts of the partnership. (Chapter 16)

Limited partnership A partnership with two types of partners: (1) limited partners who have no personal liability for the debts of the enterprise nor any right to manage the business, and (2) general partners who are responsible for management and personally liable for all debts. (Chapter 16)

Liquidated damages A contract clause specifying how much a party must pay upon breach. (Chapter 10)

Litigation The process of resolving disputes through formal court proceedings. (Chapter 3)

M

Maker The issuer of a promissory note. (Chapter 11)

Material Important or significant. Information that would affect a person's decision if he knew it. (Chapter 18)

Mediation The process of using a neutral person to aid in the settlement of a legal dispute. A mediator's decision is non-binding. (Chapter 3)

Mens rea Guilty state of mind. (Chapter 7)

Mini-trial A form of alternative dispute resolution in which the parties present short versions of their cases to a panel of three "judges." (Chapter 3)

Minor A person under the age of 18. (Chapter 9, 14)

Minute book Records of shareholder meetings and directors's meetings are kept in the corporation's minute book. (Chapter 17)

Misdemeanor A less serious crime, typically one for which the maximum penalty is incarceration for less than a year, often in a jail, as opposed to a prison. (Chapter 7)

Misrepresentation A factually incorrect statement made during contract negotiations. (Chapter 9)

Mitigation One party acts to minimize its losses when the other party breaches a contract. (Chapter 10)

Modify An appellate court order changing a lower court ruling. (Chapter 3)

Monopolization   A company acquires or maintains a monopoly through the commission of unacceptably aggressive acts. A violation of §2 of the Sherman Act. (Chapter 19)

Mortgage   A security interest in real property. (Chapter 22)

Mortgagee   A creditor who obtains a security interest in real property, typically in exchange for money given to the mortgagor to buy the property. (Chapter 22)

Mortgagor   A debtor who gives a mortgage (security interest) in real property to a creditor, typically in exchange for money used to buy the property. (Chapter 22)

Motion   A formal request that a court take some specified step during litigation. A motion to compel discovery is a request that a trial judge order the other party to respond to discovery. (Chapter 3)

Motion to suppress   A request that the court exclude evidence because it was obtained in violation of the Constitution. (Chapter 7)

Multinational enterprise   A corporation that is doing business in more than one country simultaneously. (Chapter 8)

N

NAFTA   See North American Free Trade Agreement. (Chapter 8)

National Labor Relations Board   (NLRB) The administrative agency charged with overseeing labor law. (Chapter 15)

Nationalization   A government's seizure of property or companies. (Chapter 8)

Negligence per se   Violation of a standard of care set by statute. Driving while intoxicated is illegal; thus, if a drunk driver injures a pedestrian, he has committed negligence per se. (Chapter 6)

Note   An unconditional, written promise that the maker of the instrument will pay a specific amount of money on demand or at a definite time. When issued by a corporation, a note refers to short-term debt, typically payable within five years. (Chapter 11, 17)

Novation   If there is an existing contract between A and B, a novation occurs when A agrees to release B from all liability on the contract in return for C's willingness to accept B's liability. (Chapter 10, 17)

O

Obligee   The party to a contract who is entitled to receive performance from the other party. (Chapter 10)

Obligor   The party to a contract who is required to do something for the benefit of the other party. (Chapter 10, 12)

Offeree   The party in contract negotiations who receives the first offer. (Chapter 9)

Offeror   The party in contract negotiations who makes the first offer. (Chapter 9)

P

Parol evidence   Written or oral evidence, outside the language of a contract, offered by one party to clarify interpretation of the agreement. (Chapter 10)

Partially disclosed principal   If the third party in an agency relationship knows that the agent is acting for a principal, but does not know the identity of the principal, that principal is partially disclosed. (Chapter 13)

Partnership   An association of two or more persons to carry on as co-owners of a business for profit. (Chapter 16)

Partnership at will   A partnership that has no fixed duration. A partner has the right to resign from the partnership at any time. (Chapter 16)

Partnership by estoppel   If a person who is not a partner implies that he is a partner or does not object when other people imply it, he is liable as if he really were a partner. (Chapter 16)

Patent   The right to the exclusive use of an invention for 20 years. (Chapter 21)

Payee   Someone who is owed money under the terms of an instrument. (Chapter 11)

***Per se* violation of an antitrust law**   An automatic breach. Courts will generally not consider mitigating factors. (Chapter 19)

Peremptory challenge   During voir dire, a request by one attorney that a prospective juror be excused for an unstated reason. (Chapter 3)

Perfection   A series of steps a secured party must take to protect its rights in collateral against people other than the debtor. (Chapter 12)

Personal property   All property other than real property. (Chapter 22)

Pleadings   The documents that begin a lawsuit: the complaint, the answer, the counter-claim and reply. (Chapter 3)

Precedent   An earlier case that decided the same legal issue as that presently in dispute, and which therefore will control the outcome of the current case. (Chapter 1, 4)

Predatory pricing   A violation of §2 of the Sherman Act in which a company lowers its prices below cost to drive competitors out of business. (Chapter 19)

Preemption   The doctrine, based on the Supremacy Clause, by which any federal statute takes priority whenever (1) a state statute conflicts or (2) there is no conflict but Congress indicated an intention to control the issue involved. (Chapter 5)

Preferred stock Owners of preferred stock have a right to receive dividends and liquidation proceeds of the company before common shareholders. (Chapter 17)

Preponderance of the evidence The level of proof that a plaintiff must meet to prevail in a civil lawsuit. It means that the plaintiff must offer evidence that, in sum, is slightly more persuasive than the defendant's evidence. (Chapter 3)

Prima facie "At first sight." A fact or conclusion that is presumed to be true unless someone presents evidence to disprove it. (Chapter 14)

Principal In an agency relationship, the principal is the person for whom the agent is acting. (Chapter 13)

Private law Refers to the rights and duties between individuals that they themselves have created, for example, by entering into a contract or employment relationship. (Chapter 1)

Probable cause In a search and seizure case, it means that the information available indicates that it is more likely than not that a search will uncover particular criminal evidence. (Chapter 7)

Procedural due process *See* Due Process Clause. (Chapter 5)

Procedural law The rules establishing how the legal system itself is to operate in a particular kind of case. (Chapter 1)

Proceeds Anything that a debtor obtains from the sale or disposition of collateral. Normally, proceeds refers to cash obtained from the sale of the secured property. (Chapter 12)

Product liability The potential responsibility that a manufacturer or seller has for injuries caused by defective goods. (Chapter 11)

Professional corporation A form of organization that permits professionals (such as doctors, lawyers, and accountants) to incorporate. Shareholders are not personally liable for the torts of other shareholders, or for the contract debts of the organization. (Chapter 16)

Profit The right to enter land belonging to another and take something away, such as minerals or timber. (Chapter 22)

Promissory estoppel A doctrine in which a court may enforce a promise made by the defendant even when there is no contract, if the defendant knew that the plaintiff was likely to rely on the promise, the plaintiff did in fact rely, and enforcement of it is the only way to avoid injustice. (Chapter 9)

Promissory note The maker of the instrument promises to pay a specific amount of money. (Chapter 11)

Promoter The person who creates a corporation by raising capital and undertaking the legal steps necessary for formation. (Chapter 17)

Promulgate To issue a new rule. (Chapter 4)

Prospectus Under the Securities Act of 1933, an issuer must provide this document to anyone who purchases a security in a public transaction. The prospectus contains detailed information about the issuer and its business, a description of the stock, and audited financial statements. (Chapter 18)

Proxy (1) A person whom the shareholder designates to vote in his place. (2) The written form (typically a card) that the shareholder uses to appoint a designated voter. (Chapter 17)

Proxy statement When a public company seeks proxy votes from its shareholders, it must include a proxy statement. This statement contains information about the company, such as a detailed description of management compensation. (Chapter 17)

Public law refers to the rights and obligations of governments as they deal with the nation's citizens, for example, by taxing individuals, zoning neighborhoods, and regulating advertisements. (Chapter 1)

Purchase money security interest A security interest taken by the person who sells the collateral to the debtor, or by a person who advances money so that the debtor may buy the collateral. (Chapter 12)

Q

Quantum meruit "As much as she deserves." The damages awarded in a quasi-contract case. (Chapter 9)

Quasi-contract A legal fiction in which, to avoid injustice, the court awards damages as if a contract had existed, although one did not. (Chapter 9)

Quorum The number of voters that must be present for a meeting to count. (Chapter 17)

R

Ratification When someone accepts the benefit of an unauthorized transaction or fails to repudiate it once he has learned of it, he is then bound by it. (Chapter 8, 13)

Real property Land, together with certain things associated with it, such as buildings, subsurface rights, air rights, plant life and fixtures. (Chapter 22)

Reasonable doubt The level of proof that the government must meet to convict the defendant in a criminal case. The factfinder must be persuaded to a very high degree of certainty that the defendant did what the government alleges. (Chapter 3)

Reciprocal dealing agreement An agreement under which Company *A* will purchase from Company *B* only if Company *B* also buys from Company *A*. These agreements are rule of reason violations of the Sherman Act. (Chapter 19)

Record date To vote at a shareholders meeting, a shareholder must own stock on the record date. (Chapter 12, 17)

Red herring A preliminary prospectus. (Chapter 18)

Reformation The process by which a court rewrites a contract to ensure its accuracy or viability. (Chapter 10)

Refusal to deal An agreement among competitors that they will not trade with a particular supplier or buyer. Such an agreement is a rule of reason violation of the Sherman Act. (Chapter 19)

Registration statement A document filed with the Securities and Exchange Commission under the Securities Act of 1933 by an issuer seeking to sell securities in a public transaction. (Chapter 18)

Reliance interest A remedy in a contract case that puts the injured party in the position he would have been in had the parties never entered into a contract. (Chapter 10, 18)

Remand The power of an appellate court to return a case to a lower court for additional action. (Chapter 3)

Reply A pleading, filed by the plaintiff in response to a defendant's counter-claim. (Chapter 3)

Repossess A secured party takes collateral because the debtor has defaulted on payments. (Chapter 12)

Res ipsa loquitur A doctrine of tort law holding that the facts may imply negligence when the defendant had exclusive control of the thing that caused the harm, the accident would not normally have occurred without negligence, and the plaintiff played no role in causing the injury. (Chapter 6)

Resale price maintenance A per se violation of the Sherman Act in which a manufacturer enters into an agreement with retailers about the prices they will charge. (Chapter 19)

Rescind To cancel a contract. (Chapter 9, 10, 13)

Restitution Restoring an injured party to its original position. (Chapter 9)

Restitution interest A remedy in a contract case that returns to the injured party a benefit that he has conferred on the other party, which it would be unjust to leave with that person. (Chapter 10)

Restricted security Any stock purchased in a private offering (such as one under Regulation D). (Chapter 18)

Retribution Giving a criminal defendant the punishment he deserves. (Chapter 7)

Reverse The power of an appellate court to overrule a lower court and grant judgment for the party that had lost in the lower court. (Chapter 3)

Rule of reason violation An action that breaches the antitrust laws only if it has an anticompetitive impact. (Chapter 19)

S

Scienter In a case of securities fraud, the plaintiff must prove that the defendant acted willfully, knowingly, or recklessly. (Chapter 18)

Security agreement A contract in which the debtor gives a security interest to the secured party. (Chapter 12)

Security interest An interest in personal property or fixtures that secures the performance of some obligation. (Chapter 12)

Servant An agent whose work is closely controlled by the principal. (Chapter 13)

Sexual harassment Unwanted sexual advances, comments or touching, sufficiently severe to violate Title VII of the 1964 Civil Rights Act. (Chapter 14)

Shilling A seller at auction either bids on his own goods or agrees to cross-bid with a group of other sellers. (Chapter 20)

Signatory A person, company, or nation that has signed a legal document, such as a contract, agreement, or treaty. (Chapter 8)

Slander See Defamation. (Chapter 6)

Sole proprietorship An unincorporated business owned by a single person. (Chapter 16)

Sovereign Refers to the recognized political power whom citizens obey. In the United States, the federal and all of the state governments are sovereigns. (Chapter 1)

Spam Unsolicited commercial or bulk e-mail. ("To spam" is to send such e-mail.) (Chapter 20)

Specific deterrence See Deterrence. (Chapter 7)

Stakeholders Anyone who is affected by the activities of a corporation, such as employees, customers, creditors, suppliers, shareholders, and neighbors. (Chapter 17)

Stare decisis "Let the decision stand." A basic principle of the common law, it means that precedent is usually binding. (Chapter 1)

Statute A law passed by a legislative body, such as Congress. (Chapter 1)

Statute of frauds This law provides that certain contracts are not enforceable unless in writing. (Chapter 10)

Statute of limitations A statute that determines the period within which a particular kind of lawsuit must be filed. (Chapter 10, 17)

Strict liability A tort doctrine holding to a very high standard all those who engage in ultrahazardous activity (e.g., using explosives) or who manufacture certain products. (Chapter 6)

Strike The ultimate weapon of a labor union, it occurs when all or most employees of a particular plant or employer walk off the job and refuse to work. (Chapter 15)

Subpoena   An order to appear, issued by a court or government body. (Chapter 4)

Subpoena duces tecum   An order to produce certain documents or things before a court or government body. (Chapter 4)

Substantive due process   See Due Process Clause. (Chapter 5)

Substantive law   Rules that establish the rights of parties. For example, the prohibition against slander is substantive law, as opposed to procedural law. (Chapter 1)

Summary judgment   The power of a trial court to terminate a lawsuit before a trial has begun, on the grounds that no essential facts are in dispute. (Chapter 3)

Summary jury trial   A form of alternative dispute resolution in which a small panel of jurors hears shortened, summarized versions of the evidence. (Chapter 3)

Supremacy Clause   From Article VI of the Constitution, it declares that federal statutes and treaties take priority over any state law, if there is a conflict between the two or, even absent a conflict, if Congress manifests an intent to preempt the field. (Chapter 5)

T

Takings Clause   Part of the Fifth Amendment, it ensures that when any governmental unit takes private property for public use, it must compensate the owner. (Chapter 5)

Tariff   A duty imposed on imported goods by the government of the importing nation. (Chapter 8)

Tenancy by the entirety   A form of joint ownership available only to married couples. If one member of the couple dies, the property goes automatically to the survivor. Creditors cannot attach the property, nor can one owner sell the property without the other's permission. (Chapter 22)

Tender offer   A public offer to buy a block of stock directly from shareholders. (Chapter 17)

Term partnership   When the partners agree in advance on the duration of a partnership. (Chapter 16)

Tort   A civil wrong, committed in violation of a duty that the law imposes. (Chapter 6)

Trade secret   A formula, device, process, method, or compilation of information that, when used in business, gives the owner an advantage over competitors who do not know it. (Chapter 21)

Trademark   Any combination of words and symbols that a business uses to identify its products or services and that federal law will protect. (Chapter 21)

Treasury stock   Stock that has been bought back by its issuing corporation. (Chapter 17)

Trial court   Any court in a state or federal system that holds formal hearings to determine the facts in a civil or criminal case. (Chapter 3)

Tying arrangement   A violation of the Sherman and Clayton Acts in which a seller requires that two distinct products be purchased together. The seller uses its significant power in the market for the tying product to shut out a substantial part of the market for the tied product. (Chapter 19)

U

Ultrahazardous activity   Conduct that is lawful yet unusual and much more likely to cause injury than normal commercial activity. (Chapter 6, 7)

Unconscionable contract   An agreement that a court refuses to enforce because it is fundamentally unfair as a result of unequal bargaining power by one party. (Chapter 9)

Undisclosed principal   If a third party in an agency relationship does not know that the agent is acting for a principal, that principal is undisclosed. (Chapter 13)

Unilateral contract   A binding agreement in which one party has made an offer that the other can accept only by action, not words. (Chapter 9)

V

Vertical agreement or merger   An agreement or merger between two companies at different stages of the production process, such as when a company acquires one of its suppliers or distributors. (Chapter 19)

Void agreement   An agreement that neither party may legally enforce, usually because the purpose of the bargain was illegal or because one of the parties lacked capacity to make it. (Chapter 9)

Voidable contract   An agreement that, because of some defect, may be terminated by one party, such as a minor, but not by both parties. (Chapter 9)

Voir dire   The process of selecting a jury. Attorneys for the parties and the judge may inquire of prospective jurors whether they are biased or incapable of rendering a fair and impartial verdict. (Chapter 3)

W

Warranty   A guarantee that goods will meet certain standards. (Chapter 11)

Whistleblower   Someone who discloses wrongful behavior. (Chapter 14)

Writ   An order from a government compelling someone to do a particular thing. (Chapter 1)

Table of Cases

Note: Bold page references indicate a discussion of the case.
Cases shown in this color are new in this edition.

Index